Pocket
German
Dictionary

German ➤ English   English ➤ German

INDEX

This edition published 2005 for Index Books Limited

fifth edition/fünfte Auflage 2001

© William Collins Sons & Co. Ltd. 1990
© HarperCollins Publishers 1996, 1998, 1999, 2001

HarperCollins Publishers
Westerhill Road, Bishopbriggs, Glasgow G64 2QT,
Great Britain

www.collins.co.uk

ISBN 0-00-772625-2

HarperCollins Publishers, Inc.
10 East 53rd Street, New York, NY 10022

ISBN 0-06-093752-1

Library of Congress Cataloging-in-Publication Data
has been applied for

www.harpercollins.com

Typeset by Morton Word Processing Ltd, Scarborough

Printed and bound in China by Imago

editors/Redaktion
Veronika Schnorr • Ute Nicol • Peter Terrell
Bob Grossmith • Helga Holtkamp • Horst Kopleck
Beate Wengel • John Whitlam

editorial staff/Manuskriptbearbeitung
Joyce Littlejohn • Elspeth Anderson
Christine Bahr • John Podbielski

series editor/Gesamtleitung
Lorna Sinclair Knight

INTRODUCTION

We are delighted you have decided to buy the Collins Pocket German Dictionary and hope you will enjoy and benefit from using it at home, at school, on holiday or at work.

The comprehensive wordlist provides a wealth of modern and idiomatic phrases not normally found in a dictionary this size.

In addition, the supplement provides you with guidance on using the dictionary, along with entertaining ways of improving your dictionary skills.

We hope that you will enjoy using it and that it will significantly enhance your language studies.

ZUM GEBRAUCH IHRES COLLINS TASCHENWÖRTERBUCHS

Das Wörterbuch enthält eine Fülle von Informationen, die mithilfe von unterschiedlicher Schriften und Schriftgrößen, Symbolen, Abkürzungen und Klammern vermittelt werden Die dabei verwendeten Regeln und Symbole werden in den folgenden Abschnitten erklärt.

Stichwörter
Die Wörter, die Sie im Wörterbuch nachschlagen — „Stichwörter" — sind alphabetisch geordnet. Die beiden Stichwörter oben links und rechts auf jeder Doppelseite geben da erste bzw. letzte Wort an, das auf den betreffenden Seiten behandelt wird.

Informationen zur Verwendung oder zur Form bestimmter Stichwörter stehen in Klammern hinter der Lautschrift. Sie erscheinen meist in abgekürzter Form und sind kursiv gedruckt (z. B. (*fam*), (*COMM*)).

Wo es angebracht ist, werden mit dem Stichwort verwandte Wörter im selben Artikel behandelt (z. B. **accept, acceptance**). Sie sind wie das Stichwort fett, aber etwas kleiner gedruckt.

Häufig verwendete Ausdrücke, in denen das Stichwort vorkommt (z. B. **to be cold**), sind in einer anderen Schrift halbfett gedruckt.

Lautschrift
Die Lautschrift für jedes Stichwort (zur Angabe seiner Aussprache) steht in eckiger Klammern direkt hinter dem Stichwort (z. B. **Quark** [kvark]; **knead** [ni:d]). Die Symbole der Lautschrift sind auf Seite xii erklärt.

Übersetzungen
Die Übersetzungen des Stichworts sind normal gedruckt. Wenn es mehr als eine Bedeutung oder Verwendung des Stichworts gibt, sind diese durch ein Semikolon voneinander getrennt. Vor den Übersetzungen stehen oft andere, kursiv gedruckte Wörter in Klammern Sie geben an, in welchem Zusammenhang das Stichwort erscheinen könnte (z. B. **rough** (*voice*) oder (*weather*)), oder sie sind Synonyme (z. B. **rough** (*violent*)).

Schlüsselwörter
Besonders behandelt werden bestimmte deutsche und englische Wörter, die man al „Schlüsselwörter" der jeweiligen Sprache betrachten kann. Diese Wörter komme beispielsweise sehr häufig vor oder werden unterschiedlich verwendet (z. B. **sein, auch get, that**). Mithilfe von Rauten und Ziffern können Sie die verschiedenen Wortarten une Verwendungen unterscheiden. Weitere nützliche Hinweise finden Sie kursiv und i Klammern in der jeweiligen Sprache des Benutzers.

Grammatische Informationen
Wortarten stehen in abgekürzter Form kursiv gedruckt hinter der Aussprache de Stichworts (z. B. *vt, adv, conj*).

Die unregelmäßigen Formen englischer Substantive und Verben stehen in Klammern vor der Wortart (z. B. **man** (*pl* **men**) *n*, **give** (*pt* **gave**, *pp* **given**) *vt*).

Die deutsche Rechtschreibreform

Dieses Wörterbuch folgt durchweg der reformierten deutschen Rechtschreibung. Alle Stichwörter auf der deutsch-englischen Seite, die von der Rechtschreibreform betroffen sind, sind mit ▲ gekennzeichnet. Alte Schreibungen, die sich wesentlich von der neuen Schreibung unterscheiden und an einem anderen alphabetischen Ort erscheinen, sind jedoch weiterhin aufgeführt und werden zur neuen Schreibung verwiesen. Diese alten Schreibungen sind mit △ gekennzeichnet.

USING YOUR COLLINS POCKET DICTIONARY

A wealth of information is presented in the dictionary, using various typefaces, sizes of type, symbols, abbreviations and brackets. The conventions and symbols used are explained in the following sections.

Headwords
The words you look up in a dictionary — "headwords" — are listed alphabetically. The two headwords appearing at the top left and top right of each double page indicate the first and last word dealt with on the pages in question.

Information about the usage or form of certain headwords is given in brackets after the phonetic spelling. This usually appears in abbreviated form and in italics (e.g. (*umg*), (*COMM*)).

Where appropriate, words related to headwords are grouped in the same entry (**Glück, glücken**) in a slightly smaller bold type than the headword.

Common expressions in which the headword appears are shown in a different bold roman type (e.g. **Glück haben**).

Phonetic spellings
The phonetic spelling of each headword (indicating its pronunciation) is given in square brackets immediately after the headword (e.g. **Quark** [kvark]). A list of these symbols is given on page xii.

Meanings
Headword translations are given in ordinary type and, where more than one meaning or usage exists, these are separated by a semi-colon. You will often find other words in italics in brackets before the translations. These offer suggested contexts in which the headword might appear (e.g. **eng** (*Kleidung*) or (*Freundschaft*)) or provide synonyms (e.g. **eng** (*fig: Horizont*)).

"Key" words
Special status is given to certain German and English words which are considered as "key" words in each language. They may, for example, occur very frequently or have several types of usage (e.g. **sein, auch; get, that**). A combination of lozenges and numbers helps you to distinguish different parts of speech and different meanings. Further helpful information is provided in brackets and in italics in the relevant language for the user.

Grammatical information
Parts of speech are given in abbreviated form in italics after the phonetic spellings of headwords (e.g. *vt, adv, konj*).

Genders of German nouns are indicated as follows: *m* for a masculine and *f* for a feminine and *nt* for a neuter noun. The genitive and plural forms of regular nouns are shown on the table on page xi. Nouns which do not follow these rules have the genitive and plural in brackets immediately preceding the gender (e.g. **Spaß**, (**-es**, **̈e**), *m*).

Adjectives are normally shown in their basic form (e.g. **groß** *adj*), but where they are only used attributively (i.e. before a noun) feminine and neuter endings follow in brackets (**hohe (r, s)** *adj attrib*).

German spelling reform
The German spelling reform has been fully implemented in this dictionary. All headwords on the German-English side which are affected by the spelling changes are marked with ▲. but old spellings which are markedly different from the new ones and have a different alphabetical position are still listed and are cross-referenced to the new spellings. The old spellings are marked with △.

ABKÜRZUNGEN

ABBREVIATIONS

Abkürzung	**abk, abbr**	abbreviation
Akkusativ	**acc**	accusative
Adjektiv	**adj**	adjective
Adverb	**adv**	adverb
Landwirtschaft	**AGR**	agriculture
Akkusativ	**akk**	accusative
Anatomie	**ANAT**	anatomy
Architektur	**ARCHIT**	architecture
Astrologie	**ASTROL**	astrology
Astronomie	**ASTRON**	astronomy
attributiv	**attrib**	attributive
Kraftfahrzeuge	**AUT**	automobiles
Hilfsverb	**aux**	auxiliary
Luftfahrt	**AVIAT**	aviation
besonders	**bes**	especially
Biologie	**BIOL**	biology
Botanik	**BOT**	botany
britisch	**BRIT**	British
Chemie	**CHEM**	chemistry
Film	**CINE**	cinema
Handel	**COMM**	commerce
Komparativ	**compar**	comparative
Computer	**COMPUT**	computing
Konjunktion	**conj**	conjunction
Kochen und Backen	**COOK**	cooking
zusammengesetztes Wort	**cpd**	compound
Dativ	**dat**	dative
bestimmter Artikel	**def art**	definite article
Diminutiv	**dimin**	diminutive
kirchlich	**ECCL**	ecclesiastical
Eisenbahn	**EISENB**	railways
Elektrizität	**ELEK, ELEC**	electricity
besonders	**esp**	especially
und so weiter	**etc**	et cetera
etwas	**etw**	something
Euphemismus, Hüllwort	**euph**	euphemism
Interjektion, Ausruf	**excl**	exclamation
Femininum	**f**	feminine
übertragen	**fig**	figurative
Finanzwesen	**FIN**	finance
nicht getrennt gebraucht	**fus**	(phrasal verb) inseparable
Genitiv	**gen**	genitive
Geografie	**GEOG**	geography
Geologie	**GEOL**	geology
Grammatik	**GRAM**	grammar

Geschichte	**HIST**	history
unpersönlich	**impers**	impersonal
unbestimmter Artikel	**indef art**	indefinite article
umgangssprachlich (! vulgär)	**inf(!)**	informal (! particularly offensive)
Infinitiv, Grundform	**infin**	infinitive
nicht getrennt gebraucht	**insep**	inseparable
unveränderlich	**inv**	invariable
unregelmäßig	**irreg**	irregular
jemand	**jd**	somebody
jemandem	**jdm**	(to) somebody
jemanden	**jdn**	somebody
jemandes	**jds**	somebody's
Rechtswesen	**JUR**	law
Kochen und Backen	**KOCH**	cooking
Komparativ	**kompar**	comparative
Konjunktion	**konj**	conjunction
Sprachwissenschaft	**LING**	linguistics
Literatur	**LITER**	of literature
Maskulinum	**m**	masculine
Mathematik	**MATH**	mathematics
Medizin	**MED**	medicine
Meteorologie	**MET**	meteorology
Militär	**MIL**	military
Bergbau	**MIN**	mining
Musik	**MUS**	music
Substantiv, Hauptwort	**n**	noun
nautisch, Seefahrt	**NAUT**	nautical, naval
Nominativ	**nom**	nominative
Neutrum	**nt**	neuter
Zahlwort	**num**	numeral
Objekt	**obj**	object
oder	**od**	or
sich	**o.s.**	oneself
Parlament	**PARL.**	parliament
abschätzig	**pej**	pejorative
Fotografie	**PHOT**	photography
Physik	**PHYS**	physics
Plural	**pl**	plural
Politik	**POL**	politics
Präfix, Vorsilbe	**pp**	prefix
Präposition	**präp, prep**	preposition
Typografie	**PRINT**	printing
Pronomen, Fürwort	**pron**	pronoun
Psychologie	**PSYCH**	psychology
1. Vergangenheit, Imperfekt	**pt**	past tense
Radio	**RAD**	radio
Eisenbahn	**RAIL**	railways
Religion	**REL**	religion

jemand(-en, -em)	**sb**	someone, somebody
Schulwesen	**SCH**	school
Naturwissenschaft	**SCI**	science
Singular, Einzahl	**sg**	singular
etwas	**sth**	something
Konjunktiv	**sub**	subjunctive
Subjekt	**subj**	(grammatical) subject
Superlativ	**superl**	superlative
Technik	**TECH**	technology
Nachrichtentechnik	**TEL**	telecommunications
Theater	**THEAT**	theatre
Fernsehen	**TV**	television
Typografie	**TYP**	printing
umgangssprachlich (! vulgär)	**umg(!)**	informal (! particularly offensive)
Hochschulwesen	**UNIV**	university
unpersönlich	**unpers**	impersonal
unregelmäßig	**unreg**	irregular
(nord)amerikanisch	**US**	(North) America
gewöhnlich	**usu**	usually
Verb	**vb**	verb
intransitives Verb	**vi**	intransitive verb
reflexives Verb	**vr**	reflexive verb
transitives Verb	**vt**	transitive verb
Zoologie	**ZOOL**	zoology
zusammengesetztes Wort	**zW**	compound
zwischen zwei Sprechern	**—**	change of speaker
ungefähre Entsprechung	**≈**	cultural equivalent
eingetragenes Warenzeichen	**®**	registered trademark

Warenzeichen

Note on trademarks

Wörter, die unseres Wissens eingetragene Warenzeichen darstellen, sind als solche gekennzeichnet. Es ist jedoch zu beachten, dass weder das Vorhandensein noch das Fehlen derartiger Kennzeichnungen die Rechtslage hinsichtlich eingetragener Warenzeichen berührt.

Words which we have reason to believe constitute trademarks have been designated as such. However, neither the presence nor the absence of such designation should be regarded as affecting the legal status of any trademark.

REGULAR GERMAN NOUN ENDINGS

nom		gen	pl
-ant	*m*	-anten	-anten
-anz	*f*	-anz	-anzen
-ar	*m*	-ar(e)s	-are
-chen	*nt*	-chens	-chen
-e	*f*	-	-n
-ei	*f*	-ei	-eien
-elle	*f*	-elle	-ellen
-ent	*m*	-enten	-enten
-enz	*f*	-enz	-enzen
-ette	*f*	-ette	-etten
-eur	*m*	-eurs	-eure
-euse	*f*	-euse	-eusen
-heit	*f*	-heit	-heiten
-ie	*f*	-ie	-ien
-ik	*f*	-ik	-iken
-in	*f*	-in	-innen
-ine	*f*	-ine	-inen
-ion	*f*	-ion	-ionen
-ist	*m*	-isten	-isten
-ium	*nt*	-iums	-ien
-ius	*m*	-ius	-iusse
-ive	*f*	-ive	-iven
-keit	*f*	-keit	-keiten
-lein	*nt*	-leins	-lein
-ling	*m*	-lings	-linge
-ment	*nt*	-ments	-mente
-mus	*m*	-mus	-men
-schaft	*f*	-schaft	-schaften
-tät	*f*	-tät	-täten
-tor	*m*	-tors	-toren
-ung	*f*	-ung	-ungen
-ur	*f*	-ur	-uren

PHONETIC SYMBOLS / LAUTSCHRIFT

[:] *length mark/Längezeichen* ['] *stress mark/Betonung*
[|] *glottal stop/Knacklaut*

all vowel sounds are approximate only
alle Vokallaute sind nur ungefähre Entsprechungen

bet	[b]	**B**all		[e] Metall
dim	[d]	**d**ann		[eː] geben
face	[f]	**F**ass	set	[ɛ] hässlich
go	[g]	**G**ast		[ɛː] Cousin
hit	[h]	**H**err	pity	[ɪ] Bischof
you	[j]	**j**a		[i] vital
cat	[k]	**k**alt	green	[iː] viel
lick	[l]	**L**ast	rot	[ɔ] Post
must	[m]	**M**ast	board	[ɔː]
nut	[n]	**N**uss		[o] Moral
bang	[ŋ]	la**ng**		[oː] oben
pepper	[p]	**P**akt		[õ] Champignon
red	[r]	**R**egen		[ø] ökonomisch
sit	[s]	**R**asse		[œ] gönnen
shame	[ʃ]	**Sch**al	full	[u] kulant
tell	[t]	**T**al	root	[uː] Hut
chat	[tʃ]	**tsch**üs	come	[ʌ]
vine	[v]	**w**as		[ʊ] Pult
wine	[w]			[y] physisch
loch	[x]	**B**a**ch**		[yː] für
	[ç]	i**ch**		[ʏ] Müll
zero	[z]	**H**ase	above	[ə] bitte
leisure	[ʒ]	**G**enie	girl	[əː]
join	[dʒ]			
thin	[θ]		lie	[aɪ] weit
this	[ð]		now	[au]
	[a]	**H**ast		[aʊ] Haut
hat	[æ]		day	[eɪ]
	[ɑː]	**B**a**h**n	fair	[ɛə]
farm	[ɑː]		beer	[ɪə]
	[ã]	**E**nsemble	toy	[ɔɪ]
fiancé	[ã:]			[ɔY] Heu
			pure	[uə]

[ʳ] r can be pronounced before a vowel; Bindungs-R

ZAHLEN

NUMBERS

ein(s)	1	one
zwei	2	two
drei	3	three
vier	4	four
fünf	5	five
sechs	6	six
sieben	7	seven
acht	8	eight
neun	9	nine
zehn	10	ten
elf	11	eleven
zwölf	12	twelve
dreizehn	13	thirteen
vierzehn	14	fourteen
fünfzehn	15	fifteen
sechzehn	16	sixteen
siebzehn	17	seventeen
achtzehn	18	eighteen
neunzehn	19	nineteen
zwanzig	20	twenty
einundzwanzig	21	twenty-one
zweiundzwanzig	22	twenty-two
dreißig	30	thirty
vierzig	40	forty
fünfzig	50	fifty
sechzig	60	sixty
siebzig	70	seventy
achtzig	80	eighty
neunzig	90	ninety
hundert	100	a hundred
hunderteins	101	a hundred and one
zweihundert	200	two hundred
zweihunderteins	201	two hundred and one
dreihundert	300	three hundred
dreihunderteins	301	three hundred and one
tausend	1000	a thousand
tausend(und)eins	1001	a thousand and one
fünftausend	5000	five thousand
eine Million	1000000	a million

erste(r, s)	1.	first	1st
zweite(r, s)	2.	second	2nd
dritte(r, s)	3.	third	3rd
vierte(r, s)	4.	fourth	4th
fünfte(r, s)	5.	fifth	5th
sechste(r, s)	6.	sixth	6th

siebte(r, s)	7.	seventh	7th
achte(r, s)	8.	eighth	8th
neunte(r, s)	9.	ninth	9th
zehnte(r, s)	10.	tenth	10th
elfte(r, s)	11.	eleventh	11th
zwölfte(r, s)	12.	twelfth	12th
dreizehnte(r, s)	13.	thirteenth	13th
vierzehnte(r, s)	14.	fourteenth	14th
fünfzehnte(r, s)	15.	fifteenth	15th
sechzehnte(r, s)	16.	sixteenth	16th
siebzehnte(r, s)	17.	seventeenth	17th
achtzehnte(r, s)	18.	eighteenth	18th
neunzehnte(r, s)	19.	nineteenth	19th
zwanzigste(r, s)	20.	twentieth	20th
einundzwanzigste(r, s)	21.	twenty-first	21st
dreißigste(r, s)	30.	thirtieth	30th
hundertste(r, s)	100.	hundredth	100th
hunderterste(r, s)	101.	hundred-and-first	101st
tausendste(r, s)	1000.	thousandth	1000th

Brüche usw.

Fractions etc.

ein Halb	$\frac{1}{2}$	a half	
ein Drittel	$\frac{1}{3}$	a third	
ein Viertel	$\frac{1}{4}$	a quarter	
ein Fünftel	$\frac{1}{5}$	a fifth	
null Komma fünf	0,5	(nought) point five	0.5
drei Komma vier	3,4	three point four	3.4
sechs Komma acht neun	6,89	six point eight nine	6.89
zehn Prozent	10%	ten per cent	
hundert Prozent	100%	a hundred per cent	

Beispiele

Examples

er wohnt in Nummer 10		he lives at number 10
es steht in Kapitel 7		it's in chapter 7
auf Seite 7		on page 7
er wohnt im 7. Stock		he lives on the 7th floor
er wurde 7.		he came in 7th
Maßstab eins zu zwanzigtausend		scale one to twenty thousand

UHRZEIT

THE TIME

wie viel Uhr ist es?, wie spät ist es?	*what time is it?*
es ist ...	*it's ...*
Mitternacht, zwölf Uhr nachts	midnight, twelve p.m.
ein Uhr (morgens *or* früh)	one o'clock (in the morning), one (a.m.)
fünf nach eins, ein Uhr fünf	five past one
zehn nach eins, ein Uhr zehn	ten past one
Viertel nach eins, ein Uhr fünfzehn	a quarter past one, one fifteen
fünf vor halb zwei, ein Uhr fünfundzwanzig	twenty-five past one, one twenty-five
halb zwei, ein Uhr dreißig	half past one, one thirty
fünf nach halb zwei, ein Uhr fünfunddreißig	twenty-five to two, one thirty-five
zwanzig vor zwei, ein Uhr vierzig	twenty to two, one forty
Viertel vor zwei, ein Uhr fünfundvierzig	a quarter to two, one forty-five
zehn vor zwei, ein Uhr fünfzig	ten to two, one fifty
zwölf Uhr (mittags), Mittag	twelve o'clock, midday, noon
halb eins (mittags *or* nachmittags), zwölf Uhr dreißig	half past twelve, twelve thirty (p.m.)
zwei Uhr (nachmittags)	two o'clock (in the afternoon), two (p.m.)
halb acht (abends)	half past seven (in the evening), seven thirty (p.m.)
um wie viel Uhr?	*at what time?*
um Mitternacht	at midnight
um sieben Uhr	at seven o'clock
in zwanzig Minuten	in twenty minutes
vor fünfzehn Minuten	fifteen minutes ago

DEUTSCH – ENGLISCH
GERMAN – ENGLISH

A, a

Aal [aːl] (-(e)s, -e) *m* eel
Aas [aːs] (-es, -e *od* Äser) *nt* carrion

SCHLÜSSELWORT

---

ab [ap] *präp +dat* from; **Kinder ab 12 Jahren** children from the age of 12; **ab morgen** from tomorrow; **ab sofort** as of now
♦ *adv* **1** off; **links ab** to the left; **der Knopf ist ab** the button has come off; **ab nach Hause!** off you go home
2 (*zeitlich*): **von da ab** from then on; **von heute ab** from today, as of today
3 (*auf Fahrplänen*): **München ab 12.20** leaving Munich 12.20
4: **ab und zu** *od* **an** now and then *od* again

Abänderung [ˈapˌɛndərʊŋ] *f* alteration
Abbau [ˈapbau] (-(e)s) *m* (+*gen*) dismantling; (*Verminderung*) reduction (in); (*Verfall*) decline (in); (*MIN*) mining; quarrying; (*CHEM*) decomposition; **a~en** *vt* to dismantle; (*MIN*) to mine; to quarry; (*verringern*) to reduce; (*CHEM*) to break down
abbeißen [ˈapbaɪsən] (*unreg*) *vt* to bite off
abbekommen [ˈapbəkɔmən] (*unreg*) *vt* (*Deckel, Schraube, Band*) to loosen; **etwas ~** (*beschädigt werden*) to get damaged; (: *Person*) to get injured
abbestellen [ˈapbəʃtɛlən] *vt* to cancel
abbezahlen [ˈapbətsaːlən] *vt* to pay off
abbiegen [ˈapbiːgən] (*unreg*) *vi* to turn off; (*Straße*) to bend ♦ *vt* to bend; (*verhindern*) to ward off
abbilden [ˈapbɪldən] *vt* to portray; **Abbildung** *f* illustration
abblenden [ˈapblɛndən] *vt, vi* (*AUT*) to dip (*BRIT*), to dim (*US*)
Abblendlicht [ˈapblɛntlɪçt] *nt* dipped (*BRIT*) *od* dimmed (*US*) headlights *pl*

abbrechen [ˈapbrɛçən] (*unreg*) *vt, vi* to break off; (*Gebäude*) to pull down; (*Zelt*) to take down; (*aufhören*) to stop; (*COMPUT*) to abort
abbrennen [ˈapbrɛnən] (*unreg*) *vt* to burn off; (*Feuerwerk*) to let off ♦ *vi* (*aux sein*) to burn down
abbringen [ˈapbrɪŋən] (*unreg*) *vt*: **jdn von etw ~** to dissuade sb from sth; **jdn vom Weg ~** to divert sb
abbröckeln [ˈapbrœkəln] *vt, vi* to crumble off *od* away
Abbruch [ˈapbrʊx] *m* (*von Verhandlungen etc*) breaking off; (*von Haus*) demolition; **jdm/ etw ~ tun** to harm sb/sth; **a~reif** *adj* only fit for demolition
abbrühen [ˈapbryːən] *vt* to scald; **abgebrüht** (*umg*) hard-boiled
abbuchen [ˈapbuːxən] *vt* to debit
abdanken [ˈapdaŋkən] *vi* to resign; (*König*) to abdicate; **Abdankung** *f* resignation; abdication
abdecken [ˈapdɛkən] *vt* (*Loch*) to cover; (*Tisch*) to clear; (*Plane*) to uncover
abdichten [ˈapdɪçtən] *vt* to seal; (*NAUT*) to caulk
abdrehen [ˈapdreːən] *vt* (*Gas*) to turn off; (*Licht*) to switch off; (*Film*) to shoot ♦ *vi* (*Schiff*) to change course
Abdruck [ˈapdrʊk] *m* (*Nachdrucken*) reprinting; (*Gedrucktes*) reprint; (*Gipsabdruck, Wachsabdruck*) impression; (*Fingerabdruck*) print; **a~en** *vt* to print, to publish
abdrücken [ˈapdrʏkən] *vt* (*Waffe*) to fire; (*Person*) to hug, to squeeze
Abend [ˈaːbənt] (-s, -e) *m* evening; **guten ~** good evening; **zu ~ essen** to have dinner *od* supper; **heute ~** this evening; **~brot** *nt* supper; **~essen** *nt* supper; **~garderobe** *f*

evening dress; **~kasse** *f* box office; **~kleid** *nt* evening dress; **~kurs** *m* evening classes *pl*; **~land** *nt* (*Europa*) West; **a~lich** *adj* evening; **~mahl** *nt* Holy Communion; **~rot** *nt* sunset; **a~s** *adv* in the evening

Abenteuer [ˈaːbəntɔʏər] (**-s, -**) *nt* adventure; **a~lich** *adj* adventurous; **~urlaub** *m* adventure holiday

Abenteurer (**-s, -**) *m* adventurer; **~in** *f* adventuress

aber [ˈaːbər] *konj* but; (*jedoch*) however ♦ *adv*: **das ist ~ schön** that's really nice; **nun ist ~ Schluss!** now that's enough!; **vielen Dank – ~ bitte!** thanks a lot – you're welcome; **A~glaube** *m* superstition; **~gläubisch** *adj* superstitious

aberkennen [ˈapʔɛrkɛnən] (*unreg*) *vt* (*JUR*): **jdm etw ~** to deprive sb of sth, to take sth (away) from sb

abermals [ˈaːbəmaːls] *adv* once again

Abertausend, abertausend [ˈaːbətauzənt] *indef pron* **tausend** *od* **Tausend und ~** thousands upon thousands

Abf. *abk* (= *Abfahrt*) dep.

abfahren [ˈapfaːrən] (*unreg*) *vi* to leave, to depart ♦ *vt* to take *od* cart away; (*Strecke*) to drive; (*Reifen*) to wear; (*Fahrkarte*) to use

Abfahrt [ˈapfaːrt] *f* departure; (*SKI*) descent; (*Piste*) run; **~zeit** *f* departure time

Abfall [ˈapfal] *m* waste; (*von Speisen etc*) rubbish (*BRIT*), garbage (*US*); (*Neigung*) slope; (*Verschlechterung*) decline; **~eimer** *m* rubbish bin (*BRIT*), garbage can (*US*); **a~en** (*unreg*) *vi* (*auch fig*) to fall *od* drop off; (*sich neigen*) to fall *od* drop away

abfällig [ˈapfɛlɪç] *adj* disparaging, deprecatory

abfangen [ˈapfaŋən] (*unreg*) *vt* to intercept; (*Person*) to catch; (*unter Kontrolle bringen*) to check

abfärben [ˈapfɛrbən] *vi* to lose its colour; (*Wäsche*) to run; (*fig*) to rub off

abfassen [ˈapfasən] *vt* to write, to draft

abfertigen [ˈapfɛrtɪɡən] *vt* to prepare for dispatch, to process; (*an der Grenze*) to clear; (*Kundschaft*) to attend to

Abfertigungsschalter *m* (*Flughafen*) check-in desk

abfeuern [ˈapfɔʏərn] *vt* to fire

abfinden [ˈapfɪndən] (*unreg*) *vt* to pay off ♦ *vr* to come to terms; **sich mit jdm ~/ nicht ~** to put up with/not get on with sb

Abfindung *f* (*von Gläubigern*) payment; (*Geld*) sum in settlement

abflauen [ˈapflauən] *vi* (*Wind, Erregung*) to die away, to subside; (*Nachfrage, Geschäft*) to fall *od* drop off

abfliegen [ˈapfliːɡən] (*unreg*) *vi* (*Flugzeug*) to take off; (*Passagier auch*) to fly ♦ *vt* (*Gebiet*) to fly over

abfließen [ˈapfliːsən] (*unreg*) *vi* to drain away

Abflug [ˈapfluːk] *m* departure; (*Start*) take-off; **~halle** *f* departure lounge; **~zeit** *f* departure time

Abfluss ▲ [ˈapflʊs] *m* draining away; (*Öffnung*) outlet; **~rohr** *nt* drain pipe; (*von sanitären Anlagen auch*) waste pipe

abfragen [ˈapfraːɡən] *vt* (*bes SCH*) to test orally (on)

Abfuhr [ˈapfuːr] (**-, -en**) *f* removal; (*fig*) snub, rebuff

abführen [ˈapfyːrən] *vt* to lead away; (*Gelder, Steuern*) to pay ♦ *vi* (*MED*) to have a laxative effect

Abführmittel [ˈapfyːrmɪtəl] *nt* laxative, purgative

abfüllen [ˈapfʏlən] *vt* to draw off; (*in Flaschen*) to bottle

Abgabe [ˈapɡaːbə] *f* handing in; (*von Ball*) pass; (*Steuer*) tax; (*eines Amtes*) giving up; (*einer Erklärung*) giving

Abgang [ˈapɡaŋ] *m* (*von Schule*) leaving; (*THEAT*) exit; (*Abfahrt*) departure; (*der Post, von Waren*) dispatch

Abgas [ˈapɡaːs] *nt* waste gas; (*AUT*) exhaust

abgeben [ˈapɡeːbən] (*unreg*) *vt* (*Gegenstand*) to hand *od* give in; (*Ball*) to pass; (*Wärme*) to give off; (*Amt*) to hand over; (*Schuss*) to fire; (*Erklärung, Urteil*) to give; (*darstellen, sein*) to make ♦ *vr*: **sich mit jdm/etw ~** to associate with sb/bother with sth; **jdm etw ~** (*überlassen*) to let sb have sth

abgebrüht [ˈapɡəbryːt] (*umg*) *adj* (*skrupellos*)

hard-boiled

abgehen ['apge:ən] (*unreg*) *vi* to go away, to leave; (*THEAT*) to exit; (*Knopf etc*) to come off; (*Straße*) to branch off ♦ *vt* (*Strecke*) to go *od* walk along; **etw geht jdm ab** (*fehlt*) sb lacks sth

abgelegen ['apgəle:gən] *adj* remote

abgemacht ['apgəmaxt] *adj* fixed; **~!** done!

abgeneigt ['apgənaıkt] *adj* disinclined

abgenutzt ['apgənʊtst] *adj* worn

Abgeordnete(r) ['apgə|ɔrdnətə(r)] *f(m)* member of parliament; elected representative

abgeschlossen ['apgəʃlɔsən] *adj attrib* (*Wohnung*) self-contained

abgeschmackt ['apgəʃmakt] *adj* tasteless

abgesehen ['apgəze:ən] *adj*: **es auf jdn/ etw ~ haben** to be after sb/sth; **~ von ...** apart from ...

abgespannt ['apgəʃpant] *adj* tired out

abgestanden ['apgəʃtandən] *adj* stale; (*Bier auch*) flat

abgestorben ['apgəʃtɔrbən] *adj* numb; (*BIOL, MED*) dead

abgetragen ['apgətra:gən] *adj* shabby, worn out

abgewinnen ['apgəvınən] (*unreg*) *vt*: **einer Sache etw/Geschmack ~** to get sth/ pleasure from sth

abgewöhnen ['apgəvø:nən] *vt*: **jdm/sich etw ~** to cure sb of sth/give sth up

abgrenzen ['apgrɛntsən] *vt* (*auch fig*) to mark off; to fence off

Abgrund ['apgrʊnt] *m* (*auch fig*) abyss

abhacken ['aphakən] *vt* to chop off

abhaken ['apha:kən] *vt* (*auf Papier*) to tick off

abhalten ['aphaltən] (*unreg*) *vt* (*Versammlung*) to hold; **jdn von etw ~** (*fern halten*) to keep sb away from sth; (*hindern*) to keep sb from sth

abhanden [ap'handən] *adj*: **~ kommen** to get lost

Abhandlung ['aphandlʊŋ] *f* treatise, discourse

Abhang ['aphaŋ] *m* slope

abhängen ['aphɛŋən] *vt* (*Bild*) to take down; (*Anhänger*) to uncouple; (*Verfolger*) to shake off ♦ *vi* (*unreg: Fleisch*) to hang; **von jdm/ etw ~** to depend on sb/sth

abhängig ['aphɛŋıç] *adj*: **~ (von)** dependent (on); **A~keit** *f*: **A~keit (von)** dependence (on)

abhärten ['aphɛrtən] *vt, vr* to toughen (o.s.) up; **sich gegen etw ~** to inure o.s. to sth

abhauen ['aphauən] (*unreg*) *vt* to cut off; (*Baum*) to cut down ♦ *vi* (*umg*) to clear off *od* out

abheben ['aphe:bən] (*unreg*) *vt* to lift (up); (*Karten*) to cut; (*Geld*) to withdraw, to take out ♦ *vi* (*Flugzeug*) to take off; (*Rakete*) to lift off ♦ *vr* to stand out

abheften ['apheftən] *vt* (*Rechnungen etc*) to file away

abhetzen ['aphetsən] *vr* to wear *od* tire o.s. out

Abhilfe ['aphılfə] *f* remedy; **~ schaffen** to put things right

abholen ['apho:lən] *vt* (*Gegenstand*) to fetch, to collect; (*Person*) to call for; (*am Bahnhof etc*) to pick up, to meet

abholzen ['aphɔltsən] *vt* (*Wald*) to clear

abhorchen ['aphɔrçən] *vt* (*MED*) to listen to a patient's chest

abhören ['aphø:rən] *vt* (*Vokabeln*) to test; (*Telefongespräch*) to tap; (*Tonband etc*) to listen to

Abhörgerät *nt* bug

Abitur [abi'tu:r] (**-s, -e**) *nt* German school-leaving examination; **~i'ent(in)** *m(f)* candidate for school-leaving certificate

Abitur

ℹ️ The **Abitur** is the German school-leaving examination taken in four subjects by pupils at a **Gymnasium** at the age of 18 or 19. It is necessary for entry to university.

Abk. *abk* (= *Abkürzung*) abbr.

abkapseln ['apkapsəln] *vr* to shut *od* cut o.s. off

abkaufen ['apkaufən] *vt*: **jdm etw ~** (*auch fig*) to buy sth from sb

abkehren ['apke:rən] *vt (Blick)* to avert, to turn away ♦ *vr* to turn away

abklingen ['apklıŋən] *(unreg) vi* to die away; *(Radio)* to fade out

abknöpfen ['apknœpfən] *vt* to unbutton; **jdm etw ~** *(umg)* to get sth off sb

abkochen ['apkɔxən] *vt* to boil

abkommen ['apkɔmən] *(unreg) vi* to get away; **von der Straße/von einem Plan ~** to leave the road/give up a plan; **A~ (-s, -)** *nt* agreement

abkömmlich ['apkœmlıç] *adj* available, free

abkratzen ['apkratsən] *vt* to scrape off ♦ *vi (umg)* to kick the bucket

abkühlen ['apky:lən] *vt* to cool down ♦ *vr (Mensch)* to cool down *od* off; *(Wetter)* to get cool; *(Zuneigung)* to cool

abkürzen ['apkʏrtsən] *vt* to shorten; *(Wort auch)* to abbreviate; **den Weg ~** to take a short cut

Abkürzung *f (Wort)* abbreviation; *(Weg)* short cut

abladen ['apla:dən] *(unreg) vt* to unload

Ablage ['apla:gə] *f (für Akten)* tray; *(für Kleider)* cloakroom

ablassen ['aplasən] *(unreg) vt (Wasser, Dampf)* to let off; *(vom Preis)* to knock off ♦ *vi:* **von etw ~** to give sth up, to abandon sth

Ablauf ['aplaʊf] *m (Abfluss)* drain; *(von Ereignissen)* course; *(einer Frist, Zeit)* expiry *(BRIT)*, expiration *(US)*; **a~en** *(unreg) vi (abfließen)* to drain away; *(Ereignisse)* to happen; *(Frist, Zeit, Pass)* to expire ♦ *vt (Sohlen)* to wear (down *od* out)

ablegen ['aple:gən] *vt* to put *od* lay down; *(Kleider)* to take off; *(Gewohnheit)* to get rid of; *(Prüfung)* to take, to sit; *(Zeugnis)* to give

Ableger (-s, -) *m* layer; *(fig)* branch, offshoot

ablehnen ['aple:nən] *vt* to reject; *(Einladung)* to decline, to refuse ♦ *vi* to decline, to refuse

ablehnend *adj (Haltung, Antwort)* negative; *(Geste)* disapproving; **ein ~er Bescheid** a rejection

Ablehnung *f* rejection; refusal

ableiten ['aplaɪtən] *vt (Wasser)* to divert; *(deduzieren)* to deduce; *(Wort)* to derive; **Ableitung** *f* diversion; deduction; derivation; *(Wort)* derivative

ablenken ['aplɛŋkən] *vt* to turn away, to deflect; *(zerstreuen)* to distract ♦ *vi* to change the subject; **Ablenkung** *f* distraction

ablesen ['aple:zən] *(unreg) vt* to read out; *(Messgeräte)* to read

ablichten ['aplıçtən] *vt* to photocopy

abliefern ['apli:fərn] *vt* to deliver; **etw bei jdm ~** to hand sth over to sb

Ablieferung *f* delivery

ablösen ['aplø:zən] *vt (abtrennen)* to take off, to remove; *(in Amt)* to take over from; *(Wache)* to relieve

Ablösung *f* removal; relieving

abmachen ['apmaxən] *vt* to take off; *(vereinbaren)* to agree; **Abmachung** *f* agreement

abmagern ['apma:gərn] *vi* to get thinner

Abmagerungskur *f* diet; **eine ~ machen** to go on a diet

abmarschieren ['apmarʃi:rən] *vi* to march off

abmelden ['apmɛldən] *vt (Zeitungen)* to cancel; *(Auto)* to take off the road ♦ *vr* to give notice of one's departure; *(im Hotel)* to check out; **jdn bei der Polizei ~** to register sb's departure with the police

abmessen ['apmɛsən] *(unreg) vt* to measure; **Abmessung** *f* measurement

abmontieren ['apmɔntiːrən] *vt* to take off

abmühen ['apmy:ən] *vr* to wear o.s. out

Abnahme ['apna:mə] *f (+gen)* removal; *(COMM)* buying; *(Verringerung)* decrease (in)

abnehmen ['apne:mən] *(unreg) vt* to take off, to remove; *(Führerschein)* to take away; *(Prüfung)* to hold; *(Maschen)* to decrease ♦ *vi* to decrease; *(schlanker werden)* to lose weight; **(jdm) etw ~** *(Geld)* to get sth (out of sb); *(kaufen, umg: glauben)* to buy sth (from sb); **jdm Arbeit ~** to take work off sb's shoulders

Abnehmer (-s, -) *m* purchaser, customer

Abneigung ['apnaɪgʊŋ] *f* aversion, dislike

abnorm [ap'nɔrm] *adj* abnormal

abnutzen ['apnʊtsən] *vt* to wear out; **Abnutzung** *f* wear (and tear)

Abo ['abo] (*umg*) *nt abk* = **Abonnement**

Abonnement [abɔn(ə)'mãː] (**-s, -s**) *nt* subscription; **Abonnent(in)** [abɔ'nɛnt(ɪn)] *m(f)* subscriber; **abonnieren** *vt* to subscribe to

Abordnung ['apʔɔrdnʊŋ] *f* delegation

abpacken ['appakən] *vt* to pack

abpassen ['appasən] *vt* (*Person, Gelegenheit*) to wait for

Abpfiff ['appfɪf] *m* final whistle

abplagen ['appla:gən] *vr* to wear o.s. out

abprallen ['appralən] *vi* to bounce off; to ricochet

abraten ['apra:tən] (*unreg*) *vi*: **jdm von etw ~** to advise *or* warn sb against sth

abräumen ['aprɔʏmən] *vt* to clear up *od* away

abreagieren ['apreagi:rən] *vt*: **seinen Zorn (an jdm/etw) ~** to work one's anger off (on sb/sth) ♦ *vr* to calm down

abrechnen ['aprɛçnən] *vt* to deduct, to take off ♦ *vi* to settle up; (*fig*) to get even

Abrechnung *f* settlement; (*Rechnung*) bill

Abrede ['apre:də] *f*: **etw in ~ stellen** to deny *od* dispute sth

Abreise ['apraɪzə] *f* departure; **a~n** *vi* to leave, to set off

abreißen ['apraɪsən] (*unreg*) *vt* (*Haus*) to tear down; (*Blatt*) to tear off

abrichten ['aprɪçtən] *vt* to train

abriegeln ['apri:gəln] *vt* (*Straße, Gebiet*) to seal off

Abruf ['apru:f] *m*: **auf ~** on call; **a~en** (*unreg*) *vt* (*Mensch*) to call away; (*COMM: Ware*) to request delivery of

abrunden ['aprʊndən] *vt* to round off

abrupt [a'brʊpt] *adj* abrupt

abrüsten ['apryrstən] *vi* to disarm; **Abrüstung** *f* disarmament

abrutschen ['aprʊtʃən] *vi* to slip; (*AVIAT*) to sideslip

Abs. *abk* (= *Absender*) sender, from

Absage ['apza:gə] *f* refusal; **a~n** *vt* to cancel, to call off; (*Einladung*) to turn down

♦ *vi* to cry off; (*ablehnen*) to decline

absahnen ['apza:nən] *vt* to skim ♦ *vi* (*fig*) to rake in

Absatz ['apzats] *m* (*COMM*) sales *pl*; (*Bodensatz*) deposit; (*neuer Abschnitt*) paragraph; (*Treppenabsatz*) landing; (*Schuhabsatz*) heel; **~gebiet** *nt* (*COMM*) market

abschaffen ['apʃafən] *vt* to abolish, to do away with; **Abschaffung** *f* abolition

abschalten ['apʃaltən] *vt, vi* (*auch umg*) to switch off

abschätzen ['apʃɛtsən] *vt* to estimate; (*Lage*) to assess; (*Person*) to size up

abschätzig ['apʃɛtsɪç] *adj* disparaging, derogatory

Abschaum ['apʃaʊm] (**-(e)s**) *m* scum

Abscheu ['apʃɔʏ] (**-(e)s**) *m* loathing, repugnance; **~ erregend** repulsive, loathsome; **a~lich** [ap'ʃɔʏlɪç] *adj* abominable

abschicken ['apʃɪkən] *vt* to send off

abschieben ['apʃi:bən] (*unreg*) *vt* to push away; (*Person*) to pack off; (: *POL*) to deport

Abschied ['apʃi:t] (**-(e)s, -e**) *m* parting; (*von Armee*) discharge; (**von jdm**) **~ nehmen** to say goodbye (to sb), to take one's leave (of sb); **seinen ~ nehmen** (*MIL*) to apply for discharge; **~sbrief** *m* farewell letter; **~sfeier** *f* farewell party

abschießen ['apʃi:sən] (*unreg*) *vt* (*Flugzeug*) to shoot down; (*Geschoss*) to fire

abschirmen ['apʃɪrmən] *vt* to screen

abschlagen ['apʃla:gən] (*unreg*) *vt* (*abhacken, COMM*) to knock off; (*ablehnen*) to refuse; (*MIL*) to repel

abschlägig ['apʃlɛːgɪç] *adj* negative

Abschlagszahlung *f* interim payment

Abschlepp- ['apʃlɛp] *zW*: **~dienst** *m* (*AUT*) breakdown service (*BRIT*), towing company (*US*); **a~en** *vt* (to take in) tow; **~seil** *nt* towrope

abschließen ['apʃli:sən] (*unreg*) *vt* (*Tür*) to lock; (*beenden*) to conclude, to finish; (*Vertrag, Handel*) to conclude ♦ *vr* (*sich isolieren*) to cut o.s. off; **~d** *adj* concluding

Abschluss ▲ ['apʃlʊs] *m* (*Beendigung*) close,

conclusion; (COMM: Bilanz) balancing; (von Vertrag, Handel) conclusion; **zum ~** in conclusion; **~feier** f (SCH) end of term party; **~prüfung** f final exam

abschneiden ['apʃnaɪdən] (unreg) vt to cut off ♦ vi to do, to come off

Abschnitt ['apʃnɪt] m section; (MIL) sector; (Kontrollabschnitt) counterfoil; (MATH) segment; (Zeitabschnitt) period

abschrauben ['apʃraubən] vt to unscrew

abschrecken ['apʃrɛkən] vt to deter, to put off; (mit kaltem Wasser) to plunge in cold water; **~d** adj deterrent; **~des Beispiel** warning

abschreiben ['apʃraɪbən] (unreg) vt to copy; (verloren geben) to write off; (COMM) to deduct

Abschrift ['apʃrɪft] f copy

Abschuss ▲ ['apʃus] m (eines Geschützes) firing; (Herunterschießen) shooting down; (Tötung) shooting

abschüssig ['apʃysɪç] adj steep

abschwächen ['apʃvɛçən] vt to lessen; (Behauptung, Kritik) to tone down ♦ vr to lessen

abschweifen ['apʃvaɪfən] vi to digress

abschwellen ['apʃvɛlən] (unreg) vi (Geschwulst) to go down; (Lärm) to die down

abschwören ['apʃvøːrən] vi (+dat) renounce

absehbar ['apzeːbaːr] adj foreseeable; **in ~er Zeit** in the foreseeable future; **das Ende ist ~** the end is in sight

absehen ['apzeːən] (unreg) vt (Ende, Folgen) to foresee ♦ vi: **von etw ~** to refrain from sth; (nicht berücksichtigen) to leave sth out of consideration

abseilen ['apzaɪlən] vr (Bergsteiger) to abseil (down)

abseits ['apzaɪts] adv out of the way ♦ präp +gen away from; **A~** nt (SPORT) offside

absenden ['apzɛndən] (unreg) vt to send off, to dispatch

Absender (-s, -) m sender

absetzen ['apzɛtsən] vt (niederstellen, aussteigen lassen) to put down; (abnehmen)

to take off; (COMM: verkaufen) to sell; (FIN: abziehen) to deduct; (entlassen) to dismiss; (König) to depose; (streichen) to drop; (hervorheben) to pick out ♦ vr (sich entfernen) to clear off; (sich ablagern) to be deposited

Absetzung f (FIN: Abzug) deduction; (Entlassung) dismissal; (von König) deposing

absichern ['apzɪçərn] vt to make safe; (schützen) to safeguard ♦ vr to protect o.s.

Absicht ['apzɪçt] f intention; **mit ~** on purpose; **a~lich** adj intentional, deliberate

absinken ['apzɪŋkən] (unreg) vi to sink; (Temperatur, Geschwindigkeit) to decrease

absitzen ['apzɪtsən] (unreg) vi to dismount ♦ vt (Strafe) to serve

absolut [apzoˈluːt] adj absolute; **A~ismus** m absolutism

absolvieren [apzɔlˈviːrən] vt (SCH) to complete

absonder- ['apzɔndər] zW: **~lich** adj odd, strange; **~n** vt to separate; (ausscheiden) to give off, to secrete ♦ vr to cut o.s. off; **A~ung** f separation; (MED) secretion

abspalten ['apʃpaltən] vt to split off

abspannen ['apʃpanən] vt (Pferde) to unhitch; (Wagen) to uncouple

abspeisen ['apʃpaɪzən] vt (fig) to fob off

abspenstig ['apʃpɛnstɪç] adj: **(jdm) ~ machen** to lure away (from sb)

absperren ['apʃpɛrən] vt to block od close off; (Tür) to lock; **Absperrung** f (Vorgang) blocking od closing off; (Sperre) barricade

abspielen ['apʃpiːlən] vt (Platte, Tonband) to play; (SPORT: Ball) to pass ♦ vr to happen

Absprache ['apʃpraːxə] f arrangement

absprechen ['apʃprɛçən] (unreg) vt (vereinbaren) to arrange; **jdm etw ~** to deny sb sth

abspringen ['apʃprɪŋən] (unreg) vi to jump down/off; (Farbe, Lack) to flake off; (AVIAT) to bale out; (sich distanzieren) to back out

Absprung ['apʃprʊŋ] m jump

abspülen ['apʃpyːlən] vt to rinse; (Geschirr) to wash up

abstammen ['apʃtamən] vi to be descended; (Wort) to be derived; **Abstammung** f descent; derivation

Abstand ['apʃtant] m distance; (zeitlich) interval; **davon ~ nehmen, etw zu tun** to refrain from doing sth; **mit ~ der Beste** by far the best

abstatten ['apʃtatən] vt (Dank) to give; (Besuch) to pay

abstauben ['apʃtaubən] vt, vi to dust; (umg: stehlen) to pinch; (: schnorren) to scrounge

Abstecher ['apʃtɛçər] **(-s, -)** m detour

abstehen ['apʃteːən] (unreg) vi (Ohren, Haare) to stick out; (entfernt sein) to stand away

absteigen ['apʃtaigən] (unreg) vi (vom Rad etc) to get off, to dismount; **(in die zweite Liga) ~** to be relegated (to the second division)

abstellen ['apʃtɛlən] vt (niederstellen) to put down; (entfernt stellen) to pull out; (hinstellen: Auto) to park; (ausschalten) to turn od switch off; (Missstand, Unsitte) to stop

Abstellraum m storage room

abstempeln ['apʃtɛmpəln] vt to stamp

absterben ['apʃtɛrbən] (unreg) vi to die; (Körperteil) to go numb

Abstieg ['apʃtiːk] **(-(e)s, -e)** m descent; (SPORT) relegation; (fig) decline

abstimmen ['apʃtimən] vi to vote ♦ vt: **~ (auf +akk)** (Instrument) to tune (to); (Interessen) to match (with); (Termine, Ziele) to fit in (with) ♦ vr to agree

Abstimmung f vote

Abstinenz [apsti'nɛnts] f abstinence; teetotalism; **~ler(in) (-s, -)** m(f) teetotaller

abstoßen ['apʃtoːsən] (unreg) vt to push off od away; (verkaufen) to unload; (anekeln) to repel, to repulse

abstrakt [ap'ʃtrakt] adj abstract ♦ adv abstractly, in the abstract

abstreiten ['apʃtraitən] (unreg) vt to deny

Abstrich ['apʃtriç] m (Abzug) cut; (MED) smear; **~e machen** to lower one's sights

abstufen ['apʃtuːfən] vt (Hang) to terrace; (Farben) to shade; (Gehälter) to grade

Absturz ['apʃturts] m fall; (AVIAT) crash

abstürzen ['apʃtyrtsən] vi to fall; (AVIAT) to crash

absuchen ['apzuːxən] vt to scour, to search

absurd [ap'zurt] adj absurd

Abszess ▲ [aps'tsɛs] **(-es, -e)** m abscess

Abt [apt] **(-(e)s, -e)** m abbot

Abt. abk (= Abteilung) dept.

abtasten ['aptastən] vt to feel, to probe

abtauen ['aptauən] vt, vi to thaw

Abtei [ap'tai] **(-, -en)** f abbey

Abteil [ap'tail] **(-(e)s, -e)** nt compartment; **'a~n** vt to divide up; (abtrennen) to divide off; **~ung** f (in Firma, Kaufhaus) department; (in Krankenhaus) section; (MIL) unit

abtippen ['aptipən] vt (Text) to type up

abtransportieren ['aptransportiːrən] vt to take away, to remove

abtreiben ['aptraibən] (unreg) vt (Boot, Flugzeug) to drive off course; (Kind) to abort ♦ vi to be driven off course; to abort

Abtreibung f abortion

abtrennen ['aptrɛnən] vt (lostrennen) to detach; (entfernen) to take off; (abteilen) to separate off

abtreten ['aptreːtən] (unreg) vt to wear out; (überlassen) to hand over, to cede ♦ vi to go off; (zurücktreten) to step down

Abtritt ['aptrit] m resignation

abtrocknen ['aptrɔknən] vt, vi to dry

abtun ['aptuːn] (unreg) vt (fig) to dismiss

abwägen ['apvɛːgən] (unreg) vt to weigh up

abwälzen ['apvɛltsən] vt (Schuld, Verantwortung): **~ (auf +akk)** to shift (onto)

abwandeln ['apvandəln] vt to adapt

abwandern ['apvandərn] vi to move away; (FIN) to be transferred

abwarten ['apvartən] vt to wait for ♦ vi to wait

abwärts ['apvɛrts] adv down

Abwasch ['apvaʃ] **(-(e)s)** m washing-up; **a~en** (unreg) vt (Schmutz) to wash off; (Geschirr) to wash (up)

Abwasser ['apvasər] **(-s, -wässer)** nt sewage

abwechseln ['apvɛksəln] vi, vr to alternate; (Personen) to take turns; **~d** adj alternate; **Abwechslung** f change; **abwechslungsreich** adj varied

abwegig ['apveːgiç] adj wrong

Abwehr ['apveːr] (-) f defence; (Schutz) protection; (~dienst) counterintelligence (service); **a~en** vt to ward off; (Ball) to stop

abweichen ['apvaiçən] (unreg) vi to deviate; (Meinung) to differ

abweisen ['apvaizən] (unreg) vt to turn away; (Antrag) to turn down; **~d** adj (Haltung) cold

abwenden ['apvɛndən] (unreg) vt to avert ♦ vr to turn away

abwerfen ['apvɛrfən] (unreg) vt to throw off; (Profit) to yield; (aus Flugzeug) to drop; (Spielkarte) to discard

abwerten ['apvɛrtən] vt (FIN) to devalue

abwertend adj (Worte, Sinn) pejorative

Abwertung f (von Währung) devaluation

abwesend ['apveːzənt] adj absent

Abwesenheit ['apveːzənhait] f absence

abwickeln ['apvikəln] vt to unwind; (Geschäft) to wind up

abwimmeln ['apvimlən] (umg) vt (Menschen) to get shot of

abwischen ['apviʃən] vt to wipe off od away; (putzen) to wipe

Abwurf ['apvurf] m throwing off; (von Bomben etc) dropping; (von Reiter, SPORT) throw

abwürgen ['apvYrgən] (umg) vt to scotch; (Motor) to stall

abzahlen ['aptsaːlən] vt to pay off

abzählen ['aptseːlən] vt, vi to count (up)

Abzahlung f repayment; **auf ~ kaufen** to buy on hire purchase

abzapfen ['aptsapfən] vt to draw off; **jdm Blut ~** to take blood from sb

abzäunen ['aptsɔynən] vt to fence off

Abzeichen ['aptsaiçən] nt badge; (Orden) decoration

abzeichnen ['aptsaiçnən] vt to draw, to copy; (Dokument) to initial ♦ vr to stand out; (fig: bevorstehen) to loom

abziehen ['aptsiːən] (unreg) vt to take off; (Tier) to skin; (Bett) to strip; (Truppen) to withdraw; (subtrahieren) to take away, to subtract; (kopieren) to run off ♦ vi to go away; (Truppen) to withdraw

abzielen ['aptsiːlən] vi: **~ auf** +akk to be

aimed at

Abzug ['aptsuːk] m departure; (von Truppen) withdrawal; (Kopie) copy; (Subtraktion) subtraction; (Betrag) deduction; (Rauchabzug) flue; (von Waffen) trigger

abzüglich ['aptsyːkliç] präp +gen less

abzweigen ['aptsvaigən] vi to branch off ♦ vt to set aside

Abzweigung f junction

ach [ax] excl oh; **~ ja!** (oh) yes; **~ so!** I see; **mit A~ und Krach** by the skin of one's teeth

Achse ['aksə] f axis; (AUT) axle

Achsel ['aksəl] (-, -n) f shoulder; **~höhle** f armpit

acht [axt] num eight; **~ Tage** a week; **A~¹** (-, -en) f eight; (beim Eislaufen etc) figure eight

Acht² (-, -en) f: **~ geben (auf** +akk**)** to pay attention (to); **sich in ~ nehmen (vor** +dat**)** to be careful (of), to watch out (for); **etw außer ~ lassen** to disregard sth; **a~bar** adj worthy

acht- zW: **~e(r, s)** adj eighth; **A~el** num eighth; **~en** vt to respect ♦ vi: **~en (auf** +akk**)** to pay attention (to); **~en, dass ...** to be careful that ...

ächten ['ɛçtən] vt to outlaw, to ban

Achterbahn ['axtar-] f roller coaster

acht- zW: **~fach** adj eightfold; **~geben** △ (unreg) vi siehe **Acht²**; **~hundert** num eight hundred; **~los** adj careless; **~mal** adv eight times; **~sam** adj attentive

Achtung ['axtʊŋ] f attention; (Ehrfurcht) respect ♦ excl look out!; (MIL) attention!; **alle ~!** good for you/him etc

achtzehn num eighteen

achtzig num eighty

ächzen ['ɛçtsən] vi to groan

Acker ['akər] (-s, ⁿ) m field; **a~n** vt, vi to plough; (umg) to slog away

ADAC [aːdeːˈaːtseː] abk (= Allgemeiner Deutscher Automobil-Club) ≃ AA, RAC

Adapter [aˈdaptər] (-s, -) m adapter

addieren [aˈdiːrən] vt to add (up); **Addition** [aditsiˈoːn] f addition

Adel ['aːdəl] (-s) m nobility; **a~ig** adj noble;

a~n vt to raise to the peerage
Ader ['a:dər] (-, -n) f vein
Adjektiv ['atjekti:f] (-s, -e) nt adjective
Adler ['a:dlər] (-s, -) m eagle
adlig adj noble
Adopt- zW: **a~ieren** [adɔp'ti:rən] vt to adopt; **~ion** [adɔptsi'o:n] f adoption; **~iveltern** pl adoptive parents; **~ivkind** nt adopted child
Adressbuch ▲ nt directory; (privat) address book
Adress- zW: **~e** [a'drɛsə] f address; **a~ieren** [adrɛ'si:rən] vt: **a~ieren (an** +akk) to address (to)
Adria ['a:dria] (-) f Adriatic
Advent [at'vɛnt] (-(e)s, -e) m Advent; **~skalender** m Advent calendar; **~skranz** m Advent wreath
Adverb [at'vɛrp] nt adverb
Aerobic [ae'ro:bik] nt aerobics sg
Affäre [a'fɛ:rə] f affair
Affe ['afə] (-n, -n) m monkey
Affekt [a'fɛkt] (-(e)s, -e) m: **im ~ handeln** to act in the heat of the moment; **a~iert** [afɛk'ti:rt] adj affected
Affen- zW: **a~artig** adj like a monkey; **mit a~artiger Geschwindigkeit** like a flash; **~hitze** (umg) f incredible heat
affig ['afɪç] adj affected
Afrika ['a:frika] (-s) nt Africa; **~ner(in)** [-'ka:nər(ɪn)] (-s, -) m(f) African; **a~nisch** adj African
AG [a:'ge:] abk (= Aktiengesellschaft) ≃ plc (BRIT), ≃ Inc. (US)
Agent [a'gɛnt] m agent; **~ur** f agency
Aggregat [agre'ga:t] (-(e)s, -e) nt aggregate; (TECH) unit
Aggress- zW: **~ion** [agresi'o:n] f aggression; **a~iv** [agrɛ'si:f] adj aggressive; **~ivität** [agresivi'tɛ:t] f aggressiveness
Agrarpolitik [a'gra:r-] f agricultural policy
Ägypten [ɛ'gyptən] (-s) nt Egypt; **ägyptisch** adj Egyptian
aha [a'ha:] excl aha
ähneln ['ɛ:nəln] vi +dat to be like, to resemble ♦ vr to be alike od similar
ahnen ['a:nən] vt to suspect; (Tod, Gefahr) to have a presentiment of
ähnlich ['ɛ:nlɪç] adj (+dat) similar (to); **Ä~keit** f similarity
Ahnung ['a:nʊŋ] f idea, suspicion; presentiment; **a~slos** adj unsuspecting
Ahorn ['a:hɔrn] (-s, -e) m maple
Ähre ['ɛ:rə] f ear
Aids [e:dz] nt AIDS sg
Airbag ['ɛ:əbɛk] (-s, -s) m airbag
Akademie [akade'mi:] f academy; **Aka'demiker(in)** (-s, -) m(f) university graduate; **akademisch** adj academic
akklimatisieren [aklimati'zi:rən] vr to become acclimatized
Akkord [a'kɔrt] (-(e)s, -e) m (MUS) chord; **im ~ arbeiten** to do piecework
Akkordeon [a'kɔrdeɔn] (-s, -s) nt accordion
Akku ['aku] (-s, -s) m rechargeable battery
Akkusativ ['akuzati:f] (-s, -e) m accusative
Akne ['aknə] f acne
Akrobat(in) [akro'ba:t(ɪn)] (-en, -en) m(f) acrobat
Akt [akt] (-(e)s, -e) m act; (KUNST) nude
Akte ['aktə] f file
Akten- zW: **~koffer** m attaché case; **a~kundig** adj on the files; **~schrank** m filing cabinet; **~tasche** f briefcase
Aktie ['aktsiə] f share
Aktien- zW: **~gesellschaft** f public limited company; **~index** (-(es), -e od -indices) m share index; **~kurs** m share price
Aktion [aktsi'o:n] f campaign; (Polizeiaktion, Suchaktion) action
Aktionär [aktsio'nɛ:r] (-s, -e) m shareholder
aktiv [ak'ti:f] adj active; (MIL) regular; **~ieren** [-'vi:rən] vt to activate; **A~ität** f activity
Aktualität [aktuali'tɛ:t] f topicality; (einer Mode) up-to-dateness
aktuell [aktu'ɛl] adj topical; up-to-date
Akupunktur [akupʊŋk'tu:ər] f acupuncture
Akustik [a'kʊstɪk] f acoustics pl
akut [a'ku:t] adj acute
Akzent [ak'tsɛnt] m accent; (Betonung) stress
akzeptabel [aktsɛp'ta:bl] adj acceptable
akzeptieren [aktsɛp'ti:rən] vt to accept
Alarm [a'larm] (-(e)s, -e) m alarm; **a~bereit** adj standing by; **~bereitschaft** f stand-by;

a~ieren [-'mi:rən] *vt* to alarm
Albanien [al'ba:niən] **(-s)** *nt* Albania
albanisch *adj* Albanian
albern ['albərn] *adj* silly
Albtraum ▲ ['alptraum] *m* nightmare
Album ['album] **(-s, Alben)** *nt* album
Alge ['algə] *f* algae
Algebra ['algebra] **(-)** *f* algebra
Algerier(in) [al'ge:ri:r(ın)] **(-s, -)** *m(f)* Algerian
algerisch *adj* Algerian
alias ['a:lias] *adv* alias
Alibi ['a:libi] **(-s, -s)** *nt* alibi
Alimente [ali'mɛntə] *pl* alimony *sg*
Alkohol ['alkohol] **(-s, -e)** *m* alcohol; a~frei
  adj non-alcoholic; ~iker(in)
  [alko'ho:likər(ın)] **(-s, -)** *m(f)* alcoholic;
  a~isch *adj* alcoholic; ~verbot *nt* ban on
  alcohol
All [al] **(-s)** *nt* universe
all'abendlich *adj* every evening
'allbekannt *adj* universally known

SCHLÜSSELWORT
---

alle(r, s) ['alə(r,s)] *adj* **1** (*sämtliche*) all; **wir
  alle** all of us; **alle Kinder waren da** all the
  children were there; **alle Kinder mögen ...**
  all children like ...; **alle beide** both of us/
  them; **sie kamen alle** they all came; **alles
  Gute** all the best; **alles in allem** all in all
  2 (*mit Zeit- oder Maßangaben*) every; **alle
  vier Jahre** every four years; **alle fünf
  Meter** every five metres
  ♦ *pron* everything; **alles was er sagt**
  everything he says, all that he says
  ♦ *adv* (*zu Ende, aufgebraucht*) finished; **die
  Milch ist alle** the milk's all gone, there's
  no milk left; **etw alle machen** to finish sth
  up

Allee [a'le:] *f* avenue
allein [a'laın] *adv* alone; (*ohne Hilfe*) on one's
  own, by oneself ♦ *konj* but, only; **nicht ~**
  (*nicht nur*) not only; **~ stehend** single;
  A~erziehende(r) *f(m)* single parent;
  A~gang *m*: **im A~gang** on one's own
allemal ['alə'ma:l] *adv* (*jedes Mal*) always;
  (*ohne weiteres*) with no bother; *siehe* **Mal**

allenfalls ['alən'fals] *adv* at all events;
  (*höchstens*) at most
aller- ['alər] *zW:* **~beste(r, s)** *adj* very best;
  ~dings *adv* (*zwar*) admittedly; (*gewiss*)
  certainly
Allergie [aler'gi:] *f* allergy; **al'lergisch** *adj*
  allergic
aller- *zW:* **~hand** (*umg*) *adj inv* all sorts of;
  das ist doch ~hand! that's a bit much;
  ~hand! (*lobend*) good show!; **A~'heiligen**
  nt All Saints' Day; **~höchstens** *adv* at the
  very most; **~lei** *adj inv* all sorts of;
  ~letzte(r, s) *adj* very last; **A~seelen** **(-s)**
  nt All Souls' Day; **~seits** *adv* on all sides;
  prost ~seits! cheers everyone!

Allerheiligen
---

i **Allerheiligen** (*All Saints' Day*) is
  celebrated on November 1st and is a
  public holiday in some parts of Germany
  and in Austria. **Allerseelen** (*All Souls'*
  Day) *is celebrated on November 2nd in the*
  Roman Catholic Church. It is customary to
  visit cemeteries and place lighted candles on
  the graves of relatives and friends.

Allerwelts- *in zW* (*Durchschnitts-*) common;
  (*nichts sagend*) commonplace
alles *pron* everything; **~ in allem** all in all; **~
  Gute!** all the best!
Alleskleber **(-s, -)** *m* multi-purpose glue
allgemein ['algəmaın] *adj* general; **im A~en**
  in general; **~ gültig** generally accepted;
  A~wissen *nt* general knowledge
Alliierte(r) [ali'i:rtə(r)] *m* ally
all- *zW:* **~jährlich** *adj* annual; **~mächtig**
  adj almighty; **~mählich** *adj* gradual;
  A~tag *m* everyday life; **~täglich** *adj, adv*
  daily; (*gewöhnlich*) commonplace; **~tags**
  adv on weekdays; **~'wissend** *adj*
  omniscient; **~zu** *adv* all too; **~ oft** all too
  often; **~ viel** too much
Allzweck- ['altsvɛk-] *in zW* multi-purpose
Alm [alm] **(-, -en)** *f* alpine pasture
Almosen ['almo:zən] **(-s, -)** *nt* alms *pl*
Alpen ['alpən] *pl* Alps; **~vorland** *nt* foothills
  pl of the Alps

an

Alphabet [alfaˈbeːt] (-(e)s, -e) nt alphabet;
a~isch adj alphabetical
Alptraum [ˈalptraum] = **Albtraum**

als [als] konj **1** (zeitlich) when; (gleichzeitig)
as; **damals, als ...** (in the days) when ...;
gerade, als ... just as ...
2 (in der Eigenschaft) than; **als Antwort** as
an answer; **als Kind** as a child
3 (bei Vergleichen) than; **ich kam später als
er** I came later than he (did) od later than
him; **lieber ... als ...** rather ... than ...;
nichts als Ärger nothing but trouble
4 : als ob/wenn as if

also [ˈalzo] konj so; (folglich) therefore; **~ gut**
od **schön!** okay then; **~, so was!** well
really!; **na ~!** there you are then!
Alsterwasser [ˈalstɐ-] nt shandy (BRIT),
beer and lemonade
Alt [alt] (-s, -e) m (MUS) alto
alt adj old; **alles beim A~en lassen** to leave
everything as it was
Altar [alˈtaːr] (-(e)s, -äre) m altar
Alt- zW: **~bau** m old building; **a~bekannt**
adj long-known; **~bier** nt top-fermented
German dark beer; **~eisen** nt scrap iron
Alten(wohn)heim nt old people's home
Alter [ˈaltɐ] (-s, -) nt age; (hohes) old age;
im ~ von at the age of; **a~n** vi to grow
old, to age
Alternativ- [alternaˈtiːf] in zW alternative;
~e f alternative
Alters- zW: **~grenze** f age limit; **~heim** nt
old people's home; **~rente** f old age
pension; **a~schwach** adj (Mensch) frail;
~versorgung f old age pension
Altertum [ˈaltɐtuːm] nt antiquity
alt- zW: **A~glas** nt glass for recycling;
A~glascontainer m bottle bank; **a~klug**
adj precocious; **~modisch** adj old-
fashioned; **A~papier** nt waste paper;
A~stadt f old town
Alufolie [ˈaluːfoːliə] f aluminium foil
Aluminium [aluˈmiːnium] (-s) nt aluminium,
aluminum (US)

Alzheimerkrankheit [ˈaltshaɪmɐˈkraŋkhaɪt]
f Alzheimer's (disease)
am [am] = **an dem**; **~ Schlafen** (umg)
sleeping; **~ 15. März** on March 15th; **~
besten/schönsten** best/most beautiful
Amateur [amaˈtøːr] m amateur
Amboss ▲ [ˈambɔs] (-es, -e) m anvil
ambulant [ambuˈlant] adj outpatient;
Ambulanz f outpatients sg
Ameise [ˈaːmaɪzə] f ant
Ameisenhaufen m ant hill
Amerika [aˈmeːrika] (-s) nt America;
~ner(in) [-ˈkaːnɐr(ɪn)] (-s, -) m(f) American;
a~nisch [-ˈkaːnɪʃ] adj American
Amnestie [amnɛsˈtiː] f amnesty
Ampel [ˈampəl] (-, -n) f traffic lights pl
amputieren [ampuˈtiːrən] vt to amputate
Amsel [ˈamzəl] (-, -n) f blackbird
Amt [amt] (-(e)s, ⁿer) nt office; (Pflicht) duty;
(TEL) exchange; **a~ieren** [amˈtiːrən] vi to
hold office; **a~lich** adj official
Amts- zW: **~richter** m district judge;
~stunden pl office hours; **~zeichen** nt
dialling tone; **~zeit** f period of office
amüsant [amyˈzant] adj amusing
amüsieren [amyˈziːrən] vt to amuse ♦ vr to
enjoy o.s.
Amüsierviertel nt nightclub district

an [an] präp +dat **1** (räumlich: wo?) at; (auf,
bei) on; (nahe bei) near; **an diesem Ort** at
this place; **an der Wand** on the wall; **zu
nahe an etw** too near to sth; **unten am
Fluss** down by the river; **Köln liegt am
Rhein** Cologne is on the Rhine
2 (zeitlich: wann?) on; **an diesem Tag** on
this day; **an Ostern** at Easter
3: arm an Fett low in fat; **an etw sterben**
to die of sth; **an (und für) sich** actually
♦ präp +akk **1** (räumlich: wohin?) to; **er ging
ans Fenster** he went (over) to the
window; **etw an die Wand hängen/
schreiben** to hang/write sth on the wall
2 (zeitlich: woran?): **an etw denken** to think
of sth
3 (gerichtet an) to; **ein Gruß/eine Frage**

an dich greetings/a question to you
♦ *adv* **1** (*ungefähr*) about; **an die hundert** about a hundred
2 (*auf Fahrplänen*): **Frankfurt an 18.30** arriving Frankfurt 18.30
3 (*ab*): **von dort/heute an** from there/today onwards
4 (*angeschaltet, angezogen*) on; **das Licht ist an** the light is on; **ohne etwas an** with nothing on; *siehe auch* **am**

analog [ana'lo:k] *adj* analogous; **A~ie** [-'gi:] *f* analogy
Analphabet(in) [an|alfa'be:t(ɪn)] (**-en, -en**) *m(f)* illiterate (person)
Analyse [ana'ly:zə] *f* analysis
analysieren [analy'zi:rən] *vt* to analyse
Ananas ['ananas] (**-, -** *od* **-se**) *f* pineapple
Anarchie [anar'çi:] *f* anarchy
Anatomie [anato'mi:] *f* anatomy
anbahnen ['anba:nən] *vt, vr* to open up
Anbau ['anbau] *m* (*AGR*) cultivation; (*Gebäude*) extension; **a~en** *vt* (*AGR*) to cultivate; (*Gebäudeteil*) to build on
anbehalten ['anbəhaltən] (*unreg*) *vt* to keep on
anbei [an'bai] *adv* enclosed
anbeißen ['anbaisən] (*unreg*) *vt* to bite into ♦ *vi* to bite; (*fig*) to swallow the bait; **zum A~** (*umg*) good enough to eat
anbelangen ['anbəlaŋən] *vt* to concern; **was mich anbelangt** as far as I am concerned
anbeten ['anbe:tən] *vt* to worship
Anbetracht ['anbətraxt] *m*: **in ~** +*gen* in view of
anbieten ['anbi:tən] (*unreg*) *vt* to offer ♦ *vr* to volunteer
anbinden ['anbɪndən] (*unreg*) *vt* to tie up; **kurz angebunden** (*fig*) curt
Anblick ['anblɪk] *m* sight; **a~en** *vt* to look at
anbraten ['anbra:tən] *vt* to brown
anbrechen ['anbrɛçən] (*unreg*) *vt* to start; (*Vorräte*) to break into ♦ *vi* to start; (*Tag*) to break; (*Nacht*) to fall
anbrennen ['anbrɛnən] (*unreg*) *vi* to catch fire; (*KOCH*) to burn

anbringen ['anbrɪŋən] (*unreg*) *vt* to bring; (*Ware*) to sell; (*festmachen*) to fasten
Anbruch ['anbrʊx] *m* beginning; **~ des Tages/der Nacht** dawn/nightfall
anbrüllen ['anbrʏlən] *vt* to roar at
Andacht ['andaxt] (**-, -en**) *f* devotion; (*Gottesdienst*) prayers *pl*; **andächtig** *adj* ['andɛçtɪç] devout
andauern ['andauərn] *vi* to last, to go on; **~d** *adj* continual
Anden ['andən] *pl* Andes
Andenken ['andɛŋkən] (**-s, -**) *nt* memory; souvenir
andere(r, s) ['andərə(r, z)] *adj* other; (*verschieden*) different; **ein ~s Mal** another time; **kein ~r** nobody else; **von etw ~m sprechen** to talk about something else; **~rseits** *adv* on the other hand
andermal *adv*: **ein ~** some other time
ändern ['ɛndərn] *vt* to alter, to change ♦ *vr* to change
andernfalls ['andərnfals] *adv* otherwise
anders ['andərs] *adv*: **~** (**als**) differently (from); **wer ~?** who else?; **jd/irgendwo ~** sb/somewhere else; **~ aussehen/klingen** to look/sound different; **~artig** *adj* different; **~herum** *adv* the other way round; **~wo** *adv* somewhere else; **~woher** *adv* from somewhere else
anderthalb ['andərt'halp] *adj* one and a half
Änderung ['ɛndərʊŋ] *f* alteration, change
Änderungsschneiderei *f* tailor (*who does alterations*)
anderweitig ['andər'vaitɪç] *adj* other ♦ *adv* otherwise; (*anderswo*) elsewhere
andeuten ['andɔytən] *vt* to indicate; (*Wink geben*) to hint at; **Andeutung** *f* indication; hint
Andrang ['andraŋ] *m* crush
andrehen ['andre:ən] *vt* to turn *od* switch on; **jdm etw ~** (*umg*) to unload sth onto sb
androhen ['andro:ən] *vt*: **jdm etw ~** to threaten sb with sth
aneignen ['an|aignən] *vt*: **sich** *dat* **etw ~** to acquire sth; (*widerrechtlich*) to appropriate sth

aneinander [anaɪˈnandər] *adv* at/on/to *etc* one another *od* each other; **~ geraten** to clash

Anekdote [anɛkˈdoːtə] *f* anecdote

anekeln [ˈanʔeːkəln] *vt* to disgust

anerkannt [ˈanʔɛrkant] *adj* recognized, acknowledged

anerkennen [ˈanʔɛrkɛnən] (*unreg*) *vt* to recognize, to acknowledge; (*würdigen*) to appreciate; **~d** *adj* appreciative

Anerkennung *f* recognition, acknowledgement; appreciation

anfachen [ˈanfaxən] *vt* to fan into flame; (*fig*) to kindle

anfahren [ˈanfaːrən] (*unreg*) *vt* to deliver; (*fahren gegen*) to hit; (*Hafen*) to put into; (*fig*) to bawl out ♦ *vi* to drive up; (*losfahren*) to drive off

Anfahrt [ˈanfaːrt] *f* (*~sweg, ~szeit*) journey

Anfall [ˈanfal] *m* (*MED*) attack; **a~en** (*unreg*) *vt* to attack; (*fig*) to overcome ♦ *vi* (*Arbeit*) to come up; (*Produkt*) to be obtained

anfällig [ˈanfɛlɪç] *adj* delicate; **~ für etw** prone to sth

Anfang [ˈanfaŋ] (*-(e)s, -fänge*) *m* beginning, start; **von ~ an** right from the beginning; **zu ~** at the beginning; **~ Mai** at the beginning of May; **a~en** (*unreg*) *vt, vi* to begin, to start; (*machen*) to do

Anfänger(in) [ˈanfɛŋər(ɪn)] (*-s, -*) *m(f)* beginner

anfänglich [ˈanfɛŋlɪç] *adj* initial

anfangs *adv* at first; **A~buchstabe** *m* initial *od* first letter; **A~gehalt** *nt* starting salary

anfassen [ˈanfasən] *vt* to handle; (*berühren*) to touch ♦ *vi* to lend a hand ♦ *vr* to feel

anfechten [ˈanfɛçtən] (*unreg*) *vt* to dispute

anfertigen [ˈanfɛrtɪgən] *vt* to make

anfeuern [ˈanfɔʏərn] *vt* (*fig*) to spur on

anflehen [ˈanfleːən] *vt* to implore

anfliegen [ˈanfliːgən] (*unreg*) *vt* to fly to

Anflug [ˈanfluːk] *m* (*AVIAT*) approach; (*Spur*) trace

anfordern [ˈanfɔrdərn] *vt* to demand; (*COMM*) to requisition

Anforderung *f* (*+gen*) demand (for)

Anfrage [ˈanfraːgə] *f* inquiry; **a~n** *vi* to inquire

anfreunden [ˈanfrɔʏndən] *vr* to make friends

anfügen [ˈanfyːgən] *vt* to add; (*beifügen*) to enclose

anfühlen [ˈanfyːlən] *vt, vr* to feel

anführen [ˈanfyːrən] *vt* to lead; (*zitieren*) to quote; (*umg: betrügen*) to lead up the garden path

Anführer *m* leader

Anführungszeichen *pl* quotation marks, inverted commas

Angabe [ˈangaːbə] *f* statement; (*TECH*) specification; (*umg: Prahlerei*) boasting; (*SPORT*) service

angeben [ˈangeːbən] (*unreg*) *vt* to give; (*anzeigen*) to inform on; (*bestimmen*) to set ♦ *vi* (*umg*) to boast; (*SPORT*) to serve

Angeber (-s, -) (*umg*) *m* show-off; **Angebe'rei** (*umg*) *f* showing off

angeblich [ˈangeːplɪç] *adj* alleged

angeboren [ˈangəboːrən] *adj* inborn, innate

Angebot [ˈangəboːt] *nt* offer; **~ (an +*dat*)** (*COMM*) supply (of)

angebracht [ˈangəbraxt] *adj* appropriate, in order

angegriffen [ˈangəgrɪfən] *adj* exhausted

angeheitert [ˈangəhaɪtərt] *adj* tipsy

angehen [ˈangeːən] (*unreg*) *vt* to concern; (*angreifen*) to attack; (*bitten*) **jdn ~ (um)** to approach sb (for) ♦ *vi* (*Feuer*) to light; (*umg: beginnen*) to begin; **~d** *adj* prospective

angehören [ˈangəhøːrən] *vi* (*+ dat*) to belong to; (*Partei*) to be a member of

Angehörige(r) *f(m)* relative

Angeklagte(r) [ˈangəklaːkta(r)] *f(m)* accused

Angel [ˈaŋəl] (*-, -n*) *f* fishing rod; (*Türangel*) hinge

Angelegenheit [ˈangələgənhaɪt] *f* affair, matter

Angel- *zW*: **~haken** *m* fish hook; **a~n** *vt* to catch ♦ *vi* to fish; **~n (-s)** *nt* angling, fishing; **~rute** *f* fishing rod; **~schein** *m* fishing permit

angemessen [ˈangəmɛsən] *adj* appropriate, suitable

angenehm ['angəne:m] *adj* pleasant; ~! (*bei Vorstellung*) pleased to meet you

angeregt [angəre:kt] *adj* animated, lively

angesehen ['angəze:ən] *adj* respected

angesichts ['angəzıçts] *präp +gen* in view of, considering

angespannt ['angəʃpant] *adj* (*Aufmerksamkeit*) close; (*Arbeit*) hard

Angestellte(r) ['angəʃtɛltə(r)] *f(m)* employee

angestrengt ['angəʃtrɛŋt] *adv* as hard as one can

angetan ['angəta:n] *adj*: **von jdm/etw ~ sein** to be impressed by sb/sth; **es jdm ~ haben** to appeal to sb

angetrunken ['angətrʊŋkən] *adj* tipsy

angewiesen ['angəvi:zən] *adj*: **auf jdn/etw ~ sein** to be dependent on sb/sth

angewöhnen ['angəvø:nən] *vt*: **jdm/sich etw ~** to get sb/become accustomed to sth

Angewohnheit ['angəvo:nhaıt] *f* habit

angleichen ['anglaıçən] (*unreg*) *vt, vr* to adjust

Angler ['aŋlər] (**-s, -**) *m* angler

angreifen ['angraıfən] (*unreg*) *vt* to attack; (*beschädigen*) to damage

Angreifer (**-s, -**) *m* attacker

Angriff ['angrıf] *m* attack; **etw in ~ nehmen** to make a start on sth

Angst (**-, ⁻e**) *f* fear; **jdm ist a~** sb is afraid *od* scared; **~ haben (vor +dat)** to be afraid *od* scared (of); **~ haben um jdn/etw** to be worried about sb/sth; **jdm ~ machen** to scare sb; **~hase** (*umg*) *m* chicken, scaredy-cat

ängst- ['ɛŋst] *zW*: **~igen** *vt* to frighten ♦ *vr*: **sich ~igen (vor +dat od um)** to worry (o.s.) (about); **~lich** *adj* nervous; (*besorgt*) worried; **Ä~lichkeit** *f* nervousness

anhaben ['anha:bən] (*unreg*) *vt* to have on; **er kann mir nichts ~** he can't hurt me

anhalt- ['anhalt] *zW*: **~en** (*unreg*) *vt* to stop ♦ *vi* to stop; (*andauern*) to persist; (**jdm**) **etw ~en** to hold sth up (against sb); **jdn zur Arbeit/Höflichkeit ~en** to make sb work/be polite; **~end** *adj* persistent;

A~er(in) (**-s, -**) *m(f)* hitch-hiker; **per A~er fahren** to hitch-hike; **A~spunkt** *m* clue

anhand [an'hant] *präp +gen* with

Anhang ['anhaŋ] *m* appendix; (*Leute*) family; supporters *pl*

anhäng- ['anhɛŋ] *zW*: **~en** (*unreg*) *vt* to hang up; (*Wagen*) to couple up; (*Zusatz*) to add (on); **A~er** (**-s, -**) *m* supporter; (*AUT*) trailer; (*am Koffer*) tag; (*Schmuck*) pendant; **A~erschaft** *f* supporters *pl*; **~lich** *adj* devoted; **A~lichkeit** *f* devotion; **A~sel** (**-s, -**) *nt* appendage

Anhäufung ['anhɔyfʊŋ] *f* accumulation

anheben ['anhe:bən] (*unreg*) *vt* to lift up; (*Preise*) to raise

anheizen ['anhaıtsən] *vt* (*Stimmung*) to lift; (*Moral*) to boost

Anhieb ['anhi:b] *m*: **auf ~** at the very first go; (*kurz entschlossen*) on the spur of the moment

Anhöhe ['anhø:ə] *f* hill

anhören ['anhø:rən] *vt* to listen to; (*anmerken*) to hear ♦ *vr* to sound

animieren [ani'mi:rən] *vt* to encourage, to urge on

Anis [a'ni:s] (**-es, -e**) *m* aniseed

Ank. *abk* (= *Ankunft*) arr.

Ankauf ['ankauf] *m* (*von Wertpapieren, Devisen, Waren*) purchase; **a~en** *vt* to purchase, to buy

Anker ['aŋkər] (**-s, -**) *m* anchor; **vor ~ gehen** to drop anchor

Anklage ['ankla:gə] *f* accusation; (*JUR*) charge; **~bank** *f* dock; **a~n** *vt* to accuse; **jdn (eines Verbrechens) a~n** (*JUR*) to charge sb (with a crime)

Ankläger ['ankle:gər] *m* accuser

Anklang ['anklaŋ] *m*: **bei jdm ~ finden** to meet with sb's approval

Ankleidekabine *f* changing cubicle

ankleiden ['anklaıdən] *vt, vr* to dress

anklicken ['anklıkən] *vt* (*COMPUT*) to click on

anklopfen ['anklɔpfən] *vi* to knock

anknüpfen ['anknʏpfən] *vt* to fasten *od* tie on; (*fig*) to start ♦ *vi* (*anschließen*): **~ an +akk** to refer to

ankommen ['ankɔmən] (*unreg*) *vi* to arrive;

(*näher kommen*) to approach; (*Anklang finden*): **bei jdm (gut) ~** to go down well with sb; **es kommt darauf an** it depends; (*wichtig sein*) that (is what) matters; **es darauf ~ lassen** to let things take their course; **gegen jdn/etw ~** to cope with sb/sth; **bei jdm schlecht ~** to go down badly with sb

ankreuzen ['ankrɔytsən] *vt* to mark with a cross; (*hervorheben*) to highlight

ankündigen ['ankʏndɪgən] *vt* to announce; **Ankündigung** *f* announcement

Ankunft ['ankʊnft] (**-, -künfte**) *f* arrival; **~szeit** *f* time of arrival

ankurbeln ['ankʊrbəln] *vt* (*fig*) to boost

Anlage ['anla:gə] *f* disposition; (*Begabung*) talent; (*Park*) gardens *pl*; (*Beilage*) enclosure; (*TECH*) plant; (*FIN*) investment; (*Entwurf*) layout

Anlass ▲ ['anlas] (**-es, -lässe**) *m*: **~ (zu)** cause (for); (*Ereignis*) occasion; **aus ~ +**gen on the occasion of; **~ zu etw geben** to give rise to sth; **etw zum ~ nehmen** to take the opportunity of sth

anlassen (*unreg*) *vt* to leave on; (*Motor*) to start ♦ *vr* (*umg*) to start off

Anlasser (**-s, -**) *m* (*AUT*) starter

anlässlich ▲ ['anlɛslɪç] *präp* +gen on the occasion of

Anlauf ['anlaʊf] *m* run-up; **a~en** (*unreg*) *vi* to begin; (*neuer Film*) to show; (*SPORT*) to run up; (*Fenster*) to mist up; (*Metall*) to tarnish ♦ *vt* to call at; **rot a~en** to blush; **angelaufen kommen** to come running up

anlegen ['anle:gən] *vt* to put; (*anziehen*) to put on; (*gestalten*) to lay out; (*Geld*) to invest ♦ *vi* to dock; **etw an etw** *akk* **~** to put sth against *od* on sth; **ein Gewehr ~ (auf +**akk) to aim a weapon (at); **es auf etw** *akk* **~** to be out for sth/to do sth; **sich mit jdm ~** (*umg*) to quarrel with sb

Anlegestelle *f* landing place

anlehnen ['anle:nən] *vt* to lean; (*Tür*) to leave ajar; **(sich) an etw** *akk* **~** to lean on/against sth

Anleihe ['anlaɪə] *f* (*FIN*) loan

anleiten ['anlaɪtən] *vt* to instruct;

Anleitung *f* instructions *pl*

anliegen ['anli:gən] (*unreg*) *vi* (*Kleidung*) to cling; **A~** (**-s, -**) *nt* matter; (*Wunsch*) wish; **~d** *adj* adjacent; (*beigefügt*) enclosed

Anlieger (**-s, -**) *m* resident; **„~ frei"** "residents only"

anmachen ['anmaxən] *vt* to attach; (*ELEK*) to put on; (*Zigarette*) to light; (*Salat*) to dress

anmaßen ['anma:sən] *vt*: **sich** *dat* **etw ~** (*Recht*) to lay claim to sth; **~d** *adj* arrogant

Anmaßung *f* presumption

anmelden ['anmɛldən] *vt* to announce ♦ *vr* (*sich ankündigen*) to make an appointment; (*polizeilich, für Kurs etc*) to register

Anmeldung *f* announcement; appointment; registration

anmerken ['anmɛrkən] *vt* to observe; (*anstreichen*) to mark; **sich** *dat* **nichts ~ lassen** to not give anything away

Anmerkung *f* note

anmieten ['anmi:tən] *vt* to rent; (*auch Auto*) to hire

Anmut ['anmu:t] (**-**) *f* grace; **a~en** *vt* to give a feeling; **a~ig** *adj* charming

annähen ['annɛ:ən] *vt* to sew on

annähern ['annɛ:ərn] *vr* to get closer; **~d** *adj* approximate ·

Annäherung *f* approach

Annäherungsversuch *m* advances *pl*

Annahme ['anna:mə] *f* acceptance; (*Vermutung*) assumption

annehm- ['anne:m] *zW*: **~bar** *adj* acceptable; **~en** (*unreg*) *vt* to accept; · (*Namen*) to take; (*Kind*) to adopt; (*vermuten*) to suppose, to assume ♦ *vr* (+gen) to take care (of); **A~lichkeit** *f* comfort

Annonce [a'nõ:sə] *f* advertisement

annoncieren [anõ'si:rən] *vt, vi* to advertise

annullieren [anʊ'li:rən] *vt* to annul

anonym [ano'ny:m] *adj* anonymous

Anorak ['anorak] (**-s, -s**) *m* anorak

anordnen ['an|ɔrdnən] *vt* to arrange; (*befehlen*) to order

Anordnung *f* arrangement; order

anorganisch ['an|ɔrga:nɪʃ] *adj* inorganic

anpacken ['anpakən] *vt* to grasp; (*fig*) to tackle; **mit ~** to lend a hand

anpassen ['anpasən] *vt*: **(jdm)** ~ to fit (on sb); (*fig*) to adapt ♦ *vr* to adapt

anpassungsfähig *adj* adaptable

Anpfiff ['anpfɪf] *m* (*SPORT*) (starting) whistle; kick-off; (*umg*) rocket

anprallen ['anpralən] *vi*: ~ **(gegen** *od* **an** +*akk*) to collide (with)

anprangern ['anpraŋərn] *vt* to denounce

anpreisen ['anpraɪzən] (*unreg*) *vt* to extol

Anprobe ['anpro:bə] *f* trying on

anprobieren ['anprobi:rən] *vt* to try on

anrechnen ['anrɛçnən] *vt* to charge; (*fig*) count; **jdm etw hoch** ~ to think highly of sb for sth

Anrecht ['anrɛçt] *nt*: ~ **(auf** +*akk*) right (to)

Anrede ['anre:də] *f* form of address; **a~n** *vt* to address; (*belästigen*) to accost

anregen ['anre:gən] *vt* to stimulate; **angeregte Unterhaltung** lively discussion; **~d** *adj* stimulating

Anregung *f* stimulation; (*Vorschlag*) suggestion

anreichern ['anraɪçərn] *vt* to enrich

Anreise ['anraɪzə] *f* journey; **a~n** *vi* to arrive

Anreiz ['anraɪts] *m* incentive

Anrichte ['anrɪçtə] *f* sideboard; **a~n** *vt* to serve up; **Unheil a~n** to make mischief

anrüchig ['anrʏçɪç] *adj* dubious

anrücken ['anrʏkən] *vi* to approach; (*MIL*) to advance

Anruf ['anru:f] *m* call; **~beantworter** [-bə-'antvɔrtər] **(-s, -)** *m* answering machine; **a~en** (*unreg*) *vt* to call out to; (*bitten*) to call on; (*TEL*) to ring up, to phone, to call

ans [ans] = **an das**

Ansage ['anza:gə] *f* announcement; **a~n** *vt* to announce ♦ *vr* to say one will come; **~r(in) (-s, -)** *m(f)* announcer

ansammeln ['anzaməln] *vt* (*Reichtümer*) to amass ♦ *vr* (*Menschen*) to gather, to assemble; (*Wasser*) to collect; **Ansammlung** *f* collection; (*Leute*) crowd

ansässig ['anzɛsɪç] *adj* resident

Ansatz ['anzats] *m* start; (*Haaransatz*) hairline; (*Halsansatz*) base; (*Verlängerungsstück*) extension; (*Veranschlagung*) estimate; **~punkt** *m*

starting point

anschaffen ['anʃafən] *vt* to buy, to purchase; **Anschaffung** *f* purchase

anschalten ['anʃaltən] *vt* to switch on

anschau- ['anʃau] *zW*: **~en** *vt* to look at; **~lich** *adj* illustrative; **A~ung** *f* (*Meinung*) view; **aus eigener A~ung** from one's own experience

Anschein ['anʃaɪn] *m* appearance; **allem ~ nach** to all appearances; **den ~ haben** to seem, to appear; **a~end** *adj* apparent

anschieben ['anʃi:bən] (*unreg*) *vt* to push

Anschlag ['anʃla:k] *m* notice; (*Attentat*) attack; (*COMM*) estimate; (*auf Klavier*) touch; (*Schreibmaschine*) character; **a~en** ['anʃla:gən] (*unreg*) *vt* to put up; (*beschädigen*) to chip; (*Akkord*) to strike; (*Kosten*) to estimate ♦ *vi* to hit; (*wirken*) to have an effect; (*Glocke*) to ring; **an etw** *akk* **a~en** to hit against sth

anschließen ['anʃli:sən] (*unreg*) *vt* to connect up; (*Sender*) to link up ♦ *vi*: **an etw** *akk* ~ to adjoin sth; (*zeitlich*) to follow sth ♦ *vr*: **sich jdm/etw** ~ to join sb/sth; (*beipflichten*) to agree with sb/sth; **sich an etw** *akk* ~ to adjoin sth; **~d** *adj* adjacent; (*zeitlich*) subsequent ♦ *adv* afterwards

Anschluss ▲ ['anʃlʊs] *m* (*ELEK, EISENB*) connection; (*von Wasser etc*) supply; **im ~ an** +*akk* following; **~ finden** to make friends; **~flug** *m* connecting flight

anschmiegsam ['anʃmi:kza:m] *adj* affectionate

anschnallen ['anʃnalən] *vt* to buckle on ♦ *vr* to fasten one's seat belt

anschneiden ['anʃnaɪdən] (*unreg*) *vt* to cut into; (*Thema*) to introduce

anschreiben ['anʃraɪbən] (*unreg*) *vt* to write (up); (*COMM*) to charge up; (*benachrichtigen*) to write to

anschreien ['anʃraɪən] (*unreg*) *vt* to shout at

Anschrift ['anʃrɪft] *f* address

Anschuldigung ['anʃʊldɪgʊŋ] *f* accusation

anschwellen ['anʃvelən] (*unreg*) *vi* to swell (up)

anschwindeln ['anʃvɪndəln] *vt* to lie to

ansehen ['anze:ən] (*unreg*) *vt* to look at;

jdm etw ~ to see sth (from sb's face); **jdn/etw als etw ~** to look on sb/sth as sth; **~ für** to consider; **A~** (-s) nt respect; (Ruf) reputation

ansehnlich ['anze:nlıç] adj fine-looking; (beträchtlich) considerable

ansetzen ['anzɛtsən] vt (festlegen) to fix; (entwickeln) to develop; (Fett) to put on; (Blätter) to grow; (zubereiten) to prepare ♦ vi (anfangen) to start, to begin; (Entwicklung) to set in; (dick werden) to put on weight ♦ vr (Rost etc) to start to develop; **~ an** +akk (anfügen) to fix on to; (anlegen, an Mund etc) to put to

Ansicht ['anzıçt] f (Anblick) sight; (Meinung) view, opinion; **zur ~** on approval; **meiner ~ nach** in my opinion; **~skarte** f picture postcard; **~ssache** f matter of opinion

ansonsten [an'zɔnstən] adv otherwise

anspannen ['anʃpanən] vt to harness; (Muskel) to strain; **Anspannung** f strain

anspielen ['anʃpi:lən] vi (SPORT) to start play; **auf etw** akk **~** to refer od allude to sth

Anspielung f: **~ (auf** +akk) reference (to), allusion (to)

Anspitzer ['anʃpıtsər] (-s, -) m pencil sharpener

Ansporn ['anʃpɔrn] (-(e)s) m incentive

Ansprache ['anʃpraːxə] f address

ansprechen ['anʃprɛçən] (unreg) vt to speak to; (bitten, gefallen) to appeal to ♦ vi: **(auf etw** akk**) ~** to react (to sth); **jdn auf etw** akk **(hin) ~** to ask sb about sth; **~d** adj attractive

anspringen ['anʃprıŋən] (unreg) vi (AUT) to start ♦ vt to jump at

Anspruch ['anʃprʊx] m (Recht): **~ (auf** +akk**)** claim (to); **hohe Ansprüche stellen/ haben** to demand/expect a lot; **jdn/etw in ~ nehmen** to occupy sb/take up sth; **a~slos** adj undemanding; **a~svoll** adj demanding

anstacheln ['anʃtaxəln] vt to spur on

Anstalt ['anʃtalt] (-, -en) f institution; **~en machen, etw zu tun** to prepare to do sth

Anstand ['anʃtant] m decency

anständig ['anʃtɛndıç] adj decent; (umg) proper; (groß) considerable

anstandslos adv without any ado

anstarren ['anʃtarən] vt to stare at

anstatt [an'ʃtat] präp +gen instead of ♦ konj: **~ etw zu tun** instead of doing sth

Ansteck- ['anʃtɛk] zW: **a~en** vt to pin on; (MED) to infect; (Pfeife) to light; (Haus) to set fire to ♦ vr: **ich habe mich bei ihm angesteckt** I caught it from him ♦ vi (fig) to be infectious; **a~end** adj infectious; **~ung** f infection

anstehen ['anʃteːən] (unreg) vi to queue (up) (BRIT), to line up (US)

ansteigen ['anʃtaıgən] vt (Straße) to climb; (Gelände, Temperatur, Preise) to rise.

anstelle, an Stelle [an'ʃtɛlə] präp +gen in place of etw; **~n** ['an-] (einschalten) to turn on; (Arbeit geben) to employ; (machen) to do ♦ vr to queue (up) (BRIT), to line up (US); (umg) to act

Anstellung f employment; (Posten) post, position

Anstieg ['anʃtiːk] (-(e)s, -e) m (+gen) climb; (fig: von Preisen etc) increase (in)

anstiften ['anʃtıftən] vt (Unglück) to cause; **jdn zu etw ~** to put sb up to sth

anstimmen ['anʃtımən] vt (Lied) to strike up with; (Geschrei) to set up

Anstoß ['anʃtoːs] m impetus; (Ärgernis) offence; (SPORT) kick-off; **der erste ~** the initiative; **~ nehmen an** +dat to take offence at; **a~en** (unreg) vt to push; (mit Fuß) to kick ♦ vi to knock, to bump; (mit der Zunge) to lisp; (mit Gläsern): **a~en (auf** +akk**)** to drink (to), to drink a toast (to)

anstößig ['anʃtøːsıç] adj offensive, indecent

anstreichen ['anʃtraıçən] (unreg) vt to paint

anstrengen ['anʃtrɛŋən] vt to strain; (JUR) to bring ♦ vr to make an effort; **~d** adj tiring

Anstrengung f effort

Anstrich ['anʃtrıç] m coat of paint

Ansturm ['anʃtʊrm] m rush; (MIL) attack

Antarktis [ant'|arktıs] (-) f Antarctic

antasten ['antastən] vt to touch; (Recht) to infringe upon; (Ehre) to question

Anteil ['antaıl] (-s, -e) m share; (Mitgefühl)

Spelling Reform: ▲ new spelling △ old spelling (to be phased out)

sympathy; **~ nehmen (an** +*dat*) to share (in); (*sich interessieren*) to take an interest (in); **~nahme(-)** *f* sympathy

Antenne [an'tɛnə] *f* aerial

Anti- ['anti] *in zW* anti; **~alko'holiker** *m* teetotaller; **a~autori'tär** *adj* anti-authoritarian; **~babypille** *f* contraceptive pill; **~biotikum** [antibi'o:tikʊm] **(-s, -ka)** *nt* antibiotic

antik [an'ti:k] *adj* antique; **A~e** *f* (*Zeitalter*) ancient world

Antiquariat [antikvari'a:t] **(-(e)s, -e)** *nt* secondhand bookshop

Antiquitäten [antikvi'tɛ:tən] *pl* antiques; **~händler** *m* antique dealer

Antrag ['antra:k] **(-(e)s, -träge)** *m* proposal; (*PARL*) motion; (*Gesuch*) application; **~steller(in)(-s, -)** *m(f)* claimant; (*für Kredit*) applicant

antreffen ['antrɛfən] (*unreg*) *vt* to meet

antreiben ['antraɪbən] (*unreg*) *vt* to drive on; (*Motor*) to drive

antreten ['antre:tən] (*unreg*) *vt* (*Amt*) to take up; (*Erbschaft*) to come into; (*Beweis*) to offer; (*Reise*) to start, to begin ♦ *vi* (*MIL*) to fall in; (*SPORT*) to line up; **gegen jdn ~** to play/fight (against) sb

Antrieb ['antri:p] *m* (*auch fig*) drive; **aus eigenem ~** of one's own accord

antrinken ['antrɪŋkən] (*unreg*) *vt* (*Flasche, Glas*) to start to drink from; **sich** *dat* **Mut/ einen Rausch ~** to give o.s. Dutch courage/get drunk; **angetrunken sein** to be tipsy

Antritt ['antrɪt] *m* beginning, commencement; (*eines Amts*) taking up

antun ['antu:n] (*unreg*) *vt*: **jdm etw ~** to do sth to sb; **sich** *dat* **Zwang ~** to force o.s.; **sich** *dat* **etwas ~** to (try to) take one's own life

Antwort ['antvɔrt] **(-, -en)** *f* answer, reply; **a~en** *vi* to answer, to reply

anvertrauen ['anfɛrtrauən] *vt*: **jdm etw ~** to entrust sb with sth; **sich jdm ~** to confide in sb

anwachsen ['anvaksən] (*unreg*) *vi* to grow; (*Pflanze*) to take root

Anwalt ['anvalt] **(-(e)s, -wälte)** *m* solicitor; lawyer; (*fig*) champion

Anwältin ['anvɛltɪn] *f siehe* **Anwalt**

Anwärter ['anvɛrtər] *m* candidate

anweisen ['anvaɪzən] (*unreg*) *vt* to instruct; (*zuteilen*) to assign

Anweisung *f* instruction; (*COMM*) remittance; (*Postanweisung, Zahlungsanweisung*) money order

anwend- ['anvɛnd] *zW*: **~bar** ['anvɛnt-] *adj* practicable, applicable; **~en** (*unreg*) *vt* to use, to employ; (*Gesetz, Regel*) to apply; **A~ung** *f* use; application

anwesend ['anve:zənt] *adj* present; **die A~en** those present

Anwesenheit *f* presence

anwidern ['anvi:dərn] *vt* to disgust

Anwohner(in) ['anvo:nər(ɪn)] **(-s, -)** *m(f)* neighbour

Anzahl ['antsa:l] *f*: **~ (an** +*dat*) number (of); **a~en** *vt* to pay on account; **~ung** *f* deposit, payment on account

Anzeichen ['antsaɪçən] *nt* sign, indication

Anzeige ['antsaɪgə] *f* (*Zeitungsanzeige*) announcement; (*Werbung*) advertisement; (*bei Polizei*) report; **~ erstatten gegen jdn** to report sb (to the police); **a~n** *vt* (*zu erkennen geben*) to show; (*bekannt geben*) to announce; (*bei Polizei*) to report

anziehen ['antsi:ən] (*unreg*) *vt* to attract; (*Kleidung*) to put on; (*Mensch*) to dress; (*Seil*) to pull tight; (*Schraube*) to tighten; (*Knie*) to draw up ♦ *vr* to get dressed; **~d** *adj* attractive

Anziehung *f* (*Reiz*) attraction; **~skraft** *f* power of attraction; (*PHYS*) force of gravitation

Anzug ['antsu:k] *m* suit; (*Herankommen*): **im ~ sein** to be approaching

anzüglich ['antsy:klɪç] *adj* personal; (*anstößig*) offensive; **A~keit** *f* offensiveness; (*Bemerkung*) personal remark

anzünden ['antsyndən] *vt* to light

anzweifeln ['antsvaɪfəln] *vt* to doubt

apathisch [a'pa:tɪʃ] *adj* apathetic

Apfel ['apfəl] **(-s, ⁻)** *m* apple; **~saft** *m* apple juice; **~sine** [-'zi:nə] *f* orange; **~wein** *m*

cider
Apostel [a'pɔstəl] **(-s, -)** *m* apostle
Apotheke [apo'te:kə] *f* chemist's (shop),
drugstore (*US*); **a~npflichtig** [-pflɪçtɪç] *adj*
available only at a chemist's shop (*BRIT*) or
pharmacy; **~r(in) (-s, -)** *m(f)* chemist,
druggist (*US*)

Apotheke

i The **Apotheke** *is a pharmacy selling medicines available only on prescription and toiletries. The pharmacist is qualified to give advice on medicines and treatments.*

Apparat [apa'ra:t] **(-(e)s, -e)** *m* piece of
apparatus; camera; telephone; (*RADIO, TV*)
set; **am ~!** speaking!; **~ur** [-'tu:r] *f*
apparatus
Appartement [apart(ə)'mã:] **(-s, -s)** *nt* flat
appellieren [apɛ'li:rən] *vi*: **~ (an** +*akk*) to
appeal (to)
Appetit [apɛ'ti:t] **(-(e)s, -e)** *m* appetite;
guten ~! enjoy your meal; **a~lich** *adj*
appetizing; **~losigkeit** *f* lack of appetite
Applaus [ap'laus] **(-es, -e)** *m* applause
Aprikose [apri'ko:zə] *f* apricot
April [a'prɪl] **(-(s), -e)** *m* April
Aquarell [akva'rɛl] **(-s, -e)** *nt* watercolour
Äquator [ɛ'kva:tɔr] **(-s)** *m* equator
Arab- ['arab] *zW*: **~er(in) (-s, -)** *m(f)* Arab;
~ien [a'ra:biən] **(-s)** *nt* Arabia; **a~isch**
[a'ra:bɪʃ] *adj* Arabian
Arbeit ['arbait] **(-, -en)** *f* work *no art*; (*Stelle*)
job; (*Erzeugnis*) piece of work;
(*wissenschaftliche*) dissertation; (*Klassenarbeit*)
test; **das war eine ~** that was a hard job;
a~en *vi* to work ♦ *vt* to work, to make;
~er(in) (-s, -) *m(f)* worker; (*ungelernt*)
labourer; **~erschaft** *f* workers *pl*, labour
force; **~geber (-s, -)** *m* employer;
~nehmer (-s, -) *m* employee
Arbeits- *in zW* labour; **a~am** *adj*
industrious; **~amt** *nt* employment
exchange; **~erlaubnis** *f* work permit;
a~fähig *adj* fit for work, able-bodied;
~gang *m* operation; **~kräfte** *pl*
(*Mitarbeiter*) workforce; **a~los** *adj*

unemployed, out-of-work; **~lose(r)** *f(m)*
unemployed person; **~losigkeit** *f*
unemployment; **~markt** *m* job market;
~platz *m* job; place of work; **a~scheu** *adj*
workshy; **~tag** *m* work(ing) day;
a~unfähig *adj* unfit for work; **~zeit** *f*
working hours *pl*; **~zimmer** *nt* study
Archäologe [arçɛo'lo:gə] **(-n, -n)** *m*
archaeologist
Architekt(in) [arçi'tɛkt(ɪn)] **(-en, -en)** *m(f)*
architect; **~ur** [-'tu:r] *f* architecture
Archiv [ar'çi:f] **(-s, -e)** *nt* archive
arg [ark] *adj* bad, awful ♦ *adv* awfully, very
Argentinien [argen'ti:niən] **(-s)** *nt*
Argentina, the Argentine
argentinisch *adj* Argentinian
Ärger ['ɛrgər] **(-s)** *m* (*Wut*) anger;
(*Unannehmlichkeit*) trouble; **ä~lich** *adj*
(*zornig*) angry; (*lästig*) annoying,
aggravating; **ä~n** *vt* to annoy ♦ *vr* to get
annoyed
arg- *zW*: **~listig** *adj* cunning, insidious;
~los *adj* guileless, innocent
Argument [argu'mɛnt] *nt* argument
argwöhnisch *adj* suspicious
Arie ['a:riə] *f* aria
Aristokrat [aristo'kra:t] **(-en, -en)** *m*
aristocrat; **~ie** [-'ti:] *f* aristocracy
Arktis ['arktɪs] **(-)** *f* Arctic
Arm [arm] **(-(e)s, -e)** *m* arm; (*Flussarm*)
branch
arm *adj* poor
Armatur [arma'tu:r] *f* (*ELEK*) armature;
~enbrett *nt* instrument panel; (*AUT*)
dashboard
Armband *nt* bracelet; **~uhr** *f* (wrist) watch
Arme(r) *f(m)* poor man (woman); **die ~n**
the poor
Armee [ar'me:] *f* army
Ärmel ['ɛrməl] **(-s, -)** *m* sleeve; **etw aus**
dem ~ schütteln (*fig*) to produce sth just
like that; **~kanal** *m* English Channel
ärmlich ['ɛrmlɪç] *adj* poor
armselig *adj* wretched, miserable
Armut ['armu:t] **(-)** *f* poverty
Aroma [a'ro:ma] **(-s, Aromen)** *nt* aroma;
~therapie *f* aromatherapy; **a~tisch** *adj*

[aro'ma:tɪʃ] adj aromatic

arrangieren [arãˈʒiːrən] vt to arrange ♦ vr to come to an arrangement

Arrest [aˈrɛst] (-(e)s, -e) m detention

arrogant [aroˈgant] adj arrogant

Arsch [arʃ] (-es, ᵘe) m (umg!) m arse (BRIT!), ass (US!)

Art [aːrt] (-, -en) f (Weise) way; (Sorte) kind, sort; (BIOL) species; **eine ~ (von) Frucht** a kind of fruit; **Häuser aller ~** houses of all kinds; **es ist nicht seine ~, das zu tun** it's not like him to do that; **ich mache das auf meine ~** I do that my (own) way

Arterie [arˈteːriə] f artery; **~nverkalkung** f arteriosclerosis

artig [ˈaːrtɪç] adj good, well-behaved

Artikel [arˈtiːkəl] (-s, -) m article

Artillerie [artɪləˈriː] f artillery

Artischocke [artiˈʃɔkə] f artichoke

Artist(in) [arˈtɪst(ɪn)] (-en, -en) m(f) (circus/ variety) artiste od performer

Arznei [aːrtsˈnaɪ] f medicine; **~mittel** nt medicine, medicament

Arzt [aːrtst] (-es, ᵘe) m doctor; **~helferin** f (doctor's) receptionist

Ärztin [ˈɛːrtstɪn] f doctor

ärztlich [ˈɛːrtstlɪç] adj medical

As △ [as] (-ses, -se) nt = **Ass**

Asche [ˈaʃə] f (-, -n) ash, cinder

Aschen- zW: **~bahn** f cinder track; **~becher** m ashtray

Aschermittwoch m Ash Wednesday

Äser [ˈɛːzər] pl von **Aas**

Asiat(in) [aziˈaːt(ɪn)] (-en, -en) m(f) Asian; **asiatisch** [-ˈaːtɪʃ] adj Asian

Asien [ˈaːziən] (-s) nt Asia

asozial [ˈazotsaːl] adj antisocial; (Familien) asocial

Aspekt [asˈpɛkt] (-(e)s, -e) m aspect

Asphalt [asˈfalt] (-(e)s, -e) m asphalt

Ass ▲ [as] (-es, -e) nt ace

aß etc [aːs] vb siehe **essen**

Assistent(in) [asɪsˈtɛnt(ɪn)] m(f) assistant

Assoziation [asotsiatsiˈoːn] f association

Ast [ast] (-(e)s, ᵘe) m bough, branch

ästhetisch [ɛsˈteːtɪʃ] adj aesthetic

Asthma [ˈastma] (-s) nt asthma; **~tiker(in)**

(-s, -) m(f) asthmatic

Astro- [astro] zW: **~loge** (-n, -n) m astrologer; **~lo'gie** f astrology; **~'naut** (-en, -en) m astronaut; **~'nom** (-en, -en) m astronomer; **~no'mie** f astronomy

Asyl [aˈzyːl] (-s, -e) nt asylum; (Heim) home; (Obdachlosenasyl) shelter; **~ant(in)** [azyˈlant(ɪn)] (-en, -en) m(f) asylum-seeker; **~bewerber(in)** m(f) asylum-seeker

Atelier [atəliˈeː] (-s, -s) nt studio

Atem [ˈaːtəm] (-s) m breath; **den ~ anhalten** to hold one's breath; **außer ~** out of breath; **a~beraubend** adj breathtaking; **a~los** adj breathless; **~not** f difficulty in breathing; **~pause** f breather; **~zug** m breath

Atheismus [ateˈɪsmʊs] m atheism

Atheist m atheist; **a~isch** adj atheistic

Athen [aˈteːn] (-s) nt Athens

Äthiopien [etiˈoːpiən] (-s) nt Ethiopia

Athlet [atˈleːt] (-en, -en) m athlete

Atlantik [atˈlantɪk] (-s) m Atlantic (Ocean)

Atlas [ˈatlas] (- od **-ses, -se** od **Atlanten**) m atlas

atmen [ˈaːtmən] vt, vi to breathe

Atmosphäre [atmoˈsfɛːrə] f atmosphere; **atmosphärisch** adj atmospheric

Atmung [ˈaːtmʊŋ] f respiration

Atom [aˈtoːm] (-s, -e) nt atom; **a~ar** adj atomic; **~bombe** f atom bomb; **~energie** f atomic od nuclear energy; **~kern** m atomic nucleus; **~kraftwerk** nt nuclear power station; **~krieg** m nuclear od atomic war; **~müll** m atomic waste; **~strom** m (electricity generated by) nuclear power; **~versuch** m atomic test; **~waffen** pl atomic weapons; **a~waffenfrei** adj nuclear-free; **~zeitalter** nt atomic age

Attentat [atɛnˈtaːt] (-(e)s, -e) nt: **~ (auf** +akk) (attempted) assassination (of)

Attentäter [atɛnˈtɛːtər] m (would-be) assassin

Attest [aˈtɛst] (-(e)s, -e) nt certificate

Attraktion [atraktsiˈoːn] f (Tourismus, Zirkus) attraction

attraktiv [atrakˈtiːf] adj attractive

Attrappe [aˈtrapə] f dummy

Attribut [atri'bu:t] (-(e)s, -e) *nt* (*GRAM*) attribute

ätzen ['ɛtsən] *vi* to be caustic; **~d** *adj* (*Säure*) corrosive; (*fig: Spott*) cutting

au [aʊ] *excl* ouch!; **~ ja!** oh yes!

Aubergine [ober'ʒi:nə] *f* aubergine, eggplant

auch [aʊx] *adv* **1** (*ebenfalls*) also, too, as well; **das ist auch schön** that's nice too *od* as well; **er kommt - ich auch** he's coming - so am I, me too; **auch nicht** not ... either; **ich auch nicht** nor I, me neither; **oder auch** or; **auch das noch!** not that as well! **2** (*selbst, sogar*) even; **auch wenn das Wetter schlecht ist** even if the weather is bad; **ohne auch nur zu fragen** without even asking **3** (*wirklich*) really; **du siehst müde aus - bin ich auch** you look tired - (so) I am; **so sieht es aus** it looks like it too **4** (*auch immer*): **wer auch** whoever; **was auch** whatever; **wie dem auch sei** be that as it may; **wie sehr er sich auch bemühte** however much he tried

auf [aʊf] *präp +dat* (*wo?*) on; **auf dem Tisch** on the table; **auf der Reise** on the way; **auf der Post/dem Fest** at the post office/ party; **auf der Straße** on the road; **auf dem Land/der ganzen Welt** in the country/the whole world
♦ *präp +akk* **1** (*wohin?*) on(to); **auf den Tisch** on(to) the table; **auf die Post gehen** go to the post office; **auf das Land** into the country; **etw auf einen Zettel schreiben** to write sth on a piece of paper **2** (*zeitlich*) in; **auf Deutsch** in German; **auf Lebenszeit** for my/his lifetime; **auf ihn** except for him; **auf einmal** at once; **auf seinen Vorschlag (hin)** at his suggestion
♦ *adv* **1** (*offen*) open; **auf sein** (*umg*) (*Tür, Geschäft*) to be open; **das Fenster ist auf** the window is open

2 (*hinauf*) up; **auf und ab** up and down; **auf und davon** up and away; **auf!** (*los!*) come on!
3 (*aufgestanden*) up; **auf sein** to be up; **ist er schon auf?** is he up yet?
♦ *konj*: **auf dass** (so) that

aufatmen ['aʊfʔa:tmən] *vi* to heave a sigh of relief

aufbahren ['aʊfba:rən] *vt* to lay out

Aufbau ['aʊfbaʊ] *m* (*Bauen*) building, construction; (*Struktur*) structure; (*aufgebautes Teil*) superstructure; **a~en** *vt* to erect, to build (up); (*Existenz*) to make; (*gestalten*) to construct; **a~en (auf +***dat*) (*gründen*) to found *od* base (on)

aufbauschen ['aʊfbaʊʃən] *vt* to puff out; (*fig*) to exaggerate

aufbekommen ['aʊfbəkɔmən] (*unreg*) *vt* (*öffnen*) to get open; (*Hausaufgaben*) to be given

aufbessern ['aʊfbɛsərn] *vt* (*Gehalt*) to increase

aufbewahren ['aʊfbəva:rən] *vt* to keep; (*Gepäck*) to put in the left-luggage office (*BRIT*) *od* baggage check (*US*)

Aufbewahrung *f* (safe)keeping; (*Gepäckaufbewahrung*) left-luggage office (*BRIT*), baggage check (*US*)

aufbieten ['aʊfbi:tən] (*unreg*) *vt* (*Kraft*) to summon (up); (*Armee, Polizei*) to mobilize

aufblasen ['aʊfbla:zən] (*unreg*) *vt* to blow up, to inflate ♦ *vr* (*umg*) to become bigheaded

aufbleiben ['aʊfblaɪbən] (*unreg*) *vi* (*Laden*) to remain open; (*Person*) to stay up

aufblenden ['aʊfblɛndən] *vt* (*Scheinwerfer*) to switch on full beam ♦ *vi* (*Fahrer*) to have the lights on full beam; (*AUT: Scheinwerfer*) to be on full beam

aufblicken ['aʊfblɪkən] *vi* to look up; **~ zu** to look up at; (*fig*) to look up to

aufblühen ['aʊfbly:ən] *vi* to blossom, to flourish

aufbrauchen ['aʊfbraʊxən] *vt* to use up

aufbrausen ['aʊfbraʊzən] *vi* (*fig*) to flare up; **~d** *adj* hot-tempered

aufbrechen ['aufbrɛçən] (*unreg*) *vt* to break *od* prise (*BRIT*) open ♦ *vi* to burst open; (*gehen*) to start, to set off

aufbringen ['aufbrɪŋən] (*unreg*) *vt* (*öffnen*) to open; (*in Mode*) to bring into fashion; (*beschaffen*) to procure; (*FIN*) to raise; (*ärgern*) to irritate; **Verständnis für etw ~** to be able to understand sth

Aufbruch ['aufbrʊx] *m* departure

aufbrühen ['aufbry:ən] *vt* (*Tee*) to make

aufbürden ['aufbʏrdən] *vt*: **jdm etw ~** to burden sb with sth

aufdecken ['aufdɛkən] *vt* to uncover

aufdrängen ['aufdrɛŋən] *vt*: **jdm etw ~** to force sth on sb ♦ *vr* (*Mensch*): **sich jdm ~** to intrude on sb

aufdrehen ['aufdre:ən] *vt* (*Wasserhahn etc*) to turn on; (*Ventil*) to open up

aufdringlich ['aufdrɪŋlɪç] *adj* pushy

aufeinander [auf|aɪ'nandər] *adv* on top of each other; (*schießen*) at each other; (*vertrauen*) each other; **~ folgen** to follow one another; **~ folgend** consecutive; **~ prallen** to hit one another

Aufenthalt ['auf|ɛnthalt] *m* stay; (*Verzögerung*) delay; (*EISENB*: *Halten*) stop; (*Ort*) haunt

Aufenthaltserlaubnis *f* residence permit

auferlegen ['auf|ɛrle:gən] *vt*: **(jdm) ~** to impose (upon sb)

Auferstehung ['auf|ɛrʃte:ʊŋ] *f* resurrection

aufessen ['auf|ɛsən] (*unreg*) *vt* to eat up

auffahr- ['auffa:r] *zW*: **~en** (*unreg*) *vi* (*herankommen*) to draw up; (*hochfahren*) to jump up; (*wütend werden*) to flare up; (*in den Himmel*) to ascend ♦ *vt* (*Kanonen, Geschütz*) to bring up; **~en auf** +*akk* (*Auto*) to run *od* crash into; **~end** *adj* hot-tempered; **A~t** *f* (*Hausauffahrt*) drive; (*Autobahnauffahrt*) slip road (*BRIT*), (*freeway*) entrance (*US*); **A~unfall** *m* pile-up

auffallen ['auffalən] (*unreg*) *vi* to be noticeable; **jdm ~** to strike sb

auffällig ['auffɛlɪç] *adj* conspicuous, striking

auffangen ['auffaŋən] (*unreg*) *vt* to catch; (*Funkspruch*) to intercept; (*Preise*) to peg

auffassen ['auffasən] *vt* to understand, to comprehend; (*auslegen*) to see, to view

Auffassung *f* (*Meinung*) opinion; (*Auslegung*) view, concept; (*auch:* **~sgabe**) grasp

auffindbar ['aufffɪntba:r] *adj* to be found

auffordern ['auffɔrdərn] *vt* (*befehlen*) to call upon, to order; (*bitten*) to ask

Aufforderung *f* (*Befehl*) order; (*Einladung*) invitation

auffrischen ['aufffrɪʃən] *vt* to freshen up; (*Kenntnisse*) to brush up; (*Erinnerungen*) to reawaken ♦ *vi* (*Wind*) to freshen

aufführen ['auffy:rən] *vt* (*THEAT*) to perform; (*in einem Verzeichnis*) to list, to specify ♦ *vr* (*sich benehmen*) to behave

Aufführung *f* (*THEAT*) performance; (*Liste*) specification

Aufgabe ['aufga:bə] *f* task; (*SCH*) exercise; (*Hausaufgabe*) homework; (*Verzicht*) giving up; (*von Gepäck*) registration; (*von Post*) posting; (*von Inserat*) insertion

Aufgang ['aufgaŋ] *m* ascent; (*Sonnenaufgang*) rise; (*Treppe*) staircase

aufgeben ['aufge:bən] (*unreg*) *vt* (*verzichten*) to give up; (*Paket*) to send, to post; (*Gepäck*) to register; (*Bestellung*) to give; (*Inserat*) to insert; (*Rätsel, Problem*) to set ♦ *vi* to give up

Aufgebot ['aufgəbo:t] *nt* supply; (*Eheaufgebot*) banns *pl*

aufgedunsen ['aufgədʊnzən] *adj* swollen, puffed up

aufgehen ['aufge:ən] (*unreg*) *vi* (*Sonne, Teig*) to rise; (*sich öffnen*) to open; (*klar werden*) to become clear; (*MATH*) to come out exactly; **~ (in** +*dat*) (*sich widmen*) to be absorbed (in); **in Rauch / Flammen ~** to go up in smoke/flames

aufgelegt ['aufgəle:kt] *adj*: **gut / schlecht ~ sein** to be in a good/bad mood; **zu etw ~ sein** to be in the mood for sth

aufgeregt ['aufgəre:kt] *adj* excited

aufgeschlossen ['aufgəʃlɔsən] *adj* open, open-minded

aufgeweckt ['aufgəvɛkt] *adj* bright, intelligent

aufgießen ['aufgi:sən] (*unreg*) *vt* (*Wasser*) to

pour over; (*Tee*) to infuse

aufgreifen ['aʊfɡraɪfən] (*unreg*) *vt* (*Thema*) to take up; (*Verdächtige*) to pick up, to seize

aufgrund, auf Grund [aʊf'ɡrʊnt] *präp* +*gen* on the basis of; (*wegen*) because of

aufhaben ['aʊfhaːbən] (*unreg*) *vt* to have on; (*Arbeit*) to have to do

aufhalsen ['aʊfhalzən] (*umg*) *vt*: **jdm etw ~** to saddle *od* lumber sb with sth

aufhalten ['aʊfhaltən] (*unreg*) *vt* (*Person*) to detain; (*Entwicklung*) to check; (*Tür, Hand*) to hold open; (*Augen*) to keep open ♦ *vr* (*wohnen*) to live; (*bleiben*) to stay; **sich mit etw ~** to waste time over sth

aufhängen ['aʊfhɛŋən] (*unreg*) *vt* (*Wäsche*) to hang up; (*Menschen*) to hang ♦ *vr* to hang o.s.

Aufhänger (**-s, -**) *m* (*am Mantel*) loop; (*fig*) peg

aufheben ['aʊfheːbən] (*unreg*) *vt* (*hochheben*) to raise, to lift; (*Sitzung*) to wind up; (*Urteil*) to annul; (*Gesetz*) to repeal, to abolish; (*aufbewahren*) to keep ♦ *vr* to cancel itself out; **bei jdm gut aufgehoben sein** to be well looked after at sb's; **viel A~(s) machen (von)** to make a fuss (about)

aufheitern ['aʊfhaɪtərn] *vt, vr* (*Himmel, Miene*) to brighten; (*Mensch*) to cheer up

aufhellen ['aʊfhɛlən] *vt, vr* to clear up; (*Farbe, Haare*) to lighten

aufhetzen ['aʊfhɛtsən] *vt* to stir up

aufholen ['aʊfhoːlən] *vt* to make up ♦ *vi* to catch up

aufhorchen ['aʊfhɔrçən] *vi* to prick up one's ears

aufhören ['aʊfhøːrən] *vi* to stop; **~, etw zu tun** to stop doing sth

aufklappen ['aʊfklapən] *vt* to open

aufklären ['aʊfklɛːrən] *vt* (*Geheimnis etc*) to clear up; (*Person*) to enlighten; (*sexuell*) to tell the facts of life to; (*MIL*) to reconnoitre ♦ *vr* to clear up

Aufklärung *f* (*von Geheimnis*) clearing up; (*Unterrichtung, Zeitalter*) enlightenment; (*sexuell*) sex education; (*MIL, AVIAT*) reconnaissance

aufkleben ['aʊfkleːbən] *vt* to stick on;

Aufkleber (**-s, -**) *m* sticker

aufknöpfen ['aʊfknœpfən] *vt* to unbutton

aufkommen ['aʊfkɔmən] (*unreg*) *vi* (*Wind*) to come up; (*Zweifel, Gefühl*) to arise; (*Mode*) to start; **für jdn/etw ~** to be liable *od* responsible for sb/sth

aufladen ['aʊflaːdən] (*unreg*) *vt* to load

Auflage ['aʊflaːɡə] *f* edition; (*Zeitung*) circulation; (*Bedingung*) condition

auflassen ['aʊflasən] (*unreg*) *vt* (*offen*) to leave open; (*aufgesetzt*) to leave on

auflauern ['aʊflaʊərn] *vi*: **jdm ~** to lie in wait for sb

Auflauf ['aʊflaʊf] *m* (*KOCH*) pudding; (*Menschenauflauf*) crowd

aufleben ['aʊfleːbən] *vi* (*Mensch, Gespräch*) to liven up; (*Interesse*) to revive

auflegen ['aʊfleːɡən] *vt* to put on; (*Telefon*) to hang up; (*TYP*) to print

auflehnen ['aʊfleːnən] *vt* to lean on ♦ *vr* to rebel

Auflehnung *f* rebellion

auflesen ['aʊfleːzən] (*unreg*) *vt* to pick up

aufleuchten ['aʊflɔʏçtən] *vi* to light up

auflisten ['aʊflɪstən] *vt* to list

auflockern ['aʊflɔkərn] *vt* to loosen; (*fig: Eintönigkeit etc*) to liven up

auflösen ['aʊfløːzən] *vt* to dissolve; (*Haare etc*) to loosen; (*Missverständnis*) to sort out ♦ *vr* to dissolve; to come undone; to be resolved; **(in Tränen) aufgelöst sein** to be in tears

Auflösung *f* dissolving; (*fig*) solution

aufmachen ['aʊfmaxən] *vt* to open; (*Kleidung*) to undo; (*zurechtmachen*) to do up ♦ *vr* to set out

Aufmachung *f* (*Kleidung*) outfit, get-up; (*Gestaltung*) format

aufmerksam ['aʊfmɛrkzaːm] *adj* attentive; **jdn auf etw** *akk* **~ machen** to point sth out to sb; **A~keit** *f* attention, attentiveness

aufmuntern ['aʊfmʊntərn] *vt* (*ermutigen*) to encourage; (*erheitern*) to cheer up

Aufnahme ['aʊfnaːmə] *f* reception; (*Beginn*) beginning; (*in Verein etc*) admission; (*in Liste etc*) inclusion; (*Notieren*) taking down; (*PHOT*) shot; (*auf Tonband etc*) recording;

a~fähig *adj* receptive; **~prüfung** *f*
entrance test

aufnehmen ['aʊfneːmən] (*unreg*) *vt* to
receive; (*hochheben*) to pick up; (*beginnen*)
to take up; (*in Verein etc*) to admit; (*in Liste
etc*) to include; (*fassen*) to hold; (*notieren*)
to take down; (*fotografieren*) to photograph;
(*auf Tonband, Platte*) to record; (*FIN: leihen*)
to take out; **es mit jdm ~ können** to be
able to compete with sb

aufopfern ['aʊfʔɔpfərn] *vt, vr* to sacrifice; **~d**
adj selfless

aufpassen ['aʊfpasən] *vi* (*aufmerksam sein*)
to pay attention; **auf jdn/etw ~** to look
after *od* watch sb/sth; **aufgepasst!** look
out!

Aufprall ['aʊfpral] (**-s, -e**) *m* impact; **a~en**
vi to hit, to strike

Aufpreis ['aʊfprais] *m* extra charge

aufpumpen ['aʊfpʊmpən] *vt* to pump up

aufräumen ['aʊfrɔymən] *vt, vi* (*Dinge*) to
clear away; (*Zimmer*) to tidy up

aufrecht ['aʊfrɛçt] *adj* (*auch fig*) upright;
~erhalten (*unreg*) *vt* to maintain

aufreg- ['aʊfreːg] *zW:* **~en** *vt* to excite ♦ *vr*
to get excited; **~end** *adj* exciting; **A~ung** *f*
excitement

aufreibend ['aʊfraibənt] *adj* strenuous

aufreißen ['aʊfraisən] (*unreg*) *vt* (*Umschlag*)
to tear open; (*Augen*) to open wide; (*Tür*)
to throw open; (*Straße*) to take up

aufreizen ['aʊfraitsən] *vt* to incite, to stir up;
~d *adj* exciting, stimulating

aufrichten ['aʊfrɪçtən] *vt* to put up, to
erect; (*moralisch*) to console ♦ *vr* to rise;
(*moralisch*): **sich ~ (an** +*dat*) to take heart
(from)

aufrichtig ['aʊfrɪçtɪç] *adj* sincere, honest;
A~keit *f* sincerity

aufrücken ['aʊfrʏkən] *vi* to move up;
(*beruflich*) to be promoted

Aufruf ['aʊfruːf] *m* summons; (*zur Hilfe*) call;
(*des Namens*) calling out; **a~en** (*unreg*) *vt*
(*Namen*) to call out; (*auffordern*): **jdn a~en
(zu)** to call upon sb (for)

Aufruhr ['aʊfruːr] (**-(e)s, -e**) *m* uprising,
revolt

aufrührerisch ['aʊfryːrərɪʃ] *adj* rebellious

aufrunden ['aʊfrʊndən] *vt* (*Summe*) to
round up

Aufrüstung ['aʊfrʏstʊŋ] *f* rearmament

aufrütteln ['aʊfrʏtəln] *vt* (*auch fig*) to shake
up

aufs [aʊfs] **= auf das**

aufsagen ['aʊfzaːgən] *vt* (*Gedicht*) to recite

aufsässig ['aʊfzɛsɪç] *adj* rebellious

Aufsatz ['aʊfzats] *m* (*Geschriebenes*) essay;
(*auf Schrank etc*) top

aufsaugen ['aʊfzaʊgən] (*unreg*) *vt* to soak
up

aufschauen ['aʊfʃaʊən] *vi* to look up

aufscheuchen ['aʊfʃɔyçən] *vt* to scare *od*
frighten away

aufschieben ['aʊfʃiːbən] (*unreg*) *vt* to push
open; (*verzögern*) to put off, to postpone

Aufschlag ['aʊfʃlaːk] *m* (*Ärmelaufschlag*) cuff;
(*Jackenaufschlag*) lapel; (*Hosenaufschlag*)
turn-up; (*Aufprall*) impact; (*Preisaufschlag*)
surcharge; (*Tennis*) service; **a~en** [-gən]
(*unreg*) *vt* (*öffnen*) to open; (*verwunden*) to
cut; (*hochschlagen*) to turn up; (*aufbauen:
Zelt, Lager*) to pitch, to erect; (*Wohnsitz*) to
take up ♦ *vi* (*aufprallen*) to hit; (*teurer
werden*) to go up; (*Tennis*) to serve

aufschließen ['aʊfʃliːsən] (*unreg*) *vt* to open
up, to unlock ♦ *vi* (*aufrücken*) to close up

aufschlussreich ▲ *adj* informative,
illuminating

aufschnappen ['aʊfʃnapən] *vt* (*umg*) to
pick up ♦ *vi* to fly open

aufschneiden ['aʊfʃnaidən] (*unreg*) *vt* (*Brot*)
to cut up; (*MED*) to lance ♦ *vi* to brag

Aufschneider (**-s, -**) *m* boaster, braggart

Aufschnitt ['aʊfʃnɪt] *m* (slices of) cold meat

aufschrauben ['aʊfʃraubən] *vt*
(*festschrauben*) to screw on; (*lösen*) to
unscrew

aufschrecken ['aʊfʃrɛkən] *vt* to startle ♦ *vi*
(*unreg*) to start up

aufschreiben ['aʊfʃraibən] (*unreg*) *vt* to
write down

aufschreien ['aʊfʃraiən] (*unreg*) *vi* to cry out

Aufschrift ['aʊfʃrɪft] *f* (*Inschrift*) inscription;
(*auf Etikett*) label

Aufschub ['aʊfʃuːp] (-(e)s, -schübe) *m* delay, postponement

Aufschwung ['aʊfʃvʊŋ] *m* (*Elan*) boost; (*wirtschaftlich*) upturn, boom; (*SPORT*) circle

aufsehen ['aʊfzeːən] (*unreg*) *vi* to look up; ~ **zu** to look up at; (*fig*) to look up to; **A~ (-s)** *nt* sensation,-stir; ~ **erregend** sensational

Aufseher(in) (-s, -) *m(f)* guard; (*im Betrieb*) supervisor; (*Museumsaufseher*) attendant; (*Parkaufseher*) keeper

auf sein ▲ *siehe auf*

aufsetzen ['aʊfzetsən] *vt* to put on; (*Dokument*) to draw up ♦ *vr* to sit up(right) ♦ *vi* (*Flugzeug*) to touch down

Aufsicht ['aʊfzɪçt] *f* supervision; **die ~ haben** to be in charge

Aufsichtsrat *m* (supervisory) board

aufsitzen ['aʊfzɪtsən] (*unreg*) *vi* (*aufrecht hinsitzen*) to sit up; (*aufs Pferd, Motorrad*) to mount, to get on; (*Schiff*) to run aground; **jdm ~** (*umg*) to be taken in by sb

aufsparen ['aʊfʃpaːrən] *vt* to save (up)

aufsperren ['aʊfʃperən] *vt* to unlock; (*Mund*) to open wide

aufspielen ['aʊfʃpiːlən] *vr* to show off

aufspießen ['aʊfʃpiːsən] *vt* to spear

aufspringen ['aʊfʃprɪŋən] (*unreg*) *vi* (*hochspringen*) to jump up; (*sich öffnen*) to spring open; (*Hände, Lippen*) to become chapped; **auf etw** *akk* ~ to jump onto sth

aufspüren ['aʊfʃpyːrən] *vt* to track down, to trace

aufstacheln ['aʊfʃtaxəln] *vt* to incite

Aufstand ['aʊfʃtant] *m* insurrection, rebellion; **aufständisch** ['aʊfʃtendɪʃ] *adj* rebellious, mutinous

aufstehen ['aʊfʃteːən] (*unreg*) *vi* to get up; (*Tür*) to be open

aufsteigen ['aʊfʃtaɪgən] (*unreg*) *vi* (*hochsteigen*) to climb; (*Rauch*) to rise; **auf etw** *akk* ~ to get onto sth

aufstellen ['aʊfʃtelən] *vt* (*aufrecht stellen*) to put up; (*aufreihen*) to line up; (*nominieren*) to nominate; (*formulieren: Programm etc*) to draw up; (*leisten: Rekord*) to set up

Aufstellung *f* (*SPORT*) line-up; (*Liste*) list

Aufstieg ['aʊfʃtiːk] (-(e)s, -e) *m* (*auf Berg*) ascent; (*Fortschritt*) rise; (*beruflich, SPORT*) promotion

aufstocken ['aʊfʃtɔkən] *vt* (*Kapital*) to increase

aufstoßen ['aʊfʃtoːsən] (*unreg*) *vt* to push open ♦ *vi* to belch

aufstützen ['aʊfʃtʏtsən] *vt* (*Körperteil*) to prop, to lean; (*Person*) to prop up ♦ *vr*: **sich auf etw** *akk* ~ to lean on sth

aufsuchen ['aʊfzuːxən] *vt* (*besuchen*) to visit; (*konsultieren*) to consult

Auftakt ['aʊftakt] *m* (*MUS*) upbeat; (*fig*) prelude

auftanken ['aʊftaŋkən] *vi* to get petrol (*BRIT*) od gas (*US*) ♦ *vt* to refuel

auftauchen ['aʊftaʊxən] *vi* to appear; (*aus Wasser etc*) to emerge; (*U-Boot*) to surface; (*Zweifel*) to arise

auftauen ['aʊftaʊən] *vt* to thaw ♦ *vi* to thaw; (*fig*) to relax

aufteilen ['aʊftaɪlən] *vt* to divide up; (*Raum*) to partition; **Aufteilung** *f* division; partition

Auftrag ['aʊftraːk] (-(e)s, -träge) *m* order; (*Anweisung*) commission; (*Aufgabe*) mission; **im ~ von** on behalf of; **a~en** [-gən] (*unreg*) *vt* (*Essen*) to serve; (*Farbe*) to put on; (*Kleidung*) to wear out; **jdm etw a~en** to tell sb sth; **dick a~en** (*fig*) to exaggerate; **~geber (-s, -)** *m* (*COMM*) purchaser, customer

auftreiben ['aʊftraɪbən] (*unreg*) *vt* (*umg: beschaffen*) to raise

auftreten ['aʊftreːtən] (*unreg*) *vt* to kick open ♦ *vi* to appear; (*mit Füßen*) to tread; (*sich verhalten*) to behave; **A~ (-s)** *nt* (*Vorkommen*) appearance; (*Benehmen*) behaviour

Auftrieb ['aʊftriːp] *m* (*PHYS*) buoyancy, lift; (*fig*) impetus

Auftritt ['aʊftrɪt] *m* (*des Schauspielers*) entrance; (*Szene: auch fig*) scene

aufwachen ['aʊfvaxən] *vi* to wake up

aufwachsen ['aʊfvaksən] (*unreg*) *vi* to grow up

Aufwand ['aʊfvant] (-(e)s) *m* expenditure; (*Kosten auch*) expense; (*Luxus*) show

aufwändig ▲ ['aʊfvɛndɪç] *adj* costly

aufwärmen ['aʊfvɛrmən] *vt* to warm up; (*alte Geschichten*) to rake up

aufwärts ['aʊfvɛrts] *adv* upwards; **A~entwicklung** *f* upward trend

Aufwasch ['aʊfvaʃ] *m* washing-up

aufwecken ['aʊfvɛkən] *vt* to wake up, to waken up

aufweisen ['aʊfvaɪzən] (*unreg*) *vt* to show

aufwenden ['aʊfvɛndən] (*unreg*) *vt* to expend; (*Geld*) to spend; (*Sorgfalt*) to devote

aufwendig *adj siehe* **aufwändig**

aufwerfen ['aʊfvɛrfən] (*unreg*) *vt* (*Fenster etc*) to throw open; (*Probleme*) to throw up, to raise

aufwerten ['aʊfvɛrtən] *vt* (*FIN*) to revalue; (*fig*) to raise in value

aufwickeln ['aʊfvɪkəln] *vt* (*aufrollen*) to roll up; (*umg: Haar*) to put in curlers

aufwiegen ['aʊfviːgən] (*unreg*) *vt* to make up for

Aufwind ['aʊfvɪnt] *m* up-current

aufwirbeln ['aʊfvɪrbəln] *vt* to whirl up; **Staub ~** (*fig*) to create a stir

aufwischen ['aʊfvɪʃən] *vt* to wipe up

aufzählen ['aʊftsɛːlən] *vt* to list

aufzeichnen ['aʊftsaɪçnən] *vt* to sketch; (*schriftlich*) to jot down; (*auf Band*) to record

Aufzeichnung *f* (*schriftlich*) note; (*Tonbandaufzeichnung*) recording; (*Filmaufzeichnung*) record

aufzeigen ['aʊftsaɪgən] *vt* to show, to demonstrate

aufziehen ['aʊftsiːən] (*unreg*) *vt* (*hochziehen*) to raise, to draw up; (*öffnen*) to pull open; (*Uhr*) to wind; (*umg: necken*) to tease; (*großziehen: Kinder*) to raise, to bring up; (*Tiere*) to rear

Aufzug ['aʊftsuːk] *m* (*Fahrstuhl*) lift, elevator; (*Aufmarsch*) procession, parade; (*Kleidung*) get-up; (*THEAT*) act

aufzwingen ['aʊftsvɪŋən] (*unreg*) *vt*: **jdm etw ~** to force sth upon sb

Augapfel ['aʊkʔapfəl] *m* eyeball; (*fig*) apple of one's eye

Auge ['aʊgə] (*-s*, *-n*) *nt* eye; (*Fettauge*) ·

globule of fat; **unter vier ~n** in private

Augen- *zW*: **~blick** *m* moment; **im ~blick** at the moment; **a~blicklich** *adj* (*sofort*) instantaneous; (*gegenwärtig*) present; **~braue** *f* eyebrow; **~optiker(in)** *m(f)* optician; **~weide** *f* sight for sore eyes; **~zeuge** *m* eye witness

August [aʊˈgʊst] (*-(e)s* *od* *-*, *-e*) *m* August

Auktion [aʊktsiˈoːn] *f* auction

Aula ['aʊla] (*-*, **Aulen** *od* *-s*) *f* assembly hall

SCHLÜSSELWORT

aus [aʊs] *präp +dat* **1** (*räumlich*) out of; (*von ... her*) from; **er ist aus Berlin** he's from Berlin; **aus dem Fenster** out of the window

2 (*gemacht/hergestellt aus*) made of; **ein Herz aus Stein** a heart of stone

3 (*auf Ursache deutend*) out of; **aus Mitleid** out of sympathy; **aus Erfahrung** from experience; **aus Spaß** for fun

4: **aus ihr wird nie etwas** she'll never get anywhere

♦ *adv* **1** (*zu Ende*) finished, over; **aus sein** to be over; **aus und vorbei** over and done with

2 (*ausgeschaltet, ausgezogen*) out; (*Aufschrift an Geräten*) off; **aus sein** (*nicht brennen*) to be out; (*abgeschaltet sein: Radio, Herd*) to be off; **Licht aus!** lights out!

3 (*nicht zu Hause*): **aus sein** to be out

4 (*in Verbindung mit von*): **von Rom aus** from Rome; **vom Fenster aus** out of the window; **von sich aus** (*selbstständig*) of one's own accord; **von ihm aus** as far as he's concerned

---

ausarbeiten ['aʊsʔarbaɪtən] *vt* to work out

ausarten ['aʊsʔartən] *vi* to degenerate

ausatmen ['aʊsʔaːtmən] *vi* to breathe out

ausbaden ['aʊsbaːdən] (*umg*) *vt*: **etw ~ müssen** to carry the can for sth

Ausbau ['aʊsbaʊ] *m* extension, expansion; removal; **a~en** *vt* to extend, to expand; (*herausnehmen*) to take out, to remove; **a~fähig** *adj* (*fig*) worth developing

ausbessern ['aʊsbɛsərn] *vt* to mend, to

repair
ausbeulen ['ausbɔylən] *vt* to beat out
Ausbeute ['ausbɔytə] *f* yield; (*Fische*) catch; **a~n** *vt* to exploit; (*MIN*) to work
ausbild- ['ausbɪld] *zW:* **~en** *vt* to educate; (*Lehrling, Soldat*) to instruct, to train; (*Fähigkeiten*) to develop; (*Geschmack*) to cultivate; **A~er (-s, -)** *m* instructor; **A~ung** *f* education; training, instruction; development; cultivation
ausbleiben ['ausblaɪbən] (*unreg*) *vi* (*Personen*) to stay away, not to come; (*Ereignisse*) to fail to happen, not to happen
Ausblick ['ausblɪk] *m* (*auch fig*) prospect, outlook, view
ausbrechen ['ausbrɛçən] (*unreg*) *vi* to break out ♦ *vt* to break off; **in Tränen/Gelächter ~** to burst into tears/out laughing
ausbreiten ['ausbraɪtən] *vt* to spread (out); (*Arme*) to stretch out ♦ *vr* to spread; **sich über ein Thema ~** to expand *od* enlarge on a topic
ausbrennen ['ausbrɛnən] (*unreg*) *vt* to scorch; (*Wunde*) to cauterize ♦ *vi* to burn out
Ausbruch ['ausbrux] *m* outbreak; (*von Vulkan*) eruption; (*Gefühlsausbruch*) outburst; (*von Gefangenen*) escape
ausbrüten ['ausbry:tən] *vt* (*auch fig*) to hatch
Ausdauer ['ausdauər] *f* perseverance, stamina; **a~nd** *adj* persevering
ausdehnen ['ausde:nən] *vt, vr* (*räumlich*) to expand; (*zeitlich, auch Gummi*) to stretch; (*Nebel, fig: Macht*) to extend
ausdenken ['ausdɛŋkən] (*unreg*) *vt:* **sich** *dat* **etw ~** to think sth up
Ausdruck ['ausdruk] *m* expression, phrase; (*Kundgabe, Gesichtsausdruck*) expression; (*COMPUT*) print-out, hard copy; **a~en** *vt* (*COMPUT*) to print out
ausdrücken ['ausdrykən] *vt* (*auch vr: formulieren, zeigen*) to express; (*Zigarette*) to put out; (*Zitrone*) to squeeze
ausdrücklich *adj* express, explicit
ausdrucks- *zW:* **~los** *adj* expressionless, blank; **~voll** *adj* expressive; **A~weise** *f*

mode of expression
auseinander [aus|aɪ'nandər] *adv* (*getrennt*) apart; **~ schreiben** to write as separate words; **~ bringen** to separate; **~ fallen** to fall apart; **~ gehen** (*Menschen*) to separate; (*Meinungen*) to differ; (*Gegenstand*) to fall apart; **~ halten** to tell apart; **~ nehmen** to take to pieces, to dismantle; **~ setzen** (*erklären*) to set forth, to explain; **sich ~ setzen** (*sich verständigen*) to come to terms, to settle; (*sich befassen*) to concern o.s.; **A~setzung** *f* argument
ausfahren ['ausfa:rən] (*unreg*) *vt* (*spazieren fahren: im Auto*) to take for a drive; (: *im Kinderwagen*) to take for a walk; (*liefern*) to deliver
Ausfahrt *f* (*des Zuges etc*) leaving, departure; (*Autobahnausfahrt*) exit; (*Garagenausfahrt etc*) exit, way out; (*Spazierfahrt*) drive, excursion
Ausfall ['ausfal] *m* loss; (*Nichtstattfinden*) cancellation; (*MIL*) sortie; (*radioaktiv*) fall-out; **a~en** (*unreg*) *vi* (*Zähne, Haare*) to fall *od* come out; (*nicht stattfinden*) to be cancelled; (*wegbleiben*) to be omitted; (*Person*) to drop out; (*Lohn*) to be stopped; (*nicht funktionieren*) to break down; (*Resultat haben*) to turn out; **~straße** *f* arterial road
ausfertigen ['ausfɛrtɪgən] *vt* (*förmlich: Urkunde, Pass*) to draw up; (*Rechnung*) to make out
Ausfertigung ['ausfɛrtɪgʊŋ] *f* drawing up; making out; (*Exemplar*) copy
ausfindig ['ausfɪndɪç] *adj:* **~ machen** to discover
ausfließen ['ausfli:sən] (*unreg*) *vt* (*her~*): **~ (aus)** to flow out (of); (*auslaufen: Öl etc*): **~ (aus)** to leak (out of)
Ausflucht ['ausfluxt] (**-, -flüchte**) *f* excuse
Ausflug ['ausflu:k] *m* excursion, outing; **Ausflügler** ['ausfly:klər] (**-s, -**) *m* tripper
Ausflugslokal *nt* tourist café
Ausfluss ▲ ['ausflus] *m* outlet; (*MED*) discharge
ausfragen ['ausfra:gən] *vt* to interrogate, to question
ausfressen ['ausfrɛsən] (*unreg*) *vt* to eat up;

(*aushöhlen*) to corrode; (*umg: anstellen*) to be up to

Ausfuhr ['ausfuːr] (-, -en) *f* export, exportation ♦ *in zW* export

ausführ- ['ausfyːr] *zW:* **~en** *vt* (*verwirklichen*) to carry out; (*Person*) to take out; (*Hund*) to take for a walk; (*COMM*) to export; (*erklären*) to give details of; **~lich** *adj* detailed ♦ *adv* in detail; **A~lichkeit** *f* detail; **A~ung** *f* execution, performance; (*Durchführung*) completion; (*Herstellungsart*) version; (*Erklärung*) explanation

ausfüllen ['ausfʏlən] *vt* to fill up; (*Fragebogen etc*) to fill in; (*Beruf*) to be fulfilling for

Ausgabe ['ausgaːbə] *f* (*Geld*) expenditure, outlay; (*Aushändigung*) giving out; (*Gepäckausgabe*) left-luggage office; (*Buch*) edition; (*Nummer*) issue; (*COMPUT*) output

Ausgang ['ausgaŋ] *m* way out, exit; (*Ende*) end; (*~spunkt*) starting point; (*Ergebnis*) result; (*Ausgehtag*) free time, time off; **kein ~** no exit

Ausgangs- *zW:* **~punkt** *m* starting point; **~sperre** *f* curfew

ausgeben ['ausgeːbən] (*unreg*) *vt* (*Geld*) to spend; (*austeilen*) to issue, to distribute ♦ *vr:* **sich für etw/jdn ~** to pass o.s. off as sth/ sb

ausgebucht ['ausgəbuːxt] *adj* (*Vorstellung, Flug, Maschine*) fully booked

ausgedient ['ausgədiːnt] *adj* (*Soldat*) discharged; (*verbraucht*) no longer in use; **~ haben** to have done good service

ausgefallen ['ausgəfalən] *adj* (*ungewöhnlich*) exceptional

ausgeglichen ['ausgəgliçən] *adj* (well-) balanced; **A~heit** *f* balance; (*von Mensch*) even-temperedness

ausgehen ['ausgeːən] (*unreg*) *vi* to go out; (*zu Ende gehen*) to come to an end; (*Benzin*) to run out; (*Haare, Zähne*) to fall *od* come out; (*Feuer, Ofen, Licht*) to go out; (*Strom*) to go off; (*Resultat haben*) to turn out; **mir ging das Benzin aus** I ran out of petrol (*BRIT*) *od* gas (*US*); **von etw ~** (*wegführen*) to lead away from sth; (*herrühren*) to come

from sth; (*zugrunde legen*) to proceed from sth; **wir können davon ~, dass ...** we can take as our starting point that ...; **leer ~** to get nothing

ausgelassen ['ausgəlasən] *adj* boisterous, high-spirited

ausgelastet ['ausgəlastət] *adj* fully occupied

ausgelernt ['ausgəlɛrnt] *adj* trained, qualified

ausgemacht ['ausgəmaxt] *adj* settled; (*umg: Dummkopf etc*) out-and-out, downright; **es war eine ~e Sache, dass ...** it was a foregone conclusion that ...

ausgenommen ['ausgənɔmən] *präp +gen* except ♦ *konj* except; **Anwesende sind ~** present company excepted

ausgeprägt ['ausgəprɛːkt] *adj* distinct

ausgerechnet ['ausgəreçnət] *adv* just, precisely; **~ du/heute** you of all people/ today of all days

ausgeschlossen ['ausgəflɔsən] *adj* (*unmöglich*) impossible, out of the question

ausgeschnitten ['ausgəfnitən] *adj* (*Kleid*) low-necked

ausgesprochen ['ausgəfprɔxən] *adj* (*Faulheit, Lüge etc*) out-and-out; (*unverkennbar*) marked ♦ *adv* decidedly

ausgezeichnet ['ausgətsaiçnət] *adj* excellent

ausgiebig ['ausgiːbiç] *adj* (*Gebrauch*) thorough, good; (*Essen*) generous, lavish; **~ schlafen** to have a good sleep

ausgießen ['ausgiːsən] *vt* to pour out; (*Behälter*) to empty

Ausgleich ['ausglaiç] (-(e)s, -e) *m* balance; (*Vermittlung*) reconciliation; (*SPORT*) equalization; **zum ~ einer Sache** *gen* in order to offset sth; **a~en** (*unreg*) *vt* to balance (out); to reconcile; (*Höhe*) to even up ♦ *vi* (*SPORT*) to equalize

ausgraben ['ausgraːbən] (*unreg*) *vt* to dig up; (*Leichen*) to exhume; (*fig*) to unearth

Ausgrabung *f* excavation; (*Ausgraben auch*) digging up

Ausguss ▲ ['ausgus] *m* (*Spüle*) sink; (*Abfluss*) outlet; (*Tülle*) spout

aushalten ['aushaltən] (*unreg*) *vt* to bear, to

stand; (*Geliebte*) to keep ♦ *vi* to hold out;
das ist nicht zum A~ that is unbearable
aushandeln ['aʊshandəln] *vt* to negotiate
aushändigen ['aʊshɛndɪgən] *vt*: **jdm etw ~**
to hand sth over to sb
Aushang ['aʊshaŋ] *m* notice
aushängen ['aʊshɛŋən] (*unreg*) *vt* (*Meldung*)
to put up; (*Fenster*) to take off its hinges
♦ *vi* to be displayed
ausharren ['aʊsharən] *vi* to hold out
ausheben ['aʊshe:bən] (*unreg*) *vt* (*Erde*) to
lift out; (*Grube*) to hollow out; (*Tür*) to take
off its hinges; (*Diebesnest*) to clear out; (*MIL*)
to enlist
aushecken ['aʊshɛkən] (*umg*) *vt* to cook up
aushelfen ['aʊshɛlfən] (*unreg*) *vi*: **jdm ~** to
help sb out
Aushilfe ['aʊshɪlfə] *f* help, assistance;
(*Person*) (temporary) worker
Aushilfs- *zW*: **~kraft** *f* temporary worker;
a~weise *adv* temporarily, as a stopgap
ausholen ['aʊsho:lən] *vi* to swing one's arm
back; (*zur Ohrfeige*) to raise one's hand;
(*beim Gehen*) to take long strides
aushorchen ['aʊshɔrçən] *vt* to sound out,
to pump
auskennen ['aʊskɛnən] (*unreg*) *vr* to know a
lot; (*an einem Ort*) to know one's way
about; (*in Fragen etc*) to be knowledgeable
Ausklang ['aʊsklaŋ] *m* end
auskleiden ['aʊsklaɪdən] *vr* to undress ♦ *vt*
(*Wand*) to line
ausklingen ['aʊsklɪŋən] (*unreg*) *vi* (*Ton, Lied*)
to die away; (*Fest*) to peter out
ausklopfen ['aʊsklɔpfən] *vt* (*Teppich*) to
beat; (*Pfeife*) to knock out
auskochen ['aʊskɔxən] *vt* to boil; (*MED*) to
sterilize; **ausgekocht** (*fig*) out-and-out
Auskommen (**-s**) *nt*: **sein A~ haben** to
have a regular income; **a~** (*unreg*) *vi*: **mit
jdm a~** to get on with sb; **mit etw a~** to
get by with sth
auskosten ['aʊskɔstən] *vt* to enjoy to the
full
auskundschaften ['aʊskʊntʃaftən] *vt* to
spy out; (*Gebiet*) to reconnoitre
Auskunft ['aʊskʊnft] (**-, -künfte**) *f*

information; (*nähere*) details *pl*, particulars
pl; (*Stelle*) information office; (*TEL*) directory
inquiries *sg*
auslachen ['aʊslaxən] *vt* to laugh at, to
mock
ausladen ['aʊsla:dən] (*unreg*) *vt* to unload;
(*umg*: *Gäste*) to cancel an invitation to
Auslage ['aʊsla:gə] *f* shop window (display);
~n *pl* (*Ausgabe*) outlay *sg*
Ausland ['aʊslant] *nt* foreign countries *pl*;
im ~ abroad; **ins ~** abroad
Ausländer(in) ['aʊslɛndər(ɪn)] (**-s, -**) *m(f)*
foreigner
ausländisch *adj* foreign
Auslands- *zW*: **~gespräch** *nt*
international call; **~reise** *f* trip abroad;
~schutzbrief *m* international travel cover
auslassen ['aʊslasən] (*unreg*) *vt* to leave
out; (*Wort etc auch*) to omit; (*Fett*) to melt;
(*Kleidungsstück*) to let out ♦ *vr*: **sich über
etw** *akk* **~** to speak one's mind about sth;
seine Wut *etc* **an jdm ~** to vent one's rage
etc on sb
Auslassung *f* omission
Auslauf ['aʊslaʊf] *m* (*für Tiere*) run; (*Ausfluss*)
outflow, outlet; **a~en** (*unreg*) *vi* to run out;
(*Behälter*) to leak; (*NAUT*) to put out (to
sea); (*langsam aufhören*) to run down
Ausläufer ['aʊslɔyfər] *m* (*von Gebirge*) spur;
(*Pflanze*) runner; (*MET*: *von Hoch*) ridge;
(: *von Tief*) trough
ausleeren ['aʊsle:rən] *vt* to empty
auslegen ['aʊsle:gən] *vt* (*Waren*) to lay out;
(*Köder*) to put down; (*Geld*) to lend;
(*bedecken*) to cover; (*Text etc*) to interpret
Auslegung *f* interpretation
ausleiern ['aʊslaɪərn] *vi* (*Gummi*) to wear
out
Ausleihe ['aʊslaɪə] *f* issuing; (*Stelle*) issue
desk; **a~n** (*unreg*) *vt* (*verleihen*) to lend; **sich**
dat **etw a~n** to borrow sth
Auslese ['aʊsle:zə] *f* selection; (*Elite*) elite;
(*Wein*) choice wine; **a~n** (*unreg*) *vt* to
select; (*umg*: *zu Ende lesen*) to finish
ausliefern ['aʊsli:fərn] *vt* to deliver (up), to
hand over; (*COMM*) to deliver; **jdm/etw
ausgeliefert sein** to be at the mercy of

sb/sth

ausloggen ['auslɔgən] *vi* (*COMPUT*) to log off

auslöschen ['auslœʃən] *vt* to extinguish; (*fig*) to wipe out, to obliterate

auslosen ['auslo:zən] *vt* to draw lots for

auslösen ['auslø:zən] *vt* (*Explosion, Schuss*) to set off; (*hervorrufen*) to cause, to produce; (*Gefangene*) to ransom; (*Pfand*) to redeem

ausmachen ['ausmaxən] *vt* (*Licht, Radio*) to turn off; (*Feuer*) to put out; (*entdecken*) to make out; (*vereinbaren*) to agree; (*beilegen*) to settle; (*Anteil darstellen, betragen*) to represent; (*bedeuten*) to matter; **macht es Ihnen etwas aus, wenn ...?** would you mind if ...?

ausmalen ['ausma:lən] *vt* to paint; (*fig*) to describe; **sich** *dat* **etw ~** to imagine sth

Ausmaß ['ausma:s] *nt* dimension; (*fig auch*) scale

ausmessen ['ausmesən] (*unreg*) *vt* to measure

Ausnahme ['ausna:mə] *f* exception; **~fall** *m* exceptional case; **~zustand** *m* state of emergency

ausnahms- *zW*: **~los** *adv* without exception; **~weise** *adv* by way of exception, for once

ausnehmen ['ausne:mən] (*unreg*) *vt* to take out, to remove; (*Tier*) to gut; (*Nest*) to rob; (*umg: Geld abnehmen*) to clean out; (*ausschließen*) to make an exception of ♦ *vr* to look, to appear; **~d** *adj* exceptional

ausnützen ['ausnʏtsən] *vt* (*Zeit, Gelegenheit*) to use, to turn to good account; (*Einfluss*) to use; (*Mensch, Gutmütigkeit*) to exploit

auspacken ['auspakən] *vt* to unpack

auspfeifen ['auspfaifən] (*unreg*) *vt* to hiss/boo at

ausplaudern ['ausplaudərn] *vt* to blab

ausprobieren ['ausprobi:rən] *vt* to try (out)

Auspuff ['auspuf] (**-(e)s, -e**) *m* (*TECH*) exhaust; **~rohr** *nt* exhaust (pipe)

ausradieren ['ausradi:rən] *vt* to erase, to rub out; (*fig*) to annihilate

ausrangieren ['ausrãʒi:rən] (*umg*) *vt* to chuck out

ausrauben ['ausraubən] *vt* to rob

ausräumen ['ausrɔymən] *vt* (*Dinge*) to clear away; (*Schrank, Zimmer*) to empty; (*Bedenken*) to dispel

ausrechnen ['ausreçnən] *vt* to calculate, to reckon

Ausrede ['ausre:də] *f* excuse; **a~n** *vi* to have one's say ♦ *vt*: **jdm etw a~n** to talk sb out of sth

ausreichen ['ausraiçən] *vi* to suffice, to be enough; **~d** *adj* sufficient, adequate; (*SCH*) adequate

Ausreise ['ausraizə] *f* departure; **bei der ~** when leaving the country; **~erlaubnis** *f* exit visa; **a~n** *vi* to leave the country

ausreißen ['ausraisən] (*unreg*) *vt* to tear *od* pull out ♦ *vi* (*Riss bekommen*) to tear; (*umg*) to make off, to scram

ausrenken ['ausrɛŋkən] *vt* to dislocate

ausrichten ['ausrɪçtən] *vt* (*Botschaft*) to deliver; (*Gruß*) to pass on; (*Hochzeit etc*) to arrange; (*in gerade Linie bringen*) to get in a straight line; (*angleichen*) to bring into line; (*TYP*) to justify; **ich werde es ihm ~** I'll tell him; **etwas/nichts bei jdm ~** to get somewhere/nowhere with sb

ausrotten ['ausrɔtən] *vt* to stamp out, to exterminate

Ausruf ['ausru:f] *m* (*Schrei*) cry, exclamation; (*Bekanntmachung*) proclamation; **a~en** (*unreg*) *vt* to cry out, to exclaim; to call out; **~ezeichen** *nt* exclamation mark

ausruhen ['ausru:ən] *vt, vr* to rest

ausrüsten ['ausrʏstən] *vt* to equip, to fit out

Ausrüstung *f* equipment

ausrutschen ['ausrutʃən] *vi* to slip

Aussage ['ausza:gə] *f* (*JUR*) statement; **a~n** *vt* to say, to state ♦ *vi* (*JUR*) to give evidence

ausschalten ['ausʃaltən] *vt* to switch off; (*fig*) to eliminate

Ausschank ['ausʃaŋk] (**-(e)s, -schänke**) *m* dispensing, giving out; (*COMM*) selling; (*Theke*) bar

Ausschau ['ausʃau] *f*: **~ halten (nach)** to look out (for), to watch (for); **a~en** *vi*: **a~en (nach)** to look out (for), to be on the look-out (for)

ausscheiden ['ausʃaidən] (*unreg*) *vt* to take

out; (*MED*) to secrete ♦ *vi*: ~ **(aus)** to leave; (*SPORT*) to be eliminated (from) *od* knocked out (of)

Ausscheidung *f* separation; secretion; elimination; (*aus Amt*) retirement

ausschenken ['aʊsʃɛŋkən] *vt* (*Alkohol, Kaffee*) to pour out; (*COMM*) to sell

ausschildern ['aʊsʃɪldərn] *vt* to signpost

ausschimpfen ['aʊsʃɪmpfən] *vt* to scold, to tell off

ausschlafen ['aʊsʃlaːfən] (*unreg*) *vi, vr* to have a good sleep ♦ *vt* to sleep off; **ich bin nicht ausgeschlafen** I didn't have *od* get enough sleep

Ausschlag ['aʊsʃlaːk] *m* (*MED*) rash; (*Pendelausschlag*) swing; (*Nadelausschlag*) deflection; **den ~ geben** (*fig*) to tip the balance; **a~en** [-gən] (*unreg*) *vt* to knock out; (*auskleiden*) to deck out; (*verweigern*) to decline ♦ *vi* (*Pferd*) to kick out; (*BOT*) to sprout; **a~gebend** *adj* decisive

ausschließen ['aʊsʃliːsən] (*unreg*) *vt* to shut *od* lock out; (*fig*) to exclude

ausschließlich *adj* exclusive ♦ *adv* exclusively ♦ *präp* +*gen* exclusive of, excluding

Ausschluss ▲ ['aʊsʃlʊs] *m* exclusion

ausschmücken ['aʊsʃmʏkən] *vt* to decorate; (*fig*) to embellish

ausschneiden ['aʊsʃnaɪdən] (*unreg*) *vt* to cut out; (*Büsche*) to trim

Ausschnitt ['aʊsʃnɪt] *m* (*Teil*) section; (*von Kleid*) neckline; (*Zeitungsausschnitt*) cutting; (*aus Film etc*) excerpt

ausschreiben ['aʊsʃraɪbən] (*unreg*) *vt* (*ganz schreiben*) to write out (in full); (*ausstellen*) to write (out); (*Stelle, Wettbewerb etc*) to announce, to advertise

Ausschreitung ['aʊsʃraɪtʊŋ] *f* (*usu pl*) riot

Ausschuss ▲ ['aʊsʃʊs] *m* committee, board; (*Abfall*) waste, scraps *pl*; (*COMM: auch:* ~**ware**) reject

ausschütten ['aʊsʃʏtən] *vt* to pour out; (*Eimer*) to empty; (*Geld*) to pay ♦ *vr* to shake (with laughter)

ausschweifend ['aʊsʃvaɪfənt] *adj* (*Leben*) dissipated, debauched; (*Fantasie*)

extravagant

aussehen ['aʊszeːən] (*unreg*) *vi* to look; **es sieht nach Regen aus** it looks like rain; **es sieht schlecht aus** things look bad; **A~** (**-s**) *nt* appearance

aus sein ▲ *siehe* **aus**

außen ['aʊsən] *adv* outside; (*nach* ~) outwards; ~ **ist es rot** it's red (on the) outside

Außen- *zW*: ~**dienst** *m*: **im ~dienst sein** to work outside the office; ~**handel** *m* foreign trade; ~**minister** *m* foreign minister; ~**ministerium** *nt* foreign office; ~**politik** *f* foreign policy; **a~politisch** *adj* (*Entwicklung, Lage*) foreign; ~**seite** *f* outside; ~**seiter** (**-s, -**) *m* outsider; ~**stände** *pl* outstanding debts; ~**stehende(r)** *f(m)* outsider; ~**welt** *f* outside world

außer ['aʊsər] *präp* +*dat* (*räumlich*) out of; (*abgesehen von*) except ♦ *konj* (*ausgenommen*) except; ~ **Gefahr** out of danger; ~ **Zweifel** beyond any doubt; ~ **Betrieb** out of order; ~ **Dienst** retired; ~ **Landes** abroad; ~ **sich** *dat* **sein** to be beside o.s.; ~ **sich akk geraten** to go wild; ~ **wenn** unless; ~ **dass** except; ~**dem** *konj* besides, in addition

äußere(r, s) ['ɔysərə(r,s)] *adj* outer, external

außergewöhnlich *adj* unusual

außerhalb *präp* +*gen* outside ♦ *adv* outside

äußerlich *adj* external

äußern *vt* to utter, to express; (*zeigen*) to show ♦ *vr* to give one's opinion; (*Krankheit etc*) to show itself

außerordentlich *adj* extraordinary

außerplanmäßig *adj* unscheduled

äußerst ['ɔysərst] *adv* extremely, most; ~**e(r, s)** *adj* utmost; (*räumlich*) farthest; (*Termin*) last possible; (*Preis*) highest

Äußerung *f* remark, comment

aussetzen ['aʊszɛtsən] *vt* (*Kind, Tier*) to abandon; (*Boote*) to lower; (*Belohnung*) to offer; (*Urteil, Verfahren*) to postpone ♦ *vi* (*aufhören*) to stop; (*Pause machen*) to have a break; **jdm/etw ausgesetzt sein** to be exposed to sb/sth; **an jdm/etw etwas ~** to find fault with sb/sth

Aussicht ['ausziçt] *f* view; (*in Zukunft*) prospect; **etw in ~ haben** to have sth in view

Aussichts- *zW:* **a~los** *adj* hopeless; **~punkt** *m* viewpoint; **a~reich** *adj* promising; **~turm** *m* observation tower

aussöhnen ['auszø:nən] *vt* to reconcile ♦ *vr* to reconcile o.s., to become reconciled

aussondern ['auszɔndərn] *vt* to separate, to select

aussortieren ['auszɔrti:rən] *vt* to sort out

ausspannen ['ausʃpanən] *vt* to spread *od* stretch out; (*Pferd*) to unharness; (*umg: Mädchen*) **(jdm) jdn ~** to steal sb (from sb) ♦ *vi* to relax

aussperren ['ausʃpɛrən] *vt* to lock out

ausspielen ['ausʃpi:lən] *vt* (*Karte*) to lead; (*Geldprämie*) to offer as a prize ♦ *vi* (*KARTEN*) to lead; **jdn gegen jdn ~** to play sb off against sb; **ausgespielt haben** to be finished

Aussprache ['ausʃpra:xə] *f* pronunciation; (*Unterredung*) (frank) discussion

aussprechen ['ausʃprɛçən] (*unreg*) *vt* to pronounce; (*äußern*) to say, to express ♦ *vr* (*sich äußern*): **sich ~ (über** +*akk*) to speak (about); (*sich anvertrauen*) to unburden o.s. (about *od* on); (*diskutieren*) to discuss ♦ *vi* (*zu Ende sprechen*) to finish speaking

Ausspruch ['ausʃprux] *m* saying, remark

ausspülen ['ausʃpy:lən] *vt* to wash out; (*Mund*) to rinse

Ausstand ['ausʃtant] *m* strike; **in den ~ treten** to go on strike

ausstatten ['ausʃtatən] *vt* (*Zimmer etc*) to furnish; (*Person*) to equip, to kit out

Ausstattung *f* (*Ausstatten*) provision; (*Kleidung*) outfit; (*Aufmachung*) make-up; (*Einrichtung*) furnishing

ausstechen ['ausʃtɛçən] (*unreg*) *vt* (*Augen, Rasen, Graben*) to dig out; (*Kekse*) to cut out; (*übertreffen*) to outshine

ausstehen ['ausʃte:ən] (*unreg*) *vt* to stand, to endure ♦ *vi* (*noch nicht da sein*) to be outstanding

aussteigen ['ausʃtaigən] (*unreg*) *vi* to get

out, to alight

ausstellen ['ausʃtɛlən] *vt* to exhibit, to display; (*umg: ausschalten*) to switch off; (*Rechnung etc*) to make out; (*Pass, Zeugnis*) to issue

Ausstellung *f* exhibition; (*FIN*) drawing up; (*einer Rechnung*) making out; (*eines Passes etc*) issuing

aussterben ['ausʃtɛrbən] (*unreg*) *vi* to die out

Aussteuer ['ausʃtɔyər] *f* dowry

Ausstieg ['ausʃti:k] (**-(e)s, -e**) *m* exit

ausstopfen ['ausʃtɔpfən] *vt* to stuff

ausstoßen ['ausʃto:sən] (*unreg*) *vt* (*Luft, Rauch*) to give off, to emit; (*aus Verein etc*) to expel, to exclude; (*Auge*) to poke out

ausstrahlen ['ausʃtra:lən] *vt, vi* to radiate; (*RADIO*) to broadcast

Ausstrahlung *f* radiation; (*fig*) charisma

ausstrecken ['ausʃtrɛkən] *vt, vr* to stretch out

ausstreichen ['ausʃtraiçən] (*unreg*) *vt* to cross out; (*glätten*) to smooth (out)

ausströmen ['ausʃtrø:mən] *vi* (*Gas*) to pour out, to escape ♦ *vt* to give off; (*fig*) to radiate

aussuchen ['auszu:xən] *vt* to select, to pick out

Austausch ['austauʃ] *m* exchange; **a~bar** *adj* exchangeable; **a~en** *vt* to exchange, to swap

austeilen ['austailən] *vt* to distribute, to give out

Auster ['austər] (**-, -n**) *f* oyster

austoben ['austo:bən] *vr* (*Kind*) to run wild; (*Erwachsene*) to sow one's wild oats

austragen ['austra:gən] (*unreg*) *vt* (*Post*) to deliver; (*Streit etc*) to decide; (*Wettkämpfe*) to hold

Australien [aus'tra:liən] (**-s**) *nt* Australia; **Australier(in)** (**-s, -**) *m(f)* Australian; **australisch** *adj* Australian

austreiben ['austraibən] (*unreg*) *vt* to drive out, to expel; (*Geister*) to exorcize

austreten ['austre:tən] (*unreg*) *vi* (*zur Toilette*) to be excused ♦ *vt* (*Feuer*) to tread out, to trample; (*Schuhe*) to wear out; (*Treppe*) to

wear down; **aus etw ~** to leave sth
austrinken ['aʊstrɪŋkən] (*unreg*) *vt* (*Glas*) to drain; (*Getränk*) to drink up ♦ *vi* to finish one's drink, to drink up
Austritt ['aʊstrɪt] *m* emission; (*aus Verein, Partei etc*) retirement, withdrawal
austrocknen ['aʊstrɔknən] *vt*, *vi* to dry up
ausüben ['aʊsˈyːbən] *vt* (*Beruf*) to practise, to carry out; (*Funktion*) to perform; (*Einfluss*) to exert; **einen Reiz auf jdn ~** to hold an attraction for sb; **eine Wirkung auf jdn ~** to have an effect on sb
Ausverkauf ['aʊsfɛrkaʊf] *m* sale; **a~en** *vt* to sell out; (*Geschäft*) to sell up; **a~t** *adj* (*Karten, Artikel*) sold out; (*THEAT: Haus*) full
Auswahl ['aʊsvaːl] *f*: **eine ~ (an** +*dat*) a selection (of), a choice (of)
auswählen ['aʊsvɛːlən] *vt* to select, to choose
Auswander- ['aʊsvandər] *zW*: **~er** *m* emigrant; **a~n** *vi* to emigrate; **~ung** *f* emigration
auswärtig ['aʊsvɛrtɪç] *adj* (*nicht am/vom Ort*) out-of-town; (*ausländisch*) foreign
auswärts ['aʊsvɛrts] *adv* outside; (*nach außen*) outwards; **~ essen** to eat out; **A~spiel** ['aʊsvɛrtsʃpiːl] *nt* away game
auswechseln ['aʊsvɛksəln] *vt* to change, to substitute
Ausweg ['aʊsveːk] *m* way out; **a~los** *adj* hopeless
ausweichen ['aʊsvaɪçən] (*unreg*) *vi*: **jdm/ etw ~** to move aside *od* make way for sb/ sth; (*fig*) to side-step sb/sth; **~d** *adj* evasive
ausweinen ['aʊsvaɪnən] *vr* to have a (good) cry
Ausweis ['aʊsvaɪs] (**-es, -e**) *m* identity card; passport; (*Mitgliedsausweis, Bibliotheksausweis etc*) card; **a~en** [-zən] (*unreg*) *vt* to expel, to banish ♦ *vr* to prove one's identity; **~kontrolle** *f* identity check; **~papiere** *pl* identity papers; **~ung** *f* expulsion
ausweiten ['aʊsvaɪtən] *vt* to stretch
auswendig ['aʊsvɛndɪç] *adv* by heart
auswerten ['aʊsveːrtən] *vt* to evaluate; **Auswertung** *f* evaluation, analysis; (*Nutzung*) utilization

auswirken ['aʊsvɪrkən] *vr* to have an effect; **Auswirkung** *f* effect
auswischen ['aʊsvɪʃən] *vt* to wipe out; **jdm eins ~** (*umg*) to put one over on sb
Auswuchs ['aʊsvuːks] *m* (out)growth; (*fig*) product
auszahlen ['aʊstsaːlən] *vt* (*Lohn, Summe*) to pay out; (*Arbeiter*) to pay off; (*Miterbe*) to buy out ♦ *vr* (*sich lohnen*) to pay
auszählen ['aʊstsɛːlən] *vt* (*Stimmen*) to count
auszeichnen ['aʊstsaɪçnən] *vt* to honour; (*MIL*) to decorate; (*COMM*) to price ♦ *vr* to distinguish o.s.
Auszeichnung *f* distinction; (*COMM*) pricing; (*Ehrung*) awarding of decoration; (*Ehre*) honour; (*Orden*) decoration; **mit ~** with distinction
ausziehen ['aʊstsiːən] (*unreg*) *vt* (*Kleidung*) to take off; (*Haare, Zähne, Tisch etc*) to pull out; (*nachmalen*) to trace ♦ *vr* to undress ♦ *vi* (*aufbrechen*) to leave; (*aus Wohnung*) to move out
Auszubildende(r) ['aʊstsubɪldəndə(r)] *f(m)* trainee
Auszug ['aʊstsuːk] *m* (*aus Wohnung*) removal; (*aus Buch etc*) extract; (*Konto~*) statement; (*Ausmarsch*) departure
Auto ['aʊto] (**-s, -s**) *nt* (*motor*)car; **~ fahren** to drive; **~atlas** *m* road atlas; **~bahn** *f* motorway; **~bahndreieck** *nt* motorway junction; **~bahngebühr** *f* toll; **~bahnkreuz** *nt* motorway intersection; **~bus** *m* bus; **~fähre** *f* car ferry; **~fahrer(in)** *m(f)* motorist, driver; **~fahrt** *f* drive; **a~gen** [-'geːn] *adj* autogenous; **~'gramm** *nt* autograph

---

Autobahn

i *An* **Autobahn** *is a motorway. In former West Germany there is a widespread motorway network but in the former* **DDR** *the motorways are somewhat less extensive. There is no overall speed limit but a limit of 130 km/hour is recommended and there are lower mandatory limits on certain stretches of road. As yet there are no tolls payable on*

German Autobahnen. However, a yearly toll is payable in Switzerland and tolls have been introduced in Austria.

Auto- zW: **~'mat** (**-en, -en**) m machine; **~matik** [auto'ma:tik] f (AUT) automatic; **a~'matisch** adj automatic; **a~nom** [-'no:m] adj autonomous

Autor(in) ['autɔr(ɪn)] (**-s, -en**) m(f) author

Auto- zW: **~radio** nt car radio; **~reifen** m car tyre; **~reisezug** m motorail train; **~rennen** nt motor racing

autoritär [autori'tɛ:r] adj authoritarian

Autorität f authority

Auto- zW: **~telefon** nt car phone; **~unfall** m car od motor accident; **~vermietung** m car hire (BRIT) od rental (US); **~waschanlage** f car wash

Axt [akst] (**-, ¨e**) f axe

B, b

Baby ['be:bi] (**-s, -s**) nt baby; **~nahrung** f baby food; **~sitter** (**-s, -**) m baby-sitter

Bach [bax] (**-(e)s, ¨e**) m stream, brook

Backbord (**-(e)s, -e**) nt (NAUT) port

Backe ['bakə] f cheek

backen ['bakən] (unreg) vt, vi to bake

Backenzahn m molar

Bäcker ['bɛkər(ɪn)] (**-s, -**) m baker; **~ei** f bakery; (**~eiladen**) baker's (shop)

Back- zW: **~form** f baking tin; **~obst** nt dried fruit; **~ofen** m oven; **~pflaume** f prune; **~pulver** nt baking powder; **~stein** m brick

Bad [ba:t] (**-(e)s, ¨er**) nt bath; (Schwimmen) bathe; (Ort) spa

Bade- ['ba:də] zW: **~anstalt** f (swimming) baths pl; **~anzug** m bathing suit; **~hose** f bathing od swimming trunks pl; **~kappe** f bathing cap; **~mantel** m bath(ing) robe; **~meister** m baths attendant; **b~n** vi to bathe, to have a bath ♦ vt to bath; **~ort** m spa; **~tuch** nt bath towel; **~wanne** f bath (tub); **~zimmer** nt bathroom

Bagatelle [baga'tɛlə] f trifle

Bagger ['bagər] (**-s, -**) m excavator; (NAUT) dredger; **b~n** vt, vi to excavate; to dredge

Bahn [ba:n] (**-, -en**) f railway, railroad (US); (Weg) road, way; (Spur) lane; (Rennbahn) track; (ASTRON) orbit; (Stoffbahn) length; **b~brechend** adj pioneering; **~Card** ['ba:nka:rd] (**-, -s**) ® f ≃ railcard; **~damm** m railway embankment; **b~en** vt: **sich/ jdm einen Weg b~en** to clear a way/a way for sb; **~fahrt** f railway journey; **~fracht** f rail freight; **~hof** (**-, -s**) m station; **auf dem ~hof** at the station; **~hofshalle** f station concourse; **~linie** f (railway) line; **~steig** m platform; **~übergang** m level crossing, grade crossing (US)

Bahre ['ba:rə] f stretcher

Bakterien [bak'te:riən] pl bacteria pl

Balance [ba'lã:sə] f balance, equilibrium

balan'cieren vt, vi to balance

bald [balt] adv (zeitlich) soon; (beinahe) almost; **~ig** ['baldɪç] adj early, speedy

Baldrian ['baldria:n] (**-s, -e**) m valerian

Balkan ['balka:n] (**-s**) m: **der ~** the Balkans pl

Balken ['balkən] (**-s, -**) m beam; (Tragbalken) girder; (Stützbalken) prop

Balkon [bal'kõ:] (**-s, -s** od **-e**) m balcony; (THEAT) (dress) circle

Ball [bal] (**-(e)s, ¨e**) m ball; (Tanz) dance, ball

Ballast ['balast] (**-(e)s, -e**) m ballast; (fig) weight, burden

Ballen ['balən] (**-s, -**) m bale; (ANAT) ball; **b~** vt (formen) to make into a ball; (Faust) to clench ♦ vr (Wolken etc) to build up; (Menschen) to gather

Ballett [ba'lɛt] (**-(e)s, -e**) nt ballet

Ballkleid nt evening dress

Ballon [ba'lõ:] (**-s, -s** od **-e**) m balloon

Ballspiel nt ball game

Ballungsgebiet ['baluŋsgəbi:t] nt conurbation

Baltikum ['baltikʊm] (**-s**) nt: **das ~** the Baltic States

Banane [ba'na:nə] f banana

Band¹ [bant] (**-(e)s, ¨e**) m (Buchband) volume

Band² (-(e)s, ⸚er) nt (Stoffband) ribbon, tape; (Fließband) production line; (Tonband) tape; (ANAT) ligament; **etw auf ~ aufnehmen** to tape sth; **am laufenden ~** (umg) non-stop

Band³ (-(e)s, -e) nt (Freundschaftsband etc) bond

Band⁴ [bɛnt] (-, -s) f band, group

band etc vb siehe **binden**

Bandage [ban'daːʒə] f bandage

banda'gieren vt to bandage

Bande ['bandə] f band; (Straßenbande) gang

bändigen ['bɛndɪɡən] vt (Tier) to tame; (Trieb, Leidenschaft) to control, to restrain

Bandit [ban'diːt] (-en, -en) m bandit

Band- zW: **~nudel** f (KOCH: gew pl) ribbon noodles pl; **~scheibe** f (ANAT) disc; **~wurm** m tapeworm

bange ['baŋə] adj scared; (besorgt) anxious; **jdm wird es ~** sb is becoming scared; **jdm B~ machen** to scare sb; **~n** vi: **um jdn/ etw ~n** to be anxious od worried about sb/sth

Bank¹ [baŋk] (-, ⸚e) f (Sitz~) bench; (Sand~ etc) (sand)bank, (sand)bar

Bank² [baŋk] (-, -en) f (Geldbank) bank; **~anweisung** f banker's order; **~einzug** m direct debit

Bankett [ban'kɛt] (-(e)s, -e) nt (Essen) banquet; (Straßenrand) verge (BRIT), shoulder (US)

Bankier [baŋki'eː] (-s, -s) m banker

Bank- zW: **~konto** m bank account; **~leitzahl** f bank sort code number; **~note** f banknote; **~raub** m bank robbery

Bankrott [baŋ'krɔt] (-(e)s, -e) m bankruptcy; **~ machen** to go bankrupt; **b~** adj bankrupt

Bankverbindung f banking arrangements pl; **geben Sie bitte Ihre ~ an** please give your account details

Bann [ban] (-(e)s, -e) m (HIST) ban; (Kirchenbann) excommunication; (fig: Zauber) spell; **b~en** vt (Geister) to exorcize; (Gefahr) to avert; (bezaubern) to enchant; (HIST) to banish

Banner (-s, -) nt banner, flag

Bar (-, -s) f bar

bar [baːr] adj (+gen) (unbedeckt) bare; (frei von) lacking (in); (offenkundig) utter, sheer; **~e(s) Geld** cash; **etw (in) ~ bezahlen** to pay sth (in) cash; **etw für ~e Münze nehmen** (fig) to take sth at its face value

Bär [bɛːr] (-en, -en) m bear

Baracke [ba'rakə] f hut

barbarisch [bar'baːrɪʃ] adj barbaric, barbarous

Bar- zW: **b~fuß** adj barefoot; **~geld** nt cash, ready money; **b~geldlos** adj non-cash

Barkauf m cash purchase

Barkeeper ['baːrkiːpər] (-s, -) m barman, bartender

barmherzig [barm'hɛrtsɪç] adj merciful, compassionate

Baron [ba'roːn] (-s, -e) m baron; **~in** f baroness

Barren ['barən] (-s, -) m parallel bars pl; (Goldbarren) ingot

Barriere [bari'ɛːrə] f barrier

Barrikade [bari'kaːdə] f barricade

Barsch [barʃ] (-(e)s, -e) m perch

barsch [barʃ] adj brusque, gruff

Bar- zW: **~schaft** f ready money; **~scheck** m open od uncrossed cheque (BRIT), open check (US)

Bart [baːrt] (-(e)s, ⸚e) m beard; (Schlüsselbart) bit; **bärtig** ['bɛːrtɪç] adj bearded

Barzahlung f cash payment

Base ['baːzə] f (CHEM) base; (Kusine) cousin

Basel ['baːzəl] nt Basle

Basen pl von **Base**; **Basis**

basieren [ba'ziːrən] vt to base ♦ vi to be based

Basis ['baːzɪs] (-, **Basen**) f basis

Bass ▲ [bas] (-es, ⸚e) m bass

Bassin [ba'sɛː] (-s, -s) nt pool

basteln ['bastəln] vt to make ♦ vi to do handicrafts

bat etc [baːt] vb siehe **bitten**

Bataillon [batal'joːn] (-s, -e) nt battalion

Batik ['baːtɪk] f (Verfahren) batik

Batterie [batə'riː] f battery

Bau [bau] (-(e)s) m (~en) building,

construction; (*Aufbau*) structure; (*Körperbau*) frame; (*~stelle*) building site; (*pl ~e: Tierbau*) hole, burrow; (: *MIN*) working(s); (*pl ~ten: Gebäude*) building; **sich im ~ befinden** to be under construction; **~arbeiten** *pl* building *od* construction work *sg*; **~arbeiter** *m* building worker

Bauch [baux] **(-(e)s, Bäuche)** *m* belly; (*ANAT auch*) stomach, abdomen; **~fell** *nt* peritoneum; **b~ig** *adj* bulbous; **~nabel** *m* navel; **~redner** *m* ventriloquist; **~schmerzen** *pl* stomachache; **~weh** *nt* stomachache

Baudenkmal *nt* historical monument

bauen ['bauən] *vt, vi* to build; (*TECH*) to construct; **auf jdn/etw ~** to depend *od* count upon sb/sth

Bauer[1] ['bauər] **(-n** *od* **-s, -n)** *m* farmer; (*Schach*) pawn

Bauer[2] ['bauər] **(-s, -)** *nt od m* (bird)cage

Bäuerin ['bɔyərɪn] *f* farmer; (*Frau des Bauers*) farmer's wife

bäuerlich *adj* rustic

Bauern- *zW:* **~haus** *nt* farmhouse; **~hof** *m* farm(yard)

Bau- *zW:* **b~fällig** *adj* dilapidated; **~gelände** *f* building site; **~genehmigung** *f* building permit; **~gerüst** *nt* scaffolding; **~herr** *m* purchaser; **~kasten** *m* box of bricks; **~land** *nt* building land; **b~lich** *adj* structural

Baum [baum] **(-(e)s, Bäume)** *m* tree

baumeln ['bauməln] *vi* to dangle

bäumen ['bɔymən] *vr* to rear (up)

Baum- *zW:* **~schule** *f* nursery; **~stamm** *m* tree trunk; **~stumpf** *m* tree stump; **~wolle** *f* cotton

Bau- *zW:* **~plan** *m* architect's plan; **~platz** *m* building site

bauspar- *zW:* **~en** *vi* to save with a building society; **B~kasse** *f* building society; **B~vertrag** *m* building society savings agreement

Bau- *zW:* **~stein** *m* building stone, freestone; **~stelle** *f* building site; **~teil** *nt* prefabricated part (of building); **~ten** *pl von* Bau; **~unternehmer** *m* building

contractor; **~weise** *f* (method of) construction; **~werk** *nt* building; **~zaun** *m* hoarding

Bayern ['baiərn] *nt* Bavaria

bayrisch ['baɪrɪʃ] *adj* Bavarian

Bazillus [ba'tsɪlʊs] **(-, Bazillen)** *m* bacillus

beabsichtigen [bə'apzɪçtɪgən] *vt* to intend

beacht- [bə'axt] *zW:* **~en** *vt* to take note of; (*Vorschrift*) to obey; (*Vorfahrt*) to observe; **~lich** *adj* considerable; **B~ung** *f* notice, attention, observation

Beamte(r) [bə'amtə(r)] **(-n, -n)** *m* official; (*Staatsbeamte*) civil servant; (*Bankbeamte etc*) employee

Beamtin *f siehe* Beamte(r)

beängstigend [bə'ɛŋstɪgənt] *adj* alarming

beanspruchen [bə'anʃprʊxən] *vt* to claim; (*Zeit, Platz*) to take up, to occupy; **jdn ~** to take up sb's time

beanstanden [bə'anʃtandən] *vt* to complain about, to object to

beantragen [bə'antraːgən] *vt* to apply for, to ask for

beantworten [bə'antvɔrtən] *vt* to answer; **Beantwortung** *f* (*+gen*) reply (to)

bearbeiten [bə'arbaɪtən] *vt* to work; (*Material*) to process; (*Thema*) to deal with; (*Land*) to cultivate; (*CHEM*) to treat; (*Buch*) to revise; (*umg: beeinflussen wollen*) to work on

Bearbeitung *f* processing; cultivation; treatment; revision

Bearbeitungsgebühr *f* handling charge

Beatmung [bə'aːtmʊŋ] *f* respiration

beaufsichtigen [bə'aʊfzɪçtɪgən] *vt* to supervise; **Beaufsichtigung** *f* supervision

beauftragen [bə'aʊftraːgən] *vt* to instruct; **jdn mit etw ~** to entrust sb with sth

Beauftragte(r) *f(m)* representative

bebauen [bə'baʊən] *vt* to build on; (*AGR*) to cultivate

beben ['beːbən] *vi* to tremble, to shake; **B~ (-s, -)** *nt* earthquake

Becher ['bɛçər] **(-s, -)** *m* mug; (*ohne Henkel*) tumbler

Becken ['bɛkən] **(-s, -)** *nt* basin; (*MUS*) cymbal; (*ANAT*) pelvis

bedacht [bə'daxt] *adj* thoughtful, careful; **auf etw** *akk* ~ **sein** to be concerned about sth

bedächtig [bə'dɛçtɪç] *adj* (*umsichtig*) thoughtful, reflective; (*langsam*) slow, deliberate

bedanken [bə'daŋkən] *vr*: **sich (bei jdm)** ~ to say thank you (to sb)

Bedarf [bə'darf] **(-(e)s)** *m* need, requirement; (*COMM*) demand; **je nach** ~ according to demand; **bei** ~ if necessary; ~ **an etw** *dat* **haben** to be in need of sth

Bedarfs- *zW*: ~**fall** *m* case of need; ~**haltestelle** *f* request stop

bedauerlich [bə'dauərlıç] *adj* regrettable

bedauern [bə'dauərn] *vt* to be sorry for; (*bemitleiden*) to pity; **B~ (-s)** *nt* regret; ~**swert** *adj* (*Zustände*) regrettable; (*Mensch*) pitiable, unfortunate

bedecken [bə'dɛkən] *vt* to cover

bedeckt *adj* covered; (*Himmel*) overcast

bedenken [bə'dɛŋkən] (*unreg*) *vt* to think over, to consider

Bedenken **(-s, -)** *nt* (*Überlegen*) consideration; (*Zweifel*) doubt; (*Skrupel*) scruple

bedenklich *adj* doubtful; (*bedrohlich*) dangerous, risky

Bedenkzeit *f* time to think

bedeuten [bə'dɔytən] *vt* to mean; to signify; (*wichtig sein*) to be of importance; ~**d** *adj* important; (*beträchtlich*) considerable

bedeutsam *adj* (*wichtig*) significant

Bedeutung *f* meaning; significance; (*Wichtigkeit*) importance; **b~slos** *adj* insignificant, unimportant; **b~svoll** *adj* momentous, significant

bedienen [bə'di:nən] *vt* to serve; (*Maschine*) to work, to operate ♦ *vr* (*beim Essen*) to help o.s.; **sich jds / einer Sache** ~ to make use of sb/sth

Bedienung *f* service; (*Kellnerin*) waitress; (*Verkäuferin*) shop assistant; (*Zuschlag*) service (charge)

Bedienungsanleitung *f* operating instructions *pl*

bedingen [bə'dıŋən] *vt* (*verursachen*) to cause

bedingt *adj* (*Richtigkeit, Tauglichkeit*) limited; (*Zusage, Annahme*) conditional

Bedingung *f* condition; (*Voraussetzung*) stipulation; **b~slos** *adj* unconditional

bedrängen [bə'drɛŋən] *vt* to pester, to harass

bedrohen [bə'dro:ən] *vt* to threaten; **Bedrohung** *f* threat, menace

bedrücken [bə'drʏkən] *vt* to oppress, to trouble

bedürf- [bə'dʏrf] *zW*: ~**en** (*unreg*) *vi* +*gen* to need, to require; **B~nis (-ses, -se)** *nt* need; ~**tig** *adj* in need, poor, needy

beeilen [bə'|aılən] *vr* to hurry

beeindrucken [bə'|aındrʊkən] *vt* to impress, to make an impression on

beeinflussen [bə'|aınflʊsən] *vt* to influence

beeinträchtigen [bə'|aıntrɛçtıgən] *vt* to affect adversely; (*Freiheit*) to infringe upon

beend(ig)en [bə'|ɛnd(ıg)ən] *vt* to end, to finish, to terminate

beengen [bə'|ɛŋən] *vt* to cramp; (*fig*) to hamper, to oppress

beerben [bə'|ɛrbən] *vt*: **jdn** ~ to inherit from sb

beerdigen [bə'|e:rdıgən] *vt* to bury; **Beerdigung** *f* funeral, burial

Beere ['be:rə] *f* berry; (*Traubenbeere*) grape

Beet [be:t] **(-(e)s, -e)** *nt* bed

befähigen [bə'fɛ:ıgən] *vt* to enable

befähigt *adj* (*begabt*) talented; ~ **(für)** (*fähig*) capable (of)

Befähigung *f* capability; (*Begabung*) talent, aptitude

befahrbar [bə'fa:rba:r] *adj* passable; (*NAUT*) navigable

befahren [bə'fa:rən] (*unreg*) *vt* to use, to drive over; (*NAUT*) to navigate ♦ *adj* used

befallen [bə'falən] (*unreg*) *vt* to come over

befangen [bə'faŋən] *adj* (*schüchtern*) shy, self-conscious; (*voreingenommen*) biased

befassen [bə'fasən] *vr* to concern o.s.

Befehl [bə'fe:l] **(-(e)s, -e)** *m* command, order; **b~en** (*unreg*) *vt* to order ♦ *vi* to give orders; **jdm etw b~en** to order sb to do sth; ~**sverweigerung** *f* insubordination

befestigen [bəˈfɛstɪgən] *vt* to fasten; (*stärken*) to strengthen; (*MIL*) to fortify; **~ an** +*dat* to fasten to

Befestigung *f* fastening; strengthening; (*MIL*) fortification

befeuchten [bəˈfɔʏçtən] *vt* to damp(en), to moisten

befinden [bəˈfɪndən] (*unreg*) *vr* to be; (*sich fühlen*) to feel ♦ *vt*: **jdn/etw für** *od* **als etw ~** to deem sb/sth to be sth ♦ *vi*: **~ (über** +*akk*) to decide (on), to adjudicate (on); **B~ (-s)** *nt* health, condition; (*Meinung*) view, opinion

befolgen [bəˈfɔlgən] *vt* to comply with, to follow

befördern [bəˈfœrdərn] *vt* (*senden*) to transport, to send; (*beruflich*) to promote; **Beförderung** *f* transport; promotion

befragen [bəˈfraːgən] *vt* to question

befreien [bəˈfraɪən] *vt* to set free; (*erlassen*) to exempt; **Befreiung** *f* liberation, release; (*Erlassen*) exemption

befreunden [bəˈfrɔʏndən] *vr* to make friends; (*mit Idee etc*) to acquaint o.s.

befreundet *adj* friendly

befriedigen [bəˈfriːdɪgən] *vt* to satisfy; **~d** *adj* satisfactory

Befriedigung *f* satisfaction, gratification

befristet [bəˈfrɪstət] *adj* limited

befruchten [bəˈfrʊxtən] *vt* to fertilize; (*fig*) to stimulate

Befruchtung *f*: **künstliche ~** artificial insemination

Befugnis [bəˈfuːknɪs] **(-, -se)** *f* authorization, powers *pl*

befugt *adj* authorized, entitled

Befund [bəˈfʊnt] **(-(e)s, -e)** *m* findings *pl*; (*MED*) diagnosis

befürchten [bəˈfʏrçtən] *vt* to fear; **Befürchtung** *f* fear, apprehension

befürworten [bəˈfyːrvɔrtən] *vt* to support, to speak in favour of; **Befürworter (-s, -)** *m* supporter, advocate

begabt [bəˈgaːpt] *adj* gifted

Begabung [bəˈgaːbʊŋ] *f* talent, gift

begann *etc* [bəˈgan] *vb siehe* **beginnen**

begeben [bəˈgeːbən] (*unreg*) *vr* (*gehen*) to betake o.s.; (*geschehen*) to occur; **sich ~ nach** *od* **zu** to proceed to(wards); **B~heit** *f* occurrence

begegnen [bəˈgeːgnən] *vi*: **jdm ~** to meet sb; (*behandeln*) to treat sb; **einer Sache** *dat* **~** to meet with sth

Begegnung *f* meeting

begehen [bəˈgeːən] (*unreg*) *vt* (*Straftat*) to commit; (*abschreiten*) to cover; (*Straße etc*) to use, to negotiate; (*Feier*) to celebrate

begehren [bəˈgeːrən] *vt* to desire

begehrt *adj* in demand; (*Junggeselle*) eligible

begeistern [bəˈgaɪstərn] *vt* to fill with enthusiasm, to inspire ♦ *vr*: **sich für etw ~** to get enthusiastic about sth

begeistert *adj* enthusiastic

Begierde [bəˈgiːrdə] *f* desire, passion

begierig [bəˈgiːrɪç] *adj* eager, keen

begießen [bəˈgiːsən] (*unreg*) *vt* to water; (*mit Alkohol*) to drink to

Beginn [bəˈgɪn] **(-(e)s)** *m* beginning; **zu ~** at the beginning; **b~en** (*unreg*) *vt, vi* to start, to begin

beglaubigen [bəˈglaʊbɪgən] *vt* to countersign; **Beglaubigung** *f* countersignature

begleichen [bəˈglaɪçən] (*unreg*) *vt* to settle, to pay

Begleit- [bəˈglaɪt] *zW*: **b~en** *vt* to accompany; (*MIL*) to escort; **~er (-s, -)** *m* companion; (*Freund*) escort; (*MUS*) accompanist; **~schreiben** *nt* covering letter; **~umstände** *pl* concomitant circumstances; **~ung** *f* company; (*MIL*) escort; (*MUS*) accompaniment

beglücken [bəˈglʏkən] *vt* to make happy, to delight

beglückwünschen [bəˈglʏkvʏnʃən] *vt*: **~ (zu)** to congratulate (on)

begnadigen [bəˈgnaːdɪgən] *vt* to pardon; **Begnadigung** *f* pardon, amnesty

begnügen [bəˈgnyːgən] *vr* to be satisfied, to content o.s.

begonnen *etc* [bəˈgɔnən] *vb siehe* **beginnen**

begraben [bəˈgraːbən] (*unreg*) *vt* to bury; **Begräbnis (-ses, -se)** [bəˈgrɛːpnɪs] *nt* burial, funeral

begreifen [bə'graɪfən] (*unreg*) *vt* to understand, to comprehend

begreiflich [bə'graɪflɪç] *adj* understandable

begrenzen [bə'grɛntsən] *vt* (*beschränken*) to limit

Begrenztheit [bə'grɛntstʰaɪt] *f* limitation, restriction; (*fig*) narrowness

Begriff [bə'grɪf] **(-(e)s, -e)** *m* concept, idea; **im ~ sein, etw zu tun** to be about to do sth; **schwer von ~** (*umg*) slow, dense

begriffsstutzig *adj* slow, dense

begründ- [bə'grʏnd] *zW*: **~en** *vt* (*Gründe geben*) to justify; **~et** *adj* well-founded, justified; **B~ung** *f* justification, reason

begrüßen [bə'gry:sən] *vt* to greet, to welcome; **Begrüßung** *f* greeting, welcome

begünstigen [bə'gʏnstɪgən] *vt* (*Person*) to favour; (*Sache*) to further, to promote

begutachten [bə'gu:tʔaxtən] *vt* to assess

begütert [bə'gy:tərt] *adj* wealthy, well-to-do

behaart [bə'ha:rt] *adj* hairy

behagen [bə'ha:gən] *vi*: **das behagt ihm nicht** he does not like it

behaglich [bə'ha:klɪç] *adj* comfortable, cosy; **B~keit** *f* comfort, cosiness

behalten [bə'haltən] (*unreg*) *vt* to keep, to retain; (*im Gedächtnis*) to remember

Behälter [bə'hɛltər] **(-s, -)** *m* container, receptacle

behandeln [bə'handəln] *vt* to treat; (*Thema*) to deal with; (*Maschine*) to handle

Behandlung *f* treatment; (*von Maschine*) handling

beharren [bə'harən] *vi*: **auf etw** *dat* **~** to stick *od* keep to sth

beharrlich [bə'harlɪç] *adj* (*ausdauernd*) steadfast, unwavering; (*hartnäckig*) tenacious, dogged; **B~keit** *f* steadfastness, tenacity

behaupten [bə'haʊptən] *vt* to claim, to assert, to maintain; (*sein Recht*) to defend ♦ *vr* to assert o.s.

Behauptung *f* claim, assertion

beheben [bə'he:bən] (*unreg*) *vt* to remove

behelfen [bə'hɛlfən] (*unreg*) *vr*: **sich mit etw ~** to make do with sth

behelfsmäßig *adj* improvised, makeshift;

(*vorübergehend*) temporary

behelligen [bə'hɛlɪgən] *vt* to trouble, to bother

beherbergen [bə'hɛrbɛrgən] *vt* to put up, to house

beherrsch- [bə'hɛrʃ] *zW*: **~en** *vt* (*Volk*) to rule, to govern; (*Situation*) to control; (*Sprache, Gefühle*) to master ♦ *vr* to control o.s.; **~t** *adj* controlled; **B~ung** *f* rule; control; mastery

beherzigen [bə'hɛrtsɪgən] *vt* to take to heart

beherzt *adj* courageous, brave

behilflich [bə'hɪlflɪç] *adj* helpful; **jdm ~ sein (bei)** to help sb (with)

behindern [bə'hɪndərn] *vt* to hinder, to impede

Behinderte(r) *f(m)* disabled person

Behinderung *f* hindrance; (*Körperbehinderung*) handicap

Behörde [bə'hø:rdə] *f* (*auch pl*) authorities *pl*

behördlich [bə'hø:rtlɪç] *adj* official

behüten [bə'hy:tən] *vt* to guard; **jdn vor etw** *dat* **~** to preserve sb from sth

behutsam [bə'hu:tza:m] *adj* cautious, careful; **B~keit** *f* caution, carefulness

---

SCHLÜSSELWORT

bei [baɪ] *präp* +*dat* **1** (*nahe bei*) near; (*zum Aufenthalt*) at, with; (*unter, zwischen*) among; **bei München** near Munich; **bei uns** at our place; **beim Friseur** at the hairdresser's; **bei seinen Eltern wohnen** to live with one's parents; **bei einer Firma arbeiten** to work for a firm; **etw bei sich haben** to have sth on one; **jdn bei sich haben** to have sb with one; **bei Goethe** in Goethe; **beim Militär** in the army **2** (*zeitlich*) at, on; (*während*) during; (*Zustand, Umstand*) in; **bei Nacht** at night; **bei Nebel** in fog; **bei Regen** if it rains; **bei solcher Hitze** in such heat; **bei meiner Ankuft** on my arrival; **bei der Arbeit** when I'm *etc* working; **beim Fahren** while driving

---

beibehalten ['baɪbəhaltən] (*unreg*) *vt* to keep, to retain

beibringen ['baɪbrɪŋən] (*unreg*) *vt* (*Beweis, Zeugen*) to bring forward; (*Gründe*) to adduce; **jdm etw ~** (*lehren*) to teach sb sth; (*zu verstehen geben*) to make sb understand sth; (*zufügen*) to inflict sth on sb

Beichte ['baɪçtə] *f* confession; **b~n** *vt* to confess ♦ *vi* to go to confession

beide(s) ['baɪdə(s)] *pron, adj* both; **meine ~n Brüder** my two brothers, both my brothers; **die ersten ~n** the first two; **wir ~** we two; **einer von ~n** one of the two; **alles ~s** both (of them)

beider- ['baɪdər] *zW*: **~lei** *adj inv* of both; **~seitig** *adj* mutual, reciprocal; **~seits** *adv* mutually ♦ *präp +gen* on both sides of

beieinander [baɪaɪˈnandər] *adv* together

Beifahrer ['baɪfaːrər] *m* passenger

Beifall ['baɪfal] (**-(e)s**) *m* applause; (*Zustimmung*) approval

beifügen ['baɪfyːgən] *vt* to enclose

beige ['beːʒ] *adj* beige, fawn

beigeben ['baɪgeːbən] (*unreg*) *vt* (*zufügen*) to add; (*mitgeben*) to give ♦ *vi* (*nachgeben*) to give in

Beihilfe ['baɪhɪlfə] *f* aid, assistance; (*Studienbeihilfe*) grant; (*JUR*) aiding and abetting

beikommen ['baɪkɔmən] (*unreg*) *vi +dat* to get at; (*einem Problem*) to deal with

Beil [baɪl] (**-(e)s, -e**) *nt* axe, hatchet

Beilage ['baɪlaːgə] *f* (*Buchbeilage etc*) supplement; (*KOCH*) vegetables and potatoes *pl*

beiläufig ['baɪlɔyfɪç] *adj* casual, incidental ♦ *adv* casually, by the way

beilegen ['baɪleːgən] *vt* (*hinzufügen*) to enclose, to add; (*beimessen*) to attribute, to ascribe; (*Streit*) to settle

Beileid ['baɪlaɪt] *nt* condolence, sympathy; **herzliches ~** deepest sympathy

beiliegend ['baɪliːgənt] *adj* (*COMM*) enclosed

beim [baɪm] = **bei dem**

beimessen ['baɪmɛsən] (*unreg*) *vt* (*+dat*) to attribute (to), to ascribe (to)

Bein [baɪn] (**-(e)s, -e**) *nt* leg

beinah(e) ['baɪnaː(ə)] *adv* almost, nearly

Beinbruch *m* fracture of the leg

beinhalten [bəˈɪnhaltən] *vt* to contain

Beipackzettel ['baɪpaktsetəl] *m* instruction leaflet

beipflichten ['baɪpflɪçtən] *vi*: **jdm/etw ~** to agree with sb/sth

beisammen [baɪˈzamən] *adv* together; **B~sein** (**-s**) *nt* get-together

Beischlaf ['baɪʃlaːf] *m* sexual intercourse

Beisein ['baɪzaɪn] (**-s**) *nt* presence

beiseite [baɪˈzaɪtə] *adv* to one side, aside; (*stehen*) on one side, aside; **etw ~ legen** (*sparen*) to put sth by

beisetzen ['baɪzɛtsən] *vt* to bury; **Beisetzung** *f* funeral

Beisitzer ['baɪzɪtsər] (**-s, -**) *m* (*bei Prüfung*) assessor

Beispiel ['baɪʃpiːl] (**-(e)s, -e**) *nt* example; **sich +dat an jdm ein ~ nehmen** to take sb as an example; **zum ~** for example; **b~haft** *adj* exemplary; **b~los** *adj* unprecedented; **b~sweise** *adv* for instance *od* example

beißen ['baɪsən] (*unreg*) *vt, vi* to bite; (*stechen: Rauch, Säure*) to burn ♦ *vr* (*Farben*) to clash; **~d** *adj* biting, caustic; (*fig auch*) sarcastic

Beistand ['baɪʃtant] (**-(e)s, ⁺e**) *m* support, help; (*JUR*) adviser

beistehen ['baɪʃteːən] (*unreg*) *vi*: **jdm ~** to stand by sb

beisteuern ['baɪʃtɔyərn] *vt* to contribute

Beitrag ['baɪtraːk] (**-(e)s, ⁺e**) *m* contribution; (*Zahlung*) fee, subscription; (*Versicherungsbeitrag*) premium; **b~en** ['baɪtraːgən] (*unreg*) *vt, vi*: **b~en (zu)** to contribute (to); (*mithelfen*) to help (with)

beitreten ['baɪtreːtən] (*unreg*) *vi +dat* to join

Beitritt ['baɪtrɪt] *m* joining, membership

Beiwagen ['baɪvaːgən] *m* (*Motorradbeiwagen*) sidecar

beizeiten [baɪˈtsaɪtən] *adv* in time

bejahen [bəˈjaːən] *vt* (*Frage*) to say yes to, to answer in the affirmative; (*gutheißen*) to agree with

bekämpfen [bəˈkɛmpfən] *vt* (*Gegner*) to fight; (*Seuche*) to combat ♦ *vr* to fight;

Bekämpfung f fight, struggle

bekannt [bə'kant] adj (well-)known; (nicht fremd) familiar; ~ **geben** to announce publicly; **mit jdm ~ sein** to know sb; ~ **machen** to announce; **jdn mit jdm ~ machen** to introduce sb to sb; **das ist mir ~** I know that; **es/sie kommt mir ~ vor** it/she seems familiar; **B~e(r)** f(m) acquaintance; friend; **B~enkreis** m circle of friends; **~lich** adv as is well known, as you know; **B~machung** f publication; announcement; **B~schaft** f acquaintance

bekehren [bə'ke:rən] vt to convert ♦ vr to be od become converted

bekennen [bə'kɛnən] (unreg) vt to confess; (Glauben) to profess; **Farbe ~** (umg) to show where one stands

Bekenntnis [bə'kɛntnɪs] (-ses, -se) nt admission, confession; (Religion) confession, denomination

beklagen [bə'kla:gən] vt to deplore, to lament ♦ vr to complain

bekleiden [bə'klaɪdən] vt to clothe; (Amt) to occupy, to fill

Bekleidung f clothing

beklemmen [bə'klɛmən] vt to oppress

beklommen [bə'klɔmən] adj anxious, uneasy

bekommen [bə'kɔmən] (unreg) vt to get, to receive; (Kind) to have; (Zug) to catch, to get ♦ vi: **jdm ~** to agree with sb

bekömmlich [bə'kœmlɪç] adj easily digestible

bekräftigen [bə'krɛftɪgən] vt to confirm, to corroborate

bekreuzigen [bə'krɔytsɪgən] vr to cross o.s.

bekunden [bə'kʊndən] vt (sagen) to state; (zeigen) to show

belächeln [bə'lɛçəln] vt to laugh at

beladen [bə'la:dən] (unreg) vt to load

Belag [bə'la:k] (-(e)s, ⁻e) m covering, coating; (Brotbelag) spread; (Zahnbelag) tartar; (auf Zunge) fur; (Bremsbelag) lining

belagern [bə'la:gərn] vt to besiege; **Belagerung** f siege

Belang [bə'laŋ] (-(e)s) m importance; ~**e** pl (Interessen) interests, concerns; **b~los** adj

trivial, unimportant

belassen [bə'lasən] (unreg) vt (in Zustand, Glauben) to leave; (in Stellung) to retain

belasten [bə'lastən] vt to burden; (fig: bedrücken) to trouble, to worry; (COMM: Konto) to debit; (JUR) to incriminate ♦ vr to weigh o.s. down; (JUR) to incriminate o.s.; ~**d** adj (JUR) incriminating

belästigen [bə'lɛstɪgən] vt to annoy, to pester; **Belästigung** f annoyance, pestering

Belastung [bə'lastʊŋ] f load; (fig: Sorge etc) weight; (COMM) charge, debit(ing); (JUR) incriminatory evidence

belaufen [bə'laufən] (unreg) vr: **sich ~ auf** +akk to amount to

beleben [bə'le:bən] vt (anregen) to liven up; (Konjunktur, jds Hoffnungen) to stimulate ♦ vr (Augen) to light up; (Stadt) to come to life

belebt [bə'le:pt] adj (Straße) busy

Beleg [bə'le:k] (-(e)s, -e) m (COMM) receipt; (Beweis) documentary evidence, proof; (Beispiel) example; **b~en** to cover; (Kuchen, Brot) to spread; (Platz) to reserve, to book; (Kurs, Vorlesung) to register for; (beweisen) to verify, to prove; (MIL: mit Bomben) to bomb; ~**schaft** f personnel, staff; **b~t** adj: **b~tes Brot** open sandwich

belehren [bə'le:rən] vt to instruct, to teach; **Belehrung** f instruction

beleibt [bə'laɪpt] adj stout, corpulent

beleidigen [bə'laɪdɪgən] vt to insult, to offend; **Beleidigung** f insult; (JUR) slander, libel

beleuchten [bə'lɔyçtən] vt to light, to illuminate; (fig) to throw light on

Beleuchtung f lighting, illumination

Belgien ['bɛlgiən] nt Belgium; **Belgier(in)** m(f) Belgian; **belgisch** adj Belgian

belichten [bə'lɪçtən] vt to expose

Belichtung f exposure; ~**smesser** m exposure meter

Belieben [bə'li:bən] nt: **(ganz) nach ~** (just) as you wish

beliebig [bə'li:bɪç] adj any you like ♦ adv as you like; **ein ~es Thema** any subject you like od want; ~ **viel/viele** as much/many as you like

beliebt [bə'li:pt] *adj* popular; **sich bei jdm ~ machen** to make o.s. popular with sb; **B~heit** *f* popularity

beliefern [bə'li:fərn] *vt* to supply

bellen ['belən] *vi* to bark

belohnen [bə'lo:nən] *vt* to reward; **Belohnung** *f* reward

Belüftung [bə'lʏftʊŋ] *f* ventilation

belügen [bə'ly:gən] (*unreg*) *vt* to lie to, to deceive

belustigen [bə'lʊstɪgən] *vt* to amuse; **Belustigung** *f* amusement

bemalen [bə'ma:lən] *vt* to paint

bemängeln [bə'mɛŋəln] *vt* to criticize

bemerk- [bə'mɛrk] *zW:* **~bar** *adj* perceptible, noticeable; **sich ~bar machen** (*Person*) to make *od* get o.s. noticed; (*Unruhe*) to become noticeable; **~en** *vt* (*wahrnehmen*) to notice, to observe; (*sagen*) to say, to mention; **~enswert** *adj* remarkable, noteworthy; **B~ung** *f* remark; (*schriftlich auch*) note

bemitleiden [bə'mɪtlaɪdən] *vt* to pity

bemühen [bə'my:ən] *vr* to take trouble *od* pains; **Bemühung** *f* trouble, pains *pl*, effort

benachbart [bə'naxba:rt] *adj* neighbouring

benachrichtigen [bə'na:xrɪçtɪgən] *vt* to inform; **Benachrichtigung** *f* notification, information

benachteiligen [bə'na:xtaɪlɪgən] *vt* to put at a disadvantage; to victimize

benehmen [bə'ne:mən] (*unreg*) *vr* to behave; **B~** (**-s**) *nt* behaviour

beneiden [bə'naɪdən] *vt* to envy; **~swert** *adj* enviable

benennen [bə'nɛnən] (*unreg*) *vt* to name

Bengel ['bɛŋəl] (**-s, -**) *m* (little) rascal *od* rogue

benommen [bə'nɔmən] *adj* dazed

benoten [bə'no:tən] *vt* to mark

benötigen [bə'nø:tɪgən] *vt* to need

benutzen [bə'nʊtsən] *vt* to use

Benutzer (**-s, -**) *m* user

Benutzung *f* utilization, use

Benzin [bɛnt'si:n] (**-s, -e**) *nt* (*AUT*) petrol

(*BRIT*), gas(oline) (*US*); **~kanister** *m* petrol (*BRIT*) *od* gas (*US*) can; **~tank** *m* petrol tank (*BRIT*), gas tank (*US*); **~uhr** *f* petrol (*BRIT*) *od* gas (*US*) gauge

beobachten [bə'o:baxtən] *vt* to observe; **Beobachter** (**-s, -**) *m* observer; (*eines Unfalls*) witness; (*PRESSE, TV*) correspondent; **Beobachtung** *f* observation

bepacken [bə'pakən] *vt* to load, to pack

bequem [bə'kve:m] *adj* comfortable; (*Ausrede*) convenient; (*Person*) lazy, indolent; **~en** *vr*: **sich ~en(, etw zu tun)** to condescend (to do sth); **B~lichkeit** [-'lɪçkaɪt] *f* convenience, comfort; (*Faulheit*) laziness, indolence

beraten [bə'ra:tən] (*unreg*) *vt* to advise; (*besprechen*) to discuss, to debate ♦ *vr* to consult; **gut/schlecht ~ sein** to be well/ill advised; **sich ~ lassen** to get advice

Berater (**-s, -**) *m* adviser

Beratung *f* advice; (*Besprechung*) consultation; **~sstelle** *f* advice centre

berauben [bə'raubən] *vt* to rob

berechenbar [bə'rɛçənba:r] *adj* calculable

berechnen [bə'rɛçnən] *vt* to calculate; (*COMM: anrechnen*) to charge; **~d** *adj* (*Mensch*) calculating, scheming

Berechnung *f* calculation; (*COMM*) charge

berechtigen [bə'rɛçtɪgən] *vt* to entitle; to authorize; (*fig*) to justify

berechtigt [bə'rɛçtɪçt] *adj* justifiable, justified

Berechtigung *f* authorization; (*fig*) justification

bereden [bə're:dən] *vt* (*besprechen*) to discuss; (*überreden*) to persuade ♦ *vr* to discuss

Bereich [bə'raɪç] (**-(e)s, -e**) *m* (*Bezirk*) area; (*PHYS*) range; (*Ressort, Gebiet*) sphere

bereichern [bə'raɪçərn] *vt* to enrich ♦ *vr* to get rich

bereinigen [bə'raɪnɪgən] *vt* to settle

bereisen [bə'raɪzən] *vt* (*Land*) to travel through

bereit [bə'raɪt] *adj* ready, prepared; **zu etw ~ sein** to be ready for sth; **sich ~ erklären** to declare o.s. willing; **~en** *vt* to prepare, to make ready; (*Kummer, Freude*) to cause;

~halten (*unreg*) *vt* to keep in readiness; **~legen** *vt* to lay out; **~machen** *vt*, *vr* to prepare, to get ready; **~s** *adv* already; **B~schaft** *f* readiness; (*Polizei*) alert; **B~schaftsdienst** *m* emergency service; **~stehen** (*unreg*) *vi* (*Person*) to be prepared; (*Ding*) to be ready; **~stellen** *vt* (*Kisten, Pakete etc*) to put ready; (*Geld etc*) to make available; (*Truppen, Maschinen*) to put at the ready; **~willig** *adj* willing, ready; **B~willigkeit** *f* willingness, readiness

ereuen [bəˈrɔyən] *vt* to regret

erg [berk] **(-(e)s, -e)** *m* mountain; hill; **b~ab** *adv* downhill; **~arbeiter** *m* miner; **b~auf** *adv* uphill; **~bahn** *f* mountain railway; **~bau** *m* mining

ergen [ˈbergən] (*unreg*) *vt* (*retten*) to rescue; (*Ladung*) to salvage; (*enthalten*) to contain

erg- *zW*: **~führer** *m* mountain guide; **~gipfel** *m* peak, summit; **b~ig** [ˈbergɪç] *adj* mountainous; hilly; **~kette** *f* mountain range; **~mann** (*pl* **~leute**) *m* miner; **~rettungsdienst** *m* mountain rescue team; **~rutsch** *m* landslide; **~steigen** *nt* mountaineering; **~steiger(in)** **(-s, -)** *m(f)* mountaineer, climber; **~tour** *f* mountain climb

ergung [ˈbergʊŋ] *f* (*von Menschen*) rescue; (*von Material*) recovery; (*NAUT*) salvage

erg- *zW*: **~wacht** *f* mountain rescue service; **~wanderung** *f* hike in the mountains; **~werk** *nt* mine

ericht [bəˈrɪçt] **(-(e)s, -e)** *m* report, account; **b~en** *vt*, *vi* to report; **~erstatter** **(-s, -)** *m* reporter; (*newspaper*) correspondent

erichtigen [bəˈrɪçtɪgən] *vt* to correct; **Berichtigung** *f* correction

ernstein [ˈbernʃtaɪn] *m* amber

ersten [ˈberstən] (*unreg*) *vi* to burst, to split

erüchtigt [bəˈrʏçtɪçt] *adj* notorious, infamous

erücksichtigen [bəˈrʏkzɪçtɪgən] *vt* to consider, to bear in mind; **Berücksichtigung** *f* consideration

eruf [bəˈruːf] **(-(e)s, -e)** *m* occupation, profession; (*Gewerbe*) trade; **b~en** (*unreg*)

vt: **b~en zu** to appoint to ♦ *vr*: **sich auf jdn/etw b~en** to refer *od* appeal to sb/sth ♦ *adj* competent, qualified; **b~lich** *adj* professional

Berufs- *zW*: **~ausbildung** *f* job training; **~berater** *m* careers adviser; **~beratung** *f* vocational guidance; **~geheimnis** *nt* professional secret; **~leben** *nt* professional life; **~schule** *f* vocational *od* trade school; **~sportler** [-ʃpɔrtlər] *m* professional (sportsman); **b~tätig** *adj* employed; **b~unfähig** *adj* unfit for work; **~verkehr** *m* rush-hour traffic

Berufung *f* vocation, calling; (*Ernennung*) appointment; (*JUR*) appeal; **~ einlegen** to appeal

beruhen [bəˈruːən] *vi*: **auf etw** *dat* **~** to be based on sth; **etw auf sich ~ lassen** to leave sth at that

beruhigen [bəˈruːɪgən] *vt* to calm, to pacify, to soothe ♦ *vr* (*Mensch*) to calm (o.s.) down; (*Situation*) to calm down

Beruhigung *f* soothing; (*der Nerven*) calming; **zu jds ~** (in order) to reassure sb; **~smittel** *nt* sedative

berühmt [bəˈryːmt] *adj* famous; **B~heit** *f* (*Ruf*) fame; (*Mensch*) celebrity

berühren [bəˈryːrən] *vt* to touch; (*gefühlsmäßig bewegen*) to affect; (*flüchtig erwähnen*) to mention, to touch on ♦ *vr* to meet, to touch

Berührung *f* contact

besagen [bəˈzaːgən] *vt* to mean

besänftigen [bəˈzɛnftɪgən] *vt* to soothe, to calm

Besatz [bəˈzats] **(-es, ⁼e)** *m* trimming, edging

Besatzung *f* garrison; (*NAUT, AVIAT*) crew

Besatzungsmacht *f* occupying power

beschädigen [bəˈʃɛːdɪgən] *vt* to damage; **Beschädigung** *f* damage; (*Stelle*) damaged spot

beschaffen [bəˈʃafən] *vt* to get, to acquire ♦ *adj*: **das ist so ~, dass** that is such that; **B~heit** *f* (*von Mensch*) constitution, nature

Beschaffung *f* acquisition

beschäftigen [bəˈʃɛftɪgən] *vt* to occupy;

(*beruflich*) to employ ♦ *vr* to occupy *od*
concern o.s.
beschäftigt *adj* busy, occupied
Beschäftigung *f* (*Beruf*) employment;
(*Tätigkeit*) occupation; (*Befassen*) concern
beschämen [bə'ʃɛːmən] *vt* to put to shame;
~d *adj* shameful; (*Hilfsbereitschaft*) shaming
beschämt *adj* ashamed
Bescheid [bə'ʃaɪt] (-(e)s, -e) *m* information;
(*Weisung*) directions *pl*; **~ wissen (über**
+akk) to be well-informed (about); **ich**
weiß ~ I know; **jdm ~ geben** *od* **sagen** to
let sb know
bescheiden [bə'ʃaɪdən] (*unreg*) *vr* to
content o.s. ♦ *adj* modest; **B~heit** *f*
modesty
bescheinen [bə'ʃaɪnən] (*unreg*) *vt* to shine
on
bescheinigen [bə'ʃaɪnɪgən] *vt* to certify;
(*bestätigen*) to acknowledge
Bescheinigung *f* certificate; (*Quittung*)
receipt
beschenken [bə'ʃɛŋkən] *vt*: **jdn mit etw ~**
to give sb sth as a present
bescheren [bə'ʃeːrən] *vt*: **jdm etw ~** to give
sb sth as a Christmas present; **jdn ~** to give
Christmas presents to sb
Bescherung *f* giving of Christmas
presents; (*umg*) mess
beschildern [bə'ʃɪldərn] *vt* to put signs/a
sign on
beschimpfen [bə'ʃɪmpfən] *vt* to abuse;
Beschimpfung *f* abuse; insult
Beschlag [bə'ʃlaːk] (-(e)s, ⁺e) *m*
(*Metallband*) fitting; (*auf Fenster*)
condensation; (*auf Metall*) tarnish; finish;
(*Hufeisen*) horseshoe; **jdn/etw in ~ nehmen**
od **mit ~ belegen** to monopolize sb/sth;
b~en [bə'ʃlaːgən] (*unreg*) *vt* to cover; (*Pferd*)
to shoe ♦ *vi*, *vr* (*Fenster etc*) to mist over;
b~en sein (in *od* **auf +dat)** to be well
versed (in); **b~nahmen** *vt* to seize, to
confiscate; to requisition; **~nahmung** *f*
confiscation, sequestration
beschleunigen [bə'ʃlɔʏnɪgən] *vt* to
accelerate, to speed up ♦ *vi* (*AUT*) to
accelerate; **Beschleunigung** *f* acceleration

beschließen [bə'ʃliːsən] (*unreg*) *vt* to decide
on; (*beenden*) to end, to close
Beschluss ▲ [bə'ʃlʊs] (-es, ⁺e) *m* decision,
conclusion; (*Ende*) conclusion, end
beschmutzen [bə'ʃmʊtsən] *vt* to dirty, to
soil
beschönigen [bə'ʃøːnɪgən] *vt* to gloss over
beschränken [bə'ʃrɛŋkən] *vt*, *vr*: (**sich**) **~**
(**auf +akk**) to limit *od* restrict (o.s.) (to)
beschränk- *zW*: **~t** *adj* confined,
restricted; (*Mensch*) limited, narrow-
minded; **B~ung** *f* limitation
beschreiben [bə'ʃraɪbən] (*unreg*) *vt* to
describe; (*Papier*) to write on
Beschreibung *f* description
beschriften [bə'ʃrɪftən] *vt* to mark, to label
Beschriftung *f* lettering
beschuldigen [bə'ʃʊldɪgən] *vt* to accuse;
Beschuldigung *f* accusation
Beschuss ▲ [bə'ʃʊs] *m*: **jdn/etw unter ~**
nehmen (*MIL*) to open fire on sb/sth
beschützen [bə'ʃʏtsən] *vt*: **~ (vor +dat)** to
protect (from); **Beschützer (-s, -)** *m*
protector
Beschwerde [bə'ʃveːrdə] *f* complaint;
(*Mühe*) hardship; **~n** *pl* (*Leiden*) trouble
beschweren [bə'ʃveːrən] *vt* to weight
down; (*fig*) to burden ♦ *vr* to complain
beschwerlich *adj* tiring, exhausting
beschwichtigen [bə'ʃvɪçtɪgən] *vt* to soothe,
to pacify
beschwindeln [bə'ʃvɪndəln] *vt* (*betrügen*) to
cheat; (*belügen*) to fib to
beschwingt [bə'ʃvɪŋt] *adj* in high spirits
beschwipst [bə'ʃvɪpst] (*umg*) *adj* tipsy
beschwören [bə'ʃvøːrən] (*unreg*) *vt*
(*Aussage*) to swear to; (*anflehen*) to implore;
(*Geister*) to conjure up
beseitigen [bə'zaɪtɪgən] *vt* to remove;
Beseitigung *f* removal
Besen ['beːzən] (-s, -) *m* broom; **~stiel** *m*
broomstick
besessen [bə'zɛsən] *adj* possessed
besetz- [bə'zɛts] *zW*: **~en** *vt* (*Haus, Land*) to
occupy; (*Platz*) to take, to fill; (*Posten*) to
fill; (*Rolle*) to cast; (*mit Edelsteinen*) to set; **~**
adj full; (*TEL*) engaged, busy; (*Platz*) taken;

(WC) engaged; **B~tzeichen** nt engaged tone; **B~ung** f occupation; filling; (von Rolle) casting; (die Schauspieler) cast

besichtigen [bə'zɪçtɪgən] vt to visit, to have a look at; **Besichtigung** f visit

besiegen [bə'zi:gən] vt to defeat, to overcome

besinn- [bə'zɪn] zW: **~en** (unreg) vr (nachdenken) to think, to reflect; (erinnern) to remember; **sich anders ~en** to change one's mind; **B~ung** f consciousness; **zur B~ung kommen** to recover consciousness; (fig) to come to one's senses; **~ungslos** adj unconscious

Besitz [bə'zɪts] (-es) m possession; (Eigentum) property; **b~en** (unreg) vt to possess, to own; (Eigenschaft) to have; **~er(in)** (-s, -) m(f) owner, proprietor; **~ergreifung** f occupation, seizure

besoffen [bə'zɔfən] (umg) adj drunk, stoned

besohlen [bə'zo:lən] vt to sole

Besoldung [bə'zɔldʊŋ] f salary, pay

besondere(r, s) [bə'zɔndərə(r, s)] adj special; (eigen) particular; (gesondert) separate; (eigentümlich) peculiar

Besonderheit [bə'zɔndərhaɪt] f peculiarity

besonders [bə'zɔndərs] adv especially, particularly; (getrennt) separately

besonnen [bə'zɔnən] adj sensible, level-headed

besorg- [bə'zɔrg] zW: **~en** vt (beschaffen) to acquire; (kaufen auch) to purchase; (erledigen: Geschäfte) to deal with; (sich kümmern um) to take care of; **B~nis** (-, -se) f anxiety, concern; **~t** [bə'zɔrçt] adj anxious, worried; **B~ung** f acquisition; (Kauf) purchase

bespielen [bə'ʃpi:lən] vt to record

bespitzeln [bə'ʃpɪtsəln] vt to spy on

besprechen [bə'ʃprɛçən] (unreg) vt to discuss; (Tonband etc) to record, to speak onto; (Buch) to review ♦ vr to discuss, to consult; **Besprechung** f meeting, discussion; (von Buch) review

besser ['bɛsər] adj better; **es geht ihm ~** he is feeling better; **~n** vt to make better, to improve ♦ vr to improve; (Menschen) to

reform; **B~ung** f improvement; **gute B~ung!** get well soon!; **B~wisser** (-s, -) m know-all

Bestand [bə'ʃtant] (-(e)s, ⸚e) m (Fortbestehen) duration, stability; (Kassenbestand) amount, balance; (Vorrat) stock; **~ haben, von ~ sein** to last long, to endure

beständig [bə'ʃtɛndɪç] adj (ausdauernd: auch fig) constant; (Wetter) settled; (Stoffe) resistant; (Klagen etc) continual

Bestandsaufnahme [bə'ʃtantsaʊfna:mə] f stocktaking

Bestandteil m part, component; (Zutat) ingredient

bestärken [bə'ʃtɛrkən] vt: **jdn in etw** dat **~** to strengthen od confirm sb in sth

bestätigen [bə'ʃtɛːtɪgən] vt to confirm; (anerkennen, COMM) to acknowledge; **Bestätigung** f confirmation; acknowledgement

bestatten [bə'ʃtatən] vt to bury

Bestattung f funeral

Bestattungsinstitut nt funeral director's

bestaunen [bə'ʃtaʊnən] vt to marvel at, gaze at in wonder

beste(r, s) ['bɛstə(r, s)] adj best; **so ist es am ~n** it's best that way; **am ~n gehst du gleich** you'd better go at once; **jdn zum B~n haben** to pull sb's leg; **einen Witz** etc **zum B~n geben** to tell a joke etc; **aufs B~** od **~** in the best possible way; **zu jds B~n** for the benefit of sb

bestechen [bə'ʃtɛçən] (unreg) vt to bribe; **bestechlich** adj corruptible; **Bestechung** f bribery, corruption

Besteck [bə'ʃtɛk] (-(e)s, -e) nt knife, fork and spoon, cutlery; (MED) set of instruments

bestehen [bə'ʃte:ən] (unreg) vi to be; to exist; (andauern) to last ♦ vt (Kampf, Probe, Prüfung) to pass; **~ auf** +dat to insist on; **~ aus** to consist of

bestehlen [bə'ʃte:lən] (unreg) vt: **jdn (um etw) ~** to rob sb (of sth)

besteigen [bə'ʃtaɪgən] (unreg) vt to climb, to ascend; (Pferd) to mount; (Thron) to ascend

Spelling Reform: ▲ new spelling △ old spelling (to be phased out)

Bestell- [bəˈʃtɛl] *zW:* **~buch** *nt* order book; **b~en** *vt* to order; (*kommen lassen*) to arrange to see; (*nominieren*) to name; (*Acker*) to cultivate; (*Grüße, Auftrag*) to pass on; **~formular** *nt* order form; **~nummer** *f* order code; **~ung** *f* (*COMM*) order; (*~en*) ordering

bestenfalls [ˈbɛstənˈfals] *adv* at best

bestens [ˈbɛstəns] *adv* very well

besteuern [bəˈʃtɔyərn] *vt* (*jdn, Waren*) to tax

Bestie [ˈbɛstiə] *f* (*auch fig*) beast

bestimm- [bəˈʃtɪm] *zW:* **~en** *vt* (*Regeln*) to lay down; (*Tag, Ort*) to fix; (*beherrschen*) to characterize; (*vorsehen*) to mean; (*ernennen*) to appoint; (*definieren*) to define; (*veranlassen*) to induce; **~t** *adj* (*entschlossen*) firm; (*gewiss*) certain, definite; (*Artikel*) definite ♦ *adv* (*gewiss*) definitely, for sure; **suchen Sie etwas B~tes?** are you looking for something in particular?; **B~theit** *f* firmness; certainty; **B~ung** *f* (*Verordnung*) regulation; (*Festsetzen*) determining; (*Verwendungszweck*) purpose; (*Schicksal*) fate; (*Definition*) definition; **B~ungsland** *nt* (country of) destination; **B~ungsort** *m* (place of) destination

Bestleistung *f* best performance

bestmöglich *adj* best possible

bestrafen [bəˈʃtraːfən] *vt* to punish; **Bestrafung** *f* punishment

bestrahlen [bəˈʃtraːlən] *vt* to shine on; (*MED*) to treat with X-rays

Bestrahlung *f* (*MED*) X-ray treatment, radiotherapy

Bestreben [bəˈʃtreːbən] (**-s**) *nt* endeavour, effort

bestreiten [bəˈʃtraɪtən] (*unreg*) *vt* (*abstreiten*) to dispute; (*finanzieren*) to pay for, to finance

bestreuen [bəˈʃtrɔyən] *vt* to sprinkle, to dust; (*Straße*) to grit

bestürmen [bəˈʃtʏrmən] *vt* (*mit Fragen, Bitten etc*) to overwhelm, to swamp

bestürzend [bəˈʃtʏrtsənd] *adj* (*Nachrichten*) disturbing

bestürzt [bəˈʃtʏrtst] *adj* dismayed

Bestürzung *f* consternation

Besuch [bəˈzuːx] (**-(e)s, -e**) *m* visit; (*Person*) visitor; **einen ~ machen bei jdm** to pay sb a visit *od* call; **~ haben** to have visitors; **bei jdm auf** *od* **zu ~ sein** to be visiting sb; **b~en** *vt* to visit; (*SCH etc*) to attend; **gut b~t** well-attended; **~er(in)** (**-s, -**) *m(f)* visitor, guest; **~szeit** *f* visiting hours *pl*

betätigen [bəˈtɛːtɪgən] *vt* (*bedienen*) to work, to operate ♦ *vr* to involve o.s.; **sich als etw ~** to work as sth

Betätigung *f* activity; (*beruflich*) occupation; (*TECH*) operation

betäuben [bəˈtɔybən] *vt* to stun; (*fig: Gewissen*) to still; (*MED*) to anaesthetize

Betäubung *f* (*Narkose*): **örtliche ~** local anaesthetic

Betäubungsmittel *nt* anaesthetic

Bete [ˈbeːtə] *f*: **Rote ~** beetroot (*BRIT*), beet (*US*)

beteilig- [bəˈtaɪlɪg] *zW:* **~en** *vr*: **sich ~en (an** +*dat*) to take part (in), to participate (in), to share (in); (*an Geschäft: finanziell*) to have a share (in) ♦ *vt*: **jdn ~en (an** +*dat*) to give sb a share *od* interest (in); **B~te(r)** *f(m)* (*Mitwirkender*) partner; (*finanziell*) shareholder; **B~ung** *f* participation; (*Anteil*) share, interest; (*Besucherzahl*) attendance

beten [ˈbeːtən] *vt, vi* to pray

beteuern [bəˈtɔyərn] *vt* to assert; (*Unschuld*) to protest

Beton [beˈtõː] (**-s, -s**) *m* concrete

betonen [bəˈtoːnən] *vt* to stress

betonieren [betoˈniːrən] *vt* to concrete

Betonung *f* stress, emphasis

betr. *abk* (= *betrifft*) re

Betracht [bəˈtraxt] *m*: **in ~ kommen** to be considered *od* relevant; **etw in ~ ziehen** to take sth into consideration; **außer ~ bleiben** not to be considered; **b~en** *vt* to look at; (*fig*) to look at, to consider; **~er(in)** (**-s, -**) *m(f)* observer

beträchtlich [bəˈtrɛçtlɪç] *adj* considerable

Betrachtung *f* (*Ansehen*) examination; (*Erwägung*) consideration

Betrag [bəˈtraːk] (**-(e)s, ⁼e**) *m* amount; **b~en** (*unreg*) *vt* to amount to ♦ *vr* to behave; **~en** (**-s**) *nt* behaviour

Betreff m: ~ **Ihr Schreiben vom ...** re your letter of ...

betreffen [bə'trɛfən] (unreg) vt to concern, to affect; **was mich betrifft** as for me; **~d** adj relevant, in question

betreffs [bə'trɛfs] präp +gen concerning, regarding; (COMM) re

betreiben [bə'traibən] (unreg) vt (ausüben) to practise; (Politik) to follow; (Studien) to pursue; (vorantreiben) to push ahead; (TECH: antreiben) to drive

betreten [bə'tre:tən] (unreg) vt to enter; (Bühne etc) to step onto ♦ adj embarrassed; **B~ verboten** keep off/out

Betreuer(in) [bə'trɔyər(ın)] (-s, -) m(f) (einer Person) minder; (eines Gebäudes, Arbeitsgebiets) caretaker; (SPORT) coach

Betreuung f care

Betrieb [bə'tri:p] (-(e)s, -e) m (Firma) firm, concern; (Anlage) plant; (Tätigkeit) operation; (Treiben) traffic; **außer ~ sein** to be out of order; **in ~ sein** to be in operation

Betriebs- zW: **~ausflug** m works outing; **b~bereit** adj operational; **b~fähig** adj in working order; **~ferien** pl company holidays (BRIT), company vacation sg (US); **~klima** nt (working) atmosphere; **~kosten** pl running costs; **~rat** m workers' council; **b~sicher** adj safe (to operate); **~störung** f breakdown; **~system** nt (COMPUT) operating system; **~unfall** m industrial accident; **~wirtschaft** f economics

betrinken [bə'trɪŋkən] (unreg) vr to get drunk

betroffen [bə'trɔfən] adj (bestürzt) full of consternation; **von etw ~ werden** od **sein** to be affected by sth

betrüben [bə'try:bən] vt to grieve

betrübt [bə'try:pt] adj sorrowful, grieved

Betrug [bə'tru:k] (-(e)s) m deception; (JUR) fraud

betrügen [bə'try:gən] (unreg) vt to cheat; (JUR) to defraud; (Ehepartner) to be unfaithful to ♦ vr to deceive o.s.

Betrüger (-s, -) m cheat, deceiver; **b~isch** adj deceitful; (JUR) fraudulent

betrunken [bə'trʊŋkən] adj drunk

Bett [bɛt] (-(e)s, -en) nt bed; **ins** od **zu ~ gehen** to go to bed; **~bezug** m duvet cover; **~decke** f blanket; (Daunenbett) quilt; (Überwurf) bedspread

Bettel- ['bɛtəl] zW: **b~arm** adj very poor, destitute; **~ei** [bɛtə'lai] f begging; **b~n** vi to beg

bettlägerig ['bɛtlɛːgərıç] adj bedridden

Bettlaken nt sheet

Bettler(in) ['bɛtlər(ın)] (-s, -) m(f) beggar

Bett- zW: **~tuch** ▲ nt sheet; **~vorleger** m bedside rug; **~wäsche** f bed linen; **~zeug** nt bed linen pl

beugen ['bɔygən] vt to bend; (GRAM) to inflect ♦ vr (sich fügen) to bow

Beule ['bɔylə] f bump, swelling

beunruhigen [bə'ʊnruːıgən] vt to disturb, to alarm ♦ vr to become worried

Beunruhigung f worry, alarm

beurlauben [bə'uːrlaubən] vt to give leave od a holiday to (BRIT), to grant vacation time to (US)

beurteilen [bə'ʊrtailən] vt to judge; (Buch etc) to review

Beurteilung f judgement; review; (Note) mark

Beute ['bɔytə] (-) f booty, loot

Beutel (-s, -) m bag; (Geldbeutel) purse; (Tabakbeutel) pouch

Bevölkerung [bə'fœlkərʊŋ] f population

bevollmächtigen [bə'fɔlmɛçtıgən] vt to authorize

Bevollmächtigte(r) f(m) authorized agent

bevor [bə'fo:r] konj before; **~munden** vt insep to treat like a child; **~stehen** (unreg) vi: **(jdm) ~stehen** to be in store (for sb); **~stehend** adj imminent, approaching; **~zugen** vt insep to prefer

bewachen [bə'vaxən] vt to watch, to guard

Bewachung f (Bewachen) guarding; (Leute) guard, watch

bewaffnen [bə'vafnən] vt to arm

Bewaffnung f (Vorgang) arming; (Ausrüstung) armament, arms pl

bewahren [bə'va:rən] vt to keep; **jdn vor jdm/etw ~** to save sb from sb/sth

bewähren [bə'vɛːrən] *vr* to prove o.s.; (*Maschine*) to prove its worth

bewahrheiten [bə'vaːrhaıtən] *vr* to come true

bewährt *adj* reliable

Bewährung *f* (*JUR*) probation

bewältigen [bə'vɛltɪgən] *vt* to overcome; (*Arbeit*) to finish; (*Portion*) to manage

bewandert [bə'vandərt] *adj* expert, knowledgeable

bewässern [bə'vɛsərn] *vt* to irrigate

Bewässerung *f* irrigation

bewegen [bə'veːgən] *vt, vr* to move; **jdn zu etw ~** to induce sb to do sth; **~d** *adj* touching, moving

Beweg- [bə'veːk] *zW:* **~grund** *m* motive; **b~lich** *adj* movable, mobile; (*flink*) quick; **b~t** *adj* (*Leben*) eventful; (*Meer*) rough; (*ergriffen*) touched

Bewegung *f* movement, motion; (*innere*) emotion; (*körperlich*) exercise; **~sfreiheit** *f* freedom of movement; (*fig*) freedom of action; **b~ungslos** *adj* motionless

Beweis [bə'vaıs] **(-es, -e)** *m* proof; (*Zeichen*) sign; **b~en** [-zən] (*unreg*) *vt* to prove; (*zeigen*) to show; **~mittel** *nt* evidence

Bewerb- [bə'vɛrb] *zW:* **b~en** (*unreg*) *vr* to apply (for); **~er(in)** **(-s, -)** *m(f)* applicant; **~ung** *f* application

bewerkstelligen [bə'vɛrkʃtɛlıgən] *vt* to manage, to accomplish

bewerten [bə'veːrtən] *vt* to assess

bewilligen [bə'vılıgən] *vt* to grant, to allow

Bewilligung *f* granting

bewirken [bə'vırkən] *vt* to cause, to bring about

bewirten [bə'vırtən] *vt* to feed, to entertain (to a meal)

bewirtschaften [bə'vırtʃaftən] *vt* to manage

Bewirtung *f* hospitality

bewog *etc* [bə'voːk] *vb* siehe **bewegen**

bewohn- [bə'voːn] *zW:* **~bar** *adj* habitable; **~en** *vt* to inhabit, to live in; **B~er(in)** **(-s, -)** *m(f)* inhabitant; (*von Haus*) resident

bewölkt [bə'vœlkt] *adj* cloudy, overcast

Bewölkung *f* clouds *pl*

Bewunder- [bə'vundər] *zW:* **~er** **(-s, -)** *m* admirer; **b~n** *vt* to admire; **b~nswert** *adj* admirable, wonderful; **~ung** *f* admiration

bewusst ▲ [bə'vʊst] *adj* conscious; (*absichtlich*) deliberate; **sich** *dat* **einer Sache** *gen* **~ sein** to be aware of sth; **~los** *adj* unconscious; **B~losigkeit** *f* unconsciousness; **B~sein** *nt* consciousness; **bei B~sein** conscious

bezahlen [bə'tsaːlən] *vt* to pay for

Bezahlung *f* payment

bezaubern [bə'tsaubərn] *vt* to enchant, to charm

bezeichnen [bə'tsaıçnən] *vt* (*kennzeichnen*) to mark; (*nennen*) to call; (*beschreiben*) to describe; (*zeigen*) to show, to indicate; **~d** *adj:* **~d (für)** characteristic (of), typical (of)

Bezeichnung *f* (*Zeichen*) mark, sign; (*Beschreibung*) description

bezeugen [bə'tsɔygən] *vt* to testify

Bezichtigung [bə'tsıçtıgʊŋ] *f* accusation

beziehen [bə'tsiːən] (*unreg*) *vt* (*mit Überzug*) to cover; (*Bett*) to make; (*Haus, Position*) to move into; (*Standpunkt*) to take up; (*erhalten*) to receive; (*Zeitung*) to subscribe to, to take ♦ *vr* (*Himmel*) to cloud over; **etw auf jdn/etw ~** to relate sth to sb/sth; **sich ~ auf** +*akk* to refer to

Beziehung *f* (*Verbindung*) connection; (*Zusammenhang*) relation; (*Verhältnis*) relationship; (*Hinsicht*) respect; **~en haben** (*vorteilhaft*) to have connections *od* contacts; **b~sweise** *adv* or; (*genauer gesagt auch*) that is, or rather

Bezirk [bə'tsırk] **(-(e)s, -e)** *m* district

Bezug [bə'tsuːk] **(-(e)s, ⁺e)** *m* (*Hülle*) covering; (*COMM*) ordering; (*Gehalt*) income, salary; (*Beziehung*): **~ (zu)** relation(ship) (to); **in ~ auf** +*akk* with reference to; **~ nehmen auf** +*akk* to refer to

bezüglich [bə'tsyːklıç] *präp* +*gen* concerning, referring to ♦ *adj* (*GRAM*) relative; **auf etw** *akk* **~** relating to sth

bezwecken [bə'tsvɛkən] *vt* to aim at

bezweifeln [bə'tsvaıfəln] *vt* to doubt, to query

BH *m abk von* **Büstenhalter**

Bhf. *abk (= Bahnhof)* station

Bibel ['bi:bəl] (-, -n) *f* Bible

Biber ['bi:bər] (-s, -) *m* beaver

Biblio- [bi:blio] *zW:* **~grafie** ▲ [-gra'fi:] *f* bibliography; **~thek** [-'te:k] (-, -en) *f* library; **~thekar(in)** [-te'ka:r(ɪn)] (-s, -e) *m(f)* librarian

biblisch ['bi:blɪʃ] *adj* biblical

bieder ['bi:dər] *adj* upright, worthy; *(Kleid etc)* plain

bieg- ['bi:g] *zW:* **~en** *(unreg) vt, vr* to bend ♦ *vi* to turn; **~sam** ['bi:k-] *adj* flexible; **B~ung** *f* bend, curve

Biene ['bi:nə] *f* bee

Bienenhonig *m* honey

Bienenwachs *nt* beeswax

Bier [bi:r] (-(e)s, -e) *nt* beer; **~deckel** *m* beer mat; **~garten** *m* beer garden; **~krug** *m* beer mug; **~zelt** *nt* beer tent

Biest [bi:st] (-s, -er) *(umg: pej) (Tier)* beast, creature; *(Mensch)* beast

bieten ['bi:tən] *(unreg) vt* to offer; *(bei Versteigerung)* to bid ♦ *vr (Gelegenheit):* **sich** *jdm* **~** to present itself to sb; **sich** *dat* **etw ~ lassen** to put up with sth

Bikini [bi'ki:ni] (-s, -s) *m* bikini

Bilanz [bi'lants] *f* balance; *(fig)* outcome; **~ ziehen (aus)** to take stock (of)

Bild [bɪlt] (-(e)s, -er) *nt (auch fig)* picture; photo; *(Spiegelbild)* reflection; **~bericht** *m* photographic report

bilden ['bɪldən] *vt* to form; *(erziehen)* to educate; *(ausmachen)* to constitute ♦ *vr* to arise; *(erziehen)* to educate o.s.

Bilderbuch *nt* picture book

Bilderrahmen *m* picture frame

Bild- *zW:* **~fläche** *f* screen; *(fig)* scene; **~hauer** (-s, -) *m* sculptor; **b~hübsch** *adj* lovely, pretty as a picture; **b~lich** *adj* figurative; pictorial; **~schirm** *m* television screen; *(COMPUT)* monitor; **~schirmschoner** *m (COMPUT)* screen saver; **b~schön** *adj* lovely

Bildung ['bɪldʊŋ] *f* formation; *(Wissen, Benehmen)* education

Billard ['bɪljart] (-s, -e) *nt* billiards *sg*;

~kugel *f* billiard ball

billig ['bɪlɪç] *adj* cheap; *(gerecht)* fair, reasonable; **~en** ['bɪlɪgən] *vt* to approve of

Binde ['bɪndə] *f* bandage; *(Armbinde)* band; *(MED)* sanitary towel; **~gewebe** *nt* connective tissue; **~glied** *nt* connecting link; **~hautentzündung** *f* conjunctivitis; **b~n** *(unreg) vt* to bind, to tie; **~strich** *m* hyphen

Bindfaden ['bɪnt-] *m* string

Bindung *f* bond, tie; *(Skibindung)* binding

binnen ['bɪnən] *präp (+dat od gen)* within; **B~hafen** *m* river port; **B~handel** *m* internal trade

Bio- [bio-] *in zW* bio-; **~chemie** *f* biochemistry; **~grafie** ▲ [-gra'fi:] *f* biography; **~laden** *m* wholefood shop; **~loge** [-'lo:gə] (-n, -n) *m* biologist; **~logie** [-lo'gi:] *f* biology; **b~logisch** [-'lo:gɪʃ] *adj* biological; **~top** *m od nt* biotope

---

Bioladen

ℹ️ A **Bioladen** is a shop specializing in environmentally-friendly products such as phosphate-free washing powders, recycled paper and organically-grown vegetables.

Birke ['bɪrkə] *f* birch

Birne ['bɪrnə] *f* pear; *(ELEK)* (light) bulb

SCHLÜSSELWORT

---

bis [bɪs] *präp +akk, adv* **1** *(zeitlich)* till, until; *(bis spätestens)* by; **Sie haben bis Dienstag Zeit** you have until *od* till Tuesday; **bis Dienstag muss es fertig sein** it must be ready by Tuesday; **bis auf weiteres** until further notice; **bis in die Nacht** into the night; **bis bald/gleich** see you later/soon

2 *(räumlich)* (up) to; **ich fahre bis Köln** I'm going to *od* I'm going as far as Cologne; **bis an unser Grundstück** (right *od* up) to our plot; **bis hierher** this far

3 *(bei Zahlen)* up to; **bis zu** up to

4: bis auf etw *akk (außer)* except sth; *(einschließlich)* including sth

♦ *konj* **1** *(mit Zahlen)* to; **10 bis 20** 10 to 20

2 *(zeitlich)* till, until; **bis es dunkel wird** till

---

od until it gets dark; **von ... bis ...** from ... to ...

Bischof ['bɪʃɔf] (**-s, ⸚e**) *m* bishop; **bischöflich** ['bɪʃøːflɪç] *adj* episcopal

bisher [bɪs'heːr] *adv* till now, hitherto; **~ig** *adj* till now

Biskuit [bɪs'kviːt] (**-(e)s, -s** *od* **-e**) *m od nt* (fatless) sponge

Biss ▲ [bɪs] (**-es, -e**) *m* bite

biss ▲ *etc vb siehe* **beißen**

bisschen ▲ ['bɪsçən] *adj, adv* bit

Bissen ['bɪsən] (**-s, -**) *m* bite, morsel

bissig ['bɪsɪç] *adj* (*Hund*) snappy; (*Bemerkung*) cutting, biting

bist [bɪst] *vb siehe* **sein**

bisweilen [bɪs'vaɪlən] *adv* at times, occasionally

Bitte ['bɪtə] *f* request; **b~** *excl* please; (*wie b~?*) (I beg your) pardon? ♦ *interj* (*als Antwort auf Dank*) you're welcome; **darf ich? – aber b~!** may I? – please do; **b~ schön!** it was a pleasure; **b~n** (*unreg*) *vt, vi:* **b~n (um)** to ask (for); **b~nd** *adj* pleading, imploring

bitter ['bɪtər] *adj* bitter; **~böse** *adj* very angry; **B~keit** *f* bitterness; **~lich** *adj* bitter

Blähungen ['blɛːʊŋən] *pl* (*MED*) wind *sg*

blamabel [bla'maːbəl] *adj* disgraceful

Blamage [bla'maːʒə] *f* disgrace

blamieren [bla'miːrən] *vr* to make a fool of o.s., to disgrace o.s. ♦ *vt* to let down, to disgrace

blank [blaŋk] *adj* bright; (*unbedeckt*) bare; (*sauber*) clean, polished; (*umg: ohne Geld*) broke; (*offensichtlich*) blatant

blanko ['blaŋko] *adv* blank; **B~scheck** *m* blank cheque

Blase ['blaːzə] *f* bubble; (*MED*) blister; (*ANAT*) bladder; **~balg (-(e)s, -bälge)** *m* bellows *pl*; **b~n** (*unreg*) *vt, vi* to blow; **~nentzündung** *f* cystitis

Blas- ['blaːs] *zW:* **~instrument** *nt* wind instrument; **~kapelle** *f* brass band

blass ▲ [blas] *adj* pale

Blässe ['blɛsə] (**-**) *f* paleness, pallor

Blatt [blat] (**-(e)s, ⸚er**) *nt* leaf; (*von Papier*)

sheet; (*Zeitung*) newspaper; (*KARTEN*) hand

blättern ['blɛtərn] *vi:* **in etw** *dat* **~** to leaf through sth

Blätterteig *m* flaky *od* puff pastry

blau [blaʊ] *adj* blue; (*umg*) drunk, stoned; (*KOCH*) boiled; (*Auge*) black; **~er Fleck** bruise; **Fahrt ins B~e** mystery tour; **~äugig** *adj* blue-eyed

Blech [blɛç] (**-(e)s, -e**) *nt* tin, sheet metal; (*Backblech*) baking tray; **~büchse** *f* tin, can; **~dose** *f* tin, can; **b~en** (*umg*) *vt, vi* to fork out; **~schaden** *m* (*AUT*) damage to bodywork

Blei [blaɪ] (**-(e)s, -e**) *nt* lead

Bleibe ['blaɪbə] *f* roof over one's head; **b~n** (*unreg*) *vi* to stay, to remain; **~ lassen** to leave alone; **b~nd** *adj* (*Erinnerung*) lasting; (*Schaden*) permanent

bleich [blaɪç] *adj* faded, pale; **~en** *vt* to bleach

Blei- *zW:* **b~ern** *adj* leaden; **b~frei** *adj* (*Benzin*) lead-free; **~stift** *m* pencil

Blende ['blɛndə] *f* (*PHOT*) aperture; **b~n** *vt* to blind, to dazzle; (*fig*) to hoodwink; **b~nd** (*umg*) *adj* grand; **b~nd aussehen** to look smashing

Blick [blɪk] (**-(e)s, -e**) *m* (*kurz*) glance, glimpse; (*Anschauen*) look; (*Aussicht*) view; **b~en** *vi* to look; **sich b~en lassen** to put in an appearance; **~fang** *m* eye-catcher

blieb [bliːp] *etc vb siehe* **bleiben**

blind [blɪnt] *adj* blind; (*Glas etc*) dull; **~er Passagier** stowaway; **B~darm** *m* appendix; **B~darmentzündung** *f* appendicitis; **B~enschrift** ['blɪndən-] *f* Braille; **B~heit** *f* blindness; **~lings** *adv* blindly

blink- ['blɪŋk] *zW:* **~en** *vi* to twinkle, to sparkle; (*Licht*) to flash, to signal; (*AUT*) to indicate ♦ *vt* to flash, to signal; **B~er (-s, -)** *m* (*AUT*) indicator; **B~licht** *nt* (*AUT*) indicator; (*an Bahnübergängen usw*) flashing light

blinzeln ['blɪntsəln] *vi* to blink, to wink

Blitz [blɪts] (**-es, -e**) *m* (flash of) lightning; **~ableiter** *m* lightning conductor; **b~en** *vi* (*aufleuchten*) to flash, to sparkle; **es b~t**

(MET) there's a flash of lightning; **~licht** nt flashlight; **b~schnell** adj lightning ♦ adv (as) quick as a flash

Block [blɔk] (-(e)s, ⁿe) m block; (von Papier) pad; **~ade** [blɔˈkaːdə] f blockade; **~flöte** f recorder; **b~frei** adj (POL) unaligned; **~haus** nt log cabin; **b~ieren** [blɔˈkiːrən] vt to block ♦ vi (Räder) to jam; **~schrift** f block letters pl

blöd [bløːt] adj silly, stupid; **~eln** [ˈbløːdəln] (umg) vi to act the goat (fam), to fool around; **B~sinn** m nonsense; **~sinnig** adj silly, idiotic

blond [blɔnt] adj blond, fair-haired

<hr>

SCHLÜSSELWORT

bloß [bloːs] adj 1 (unbedeckt) bare; (nackt) naked; **mit der bloßen Hand** with one's bare hand; **mit bloßem Auge** with the naked eye

2 (alleinig, nur) mere; **der bloße Gedanke** the very thought; **bloßer Neid** sheer envy ♦ adv only, merely; **lass das bloß!** just don't do that!; **wie ist das bloß passiert?** how on earth did that happen?

<hr>

Blöße [ˈbløːsə] f bareness; nakedness; (fig) weakness

bloßstellen vt to show up

blühen [ˈblyːən] vi to bloom (lit), to be in bloom; (fig) to flourish; **~d** adj (Pflanze) blooming; (Aussehen) blooming, radiant; (Handel) thriving, booming

Blume [ˈbluːmə] f flower; (von Wein) bouquet

Blumen- zW: **~kohl** m cauliflower; **~topf** m flowerpot; **~zwiebel** f bulb

Bluse [ˈbluːzə] f blouse

Blut [bluːt] (-(e)s) nt blood; **b~arm** adj anaemic; (fig) penniless; **b~befleckt** adj bloodstained; **~bild** nt blood count; **~druck** m blood pressure

Blüte [ˈblyːtə] f blossom; (fig) prime

Blut- zW: **b~en** vi to bleed; **~er** m (MED) haemophiliac; **~erguss** ▲ m haemorrhage; (auf Haut) bruise

Blütezeit f flowering period; (fig) prime

Blut- zW: **~gruppe** f blood group; **b~ig** adj bloody; **b~jung** adj very young; **~probe** f blood test; **~spender** m blood donor; **~transfusion** f (MED) blood transfusion; **~ung** f bleeding, haemorrhage; **~vergiftung** f blood poisoning; **~wurst** f black pudding

Bö [bøː] (-, -en) f squall

Bock [bɔk] (-(e)s, ⁿe) m buck, ram; (Gestell) trestle, support; (SPORT) buck; **~wurst** f type of pork sausage

Boden [ˈboːdən] (-s, ⁿ) m ground; (Fußboden) floor; (Meeresboden, Fassboden) bottom; (Speicher) attic; **b~los** adj bottomless; (umg) incredible; **~nebel** m ground mist; **~personal** nt (AVIAT) ground staff; **~schätze** pl mineral resources; **~see** m: **der ~see** Lake Constance; **~turnen** nt floor exercises pl

Böe [ˈbøːə] f squall

Bogen [ˈboːgən] (-s, -) m (Biegung) curve; (ARCHIT) arch; (Waffe, MUS) bow; (Papier) sheet

Bohne [ˈboːnə] f bean

bohnern vt to wax, to polish

Bohnerwachs nt floor polish

Bohr- [ˈboːr] zW: **b~en** vt to bore; **~er** (-s, -) m drill; **~insel** f oil rig; **~maschine** f drill; **~turm** m derrick

Boiler [ˈbɔylər] (-s, -) m (hot-water) tank

Boje [ˈboːjə] f buoy

Bolzen [ˈbɔltsən] (-s, -) m bolt

bombardieren [bɔmbarˈdiːrən] vt to bombard; (aus der Luft) to bomb

Bombe [ˈbɔmbə] f bomb

Bombenangriff m bombing raid

Bombenerfolg (umg) m smash hit

Bon [bɔŋ] (-s, -s) m voucher, chit

Bonbon [bõˈbõː] (-s, -s) m od sweet

Boot [boːt] (-(e)s, -e) nt boat

Bord [bɔrt] (-(e)s, -e) m (AVIAT, NAUT) board ♦ nt (Brett) shelf; **an ~** on board

Bordell [bɔrˈdɛl] (-s, -e) nt brothel

Bordstein m kerb(stone)

borgen [ˈbɔrgən] vt to borrow; **jdm etw ~** to lend sb sth

borniert [bɔrˈniːrt] adj narrow-minded

Börse ['bœːrzə] f stock exchange; (*Geldbörse*) purse; **~nmakler** m stockbroker

Borte ['bɔrtə] f edging; (*Band*) trimming

bös [bøːs] adj = **böse**

bösartig ['bøːz-] adj malicious

Böschung ['bœʃʊŋ] f slope; (*Uferböschung etc*) embankment

böse ['bøːzə] adj bad, evil; (*zornig*) angry

boshaft ['boːshaft] adj malicious, spiteful

Bosheit f malice, spite

Bosnien ['bɔsniən] (**-s**) nt Bosnia; **~ und Herzegowina** [-hɛrtsə'goːvina] nt Bosnia (and) Herzegovina

böswillig ['bøːsvɪlɪç] adj malicious

bot etc [boːt] vb siehe **bieten**

Botanik [bo'taːnɪk] f botany; **botanisch** adj botanical

Bot- ['boːt] zW: **~e (-n, -n)** m messenger; **~schaft** f message, news; (*POL*) embassy; **~schafter (-s, -)** m ambassador

Bottich ['bɔtɪç] (**-(e)s, -e**) m vat, tub

Bouillon [bu'ljõ] (**-, -s**) f consommé

Bowle ['boːlə] f punch

Box- ['bɔks] zW: **b~en** vi to box; **~er (-s, -)** m boxer; **~kampf** m boxing match

boykottieren [bɔykɔ'tiːrən] vt to boycott

brach etc [braːx] vb siehe **brechen**

brachte etc ['braxtə] vb siehe **bringen**

Branche ['brãːʃə] f line of business

Branchenverzeichnis nt Yellow Pages® pl

Brand [brant] (**-(e)s, ⁼e**) m fire; (*MED*) gangrene; **b~en** ['brandən] vi to surge; (*Meer*) to break; **b~marken** vt to brand; (*fig*) to stigmatize; **~salbe** f ointment for burns; **~stifter** [-ʃtɪftər] m arsonist, fire raiser; **~stiftung** f arson; **~ung** f surf

Branntwein ['brantvaɪn] m brandy

Brasilien [bra'ziːliən] nt Brazil

Brat- ['braːt] zW: **~apfel** m baked apple; **b~en** (*unreg*) vt to roast; to fry; **~en (-s, -)** m roast, joint; **~hähnchen** nt roast chicken; **~huhn** nt roast chicken; **~kartoffeln** pl fried od roast potatoes; **~pfanne** f frying pan

Bratsche ['braːtʃə] f viola

Bratspieß m spit

Bratwurst f grilled/fried sausage

Brauch [braʊx] (**-(e)s, Bräuche**) m custom; **b~bar** adj usable, serviceable; (*Person*) capable; **b~en** vt (*bedürfen*) to need; (*müssen*) to have to; (*umg: verwenden*) to use

Braue ['braʊə] f brow

brauen ['braʊən] vt to brew

Braue'rei f brewery

braun [braʊn] adj brown; (*von Sonne auch*) tanned; **~ gebrannt** tanned

Bräune ['brɔynə] (**-**) f brownness; (*Sonnenbräune*) tan; **b~n** vt to make brown; (*Sonne*) to tan

Brause ['braʊzə] f shower bath; (*von Gießkanne*) rose; (*Getränk*) lemonade; **b~n** vi to roar; (*auch vr: duschen*) to take a shower

Braut [braʊt] (**-, Bräute**) f bride; (*Verlobte*) fiancée

Bräutigam ['brɔytigam] (**-s, -e**) m bridegroom; fiancé

Brautpaar nt bride and (bride)groom, bridal pair

brav [braːf] adj (*artig*) good; (*ehrenhaft*) worthy, honest

bravo ['braːvo] excl well done

BRD ['beː'ʔɛr'deː] (**-**) f abk = **Bundesrepublik Deutschland**

BRD

ⓘ The **BRD** (*Bundesrepublik Deutschland*) is the official name for the Federal Republic of Germany. It comprises 16 **Länder** (see **Land**). It was formerly the name given to West Germany as opposed to East Germany (the **DDR**). The two Germanies were reunited on 3rd October 1990.

Brech- ['brɛç] zW: **~eisen** nt crowbar; **b~en** (*unreg*) vt, vi to break; (*Licht*) to refract; (*fig: Mensch*) to crush; (*speien*) to vomit; **~reiz** m nausea, retching

Brei [braɪ] (**-(e)s, -e**) m (*Masse*) pulp; (*KOCH*) gruel; (*Haferbrei*) porridge

breit [braɪt] adj wide, broad; **sich ~ machen** to spread o.s. out; **B~e** f width; (*bes bei*

Maßangaben) breadth; (*GEOG*) latitude; **~en**
vt: **etw über etw** *akk* **~en** fo spread sth
over sth; **B~engrad** *m* degree of latitude;
~treten *(unreg)* *(umg)* *vt* to go on about

Brems- ['brɛms] *zW:* **~belag** *m* brake
lining; **~e** [-zə] *f* brake; (*ZOOL*) horsefly;
b~en [-zən] *vi* to brake ♦ *vt* (*Auto*) to brake;
(fig) to slow down; **~flüssigkeit** *f* brake
fluid; **~licht** *nt* brake light; **~pedal** *nt*
brake pedal; **~spur** *f* skid mark(s *pl*); **~weg**
m braking distance

Brenn- ['brɛn] *zW:* **b~bar** *adj* inflammable;
b~en *(unreg)* *vi* to burn, to be on fire;
(Licht, Kerze etc) to burn ♦ *vt* (*Holz etc*) to
burn; (*Ziegel, Ton*) to fire; (*Kaffee*) to roast;
darauf b~en, etw zu tun to be dying to
do sth; **~nessel** ▲ *f* stinging nettle;
~punkt *m* (*PHYS*) focal point; (*Mittelpunkt*)
focus; **~stoff** *m* fuel

brenzlig ['brɛntslɪç] *adj (fig)* precarious

Bretagne [brə'tanjə] *f:* **die ~** Brittany

Brett [brɛt] **(-(e)s, -er)** *nt* board, plank;
(Bord) shelf; (*Spielbrett*) board; **~er** *pl* (*SKI*)
skis; (*THEAT*) boards; **schwarzes ~** notice
board; **~erzaun** *m* wooden fence; **~spiel**
nt board game

Brezel ['breːtsəl] **(-, -n)** *f* pretzel

brichst *etc* [brɪçst] *vb siehe* **brechen**

Brief [briːf] **(-(e)s, -e)** *m* letter; **~freund** *m*
penfriend; **~kasten** *m* letterbox; **b~lich**
adj, adv by letter; **~marke** *f* (*postage*)
stamp; **~papier** *nt* notepaper; **~tasche** *f*
wallet; **~träger** *m* postman; **~umschlag**
m envelope; **~waage** *f* letter scales;
~wechsel *m* correspondence

briet *etc* [briːt] *vb siehe* **braten**

Brikett [bri'kɛt] **(-s, -s)** *nt* briquette

Brillant [brɪl'jant] *adj (fig)* brilliant; **B~ (-en,
-en)** *m* brilliant, diamond

Brille ['brɪlə] *f* spectacles *pl*; (*Schutzbrille*)
goggles *pl*; (*Toilettenbrille*) (toilet) seat;
~ngestell *nt* (spectacle) frames

bringen ['brɪŋən] *(unreg)* *vt* to bring;
(mitnehmen, begleiten) to take; (*einbringen:
Profit*) to bring in; (*veröffentlichen:
Profit*) to publish; (*THEAT, CINE*) to show; (*RADIO, TV*) to
broadcast; (*in einen Zustand versetzen*) to

get; (*umg: tun können*) to manage; **jdn
dazu ~, etw zu tun** to make sb do sth; **jdn
nach Hause ~** to take sb home; **jdn um
etw ~** to make sb lose sth; **jdn auf eine
Idee ~** to give sb an idea

Brise ['briːzə] *f* breeze

Brit- ['briːt] *zW:* **~e** *m* Briton; **~in** *f* Briton;
b~isch *adj* British

bröckelig ['brœkəlɪç] *adj* crumbly

Brocken ['brɔkən] **(-s, -)** *m* piece, bit;
(Felsbrocken) lump of rock

brodeln ['broːdəln] *vi* to bubble

Brokkoli ['brɔkoli] *pl* (*BOT*) broccoli

Brombeere ['brɔmbeːrə] *f* blackberry,
bramble (*BRIT*)

Bronchien ['brɔnçiən] *pl* bronchia(l tubes)
pl

Bronchitis [brɔn'çiːtɪs] **(-)** *f* bronchitis

Bronze ['brõːsə] *f* bronze

Brosche ['brɔʃə] *f* brooch

Broschüre [brɔ'ʃyːrə] *f* pamphlet

Brot [broːt] **(-(e)s, -e)** *nt* bread; (*Laib*) loaf

Brötchen ['brøːtçən] *nt* roll

Bruch [brʊx] **(-(e)s, ᵉe)** *m* breakage;
(zerbrochene Stelle) break; (*fig*) split, breach;
(MED: Eingeweidebruch) rupture, hernia;
(Beinbruch etc) fracture; (*MATH*) fraction

brüchig ['brʏçɪç] *adj* brittle, fragile; (*Haus*)
dilapidated

Bruch- *zW:* **~landung** *f* crash landing;
~strich *m* (*MATH*) line; **~stück** *nt*
fragment; **~teil** *m* fraction; **~zahl** [brʊxtsaːl]
f (*MATH*) fraction

Brücke ['brʏkə] *f* bridge; (*Teppich*) rug

Bruder ['bruːdər] **(-s, ᵘ)** *m* brother;
brüderlich *adj* brotherly

Brühe ['bryːə] *f* broth, stock; (*pej*) muck

brüllen ['brʏlən] *vi* to bellow, to roar

brummen ['brʊmən] *vi* (*Bär, Mensch etc*) to
growl; (*Insekt*) to buzz; (*Motoren*) to roar;
(murren) to grumble

brünett [brʏ'nɛt] *adj* brunette, dark-haired

Brunnen ['brʊnən] **(-s, -)** *m* fountain; (*tief*)
well; (*natürlich*) spring

Brust [brʊst] **(-, ᵘe)** *f* breast; (*Männerbrust*)
chest

brüsten ['brʏstən] *vr* to boast

Brust- *zW:* **~kasten** *m* chest; **~schwimmen** *nt* breast-stroke
Brüstung ['brystʊŋ] *f* parapet
Brut [bruːt] (-, -en) *f* brood; (*Brüten*) hatching
brutal [bru'taːl] *adj* brutal
Brutali'tät *f* brutality
brüten ['bryːtən] *vi* (*auch fig*) to brood
Brutkasten *m* incubator
brutto ['brʊto] *adv* gross; **B~einkommen** *nt* gross salary; **B~gehalt** *nt* gross salary; **B~gewicht** *nt* gross weight; **B~lohn** *m* gross wages *pl*; **B~sozialprodukt** *nt* gross national product
BSE *f abk* (= *Bovine Spongiforme Enzephalopathie*) BSE
Bube ['buːbə] (-n, -n) *m* (*Schurke*) rogue; (*KARTEN*) jack
Buch [buːx] (-(e)s, ⁺er) *nt* book; (*COMM*) account book; **~binder** *m* bookbinder; **~drucker** *m* printer
Buche *f* beech tree
buchen *vt* to book; (*Betrag*) to enter
Bücher- ['byːçər] *zW:* **~brett** *nt* book-shelf; **~ei** [-'raɪ] *f* library; **~regal** *nt* book-shelves *pl*, bookcase; **~schrank** *m* book-case
Buch- *zW:* **~führung** *f* book-keeping, accounting; **~halter(in)** (-s, -) *m(f)* book-keeper; **~handel** *m* book trade; **~händler(in)** *m(f)* bookseller; **~handlung** *f* bookshop
Büchse ['byksə] (-, -n) *f* tin, can; (*Holzbüchse*) box; (*Gewehr*) rifle; **~nfleisch** *nt* tinned meat; **~nmilch** *f* (*KOCH*) evaporated milk, tinned milk; **~nöffner** *m* tin *od* can opener
Buchstabe (-ns, -n) *m* letter (of the alphabet)
buchstabieren [buːxʃta'biːrən] *vt* to spell
buchstäblich ['buːxʃtɛːplɪç] *adj* literal
Bucht ['bʊxt] (-, -en) *f* bay
Buchung ['buːxʊŋ] *f* booking; (*COMM*) entry
Buckel ['bʊkəl] (-s, -) *m* hump
bücken ['bʏkən] *vr* to bend
Bude ['buːdə] *f* booth, stall; (*umg*) digs *pl* (*BRIT*)
Büfett [by'fɛt] (-s, -s) *nt* (*Anrichte*) sideboard;

(*Geschirrschrank*) dresser; **kaltes ~** cold buffet
Büffel ['bʏfəl] (-s, -) *m* buffalo
Bug [buːk] (-(e)s, -e) *m* (*NAUT*) bow; (*AVIAT*) nose
Bügel ['byːgəl] (-s, -) *m* (*Kleider~*) hanger; (*Steig~*) stirrup; (*Brillen~*) arm; **~brett** *nt* ironing board; **~eisen** *nt* iron; **~falte** *f* crease; **b~frei** *adj* crease-resistant, noniron; **b~n** *vt, vi* to iron
Bühne ['byːnə] *f* stage; **~nbild** *nt* set, scenery
Buhruf ['buːruːf] *m* boo
buk *etc* [buːk] *vb siehe* **backen**
Bulgarien [bul'gaːriən] *nt* Bulgaria
Bull- ['bʊl] *zW:* **~auge** *nt* (*NAUT*) porthole; **~dogge** *f* bulldog; **~dozer** ['bʊldoːzər] (-s, -) *m* bulldozer; **~e** (-n, -n) *m* bull
Bumerang ['buːməraŋ] (-s, -e) *m* boomerang
Bummel ['bʊməl] (-s, -) *m* stroll; (*Schaufensterbummel*) window-shopping; **~ant** [-'lant] *m* slowcoach; **~ei** [-'laɪ] *f* wandering; dawdling; skiving; **b~n** *vi* to wander, to stroll; (*trödeln*) to dawdle; (*faulenzen*) to skive, to loaf around; **~streik** ['bʊməlʃtraɪk] *m* go-slow
Bund¹ [bʊnt] (-(e)s, ⁺e) *m* (*Freundschaftsbund etc*) bond; (*Organisation*) union; (*POL*) confederacy; (*Hosenbund, Rockbund*) waistband
Bund² (-(e)s, -e) *nt* bunch; (*Strohbund*) bundle
Bündel ['bʏndəl] (-s, -) *nt* bundle, bale; **b~n** *vt* to bundle
Bundes- ['bʊndəs] *in zW* Federal; **~bürger** *m* German citizen; **~hauptstadt** *f* Federal capital; **~kanzler** *m* Federal Chancellor; **~land** *nt* Land; **~liga** *f* football league; **~präsident** *m* Federal President; **~rat** *m* upper house of German Parliament; **~regierung** *f* Federal government; **~republik** *f* Federal Republic (of Germany); **~staat** *m* Federal state; **~straße** *f* Federal road; **~tag** *m* German Parliament; **~wehr** *f* German Armed Forces *pl*; **b~weit** *adj* nationwide

Bundespräsident

ⓘ The **Bundespräsident** is the head of state of the Federal Republic of Germany. He is elected every 5 years - no-one can be elected more than twice - by the members of the **Bundesversammlung**, a body formed especially for this purpose. His role is to represent Germany at home and abroad. In Switzerland the **Bundespräsident** is the head of the government, known as the **Bundesrat**. The **Bundesrat** is the Upper House of the German Parliament whose 68 members are nominated by the parliaments of the **Länder**. Its most important function is to approve federal laws concerned with the jurisdiction of the **Länder**; it can raise objections to other laws, but can be outvoted by the **Bundestag**. In Austria the **Länder** are also represented in the **Bundesrat**.

Bundestag

ⓘ The **Bundestag** is the Lower House of the German Parliament and is elected by the people by proportional representation. There are 672 MPs, half of them elected directly from the first vote (**Erststimme**), and half from the regional list of parliamentary candidates resulting from the second vote (**Zweitstimme**). The **Bundestag** exercises parliamentary control over the government.

Bündnis ['byntnɪs] (**-ses, -se**) nt alliance
bunt [bʊnt] adj coloured; (gemischt) mixed; **jdm wird es zu ~** it's getting too much for sb; **B~stift** m coloured pencil, crayon
Burg [bʊrk] (**-, -en**) f castle, fort
Bürge ['byrgə] (**-n, -n**) m guarantor; **b~n** vi: **b~n für** to vouch for
Bürger(in) ['byrgər(ɪn)] (**-s, -**) m(f) citizen; member of the middle class; **~krieg** m civil war; **b~lich** adj (Rechte) civil; (Klasse) middle-class; (pej) bourgeois; **~meister** m

mayor; **~recht** nt civil rights pl; **~schaft** f (Vertretung) City Parliament; **~steig** m pavement
Bürgschaft f surety; **~ leisten** to give security
Büro [by'roː] (**-s, -s**) nt office; **~angestellte(r)** f(m) office worker; **~klammer** f paper clip; **~kra'tie** f bureaucracy; **b~'kratisch** adj bureaucratic; **~schluss** ▲ m office closing time
Bursche ['bʊrʃə] (**-n, -n**) m lad, fellow; (Diener) servant
Bürste ['byrstə] f brush; **b~n** vt to brush
Bus [bʊs] (**-ses, -se**) m bus; **~bahnhof** m bus/coach (BRIT) station
Busch [bʊʃ] (**-(e)s, ⁼e**) m bush, shrub
Büschel ['byʃəl] (**-s, -**) nt tuft
buschig adj bushy
Busen ['buːzən] (**-s, -**) m bosom; (Meerbusen) inlet, bay
Bushaltestelle f bus stop
Buße ['buːsə] f atonement, penance; (Geld) fine
büßen ['byːsən] vi to do penance, to atone ♦ vt to do penance for, to atone for
Bußgeld ['buːsɡɛlt] nt fine; **~bescheid** m notice of payment due (for traffic offence etc)
Büste ['bystə] f bust; **~nhalter** m bra
Butter ['bʊtər] (**-**) f butter; **~blume** f buttercup; **~brot** nt (piece of) bread and butter; (umg) sandwich; **~brotpapier** nt greaseproof paper; **~dose** f butter dish; **~milch** f buttermilk; **b~weich** ['bʊtərvaɪç] adj soft as butter; (fig, umg) soft
b. w. abk (= bitte wenden) p.t.o.
bzgl. abk (= bezüglich) re
bzw. abk = **beziehungsweise**

C, c

ca. [ka] abk (= circa) approx.
Café [ka'feː] (**-s, -s**) nt café
Cafeteria [kafete'riːa] (**-, -s**) f cafeteria
Camcorder (**-s, -**) m camcorder
Camp- ['kɛmp] zW: **c~en** vi to camp; **~er**

(-s, -) *m* camper; **~ing** (-s) *nt* camping;
~ingführer *m* camping guide (book);
~ingkocher *m* camping stove; **~ingplatz**
m camp(ing) site
CD-Spieler *m* CD (player)
Cello ['tʃɛlo] (-s, -s *od* **Celli**) *nt* cello
Celsius ['tsɛlzius] (-) *nt* centigrade
Cent [sɛnt] (-s, -s) *m* cent
Champagner [ʃam'panjər] (-s, -) *m*
champagne
Champignon ['ʃampinjõ] (-s, -s) *m* button
mushroom
Chance ['ʃãːs(ə)] *f* chance, opportunity
Chaos ['kaːɔs] (-, -) *nt* chaos; **chaotisch**
[ka'oːtiʃ] *adj* chaotic
Charakter [ka'raktər, *pl* karak'teːrə] (-s, -e) *m*
character; **c~fest** *adj* of firm character,
strong; **c~i'sieren** *vt* to characterize;
c~istisch [karakte'rɪstiʃ] *adj*: **c~istisch (für)**
characteristic (of), typical (of); **c~los** *adj*
unprincipled; **~losigkeit** *f* lack of principle;
~schwäche *f* weakness of character;
~stärke *f* strength of character; **~zug** *m*
characteristic, trait
charmant [ʃar'mant] *adj* charming
Charme [ʃarm] (-s) *m* charm
Charterflug ['tʃartərfluːk] *m* charter flight
Chauffeur [ʃɔ'føːr] *m* chauffeur
Chauvinist [ʃovi'nɪst] *m* chauvinist, jingoist
Chef [ʃɛf] (-s, -s) *m* head; (*umg*) boss; **~arzt**
m senior consultant; **~in** (*umg*) *f* boss
Chemie [çe'miː] (-) *f* chemistry; **~faser** *ff*
man-made fibre
Chemikalie [çemi'kaːliə] *f* chemical
Chemiker ['çeːmikər] (-s, -) *m* (industrial)
chemist
chemisch ['çeːmiʃ] *adj* chemical; **~e**
Reinigung dry cleaning
Chicorée ['ʃikoreː] (-s) *m od f* chicory
Chiffre ['ʃifrə] *f* (*Geheimzeichen*) cipher; (*in*
Zeitung) box number
Chile ['tʃiːle] *nt* Chile
Chin- ['çiːn] *zW*: **~ant** China; **~akohl** *m*
Chinese leaves; **~ese** [-'neːzə] *m* Chinese;
~esin *f* Chinese; **c~esisch** *adj* Chinese
Chip [tʃip] (-s, -s) *m* (*Kartoffelchips* crisp
(*BRIT*), chip (*US*); (*COMPUT*) chip; **~karte** *f*

smart card
Chirurg [çi'rʊrg] (-en, -en) *m* surgeon; **~ie**
[-'giː] *f* surgery; **c~isch** *adj* surgical
Chlor [kloːr] (-s) *nt* chlorine; **~o'form** (-s) *nt*
chloroform
cholerisch [ko'leːriʃ] *adj* choleric
Chor [koːr] (-(e)s, ⁺e) *m* choir; (*Musikstück*,
THEAT) chorus; **~al** [ko'raːl] (-s, -äle) *m*
chorale
Choreograf ▲ [koreo'graːf] (-en, -en) *m*
choreographer
Christ [krɪst] (-en, -en) *m* Christian; **~baum**
m Christmas tree; **~entum** *nt* Christianity;
~in *f* Christian; **~kind** *nt* ≈ Father
Christmas; (*Jesus*) baby Jesus; **c~lich** *adj*
Christian; **~us** (-) *m* Christ
Chrom [kroːm] (-s) *nt* chromium; chrome
Chron- ['kroːn] *zW*: **~ik** *f* chronicle; **c~isch**
adj chronic; **c~ologisch** [-o'loːgiʃ] *adj*
chronological
circa ['tsɪrka] *adv* about, approximately
Clown [klaʊn] (-s, -s) *m* clown
Cocktail ['kɔkteːl] (-s, -s) *m* cocktail
Cola ['koːla] (-, -s) *f* Coke ®
Computer [kɔm'pjuːtər] (-s, -) *m* computer;
~spiel *nt* computer game
Cord [kɔrt] (-s) *m* cord, corduroy
Couch [kaʊtʃ] (-, -es *od* -en) *f* couch
Coupon [ku'põː] (-s, -s) *m* = **Kupon**
Cousin [ku'zɛ̃ː] (-s, -s) *m* cousin; **~e**
[ku'ziːnə] *f* cousin
Creme [krɛːm] (-, -s) *f* cream; (*Schuhcreme*)
polish; (*Zahncreme*) paste; (*KOCH*) mousse;
c~farben *adj* cream(-coloured)
cremig ['kreːmiç] *adj* creamy
Curry ['kari] (-s) *m od adj* curry powder;
~pulver *nt* curry powder; **~wurst** *f* curried
sausage

D, d

da [daː] *adv* **1** (*örtlich*) there; (*hier*) here; **da**
draußen out there; **da sein** to be there; **da**

Rechtschreibreform: ▲ *neue Schreibung* △ *alte Schreibung (auslaufend)*

bin ich here I am; **da, wo** where; **ist noch Milch da?** is there any milk left? **2** (*zeitlich*) then; (*folglich*) so **3:** **da haben wir Glück gehabt** we were lucky there; **da kann man nichts machen** nothing can be done about it ♦ *konj* (*weil*) as, since

dabehalten (*unreg*) *vt* to keep

dabei [da'baɪ] *adv* (*räumlich*) close to it; (*noch dazu*) besides; (*zusammen mit*) with them; (*zeitlich*) during this; (*obwohl doch*) but, however; **was ist schon ~?** what of it?; **es ist doch nichts ~, wenn ...** it doesn't matter if ...; **bleiben wir ~** let's leave it at that; **es bleibt ~** that's settled; **das Dumme/Schwierige ~** the stupid/difficult part of it; **er war gerade ~ zu gehen** he was just leaving; **~ sein** (*anwesend*) to be present; (*beteiligt*) to be involved; **~stehen** (*unreg*) *vi* to stand around

Dach [dax] (*-(e)s, ¨er*) *nt* roof; **~boden** *m* attic, loft; **~decker** (*-s, -*) *m* slater, tiler; **~fenster** *nt* skylight; **~gepäckträger** *m* roof rack; **~luke** *f* skylight; **~pappe** *f* roofing felt; **~rinne** *f* gutter

Dachs [daks] (*-es, -e*) *m* badger

dachte *etc* ['daxtə] *vb siehe* **denken**

Dackel ['dakəl] (*-s, -*) *m* dachshund

dadurch [da'dʊrç] *adv* (*räumlich*) through it; (*durch diesen Umstand*) thereby, in that way; (*deshalb*) because of that, for that reason ♦ *konj*: **~, dass** because

dafür [da'fy:r] *adv* for it; (*anstatt*) instead; **er kann nichts ~** he can't help it; **er ist bekannt ~** he is well-known for that; **was bekomme ich ~?** what will I get for it?

dagegen [da'ge:gən] *adv* against it; (*im Vergleich damit*) in comparison with it; (*bei Tausch*) for it/them ♦ *konj* however; **ich habe nichts ~** I don't mind; **ich war ~** I was against it; **~ kann man nichts tun** one can't do anything about it; **~halten** (*unreg*) *vt* (*vergleichen*) to compare with it; (*entgegnen*) to object to it; **~sprechen** (*unreg*) *vi*: **es spricht nichts ~** there's no reason why not

daheim [da'haɪm] *adv* at home; **D~ (-s)** *nt* home

daher [da'he:r] *adv* (*räumlich*) from there; (*Ursache*) from that ♦ *konj* (*deshalb*) that's why

dahin [da'hɪn] *adv* (*räumlich*) there; (*zeitlich*) then; (*vergangen*) gone; **~ gehend** on this matter; **~'gegen** *konj* on the other hand; **~gestellt** *adv*: **~gestellt bleiben** to remain to be seen; **~gestellt sein lassen** to leave open *od* undecided

dahinten [da'hɪntən] *adv* over there

dahinter [da'hɪntər] *adv* behind it; **~ kommen** to get to the bottom of it

dalli ['dali] (*umg*) *adv* chop chop

damalig ['da:ma:lɪç] *adj* of that time, then

damals ['da:ma:ls] *adv* at that time, then

Dame ['da:mə] *f* lady; (*SCHACH, KARTEN*) queen; (*Spiel*) draughts *sg*; **~nbinde** *f* sanitary towel *od* napkin (US); **d~nhaft** *adj* ladylike; **~ntoilette** *f* ladies' toilet *od* restroom (US); **~nwahl** *f* ladies' excuse-me

damit [da'mɪt] *adv* with it; (*begründend*) by that ♦ *konj* in order that, in order to; **was meint er ~?** what does he mean by that?; **genug ~!** that's enough!

dämlich ['dɛ:mlɪç] (*umg*) *adj* silly, stupid

Damm [dam] (*-(e)s, ¨e*) *m* dyke; (*Staudamm*) dam; (*Hafendamm*) mole; (*Bahndamm, Straßendamm*) embankment

dämmen ['dɛmən] *vt* (*Wasser*) to dam up; (*Schmerzen*) to keep back

dämmer- *zW*: **~ig** *adj* dim, faint; **~n** *vi* (*Tag*) to dawn; (*Abend*) to fall; **D~ung** *f* twilight; (*Morgendämmerung*) dawn; (*Abenddämmerung*) dusk

Dampf [dampf] (*-(e)s, ¨e*) *m* steam; (*Dunst*) vapour; **d~en** *vi* to steam

dämpfen ['dɛmpfən] *vt* (*KOCH*) to steam; (*bügeln*) to iron with a damp cloth; (*fig*) to dampen, to subdue

Dampf- *zW*: **~schiff** *nt* steamship; **~walze** *f* steamroller

danach [da'na:x] *adv* after that; (*zeitlich*) after that, afterwards; (*gemäß*) accordingly; according to which; according to that; **er sieht ~ aus** he looks it

Däne ['dɛːnə] **(-n, -n)** *m* Dane

daneben [da'neːbən] *adv* beside it; (*im Vergleich*) in comparison; **~benehmen** (*unreg*) *vr* to misbehave; **~gehen** (*unreg*) *vi* to miss; (*Plan*) to fail

Dänemark ['dɛːnəmark] *nt* Denmark; **Dänin** *f* Dane; **dänisch** *adj* Danish

Dank [daŋk] **(-(e)s)** *m* thanks *pl*; **vielen** *od* **schönen ~** many thanks; **jdm ~ sagen** to thank sb; **d~** *präp* (+*dat od gen*) thanks to; **d~bar** *adj* grateful; (*Aufgabe*) rewarding; **~barkeit** *f* gratitude; **d~e** *excl* thank you, thanks; **d~en** *vi* +*dat* to thank; **d~enswert** *adj* (*Arbeit*) worthwhile; rewarding; (*Bemühung*) kind; **d~sagen** *vi* to express one's thanks

dann [dan] *adv* then; **~ und wann** now and then

daran [da'ran] *adv* on it; (*stoßen*) against it; **es liegt ~, dass ...** the cause of it is that ...; **gut/schlecht ~ sein** to be well-/badly off; **das Beste/Dümmste ~** the best/ stupidest thing about it; **ich war nahe ~ zu ...** I was on the point of ...; **er ist ~ gestorben** he died from it *od* of it; **~gehen** (*unreg*) *vi* to start; **~setzen** *vt* to stake

darauf [da'rauf] *adv* (*räumlich*) on it; (*zielgerichtet*) towards it; (*danach*) afterwards; **es kommt ganz ~ an, ob ...** it depends whether ...; **die Tage ~** the days following *od* thereafter; **am Tag ~** the next day; **~ folgend** (*Tag, Jahr*) next, following; **~ legen** to lay *od* put on top

daraus [da'raus] *adv* from it; **was ist ~ geworden?** what became of it?; **~ geht hervor, dass ...** this means that ...

Darbietung ['daːrbiːtʊŋ] *f* performance

darf *etc* [darf] *vb siehe* **dürfen**

darin [da'rɪn] *adv* in (there), in it

darlegen ['daːrleːgən] *vt* to explain, to expound, to set forth; **Darlegung** *f* explanation

Darleh(e)n **(-s, -)** *nt* loan

Darm [darm] **(-(e)s, ⁻e)** *m* intestine; (*Wurstdarm*) skin; **~grippe** *f* (*MED*) gastric influenza *od* flu

darstell- ['daːrʃtɛl] *zW:* **~en** *vt* (*abbilden, bedeuten*) to represent; (*THEAT*) to act; (*beschreiben*) to describe ♦ *vr* to appear to be; **D~er(in)** **(-s, -)** *m(f)* actor (actress); **D~ung** *f* portrayal, depiction

darüber [da'ryːbər] *adv* (*räumlich*) over it, above it; (*fahren*) over it; (*mehr*) more; (*währenddessen*) meanwhile; (*sprechen, streiten*) about it; **~ geht nichts** there's nothing like it

darum [da'rʊm] *adv* (*räumlich*) round it ♦ *konj* that's why; **er bittet ~** he is pleading for it; **es geht ~, dass ...** the thing is that ...; **er würde viel ~ geben, wenn ...** he would give a lot to ...; **ich tue es ~, weil ...** I am doing it because ...

darunter [da'rʊntər] *adv* (*räumlich*) under it; (*dazwischen*) among them; (*weniger*) less; **ein Stockwerk ~** one floor below (it); **was verstehen Sie ~?** what do you understand by that?

das [das] *def art* the ♦ *pron* that

Dasein ['daːzain] **(-s)** *nt* (*Leben*) life; (*Anwesenheit*) presence; (*Bestehen*) existence

da sein ▲ *siehe* **da**

dass ▲ [das] *konj* that

dasselbe [das'zɛlbə] *art, pron* the same

dastehen ['daːʃteːən] (*unreg*) *vi* to stand there

Datei [da'tai] *f* file

Daten- ['daːtən] *zW:* **~bank** *f* data base; **~schutz** *m* data protection; **~verarbeitung** *f* data processing

datieren [da'tiːrən] *vt* to date

Dativ ['daːtiːf] **(-s, -e)** *m* dative (case)

Dattel ['datəl] **(-, -n)** *f* date

Datum ['daːtʊm] **(-s, Daten)** *nt* date; **Daten** *pl* (*Angaben*) data *pl*

Dauer ['dauər] **(-, -n)** *f* duration; (*gewisse Zeitspanne*) length; (*Bestand, Fortbestehen*) permanence; **es war nur von kurzer ~** it didn't last long; **auf die ~** in the long run; (*auf längere Zeit*) indefinitely; **~auftrag** *m* standing order; **d~haft** *adj* lasting, durable; **~karte** *f* season ticket; **~lauf** *m* jog(ging); **d~n** *vi* to last; **es hat sehr lang gedauert, bis er ...** it took him a long time to ...;

d~nd adj constant; **~parkplatz** m long-stay car park; **~welle** f perm, permanent wave; **~wurst** f German salami; **~zustand** m permanent condition

Daumen ['daumən] (**-s, -**) m thumb

Daune ['daunə] f down; **~ndecke** f down duvet, down quilt

davon [da'fɔn] adv of it; (räumlich) away; (weg von) from it; (Grund) because of it; **das kommt ~!** that's what you get; **~ abgesehen** apart from that; **~ sprechen/wissen** to talk/know of od about it; **was habe ich ~?** what's the point?; **~kommen** (unreg) vi to escape; **~laufen** (unreg) vi to run away

davor [da'fo:r] adv (räumlich) in front of it; (zeitlich) before (that); **~ warnen** to warn about it

dazu [da'tsu:] adv (legen, stellen) by it; (essen, singen) with it; **und ~ noch** and in addition; **ein Beispiel/seine Gedanken ~** one example for/his thoughts on this; **wie komme ich denn ~?** why should I?; **~ fähig sein** to be capable of it; **sich ~ äußern** to say something on it; **~gehören** vi to belong to it; **~kommen** (unreg) vi (Ereignisse) to happen too; (an einen Ort) to come along

dazwischen [da'tsvɪʃən] adv in between; (räumlich auch) between (them); (zusammen mit) among them; **~kommen** (unreg) vi (hineingeraten) to get caught in it; **es ist etwas ~gekommen** something cropped up; **~reden** vi (unterbrechen) to interrupt; (sich einmischen) to interfere; **~treten** (unreg) vi to intervene

---

DDR

ℹ️ *The DDR (Deutsche Demokratische Republik) was the name by which the former Communist German Democratic Republic was known. It was founded in 1949 from the Soviet-occupied zone. After the Berlin Wall was built in 1961 it was virtually sealed off from the West. Mass demonstrations and demands for reform forced the opening of the borders in 1989*

and the DDR merged in 1990 with the BRD.

Debatte [de'batə] f debate

Deck [dɛk] (**-(e)s, -s** od **-e**) nt deck; **an ~ gehen** to go on deck

Decke f cover; (Bettdecke) blanket; (Tischdecke) tablecloth; (Zimmerdecke) ceiling; **unter einer ~ stecken** to be hand in glove; **~I** (**-s, -**) m lid; **d~n** vt to cover ♦ vr to coincide

Deckung f (Schützen) covering; (Schutz) cover; (SPORT) defence; (Übereinstimmen) agreement

Defekt [de'fɛkt] (**-(e)s, -e**) m fault, defect; **d~** adj faulty

defensiv [defɛn'si:f] adj defensive

definieren [defi'ni:rən] vt to define;

Definition [definitsi'o:n] f definition

Defizit ['de:fitsit] (**-s, -e**) nt deficit

deftig ['dɛftɪç] adj (Essen) large; (Witz) coarse

Degen ['de:gən] (**-s, -**) m sword

degenerieren [degene'ri:rən] vi to degenerate

dehnbar ['de:nba:r] adj elastic; (fig: Begriff) loose

dehnen vt, vr to stretch

Deich [daɪç] (**-(e)s, -e**) m dyke, dike

deichseln (umg) vt (fig) to wangle

dein(e) [daɪn(ə)] adj your; **~e(r, s)** pron yours; **~er** (gen von du) pron of you; **~erseits** adv on your part; **~esgleichen** pron people like you; **~etwegen** adv (für dich) for your sake; (wegen dir) on your account; **~etwillen** adv: **um ~etwillen =** **deinetwegen; ~ige** pron: **der/die/das ~ige** od **D~ige** yours

Deklination [deklinatsi'o:n] f declension

deklinieren [dekli'ni:rən] vt to decline

Dekolleté, Dekolletee ▲ [dekɔl'te:] (**-s, -s**) nt low neckline

Deko- [deko] zW: **~rateur** [-ra'tø:r] m window dresser; **~ration** [-ratsi'o:n] f decoration; (in Laden) window dressing; **d~rativ** [-ra'ti:f] adj decorative; **d~rieren** [-'ri:rən] vt to decorate; (Schaufenster) to dress

Delegation [delegatsi'o:n] *f* delegation

delegieren [dele'gi:rən] *vt*: ~ **an** +*akk* (*Aufgaben*) to delegate to

Delfin ▲ [dɛl'fi:n] **(-s, -e)** *m* dolphin

delikat [deli'ka:t] *adj* (*zart, heikel*) delicate; (*köstlich*) delicious

Delikatesse [delika'tɛsə] *f* delicacy; **~n** *pl* (*Feinkost*) delicatessen food; **~ngeschäft** *nt* delicatessen

Delikt [de'lɪkt] **(-(e)s, -e)** *nt* (*JUR*) offence

Delle [ˈdɛlə] (*umg*) *f* dent

Delphin △ [dɛl'fi:n] **(-s, -e)** *m* = **Delfin**

dem [de(:)m] *art dat von* **der**

Demagoge [dema'go:gə] **(-n, -n)** *m* demagogue

dementieren [demɛn'ti:rən] *vt* to deny

dem- *zW*: **~gemäß** *adv* accordingly; **~nach** *adv* accordingly; **~nächst** *adv* shortly

Demokrat [demo'kra:t] **(-en, -en)** *m* democrat; **~ie** [-'ti:] *f* democracy; **d~isch** *adj* democratic; **d~isieren** [-i'zi:rən] *vt* to democratize

demolieren [demo'li:rən] *vt* to demolish

Demon- [demɔn] *zW*: **~strant(in)** [-'strant(ɪn)] *m(f)* demonstrator; **~stration** [-stratsi'o:n] *f* demonstration; **d~strativ** [-stra'ti:f] *adj* demonstrative; (*Protest*) pointed; **d~strieren** [-'stri:rən] *vt, vi* to demonstrate

Demoskopie [demosko'pi:] *f* public opinion research

Demut [ˈde:mu:t] **(-)** *f* humility

demütig [ˈde:my:tɪç] *adj* humble; **~en** [ˈde:my:tɪgən] *vt* to humiliate; **D~ung** *f* humiliation

demzufolge [ˈde:mtsu'fɔlgə] *adv* accordingly

den [de(:)n] *art akk von* **der**

denen [ˈde:nən] *pron dat pl von* **der**; **die**; **das**

Denk- [dɛŋk] *zW*: **d~bar** *adj* conceivable; **~en (-s)** *nt* thinking; **d~en** (*unreg*) *vt, vi* to think; **d~faul** *adj* lazy; **~fehler** *m* logical error; **~mal (-s, ⁼er)** *nt* monument; **~malschutz** *m* protection of historical monuments; **unter ~malschutz stehen** to be classified as a historical monument; **d~würdig** *adj* memorable; **~zettel** *m*: **jdm**

einen ~zettel verpassen to teach sb a lesson

denn [dɛn] *konj* for ♦ *adv* then; (*nach Komparativ*) than; **warum ~?** why?

dennoch [ˈdɛnɔx] *konj* nevertheless

Denunziant [denuntsi'ant(ɪn)] *m* informer

Deodorant [deʔodo'rant] **(-s, -s** *od* **-e)** *nt* deodorant

Deponie [depo'ni:] *f* dump

deponieren [depo'ni:rən] *vt* (*COMM*) to deposit

Depot [de'po:] **(-s, -s)** *nt* warehouse; (*Busdepot, EISENB*) depot; (*Bankdepot*) strongroom, safe (*US*)

Depression [deprɛsi'o:n] *f* depression; **depres'siv** *adj* depressive

deprimieren [depri'mi:rən] *vt* to depress

┌─────────────────────┐
│ *SCHLÜSSELWORT* │
└─────────────────────┘

der [de(:)r] (*f* **die**, *nt* **das**, *gen* **des, der, des**, *dat* **dem, der, dem**, *akk* **den, die, das**, *pl* **die**) *def art* the; **der Rhein** the Rhine; **der Klaus** (*umg*) Klaus; **die Frau** (*im Allgemeinen*) women; **der Tod/das Leben** death/life; **der Fuß des Berges** the foot of the hill; **gib es der Frau** give it to the woman; **er hat sich die Hand verletzt** he has hurt his hand

♦ *relativ pron* (*bei Menschen*) who, that; (*bei Tieren, Sachen*) which, that; **der Mann, den ich gesehen habe** the man who *od* whom *od* that I saw

♦ *demonstrativ pron* he/she/it; (*jener, dieser*) that; (*pl*) those; **der/die war es** it was him/her; **der mit der Brille** the one with glasses; **ich will den (da)** I want that one

---

derart [ˈde:rʔa:rt] *adv* so; (*solcher Art*) such; **~ig** *adj* such, this sort of

derb [dɛrp] *adj* sturdy; (*Kost*) solid; (*grob*) coarse

der- *zW*: **~'gleichen** *pron* such; **~'jenige** *pron* he; she; it; the one (who); that (which); **~'maßen** *adv* to such an extent, so; **~'selbe** *art, pron* the same; **~'weil(en)** *adv* in the meantime; **~'zeitig** *adj* present, current; (*damalig*) then

---

des [dɛs] *art gen von* **der**

desertieren [dezɛrˈtiːrən] *vi* to desert

desgleichen [dɛsˈɡlaɪçən] *adv* likewise, also

deshalb [ˈdɛshalp] *adv* therefore, that's why

Desinfektion [dɛzɪnfɛktsiˈoːn] *f* disinfection; **~smittel** *nt* disinfectant

desinfizieren [dɛzɪnfiˈtsiːrən] *vt* to disinfect

dessen [ˈdɛsən] *pron gen von* **der**; **das**; **~ ungeachtet** nevertheless, regardless

Dessert [dɛˈsɛːr] **(-s, -s)** *nt* dessert

destillieren [dɛstɪˈliːrən] *vt* to distil

desto [ˈdɛsto] *adv* all the, so much the; **~ besser** all the better

deswegen [ˈdɛsveːɡən] *konj* therefore, hence

Detail [deˈtaɪ] **(-s, -s)** *nt* detail

Detektiv [detɛkˈtiːf] **(-s, -e)** *m* detective

deut- [ˈdɔʏt] *zW:* **~en** *vt* to interpret, to explain ♦ *vi:* **~en (auf** +*akk*) to point (to *od* at); **~lich** *adj* clear; (*Unterschied*) distinct; **D~lichkeit** *f* clarity; distinctness

Deutsch [dɔʏtʃ] *nt* German

deutsch *adj* German; **auf D~** in German; **D~e Demokratische Republik** (*HIST*) German Democratic Republic, East Germany; **~es Beefsteak** ≈ hamburger; **D~e(r)** *mf* German; **ich bin D~er** I am German; **D~land** *nt* Germany

Devise [deˈviːzə] *f* motto, device; **~n** *pl* (*FIN*) foreign currency, foreign exchange

Dezember [deˈtsɛmbər] **(-s, -)** *m* December

dezent [deˈtsɛnt] *adj* discreet

dezimal [detsiˈmaːl] *adj* decimal; **D~system** *nt* decimal system

d. h. *abk* (= *das heißt*) i.e.

Dia [ˈdiːa] **(-s, -s)** *nt* (*PHOT*) slide, transparency

Diabetes [diaˈbeːtɛs] **(-, -)** *m* (*MED*) diabetes

Diagnose [diaˈɡnoːzə] *f* diagnosis

diagonal [diaɡoˈnaːl] *adj* diagonal

Dialekt [diaˈlɛkt] **(-(e)s, -e)** *m* dialect; **d~isch** *adj* dialectal; (*Logik*) dialectical

Dialog [diaˈloːk] **(-(e)s, -e)** *m* dialogue

Diamant [diaˈmant] *m* diamond

Diaprojektor [ˈdiːaprojɛktɔr] *m* slide projector

Diät [diˈɛːt] **(-, -en)** *f* diet

dich [dɪç] (*akk von du*) *pron* you; yourself

dicht [dɪçt] *adj* dense; (*Nebel*) thick; (*Gewebe*) close; (*undurchlässig*) (water)tight; (*fig*) concise ♦ *adv:* **~ an/bei** close to; **~ bevölkert** densely *od* heavily populated; **D~e** *f* density; thickness; closeness; (water)tightness; (*fig*) conciseness

dichten *vt* (*dicht machen*) to make watertight, to seal; (*NAUT*) to caulk; (*LITER*) to compose, to write ♦ *vi* to compose, to write

Dichter(in) **(-s, -)** *m(f)* poet; (*Autor*) writer; **d~isch** *adj* poetical

dichthalten (*unreg*) (*umg*) *vi* to keep one's mouth shut

Dichtung *f* (*TECH*) washer; (*AUT*) gasket; (*Gedichte*) poetry; (*Prosa*) (piece of) writing

dick [dɪk] *adj* thick; (*fett*) fat; **durch ~ und dünn** through thick and thin; **D~darm** *m* (*ANAT*) colon; **D~e** *f* thickness; fatness; **~flüssig** *adj* viscous; **D~icht** **(-s, -e)** *nt* thicket; **D~kopf** *m* mule; **D~milch** *f* soured milk

die [diː] *def art siehe* **der**

Dieb(in) [diːp, ˈdiːbɪn] **(-(e)s, -e)** *m(f)* thief; **d~isch** *adj* thieving; (*umg*) immense; **~stahl** **(-(e)s, ⁺e)** *m* theft; **~stahlversicherung** *f* insurance against theft

Diele [ˈdiːlə] *f* (*Brett*) board; (*Flur*) hall, lobby

dienen [ˈdiːnən] *vi:* **(jdm) ~** to serve (sb)

Diener **(-s, -)** *m* servant; **~in** *f* (maid)servant; **~schaft** *f* servants *pl*

Dienst [diːnst] **(-(e)s, -e)** *m* service; **außer ~** retired; **~ haben** to be on duty; **~ habend** (*Arzt*) on duty

Dienstag [ˈdiːnstaːk] *m* Tuesday; **d~s** *adv* on Tuesdays

Dienst- *zW:* **~bote** *m* servant; **~geheimnis** *nt* official secret; **~gespräch** *nt* business call; **~leistung** *f* service; **d~lich** *adj* official; **~mädchen** *nt* (house)maid; **~reise** *f* business trip; **~stelle** *f* office; **~vorschrift** *f* official regulations *pl*; **~weg** *m* official channels *pl*; **~zeit** *f* working hours *pl*; (*MIL*) period of service

dies [diːs] *pron (demonstrativ: sg)* this; (: *pl*)
these; **~bezüglich** *adj (Frage)* on this
matter; **~e(r, s)** ['diːzə(r, s)] *pron* this (one)

Diesel ['diːzəl] *m (Kraftstoff)* diesel

dieselbe [diː'zɛlbə] *pron, art* the same

Dieselmotor *m* diesel engine

diesig ['diːzɪç] *adj* drizzly

dies- *zW:* **~jährig** *adj* this year's; **~mal** *adv*
this time; **~seits** *präp +gen* on this side;
D~seits (-) *nt* this life

Dietrich ['diːtrɪç] (-s, -e) *m* picklock

diffamieren [dɪfa'miːrən] *(pej) vt* to defame

Differenz [dɪfə'rɛnts] (-, -en) *f (Unterschied)*
difference; **~en** *pl (Meinungsverschiedenheit)*
difference (of opinion); **d~ieren** *vt* to
make distinctions in; **d~iert** *adj (Mensch
etc)* complex

differenzial ▲ [dɪferentsia:l] *adj* differential;
D~rechnung *f* differential calculus

digital [digi'taːl] *adj* digital; **D~fernsehen** *f*
digital TV

Dikt- [dɪkt] *zW:* **~afon**, **~aphon** [-a'foːn] *nt*
dictaphone; **~at** [-'taːt] (-(e)s, -e) *nt*
dictation; **~ator** [-'taːtɔr] *m* dictator;
d~atorisch [-a'toːrɪʃ] *adj* dictatorial; **~atur**
[-a'tuːr] *f* dictatorship; **d~ieren** [-'tiːrən] *vt*
to dictate

Dilemma [di'lema] (-s, -s *od* -ta) *nt*
dilemma

Dilettant [dile'tant] *m* dilettante, amateur;
d~isch *adj* amateurish, dilettante

Dimension [dimɛnzi'oːn] *f* dimension

DIN *f abk (= Deutsche Industrie-Norm)*
German Industrial Standard

Ding [dɪŋ] (-(e)s, -e) *nt* thing, object;
d~lich *adj* real, concrete; **~s(bums)**
['dɪŋks(bʊms)] (-) *(umg) nt* thingummybob

Diplom [di'ploːm] (-(e)s, -e) *nt* diploma,
certificate; **~at** [-'maːt] (-en, -en) *m*
diplomat; **~atie** [-a'tiː] *f* diplomacy;
d~atisch [-'maːtɪʃ] *adj* diplomatic;
~ingenieur *m* qualified engineer

dir [diːr] *(dat von* **du***) pron* (to) you

direkt [di'rɛkt] *adj* direct; **D~flug** *m* direct
flight; **D~or** *m* director; *(SCH)* principal,
headmaster; **D~übertragung** *f* live
broadcast

Dirigent [diri'gɛnt(ɪn)] *m* conductor

dirigieren [diri'giːrən] *vt* to direct; *(MUS)* to
conduct

Diskette [dɪs'ketə] *f* diskette, floppy disk

Diskont [dɪs'kɔnt] (-s, -e) *m* discount; **~satz**
m rate of discount

Diskothek [dɪsko'teːk] (-, -en) *f*
disco(theque)

diskret [dɪs'kreːt] *adj* discreet; **D~ion** *f*
discretion

diskriminieren [dɪskrimi'niːrən] *vt* to
discriminate against

Diskussion [dɪskʊsi'oːn] *f* discussion;
debate; **zur ~ stehen** to be under
discussion

diskutieren [dɪsku'tiːrən] *vt, vi* to discuss; to
debate

Distanz [dɪs'tants] *f* distance; **distan'zieren**
vr: **sich von jdm/etw d~ieren** to distance
o.s. from sb/sth

Distel ['dɪstəl] (-, -n) *f* thistle

Disziplin [dɪstsi'pliːn] *f* discipline

Dividende [divi'dɛndə] *f* dividend

dividieren [divi'diːrən] *vt:* **(durch etw) ~** to
divide (by sth)

DM [deː'|ɛm] *abk (= Deutsche Mark)* German
Mark

D-Mark ['deːmark] *f* D Mark, German
Mark

SCHLÜSSELWORT
---

doch [dɔx] *adv* **1** *(dennoch)* after all; *(sowieso)*
anyway; **er kam doch noch** he came after
all; **du weißt es ja doch besser** you know
better than I do anyway; **und doch ...** and
yet ...

2 *(als bejahende Antwort)* yes I do/it does
etc; **das ist nicht wahr - doch!** that's not
true - yes it is!

3 *(auffordernd):* **komm doch** do come; **lass
ihn doch** just leave him; **nicht doch!** oh
no!

4: sie ist doch noch so jung but she's still
so young; **Sie wissen doch, wie das ist** you
know how it is (, don't you?); **wenn
doch** if only

♦ *konj (aber)* but; *(trotzdem)* all the same;

und doch hat er es getan but still he did it

Docht [dɔxt] (-(e)s, -e) m wick

Dock [dɔk] (-s, -s od -e) nt dock

Dogge ['dɔgə] f bulldog

Dogma ['dɔgma] (-s, -men) nt dogma; **d~tisch** adj dogmatic

Doktor ['dɔktɔr, pl -'toːrən] (-s, -en) m doctor

Dokument [doku'mɛnt] nt document

Dokumentar- [dokumɛn'taːr] zW: **~bericht** m documentary; **~film** m documentary (film); **d~isch** adj documentary

Dolch [dɔlç] (-(e)s, -e) m dagger

dolmetschen ['dɔlmɛtʃən] vt, vi to interpret; **Dolmetscher(in)** (-s, -) m(f) interpreter

Dom [doːm] (-(e)s, -e) m cathedral

dominieren [domi'niːrən] vt to dominate ♦ vi to predominate

Donau ['doːnau] f Danube

Donner ['dɔnər] (-s, -) m thunder; **d~n** vi unpers to thunder

Donnerstag ['dɔnərstaːk] m Thursday

doof [doːf] (umg) adj daft, stupid

Doppel ['dɔpəl] (-s, -) nt duplicate; (SPORT) doubles; **~bett** nt double bed; **d~deutig** adj ambiguous; **~fenster** nt double glazing; **~gänger** (-s, -) m double; **~punkt** m colon; **~stecker** m two-way adaptor; **d~t** adj double; **in d~ter Ausführung** in duplicate; **~verdiener** m person with two incomes; (pl: Paar) two-income family; **~zentner** m 100 kilograms; **~zimmer** nt double room

Dorf [dɔrf] (-(e)s, ⁻er) nt village; **~bewohner** m villager

Dorn [dɔrn] (-(e)s, -en) m (BOT) thorn; **d~ig** adj thorny

Dörrobst ['dœro:pst] nt dried fruit

Dorsch [dɔrʃ] (-(e)s, -e) m cod

dort [dɔrt] adv there; **~ drüben** over there; **~her** adv from there; **~hin** adv (to) there; **~ig** adj of that place; in that town

Dose ['doːzə] f box; (Blechdose) tin, can

Dosen pl von **Dose**; **Dosis**

Dosenöffner m tin od can opener

Dosis ['doːzɪs] (-, Dosen) f dose

Dotter ['dɔtər] (-s, -) m (egg) yolk

Drache ['draxə] (-n, -n) m (Tier) dragon

Drachen (-s, -) m kite; **~fliegen** (-s) nt hang-gliding

Draht [draːt] (-(e)s, ⁻e) m wire; **auf ~ sein** to be on the ball; **d~ig** adj (Mann) wiry; **~seil** nt cable; **~seilbahn** f cable railway, funicular

Drama ['draːma] (-s, Dramen) nt drama, play; **~tiker** [-'maːtikər] (-s, -) m dramatist; **d~tisch** [-'maːtɪʃ] adj dramatic

dran [dran] (umg) adv: **jetzt bin ich ~!** it's my turn now; siehe **daran**

Drang [draŋ] (-(e)s, ⁻e) m (Trieb): **~ (nach)** impulse (for), urge (for), desire (for); (Druck) pressure

drängeln ['drɛŋəln] vt, vi to push, to jostle

drängen ['drɛŋən] vt (schieben) to push, to press; (antreiben) to urge ♦ vi (eilig sein) to be urgent; (Zeit) to press; **auf etw** akk **~** to press for sth

drastisch ['drastɪʃ] adj drastic

drauf [drauf] (umg) adv = **darauf**; **D~gänger** (-s, -) m daredevil

draußen ['drausən] adv outside

Dreck [drɛk] (-(e)s) m mud, dirt; **d~ig** adj dirty, filthy

Dreh- ['dreː] zW: **~arbeiten** pl (CINE) shooting sg; **~bank** f lathe; **~buch** nt (CINE) script; **d~en** vt to turn, to rotate; (Zigaretten) to roll; (Film) to shoot ♦ vi to turn, to rotate ♦ vr to turn; (handeln von): **es d~t sich um ...** it's about ...; **~orgel** f barrel organ; **~tür** f revolving door; **~ung** f (Rotation) rotation; (Umdrehung, Wendung) turn; **~zahl** f rate of revolutions; **~zahlmesser** m rev(olution) counter

drei [drai] num three; **~ viertel** three quarters; **D~eck** nt triangle; **~eckig** adj triangular; **~einhalb** num three and a half; **~erlei** adj inv of three kinds; **~fach** adj triple, treble ♦ adv three times; **~hundert** num three hundred; **D~'königsfest** nt Epiphany; **~mal** adv three times; **~malig** adj three times

dreinreden ['draɪnre:dən] *vi:* **jdm ~**
(*dazwischenreden*) to interrupt sb; (*sich einmischen*) to interfere with sb

Dreirad *nt* tricycle

dreißig ['draɪsɪç] *num* thirty

dreist [draɪst] *adj* bold, audacious

drei- *zW:* **~viertel** △ *num siehe* **drei**;
D~viertelstunde *f* three-quarters of an hour; **~zehn** *num* thirteen

dreschen ['drɛʃən] (*unreg*) *vt* (*Getreide*) to thresh; (*umg: verprügeln*) to beat up

dressieren [drɛ'si:rən] *vt* to train

drillen ['drɪlən] *vt* (*bohren*) to drill, to bore; (*MIL*) to drill; (*fig*) to train

Drilling *m* triplet

drin [drɪn] (*umg*) *adv* = **darin**

dringen ['drɪŋən] (*unreg*) *vi* (*Wasser, Licht, Kälte*): **~ (durch/in** +*akk*) to penetrate (through/into); **auf etw** *akk* **~** to insist on sth

dringend ['drɪŋənt] *adj* urgent

Dringlichkeit *f* urgency

drinnen ['drɪnən] *adv* inside, indoors

dritte(r, s) ['drɪtə(r, s)] *adj* third; **D~ Welt** Third World; **D~s Reich** Third Reich; **D~l** (**-s, -**) *nt* third; **~ns** *adv* thirdly

DRK [de:ɛr'ka:] *nt abk* (= *Deutsches Rotes Kreuz*) German Red Cross

droben ['dro:bən] *adv* above, up there

Droge ['dro:gə] *f* drug

drogen *zW:* **~abhängig** *adj* addicted to drugs; **D~händler** *m* drug pedlar, pusher

Drogerie [dro:gə'ri:] *f* chemist's shop

> **Drogerie**
>
> *i* The **Drogerie** as opposed to the **Apotheke** sells medicines not requiring a prescription. It tends to be cheaper and also sells cosmetics, perfume and toiletries.

Drogist [dro'gɪst] *m* pharmacist, chemist

drohen ['dro:ən] *vi:* (**jdm**) **~** to threaten (sb)

dröhnen ['drø:nən] *vi* (*Motor*) to roar; (*Stimme, Musik*) to ring, to resound

Drohung ['dro:ʊŋ] *f* threat

drollig ['drɔlɪç] *adj* droll

Drossel ['drɔsəl] (**-, -n**) *f* thrush

drüben ['dry:bən] *adv* over there, on the other side

drüber ['dry:bər] (*umg*) *adv* = **darüber**

Druck [drʊk] (**-(e)s, -e**) *m* (*PHYS: Zwang*) pressure; (*TYP: Vorgang*) printing; (*: Produkt*) print; (*fig: Belastung*) burden, weight; **~buchstabe** *m* block letter

drücken ['drʏkən] *vt* (*Knopf, Hand*) to press; (*zu eng sein*) to pinch; (*fig: Preise*) to keep down; (*: belasten*) to oppress, to weigh down ♦ *vi* to press; to pinch ♦ *vr:* **sich vor etw** *dat* **~** to get out of (doing) sth; **~d** *adj* oppressive

Drucker (**-s, -**) *m* printer

Drücker (**-s, -**) *m* button; (*Türdrücker*) handle; (*Gewehrdrücker*) trigger

Druck- *zW:* **~erei** *f* printing works, press; **~erschwärze** *f* printer's ink; **~fehler** *m* misprint; **~knopf** *m* press stud, snap fastener; **~sache** *f* printed matter; **~schrift** *f* block *od* printed letters *pl*

drum [drʊm] (*umg*) *adv* = **darum**

drunten ['drʊntən] *adv* below, down there

Drüse ['dry:zə] *f* gland

Dschungel ['dʒʊŋəl] (**-s, -**) *m* jungle

du [du:] (*nom*) *pron* you; **~ sagen** = **duzen**

Dübel ['dy:bəl] (**-s, -**) *m* Rawlplug ®

ducken ['dʊkən] *vt* (*Kopf, Person*) to duck; (*fig*) to take down a peg or two ♦ *vr* to duck

Duckmäuser ['dʊkmɔyzər] (**-s, -**) *m* yes man

Dudelsack ['du:dəlzak] *m* bagpipes *pl*

Duell [du'ɛl] (**-s, -e**) *nt* duel

Duft [dʊft] (**-(e)s, ᵉe**) *m* scent, odour; **d~en** *vi* to smell, to be fragrant; **d~ig** *adj* (*Stoff, Kleid*) delicate, diaphanous

dulden ['dʊldən] *vt* to suffer; (*zulassen*) to tolerate ♦ *vi* to suffer

dumm [dʊm] *adj* stupid; (*ärgerlich*) annoying; **der D~e sein** to be the loser; **~erweise** *adv* stupidly; **D~heit** *f* stupidity; (*Tat*) blunder, stupid mistake; **D~kopf** *m* blockhead

dumpf [dʊmpf] *adj* (*Ton*) hollow, dull; (*Luft*)

musty; (*Erinnerung, Schmerz*) vague

Düne ['dy:nə] *f* dune

düngen ['dyŋən] *vt* to manure

Dünger (-s, -) *m* dung, manure; (*künstlich*) fertilizer

dunkel ['dʊŋkəl] *adj* dark; (*Stimme*) deep; (*Ahnung*) vague; (*rätselhaft*) obscure; (*verdächtig*) dubious, shady; **im D~n tappen** (*fig*) to grope in the dark

Dunkel- *zW:* **~heit** *f* darkness; (*fig*) obscurity; **~kammer** *f* (*PHOT*) darkroom; **d~n** *vi unpers* to grow dark; **~ziffer** *f* estimated number of unreported cases

dünn [dʏn] *adj* thin; **~flüssig** *adj* watery, thin

Dunst [dʊnst] (**-es**, **ᵘe**) *m* vapour; (*Wetter*) haze

dünsten ['dʏnstən] *vt* to steam

dunstig ['dʊnstɪç] *adj* vaporous; (*Wetter*) hazy, misty

Duplikat [dupli'ka:t] (**-(e)s**, **-e**) *nt* duplicate

Dur [du:r] (**-**, **-**) *nt* (*MUS*) major

SCHLÜSSELWORT

durch [dʊrç] *präp +akk* **1** (*hindurch*) through; **durch den Urwald** through the jungle; **durch die ganze Welt reisen** to travel all over the world

2 (*mittels*) through, by (means of); (*aufgrund*) due to, owing to; **Tod durch Herzschlag/den Strang** death from a heart attack/by hanging; **durch die Post** by post; **durch seine Bemühungen** through his efforts

♦ *adv* **1** (*hindurch*) through; **die ganze Nacht durch** all through the night; **die ganze Sommer durch** during the summer; **8 Uhr durch** past 8 o'clock; **durch und durch** completely

2 (*durchgebraten etc*): **(gut) durch** well-done

---

durch- *zW:* **~arbeiten** *vt, vi* to work through ♦ *vr* to work one's way through; **~'aus** *adv* completely; (*unbedingt*) definitely; **~aus nicht** absolutely not

Durchblick ['dʊrçblɪk] *m* view; (*fig*) comprehension; **d~en** *vi* to look through;

(*umg: verstehen*): **(bei etw) d~en** to understand (sth); **etw d~en lassen** (*fig*) to hint at sth

durchbrechen ['dʊrçbrɛçən] (*unreg*) *vt, vi* to break

durch'brechen ['dʊrçbrɛçən] (*unreg*) *vt insep* (*Schranken*) to break through; (*Schallmauer*) to break; (*Gewohnheit*) to break free from

durchbrennen ['dʊrçbrɛnən] (*unreg*) *vi* (*Draht, Sicherung*) to burn through; (*umg*) to run away

durchbringen (*unreg*) *vt* (*Kranken*) to pull through; (*umg: Familie*) to support; (*durchsetzen: Antrag, Kandidat*) to get through; (*vergeuden: Geld*) to get through, to squander

Durchbruch ['dʊrçbrʊx] *m* (*Öffnung*) opening; (*MIL*) breach; (*von Gefühlen etc*) eruption; (*der Zähne*) cutting; (*fig*) breakthrough; **zum ~ kommen** to break through

durch- *zW:* **~dacht** [-'daxt] *adj* well thought-out; **~'denken** (*unreg*) *vt* to think out; **~drehen** *vt* (*Fleisch*) to mince ♦ *vi* (*umg*) to crack up

durcheinander [dʊrçaɪ'nandər] *adv* in a mess, in confusion; (*umg: verwirrt*) confused; **~ bringen** to mess up; (*verwirren*) to confuse; **~ reden** to talk at the same time; **D~** (**-s**) *nt* (*Verwirrung*) confusion; (*Unordnung*) mess

durch- *zW:* **~fahren** (*unreg*) *vi* (*~ Tunnel usw*) to drive through; (*ohne Unterbrechung*) to drive straight through; (*ohne anzuhalten*): **der Zug fährt bis Hamburg ~** the train runs direct to Hamburg; (*ohne Umsteigen*): **können wir ~fahren?** can we go direct?, can we go non-stop?; **D~fahrt** *f* transit; (*Verkehr*) thoroughfare; **D~fall** *m* (*MED*) diarrhoea; **~fallen** (*unreg*) *vi* to fall through; (*in Prüfung*) to fail; **~finden** (*unreg*) *vr* to find one's way through; **~fragen** *vr* to find one's way by asking

durchführ- ['dʊrçfy:r] *zW:* **~bar** *adj* feasible, practicable; **~en** *vt* to carry out; **D~ung** *f* execution, performance

---

Durchgang ['dʊrçgaŋ] *m* passage(way); (*bei Produktion, Versuch*) run; (*SPORT*) round; (*bei Wahl*) ballot; „**~ verboten"** "no thoroughfare"

Durchgangsverkehr *m* through traffic

durchgefroren ['dʊrçgəfroːrən] *adj* (*Mensch*) frozen stiff

durchgehen ['dʊrçgeːən] (*unreg*) *vt* (*behandeln*) to go over ♦ *vi* to go through; (*ausreißen: Pferd*) to break loose; (*Mensch*) to run away; **mein Temperament ging mit mir durch** my temper got the better of me; **jdm etw ~ lassen** to let sb get away with sth; **~d** *adj* (*Zug*) through; (*Öffnungszeiten*) continuous

durch- *zW:* **~greifen** (*unreg*) *vi* to take strong action; **~halten** (*unreg*) *vi* to last out ♦ *vt* to keep up; **~kommen** (*unreg*) *vi* to get through; (*überleben*) to pull through; **~'kreuzen** *vt insep* to thwart, to frustrate; **~lassen** (*unreg*) *vt* (*Person*) to let through; (*Wasser*) to let in; **~lesen** (*unreg*) *vt* to read through; **~'leuchten** *vt insep* to X-ray; **~machen** *vt* to go through; **die Nacht ~machen** to make a night of it

Durchmesser (**-s, -**) *m* diameter

durch- *zW:* **~'nässen** *vt insep* to soak (through); **~nehmen** (*unreg*) *vt* to go over; **~nummerieren** ▲ *vt* to number consecutively; **~queren** [dʊrç'kveːrən] *vt insep* to cross; **D~reise** *f* transit; **auf der D~reise** passing through; (*Güter*) in transit; **~ringen** (*unreg*) *vr* to reach a decision after a long struggle

durchs [dʊrçs] = **durch das**

Durchsage ['dʊrçzaːgə] *f* intercom *od* radio announcement

durchschauen ['dʊrçʃauən] *vi* to look *od* see through; (*Person, Lüge*) to see through

durchscheinen ['dʊrçʃaɪnən] (*unreg*) *vi* to shine through; **~d** *adj* translucent

Durchschlag ['dʊrçʃlaːk] *m* (*Doppel*) carbon copy; (*Sieb*) strainer; **d~en** [-gən] (*unreg*) *vt* (*entzweischlagen*) to split (in two); (*sieben*) to sieve ♦ *vi* (*zum Vorschein kommen*) to emerge, to come out ♦ *vr* to

get by

durchschlagend *adj* resounding

durchschneiden ['dʊrçʃnaɪdən] (*unreg*) *vt* to cut through

Durchschnitt ['dʊrçʃnɪt] *m* (*Mittelwert*) average; **über/unter dem ~** above/below average; **im ~** on average; **d~lich** *adj* average ♦ *adv* on average

Durchschnittswert *m* average

durch- *zW:* **D~schrift** *f* copy; **~sehen** (*unreg*) *vt* to look through; **~setzen** *vt* to enforce ♦ *vr* (*Erfolg haben*) to succeed; (*sich behaupten*) to get one's way; **seinen Kopf ~setzen** to get one's way; **~'setzen** *vt insep* to mix

Durchsicht ['dʊrçzɪçt] *f* looking through, checking; **d~ig** *adj* transparent

durch- *zW:* **'~sprechen** (*unreg*) *vt* to talk over; '**~stehen** (*unreg*) *vt* to live through; **~stellen** *vt* (*an Telefon*) to put through; **~stöbern** (*auch untr*) *vt* (*Kisten*) to rummage through, to rifle through; (*Haus, Wohnung*) to ransack; '**~streichen** (*unreg*) *vt* to cross out; **~'suchen** *vt insep* to search; **D~'suchung** *f* search; **~'wachsen** *adj* (*Speck*) streaky; (*fig: mittelmäßig*) so-so; **D~wahl** *f* (*TEL*) direct dialling; **~weg** *adv* throughout, completely; **~ziehen** (*unreg*) *vt* (*Faden*) to draw through ♦ *vi* to pass through; **D~zug** *m* (*Luft*) draught; (*von Truppen, Vögeln*) passage

---
SCHLÜSSELWORT
---

dürfen ['dʏrfən] (*unreg*) *vi* **1** (*Erlaubnis haben*) to be allowed to; **ich darf das** I'm allowed to (do that); **darf ich?** may I?; **darf ich ins Kino?** can *od* may I go to the cinema?; **es darf geraucht werden** you may smoke

2 (*in Verneinungen*): **er darf das nicht** he's not allowed to (do that); **das darf nicht geschehen** that must not happen; **da darf sie sich nicht wundern** that shouldn't surprise her

3 (*in Höflichkeitsformeln*): **darf ich Sie bitten, das zu tun?** may *od* could I ask you to do that?; **was darf es sein?** what can I do for you?

4 (*können*): **das dürfen Sie mir glauben**
you can believe me
5 (*Möglichkeit*): **das dürfte genug sein** that
should be enough; **es dürfte Ihnen
bekannt sein, dass ...** as you will
probably know ...

dürftig ['dʏrftɪç] *adj* (*ärmlich*) needy, poor;
(*unzulänglich*) inadequate
dürr [dʏr] *adj* dried-up; (*Land*) arid; (*mager*)
skinny, gaunt; **D~e** *f* aridity; (*Zeit*) drought;
(*Magerkeit*) skinniness
Durst [dʊrst] (-(e)s) *m* thirst; ~ **haben** to be
thirsty; **d~ig** *adj* thirsty
Dusche ['duʃə] *f* shower; **d~en** *vi, vr* to
have a shower
Düse ['dy:zə] *f* nozzle; (*Flugzeugdüse*) jet
Düsen- *zW*: ~**antrieb** *m* jet propulsion;
~**flugzeug** *nt* jet (plane); ~**jäger** *m* jet
fighter
Dussel ['dʊsəl] (-s, -) (*umg*) *m* twit
düster ['dy:star] *adj* dark; (*Gedanken,
Zukunft*) gloomy
Dutzend ['dʊtsənt] (-s, -e) *nt* dozen; ~**(e)** *od*
d~(e) Mal(e) a dozen times
duzen ['du:tsən] *vt*: (**jdn**) ~ to use the
familiar form of address "du" (to *od* with
sb)

┌─────────────────┐
│ **duzen** │
└─────────────────┘

i *There are two different forms of address
in Germany: du and Sie.* **Duzen** *means
addressing someone as 'du' - used with
children, family and close friends - and*
siezen *means addressing someone as 'Sie' -
used for all grown-ups and older teenagers.
Students almost always use 'du' to each
other.*

Dynamik [dy'na:mɪk] *f* (*PHYS*) dynamics *sg*;
(*fig: Schwung*) momentum; (*von Mensch*)
dynamism; **dynamisch** *adj* (*auch fig*)
dynamic
Dynamit [dyna'mi:t] (-s) *nt* dynamite
Dynamo [dy'na:mo] (-s, -s) *m* dynamo
DZ *nt abk* = **Doppelzimmer**
D-Zug ['de:tsu:k] *m* through train

E, e

Ebbe ['ɛbə] *f* low tide
eben ['e:bən] *adj* level, flat; (*glatt*) smooth
♦ *adv* just; (*bestätigend*) exactly; ~
deswegen just because of that; ~**bürtig**
adj: **jdm** ~**bürtig sein** to be sb's equal;
E~e *f* plain; (*fig*) level; ~**falls** *adv* likewise;
~**so** *adv* just as
Eber ['e:bar] (-s, -) *m* boar
ebnen ['e:bnən] *vt* to level
Echo ['ɛço] (-s, -s) *nt* echo
echt [ɛçt] *adj* genuine; (*typisch*) typical;
E~heit *f* genuineness
Eck- ['ɛk] *zW*: ~**ball** *m* corner (kick); ~**e** *f*
corner; (*MATH*) angle; **e~ig** *adj* angular;
~**zahn** *m* eye tooth
ECU ['e:ky:] (-, -s) *m* (*FIN*) ECU
edel ['e:dəl] *adj* noble; **E~metall** *nt* rare
metal; **E~stahl** *m* high-grade steel;
E~stein *m* precious stone
EDV [e:de:'fau] (-) *f abk* (= *elektronische
Datenverarbeitung*) electronic data
processing
Efeu ['e:fɔy] (-s) *m* ivy
Effekt [ɛ'fɛkt] (-s, -e) *m* effect
Effekten [ɛ'fɛktən] *pl* stocks
effektiv [ɛfɛk'ti:f] *adj* effective, actual
EG [e:'ge:] *f abk* (= *Europäische Gemeinschaft*)
EC
egal [e'ga:l] *adj* all the same
Ego- [e:go] *zW*: ~**ismus** [-'ɪsmʊs] *m*
selfishness, egoism; ~**ist** [-'ɪst] *m* egoist;
e~istisch *adj* selfish, egoistic
Ehe ['e:ə] *f* marriage
ehe *konj* before
Ehe- *zW*: ~**beratung** *f* marriage guidance
(counselling); ~**bruch** *m* adultery; ~**frau** *f*
married woman; wife; ~**leute** *pl* married
people; **e~lich** *adj* matrimonial; (*Kind*)
legitimate
ehemalig *adj* former
ehemals *adv* formerly
Ehe- *zW*: ~**mann** *m* married man; husband;
~**paar** *nt* married couple

eher ['e:ər] *adv (früher)* sooner; *(lieber)* rather, sooner; *(mehr)* more

Ehe- *zW:***~ring** *m* wedding ring; **~schließung** *f* marriage ceremony

eheste(r, s) ['e:əstə(r, s)] *adj (früheste)* first, earliest; **am ~n** *(liebsten)* soonest; *(meist)* most; *(wahrscheinlichst)* most probably

Ehr- ['e:r] *zW:***e~bar** *adj* honourable, respectable;**~e** *f* honour;**e~en** *vt* to honour

Ehren- ['e:rən] *zW:***e~amtlich** *adj* honorary;**~gast** *m* guest of honour; **e~haft** *adj* honourable;**e~lich** *adj* honest;**~platz** *m* place of honour *od (US)* honor;**~runde** *f* lap of honour;**~sache** *f* point of honour;**e~voll** *adj* honourable;**~wort** *nt* word of honour

Ehr- *zW:***~furcht** *f* awe, deep respect; **e~fürchtig** *adj* reverent;**~gefühl** *nt* sense of honour;**~geiz** *m* ambition;**e~geizig** *adj* ambitious;**e~lich** *adj* honest;**~lichkeit** *f* honesty;**e~los** *adj* dishonourable;**~ung** *f* honour(ing);**e~würdig** *adj* venerable

Ei [aɪ] (-(e)s, -er) *nt* egg

Eich- *zW:***~e** ['aɪçə] *f* oak (tree);**~l** (-, -n) *f* acorn;**~hörnchen** *nt* squirrel

Eichmaß *nt* standard

Eid [aɪt] (-(e)s, -e) *m* oath

Eidechse ['aɪdɛksə] *f* lizard

eidesstattlich *adj:* **~e Erklärung** affidavit

Eidgenosse *m* Swiss

Eier- *zW:***~becher** *m* eggcup;**~kuchen** *m* omelette; pancake;**~likör** *m* advocaat; **~schale** *f* eggshell;**~stock** *m* ovary;**~uhr** *f* egg timer

Eifer ['aɪfər] (-s) *m* zeal, enthusiasm;**~sucht** *f* jealousy;**e~süchtig** *adj:* **e~süchtig (auf** **+akk)** jealous (of)

eifrig ['aɪfrɪç] *adj* zealous, enthusiastic

Eigelb ['aɪgɛlp] (-(e)s, -) *nt* egg yolk

eigen ['aɪgən] *adj* own; *(~artig)* peculiar; **mit der/dem ihm ~en ...** with that ... peculiar to him; **sich** *dat* **etw zu E~ machen** to make sth one's own;**E~art** *f* peculiarity; characteristic;**~artig** *adj* peculiar; **E~bedarf** *m:* **zum E~bedarf** for (one's own) personal use/domestic requirements; **der Vermieter machte E~bedarf geltend** the landlord showed he needed the house/flat for himself;**~händig** *adj* with one's own hand;**E~heim** *nt* owner-occupied house;**E~heit** *f* peculiarity; **~mächtig** *adj* high-handed;**E~name** *m* proper name;**~s** *adv* expressly, on purpose;**E~schaft** *f* quality, property, attribute;**E~sinn** *m* obstinacy;**~sinnig** *adj* obstinate;**~tlich** *adj* actual, real ♦ *adv* actually, really;**E~tor** *nt* own goal;**E~tum** *nt* property;**E~tümer(in)** (-s, -) *m(f)* owner, proprietor;**~tümlich** *adj* peculiar; **E~tümlichkeit** *f* peculiarity; **E~tumswohnung** *f* freehold flat

eignen ['aɪgnən] *vr* to be suited;**Eignung** *f* suitability

Eil- ['aɪl] *zW:***~bote** *m* courier;**~brief** *m* express letter;**~e** *f* haste; **es hat keine ~e** there's no hurry;**e~en** *vi (Mensch)* to hurry; *(dringend sein)* to be urgent;**e~ends** *adv* hastily;**~gut** *nt* express goods *pl*, fast freight *(US)*;**e~ig** *adj* hasty, hurried; *(dringlich)* urgent; **es e~ig haben** to be in a hurry;**~zug** *m* semi-fast train, limited stop train

Eimer ['aɪmər] (-s, -) *m* bucket, pail

ein ['aɪn] *adv:* **nicht ~ noch aus wissen** not to know what to do

ein(e) ['aɪn(ə)] *num* one ♦ *indef art* a, an

einander [aɪ'nandər] *pron* one another, each other

einarbeiten ['aɪnˌarbaɪtən] *vt* to train ♦ *vr:* **sich in etw** *akk* **~** to familiarize o.s. with sth

einatmen ['aɪnˌaːtmən] *vt, vi* to inhale, to breathe in

Einbahnstraße ['aɪnbaːnʃtrasə] *f* one-way street

Einband ['aɪnbant] *m* binding, cover

einbauen ['aɪnbauən] *vt* to build in; *(Motor)* to install, to fit

Einbaumöbel *pl* built-in furniture *sg*

einbegriffen ['aɪnbəgrɪfən] *adj* included

einberufen ['aɪnbəruːfən] *(unreg) vt* to convene; *(MIL)* to call up

Einbettzimmer *nt* single room

einbeziehen ['aɪnbətsiːən] *(unreg) vt* to

include

einbiegen ['aɪnbiːɡən] (*unreg*) *vi* to turn

einbilden ['aɪnbɪldən] *vt*: **sich** *dat* **etw ~ to** imagine sth

Einbildung *f* imagination; (*Dünkel*) conceit; **~skraft** *f* imagination

Einblick ['aɪnblɪk] *m* insight

einbrechen ['aɪnbrɛçən] (*unreg*) *vi* (*in Haus*) to break in; (*Nacht*) to fall; (*Winter*) to set in; (*durchbrechen*) to break; **~ in** +*akk* (*MIL*) to invade

Einbrecher (-s, -) *m* burglar

einbringen ['aɪnbrɪŋən] (*unreg*) *vt* to bring in; (*Geld, Vorteil*) to yield; (*mitbringen*) to contribute

Einbruch ['aɪnbrʊx] *m* (*Hauseinbruch*) break-in, burglary; (*Eindringen*) invasion; (*des Winters*) onset; (*Durchbrechen*) break; (*MET*) approach; (*MIL*) penetration; **(bei/vor) ~ der Nacht** at/before nightfall; **e~sicher** *adj* burglar-proof

einbürgern ['aɪnbʏrɡərn] *vt* to naturalize ♦ *vr* to become adopted

einbüßen ['aɪnbyːsən] *vt* to lose, to forfeit

einchecken ['aɪntʃɛkən] *vt, vi* to check in

eincremen ['aɪnkreːmən] *vt* to put cream on

eindecken ['aɪndɛkən] *vr*: **sich (mit etw) ~** to lay in stocks (of sth); to stock up (with sth)

eindeutig ['aɪndɔytɪç] *adj* unequivocal

eindringen ['aɪndrɪŋən] (*unreg*) *vi*: **~ (in** +*akk*) to force one's way in(to); (*in Haus*) to break in(to); (*in Land*) to invade; (*Gas, Wasser*) to penetrate; **(auf jdn) ~** (*mit Bitten*) to pester (sb)

eindringlich *adj* forcible, urgent

Eindringling *m* intruder

Eindruck ['aɪndrʊk] *m* impression

eindrücken ['aɪndrʏkən] *vt* to press in

eindrucksvoll *adj* impressive

eine(r, s) *pron* one; (*jemand*) someone

eineiig ['aɪn|aɪç] *adj* (*Zwillinge*) identical

eineinhalb ['aɪn|aɪn'halp] *num* one and a half

einengen ['aɪn|ɛŋən] *vt* to confine, to restrict

einer- ['aɪnər] *zW*: **'E~'lei (-s)** *nt* sameness; **'~'lei** *adj* (*gleichartig*) the same kind of; **es ist mir ~lei** it is all the same to me; **~seits** *adv* on the one hand

einfach ['aɪnfax] *adj* simple; (*nicht mehrfach*) single ♦ *adv* simply; **E~heit** *f* simplicity

einfädeln ['aɪnfɛːdəln] *vt* (*Nadel, Faden*) to thread; (*fig*) to contrive

einfahren ['aɪnfaːrən] (*unreg*) *vt* to bring in; (*Barriere*) to knock down; (*Auto*) to run in ♦ *vi* to drive in; (*Zug*) to pull in; (*MIN*) to go down

Einfahrt *f* (*Vorgang*) driving in; pulling in; (*MIN*) descent; (*Ort*) entrance

Einfall ['aɪnfal] *m* (*Idee*) idea, notion; (*Lichteinfall*) incidence; (*MIL*) raid; **e~en** (*unreg*) *vi* (*Licht*) to fall; (*MIL*) to raid; (*einstürzen*) to fall in, to collapse; (*einstimmen*) to join in (with sth); **(in etw** *akk*) **e~en** to join in (with sth); **etw fällt jdm ein** sth occurs to sb; **das fällt mir gar nicht ein** I wouldn't dream of it; **sich** *dat* **etw e~en lassen** to have a good idea

einfältig ['aɪnfɛltɪç] *adj* simple(-minded)

Einfamilienhaus [aɪnfa'miːliənhaʊs] *nt* detached house

einfarbig ['aɪnfarbɪç] *adj* all one colour; (*Stoff etc*) self-coloured

einfetten ['aɪnfɛtən] *vt* to grease

einfließen ['aɪnfliːsən] (*unreg*) *vi* to flow in

einflößen ['aɪnfløːsən] *vt*: **jdm etw ~** to give sb sth; (*fig*) to instil sth in sb

Einfluss ▲ ['aɪnflʊs] *m* influence; **~bereich** *m* sphere of influence

einförmig ['aɪnfœrmɪç] *adj* uniform; **E~keit** *f* uniformity

einfrieren ['aɪnfriːrən] (*unreg*) *vi* to freeze (up) ♦ *vt* to freeze

einfügen ['aɪnfyːɡən] *vt* to fit in; (*zusätzlich*) to add

Einfuhr ['aɪnfuːr] (-) *f* import; **~beschränkung** *f* import restrictions *pl*; **~bestimmungen** *pl* import regulations

einführen ['aɪnfyːrən] *vt* to bring in; (*Mensch, Sitten*) to introduce; (*Ware*) to import

Einführung *f* introduction

Spelling Reform: ▲ *new spelling* △ *old spelling (to be phased out)*

Eingabe ['aɪngaːbə] *f* petition; (*COMPUT*) input

Eingang ['aɪngaŋ] *m* entrance; (*COMM: Ankunft*) arrival; (*Erhalt*) receipt

eingeben ['aɪngeːbən] (*unreg*) *vt* (*Arznei*) to give; (*Daten etc*) to enter

eingebildet ['aɪngəbɪldət] *adj* imaginary; (*eitel*) conceited

Eingeborene(r) ['aɪngəboːrənə(r)] *f(m)* native

Eingebung *f* inspiration

eingefleischt ['aɪngəflaɪʃt] *adj* (*Gewohnheit, Vorurteile*) deep-rooted

eingehen ['aɪngeːən] (*unreg*) *vi* (*Aufnahme finden*) to come in; (*Sendung, Geld*) to be received; (*Tier, Pflanze*) to die; (*Firma*) to fold; (*schrumpfen*) to shrink ♦ *vt* to enter into; (*Wette*) to make; **auf etw** *akk* **~** to go into sth; **auf jdn ~** to respond to sb; **jdm ~** (*verständlich sein*) to be comprehensible to sb; **~d** *adj* exhaustive, thorough

Eingemachte(s) ['aɪngəmaːxtə(s)] *nt* preserves *pl*

eingenommen ['aɪngənɔmən] *adj*: **~ (von)** fond (of), partial (to); **~ (gegen)** prejudiced (against)

eingeschrieben ['aɪngəʃriːbən] *adj* registered

eingespielt ['aɪngəʃpiːlt] *adj*: **aufeinander ~ sein** to be in tune with each other

Eingeständnis ['aɪngəʃtɛntnɪs] (**-ses, -se**) *nt* admission, confession

eingestehen ['aɪngəʃteːən] (*unreg*) *vt* to confess

eingestellt ['aɪngəʃtɛlt] *adj*: **auf etw ~ sein** to be prepared for sth

eingetragen ['aɪngətraːgən] *adj* (*COMM*) registered

Eingeweide ['aɪngəvaɪdə] (**-s, -**) *nt* innards *pl*, intestines *pl*

Eingeweihte(r) ['aɪngəvaɪtə(r)] *f(m)* initiate

eingewöhnen ['aɪngəvøːnən] *vr*: **sich ~ in** +*akk* to settle (down) in

eingleisig ['aɪnglaɪzɪç] *adj* single-track

eingreifen ['aɪngraɪfən] (*unreg*) *vi* to intervene, to interfere; (*Zahnrad*) to mesh

Eingriff ['aɪngrɪf] *m* intervention,

interference; (*Operation*) operation

einhaken ['aɪnhaːkən] *vt* to hook in ♦ *vr*: **sich bei jdm ~** to link arms with sb ♦ *vi* (*sich einmischen*) to intervene

Einhalt ['aɪnhalt] *m*: **~ gebieten** +*dat* to put a stop to; **e~en** (*unreg*) *vt* (*Regel*) to keep ♦ *vi* to stop

einhändigen ['aɪnhɛndɪgən] *vt* to hand in

einhängen ['aɪnhɛŋən] *vt* to hang; (*Telefon*) to hang up ♦ *vi* (*TEL*) to hang up; **sich bei jdm ~** to link arms with sb

einheimisch ['aɪnhaɪmɪʃ] *adj* native; **E~e(r)** *f(m)* local

Einheit ['aɪnhaɪt] *f* unity; (*Maß, MIL*) unit; **e~lich** *adj* uniform; **~spreis** *m* standard price

einholen ['aɪnhoːlən] *vt* (*Tau*) to haul in; (*Fahne, Segel*) to lower; (*Vorsprung aufholen*) to catch up with; (*Verspätung*) to make up; (*Rat, Erlaubnis*) to ask ♦ *vi* (*einkaufen*) to shop

einhüllen ['aɪnhʏlən] *vt* to wrap up

einhundert ['aɪnˈhʊndərt] *num* one hundred, a hundred

einig ['aɪnɪç] *adj* (*vereint*) united; **~ gehen** to agree; **sich** *dat* **~ sein** to be in agreement; **~ werden** to agree

einige(r, s) ['aɪnɪgə(r, s)] *adj, pron* some ♦ *pl* some; (*mehrere*) several; **~ Mal** a few times

einigen *vt* to unite ♦ *vr*: **sich ~ (auf** +*akk*) to agree (on)

einigermaßen *adv* somewhat; (*leidlich*) reasonably

einig- *zW*: **E~keit** *f* unity; (*Übereinstimmung*) agreement; **E~ung** *f* agreement; (*Vereinigung*) unification

einkalkulieren ['aɪnkalkuliːrən] *vt* to take into account, to allow for

Einkauf ['aɪnkaʊf] *m* purchase; **e~en** *vt* to buy ♦ *vi* to shop; **e~en gehen** to go shopping

Einkaufs- *zW*: **~bummel** *m* shopping spree; **~korb** *m* shopping basket; **~wagen** *m* shopping trolley; **~zentrum** *nt* shopping centre

einklammern ['aɪnklamərn] *vt* to put in brackets, to bracket

Einklang ['aɪnklaŋ] m harmony

einklemmen ['aɪnklɛmən] vt to jam

einkochen ['aɪnkɔxən] vt to boil down; (Obst) to preserve, to bottle

Einkommen ['aɪnkɔmən] (-s, -) nt income; **~(s)steuer** f income tax

Einkünfte ['aɪnkʏnftə] pl income sg, revenue sg

einladen ['aɪnlaːdən] (unreg) vt (Person) to invite; (Gegenstände) to load; **jdn ins Kino ~** to take sb to the cinema

Einladung f invitation

Einlage ['aɪnlaːgə] f (Programm~) interlude; (Spar~) deposit; (Schuh~) insole; (Fußstütze) support; (Zahn~) temporary filling; (KOCH) noodles pl, vegetables pl etc in soup

einlagern ['aɪnlaːgərn] vt to store

Einlass ▲ ['aɪnlas] (-es, ̈e) m (Zutritt) admission

einlassen ['aɪnlasən] (unreg) vt to let in; (einsetzen) to set in ♦ vr: **sich mit jdm/auf etw** akk **~** to get involved with sb/sth

Einlauf ['aɪnlauf] m arrival; (von Pferden) finish; (MED) enema; **e~en** (unreg) vi to arrive, to come in; (in Hafen) to enter; (SPORT) to finish; (Wasser) to run in; (Stoff) to shrink ♦ vt (Schuhe) to break in ♦ vr (SPORT) to warm up; (Motor, Maschine) to run in; **jdm das Haus e~en** to invade sb's house

einleben ['aɪnleːbən] vr to settle down

einlegen ['aɪnleːgən] vt (einfügen: Blatt, Sohle) to insert; (KOCH) to pickle; (Pause) to have; (Protest) to make; (Veto) to use; (Berufung) to lodge; (AUT: Gang) to engage

einleiten ['aɪnlaɪtən] vt to introduce, to start; (Geburt) to induce; **Einleitung** f introduction; induction

einleuchten ['aɪnlɔʏçtən] vi: (jdm) **~** to be clear od evident (to sb); **~d** adj clear

einliefern ['aɪnliːfərn] vt: **~ (in** +akk) to take (into)

Einlieferungsschein m certificate of posting

Einliegerwohnung ['aɪnliːgərvoːnuŋ] f self-contained flat; (für Eltern, Großeltern) granny flat

einloggen ['aɪnlɔgən] vi (COMPUT) to log on

einlösen ['aɪnløːzən] vt (Scheck) to cash; (Schuldschein, Pfand) to redeem; (Versprechen) to keep

einmachen ['aɪnmaxən] vt to preserve

einmal ['aɪnmaːl] adv once; (erstens) first; (zukünftig) sometime; **nehmen wir ~ an** just let's suppose; **noch ~** once more; **nicht ~** not even; **auf ~** all at once; **es war ~** once upon a time there was/were; **E~eins** nt multiplication tables pl; **~ig** adj unique; (einmal erforderlich) single; (prima) fantastic

Einmarsch ['aɪnmarʃ] m entry; (MIL) invasion; **e~ieren** vi to march in

einmischen ['aɪnmɪʃən] vr: **sich ~ (in** +akk) to interfere (with)

einmütig ['aɪnmyːtɪç] adj unanimous

Einnahme ['aɪnnaːmə] f (von Medizin) taking; (MIL) capture, taking; **~n** pl (Geld) takings, revenue sg; **~quelle** f source of income

einnehmen ['aɪnneːmən] (unreg) vt to take; (Stellung, Raum) to take up; **~ für/gegen** to persuade in favour of/against; **~d** adj charming

einordnen ['aɪnɔrdnən] vt to arrange, to fit in ♦ vr to adapt; (AUT) to get into lane

einpacken ['aɪnpakən] vt to pack (up)

einparken ['aɪnparkən] vt to park

einpendeln ['aɪnpɛndəln] vr to even out

einpflanzen ['aɪnpflantsən] vt to plant; (MED) to implant

einplanen ['aɪnplaːnən] vt to plan for

einprägen ['aɪnpreːgən] vt to impress, to imprint; (beibringen): **(jdm) ~** to impress (on sb); **sich** dat **etw ~** to memorize sth

einrahmen ['aɪnraːmən] vt to frame

einräumen ['aɪnrɔʏmən] vt (ordnend) to put away; (überlassen: Platz) to give up; (zugestehen) to admit, to concede

einreden ['aɪnreːdən] vt: **jdm/sich etw ~** to talk sb/o.s. into believing sth

einreiben ['aɪnraɪbən] (unreg) vt to rub in

einreichen ['aɪnraɪçən] vt to hand in; (Antrag) to submit

Einreise ['aɪnraɪzə] f entry;

~bestimmungen pl entry regulations;
~erlaubnis f entry permit;
~genehmigung f entry permit; **e~n** vi:
(in ein Land) e~n to enter (a country)

einrichten ['aɪnrɪçtən] vt (Haus) to furnish;
(schaffen) to establish, to set up;
(arrangieren) to arrange; (möglich machen)
to manage ♦ vr (in Haus) to furnish one's
house; **sich ~ (auf +akk)** (sich vorbereiten)
to prepare o.s. (for); (sich anpassen) to adapt
(to)

Einrichtung f (Wohnungseinrichtung)
furnishings pl; (öffentliche Anstalt)
organization; (Dienste) service

einrosten ['aɪnrɔstən] vi to get rusty

einrücken ['aɪnrʏkən] vi (MIL: in Land) to
move in

Eins [aɪns] (-, -en) f one; **e~** num one; **es ist
mir alles e~** it's all one to me

einsam ['aɪnzaːm] adj lonely, solitary;
E~keit f loneliness, solitude

einsammeln ['aɪnzaməln] vt to collect

Einsatz ['aɪnzats] m (Teil) inset; (an Kleid)
insertion; (Verwendung) use, employment;
(Spieleinsatz) stake; (Risiko) risk; (MIL)
operation; (MUS) entry; **im ~** in action;
e~bereit adj ready for action

einschalten ['aɪnʃaltən] vt (einfügen) to
insert; (Pause) to make; (ELEK) to switch on;
(Anwalt) to bring in ♦ vr (dazwischentreten)
to intervene

einschärfen ['aɪnʃɛrfən] vt: **jdm etw ~** to
impress sth (up)on sb

einschätzen ['aɪnʃɛtsən] vt to estimate, to
assess ♦ vr to rate o.s.

einschenken ['aɪnʃɛŋkən] vt to pour out

einschicken ['aɪnʃɪkən] vt to send in

einschl. abk (= einschließlich) incl.

einschlafen ['aɪnʃlaːfən] (unreg) vi to fall
asleep, to go to sleep

einschläfernd ['aɪnʃlɛːfərnt] adj (MED)
soporific; (langweilig) boring; (Stimme)
lulling

Einschlag ['aɪnʃlaːk] m impact; (fig:
Beimischung) touch, hint; **e~en** [-gən]
(unreg) vt to knock in; (Fenster) to smash, to
break; (Zähne, Schädel) to smash in; (AUT:

Räder) to turn; (kürzer machen) to take up;
(Ware) to pack, to wrap up; (Weg, Richtung)
to take ♦ vi to hit; (sich einigen) to agree;
(Anklang finden) to work, to succeed; **in etw
akk/auf jdn e~en** to hit sth/sb

einschlägig ['aɪnʃlɛːgɪç] adj relevant

einschließen ['aɪnʃliːsən] (unreg) vt (Kind) to
lock in; (Häftling) to lock up; (Gegenstand)
to lock away; (Bergleute) to cut off;
(umgeben) to surround; (MIL) to encircle;
(fig) to include, to comprise ♦ vr to lock
o.s. in

einschließlich adv inclusive ♦ präp +gen
inclusive of, including

einschmeicheln ['aɪnʃmaɪçəln] vr: **sich ~
(bei)** to ingratiate o.s. (with)

einschnappen ['aɪnʃnapən] vi (Tür) to click
to; (fig) to be touchy; **eingeschnappt sein**
to be in a huff

einschneidend ['aɪnʃnaɪdənt] adj drastic

Einschnitt ['aɪnʃnɪt] m cutting; (MED)
incision; (Ereignis) decisive point

einschränken ['aɪnʃrɛŋkən] vt to limit, to
restrict; (Kosten) to cut down, to reduce
♦ vr to cut down (on expenditure);
Einschränkung f restriction, limitation;
reduction; (von Behauptung) qualification

Einschreib- ['aɪnʃraɪb] zW:**~(e)brief** m
recorded delivery letter; **e~en** (unreg) vt to
write in; (Post) to send recorded delivery
♦ vr to register; (UNIV) to enrol; **~en** nt
recorded delivery letter

einschreiten ['aɪnʃraɪtən] (unreg) vi to step
in, to intervene; **~ gegen** to take action
against

einschüchtern ['aɪnʃʏçtərn] vt to intimidate

einschulen ['aɪnʃuːlən] vt: **eingeschult
werden** (Kind) to start school

einsehen ['aɪnzeːən] (unreg) vt (hineinsehen
in) to realize; (Akten) to have a look at;
(verstehen) to see; **E~** (-s) nt
understanding; **ein E~ haben** to show
understanding

einseitig ['aɪnzaɪtɪç] adj one-sided

Einsend- ['aɪnzɛnd] zW:**e~en** (unreg) vt to
send in; **~er** (-s, -) m sender, contributor;
~ung f sending in

einsetzen ['aɪnzɛtsən] vt to put (in); (in Amt) to appoint, to install; (Geld) to stake; (verwenden) to use; (MIL) to employ ♦ vi (beginnen) to set in; (MUS) to enter, to come in ♦ vr to work hard; **sich für jdn/ etw ~** to support sb/sth

Einsicht ['aɪnzɪçt] f insight; (in Akten) look, inspection; **zu der ~ kommen, dass ...** to come to the conclusion that ...; **e~ig** adj (Mensch) judicious; **e~slos** adj unreasonable; **e~svoll** adj understanding

einsilbig ['aɪnzɪlbɪç] adj (auch fig) monosyllabic; (Mensch) uncommunicative

einspannen ['aɪnʃpanən] vt (Papier) to insert; (Pferde) to harness; (umg: Person) to rope in

Einsparung ['aɪnʃpaːrʊŋ] f economy, saving

einsperren ['aɪnʃpɛrən] vt to lock up

einspielen ['aɪnʃpiːlən] vr (SPORT) to warm up ♦ vt (Film: Geld) to bring in; (Instrument) to play in; **sich aufeinander ~** to become attuned to each other; **gut eingespielt** running smoothly

einsprachig ['aɪnʃpraːxɪç] adj monolingual

einspringen ['aɪnʃprɪŋən] (unreg) vi (aushelfen) to help out, to step into the breach

Einspruch ['aɪnʃprʊx] m protest, objection; **~srecht** nt veto

einspurig ['aɪnʃpuːrɪç] adj (EISENB) single-track; (AUT) single-lane

einst [aɪnst] adv once; (zukünftig) one day, some day

einstecken ['aɪnʃtɛkən] vt to stick in, to insert; (Brief) to post; (ELEK: Stecker) to plug in; (Geld) to pocket; (mitnehmen) to take; (überlegen sein) to put in the shade; (hinnehmen) to swallow

einstehen ['aɪnʃteːən] (unreg) vi: **für jdn/ etw ~** to guarantee sb/sth; (verantworten): **für etw ~** to answer for sth

einsteigen ['aɪnʃtaɪgən] (unreg) vi to get in od on; (in Schiff) to go on board; (sich beteiligen) to come in; (hineinklettern) to climb in

einstellen ['aɪnʃtɛlən] vt (aufhören) to stop; (Geräte) to adjust; (Kamera etc) to focus;

(Sender, Radio) to tune in; (unterstellen) to put; (in Firma) to employ, to take on ♦ vi (Firma) to take on staff/workers ♦ vr (anfangen) to set in; (kommen) to arrive; **sich auf jdn ~** to adapt to sb; **sich auf etw** akk **~** to prepare o.s. for sth

Einstellung f (Aufhören) suspension; adjustment; focusing; (von Arbeiter etc) appointment; (Haltung) attitude

Einstieg ['aɪnʃtiːk] (-(e)s, -e) m entry; (fig) approach

einstig ['aɪnstɪç] adj former

einstimmig ['aɪnʃtɪmɪç] adj unanimous; (MUS) for one voice

einstmals adv once, formerly

einstöckig ['aɪnʃtœkɪç] adj two-storeyed

Einsturz ['aɪnʃtʊrts] m collapse

einstürzen ['aɪnʃtʏrtsən] vi to fall in, to collapse

einst- zW: **~weilen** adv meanwhile; (vorläufig) temporarily, for the time being; **~weilig** adj temporary

eintägig ['aɪntɛːgɪç] adj one-day

eintauschen ['aɪntaʊʃən] vt: **~ (gegen** od **für)** to exchange (for)

eintausend ['aɪntaʊzənt] num one thousand

einteilen ['aɪntaɪlən] vt (in Teile) to divide (up); (Menschen) to assign

einteilig adj one-piece

eintönig ['aɪntøːnɪç] adj monotonous

Eintopf ['aɪntɔpf] m stew

Eintracht ['aɪntraxt] (-) f concord, harmony; **einträchtig** ['aɪntrɛçtɪç] adj harmonious

Eintrag ['aɪntraːk] (-(e)s, ˣe) m entry; **amtlicher ~** entry in the register; **e~en** [-gən] (unreg) vt (in Buch) to enter; (Profit) to yield ♦ vr to put one's name down

einträglich ['aɪntrɛːklɪç] adj profitable

eintreffen ['aɪntrɛfən] (unreg) vi to happen; (ankommen) to arrive

eintreten ['aɪntreːtən] (unreg) vi to occur; (sich einsetzen) to intercede ♦ vt (Tür) to kick open; **~ in** +akk to enter; (in Klub, Partei) to join

Eintritt ['aɪntrɪt] m (Betreten) entrance; (Anfang) commencement; (in Klub etc)

Spelling Reform: ▲ new spelling △ old spelling (to be phased out)

joining

Eintritts- *zW:* **~geld** *nt* admission charge; **~karte** *f* (admission) ticket; **~preis** *m* admission charge

einüben ['aɪnˌyːbən] *vt* to practise

Einvernehmen ['aɪnfɛrneːmən] **(-s, -)** *nt* agreement, harmony

einverstanden ['aɪnfɛrʃtandən] *excl* agreed, okay ♦ *adj:* **~ sein** to agree, to be agreed

Einverständnis ['aɪnfɛrʃtɛntnɪs] *nt* understanding; (*gleiche Meinung*) agreement

Einwand ['aɪnvant] **(-(e)s, ⁼e)** *m* objection

Einwand- *zW:* **~erer** ['aɪnvandərər] *m* immigrant; **e~ern** *vi* to immigrate; **~erung** *f* immigration

einwandfrei *adj* perfect ♦ *adv* absolutely

Einweg- ['aɪnveːg] *zW:* **~flasche** *f* no-deposit bottle; **~spritze** *f* disposable syringe

einweichen ['aɪnvaɪçən] *vt* to soak

einweihen ['aɪnvaɪən] *vt* (*Kirche*) to consecrate; (*Brücke*) to open; (*Gebäude*) to inaugurate; **~ (in** +*akk*) (*Person*) to initiate (in); **Einweihung** *f* consecration; opening; inauguration; initiation

einweisen ['aɪnvaɪzən] (*unreg*) *vt* (*in Amt*) to install; (*in Arbeit*) to introduce; (*in Anstalt*) to send

einwenden ['aɪnvɛndən] (*unreg*) *vt:* **etwas ~ gegen** to object to, to oppose

einwerfen ['aɪnvɛrfən] (*unreg*) *vt* to throw in; (*Brief*) to post; (*Geld*) to put in, to insert; (*Fenster*) to smash; (*äußern*) to interpose

einwickeln ['aɪnvɪkəln] *vt* to wrap up; (*fig: umg*) to outsmart

einwilligen ['aɪnvɪlɪɡən] *vi:* **~ (in** +*akk*) to consent (to), to agree (to); **Einwilligung** *f* consent

einwirken ['aɪnvɪrkən] *vi:* **auf jdn/etw ~** to influence sb/sth

Einwohner ['aɪnvoːnər] **(-s, -)** *m* inhabitant; **~meldeamt** *nt* registration office; **~schaft** *f* population, inhabitants *pl*

Einwurf ['aɪnvʊrf] *m* (*Öffnung*) slot; (*von Münze*) insertion; (*von Brief*) posting; (*Einwand*) objection; (*SPORT*) throw-in

Einzahl ['aɪntsaːl] *f* singular; **e~en** *vt* to pay

in; **~ung** *f* paying in; **~ungsschein** *m* paying-in slip, deposit slip

einzäunen ['aɪntsɔʏnən] *vt* to fence in

Einzel ['aɪntsəl] **(-s, -)** *nt* (*TENNIS*) singles; **~fahrschein** *m* one-way ticket; **~fall** *m* single instance, individual case; **~handel** *m* retail trade; **~handelspreis** *m* retail price; **~heit** *f* particular, detail; **~kind** *nt* only child; **e~n** *adj* single; (*vereinzelt*) the odd ♦ *adv* singly; **e~n angeben** to specify; **der/die E~ne** the individual; **das E~ne** the particular; **ins E~ne gehen** to go into detail(s); **~teil** *nt* component (part); **~zimmer** *nt* single room; **~zimmerzuschlag** *m* single room supplement

einziehen ['aɪntsiːən] (*unreg*) *vt* to draw in, to take in; (*Kopf*) to duck; (*Fühler, Antenne, Fahrgestell*) to retract; (*Steuern, Erkundigungen*) to collect; (*MIL*) to draft, to call up; (*aus dem Verkehr ziehen*) to withdraw; (*konfiszieren*) to confiscate ♦ *vi* to move in; (*Friede, Ruhe*) to come; (*Flüssigkeit*) to penetrate

einzig ['aɪntsɪç] *adj* only; (*ohnegleichen*) unique; **das E~e** the only thing; **der/die E~e** the only one; **~artig** *adj* unique

Einzug ['aɪntsuːk] *m* entry, moving in

Eis [aɪs] **(-es, -)** *nt* ice; (*Speiseeis*) ice cream; **~bahn** *f* ice *od* skating rink; **~bär** *m* polar bear; **~becher** *m* sundae; **~bein** *nt* pig's trotters *pl*; **~berg** *m* iceberg; **~café** *nt* ice-cream parlour (*BRIT*) *od* parlor (*US*); **~decke** *f* sheet of ice; **~diele** *f* ice-cream parlour

Eisen ['aɪzən] **(-s, -)** *nt* iron

Eisenbahn *f* railway, railroad (*US*); **~er (-s, -)** *m* railwayman, railway employee, railroader (*US*); **~schaffner** *m* railway guard; **~wagen** *m* railway carriage

Eisenerz *nt* iron ore

eisern ['aɪzərn] *adj* iron; (*Gesundheit*) robust; (*Energie*) unrelenting; (*Reserve*) emergency

Eis- *zW:* **e~frei** *adj* clear of ice; **~hockey** *nt* ice hockey; **e~ig** ['aɪzɪç] *adj* icy; **e~kalt** *adj* icy cold; **~kunstlauf** *m* figure skating; **~laufen** *nt* ice skating; **~pickel** *m* ice axe; **~schrank** *m* fridge, icebox (*US*); **~würfel**

m ice cube; **~zapfen** *m* icicle; **~zeit** *f* ice age

eitel ['aɪtəl] *adj* vain; **E~keit** *f* vanity

Eiter ['aɪtər] **(-s)** *m* pus; **e~ig** *adj* suppurating; **e~n** *vi* to suppurate

Eiweiß **(-es, -e)** *nt* white of an egg; (*CHEM*) protein

Ekel[1] ['e:kəl] **(-s, -)** *nt* (*umg: Mensch*) nauseating person

Ekel[2] ['e:kəl] **(-s)** *m* nausea, disgust; **~erregend** nauseating, disgusting; **e~haft** *adj* nauseating, disgusting; **e~ig** *adj* nauseating, disgusting; **e~n** *vt* to disgust ♦ *vr*: **sich e~n (vor** +*dat*) to loathe, to be disgusted (at); **es e~t jdn** *od* **jdm** sb is disgusted; **eklig** *adj* nauseating, disgusting

Ekstase [ɛkˈstaːzə] *f* ecstasy

Ekzem [ɛkˈtseːm] **(-s, -e)** *nt* (*MED*) eczema

Elan [eˈlãː] **(-s)** *m* elan

elastisch [eˈlastɪʃ] *adj* elastic

Elastizität [elastitsiˈtɛːt] *f* elasticity

Elch [ɛlç] **(-(e)s, -e)** *m* elk

Elefant [eleˈfant] *m* elephant

elegant [eleˈgant] *adj* elegant

Eleganz [eleˈgants] *f* elegance

Elek- [eˈlɛk] *zW*: **~triker** [-trikər] **(-s, -)** *m* electrician; **e~trisch** [-trɪʃ] *adj* electric; **e~trisieren** [-triˈziːrən] *vt* (*auch fig*) to electrify; (*Mensch*) to give an electric shock to ♦ *vr* to get an electric shock; **~trizität** [tritsiˈtɛːt] *f* electricity; **~trizitätswerk** *nt* power station; (*Gesellschaft*) electric power company

Elektro- [eˈlɛktro] *zW*: **~de** [-ˈtroːdə] *f* electrode; **~gerät** *nt* electrical appliance; **~herd** *m* electric cooker; **~n** **(-s, -en)** *nt* electron; **~nik** *f* electronics *sg*; **e~nisch** *adj* electronic; **~rasierer** *m* electric razor; **~technik** *f* electrical engineering

Element [eleˈment] **(-s, -e)** *nt* element; (*ELEK*) cell, battery; **e~ar** [-ˈtaːr] *adj* elementary; (*naturhaft*) elemental

Elend ['eːlɛnt] **(-(e)s)** *nt* misery; **e~** *adj* miserable; **~sviertel** *nt* slum

elf [ɛlf] *num* eleven; **E~ (-, -en)** *f* (*SPORT*) eleven

Elfe *f* elf

Elfenbein *nt* ivory

Elfmeter *m* (*SPORT*) penalty (kick)

Elite [eˈliːtə] *f* elite

Ell- *zW*: **~bogen** *m* elbow; **~e** ['ɛlə] *f* ell; (*Maß*) yard; **~enbogen** *m* elbow; **~(en)bogenfreiheit** *f* (*fig*) elbow room

Elsass ▲ ['ɛlzas] **(- od -es)** *nt*: **das ~** Alsace

Elster ['ɛlstər] **(-, -n)** *f* magpie

Eltern ['ɛltərn] *pl* parents; **~beirat** *m* (*SCH*) ≈ PTA (*BRIT*), parents' council; **~haus** *nt* home; **e~los** *adj* parentless

E-Mail ['iːmeːl] **(-, -s)** *f* E-mail; **~-Adresse** *f* e-mail address

Emaille [eˈmaljə] **(-s, -s)** *nt* enamel

emaillieren [emaˈjiːrən] *vt* to enamel

Emanzipation [emantsipatsiˈoːn] *f* emancipation

emanzipieren *vt* to emancipate

Embryo ['ɛmbryo] **(-s, -s** *od* **Embryonen)** *m* embryo

Emi- *zW*: **~'grant(in)** *m(f)* emigrant; **~gration** *f* emigration; **e~grieren** *vi* to emigrate

Emissionen [emɪsiˈoːnən] *fpl* emissions

Empfang [ɛmˈpfaŋ] **(-(e)s, ⁼e)** *m* reception; (*Erhalten*) receipt; **in ~ nehmen** to receive; **e~en** (*unreg*) *vt* to receive ♦ *vi* (*schwanger werden*) to conceive

Empfäng- [ɛmˈpfɛŋ] *zW*: **~er (-s, -)** *m* receiver; (*COMM*) addressee, consignee; **~erabschnitt** *m* receipt slip; **e~lich** *adj* receptive, susceptible; **~nis (-, -se)** *f* conception; **~nisverhütung** *f* contraception

Empfangs- *zW*: **~bestätigung** *f* acknowledgement; **~dame** *f* receptionist; **~schein** *m* receipt; **~zimmer** *nt* reception room

empfehlen [ɛmˈpfeːlən] (*unreg*) *vt* to recommend ♦ *vr* to take one's leave; **~swert** *adj* recommendable

Empfehlung *f* recommendation

empfiehlst *etc* [ɛmˈpfiːlst] *vb siehe* **empfehlen**

empfind- [ɛmˈpfɪnt] *zW*: **~en** [-dən] (*unreg*) *vt* to feel; **~lich** *adj* sensitive; (*Stelle*) sore; (*reizbar*) touchy; **~sam** *adj* sentimental;

E~ung [-dʊŋ] *f* feeling, sentiment

empfohlen *etc* [ɛm'pfo:lən] *vb siehe*
empfehlen

empor [ɛm'po:r] *adv* up, upwards

empören [ɛm'pø:rən] *vt* to make indignant;
to shock ♦ *vr* to become indignant; **~d** *adj*
outrageous

Emporkömmling [ɛm'po:rkœmlɪŋ] *m*
upstart, parvenu

Empörung *f* indignation

emsig ['ɛmzɪç] *adj* diligent, busy

End- ['ɛnt] *in zW* final; **~e** (**-s, -n**) *nt* end;
am ~e at the end; (*schließlich*) in the end;
am ~e sein to be at the end of one's
tether; **~e Dezember** at the end of
December; **zu ~e sein** to be finished;
e~en *vi* to end; **e~gültig** ['ɛnt-] *adj* final,
definite

Endivie [ɛn'di:viə] *f* endive

End- *zW:* **e~lich** *adj* final; (*MATH*) finite
♦ *adv* finally; **e~lich!** at last!; **komm e~lich!**
come on!; **e~los** *adj* endless, infinite;
~spiel *nt* final(s); **~spurt** *m* (*SPORT*) final
spurt; **~station** *f* terminus; **~ung** *f* ending

Energie [enɛr'gi:] *f* energy; **~bedarf** *m*
energy requirement; **e~los** *adj* lacking in
energy, weak; **~verbrauch** *m* energy
consumption; **~versorgung** *f* supply of
energy; **~wirtschaft** *f* energy industry

energisch [e'nɛrgɪʃ] *adj* energetic

eng [ɛŋ] *adj* narrow; (*Kleidung*) tight; (*fig:
Horizont*) narrow, limited; (*Freundschaft,
Verhältnis*) close; **~ an etw** *dat* close to sth

Engagement [ãgaʒə'mã:] (**-s, -s**) *nt*
engagement; (*Verpflichtung*) commitment

engagieren [ãga'ʒi:rən] *vt* to engage ♦ *vr* to
commit o.s.

Enge ['ɛŋə] *f* (*auch fig*) narrowness;
(*Landenge*) defile; (*Meerenge*) straits *pl*; **jdn
in die ~ treiben** to drive sb into a corner

Engel ['ɛŋəl] (**-s, -**) *m* angel; **e~haft** *adj*
angelic

England ['ɛŋlant] *nt* England;
Engländer(in) *m(f)* Englishman(-woman);
englisch *adj* English

Engpass ▲ *m* defile, pass; (*fig, Verkehr*)
bottleneck

en gros [ã'gro] *adv* wholesale

engstirnig ['ɛŋʃtɪrnɪç] *adj* narrow-minded

Enkel ['ɛŋkəl] (**-s, -**) *m* grandson; **~in** *f*
granddaughter; **~kind** *nt* grandchild

enorm [e'nɔrm] *adj* enormous

Ensemble [ã'sãbəl] (**-s, -s**) *nt* company,
ensemble

entbehr- [ɛnt'be:r-] *zW:* **~en** *vt* to do
without, to dispense with; **~lich** *adj*
superfluous; **E~ung** *f* deprivation

entbinden [ɛnt'bɪndən] (*unreg*) *vt* (+*gen*) to
release (from); (*MED*) to deliver ♦ *vi* (*MED*)
to give birth; **Entbindung** *f* release; (*MED*)
confinement; **Entbindungsheim** *nt*
maternity hospital

entdeck- [ɛnt'dɛk] *zW:* **~en** *vt* to discover;
E~er (**-s, -**) *m* discoverer; **E~ung** *f*
discovery

Ente ['ɛntə] *f* duck; (*fig*) canard, false report

enteignen [ɛnt'aignən] *vt* to expropriate;
(*Besitzer*) to dispossess

enterben [ɛnt'ɛrbən] *vt* to disinherit

entfallen [ɛnt'falən] (*unreg*) *vi* to drop, to
fall; (*wegfallen*) to be dropped; **jdm ~**
(*vergessen*) to slip sb's memory; **auf jdn ~**
to be allotted to sb

entfalten [ɛnt'faltən] *vt* to unfold; (*Talente*)
to develop ♦ *vr* to open; (*Mensch*) to
develop one's potential; **Entfaltung** *f*
unfolding; (*von Talenten*) development

entfern- [ɛnt'fɛrn] *zW:* **~en** *vt* to remove;
(*hinauswerfen*) to expel ♦ *vr* to go away, to
withdraw; **~t** *adj* distant; **weit davon ~t
sein, etw zu tun** to be far from doing sth;
E~ung *f* distance; (*Wegschaffen*) removal

entfremden [ɛnt'frɛmdən] *vt* to estrange, to
alienate; **Entfremdung** *f* alienation,
estrangement

entfrosten [ɛnt'frɔstən] *vt* to defrost

Entfroster (**-s, -**) *m* (*AUT*) defroster

entführ- [ɛnt'fy:r] *zW:* **~en** *vt* to carry off,
to abduct; to kidnap; **E~er** *m* kidnapper;
E~ung *f* abduction; kidnapping

entgegen [ɛnt'ge:gən] *präp* +*dat* contrary to,
against ♦ *adv* towards; **~bringen** (*unreg*) *vt*
to bring; **jdm etw ~bringen** (*fig*) to show
sb sth; **~gehen** (*unreg*) *vi* +*dat* to go to

meet, to go towards; **~gesetzt** adj
opposite; (widersprechend) opposed;
~halten (unreg) vt (fig) to object;
E~kommen nt obligingness; **~kommen**
(unreg) vi +dat to approach; to meet; (fig)
to accommodate; **~kommend** adj
obliging; **~nehmen** (unreg) vt to receive,
to accept; **~sehen** (unreg) vi +dat to await;
~setzen vt to oppose; **~treten** (unreg) vi
+dat to step up to; (fig) to oppose, to
counter; **~wirken** vi +dat to counteract
entgegnen [ɛnt'geːgnən] vt to reply, to
retort
entgehen [ɛnt'geːən] (unreg) vi (fig): **jdm ~**
to escape sb's notice; **sich** dat **etw ~**
lassen to miss sth
Entgelt [ɛnt'gɛlt] **(-(e)s, -e)** nt
compensation, remuneration
entgleisen [ɛnt'glaɪzən] vi (EISENB) to be
derailed; (fig: Person) to misbehave; **~**
lassen to derail
entgräten [ɛnt'grɛːtən] vt to fillet, to bone
Enthaarungscreme [ɛnt'haːrʊŋs-] f hair-
removing cream
enthalten [ɛnt'haltən] (unreg) vt to contain
♦ vr: **sich (von etw) ~** to abstain (from
sth), to refrain (from sth)
enthaltsam [ɛnt'haltzaːm] adj abstinent,
abstemious
enthemmen [ɛnt'hɛmən] vt: **jdn ~** to free
sb from his inhibitions
enthüllen [ɛnt'hʏlən] vt to reveal, to unveil
Enthusiasmus [ɛntuzi'asmʊs] m
enthusiasm
entkommen [ɛnt'kɔmən] (unreg) vi: **~ (aus**
od +dat**)** to get away (from), to escape
(from)
entkräften [ɛnt'krɛftən] vt to weaken, to
exhaust; (Argument) to refute
entladen [ɛnt'laːdən] (unreg) vt to unload;
(ELEK) to discharge ♦ vr (ELEK: Gewehr) to
discharge; (Ärger etc) to vent itself
entlang [ɛnt'laŋ] adv along; **~ dem Fluss,**
den Fluss ~ along the river; **~gehen**
(unreg) vi to walk along
entlarven [ɛnt'larfən] vt to unmask, to
expose

entlassen [ɛnt'lasən] (unreg) vt to
discharge; (Arbeiter) to dismiss;
Entlassung f discharge; dismissal
entlasten [ɛnt'lastən] vt to relieve; (Achse) to
relieve the load on; (Angeklagten) to
exonerate; (Konto) to clear
Entlastung f relief; (COMM) crediting
Entlastungszug m relief train
entlegen [ɛnt'leːgən] adj remote
entlocken [ɛnt'lɔkən] vt: **(jdm etw) ~** to
elicit (sth from sb)
entmutigen [ɛnt'muːtɪgən] vt to discourage
entnehmen [ɛnt'neːmən] (unreg) vt (+dat) to
take out (of), to take (from); (folgern) to
infer (from)
entreißen [ɛnt'raɪsən] (unreg) vt: **jdm etw ~**
to snatch sth (away) from sb
entrichten [ɛnt'rɪçtən] vt to pay
entrosten [ɛnt'rɔstən] vt to remove rust
from
entrümpeln [ɛnt'rʏmpəln] vt to clear out
entrüst- [ɛnt'rʏst] zW: **~en** vt to incense, to
outrage ♦ vr to be filled with indignation;
~et adj indignant, outraged; **E~ung** f
indignation
entschädigen [ɛnt'ʃɛːdɪgən] vt to
compensate; **Entschädigung** f
compensation
entschärfen [ɛnt'ʃɛrfən] vt to defuse; (Kritik)
to tone down
Entscheid [ɛnt'ʃaɪt] **(-(e)s, -e)** m decision;
e~en [-dən] (unreg) vt, vi, vr to decide;
e~end adj decisive; (Stimme) casting;
~ung f decision
entschieden [ɛnt'ʃiːdən] adj decided;
(entschlossen) resolute; **E~heit** f firmness,
determination
entschließen [ɛnt'ʃliːsən] (unreg) vr to
decide
entschlossen [ɛnt'ʃlɔsən] adj determined,
resolute; **E~heit** f determination
Entschluss ▲ [ɛnt'ʃlʊs] m decision;
e~freudig adj decisive; **~kraft** f
determination, decisiveness
entschuldigen [ɛnt'ʃʊldɪgən] vt to excuse
♦ vr to apologize
Entschuldigung f apology; (Grund)

excuse; **jdn um ~ bitten** to apologize to sb;
~! excuse me; (*Verzeihung*) sorry

entsetz- [ɛntˈzɛts] *zW:* **~en** *vt* to horrify;
(*MIL*) to relieve ♦ *vr* to be horrified *od*
appalled; **E~en (-s)** *nt* horror, dismay;
~lich *adj* dreadful, appalling; **~t** *adj*
horrified

Entsorgung [ɛntˈzɔrɡʊŋ] *f* (*von Kraftwerken,
Chemikalien*) (waste) disposal

entspannen [ɛntˈʃpanən] *vt, vr* (*Körper*) to
relax; (*POL: Lage*) to ease

Entspannung *f* relaxation, rest; (*POL*)
détente; **~spolitik** *f* policy of détente

entsprechen [ɛntˈʃprɛçən] (*unreg*) *vi* +*dat* to
correspond to; (*Anforderungen, Wünschen*) to
meet, to comply with; **~d** *adj* appropriate
♦ *adv* accordingly

entspringen [ɛntˈʃprɪŋən] (*unreg*) *vi* (+*dat*)
to spring (from)

entstehen [ɛntˈʃteːən] (*unreg*) *vi:* **~ (aus** *od*
durch) to arise (from), to result (from)

Entstehung *f* genesis, origin

entstellen [ɛntˈʃtɛlən] *vt* to disfigure;
(*Wahrheit*) to distort

entstören [ɛntˈʃtøːrən] *vt* (*RADIO*) to
eliminate interference from

enttäuschen [ɛntˈtɔyʃən] *vt* to disappoint;
Enttäuschung *f* disappointment

entwaffnen [ɛntˈvafnən] *vt* (*lit, fig*) to
disarm

entwässern [ɛntˈvɛsərn] *vt* to drain;
Entwässerung *f* drainage

entweder [ɛntˈveːdər] *konj* either

entwenden [ɛntˈvɛndən] (*unreg*) *vt* to
purloin, to steal

entwerfen [ɛntˈvɛrfən] (*unreg*) *vt* (*Zeichnung*)
to sketch; (*Modell*) to design; (*Vortrag,
Gesetz etc*) to draft

entwerten [ɛntˈveːrtən] *vt* to devalue;
(*stempeln*) to cancel

Entwerter (-s, -) *m* ticket punching
machine

entwickeln [ɛntˈvɪkəln] *vt, vr* (*auch PHOT*) to
develop; (*Mut, Energie*) to show (o.s.), to
display (o.s.)

Entwicklung [ɛntˈvɪklʊŋ] *f* development;
(*PHOT*) developing

Entwicklungs- *zW:* **~hilfe** *f* aid for
developing countries; **~land** *nt* developing
country

entwöhnen [ɛntˈvøːnən] *vt* to wean;
(*Süchtige*): (**einer Sache** *dat od* **von etw) ~**
to cure (of sth)

Entwöhnung *f* weaning; cure, curing

entwürdigend [ɛntˈvvrdɪɡənt] *adj*
degrading

Entwurf [ɛntˈvʊrf] *m* outline, design;
(*Vertragsentwurf, Konzept*) draft

entziehen [ɛntˈtsiːən] (*unreg*) *vt* (+*dat*) to
withdraw (from), to take away (from);
(*Flüssigkeit*) to draw (from), to extract
(from) ♦ *vr* (+*dat*) to escape (from); (*jds
Kenntnis*) to be outside *od* beyond; (*der
Pflicht*) to shirk (from)

Entziehung *f* withdrawal; **~sanstalt** *f*
drug addiction/alcoholism treatment
centre; **~skur** *f* treatment for drug
addiction/alcoholism

entziffern [ɛntˈtsɪfərn] *vt* to decipher; to
decode

entzücken [ɛntˈtsykən] *vt* to delight; **E~
(-s)** *nt* delight; **~d** *adj* delightful, charming

entzünden [ɛntˈtsyndən] *vt* to light, to set
light to; (*fig, MED*) to inflame; (*Streit*) to
spark off ♦ *vr* (*auch fig*) to catch fire; (*Streit*)
to start; (*MED*) to become inflamed

Entzündung *f* (*MED*) inflammation

entzwei [ɛntˈtsvaɪ] *adv* broken; in two;
~brechen (*unreg*) *vt, vi* to break in two;
~en *vr* to set at odds ♦ *vr* to fall out;
~gehen (*unreg*) *vi* to break (in two)

Enzian [ˈɛntsiaːn] **(-s, -e)** *m* gentian

Epidemie [epideˈmiː] *f* epidemic

Epilepsie [epileˈpsiː] *f* epilepsy

Episode [epiˈzoːdə] *f* episode

Epoche [eˈpɔxə] *f* epoch; **~ machend**
epoch-making

Epos [ˈeːpɔs] **(-s, Epen)** *nt* epic (poem)

er [eːr] (*nom*) *pron* he; it

erarbeiten [ɛrˈarbaɪtən] *vt* to work for, to
acquire; (*Theorie*) to work out

erbarmen [ɛrˈbarmən] *vr* (+*gen*) to have pity
od mercy (on); **E~ (-s)** *nt* pity

erbärmlich [ɛrˈbɛrmlɪç] *adj* wretched,

pitiful; **E~keit** f wretchedness

rbarmungslos [ɛr'barmʊŋsloːs] adj
pitiless, merciless

rbau- [ɛr'bau] zW: **~en** vt to build, to
erect; (fig) to edify; **E~er** (-s, -) m builder;
~lich adj edifying

rbe1 ['ɛrbə] (-n, -n) m heir

rbe2 ['ɛrbə] nt inheritance; (fig) heritage

rben vt to inherit

rbeuten [ɛr'bɔytən] vt to carry off; (MIL) to
capture

rb- [ɛrb] zW: **~faktor** m gene; **~folge** f
(line of) succession; **~in** f heiress

rbittern [ɛr'bɪtərn] vt to embitter;
(erzürnen) to incense

rbittert [ɛr'bɪtərt] adj (Kampf) fierce, bitter

rblassen [ɛr'blasən] vi to (turn) pale

rblich ['ɛrplɪç] adj hereditary

rblinden [ɛr'blɪndən] vi to go blind

rbrechen [ɛr'brɛçən] (unreg) vt, vr to vomit

rbschaft f inheritance, legacy

rbse ['ɛrpsə] f pea

rbstück nt heirloom

rd- ['ɛːrd] zW: **~achse** f earth's axis; **~atmo-
sphäre** f earth's atmosphere; **~beben**
nt earthquake; **~beere** f strawberry;
~boden m ground; **~e** f earth; **zu ebe-
ner ~e** at ground level; **e~en** vt (ELEK) to
earth

rdenklich [ɛr'dɛŋklɪç] adj conceivable

rd- zW: **~gas** nt natural gas; **~geschoss**
▲ nt ground floor; **~kunde** f geography;
~nuss ▲ f peanut; **~öl** nt (mineral) oil

rdrosseln [ɛr'drɔsəln] vt to strangle, to
throttle

rdrücken [ɛr'drʏkən] vt to crush

rd- zW: **~rutsch** m landslide; **~teil** m
continent

rdulden [ɛr'dʊldən] vt to endure, to suffer

reignen [ɛr'aignən] vr to happen

reignis [ɛr'|aignɪs] (-ses, -se) nt event;
e~los adj uneventful; **e~reich** adj eventful

rerbt [ɛr'ɛrpt] adj (Haus) inherited;
(Krankheit) hereditary

rfahren [ɛr'faːrən] (unreg) vt to learn, to
find out; (erleben) to experience ♦ adj
experienced

Erfahrung f experience; **e~sgemäß** adv
according to experience

erfassen [ɛr'fasən] vt to seize; (fig:
einbeziehen) to include, to register;
(verstehen) to grasp

erfind- [ɛr'fɪnd] zW: **~en** (unreg) vt to
invent; **E~er** (-s, -) m inventor; **~erisch**
adj inventive; **E~ung** f invention

Erfolg [ɛr'fɔlk] (-(e)s, -e) m success; (Folge)
result; **~ versprechend** promising; **e~en**
[-gən] vi to follow; (sich ergeben) to result;
(stattfinden) to take place; (Zahlung) to be
effected; **e~los** adj unsuccessful;
~losigkeit f lack of success; **e~reich** adj
successful

erforderlich adj requisite, necessary

erfordern [ɛr'fɔrdərn] vt to require, to
demand

erforschen [ɛr'fɔrʃən] vt (Land) to explore;
(Problem) to investigate; (Gewissen) to
search; **Erforschung** f exploration;
investigation; searching

erfreuen [ɛr'frɔyən] vr: **sich ~ an** +dat to
enjoy ♦ vt to delight; **sich einer Sache** gen
~ to enjoy sth

erfreulich [ɛr'frɔylɪç] adj pleasing, gratifying;
~erweise adv happily, luckily

erfrieren [ɛr'friːrən] (unreg) vi to freeze (to
death); (Glieder) to get frostbitten;
(Pflanzen) to be killed by frost

erfrischen [ɛr'frɪʃən] vt to refresh;
Erfrischung f refreshment

Erfrischungs- zW: **~getränk** nt (liquid)
refreshment; **~raum** m snack bar, cafeteria

erfüllen [ɛr'fʏlən] vt (Raum etc) to fill; (fig:
Bitte etc) to fulfil ♦ vr to come true

ergänzen [ɛr'gɛntsən] vt to supplement, to
complete ♦ vr to complement one another;
Ergänzung f completion; (Zusatz)
supplement

ergeben [ɛr'geːbən] (unreg) vt to yield, to
produce ♦ vr to surrender; (folgen) to result
♦ adj devoted, humble

Ergebnis [ɛr'geːpnɪs] (-ses, -se) nt result;
e~los adj without result, fruitless

ergehen [ɛr'geːən] (unreg) vi to be issued, to
go out ♦ vi unpers: **es ergeht ihm gut/**

schlecht he's faring *od* getting on well/badly ♦ *vr*: **sich in etw** *dat* ~ to indulge in sth; **etw über sich ~ lassen** to put up with sth

ergiebig [ɛr'gi:bɪç] *adj* productive

Ergonomie [ɛrgono'mi:] *f* ergonomics *sg*

Ergonomik [ɛrgo'no:mɪk] *f* = **Ergonomie**

ergreifen [ɛr'graifən] (*unreg*) *vt* (*auch fig*) to seize; (*Beruf*) to take up; (*Maßnahmen*) to resort to; (*rühren*) to move; **~d** *adj* moving, touching

ergriffen [ɛr'grɪfən] *adj* deeply moved

Erguss ▲ [ɛr'gʊs] *m* discharge; (*fig*) outpouring, effusion

erhaben [ɛr'ha:bən] *adj* raised, embossed; (*fig*) exalted, lofty; **über etw** *akk* ~ **sein** to be above sth

erhalten [ɛr'haltən] (*unreg*) *vt* to receive; (*bewahren*) to preserve, to maintain; **gut ~** in good condition

erhältlich [ɛr'hɛltlɪç] *adj* obtainable, available

Erhaltung *f* maintenance, preservation

erhärten [ɛr'hɛrtən] *vt* to harden; (*These*) to substantiate, to corroborate

erheben [ɛr'he:bən] (*unreg*) *vt* to raise; (*Protest, Forderungen*) to make; (*Fakten*) to ascertain, to establish ♦ *vr* to rise (up)

erheblich [ɛr'he:plɪç] *adj* considerable

erheitern [ɛr'haitərn] *vt* to amuse, to cheer (up)

Erheiterung *f* exhilaration; **zur allgemeinen ~** to everybody's amusement

erhitzen [ɛr'hɪtsən] *vt* to heat ♦ *vr* to heat up; (*fig*) to become heated

erhoffen [ɛr'hɔfən] *vt* to hope for

erhöhen [ɛr'hø:ən] *vt* to raise; (*verstärken*) to increase

erhol- [ɛr'ho:l] *zW*: **~en** *vr* to recover; (*entspannen*) to have a rest; **~sam** *adj* restful; **E~ung** *f* recovery; relaxation, rest; **~ungsbedürftig** *adj* in need of a rest, run-down; **E~ungsgebiet** *nt* ≈ holiday area; **E~ungsheim** *nt* convalescent home

erhören [ɛr'hø:rən] *vt* (*Gebet etc*) to hear; (*Bitte etc*) to yield to

erinnern [ɛr|'ɪnərn] *vt*: ~ **(an** +*akk*) to remind (of) ♦ *vr*: **sich (an** *akk* **etw)** ~ to remember (sth)

Erinnerung *f* memory; (*Andenken*) reminder

erkältet [ɛr'kɛltət] *adj* with a cold; ~ **sein** to have a cold

Erkältung *f* cold

erkennbar *adj* recognizable

erkennen [ɛr'kɛnən] (*unreg*) *vt* to recognize; (*sehen, verstehen*) to see

erkennt- *zW*: **~lich** *adj*: **sich ~lich zeigen** to show one's appreciation; **E~lichkeit** *f* gratitude; (*Geschenk*) token of one's gratitude; **E~nis** (-, -se) *f* knowledge; (*das Erkennen*) recognition; (*Einsicht*) insight; **zur E~nis kommen** to realize

Erkennung *f* recognition

Erkennungszeichen *nt* identification

Erker ['ɛrkər] (-s, -) *m* bay

erklär- [ɛr'klɛ:r] *zW*: **~bar** *adj* explicable; **~en** *vt* to explain; **~lich** *adj* explicable; (*verständlich*) understandable; **E~ung** *f* explanation; (*Aussage*) declaration

erkranken [ɛr'kraŋkən] *vi* to fall ill; **Erkrankung** *f* illness

erkund- [ɛr'kʊnd] *zW*: **~en** *vt* to find out, to ascertain; (*bes MIL*) to reconnoitre, to scout; **~igen** *vr*: **sich ~igen (nach)** to inquire (about); **E~igung** *f* inquiry; **E~ung** *f* reconnaissance, scouting

erlahmen [ɛr'la:mən] *vi* to tire; (*nachlassen*) to flag, to wane

erlangen [ɛr'laŋən] *vt* to attain, to achieve

Erlass ▲ [ɛr'las] (-es, ᵘe) *m* decree; (*Aufhebung*) remission

erlassen (*unreg*) *vt* (*Verfügung*) to issue; (*Gesetz*) to enact; (*Strafe*) to remit; **jdm etw** ~ to release sb from sth

erlauben [ɛr'laubən] *vt*: (**jdm etw**) ~ to allow *od* permit (sb (to do) sth) ♦ *vr* to permit o.s., to venture

Erlaubnis [ɛr'laupnɪs] (-, -se) *f* permission; (*Schriftstück*) permit

erläutern [ɛr'lɔytərn] *vt* to explain; **Erläuterung** *f* explanation

erleben [ɛr'le:bən] *vt* to experience; (*Zeit*) to live through; (*miterleben*) to witness; (*noch* *miterleben*) to live to see

Erlebnis [ɛrˈleːpnɪs] **(-ses, -se)** nt experience

erledigen [ɛrˈleːdɪɡən] vt to take care of, to deal with; (*Antrag etc*) to process; (*umg: erschöpfen*) to wear out; (: *ruinieren*) to finish; (: *umbringen*) to do in

erleichtern [ɛrˈlaɪçtɐn] vt to make easier; (*fig: Last*) to lighten; (*lindern, beruhigen*) to relieve; **Erleichterung** f facilitation; lightening; relief

erleiden [ɛrˈlaɪdən] (*unreg*) vt to suffer, to endure

erlernen [ɛrˈlɛrnən] vt to learn, to acquire

erlesen [ɛrˈleːzən] adj select, choice

erleuchten [ɛrˈlɔyçtən] vt to illuminate; (*fig*) to inspire

Erleuchtung f (*Einfall*) inspiration

Erlös [ɛrˈløːs] **(-es, -e)** m proceeds pl

erlösen [ɛrˈløːzən] vt to redeem, to save; **Erlösung** f release; (*REL*) redemption

ermächtigen [ɛrˈmɛçtɪɡən] vt to authorize, to empower; **Ermächtigung** f authorization; authority

ermahnen [ɛrˈmaːnən] vt to exhort, to admonish; **Ermahnung** f admonition, exhortation

ermäßigen [ɛrˈmɛsɪɡən] vt to reduce; **Ermäßigung** f reduction

ermessen [ɛrˈmɛsən] (*unreg*) vt to estimate, to gauge; **E~ (-s)** nt estimation; discretion; **in jds E~ liegen** to lie within sb's discretion

ermitteln [ɛrˈmɪtəln] vt to determine; (*Täter*) to trace ♦ vi: **gegen jdn ~** to investigate sb **Ermittlung** [ɛrˈmɪtlʊŋ] f determination; (*Polizeiermittlung*) investigation

ermöglichen [ɛrˈmøːɡlɪçən] vt (*+dat*) to make possible (for)

ermorden [ɛrˈmɔrdən] vt to murder

ermüden [ɛrˈmyːdən] vt, vi to tire; (*TECH*) to fatigue; **~d** adj tiring; (*fig*) wearisome **Ermüdung** f fatigue

ermutigen [ɛrˈmuːtɪɡən] vt to encourage

ernähr- [ɛrˈnɛːr] zW: **~en** vt to feed, to nourish; (*Familie*) to support ♦ vr to support o.s., to earn a living; **sich ~en von** to live

on; **E~er (-s, -)** m breadwinner; **E~ung** f nourishment; nutrition; (*Unterhalt*) maintenance

ernennen [ɛrˈnɛnən] (*unreg*) vt to appoint; **Ernennung** f appointment

erneu- [ɛrˈnɔy] zW: **~ern** vt to renew; to restore; to renovate; **E~erung** f renewal; restoration; renovation; **~t** adj renewed, fresh ♦ adv once more

ernst [ɛrnst] adj serious; **~ gemeint** meant in earnest, serious; **E~ (-es)** m seriousness; **das ist mein E~** I'm quite serious; **im E~** in earnest; **E~ machen mit etw** to put sth into practice; **E~fall** m emergency; **~haft** adj serious; **E~haftigkeit** f seriousness; **~lich** adj serious

Ernte [ˈɛrntə] f harvest; **e~n** vt to harvest; (*Lob etc*) to earn

ernüchtern [ɛrˈnʏçtɐn] vt to sober up; (*fig*) to bring down to earth

Erober- [ɛrˈoːbɐr] zW: **~er (-s, -)** m conqueror; **e~n** vt to conquer; **~ung** f conquest

eröffnen [ɛrˈœfnən] vt to open ♦ vr to present itself; **jdm etw ~** to disclose sth to sb

Eröffnung f opening

erörtern [ɛrˈœrtɐn] vt to discuss

Erotik [eˈroːtɪk] f eroticism; **erotisch** adj erotic

erpress- [ɛrˈprɛs] zW: **~en** vt (*Geld etc*) to extort; (*Mensch*) to blackmail; **E~er (-s, -)** m blackmailer; **E~ung** f extortion; blackmail

erprobt [ɛrˈproːpt] adj (*Gerät, Medikamente*) proven, tested

erraten [ɛrˈraːtən] (*unreg*) vt to guess

erreg- [ɛrˈreːɡ] zW: **~en** vt to excite; (*ärgern*) to infuriate; (*hervorrufen*) to arouse, to provoke ♦ vr to get excited od worked up; **E~er (-s, -)** m causative agent; **E~ung** f excitement

erreichbar adj accessible, within reach

erreichen [ɛrˈraɪçən] vt to reach; (*Zweck*) to achieve; (*Zug*) to catch

errichten [ɛrˈrɪçtən] vt to erect, to put up; (*gründen*) to establish, to set up

erringen [ɛrˈrɪŋən] (*unreg*) *vt* to gain, to win

erröten [ɛrˈrøːtən] *vi* to blush, to flush

Errungenschaft [ɛrˈrʊŋənʃaft] *f* achievement; (*umg: Anschaffung*) acquisition

Ersatz [ɛrˈzats] (**-es**) *m* substitute; replacement; (*Schadenersatz*) compensation; (*MIL*) reinforcements *pl*; **~dienst** *m* (*MIL*) alternative service; **~reifen** *m* (*AUT*) spare tyre; **~teil** *nt* spare (part)

erschaffen [ɛrˈʃafən] (*unreg*) *vt* to create

erscheinen [ɛrˈʃaɪnən] (*unreg*) *vi* to appear; **Erscheinung** *f* appearance; (*Geist*) apparition; (*Gegebenheit*) phenomenon; (*Gestalt*) figure

erschießen [ɛrˈʃiːsən] (*unreg*) *vt* to shoot (dead)

erschlagen [ɛrˈʃlaːgən] (*unreg*) *vt* to strike dead

erschöpf- [ɛrˈʃœpf] *zW*: **~en** *vt* to exhaust; **~end** *adj* exhaustive, thorough; **E~ung** *f* exhaustion

erschrecken [ɛrˈʃrɛkən] *vt* to startle, to frighten ♦ *vi* to be frightened *od* startled; **~d** *adj* alarming, frightening

erschrocken [ɛrˈʃrɔkən] *adj* frightened, startled

erschüttern [ɛrˈʃʏtərn] *vt* to shake; (*fig*) to move deeply; **Erschütterung** *f* shaking; shock

erschweren [ɛrˈʃveːrən] *vt* to complicate

erschwinglich *adj* within one's means

ersetzen [ɛrˈzɛtsən] *vt* to replace; **jdm Unkosten** *etc* **~** to pay sb's expenses *etc*

ersichtlich [ɛrˈzɪçtlɪç] *adj* evident, obvious

ersparen [ɛrˈʃpaːrən] *vt* to (*Ärger etc*) to spare; (*Geld*) to save

Ersparnis (**-, -se**) *f* saving

erst [eːrst] *adv* **1** first; **mach erst mal die Arbeit fertig** finish your work first; **wenn du das erst mal hinter dir hast** once you've got that behind you
2 (*nicht früher als, nur*) only; (*nicht bis*) not till; **erst gestern** only yesterday; **erst morgen** not until tomorrow; **erst als** only when, not until; **wir fahren erst später**

we're not going until later; **er ist (gerade) erst angekommen** he's only just arrived
3: **wäre er doch erst zurück!** if only he were back!

erstatten [ɛrˈʃtatən] *vt* (*Kosten*) to (re)pay; **Anzeige** *etc* **gegen jdn ~** to report sb; **Bericht ~** to make a report

Erstattung *f* (*von Kosten*) refund

Erstaufführung [ˈeːrstˈaʊffyːrʊŋ] *f* first performance

erstaunen [ɛrˈʃtaʊnən] *vt* to astonish ♦ *vi* to be astonished; **E~** (**-s**) *nt* astonishment

erstaunlich *adj* astonishing

erst- [ˈeːrst] *zW*: **E~ausgabe** *f* first edition; **~beste(r, s)** *adj* first that comes along; **~e(r, s)** *adj* first

erstechen [ɛrˈʃtɛçən] (*unreg*) *vt* to stab (to death)

erstehen [ɛrˈʃteːən] (*unreg*) *vt* to buy ♦ *vi* to (a)rise

erstens [ˈeːrstəns] *adv* firstly, in the first place

ersticken [ɛrˈʃtɪkən] *vt* (*auch fig*) to stifle; (*Mensch*) to suffocate; (*Flammen*) to smother ♦ *vi* (*Mensch*) to suffocate; (*Feuer*) to be smothered; **in Arbeit ~** to be snowed under with work

erst- *zW*: **~klassig** *adj* first-class; **~malig** *adj* first; **~mals** *adv* for the first time

erstrebenswert [ɛrˈʃtreːbənsveːrt] *adj* desirable, worthwhile

erstrecken [ɛrˈʃtrɛkən] *vr* to extend, to stretch

ersuchen [ɛrˈzuːxən] *vt* to request

ertappen [ɛrˈtapən] *vt* to catch, to detect

erteilen [ɛrˈtaɪlən] *vt* to give

Ertrag [ɛrˈtraːk] (**-(e)s, ▾e**) *m* yield; (*Gewinn*) proceeds *pl*

ertragen [ɛrˈtraːgən] (*unreg*) *vt* to bear, to stand

erträglich [ɛrˈtrɛːklɪç] *adj* tolerable, bearable

ertrinken [ɛrˈtrɪŋkən] (*unreg*) *vi* to drown; **E~** (**-s**) *nt* drowning

erübrigen [ɛrˈyːbrɪgən] *vt* to spare ♦ *vr* to be unnecessary

erwachen [ɛrˈvaxən] *vi* to awake

erwachsen [ɛr'vaksən] *adj* grown-up;
E~e(r) *f(m)* adult; **E~enbildung** *f* adult
education

erwägen [ɛr've:gən] *(unreg) vt* to consider;
Erwägung *f* consideration

erwähn- [ɛr've:n] *vt* to mention;
~**enswert** *adj* worth mentioning; **E~ung** *f*
mention

erwärmen [ɛr'vɛrmən] *vt* to warm, to heat
♦ *vr* to get warm, to warm up; **sich ~ für**
to warm to

Erwarten *nt*: **über meinen/unseren** *usw* ~
beyond my/our *etc* expectations; **wider** ~
contrary to expectations

erwarten [ɛr'vartən] *vt* to expect; *(warten
auf)* to wait for; **etw kaum ~ können** to be
hardly able to wait for sth

Erwartung *f* expectation

erwartungsgemäß *adv* as expected

erwartungsvoll *adj* expectant

erwecken [ɛr'vɛkən] *vt* to rouse, to awake;
den Anschein ~ to give the impression

Erweis [ɛr'vais] (-es, -e) *m* proof; **e~en**
(unreg) vt to prove ♦ *vr*: **sich e~en (als)** to
prove (to be); **jdm einen Gefallen/Dienst
e~en** to do sb a favour/service

Erwerb [ɛr'vɛrp] (-(e)s, -e) *m* acquisition;
(Beruf) trade; **e~en** [-bən] *(unreg) vt* to
acquire

erwerbs- *zW*: ~**los** *adj* unemployed;
E~quelle *f* source of income; ~**tätig** *adj*
(gainfully) employed

erwidern [ɛr'vi:dərn] *vt* to reply; *(vergelten)*
to return

erwischen [ɛr'vɪʃən] *(umg) vt* to catch, to
get

erwünscht [ɛr'vʏnʃt] *adj* desired

erwürgen [ɛr'vʏrgən] *vt* to strangle

Erz [e:rts] (-es, -e) *nt* ore

erzähl- [ɛr'tsɛ:l] *zW*: ~**en** *vt* to tell ♦ *vi*: **sie
kann gut ~en** she's a good story-teller;
E~er (-s, -) *m* narrator; **E~ung** *f* story, tale

Erzbischof *m* archbishop

erzeug- [ɛr'tsɔyg] *zW*: ~**en** *vt* to produce;
(Strom) to generate; **E~nis** (-ses, -se) *nt*
product, produce; **E~ung** *f* production,
generation

erziehen [ɛr'tsi:ən] *(unreg) vt* to bring up;
(bilden) to educate, to train; **Erzieher(in)**
(-s, -) *m(f) (Berufsbezeichnung)* teacher;
Erziehung *f* bringing up; *(Bildung)*
education; **Erziehungsbeihilfe** *f*
educational grant;
Erziehungsberechtigte(r) *f(m)* parent;
guardian

erzielen [ɛr'tsi:lən] *vt* to achieve, to obtain;
(Tor) to score

erzwingen [ɛr'tsvɪŋən] *(unreg) vt* to force, to
obtain by force

es [ɛs] *(nom, akk) pron* it

Esel ['e:zəl] (-s, -) *m* donkey, ass

Eskalation [ɛskalatsi'o:n] *f* escalation

ess- ▲ ['ɛs] *zW*: ~**bar** ['ɛsba:r] *adj* eatable,
edible; **E~besteck** *nt* knife, fork and
spoon; **E~ecke** *f* dining area

essen ['ɛsən] *(unreg) vt, vi* to eat; **E~** (-s, -)
nt meal; food

Essig ['ɛsɪç] (-s, -e) *m* vinegar

Ess- ▲ *zW*: ~**kastanie** *f* sweet chestnut;
~**löffel** *m* tablespoon; ~**tisch** *m* dining
table; ~**waren** *pl* foodstuffs, provisions;
~**zimmer** *nt* dining room

etablieren [eta'bli:rən] *vr* to become
established; to set up in business

Etage [e'ta:ʒə] *f* floor, storey; ~**nbetten** *pl*
bunk beds; ~**nwohnung** *f* flat

Etappe [e'tapə] *f* stage

Etat [e'ta:] (-s, -s) *m* budget

etc *abk* (= *et cetera*) etc

Ethik ['e:tɪk] *f* ethics *sg*; **ethisch** *adj* ethical

Etikett [eti'kɛt] (-(e)s, -e) *nt* label; tag; ~**e** *f*
etiquette, manners *pl*

etliche ['ɛtlɪçə] *pron pl* some, quite a few; ~**s**
pron a thing or two

Etui [et'vi:] (-s, -s) *nt* case

etwa ['ɛtva] *adv (ungefähr)* about; *(vielleicht)*
perhaps; *(beispielsweise)* for instance; **nicht**
~ by no means; ~**ig** ['ɛtvaɪç] *adj* possible

etwas *pron* something; anything; *(ein wenig)*
a little ♦ *adv* a little

euch [ɔyç] *pron (akk von ihr)* you; yourselves;
(dat von ihr) (to) you

euer ['ɔyər] *pron (gen von ihr)* of you ♦ *adj*
your

Eule [ˈɔylə] *f* owl

eure [ˈɔyrə] *adj f siehe* **euer**

eure(r, s) [ˈɔyrə(r, s)] *pron* yours; **~rseits**
adv on your part; **~s** *adj nt siehe* **euer**;
~sgleichen *pron* people like you;
~twegen *adv (für euch)* for your sakes;
(wegen euch) on your account; **~twillen**
adv: **um ~twillen** = **euretwegen**

eurige [ˈɔyrɪgə] *pron*: **der/die/das ~** *od* **E~**
yours

Euro [ˈɔyroː] **(-, -s)** *m (FIN)* euro

Euro- *zW*: **~pa** [ɔyˈroːpa] *nt* Europe;
~päer(in) [ɔyroˈpɛːər(ɪn)] *m(f)* European;
e~päisch *adj* European; **~pameister**
[ɔyˈroːpa-] *m* European champion;
~paparlament *nt* European Parliament;
~scheck *m (FIN)* eurocheque

Euter [ˈɔytər] **(-s, -)** *nt* udder

ev. *abk* = **evangelisch**

evakuieren [evakuˈiːrən] *vt* to evacuate

evangelisch [evaŋˈgeːlɪʃ] *adj* Protestant

Evangelium [evaŋˈgeːlium] *nt* gospel

eventuell [eventuˈɛl] *adj* possible ♦ *adv*
possibly, perhaps

evtl. *abk* = **eventuell**

EWG [eːveːˈgeː] **(-)** *f abk (= Europäische
Wirtschaftsgemeinschaft)* EEC, Common
Market

ewig [ˈeːvɪç] *adj* eternal; **E~keit** *f* eternity

EWU [eːveːˈʔuː] *f abk (= Europäische
Währungsunion)* EMU

exakt [ɛˈksakt] *adj* exact

Examen [ɛˈksaːmən] **(-s, -** *od* **Examina)** *nt*
examination

Exemplar [ɛksɛmˈplaːr] **(-s, -e)** *nt* specimen;
(Buchexemplar) copy; **e~isch** *adj* exemplary

Exil [ɛˈksiːl] **(-s, -e)** *nt* exile

Existenz [ɛksɪsˈtɛnts] *f* existence; *(Unterhalt)*
livelihood, living; *(pej: Mensch)* character;
~minimum (-s) *nt* subsistence level

existieren [ɛksɪsˈtiːrən] *vi* to exist

exklusiv [ɛkskluˈziːf] *adj* exclusive; **~e** *adv*
exclusive of, not including ♦ *präp* +*gen*
exclusive of, not including

exotisch [ɛˈksoːtɪʃ] *adj* exotic

Expedition [ɛkspeditsiˈoːn] *f* expedition

Experiment [ɛksperiˈment] *nt* experiment;

e~ell [-ˈtɛl] *adj* experimental; **e~ieren**
[-ˈtiːrən] *vi* to experiment

Experte [ɛksˈpɛrtə] **(-n, -n)** *m* expert,
specialist; **Expertin** *f* expert, specialist

explo- [ɛksplo] *zW*: **~dieren** [-ˈdiːrən] *vi* to
explode; **E~sion** [-ziˈoːn] *f* explosion; **~siv**
[-ˈziːf] *adj* explosive

Export [ɛksˈpɔrt] **(-(e)s, -e)** *m* export; **~eur**
[-ˈtøːr] *m* exporter; **~handel** *m* export
trade; **e~ieren** [-ˈtiːrən] *vt* to export; **~land**
nt exporting country

Express- ▲ [ɛksˈprɛs] *zW*: **~gut** *nt* express
goods *pl*, express freight; **~zug** *m* express
(train)

extra [ˈɛkstra] *adj inv (umg: gesondert)*
separate; *(besondere)* extra ♦ *adv (gesondert)*
separately; *(speziell)* specially; *(absichtlich)*
on purpose; *(vor Adjektiven, zusätzlich)* extra;
E~ **(-s, -s)** *nt* extra; **E~ausgabe** *f* special
edition; **E~blatt** *nt* special edition

Extrakt [ɛksˈtrakt] **(-(e)s, -e)** *m* extract

extravagant [ɛkstravaˈgant] *adj* extravagant

extrem [ɛksˈtreːm] *adj* extreme; **~istisch**
[-ˈmɪstɪʃ] *adj (POL)* extremist; **E~itäten**
[-miˈtɛːtən] *pl* extremities

exzentrisch [ɛksˈtsɛntrɪʃ] *adj* eccentric

EZ *nt abk* = **Einzelzimmer**

EZB *f abk (= Europäische Zentralbank)* ECB

F, f

Fa. *abk (= Firma)* firm; *(in Briefen)* Messrs

Fabel [ˈfaːbəl] **(-, -n)** *f* fable; **f~haft** *adj*
fabulous, marvellous

Fabrik [faˈbriːk] *f* factory; **~ant** [-ˈkant] *m*
(Hersteller) manufacturer; *(Besitzer)*
industrialist; **~arbeiter** *m* factory worker;
~at [-ˈkaːt] **(-(e)s, -e)** *nt* manufacture,
product; **~gelände** *nt* factory site

Fach [fax] **(-(e)s, er)** *nt* compartment;
(Sachgebiet) subject; **ein Mann vom ~** an
expert; **~arbeiter** *m* skilled worker; **~arzt**
m (medical) specialist; **~ausdruck** *m*
technical term

Fächer [ˈfɛçər] **(-s, -)** *m* fan

Fach- *zW*: **~geschäft** *nt* specialist shop;

~hochschule f technical college; **~kraft** f skilled worker, trained employee; **f~kundig** adj expert, specialist; **f~lich** adj professional; expert; **~mann** (pl **-leute**) m specialist; **f~männisch** adj professional; **~schule** f technical college; **f~simpeln** vi to talk shop; **~werk** nt timber frame

Fackel ['fakəl] (**-**, **-n**) f torch

fad(e) [faːt, 'faːdə] adj insipid; (langweilig) dull

Faden ['faːdən] (**-s**, **ꞏ**) m thread; **f~scheinig** adj (auch fig) threadbare

fähig ['fɛːɪç] adj: **~** (**zu** od +gen) capable (of); able (to); **F~keit** f ability

fahnden ['faːndən] vi: **~ nach** to search for; **Fahndung** f search

Fahndungsliste f list of wanted criminals, wanted list

Fahne ['faːnə] f flag, standard; **eine ~ haben** (umg) to smell of drink; **~nflucht** f desertion

Fahr- ['faːr] zW: **~ausweis** m ticket; **~bahn** f carriageway (BRIT), roadway

Fähre ['fɛːrə] f ferry

fahren ['faːrən] (unreg) vt to drive; (Rad) to ride; (befördern) to drive, to take; (Rennen) to drive in ♦ vi (sich bewegen) to go; (Schiff) to sail; (abfahren) to leave; **mit dem Auto/ Zug ~** to go od travel by car/train; **mit der Hand ~ über** +akk to pass one's hand over

Fahr- zW: **~er(in)** (**-s**, **-**) m(f) driver; **~erflucht** f hit-and-run; **~gast** m passenger; **~geld** nt fare; **~karte** f ticket; **~kartenausgabe** f ticket office; **~kartenautomat** m ticket machine; **~kartenschalter** m ticket office; **f~lässig** adj negligent; **f~lässige Tötung** manslaughter; **~lehrer** m driving instructor; **~plan** m timetable; **f~planmäßig** adj scheduled; **~preis** m fare; **~prüfung** f driving test; **~rad** nt bicycle; **~radweg** m cycle lane; **~schein** m ticket; **~scheinentwerter** m (automatic) ticket stamping machine

Fährschiff ['fɛːrʃɪf] nt ferry(boat)

Fahr- zW: **~schule** f driving school; **~spur** f lane; **~stuhl** m lift (BRIT), elevator (US)

Fahrt [faːrt] (**-**, **-en**) f journey; (kurz) trip;

(AUT) drive; (Geschwindigkeit) speed; **gute ~!** have a good journey

Fährte ['fɛːrtə] f track, trail

Fahrt- zW: **~kosten** pl travelling expenses; **~richtung** f course, direction

Fahrzeit f time for the journey

Fahrzeug nt vehicle; **~brief** m log book; **~papiere** pl vehicle documents

fair [fɛːr] adj fair

Fakt [fakt] (**-(e)s**, **-en**) m fact

Faktor ['faktɔr] m factor

Fakultät [fakʊlˈtɛːt] f faculty

Falke ['falkə] (**-n**, **-n**) m falcon

Fall [fal] (**-(e)s**, **ꞏe**) m (Sturz) fall; (Sachverhalt, JUR, GRAM) case; **auf jeden ~**, **auf alle Fälle** in any case; (bestimmt) definitely; **auf keinen ~!** no way!

Falle f trap

fallen (unreg) vi to fall; **etw ~ lassen** to drop sth; (Bemerkung) to make sth; (Plan) to abandon sth, to drop sth

fällen ['fɛlən] vt (Baum) to fell; (Urteil) to pass

fällig ['fɛlɪç] adj due

falls [fals] adv in case, if

Fallschirm m parachute; **~springer** m parachutist

falsch [falʃ] adj false; (unrichtig) wrong

fälschen ['fɛlʃən] vt to forge

fälsch- zW: **f~lich** adj false; **~licherweise** adv mistakenly; **F~ung** f forgery

Falte ['faltə] f (Knick) fold, crease; (Hautfalte) wrinkle; (Rockfalte) pleat; **f~n** vt to fold; (Stirn) to wrinkle

faltig ['faltɪç] adj (Hände, Haut) wrinkled; (zerknittert: Rock) creased

familiär [famɪliˈɛːr] adj familiar

Familie [faˈmiːliə] f family

Familien- zW: **~betrieb** m family business; **~kreis** m family circle; **~mitglied** nt member of the family; **~name** m surname; **~stand** m marital status

Fanatiker [faˈnaːtikər] (**-s**, **-**) m fanatic; **fanatisch** adj fanatical

fand etc [fant] vb siehe **finden**

Fang [faŋ] (**-(e)s**, **ꞏe**) m catch; (Jagen) hunting; (Kralle) talon, claw; **f~en** (unreg) vt to catch ♦ vr to get caught; (Flugzeug) to level out; (*Mensch: nicht fallen*) to steady o.s.; (*fig*) to compose o.s.; (*in Leistung*) to get back on form

Fantasie ▲ [fanta'zi:] *f* imagination; **f~los** *adj* unimaginative; **f~ren** *vi* to fantasize; **f~voll** *adj* imaginative

fantastisch ▲ [fan'tastɪʃ] *adj* fantastic

Farb- ['farb] *zW:* **~abzug** *m* colour print; **~aufnahme** *f* colour photograph; **~band** *m* typewriter ribbon; **~e** *f* colour; (*zum Malen etc*) paint; (*Stoffarbe*) dye; **f~echt** *adj* colourfast

färben ['fɛrbən] *vt* to colour; (*Stoff, Haar*) to dye

farben- ['farbən] *zW:* **~blind** *adj* colourblind; **~freudig** *adj* colourful; **~froh** *adj* colourful, gay

Farb- *zW:* **~fernsehen** *nt* colour television; **~film** *m* colour film; **~foto** *nt* colour photograph; **f~ig** *adj* coloured; **~ige(r)** *f(m)* coloured (person); **~kasten** *m* paintbox; **f~lich** *adj* colour; **f~los** *adj* colourless; **~stift** *m* coloured pencil; **~stoff** *m* dye; **~ton** *m* hue, tone

Färbung ['fɛrbʊŋ] *f* colouring; (*Tendenz*) bias

Farn [farn] (-(e)s, -e) *m* fern; bracken

Fasan [fa'za:n] (-(e)s, -e(n)) *m* pheasant

Fasching ['faʃɪŋ] (-s, -e *od* -s) *m* carnival

Faschismus [fa'ʃɪsmʊs] *m* fascism

Faschist *m* fascist

Faser ['fa:zər] (-, -n) *f* fibre; **f~n** *vi* to fray

Fass ▲ [fas] (-es, ⁺er) *nt* vat, barrel; (*für Öl*) drum; **Bier vom ~** draught beer

Fassade [fa'sa:də] *f* façade

fassen ['fasən] *vt* (*ergreifen*) to grasp, to take; (*inhaltlich*) to hold; (*Entschluss etc*) to take; (*verstehen*) to understand; (*Ring etc*) to set; (*formulieren*) to formulate, to phrase ♦ *vr* to calm down; **nicht zu ~** unbelievable

Fassung ['fasʊŋ] *f* (*Umrahmung*) mounting; (*Lampenfassung*) socket; (*Wortlaut*) version; (*Beherrschung*) composure; **jdn aus der ~ bringen** to upset sb; **f~slos** *adj* speechless

fast [fast] *adv* almost, nearly

fasten ['fastən] *vi* to fast; **F~zeit** *f* Lent

Fastnacht *f* Shrove Tuesday; carnival

faszinieren [fastsi'ni:rən] *vt* to fascinate

fatal [fa'ta:l] *adj* fatal; (*peinlich*) embarrassing

faul [faʊl] *adj* rotten; (*Person*) lazy; (*Ausreden*) lame; **daran ist etwas ~** there's something fishy about it; **~en** *vi* to rot; **~enzen** *vi* to idle; **F~enzer** (-s, -) *m* idler, loafer; **F~heit** *f* laziness; **~ig** *adj* putrid

Faust ['faʊst] (-, Fäuste) *f* fist; **auf eigene ~** off one's own bat; **~handschuh** *m* mitten

Favorit [favo'ri:t] (-en, -en) *m* favourite

Fax [faks] (-, -(e)) *nt* fax

faxen ['faksən] *vt* to fax; **jdm etw ~** to fax sth to sb

FCKW *m abk* (= *Fluorchlorkohlenwasserstoff*) CFC

Februar ['fe:brua:r] (-(s), -e) *m* February

fechten ['fɛçtən] (*unreg*) *vi* to fence

Feder ['fe:dər] (-, -n) *f* feather; (*Schreibfeder*) pen nib; (*TECH*) spring; **~ball** *m* shuttlecock; **~bett** *nt* continental quilt; **~halter** *m* penholder, pen; **f~leicht** *adj* light as a feather; **f~n** *vi* (*nachgeben*) to be springy; (*sich bewegen*) to bounce ♦ *vt* to spring; **~ung** *f* (*AUT*) suspension

Fee [fe:] *f* fairy

fegen ['fe:gən] *vt* to sweep

fehl [fe:l] *adj:* **~ am Platz** *od* **Ort** out of place; **F~betrag** *m* deficit; **~en** *vi* to be wanting *od* missing; (*abwesend sein*) to be absent; **etw ~t jdm** sth lacks sb; **du ~st mir** I miss you; **was ~t ihm?** what's wrong with him?; **F~er** (-s, -) *m* mistake, error; (*Mangel, Schwäche*) fault; **~erfrei** *adj* faultless; without any mistakes; **~erhaft** *adj* incorrect; faulty; **~erlos** *adj* flawless, perfect; **F~geburt** *f* miscarriage; **~gehen** (*unreg*) *vi* to go astray; **F~griff** *m* blunder; **F~konstruktion** *f* badly designed thing; **~schlagen** (*unreg*) *vi* to fail; **F~start** *m* (*SPORT*) false start; **F~zündung** *f* (*AUT*) misfire, backfire

Feier ['faɪər] (-, -n) *f* celebration; **~abend** *m* time to stop work; **~abend machen** to stop, to knock off; **jetzt ist ~abend!** that's enough!; **f~lich** *adj* solemn; **~lichkeit** *f* solemnity; **~lichkeiten** *pl* (*Veranstaltungen*) festivities; **f~n** *vt, vi* to celebrate; **~tag** *m* holiday

feig(e) [faɪk, 'faɪɡə] adj cowardly

Feige ['faɪɡə] f fig

Feigheit f cowardice

Feigling m coward

Feile ['faɪlə] f file

feilschen ['faɪlʃən] vi to haggle

fein [faɪn] adj fine; (vornehm) refined; (Gehör etc) keen; **~!** great!

Feind [faɪnt] (-(e)s, -e) m enemy; **f~lich** adj hostile; **~schaft** f enmity; **f~selig** adj hostile

Fein- zW: **f~fühlig** adj sensitive; **~gefühl** nt delicacy, tact; **~heit** f fineness; refinement; keenness; **~kostgeschäft** nt delicatessen (shop); **~schmecker** (-s, -) m gourmet; **~wäsche** f delicate clothing (when washing); **~waschmittel** nt mild detergent

Feld [fɛlt] (-(e)s, -er) nt field; (SCHACH) square; (SPORT) pitch; **~herr** m commander; **~stecher** (-s, -) m binoculars pl; **~weg** m path; **~zug** m (fig) campaign

Felge ['fɛlɡə] f (wheel) rim

Fell [fɛl] (-(e)s, -e) nt fur; coat; (von Schaf) fleece; (von toten Tieren) skin

Fels [fɛls] (-en, -en) m rock; (Klippe) cliff

Felsen ['fɛlzən] (-s, -) m = Fels; **f~fest** adj firm

feminin [femi'niːn] adj feminine

Fenster ['fɛnstər] (-s, -) nt window; **~bank** f windowsill; **~laden** m shutter; **~leder** nt chamois (leather); **~scheibe** f windowpane

Ferien ['feːriən] pl holidays, vacation sg (US); **~ haben** to be on holiday; **~bungalow** [-bʊŋɡalo] (-s, -s) m holiday bungalow; **~haus** nt holiday home; **~kurs** m holiday course; **~lager** nt holiday camp; **~reise** f holiday; **~wohnung** f holiday apartment

Ferkel ['fɛrkəl] (-s, -) nt piglet

fern [fɛrn] adj, adv far-off, distant; **~ von hier** a long way (away) from here; **der F~e Osten** the Far East; **~ halten** to keep away; **F~bedienung** f remote control; **F~e** f distance; **~er** adj further ♦ adv further; (weiterhin) in future; **F~gespräch** nt trunk call; **F~glas** nt binoculars pl; **F~licht** nt

(AUT) full beam; **F~rohr** nt telescope; **F~ruf** m (förmlich) telephone number; **F~schreiben** nt telex; **F~sehapparat** m television set; **F~sehen** (-s) nt television; **im F~sehen** on television; **~sehen** (unreg) vi to watch television; **F~seher** m television; **F~sehturm** m television tower; **F~sprecher** m telephone; **F~steuerung** f remote control; **F~straße** f ≈ 'A' road (BRIT), highway (US); **F~verkehr** m long-distance traffic

Ferse ['fɛrzə] f heel

fertig ['fɛrtɪç] adj (bereit) ready; (beendet) finished; (gebrauchsfertig) ready-made; **~ bringen** (fähig sein) to be capable of; **~ machen** (beenden) to finish; (umg: Person) to finish; (: körperlich) to exhaust; (: moralisch) to get down; **sich ~ machen** to get ready; **~ stellen** to complete; **F~gericht** nt precooked meal; **F~haus** nt kit house, prefab; **F~keit** f skill

Fessel ['fɛsəl] (-, -n) f fetter; **f~n** vt to bind; (mit ~n) to fetter; (fig) to spellbind; **f~nd** adj fascinating, captivating

Fest [fɛst] (-(e)s, -e) nt party; festival; **frohes ~!** Happy Christmas!

fest [fɛst] adj firm; (Nahrung) solid; (Gehalt) regular; **~e Kosten** fixed cost ♦ adv (schlafen) soundly); **~ angestellt** permanently employed; **~binden** (unreg) vt to tie, to fasten; **~bleiben** (unreg) vi to stand firm; **F~essen** nt banquet; **~halten** (unreg) vt to seize, to hold fast; (Ereignis) to record ♦ vr: **sich ~halten (an** +dat) to hold on (to); **~igen** vt to strengthen; **F~igkeit** f strength; **F~ival** ['fɛstɪval] (-s, -s) nt festival; **F~land** nt mainland; **~legen** vt to fix ♦ vr to commit o.s.; **~lich** adj festive; **~liegen** (unreg) vi (~stehen: Termin) to be confirmed, to be fixed; **~machen** vt to fasten; (Termin etc) to fix; **F~nahme** f arrest; **~nehmen** (unreg) vt to arrest; **F~preis** m (COMM) fixed price; **F~rede** f address; **~setzen** vt to fix, to settle; **F~spiele** pl (Veranstaltung) festival sg; **~stehen** (unreg) vi to be certain; **~stellen** vt to establish; (sagen) to remark; **F~tag** m

feast day, holiday; **F~ung** f fortress;
F~wochen pl festival sg

Fett [fɛt] (-(e)s, -e) nt fat, grease
fett adj fat; (Essen etc) greasy; (TYP) bold;
~arm adj low fat; **~en** vt to grease;
F~fleck m grease stain; **~ig** adj greasy,
fatty

Fetzen ['fɛtsən] (-s, -) m scrap

feucht [fɔʏçt] adj damp; (Luft) humid;
F~igkeit f dampness; humidity;
F~igkeitscreme f moisturising cream

Feuer ['fɔʏər] (-s, -) nt fire; (zum Rauchen) a
light; (fig: Schwung) spirit; **~alarm** m fire
alarm; **f~fest** adj fireproof; **~gefahr** f
danger of fire; **f~gefährlich** adj
inflammable; **~leiter** f fire escape ladder;
~löscher (-s, -) m fire extinguisher;
~melder (-s, -) m fire alarm; **f~n** vt, vi
(auch fig) to fire; **~stein** m flint; **~treppe** f
fire escape; **~wehr** (-, -en) f fire brigade;
~wehrauto nt fire engine; **~wehrmann**
m fireman; **~werk** nt fireworks pl; **~zeug**
nt (cigarette) lighter

Fichte ['fɪçtə] f spruce, pine

Fieber ['fiːbər] (-s, -) nt fever, temperature;
f~haft adj feverish; **~thermometer** nt
thermometer; **fiebrig** adj (Erkältung)
feverish

fiel etc [fiːl] vb siehe **fallen**

fies [fiːs] (umg) adj nasty

Figur [fi'guːr] (-, -en) f figure; (Schachfigur)
chessman, chess piece

Filet [fi'leː] (-s, -s) nt (KOCH) fillet

Filiale [fili'aːlə] f (COMM) branch

Film [fɪlm] (-(e)s, -e) m film; **~aufnahme** f
shooting; **f~en** vt, vi to film; **~kamera** f
cine camera

Filter ['fɪltər] (-s, -) m filter; **f~n** vt to filter;
~papier nt filter paper; **~zigarette** f
tipped cigarette

Filz [fɪlts] (-es, -e) m felt; **f~en** vt (umg) to
frisk ♦ vi (Wolle) to mat; **~stift** m felt-tip
pen

Finale [fi'naːlə] (-s, -(s)) nt finale; (SPORT)
final(s)

Finanz [fi'nants] f finance; **~amt** nt Inland
Revenue office; **~beamte(r)** m revenue

office, **f~iell** [-tsi'ɛl] adj financial; **f~ieren**
[-'tsiːrən] vt to finance; **f~kräftig** adj
financially strong; **~minister** m Chancellor
of the Exchequer (BRIT), Minister of Finance

Find- ['fɪnt] zW: **f~en** (unreg) vt to find;
(meinen) to think ♦ vr to be (found); (sich
fassen) to compose o.s.; **ich f~e nichts
dabei, wenn ...** I don't see what's wrong if
...; **das wird sich f~en** things will work
out; **~er** (-s, -) m finder; **~erlohn** m
reward (for sb who finds sth); **f~ig** adj
resourceful

fing etc [fɪŋ] vb siehe **fangen**

Finger ['fɪŋər] (-s, -) m finger; **~abdruck** m
fingerprint; **~nagel** m fingernail; **~spitze** f
fingertip

fingiert adj made-up, fictitious

Fink [fɪŋk] (-en, -en) m finch

Finn- [fɪn] zW: **~e** (-n, -n) m Finn; **~in** f
Finn; **f~isch** adj Finnish; **~land** nt Finland

finster ['fɪnstər] adj dark, gloomy;
(verdächtig) dubious; (verdrossen) grim;
(Gedanke) dark; **F~nis** (-) f darkness, gloom

Firma ['fɪrma] (-, -men) f firm

Firmen- ['fɪrmən] zW: **~inhaber** m owner
of firm; **~schild** nt (shop) sign; **~wagen**
m company car; **~zeichen** nt trademark

Fisch [fɪʃ] (-(e)s, -e) m fish; **~e** pl (ASTROL)
Pisces sg; **f~en** vt, vi to fish; **~er** (-s, -) m
fisherman; **~erei** f fishing, fishery; **~fang**
m fishing; **~geschäft** nt fishmonger's
(shop); **~gräte** f fishbone; **~stäbchen**
[-stɛːpçən] nt fish finger (BRIT), fish stick (US)

fit [fɪt] adj fit; **F~ness** ▲ (-, -) f (physical)
fitness

fix [fɪks] adj fixed; (Person) alert, smart; **~ und
fertig** finished; (erschöpft) done in;
F~er(in) m(f) (umg) junkie; **F~erstube** f
(umg) junkies centre; **~ieren** [fɪ'ksiːrən] vt
to fix; (anstarren) to stare at

flach [flax] adj flat; (Gefäß) shallow

Fläche ['flɛçə] f area; (Oberfläche) surface

Flachland nt lowland

flackern ['flakərn] vi to flare, to flicker

Flagge ['flagə] f flag; **f~n** vi to fly a flag

flämisch ['flɛːmɪʃ] adj (LING) Flemish

Flamme ['flamə] f flame

Flandern ['flandərn] nt Flanders

Flanke ['flaŋkə] f flank; (SPORT: Seite) wing

Flasche ['flaʃə] f bottle; (umg: Versager) wash-out

Flaschen- zW:**~bier** nt bottled beer; **~öffner** m bottle opener;**~zug** m pulley

flatterhaft adj flighty, fickle

flattern ['flatərn] vi to flutter

flau [flau] adj weak, listless; (Nachfrage) slack; **jdm ist ~** sb feels queasy

Flaum [flaum] (-(e)s) m (Feder) down; (Haare) fluff

flauschig ['flauʃɪç] adj fluffy

Flaute ['flautə] f calm; (COMM) recession

Flechte ['flɛçtə] f plait; (MED) dry scab; (BOT) lichen;**f~n** (unreg) vt to plait; (Kranz) to twine

Fleck [flɛk] (-(e)s, -e) m spot; (Schmutzfleck) stain; (Stofffleck) patch; (Makel) blemish; **nicht vom ~ kommen** (auch fig) not to get any further; **vom ~ weg** straight away

Flecken (-s, -) m = Fleck;**f~los** adj spotless;**~mittel** nt stain remover; **~wasser** nt stain remover

Fledermaus ['fle:dərmaus] f bat

Flegel ['fle:gəl] (-s, -) m (Mensch) lout; **f~haft** adj loutish, unmannerly;**~jahre** pl adolescence sg

flehen ['fle:ən] vi to implore;**~tlich** adj imploring

Fleisch [flaɪʃ] (-(e)s) nt flesh; (Essen) meat; **~brühe** f beef tea, meat stock;**~er** (-s, -) m butcher;**~erei** f butcher's (shop);**f~ig** adj fleshy;**f~los** adj meatless, vegetarian

Fleiß [flaɪs] (-es) m diligence, industry;**f~ig** adj diligent, industrious

fletschen ['flɛtʃən] vt (Zähne) to show

flexibel [flɛ'ksi:bəl] adj flexible

Flicken ['flɪkən] (-s, -) m patch;**f~** vt to mend

Flieder ['fli:dər] (-s, -) m lilac

Fliege ['fli:gə] f fly; (Kleidung) bow tie;**f~n** (unreg) vt, vi to fly; **auf jdn/etw f~n** (umg) to be mad about sb/sth;**~npilz** m toadstool;**~r** (-s, -) m flier, airman

fliehen ['fli:ən] (unreg) vi to flee

Fliese ['fli:zə] f tile

Fließ- ['fli:s] zW:**~band** nt production od assembly line;**f~en** (unreg) vi to flow; **f~end** adj flowing; (Rede, Deutsch) fluent; (Übergänge) smooth

flimmern ['flɪmərn] vi to glimmer

flink [flɪŋk] adj nimble, lively

Flinte ['flɪntə] f rifle; shotgun

Flitterwochen pl honeymoon sg

flitzen ['flɪtsən] vi to flit

Flocke ['flɔkə] f flake

flog etc [flo:k] vb siehe **fliegen**

Floh [flo:] (-(e)s, ⸚e) m flea;**~markt** m flea market

florieren [flo'ri:rən] vi to flourish

Floskel ['flɔskəl] (-, -n) f set phrase

Floß [flɔs] (-es, ⸚e) nt raft, float

floss ▲ etc vb siehe **fließen**

Flosse ['flɔsə] f fin

Flöte ['flø:tə] f flute; (Blockflöte) recorder

flott [flɔt] adj lively; (elegant) smart; (NAUT) afloat;**F~e** f fleet, navy

Fluch [flu:x] (-(e)s, ⸚e) m curse;**f~en** vi to curse, to swear

Flucht [fluxt] (-, -en) f flight; (Fensterflucht) row; (Zimmerflucht) suite;**f~artig** adj hasty

flücht- ['flʏçt] zW:**~en** vi, vr to flee, to escape;**~ig** adj fugitive; (vergänglich) transitory; (oberflächlich) superficial; (eilig) fleeting;**F~igkeitsfehler** m careless slip; **F~ling** m fugitive, refugee

Flug [flu:k] (-(e)s, ⸚e) m flight;**~blatt** nt pamphlet

Flügel ['fly:gəl] (-s, -) m wing; (MUS) grand piano

Fluggast m airline passenger

Flug- zW:**~gesellschaft** f airline (company);**~hafen** m airport;**~lärm** m aircraft noise;**~linie** f airline;**~plan** m flight schedule;**~platz** m airport; (klein) airfield;**~reise** f flight;**~schein** m (Ticket) plane ticket; (Pilotenschein) pilot's licence; **~steig** [-staɪk] (-(e)s, -e) m gate; **~verbindung** f air connection;**~verkehr** m air traffic;**~zeug** nt (aero)plane, airplane (US);**~zeugentführung** f hijacking of a plane;**~zeughalle** f hangar;**~zeugträger**

m aircraft carrier

Flunder ['flʊndər] (-, -n) *f* flounder

flunkern ['flʊŋkərn] *vi* to fib, to tell stories

Fluor ['fluːər] (-s) *nt* fluorine

Flur [fluːr] (-(e)s, -e) *m* hall; (*Treppenflur*) staircase

Fluss ▲ [flʊs] (-es, ⸚e) *m* river; (*Fließen*) flow

flüssig ['flʏsɪç] *adj* liquid; ~ **machen** (*Geld*) to make available; **F~keit** *f* liquid; (*Zustand*) liquidity

flüstern ['flʏstərn] *vt, vi* to whisper

Flut [fluːt] (-, -en) *f* (*auch fig*) flood; (*Gezeiten*) high tide; **f~en** *vi* to flood; **~licht** *nt* floodlight

Fohlen ['foːlən] (-s, -) *nt* foal

Föhn¹ [føːn] (-(e)s, -e) *m* (*warmer Fallwind*) föhn

Föhn² (-(e)s, -e) ▲ (*Haartrockner*) hair-dryer; **f~en ▲** *vt* to (blow) dry; **~frisur ▲** *f* blow-dry hairstyle

Folge ['fɔlgə] *f* series, sequence; (*Fortsetzung*) instalment; (*Auswirkung*) result; **in rascher ~** in quick succession; **etw zur ~ haben** to result in sth; **~n haben** to have consequences; **einer Sache** *dat* **~ leisten** to comply with sth; **f~n** *vi* +*dat* to follow; (*gehorchen*) to obey; **jdm f~n können** (*fig*) to follow *od* understand sb; **f~nd** *adj* following; **f~ndermaßen** *adv* as follows, in the following way; **f~rn** *vt*: **f~rn (aus)** to conclude (from); **~rung** *f* conclusion

folglich ['fɔlklɪç] *adv* consequently

folgsam ['fɔlkzaːm] *adj* obedient

Folie ['foːliə] *f* foil

Folklore ['fɔlkloːar] *f* folklore

Folter ['fɔltər] (-, -n) *f* torture; (*Gerät*) rack; **f~n** *vt* to torture

Fön [føːn] (-(e)s, -e) ® *m* hair dryer

Fondue [fõdyː] (-s, -s *od* -, -s) *nt od f* (*KOCH*) fondue

fönen △ *vt siehe* **föhnen**

Fönfrisur △ *f siehe* **Föhnfrisur**

Fontäne [fɔnˈtɛːnə] *f* fountain

Förder- [ˈfœrdər] *zW:* **~band** *nt* conveyor belt; **~korb** *m* pit cage; **f~lich** *adj* beneficial

fordern ['fɔrdərn] *vt* to demand

fördern ['fœrdərn] *vt* to promote; (*unterstützen*) to help; (*Kohle*) to extract

Forderung ['fɔrdərʊŋ] *f* demand

Förderung ['fœrdərʊŋ] *f* promotion; help; extraction

Forelle [foˈrɛlə] *f* trout

Form [fɔrm] (-, -en) *f* shape; (*Gestaltung*) form; (*Gussform*) mould; (*Backform*) baking tin; **in ~ sein** to be in good form *od* shape; **in ~ von** in the shape of

Formali'tät *f* formality

Format [fɔrˈmaːt] (-(e)s, -e) *nt* format; (*fig*) distinction

formbar *adj* malleable

Formblatt *nt* form

Formel (-, -n) *f* formula

formell [fɔrˈmɛl] *adj* formal

formen *vt* to form, to shape

Formfehler *m* faux pas, gaffe; (*JUR*) irregularity

formieren [fɔrˈmiːrən] *vt* to form ♦ *vr* to form up

förmlich ['fœrmlɪç] *adj* formal; (*umg*) real; **F~keit** *f* formality

formlos *adj* shapeless; (*Benehmen etc*) informal

Formular [fɔrmuˈlaːr] (-s, -e) *nt* form

formulieren [fɔrmuˈliːrən] *vt* to formulat

forsch [fɔrʃ] *adj* energetic, vigorous

forsch- *zW:* **~en** *vi:* **~en (nach)** to searc (for); (*wissenschaftlich*) to (do) research; **~end** *adj* searching; **F~er** (-s, -) *m* research scientist; (*Naturforscher*) explore **F~ung** *f* research

Forst [fɔrst] (-(e)s, -e) *m* forest

Förster ['fœrstər] (-s, -) *m* forester; (*für W* gamekeeper

fort [fɔrt] *adv* away; (*verschwunden*) gone, (*vorwärts*) on; **und so ~** and so on; **in einem ~** on and on; **~bestehen** (*unreg* to survive; **~bewegen** *vt, vr* to move away; **~bilden** *vr* to continue one's education; **~bleiben** (*unreg*) *vi* to stay away; **F~dauer** *f* continuance; **~fahre** (*unreg*) *vi* to depart; (*~setzen*) to go on, continue; **~führen** *vt* to continue, to c on; **~gehen** (*unreg*) *vi* to go away;

~**geschritten** adj advanced; ~**pflanzen** vr to reproduce; **F~pflanzung** f reproduction

fort- zW: ~**schaffen** vt to remove; ~**schreiten** (unreg) vi to advance

Fortschritt ['fɔrtʃrɪt] m advance; ~**e machen** to make progress; **f~lich** adj progressive

fort- zW: ~**setzen** vt to continue; **F~setzung** f continuation; (folgender Teil) instalment; **F~setzung folgt** to be continued; ~**während** adj incessant, continual

Foto ['fo:to] (-s, -s) nt photo(graph); ~**apparat** m camera; ~'**graf** m photographer; ~**gra'fie** f photography; (Bild) photograph; **f~gra'fieren** vt to photograph ♦ vi to take photographs; ~**kopie** f photocopy

Fr. abk (= Frau) Mrs, Ms

Fracht [fraxt] (-, -en) f freight; (NAUT) cargo; (Preis) carriage; ~ **zahlt Empfänger** (COMM) carriage forward; ~**er** (-s, -) m freighter, cargo boat; ~**gut** nt freight

Frack [frak] (-(e)s, ⸚e) m tails pl

Frage ['fra:gə] (-, -n) f question; **jdm eine ~ stellen** to ask sb a question, to put a question to sb; siehe **infrage**; ~**bogen** m questionnaire; **f~n** vt, vi to ask; ~**zeichen** nt question mark

fraglich adj questionable, doubtful

fraglos adv unquestionably

Fragment [fra'gment] nt fragment

fragwürdig ['fra:kvyrdɪç] adj questionable, dubious

Fraktion [fraktsi'o:n] f parliamentary party

frankieren [fraŋ'ki:rən] vt to stamp, to frank

franko ['fraŋko] adv post-paid; carriage paid

Frankreich ['fraŋkraiç] (-s) nt France

Franzose [fran'tso:zə] m Frenchman; **Französin** [fran'tsø:zɪn] f Frenchwoman; **französisch** adj French

fraß etc [fras] vb siehe **fressen**

Fratze ['fratsə] f grimace

Frau [frau] (-, -en) f woman; (Ehefrau) wife; (Anrede) Mrs, Ms; ~ **Doktor** Doctor

Frauen- zW: ~**arzt** m gynaecologist; ~**bewegung** f feminist movement; ~**haus**

nt women's refuge; ~**zimmer** nt female, broad (US)

Fräulein ['frɔylain] nt young lady; (Anrede) Miss, Ms

fraulich ['fraulɪç] adj womanly

frech [freç] adj cheeky, impudent; **F~heit** f cheek, impudence

frei [frai] adj free; (Stelle, Sitzplatz) free, vacant; (Mitarbeiter) freelance; (unbekleidet) bare; **von etw ~ sein** to be free of sth; **im F~en** in the open air; ~ **sprechen** to talk without notes; ~**es Haus** (COMM) carriage paid; ~**er Wettbewerb** (COMM) fair/open competition; **F~bad** nt open-air swimming pool; ~**bekommen** (unreg) vt: **einen Tag ~bekommen** to get a day off; ~**beruflich** adj self-employed; ~**gebig** adj generous; ~**halten** (unreg) vt to keep free; ~**händig** adv (fahren) with no hands; **F~heit** f freedom; ~**heitlich** adj liberal; **F~heitsstrafe** f prison sentence; **F~karte** f free ticket; ~**lassen** (unreg) vt to (set) free; ~**legen** vt to expose; ~**lich** adv certainly, admittedly; **ja ~lich** yes of course; **F~lichtbühne** f open-air theatre; **F~lichtmuseum** nt open-air museum; ~**machen** vt (Post) to frank ♦ vr to arrange to be free; (entkleiden) to undress; **Tage ~machen** to take days off; ~**nehmen** ▲ (unreg) vt: **sich** dat **einen Tag ~nehmen** to take a day off; ~**sprechen** (unreg) vt: ~**sprechen (von)** to acquit (of); **F~spruch** m acquittal; ~**stehen** (unreg) vi: **es steht dir ~, das zu tun** you're free to do that; (leer stehen: Wohnung, Haus) to lie/stand empty; ~**stellen** vt: **jdm etw ~stellen** to leave sth (up) to sb; **F~stoß** m free kick

Freitag m Friday; **f~s** adv on Fridays

frei- zW: ~**willig** adj voluntary; **F~zeit** f spare od free time; **F~zeitpark** m amusement park; **F~zeitzentrum** nt leisure centre; ~**zügig** adj liberal, broad-minded; (mit Geld) generous

fremd [fremt] adj (unvertraut) strange; (ausländisch) foreign; (nicht eigen) someone else's; **etw ist jdm ~** sth is foreign to sb; ~**artig** adj strange; **F~enführer** ['fremdən-]

m (tourist) guide; **F~enverkehr** m tourism; **F~enverkehrsamt** nt tourist board; **F~enzimmer** nt guest room; **F~körper** m foreign body; **~ländisch** adj foreign; **F~sprache** f foreign language; **F~wort** nt foreign word

Frequenz ['fre:kvɛnts] f (RADIO) frequency

fressen ['frɛsən] (unreg) vt, vi to eat

Freude ['frɔydə] f joy, delight

freudig adj joyful, happy

freuen ['frɔyən] vt unpers to make happy od pleased ♦ vr to be glad od happy; **freut mich!** pleased to meet you; **sich auf etw** akk ~ to look forward to sth; **sich über etw** akk ~ to be pleased about sth

Freund ['frɔynt] (-(e)s, -e) m friend; boyfriend; **~in** [-dɪn] f friend; girlfriend; **f~lich** adj kind, friendly; **f~licherweise** adv kindly; **~lichkeit** f friendliness, kindness; **~schaft** f friendship; **f~schaftlich** adj friendly

Frieden ['fri:dən] (-s, -) m peace; **im ~** in peacetime

Friedens- zW: **~schluss** ▲ m peace agreement; **~vertrag** m peace treaty; **~zeit** f peacetime

fried- ['fri:t] zW: **~fertig** adj peaceable; **F~hof** m cemetery; **~lich** adj peaceful

frieren ['fri:rən] (unreg) vt, vi to freeze; **ich friere, es friert mich** I'm freezing, I'm cold

Frikadelle [frika'dɛlə] f rissole

Frikassee [frika'se:] (-s, -s) nt (KOCH) fricassee

frisch [frɪʃ] adj fresh; (lebhaft) lively; **~ gestrichen!** wet paint; **sich ~ machen** to freshen (o.s.) up; **F~e** f freshness; liveliness; **F~haltefolie** f cling film

Friseur [fri'zø:r] m hairdresser

Friseuse [fri'zø:zə] f hairdresser

frisieren [fri'zi:rən] vt to do (one's) hair; (fig: Abrechnung) to fiddle, to doctor ♦ vr to do one's hair

Frisiersalon m hairdressing salon

frisst ▲ [frɪst] vb siehe **fressen**

Frist [frɪst] (-, -en) f period; (Termin) deadline; **f~gerecht** adj within the stipulated time od period; **f~los** adj

(Entlassung) instant

Frisur [fri'zu:r] f hairdo, hairstyle

frivol [fri'vo:l] adj frivolous

froh [fro:] adj happy, cheerful; **ich bin ~, dass ...** I'm glad that ...

fröhlich ['frø:lɪç] adj merry, happy; **F~keit** f merriness, gaiety

fromm [frɔm] adj pious, good; (Wunsch) idle; **Frömmigkeit** ['frœmɪçkaɪt] f piety

Fronleichnam [fro:n'laɪçna:m] (-(e)s) m Corpus Christi

Front [frɔnt] (-, -en) f front; **f~al** [frɔn'ta:l] adj frontal

fror etc [fro:r] vb siehe **frieren**

Frosch [frɔʃ] (-(e)s, ⁼e) m frog; (Feuerwerk) squib; **~mann** m frogman; **~schenkel** m frog's leg

Frost [frɔst] (-(e)s, ⁼e) m frost; **~beule** f chilblain

frösteln ['frœstəln] vi to shiver

frostig adj frosty

Frostschutzmittel nt antifreeze

Frottier(hand)tuch [frɔ'ti:r(hant)tu:x] nt towel

Frucht [frʊxt] (-, ⁼e) f (auch fig) fruit; (Getreide) corn; **f~bar** adj fruitful, fertile; **~barkeit** f fertility; **f~ig** adj (Geschmack) fruity; **f~los** adj fruitless; **~saft** m fruit juic

früh [fry:] adj, adv early; **heute ~** this morning; **F~aufsteher** (-s, -) m early rise **F~e** f early morning; **~er** adj earlier; (ehemalig) former ♦ adv formerly; **~er war das anders** that used to be different; **~estens** adv at the earliest; **F~jahr** nt, **F~ling** m spring; **~reif** adj precocious; **F~stück** nt breakfast; **~stücken** vi to (have) breakfast; **F~stücksbüfett** nt breakfast buffet; **~zeitig** adj early; (pej) untimely

frustrieren [frʊs'tri:rən] vt to frustrate

Fuchs [fʊks] (-es, ⁼e) m fox; **f~en** (umg) v to rile, to annoy; **f~teufelswild** adj hopping mad

Fuge ['fu:gə] f joint; (MUS) fugue

fügen ['fy:gən] vt to place, to join ♦ vr: sic **~ (in** +dat) to be obedient (to); (anpasser to adapt oneself (to) ♦ vr unpers to happe

fühl- zW: **~bar** adj perceptible, noticeable; **~en** vt, vi, vr to feel; **F~er** (-s, -) m feeler

fuhr etc [fu:r] vb siehe **fahren**

führen ['fy:rən] vt to lead; (Geschäft) to run; (Name) to bear; (Buch) to keep ♦ vi to lead ♦ vr to behave

Führer ['fy:rər] (-s, -) m leader; (Fremdenführer) guide; **~schein** m driving licence

Führung ['fy:rʊŋ] f leadership; (eines Unternehmens) management; (MIL) command; (Benehmen) conduct; (Museumsführung) conducted tour; **~zeugnis** nt certificate of good conduct

Fülle ['fʏlə] f wealth, abundance; **f~n** vt to fill; (KOCH) to stuff ♦ vr to fill (up)

Füll- zW: **~er** (-s, -) m fountain pen; **~federhalter** m fountain pen; **~ung** f filling; (Holzfüllung) panel

fummeln ['fʊməln] (umg) vi to fumble

Fund [fʊnt] (-(e)s, -e) m find

Fundament [fʊnda'mɛnt] nt foundation; **fundamen'tal** adj fundamental

Fund- zW: **~büro** nt lost property office, lost and found (US); **~grube** f (fig) treasure trove

fundiert [fʊn'di:rt] adj sound

fünf [fʏnf] num five; **~hundert** num five hundred; **~te(r, s)** adj fifth; **F~tel** (-s, -) nt fifth; **~zehn** num fifteen; **~zig** num fifty

Funk [fʊŋk] (-s) m radio, wireless; **F~e** (-ns, -n) m (auch fig) spark; **F~eln** vi to sparkle; **~en** (-s, -) m (auch fig) spark; **f~en** vi (durch Funk) to signal, to radio; (umg: richtig funktionieren) to work ♦ vt (Funken sprühen) to shower with sparks; **~er** (-s, -) m radio operator; **~gerät** nt radio set; **~rufempfänger** m pager, paging device; **~streife** f police radio patrol; **~telefon** nt cellphone

Funktion [fʊŋktsi'o:n] f function; **f~ieren** [-'ni:rən] vi to work, to function

für [fy:r] präp +akk for; **was ~** what kind od sort of; **das F~ und Wider** the pros and cons pl; **Schritt ~ Schritt** step by step

Furche ['fʊrçə] f furrow

Furcht [fʊrçt] (-) f fear; **f~bar** adj terrible, frightful

fürchten ['fʏrçtən] vt to be afraid of, to fear ♦ vr: **sich ~ (vor** +dat) to be afraid (of)

fürchterlich adj awful

furchtlos adj fearless

füreinander [fy:r|aɪ'nandər] adv for each other

Furnier [fʊr'ni:r] (-s, -e) nt veneer

fürs [fy:rs] = **für das**

Fürsorge ['fy:rzɔrgə] f care; (Sozialfürsorge) welfare; **~r(in)** (-s, -) m(f) welfare worker; **~unterstützung** f social security, welfare benefit (US); **fürsorglich** adj attentive, caring

Fürsprache f recommendation; (um Gnade) intercession

Fürsprecher m advocate

Fürst [fʏrst] (-en, -en) m prince; **~entum** nt principality; **~in** f princess; **f~lich** adj princely

Fuß [fu:s] (-es, ⸚e) m foot; (von Glas, Säule etc) base; (von Möbel) leg; **zu ~** on foot; **~ball** m football; **~ballplatz** m football pitch; **~ballspiel** nt football match; **~ballspieler** m footballer; **~boden** m floor; **~bremse** f (AUT) footbrake; **~ende** nt foot; **~gänger(in)** (-s, -) m(f) pedestrian; **~gängerzone** f pedestrian precinct; **~nagel** m toenail; **~note** f footnote; **~spur** f footprint; **~tritt** m kick; (Spur) footstep; **~weg** m footpath

Futter ['fʊtər] (-s, -) nt fodder, feed; (Stoff) lining; **~al** [-'ra:l] (-s, -e) nt case

füttern ['fʏtərn] vt to feed; (Kleidung) to line

Futur [fu'tu:r] (-s, -e) nt future

G, g

g abk = **Gramm**

gab etc [ga:p] vb siehe **geben**

Gabe ['ga:bə] f gift

Gabel ['ga:bəl] (-, -n) f fork; **~ung** f fork

gackern ['gakərn] vi to cackle

gaffen ['gafən] vi to gape

Gage ['ga:ʒə] f fee; salary

gähnen ['gɛ:nən] vi to yawn

Galerie [galə'ri:] *f* gallery

Galgen ['galgən] **(-s, -)** *m* gallows *sg*; **~frist** *f* respite; **~humor** *m* macabre humour

Galle ['galə] *f* gall; (*Organ*) gall bladder; **~nstein** *m* gallstone

gammeln ['gaməln] (*umg*) *vi* to bum around; **Gammler(in) (-s, -)** (*pej*) *m(f)* layabout, loafer (*inf*)

Gämse ▲ ['gɛmzə] *f* chamois

Gang [gaŋ] **(-(e)s, ¬e)** *m* walk; (*Botengang*) errand; (*~art*) gait; (*Abschnitt eines Vorgangs*) operation; (*Essensgang, Ablauf*) course; (*Flur etc*) corridor; (*Durchgang*) passage; (*TECH*) gear; **in ~ bringen** to start up; (*fig*) to get off the ground; **in ~ sein** to be in operation; (*fig*) to be under way

gang *adj*: **~ und gäbe** usual, normal

gängig ['gɛŋɪç] *adj* common, current; (*Ware*) in demand, selling well

Gangschaltung *f* gears *pl*

Ganove [ga'no:və] **(-n, -n)** (*umg*) *m* crook

Gans [gans] **(-, ¬e)** *f* goose

Gänse- ['gɛnzə] *zW*: **~blümchen** *nt* daisy; **~füßchen** (*umg*) *pl* (*Anführungszeichen*) inverted commas; **~haut** *f* goose pimples *pl*; **~marsch** *m*: **im ~marsch** in single file; **~rich (-s, -e)** *m* gander

ganz [gants] *adj* whole; (*vollständig*) complete ♦ *adv* quite; (*völlig*) completely; **~ Europa** all Europe; **sein ~es Geld** all his money; **~ und gar nicht** not at all; **es sieht ~ so aus** it really looks like it; **aufs G~e gehen** to go for the lot

gänzlich ['gɛntslɪç] *adj* complete, entire ♦ *adv* completely, entirely

Ganztagsschule *f* all-day school

gar [ga:r] *adj* cooked, done ♦ *adv* quite; **~ nicht/nichts/keiner** not/nothing/nobody at all; **~ nicht schlecht** not bad at all

Garage [ga'ra:ʒə] *f* garage

Garantie [garan'ti:] *f* guarantee; **g~ren** *vt* to guarantee; **er kommt g~rt** he's guaranteed to come

Garbe ['garbə] *f* sheaf

Garde ['gardə] *f* guard

Garderobe [gardə'ro:bə] *f* wardrobe; (*Abgabe*) cloakroom; **~nfrau** *f* cloakroom

attendant

Gardine [gar'di:nə] *f* curtain

garen ['ga:rən] *vt, vi* to cook

gären ['gɛ:rən] (*unreg*) *vi* to ferment

Garn [garn] **(-(e)s, -e)** *nt* thread; yarn (*auch fig*)

Garnele [gar'ne:lə] *f* shrimp, prawn

garnieren [gar'ni:rən] *vt* to decorate; (*Speisen, fig*) to garnish

Garnison [garni'zo:n] **(-, -en)** *f* garrison

Garnitur [garni'tu:r] *f* (*Satz*) set; (*Unterwäsche*) set of (matching) underwear; **erste ~** (*fig*) top rank; **zweite ~** (*fig*) second rate

garstig ['garstɪç] *adj* nasty, horrid

Garten ['gartən] **(-s, ¬)** *m* garden; **~arbeit** *f* gardening; **~gerät** *nt* gardening tool; **~lokal** *nt* beer garden; **~tür** *f* garden gate

Gärtner(in) ['gɛrtnər(ɪn)] **(-s, -)** *m(f)* gardener; **~ei** [-'raɪ] *f* nursery; (*Gemüsegärtnerei*) market garden (*BRIT*), truck farm (*US*)

Gärung ['gɛ:rʊŋ] *f* fermentation

Gas [ga:s] **(-es, -e)** *nt* gas; **~ geben** (*AUT*) to accelerate, to step on the gas; **~hahn** *m* gas tap; **~herd** *m* gas cooker; **~kocher** *m* gas cooker; **~leitung** *f* gas pipe; **~pedal** *nt* accelerator, gas pedal

Gasse ['gasə] *f* lane, alley

Gast [gast] **(-es, ¬e)** *m* guest; (*in Lokal*) patron; **bei jdm zu ~ sein** to be sb's guest; **~arbeiter(in)** *m(f)* foreign worker

Gäste- ['gɛstə] *zW*: **~buch** *nt* visitors' book, guest book; **~zimmer** *nt* guest *od* spare room

Gast- *zW*: **g~freundlich** *adj* hospitable; **~geber (-s, -)** *m* host; **~geberin** *f* hostess; **~haus** *nt* hotel, inn; **~hof** *m* hotel, inn; **g~ieren** [-'ti:rən] *vi* (*THEAT*) to (appear as a) guest; **g~lich** *adj* hospitable; **~rolle** *f* guest role; **~spiel** *nt* (*THEAT*) guest performance; **~stätte** *f* restaurant; pub; **~wirt** *m* innkeeper; **~wirtschaft** *f* hotel, inn

Gaswerk *nt* gasworks *sg*

Gaszähler *m* gas meter

Gatte ['gatə] **(-n, -n)** *m* husband, spouse

Gattin *f* wife, spouse

Gattung ['gatʊŋ] f genus; kind
Gaudi ['gaʊdi] (*umg: SÜDD, ÖSTERR*) nt od f fun
Gaul [gaʊl] (-(e)s, Gäule) m horse; nag
Gaumen ['gaʊmən] (-s, -) m palate
Gauner ['gaʊnər] (-s, -) m rogue; ~**ei** [-'raɪ] f swindle
geb. abk = **geboren**
Gebäck [gə'bɛk] (-(e)s, -e) nt pastry
gebacken [gə'bakən] adj baked; (*gebraten*) fried
Gebälk [gə'bɛlk] (-(e)s) nt timberwork
Gebärde [gə'bɛːrdə] f gesture; g~**n** vr to behave
gebären [gə'bɛːrən] (*unreg*) vt to give birth to, to bear
Gebärmutter f uterus, womb
Gebäude [gə'bɔʏdə] (-s, -) nt building; ~**komplex** m (building) complex
geben ['geːbən] (*unreg*) vt, vi to give; (*Karten*) to deal ♦ vb unpers: **es gibt** there is/are; there will be ♦ vr (*sich verhalten*) to behave, to act; (*aufhören*) to abate; **jdm etw** ~ to give sb sth od sth to sb; **was gibts?** what's up?; **was gibt es im Kino?** what's on at the cinema?; **sich geschlagen** ~ to admit defeat; **das wird sich schon** ~ that'll soon sort itself out
Gebet [gə'beːt] (-(e)s, -e) nt prayer
gebeten [gə'beːtən] vb siehe **bitten**
Gebiet [gə'biːt] (-(e)s, -e) nt area; (*Hoheitsgebiet*) territory; (*fig*) field; g~**en** (*unreg*) vt to command, to demand; g~**erisch** adj imperious
Gebilde [gə'bɪldə] (-s, -) nt object
gebildet [gə'bɪldət] adj cultured, educated
Gebirge [gə'bɪrgə] (-s, -) nt mountain chain
Gebiss [gə'bɪs] (-es, -e) nt teeth pl; (*künstlich*) dentures pl
gebissen vb siehe **beißen**
geblieben [gə'bliːbən] vb siehe **bleiben**
geblümt [gə'blyːmt] adj (*Kleid, Stoff, Tapete*) floral
geboren [gə'boːrən] adj born; (*Frau*) née
geborgen [gə'bɔrgən] adj secure, safe
Gebot [gə'boːt] (-(e)s, -e) nt command; (*REL*) commandment; (*bei Auktion*) bid

geboten [gə'boːtən] vb siehe **bieten**
Gebr. abk (= *Gebrüder*) Bros.
gebracht [gə'braxt] vb siehe **bringen**
gebraten [gə'braːtən] adj fried
Gebrauch [gə'braʊx] (-(e)s, Gebräuche) m use; (*Sitte*) custom; g~**en** vt to use
gebräuchlich [gə'brɔʏçlɪç] adj usual, customary
Gebrauchs- zW: ~**anweisung** f directions pl for use; g~**fertig** adj ready for use; ~**gegenstand** m commodity
gebraucht [gə'braʊxt] adj used; G~**wagen** m secondhand od used car
gebrechlich [gə'brɛçlɪç] adj frail
Gebrüder [gə'bryːdər] pl brothers
Gebrüll [gə'brʏl] (-(e)s) nt roaring
Gebühr [gə'byːr] (-, -en) f charge, fee; **nach** ~ fittingly; **über** ~ unduly; g~**en** vi: **jdm** g~**en** to be sb's due od due to sb ♦ vr to be fitting; g~**end** adj fitting, appropriate ♦ adv fittingly, appropriately
Gebühren- zW: ~**einheit** f (*TEL*) unit; ~**erlass** ▲ m remission of fees; ~**ermäßigung** f reduction of fees; g~**frei** adj free of charge; ~**ordnung** f scale of charges, tariff; g~**pflichtig** adj subject to a charge
gebunden [gə'bʊndən] vb siehe **binden**
Geburt [gə'buːrt] (-, -en) f birth
Geburtenkontrolle f birth control
Geburtenregelung f birth control
gebürtig [gə'bʏrtɪç] adj born in, native of; ~**e Schweizerin** native of Switzerland
Geburts- zW: ~**anzeige** f birth notice; ~**datum** nt date of birth; ~**jahr** nt year of birth; ~**ort** m birthplace; ~**tag** m birthday; ~**urkunde** f birth certificate
Gebüsch [gə'bʏʃ] (-(e)s, -e) nt bushes pl
gedacht [gə'daxt] vb siehe **denken**
Gedächtnis [gə'dɛçtnɪs] (-ses, -se) nt memory; ~**feier** f commemoration
Gedanke [gə'daŋkə] (-ns, -n) m thought; **sich über etw** akk ~**n machen** to think about sth
Gedanken- zW: ~**austausch** m exchange of ideas; g~**los** adj thoughtless; ~**strich** m dash; ~**übertragung** f thought

Spelling Reform: ▲ *new spelling* △ *old spelling (to be phased out)*

transference, telepathy

Gedeck [gə'dɛk] **(-(e)s, -e)** *nt* cover(ing); (*Speisenfolge*) menu; **ein ~ auflegen** to lay a place

gedeihen [gə'daɪən] (*unreg*) *vi* to thrive, to prosper

Gedenken *nt*: **zum ~ an jdn** in memory of sb

gedenken [gə'dɛŋkən] (*unreg*) *vi* +*gen* (*beabsichtigen*) to intend; (*sich erinnern*) to remember

Gedenk- *zW*: **~feier** *f* commemoration; **~minute** *f* minute's silence; **~stätte** *f* memorial; **~tag** *m* remembrance day

Gedicht [gə'dɪçt] **(-(e)s, -e)** *nt* poem

gediegen [gə'di:gən] *adj* (good) quality; (*Mensch*) reliable, honest

Gedränge [gə'drɛŋə] **(-s)** *nt* crush, crowd

gedrängt *adj* compressed; **~ voll** packed

gedrückt [gə'drʏkt] *adj* (*deprimiert*) low, depressed

gedrungen [gə'drʊŋən] *adj* thickset, stocky

Geduld [gə'dʊlt] *f* patience; **g~en** [gə'dʊldən] *vr* to be patient; **g~ig** *adj* patient, forbearing; **~sprobe** *f* trial of (one's) patience

gedurft [gə'dʊrft] *vb siehe* **dürfen**

geehrt [gə'|e:rt] *adj*: **Sehr ~e Frau X!** Dear Mrs X

geeignet [gə'|aɪgnət] *adj* suitable

Gefahr [gə'fa:r] **(-, -en)** *f* danger; **~ laufen, etw zu tun** to run the risk of doing sth; **auf eigene ~** at one's own risk

gefährden [gə'fɛːrdən] *vt* to endanger

Gefahren- *zW*: **~quelle** *f* source of danger; **~zulage** *f* danger money

gefährlich [gə'fɛːrlɪç] *adj* dangerous

Gefährte [gə'fɛːrtə] **(-n, -n)** *m* companion; (*Lebenspartner*) partner

Gefährtin [gə'fɛːrtɪn] *f* (female) companion; (*Lebenspartner*) (female) partner

Gefälle [gə'fɛlə] **(-s, -)** *nt* gradient, incline

Gefallen[1] [gə'falən] **(-s, -)** *m* favour

Gefallen[2] [gə'falən] **(-s)** *nt* pleasure; **an etw** *dat* **~finden** to derive pleasure from sth

gefallen *pp von* **fallen ♦** *vi*: **jdm ~** to please

sb; **er/es gefällt mir** I like him/it; **das gefällt mir an ihm** that's one thing I like about him; **sich** *dat* **etw ~ lassen** to put up with sth

gefällig [gə'fɛlɪç] *adj* (*hilfsbereit*) obliging; (*erfreulich*) pleasant; **G~keit** *f* favour; helpfulness; **etw aus G~keit tun** to do sth out of the goodness of one's heart

gefangen [gə'faŋən] *adj* captured; (*fig*) captivated; **~ halten** to keep prisoner; **~ nehmen** to take prisoner; **G~e(r)** *f(m)* prisoner, captive; **G~nahme** *f* capture; **G~schaft** *f* captivity

Gefängnis [gə'fɛŋnɪs] **(-ses, -se)** *nt* prison; **~strafe** *f* prison sentence; **~wärter** *m* prison warder; **~zelle** *f* prison cell

Gefäß [gə'fɛːs] **(-es, -e)** *nt* vessel; (*auch* ANAT) container

gefasst ▲ [gə'fast] *adj* composed, calm; **auf etw** *akk* **~ sein** to be prepared *od* ready for sth

Gefecht [gə'fɛçt] **(-(e)s, -e)** *nt* fight; (MIL) engagement

Gefieder [gə'fi:dər] **(-s, -)** *nt* plumage, feathers *pl*

gefleckt [gə'flɛkt] *adj* spotted, mottled

geflogen [gə'flo:gən] *vb siehe* **fliegen**

geflossen [gə'flɔsən] *vb siehe* **fließen**

Geflügel [gə'fly:gəl] **(-s)** *nt* poultry

Gefolgschaft [gə'fɔlkʃaft] *f* following

gefragt [ge'fra:kt] *adj* in demand

gefräßig [gə'frɛːsɪç] *adj* voracious

Gefreite(r) [gə'fraɪtə(r)] *m* lance corporal; (NAUT) able seaman; (AVIAT) aircraftman

Gefrierbeutel *m* freezer bag

gefrieren [gə'fri:rən] (*unreg*) *vi* to freeze

Gefrier- *zW*: **~fach** *nt* icebox; **~fleisch** *nt* frozen meat; **g~getrocknet** [-gətrɔknət] *adj* freeze-dried; **~punkt** *m* freezing point; **~schutzmittel** *nt* antifreeze; **~truhe** *f* deep-freeze

gefroren [gə'fro:rən] *vb siehe* **frieren**

Gefühl [gə'fy:l] **(-(e)s, -e)** *nt* feeling; **etw im ~ haben** to have a feel for sth; **g~los** *adj* unfeeling

gefühls- *zW*: **~betont** *adj* emotional; **G~duselei** [-du:zə'laɪ] *f* over-sentimentality;

~**mäßig** adj instinctive
gefüllt [gə'fʏlt] adj (KOCH) stuffed
gefunden [gə'fʊndən] vb siehe **finden**
gegangen [gə'gaŋən] vb siehe **gehen**
gegeben [gə'ge:bən] vb siehe **geben** ♦ adj
given; **zu ~er Zeit** in good time
gegebenenfalls [gə'ge:bənənfals] adv if
need be

gegen ['ge:gən] präp +akk **1** against; **nichts
gegen jdn haben** to have nothing against
sb; **X gegen Y** (SPORT, JUR) X versus Y; **ein
Mittel gegen Schnupfen** something for
colds
2 (in Richtung auf) towards; **gegen Osten**
to(wards) the east; **gegen Abend** towards
evening; **gegen einen Baum fahren** to
drive into a tree
3 (ungefähr) round about; **gegen 3 Uhr**
around 3 o'clock
4 (gegenüber) towards; (ungefähr) around;
gerecht gegen alle fair to all
5 (im Austausch für) for; **gegen bar** for cash;
gegen Quittung against a receipt
6 (verglichen mit) compared with

Gegenangriff m counter-attack
Gegenbeweis m counter-evidence
Gegend ['ge:gənt] (-, -en) f area, district
Gegen- zW: ~**ei'nander** adv against one
another; ~**fahrbahn** f oncoming
carriageway; ~**frage** f counter-question;
~**gewicht** nt counterbalance; ~**gift** nt
antidote; ~**leistung** f service in return;
~**maßnahme** f countermeasure; ~**mittel**
nt antidote, cure; ~**satz** m contrast; ~**sätze
überbrücken** to overcome differences;
g~sätzlich adj contrary, opposite;
(widersprüchlich) contradictory; **g~seitig** adj
mutual, reciprocal; **sich g~seitig helfen** to
help each other; ~**spieler** m opponent;
~**sprechanlage** f (two-way) intercom;
~**stand** m object; ~**stimme** f vote against;
~**stoß** m counterblow; ~**stück** nt
counterpart; ~**teil** nt opposite; **im ~teil** on
the contrary; **g~teilig** adj opposite,

contrary
gegenüber [ge:gən'|y:bər] präp +dat
opposite; (zu) to(wards); (angesichts) in the
face of ♦ adv opposite; **G~** (-s, -) nt person
opposite; ~**liegen** (unreg) vr to face each
other; ~**stehen** (unreg) vr to be opposed
(to each other); ~**stellen** vt to confront;
(fig) to contrast; **G~stellung** f
confrontation; (fig) contrast; ~**treten**
(unreg) vi +dat to face
Gegen- zW: ~**verkehr** m oncoming traffic;
~**vorschlag** m counterproposal; ~**wart** f
present; **g~wärtig** adj present ♦ adv at
present; **das ist mir nicht mehr g~wärtig**
that has slipped my mind; ~**wert** m
equivalent; ~**wind** m headwind;
g~zeichnen vt, vi to countersign
gegessen [gə'gesən] vb siehe **essen**
Gegner ['ge:gnər] (-s, -) m opponent;
g~isch adj opposing
gegr. abk (= gegründet) est.
gegrillt [gə'grɪlt] adj grilled
Gehackte(s) [ge'hakta(s)] nt mince(d meat)
Gehalt¹ [gə'halt] (-(e)s, -e) m content
Gehalt² [gə'halt] (-(e)s, ⸗er) nt salary
Gehalts- zW: ~**empfänger** m salary
earner; ~**erhöhung** f salary increase;
~**zulage** f salary increment
gehaltvoll [gə'haltfɔl] adj (nahrhaft)
nutritious
gehässig [gə'hɛsɪç] adj spiteful, nasty
Gehäuse [gə'hɔyzə] (-s, -) nt case; casing;
(von Apfel etc) core
Gehege [gə'he:gə] (-s, -) nt reserve; (im Zoo)
enclosure
geheim [gə'haɪm] adj secret; ~ **halten** to
keep secret; **G~dienst** m secret service,
intelligence service; **G~nis** (-ses, -se) nt
secret; mystery; ~**nisvoll** adj mysterious;
G~polizei f secret police
gehemmt [gə'hɛmt] adj inhibited, self-
conscious
gehen ['ge:ən] (unreg) vt, vi to go; (zu Fuß ~)
to walk ♦ vb unpers: **wie geht es (dir)?**
how are you od things?; ~ **nach** (Fenster) to
face; **mir/ihm geht es gut** I'm/he's (doing)
fine; **geht das?** is that possible?; **gehts**

noch? can you manage?; **es geht** not too bad, O.K.; **das geht nicht** that's not on; **es geht um etw** it has to do with sth, it's about sth; **sich ~ lassen** (*unbeherrscht sein*) to lose control (of o.s.); **jdn ~ lassen** to let/leave sb alone; **lass mich ~!** leave me alone!

geheuer [gə'hɔyər] *adj:* **nicht ~** eerie; (*fragwürdig*) dubious

Gehilfe [gə'hɪlfə] (**-n, -n**) *m* assistant; **Gehilfin** *f* assistant

Gehirn [gə'hɪrn] (**-(e)s, -e**) *nt* brain; **~erschütterung** *f* concussion; **~hautentzündung** *f* meningitis

gehoben [gə'ho:bən] *pp von* **heben** ♦ *adj* (*Position*) elevated; high

geholfen [gə'hɔlfən] *vb siehe* **helfen**

Gehör [gə'hø:r] (**-(e)s**) *nt* hearing; **musikalisches ~** ear; **~ finden** to gain a hearing; **jdm ~ schenken** to give sb a hearing

gehorchen [gə'hɔrçən] *vi +dat* to obey

gehören [gə'hø:rən] *vi* to belong ♦ *vr unpers* to be right od proper

gehörig *adj* proper; **~ zu** od +dat belonging to; part of

gehörlos *adj* deaf

gehorsam [gə'ho:rza:m] *adj* obedient; **G~ (-s)** *m* obedience

Geh- ['ge:-] *zW:* **~steig** *m* pavement, sidewalk (*US*); **~weg** *m* pavement, sidewalk (*US*)

Geier ['gaɪər] (**-s, -**) *m* vulture

Geige ['gaɪgə] *f* violin; **~r (-s, -)** *m* violinist

geil [gaɪl] *adj* randy (*BRIT*), horny (*US*)

Geisel ['gaɪzəl] (**-, -n**) *f* hostage

Geist [gaɪst] (**-(e)s, -er**) *m* spirit; (*Gespenst*) ghost; (*Verstand*) mind

geisterhaft *adj* ghostly

Geistes- *zW:* **g~abwesend** *adj* absent-minded; **~blitz** *m* brainwave; **~gegenwart** *f* presence of mind; **g~krank** *adj* mentally ill; **~kranke(r)** *f(m)* mentally ill person; **~krankheit** *f* mental illness; **~wissenschaften** *pl* the arts; **~zustand** *m* state of mind

geist- *zW:* **~ig** *adj* intellectual; mental;

(*Getränke*) alcoholic; **~ig behindert** mentally handicapped; **~lich** *adj* spiritual; religious; clerical; **G~liche(r)** *m* clergyman; **G~lichkeit** *f* clergy; **~los** *adj* uninspired, dull; **~reich** *adj* clever; witty; **~voll** *adj* intellectual; (*weise*) wise

Geiz [gaɪts] (**-es**) *m* miserliness, meanness; **g~en** *vi* to be miserly; **~hals** *m* miser; **g~ig** *adj* miserly, mean; **~kragen** *m* miser

gekannt [gə'kant] *vb siehe* **kennen**

gekonnt [gə'kɔnt] *adj* skilful ♦ *vb siehe* **können**

gekünstelt [gə'kynstəlt] *adj* artificial, affected

Gel [ge:l] (**-s, -e**) *nt* gel

Gelächter [gə'lɛçtər] (**-s, -**) *nt* laughter

geladen [gə'la:dən] *adj* loaded; (*ELEK*) live; (*fig*) furious

gelähmt [gə'lɛ:mt] *adj* paralysed

Gelände [gə'lɛndə] (**-s, -**) *nt* land, terrain; (*von Fabrik, Sportgelände*) grounds *pl*; (*Bau~*) site; **~lauf** *m* cross-country race

Geländer [gə'lɛndər] (**-s, -**) *nt* railing; (*Treppengeländer*) banister(s)

gelangen [gə'laŋən] *vi:* **~ (an** +*akk* od **zu)** to reach; (*erwerben*) to attain; **in jds Besitz** *akk* ~ to come into sb's possession

gelangweilt [gə'laŋvaɪlt] *adj* bored

gelassen [gə'lasən] *adj* calm, composed; **G~heit** *f* calmness, composure

Gelatine [ʒela'ti:nə] *f* gelatine

geläufig [gə'lɔyfɪç] *adj* (*üblich*) common; **das ist mir nicht ~** I'm not familiar with that

gelaunt [gə'launt] *adj:* **schlecht/gut ~** in a bad/good mood; **wie ist er ~?** what sort of mood is he in?

gelb [gɛlp] *adj* yellow; (*Ampellicht*) amber; **~lich** *adj* yellowish; **G~sucht** *f* jaundice

Geld [gɛlt] (**-(e)s, -er**) *nt* money; **etw zu ~ machen** to sell sth off; **~anlage** *f* investment; **~automat** *m* cash dispenser; **~beutel** *m* purse; **~börse** *f* purse; **~geber (-s, -)** *m* financial backer; **g~gierig** *adj* avaricious; **~schein** *m* banknote; **~schrank** *m* safe, strongbox; **~strafe** *f* fine; **~stück** *nt* coin; **~wechsel**

m exchange (of money)

Gelee [ʒeˈleː] (**-s, -s**) *nt od m* jelly

gelegen [gəˈleːgən] *adj* situated; (*passend*) convenient, opportune ♦ *vb siehe* **liegen**; **etw kommt jdm** ~ sth is convenient for sb

Gelegenheit [gəˈleːgənhaɪt] *f* opportunity; (*Anlaß*) occasion; **bei jeder** ~ at every opportunity; **~sarbeit** *f* casual work; **~skauf** *m* bargain

gelegentlich [gəˈleːgəntlɪç] *adj* occasional ♦ *adv* occasionally; (*bei Gelegenheit*) some time (or other) ♦ *präp +gen* on the occasion of

gelehrt [gəˈleːrt] *adj* learned; **G~e(r)** *f(m)* scholar; **G~heit** *f* scholarliness

Geleise [gəˈlaɪzə] (**-s, -**) *nt* = **Gleis**

Geleit [gəˈlaɪt] (**-(e)s, -e**) *nt* escort; **g~en** *vt* to escort

Gelenk [gəˈlɛŋk] (**-(e)s, -e**) *nt* joint; **g~ig** supple

gelernt [gəˈlɛrnt] *adj* skilled

Geliebte(r) [gəˈliːptə(r)] *f(m)* sweetheart, beloved

geliehen [gəˈliːən] *vb siehe* **leihen**

gelind(e) [gəˈlɪnd(ə)] *adj* mild, light; (*fig: Wut*) fierce; **~gesagt** to put it mildly

gelingen [gəˈlɪŋən] (*unreg*) *vi* to succeed; **es ist mir gelungen, etw zu tun** I succeeded in doing sth

geloben [gəˈloːbən] *vt, vi* to vow, to swear

gelten [ˈgɛltən] (*unreg*) *vt* (*wert sein*) to be worth ♦ *vi* (*gültig sein*) to be valid; (*erlaubt sein*) to be allowed ♦ *vb unpers*: **es gilt, etw zu tun** it is necessary to do sth; **jdm viel/wenig** ~ to mean a lot/not to mean much to sb; **was gilt die Wette?** what do you bet?; **etw** ~ **lassen** to accept sth; **als** *od* **für etw** ~ to be considered to be sth; **jdm** *od* **für jdn** ~ (*betreffen*) to apply to *od* for sb; **~d** *adj* prevailing; **etw ~d machen** to assert sth; **sich ~d machen** to make itself/o.s. felt

Geltung [ˈgɛltʊŋ] *f*: ~ **haben** to have validity; **sich/etw** *dat* ~ **verschaffen** to establish one's position/the position of sth; **etw zur** ~ **bringen** to show sth to its best advantage; **zur** ~ **kommen** to be seen/

heard *etc* to its best advantage

Geltungsbedürfnis *nt* desire for admiration

Gelübde [gəˈlʏpdə] (**-s, -**) *nt* vow

gelungen [gəˈlʊŋən] *adj* successful

gemächlich [gəˈmɛːçlɪç] *adj* leisurely

Gemahl [gəˈmaːl] (**-(e)s, -e**) *m* husband; ~**in** *f* wife

Gemälde [gəˈmɛːldə] (**-s, -**) *nt* picture, painting

gemäß [gəˈmɛːs] *präp +dat* in accordance with ♦ *adj (+dat)* appropriate (to)

gemäßigt *adj* moderate; (*Klima*) temperate

gemein [gəˈmaɪn] *adj* common; (*niederträchtig*) mean; **etw** ~ **haben (mit)** to have sth in common (with)

Gemeinde [gəˈmaɪndə] *f* district, community; (*Pfarrgemeinde*) parish; (*Kirchengemeinde*) congregation; ~**steuer** *f* local rates *pl*; ~**verwaltung** *f* local administration; ~**wahl** *f* local election

Gemein- *zW*: **g~gefährlich** *adj* dangerous to the public; ~**heit** *f* commonness; mean thing to do/to say; **g~nützig** *adj* charitable; **g~nütziger Verein** non-profit-making organization; **g~sam** *adj* joint, common (*AUCH MATH*) ♦ *adv* together, jointly; **g~same Sache mit jdm machen** to be in cahoots with sb; **etw g~sam haben** to have sth in common; ~**samkeit** *f* community, having in common; ~**schaft** *f* community; **in ~schaft mit** jointly *od* together with; **g~schaftlich** *adj* = **gemeinsam**; ~**schaftsarbeit** *f* teamwork; team effort; ~**sinn** *m* public spirit

Gemenge [gəˈmɛŋə] (**-s, -**) *nt* mixture; (*Handgemenge*) scuffle

gemessen [gəˈmɛsən] *adj* measured

Gemetzel [gəˈmɛtsəl] (**-s, -**) *nt* slaughter, carnage, butchery

Gemisch [gəˈmɪʃ] (**-es, -e**) *nt* mixture; **g~t** *adj* mixed

gemocht [gəˈmɔxt] *vb siehe* **mögen**

Gemse △ [ˈgɛmzə] *f siehe* **Gämse**

Gemurmel [gəˈmʊrməl] (**-s**) *nt* murmur(ing)

Gemüse [gəˈmyːzə] (**-s, -**) *nt* vegetables *pl*; ~**garten** *m* vegetable garden; ~**händler** *m* greengrocer

gemusst ▲ [gə'must] *vb siehe* **müssen**

gemustert [gə'mustərt] *adj* patterned

Gemüt [gə'my:t] (-(e)s, -er) *nt* disposition, nature; person; **sich** *dat* **etw zu ~e führen** (*umg*) to indulge in sth; **die ~er erregen** to arouse strong feelings; **g~lich** *adj* comfortable, cosy; (*Person*) good-natured; **~lichkeit** *f* comfortableness, cosiness; amiability

Gemüts- *zW:* **~mensch** *m* sentimental person; **~ruhe** *f* composure; **~zustand** *m* state of mind

Gen [ge:n] (-s, -e) *nt* gene

genannt [gə'nant] *vb siehe* **nennen**

genau [gə'nau] *adj* exact, precise ♦ *adv* exactly, precisely; **etw ~ nehmen** to take sth seriously; **G~igkeit** *f* exactness, accuracy; **~so** *adv* just the same; **~so gut** just as good

genehm [gə'ne:m] *adj* agreeable, acceptable; **~igen** *vt* to approve, to authorize; **sich** *dat* **etw ~igen** to indulge in sth; **G~igung** *f* approval, authorization; (*Schriftstück*) permit

General [gene'ra:l] (-s, -e *od* ∸e) *m* general; **~direktor** *m* director general; **~konsulat** *nt* consulate general; **~probe** *f* dress rehearsal; **~streik** *m* general strike; **g~überholen** *vt* to overhaul thoroughly; **~versammlung** *f* general meeting

Generation [generatsi'o:n] *f* generation

Generator [gene'ra:tɔr] *m* generator, dynamo

generell [gena'rɛl] *adj* general

genesen [ge'ne:zən] (*unreg*) *vi* to convalesce, to recover; **Genesung** *f* recovery, convalescence

genetisch [ge'ne:tiʃ] *adj* genetic

Genf ['gɛnf] *nt* Geneva; **der ~er See** Lake Geneva

genial [geni'a:l] *adj* brilliant

Genick [gə'nik] (-(e)s, -e) *nt* (back of the) neck

Genie [ʒe'ni:] (-s, -s) *nt* genius

genieren [ʒe'ni:rən] *vt* to bother ♦ *vr* to feel

awkward *od* self-conscious

genieß- *zW:* **~bar** *adj* edible; drinkable; **~en** [gə'ni:sən] (*unreg*) *vt* to enjoy; to eat; to drink; **G~er** (-s, -) *m* epicure; pleasure lover; **~erisch** *adj* appreciative ♦ *adv* with relish

genmanipuliert ['ge:nmanipuli:rt] *adj* genetically modified

genommen [gə'nɔmən] *vb siehe* **nehmen**

Genosse [gə'nɔsə] (-n, -n) *m* (*bes POL*) comrade, companion; **~nschaft** *f* cooperative (association)

Genossin *f* (*bes POL*) comrade, companion

Gentechnik ['gɛntɛçnɪk] *f* genetic engineering

genug [gə'nu:k] *adv* enough

Genüge [gə'ny:gə] *f:* **jdm/etw ~ tun** *od* **leisten** to satisfy sb/sth; **g~n** *vi* (+*dat*) to be enough (for); **g~nd** *adj* sufficient

genügsam [gə'ny:kza:m] *adj* modest, easily satisfied; **G~keit** *f* moderation

Genugtuung [gə'nu:ktu:ʊŋ] *f* satisfaction

Genuss ▲ [gə'nʊs] (-es, ∸e) *m* pleasure; (*Zusichnehmen*) consumption; **in den ~ von etw kommen** to receive the benefit of sth

genüsslich ▲ [gə'nʏslɪç] *adv* with relish

Genussmittel ▲ *pl* (semi-)luxury items

geöffnet [gə'œfnət] *adj* open

Geograf ▲ [geo'gra:f] (-en, -en) *m* geographer; **Geogra'fie** ▲ *f* geography; **g~isch** *adj* geographical

Geologe [geo'lo:gə] (-n, -n) *m* geologist; **Geolo'gie** *f* geology

Geometrie [geome'tri:] *f* geometry

Gepäck [gə'pɛk] (-(e)s) *nt* luggage, baggage; **~abfertigung** *f* luggage office; **~annahme** *f* luggage office; **~aufbewahrung** *f* left-luggage office (*BRIT*), baggage check (*US*); **~aufgabe** *f* luggage office; **~ausgabe** *f* luggage office; (*AVIAT*) luggage reclaim; **~netz** *nt* luggage rack; **~träger** *m* porter; (*Fahrrad*) carrier; **~versicherung** *f* luggage insurance; **~wagen** *m* luggage van (*BRIT*), baggage car (*US*)

gepflegt [gə'pfle:kt] *adj* well-groomed; (*Park etc*) well looked after

Gerade [gə'ra:də] f straight line; **g~'aus** adv straight ahead; **g~he'raus** adv straight out, bluntly; **g~stehen** (unreg) vi: **für jdn/etw g~stehen** to be answerable for sb('s actions)/sth; **g~wegs** adv direct, straight; **g~zu** adv (beinahe) virtually, almost

---
SCHLÜSSELWORT
---

gerade [gə'ra:də] adj straight; (aufrecht) upright; **eine gerade Zahl** an even number

♦ adv 1 (genau) just, exactly; (speziell) especially; **gerade deshalb** that's just od exactly why; **das ist es ja gerade!** that's just it!; **gerade du** you especially; **warum gerade ich?** why me (of all people)?; **jetzt gerade nicht!** not now!; **gerade neben** right next to

2 (eben, soeben) just; **er wollte gerade aufstehen** he was just about to get up; **gerade erst** only just; **gerade noch** (only) just

---

gerannt [gə'rant] vb siehe **rennen**
Gerät [gə'rɛ:t] (-(e)s, -e) nt device; (Werkzeug) tool; (SPORT) apparatus; (Zubehör) equipment no pl
geraten [gə'ra:tən] (unreg) vi (gedeihen) to thrive; (gelingen): **(jdm) ~** to turn out well (for sb); **gut/schlecht ~** to turn out well/ badly; **an jdn ~** to come across sb; **in etw** akk **~** to get into sth; **nach jdm ~** to take after sb
Geratewohl [gəra:tə'vo:l] nt: **aufs ~** on the off chance; (bei Wahl) at random
geräuchert [gə'rɔyçərt] adj smoked
geräumig [gə'rɔymiç] adj roomy
Geräusch [gə'rɔyʃ] (-(e)s, -e) nt sound, noise; **g~los** adj silent
gerben ['gɛrbən] vt to tan
gerecht [gə'rɛçt] adj just, fair; **jdm/etw ~ werden** to do justice to sb/sth; **G~igkeit** f justice, fairness
Gerede [gə're:də] (-s) nt talk, gossip
geregelt [gə're:gəlt] adj (Arbeit) steady, regular; (Mahlzeiten) regular, set

gereizt [gə'raɪtst] adj irritable; **G~heit** f irritation
Gericht [gə'rɪçt] (-(e)s, -e) nt court; (Essen) dish; **mit jdm ins ~ gehen** (fig) to judge sb harshly; **das Jüngste ~** the Last Judgement; **g~lich** adj judicial, legal ♦ adv judicially, legally
Gerichts- zW: **~barkeit** f jurisdiction; **~hof** m court (of law); **~kosten** pl (legal) costs; **~medizin** f forensic medicine; **~saal** m courtroom; **~verfahren** nt legal proceedings pl; **~verhandlung** f trial; **~vollzieher** m bailiff
gerieben [gə'ri:bən] adj grated; (umg: schlau) smart, wily ♦ vb siehe **reiben**
gering [gə'rɪŋ] adj slight, small; (niedrig) low; (Zeit) short; **~fügig** adj slight, trivial; **~schätzig** adj disparaging
geringste(r, s) adj slightest, least; **~nfalls** adv at the very least
gerinnen [gə'rɪnən] (unreg) vi to congeal; (Blut) to clot; (Milch) to curdle
Gerippe [gə'rɪpə] (-s, -) nt skeleton
gerissen [gə'rɪsən] adj wily, smart
geritten [gə'rɪtən] vb siehe **reiten**
gern(e) ['gɛrn(ə)] adv willingly, gladly; **~ haben, ~ mögen** to like; **etwas ~ tun** to like doing something; **ich möchte ~ ...** I'd like ...; **ja, ~** yes, please; yes, I'd like to; **~ geschehen** it's a pleasure
gerochen [gə'rɔxən] vb siehe **riechen**
Geröll [gə'rœl] (-(e)s, -e) nt scree
Gerste ['gɛrstə] f barley; **~nkorn** nt (im Auge) stye
Geruch [gə'rʊx] (-(e)s, ⁺e) m smell, odour; **g~los** adj odourless
Gerücht [gə'rʏçt] (-(e)s, -e) nt rumour
geruhsam [gə'ru:za:m] adj (Leben) peaceful; (Nacht, Zeit) peaceful, restful; (langsam: Arbeitsweise, Spaziergang) leisurely
Gerümpel [gə'rʏmpəl] (-s) nt junk
Gerüst [gə'rʏst] (-(e)s, -e) nt (Baugerüst) scaffold(ing); frame
gesalzen [gə'zaltsən] pp von **salzen** ♦ adj (umg: Preis, Rechnung) steep
gesamt [gə'zamt] adj whole, entire; (Kosten) total; (Werke) complete; **im G~en** all in all;

~deutsch *adj* all-German; **G~eindruck** *m* general impression; **G~heit** *f* totality, whole; **G~schule** *f* ≈ comprehensive school

---

> **Gesamtschule**
>
> *i* The Gesamtschule *is a comprehensive school for pupils of different abilities. Traditionally pupils go to either a* Gymnasium, Realschule *or* Hauptschule, *depending on ability. The* Gesamtschule *seeks to avoid the elitism of many* Gymnasien. *However, these schools are still very controversial, with many parents still preferring the traditional education system.*

---

gesandt [gəˈzant] *vb siehe* **senden**
Gesandte(r) [gəˈzantə(r)] *m* envoy
Gesandtschaft [gəˈzantʃaft] *f* legation
Gesang [gəˈzaŋ] **(-(e)s, -̈e)** *m* song; (*Singen*) singing; **~buch** *nt* (*REL*) hymn book
Gesäß [gəˈzɛːs] **(-es, -e)** *nt* seat, bottom
Geschäft [gəˈʃɛft] **(-(e)s, -e)** *nt* business; (*Laden*) shop; (*~sabschluß*) deal; **g~ig** *adj* active, busy; (*pej*) officious; **g~lich** *adj* commercial ♦ *adv* on business
Geschäfts- *zW:* **~bedingungen** *pl* terms pl of business; **~bericht** *m* financial report; **~frau** *f* businesswoman; **~führer** *m* manager; (*Klub*) secretary; **~geheimnis** *nt* trade secret; **~jahr** *nt* financial year; **~lage** *f* business conditions pl; **~mann** *m* businessman; **g~mäßig** *adj* businesslike; **~partner** *m* business partner; **~reise** *f* business trip; **~schluss** ▲ *m* closing time; **~stelle** *f* office, place of business; **g~tüchtig** *adj* business-minded; **~viertel** *nt* business quarter; shopping centre; **~wagen** *m* company car; **~zeit** *f* business hours pl
geschehen [gəˈʃeːən] (*unreg*) *vi* to happen; **es war um ihn ~** that was the end of him
gescheit [gəˈʃait] *adj* clever
Geschenk [gəˈʃɛŋk] **(-(e)s, -e)** *nt* present, gift
Geschichte [gəˈʃɪçtə] *f* story; (*Sache*) affair;

(*Historie*) history
geschichtlich *adj* historical
Geschick [gəˈʃɪk] **(-(e)s, -e)** *nt* aptitude; (*Schicksal*) fate; **~lichkeit** *f* skill, dexterity; **g~t** *adj* skilful
geschieden [gəˈʃiːdən] *adj* divorced
geschienen [gəˈʃiːnən] *vb siehe* **scheinen**
Geschirr [gəˈʃɪr] **(-(e)s, -e)** *nt* crockery; pots and pans pl; (*Pferdegeschirr*) harness; **~spülmaschine** *f* dishwasher; **~spülmittel** *nt* washing-up liquid; **~tuch** *nt* dish cloth
Geschlecht [gəˈʃlɛçt] **(-(e)s, -er)** *nt* sex; (*GRAM*) gender; (*Gattung*) race; family; **g~lich** *adj* sexual
Geschlechts- *zW:* **~krankheit** *f* venereal disease; **~teil** *nt* genitals pl; **~verkehr** *m* sexual intercourse
geschlossen [gəˈʃlɔsən] *adj* shut ♦ *vb siehe* **schließen**
Geschmack [gəˈʃmak] **(-(e)s, -̈e)** *m* taste; **nach jds ~** to sb's taste; **~ finden an etw** *dat* to (come to) like sth; **g~los** *adj* tasteless; (*fig*) in bad taste; **~ssinn** *m* sense of taste; **g~voll** *adj* tasteful
geschmeidig [gəˈʃmaidɪç] *adj* supple; (*formbar*) malleable
Geschnetzelte(s) [gəˈʃnɛtsəltə(s)] *nt* (*KOCH*) strips of meat stewed to produce a thick sauce
geschnitten [gəˈʃnɪtən] *vb siehe* **schneiden**
Geschöpf [gəˈʃœpf] **(-(e)s, -e)** *nt* creature
Geschoss ▲ [gəˈʃɔs] **(-es, -e)** *nt* (*MIL*) projectile, missile; (*Stockwerk*) floor
geschossen [gəˈʃɔsən] *vb siehe* **schießen**
geschraubt [gəˈʃraupt] *adj* stilted, artificial
Geschrei [gəˈʃrai] **(-s)** *nt* cries pl, shouting; (*fig: Aufheben*) noise, fuss
geschrieben [gəˈʃriːbən] *vb siehe* **schreiben**
Geschütz [gəˈʃʏts] **(-es, -e)** *nt* gun, cannon; **ein schweres ~ auffahren** (*fig*) to bring out the big guns
geschützt *adj* protected
Geschw. *abk siehe* **Geschwister**
Geschwätz [gəˈʃvɛts] **(-es)** *nt* chatter, gossip; **g~ig** *adj* talkative
geschweige [gəˈʃvaigə] *adv:* **~ (denn)** let

alone, not to mention
geschwind [gə'ʃvɪnt] *adj* quick, swift;
G~igkeit [-dɪçkaɪt] *f* speed, velocity;
G~igkeitsbeschränkung *f* speed limit;
G~igkeitsüberschreitung *f* exceeding
the speed limit
Geschwister [gə'ʃvɪstər] *pl* brothers and
sisters
geschwommen [gə'ʃvɔmən] *vb siehe*
schwimmen
Geschworene(r) [gə'ʃvoːrənə(r)] *f(m)* juror;
~n *pl* jury
Geschwulst [gə'ʃvʊlst] **(-, ~e)** *f* swelling;
growth, tumour
geschwungen [gə'ʃvʊŋən] *pp von*
schwingen ♦ *adj* curved, arched
Geschwür [gə'ʃvyːr] **(-(e)s, -e)** *nt* ulcer
Gesell- [gə'zɛl] *zW:* **~e (-n, -n)** *m* fellow;
(*Handwerkgeselle*) journeyman; **g~ig** *adj*
sociable; **~igkeit** *f* sociability; **~schaft** *f*
society; (*Begleitung, COMM*) company;
(*Abendgesellschaft etc*) party; **g~schaftlich**
adj social; **~schaftsordnung** *f* social
structure; **~schaftsschicht** *f* social
stratum
gesessen [gə'zɛsən] *vb siehe* **sitzen**
Gesetz [gə'zɛts] **(-es, -e)** *nt* law; **~buch** *nt*
statute book; **~entwurf** *m* (draft) bill;
~gebung *f* legislation; **g~lich** *adj* legal,
lawful; **g~licher Feiertag** statutory holiday;
g~los *adj* lawless; **g~mäßig** *adj* lawful;
g~t *adj* (*Mensch*) sedate; **g~widrig** *adj*
illegal, unlawful
Gesicht [gə'zɪçt] **(-(e)s, -er)** *nt* face; **das
zweite ~** second sight; **das ist mir nie zu
~ gekommen** I've never laid eyes on that
Gesichts- *zW:* **~ausdruck** *m* (facial)
expression; **~creme** *f* face cream; **~farbe**
f complexion; **~punkt** *m* point of view;
~wasser *nt* face lotion; **~züge** *pl* features
Gesindel [gə'zɪndəl] **(-s)** *nt* rabble
gesinnt [gə'zɪnt] *adj* disposed, minded
Gesinnung [gə'zɪnʊŋ] *f* disposition; (*Ansicht*)
views *pl*
gesittet [gə'zɪtət] *adj* well-mannered
Gespann [gə'ʃpan] **(-(e)s, -e)** *nt* team;
(*umg*) couple

gespannt *adj* tense, strained; (*begierig*)
eager; **ich bin ~, ob** I wonder if *od*
whether; **auf etw/jdn ~ sein** to look
forward to sth/meeting sb
Gespenst [gə'ʃpɛnst] **(-(e)s, -er)** *nt* ghost,
spectre
gesperrt [gə'ʃpɛrt] *adj* closed off
Gespött [gə'ʃpœt] **(-(e)s)** *nt* mockery; **zum ~
werden** to become a laughing stock
Gespräch [gə'ʃprɛːç] **(-(e)s, -e)** *nt*
conversation; discussion(s); (*Anruf*) call;
g~ig *adj* talkative
gesprochen [gə'ʃprɔxən] *vb siehe* **sprechen**
gesprungen [gə'ʃprʊŋən] *vb siehe* **springen**
Gespür [gə'ʃpyːr] **(-s)** *nt* feeling
Gestalt [gə'ʃtalt] **(-, -en)** *f* form, shape;
(*Person*) figure; **in ~ von** in the form of; **~
annehmen** to take shape; **g~en** *vt* (*formen*)
to shape, to form; (*organisieren*) to arrange,
to organize ♦ *vr:* **sich g~en (zu)** to turn out
(to be); **~ung** *f* formation; organization
gestanden [gə'ʃtandən] *vb siehe* **stehen**
Geständnis [gə'ʃtɛntnɪs] **(-ses, -se)** *nt*
confession
Gestank [gə'ʃtaŋk] **(-(e)s)** *m* stench
gestatten [gə'ʃtatən] *vt* to permit, to allow;
~ Sie? may I?; **sich** *dat* **, etw zu tun** to
take the liberty of doing sth
Geste ['gɛstə] *f* gesture
gestehen [gə'ʃteːən] (*unreg*) *vt* to confess
Gestein [gə'ʃtaɪn] **(-(e)s, -e)** *nt* rock
Gestell [gə'ʃtɛl] **(-(e)s, -e)** *nt* frame; (*Regal*)
rack, stand
gestern ['gɛstərn] *adv* yesterday; **~ Abend/
Morgen** yesterday evening/morning
Gestirn [gə'ʃtɪrn] **(-(e)s, -e)** *nt* star;
(*Sternbild*) constellation
gestohlen [gə'ʃtoːlən] *vb siehe* **stehlen**
gestorben [gə'ʃtɔrbən] *vb siehe* **sterben**
gestört [gə'ʃtøːrt] *adj* disturbed
gestreift [gə'ʃtraɪft] *adj* striped
gestrichen [gə'ʃtrɪçən] *adj* cancelled
gestrig ['gɛstrɪç] *adj* yesterday's
Gestrüpp [gə'ʃtrʏp] **(-(e)s, -e)** *nt*
undergrowth
Gestüt [gə'ʃtyːt] **(-(e)s, -e)** *nt* stud farm
Gesuch [gə'zuːx] **(-(e)s, -e)** *nt* petition;

(*Antrag*) application; **g~t** *adj* (*COMM*) in demand; wanted; (*fig*) contrived

gesund [gə'zʊnt] *adj* healthy; **wieder ~ werden** to get better; **G~heit** *f* health(iness); **G~heit!** bless you!; **~heitlich** *adj* health *attrib*, physical ♦ *adv*: **wie geht es Ihnen ~heitlich?** how's your health?; **~heitsschädlich** *adj* unhealthy; **G~heitswesen** *nt* health service; **G~heitszustand** *m* state of health

gesungen [gə'zʊŋən] *vb siehe* **singen**

getan [gə'ta:n] *vb siehe* **tun**

Getöse [gə'tø:zə] (**-s**) *nt* din, racket

Getränk [gə'trɛŋk] (**-(e)s, -e**) *nt* drink; **~ekarte** *f* wine list

getrauen [gə'trauən] *vr* to dare, to venture

Getreide [gə'traidə] (**-s, -**) *nt* cereals *pl*, grain; **~speicher** *m* granary

getrennt [gə'trɛnt] *adj* separate

Getriebe [gə'tri:bə] (**-s, -**) *nt* (*Leute*) bustle; (*AUT*) gearbox

getrieben *vb siehe* **treiben**

getroffen [gə'trɔfən] *vb siehe* **treffen**

getrost [gə'tro:st] *adv* without any bother

getrunken [gə'trʊŋkən] *vb siehe* **trinken**

Getue [gə'tu:ə] (**-s**) *nt* fuss

geübt [gə'y:pt] *adj* experienced

Gewächs [gə'vɛks] (**-es, -e**) *nt* growth; (*Pflanze*) plant

gewachsen [gə'vaksən] *adj*: **jdm/etw ~ sein** to be sb's equal/equal to sth

Gewächshaus *nt* greenhouse

gewagt [gə'va:kt] *adj* daring, risky

gewählt [gə'vɛ:lt] *adj* (*Sprache*) refined, elegant

Gewähr [gə'vɛ:r] (**-**) *f* guarantee; **keine ~ übernehmen für** to accept no responsibility for; **g~en** *vt* to grant; (*geben*) to provide; **g~leisten** *vt* to guarantee

Gewahrsam [gə'va:rza:m] (**-s, -e**) *m* safekeeping; (*Polizeigewahrsam*) custody

Gewalt [gə'valt] (**-, -en**) *f* power; (*große Kraft*) force; (**~taten**) violence; **mit aller ~** with all one's might; **~anwendung** *f* use of force; **g~ig** *adj* tremendous; (*Irrtum*) huge; **~marsch** *m* forced march; **g~sam** *adj* forcible; **g~tätig** *adj* violent

Gewand [gə'vant] (**-(e)s, ^er**) *nt* gown, robe

gewandt [gə'vant] *adj* deft, skilful; (*erfahren*) experienced; **G~heit** *f* dexterity, skill

gewann *etc* [gə'va:n] *vb siehe* **gewinnen**

Gewässer [gə'vɛsər] (**-s, -**) *nt* waters *pl*

Gewebe [gə've:bə] (**-s, -**) *nt* (*Stoff*) fabric; (*BIOL*) tissue

Gewehr [gə've:r] (**-(e)s, -e**) *nt* gun; rifle; **~lauf** *m* rifle barrel

Geweih [gə'vai] (**-(e)s, -e**) *nt* antlers *pl*

Gewerb- [gə'vɛrb-] *zW*: **~e** (**-s, -**) *nt* trade, occupation; **Handel und ~e** trade and industry; **~eschule** *f* technical school; **~ezweig** *m* line of trade

Gewerkschaft [gə'vɛrkʃaft] *f* trade union; **~ler** (**-s, -**) *m* trade unionist; **~sbund** *m* trade unions federation

gewesen [gə've:zən] *pp von* **sein**

Gewicht [gə'vɪçt] (**-(e)s, -e**) *nt* weight; (*fig*) importance

gewieft [gə'vi:ft] *adj* shrewd, cunning

gewillt [gə'vɪlt] *adj* willing, prepared

Gewimmel [gə'vɪməl] (**-s**) *nt* swarm

Gewinde [gə'vɪndə] (**-s, -**) *nt* (*Kranz*) wreath; (*von Schraube*) thread

Gewinn [gə'vɪn] (**-(e)s, -e**) *m* profit; (*bei Spiel*) winnings *pl*; **~ bringend** profitable; **etw mit ~ verkaufen** to sell sth at a profit; **~- und Verlustrechnung** (*COMM*) profit and loss account; **~beteiligung** *f* profit-sharing; **g~en** (*unreg*) *vt* to win; (*erwerben*) to gain; (*Kohle, Öl*) to extract ♦ *vi* to win; (*profitieren*) to gain; **an etw** *dat* **g~en** to gain (in) sth; **g~end** *adj* (*Lächeln, Aussehen*) winning, charming; **~er(in)** (**-s, -**) *m(f)* winner; **~spanne** *f* profit margin; **~ung** *f* winning; gaining; (*von Kohle etc*) extraction

Gewirr [gə'vɪr] (**-(e)s, -e**) *nt* tangle; (*von Straßen*) maze

gewiss ▲ [gə'vɪs] *adj* certain ♦ *adv* certainly

Gewissen [gə'vɪsən] (**-s, -**) *nt* conscience; **g~haft** *adj* conscientious; **g~los** *adj* unscrupulous

Gewissens- *zW*: **~bisse** *pl* pangs of conscience, qualms; **~frage** *f* matter of conscience; **~konflikt** *m* moral conflict

gewissermaßen [gəvɪsər'ma:sən] *adv* more

or less, in a way

Gewissheit ▲ [gə'vɪshaɪt] f certainty

Gewitter [gə'vɪtər] (-s, -) nt thunderstorm; **g~n** unpers: **es g~t** there's a thunderstorm

gewitzt [gə'vɪtst] adj shrewd, cunning

gewogen [gə'vo:gən] adj (+dat) well-disposed (towards)

gewöhnen [gə'vø:nən] vt: **jdn an etw** akk **~** to accustom sb to sth; (erziehen zu) to teach sb sth ♦ vr: **sich an etw** akk **~** to get used od accustomed to sth

Gewohnheit [gə'vo:nhaɪt] f habit; (Brauch) custom; **aus ~** from habit; **zur ~ werden** to become a habit

Gewohnheits- zW: **~mensch** m creature of habit; **~recht** nt common law

gewöhnlich [gə'vø:nlɪç] adj usual; ordinary; (pej) common; **wie ~** as usual

gewohnt [gə'vo:nt] adj usual; **etw ~ sein** to be used to sth

Gewöhnung f: **~ (an** +akk) getting accustomed (to)

Gewölbe [gə'vœlbə] (-s, -) nt vault

gewollt [gə'vɔlt] adj affected, artificial

gewonnen [gə'vɔnən] vb siehe **gewinnen**

geworden [gə'vɔrdən] vb siehe **werden**

geworfen [gə'vɔrfən] vb siehe **werfen**

Gewühl [gə'vy:l] (-(e)s) nt throng

Gewürz [gə'vyrts] (-es, -e) nt spice, seasoning; **g~t** adj spiced

gewusst ▲ [gə'vʊst] vb siehe **wissen**

Gezeiten [gə'tsaɪtən] pl tides

gezielt [gə'tsi:lt] adj with a particular aim in mind, purposeful; (Kritik) pointed

gezogen [gə'tso:gən] vb siehe **ziehen**

Gezwitscher [gə'tsvɪtʃər] (-s) nt twitter(ing), chirping

gezwungen [gə'tsvʊŋən] adj forced; **~ermaßen** adv of necessity

ggf. abk von **gegebenenfalls**

gibst etc [gi:pst] vb siehe **geben**

Gicht [gɪçt] (-) f gout

Giebel ['gi:bəl] (-s, -) m gable; **~dach** nt gable(d) roof; **~fenster** nt gable window

Gier [gi:r] (-) f greed; **g~ig** adj greedy

gießen ['gi:sən] (unreg) vt to pour; (Blumen)

to water; (Metall) to cast; (Wachs) to mould

Gießkanne f watering can

Gift [gɪft] (-(e)s, -e) nt poison; **g~ig** adj poisonous; (fig: boshaft) venomous; **~müll** m toxic waste; **~stoff** m toxic substance; **~zahn** m fang

ging etc [gɪŋ] vb siehe **gehen**

Gipfel ['gɪpfəl] (-s, -) m summit, peak; (fig: Höhepunkt) height; **g~n** vi to culminate; **~treffen** nt summit (meeting)

Gips [gɪps] (-es, -e) m plaster; (MED) plaster (of Paris); **~abdruck** m plaster cast; **g~en** vt to plaster; **~verband** m plaster (cast)

Giraffe [gi'rafə] f giraffe

Girlande [gɪr'landə] f garland

Giro ['ʒi:ro] (-s, -s) nt giro; **~konto** nt current account

Gitarre [gi'tarə] f guitar

Gitter ['gɪtər] (-s, -) nt grating, bars pl; (für Pflanzen) trellis; (Zaun) railing(s); **~bett** nt cot; **~fenster** nt barred window; **~zaun** m railing(s)

Glanz [glants] (-es) m shine, lustre; (fig) splendour

glänzen ['glɛntsən] vi to shine (also fig), to gleam ♦ vt to polish; **~d** adj shining; (fig) brilliant

Glanz- zW: **~leistung** f brilliant achievement; **g~los** adj dull; **~zeit** f heyday

Glas [gla:s] (-es, ˝er) nt glass; **~er** (-s, -) m glazier; **~faser** f fibreglass; **g~ieren** [gla'zi:rən] vt to glaze; **g~ig** adj glassy; **~scheibe** f pane; **~ur** [gla'zu:r] f glaze; (KOCH) icing

glatt [glat] adj smooth; (rutschig) slippery; (Absage) flat; (Lüge) downright; **Glätte** f smoothness; slipperiness

Glatteis nt (black) ice; **jdn aufs ~ führen** (fig) to take sb for a ride

glätten vt to smooth out

Glatze ['glatsə] f bald head; **eine ~ bekommen** to go bald

Glaube ['glaubə] (-ns, -n) m: **~ (an** +akk) faith (in); belief (in); **g~n** vt, vi to believe; to think; **jdm g~n** to believe sb; **an etw** akk **g~n** to believe in sth; **daran g~n müssen**

(umg) to be for it
glaubhaft ['glaʊbhaft] *adj* credible
gläubig ['glɔʏbɪç] *adj (REL)* devout; *(vertrauensvoll)* trustful; **G~e(r)** *f(m)* believer; **die G~en** the faithful; **G~er** (-s, -) *m* creditor
glaubwürdig ['glaʊbvʏrdɪç] *adj* credible; *(Mensch)* trustworthy; **G~keit** *f* credibility; trustworthiness
gleich [glaɪç] *adj* equal; *(identisch)* (the) same, identical ♦ *adv* equally; *(sofort)* straight away; *(bald)* in a minute; **es ist mir ~** it's all the same to me; **~ bleibend** constant; **~ gesinnt** like-minded; **2 mal 2 ~ 4** 2 times 2 is *od* equals 4; **~ groß** the same size; **~ nach/an** right after/at; **~altrig** *adj* of the same age; **~artig** *adj* similar; **~bedeutend** *adj* synonymous; **G~berechtigung** *f* equal rights *pl*; **~en** *(unreg) vi:* **jdm/etw ~en** to be like sb/sth ♦ *vr* to be alike; **~falls** *adv* likewise; **danke ~falls!** the same to you; **G~förmigkeit** *f* uniformity; **G~gewicht** *nt* equilibrium, balance; **~gültig** *adj* indifferent; *(unbedeutend)* unimportant; **G~gültigkeit** *f* indifference; **G~heit** *f* equality; **~kommen** *(unreg) vi +dat* to be equal to; **~mäßig** *adj* even, equal; **~sam** *adv* as it were; **G~schritt** *m:* **im G~schritt gehen** to walk in step; **~stellen** *vt (rechtlich etc)* to treat as (an) equal; **G~strom** *m (ELEK)* direct current; **~tun** *(unreg) vi:* **es jdm ~tun** to match sb; **G~ung** *f* equation; **~viel** *adv* no matter; **~wertig** *adj (Geld)* of the same value; *(Gegner)* evenly matched; **~zeitig** *adj* simultaneous
Gleis [glaɪs] (-es, -e) *nt* track, rails *pl*; *(Bahnsteig)* platform
gleiten ['glaɪtən] *(unreg) vi* to glide; *(rutschen)* to slide
Gleitzeit *f* flex(i)time
Gletscher ['glɛtʃər] (-s, -) *m* glacier; **~spalte** *f* crevasse
Glied [gliːt] (-(e)s, -er) *nt* member; *(Arm, Bein)* limb; *(von Kette)* link; *(MIL)* rank(s); **g~ern** [-dərn] *vt* to organize, to structure; **~erung** *f* structure, organization

glimmen ['glɪmən] *(unreg) vi* to glow, to gleam
glimpflich ['glɪmpflɪç] *adj* mild, lenient; **~ davonkommen** to get off lightly
glitschig ['glɪtʃɪç] *adj (Fisch, Weg)* slippery
glitzern ['glɪtsərn] *vi* to glitter; to twinkle
global [glo'baːl] *adj* global
Globus ['gloːbʊs] (- *od* -ses, Globen *od* -s *m* globe
Glocke ['glɔkə] *f* bell; **etw an die große ~ hängen** *(fig)* to shout sth from the rooftop
Glocken- *zW:* **~blume** *f* bellflower; **~geläut** *nt* peal of bells; **~spiel** *nt* chime(s); *(MUS)* glockenspiel; **~turm** *m* b tower
Glosse ['glɔsə] *f* comment
glotzen ['glɔtsən] *(umg) vi* to stare
Glück [glʏk] (-(e)s) *nt* luck, fortune; *(Freud* happiness; **~ haben** to be lucky; **viel ~!** good luck!; **zum ~** fortunately; **g~en** *vi* t succeed; **es g~te ihm, es zu bekommen** he succeeded in getting it
gluckern ['glʊkərn] *vi* to glug
glück- *zW:* **~lich** *adj* fortunate; *(froh)* happy; **~licherweise** *adv* fortunately; **~'selig** *adj* blissful
Glücks- *zW:* **~fall** *m* stroke of luck; **~kin** *nt* lucky person; **~sache** *f* matter of luck **~spiel** *nt* game of chance
Glückwunsch *m* congratulations *pl*, best wishes *pl*
Glüh- [glyː] *zW:* **~birne** *f* light bulb; **g~e** *vi* to glow; **~wein** *m* mulled wine; **~würmchen** *nt* glow-worm
Glut [gluːt] (-, -en) *f (Röte)* glow; *(Feuerglu* fire; *(Hitze)* heat; *(fig)* ardour
GmbH [geːʔɛmbeː'haː] *f abk (= Gesellschaft m beschränkter Haftung)* limited company, Ltd
Gnade ['gnaːdə] *f (Gunst)* favour; *(Erbarmer* mercy; *(Milde)* clemency
Gnaden- *zW:* **~frist** *f* reprieve, respite; **g~los** *adj* merciless; **~stoß** *m* coup de grâce
gnädig ['gnɛːdɪç] *adj* gracious; *(voll Erbarme* merciful
Gold [gɔlt] (-(e)s) *nt* gold; **g~en** *adj* golde **~fisch** *m* goldfish; **~grube** *f* goldmine;

g~ig ['gɔldɪç] (*umg*) *adj* (*fig: allerliebst*) sweet, adorable; **~regen** *m* laburnum; **~schmied** *m* goldsmith

Golf[1] [gɔlf] (-(e)s, -e) *m* gulf

Golf[2] [gɔlf] *nt* golf; **~platz** *m* golf course; **~schläger** *m* golf club

Golfstrom *m* Gulf Stream

Gondel ['gɔndəl] (-, -n) *f* gondola; (*Seilbahn*) cable car

gönnen ['gœnən] *vt*: **jdm etw ~** not to begrudge sb sth; **sich** *dat* **etw ~** to allow o.s. sth

Gönner (-s, -) *m* patron; **g~haft** *adj* patronizing

Gosse ['gɔsə] *f* gutter

Gott [gɔt] (-es, ⁺er) *m* god; **mein ~!** for heaven's sake!; **um ~es Willen!** for heaven's sake!; **grüß ~!** hello; **~ sei Dank!** thank God!; **~heit** *f* deity

Göttin ['gœtɪn] *f* goddess

göttlich *adj* divine

gottlos *adj* godless

Götze ['gœtsə] (-n, -n) *m* idol

Grab [gra:p] (-(e)s, ⁺er) *nt* grave; **g~en** ['gra:bən] (*unreg*) *vt* to dig; **~en** (-s, ⁺) *m* ditch; (*MIL*) trench; **~stein** *m* gravestone

Grad [gra:t] (-(e)s, -e) *m* degree

Graf [gra:f] (-en, -en) *m* count, earl

Grafiker(in) ▲ ['gra:fɪkər(ɪn)] (-s, -) *m(f)* graphic designer

grafisch ▲ ['gra:fɪʃ] *adj* graphic

Gram [gra:m] (-(e)s) *m* grief, sorrow

grämen ['grɛ:mən] *vr* to grieve

Gramm [gram] (-s, -e) *nt* gram(me)

Grammatik [gra'matɪk] *f* grammar

Granat [gra'na:t] (-(e)s, -e) *m* (*Stein*) garnet

Granate *f* (*MIL*) shell; (*Handgranate*) grenade

Granit [gra'ni:t] (-s, -e) *m* granite

Gras [gra:s] (-es, ⁺er) *nt* grass; **g~en** ['gra:zən] *vi* to graze; **~halm** *m* blade of grass

grassieren [gra'si:rən] *vi* to be rampant, to rage

grässlich ▲ ['grɛslɪç] *adj* horrible

Grat [gra:t] (-(e)s, -e) *m* ridge

Gräte ['grɛ:tə] *f* fishbone

gratis ['gra:tɪs] *adj, adv* free (of charge);

G~probe *f* free sample

Gratulation [gratulatsi'o:n] *f* congratulation(s)

gratulieren [gratu'li:rən] *vi*: **jdm ~ (zu etw)** to congratulate sb (on sth); **(ich) gratuliere!** congratulations!

grau [grau] *adj* grey

Gräuel ▲ ['grɔyəl] (-s, -) *m* horror, revulsion; **etw ist jdm ein ~** sb loathes sth

Grauen (-s) *nt* horror; **g~** *vi unpers*: **es graut jdm vor etw** sb dreads sth, sb is afraid of sth ♦ *vr*: **sich g~ vor** to dread, to have a horror of; **g~haft** *adj* horrible

grauhaarig *adj* grey-haired

gräulich ▲ ['grɔylɪç] *adj* horrible

grausam ['grauza:m] *adj* cruel; **G~keit** *f* cruelty

Grausen ['grauzən] (-s) *nt* horror; **g~** *vb* = **grauen**

gravieren [gra'vi:rən] *vt* to engrave; **~d** *adj* grave

graziös [gratsi'ø:s] *adj* graceful

greifbar *adj* tangible, concrete; **in ~er Nähe** within reach

greifen ['graifən] (*unreg*) *vt* to seize; to grip; **nach etw ~** to reach for sth; **um sich ~** (*fig*) to spread; **zu etw ~** (*fig*) to turn to sth

Greis [grais] (-es, -e) *m* old man; **g~enhaft** *adj* senile; **~in** *f* old woman

grell [grɛl] *adj* harsh

Grenz- ['grɛnts] *zW*: **~beamte(r)** *m* frontier official; **~e** *f* boundary; (*Staatsgrenze*) frontier; (*Schranke*) limit; **g~en** *vi*: **g~en (an** +*akk*) to border (on); **g~enlos** *adj* boundless; **~fall** *m* borderline case; **~kontrolle** *f* border control; **~übergang** *m* frontier crossing

Greuel △ ['grɔyəl] (-s, -) *m siehe* **Gräuel**

greulich △ *adj siehe* **gräulich**

Griech- ['gri:ç] *zW*: **~e** (-n, -n) *m* Greek; **~enland** *nt* Greece; **~in** *f* Greek; **g~isch** *adj* Greek

griesgrämig ['gri:sgrɛ:mɪç] *adj* grumpy

Grieß [gri:s] (-es, -e) *m* (*KOCH*) semolina

Griff [grɪf] (-(e)s, -e) *m* grip; (*Vorrichtung*) handle; **g~bereit** *adj* handy

Grill [grɪl] *m* grill; **~e** *f* cricket; **g~en** *vt* to grill; **~fest** *nt* barbecue party

Grimasse [gri'masə] *f* grimace

grimmig ['grɪmɪç] *adj* furious; (*heftig*) fierce, severe

grinsen ['grɪnzən] *vi* to grin

Grippe ['grɪpə] *f* influenza, flu

grob [gro:p] *adj* coarse, gross; (*Fehler, Verstoß*) gross; **G~heit** *f* coarseness; coarse expression

grölen ['grø:lən] (*pej*) *vt* to bawl, to bellow

Groll [grɔl] **(-(e)s)** *m* resentment; **g~en** *vi* (*Donner*) to rumble; **g~en (mit** *od* +*dat*) to bear ill will (towards)

groß [gro:s] *adj* big, large; (*hoch*) tall; (*fig*) great ♦ *adv* greatly; **im G~en und Ganzen** on the whole; **bei jdm ~ geschrieben werden** to be high on sb's list of priorities; **~artig** *adj* great, splendid; **G~aufnahme** *f* (*CINE*) close-up; **G~britannien** *nt* Great Britain

Größe ['grø:sə] *f* size; (*Höhe*) height; (*fig*) greatness

Groß- *zW*: **~einkauf** *m* bulk purchase; **~eltern** *pl* grandparents; **g~enteils** *adv* mostly; **~format** *nt* large size; **~handel** *m* wholesale trade; **~händler** *m* wholesaler; **~macht** *f* great power; **~mutter** *f* grandmother; **~rechner** *m* mainframe (computer); **g~schreiben** (*unreg*) *vt* (*Wort*) to write in block capitals; *siehe* **groß**; **g~spurig** *adj* pompous; **~stadt** *f* city, large town

größte(r, s) [grø:stə(r, s)] *adj superl von* **groß**; **größtenteils** *adv* for the most part

Groß- *zW*: **g~tun** (*unreg*) *vi* to boast; **~vater** *m* grandfather; **g~ziehen** (*unreg*) *vt* to raise; **g~zügig** *adj* generous; (*Planung*) on a large scale

grotesk [gro'tɛsk] *adj* grotesque

Grotte ['grɔtə] *f* grotto

Grübchen ['gry:pçən] *nt* dimple

Grube ['gru:bə] *f* pit; mine

grübeln ['gry:bəln] *vi* to brood

Gruft [gruft] **(-, ¨e)** *f* tomb, vault

grün [gry:n] *adj* green; **der ~e Punkt** *green spot symbol on recyclable packaging*

---

grüner Punkt

i The **grüner Punkt** is a green spot which appears on packaging that should be kept separate from normal household refuse to be recycled through the recycling company, DSD (Duales System Deutschland). The recycling is financed by licences bought by the packaging manufacturer from DSD. These costs are often passed on to the consumer.

Grünanlage *f* park

Grund [grʊnt] **(-(e)s, ¨e)** *m* ground; (*von See, Gefäß*) bottom; (*fig*) reason; **im ~e genommen** basically; *siehe* **aufgrund**; **~ausbildung** *f* basic training; **~besitz** *m* land(ed property), real estate; **~buch** *nt* land register

gründen [grʏndən] *vt* to found ♦ *vr*: **sich ~ (auf** +*dat*) to be based (on); **~ auf** +*akk* to base on; **Gründer (-s, -)** *m* founder

Grund- *zW*: **~gebühr** *f* basic charge; **~gesetz** *nt* constitution; **~lage** *f* foundation; **g~legend** *adj* fundamental

gründlich *adj* thorough

Grund- *zW*: **g~los** *adj* groundless; **~regel** *f* basic rule; **~riss** ▲ *m* plan; (*fig*) outline; **~satz** *m* principle; **g~sätzlich** *adj* fundamental; (*Frage*) of principle ♦ *adv* fundamentally; (*prinzipiell*) on principle; **~schule** *f* elementary school; **~stein** *m* foundation stone; **~stück** *nt* estate; plot

Grundwasser *nt* ground water

Grundschule

i The **Grundschule** is a primary school which children attend for 4 years from the age of 6 to 10. There are no formal examinations in the **Grundschule** but parents receive a report on their child's progress twice a year. Many children attend a **Kindergarten** from 3-6 years before going to the **Grundschule**, though no formal instruction takes place in the **Kindergarten**.

Grünstreifen *m* central reservation

grunzen ['grʊntsən] *vi* to grunt

Gruppe ['grʊpə] *f* group; **~nermäßigung** *f* group reduction; **g~nweise** *adv* in groups

gruppieren [grʊ'piːrən] *vt, vr* to group

gruselig *adj* creepy

gruseln ['gruːzəln] *vi unpers*: **es gruselt jdm vor etw** sth gives sb the creeps ♦ *vr* to have the creeps

Gruß [gruːs] **(-es, ⸚e)** *m* greeting; (*MIL*) salute; **viele Grüße** best wishes; **mit freundlichen Grüßen** yours sincerely; **Grüße an** +*akk* regards to

grüßen ['gryːsən] *vt* to greet; (*MIL*) to salute; **jdn von jdm ~** to give sb sb's regards; **jdn ~ lassen** to send sb one's regards

gucken ['gʊkən] *vi* to look

gültig ['gʏltɪç] *adj* valid; **G~keit** *f* validity

Gummi ['gʊmi] **(-s, -s)** *nt od m* rubber; (*~harze*) gum; **~band** *nt* rubber od elastic band; (*Hosenband*) elastic; **~bärchen** *nt* ≈ jelly baby (*BRIT*); **~baum** *m* rubber plant; **g~eren** [gʊ'miːrən] *vt* to gum; **~stiefel** *m* rubber boot

günstig ['gʏnstɪç] *adj* convenient; (*Gelegenheit*) favourable; **das habe ich ~ bekommen** it was a bargain

Gurgel ['gʊrgəl] **(-, -n)** *f* throat; **g~n** *vi* to gurgle; (*im Mund*) to gargle

Gurke ['gʊrkə] *f* cucumber; **saure ~** pickled cucumber, gherkin

Gurt [gʊrt] **(-(e)s, -e)** *m* belt

Gürtel ['gʏrtəl] **(-s, -)** *m* belt; (*GEOG*) zone; **~reifen** *m* radial tyre

GUS *f abk* (= *Gemeinschaft unabhängiger Staaten*) CIS

Guss [gʊs] **(-es, ⸚e)** *m* casting; (*Regenguss*) downpour; (*KOCH*) glazing; **~eisen** *nt* cast iron

---

gut *adj* good; **alles Gute** all the best; **also gut** all right then
♦ *adv* well; **gut gehen** to work, to come off; **es geht jdm gut** sb's doing fine; **gut gemeint** well meant; **gut schmecken** to

taste good; **jdm gut tun** to do sb good; **gut, aber ...** OK, but ...; **(na) gut, ich komme** all right, I'll come; **gut drei Stunden** a good three hours; **das kann gut sein** that may well be; **lass es gut sein** that'll do

---

Gut [guːt] **(-(e)s, ⸚er)** *nt* (*Besitz*) possession; **Güter** *pl* (*Waren*) goods; **~achten (-s, -)** *nt* (expert) opinion; **~achter (-s, -)** *m* expert; **g~artig** *adj* good-natured; (*MED*) benign; **g~bürgerlich** *adj* (*Küche*) (good) plain; **~dünken** *nt*: **nach ~dünken** at one's discretion

Güte ['gyːtə] *f* goodness, kindness; (*Qualität*) quality

Güter- *zW*: **~abfertigung** *f* (*EISENB*) goods office; **~bahnhof** *m* goods station; **~wagen** *m* goods waggon (*BRIT*), freight car (*US*); **~zug** *m* goods train (*BRIT*), freight train (*US*)

Gütezeichen *nt* quality mark; ≈ kite mark

gut- *zW*: **~gehen** △ (*unreg*) *vi unpers siehe* **gut**; **~gemeint** △ *adj siehe* **gut**; **~gläubig** *adj* trusting; **G~haben (-s)** *nt* credit; **~heißen** (*unreg*) *vt* to approve (of)

gütig ['gyːtɪç] *adj* kind

Gut- *zW*: **g~mütig** *adj* good-natured; **~schein** *m* voucher; **g~schreiben** (*unreg*) *vt* to credit; **~schrift** *f* (*Betrag*) credit; **g~tun** △ (*unreg*) *vi siehe* **gut**; **g~willig** *adj* willing

Gymnasium [gym'naːziʊm] *nt* grammar school (*BRIT*), high school (*US*)

Gymnasium

---

❶ The Gymnasium is a selective secondary school. After nine years of study pupils sit the Abitur so they can go on to higher education. Pupils who successfully complete six years at a Gymnasium automatically gain the mittlere Reife.

Gymnastik [gym'nastɪk] *f* exercises *pl*, keep fit

H, h

Haag [haːk] *m*: **Den ~** the Hague

Haar [haːr] (-(e)s, -e) *nt* hair; **um ein ~** nearly; **an den ~en herbeigezogen** (*umg*: *Vergleich*) very far-fetched; **~bürste** *f* hairbrush; **h~en** *vi, vr* to lose hair; **~esbreite** *f*: **um ~esbreite** by a hair's-breadth; **~festiger** (-s, -) *m* (hair) setting lotion; **h~genau** *adv* precisely; **h~ig** *adj* hairy; (*fig*) nasty; **~klammer** *f* hairgrip; **~nadel** *f* hairpin; **h~scharf** *adv* (*beobachten*) very sharply; (*daneben*) by a hair's breadth; **~schnitt** *m* haircut; **~spange** *f* hair slide; **h~sträubend** *adj* hair-raising; **~teil** *nt* hairpiece; **~waschmittel** *nt* shampoo

Habe ['haːbə] (-) *f* property

haben ['haːbən] (*unreg*) *vt, vb aux* to have; **Hunger/Angst ~** to be hungry/afraid; **woher hast du das?** where did you get that from?; **was hast du denn?** what's the matter (with you)?; **du hast zu schweigen** you're to be quiet; **ich hätte gern** I would like; **H~** (-s, -) *nt* credit

Habgier *f* avarice; **h~ig** *adj* avaricious

Habicht ['haːbɪçt] (-s, -e) *m* hawk

Habseligkeiten ['haːpzeːlɪçkaɪtən] *pl* belongings

Hachse ['haksə] *f* (*KOCH*) knuckle

Hacke ['hakə] *f* hoe; (*Ferse*) heel; **h~n** *vt* to hack, to chop; (*Erde*) to hoe

Hackfleisch *nt* mince, minced meat

Hafen ['haːfən] (-s, ") *m* harbour, port; **~arbeiter** *m* docker; **~rundfahrt** *f* boat trip round the harbour; **~stadt** *f* port

Hafer ['haːfər] (-s, -) *m* oats *pl*; **~flocken** *pl* rolled oats; **~schleim** *m* gruel

Haft [haft] (-) *f* custody; **h~bar** *adj* liable, responsible; **~befehl** *m* warrant (for arrest); **h~en** *vi* to stick, to cling; **h~en für** to be liable *od* responsible for; **h~en bleiben (an** +*dat*) to stick (to); **Häftling** *m* prisoner; **~pflicht** *f* liability; **~pflichtversicherung** *f* (*AUT*) third party

insurance; **~schalen** *pl* contact lenses; **~ung** *f* liability; **~ungsbeschränkung** *f* limitation of liability

Hagebutte ['haːgəbutə] *f* rose hip

Hagel ['haːgəl] (-s) *m* hail; **h~n** *vi unpers* to hail

hager ['haːgər] *adj* gaunt

Hahn [haːn] (-(e)s, "e) *m* cock; (*Wasserhahn*) tap, faucet (*US*)

Hähnchen ['hɛːnçən] *nt* cockerel; (*KOCH*) chicken

Hai(fisch) ['haɪ(fɪʃ)] (-(e)s, -e) *m* shark

häkeln ['hɛːkəln] *vt* to crochet

Haken ['haːkən] (-s, -) *m* hook; (*fig*) catch; **~kreuz** *nt* swastika; **~nase** *f* hooked nose

halb [halp] *adj* half; **~ eins** half past twelve; **~ offen** half-open; **ein ~es Dutzend** half a dozen; **H~dunkel** *nt* semi-darkness

halber ['halbər] *präp* +*gen* (*wegen*) on account of; (*für*) for the sake of

Halb- *zW*: **~heit** *f* half-measure; **h~ieren** *vt* to halve; **~insel** *f* peninsula; **~jahr** *nt* six months; (*auch*: *COMM*) half-year; **h~jährlich** *adj* half-yearly; **~kreis** *m* semicircle; **~leiter** *m* semiconductor; **~mond** *m* half-moon; (*fig*) crescent; **~pension** *f* half-board; **~schuh** *m* shoe; **h~tags** *adv*: **h~tags arbeiten** to work part-time, to work mornings/afternoons; **h~wegs** *adv* halfway; **h~wegs besser** more or less better; **~zeit** *f* (*SPORT*) half; (*Pause*) half-time

Halde ['haldə] *f* (*Kohlen*) heap

half [half] *vb siehe* **helfen**

Hälfte ['hɛlftə] *f* half

Halfter ['halftər] (-s, -) *m od nt* (*für Tiere*) halter

Halle ['halə] *f* hall; (*AVIAT*) hangar; **h~n** *vi* to echo, to resound; **~nbad** *nt* indoor swimming pool

hallo [ha'loː] *excl* hello

Halluzination [halutsinatsi'oːn] *f* hallucination

Halm ['halm] (-(e)s, -e) *m* blade; stalk

Halogenlampe [halo'geːnlampə] *f* halogen lamp

Hals [hals] (**-es**, **ᵘe**) m neck; (*Kehle*) throat; ~
über Kopf in a rush; **~band** nt (*von Hund*)
collar; **~kette** f necklace; **~-Nasen-
Ohren-Arzt** m ear, nose and throat
specialist; **~schmerzen** pl sore throat sg;
~tuch nt scarf

Halt [halt] (**-(e)s**, **-e**) m stop; (*fester* ~) hold;
(*innerer* ~) stability; ~ od **h~!** stop!, halt!; ~
machen to stop; **h~bar** adj durable;
(*Lebensmittel*) non-perishable; (*MIL, fig*)
tenable; **~barkeit** f durability; (non-)
perishability

halten ['haltən] (*unreg*) vt to keep;
(*festhalten*) to hold ♦ vi to hold; (*frisch
bleiben*) to keep; (*stoppen*) to stop ♦ vr
(*frisch bleiben*) to keep; (*sich behaupten*) to
hold out; ~ **für** to regard as; ~ **von** to think
of; **an sich** ~ to restrain o.s.; **sich rechts/
links** ~ to keep to the right/left

Halte- zW: **~stelle** f stop; **~verbot** nt: **hier
ist ~verbot** there's no waiting here

Halt- zW: **h~los** adj unstable; **h~machen**
△ vi siehe **Halt**; **~ung** f posture; (*fig*)
attitude; (*Selbstbeherrschung*) composure

Halunke [ha'lʊŋkə] (**-n**, **-n**) m rascal

hämisch ['hɛːmɪʃ] adj malicious

Hammel ['haml] (**-s**, **ᵛ** od **-**) m wether;
~fleisch nt mutton

Hammer ['hamər] (**-s**, **ᵛ**) m hammer

hämmern ['hɛmərn] vt, vi to hammer

Hämorr(ho)iden [hɛmɔro'iːdən,hɛmɔ'riːdn]
pl haemorrhoids

Hamster ['hamstər] (**-s**, **-**) m hamster; **~ei**
[-'raɪ] f hoarding; **h~n** vi to hoard

Hand [hant] (**-**, **ᵘe**) f hand; **~arbeit** f
manual work; (*Nadelarbeit*) needlework;
~ball m (*SPORT*) handball; **~bremse** f
handbrake; **~buch** nt handbook, manual

Händedruck ['hɛndədrʊk] m handshake

Handel ['handəl] (**-s**) m trade; (*Geschäft*)
transaction

Handeln ['handəln] (**-s**) nt action

handeln vi to trade; (*agieren*) to act ♦ vr
unpers: **sich ~ um** to be a question of, to
be about; ~ **von** to be about

Handels- zW: **~bilanz** f balance of trade;

~kammer f chamber of commerce;
~reisende(r) m commercial traveller;
~schule f business school; **h~üblich** adj
customary; (*Preis*) going attrib; **~vertreter**
m sales representative

Hand- zW: **~feger** (**-s**, **-**) m hand brush;
h~fest adj hefty; **h~gearbeitet** adj
handmade; **~gelenk** nt wrist; **~gemenge**
nt scuffle; **~gepäck** nt hand luggage;
h~geschrieben adj handwritten;
h~greiflich adj palpable; **h~greiflich
werden** to become violent; **~griff** m flick
of the wrist; **h~haben** vt insep to handle

Händler ['hɛndlər] (**-s**, **-**) m trader, dealer

handlich ['hantlɪç] adj handy

Handlung ['handlʊŋ] f act(ion); (*in Buch*)
plot; (*Geschäft*) shop

Hand- zW: **~schelle** f handcuff; **~schrift** f
handwriting; (*Text*) manuscript; **~schuh** m
glove; **~stand** m (*SPORT*) handstand;
~tasche f handbag; **~tuch** nt towel;
~umdrehen nt: **im ~umdrehen** in the
twinkling of an eye; **~werk** nt trade, craft;
~werker (**-s**, **-**) m craftsman, artisan;
~werkzeug nt tools pl

Handy ['hændɪ] (**-s**, **-s**) nt mobile
(telephone)

Hanf [hanf] (**-(e)s**) m hemp

Hang [haŋ] (**-(e)s**, **ᵘe**) m inclination;
(*Abhang*) slope

Hänge- ['hɛŋə] in zW hanging; **~brücke** f
suspension bridge; **~matte** f hammock

hängen ['hɛŋən] (*unreg*) vi to hang ♦ vt: **etw
(an etw** akk) ~ to hang sth (on sth); ~ **an**
+dat (fig) to be attached to; **sich ~ an** +akk
to hang on to, to cling to; ~ **bleiben** to be
caught; (*fig*) to remain, to stick; ~ **bleiben
an** +dat to catch od get caught on; ~
lassen (*vergessen*) to leave; **den Kopf ~
lassen** to get downhearted

Hannover [ha'noːfar] (**-s**) nt Hanover

hänseln ['hɛnzəln] vt to tease

Hansestadt ['hanzəʃtat] f Hanse town

hantieren [han'tiːrən] vi to work, to be
busy; **mit etw ~** to handle sth

hapern ['haːpərn] vi unpers: **es hapert an
etw** dat there is a lack of sth

Happen ['hapən] **(-s, -)** *m* mouthful

Harfe ['harfə] *f* harp

Harke ['harkə] *f* rake; **h~n** *vt, vi* to rake

harmlos ['harmloːs] *adj* harmless; **H~igkeit** *f* harmlessness

Harmonie [harmo'niː] *f* harmony; **h~ren** *vi* to harmonize

harmonisch [har'moːnɪʃ] *adj* harmonious

Harn ['harn] **(-(e)s, -e)** *m* urine; **~blase** *f* bladder

Harpune [har'puːnə] *f* harpoon

harren ['harən] *vi:* **~ (auf** +*akk*) to wait (for)

hart [hart] *adj* hard; *(fig)* harsh; **~ gekocht** hard-boiled

Härte ['hɛrtə] *f* hardness; *(fig)* harshness

hart- *zW:* **~herzig** *adj* hard-hearted; **~näckig** *adj* stubborn

Harz [haːrts] **(-es, -e)** *nt* resin

Haschee [ha'ʃeː] **(-s, -s)** *nt* hash

Haschisch ['haʃɪʃ] **(-)** *nt* hashish

Hase ['haːzə] **(-n, -n)** *m* hare

Haselnuss ▲ ['haːzəlnʊs] *f* hazelnut

Hasenscharte *f* harelip

Hass ▲ [has] **(-es)** *m* hate, hatred

hassen ['hasən] *vt* to hate

hässlich ['hɛslɪç] *adj* ugly; *(gemein)* nasty; **H~keit** *f* ugliness; nastiness

Hast [hast] *f* haste

hast *vb siehe* **haben**

hasten *vi* to rush

hastig *adj* hasty

hat [hat] *vb siehe* **haben**

hatte *etc* ['hatə] *vb siehe* **haben**

Haube ['haʊbə] *f* hood; *(Mütze)* cap; *(AUT)* bonnet, hood *(US)*

Hauch [haʊx] **(-(e)s, -e)** *m* breath; *(Lufthauch)* breeze; *(fig)* trace; **h~dünn** *adj* extremely thin

Haue ['haʊə] *f* hoe, pick; *(umg)* hiding; **h~n** *(unreg) vt* to hew, to cut; *(umg)* to thrash

Haufen ['haʊfən] **(-s, -)** *m* heap; *(Leute)* crowd; **ein ~ (x)** *(umg)* loads *od* a lot (of x); **auf einem ~** in one heap

häufen ['hɔʏfən] *vt* to pile up ♦ *vr* to accumulate

haufenweise *adv* in heaps; in droves; **etw ~ haben** to have piles of sth

häufig ['hɔʏfɪç] *adj* frequent ♦ *adv* frequently; **H~keit** *f* frequency

Haupt [haʊpt] **(-(e)s, Häupter)** *nt* head; *(Oberhaupt)* chief ♦ *in zW* main; **~bahnhof** *m* central station; **h~beruflich** *adv* as one's main occupation; **~darsteller(in)** *m(f)* leading actor (actress); **~fach** *nt* (*SCH, UNIV*) main subject, major *(US)*; **~gericht** *nt* (*KOCH*) main course

Häuptling ['hɔʏptlɪŋ] *m* chief(tain)

Haupt- *zW:* **~mann** *(pl* **-leute)** *m* (*MIL*) captain; **~person** *f* central figure; **~quartier** *nt* headquarters *pl;* **~rolle** *f* leading part; **~sache** *f* main thing; **h~sächlich** *adj* ♦ *adv* chiefly; **~saison** *f* high season, peak season; **~schule** *f* ≈ secondary school; **~stadt** *f* capital; **~straße** *f* main street; **~verkehrszeit** *f* rush-hour, peak traffic hours *pl*

Hauptschule

ℹ The Hauptschule is *a non-selective school which pupils may attend after the* Grundschule. *They complete five years of study and most go on to do some vocational training.*

Haus [haʊs] **(-es, Häuser)** *nt* house; **~ halten** *(sparen)* to economize; **nach ~e** home; **zu ~e** at home; **~apotheke** *f* medicine cabinet; **~arbeit** *f* housework; *(SCH)* homework; **~arzt** *m* family doctor; **~aufgabe** *f* (*SCH*) homework; **~besitzer(in)** *m(f)* house owner; **~besuch** *m* (*von Arzt*) house call; **~durchsuchung** *f* police raid; **h~eigen** *adj* belonging to a/ the hotel/firm

Häuser- ['hɔʏzər] *zW:* **~block** *m* block (of houses); **~makler** *m* estate agent *(BRIT)*, real estate agent *(US)*

Haus- *zW:* **~flur** *m* hallway; **~frau** *f* housewife; **h~gemacht** *adj* home-made; **~halt** *m* household; *(POL)* budget; **h~halten** *(unreg) vi* △ *siehe* **Haus**; **~hälterin** *f* housekeeper; **~haltsgeld** *nt* housekeeping (money); **~haltsgerät** *nt*

---

domestic appliance; **~herr** m host;
(*Vermieter*) landlord; **h~hoch** adv: **h~hoch
verlieren** to lose by a mile

hausieren [hau'ziːrən] vi to peddle

Hausierer (-s, -) m pedlar (*BRIT*), peddler
(*US*)

häuslich ['hɔyslıç] adj domestic

Haus- ~meister m caretaker, janitor;
~nummer f street number; **~ordnung** f
house rules pl; **~putz** m house cleaning;
~schlüssel m front door key; **~schuh** m
slipper; **~tier** nt pet; **~tür** f front door;
~wirt m landlord; **~wirtschaft** f domestic
science; **~zelt** nt frame tent

Haut [haut] (-, Häute) f skin; (*Tierhaut*) hide;
~creme f skin cream; **h~eng** adj skin-
tight; **~farbe** f complexion; **h~krebs** m skin
cancer

Haxe ['haksə] f = **Hachse**

Hbf. abk = **Hauptbahnhof**

Hebamme ['heːpˌamə] f midwife

Hebel ['heːbəl] (-s, -) m lever

heben ['heːbən] (*unreg*) vt to raise, to lift

Hecht [hɛçt] (-(e)s, -e) m pike

Heck [hɛk] (-(e)s, -e) nt stern; (*von Auto*)
rear

Hecke ['hɛkə] f hedge

Heckenschütze m sniper

Heckscheibe f rear window

Heer [heːr] (-(e)s, -e) nt army

Hefe ['heːfə] f yeast

Heft [hɛft] (-(e)s, -e) nt exercise book;
(*Zeitschrift*) number; (*von Messer*) haft;
h~en vt: **h~en an** (an +akk) to fasten (to);
(*nähen*) to tack ((on) to); **etw an etw** akk
h~en to fasten sth to sth; **~er** (-s, -) m
folder

heftig adj fierce, violent; **H~keit** f
fierceness, violence

Heft- ~klammer f paper clip;
~pflaster nt sticking plaster; **~zwecke** f
drawing pin

hegen ['heːgən] vt (*Wild, Bäume*) to care for,
to tend; (*fig, geh: empfinden: Wunsch*) to
cherish; (: *Misstrauen*) to feel

ehl [heːl] m od nt: **kein(en) ~ aus etw
machen** to make no secret of sth; **~er** (-s,

-) m receiver (of stolen goods), fence

Heide[1] ['haıdə] (-n, -n) m heathen, pagan

Heide[2] ['haıdə] f heath, moor; **~kraut** nt
heather

Heidelbeere f bilberry

Heidentum nt paganism

Heidin f heathen, pagan

heikel ['haıkəl] adj awkward, thorny

Heil [haıl] (-(e)s) nt well-being; (*Seelenheil*)
salvation; **h~** adj in one piece, intact; **~and**
(-(e)s, -e) m saviour; **h~bar** adj curable;
h~en vt to cure ♦ vi to heal; **h~froh** adj
very relieved

heilig ['haılıç] adj holy; **~ sprechen** to
canonize; **H~abend** m Christmas Eve;
H~e(r) f(m) saint; **~en** vt to sanctify, to
hallow; **H~enschein** m halo; **H~keit** f
holiness; **H~tum** nt shrine; (*Gegenstand*)
relic

Heil- ~los adj unholy; (*fig*) hopeless;
~mittel nt remedy; **~praktiker(in)** m(f)
non-medical practitioner; **h~sam** adj (*fig*)
salutary; **~sarmee** f Salvation Army; **~ung**
f cure

Heim [haım] (-(e)s, -e) nt home; **h~** adv
home

Heimat ['haımaːt] (-, -en) f home (town/
country etc); **~land** nt homeland; **h~lich**
adj native, home attrib; (*Gefühle*) nostalgic;
h~los adj homeless; **~ort** m home town/
area

Heim- ~computer m home computer;
h~fahren (*unreg*) vi to drive home; **~fahrt**
f journey home; **h~gehen** (*unreg*) vi to go
home; (*sterben*) to pass away; **h~isch** adj
(*gebürtig*) native; **sich h~isch fühlen** to feel
at home; **~kehr** (-, -en) f homecoming;
h~kehren vi to return home; **h~lich** adj
secret; **~lichkeit** f secrecy; **~reise** f
journey home; **~spiel** nt (*SPORT*) home
game; **h~suchen** vt to afflict; (*Geist*) to
haunt; **~trainer** m exercise bike;
h~tückisch adj malicious; **~weg** m way
home; **~weh** nt homesickness; **~werker**
(-s, -) m handyman; **h~zahlen** vt: **jdm etw
h~zahlen** to pay sb back for sth

Heirat ['haıraːt] (-, -en) f marriage; **h~en** vt

to marry ♦ *vi* to marry, to get married ♦ *vr* to get married; **~santrag** *m* proposal

heiser ['haɪzər] *adj* hoarse; **H~keit** *f* hoarseness

heiß [haɪs] *adj* hot; **~e(s) Eisen** (*umg*) hot potato; **~blütig** *adj* hot-blooded

heißen ['haɪsən] (*unreg*) *vi* to be called; (*bedeuten*) to mean ♦ *vt* to command; (*nennen*) to name ♦ *vi unpers*: **es heißt** it says; it is said; **das heißt** that is (to say)

Heiß- *zW*: **~hunger** *m* ravenous hunger; **h~laufen** (*unreg*) *vi*, *vr* to overheat

heiter ['haɪtər] *adj* cheerful; (*Wetter*) bright; **H~keit** *f* cheerfulness; (*Belustigung*) amusement

Heiz- ['haɪts] *zW*: **h~bar** *adj* heated; (*Raum*) with heating; **h~en** *vt* to heat; **~körper** *m* radiator; **~öl** *nt* fuel oil; **~sonne** *f* electric fire; **~ung** *f* heating

hektisch ['hɛktɪʃ] *adj* hectic

Held [hɛlt] (**-en, -en**) *m* hero; **h~enhaft** *adj* heroic; **~in** *f* heroine

helfen ['hɛlfən] (*unreg*) *vi* to help; (*nützen*) to be of use ♦ *vb unpers*: **es hilft nichts, du musst ...** it's no use, you'll have to ...; **jdm (bei etw) ~** to help sb (with sth); **sich** *dat* **zu ~ wissen** to be resourceful

Helfer (**-s, -**) *m* helper, assistant; **~shelfer** *m* accomplice

hell [hɛl] *adj* clear, bright; (*Farbe, Bier*) light; **~blau** *adj* light blue; **~blond** *adj* ash blond; **H~e** (**-**) *f* clearness, brightness; **~hörig** *adj* (*Wand*) paper-thin; **~hörig werden** (*fig*) to prick up one's ears; **H~seher** *m* clairvoyant; **~wach** *adj* wide-awake

Helm ['hɛlm] (**-(e)s, -e**) *m* (*auf Kopf*) helmet

Hemd [hɛmt] (**-(e)s, -en**) *nt* shirt; (*Unterhemd*) vest; **~bluse** *f* blouse

hemmen ['hɛmən] *vt* to check, to hold up; **gehemmt sein** to be inhibited; **Hemmung** *f* check; (*PSYCH*) inhibition; **hemmungslos** *adj* unrestrained, without restraint

Hengst [hɛŋst] (**-es, -e**) *m* stallion

Henkel ['hɛŋkəl] (**-s, -**) *m* handle

Henker (**-s, -**) *m* hangman

Henne ['hɛnə] *f* hen

SCHLÜSSELWORT

her [heːr] *adv* **1** (*Richtung*): **komm her zu mir** come here (to me); **von England her** from England; **von weit her** from a long way away; **her damit!** hand it over!; **wo hat er das her?** where did he get that from?
2 (*Blickpunkt*): **von der Form her** as far as the form is concerned
3 (*zeitlich*): **das ist 5 Jahre her** that was 5 years ago; **wo bist du her?** where do you come from?; **ich kenne ihn von früher her** I know him from before

herab [hɛˈrap] *adv* down(ward(s)); **~hängen** (*unreg*) *vi* to hang down; **~lassen** (*unreg*) *vt* to let down ♦ *vr* to condescend; **~lassend** *adj* condescending; **~setzen** *vt* to lower, to reduce; (*fig*) to belittle, to disparage

heran [hɛˈran] *adv*: **näher ~!** come up closer!; **~ zu mir!** come up to me!; **~bringen** (*unreg*) *vt*: **~bringen (an** +*akk*) to bring up (to); **~fahren** (*unreg*) *vi*: **~fahren (an** +*akk*) to drive up (to); **~kommen** (*unreg*) *vi*: **(an jdn/etw) ~kommen** to approach (sb/sth), to come near to (sb/sth); **~machen** *vr*: **sich an jdn ~machen** to make up to sb; **~treten** (*unreg*) *vi*: **mit etw an jdn ~treten** to approach sb with sth; **~wachsen** (*unreg*) *vi* to grow up; **~ziehen** (*unreg*) *vt* to pull nearer; (*aufziehen*) to raise; (*ausbilden*) to train; **jdn zu etw ~ziehen** to call upon sb to help in sth

herauf [hɛˈrauf] *adv* up(ward(s)), up here; **~beschwören** (*unreg*) *vt* to conjure up, to evoke; **~bringen** (*unreg*) *vt* to bring up; **~setzen** *vt* (*Preise, Miete*) to raise, put up

heraus [hɛˈraus] *adv* out; **~bekommen** (*unreg*) *vt* to get out; (*fig*) to find *od* figure out; **~bringen** (*unreg*) *vt* to bring out; (*Geheimnis*) to elicit; **~finden** (*unreg*) *vt* to find out; **~fordern** (*unreg*) *vt* to challenge; **H~forderung** *f* challenge; provocation; **~geben** (*unreg*) *vt* to hand over, to surrender; (*zurückgeben*) to give back; (*Buch*) to edit; (*veröffentlichen*) to publish; **H~geber** (**-s, -**) *m* editor; (*Verleger*) publisher; **~gehen** (*unreg*) *vi*: **aus sich ~gehen** to come out of one's shell; **~halten** (*unreg*) *vr*: **sich aus etw ~halten** to keep out of sth; **~hängen**[1] *vt* to hang out; **~hängen**[2] (*unreg*) *vt* to hang out; **~holen** *vt*: **~holen (aus)** to get out (of); **~kommen** (*unreg*) *vi* to come out; **dabei kommt nichts ~** nothing will come of it; **~nehmen** (*unreg*) *vt* to remove (from), take out (of); **sich** *dat* **etw ~nehmen** to take liberties; **~reißen** (*unreg*) *vt* to tear out; to pull out; **~rücken** *vt* (*Geld*) to fork out, to hand over; **mit etw ~rücken** (*fig*) to come out with sth; **~stellen** *vr*: **sich ~stellen (als)** to turn out (to be); **~suchen** *vt*: **sich aus jdn/etw ~suchen** to pick sb/sth out; **~ziehen** (*unreg*) *vt* to pull out, to extract

herb [hɛrp] *adj* (slightly) bitter, acid; (*Wein*) dry; (*fig: schmerzlich*) bitter

herbei [hɛr'baɪ] *adv* (over) here; **~führen** *vt* to bring about; **~schaffen** *vt* to procure

herbemühen ['heːrbəmyːən] *vr* to take the trouble to come

Herberge ['hɛrbɛrgə] *f* shelter; hostel, inn

Herbergsmutter *f* warden

Herbergsvater *m* warden

herbitten (*unreg*) *vt* to ask to come (here)

Herbst [hɛrpst] (**-(e)s, -e**) *m* autumn, fall (*US*); **h~lich** *adj* autumnal

Herd [heːrt] (**-(e)s, -e**) *m* cooker; (*fig, MED*) focus, centre

Herde ['heːrdə] *f* herd; (*Schafherde*) flock

herein [hɛ'raɪn] *adv* in (here), here; **~!** come in!; **~bitten** (*unreg*) *vt* to ask in; **~brechen** (*unreg*) *vi* to set in; **~bringen** (*unreg*) *vt* to bring in; **~fallen** (*unreg*) *vi* to be caught, to be taken in; **~fallen auf** +*akk* to fall for; **~kommen** (*unreg*) *vi* to come in; **~lassen** (*unreg*) *vt* to admit; **~legen** *vt*: **jdn ~legen** to take sb in; **~platzen** (*umg*) *vi* to burst in

Her- *zW*: **~fahrt** *f* journey here; **h~fallen** *vi*: **h~fallen über** +*akk* to fall upon; **~gang** *m* course of events; **h~geben**

(*unreg*) *vt* to give, to hand (over); **sich zu etw h~geben** to lend one's name to sth; **h~gehen** (*unreg*) *vi*: **hinter jdm h~gehen** to follow sb; **es geht hoch h~** there are a lot of goings-on; **h~halten** (*unreg*) *vt* to hold out; **h~halten müssen** (*umg*) to have to suffer; **h~hören** *vi* to listen

Hering ['heːrɪŋ] (**-s, -e**) *m* herring

her- [hɛr] *zW*: **~kommen** (*unreg*) *vi* to come; **komm mal ~!** come here!; **~kömmlich** *adj* traditional; **H~kunft** (**-, -künfte**) *f* origin; **H~kunftsland** *nt* country of origin; **H~kunftsort** *m* place of origin; **~laufen** (*unreg*) *vi*: **~laufen hinter** +*dat* to run after

hermetisch [hɛr'meːtɪʃ] *adj* hermetic ♦ *adv* hermetically

her'nach *adv* afterwards

Heroin [hero'iːn] (**-s**) *nt* heroin

Herr [hɛr] (**-(e)n, -en**) *m* master; (*Mann*) gentleman; (*REL*) Lord; (*vor Namen*) Mr.; **mein ~!** sir!; **meine ~en!** gentlemen!

Herren- *zW*: **~haus** *nt* mansion; **~konfektion** *f* menswear; **h~los** *adj* ownerless; **~toilette** *f* men's toilet *od* restroom (*US*)

herrichten ['heːrrɪçtən] *vt* to prepare

Herr- *zW*: **~in** *f* mistress; **h~isch** *adj* domineering; **h~lich** *adj* marvellous, splendid; **~lichkeit** *f* splendour, magnificence; **~schaft** *f* power, rule; (*~ und ~in*) master and mistress; **meine ~schaften!** ladies and gentlemen!

herrschen ['hɛrʃən] *vi* to rule; (*bestehen*) to prevail, to be

Herrscher(in) (**-s, -**) *m(f)* ruler

her- *zW*: **~rühren** *vi* to arise, to originate; **~sagen** *vt* to recite; **~stellen** *vt* to make, to manufacture; **H~steller** (**-s, -**) *m* manufacturer; **H~stellung** *f* manufacture

herüber [hɛ'ryːbɐr] *adv* over (here), across

herum [hɛ'rʊm] *adv* about, (a)round; **um etw ~** around sth; **~führen** *vt* to show around; **~gehen** (*unreg*) *vi* to walk about; **um etw ~gehen** to walk *od* go round sth; **~kommen** (*unreg*) *vi* (*um Kurve etc*) to come round, to turn (round); **~kriegen**

(*umg*) *vt* to bring *od* talk around; **~lungern**
(*umg*) *vi* to hang about *od* around;
~sprechen (*unreg*) *vr* to get around, to be
spread; **~treiben** *vi, vr* to drift about;
~ziehen *vi, vr* to wander about

herunter [heˈrʊntər] *adv* downward(s),
down (there); **~gekommen** *adj* run-down;
~kommen (*unreg*) *vi* to come down; (*fig*)
to come down in the world; **~laden** *unreg*
vt (*COMPUT*) to download; **~machen** *vt* to
take down; (*schimpfen*) to have a go at

hervor [herˈfoːr] *adv* out, forth; **~bringen**
(*unreg*) *vt* to produce; (*Wort*) to utter;
~gehen (*unreg*) *vi* to emerge, to result;
~heben (*unreg*) *vt* to stress; (*als Kontrast*) to
set off; **~ragend** *adj* (*fig*) excellent; **~rufen**
(*unreg*) *vt* to cause, to give rise to; **~treten**
(*unreg*) *vi* to come out (from behind/
between/below); (*Adern*) to be prominent

Herz [herts] (**-ens, -en**) *nt* heart; (*KARTEN*)
hearts *pl*; **~anfall** *m* heart attack; **~fehler**
m heart defect; **h~haft** *adj* hearty

herziehen [ˈheːrtsiːən] (*unreg*) *vi*: **über jdn/
etw ~** (*umg*) to pull sb/sth to pieces (*inf*)

Herz- *zW*: **~infarkt** *m* heart attack;
~klopfen *nt* palpitation; **h~lich** *adj*
cordial; **h~lichen Glückwunsch**
congratulations *pl*; **h~liche Grüße** best
wishes; **h~los** *adj* heartless

Herzog [ˈhertsoːk] (**-(e)s, ᵉe**) *m* duke; **~tum**
nt duchy

Herz- *zW*: **~schlag** *m* heartbeat; (*MED*)
heart attack; **~stillstand** *m* cardiac arrest;
h~zerreißend *adj* heartrending

Hessen [ˈhesən] (**-s**) *nt* Hesse

hessisch *adj* Hessian

Hetze [ˈhetsə] *f* (*Eile*) rush; **h~n** *vt* to hunt;
(*verfolgen*) to chase ♦ *vi* (*eilen*) to rush;
jdn/etw auf jdn/etw h~n to set sb/sth on
sb/sth; **h~n gegen** to stir up feeling
against; **h~n zu** to agitate for

Heu [hɔy] (**-(e)s**) *nt* hay; **Geld wie ~** stacks
of money

Heuch- [ˈhɔyç] *zW*: **~elei** [-əˈlaɪ] *f* hypocrisy;
h~eln *vt* to pretend, to feign ♦ *vi* to be
hypocritical; **~ler(in)** (**-s, -**) *m(f)* hypocrite;
h~lerisch *adj* hypocritical

heulen [ˈhɔylən] *vi* to howl; to cry

Heurige(r) [ˈhɔyrɪgə(r)] *m* new wine

Heu- *zW*: **~schnupfen** *m* hay fever;
~schrecke *f* grasshopper; locust

heute [ˈhɔytə] *adv* today; **~ Abend/früh** this
evening/morning

heutig [ˈhɔytɪç] *adj* today's

heutzutage [ˈhɔyttsutaːgə] *adv* nowadays

Hexe [ˈheksə] *f* witch; **h~n** *vi* to practise
witchcraft; **ich kann doch nicht h~n** I can't
work miracles; **~nschuss** ▲ *m* lumbago;
~rei *f* witchcraft

Hieb [hiːp] (**-(e)s, -e**) *m* blow; (*Wunde*) cut,
gash; (*Stichelei*) cutting remark; **~e**
bekommen to get a thrashing

hielt *etc* [hiːlt] *vb siehe* **halten**

hier [hiːr] *adv* here; **~ behalten** to keep
here; **~ bleiben** to stay here; **~ lassen** to
leave here; **~auf** *adv* thereupon; (*danach*)
after that; **~bei** *adv* herewith, enclosed;
~durch *adv* by this means; (*örtlich*)
through here; **~her** *adv* this way, here;
~hin *adv* here; **~mit** *adv* hereby; **~nach**
adv hereafter; **~von** *adv* about this, hereof;
~zulande, ~ zu Lande *adv* in this
country

hiesig [ˈhiːzɪç] *adj* of this place, local

hieß *etc* [hiːs] *vb siehe* **heißen**

Hilfe [ˈhɪlfə] *f* help; aid; **erste ~** first aid; **~!**
help!

Hilf- *zW*: **h~los** *adj* helpless; **~losigkeit** *f*
helplessness; **h~reich** *adj* helpful

Hilfs- *zW*: **~arbeiter** *m* labourer;
h~bedürftig *adj* needy; **h~bereit** *adj*
ready to help; **~kraft** *f* assistant, helper

hilfst [hɪlfst] *vb siehe* **helfen**

Himbeere [ˈhɪmbeːrə] *f* raspberry

Himmel [ˈhɪməl] (**-s, -**) *m* sky; (*REL, auch fig*)
heaven; **~bett** *nt* four-poster bed; **h~blau**
adj sky-blue; **~fahrt** *f* Ascension;
~srichtung *f* direction

himmlisch [ˈhɪmlɪʃ] *adj* heavenly

SCHLÜSSELWORT

hin [hɪn] *adv* **1** (*Richtung*): **hin und zurück**
there and back; **hin und her** to and fro;
bis zur Mauer hin up to the wall; **wo ist**

er hin? where has he gone?; **Geld hin, Geld her** money or no money

2 (auf ... hin): **auf meine Bitte hin** at my request; **auf seinen Rat hin** on the basis of his advice

3 : mein Glück ist hin my happiness has gone

hinab [hɪ'nap] *adv* down;~**gehen** (*unreg*) *vi* to go down;~**sehen** (*unreg*) *vi* to look down

hinauf [hɪ'nauf] *adv* up;~**arbeiten** *vr* to work one's way up;~**steigen** (*unreg*) *vi* to climb

hinaus [hɪ'naus] *adv* out;~**gehen** (*unreg*) *vi* to go out; ~**gehen über** +*akk* to exceed; ~**laufen** (*unreg*) *vi* to run out; ~**laufen auf** +*akk* to come to, to amount to; ~**schieben** (*unreg*) *vt* to put off, to postpone;~**werfen** (*unreg*) *vt* (*Gegenstand, Person*) to throw out;~**wollen** *vi* to want to go out; ~**wollen auf** +*akk* to drive at, to get at

Hinblick ['hɪnblɪk] *m*: **in** *od* **im** ~ **auf** +*akk* in view of

hinder- ['hɪndər] *zW*:~**lich** *adj*: ~**lich sein** to be a hindrance *od* nuisance;~**n** *vt* to hinder, to hamper; **jdn an etw** *dat* ~**n** to prevent sb from doing sth;**H~nis** (-ses, -se) *nt* obstacle;**H~nisrennen** *nt* steeplechase

hindeuten ['hɪndɔʏtən] *vi*: ~ **auf** +*akk* to point to

hindurch [hɪn'dʊrç] *adv* through; across; (*zeitlich*) through(out)

hinein [hɪ'naɪn] *adv* in;~**fallen** (*unreg*) *vi* to fall in; ~**fallen in** +*akk* to fall into;~**gehen** (*unreg*) *vi* to go in; ~**gehen in** +*akk* to go into, to enter;~**geraten** (*unreg*) *vi*: ~**geraten in** +*akk* to get into;~**passen** *vi* to fit in; ~**passen in** +*akk* to fit into; (*fig*) to fit in with;~**steigern** *vr* to get worked up; ~**versetzen** *vr*: **sich** ~**versetzen in** +*akk* to put o.s. in the position of;~**ziehen** (*unreg*) *vt* to pull in

hin- ['hɪn] *zW*:~**fahren** (*unreg*) *vi* to go; to drive ♦ *vt* to take; to drive;**H~fahrt** *f*

journey there;~**fallen** (*unreg*) *vi* to fall (down);~**fällig** *adj* frail; (*fig: ungültig*) invalid;**H~flug** *m* outward flight;**H~gabe** *f* devotion;~**geben** (*unreg*) *vr* +*dat* to give o.s. up to, to devote o.s. to;~**gehen** (*unreg*) *vi* to go; (*Zeit*) to pass;~**halten** (*unreg*) *vt* to hold out; (*warten lassen*) to put off, to stall

hinken ['hɪŋkən] *vi* to limp; (*Vergleich*) to be unconvincing

hinkommen (*unreg*) *vi* (*an Ort*) to arrive

hin- ['hɪn] *zW*:~**legen** *vt* to put down ♦ *vr* to lie down;~**nehmen** (*unreg*) *vt* (*fig*) to put up with, to take;**H~reise** *f* journey out;~**reißen** (*unreg*) *vt* to carry away, to enrapture; **sich** ~**reißen lassen, etw zu tun** to get carried away and do sth;

~**richten** *vt* to execute;**H~richtung** *f* execution;~**setzen** *vt* to put down ♦ *vr* to sit down;~**sichtlich** *präp* +*gen* with regard to;~**stellen** *vt* to put (down) ♦ *vr* to place o.s.

hinten ['hɪntən] *adv* at the back; behind; ~**herum** *adv* round the back; (*fig*) secretly

hinter ['hɪntər] *präp* (+*dat od akk*) behind; (: *nach*) after; ~ **jdm her sein** to be after sb;**H~achse** *f* rear axle;**H~bliebene(r)** *f(m)* surviving relative;~**e(r, s)** *adj* rear, back;~**einander** *adv* one after the other; **H~gedanke** *m* ulterior motive;~**gehen** (*unreg*) *vt* to deceive;**H~grund** *m* background;**H~halt** *m* ambush;~**hältig** *adj* underhand, sneaky;~**her** *adv* afterwards *od* after;**H~hof** *m* backyard; **H~kopf** *m* back of one's head;~**lassen** (*unreg*) *vt* to leave;~**legen** *vt* to deposit; **H~list** *f* cunning, trickery; (*Handlung*) trick, dodge;~**listig** *adj* cunning, crafty; **H~mann** *m* person behind;**H~rad** *nt* back wheel;**H~radantrieb** *m* (*AUT*) rear wheel drive;~**rücks** *adv* from behind; **H~tür** *f* back door; (*fig: Ausweg*) loophole; ~'**ziehen** (*unreg*) *vt* (*Steuern*) to evade

hinüber [hɪ'ny:bər] *adv* across, over; ~**gehen** (*unreg*) *vi* to go over *od* across

hinunter [hɪ'nʊntər] *adv* down;~**bringen** (*unreg*) *vt* to take down;~**schlucken** *vt*

(auch fig) to swallow; **~steigen** *(unreg)* vi
to descend

Hinweg ['hɪnveːk] m journey out

hinweghelfen [hɪn'vɛk-] *(unreg)* vi: **jdm
über etw** *akk* ~ to help sb to get over sth

hinwegsetzen [hɪn'vɛk-] vr: **sich** ~ **über**
+*akk* to disregard

hin- ['hɪn] zW: **H~weis (-es, -e)** m
(Andeutung) hint; *(Anweisung)* instruction;
(Verweis) reference; **~weisen** *(unreg)* vi:
~weisen auf +*akk* *(anzeigen)* to point to;
(sagen) to point out, to refer to; **~werfen**
(unreg) vt to throw down; **~ziehen** *(unreg)*
vr *(fig)* to drag on

hinzu [hɪn'tsuː] adv in addition; **~fügen** vt
to add; **~kommen** *(unreg)* vi *(Mensch)* to
arrive, to turn up; *(Umstand)* to ensue

Hirn [hɪrn] **(-(e)s, -e)** nt brain(s); **~gespinst**
(-(e)s, -e) nt fantasy

Hirsch [hɪrʃ] **(-(e)s, -e)** m stag

Hirt ['hɪrt] **(-en, -en)** m herdsman; *(Schafhirt,
fig)* shepherd

hissen ['hɪsən] vt to hoist

Historiker [hɪs'toːrikər] **(-s, -)** m historian

historisch [hɪs'toːrɪʃ] adj historical

Hitze ['hɪtsə] **(-)** f heat; **h~beständig** adj
heat-resistant; **h~frei** adj: **h~frei haben** to
have time off school because of excessively
hot weather; **~welle** f heat wave

hitzig ['hɪtsɪç] adj hot-tempered; *(Debatte)*
heated

Hitzkopf m hothead

Hitzschlag m heatstroke

hl. abk von **heilig**

H-Milch ['haːmɪlç] f long-life milk

Hobby ['hɔbi] **(-s, -s)** nt hobby

Hobel ['hoːbəl] **(-s, -)** m plane; **~bank** f
carpenter's bench; **h~n** vt, vi to plane;
~späne pl wood shavings

Hoch (-s, -s) nt *(Ruf)* cheer; *(MET)*
anticyclone

hoch [hoːx] *(attrib* **hohe(r, s))** adj high;
♦ adv: ~ **achten** to respect; ~ **begabt**
extremely gifted; ~ **dotiert** highly paid;
H~achtung f respect, esteem;
~achtungsvoll adv yours faithfully;
H~amt nt high mass; **~arbeiten** vr to

work one's way up; **H~betrieb** m intense
activity; *(COMM)* peak time; **H~burg** f
stronghold; **H~deutsch** nt High German;
H~druck m high pressure; **H~ebene** f
plateau; **H~form** f top form; **H~gebirge**
nt high mountains pl; **H~glanz** m *(PHOT)*
high gloss print; **etw auf H~glanz bringen**
to make sth sparkle like new; **~halten**
(unreg) vt to hold up; *(fig)* to uphold, to
cherish; **H~haus** nt multi-storey building;
~heben *(unreg)* vt to lift (up);
H~konjunktur f boom; **H~land** nt
highlands pl; **~leben** vi: **jdn ~leben
lassen** to give sb three cheers; **H~mut** m
pride; **~mütig** adj proud, haughty; **~näsig**
adj stuck-up, snooty; **H~ofen** m blast
furnace; **~prozentig** adj *(Alkohol)* strong;
H~rechnung f projection; **H~saison** f
high season; **H~schule** f college;
university; **H~sommer** m middle of
summer; **H~spannung** f high tension;
H~sprung m high jump

höchst [høːçst] adv highly, extremely

Hochstapler ['hoːxstaːplər] **(-s, -)** m
swindler

höchste(r, s) adj highest; *(äußerste)*
extreme

Höchst- zW: **h~ens** adv at the most;
~geschwindigkeit f maximum speed;
h~persönlich adv in person; **~preis** m
maximum price; **h~wahrscheinlich** adv
most probably

Hoch- zW: **~verrat** m high treason;
~wasser nt high water; *(Überschwemmung)*
floods pl

Hochzeit ['hɔxtsaɪt] **(-, -en)** f wedding;
~sreise f honeymoon

hocken ['hɔkən] vi, vr to squat, to crouch

Hocker (-s, -) m stool

Höcker ['hœkər] **(-s, -)** m hump

Hoden ['hoːdən] **(-s, -)** m testicle

Hof [hoːf] **(-(e)s, ⁺e)** m *(Hinterhof)* yard;
(Bauernhof) farm; *(Königshof)* court

hoff- ['hɔf] zW: **~en** vi: **~en (auf** +*akk)* to
hope (for); **~entlich** adv I hope, hopefully;
H~nung f hope

Hoffnungs- zW: **h~los** adj hopeless;

~losigkeit f hopelessness; **h~voll** adj hopeful

höflich ['hø:flɪç] adj polite, courteous; **H~keit** f courtesy, politeness

hohe(r, s) ['ho:ə(r, s)] adj attrib siehe **hoch**

Höhe ['hø:ə] f height; (Anhöhe) hill

Hoheit ['ho:haɪt] f (POL) sovereignty; (Titel) Highness

Hoheits- zW: **~gebiet** nt sovereign territory; **~gewässer** nt territorial waters pl

Höhen- ['hø:ən] zW: **~luft** f mountain air; **~messer (-s, -)** m altimeter; **~sonne** f sun lamp; **~unterschied** m difference in altitude

Höhepunkt m climax

höher adj, adv higher

hohl [ho:l] adj hollow

Höhle ['hø:lə] f cave, hole; (Mundhöhle) cavity; (fig, ZOOL) den

Hohlmaß nt measure of volume

Hohn [ho:n] **(-(e)s)** m scorn

höhnisch adj scornful, taunting

holen ['ho:lən] vt to get, to fetch; (Atem) to take; **jdn/etw ~ lassen** to send for sb/sth

Holland ['hɔlant] nt Holland; **Holländer** ['hɔlɛndər] m Dutchman; **holländisch** adj Dutch

Hölle ['hœlə] f hell

höllisch ['hœlɪʃ] adj hellish, infernal

holperig ['hɔlpərɪç] adj rough, bumpy

Holunder [ho'lʊndər] **(-s, -)** m elder

Holz [hɔlts] **(-es, ⁻er)** nt wood

hölzern ['hœltsərn] adj (auch fig) wooden

Holz- zW: **~fäller (-s, -)** m lumberjack, woodcutter; **h~ig** adj woody; **~kohle** f charcoal; **~schuh** m clog; **~weg** m (fig) wrong track; **~wolle** f fine wood shavings pl

Homöopathie [homøopa'ti:] f homeopathy

homosexuell [homozɛksu'ɛl] adj homosexual

Honig ['ho:nɪç] **(-s, -e)** m honey; **~melone** f (BOT, KOCH) honeydew melon; **~wabe** f honeycomb

Honorar [hono'ra:r] **(-s, -e)** nt fee

Hopfen ['hɔpfən] **(-s, -)** m hops pl

hopsen ['hɔpsən] vi to hop

Hörapparat m hearing aid

hörbar adj audible

horchen ['hɔrçən] vi to listen; (pej) to eavesdrop

Horde ['hɔrdə] f horde

hör- ['hø:r] zW: **~en** vt, vi to hear; **Musik/ Radio ~en** to listen to music/the radio; **H~er (-s, -)** m hearer; (RADIO) listener; (UNIV) student; (Telefonhörer) receiver; **H~funk (-s)** m radio; **~geschädigt** [-gəʃɛ:dɪçt] adj hearing-impaired

Horizont [hori'tsɔnt] **(-(e)s, -e)** m horizon; **h~al** [-'ta:l] adj horizontal

Hormon [hɔr'mo:n] **(-s, -e)** nt hormone

Hörmuschel f (TEL) earpiece

Horn [hɔrn] **(-(e)s, ⁻er)** nt horn; **~haut** f horny skin

Hornisse [hɔr'nɪsə] f hornet

Horoskop [horo'sko:p] **(-s, -e)** nt horoscope

Hörspiel nt radio play

Hort [hɔrt] **(-(e)s, -e)** m (SCH) day centre for schoolchildren whose parents are at work

horten ['hɔrtən] vt to hoard

Hose ['ho:zə] f trousers pl, pants pl (US)

Hosen- zW: **~anzug** m trouser suit; **~rock** m culottes pl; **~tasche** f (trouser) pocket; **~träger** m braces pl (BRIT), suspenders pl (US)

Hostie ['hɔstiə] f (REL) host

Hotel [ho'tɛl] **(-s, -s)** nt hotel; **~ier (-s, -s)** [hotɛli'e:] m hotelkeeper, hotelier; **~verzeichnis** nt hotel register

Hubraum m (AUT) cubic capacity

hübsch [hypʃ] adj pretty, nice

Hubschrauber ['hu:pʃraʊbər] **(-s, -)** m helicopter

Huf ['hu:f] **(-(e)s, -e)** m hoof; **~eisen** nt horseshoe

Hüft- ['hʏft] zW: **~e** f hip; **~gürtel** m girdle; **~halter (-s, -)** m girdle

Hügel ['hy:gəl] **(-s, -)** m hill; **h~ig** adj hilly

Huhn [hu:n] **(-(e)s, ⁻er)** nt hen; (KOCH) chicken

Hühner- ['hy:nər] zW: **~auge** nt corn; **~brühe** f chicken broth

Hülle ['hʏlə] f cover(ing); wrapping; **in ~**

und Fülle galore; **h~n** *vt:* **h~n (in** +*akk*) to cover (with); to wrap (in)

Hülse ['hʏlzə] *f* husk, shell; **~nfrucht** *f* pulse

human [hu'maːn] *adj* humane; **~i'tär** *adj* humanitarian; **H~i'tät** *f* humanity

Hummel ['hʊməl] **(-, -n)** *f* bumblebee

Hummer ['hʊmər] **(-s, -)** *m* lobster

Humor [hu'moːr] **(-s, -e)** *m* humour; **~ haben** to have a sense of humour; **~ist** [-'rɪst] *m* humorist; **h~voll** *adj* humorous

humpeln ['hʊmpəln] *vi* to hobble

Humpen ['hʊmpən] **(-s, -)** *m* tankard

Hund [hʊnt] **(-(e)s, -e)** *m* dog

Hunde- ['hʊndə] *zW:* **~hütte** *f* (dog) kennel; **h~müde** (*umg*) *adj* dog-tired

hundert ['hʊndərt] *num* hundred; **H~'jahrfeier** *f* centenary; **~prozentig** *adj, adv* one hundred per cent

Hundesteuer *f* dog licence fee

Hündin ['hʏndɪn] *f* bitch

Hunger ['hʊŋər] **(-s)** *m* hunger; **~ haben** to be hungry; **h~n** *vi* to starve; **~snot** *f* famine

hungrig ['hʊŋrɪç] *adj* hungry

Hupe ['huːpə] *f* horn; **h~n** *vi* to hoot, to sound one's horn

hüpfen ['hʏpfən] *vi* to hop; to jump

Hürde ['hʏrdə] *f* hurdle; (*für Schafe*) pen; **~nlauf** *m* hurdling

Hure ['huːrə] *f* whore

hurtig ['hʊrtɪç] *adj* brisk, quick ♦ *adv* briskly, quickly

huschen ['hʊʃən] *vi* to flit; to scurry

Husten ['huːstən] **(-s)** *m* cough; **h~** *vi* to cough; **~anfall** *m* coughing fit; **~bonbon** *m od nt* cough drop; **~saft** *m* cough mixture

Hut¹ [huːt] **(-(e)s, ⁼e)** *m* hat

Hut² [huːt] **(-)** *f* care; **auf der ~ sein** to be on one's guard

hüten ['hyːtən] *vt* to guard ♦ *vr* to watch out; **sich ~, zu** to take care not to; **sich ~ (vor)** to beware (of), to be on one's guard (against)

Hütte ['hʏtə] *f* hut; cottage; (*Eisen~*) forge

Hütten- *zW:* **~käse** *m* (*KOCH*) cottage cheese; **~schuh** *m* slipper sock

Hydrant [hy'drant] *m* hydrant

hydraulisch [hy'draʊlɪʃ] *adj* hydraulic

Hygiene [hygi'eːnə] **(-)** *f* hygiene

hygienisch [hygi'eːnɪʃ] *adj* hygienic

Hymne ['hʏmnə] *f* hymn; anthem

Hypno- [hʏp'noː] *zW:* **~se** *f* hypnosis; **h~tisch** *adj* hypnotic; **~tiseur** [-ti'zøːr] *m* hypnotist; **h~ti'sieren** *vt* to hypnotize

Hypothek [hypo'teːk] **(-, -en)** *f* mortgage

Hypothese [hypo'teːzə] *f* hypothesis

Hysterie [hyste'riː] *f* hysteria

hysterisch [hʏs'teːrɪʃ] *adj* hysterical

I, i

ICE [iːtseː'|eː] *m abk* = **Intercity-Expresszug**

Ich **(-(s), -(s))** *nt* self; (*PSYCH*) ego

ich [ɪç] *pron* I; **~ bins!** it's me!

Icon ['aɪkɔn] **(-s, -s)** *nt* (*COMPUT*) icon

Ideal [ide'aːl] **(-s, -e)** *nt* ideal; **ideal** *adj* ideal; **idealistisch** [-'lɪstɪʃ] *adj* idealistic

Idee [i'deː, *pl* i'deːən] *f* idea

identifizieren [identifi'tsiːrən] *vt* to identify

identisch [i'dentɪʃ] *adj* identical

Identität [identi'tɛːt] *f* identity

Ideo- [ideo'] *zW:* **~loge** [-'loːgə] **(-n, -n)** *m* ideologist; **~logie** [-lo'giː] *f* ideology; **ideologisch** [-'loːgɪʃ] *adj* ideological

Idiot [idi'oːt] **(-en, -en)** *m* idiot; **idiotisch** *adj* idiotic

idyllisch [i'dʏlɪʃ] *adj* idyllic

Igel ['iːgəl] **(-s, -)** *m* hedgehog

ignorieren [ɪgno'riːrən] *vt* to ignore

ihm [iːm] (*dat von* **er, es**) *pron* (to) him; (to) it

ihn [iːn] (*akk von* **er, es**) *pron* him; it; **~en** (*dat von* **sie** *pl*) *pron* (to) them; **Ihnen** (*dat von* **Sie** *pl*) *pron* (to) you

SCHLÜSSELWORT

ihr [iːr] *pron* **1** (*nom pl*) you; **ihr seid es** it's you

2 (*dat von* **sie**) to her; **gib es ihr** give it to her; **er steht neben ihr** he is standing beside her

♦ *possessiv pron* **1** (*sg*) her; (: *bei Tieren,*

Dingen) its; **ihr Mann** her husband **2** (*pl*) their; **die Bäume und ihre Blätter** the trees and their leaves

ihr(e) [iːr] *adj* (*sg*) her, its; (*pl*) their; **Ihr(e)** *adj* your

ihre(r, s) *pron* (*sg*) hers, its; (*pl*) theirs; **Ihre(r, s)** *pron* yours; **~r** (*gen von* **sie** *sg/pl*) *pron* of her/them; **Ihrer** (*gen von* **Sie**) *pron* of you; **~rseits** *adv* for her/their part; **~sgleichen** *pron* people like her/them; (*von Dingen*) others like it; **~twegen** *adv* (*für sie*) for her/its/their sake; (*wegen ihr*) on her/its/their account; **~twillen** *adv*: **um ~twillen = ihretwegen**

ihrige [ˈiːrɪɡə] *pron*: **der/die/das ~** *od* **I~** hers; its; theirs

illegal [ˈɪleɡaːl] *adj* illegal

Illusion [ɪluziˈoːn] *f* illusion

illusorisch [ɪluˈzoːrɪʃ] *adj* illusory

illustrieren [ɪlʊsˈtriːrən] *vt* to illustrate

Illustrierte *f* magazine

im [ɪm] = **in dem**

Imbiss ▲ [ˈɪmbɪs] (**-es, -e**) *m* snack; **~stube** *f* snack bar

imitieren [imiˈtiːrən] *vt* to imitate

Imker [ˈɪmkər] (**-s, -**) *m* beekeeper

immatrikulieren [ɪmatrikuˈliːrən] *vi, vr* to register

immer [ˈɪmər] *adv* always; **~ wieder** again and again; **~ noch** still; **~ noch nicht** still not; **für ~** forever; **~ wenn ich ...** every time I ...; **~ schöner/trauriger** more and more beautiful/sadder and sadder; **was/ wer (auch) ~** whatever/whoever; **~hin** *adv* all the same; **~zu** *adv* all the time

Immobilien [ɪmoˈbiːliən] *pl* real estate *sg*; **~makler** *m* estate agent (*BRIT*), realtor (*US*)

immun [ɪˈmuːn] *adj* immune; **Immunität** [-iˈtɛːt] *f* immunity; **Immunsystem** *nt* immune system

Imperfekt [ˈɪmpɛrfɛkt] (**-s, -e**) *nt* imperfect (tense)

Impf- [ˈɪmpf] *zW*: **impfen** *vt* to vaccinate; **~stoff** *m* vaccine, serum; **~ung** *f* vaccination

imponieren [ɪmpoˈniːrən] *vi* +*dat* to impress

Import [ɪmˈpɔrt] (**-(e)s, -e**) *m* import; **~eur** *m* importer; **importieren** *vt* to import

imposant [ɪmpoˈzant] *adj* imposing

impotent [ˈɪmpotɛnt] *adj* impotent

imprägnieren [ɪmprɛˈɡniːrən] *vt* to (water)proof

improvisieren [ɪmproviˈziːrən] *vt, vi* to improvise

Impuls [ɪmˈpʊls] (**-es, -e**) *m* impulse; **impulsiv** [-ˈziːf] *adj* impulsive

imstande, im Stande [ɪmˈʃtandə] *adj*: **~ sein** to be in a position; (*fähig*) to be able

in [ɪn] *präp* +*akk* **1** (*räumlich: wohin?*) in, into; **in die Stadt** into town; **in die Schule gehen** to go to school

2 (*zeitlich*): **bis ins 20. Jahrhundert** into *od* up to the 20th century

♦ *präp* +*dat* **1** (*räumlich: wo*) in; **in der Stadt** in town; **in der Schule sein** to be at school

2 (*zeitlich: wann*): **in diesem Jahr** this year; (*in jenem Jahr*) in that year; **heute in zwei Wochen** two weeks today

Inanspruchnahme [ɪnˈanʃprʊxnaːmə] *f* (+*gen*) demands *pl* (on)

Inbegriff [ˈɪnbəɡrɪf] *m* embodiment, personification; **inbegriffen** *adv* included

indem [ɪnˈdeːm] *konj* while; **~ man etw macht** (*dadurch*) by doing sth

Inder(in) [ˈɪndər(ɪn)] *m(f)* Indian

indes(sen) [ɪnˈdɛs(ən)] *adv* however; (*inzwischen*) meanwhile ♦ *konj* while

Indianer(in) [ɪndiˈaːnər(ɪn)] (**-s, -**) *m(f)* American Indian, native American; **indianisch** *adj* Red Indian

Indien [ˈɪndiən] *nt* India

indirekt [ˈɪndirɛkt] *adj* indirect

indisch [ˈɪndɪʃ] *adj* Indian

indiskret [ˈɪndɪskreːt] *adj* indiscreet

indiskutabel [ˈɪndɪskutaːbəl] *adj* out of the question

individuell [ɪndividuˈɛl] *adj* individual

Individuum [ɪndiˈviːduʊm] (**-s, -en**) *nt* individual

Indiz [ɪnˈdiːts] (**-es, -ien**) *nt* (*JUR*) clue; **~ (für)** sign (of)

industrialisieren [ɪndʊstriˈaliˈziːrən] *vt* to industrialize

Industrie [ɪndʊsˈtriː] *f* industry ♦ *in zW* industrial; **~gebiet** *nt* industrial area; **~~ und Handelskammer** *f* chamber of commerce; **~zweig** *m* branch of industry

ineinander [ɪnʔaɪˈnandər] *adv* in(to) one another *od* each other

Infarkt [ɪnˈfarkt] (**-(e)s, -e**) *m* coronary (thrombosis)

Infektion [ɪnfɛktsiˈoːn] *f* infection; **~skrankheit** *f* infectious disease

Infinitiv [ˈɪnfinitiːf] (**-s, -e**) *m* infinitive

infizieren [ɪnfiˈtsiːrən] *vt* to infect ♦ *vr*: **sich (bei jdm) ~** to be infected (by sb)

Inflation [ɪnflatsiˈoːn] *f* inflation

inflationär [ɪnflatsioˈnɛːr] *adj* inflationary

infolge [ɪnˈfɔlgə] *präp +gen* as a result of, owing to; **~dessen** [-ˈdɛsən] *adv* consequently

Informatik [ɪnfɔrˈmaːtɪk] *f* information studies *pl*

Information [ɪnfɔrmatsiˈoːn] *f* information *no pl*

informieren [ɪnfɔrˈmiːrən] *vt* to inform ♦ *vr*: **sich ~ (über +akk)** to find out (about)

infrage, in Frage *adv*: **~ stellen** to question sth; **nicht ~ kommen** to be out of the question

Ingenieur [ɪnʒeniˈøːr] *m* engineer; **~schule** *f* school of engineering

Ingwer [ˈɪŋvər] (**-s**) *m* ginger

Inh. *abk* (= *Inhaber*) prop.; (= *Inhalt*) contents

Inhaber(in) [ˈɪnhaːbər(ɪn)] (**-s, -**) *m(f)* owner; (*Hausinhaber*) occupier; (*Lizenzinhaber*) licensee, holder; (*FIN*) bearer

inhaftieren [ɪnhafˈtiːrən] *vt* to take into custody

inhalieren [ɪnhaˈliːrən] *vt, vi* to inhale

Inhalt [ˈɪnhalt] (**-(e)s, -e**) *m* contents *pl*; (*eines Buchs etc*) content; (*MATH*) area; volume; **inhaltlich** *adj* as regards content

Inhalts- *zW*: **~angabe** *f* summary; **~verzeichnis** *nt* table of contents

inhuman [ˈɪnhumaːn] *adj* inhuman

Initiative [initsiaˈtiːvə] *f* initiative

inklusive [ɪnkluˈziːvə] *präp +gen* inclusive of ♦ *adv* inclusive

In-Kraft-Treten [ɪnˈkrafttreːtən] (**-s**) *nt* coming into force

Inland [ˈɪnlant] (**-(e)s**) *nt* (*GEOG*) inland; (*POL, COMM*) home (country); **~flug** *m* domestic flight

inmitten [ɪnˈmɪtən] *präp +gen* in the middle of; **~ von** amongst

innehaben [ˈɪnahaːbən] (*unreg*) *vt* to hold

innen [ˈɪnən] *adv* inside; **Innenarchitekt** *m* interior designer; **Inneneinrichtung** *f* (interior) furnishings *pl*; **Innenhof** *m* inner courtyard; **Innenminister** *m* minister of the interior, Home Secretary (*BRIT*); **Innenpolitik** *f* domestic policy; **~politisch** *adj* (*Entwicklung, Lage*) internal, domestic; **Innenstadt** *f* town/city centre

inner- [ˈɪnər] *zW*: **~e(r, s)** *adj* inner; (*im Körper, inländisch*) internal; **Innere(s)** *nt* inside; (*Mitte*) centre; (*fig*) heart; **Innereien** [-ˈraɪən] *pl* innards; **~halb** *adv* within; (*räumlich*) inside ♦ *präp +gen* within; inside; **~lich** *adj* internal; (*geistig*) inward; **~ste(r, s)** *adj* innermost; **Innerste(s)** *nt* heart

innig [ˈɪnɪç] *adj* (*Freundschaft*) close

inoffiziell [ˈɪnʔofitsiɛl] *adj* unofficial

ins [ɪns] = **in das**

Insasse [ˈɪnzasə] (**-n, -n**) *m* (*Anstalt*) inmate; (*AUT*) passenger

Insassenversicherung *f* passenger insurance

insbesondere [ɪnsbəˈzɔndərə] *adv* (e)specially

Inschrift [ˈɪnʃrɪft] *f* inscription

Insekt [ɪnˈzɛkt] (**-(e)s, -en**) *nt* insect

Insektenschutzmittel *nt* insect repellent

Insel [ˈɪnzəl] (**-, -n**) *f* island

Inser- *zW*: **~at** [ɪnzeˈraːt] (**-(e)s, -e**) *nt* advertisement; **~ent** [ɪnzeˈrɛnt] *m* advertiser; **inserieren** [ɪnzeˈriːrən] *vt, vi* to advertise

insgeheim [ɪnsgəˈhaɪm] *adv* secretly

insgesamt [ɪnsgəˈzamt] *adv* altogether, all in all

insofern [ɪnzo'fɛrn] adv in this respect ♦ konj if; (deshalb) (and) so; ~ **als** in so far as

insoweit [ɪnzo'vaɪt] = **insofern**

Installateur [ɪnstala'tøːr] m electrician; plumber

Instandhaltung [ɪn'ʃtanthaltʊŋ] f maintenance

inständig [ɪn'ʃtɛndɪç] adj urgent

Instandsetzung [ɪn'ʃtant-] f overhaul; (eines Gebäudes) restoration

Instanz [ɪn'ʃtants] f authority; (JUR) court

Instinkt [ɪn'ʃtɪŋkt] (-(e)s, -e) m instinct; **instinktiv** [-'tiːf] adj instinctive

Institut [ɪnsti'tuːt] (-(e)s, -e) nt institute

Instrument [ɪnstru'mɛnt] nt instrument

Intell- [ɪntɛl] zW: **i~ektuell** [-ɛktu'ɛl] adj intellectual; **intelligent** [-i'gɛnt] adj intelligent; **~igenz** [-i'gɛnts] f intelligence; (Leute) intelligentsia pl

Intendant [ɪntɛn'dant] m director

intensiv [ɪntɛn'ziːf] adj intensive; **Intensivstation** f intensive care unit

Intercity- [ɪntər'sɪti] zW: **~-Expresszug ▲** m high-speed train; **~-Zug** m intercity (train); **~-Zuschlag** m intercity supplement

Interess- zW: **i~ant** [ɪntere'sant] adj interesting; **i~anterweise** adv interestingly enough; **~e** [ɪnte'resə] (-s, -n) nt interest; **~e haben an** +dat to be interested in; **~ent** [ɪntere'sɛnt] m interested party; **i~ieren** [ɪntere'siːrən] vt to interest ♦ vr: **sich i~ieren für** to be interested in

intern [ɪn'tɛrn] adj (Angelegenheiten, Regelung) internal; (Besprechung) private

Internat [ɪntər'naːt] (-(e)s, -e) nt boarding school

inter- [ɪntər] zW: **~national** [-natsio'naːl] adj international; **I~net** ['ɪntərnɛt] (-s) nt: **das I~net** the Internet; **I~net-Anbieter** m Internet Service Provider, ISP; **I~net-Café** nt Internet café; **~pretieren** [-pre'tiːrən] vt to interpret; **I~vall** [-'val] (-s, -e) nt interval; **I~view** ['-vjuː] (-s, -s) nt interview; **~viewen** ['-vjuːən] vt to interview

intim [ɪn'tiːm] adj intimate; **Intimität** f intimacy

intolerant ['ɪntolerant] adj intolerant

Intrige [ɪn'triːgə] f intrigue, plot

Invasion [ɪnvazi'oːn] f invasion

Inventar [ɪnvɛn'taːr] (-s, -e) nt inventory

Inventur [ɪnvɛn'tuːr] f stocktaking; ~ **machen** to stocktake

investieren [ɪnvɛs'tiːrən] vt to invest

inwie- [ɪnvi'] zW: **~fern** adv how far, to what extent; **~weit** adv how far, to what extent

inzwischen [ɪn'tsvɪʃən] adv meanwhile

Irak [i'raːk] (-s) m: **der ~** Iraq; **irakisch** adj Iraqi

Iran [i'raːn] (-s) m: **der ~** Iran; **iranisch** adj Iranian

irdisch ['ɪrdɪʃ] adj earthly

Ire ['iːrə] (-n, -n) m Irishman

irgend ['ɪrgənt] adv at all; **wann/was/wer ~** whenever/whatever/whoever; **~etwas** pron something/anything; **~jemand** pron somebody/anybody; **~ein(e, s)** adj some, any; **~einmal** adv sometime or other; (fragend) ever; **~wann** adv sometime; **~wie** adv somehow; **~wo** adv somewhere; anywhere; **~wohin** adv somewhere; anywhere

Irin ['iːrɪn] f Irishwoman

Irland ['ɪrlant] (-s) nt Ireland

Ironie [iro'niː] f irony; **ironisch** [i'roːnɪʃ] adj ironic(al)

irre ['ɪrə] adj crazy, mad; **Irre(r)** f(m) lunatic; **~führen** vt to mislead; **~machen** vt to confuse; **~n** vi to be mistaken; (umherirren) to wander, to stray ♦ vr to be mistaken; **Irrenanstalt** f lunatic asylum

Irr- zW: **~garten** m maze; **i~ig** ['ɪrɪç] adj incorrect, wrong; **i~itieren** [ɪri'tiːrən] vt (verwirren) to confuse; (ärgern) to irritate; (stören) to annoy; **irrsinnig** adj mad, crazy; (umg) terrific; **~tum** (-s, -tümer) m mistake, error; **irrtümlich** adj mistaken

Island ['iːslant] (-s) nt Iceland

Isolation [izolatsi'oːn] f isolation; (ELEK) insulation

Isolier- [izo'liːr] zW: **~band** nt insulating tape; **isolieren** vt to isolate; (ELEK) to insulate; **~station** f (MED) isolation ward;

~ung f isolation; (ELEK) insulation
Israel ['ɪsraeːl] (-s) nt Israel; **~i** (-s, -s) [-'eːli]
m Israeli; **israelisch** adj Israeli
isst ▲ [ɪst] vb siehe **essen**
ist [ɪst] vb siehe **sein**
Italien [i'taːliən] (-s) nt Italy; **~er(in)** (-s)
m(f) Italian; **italienisch** adj Italian
i. V. abk = in Vertretung

J, j

ja [jaː] adv 1 yes; **haben Sie das gesehen? -
ja** did you see it? - yes(, I did); **ich glaube
ja** (yes) I think so
2 (fragend) really?; **ich habe gekündigt -
ja?** I've quit - have you?; **du kommst, ja?**
you're coming, aren't you?
3: **sei ja vorsichtig** do be careful; **Sie
wissen ja, dass ...** as you know, ...; **tu
das ja nicht!** don't do that!; **ich habe es
ja gewusst** I just knew it!; **ja, also ...** well
you see ...

Jacht [jaxt] (-, -en) f yacht
Jacke ['jakə] f jacket; (Wolljacke) cardigan
Jackett [ʒa'ket] (-s, -s od -e) nt jacket
Jagd [jaːkt] (-, -en) f hunt; (Jagen) hunting;
~beute f kill; **~flugzeug** nt fighter;
~hund m hunting dog
jagen ['jaːgən] vi to hunt; (eilen) to race ♦ vt
to hunt; (wegjagen) to drive (off); (verfolgen)
to chase
Jäger ['jeːgər] (-s, -) m hunter; **~schnitzel**
nt (KOCH) pork in a spicy sauce with
mushrooms
jäh [jeː] adj sudden, abrupt; (steil) steep,
precipitous
Jahr [jaːr] (-(e)s, -e) nt year; **j~elang** adv for
years
Jahres- zW: **~abonnement** nt annual
subscription; **~abschluss** ▲ m end of the
year; (COMM) annual statement of account;
~beitrag m annual subscription; **~karte** f

yearly season ticket; **~tag** m anniversary;
~wechsel m turn of the year; **~zahl** f
date; year; **~zeit** f season
Jahr- zW: **~gang** m age group; (von Wein)
vintage; **~'hundert** (-s, -e) nt century;
jährlich ['jeːrlɪç] adj, adv yearly; **~markt** m
fair; **~tausend** nt millennium; **~'zehnt** nt
decade
Jähzorn ['jeːtsɔrn] m sudden anger; hot
temper; **j~ig** adj hot-tempered
Jalousie [ʒalu'ziː] f venetian blind
Jammer ['jamər] (-s) m misery; **es ist ein ~,
dass ...** it is a crying shame that ...
jämmerlich ['jemərlɪç] adj wretched,
pathetic
jammern vi to wail ♦ vt unpers: **es jammert
jdn** it makes sb feel sorry
Januar ['januaːr] (-(s), -e) m January
Japan ['jaːpan] (-s) nt Japan; **~er(in)**
[-'paːnər(ɪn)] (-s) m(f) Japanese; **j~isch** adj
Japanese
jäten ['jeːtən] vt: **Unkraut ~** to weed
jauchzen ['jauxtsən] vi to rejoice
jaulen ['jaulən] vi to howl
jawohl [ja'voːl] adv yes (of course)
Jawort ['jaːvɔrt] nt consent
Jazz [dʒæz] (-) m Jazz

je [jeː] adv 1 (jemals) ever; **hast du so was je
gesehen?** did you ever see anything like
it?
2 (jeweils) every, each; **sie zahlten je 3
Mark** they paid 3 marks each
♦ konj 1: **je nach** depending on; **je
nachdem** it depends; **je nachdem, ob ...**
depending on whether ...
2: **je eher, desto** od **umso besser** the
sooner the better ·

Jeans [dʒiːnz] pl jeans
jede(r, s) ['jeːdə(r, s)] adj every, each ♦ pron
everybody; (~ Einzelne) each; **~s Mal** every
time, each time; **ohne ~ x** without any x
jedenfalls adv in any case
jedermann pron everyone
jederzeit adv at any time

jedoch [je'dɔx] *adv* however

jeher ['je:he:r] *adv*: **von/seit ~** always

jemals ['je:ma:ls] *adv* ever

jemand ['je:mant] *pron* somebody; anybody

jene(r, s) ['je:nə(r, s)] *adj* that ♦ *pron* that one

jenseits ['je:nzaits] *adv* on the other side ♦ *präp* +*gen* on the other side of, beyond

Jenseits *nt*: **das ~** the hereafter, the beyond

jetzig ['jetsiç] *adj* present

jetzt [jetst] *adv* now

jeweilig *adj* respective

jeweils *adv*: **~ zwei zusammen** two at a time; **zu ~ 5 DM** at 5 marks each; **~ das Erste** the first each time

Jh. *abk* = **Jahrhundert**

Job [dʒɔp] (**-s, -s**) *m* (*umg*) job; **j~ben** ['dʒɔbən] *vi* (*umg*) to work

Jockei ['dʒɔke] (**-s, -s**) *m* jockey

Jod [jo:t] (**-(e)s**) *nt* iodine

jodeln ['jo:dəln] *vi* to yodel

joggen ['dʒɔgən] *vi* to jog

Jog(h)urt ['jo:gurt] (**-s, -s**) *m od nt* yogurt

Johannisbeere [jo'hanisbe:rə] *f* redcurrant; **schwarze ~** blackcurrant

johlen ['jo:lən] *vi* to yell

jonglieren [ʒõ'gli:rən] *vi* to juggle

Journal- [ʒurnal] *zW*: **~ismus** [-'lismus] *m* journalism; **~ist(in)** [-'list(in)] *m(f)* journalist; **journa'listisch** *adj* journalistic

Jubel ['ju:bəl] (**-s**) *m* rejoicing; **j~n** *vi* to rejoice

Jubiläum [jubi'lɛːʊm] (**-s, Jubiläen**) *nt* anniversary; jubilee

jucken ['jukən] *vi* to itch ♦ *vt*: **es juckt mich am Arm** my arm is itching

Juckreiz ['jukraits] *m* itch

Jude ['ju:də] (**-n, -n**) *m* Jew

Juden- *zW*: **~tum** (**-s**) *nt* Judaism; Jewry; **~verfolgung** *f* persecution of the Jews

Jüdin ['jy:dɪn] *f* Jewess

jüdisch ['jy:dɪʃ] *adj* Jewish

Jugend ['ju:gənt] (**-**) *f* youth; **j~frei** *adj* (*CINE*) U (*BRIT*), G (*US*), suitable for children; **~herberge** *f* youth hostel; **~herbergsausweis** *m* youth hostelling

card; **j~lich** *adj* youthful; **~liche(r)** *f(m)* teenager, young person

Jugoslaw- [jugo'sla:v] *zW*: **~ien** (**-s**) *nt* Yugoslavia; **j~isch** *adj* Yugoslavian

Juli ['ju:li] (**-(s), -s**) *m* July

jun. *abk* (= *junior*) jr.

jung [jʊŋ] *adj* young; **J~e** (**-n, -n**) *m* boy, lad ♦ *nt* young animal; **J~en** *pl* (*von Tier*) young *pl*

Jünger ['jvŋər] (**-s, -**) *m* disciple

jünger *adj* younger

Jung- *zW*: **~frau** *f* virgin; (*ASTROL*) Virgo; **~geselle** *m* bachelor; **~gesellin** *f* unmarried woman

jüngst [jvŋst] *adv* lately, recently; **~e(r, s)** *adj* youngest; (*neueste*) latest

Juni ['ju:ni] (**-(s), -s**) *m* June

Junior ['ju:niɔr] (**-s, -en**) *m* junior

Jurist [ju'rist] *m* jurist, lawyer; **j~isch** *adj* legal

Justiz [jus'ti:ts] (**-**) *f* justice; **~beamte(r)** *m* judicial officer; **~irrtum** *m* miscarriage of justice; **~minister** *m* ≃ Lord (High) Chancellor (*BRIT*), ≃ Attorney General (*US*)

Juwel [ju've:l] (**-s, -en**) *nt od m* jewel

Juwelier [juve'li:r] (**-s, -e**) *m* jeweller; **~geschäft** *nt* jeweller's (shop)

Jux [juks] (**-es, -e**) *m* joke, lark

K, k

Kabarett [kaba'ret] (**-s, -e** *od* **-s**) *nt* cabaret; **~ist** [-'tist] *m* cabaret artiste

Kabel ['ka:bəl] (**-s, -**) *nt* (*ELEK*) wire; (*stark*) cable; **~fernsehen** *nt* cable television

Kabeljau ['ka:bəljau] (**-s, -e** *od* **-s**) *m* cod

Kabine [ka'bi:nə] *f* cabin; (*Zelle*) cubicle

Kabinenbahn *f* cable railway

Kabinett [kabi'net] (**-s, -e**) *nt* (*POL*) cabinet

Kachel ['kaxəl] (**-, -n**) *f* tile; **k~n** *vt* to tile; **~ofen** *m* tiled stove

Käfer ['kɛ:fər] (**-s, -**) *m* beetle

Kaffee ['kafe] (**-s, -s**) *m* coffee; **~haus** *nt* café; **~kanne** *f* coffeepot; **~löffel** *m* coffee spoon

Käfig ['kɛ:fiç] (**-s, -e**) *m* cage

kahl [kaːl] *adj* bald; **~ geschoren** shaven, shorn; **~köpfig** *adj* bald-headed

Kahn [kaːn] (-(e)s, ᵉe) *m* boat, barge

Kai [kaɪ] (-s, -e *od* -s) *m* quay

Kaiser ['kaɪzər] (-s, -) *m* emperor; **~in** *f* empress; **k~lich** *adj* imperial; **~reich** *nt* empire; **~schnitt** *m* (*MED*) Caesarian (section)

Kakao [ka'kaːo] (-s, -s) *m* cocoa

Kaktee [kak'teː(ə)] (-, -n) *f* cactus

Kaktus ['kaktʊs] (-, -teen) *m* cactus

Kalb [kalp] (-(e)s, ᵉer) *nt* calf; **k~en** ['kalbən] *vi* to calve; **~fleisch** *nt* veal; **~sleder** *nt* calf(skin)

Kalender [ka'lɛndər] (-s, -) *m* calendar; (*Taschenkalender*) diary

Kaliber [ka'liːbər] (-s, -) *nt* (*auch fig*) calibre

Kalk [kalk] (-(e)s, -e) *m* lime; (*BIOL*) calcium; **~stein** *m* limestone

kalkulieren [kalku'liːrən] *vt* to calculate

Kalorie [kalo'riː] *f* calorie

kalt [kalt] *adj* cold; **mir ist (es) ~** I am cold; **~ bleiben** (*fig*) to remain unmoved; **~ stellen** to chill; **~blütig** *adj* cold-blooded; (*ruhig*) cool

Kälte ['kɛltə] (-) *f* cold; coldness; **~grad** *m* degree of frost *od* below zero; **~welle** *f* cold spell

kalt- *zW*: **~herzig** *adj* cold-hearted; **~schnäuzig** *adj* cold, unfeeling; **~stellen** *vt* (*fig*) to leave out in the cold

kam *etc* [kaːm] *vb siehe* **kommen**

Kamel [ka'meːl] (-(e)s, -e) *nt* camel

Kamera ['kamera] (-, -s) *f* camera

Kamerad [kamə'raːt] (-en, -en) *m* comrade, friend; **~schaft** *f* comradeship; **k~schaftlich** *adj* comradely

Kameramann (-(e)s, -männer) *m* cameraman

Kamille [ka'mɪlə] *f* camomile; **~ntee** *m* camomile tea

Kamin [ka'miːn] (-s, -e) *m* (*außen*) chimney; (*innen*) fireside, fireplace; **~kehrer** (-s, -) *m* chimney sweep

Kamm [kam] (-(e)s, ᵉe) *m* comb; (*Bergkamm*) ridge; (*Hahnenkamm*) crest

kämmen ['kɛmən] *vt* to comb ♦ *vr* to comb one's hair

Kammer ['kamər] (-, -n) *f* chamber; small bedroom

Kammerdiener *m* valet

Kampagne [kam'panjə] *f* campaign

Kampf [kampf] (-(e)s, ᵉe) *m* fight, battle; (*Wettbewerb*) contest; (*fig: Anstrengung*) struggle; **k~bereit** *adj* ready for action

kämpfen ['kɛmpfən] *vi* to fight

Kämpfer (-s, -) *m* fighter, combatant

Kampf- *zW*: **~handlung** *f* action; **k~los** *adj* without a fight; **~richter** *m* (*SPORT*) referee; (*TENNIS*) umpire; **~stoff** *m*: **chemischer/biologischer ~stoff** chemical/biological weapon

Kanada ['kanada] (-s) *nt* Canada; **Kanadier(in)** (-s, -) [kə'naːdiər(ɪn)] *m(f)* Canadian; **ka'nadisch** *adj* Canadian

Kanal [ka'naːl] (-s, Kanäle) *m* (*Fluss*) canal; (*Rinne, Ärmelkanal*) channel; (*für Abfluss*) drain; **~inseln** *pl* Channel Islands; **~isation** [-izatsi'oːn] *f* sewage system; **~tunnel** *m*: **der ~tunnel** the Channel Tunnel

Kanarienvogel [ka'naːriənfoːgəl] *m* (*ZOOL*) canary

kanarisch [ka'naːrɪʃ] *adj*: **K~e Inseln** Canary Islands, Canaries

Kandi- [kandi] *zW*: **~dat** [-'daːt] (-en, -en) *m* candidate; **~datur** [-da'tuːr] *f* candidature, candidacy; **k~dieren** [-'diːrən] *vi* to stand, to run

Kandis(zucker) ['kandɪs(tsʊkər)] (-) *m* candy

Känguru ▲ ['kɛŋguru] (-s, -s) *nt* kangaroo

Kaninchen [ka'niːnçən] *nt* rabbit

Kanister [ka'nɪstər] (-s, -) *m* can, canister

Kännchen ['kɛnçən] *nt* pot

Kanne ['kanə] *f* (*Krug*) jug; (*Kaffeekanne*) pot; (*Milchkanne*) churn; (*Gießkanne*) can

kannst *etc* [kanst] *vb siehe* **können**

Kanone [ka'noːnə] *f* gun; (*HIST*) cannon; (*fig: Mensch*) ace

Kantate [kan'taːtə] *f* cantaga

Kante ['kantə] *f* edge

Kantine [kan'tiːnə] *f* canteen

Kanton [kan'toːn] (-s, -e) *m* canton

| Kanton |

(i) **Kanton** is the term for a state or region of Switzerland. Under the Swiss constitution the **Kantone** enjoy considerable autonomy. The Swiss **Kantone** are Aargau, Appenzell, Basel, Bern, Fribourg, Geneva, Glarus, Graubünden, Luzern, Neuchâtel, St. Gallen, Schaffhausen, Schwyz, Solothurn, Ticino, Thurgau, Unterwalden, Uri, Valais, Vaud, Zug and Zürich.

Kanu ['ka:nu] **(-s, -s)** nt canoe
Kanzel ['kantsəl] **(-, -n)** f pulpit
Kanzler ['kantslər] **(-s, -)** m chancellor
Kap [kap] **(-s, -s)** nt cape (GEOG)
Kapazität [kapatsi'tε:t] f capacity; (Fachmann) authority
Kapelle [ka'pelə] f (Gebäude) chapel; (MUS) band
kapieren [ka'pi:rən] (umg) vt, vi to get, to understand
Kapital [kapi'ta:l] **(-s, -e** od **-ien)** nt capital; **~anlage** f investment; **~ismus** [-'lısmʊs] m capitalism; **~ist** [-'lıst] m capitalist; **k~istisch** adj capitalist
Kapitän [kapi'tε:n] **(-s, -e)** m captain
Kapitel [ka'pıtəl] **(-s, -)** nt chapter
Kapitulation [kapitulatsi'o:n] f capitulation
kapitulieren [kapitu'li:rən] vi to capitulate
Kappe ['kapə] f cap; (Kapuze) hood
kappen vt to cut
Kapsel ['kapsəl] **(-, -n)** f capsule
kaputt [ka'pʊt] (umg) adj kaput, broken; (Person) exhausted, finished; **am Auto ist etwas ~** there's something wrong with the car; **~gehen** (unreg) vi to break; (Schuhe) to fall apart; (Firma) to go bust; (Stoff) to wear out; (sterben) to cop it (umg); **~machen** vt to break; (Mensch) to exhaust, to wear out
Kapuze [ka'pu:tsə] f hood
Karamell ▲ [kara'mεl] **(-s)** m caramel; **~bonbon** m od nt toffee
Karate [ka'ra:tə] **(-s)** nt karate
Karawane [kara'va:nə] f caravan

Kardinal [kardi'na:l] **(-s, Kardinäle)** m cardinal;**~zahl** f cardinal number
Karfreitag [ka:r'fraıta:k] m Good Friday
karg [kark] adj (Landschaft, Boden) barren; (Lohn) meagre
kärglich ['kεrklıç] adj poor, scanty
Karibik [ka'ri:bık] **(-)** f: **die ~** the Caribbean
karibisch [ka'ri:bıʃ] adj: **K~e Inseln** Caribbean Islands
kariert [ka'ri:rt] adj (Stoff) checked; (Papier) squared
Karies ['ka:ries] **(-)** f caries
Karikatur [karika'tu:r] f caricature;**~ist** [-'rıst] m cartoonist
Karneval ['karnəval] **(-s, -e** od **-s)** m carnival

| Karneval |

(i) **Karneval** is the time immediately before Lent when people gather to eat, drink and generally have fun before the fasting begins. **Rosenmontag**, the day before Shrove Tuesday, is the most important day of **Karneval** on the Rhine. Most firms take a day's holiday on that day to enjoy the celebrations. In South Germany and Austria **Karneval** is called **Fasching**.

Karo ['ka:ro] **(-s, -s)** nt square; (KARTEN) diamonds
Karosserie [karɔsə'ri:] f (AUT) body(work)
Karotte [ka'rɔtə] f carrot
Karpfen ['karpfən] **(-s, -)** m carp
Karre ['karə] f cart, barrow
Karren (-s, -) m cart, barrow
Karriere [kari'ε:rə] f career; **~ machen** to get on, to get to the top; **~macher (-s, -)** m careerist
Karte ['kartə] f card; (Landkarte) map; (Speisekarte) menu; (Eintrittskarte, Fahrkarte) ticket; **alles auf eine ~ setzen** to put all one's eggs in one basket
Kartei [kar'taı] f card index; **~karte** f index card
Kartell [kar'tεl] **(-s, -e)** nt cartel
Karten- zW: **~spiel** nt card game; pack of cards; **~telefon** nt cardphone;

~vorverkauf *m* advance booking office

Kartoffel [kar'tɔfəl] **(-, -n)** *f* potato; **~brei** *m* mashed potatoes *pl*; **~mus** *nt* mashed potatoes *pl*; **~püree** *nt* mashed potatoes *pl*; **~salat** *m* potato salad

Karton [kar'tõ:] **(-s, -s)** *m* cardboard; (*Schachtel*) cardboard box; **k~iert** [karto'ni:rt] *adj* hardback

Karussell [karu'sɛl] **(-s, -s)** *nt* roundabout (*BRIT*), merry-go-round

Karwoche ['ka:rvɔxə] *f* Holy Week

Käse ['kɛ:zə] **(-s, -)** *m* cheese; **~glocke** *f* cheese (plate) cover; **~kuchen** *m* cheesecake

Kaserne [ka'zɛrnə] *f* barracks *pl*; **~nhof** *m* parade ground

Kasino [ka'zi:no] **(-s, -s)** *nt* club; (*MIL*) officers' mess; (*Spielkasino*) casino

Kaskoversicherung ['kasko-] *f* (*Teilkasko*) ≈ third party, fire and theft insurance; (*Vollkasko*) ≈ fully comprehensive insurance

Kasse ['kasə] *f* (*Geldkasten*) cashbox; (*in Geschäft*) till, cash register; cash desk, checkout; (*Kinokasse, Theaterkasse etc*) box office; ticket office; (*Krankenkasse*) health insurance; (*Sparkasse*) savings bank; **~machen** to count the money; **getrennte ~ führen** to pay separately; **an der ~** (*in Geschäft*) at the desk; **gut bei ~ sein** to be in the money

Kassen- *zW*: **~arzt** *m* panel doctor (*BRIT*); **~bestand** *m* cash balance; **~patient** *m* panel patient (*BRIT*); **~prüfung** *f* audit; **~sturz** *m*: **~sturz machen** to check one's money; **~zettel** *m* receipt

Kassette [ka'sɛtə] *f* small box; (*Tonband, PHOT*) cassette; (*Bücherkassette*) case

Kassettenrekorder **(-s, -)** *m* cassette recorder

kassieren [ka'si:rən] *vt* to take ♦ *vi*: **darf ich ~?** would you like to pay now?

Kassierer [ka'si:rər] **(-s, -)** *m* cashier; (*von Klub*) treasurer

Kastanie [kas'ta:niə] *f* chestnut; (*Baum*) chestnut tree

Kasten ['kastən] **(-s, ⁖)** *m* (*auch SPORT*) box; case; (*Truhe*) chest

kastrieren [kas'tri:rən] *vt* to castrate

Katalog [kata'lo:k] **(-(e)s, -e)** *m* catalogue

Katalysator [kataly'za:tɔr] *m* catalyst; (*AUT*) catalytic converter

katastrophal [katastro'fa:l] *adj* catastrophic

Katastrophe [kata'stro:fə] *f* catastrophe, disaster

Kat-Auto ['kat|auto] *nt* car fitted with a catalytic converter

Kategorie [katego'ri:] *f* category

kategorisch [kate'go:rɪʃ] *adj* categorical

Kater ['ka:tər] **(-s, -)** *m* tomcat; (*umg*) hangover

kath. *abk* (= *katholisch*) Cath.

Kathedrale [kate'dra:lə] *f* cathedral

Katholik [kato'li:k] **(-en, -en)** *m* Catholic

katholisch [ka'to:lɪʃ] *adj* Catholic

Kätzchen ['kɛtsçən] *nt* kitten

Katze ['katsə] *f* cat; **für die Katz** (*umg*) in vain, for nothing

Katzen- *zW*: **~auge** *nt* cat's eye; (*Fahrrad*) rear light; **~sprung** (*umg*) *m* stone's throw; short journey

Kauderwelsch ['kaudərvɛlʃ] **(-(s))** *nt* jargon; (*umg*) double Dutch

kauen ['kauən] *vt, vi* to chew

kauern ['kauərn] *vi* to crouch down; (*furchtsam*) to cower

Kauf [kauf] **(-(e)s, Käufe)** *m* purchase, buy; (*~en*) buying; **ein guter ~** a bargain; **etw in ~ nehmen** to put up with sth; **k~en** *vt* to buy

Käufer(in) ['kɔyfər(ɪn)] **(-s, -)** *m(f)* buyer

Kauf- *zW*: **~frau** *f* businesswoman; **~haus** *nt* department store; **~kraft** *f* purchasing power

käuflich ['kɔyflɪç] *adj* purchasable, for sale; (*pej*) venal ♦ *adv*: **~ erwerben** to purchase

Kauf- *zW*: **k~lustig** *adj* interested in buying; **~mann** (*pl* **-leute**) *m* businessman; shopkeeper; **k~männisch** *adj* commercial; **k~männischer Angestellter** office worker; **~preis** *m* purchase price; **~vertrag** *m* bill of sale

Kaugummi ['kaugumi] *m* chewing gum

Kaulquappe ['kaulkvapə] *f* tadpole

kaum [kaum] *adv* hardly, scarcely

Kaution [kauts'o:n] f deposit; (JUR) bail

Kauz [kauts] (-es, Käuze) m owl; (fig) queer fellow

Kavalier [kava'li:r] (-s, -e) m gentleman, cavalier; **~sdelikt** nt peccadillo

Kaviar ['ka:viar] m caviar

keck [kɛk] adj daring, bold

Kegel ['ke:gəl] (-s, -) m skittle; (MATH) cone; **~bahn** f skittle alley; bowling alley; **k~n** vi to play skittles

Kehle ['ke:lə] f throat

Kehlkopf m larynx

Kehre ['ke:rə] f turn(ing), bend; **k~n** vt, vi (wenden) to turn; (mit Besen) to sweep; **sich an etw** dat **nicht k~n** not to heed sth

Kehricht ['ke:rɪçt] (-s) m sweepings pl

Kehrseite f reverse, other side; wrong side; bad side

kehrtmachen vi to turn about, to about-turn

keifen ['kaifən] vi to scold, to nag

Keil [kail] (-(e)s, -e) m wedge; (MIL) arrowhead; **~riemen** m (AUT) fan belt

Keim [kaim] (-(e)s, -e) m bud; (MED, fig) germ; **k~en** vi to germinate; **k~frei** adj sterile; **~zelle** f (fig) nucleus

kein [kain] adj no, not ... any; **~e(r, s)** pron no one, nobody; none; **~erlei** adj attrib no ... whatsoever

keinesfalls adv on no account

keineswegs adv by no means

keinmal adv not once

Keks [ke:ks] (-es, -e) m od nt biscuit

Kelch [kɛlç] (-(e)s, -e) m cup, goblet, chalice

Kelle ['kɛlə] f (Suppenkelle) ladle; (Maurerkelle) trowel

Keller ['kɛlər] (-s, -) m cellar

Kellner(in) ['kɛlnər(ɪn)] (-s, -) m(f) waiter (-tress)

keltern ['kɛltərn] vt to press

kennen ['kɛnən] (unreg) vt to know; **~ lernen** ▲ to get to know; **sich ~ lernen** to get to know each other; (zum ersten Mal) to meet

Kenner (-s, -) m connoisseur

kenntlich adj distinguishable, discernible;

etw **~ machen** to mark sth

Kenntnis (-, -se) f knowledge no pl; **etw zur ~ nehmen** to note sth; **von etw ~ nehmen** to take notice of sth; **jdn in ~ setzen** to inform sb

Kenn- zW: **~zeichen** nt mark, characteristic; **k~zeichnen** vt insep to characterize; **~ziffer** f reference number

kentern ['kɛntərn] vi to capsize

Keramik [ke'ra:mɪk] (-, -en) f ceramics pl, pottery

Kerbe ['kɛrbə] f notch, groove

Kerker ['kɛrkər] (-s, -) m prison

Kerl [kɛrl] (-s, -e) m chap, bloke (BRIT), guy

Kern [kɛrn] (-(e)s, -e) m (Obstkern) pip, stone; (Nusskern) kernel; (Atomkern) nucleus; (fig) heart, core; **~energie** f nuclear energy; **~forschung** f nuclear research; **~frage** f central issue; **k~gesund** adj thoroughly healthy, fit as a fiddle; **k~ig** adj (kraftvoll) robust; (Ausspruch) pithy; **~kraftwerk** nt nuclear power station; **k~los** adj seedless, without pips; **~physik** f nuclear physics sg; **~spaltung** f nuclear fission; **~waffen** pl nuclear weapons

Kerze ['kɛrtsə] f candle; (Zündkerze) plug; **k~ngerade** adj straight as a die; **~nständer** m candle holder

kess ▲ [kɛs] adj saucy

Kessel ['kɛsəl] (-s, -) m kettle; (von Lokomotive etc) boiler; (GEOG) depression; (MIL) encirclement

Kette ['kɛtə] f chain; **k~n** vt to chain; **~nrauchen** (-s) nt chain smoking; **~nreaktion** f chain reaction

Ketzer ['kɛtsər] (-s, -) m heretic

keuchen ['kɔyçən] vi to pant, to gasp

Keuchhusten m whooping cough

Keule ['kɔylə] f club; (KOCH) leg

keusch [kɔyʃ] adj chaste; **K~heit** f chastity

kfm. abk = **kaufmännisch**

Kfz [ka:ɛf'tset] nt abk = **Kraftfahrzeug**

KG [ka:'ge:] (-, -s) f abk (= Kommanditgesellschaft) limited partnership

kg abk = **Kilogramm**

kichern ['kɪçərn] vi to giggle

kidnappen ['kɪtnɛpən] *vt* to kidnap
Kiefer¹ ['kiːfər] (-s, -) *m* jaw
Kiefer² ['kiːfər] (-, -n) *f* pine; **~nzapfen** *m* pine cone
Kiel [kiːl] (-(e)s, -e) *m* (*Federkiel*) quill; (*NAUT*) keel
Kieme ['kiːmə] *f* gill
Kies [kiːs] (-es, -e) *m* gravel
Kilo ['kiːlo] *nt* kilo; **~gramm** [kilo'gram] *nt* kilogram; **~meter** [kilo'meːtər] *m* kilometre; **~meterzähler** *m* milometer
Kind [kɪnt] (-(e)s, -er) *nt* child; **von ~ auf** from childhood
Kinder- ['kɪndər] *zW:* **~betreuung** *f* crèche; **~ei** [-'raɪ] *f* childishness; **~garten** *m* nursery school, playgroup; **~gärtnerin** *f* nursery school teacher; **~geld** *nt* child benefit (*BRIT*); **~heim** *nt* children's home; **~krippe** *f* crèche; **~lähmung** *f* poliomyelitis; **k~leicht** *adj* childishly easy; **k~los** *adj* childless; **~mädchen** *nt* nursemaid; **k~reich** *adj* with a lot of children; **~sendung** *f* (*RADIO, TV*) children's programme; **~sicherung** *f* (*AUT*) childproof safety catch; **~spiel** *nt* (*fig*) child's play; **~tagesstätte** *f* day nursery; **~wagen** *m* pram, baby carriage (*US*); **~zimmer** *nt* (*für ~*) children's room; (*für Säugling*) nursery

---
Kindergarten

ⓘ A **Kindergarten** *is a nursery school for children aged between 3 and 6 years. The children sing and play but do not receive any formal instruction. Most Kindergärten are financed by the town or the church with parents paying a monthly contribution towards the cost.*

Kind- *zW:* **~heit** *f* childhood; **k~isch** *adj* childish; **k~lich** *adj* childlike
Kinn [kɪn] (-(e)s, -e) *nt* chin; **~haken** *m* (*BOXEN*) uppercut
Kino ['kiːno] (-s, -s) *nt* cinema; **~besucher** *m* cinema-goer; **~programm** *nt* film programme
Kiosk [ki'ɔsk] (-(e)s, -e) *m* kiosk

Kippe ['kɪpə] *f* cigarette end; (*umg*) fag; **auf der ~ stehen** (*fig*) to be touch and go
kippen *vi* to topple over, to overturn ♦ *vt* to tilt
Kirch- ['kɪrç] *zW:* **~e** *f* church; **~enlied** *nt* hymn; **~ensteuer** *f* church tax; **~gänger** (-s, -) *m* churchgoer; **~hof** *m* churchyard; **k~lich** *adj* ecclesiastical
Kirmes ['kɪrməs] (-, -sen) *f* fair
Kirsche ['kɪrʃə] *f* cherry
Kissen ['kɪsən] (-s, -) *nt* cushion; (*Kopfkissen*) pillow; **~bezug** *m* pillowslip
Kiste ['kɪstə] *f* box; chest
Kitsch [kɪtʃ] (-(e)s) *m* kitsch; **k~ig** *adj* kitschy
Kitt [kɪt] (-(e)s, -e) *m* putty
Kittel (-s, -) *m* overall, smock
kitten *vt* to putty; (*fig: Ehe etc*) to cement
kitzelig ['kɪtsəlɪç] *adj* (*auch fig*) ticklish
kitzeln *vi* to tickle
Kiwi ['kiːvi] (-, -s) *f* (*BOT, KOCH*) kiwi fruit
KKW [kaːkaːˈveː] *nt abk* = **Kernkraftwerk**
Klage ['klaːgə] *f* complaint; (*JUR*) action; **k~n** *vi* (*wehklagen*) to lament, to wail; (*sich beschweren*) to complain; (*JUR*) to take legal action
Kläger(in) ['klɛːgər(ɪn)] (-s, -) *m(f)* plaintiff
kläglich ['klɛːklɪç] *adj* wretched
klamm [klam] *adj* (*Finger*) numb; (*feucht*) damp
Klammer ['klamər] (-, -n) *f* clamp; (*in Text*) bracket; (*Büro~*) clip; (*Wäsche~*) peg; (*Zahn~*) brace; **k~n** *vr:* **sich k~n an** +*akk* to cling to
Klang [klaŋ] (-(e)s, -̈e) *m* sound; **k~voll** *adj* sonorous
Klappe ['klapə] *f* valve; (*Ofen~*) damper; (*umg: Mund*) trap; **k~n** *vi* (*Geräusch*) to click; (*Sitz etc*) to tip ♦ *vt* to tip ♦ *vb unpers* to work
Klapper ['klapər] (-, -n) *f* rattle; **k~ig** *adj* run-down, worn-out; **k~n** *vi* to clatter, to rattle; **~schlange** *f* rattlesnake; **~storch** *m* stork
Klapp- *zW:* **~messer** *nt* jackknife; **~rad** *nt* collapsible bicycle; **~stuhl** *m* folding chair; **~tisch** *m* folding table
Klaps [klaps] (-es, -e) *m* slap

klar [klaːr] adj clear; (NAUT) ready for sea; (MIL) ready for action; **sich** dat **(über etw** akk**) ~ werden** to get (sth) clear in one's mind; **sich** dat **im K~en sein über** +akk to be clear about; **ins K~e kommen** to get clear; **(na) ~!** of course!; **~ sehen** to see clearly

Kläranlage f purification plant

klären ['klɛːrən] vt (Flüssigkeit) to purify; (Probleme) to clarify ♦ vr to clear (itself) up

Klarheit f clarity

Klarinette [klari'nɛtə] f clarinet

klar- zW: **~legen** vt to clear up, to explain; **~machen** vt (Schiff) to get ready for sea; **jdm etw ~machen** to make sth clear to sb; **~sehen** △ (unreg) vi siehe **klar**; **K~sichtfolie** f transparent film; **~stellen** vt to clarify

Klärung ['klɛːrʊŋ] f (von Flüssigkeit) purification; (von Probleme) clarification

klarwerden △ (unreg) vi siehe **klar**

Klasse ['klasə] f class; (SCH) class, form

klasse (umg) adj smashing

Klassen- zW: **~arbeit** f test; **~gesellschaft** f class society; **~lehrer** m form master; **k~los** adj classless; **~sprecher(in)** m(f) form prefect; **~zimmer** nt classroom

klassifizieren [klasifi'tsiːrən] vt to classify

Klassik ['klasɪk] f (Zeit) classical period; (Stil) classicism; **~er (-s, -)** m classic

klassisch adj (auch fig) classical

Klatsch [klatʃ] **(-(e)s, -e)** m smack, crack; (Gerede) gossip; **~base** f gossip, scandalmonger; **~e** (umg) f crib; **k~en** vi (Geräusch) to clash; (reden) to gossip; (applaudieren) to applaud, to clap ♦ vt: **jdm Beifall k~en** to applaud sb; **~mohn** m (corn) poppy; **k~nass** ▲ adj soaking wet

Klaue ['klauə] f claw; (umg: Schrift) scrawl; **k~n** (umg) vt to pinch

Klausel ['klauzəl] **(-, -n)** f clause

Klausur [klau'zuːr] f seclusion; **~arbeit** f examination paper

Klavier [kla'viːr] **(-s, -e)** nt piano

Kleb- ['kleːb] zW: **k~en** ['kleːbən] vt, vi: **k~en (an** +akk**)** to stick (to); **k~rig** adj

sticky; **~stoff** m glue; **~streifen** m adhesive tape

kleckern ['klekərn] vi to make a mess ♦ vt to spill

Klecks [kleks] **(-es, -e)** m blot, stain

Klee [kleː] **(-s)** m clover; **~blatt** nt cloverleaf; (fig) trio

Kleid [klait] **(-(e)s, -er)** nt garment; (Frauenkleid) dress; **~er** pl (~ung) clothes; **k~en** ['klaidən] vt to clothe, to dress; to suit ♦ vr to dress

Kleider- ['klaidər] zW: **~bügel** m coat hanger; **~bürste** f clothes brush; **~schrank** m wardrobe

Kleid- zW: **k~sam** adj flattering; **~ung** f clothing; **~ungsstück** nt garment

klein [klain] adj little, small; **~ hacken** to chop, to mince; **~ schneiden** to chop up; **K~e(r, s)** mf little one; **K~format** nt small size; **im K~format** small-scale; **K~geld** nt small change; **K~igkeit** f trifle; **K~kind** nt infant; **K~kram** m details pl; **k~laut** adj dejected, quiet; **~lich** adj petty, paltry; **K~od** ['klainoːt] **(-s, -odien)** nt gem, jewel; treasure; **K~stadt** f small town; **~städtisch** adj provincial; **~stmöglich** adj smallest possible

Kleister ['klaistər] **(-s, -)** m paste

Klemme ['klemə] f clip; (MED) clamp; (fig) jam; **k~n** vt (festhalten) to jam; (quetschen) to pinch, to nip ♦ vr to catch o.s.; (sich hineinzwängen) to squeeze o.s. ♦ vi (Tür) to stick, to jam; **sich hinter jdn/etw k~n** to get on to sb/down to sth

Klempner ['klempnər] **(-s, -)** m plumber

Klerus ['kleːrus] **(-)** m clergy

Klette ['kletə] f burr

Kletter- ['kletər] zW: **~er (-s, -)** m climber; **k~n** vi to climb; **~pflanze** f creeper

klicken ['klɪkən] vi (COMPUT) to click

Klient(in) [kli'ent(in)] m(f) client

Klima ['kliːma] **(-s, -s** od **-te)** nt climate; **~anlage** f air conditioning; **~wechsel** m change of air

klimpern ['klɪmpərn] (umg) vi (mit Münzen, Schlüsseln) to jingle; (auf Klavier) to plonk (away)

Klinge ['klɪŋə] f blade; sword

Klingel ['klɪŋəl] (-, -n) f bell; **~beutel** m collection bag; **k~n** vi to ring

klingen ['klɪŋən] (unreg) vi to sound; (Gläser) to clink

Klinik ['kli:nɪk] f hospital, clinic

Klinke ['klɪŋkə] f handle

Klippe ['klɪpə] f cliff; (im Meer) reef; (fig) hurdle

klipp und klar ['klɪp|ʊntkla:r] adj clear and concise

klirren ['klɪrən] vi to clank, to jangle; (Gläser) to clink; **~de Kälte** biting cold

Klischee [klɪ'ʃe:] (-s, -s) nt (Druckplatte) plate, block; (fig) cliché; **~vorstellung** f stereotyped idea

Klo [klo:] (-s, -s) (umg) nt loo (BRIT), john (US)

Kloake [klo'a:kə] f sewer

klobig ['klo:bɪç] adj clumsy

Klon [klo:n] (-s, -e) m clone

klonen ['klo:nən] vti to clone

Klopapier (umg) nt loo paper (BRIT)

klopfen ['klɔpfən] vi to knock; (Herz) to thump ♦ vt to beat; **es klopft** somebody's knocking; **jdm auf die Schulter ~** to tap sb on the shoulder

Klopfer (-s, -) m (Teppichklopfer) beater; (Türklopfer) knocker

Klops [klɔps] (-es, -e) m meatball

Klosett [klo'zɛt] (-s, -e od -s) nt lavatory, toilet; **~papier** nt toilet paper

Kloß [klo:s] (-es, ⁺e) m (im Hals) lump; (KOCH) dumpling

Kloster ['klo:stər] (-s, ⁺) nt (Männerkloster) monastery; (Frauenkloster) convent; **klösterlich** ['klø:stərlɪç] adj monastic; convent cpd

Klotz [klɔts] (-es, ⁺e) m log; (Hackklotz) block; **ein ~ am Bein** (fig) a drag, a millstone round (sb's) neck

Klub [klʊp] (-s, -s) m club; **~sessel** m easy chair

Kluft [klʊft] (-, ⁺e) f cleft, gap; (GEOG) gorge, chasm

klug [klu:k] adj clever, intelligent; **K~heit** f cleverness, intelligence

Klumpen ['klʊmpən] (-s, -) m (Erd~) clod;

(Blut~) clot; (Gold~) nugget; (KOCH) lump

km abk = **Kilometer**

knabbern ['knabərn] vt, vi to nibble

Knabe ['kna:bə] (-n, -n) m boy

Knäckebrot ['knɛkəbro:t] nt crispbread

knacken ['knakən] vt, vi (auch fig) to crack

Knacks [knaks] (-es, -e) m crack; (fig) defect

Knall [knal] (-(e)s, -e) m bang; (Peitschenknall) crack; **~ und Fall** (umg) unexpectedly; **~bonbon** nt cracker; **k~en** vi to bang; to crack; **k~rot** adj bright red

knapp [knap] adj tight; (Geld) scarce; (Sprache) concise; **eine ~e Stunde** just under an hour; **~ unter/neben** just under/ by; **K~heit** f tightness; scarcity; conciseness

knarren ['knarən] vi to creak

Knast [knast] (-(e)s) (umg) m (Haftstrafe) porridge (inf), time (inf); (Gefängnis) slammer (inf), clink (inf)

knattern ['knatərn] vi to rattle; (Maschinengewehr) to chatter

Knäuel ['knɔyəl] (-s, -) m od nt (Wollknäuel) ball; (Menschenknäuel) knot

Knauf [knaʊf] (-(e)s, Knäufe) m knob; (Schwertknauf) pommel

Knebel ['kne:bəl] (-s, -) m gag

kneifen ['knaɪfən] (unreg) vt to pinch ♦ vi to pinch; (sich drücken) to back out; **vor etw ~** to dodge sth

Kneipe ['knaɪpə] (umg) f pub

kneten ['kne:tən] vt to knead; (Wachs) to mould

Knick [knɪk] (-(e)s, -e) m (Sprung) crack; (Kurve) bend; (Falte) fold; **k~en** vt, vi (springen) to crack; (brechen) to break; (Papier) to fold; **geknickt sein** to be downcast

Knicks [knɪks] (-es, -e) m curtsey

Knie [kni:] (-s, -) nt knee; **~beuge** f knee bend; **~bundhose** f knee breeches; **~gelenk** nt knee joint; **~kehle** f back of the knee; **k~n** vi to kneel; **~scheibe** f kneecap; **~strumpf** m knee-length sock

Kniff [knɪf] (-(e)s, -e) m (fig) trick, knack; **k~elig** adj tricky

knipsen ['knɪpsən] vt (Fahrkarte) to punch; (PHOT) to take a snap of, to snap ♦ vi to take a snap od snaps

Knirps [knɪrps] (-es, -e) m little chap; (®: Schirm) telescopic umbrella

knirschen ['knɪrʃən] vi to crunch; **mit den Zähnen ~** to grind one's teeth

knistern ['knɪstərn] vi to crackle

Knitter- ['knɪtər] zW: **~falte** f crease; **k~frei** adj non-crease; **k~n** vi to crease

Knoblauch ['knoːplaʊx] (-(e)s) m garlic; **~zehe** f (KOCH) clove of garlic

Knöchel ['knœçəl] (-s, -) m knuckle; (Fußknöchel) ankle

Knochen ['knɔxən] (-s, -) m bone; **~bruch** m fracture; **~gerüst** nt skeleton; **~mark** nt bone marrow

knöchern ['knœçərn] adj bone

knochig ['knɔxɪç] adj bony

Knödel ['knøːdəl] (-s, -) m dumpling

Knolle ['knɔlə] f tuber

Knopf [knɔpf] (-(e)s, ⁻e) m button; (Kragenknopf) stud

knöpfen ['knœpfən] vt to button

Knopfloch nt buttonhole

Knorpel ['knɔrpəl] (-s, -) m cartilage, gristle; **k~ig** adj gristly

Knospe ['knɔspə] f bud

Knoten ['knoːtən] (-s, -) m knot; (BOT) node; (MED) lump; **k~** vt to knot; **~punkt** m junction

Knüller ['knʏlər] (-s, -) (umg) m hit; (Reportage) scoop

knüpfen ['knʏpfən] vt to tie; (Teppich) to knot; (Freundschaft) to form

Knüppel ['knʏpəl] (-s, -) m cudgel; (Polizeiknüppel) baton, truncheon; (AVIAT) (joy)stick

knurren ['knʊrən] vi (Hund) to snarl, to growl; (Magen) to rumble; (Mensch) to mutter

knusperig ['knʊspərɪç] adj crisp; (Keks) crunchy

k. o. [kaːˈoː] adj knocked out; (fig) done in

Koalition [koalitsiˈoːn] f coalition

Kobold ['koːbɔlt] (-(e)s, -e) m goblin, imp

Koch [kɔx] (-(e)s, ⁻e) m cook; **~buch** nt cook(ery) book; **k~en** vt, vi to cook; (Wasser) to boil; **~er** (-s, -) m stove, cooker; **~gelegenheit** f cooking facilities pl

Köchin ['kœçɪn] f cook

Koch- zW: **~löffel** m kitchen spoon; **~nische** f kitchenette; **~platte** f hotplate; **~salz** nt cooking salt; **~topf** m saucepan, pot

Köder ['køːdər] (-s, -) m bait, lure

ködern vt (Tier) to trap with bait; (Person) to entice, to tempt

Koexistenz [koɛksɪsˈtɛnts] f coexistence

Koffein [kɔfeˈiːn] (-s) nt caffeine; **k~frei** adj decaffeinated

Koffer ['kɔfər] (-s, -) m suitcase; (Schrankkoffer) trunk; **~kuli** m (luggage) trolley; **~radio** nt portable radio; **~raum** m (AUT) boot (BRIT), trunk (US)

Kognak ['kɔnjak] (-s, -s) m brandy, cognac

Kohl [koːl] (-(e)s, -e) m cabbage

Kohle ['koːlə] f coal; (Holzkohle) charcoal; (CHEM) carbon; **~hydrat** (-(e)s, -e) nt carbohydrate

Kohlen- zW: **~dioxid** (-(e)s, -e) nt carbon dioxide; **~händler** m coal merchant, coalman; **~säure** f carbon dioxide; **~stoff** m carbon

Kohlepapier nt carbon paper

Koje ['koːjə] f cabin; (Bett) bunk

Kokain [kokaˈiːn] (-s) nt cocaine

kokett [koˈkɛt] adj coquettish, flirtatious

Kokosnuss ▲ ['koːkɔsnʊs] f coconut

Koks [koːks] (-es, -e) m coke

Kolben ['kɔlbən] (-s, -) m (Gewehrkolben) rifle butt; (Keule) club; (CHEM) flask; (TECH) piston; (Maiskolben) cob

Kolik ['koːlɪk] f colic, the gripes pl

Kollaps [kɔˈlaps] (-es, -e) m collapse

Kolleg [kɔˈleːk] (-s, -s od -ien) nt lecture course; **~e** [kɔˈleːgə] (-n, -n) m colleague; **~in** f colleague; **~ium** nt working party; (SCH) staff

Kollekte [kɔˈlɛktə] f (REL) collection

kollektiv [kɔlɛkˈtiːf] adj collective

Köln [kœln] (-s) nt Cologne

Kolonie [koloˈniː] f colony

kolonisieren [koloni'zi:rən] *vt* to colonize

Kolonne [ko'lɔnə] *f* column; (*von Fahrzeugen*) convoy

Koloss ▲ [ko'lɔs] (**-es, -e**) *m* colossus; **kolo'ssal** *adj* colossal

Kölsch [kœlʃ] (**-, -**) *nt* (*Bier*) ≈ (strong) lager

Kombi- ['kɔmbi] *zW:* **~nation** [-natsi'o:n] *f* combination; (*Vermutung*) conjecture; (*Hemdhose*) combinations *pl;* **k~nieren** [-'ni:rən] *vt* to combine ♦ *vi* to deduce, to work out; (*vermuten*) to guess; **~wagen** *m* station wagon; **~zange** *f* (pair of) pliers *pl*

Komet [ko'me:t] (**-en, -en**) *m* comet

Komfort [kɔm'fo:r] (**-s**) *m* luxury

Komik ['ko:mik] *f* humour, comedy; **~er** (**-s, -**) *m* comedian

komisch ['ko:miʃ] *adj* funny

Komitee [komi'te:] (**-s, -s**) *nt* committee

Komma ['kɔma] (**-s, -s** *od* **-ta**) *nt* comma; **2 ~ 3** 2 point 3

Kommand- [ko'mand] *zW:* **~ant** [-'dant] *m* commander, commanding officer; **k~ieren** [-'di:rən] *vt, vi* to command; **~o** (**-s, -s**) *nt* command, order; (*Truppe*) detachment, squad; **auf ~o** to order

kommen ['kɔmən] (*unreg*) *vi* to come; (*näher kommen*) to approach; (*passieren*) to happen; (*gelangen, geraten*) to get; (*Blumen, Zähne, Tränen etc*) to appear; (*in die Schule, das Zuchthaus etc*) to go; **~ lassen** to send for; **das kommt in den Schrank** that goes in the cupboard; **zu sich ~** to come round *od* to; **zu etw ~** to acquire sth; **um etw ~** to lose sth; **nichts auf jdn/etw ~ lassen** to have nothing said against sb/sth; **jdm frech ~** to get cheeky with sb; **auf jeden vierten kommt ein Platz** there's one place for every fourth person; **wer kommt zuerst?** who's first?; **unter ein Auto ~** to be run over by a car; **wie hoch kommt das?** what does that cost?; **komm gut nach Hause!** safe journey (home); **~den Sonntag** next Sunday; **K~** (**-s**) *nt* coming

Kommentar [kɔmen'ta:r] *m* commentary; **kein ~** no comment; **k~los** *adj* without comment

Kommentator [kɔmen'ta:tɔr] *m* (*TV*)
commentator

kommentieren [kɔmen'ti:rən] *vt* to comment on

kommerziell [kɔmertsi'ɛl] *adj* commercial

Kommilitone [kɔmili'to:nə] (**-n, -n**) *m* fellow student

Kommissar [kɔmi'sa:r] *m* police inspector

Kommission [kɔmi'sio:n] *f* (*COMM*) commission; (*Ausschuss*) committee

Kommode [kɔ'mo:də] *f* (chest of) drawers

kommunal [kɔmu'na:l] *adj* local; (*von Stadt auch*) municipal

Kommune [kɔ'mu:nə] *f* commune

Kommunikation [kɔmunikatsi'o:n] *f* communication

Kommunion [kɔmuni'o:n] *f* communion

Kommuniqué, Kommunikee ▲ [kɔmyni'ke:] (**-s, -s**) *nt* communiqué

Kommunismus [kɔmu'nismʊs] *m* communism

Kommunist(in) [kɔmu'nist(in)] *m(f)* communist; **k~isch** *adj* communist

kommunizieren [kɔmuni'tsi:rən] *vi* to communicate

Komödie [ko'mø:diə] *f* comedy

Kompagnon [kɔmpan'jõ:] (**-s, -s**) *m* (*COMM*) partner

kompakt [kɔm'pakt] *adj* compact

Kompanie [kɔmpa'ni:] *f* company

Kompass ▲ ['kɔmpas] (**-es, -e**) *m* compass

kompatibel [kɔmpa'ti:bəl] *adj* compatible

kompetent [kɔmpe'tent] *adj* competent

Kompetenz *f* competence, authority

komplett [kɔm'plet] *adj* complete

Komplex [kɔm'pleks] (**-es, -e**) *m* (*Gebäudekomplex*) complex

Komplikation [kɔmplikatsi'o:n] *f* complication

Kompliment [kɔmpli'ment] *nt* compliment

Komplize [kɔm'pli:tsə] (**-n, -n**) *m* accomplice

kompliziert [kɔmpli'tsi:rt] *adj* complicated

komponieren [kɔmpo'ni:rən] *vt* to compose

Komponist [kɔmpo'nist(in)] *m* composer

Komposition [kɔmpozitsi'o:n] *f* composition

Kompost [kɔm'pɔst] (**-(e)s, -e**) *m* compost

Kompott [kɔm'pɔt] (-(e)s, -e) nt stewed fruit

Kompromiss ▲ [kɔmpro'mɪs] (-es, -e) m compromise; **k~bereit** adj willing to compromise

Kondens- [kɔn'dɛns] zW: **~ation** [kɔndenzatsi'oːn] f condensation; **k~ieren** [kɔnden'ziːrən] vt to condense; **~milch** f condensed milk

Kondition [kɔnditsi'oːn] f (COMM, FIN) condition; (Durchhaltevermögen) stamina; (körperliche Verfassung) physical condition, state of health

Konditionstraining [kɔnditsi'oːnstreːnɪŋ] nt fitness training

Konditor [kɔn'diːtɔr] m pastry cook; **~ei** [-'raɪ] f café; cake shop

Kondom [kɔn'doːm] (-s, -e) nt condom

Konferenz [kɔnfe'rɛnts] f conference, meeting

Konfession [kɔnfesi'oːn] f (religious) denomination; **k~ell** [-'nɛl] adj denominational; **k~slos** adj non-denominational

Konfirmand [kɔnfɪr'mant] m candidate for confirmation

Konfirmation [kɔnfɪrmatsi'oːn] f (REL) confirmation

konfirmieren [kɔnfɪr'miːrən] vt to confirm

konfiszieren [kɔnfɪs'tsiːrən] vt to confiscate

Konfitüre [kɔnfi'tyːrə] f jam

Konflikt [kɔn'flɪkt] (-(e)s, -e) m conflict

konfrontieren [kɔnfrɔn'tiːrən] vt to confront

konfus [kɔn'fuːs] adj confused

Kongress ▲ [kɔn'grɛs] (-es, -e) m congress; **~zentrum** nt conference centre

Kongruenz [kɔngru'ɛnts] f agreement, congruence

König ['køːnɪç] (-(e)s, -e) m king; **~in** ['køːnɪgɪn] f queen; **k~lich** adj royal; **~reich** nt kingdom

Konjugation [kɔnjugatsi'oːn] f conjugation

konjugieren [kɔnju'giːrən] vt to conjugate

Konjunktion [kɔnjuŋktsi'oːn] f conjunction

Konjunktiv ['kɔnjuŋktiːf] (-s, -e) m subjunctive

Konjunktur [kɔnjuŋk'tuːr] f economic

situation; (Hochkonjunktur) boom

konkret [kɔn'kreːt] adj concrete

Konkurrent(in) [kɔnkʊ'rɛnt(ɪn)] m(f) competitor

Konkurrenz [kɔnkʊ'rɛnts] f competition; **k~fähig** adj competitive; **~kampf** m competition; rivalry, competitive situation

konkurrieren [kɔnkʊ'riːrən] vi to compete

Konkurs [kɔn'kʊrs] (-es, -e) m bankruptcy

Können (-s) nt ability

SCHLÜSSELWORT
---

können ['kœnən] (pt konnte, pp gekonnt od (als Hilfsverb) können) vt, vi **1** to be able to; **ich kann es machen** I can do it, I am able to do it; **ich kann es nicht machen** I can't do it, I'm not able to do it; **ich kann nicht ...** I can't ..., I cannot ...; **ich kann nicht mehr** I can't go on

2 (wissen, beherrschen) to know; **können Sie Deutsch?** can you speak German?; **er kann gut Englisch** he speaks English well; **sie kann keine Mathematik** she can't do mathematics

3 (dürfen) to be allowed to; **kann ich gehen?** can I go?; **könnte ich ...?** could I ...?; **kann ich mit?** (umg) can I come with you?

4 (möglich sein): **Sie könnten Recht haben** you may be right; **das kann sein** that's possible; **kann sein** maybe

---

Könner m expert

konnte etc ['kɔntə] vb siehe **können**

konsequent [kɔnze'kvɛnt] adj consistent

Konsequenz [kɔnze'kvɛnts] f consistency; (Folgerung) conclusion

Konserv- [kɔn'zɛrv] zW: **k~ativ** [-a'tiːf] adj conservative; **~ative(r)** [-a'tiːvə(r)] f(m) (POL) conservative; **~e** f tinned food; **~enbüchse** f tin, can; **k~ieren** [-'viːrən] vt to preserve; **~ierung** f preservation; **~ierungsstoff** m preservatives

Konsonant [kɔnzo'nant] m consonant

konstant [kɔn'stant] adj constant

konstru- zW: **~ieren** [kɔnstru'iːrən] vt to construct; **K~kteur** [kɔnstrʊk'tøːr] m

designer; **K~ktion** [kənstrʊktsi'oːn] f
construction; **~ktiv** [kɔnstrʊk'tiːf] *adj*
constructive

Konsul ['kɔnzʊl] (-s, -n) *m* consul; **~at** [-'laːt]
nt consulate

konsultieren [kɔnzʊl'tiːrən] *vt* to consult

Konsum [kɔn'zuːm] (-s) *m* consumption;
~artikel *m* consumer article; **~ent** [-'ment]
m consumer; **k~ieren** [-'miːrən] *vt* to
consume

Kontakt [kɔn'takt] (-(e)s, -e) *m* contact;
k~arm *adj* unsociable; **k~freudig** *adj*
sociable; **~linsen** *pl* contact lenses

kontern ['kɔntərn] *vt, vi* to counter

Kontinent [kɔnti'nent] *m* continent

Kontingent [kɔntɪŋ'gent] (-(e)s, -e) *nt*
quota; (*Truppenkontingent*) contingent

kontinuierlich [kɔntinu'iːrlɪç] *adj*
continuous

Konto ['kɔnto] (-s, Konten) *nt* account;
~auszug *m* statement (of account);
~inhaber(in) *m(f)* account holder; **~stand**
m balance

Kontra ['kɔntra] (-s, -s) *nt* (*KARTEN*) double;
jdm ~ geben (*fig*) to contradict sb;
~bass ▲ *m* double bass; **~hent** *m* (*COMM*)
contracting party; **~punkt** *m* counterpoint

Kontrast [kɔn'trast] (-(e)s, -e) *m* contrast

Kontroll- [kɔn'trɔl] *zW:* **~e** *f* control,
supervision; (*Passkontrolle*) passport control;
~eur [-'løːr] *m* inspector; **k~ieren** [-'liːrən]
vt to control, to supervise; (*nachprüfen*) to
check

Konvention [kɔnventsi'oːn] *f* convention;
k~ell [-'nɛl] *adj* conventional

Konversation [kɔnverzatsi'oːn] *f*
conversation; **~slexikon** *nt*
encyclop(a)edia

Konvoi ['kɔnvɔy] (-s, -s) *m* convoy

Konzentration [kɔntsentratsi'oːn] *f*
concentration

Konzentrationslager *nt* concentration
camp

konzentrieren [kɔntsen'triːrən] *vt, vr* to
concentrate

konzentriert *adj* concentrated ♦ *adv*
(*zuhören, arbeiten*) intently

Konzern [kɔn'tsern] (-s, -e) *m* combine

Konzert [kɔn'tsert] (-(e)s, -e) *nt* concert;
(*Stück*) concerto; **~saal** *m* concert hall

Konzession [kɔntsesi'oːn] *f* licence;
(*Zugeständnis*) concession

Konzil [kɔn'tsiːl] (-s, -e *od* -len) *nt* council

kooperativ [koopera'tiːf] *adj* cooperative

koordinieren [koɔrdi'niːrən] *vt* to
coordinate

Kopf [kɔpf] (-(e)s, ⸚e) *m* head; **~haut** *f*
scalp; **~hörer** *m* headphones *pl*; **~kissen**
nt pillow; **k~los** *adj* panic-stricken;
k~rechnen *vi* to do mental arithmetic;
~salat *m* lettuce; **~schmerzen** *pl*
headache *sg*; **~sprung** *m* header, dive;
~stand *m* headstand; **~stütze** *f* (*im Auto
etc*) headrest, head restraint; **~tuch** *nt*
headscarf; **~weh** *nt* headache;
~zerbrechen *nt*: **jdm ~zerbrechen
machen** to be a headache for sb

Kopie [ko'piː] *f* copy; **k~ren** *vt* to copy

Kopiergerät *nt* photocopier

Koppel¹ ['kɔpəl] (-, -n) *f* (*Weide*) enclosure

Koppel² ['kɔpəl] (-s, -) *nt* (*Gürtel*) belt

koppeln *vt* to couple

Koppelung *f* coupling

Koralle [ko'ralə] *f* coral

Korb [kɔrp] (-(e)s, ⸚e) *m* basket; **jdm einen
~ geben** (*fig*) to turn sb down; **~ball** *m*
basketball; **~stuhl** *m* wicker chair

Kord [kɔrt] (-(e)s, -e) *m* cord, corduroy

Kordel ['kɔrdəl] (-, -n) *f* cord, string

Kork [kɔrk] (-(e)s, -e) *m* cork; **~en** (-s, -) *m*
stopper, cork; **~enzieher** (-s, -) *m*
corkscrew

Korn [kɔrn] (-(e)s, ⸚er) *nt* corn, grain;
(*Gewehr*) sight

Körper ['kœrpər] (-s, -) *m* body; **~bau** *m*
build; **k~behindert** *adj* disabled; **~geruch**
m body odour; **~gewicht** *nt* weight;
~größe *f* height; **k~lich** *adj* physical;
~pflege *f* personal hygiene; **~schaft** *f*
corporation; **~schaftssteuer** *f* corporation
tax; **~teil** *m* part of the body;
~verletzung *f* bodily *od* physical injury

korpulent [kɔrpu'lent] *adj* corpulent

korrekt [kɔ'rekt] *adj* correct; **K~ur** [-'tuːr] *f*

(*eines Textes*) proofreading; (*Text*) proof; (*SCH*) marking, correction

Korrespond- [kɔrɛspɔnd] *zW:* **~ent(in)** [-'dɛnt(ɪn)] *m(f)* correspondent; **~enz** [-'dɛnts] *f* correspondence; **k~ieren** [-'diːrən] *vi* to correspond

Korridor ['kɔridoːr] (**-s, -e**) *m* corridor

korrigieren [kɔri'giːrən] *vt* to correct

Korruption [kɔruptsi'oːn] *f* corruption

Kose- ['koːzə] *zW:* **~form** *f* pet form; **~name** *m* pet name; **~wort** *nt* term of endearment

Kosmetik [kɔs'meːtɪk] *f* cosmetics *pl;* **~erin** *f* beautician

kosmetisch *adj* cosmetic; (*Chirurgie*) plastic

kosmisch ['kɔsmɪʃ] *adj* cosmic

Kosmo- [kɔsmo] *zW:* **~naut** [-'naut] (**-en, -en**) *m* cosmonaut; **k~politisch** *adj* cosmopolitan; **~s** (**-**) *m* cosmos

Kost [kɔst] (**-**) *f* (*Nahrung*) food; (*Verpflegung*) board; **k~bar** *adj* precious; (*teuer*) costly, expensive; **~barkeit** *f* preciousness; costliness, expensiveness; (*Wertstück*) valuable

Kosten *pl* cost(s); (*Ausgaben*) expenses; **auf ~ von** at the expense of; **k~** *vt* to cost; (*versuchen*) to taste ♦ *vi* to taste; **was kostet ...?** what does ... cost?, how much is ...?; **~anschlag** *m* estimate; **k~los** *adj* free (of charge)

köstlich ['kœstlɪç] *adj* precious; (*Einfall*) delightful; (*Essen*) delicious; **sich ~ amüsieren** to have a marvellous time

Kostprobe *f* taste; (*fig*) sample

kostspielig *adj* expensive

Kostüm [kɔs'tyːm] (**-s, -e**) *nt* costume; (*Damenkostüm*) suit; **~fest** *nt* fancy-dress party; **k~ieren** [kɔsty'miːrən] *vt, vr* to dress up; **~verleih** *m* costume agency

Kot [koːt] (**-(e)s**) *m* excrement

Kotelett [kɔtə'lɛt] (**-(e)s, -e** *od* **-s**) *nt* cutlet, chop; **~en** *pl* (*Bart*) sideboards

Köter ['køːtər] (**-s, -**) *m* cur

Kotflügel *m* (*AUT*) wing

kotzen ['kɔtsən] (*umg!*) *vi* to puke (*umg*), to throw up (*umg*)

Krabbe ['krabə] *f* shrimp; **k~ln** *vi* to crawl

Krach [krax] (**-(e)s, -s** *od* **-e**) *m* crash; (*andauernd*) noise; (*umg: Streit*) quarrel, argument; **k~en** *vi* to crash; (*beim Brechen*) to crack ♦ *vr* (*umg*) to argue, to quarrel

krächzen ['krɛçtsən] *vi* to croak

Kraft [kraft] (**-, ⁺e**) *f* strength; power; force; (*Arbeitskraft*) worker; **in ~ treten** to come into force; **k~ präp** +*gen* by virtue of; **~fahrer** *m* (motor) driver; **~fahrzeug** *nt* motor vehicle; **~fahrzeugbrief** *m* logbook; **~fahrzeugsteuer** *f* ≈ road tax; **~fahrzeugversicherung** *f* car insurance

kräftig ['krɛftɪç] *adj* strong; **~en** *vt* to strengthen

Kraft- *zW:* **k~los** *adj* weak; powerless; (*JUR*) invalid; **~probe** *f* trial of strength; **~stoff** *m* fuel; **k~voll** *adj* vigorous; **~werk** *nt* power station

Kragen ['kraːgən] (**-s, -**) *m* collar; **~weite** *f* collar size

Krähe ['krɛːə] *f* crow; **k~n** *vi* to crow

Kralle ['kralə] *f* claw; (*Vogelkralle*) talon; **k~n** *vt* to clutch; (*krampfhaft*) to claw

Kram [kraːm] (**-(e)s**) *m* stuff, rubbish; **k~en** *vi* to rummage; **~laden** (*pej*) *m* small shop

Krampf [krampf] (**-(e)s, ⁺e**) *m* cramp; (*zuckend*) spasm; **~ader** *f* varicose vein; **k~haft** *adj* convulsive; (*fig: Versuche*) desperate

Kran [kraːn] (**-(e)s, ⁺e**) *m* crane; (*Wasserkran*) tap, faucet (*US*)

krank [kraŋk] *adj* ill, sick; **K~e(r)** *f(m)* sick person, invalid; patient; **~en** *vi:* **an etw** *dat* **~en** (*fig*) to suffer from sth

kränken ['krɛŋkən] *vt* to hurt

Kranken- *zW:* **~geld** *nt* sick pay; **~gymnastik** *f* physiotherapy; **~haus** *nt* hospital; **~kasse** *f* health insurance; **~pfleger** *m* nursing orderly; **~schein** *m* health insurance card; **~schwester** *f* nurse; **~versicherung** *f* health insurance; **~wagen** *m* ambulance

Krank- *zW:* **k~haft** *adj* diseased; (*Angst etc*) morbid; **~heit** *f* illness; disease; **~heitserreger** *m* disease-causing agent

kränklich ['krɛŋklɪç] *adj* sickly

Kränkung *f* insult, offence

Kranz [krants] (**-es, ⸚e**) *m* wreath, garland
krass ▲ [kras] *adj* crass
Krater ['kra:tər] (**-s, -**) *m* crater
Kratz- ['krats] *zW*: **~bürste** *f* (*fig*) crosspatch; **k~en** *vt, vi* to scratch; **~er** (**-s, -**) *m* scratch; (*Werkzeug*) scraper
Kraul [kraʊl] (**-s**) *nt* crawl; **~ schwimmen** to do the crawl; **k~en** *vi* (*schwimmen*) to do the crawl ♦ *vt* (*streicheln*) to fondle
kraus [kraʊs] *adj* crinkly; (*Haar*) frizzy; (*Stirn*) wrinkled
Kraut [kraʊt] (**-(e)s, Kräuter**) *nt* plant; (*Gewürz*) herb; (*Gemüse*) cabbage
Krawall [kra'val] (**-s, -e**) *m* row, uproar
Krawatte [kra'vatə] *f* tie
kreativ [krea'ti:f] *adj* creative
Krebs [kre:ps] (**-es, -e**) *m* crab; (*MED, ASTROL*) cancer; **k~krank** *adj* suffering from cancer
Kredit [kre'di:t] (**-(e)s, -e**) *m* credit; **~institut** *nt* bank; **~karte** *f* credit card
Kreide ['kraɪdə] *f* chalk; **k~bleich** *adj* as white as a sheet
Kreis [kraɪs] (**-es, -e**) *m* circle; (*Stadtkreis etc*) district; **im ~ gehen** (*auch fig*) to go round in circles
kreischen ['kraɪʃən] *vi* to shriek, to screech
Kreis- *zW*: **~el** ['kraɪzəl] (**-s, -**) *m* top; (*~verkehr*) roundabout (*BRIT*), traffic circle (*US*); **k~en** ['kraɪzən] *vi* to spin; **~lauf** *m* (*MED*) circulation; (*fig: der Natur etc*) cycle; **~säge** *f* circular saw; **~stadt** *f* county town; **~verkehr** *m* roundabout traffic
Krematorium [krema'to:riʊm] *nt* crematorium
Kreml ['kre:ml] (**-s**) *m* Kremlin
krepieren [kre'pi:rən] (*umg*) *vi* (*sterben*) to die, to kick the bucket
Krepp [krɛp] (**-s, -s** *od* **-e**) *m* crepe; **~papier** ▲ *nt* crepe paper
Kresse ['krɛsə] *f* cress
Kreta ['kre:ta] (**-s**) *nt* Crete
Kreuz [krɔʏts] (**-es, -e**) *nt* cross; (*ANAT*) small of the back; (*KARTEN*) clubs; **k~en** *vt, vr* to cross ♦ *vi* (*NAUT*) to cruise; **~er** (**-s, -**) *m* (*Schiff*) cruiser; **~fahrt** *f* cruise; **~feuer** *nt* (*fig*): **ins ~feuer geraten** to be under fire from all sides; **~gang** *m* cloisters *pl*; **k~igen** *vt* to crucify; **~igung** *f* crucifixion; **~ung** *f* (*Verkehrskreuzung*) crossing, junction; (*Züchten*) cross; **~verhör** *nt* cross-examination; **~weg** *m* crossroads; (*REL*) Way of the Cross; **~worträtsel** *nt* crossword puzzle; **~zug** *m* crusade
Kriech- ['kri:ç] *zW*: **k~en** (*unreg*) *vi* to crawl, to creep; (*pej*) to grovel, to crawl; **~er** (**-s, -**) *m* crawler; **~spur** *f* crawler lane; **~tier** *nt* reptile
Krieg [kri:k] (**-(e)s, -e**) *m* war
kriegen ['kri:gən] (*umg*) *vt* to get
Kriegs- *zW*: **~erklärung** *f* declaration of war; **~fuß** *m*: **mit jdm / etw auf ~fuß stehen** to be at loggerheads with sb/to have difficulties with sth; **~gefangene(r)** *m* prisoner of war; **~gefangenschaft** *f* captivity; **~gericht** *nt* court-martial; **~schiff** *nt* warship; **~verbrecher** *m* war criminal; **~versehrte(r)** *m* person disabled in the war; **~zustand** *m* state of war
Krim [krɪm] (**-**) *f* Crimea
Krimi ['kri:mi] (**-s, -s**) (*umg*) *m* thriller
Kriminal- [krimi'na:l] *zW*: **~beamte(r)** *m* detective; **~i'tät** *f* criminality; **~'polizei** *f* ≃ Criminal Investigation Department (*BRIT*), Federal Bureau of Investigation (*US*); **~ro'man** *m* detective story
kriminell [kri:mi'nɛl] *adj* criminal; **K~e(r)** *m* criminal
Krippe ['krɪpə] *f* crib; (*Kinderkrippe*) crèche
Krise ['kri:zə] *f* crisis; **k~ln** *vi*: **es k~lt** there's a crisis
Kristall [krɪs'tal] (**-s, -e**) *m* crystal ♦ *nt* (*Glas*) crystal
Kriterium [kri'te:riʊm] *nt* criterion
Kritik [kri'ti:k] *f* criticism; (*Zeitungskritik*) review, write-up; **~er** ['kri:tikər] (**-s, -**) *m* critic; **k~los** *adj* uncritical
kritisch ['kri:tɪʃ] *adj* critical
kritisieren [kriti'zi:rən] *vt, vi* to criticize
kritzeln ['krɪtsəln] *vt, vi* to scribble, to scrawl
Kroatien [kro'a:tsiən] *nt* Croatia
Krokodil [kroko'di:l] (**-s, -e**) *nt* crocodile
Krokus ['kro:kʊs] (**-, -** *od* **-se**) *m* crocus
Krone ['kro:nə] *f* crown; (*Baumkrone*) top
krönen ['krø:nən] *vt* to crown

Kron- zW: **~korken** m bottle top; **~leuchter** m chandelier; **~prinz** m crown prince

Krönung ['krøːnʊŋ] f coronation

Kropf [krɔpf] **(-(e)s, ⁼e)** m (MED) goitre; (von Vogel) crop

Kröte ['krøːtə] f toad

Krücke ['krykə] f crutch

Krug [kruːk] **(-(e)s, ⁼e)** m jug; (Bierkrug) mug

Krümel ['kryːməl] **(-s, -)** m crumb; **k~n** vt, vi to crumble

krumm [krʊm] adj (auch fig) crooked; (kurvig) curved; **jdm etw ~ nehmen** to take sth amiss; **~beinig** adj bandy-legged; **~lachen** (umg) vr to laugh o.s. silly

Krümmung ['krʏmʊŋ] f bend, curve

Krüppel ['krʏpəl] **(-s, -)** m cripple

Kruste ['krʊstə] f crust

Kruzifix [krutsi'fɪks] **(-es, -e)** nt crucifix

Kübel ['kyːbəl] **(-s, -)** m tub; (Eimer) pail

Kubikmeter [ku'biːkmeːtər] m cubic metre

Küche ['kʏçə] f kitchen; (Kochen) cooking, cuisine

Kuchen ['kuːxən] **(-s, -)** m cake; **~form** f baking tin; **~gabel** f pastry fork

Küchen- zW: **~herd** m cooker, stove; **~schabe** f cockroach; **~schrank** m kitchen cabinet

Kuckuck ['kʊkʊk] **(-s, -e)** m cuckoo; **~suhr** f cuckoo clock

Kugel ['kuːgəl] **(-, -n)** f ball; (MATH) sphere; (MIL) bullet; (Erdkugel) globe; (SPORT) shot; **k~förmig** adj spherical; **~lager** nt ball bearing; **k~rund** adj (Gegenstand) round; (umg: Person) tubby; **~schreiber** m ballpoint (pen), Biro ®; **k~sicher** adj bulletproof; **~stoßen** **(-s)** nt shot put

Kuh [kuː] **(-, ⁼e)** f cow

kühl [kyːl] adj (auch fig) cool; **K~anlage** f refrigeration plant; **K~e** **(-)** f coolness; **~en** vt to cool; **K~er** **(-s, -)** m (AUT) radiator; **K~erhaube** f (AUT) bonnet (BRIT), hood (US); **K~raum** m cold storage chamber; **K~schrank** m refrigerator; **K~truhe** f freezer; **K~ung** f cooling; **K~wasser** nt radiator water

kühn [kyːn] adj bold, daring; **K~heit** f boldness

Kuhstall m byre, cattle shed

Küken ['kyːkən] **(-s, -)** nt chicken

kulant [ku'lant] adj obliging

Kuli ['kuːli] **(-s, -s)** m coolie; (umg: Kugelschreiber) Biro ®

kullern ['kʊlərn] vi to roll

Kult [kʊlt] **(-(e)s, -e)** m worship, cult; **mit etw einen ~ treiben** to make a cult out of sth

kultivieren [kʊlti'viːrən] vt to cultivate

kultiviert adj cultivated, refined

Kultur [kʊl'tuːr] f culture; civilization; (des Bodens) cultivation; (umg) m philistine, low-brow; **~beutel** m toilet bag; **k~ell** [-u'rɛl] adj cultural; **~ministerium** nt ministry of education and the arts

Kümmel ['kʏməl] **(-s, -)** m caraway seed; (Branntwein) kümmel

Kummer ['kʊmər] **(-s)** m grief, sorrow

kümmerlich ['kʏmərlɪç] adj miserable, wretched

kümmern ['kʏmərn] vt to concern ♦ vr: **sich um jdn ~** to look after sb; **das kümmert mich nicht** that doesn't worry me; **sich um etw ~** to see to sth

Kumpel ['kʊmpəl] **(-s, -)** (umg) m mate

kündbar ['kʏntbaːr] adj redeemable, recallable; (Vertrag) terminable

Kunde¹ ['kʊndə] **(-n, -n)** m customer

Kunde² ['kʊndə] f (Botschaft) news

Kunden- zW: **~dienst** m after-sales service; **~konto** nt charge account; **~nummer** f customer number

Kund- zW: **k~geben** (unreg) vt to announce; **~gebung** f announcement; (Versammlung) rally

Künd- ['kʏnd] zW: **k~igen** vi to give in one's notice ♦ vt to cancel; **jdm k~igen** to give sb his notice; **die Stellung/Wohnung k~igen** to give notice that one is leaving one's job/house; **jdm die Stellung/Wohnung k~igen** to give sb notice to leave his/her job/house; **~igung** f notice; **~igungsfrist** f period of notice; **~igungsschutz** m protection against wrongful dismissal

Kundin f customer

Kundschaft f customers pl, clientele

künftig ['kʏnftɪç] adj future ♦ adv in future

Kunst [kʊnst] (-, ⁻e) f art; (Können) skill; **das ist doch keine ~** it's easy; **~dünger** m artificial manure; **~faser** f synthetic fibre; **~fertigkeit** f skilfulness; **~gegenstand** m art object; **~gerecht** adj skilful; **~geschichte** f history of art; **~gewerbe** nt arts and crafts pl; **~griff** m trick, knack; **~händler** m art dealer

Künstler(in) ['kʏnstlər(ɪn)] (-s, -) m(f) artist; **k~isch** adj artistic; **~name** m pseudonym

künstlich ['kʏnstlɪç] adj artificial

Kunst- zW: **~sammler** (-s, -) m art collector; **~seide** f artificial silk; **~stoff** m synthetic material; **~stück** nt trick; **~turnen** nt gymnastics sg; **k~voll** adj artistic; **~werk** nt work of art

kunterbunt ['kʊntərbʊnt] adj higgledy-piggledy

Kupee ▲ [ku'pe:] (-s, -s) nt coupé

Kupfer ['kʊpfər] (-s) nt copper; **k~n** adj copper

Kupon [ku'põː, -'pɔŋ] (-s, -s) m coupon; (Stoff~) length of cloth

Kuppe ['kʊpə] f (Bergkuppe) top; (Fingerkuppe) tip

Kuppel (-, -n) f dome; **k~n** vi (JUR) to procure; (AUT) to declutch ♦ vt to join

Kupplung f coupling; (AUT) clutch

Kur [kuːr] (-, -en) f cure, treatment

Kür [kyːr] (-, -en) f (SPORT) free exercises pl

Kurbel ['kʊrbəl] (-, -n) f crank, winder; (AUT) starting handle; **~welle** f crankshaft

Kürbis ['kʏrbɪs] (-ses, -se) m pumpkin; (exotisch) gourd

Kurgast m visitor (to a health resort)

kurieren [ku'riːrən] vt to cure

kurios [kuri'oːs] adj curious, odd; **K~i'tät** f curiosity

Kurort m health resort

Kurs [kʊrs] (-es, -e) m course; (FIN) rate; **~buch** nt timetable; **k~ieren** [kʊr'ziːrən] vi to circulate; **k~iv** [kʊr'ziːf] adv in italics; **~us** ['kʊrzʊs] (-, **Kurse**) m course; **~wagen**

m (EISENB) through carriage

Kurtaxe [-taksə] (-, -n) f visitors' tax (at health resort or spa)

Kurve ['kʊrvə] f curve; (Straßenkurve) curve, bend; **kurvig** adj (Straße) bendy

kurz [kʊrts] adj short; **~ gesagt** in short; **~ halten** to keep short; **zu ~ kommen** to come off badly; **den Kürzeren ziehen** to get the worst of it; **K~arbeit** f short-time work; **~ärm(e)lig** adj short-sleeved

Kürze ['kʏrtsə] f shortness, brevity; **k~n** vt to cut short; (in der Länge) to shorten; (Gehalt) to reduce

kurz- zW: **~erhand** adv on the spot; **~fristig** adj short-term; **K~geschichte** f short story; **~halten** △ (unreg) vt siehe **kurz**; **~lebig** adj short-lived

kürzlich ['kʏrtslɪç] adv lately, recently

Kurz- zW: **~schluss** ▲ m (ELEK) short circuit; **k~sichtig** adj short-sighted

Kürzung f (eines Textes) abridgement; (eines Theaterstück, des Gehalts) cut

Kurzwelle f short wave

kuscheln ['kʊʃəln] vr to snuggle up

Kusine [ku'ziːnə] f cousin

Kuss ▲ [kʊs] (-es, ⁻e) m kiss

küssen ['kʏsən] vt, vr to kiss

Küste ['kʏstə] f coast, shore

Küstenwache f coastguard

Küster ['kʏstər] (-s, -) m sexton, verger

Kutsche ['kʊtʃə] f coach, carriage; **~r** (-s, -) m coachman

Kutte ['kʊtə] f habit

Kuvert [ku'vɛrt] (-s, -e od -s) nt envelope; cover

KZ nt abk von **Konzentrationslager**

L, l

l abk = **Liter**

labil [la'biːl] adj (MED: Konstitution) delicate

Labor [la'boːr] (-s, -e od -s) nt lab; **~ant(in)** m(f) lab(oratory) assistant

Labyrinth [laby'rɪnt] (-s, -e) nt labyrinth

Lache ['laxə] f (Flüssigkeit) puddle; (von Blut, Benzin etc) pool

lächeln ['lɛçəln] vi to smile; **L~** (**-s**) nt smile
lachen ['laxən] vi to laugh
lächerlich ['lɛçərlɪç] adj ridiculous
Lachgas nt laughing gas
lachhaft adj laughable
Lachs [laks] (**-es, -e**) m salmon
Lack [lak] (**-(e)s, -e**) m lacquer, varnish; (von Auto) paint; **l~ieren** [la'ki:rən] vt to varnish; (Auto) to spray; **~ierer** [la'ki:rər] (**-s, -**) m varnisher
Laden ['la:dən] (**-s, ¨**) m shop; (Fensterladen) shutter
laden ['la:dən] (unreg) vt (Lasten) to load; (JUR) to summon; (einladen) to invite
Laden- zW: **~dieb** m shoplifter; **~diebstahl** m shoplifting; **~schluss** ▲ m closing time; **~tisch** m counter
Laderaum m freight space; (AVIAT, NAUT) hold
Ladung ['la:dʊŋ] f (Last) cargo, load; (Beladen) loading; (JUR) summons; (Einladung) invitation; (Sprengladung) charge
Lage ['la:gə] f position, situation; (Schicht) layer; **in der ~ sein** to be in a position
Lageplan m ground plan
Lager ['la:gər] (**-s, -**) nt camp; (COMM) warehouse; (Schlaflager) bed; (von Tier) lair; (TECH) bearing; **~bestand** m stocks pl; **~feuer** nt campfire; **~haus** nt warehouse, store
lagern ['la:gərn] vi (Dinge) to be stored; (Menschen) to camp ♦ vt to store; (betten) to lay down; (Maschine) to bed
Lagune [la'gu:nə] f lagoon
lahm [la:m] adj lame; **~ legen** to paralyse; **~en** vi to be lame
Lähmung f paralysis
Laib [laɪp] (**-s, -e**) m loaf
Laie ['laɪə] (**-n, -n**) m layman; **l~nhaft** adj amateurish
Laken ['la:kən] (**-s, -**) nt sheet
Lakritze [la'krɪtsə] f liquorice
lallen ['lalən] vt, vi to slur; (Baby) to babble
Lamelle [la'mɛlə] f lamella; (ELEK) lamina; (TECH) plate
Lametta [la'mɛta] (**-s**) nt tinsel

Lamm [lam] (**-(e)s, ¨er**) nt lamb
Lampe ['lampə] f lamp
Lampen- zW: **~fieber** nt stage fright; **~schirm** m lampshade
Lampion [lampi'õː] (**-s, -s**) m Chinese lantern
Land [lant] (**-(e)s, ¨er**) nt land; (Nation, nicht Stadt) country; (Bundesland) state; **auf dem ~(e)** in the country; siehe **hierzulande**; **~besitz** m landed property; **~ebahn** f runway; **l~en** ['landən] vt, vi to land

┌─────────────────────────────────────┐
│ **Land** │
└─────────────────────────────────────┘

ⓘ A **Land** (plural **Länder**) is a member state of the BRD and of Austria. There are 16 **Länder** in Germany, namely Baden-Württemberg, Bayern, Berlin, Brandenburg, Bremen, Hamburg, Hessen, Mecklenburg-Vorpommern, Niedersachsen, Nordrhein-Westfalen, Rheinland-Pfalz, Saarland, Sachsen, Sachsen-Anhalt, Schleswig-Holstein and Thüringen. Each **Land** has its own parliament and constitution. The 9 **Länder** of Austria are Vorarlberg, Tirol, Salzburg, Oberösterreich, Niederösterreich, Kärnten, Steiermark, Burgenland and Wien.

Landes- ['landəs] zW: **~farben** pl national colours; **~innere(s)** nt inland region; **~sprache** f national language; **l~üblich** adj customary; **~verrat** m high treason; **~währung** f national currency; **l~weit** adj nationwide
Land- zW: **~haus** nt country house; **~karte** f map; **~kreis** m administrative region; **l~läufig** adj customary
ländlich ['lɛntlɪç] adj rural
Land- zW: **~schaft** f countryside; (KUNST) landscape; **~schaftsschutzgebiet** nt nature reserve; **~sitz** m country seat; **~straße** f country road; **~streicher** (**-s, -**) m tramp; **~strich** m region
Landung ['landʊŋ] f landing; **~sbrücke** f jetty, pier
Land- zW: **~weg** m: etw auf dem **~weg** befördern to transport sth by land; **~wirt**

m farmer; **~wirtschaft** *f* agriculture;
~zunge *f* spit

lang [laŋ] *adj* long; *(Mensch)* tall; **~atmig** *adj*
long-winded; **~e** *adv* for a long time;
(dauern, brauchen) a long time

Länge ['lɛŋə] *f* length; *(GEOG)* longitude

langen ['laŋən] *vi (ausreichen)* to do, to
suffice; *(fassen)*: **~ (nach)** to reach (for)
♦ *vt*: **jdm etw ~** to hand *od* pass sb sth; **es
langt mir** I've had enough

Längengrad *m* longitude

Längenmaß *nt* linear measure

lang- *zW*: **L~eweile** *f* boredom; **~fristig**
adj long-term; **~jährig** *adj (Freundschaft,
Gewohnheit)* long-standing; **L~lauf** *m (SKI)*
cross-country skiing

länglich *adj* longish

längs [lɛŋs] *präp (+gen od dat)* along ♦ *adv*
lengthwise

lang- *zW*: **~sam** *adj* slow; **L~samkeit** *f*
slowness; **L~schläfer(in)** *m(f)* late riser

längst [lɛŋst] *adv*: **das ist ~ fertig** that was
finished a long time ago, that has been
finished for a long time; **~e(r, s)** *adj*
longest

lang- *zW*: **~weilen** *vt* to bore ♦ *vr* to be
bored; **~weilig** *adj* boring, tedious;
L~welle *f* long wave; **~wierig** *adj* lengthy,
long-drawn-out

Lanze ['lantsə] *f* lance

Lappalie [la'pa:liə] *f* trifle

Lappen ['lapən] *(-s, -)* *m* cloth, rag; *(ANAT)*
lobe

läppisch ['lɛpɪʃ] *adj* foolish

Lapsus ['lapsus] *(-, -)* *m* slip

Laptop ['lɛptɔp] *(-s, -s)* *m* laptop
(computer)

Lärche ['lɛrçə] *f* larch

Lärm [lɛrm] *(-(e)s)* *m* noise; **l~en** *vi* to be
noisy, to make a noise

Larve ['larfə] *f (BIOL)* larva

lasch [laʃ] *adj* slack

Laser ['le:zər] *(-s, -)* *m* laser

SCHLÜSSELWORT

lassen ['lasən] *(pt* **ließ**, *pp* **gelassen** *od (als
Hilfsverb)* **lassen**) *vt* **1** *(unterlassen)* to stop;

(momentan) to leave; **lass das (sein)!** don't
(do it)!; *(hör auf)* stop it!; **lass mich!** leave
me alone; **lassen wir das!** let's leave it; **er
kann das Trinken nicht lassen** he can't
stop drinking

2 *(zurücklassen)* to leave; **etw lassen, wie
es ist** to leave sth (just) as it is

3 *(überlassen)*: **jdn ins Haus lassen** to let
sb into the house

♦ *vi*: **lass mal, ich mache das schon** leave
it, I'll do it

♦ *Hilfsverb* **1** *(veranlassen)*: **etw machen
lassen** to have *od* get sth done; **sich** *dat*
etw schicken lassen to have sth sent (to
one)

2 *(zulassen)*: **jdn etw wissen lassen** to let
sb know sth; **das Licht brennen lassen** to
leave the light on; **jdn warten lassen** to
keep sb waiting; **das lässt sich machen**
that can be done

3: **lass uns gehen** let's go

---

lässig ['lɛsɪç] *adj* casual; **L~keit** *f* casualness

Last [last] *(-, -en)* *f* load, burden; *(NAUT,
AVIAT)* cargo; *(meist pl: Gebühr)* charge; **jdm
zur ~ fallen** to be a burden to sb; **~auto**
nt lorry, truck; **l~en** *vi*: **l~en auf** *+dat* to
weigh on; **~enaufzug** *m* goods lift *od*
elevator *(US)*

Laster ['lastər] *(-s, -)* *nt* vice

lästern ['lɛstərn] *vt, vi (Gott)* to blaspheme;
(schlecht sprechen) to mock

Lästerung *f* jibe; *(Gotteslästerung)*
blasphemy

lästig ['lɛstɪç] *adj* troublesome, tiresome

Last- *zW*: **~kahn** *m* barge; **~kraftwagen**
m heavy goods vehicle; **~schrift** *f* debit;
~wagen *m* lorry, truck; **~zug** *m* articulated
lorry

Latein [la'taɪn] *(-s)* *nt* Latin; **~amerika** *nt*
Latin America

latent [la'tɛnt] *adj* latent

Laterne [la'tɛrnə] *f* lantern; *(Straßenlaterne)*
lamp, light; **~npfahl** *m* lamppost

latschen ['la:tʃən] *(umg)* *vi (gehen)* to
wander, to go; *(lässig)* to slouch

Latte ['latə] *f* lath; *(SPORT)* goalpost; *(quer)*

Rechtschreibreform: ▲ *neue Schreibung* △ *alte Schreibung (auslaufend)* crossbar

Latzhose ['latsho:zə] f dungarees pl

lau [lau] adj (Nacht) balmy; (Wasser) lukewarm

Laub [laup] (-(e)s) nt foliage;**~baum** m deciduous tree;**~frosch** m tree frog; **~säge** f fretsaw

Lauch [laux] (-(e)s, -e) m leek

Lauer ['lauər] f: **auf der ~ sein** od **liegen** to lie in wait;**l~n** vi to lie in wait; (Gefahr) to lurk

Lauf [lauf] (-(e)s, Läufe) m run; (Wettlauf) race; (Entwicklung, ASTRON) course; (Gewehrlauf) barrel; **einer Sache** dat **ihren ~ lassen** to let sth take its course;**~bahn** f career

laufen ['laufən] (unreg) vt, vi to run; (umg: gehen) to walk;**~d** adj running; (Monat, Ausgaben) current; **auf dem ~den sein/halten** to be/keep up to date; **am ~den Band** (fig) continuously

Läufer ['lɔyfər] (-s, -) m (Teppich, SPORT) runner; (Fußball) half-back; (Schach) bishop

Lauf- zW:**~masche** f run, ladder (BRIT); **~pass** ▲ m: **jdm den ~pass geben** (umg) to send sb packing (inf);**~stall** m playpen; **~steg** m catwalk;**~werk** nt (COMPUT) disk drive

Lauge ['laugə] f soapy water; (CHEM) alkaline solution

Laune ['launə] f mood, humour; (Einfall) caprice; (schlechte) temper;**l~nhaft** adj capricious, changeable

launisch adj moody; bad-tempered

Laus [laus] (-, Läuse) f louse

lauschen ['lauʃən] vi to eavesdrop, to listen in

lauschig ['lauʃɪç] adj snug

lausig ['lauzɪç] (umg: pej) adj measly; (Kälte) perishing

laut [laut] adj loud ♦ adv loudly; (lesen) aloud ♦ präp (+gen od dat) according to;**L~** (-(e)s, -e) m sound

Laute ['lautə] f lute

lauten ['lautən] vi to say; (Urteil) to be

läuten ['lɔytən] vt, vi to ring, to sound

lauter ['lautər] adj (Wasser) clear, pure;

(Wahrheit, Charakter) honest ♦ adj inv (Freude, Dummheit etc) sheer ♦ adv nothing but, only

laut- zW:**~hals** adv at the top of one's voice;**~los** adj noiseless, silent;**L~schrift** f phonetics pl;**L~sprecher** m loudspeaker; **~stark** adj vociferous;**L~stärke** f (RADIO) volume

lauwarm ['lauvarm] adj (auch fig) lukewarm

Lavendel [la'vɛndəl] (-s, -) m lavender

Lawine [la'vi:nə] f avalanche;**~ngefahr** f danger of avalanches

lax [laks] adj lax .

Lazarett [latsa'rɛt] (-(e)s, -e) nt (MIL) hospital, infirmary

leasen ['li:zən] vt to lease

Leben (-s, -) nt life

leben ['le:bən] vt, vi to live;**~d** adj living; **~dig** [le'bɛndɪç] adj living, alive; (lebhaft) lively;**L~digkeit** f liveliness

Lebens- zW:**~art** f way of life; **~erwartung** f life expectancy;**l~fähig** adj able to live;**~freude** f zest for life; **~gefahr** f: **~gefahr!** danger!; **in ~gefahr** dangerously ill;**l~gefährlich** adj dangerous; (Verletzung) critical; **~haltungskosten** pl cost of living sg; **~jahr** nt year of life;**l~länglich** adj (Strafe) for life;**~lauf** m curriculum vitae;**~mittel** pl food sg;**~mittelgeschäft** nt grocer's (shop);**~mittelvergiftung** f (MED) food poisoning;**l~müde** adj tired of life; **~retter** m lifesaver;**~standard** m standard of living;**~unterhalt** m livelihood;**~versicherung** f life insurance; **~wandel** m way of life;**~weise** f lifestyle, way of life;**l~wichtig** adj vital, essential; **~zeichen** nt sign of life

Leber ['le:bər] (-, -n) f liver;**~fleck** m mole; **~tran** m cod-liver oil;**~wurst** f liver sausage

Lebewesen nt creature

leb- ['le:p] zW:**~haft** adj lively, vivacious; **L~kuchen** m gingerbread;**~los** adj lifeless

Leck [lɛk] (-(e)s, -e) nt leak;**l~** adj leaky, leaking;**l~en** vi (Loch haben) to leak; (schlecken) to lick ♦ vt to lick

lecker ['lɛkər] *adj* delicious, tasty; **L~bissen** *m* dainty morsel

Leder ['le:dər] (**-s, -**) *nt* leather; **~hose** *f* lederhosen; **l~n** *adj* leather; **~waren** *pl* leather goods

ledig ['le:dɪç] *adj* single; **einer Sache** *gen* **~ sein** to be free of sth; **~lich** *adv* merely, solely

leer [le:r] *adj* empty; vacant; **~ machen** to empty; **~ stehend** empty; **L~e (-)** *f* emptiness; **~en** *vt, vr* to empty; **L~gewicht** *nt* weight when empty; **L~gut** *nt* empties *pl*; **L~lauf** *m* neutral; **L~ung** *f* emptying; (*Post*) collection

legal [le'ga:l] *adj* legal, lawful; **~i'sieren** *vt* to legalize

legen ['le:gən] *vt* to lay, to put, to place; (*Ei*) to lay ♦ *vr* to lie down; (*fig*) to subside

Legende [le'gɛndə] *f* legend

leger [le'ʒe:r] *adj* casual

Legierung [le'gi:rʊŋ] *f* alloy

Legislative [legɪsla'ti:və] *f* legislature

legitim [legi'ti:m] *adj* legitimate

legitimieren [legiti'mi:rən] *vt* to legitimate ♦ *vr* to prove one's identity

Lehm [le:m] (**-(e)s, -e**) *m* loam; **l~ig** *adj* loamy

Lehne ['le:nə] *f* arm; back; **l~n** *vt, vr* to lean

Lehnstuhl *m* armchair

Lehr- *zW*: **~amt** *nt* teaching profession; **~buch** *nt* textbook

Lehre ['le:rə] *f* teaching, doctrine; (*beruflich*) apprenticeship; (*moralisch*) lesson; (*TECH*) gauge; **l~n** *vt* to teach

Lehrer(in) (**-s, -**) *m(f)* teacher; **~zimmer** *nt* staff room

Lehr- *zW*: **~gang** *m* course; **~jahre** *pl* apprenticeship *sg*; **~kraft** *f* (*förmlich*) teacher; **~ling** *m* apprentice; **~plan** *m* syllabus; **l~reich** *adj* instructive; **~stelle** *f* apprenticeship; **~zeit** *f* apprenticeship

Leib [laɪp] (**-(e)s, -er**) *m* body; **halt ihn mir vom ~!** keep him away from me!; **l~haftig** *adj* personified; (*Teufel*) incarnate; **l~lich** *adj* bodily; (*Vater etc*) own; **~schmerzen** *pl* stomach pains; **~wache** *f* bodyguard

Leiche ['laɪçə] *f* corpse; **~nhalle** *f* mortuary; **~nwagen** *m* hearse

Leichnam ['laɪçna:m] (**-(e)s, -e**) *m* corpse

leicht [laɪçt] *adj* light; (*einfach*) easy; **jdm ~ fallen** to be easy for sb; **es sich** *dat* **~ machen** to make things easy for o.s.; **L~athletik** *f* athletics *sg*; **~fertig** *adj* frivolous; **~gläubig** *adj* gullible, credulous; **~hin** *adv* lightly; **L~igkeit** *f* easiness; **mit L~igkeit** with ease; **L~sinn** *m* carelessness; **~sinnig** *adj* careless

Leid [laɪt] (**-(e)s**) *nt* grief, sorrow; **es tut mir/ihm ~** I am/he is sorry; **er/das tut mir ~** I am sorry for him/it; **l~** *adj*: **etw l~ haben** *od* **sein** to be tired of sth; **l~en** (*unreg*) *vt* to suffer; (*erlauben*) to permit ♦ *vi* to suffer; **jdn/etw nicht l~en können** not to be able to stand sb/sth; **~en** ['laɪdən] (**-s, -**) *nt* suffering; (*Krankheit*) complaint; **~enschaft** *f* passion; **l~enschaftlich** *adj* passionate

leider ['laɪdər] *adv* unfortunately; **ja, ~** yes, I'm afraid so; **~ nicht** I'm afraid not

leidig ['laɪdɪç] *adj* worrying, troublesome

leidlich ['laɪtlɪç] *adj* tolerable ♦ *adv* tolerably

Leid- *zW*: **~tragende(r)** *f(m)* bereaved; (*Benachteiligter*) one who suffers; **~wesen** *nt*: **zu jds ~wesen** to sb's disappointment

Leier ['laɪər] (**-, -n**) *f* lyre; (*fig*) old story; **~kasten** *m* barrel organ

Leihbibliothek *f* lending library

Leihbücherei *f* lending library

leihen ['laɪən] (*unreg*) *vt* to lend; **sich** *dat* **etw ~** to borrow sth

Leih- *zW*: **~gebühr** *f* hire charge; **~haus** *nt* pawnshop; **~wagen** *m* hired car

Leim [laɪm] (**-(e)s, -e**) *m* glue; **l~en** *vt* to glue

Leine ['laɪnə] *f* line, cord; (*Hundeleine*) leash, lead

Leinen *nt* linen; **l~** *adj* linen

Leinwand *f* (*KUNST*) canvas; (*CINE*) screen

leise ['laɪzə] *adj* quiet; (*sanft*) soft, gentle

Leiste ['laɪstə] *f* ledge; (*Zierleiste*) strip; (*ANAT*) groin

leisten ['laɪstən] *vt* (*Arbeit*) to do; (*Gesellschaft*) to keep; (*Ersatz*) to supply; (*vollbringen*) to achieve; **sich** *dat* **etw ~**

können to be able to afford sth
Leistung f performance; (gute)
achievement; **~sdruck** m pressure;
l~sfähig adj efficient
Leitartikel m leading article
Leitbild nt model
leiten ['laɪtən] vt to lead; (Firma) to manage;
(in eine Richtung) to direct; (ELEK) to conduct
Leiter[1] ['laɪtər] (-s, -) m leader, head; (ELEK)
conductor
Leiter[2] ['laɪtər] (-, -n) f ladder
Leitfaden m guide
Leitplanke f crash barrier
Leitung f (Führung) direction; (CINE, THEAT
etc) production; (von Firma) management;
directors pl; (Wasserleitung) pipe; (Kabel)
cable; **eine lange ~ haben** to be slow on
the uptake
Leitungs- zW: **~draht** m wire; **~rohr** nt
pipe; **~wasser** nt tap water
Lektion [lɛktsi'oːn] f lesson
Lektüre [lɛk'tyːrə] f (Lesen) reading;
(Lesestoff) reading matter
Lende ['lɛndə] f loin; **~nstück** nt fillet
lenk- ['lɛŋk] zW: **~bar** adj (Fahrzeug)
steerable; (Kind) manageable; **~en** vt to
steer; (Kind) to guide; (Blick,
Aufmerksamkeit): **~en (auf** +akk) to direct
(at); **L~rad** nt steering wheel;
L~radschloss ▲ nt steering (wheel) lock;
L~stange f handlebars pl; **L~ung** f
steering
Lepra ['leːpra] (-) f leprosy
Lerche ['lɛrçə] f lark
lernbegierig adj eager to learn
lernen ['lɛrnən] vt to learn
lesbar ['leːsbaːr] adj legible
Lesbierin ['lɛsbiərɪn] f lesbian
lesbisch ['lɛsbɪʃ] adj lesbian
Lese ['leːzə] f (Wein) harvest
Lesebrille f reading glasses
Lesebuch nt reading book, reader
lesen (unreg) vt, vi to read; (ernten) to
gather, to pick
Leser(in) (-s, -) m(f) reader; **~brief** m
reader's letter; **l~lich** adj legible
Lesezeichen nt bookmark

Lesung ['leːzʊŋ] f (PARL) reading
letzte(r, s) ['lɛtstə(r, s)] adj last; (neueste)
latest; **zum ~n Mal** for the last time; **~ns**
adv lately; **~re(r, s)** adj latter
Leuchte ['lɔʏçtə] f lamp, light; **l~n** vi to
shine, to gleam; **~r** (-s, -) m candlestick
Leucht- zW: **~farbe** f fluorescent colour;
~rakete f flare; **~reklame** f neon sign;
~röhre f strip light; **~turm** m lighthouse
leugnen ['lɔʏɡnən] vt to deny
Leukämie [lɔʏkɛ'miː] f leukaemia
Leukoplast [lɔʏko'plast] (®; **-(e)s, -e)** nt
Elastoplast ®
Leumund ['lɔʏmʊnt] (**-(e)s, -e)** m
reputation
Leumundszeugnis nt character reference
Leute ['lɔʏtə] pl people pl
Leutnant ['lɔʏtnant] (**-s, -s** od **-e)** m
lieutenant
leutselig ['lɔʏtzeːlɪç] adj amiable
Lexikon ['lɛksɪkɔn] (**-s, Lexiken** od **Lexika)**
nt encyclop(a)edia
Libelle [li'bɛlə] f dragonfly; (TECH) spirit level
liberal [libe'raːl] adj liberal; **L~e(r)** f(m)
liberal
Licht [lɪçt] (**-(e)s, -er)** nt light; **~bild** nt
photograph; (Dia) slide; **~blick** m cheering
prospect; **l~empfindlich** adj sensitive to
light; **l~en** vt to clear; (Anker) to weigh ♦ vr
to clear up; (Haar) to thin; **l~erloh** adv:
l~erloh brennen to be ablaze; **~hupe** f
flashing of headlights; **~jahr** nt light year;
~maschine f dynamo; **~schalter** m light
switch; **~schutzfaktor** m protection factor
Lichtung f clearing, glade
Lid [liːt] (**-(e)s, -er)** nt eyelid; **~schatten** m
eyeshadow
lieb [liːp] adj dear; **das ist ~ von dir** that's
kind of you; **~ gewinnen** to get fond of; **~**
haben to be fond of; **~äugeln** ['liːbɔʏɡəln]
vi insep: **mit etw ~äugeln** to have one's
eye on sth; **mit dem Gedanken ~äugeln,**
etw zu tun to toy with the idea of doing
sth
Liebe ['liːbə] f love; **l~bedürftig** adj:
l~bedürftig sein to need love; **l~n** vt to
love; to like

liebens- *zW:* **~wert** *adj* loveable; **~würdig** *adj* kind; **~würdigerweise** *adv* kindly; **L~würdigkeit** *f* kindness

lieber ['liːbər] *adv* rather, preferably; **ich gehe ~ nicht** I'd rather not go; *siehe auch* **gern**; **lieb**

Liebes- *zW:* **~brief** *m* love letter; **~kummer** *m:* **~kummer haben** to be lovesick; **~paar** *nt* courting couple, lovers *pl*

liebevoll *adj* loving

lieb- [liːp] *zW:* **~gewinnen** △ *(unreg) vt siehe* **lieb**; **~haben** △ *(unreg) vt siehe* **lieb**; **L~haber (-s, -)** *m* lover; **L~habe'rei** *f* hobby; **~kosen** ['liːpkoːzən] *vt insep* to caress; **~lich** *adj* lovely, charming; **L~ling** *m* darling; **L~lings-** *in zW* favourite; **~los** *adj* unloving; **L~schaft** *f* love affair

Lied [liːt] **(-(e)s, -er)** *nt* song; (*REL*) hymn; **~erbuch** ['liːdər-] *nt* songbook; hymn book

liederlich ['liːdərlɪç] *adj* slovenly; (*Lebenswandel*) loose, immoral; **L~keit** *f* slovenliness; immorality

lief *etc* [liːf] *vb siehe* **laufen**

Lieferant [liːfə'rant] *m* supplier

Lieferbedingungen *pl* terms of delivery

liefern ['liːfərn] *vt* to deliver; (*versorgen mit*) to supply; (*Beweis*) to produce

Liefer- *zW:* **~schein** *m* delivery note; **~termin** *m* delivery date; **~ung** *f* delivery; supply; **~wagen** *m* van; **~zeit** *f* delivery period

Liege ['liːgə] *f* bed

liegen ['liːgən] *(unreg) vi* to lie; (*sich befinden*) to be; **mir liegt nichts/viel daran** it doesn't matter to me/it matters a lot to me; **es liegt bei Ihnen, ob ...** it's up to you whether ...; **Sprachen ~ mir nicht** languages are not my line; **~ woran liegt es?** what's the cause?; **~ bleiben** (*im Bett*) to stay in bed; (*nicht aufstehen*) to stay lying down; (*vergessen werden*) to be left (behind); **~ lassen** (*vergessen*) to leave behind

Liege- *zW:* **~sitz** *m* (*AUT*) reclining seat; **~stuhl** *m* deck chair; **~wagen** *m* (*EISENB*) couchette

Lift [lɪft] **(-(e)s, -e** *od* **-s)** *m* lift

Likör [li'køːr] **(-s, -e)** *m* liqueur

lila ['liːla] *adj inv* purple, lilac; **L~ (-s, -s)** *nt* (*Farbe*) purple, lilac

Lilie ['liːliə] *f* lily

Limonade [limo'naːdə] *f* lemonade

Limone [li'moːnə] *f* lime

Linde ['lɪndə] *f* lime tree, linden

lindern ['lɪndərn] *vt* to alleviate, to soothe; **Linderung** *f* alleviation

Lineal [line'aːl] **(-s, -e)** *nt* ruler

Linie ['liːniə] *f* line

Linien- *zW:* **~blatt** *nt* ruled sheet; **~flug** *m* scheduled flight; **~richter** *m* linesman

linieren [li'niːrən] *vt* to line

Linke ['lɪŋkə] *f* left side; left hand; (*POL*) left

linkisch *adj* awkward, gauche

links [lɪŋks] *adv* left; to *od* on the left; **~ von mir** on *od* to my left; **L~händer(in) (-s, -)** *m(f)* left-handed person; **L~kurve** *f* left-hand bend; **L~verkehr** *m* driving on the left

Linoleum [li'noːleʊm] **(-s)** *nt* lino(leum)

Linse ['lɪnzə] *f* lentil; (*optisch*) lens *sg*

Lippe ['lɪpə] *f* lip; **~nstift** *m* lipstick

lispeln ['lɪspəln] *vi* to lisp

Lissabon ['lɪsabɔn] **(-s)** *nt* Lisbon

List [lɪst] **(-, -en)** *f* cunning; trick, ruse

Liste ['lɪstə] *f* list

listig ['lɪstɪç] *adj* cunning, sly

Liter ['liːtər] **(-s, -)** *nt od m* litre

literarisch [lite'raːrɪʃ] *adj* literary

Literatur [litera'tuːr] *f* literature

Litfaßsäule ['lɪtfaszɔʏlə] *f* advertising pillar

Liturgie [litur'giː] *f* liturgy

liturgisch [li'tʊrgɪʃ] *adj* liturgical

Litze ['lɪtsə] *f* braid; (*ELEK*) flex

Lizenz [li'tsɛnts] *f* licence

Lkw [ɛlkaː'veː] **(-(s), -(s))** *m abk =* **Lastkraftwagen**

Lob [loːp] **(-(e)s)** *nt* praise

Lobby ['lɔbi] *f* lobby

loben ['loːbən] *vt* to praise; **~swert** *adj* praiseworthy

löblich ['løːplɪç] *adj* praiseworthy, laudable

Loch [lɔx] **(-(e)s, ⁺er)** *nt* hole; **l~en** *vt* to punch holes in; **~er (-s, -)** *m* punch

löcherig ['lœçərɪç] adj full of holes
Lochkarte f punch card
Lochstreifen m punch tape
Locke ['lɔkə] f lock, curl; **l~n** vt to entice; (Haare) to curl; **~nwickler (-s, -)** m curler
locker ['lɔkər] adj loose; **~lassen** (unreg) vi: **nicht ~lassen** not to let up; **~n** vt to loosen
lockig ['lɔkɪç] adj curly
lodern ['lo:dərn] vi to blaze
Löffel ['lœfəl] **(-s, -)** m spoon
löffeln vt to spoon
Loge ['lo:ʒə] f (THEAT) box; (Freimaurer) (masonic) lodge; (Pförtnerloge) office
Logik ['lo:gɪk] f logic
logisch ['lo:gɪʃ] adj logical
Logopäde [logo'pɛ:də] **(-n, -n)** m speech therapist
Lohn [lo:n] **(-(e)s, ⁓e)** m reward; (Arbeitslohn) pay, wages pl; **~büro** nt wages office; **~empfänger** m wage earner
lohnen ['lo:nən] vr unpers to be worth it ♦ vt: **(jdm etw) ~** to reward (sb for sth); **~d** adj worthwhile
Lohn- zW: **~erhöhung** f pay rise; **~steuer** f income tax; **~steuerkarte** f (income) tax card; **~streifen** m pay slip; **~tüte** f pay packet
Lokal [lo'ka:l] **(-(e)s, -e)** nt pub(lic house)
lokal adj local; **~i'sieren** vt to localize
Lokomotive [lokomo'ti:və] f locomotive
Lokomotivführer m engine driver
Lorbeer ['lɔrbe:r] **(-s, -en)** m (auch fig) laurel; **~blatt** nt (KOCH) bay leaf
Los [lo:s] **(-es, -e)** nt (Schicksal) lot, fate; (Lotterielos) lottery ticket
los [lo:s] adj (locker) loose; **~!** go on!; **etw ~ sein** to be rid of sth; **was ist ~?** what's the matter?; **dort ist nichts/viel ~** there's nothing/a lot going on there; **~binden** (unreg) vt to untie
Löschblatt ['lœʃblat] nt sheet of blotting paper
löschen ['lœʃən] vt (Feuer, Licht) to put out, to extinguish; (Durst) to quench; (COMM) to cancel; (COMPUT) to delete; (Tonband) to erase; (Fracht) to unload ♦ vi (Feuerwehr) to

put out a fire; (Tinte) to blot
Lösch- zW: **~fahrzeug** nt fire engine; fire boat; **~gerät** nt fire extinguisher; **~papier** nt blotting paper
lose ['lo:zə] adj loose
Lösegeld nt ransom
losen ['lo:zən] vi to draw lots
lösen ['lø:zən] vt to loosen; (Rätsel etc) to solve; (Verlobung) to call off; (CHEM) to dissolve; (Partnerschaft) to break up; (Fahrkarte) to buy ♦ vr (aufgehen) to come loose; (Zucker etc) to dissolve; (Problem, Schwierigkeit) to (re)solve itself
los- zW: **~fahren** (unreg) vi to leave; **~gehen** (unreg) vi to set out; (anfangen) to start; (Bombe) to go off; **auf jdn ~gehen** to go for sb; **~kaufen** vt (Gefangene, Geißeln) to pay ransom for; **~kommen** (unreg) vi: **von etw ~kommen** to get away from sth; **~lassen** (unreg) vt (Seil) to let go of; (Schimpfe) to let loose; **~laufen** (unreg) vi to run off
löslich ['lø:slɪç] adj soluble; **L~keit** f solubility
los- zW: **~lösen** vt: **(sich) ~lösen** to free (o.s.); **~machen** vt to loosen; (Boot) to unmoor ♦ vr to get away; **~schrauben** vt to unscrew
Losung ['lo:zʊŋ] f watchword, slogan
Lösung ['lø:zʊŋ] f (Lockermachen) loosening; (eines Rätsels, CHEM) solution; **~smittel** nt solvent
los- zW: **~werden** (unreg) vt to get rid of; **~ziehen** (unreg) (umg) vi (sich aufmachen) to set off
Lot [lo:t] **(-(e)s, -e)** nt plumbline; **im ~** vertical; (fig) on an even keel
löten ['lø:tən] vt to solder
Lothringen ['lo:trɪŋən] **(-s)** nt Lorraine
Lotse ['lo:tsə] **(-n, -n)** m pilot; (AVIAT) air traffic controller; **l~n** vt to pilot; (umg) to lure
Lotterie [lɔtə'ri:] f lottery
Lotto ['lɔto] **(-s, -s)** nt national lottery; **~zahlen** pl winning lottery numbers
Löwe ['lø:və] **(-n, -n)** m lion; (ASTROL) Leo; **~nanteil** m lion's share; **~nzahn** m

---

Spelling Reform: ▲ *new spelling* △ *old spelling (to be phased out)*

dandelion

loyal [loaˈjaːl] *adj* loyal; **L~ität** *f* loyalty

Luchs [lʊks] (**-es, -e**) *m* lynx

Lücke [ˈlʏkə] *f* gap

Lücken- *zW:* **~büßer** (**-s, -**) *m* stopgap; **l~haft** *adj* full of gaps; (*Versorgung, Vorräte etc*) inadequate; **l~los** *adj* complete

Luft [lʊft] (**-, ⁻e**) *f* air; (*Atem*) breath; **in der ~ liegen** to be in the air; **jdn wie ~ behandeln** to ignore sb; **~angriff** *m* air raid; **~ballon** *m* balloon; **~blase** *f* air bubble; **l~dicht** *adj* airtight; **~druck** *m* atmospheric pressure

lüften [ˈlʏftən] *vt* to air; (*Hut*) to lift, to raise ♦ *vi* to let some air in

Luft- *zW:* **~fahrt** *f* aviation; **~fracht** *f* air freight; **l~gekühlt** *adj* air-cooled; **~gewehr** *nt* air rifle, airgun; **l~ig** *adj* (*Ort*) breezy; (*Raum*) airy; (*Kleider*) summery; **~kissenfahrzeug** *nt* hovercraft; **~kurort** *m* health resort; **l~leer** *adj*: **l~leerer Raum** vacuum; **~linie** *f*: **in der ~linie** as the crow flies; **~loch** *nt* air hole; (*AVIAT*) air pocket; **~matratze** *f* Lilo ® (*BRIT*) air mattress; **~pirat** *m* hijacker; **~post** *f* airmail; **~pumpe** *f* air pump; **~röhre** *f* (*ANAT*) windpipe; **~schlange** *f* streamer; **~schutzkeller** *m* air-raid shelter; **~verkehr** *m* air traffic; **~verschmutzung** *f* air pollution; **~waffe** *f* air force; **~zug** *m* draught

Lüge [ˈlyːgə] *f* lie; **jdn/etw ~n strafen** to give the lie to sb/sth; **l~n** (*unreg*) *vi* to lie

Lügner(in) (**-s, -**) *m(f)* liar

Luke [ˈluːkə] *f* dormer window; hatch

Lump [lʊmp] (**-en, -en**) *m* scamp, rascal

Lumpen [ˈlʊmpən] (**-s, -**) *m* rag

lumpen [ˈlʊmpən] *vi*: **sich nicht ~ lassen** not to be mean

lumpig [ˈlʊmpɪç] *adj* shabby

Lupe [ˈluːpə] *f* magnifying glass; **unter die ~ nehmen** (*fig*) to scrutinize

Lust [lʊst] (**-, ⁻e**) *f* joy, delight; (*Neigung*) desire; **~ haben zu** *od* **auf etw** *akk* / **etw zu tun** to feel like sth/doing sth

lüstern [ˈlʏstərn] *adj* lustful, lecherous

lustig [ˈlʊstɪç] *adj* (*komisch*) amusing, funny;

(*fröhlich*) cheerful

Lust- *zW:* **l~los** *adj* unenthusiastic; **~mord** *m* sex(ual) murder; **~spiel** *nt* comedy

lutschen [ˈlʊtʃən] *vt, vi* to suck; **am Daumen ~** to suck one's thumb

Lutscher (**-s, -**) *m* lollipop

luxuriös [lʊksuriˈøːs] *adj* luxurious

Luxus [ˈlʊksʊs] (**-**) *m* luxury; **~artikel** *pl* luxury goods; **~hotel** *nt* luxury hotel

Luzern [luˈtsɛrn] (**-s**) *nt* Lucerne

Lymphe [ˈlʏmfə] *f* lymph

lynchen [ˈlʏnçən] *vt* to lynch

Lyrik [ˈlyːrɪk] *f* lyric poetry; **~er** (**-s, -**) *m* lyric poet

lyrisch [ˈlyːrɪʃ] *adj* lyrical

M, m

m *abk* = **Meter**

Machart *f* make

machbar *adj* feasible

SCHLÜSSELWORT
---

machen [ˈmaxən] *vt* **1** to do; (*herstellen, zubereiten*) to make; **was machst du da?** what are you doing (there)?; **das ist nicht zu machen** that can't be done; **das Radio leiser machen** to turn the radio down; **aus Holz gemacht** made of wood

2 (*verursachen, bewirken*) to make; **jdm Angst machen** to make sb afraid; **das macht die Kälte** it's the cold that does that

3 (*ausmachen*) to matter; **das macht nichts** that doesn't matter; **die Kälte macht mir nichts** I don't mind the cold

4 (*kosten, ergeben*) to be; **3 und 5 macht 8** 3 and 5 is *od* are 8; **was *od* wie viel macht das?** how much does that make?

5 was macht die Arbeit? how's the work going?; **was macht dein Bruder?** how is your brother doing?; **das Auto machen lassen** to have the car done; **machs gut!** take care!; (*viel Glück*) good luck!

♦ *vi*: **mach schnell!** hurry up!; **Schluss machen** to finish (off); **mach schon!** come on!; **das macht müde** it makes you tired; **in etw** *dat* **machen** to be *od* deal in sth ♦ *vr* to come along (nicely); **sich an etw** *akk* **machen** to set about sth; **sich verständlich machen** to make o.s. understood; **sich** *dat* **viel aus jdm/etw machen** to like sb/sth

Macht [maxt] (-, ‐ᵉe) *f* power; **~haber** (-s, -) *m* ruler

mächtig ['mɛçtɪç] *adj* powerful, mighty; (*umg: ungeheuer*) enormous

Macht- *zW:* **m~los** *adj* powerless; **~probe** *f* trial of strength; **~wort** *nt:* **ein ~wort sprechen** to exercise one's authority

Mädchen ['mɛːtçən] *nt* girl; **m~haft** *adj* girlish; **~name** *m* maiden name

Made ['maːdə] *f* maggot

madig ['maːdɪç] *adj* maggoty; **jdm etw ~ machen** to spoil sth for sb

mag *etc* [maːk] *vb siehe* **mögen**

Magazin [magaˈtsiːn] (-s, -e) *nt* magazine

Magen ['maːɡən] (-s, - *od* ‐ᵉ) *m* stomach; **~geschwür** *nt* (*MED*) stomach ulcer; **~schmerzen** *pl* stomachache *sg*

mager ['maːɡər] *adj* lean; (*dünn*) thin; **M~keit** *f* leanness; thinness

Magie [maˈɡiː] *f* magic

magisch ['maːɡɪʃ] *adj* magical

Magnet [maˈɡneːt] (-s *od* -en, -en) *m* magnet; **m~isch** *adj* magnetic; **~nadel** *f* magnetic needle

mähen ['mɛːən] *vt, vi* to mow

Mahl [maːl] (-(e)s, -e) *nt* meal; **m~en** (*unreg*) *vt* to grind; **~zeit** *f* meal ♦ *excl* enjoy your meal

Mahnbrief *m* reminder

Mähne ['mɛːnə] *f* mane

mahn- ['maːn] *zW:* **~en** *vt* to remind; (*warnend*) to warn; (*wegen Schuld*) to demand payment from; **M~mal** *nt* memorial; **M~ung** *f* reminder; admonition, warning

Mai [maɪ] (-(e)s, -e) *m* May; **~glöckchen** *nt* lily of the valley

Mailand ['maɪlant] *nt* Milan

mailändisch *adj* Milanese

mailen ['meːlən] *vti* to e-mail

Mais [maɪs] (-es, -e) *m* maize, corn (*US*); **~kolben** *m* corncob; **~mehl** *nt* (*KOCH*) corn meal

Majestät [majɛsˈtɛːt] *f* majesty; **m~isch** *adj* majestic

Majonäse ▲ [majoˈnɛːzə] *f* mayonnaise

Major [maˈjoːr] (-s, -e) *m* (*MIL*) major; (*AVIAT*) squadron leader

Majoran [majoˈraːn] (-s, -e) *m* marjoram

makaber [maˈkaːbər] *adj* macabre

Makel ['maːkəl] (-s, -) *m* blemish; (*moralisch*) stain; **m~los** *adj* immaculate, spotless

mäkeln ['mɛːkəln] *vi* to find fault

Makler(in) ['maːklər(ɪn)] (-s, -) *m(f)* broker

Makrele [maˈkreːlə] *f* mackerel

Mal [maːl] (-(e)s, -e) *nt* mark, sign; (*Zeitpunkt*) time; **ein für alle ~** once and for all; **m~** *adv* times; (*umg*) *siehe* **einmal** ♦ *suffix:* **-m~** -times

malen *vt, vi* to paint

Maler (-s, -) *m* painter; **Male'rei** *f* painting; **m~isch** *adj* picturesque

Malkasten *m* paintbox

Mallorca [maˈjɔrka, maˈlɔrka] (-s) *nt* Majorca

malnehmen (*unreg*) *vt, vi* to multiply

Malz [malts] (-es) *nt* malt; **~bier** *nt* (*KOCH*) malt beer; **~bonbon** *nt* cough drop; **~kaffee** *m* malt coffee

Mama ['mamaː] (-, -s) (*umg*) *f* mum(my) (*BRIT*), mom(my) (*US*)

Mami ['mami] (-, -s) = **Mama**

Mammut ['mamʊt] (-s, -e *od* -s) *nt* mammoth

man [man] *pron* one, you; **~ sagt, ...** they *od* people say ...; **wie schreibt ~ das?** how do you write it?, how is it written?

Manager(in) ['mɛnɪdʒər(ɪn)] (-s, -) *m(f)* manager

manch [manç] (*unver*) *pron* many a

manche(r, s) ['mançə(r, s)] *adj* many a; (*pl: einige*) a number of ♦ *pron* some

mancherlei [mançər'laɪ] *adj inv* various ♦ *pron inv* a variety of things

manchmal *adv* sometimes

Mandant(in) [man'dant(ɪn)] *m(f)* (*JUR*) client

Mandarine [manda'riːnə] *f* mandarin,

tangerine

Mandat [man'da:t] (-(e)s, -e) *nt* mandate

Mandel ['mandəl] (-, -n) *f* almond; (*ANAT*) tonsil; **~entzündung** *f* (*MED*) tonsillitis

Manege [ma'ne:ʒə] *f* ring, arena

Mangel ['maŋəl] (-s, ⁺) *m* lack; (*Knappheit*) shortage; (*Fehler*) defect, fault; **~ an** +*dat* shortage of; (*Erscheinung* *f* deficiency symptom; **m~haft** *adj* poor; (*fehlerhaft*) defective, faulty; **m~n** *vi unpers*: **es m~t jdm an etw** *dat* sb lacks sth ♦ *vt* (*Wäsche*) to mangle

mangels *präp* +*gen* for lack of

Manie [ma'ni:] *f* mania

Manier [ma'ni:r] (-) *f* manner; style; (*pej*) mannerism; **~en** *pl* (*Umgangsformen*) manners; **m~lich** *adj* well-mannered

Manifest [mani'fɛst] (-es, -e) *nt* manifesto

Maniküre [mani'ky:rə] *f* manicure

manipulieren [manipu'li:rən] *vt* to manipulate

Manko ['maŋko] (-s, -s) *nt* deficiency; (*COMM*) deficit

Mann [man] (-(e)s, ⁺er) *m* man; (*Ehemann*) husband; (*NAUT*) hand; **seinen ~ stehen** to hold one's own

Männchen ['mɛnçən] *nt* little man; (*Tier*) male

Mannequin [manə'kɛ̃:] (-s, -s) *nt* fashion model

männlich ['mɛnlıç] *adj* (*BIOL*) male; (*fig*, *GRAM*) masculine

Mannschaft *f* (*SPORT*, *fig*) team; (*AVIAT*, *NAUT*) crew; (*MIL*) other ranks *pl*

Manöver [ma'nø:vər] (-s, -) *nt* manoeuvre

manövrieren [manø'vri:rən] *vt*, *vi* to manoeuvre

Mansarde [man'zardə] *f* attic

Manschette [man'ʃɛta] *f* cuff; (*TECH*) collar; sleeve; **~nknopf** *m* cufflink

Mantel ['mantəl] (-s, ⁺) *m* coat; (*TECH*) casing, jacket

Manuskript [manu'skrıpt] (-(e)s, -e) *nt* manuscript

Mappe ['mapə] *f* briefcase; (*Aktenmappe*) folder

Märchen ['mɛːrçən] *nt* fairy tale; **m~haft**

adj fabulous; **~prinz** *m* Prince Charming

Margarine [marga'ri:nə] *f* margarine

Margerite [margə'ri:tə] *f* (*BOT*) marguerite

Marienkäfer [ma'ri:ənkɛːfər] *m* ladybird

Marine [ma'ri:nə] *f* navy; **m~blau** *adj* navy blue

marinieren [mari'ni:rən] *vt* to marinate

Marionette [mario'nɛtə] *f* puppet

Mark¹ [mark] (-, -) *f* (*Münze*) mark

Mark² [mark] (-(e)s) *nt* (*Knochenmark*) marrow; **jdm durch ~ und Bein gehen** to go right through sb

markant [mar'kant] *adj* striking

Marke ['markə] *f* mark; (*Warensorte*) brand; (*Fabrikat*) make; (*Rabatt~*, *Brief~*) stamp; (*Essen~*) ticket; (*aus Metall etc*) token, disc

Markenartikel *m* proprietary article

markieren [mar'ki:rən] *vt* to mark; (*umg*) to act ♦ *vi* (*umg*) to act it

Markierung *f* marking

Markise [mar'ki:zə] *f* awning

Markstück *nt* one-mark piece

Markt [markt] (-(e)s, ⁺e) *m* market; **~forschung** *f* market research; **~lücke** *f* (*COMM*) opening, gap in the market; **~platz** *m* market place; **m~üblich** *adj* (*Preise*, *Mieten*) standard, usual; **~wert** *m* (*COMM*) market value; **~wirtschaft** *f* market economy

Marmelade [marmə'la:də] *f* jam

Marmor ['marmɔr] (-s, -e) *m* marble; **m~ieren** [-'ri:rən] *vt* to marble

Marokko [ma'rɔko] (-s) *nt* Morocco

Marone [ma'ro:nə] (-, -n *od* **Maroni**) *f* chestnut

Marotte [ma'rɔtə] *f* fad, quirk

Marsch¹ [marʃ] (-, -en) *f* marsh

Marsch² [marʃ] (-(e)s, ⁺e) *m* march ♦ *excl* march!; **~befehl** *m* marching orders *pl*; **m~bereit** *adj* ready to move; **m~ieren** [mar'ʃi:rən] *vi* to march

Märtyrer(in) ['mɛrtyrər(ın)] (-s, -) *m(f)* martyr

März [mɛrts] (-(es), -e) *m* March

Marzipan [martsi'pa:n] (-s, -e) *nt* marzipan

Masche ['maʃə] *f* mesh; (*Strickmasche*) stitch; **das ist die neueste ~** that's the

latest thing; **~ndraht** m wire mesh;
m~nfest adj run-resistant

Maschine [maˈʃiːnə] f machine; (Motor)
engine; (Schreibmaschine) typewriter; **~
schreiben** to type; **m~ll** [maʃiˈnɛl] adj
machine(-); mechanical

Maschinen- zW: **~bauer** m mechanical
engineer; **~gewehr** nt machine gun;
~pistole f submachine gun; **~schaden** m
mechanical fault; **~schlosser** m fitter;
~schrift f typescript

Maschinist [maʃiˈnɪst] m engineer

Maser [ˈmaːzər] (-, -n) f (von Holz) grain; **~n**
pl (MED) measles sg

Maske [ˈmaskə] f mask; **~nball** m fancy-
dress ball

maskieren [masˈkiːrən] vt to mask;
(verkleiden) to dress up ♦ vr to disguise o.s.;
to dress up

Maskottchen [masˈkɔtçən] nt (lucky)
mascot

Maß¹ [maːs] (-es, -e) nt measure;
(Mäßigung) moderation; (Grad) degree,
extent; **~ halten** to exercise moderation

Maß² [maːs] (-, -(e)) f litre of beer

Massage [maˈsaːʒə] f massage

Maßanzug m made-to-measure suit

Maßarbeit f (fig) neat piece of work

Masse [ˈmasə] f mass

Maßeinheit f unit of measurement

Massen- zW: **~artikel** m mass-produced
article; **~grab** nt mass grave; **m~haft** adj
loads of; **~medien** pl mass media pl;
~veranstaltung f mass meeting;
m~weise adv on a large scale

Masseur [maˈsøːr] m masseur; **~in** f
masseuse

maßgebend adj authoritative

maßhalten △ (unreg) vi siehe **Maß¹**

massieren [maˈsiːrən] vt to massage; (MIL)
to mass

massig [ˈmasɪç] adj massive; (umg) massive
amount of

mäßig [ˈmɛːsɪç] adj moderate; **~en**
[ˈmɛːsɪgən] vt to restrain, to moderate;
M~keit f moderation

Massiv (-s, -e) nt massif

massiv [maˈsiːf] adj solid; (fig) heavy, rough

Maß- zW: **~krug** m tankard; **m~los** adj
extreme; **~nahme** f measure, step; **~stab**
m rule, measure; (fig) standard; (GEOG)
scale; **m~voll** adj moderate

Mast [mast] (-(e)s, -e(n)) m mast; (ELEK)
pylon

mästen [ˈmɛstən] vt to fatten

Material [materiˈaːl] (-s, -ien) nt material(s);
~fehler m material defect; **~ismus** [-
ˈlɪsmʊs] m materialism; **m~istisch** [-ˈlɪstɪʃ]
adj materialistic

Materie [maˈteːriə] f matter, substance

materiell [materiˈel] adj material

Mathematik [matemaˈtiːk] f mathematics
sg; **~er(in)** [mateˈmaːtikər(ɪn)] (-s, -) m(f)
mathematician

mathematisch [mateˈmaːtɪʃ] adj
mathematical

Matjeshering [ˈmatjəsheːrɪŋ] m (KOCH)
young herring

Matratze [maˈtratsə] f mattress

Matrixdrucker [ˈmaːtrɪks-] m dot-matrix
printer

Matrose [maˈtroːzə] (-n, -n) m sailor

Matsch [matʃ] (-(e)s) m mud;
(Schneematsch) slush; **m~ig** adj muddy;
slushy

matt [mat] adj weak; (glanzlos) dull; (PHOT)
matt; (SCHACH) mate

Matte [ˈmatə] f mat

Mattscheibe f (TV) screen

Mauer [ˈmaʊər] (-, -n) f wall; **m~n** vi to
build; to lay bricks ♦ vt to build

Maul [maʊl] (-(e)s, Mäuler) nt mouth;
m~en (umg) vi to grumble; **~esel** m mule;
~korb m muzzle; **~sperre** f lockjaw;
~tasche f (KOCH) pasta envelopes stuffed
and used in soup; **~tier** nt mule; **~wurf** m
mole

Maurer [ˈmaʊrər] (-s, -) m bricklayer

Maus [maʊs] (-, Mäuse) f (auch COMPUT)
mouse

Mause- [ˈmaʊzə] zW: **~falle** f mousetrap;
m~n vi to catch mice ♦ vt (umg) to pinch;
m~tot adj stone dead

Maut- [ˈmaʊt] zW: **~gebühr** f toll (charge);

~**straße** f toll road

maximal [maksi'ma:l] adj maximum ♦ adv at most

Mayonnaise [majɔ'nɛːzə] f mayonnaise

Mechan- [me'ça:n] zW: ~**ik** f mechanics sg; (Getriebe) mechanics pl; ~**iker** (-s, -) m mechanic, engineer; **m~isch** adj mechanical; ~**ismus** m mechanism

meckern ['mɛkərn] vi to bleat; (umg) to moan

Medaille [me'daljə] f medal

Medaillon [medal'jõ:] (-s, -s) nt (Schmuck) locket

Medikament [medika'ment] nt medicine

Meditation [meditatsi'o:n] f meditation

meditieren [medi'ti:rən] vi to meditate

Medizin [medi'tsi:n] (-, -en) f medicine; **m~isch** adj medical

Meer [me:r] (-(e)s, -e) nt sea; ~**enge** f straits pl; ~**esfrüchte** pl seafood sg; ~**esspiegel** m sea level; ~**rettich** m horseradish; ~**schweinchen** nt guinea-pig

Mehl [me:l] (-(e)s, -e) nt flour; **m~ig** adj floury; ~**schwitze** f (KOCH) roux; ~**speise** f (KOCH) flummery

mehr [me:r] adj, adv more; ~**deutig** adj ambiguous; ~**ere** adj several; ~**eres** pron several things; ~**fach** adj multiple; (wiederholt) repeated; **M~fahrtenkarte** f multi-journey ticket; **M~heit** f majority; ~**malig** adj repeated; ~**mals** adv repeatedly; ~**stimmig** adj for several voices; ~**stimmig singen** to harmonize; **M~wertsteuer** f value added tax; **M~zahl** f majority; (GRAM) plural

Mehrzweck- in zW multipurpose

meiden ['maidən] (unreg) vt to avoid

Meile ['mailə] f mile; ~**nstein** m milestone; **m~nweit** adj for miles

mein(e) [main] adj my; ~**e(r, s)** pron mine

Meineid ['main|ait] m perjury

meinen ['mainən] vi to think ♦ vt to think; (sagen) to say; (sagen wollen) to mean; **das will ich ~** I should think so

mein- zW: ~**erseits** adv for my part; ~**etwegen** adv (für mich) for my sake; (wegen mir) on my account; (von mir aus) as far as I'm concerned; I don't care od mind; ~**etwillen** adv: **um ~etwillen** for my sake, on my account

Meinung ['mainʊŋ] f opinion; **ganz meine** ~ I quite agree; **jdm die ~ sagen** to give sb a piece of one's mind

Meinungs- zW: ~**austausch** m exchange of views; ~**umfrage** f opinion poll; ~**verschiedenheit** f difference of opinion

Meise ['maizə] f tit(mouse)

Meißel ['maisəl] (-s, -) m chisel

meist [maist] adj, adv mostly; **am ~en** the most; ~**ens** adv generally, usually

Meister ['maistər] (-s, -) m master; (SPORT) champion; **m~haft** adj masterly; **m~n** vt (Schwierigkeiten etc) to overcome, conquer; ~**schaft** f mastery; (SPORT) championship; ~**stück** nt masterpiece; ~**werk** nt masterpiece

Melancholie [melaŋko'li:] f melancholy; **melancholisch** [melaŋ'ko:lɪʃ] adj melancholy

Melde- ['meldə] zW: ~**frist** f registration period; **m~n** vt to report ♦ vr to report; (SCH) to put one's hand up; (freiwillig) to volunteer; (auf etw, am Telefon) to answer; **sich m~n bei** to report to; to register with; **sich zu Wort m~n** to ask to speak; ~**pflicht** f obligation to register with the police; ~**schluss** ▲ m closing date; ~**stelle** f registration office

Meldung ['meldʊŋ] f announcement; (Bericht) report

meliert [me'li:rt] adj (Haar) greying; (Wolle) flecked

melken ['mɛlkən] (unreg) vt to milk

Melodie [melo'di:] f melody, tune

melodisch [me'lo:dɪʃ] adj melodious, tuneful

Melone [me'lo:nə] f melon; (Hut) bowler (hat)

Membran [mem'bra:n] (-, -en) f (TECH) diaphragm

Memoiren [memo'a:rən] pl memoirs

Menge ['mɛŋə] f quantity; (Menschenmenge) crowd; (große Anzahl) lot (of); **m~n** vt to mix ♦ vr: **sich m~n in** +akk to meddle

with; **~nlehre** f (MATH) set theory;
~nrabatt m bulk discount

Mensch [mɛnʃ] (**-en, -en**) m human being,
man; person ♦ excl hey!; **kein ~** nobody

Menschen- zW: **~affe** m (ZOOL) ape;
m~freundlich adj philanthropical;
~kenner m judge of human nature;
m~leer adj deserted; **m~möglich** adj
humanly possible; **~rechte** pl human
rights; **m~unwürdig** adj beneath human
dignity; **~verstand** m: **gesunder
~verstand** common sense

Mensch- zW: **~heit** f humanity, mankind;
m~lich adj human; (human) humane;
~lichkeit f humanity

Menstruation [mɛnstruatsi'o:n] f
menstruation

Mentalität [mɛntali'tɛ:t] f mentality

Menü [me'ny:] (**-s, -s**) nt (auch COMPUT)
menu

Merk- ['mɛrk] zW: **~blatt** nt instruction
sheet od leaflet; **m~en** vt to notice; **sich**
dat **etw m~en** to remember sth; **m~lich**
adj noticeable; **~mal** nt sign, characteristic;
m~würdig adj odd

messbar ▲ ['mɛsbaːr] adj measurable

Messbecher ▲ m measuring jug

Messe ['mɛsə] f fair; (ECCL) mass; **~gelände**
nt exhibition centre; **~halle** f pavilion at a
fair

messen (unreg) vt to measure ♦ vr to
compete

Messer (**-s, -**) nt knife; **~spitze** f knife
point; (in Rezept) pinch

Messestand m stall at a fair

Messgerät ▲ nt measuring device, gauge

Messing ['mɛsɪŋ] (**-s**) nt brass

Metall [me'tal] (**-s, -e**) nt metal; **m~isch** adj
metallic

Meter ['me:tər] (**-s, -**) nt od m metre; **~maß**
nt tape measure

Methode [me'to:də] f method;
methodisch adj methodical

Metropole [metro'po:lə] f metropolis

Metzger ['mɛtsgər] (**-s, -**) m butcher; **~ei**
[-'raɪ] f butcher's (shop)

Meute ['mɔʏtə] f pack; **~'rei** f mutiny;

m~rn vi to mutiny

miauen [mi'aʊən] vi to miaow

mich [mɪç] (akk von **ich**) pron me; myself

Miene ['mi:nə] f look, expression

mies [mi:s] (umg) adj lousy

Miet- ['mi:t] zW: **~auto** nt hired car; **~e** f
rent; **zur ~e wohnen** to live in rented
accommodation; **m~en** vt to rent; (Auto)
to hire; **~er(in)** (**-s, -**) m(f) tenant; **~shaus**
nt tenement, block of (rented) flats;
~vertrag m lease

Migräne [mi'grɛ:nə] f migraine

Mikro- ['mikro] zW: **~fon, ~phon**
[-'fo:n] (**-s, -e**) nt microphone; **~skop**
[-'sko:p] (**-s, -e**) nt microscope;
m~skopisch adj microscopic;
~wellenherd m microwave (oven)

Milch [mɪlç] (**-**) f milk; **~glas** nt frosted
glass; **m~ig** adj milky; **~kaffee** m white
coffee; **~mann** (pl **-männer**) m milkman;
~mixgetränk nt (KOCH) milkshake;
~pulver nt powdered milk; **~straße** f
Milky Way; **~zahn** m milk tooth

mild [mɪlt] adj mild; (Richter) lenient;
(freundlich) kind, charitable; **M~e** f
mildness; leniency; **~ern** vt to mitigate, to
soften; (Schmerz) to alleviate; **~ernde
Umstände** extenuating circumstances

Milieu [mili'ø:] (**-s, -s**) nt background,
environment; **m~geschädigt** adj
maladjusted

Mili- [mili] zW: **m~tant** [-'tant] adj militant;
~tär [-'tɛ:r] (**-s**) nt military, army;
~'tärgericht nt military court; **m~'tärisch**
adj military

Milli- ['mili] zW: **~ardär** [-ar'dɛ:r] m
multimillionaire; **~arde** [-'ardə] f milliard;
billion (BES US); **~meter** m millimetre;
~meterpapier nt graph paper

Million [mɪli'o:n] (**-, -en**) f million; **~är**
[-o'nɛ:r] m millionaire

Milz [mɪlts] (**-, -en**) f spleen

Mimik ['mi:mɪk] f mime

Mimose [mi'mo:zə] f mimosa; (fig) sensitive
person

minder ['mɪndər] adj inferior ♦ adv less;
M~heit f minority; **~jährig** adj minor;

M~jährige(r) *f(m)* minor; ~n *vt, vr* to decrease, to diminish; M~ung *f* decrease; ~wertig *adj* inferior; M~wertigkeitskomplex *m* inferiority complex

Mindest- ['mɪndəst] *zW:* ~alter *nt* minimum age; ~betrag *m* minimum amount; m~e(r, s) *adj* least; zum ~en *od* m~en *adv* at least; ~haltbarkeitsdatum *nt* best-before date; ~lohn *m* minimum wage; ~maß *nt* minimum

Mine ['mi:nə] *f* mine; (*Bleistiftmine*) lead; (*Kugelschreibermine*) refill

Mineral [mine'ra:l] (-s, -e *od* -ien) *nt* mineral; m~isch *adj* mineral; ~wasser *nt* mineral water

Miniatur [minia'tu:r] *f* miniature

Mini- *zW:* ~golf ['mɪnɪgɔlf] *nt* miniature golf, crazy golf; m~mal [mini'ma:l] *adj* minimal; ~mum ['mi:nimʊm] *nt* minimum; ~rock *nt* miniskirt

Minister [mi'nɪstər] (-s, -) *m* minister; m~iell *adj* ministerial; ~ium *nt* ministry; ~präsident *m* prime minister

Minus ['mi:nʊs] (-, -) *nt* deficit

minus *adv* minus; M~zeichen *nt* minus sign

Minute [mi'nu:tə] *f* minute

Minze ['mɪntsə] *f* mint

mir [mi:r] (*dat von* ich) *pron* (to) me; ~ nichts, dir nichts just like that

Misch- ['mɪʃ] *zW:* ~brot *nt* bread made from more than one kind of flour; ~ehe *f* mixed marriage; m~en *vt* to mix; ~ling *m* half-caste; ~ung *f* mixture

miserabel [mizə'ra:bəl] (*umg*) *adj* (*Essen, Film*) dreadful

Miss- ▲ ['mɪs] *zW:* ~behagen *nt* discomfort, uneasiness; ~bildung *f* deformity; m~'billigen *vt insep* to disapprove of; ~brauch *m* abuse; (*falscher Gebrauch*) misuse; m~'brauchen *vt insep* to abuse; jdn zu *od* für etw m~brauchen to use sb for *od* to do sth; ~erfolg *m* failure; ~fallen (-s) *nt* displeasure; m~'fallen (*unreg*) *vi insep:* jdm m~fallen

to displease sb; ~geschick *nt* misfortune; m~glücken [mɪs'glʏkən] *vi insep* to fail; jdm m~glückt etw sb does not succeed with sth; ~griff *m* mistake; ~gunst *f* envy; m~günstig *adj* envious; m~'handeln *vt insep* to ill-treat; ~'handlung *f* ill-treatment

Mission [mɪsi'o:n] *f* mission; ~ar(in) *m(f)* missionary

Miss- ▲ *zW:* ~klang *m* discord; ~kredit *m* discredit; m~lingen [mɪs'lɪŋən] (*unreg*) *vi insep* to fail; ~mut *m* sullenness; m~mutig *adj* sullen; m~'raten (*unreg*) *vi insep* to turn out badly ♦ *adj* ill-bred; ~stand *m* bad state of affairs; abuse; m~'trauen *vi insep* to mistrust; ~trauen (-s) *nt* distrust, suspicion; ~trauensantrag *m* (*POL*) motion of no confidence; m~trauisch *adj* distrustful, suspicious; ~verhältnis *nt* disproportion; ~verständnis *nt* misunderstanding; m~verstehen (*unreg*) *vt insep* to misunderstand; ~wirtschaft *f* mismanagement

Mist [mɪst] (-(e)s) *m* dung; dirt; (*umg*) rubbish

Mistel (-, -n) *f* mistletoe

Misthaufen *m* dungheap

mit [mɪt] *präp +dat* with; (~tels) by ♦ *adv* along, too; ~ der Bahn by train; ~ 10 Jahren at the age of 10; wollen Sie ~? do you want to come along?

Mitarbeit ['mɪtarbaɪt] *f* cooperation; m~en *vi* to cooperate, to collaborate; ~er(in) *m(f)* collaborator; co-worker ♦ *pl* (*Personal*) staff

Mit- *zW:* ~bestimmung *f* participation in decision-making; m~bringen (*unreg*) *vt* to bring along

miteinander [mɪtaɪ'nandər] *adv* together, with one another

miterleben *vt* to see, to witness

Mitesser ['mɪtɛsər] (-s, -) *m* blackhead

mitfahr- *zW:* ~en *vi* to accompany; (*auf Reise auch*) to travel with; M~gelegenheit *f* lift; M~zentrale *f* agency for arranging lifts

mitfühlend *adj* sympathetic, compassionate

Mit- *zW*: **m~geben** (*unreg*) *vt* to give;
~**gefühl** *nt* sympathy; **m~gehen** (*unreg*) *vi*
to go/come along; **m~genommen** *adj*
done in, in a bad way; **m~gift** *f* dowry

Mitglied ['mɪtgliːt] *nt* member; ~**sbeitrag**
m membership fee; ~**schaft** *f* membership

Mit- *zW*: **m~halten** (*unreg*) *vi* to keep up;
m~helfen (*unreg*) *vi* to help; ~**hilfe** *f* help,
assistance; **m~hören** *vt* to listen in to;
m~kommen (*unreg*) *vi* to come along;
(*verstehen*) to keep up, to follow; ~**läufer**
m hanger-on; (*POL*) fellow traveller

Mitleid *nt* sympathy; (*Erbarmen*)
compassion; **m~ig** *adj* sympathetic;
m~slos *adj* pitiless, merciless

Mit- *zW*: **m~machen** *vt* to join in, to take
part in; ~**mensch** *m* fellow man;
m~nehmen (*unreg*) *vt* to take along/away;
(*anstrengen*) to wear out, to exhaust; **zum
~nehmen** to take away; **m~reden** *vi*: **bei
etw m~reden** to have a say in sth;
m~reißen (*unreg*) *vt* to carry away/along;
(*fig*) to thrill, captivate

mitsamt [mɪt'zamt] *präp +dat* together with

Mitschuld *f* complicity; **m~ig** *adj*: **m~ig
(an +*dat*)** implicated (in); (*an Unfall*) partly
responsible (for)

Mit- *zW*: ~**schüler(in)** *m(f)* schoolmate;
m~spielen *vi* to join in, to take part;
~**spieler(in)** *m(f)* partner

Mittag ['mɪtaːk] (**-(e)s, -e**) *m* midday,
lunchtime; (**zu**) ~ **essen** to have lunch;
heute/morgen ~ today/tomorrow at
lunchtime *od* noon; ~**essen** *nt* lunch,
dinner

mittags *adv* at lunchtime *od* noon;
M~pause *f* lunch break; **M~schlaf** *m*
early afternoon nap, siesta

Mittäter(in) ['mɪttɛːtər(ɪn)] *m(f)* accomplice

Mitte ['mɪtə] *f* middle; (*POL*) centre; **aus
unserer** ~ from our midst

mitteilen ['mɪttaɪlən] *vt*: **jdm etw** ~ to
inform sb of sth, to communicate sth to sb

Mitteilung *f* communication

Mittel ['mɪtəl] (**-s -**) *nt* means; method;
(*MATH*) average; (*MED*) medicine; **ein** ~ **zum
Zweck** a means to an end; ~**alter** *nt*

Middle Ages *pl*; **m~alterlich** *adj*
mediaeval; ~**ding** *nt* cross; ~**europa** *nt*
Central Europe; ~**gebirge** *nt* low mountain
range; **m~mäßig** *adj* mediocre, middling;
~**mäßigkeit** *f* mediocrity; ~**meer** *nt*
Mediterranean; ~**ohrentzündung** *f*
inflammation of the middle ear; ~**punkt** *m*
centre; ~**stand** *m* middle class; ~**streifen**
m central reservation; ~**stürmer** *m* centre-
forward; ~**weg** *m* middle course; ~**welle** *f*
(*RADIO*) medium wave

mitten ['mɪtən] *adv* in the middle; ~ **auf der
Straße/in der Nacht** in the middle of the
street/night

Mitternacht ['mɪtərnaxt] *f* midnight

mittlere(r, s) ['mɪtlərə(r, s)] *adj* middle;
(*durchschnittlich*) medium, average; ~ **Reife**
≃ O-levels

> **mittlere Reife**
>
> *i* The **mittlere Reife** *is the standard
> certificate gained at a* **Realschule** *or*
> **Gymnasium** *on successful completion of 6
> years' education there. If a pupil at a*
> **Realschule** *attains good results in several
> subjects he is allowed to enter the 11th
> class of a* **Gymnasium** *to study for the*
> **Abitur***.*

---

mittlerweile ['mɪtlər'vaɪlə] *adv* meanwhile

Mittwoch ['mɪtvɔx] (**-(e)s, -e**) *m*
Wednesday; **m~s** *adv* on Wednesdays

mitunter [mɪt'ʊntər] *adv* occasionally,
sometimes

Mit- *zW*: **m~verantwortlich** *adj* jointly
responsible; **m~wirken** *vi*: **m~wirken (bei)**
to contribute (to); (*THEAT*) to take part (in);
~**wirkung** *f* contribution; participation

Mobbing ['mɔbɪŋ] (**-s**) *nt* workplace
bullying

Möbel ['møːbəl] *pl* furniture *sg*; ~**wagen** *m*
furniture *od* removal van

mobil [mo'biːl] *adj* mobile; (*MIL*) mobilized;
M~iar [mobili'aːr] (**-s, -e**) *nt* furnishings *pl*;
M~machung *f* mobilization; **M~telefon**
nt mobile phone

möblieren [mø'bliːrən] *vt* to furnish;

möbliert wohnen to live in furnished accommodation

möchte *etc* ['mϾçtǝ] *vb siehe* **mögen**

Mode ['moːdǝ] *f* fashion

Modell [mo'dɛl] **(-s, -e)** *nt* model; **m~ieren** [-'liːrǝn] *vt* to model

Modenschau *f* fashion show

moderig ['moːdǝrıç] *adj* (*Keller*) musty; (*Luft*) stale

modern [mo'dɛrn] *adj* modern; (*modisch*) fashionable; **~isieren** *vt* to modernize

Mode- *zW*: **~schau** *f* fashion show; **~schmuck** *m* fashion jewellery; **~schöpfer(in)** *m(f)* fashion designer; **~wort** *nt* fashionable word, buzz word

modisch ['moːdıʃ] *adj* fashionable

Mofa ['moːfa] **(-s, -s)** *nt* small moped

mogeln ['moːgǝln] (*umg*) *vi* to cheat

SCHLÜSSELWORT

mögen ['møːgǝn] (*pt* **mochte**, *pp* **gemocht** *od* (*als Hilfsverb*) **mögen**) *vt, vi* to like; **magst du/mögen Sie ihn?** do you like him?; **ich möchte ...** I would like ..., I'd like ...; **er möchte in die Stadt** he'd like to go into town; **ich möchte nicht, dass du ...** I wouldn't like you to ...; **ich mag nicht mehr** I've had enough

♦ *Hilfsverb* to like to; (*wollen*) to want; **möchtest du etwas essen?** would you like something to eat?; **sie mag nicht bleiben** she doesn't want to stay; **das mag wohl sein** that may well be; **was mag das heißen?** what might that mean?; **Sie möchten zu Hause anrufen** could you please call home?

---

möglich ['møːklıç] *adj* possible; **~erweise** *adv* possibly; **M~keit** *f* possibility; **nach M~keit** if possible; **~st** *adv* as ... as possible

Mohn [moːn] **(-(e)s, -e)** *m* (*~blume*) poppy; (*~samen*) poppy seed

Möhre ['møːrǝ] *f* carrot

Mohrrübe ['moːryːbǝ] *f* carrot

mokieren [mo'kiːrǝn] *vr*: **sich ~ über** +*akk* to make fun of

Mole ['moːlǝ] *f* (harbour) mole

Molekül [mole'kyːl] **(-s, -e)** *nt* molecule

Molkerei [mɔlkǝ'raı] *f* dairy

Moll [mɔl] **(-, -)** *nt* (MUS) minor (key)

mollig *adj* cosy; (*dicklich*) plump

Moment [mo'mɛnt] **(-(e)s, -e)** *m* moment ♦ *nt* factor; **im ~** at the moment; **~ (mal)!** just a moment; **m~an** [-'taːn] *adj* momentary ♦ *adv* at the moment

Monarch [mo'narç] **(-en, -en)** *m* monarch; **~ie** [monar'çiː] *f* monarchy

Monat ['moːnat] **(-(e)s, -e)** *m* month; **m~elang** *adv* for months; **m~lich** *adj* monthly

Monats- *zW*: **~gehalt** *nt*: **das dreizehnte ~gehalt** Christmas bonus (*of one month's salary*); **~karte** *f* monthly ticket

Mönch [mœnç] **(-(e)s, -e)** *m* monk

Mond [moːnt] **(-(e)s, -e)** *m* moon; **~finsternis** *f* eclipse of the moon; **m~hell** *adj* moonlit; **~landung** *f* moon landing; **~schein** *m* moonlight

Mono- [mono] *in zW* mono; **~log** [-'loːk] **(-s, -e)** *m* monologue; **~pol** [-'poːl] **(-s, -e)** *nt* monopoly; **m~polisieren** [-poli'ziːrǝn] *vt* to monopolize; **m~ton** [-'toːn] *adj* monotonous; **~tonie** [-to'niː] *f* monotony

Montag ['moːntaːk] **(-(e)s, -e)** *m* Monday

Montage [mɔn'taːʒǝ] *f* (PHOT *etc*) montage; (TECH) assembly; (*Einbauen*) fitting

Monteur [mɔn'tøːr] *m* fitter

montieren [mɔn'tiːrǝn] *vt* to assemble

Monument [monu'mɛnt] *nt* monument; **m~al** [-'taːl] *adj* monumental

Moor [moːr] **(-(e)s, -e)** *nt* moor

Moos [moːs] **(-es, -e)** *nt* moss

Moped ['moːpɛt] **(-s, -s)** *nt* moped

Moral [mo'raːl] **(-, -en)** *f* morality; (*einer Geschichte*) moral; **m~isch** *adj* moral

Morast [mo'rast] **(-(e)s, -e)** *m* morass, mire; **m~ig** *adj* boggy

Mord [mɔrt] **(-(e)s, -e)** *m* murder; **~anschlag** *m* murder attempt

Mörder(in) ['mœrdǝr(ın)] **(-s, -)** *m(f)* murderer (murderess)

mörderisch *adj* (*fig*: *schrecklich*) terrible, dreadful ♦ *adv* (*umg*: *entsetzlich*) terribly, dreadfully

---

Mord- zW: **~kommission** f murder squad; **~glück** (umg) nt amazing luck; **m~smäßig** (umg) adj terrific, enormous; **~verdacht** m suspicion of murder; **~waffe** f murder weapon

morgen ['mɔrgən] adv tomorrow; **~ früh** tomorrow morning; **M~** (-s, -) nt morning; **M~mantel** m dressing gown; **M~rock** m dressing gown; **M~röte** f dawn; **~s** adv in the morning

morgig ['mɔrgɪç] adj tomorrow's; **der ~e Tag** tomorrow

Morphium ['mɔrfiʊm] nt morphine

morsch [mɔrʃ] adj rotten

Morsealphabet ['mɔrzə|alfabeːt] nt Morse code

morsen vi to send a message by Morse code

Mörtel ['mœrtəl] (-s, -) m mortar

Mosaik [moza'iːk] (-s, -en od -e) nt mosaic

Moschee [mɔ'ʃeː] (-, -n) f mosque

Moskito [mɔs'kiːto] (-s, -s) m mosquito

Most [mɔst] (-(e)s, -e) m (unfermented) fruit juice; (Apfelwein) cider

Motel [mo'tɛl] (-s, -s) nt motel

Motiv [mo'tiːf] (-s, -e) nt motive; (MUS) theme; **~ation** [-vatsi'oːn] f motivation; **m~ieren** [moti'viːrən] vt to motivate

Motor ['moːtɔr, pl mo'toːrən] (-s, -en) m engine; (bes ELEK) motor; **~boot** nt motorboat; **~haube** f (von Auto) bonnet (BRIT), hood (US); **m~isieren** vt to motorize; **~öl** nt engine oil; **~rad** nt motorcycle; **~roller** m (motor) scooter; **~schaden** m engine trouble od failure

Motte ['mɔtə] f moth; **~nkugel** f mothball(s)

Motto ['mɔto] (-s, -s) nt motto

Möwe ['møːvə] f seagull

Mücke ['mʏkə] f midge, gnat; **~nstich** m midge od gnat bite

müde ['myːdə] adj tired

Müdigkeit ['myːdɪçkaɪt] f tiredness

Muffel (-s, -) (umg) m killjoy, sourpuss

muffig adj (Luft) musty

Mühe ['myːə] f trouble, pains pl; **mit Müh und Not** with great difficulty; **sich** dat **~**

geben to go to a lot of trouble; **m~los** adj without trouble, easy; **m~voll** adj laborious, arduous

Mühle ['myːlə] f mill; (Kaffeemühle) grinder

Müh- zW: **~sal** (-, -e) f tribulation; **m~sam** adj arduous, troublesome; **m~selig** adj arduous, laborious

Mulde ['mʊldə] f hollow, depression

Mull [mʊl] (-(e)s, -e) m thin muslin

Müll [mʏl] (-(e)s) m refuse; **~abfuhr** f rubbish disposal; (Leute) dustmen pl; **~abladeplatz** m rubbish dump; **~binde** f gauze bandage; **~eimer** m dustbin, garbage can (US); **~haufen** m rubbish heap; **~schlucker** (-s, -) m garbage disposal unit; **~tonne** f dustbin **~verbrennungsanlage** f incinerator

mulmig ['mʊlmɪç] adj rotten; (umg) dodgy; **jdm ist ~** sb feels funny

multiplizieren [mʊltipli'tsiːrən] vt to multiply

Mumie ['muːmiə] f mummy

Mumm [mʊm] (-s) (umg) m gumption, nerve

Mumps [mʊmps] (-) m od f (MED) mumps

München ['mʏnçən] (-s) nt Munich

Mund [mʊnt] (-(e)s, ᵘer) m mouth; **~art** f dialect

münden ['mʏndən] vi: **~ in** +akk to flow into

Mund- zW: **m~faul** adj taciturn; **~geruch** m bad breath; **~harmonika** f mouth organ

mündig ['mʏndɪç] adj of age; **M~keit** f majority

mündlich ['mʏntlɪç] adj oral

Mundstück nt mouthpiece; (Zigarettenmundstück) tip

Mündung ['mʏndʊn] f (von Fluss) mouth; (Gewehr) muzzle

Mund- zW: **~wasser** nt mouthwash; **~werk** nt: **ein großes ~werk haben** to have a big mouth; **~winkel** m corner of the mouth

Munition [munitsi'oːn] f ammunition; **~slager** nt ammunition dump

munkeln ['mʊŋkəln] vi to whisper, to

mutter

Münster ['mʏnstər] **(-s, -)** *nt* minster

munter ['muntər] *adj* lively

Münze ['mʏntsə] *f* coin; **m~n** *vt* to coin, to mint; **auf jdn gemünzt sein** to be aimed at sb

Münzfernsprecher ['mʏntsfernʃpreçər] *m* callbox (*BRIT*), pay phone

mürb(e) ['mʏrb(ə)] *adj* (*Gestein*) crumbly; (*Holz*) rotten; (*Gebäck*) crisp; **jdn ~ machen** to wear sb down; **M~eteig** ['mʏrbətaɪç] *m* shortcrust pastry

murmeln ['murməln] *vt, vi* to murmur, to mutter

murren ['murən] *vi* to grumble, to grouse

mürrisch ['mʏrɪʃ] *adj* sullen

Mus [muːs] **(-es, -e)** *nt* purée

Muschel ['muʃəl] **(-, -n)** *f* mussel; (*~schale*) shell; (*Telefonmuschel*) receiver

Muse ['muːzə] *f* muse

Museum [muˈzeːʊm] **(-s, Museen)** *nt* museum

Musik [muˈziːk] *f* music; (*Kapelle*) band; **m~alisch** [-kaːlɪʃ] *adj* musical; **~ant(in)** [-ˈkant(ɪn)] **(-en, -en)** *m(f)* musician; **~box** *f* jukebox; **~er** **(-s, -)** *m* musician; **~hochschule** *f* college of music; **~instrument** *nt* musical instrument

musisch ['muːzɪʃ] *adj* (*Mensch*) artistic

musizieren [muziˈtsiːrən] *vi* to make music

Muskat [musˈkaːt] **(-(e)s, -e)** *m* nutmeg

Muskel ['muskəl] **(-s, -n)** *m* muscle; **~kater** *m*: **~kater haben** to be stiff

Muskulatur [muskulaˈtuːr] *f* muscular system

muskulös [muskuˈløːs] *adj* muscular

Müsli ['myːsli] **(-s, -)** *nt* (*KOCH*) muesli

Muss ▲ [mus] **(-)** *nt* necessity, must

Muße ['muːsə] **(-)** *f* leisure

---SCHLÜSSELWORT---

müssen ['mʏsən] (*pt* **musste**, *pp* **gemusst** *od* (*als Hilfsverb*) **müssen**) *vi* **1** (*Zwang*) must (*nur im Präsens*), to have to; **ich muss es tun** I must do it, I have to do it; **ich musste es tun** I had to do it; **er muss es**

nicht tun he doesn't have to do it; **muss ich?** must I?, do I have to?; **wann müsst ihr zur Schule?** when do you have to go to school?; **er hat gehen müssen** he (has) had to go; **muss das sein?** is that really necessary?; **ich muss mal** (*umg*) I need the toilet

2 (*sollen*): **das musst du nicht tun!** you oughtn't to *od* shouldn't do that; **Sie hätten ihn fragen müssen** you should have asked him

3: **es muss geregnet haben** it must have rained; **es muss nicht wahr sein** it needn't be true

---

müßig ['myːsɪç] *adj* idle

Muster ['mustər] **(-s, -)** *nt* model; (*Dessin*) pattern; (*Probe*) sample; **m~gültig** *adj* exemplary; **m~n** *vt* (*Tapete*) to pattern; (*fig, MIL*) to examine; (*Truppen*) to inspect; **~ung** *f* (*von Stoff*) pattern; (*MIL*) inspection

Mut [muːt] *m* courage; **nur ~!** cheer up!; **jdm ~ machen** to encourage sb; **m~ig** *adj* courageous; **m~los** *adj* discouraged, despondent

mutmaßlich ['muːtmaːslɪç] *adj* presumed
♦ *adv* probably

Mutprobe *f* test *od* trial of courage

Mutter¹ ['mutər] **(-, ᵉ)** *f* mother

Mutter² ['mutər] **(-, -n)** *f* (*Schraubenmutter*) nut

mütterlich ['mʏtərlɪç] *adj* motherly; **~erseits** *adv* on the mother's side

Mutter- *zW*: **~liebe** *f* motherly love; **~mal** *nt* birthmark; **~milch** *f* mother's milk; **~schaft** *f* motherhood, maternity; **~schutz** *m* maternity regulations; **'~'seelen|allein** *adj* all alone; **~sprache** *f* native language; **~tag** *m* Mother's Day

Mutti ['muti] **(-, -s)** *f* mum(my) (*BRIT*), mom(my) (*US*)

mutwillig ['muːtvɪlɪç] *adj* malicious, deliberate

Mütze ['mʏtsə] *f* cap

MwSt *abk* (= *Mehrwertsteuer*) VAT

mysteriös [mʏsteriˈøːs] *adj* mysterious

Mythos ['myːtɔs] **(-, Mythen)** *m* myth⸱

N, n

na [na] *excl* well; **~ gut** okay then
Nabel ['na:bəl] **(-s, -)** *m* navel; **~schnur** *f*
umbilical cord

SCHLÜSSELWORT

nach [na:x] *präp +dat* **1** (*örtlich*) to; **nach
Berlin** to Berlin; **nach links/rechts** (to the)
left/right; **nach oben/hinten** up/back
2 (*zeitlich*) after; **einer nach dem anderen**
one after the other; **nach Ihnen!** after
you!; **zehn (Minuten) nach drei** ten
(minutes) past three
3 (*gemäß*) according to; **nach dem Gesetz**
according to the law; **dem Namen nach**
judging by his/her name; **nach allem, was
ich weiß** as far as I know
♦ *adv*: **ihm nach!** after him!; **nach und
nach** gradually, little by little; **nach wie
vor** still

nachahmen ['na:xˌʔa:mən] *vt* to imitate
Nachbar(in) ['na:xba:r(ɪn)] **(-s, -en)** *m(f)*
neighbour; **~haus** *nt*: **im ~haus** next door;
n~lich *adj* neighbourly; **~schaft** *f*
neighbourhood; **~staat** *m* neighbouring
state
nach- *zW*: **~bestellen** *vt*: **50 Stück
~bestellen** to order another 50;
N~bestellung *f* (*COMM*) repeat order;
N~bildung *f* imitation, copy; **~blicken** *vi*
to gaze after; **~datieren** *vt* to postdate
nachdem [na:x'de:m] *konj* after; (*weil*) since;
je ~ (ob) it depends (whether)
nachdenken (*unreg*) *vi*: **~ über** +akk to
think about; **N~ (-s)** *nt* reflection,
meditation
nachdenklich *adj* thoughtful, pensive
Nachdruck ['na:xdrʊk] *m* emphasis; (*TYP*)
reprint, reproduction
nachdrücklich ['na:xdrʏklɪç] *adj* emphatic
nacheinander [na:xʔaɪ'nandər] *adv* one
after the other
nachempfinden ['na:xʔɛmpfɪndən] (*unreg*)

vt: **jdm etw ~** to feel sth with sb
Nacherzählung ['na:xʔɛrtse:lʊŋ] *f*
reproduction (of a story)
Nachfahr ['na:xfa:r] **(-s, -en)** *m* descendant
Nachfolge ['na:xfɔlgə] *f* succession; **n~n** *vi*
+dat to follow; **~r(in) (-s, -)** *m(f)* successor
nachforschen *vt, vi* to investigate
Nachforschung *f* investigation
Nachfrage ['na:xfra:gə] *f* inquiry; (*COMM*)
demand; **n~n** *vi* to inquire
nach- *zW*: **~füllen** *vt* to refill; **~geben**
(*unreg*) *vi* to give way, to yield; **N~gebühr**
f (*POST*) excess postage
nachgehen ['na:xge:ən] (*unreg*) *vi* (+dat) to
follow; (*erforschen*) to inquire (into); (*Uhr*)
to be slow
Nachgeschmack ['na:xgəʃmak] *m*
aftertaste
nachgiebig ['na:xgi:bɪç] *adj* soft,
accommodating; **N~keit** *f* softness
nachhaltig ['na:xhaltɪç] *adj* lasting;
(*Widerstand*) persistent
nachhause *adv* (*österreichisch, schweizerisch*)
home
nachhelfen ['na:xhɛlfən] (*unreg*) *vi* +dat to
assist, to help
nachher [na:x'he:r] *adv* afterwards
Nachhilfeunterricht ['na:xhɪlfəʊntərrɪçt]
m extra tuition
nachholen ['na:xho:lən] *vt* to catch up
with; (*Versäumtes*) to make up for
Nachkomme ['na:xkɔmə] **(-, -n)** *m*
descendant
nachkommen (*unreg*) *vi* to follow; (*einer
Verpflichtung*) to fulfil; **N~schaft** *f*
descendants *pl*
Nachkriegszeit *f* postwar period
Nach- *zW*: **~lass** ▲ **(-es, -lässe)** *m*
(*COMM*) discount, rebate; (*Erbe*) estate;
n~lassen (*unreg*) *vt* (*Strafe*) to remit;
(*Summe*) to take off; (*Schulden*) to cancel
♦ *vi* to decrease, to ease off; (*Sturm*) to die
down, to ease off; (*schlechter werden*) to
deteriorate; **er hat n~gelassen** he has got
worse; **n~lässig** *adj* negligent, careless
nachlaufen ['na:xlaʊfən] (*unreg*) *vi* +dat to
run after, to chase

nachlösen ['naːxløːzən] *vi (Zuschlag)* to pay on the train, pay at the other end; *(zur Weiterfahrt)* to pay the supplement

nachmachen ['naːxmaxən] *vt* to imitate, to copy; *(fälschen)* to counterfeit

Nachmittag ['naːxmɪtaːk] *m* afternoon; **am ~** in the afternoon; **n~s** *adv* in the afternoon

Nach- *zW:* **~nahme** *f* cash on delivery; **per ~nahme** C.O.D.; **~name** *m* surname; **~porto** *nt* excess postage

nachprüfen ['naːxpryːfən] *vt* to check, to verify

nachrechnen ['naːxrɛçnən] *vt* to check

nachreichen ['naːxraɪçən] *vt (Unterlagen)* to hand in later

Nachricht ['naːxrɪçt] *(-, -en) f* (piece of) news; *(Mitteilung)* message; **~en** *pl* *(Neuigkeiten)* news

Nachrichten- *zW:* **~agentur** *f* news agency; **~dienst** *m (MIL)* intelligence service; **~sprecher(in)** *m(f)* newsreader; **~technik** *f* telecommunications *sg*

Nachruf ['naːxruːf] *m* obituary

nachsagen ['naːxzaːgən] *vt* to repeat; **jdm etw ~** to say sth of sb

Nachsaison ['naːxzɛzõ:] *f* off-season

nachschicken ['naːxʃɪkən] *vt* to forward

nachschlagen ['naːxʃlaːgən] *(unreg) vt* to look up

Nachschlagewerk *nt* reference book

Nachschlüssel *m* duplicate key

Nachschub ['naːxʃuːp] *m* supplies *pl*; *(Truppen)* reinforcements *pl*

nachsehen ['naːxzeːən] *(unreg) vt (prüfen)* to check ♦ *vi (erforschen)* to look and see; **jdm etw ~** to forgive sb sth; **das N~ haben** to come off worst

Nachsendeantrag *m application to have one's mail forwarded*

nachsenden ['naːxzɛndən] *(unreg) vt* to send on, to forward

nachsichtig *adj* indulgent, lenient

nachsitzen ['naːxzɪtsən] *(unreg) vi:* **~ (müssen)** *(SCH)* to be kept in

Nachspeise ['naːxʃpaɪzə] *f* dessert, sweet, pudding

Nachspiel ['naːxʃpiːl] *nt* epilogue; *(fig)* sequel

nachsprechen ['naːxʃprɛçən] *(unreg) vt:* **(jdm) ~** to repeat (after sb)

nächst [nɛːçst] *präp +dat (räumlich)* next to; *(außer)* apart from; **~beste(r, s)** *adj* first that comes along; *(zweitbeste)* next best; **N~e(r)** *f(m)* neighbour; **~e(r, s)** *adj* next; *(~gelegen)* nearest

nachstellen ['naːxʃtɛlən] *vt (TECH: neu einstellen)* to adjust

nächst *zW:* **N~enliebe** *f* love for one's fellow men; **~ens** *adv* shortly, soon; **~liegend** *adj* nearest; *(fig)* obvious; **~möglich** *adj* next possible

Nacht [naxt] *(-, ⁿe) f* night; **~dienst** *m* night shift

Nachteil ['naːxtaɪl] *m* disadvantage; **n~ig** *adj* disadvantageous

Nachthemd *nt (Herrennachthemd)* nightshirt; *(Damennachthemd)* nightdress

Nachtigall ['naxtɪgal] *(-, -en) f* nightingale

Nachtisch ['naːxtɪʃ] *m* = Nachspeise

Nachtklub *m* night club

Nachtleben *nt* nightlife

nächtlich ['nɛçtlɪç] *adj* nightly

Nachtlokal *nt* night club

Nach- *zW:* **~trag** *(-(e)s, -träge) m* supplement; **n~tragen** *(unreg) vt* to carry; *(zufügen)* to add; **jdm etw n~tragen** to hold sth against sb; **n~träglich** *adj* later, subsequent; additional ♦ *adv* later, subsequently; additionally; **n~trauern** *vi:* **jdm/etw n~trauern** to mourn the loss of sb/sth

Nacht- *zW:* **n~s** *adv* at *od* by night; **~schicht** *f* nightshift; **~schwester** *f* night nurse; **~tarif** *m* off-peak tariff; **~tisch** *m* bedside table; **~wächter** *m* night watchman

Nach- *zW:* **~untersuchung** *f* checkup; **n~wachsen** *(unreg) vi* to grow again; **~wahl** *f (POL)* ≈ by-election

Nachweis ['naːxvaɪs] *(-es, -e) m* proof; **n~bar** *adj* provable, demonstrable; **n~en** *(unreg) vt* to prove; **jdm etw n~en** to point sth out to sb; **n~lich** *adj* evident, demonstrable

nach- *zW:* **~wirken** *vi* to have after-effects; **N~wirkung** *f* aftereffect; **N~wort** *nt* epilogue; **N~wuchs** *m* offspring; *(beruflich etc)* new recruits *pl;* **~zahlen** *vt, vi* to pay extra; **N~zahlung** *f* additional payment; *(zurückdatiert)* back pay; **~ziehen** *(unreg) vt (hinter sich herziehen: Bein)* to drag; **N~zügler (-s, -)** *m* straggler

Nacken ['nakən] **(-s, -)** *m* nape of the neck

nackt [nakt] *adj* naked; *(Tatsachen)* plain, bare; **N~badestrand** *m* nudist beach; **N~heit** *f* nakedness

Nadel ['na:dəl] **(-, -n)** *f* needle; *(Stecknadel)* pin; **~öhr** *nt* eye of a needle; **~wald** *m* coniferous forest

Nagel ['na:gəl] **(-s, ⸚)** *m* nail; **~bürste** *f* nailbrush; **~feile** *f* nailfile; **~lack** *m* nail varnish od polish *(BRIT);* **n~n** *vt, vi* to nail; **n~neu** *adj* brand-new; **~schere** *f* nail scissors *pl*

nagen ['na:gən] *vt, vi* to gnaw

Nagetier ['na:gəti:r] *nt* rodent

nah(e) ['na:(ə)] *adj (räumlich)* near(by); *(Verwandte)* near; *(Freunde)* close; *(zeitlich)* near, close ♦ *adv* near(by); near, close; *(verwandt)* closely ♦ *präp (+dat)* near (to), close to; **der Nahe Osten** the Near East; **~ gehen** *(+dat)* to grieve; **~ kommen** *(+dat)* to get close (to); **jdm etw ~ legen** to suggest sth to sb; **~ liegen** to be obvious; **~ liegend** obvious; **~ stehen** *(+dat)* to be close (to); **einer Sache ~ stehen** to sympathize with sth; **~ stehend** close; **jdm (zu) ~ treten** to offend sb

Nahaufnahme *f* close-up

Nähe ['nɛ:ə] **(-)** *f* nearness, proximity; *(Umgebung)* vicinity; **in der ~** close by; at hand; **aus der ~** from close to

nah(e)bei *adv* nearby

nahen *vi, vr* to approach, to draw near

nähen ['nɛ:ən] *vt, vi* to sew

näher *adj, adv* nearer; *(Erklärung, Erkundigung)* more detailed; **(sich) ~ kommen** to get closer; **N~e(s)** *nt* details *pl,* particulars *pl*

Naherholungsgebiet *nt* recreational area

(close to a town)

nähern *vr* to approach

nahezu *adv* nearly

Nähgarn *nt* thread

Nahkampf *m* hand-to-hand fighting

Nähkasten *m* sewing basket, workbox

nahm *etc* [na:m] *vb siehe* **nehmen**

Nähmaschine *f* sewing machine

Nähnadel *f* needle

nähren ['nɛ:rən] *vt* to feed ♦ *vr (Person)* to feed o.s.; *(Tier)* to feed

nahrhaft ['na:rhaft] *adj* nourishing, nutritious

Nahrung ['na:rʊŋ] *f* food; *(fig auch)* sustenance

Nahrungs- *zW:* **~mittel** *nt* foodstuffs *pl;* **~mittelindustrie** *f* food industry; **~suche** *f* search for food

Nährwert *m* nutritional value

Naht [na:t] **(-, ⸚e)** *f* seam; *(MED)* suture; *(TECH)* join; **n~los** *adj* seamless; **n~los ineinander übergehen** to follow without a gap

Nah- *zW:* **~verkehr** *m* local traffic; **~verkehrszug** *m* local train; **~ziel** *nt* immediate objective

Name ['na:mə] **(-ns, -n)** *m* name; **im ~n von** on behalf of; **n~ns** *adv* by the name of; **~nstag** *m* name day, saint's day; **n~ntlich** *adj* by name ♦ *adv* particularly, especially

---

Namenstag

i In Catholic areas of Germany the **Namenstag** is often a more important celebration than a birthday. This is the day dedicated to the saint after whom a person is called, and on that day the person receives presents and invites relatives and friends round to celebrate.

---

namhaft ['na:mhaft] *adj (berühmt)* famed, renowned; *(beträchtlich)* considerable; **~ machen** to name

nämlich ['nɛ:mlɪç] *adv* that is to say, namely; *(denn)* since

nannte *etc* ['nantə] *vb siehe* **nennen**

Napf [napf] **(-(e)s, ⸚e)** *m* bowl, dish

Narbe ['narbə] *f* scar; **narbig** *adj* scarred

Narkose [nar'ko:zə] *f* anaesthetic

Narr [nar] **(-en, -en)** *m* fool; **n~en** *vt* to fool; **Närrin** ['nɛrɪn] *f* fool; **närrisch** *adj* foolish, crazy

Narzisse [nar'tsɪsə] *f* narcissus; daffodil

naschen ['naʃən] *vt, vi* to nibble; *(heimlich kosten)* to pinch a bit

naschhaft *adj* sweet-toothed

Nase ['na:zə] *f* nose

Nasen- *zW:* **~bluten (-s)** *nt* nosebleed; **~loch** *nt* nostril; **~tropfen** *pl* nose drops

naseweis *adj* pert, cheeky; *(neugierig)* nosey

Nashorn ['na:shɔrn] *nt* rhinoceros

nass ▲ [nas] *adj* wet

Nässe ['nɛsə] **(-)** *f* wetness; **n~n** *vt* to wet

nasskalt ▲ *adj* wet and cold

Nassrasur ▲ *f* wet shave

Nation [natsi'o:n] *f* nation

national [natsio'na:l] *adj* national; **N~feiertag** *m* national holiday; **N~hymne** *f* national anthem; **~isieren** [-i'zi:rən] *vt* to nationalize; **N~ismus** [-'ɪsmʊs] *m* nationalism; **~istisch** [-'ɪstɪʃ] *adj* nationalistic; **N~ität** *f* nationality; **N~mannschaft** *f* national team; **N~sozialismus** *m* national socialism

Natron ['na:trɔn] **(-s)** *nt* soda

Natter ['natər] **(-, -n)** *f* adder

Natur [na'tu:r] *f* nature; *(körperlich)* constitution; **~ell (-es, -e)** *nt* disposition; **~erscheinung** *f* natural phenomenon *od* event; **n~farben** *adj* natural coloured; **n~gemäß** *adj* natural; **~gesetz** *nt* law of nature; **n~getreu** *adj* true to life; **~katastrophe** *f* natural disaster

natürlich [na'ty:rlɪç] *adj* natural ♦ *adv* naturally; **ja, ~!** yes, of course; **N~keit** *f* naturalness

Natur- *zW:* **~park** *m* ≈ national park; **~produkt** *nt* natural product; **n~rein** *adj* natural, pure; **~schutz** *m* nature conservation; **unter ~schutz stehen** to be legally protected; **~schutzgebiet** *nt* nature reserve; **~wissenschaft** *f* natural science; **~wissenschaftler(in)** *m(f)* scientist

nautisch ['naʊtɪʃ] *adj* nautical

Nazi ['na:tsi] **(-s, -s)** *m* Nazi

NB *abk* (= *nota bene*) nb

n. Chr. *abk* (= *nach Christus*) A.D.

Nebel ['ne:bəl] **(-s, -)** *m* fog, mist; **n~ig** *adj* foggy, misty; **~scheinwerfer** *m* fog lamp

neben ['ne:bən] *präp* (+*akk od dat*) next to; (+*dat: außer*) apart from, besides; **~an** [ne:-bən'an] *adv* next door; **N~anschluss** ▲ *m* (*TEL*) extension; **N~ausgang** *m* side exit; **~bei** [ne:bən'baɪ] *adv* at the same time; *(außerdem)* additionally; *(beiläufig)* incidentally; **N~beruf** *m* second job; **N~beschäftigung** *f* second job; **N~buhler(in)** **(-s, -)** *m(f)* rival; **~einander** [ne:bən|aɪ'nandər] *adv* side by side; **~einander legen** to put next to each other; **N~eingang** *m* side entrance; **N~fach** *nt* subsidiary subject; **N~fluss** ▲ *m* tributary; **N~gebäude** *nt* annexe; **N~geräusch** *nt* (*RADIO*) atmospherics *pl*, interference; **~her** [ne:bən'he:r] *adv* *(zusätzlich)* besides; *(gleichzeitig)* at the same time; *(daneben)* alongside; **N~kosten** *pl* extra charges, extras; **N~produkt** *nt* by-product; **N~sache** *f* trifle, side issue; **~sächlich** *adj* minor, peripheral; **N~saison** *f* low season; **N~straße** *f* side street; **N~verdienst** *m* secondary income; **N~wirkung** *f* side effect; **N~zimmer** *nt* adjoining room

neblig ['ne:blɪç] *adj* foggy, misty

Necessaire [nese'sɛ:r] **(-s, -s)** *nt* (*Nähnecessaire*) needlework box; (*Nagelnecessaire*) manicure case

necken ['nɛkən] *vt* to tease

Neckerei [nɛkə'raɪ] *f* teasing

Neffe ['nɛfə] **(-n, -n)** *m* nephew

negativ ['ne:gati:f] *adj* negative; **N~ (-s, -e)** *nt* (*PHOT*) negative

Neger ['ne:gər] **(-s, -)** *m* negro; **~in** *f* negress

nehmen ['ne:mən] (*unreg*) *vt* to take; **jdn zu sich ~** to take sb in; **sich ernst ~** to take o.s. seriously; **nimm dir doch bitte** please help yourself

Neid [naɪt] (-(e)s) *m* envy; **~er** (-s, -) *m* envier; **n~isch** ['naɪdɪʃ] *adj* envious, jealous

neigen ['naɪgən] *vt* to incline, to lean; (*Kopf*) to bow ♦ *vi*: **zu etw ~** to tend to sth

Neigung *f* (*des Geländes*) slope; (*Tendenz*) tendency, inclination; (*Vorliebe*) liking; (*Zuneigung*) affection

nein [naɪn] *adv* no

Nektarine [nɛkta'riːnə] *f* (*Frucht*) nectarine

Nelke ['nɛlkə] *f* carnation, pink; (*Gewürz*) clove

Nenn- ['nɛn] *zW*: **n~en** (*unreg*) *vt* to name; (*mit Namen*) to call; **wie n~t man ...?** what do you call ...?; **n~enswert** *adj* worth mentioning; **~er** (-s, -) *m* denominator; **~wert** *m* nominal value; (*COMM*) par

Neon ['neːɔn] (-s) *nt* neon; **~licht** *nt* neon light; **~röhre** *f* neon tube

Nerv [nɛrf] (-s, -en) *m* nerve; **jdm auf die ~en gehen** to get on sb's nerves; **n~enaufreibend** *adj* nerve-racking; **~enbündel** *nt* bundle of nerves; **~enheilanstalt** *f* mental home; **n~enkrank** *adj* mentally ill; **~ensäge** (*umg*) *f* pain (in the neck) (*umg*); **~ensystem** *nt* nervous system; **~enzusammenbruch** *m* nervous breakdown; **~lich** *adj* (*Belastung*) affecting the nerves; **n~ös** [nɛr'vøːs] *adj* nervous; **~osität** *f* nervousness; **n~tötend** *adj* nerve-racking; (*Arbeit*) soul-destroying

Nerz [nɛrts] (-es, -e) *m* mink

Nessel ['nɛsəl] (-, -n) *f* nettle

Nessessär ▲ [nese'sɛːr] (-s, -s) *nt* = **Necessaire**

Nest [nɛst] (-(e)s, -er) *nt* nest; (*umg: Ort*) dump

nett [nɛt] *adj* nice; (*freundlich*) nice, kind; **~erweise** *adv* kindly

netto ['nɛto:] *adv* net

Netz [nɛts] (-es, -e) *nt* net; (*Gepäcknetz*) rack; (*Einkaufsnetz*) string bag; (*Spinnennetz*) web; (*System*) network; **jdm ins ~ gehen** (*fig*) to fall into sb's trap; **~anschluss** ▲ *m* mains connection

Netzhaut *f* retina

neu [nɔy] *adj* new; (*Sprache, Geschichte*) modern; **seit ~estem** (since) recently; **die ~esten Nachrichten** the latest news; **schreiben** to rewrite, to write again; **N~anschaffung** *f* new purchase *od* acquisition; **~artig** *adj* new kind of; **N~bau** *m* new building; **N~e(r)** *f(m)* the new man/woman; **~erdings** *adv* (*kürzlich*) (since) recently; (*von ~em*) again; **N~erscheinung** *f* (*Buch*) new publication; (*Schallplatte*) new release; **N~erung** *f* innovation, new departure; **N~gier** *f* curiosity; **~gierig** *adj* curious; **N~heit** *f* newness; novelty; **N~igkeit** *f* news *sg*; **N~jahr** *nt* New Year; **~lich** *adv* recently, the other day; **N~ling** *m* novice; **N~mond** *m* new moon

neun [nɔyn] *num* nine; **~zehn** *num* nineteen; **~zig** *num* ninety

neureich *adj* nouveau riche; **N~e(r)** *f(m)* nouveau riche

neurotisch *adj* neurotic

Neuseeland [nɔy'zeːlant] *nt* New Zealand; **Neuseeländer(in)** [nɔy'zeːlɛndər(ɪn)] *m(f)* New Zealander

neutral [nɔy'traːl] *adj* neutral; **~i'sieren** *vt* to neutralize

Neutrum ['nɔytrʊm] (-s, -a *od* -en) *nt* neuter

Neu- *zW*: **~wert** *m* purchase price; **n~wertig** *adj* (as) new, not used; **~zeit** *f* modern age; **n~zeitlich** *adj* modern, recent

---

SCHLÜSSELWORT

nicht [nɪçt] *adv* **1** (*Verneinung*) not; **er ist es nicht** it's not him, it isn't him; **er raucht nicht** (*gerade*) he isn't smoking; (*gewöhnlich*) he doesn't smoke; **ich kann das nicht - ich auch nicht** I can't do it - neither *od* nor can I; **es regnet nicht mehr** it's not raining any more; **nicht rostend** stainless

2 (*Bitte, Verbot*): **nicht!** don't!, no!; **nicht berühren!** do not touch!; **nicht doch!** don't!

3 (*rhetorisch*): **du bist müde, nicht (wahr)?** you're tired, aren't you?; **das ist schön,**

nicht (wahr)? it's nice, isn't it?
4: was du nicht sagst! the things you say!

Nichtangriffspakt [nɪçt'|angrɪfspakt] *m*
non-aggression pact
Nichte ['nɪçtə] *f* niece
nichtig ['nɪçtɪç] *adj* (*ungültig*) null, void;
(*wertlos*) futile
Nichtraucher(in) *m(f)* non-smoker
nichts [nɪçts] *pron* nothing; **für ~ und
wieder ~** for nothing at all; **~ sagend**
meaningless; **N~ (-)** *nt* nothingness; (*pej*:
Person) nonentity
Nichtschwimmer *m* non-swimmer
nichts- *zW*: **~desto'weniger** *adv*
nevertheless; **N~nutz (-es, -e)** *m* good-
for-nothing; **~nutzig** *adj* worthless, useless;
N~tun (-s) *nt* idleness
Nichtzutreffende(s) *nt*: **~s** *od* **nicht
Zutreffendes (bitte) streichen!** (please)
delete where appropriate
Nickel ['nɪkəl] **(-s)** *nt* nickel
nicken ['nɪkən] *vi* to nod
Nickerchen ['nɪkərçən] *nt* nap
nie [niː] *adv* never; **~ wieder** *od* **mehr** never
again; **~ und nimmer** never ever
nieder ['niːdər] *adj* low; (*gering*) inferior
♦ *adv* down; **N~gang** *m* decline;
~gedrückt *adj* (*deprimiert*) dejected,
depressed; **~gehen** (*unreg*) *vi* to descend;
(*AVIAT*) to come down; (*Regen*) to fall;
(*Boxer*) to go down; **~geschlagen** *adj*
depressed, dejected; **N~lage** *f* defeat;
N~lande *pl* Netherlands; **N~länder(in)**
m(f) Dutchman(-woman); **~ländisch** *adj*
Dutch; **~lassen** (*unreg*) *vr* (*sich setzen*) to
sit down; (*an Ort*) to settle (down); (*Arzt,
Rechtsanwalt*) to set up a practice;
N~lassung *f* settlement; (*COMM*) branch;
~legen *vt* to lay down; (*Arbeit*) to stop;
(*Amt*) to resign; **N~sachsen** *nt* Lower
Saxony; **N~schlag** *m* (*MET*) precipitation;
rainfall; **~schlagen** (*unreg*) *vt* (*Gegner*) to
beat down; (*Gegenstand*) to knock down;
(*Augen*) to lower; (*Aufstand*) to put down
♦ *vr* (*CHEM*) to precipitate; **~trächtig** *adj*
base, mean; **N~trächtigkeit** *f* meanness,

baseness; outrage; **N~ung** *f* (*GEOG*)
depression; (*Mündungsgebiet*) flats *pl*
niedlich ['niːtlɪç] *adj* sweet, cute
niedrig ['niːdrɪç] *adj* low; (*Stand*) lowly,
humble; (*Gesinnung*) mean
niemals ['niːmaːls] *adv* never
niemand ['niːmant] *pron* nobody, no-one
Niemandsland ['niːmantslant] *nt* no-
man's-land
Niere ['niːrə] *f* kidney
nieseln ['niːzəln] *vi* to drizzle
niesen ['niːzən] *vi* to sneeze
Niete ['niːtə] *f* (*TECH*) rivet; (*Los*) blank;
(*Reinfall*) flop; (*Mensch*) failure; **n~n** *vt* to
rivet

St. Nikolaus

i On December 6th, **St. Nikolaus** visits
German children to reward those who
have been good by filling shoes they have
left out with sweets and small presents.

Nikotin [niko'tiːn] **(-s)** *nt* nicotine
Nilpferd [niːl-] *nt* hippopotamus
Nimmersatt ['nɪmərzat] **(-(e)s, -e)** *m*
glutton
nimmst *etc* [nɪmst] *vb siehe* **nehmen**
nippen ['nɪpən] *vt, vi* to sip
nirgend- ['nɪrgənt] *zW*: **~s** *adv* nowhere;
~wo *adv* nowhere; **~wohin** *adv* nowhere
Nische ['niːʃə] *f* niche
nisten ['nɪstən] *vi* to nest
Niveau [ni'voː] **(-s, -s)** *nt* level
Nixe ['nɪksə] *f* water nymph
nobel ['noːbəl] *adj* (*großzügig*) generous;
(*elegant*) posh (*inf*)

SCHLÜSSELWORT

noch [nɔx] *adv* **1** (*weiterhin*) still; **noch nicht**
not yet; **noch nie** never (yet); **noch immer**
od **immer noch** still; **bleiben Sie doch
noch** stay a bit longer
2 (*in Zukunft*) still, yet; **das kann noch
passieren** that might still happen; **er wird
noch kommen** he'll come (yet)
3 (*nicht später als*): **noch vor einer Woche**
only a week ago; **noch am selben Tag** the

---

very same day; **noch im 19. Jahrhundert** as late as the 19th century; **noch heute** today

4 (zusätzlich): **wer war noch da?** who else was there?; **noch einmal** once more, again; **noch dreimal** three more times; **noch einer** another one

5 (bei Vergleichen): **noch größer** even bigger; **das ist noch besser** that's better still; **und wenn es noch so schwer ist** however hard it is

6: **Geld noch und noch** heaps (and heaps) of money; **sie hat noch und noch versucht, ...** she tried again and again to ...

♦ konj: **weder A noch B** neither A nor B

noch- zW: **~mal** ['nɔxmaːl] adv again, once more; **~malig** ['nɔxmaːlɪç] adj repeated; **~mals** adv again, once more

Nominativ ['noːminatiːf] (-s, -e) m nominative

nominell [nomiˈnɛl] adj nominal

Nonne ['nɔnə] f nun

Nord(en) ['nɔrd(ən)] (-s) m north

Nord'irland nt Northern Ireland

nordisch adj northern

nördlich ['nœrtlɪç] adj northerly, northern ♦ präp +gen (to the) north of; **~ von** (to the) north of

Nord- zW: **~pol** m North Pole; **~rhein-Westfalen** nt North Rhine-Westphalia; **~see** f North Sea; **n~wärts** adv northwards

nörgeln ['nœrgəln] vi to grumble; **Nörgler** (-s, -) m grumbler

Norm [nɔrm] (-, -en) f norm; (Größenvorschrift) standard; **n~al** [nɔrˈmaːl] adj normal; **~al(benzin)** nt ≈ 2-star petrol (BRIT), regular petrol (US); **n~alerweise** adv normally; **n~ali'sieren** vt to normalize ♦ vr to return to normal

normen vt to standardize

Norwegen ['nɔrveːgən] nt Norway; **norwegisch** adj Norwegian

Nostalgie [nɔstalˈgiː] f nostalgia

Not [noːt] (-, ⁎e) f need; (Mangel) want;

(Mühe) trouble; (Zwang) necessity; **~ leidend** needy; **zur ~** if necessary; (gerade noch) just about

Notar [noˈtaːr] (-s, -e) m notary; **n~i'ell** adj notarial

Not- zW: **~arzt** m emergency doctor; **~ausgang** m emergency exit; **~behelf** (-s, -e) m makeshift; **~bremse** f emergency brake; **~dienst** m (Bereitschaftsdienst) emergency service; **n~dürftig** adj scanty; (behelfsmäßig) makeshift

Note ['noːtə] f note; (SCH) mark (BRIT), grade (US)

Noten- zW: **~blatt** nt sheet of music; **~schlüssel** m clef; **~ständer** m music stand

Not- zW: **~fall** m (case of) emergency; **n~falls** adv if need be; **n~gedrungen** adj necessary, unavoidable; **etw n~gedrungen machen** to be forced to do sth

notieren [noˈtiːrən] vt to note; (COMM) to quote

Notierung f (COMM) quotation

nötig ['nøːtɪç] adj necessary; **etw ~ haben** to need sth; **~en** [-gən] vt to compel, to force; **~enfalls** adv if necessary

Notiz [noˈtiːts] (-, -en) f note; (Zeitungsnotiz) item; **~ nehmen** to take notice; **~block** m notepad; **~buch** nt notebook

Not- zW: **~lage** f crisis, emergency; **n~landen** vi to make a forced od emergency landing; **n~leidend** △ adj siehe **Not**; **~lösung** f temporary solution; **~lüge** f white lie

notorisch [noˈtoːrɪʃ] adj notorious

Not- zW: **~ruf** m emergency call; **~rufsäule** f emergency telephone; **~stand** m state of emergency; **~unterkunft** f emergency accommodation; **~verband** m emergency dressing; **~wehr** (-) f self-defence; **n~wendig** adj necessary; **~wendigkeit** f necessity

Novelle [noˈvɛlə] f short novel; (JUR) amendment

November [noˈvɛmbər] (-s, -) m November

Nu [nuː] m: **im ~** in an instant

Nuance [ny'ã:sə] *f* nuance
nüchtern ['nʏçtərn] *adj* sober; (*Magen*) empty; (*Urteil*) prudent; **N~heit** *f* sobriety
Nudel ['nu:dəl] (-, -n) *f* noodle; **~n** *pl* (*Teigwaren*) pasta *sg*; (*in Suppe*) noodles
Null [nʊl] (-, -en) *f* nought, zero; (*pej: Mensch*) washout; **n~** *num* zero; (*Fehler*) no; **n~ Uhr** midnight; **n~ und nichtig** null and void; **~punkt** *m* zero; **auf dem ~punkt** at zero
numerisch [nu'me:rɪʃ] *adj* numerical
Nummer ['nʊmər] (-, -n) *f* number; (*Größe*) size; **n~ieren** ▲ *vt* to number; **~nschild** *nt* (*AUT*) number *od* license (*US*) plate
nun [nu:n] *adv* now ♦ *excl* well; **das ist ~ mal so** that's the way it is
nur [nu:r] *adv* just, only; **wo bleibt er ~?** (just) where is he?
Nürnberg ['nʏrnbɛrk] (-s) *nt* Nuremberg
Nuss ▲ [nʊs] (-, ᵉe) *f* nut; **~baum** *m* walnut tree; **~knacker** (-s, -) *m* nutcracker
nutz [nʊts] *adj:* **zu nichts ~ sein** to be no use for anything; **~bringend** *adj* (*Verwendung*) profitable
nütze ['nʏtsə] *adj* = nutz
Nutzen (-s) *m* usefulness; (*Gewinn*) profit; **von ~ sein** to be of use ♦ *vt:* **etw zu etw n~** to use sth for sth ♦ **was nutzt es?** what's the use?, what use is it?
nützen *vi, vt* = nutzen
nützlich ['nʏtslɪç] *adj* useful; **N~keit** *f* usefulness
Nutz- *zW:* **n~los** *adj* useless; **~losigkeit** *f* uselessness; **~nießer** (-s, -) *m* beneficiary
Nylon ['naɪlɔn] (-(s)) *nt* nylon

O, o

Oase [o'a:zə] *f* oasis
ob [ɔp] *konj* if, whether; **~ das wohl wahr ist?** can that be true?; **und ~!** you bet!
obdachlos *adj* homeless
Obdachlose(r) *f(m)* homeless person; **~nasyl** *nt* shelter for the homeless
Obduktion [ɔpdʊktsi'o:n] *f* post-mortem
obduzieren [ɔpdu'tsi:rən] *vt* to do a post-

mortem on
O-Beine ['o:baɪnə] *pl* bow *od* bandy legs
oben ['o:bən] *adv* above; (*in Haus*) upstairs; **~ erwähnt, ~ gennant** above-mentioned; **nach ~** up; **von ~** down; **~ ohne** topless; **jdn von ~ bis unten ansehen** to look sb up and down; **~an** *adv* at the top; **~auf** *adv* up above, on the top ♦ *adj* (*munter*) in form; **~drein** *adv* into the bargain
Ober ['o:bər] (-s, -) *m* waiter; **die ~en** *pl* (*umg*) the bosses; (*ECCL*) the superiors; **~arm** *m* upper arm; **~arzt** *m* senior physician; **~aufsicht** *f* supervision; **~bayern** *nt* Upper Bavaria; **~befehl** *m* supreme command; **~befehlshaber** *m* commander-in-chief; **~bekleidung** *f* outer clothing; **~'bürgermeister** *m* lord mayor; **~deck** *nt* upper *od* top deck; **o~e(r, s)** *adj* upper; **~fläche** *f* surface; **o~flächlich** *adj* superficial; **~geschoss** ▲ *nt* upper storey; **o~halb** *adv* above ♦ *präp +gen* above; **~haupt** *nt* head, chief; **~haus** *nt* (*POL*) upper house, House of Lords (*BRIT*); **~hemd** *nt* shirt; **~herrschaft** *f* supremacy, sovereignty; **~in** *f* matron; (*ECCL*) Mother Superior; **~kellner** *m* head waiter; **~kiefer** *m* upper jaw; **~körper** *m* upper part of body; **~leitung** *f* direction; (*ELEK*) overhead cable; **~licht** *nt* skylight; **~lippe** *f* upper lip; **~schenkel** *m* thigh; **~schicht** *f* upper classes *pl*; **~schule** *f* grammar school (*BRIT*), high school (*US*); **~schwester** *f* (*MED*) matron
Oberst ['o:bərst] (-en *od* -s, -en *od* -e) *m* colonel; **o~e(r, s)** *adj* very top, top-most
Ober- *zW:* **~stufe** *f* upper school; **~teil** *nt* upper part; **~weite** *f* bust/chest measurement
obgleich [ɔp'glaɪç] *konj* although
Obhut ['ɔphu:t] (-) *f* care, protection; **in jds ~ sein** to be in sb's care
obig ['o:bɪç] *adj* above
Objekt [ɔp'jɛkt] (-(e)s, -e) *nt* object; **~iv** [-'ti:f] (-s, -e) *nt* lens; **o~iv** *adj* objective; **~ivi'tät** *f* objectivity
Oblate [o'bla:tə] *f* (*Gebäck*) wafer; (*ECCL*) host

obligatorisch [obliga'to:rɪʃ] *adj* compulsory, obligatory

Obrigkeit ['o:brɪçkaɪt] *f* (*Behörden*) authorities *pl*, administration; (*Regierung*) government

obschon [ɔp'ʃoːn] *konj* although

Observatorium [ɔpzɛrva'to:riʊm] *nt* observatory

obskur [ɔps'ku:r] *adj* obscure; (*verdächtig*) dubious

Obst [o:pst] (**-(e)s**) *nt* fruit; **~baum** *m* fruit tree; **~garten** *m* orchard; **~händler** *m* fruiterer, fruit merchant; **~kuchen** *m* fruit tart

obszön [ɔps'tsø:n] *adj* obscene; **O~i'tät** *f* obscenity

obwohl [ɔp'vo:l] *konj* although

Ochse ['ɔksə] (**-n, -n**) *m* ox; **o~n** (*umg*) *vt, vi* to cram, to swot (BRIT)

Ochsenschwanzsuppe *f* oxtail soup

Ochsenzunge *f* oxtongue

öd(e) ['ø:d(ə)] *adj* (*Land*) waste, barren; (*fig*) dull; **Ö~** *f* desert, waste(land); (*fig*) tedium

oder ['o:dər] *konj* or; **das stimmt, ~?** that's right, isn't it?

Ofen ['o:fən] (**-s, ⁻**) *m* oven; (*Heizofen*) fire, heater; (*Kohlenofen*) stove; (*Hochofen*) furnace; (*Herd*) cooker, stove; **~rohr** *nt* stovepipe

offen ['ɔfən] *adj* open; (*aufrichtig*) frank; (*Stelle*) vacant; **~ bleiben** (*Fenster*) to stay open; (*Frage, Entscheidung*) to remain open; **~ halten** to keep open; **~ lassen** to leave open; **~ stehen** to be open; (*Rechnung*) to be unpaid; **es steht Ihnen ~, es zu tun** you are at liberty to do it; **~ gesagt** to be honest; **~bar** *adj* obvious; **~baren** [ɔfən'ba:rən] *vt* to reveal, to manifest; **O~'barung** *f* (REL) revelation; **O~heit** *f* candour, frankness; **~herzig** *adj* candid, frank; (*Kleid*) revealing; **~kundig** *adj* well-known; (*klar*) evident; **~sichtlich** *adj* evident, obvious

offensiv [ɔfɛn'zi:f] *adj* offensive; **O~e** [-'zi:və] *f* offensive

öffentlich ['œfəntlɪç] *adj* public; **Ö~keit** *f* (*Leute*) public; (*einer Versammlung etc*) public nature; **in aller Ö~keit** in public; **an die Ö~keit dringen** to reach the public ear

offiziell [ɔfitsi'ɛl] *adj* official

Offizier [ɔfi'tsi:r] (**-s, -e**) *m* officer; **~skasino** *nt* officers' mess

öffnen ['œfnən] *vt, vr* to open; **jdm die Tür ~** to open the door for sb

Öffner ['œfnər] (**-s, -**) *m* opener

Öffnung ['œfnʊŋ] *f* opening; **~szeiten** *pl* opening times

oft [ɔft] *adv* often

öfter ['œftər] *adv* more often *od* frequently; **~s** *adv* often, frequently

oh [o:] *excl* oh; **~ je!** oh dear

OHG *abk* (= *Offene Handelsgesellschaft*) general partnership

ohne ['o:nə] *präp +akk* without ♦ *konj* without; **das ist nicht ~** (*umg*) it's not bad; **~ weiteres** without a second thought; (*sofort*) immediately; **~ zu fragen** without asking; **~ dass er es wusste** without him knowing it; **~dies** [o:nə'di:s] *adv* anyway; **~gleichen** [o:nə'glaɪçən] *adj* unsurpassed, without equal; **~hin** [o:nə'hɪn] *adv* anyway, in any case

Ohnmacht ['o:nmaxt] *f* faint; (*fig*) impotence; **in ~ fallen** to faint

ohnmächtig ['o:nmɛçtɪç] *adj* in a faint, unconscious; (*fig*) weak, impotent; **sie ist ~** she has fainted

Ohr [o:r] (**-(e)s, -en**) *nt* ear

Öhr [ø:r] (**-(e)s, -e**) *nt* eye

Ohren- *zW*: **~arzt** *m* ear specialist; **o~betäubend** *adj* deafening; **~schmalz** *nt* earwax; **~schmerzen** *pl* earache *sg*

Ohr- *zW*: **~feige** *f* slap on the face; box on the ears; **o~feigen** *vt*: **jdn o~feigen** to slap sb's face; to box sb's ears; **~läppchen** *nt* ear lobe; **~ring** *m* earring; **~wurm** *m* earwig; (MUS) catchy tune

Öko- [øko] *zW*: **~laden** *m* wholefood shop; **ö~logisch** [-'lo:gɪʃ] *adj* ecological; **ö~nomisch** [-'no:mɪʃ] *adj* economical

Oktober [ɔk'to:bər] (**-s, -**) *m* October; **~fest** *nt* Munich beer festival

---

Spelling Reform: ▲ *new spelling* △ *old spelling (to be phased out)*

Oktoberfest

ⓘ *The annual beer festival, the* **Oktoberfest***, takes place in Munich at the end of September in a huge area where beer tents and various amusements are set up. People sit at long wooden tables, drink beer from enormous beer mugs, eat pretzels and listen to brass bands. It is a great attraction for tourists and locals alike.*

ökumenisch [øku'me:nɪʃ] *adj* ecumenical

Öl [ø:l] *(-(e)s, -e) nt* oil; **~baum** *m* olive tree; **ö~en** *vt* to oil; (*TECH*) to lubricate; **~farbe** *f* oil paint; **~feld** *nt* oilfield; **~film** *m* film of oil; **~heizung** *f* oil-fired central heating; **ö~ig** *adj* oily; **~industrie** *f* oil industry

oliv [o'li:f] *adj* olive-green; **O~e** *f* olive

Öl- *zW:* **~messstab** ▲ *m* dipstick; **~sardine** *f* sardine; **~stand** *m* oil level; **~standanzeiger** *m* (*AUT*) oil gauge; **~tanker** *m* oil tanker; **~ung** *f* lubrication; oiling; (*ECCL*) anointment; **die Letzte ~ung** Extreme Unction; **~wechsel** *m* oil change

Olymp- [o'lʏmp] *zW:* **~iade** [olʏmpi'a:də] *f* Olympic Games *pl*; **~iasieger(in)** [-iazi:gər(ɪn)] *m(f)* Olympic champion; **~iateilnehmer(in)** *m(f)* Olympic competitor; **o~isch** *adj* Olympic

Ölzeug *nt* oilskins *pl*

Oma ['o:ma] *(-, -s) (umg) f* granny

Omelett [ɔm(ə)'let] *(-(e)s, -s) nt* omelet(te)

ominös [omi'nø:s] *adj* (*unheilvoll*) ominous

Onanie [ona'ni:] *f* masturbation; **o~ren** *vi* to masturbate

Onkel ['ɔŋkəl] *(-s, -) m* uncle

Opa ['o:pa] *(-s, -s) (umg) m* grandpa

Oper ['o:pər] *(-, -n) f* opera; opera house

Operation [operatsi'o:n] *f* operation; **~ssaal** *m* operating theatre

Operette [ope'retə] *f* operetta

operieren [ope'ri:rən] *vt* to operate on ♦ *vi* to operate

Opern- *zW:* **~glas** *nt* opera glasses *pl*; **~haus** *nt* opera house

Opfer ['ɔpfər] *(-s, -) nt* sacrifice; (*Mensch*) victim; **o~n** *vt* to sacrifice; **~ung** *f* sacrifice

opponieren [ɔpo'ni:rən] *vi:* **gegen jdn/etw ~** to oppose sb/sth

Opportunist [ɔpɔrtu'nɪst] *m* opportunist

Opposition [ɔpozitsi'o:n] *f* opposition; **o~ell** *adj* opposing

Optik ['ɔptɪk] *f* optics *sg;* **~er** *(-s, -) m* optician

optimal [ɔpti'ma:l] *adj* optimal, optimum

Optimismus [ɔpti'mɪsmʊs] *m* optimism

Optimist [ɔpti'mɪst] *m* optimist; **o~isch** *adj* optimistic

optisch ['ɔptɪʃ] *adj* optical

Orakel [o'ra:kəl] *(-s, -) nt* oracle

oral [o'ra:l] *adj* (*MED*) oral

Orange [o'rã:ʒə] *f* orange; **o~** *adj* orange; **~ade** [orã'ʒa:də] *f* orangeade; **~at** [orã'ʒa:t] *(-s, -e) nt* candied peel

Orchester [ɔr'kɛstər] *(-s, -) nt* orchestra

Orchidee [ɔrçi'de:ə] *f* orchid

Orden ['ɔrdən] *(-s, -) m* (*ECCL*) order; (*MIL*) decoration; **~sschwester** *f* nun

ordentlich ['ɔrdəntlɪç] *adj* (*anständig*) decent, respectable; (*geordnet*) tidy, neat; (*umg: annehmbar*) not bad; (: *tüchtig*) real, proper ♦ *adv* properly; **~er Professor** (full) professor; **O~keit** *f* respectability; tidiness, neatness

ordinär [ɔrdi'nɛ:r] *adj* common, vulgar

ordnen ['ɔrdnən] *vt* to order, to put in order

Ordner *(-s, -) m* steward; (*COMM*) file

Ordnung *f* order; (*Ordnen*) ordering; (*Geordnetsein*) tidiness; **~ machen** to tidy up; **in ~!** okay!

Ordnungs- *zW:* **o~gemäß** *adj* proper, according to the rules; **o~liebend** *adj* orderly, methodical; **~strafe** *f* fine; **o~widrig** *adj* contrary to the rules, irregular; **~widrigkeit** [-vɪdrɪçkaɪt] *f* infringement (*of law or rule*); **~zahl** *f* ordinal number

Organ [ɔr'ga:n] *(-s, -e) nt* organ; (*Stimme*) voice; **~isation** [-izatsi'o:n] *f* organization; **~isator** [i'za:tɔr] *m* organizer; **o~isch** *adj* organic; **o~isieren** [-i'zi:rən] *vt* to organize, to arrange; (*umg: beschaffen*) to acquire ♦ *vr* to organize; **~ismus** [-'nɪsmʊs] *m*

organism; **~ist** [-'nɪst] *m* organist;
~spende *f* organ donation;
~spenderausweis *m* donor card
Orgasmus [ɔr'gasmus] *m* orgasm
Orgel ['ɔrgəl] (-, -n) *f* organ
Orgie ['ɔrgiə] *f* orgy
Orient ['oːriɛnt] (-s) *m* Orient, east;
o~alisch [-'taːlɪʃ] *adj* oriental
orientier- *zW:* **~en** [-'tiːrən] *vt* (*örtlich*) to
locate; (*fig*) to inform ♦ *vr* to find one's way
od bearings; to inform o.s.; **O~ung** [-'tiːruŋ]
f orientation; (*fig*) information;
O~ungssinn *m* sense of direction;
O~ungsstufe *f* period during which pupils
are selected for different schools

> ┌─────────────────────────┐
> │ **Orientierungsstufe** │
> └─────────────────────────┘
>
> ⓘ The **Orientierungsstufe** is the name
> given to the first two years spent in a
> **Realschule** or **Gymnasium**, during which
> a child is assessed as to his or her
> suitability for that type of school. At the
> end of two years it may be decided to
> transfer the child to a school more suited to
> his or her ability.

original [origi'naːl] *adj* original; **O~** (-s, -e)
nt original; **O~fassung** *f* original version;
O~i'tät *f* originality
originell [origi'nɛl] *adj* original
Orkan [ɔr'kaːn] (-(e)s, -e) *m* hurricane;
o~artig *adj* (*Wind*) gale-force; (*Beifall*)
thunderous
Ornament [ɔrna'mɛnt] *nt* decoration,
ornament; **o~al** [-'taːl] *adj* decorative,
ornamental
Ort [ɔrt] (-(e)s, -e *od* ⁺er) *m* place; **an ~ und
Stelle** on the spot; **o~en** *vt* to locate
ortho- [ɔrto] *zW:* **~dox** [-'dɔks] *adj* orthodox;
O~grafie ▲ [-gra'fiː] *f* spelling,
orthography; **~'grafisch** ▲ *adj*
orthographic; **O~päde** [-'pɛːdə] (-n, -n) *m*
orthopaedist; **O~pädie** [-pɛ'diː] *f*
orthopaedics *sg;* **~'pädisch** *adj*
orthopaedic
örtlich ['œrtlɪç] *adj* local; **Ö~keit** *f* locality
ortsansässig *adj* local

Ortschaft *f* village, small town
Orts- *zW:* **o~fremd** *adj* non-local;
~gespräch *nt* local (phone)call; **~name**
m place name; **~netz** *nt* (*TEL*) local
telephone exchange area; **~tarif** *m* (*TEL*)
tariff for local calls; **~zeit** *f* local time
Ortung *f* locating
Öse ['øːzə] *f* loop, eye
Ost'asien [ɔs'taːziən] *nt* Eastern Asia
Osten ['ɔstən] (-s) *m* east
Oster- ['oːstar] *zW:* **~ei** *nt* Easter egg; **~fest**
nt Easter; **~glocke** *f* daffodil; **~hase** *m*
Easter bunny; **~montag** *m* Easter Monday;
~n (-s, -) *nt* Easter
Österreich ['øːstəraɪç] (-s) *nt* Austria;
~er(in) (-s, -) *m(f)* Austrian; **ö~isch** *adj*
Austrian
Ostküste *f* east coast
östlich ['œstlɪç] *adj* eastern, easterly
Ostsee *f:* **die ~** the Baltic (Sea)
Ouvertüre [uver'tyːrə] *f* overture
oval [o'vaːl] *adj* oval
Ovation [ovatsi'oːn] *f* ovation
Oxid, Oxyd [ɔ'ksyːt] (-(e)s, -e) *nt* oxide;
o~ieren *vt, vi* to oxidize; **~ierung** *f*
oxidization
Ozean ['oːtseaːn] (-s, -e) *m* ocean;
~dampfer *m* (ocean-going) liner
Ozon [o'tsoːn] (-s) *nt* ozone; **~loch** *nt* ozone
hole; **~schicht** *f* ozone layer

P, p

Paar [paːr] (-(e)s, -e) *nt* pair; (*Ehepaar*)
couple; **ein p~ a** few; **ein p~ Mal** a few
times; **p~en** *vt, vr* to couple; (*Tiere*) to
mate; **~lauf** *m* pair skating; **~ung** *f*
combination; mating; **p~weise** *adv* in
pairs; in couples
Pacht [paxt] (-, -en) *f* lease; **p~en** *vt* to
lease
Pächter ['pɛçtər] (-s, -) *m* leaseholder,
tenant
Pack¹ [pak] (-(e)s, -e *od* ⁺e) *m* bundle,
pack
Pack² [pak] (-(e)s, -e) *nt* (*pej*) mob, rabble

Päckchen ['pɛkçən] *nt* small package; (*Zigaretten*) packet; (*Postpäckchen*) small parcel

Pack- *zW:* **p~en** *vt* to pack; (*fassen*) to grasp, to seize; (*umg: schaffen*) to manage; (*fig: fesseln*) to grip; **~en** (-s, -) *m* bundle; (*fig: Menge*) heaps of; **~esel** *m* (*auch fig*) packhorse; **~papier** *nt* brown paper, wrapping paper; **~ung** *f* packet; (*Pralinenpackung*) box; (*MED*) compress; **~ungsbeilage** *f* enclosed instructions *pl* for use

Pädagog- [pɛda'goːg] *zW:* **~e** (-n, -n) *m* teacher; **~ik** *f* education; **p~isch** *adj* educational, pedagogical

Paddel ['padəl] (-s, -) *nt* paddle; **~boot** *nt* canoe; **p~n** *vi* to paddle

Page ['paːʒə] (-n, -n) *m* page

Paket [pa'keːt] (-(e)s, -e) *nt* packet; (*Postpaket*) parcel; **~karte** *f* dispatch note; **~post** *f* parcel post; **~schalter** *m* parcels counter

Pakt [pakt] (-(e)s, -e) *m* pact

Palast [pa'last] (-es, **Paläste**) *m* palace

Palästina [palɛ'stiːna] (-s) *nt* Palestine

Palme ['palmə] *f* palm (tree)

Pampelmuse ['pampəlmuːzə] *f* grapefruit

panieren [pa'niːrən] *vt* (*KOCH*) to bread

Paniermehl [pa'niːrmeːl] *nt* breadcrumbs *pl*

Panik ['paːnɪk] *f* panic

panisch ['paːnɪʃ] *adj* panic-stricken

Panne ['panə] *f* (*AUT etc*) breakdown; (*Missgeschick*) slip; **~nhilfe** *f* breakdown service

panschen ['panʃən] *vi* to splash about ♦ *vt* to water down

Pantoffel [pan'tɔfəl] (-s, -n) *m* slipper

Pantomime [panto'miːmə] *f* mime

Panzer ['pantsər] (-s, -) *m* armour; (*Platte*) armour plate; (*Fahrzeug*) tank; **~glas** *nt* bulletproof glass; **p~n** *vt* to armour ♦ *vr* (*fig*) to arm o.s.

Papa [pa'paː] (-s, -s) (*umg*) *m* dad, daddy

Papagei [papa'gaɪ] (-s, -en) *m* parrot

Papier [pa'piːr] (-s, -e) *nt* paper; (*Wertpapier*) security; **~fabrik** *f* paper mill; **~geld** *nt* paper money; **~korb** *m* wastepaper basket;

~taschentuch *nt* tissue

Papp- ['pap] *zW:* **~deckel** *m* cardboard; **~e** *f* cardboard; **~el** (-, -n) *f* poplar; **p~en** (*umg*) *vt, vi* to stick; **p~ig** *adj* sticky

Paprika ['paprika] (-s, -s) *m* (*Gewürz*) paprika; (*~schote*) pepper

Papst [paːpst] (-(e)s, **ᵉe**) *m* pope

päpstlich ['pɛːpstlɪç] *adj* papal

Parabel [pa'raːbəl] (-, -n) *f* parable; (*MATH*) parabola

Parabolantenne [parabo'lantenə] *f* satellite dish

Parade [pa'raːdə] *f* (*MIL*) parade, review; (*SPORT*) parry

Paradies [para'diːs] (-es, -e) *nt* paradise; **p~isch** *adj* heavenly

Paradox [para'dɔks] (-es, -e) *nt* paradox; **p~** *adj* paradoxical.

Paragraf ▲ [para'graːf] (-en, -en) *m* paragraph; (*JUR*) section

parallel [para'leːl] *adj* parallel; **P~e** *f* parallel

Parasit [para'ziːt] (-en, -en) *m* (*auch fig*) parasite

parat [pa'raːt] *adj* ready.

Pärchen ['pɛːrçən] *nt* couple

Parfüm [par'fyːm] (-s, -s *od* -e) *nt* perfume; **~erie** [-ə'riː] *f* perfumery; **p~frei** *adj* non-perfumed; **p~ieren** *vt* to scent, to perfume

parieren [pa'riːrən] *vt* to parry ♦ *vi* (*umg*) to obey

Paris [pa'riːs] (-) *nt* Paris; **~er** *adj* Parisian ♦ *m* Parisian; **~erin** *f* Parisian

Park [park] (-s, -s) *m* park; **~anlage** *f* park; (*um Gebäude*) grounds *pl*; **p~en** *vt, vi* to park; **~ett** (-(e)s, -e) *nt* parquet (floor); (*THEAT*) stalls *pl*; **~gebühr** *f* parking fee; **~haus** *nt* multi-storey car park; **~lücke** *f* parking space; **~platz** *m* parking place; car park, parking lot (*US*); **~scheibe** *f* parking disc; **~schein** *m* car park ticket; **~uhr** *f* parking meter; **~verbot** *nt* parking ban

Parlament [parla'mɛnt] *nt* parliament; **~arier** [-'taːriər] (-s, -) *m* parliamentarian; **p~arisch** [-'taːrɪʃ] *adj* parliamentary

Parlaments- *zW:* **~beschluss** ▲ *m* vote of parliament; **~mitglied** *nt* member of parliament; **~sitzung** *f* sitting (of parliament)

Parodie [paro'di:] f parody; **p~ren** vt to parody

Parole [pa'ro:lə] f password; (Wahlspruch) motto

Partei [par'tai] f party; ~ **ergreifen für jdn** to take sb's side; **p~isch** adj partial, bias(s)ed; **p~los** adj neutral, impartial; ~**mitglied** nt party member; ~**programm** nt (party) manifesto; ~**tag** m party conference

Parterre [par'tɛr] (-s, -s) nt ground floor; (THEAT) stalls pl

Partie [par'ti:] f part; (Spiel) game; (Ausflug) outing; (Mann, Frau) catch; (COMM) lot; **mit von der ~ sein** to join in

Partizip [parti'tsi:p] (-s, -ien) nt participle

Partner(in) ['partnər(in)] (-s, -) m(f) partner; ~**schaft** f partnership; (von Städten) twinning; **p~schaftlich** adj as partners; ~**stadt** f twin town

Party ['pa:rti] (-, -s) f party

Pass ▲ [pas] (-es, ⁼e) m pass; (Ausweis) passport

passabel [pa'sa:bəl] adj passable, reasonable

Passage [pa'sa:ʒə] f passage

Passagier [pasa'ʒi:r] (-s, -e) m passenger; ~**flugzeug** nt airliner

Passamt ▲ nt passport office

Passant [pa'sant] m passer-by

Passbild ▲ nt passport photograph

passen ['pasən] vi to fit; (Farbe) to go; (auf Frage, KARTEN, SPORT) to pass; **das passt mir nicht** that doesn't suit me; ~ **zu** (Farbe, Kleider) to go with; **er passt nicht zu dir** he's not right for you; **~d** adj suitable; (zusammenpassend) matching; (angebracht) fitting; (Zeit) convenient

passier- [pa'si:r] zW: ~**bar** adj passable; ~**en** vt to pass; (durch Sieb) to strain ♦ vi to happen; **P~schein** m pass, permit

Passion [pasi'o:n] f passion; **p~iert** [-'ni:rt] adj enthusiastic, passionate; ~**sspiel** nt Passion Play

passiv ['pasi:f] adj passive; **P~** (-s, -e) nt passive; **P~a** pl (COMM) liabilities; **P~i'tät** f

passiveness; **P~rauchen** nt passive smoking

Pass- ▲ zW: ~**kontrolle** f passport control; ~**stelle** f passport office; ~**straße** f (mountain) pass

Paste ['pastə] f paste

Pastete [pas'te:tə] f pie

pasteurisieren [pastøri'zi:rən] vt to pasteurize

Pastor ['pastɔr] m vicar; pastor, minister

Pate ['pa:tə] (-n, -n) m godfather; ~**nkind** nt godchild

Patent [pa'tɛnt] (-(e)s, -e) nt patent; (MIL) commission; **p~** adj clever; ~**amt** nt patent office

Patentante f godmother

patentieren [patɛn'ti:rən] vt to patent

Patentinhaber m patentee

pathetisch [pa'te:tiʃ] adj emotional; bombastic

Pathologe [pato'lo:gə] (-n, -n) m pathologist

pathologisch adj pathological

Pathos ['pa:tɔs] (-) nt emotiveness, emotionalism

Patient(in) [patsi'ɛnt(in)] m(f) patient

Patin ['pa:tin] f godmother

Patriot [patri'o:t] (-en, -en) m patriot; **p~isch** adj patriotic; ~**ismus** [-'tismʊs] m patriotism

Patrone [pa'tro:nə] f cartridge

Patrouille [pa'trʊljə] f patrol

patrouillieren [patrʊl'ji:rən] vi to patrol

patsch [patʃ] excl splash; **P~e** (umg) f (Bedrängnis) mess, jam; ~**en** vi to smack, to slap; (im Wasser) to splash; ~**nass** ▲ adj soaking wet

patzig ['patsiç] (umg) adj cheeky, saucy

Pauke ['paʊkə] f kettledrum; **auf die ~ hauen** to live it up

pauken vt (intensiv lernen) to swot up (inf) ♦ vi to swot (inf), cram (inf)

pausbäckig ['paʊsbɛkiç] adj chubby-cheeked

pauschal [paʊ'ʃa:l] adj (Kosten) inclusive; (Urteil) sweeping; **P~e** f flat rate; **P~gebühr** f flat rate; **P~preis** m all-in

price; **P~reise** f package tour; **P~summe**
f lump sum

Pause ['pauzə] f break; (*THEAT*) interval;
(*Innehalten*) pause; (*Kopie*) tracing

pausen vt to trace; **~los** adj non-stop;
P~zeichen nt call sign; (*MUS*) rest

Pauspapier ['pauspapiːr] nt tracing paper

Pavillon ['paviljõ] (**-s, -s**) m pavilion

Pazif- [pa'tsiːf] zW: **~ik** (**-s**) m Pacific;
p~istisch adj pacifist

Pech [pɛç] (**-s, -e**) nt pitch; (*fig*) bad luck; **~**
haben to be unlucky; **p~schwarz** adj
pitch-black; **~strähne** (*umg*) m unlucky
patch; **~vogel** (*umg*) m unlucky person

Pedal [pe'daːl] (**-s, -e**) nt pedal

Pedant [pe'dant] m pedant; **~e'rie** f
pedantry; **p~isch** adj pedantic

Pediküre [pedi'kyːrə] f (*Fußpflege*) pedicure

Pegel ['peːgəl] (**-s, -**) m water gauge;
~stand m water level

peilen ['paɪlən] vt to get a fix on

Pein [paɪn] (**-**) f agony, pain; **p~igen** vt to
torture; (*plagen*) to torment; **p~lich** adj
(*unangenehm*) embarrassing, awkward,
painful; (*genau*) painstaking

Peitsche ['paɪtʃə] f whip; **p~n** vt to whip;
(*Regen*) to lash

Pelle ['pɛlə] f skin; **p~n** vt to skin, to peel

Pellkartoffeln pl jacket potatoes

Pelz [pɛlts] (**-es, -e**) m fur

Pendel ['pɛndəl] (**-s, -**) nt pendulum; **p~n** vi
(*Zug, Fähre etc*) to operate a shuttle service;
(*Mensch*) to commute; **~verkehr** m shuttle
traffic; (*für Pendler*) commuter traffic

Pendler ['pɛndlər] (**-s, -**) m commuter

penetrant [pene'trant] adj sharp; (*Person*)
pushing

Penis ['peːnɪs] (**-, -se**) m penis

pennen ['pɛnən] (*umg*) vi to kip

Penner (*umg: pej*) m (*Landstreicher*) tramp

Pension [pɛnzi'oːn] f (*Geld*) pension;
(*Ruhestand*) retirement; (*für Gäste*) boarding
od guesthouse; **~är(in)** [-'nɛːr(ɪn)] (**-s, -e**)
m(f) pensioner; **p~ieren** vt to pension off;
p~iert adj retired; **~ierung** f retirement;
~sgast m boarder, paying guest

Pensum ['pɛnzʊm] (**-s, Pensen**) nt quota;

(*SCH*) curriculum

per [pɛr] präp +akk by, per; (*pro*) per; (*bis*) by

Perfekt ['pɛrfɛkt] (**-(e)s, -e**) nt perfect; **p~**
adj perfect

perforieren [pɛrfo'riːrən] vt to perforate

Pergament [pɛrga'mɛnt] nt parchment;
~papier nt greaseproof paper

Periode [peri'oːdə] f period; **periodisch** adj
periodic; (*dezimal*) recurring

Perle ['pɛrlə] f (*auch fig*) pearl; **p~n** vi to
sparkle; (*Tropfen*) to trickle

Perl- ['pɛrl] zW: **~mutt** (**-s**) nt mother-of-
pearl; **~wein** m sparkling wine

perplex [pɛr'plɛks] adj dumbfounded

Person [pɛr'zoːn] (**-, -en**) f person; **ich für**
meine ~ ... personally I ...

Personal [pɛrzo'naːl] (**-s**) nt personnel;
(*Bedienung*) servants pl; **~ausweis** m
identity card; **~computer** m personal
computer; **~ien** [-iən] pl particulars;
~mangel m undermanning; **~pronomen**
nt personal pronoun

personell [pɛrzo'nɛl] adj (*Veränderungen*)
personnel

Personen- zW: **~aufzug** m lift, elevator
(*US*); **~kraftwagen** m private motorcar;
~schaden m injury to persons; **~zug** m
stopping train; passenger train

personifizieren [pɛrzonifi'tsiːrən] vt to
personify

persönlich [pɛr'zøːnlɪç] adj personal ♦ adv
in person; personally; **P~keit** f personality

Perspektive [pɛrspɛk'tiːvə] f perspective

Perücke [pe'rykə] f wig

pervers [pɛr'vɛrs] adj perverse

Pessimismus [pɛsi'mɪsmʊs] m pessimism

Pessimist [pɛsi'mɪst] m pessimist; **p~isch**
adj pessimistic

Pest [pɛst] (**-**) f plague

Petersilie [petɛr'ziːliə] f parsley

Petroleum [pe'troːleʊm] (**-s**) nt paraffin,
kerosene (*US*)

Pfad [pfaːt] (**-(e)s, -e**) m path; **~finder** (**-s,**
-) m boy scout; **~finderin** f girl guide

Pfahl [pfaːl] (**-(e)s, ⁔e**) m post, stake

Pfand [pfant] (**-(e)s, ⁔er**) nt pledge, security;
(*Flaschenpfand*) deposit; (*im Spiel*) forfeit;

~brief m bond
pfänden ['pfɛndən] vt to seize, to distrain
Pfänderspiel nt game of forfeits
Pfandflasche f returnable bottle
Pfandschein m pawn ticket
Pfändung ['pfɛnduŋ] f seizure, distraint
Pfanne ['pfanə] f (frying) pan
Pfannkuchen m pancake; (Berliner) doughnut
Pfarr- ['pfar] zW: **~ei** f parish; **~er** (-s, -) m priest; (evangelisch) vicar; minister; **~haus** nt vicarage; manse
Pfau [pfau] (-(e)s), -en m peacock; **~enauge** nt peacock butterfly
Pfeffer ['pfɛfər] (-s, -) m pepper; **~kuchen** m gingerbread; **~minz** (-es, -e) nt peppermint; **~mühle** f pepper mill; **p~n** vt to pepper; (umg: werfen) to fling; **gepfefferte Preise/Witze** steep prices/ spicy jokes
Pfeife ['pfaifə] f whistle; (Tabakpfeife, Orgelpfeife) pipe; **p~n** (unreg) vt, vi to whistle; **~r** (-s, -) m piper
Pfeil [pfail] (-(e)s), -e m arrow
Pfeiler ['pfailər] (-s, -) m pillar, prop; (Brückenpfeiler) pier
Pfennig ['pfɛniç] (-(e)s), -e m pfennig (hundredth part of a mark)
Pferd [pfeːrt] (-(e)s), -e nt horse
Pferde- ['pfeːrdə] zW: **~rennen** nt horse race; horse racing; **~schwanz** m (Frisur) ponytail; **~stall** m stable
Pfiff [pfif] (-(e)s), -e m whistle
Pfifferling ['pfifərliŋ] m yellow chanterelle (mushroom); **keinen ~ wert** not worth a thing
pfiffig adj sly, sharp
Pfingsten ['pfiŋstən] (-, -) nt Whitsun (BRIT), Pentecost
Pfirsich ['pfirziç] (-s, -e) m peach
Pflanz- ['pflants] zW: **~e** f plant; **p~en** vt to plant; **~enfett** nt vegetable fat; **p~lich** adj vegetable; **~ung** f plantation
Pflaster ['pflastər] (-s, -) nt plaster; (Straße) pavement; **p~n** vt to pave; **~stein** m paving stone
Pflaume ['pflaumə] f plum

Pflege ['pfleːgə] f care; (von Idee) cultivation; (Krankenpflege) nursing; **in ~ sein** (Kind) to be fostered out; **p~bedürftig** adj needing care; **~eltern** pl foster parents; **~heim** nt nursing home; **~kind** nt foster child; **p~leicht** adj easy-care; **~mutter** f foster mother; **p~n** vt to look after; (Kranke) to nurse; (Beziehungen) to foster; **~r** (-s, -) m orderly; male nurse; **~rin** f nurse, attendant; **~vater** m foster father
Pflicht [pfliçt] (-, -en) f duty; (SPORT) compulsory section; **p~bewusst ▲** adj conscientious; **~fach** nt (SCH) compulsory subject; **~gefühl** nt sense of duty; **p~gemäß** adj dutiful ♦ adv as in duty bound; **~versicherung** f compulsory insurance
pflücken ['pflykən] vt to pick; (Blumen) to pick, to pluck
Pflug [pfluːk] (-(e)s), ⁻e m plough
pflügen ['pflyːgən] vt to plough
Pforte ['pfɔrtə] f gate; door
Pförtner ['pfœrtnər] (-s, -) m porter, doorkeeper, doorman
Pfosten ['pfɔstən] (-s, -) m post
Pfote ['pfoːtə] f paw; (umg: Schrift) scrawl
Pfropfen (-s, -) m (Flaschenpfropfen) stopper; (Blutpfropfen) clot
pfui [pfui] excl ugh!
Pfund [pfunt] (-(e)s), -e nt pound
pfuschen ['pfuʃən] (umg) vi to be sloppy; **jdm ins Handwerk ~** to interfere in sb's business
Pfuscher ['pfuʃər] (-s, -) (umg) m sloppy worker; (Kurpfuscher) quack; **~ei** (umg) f sloppy work; quackery
Pfütze ['pfʏtsə] f puddle
Phänomen [fɛnoˈmeːn] (-s, -e) nt phenomenon
phänomenal [-ˈnaːl] adj phenomenal
Phantasie etc [fantaˈziː] f = **Fantasie** etc
phantastisch [fanˈtastiʃ] adj = **fantastisch**
Phase ['faːzə] f phase
Philologie [filoloˈɡiː] f philology
Philosoph [filoˈzoːf] (-en, -en) m philosopher; **~ie** [-ˈfiː] f philosophy; **p~isch** adj philosophical

phlegmatisch [flɛˈgmaːtɪʃ] *adj* lethargic

Phonetik [foˈneːtɪk] *f* phonetics *sg*

phonetisch *adj* phonetic

Phosphor [ˈfɔsfɔr] **(-s)** *m* phosphorus

Photo *etc* [ˈfoːto] **(-s, -s)** *nt* = **Foto** *etc*

Phrase [ˈfraːzə] *f* phrase; *(pej)* hollow phrase

pH-Wert [peːˈhaːveːrt] *m* pH-value

Physik [fyˈziːk] *f* physics *sg*; **p~alisch** [-ˈkaːlɪʃ] *adj* of physics; **~er(in)** [ˈfyːzɪkər(ɪn)] **(-s, -)** *m(f)* physicist

Physiologie [fyzioloˈgiː] *f* physiology

physisch [ˈfyːzɪʃ] *adj* physical

Pianist(in) [piaˈnɪst(ɪn)] *m(f)* pianist

Pickel [ˈpɪkəl] **(-s, -)** *m* pimple; *(Werkzeug)* pickaxe; *(Bergpickel)* ice axe; **p~ig** *adj* pimply, spotty

picken [ˈpɪkən] *vi* to pick, to peck

Picknick [ˈpɪknɪk] **(-s, -e** *od* **-s)** *nt* picnic; **~ machen** to have a picnic

piepen [ˈpiːpən] *vi* to chirp

piepsen [ˈpiːpsən] *vi* to chirp

Piepser *(umg)* *m* pager, paging device

Pier [piːər] **(-s, -s** *od* **-e)** *m od f* pier

Pietät [pieˈtɛːt] *f* piety, reverence; **p~los** *adj* impious, irreverent

Pigment [pɪgˈmɛnt] *nt* pigment

Pik [piːk] **(-s, -s)** *nt (KARTEN)* spades

pikant [piˈkant] *adj* spicy, piquant; *(anzüglich)* suggestive

Pilger [ˈpɪlgər] **(-s, -)** *m* pilgrim; **~fahrt** *f* pilgrimage

Pille [ˈpɪlə] *f* pill

Pilot [piˈloːt] **(-en, -en)** *m* pilot

Pilz [pɪlts] **(-es, -e)** *m* fungus; *(essbar)* mushroom; *(giftig)* toadstool; **~krankheit** *f* fungal disease

Pinguin [ˈpɪŋguiːn] **(-s, -e)** *m* penguin

Pinie [ˈpiːniə] *f* pine

pinkeln [ˈpɪŋkəln] *(umg)* *vi* to pee

Pinnwand [ˈpɪnvant] *f* noticeboard

Pinsel [ˈpɪnzəl] **(-s, -)** *m* paintbrush

Pinzette [pɪnˈtsɛtə] *f* tweezers *pl*

Pionier [pioˈniːr] **(-s, -e)** *m* pioneer; *(MIL)* sapper, engineer

Pirat [piˈraːt] **(-en, -en)** *m* pirate

Piste [ˈpɪstə] *f (SKI)* run, piste; *(AVIAT)* runway

Pistole [pɪsˈtoːlə] *f* pistol

Pizza [ˈpɪtsa] **(-, -s)** *f* pizza

Pkw [peːkaːˈveː] **(-(s), -(s))** *m abk* = **Personenkraftwagen**

plädieren [plɛˈdiːrən] *vi* to plead

Plädoyer [plɛdoaˈjeː] **(-s, -s)** *nt* speech for the defence; *(fig)* plea

Plage [ˈplaːgə] *f* plague; *(Mühe)* nuisance; **~geist** *m* pest, nuisance; **p~n** *vt* to torment ♦ *vr* to toil, to slave

Plakat [plaˈkaːt] **(-(e)s, -e)** *nt* placard; poster

Plan [plaːn] **(-(e)s, ˆe)** *m* plan; *(Karte)* map

Plane *f* tarpaulin

planen *vt* to plan; *(Mord etc)* to plot

Planer **(-s, -)** *m* planner

Planet [plaˈneːt] **(-en, -en)** *m* planet

planieren [plaˈniːrən] *vt* to plane, to level

Planke [ˈplaŋkə] *f* plank

plan- [ˈplaːn] *zW:* **~los** *adj (Vorgehen)* unsystematic; *(Umherlaufen)* aimless; **~mäßig** *adj* according to plan; systematic; *(EISENB)* scheduled

Plansoll **(-s)** *nt* output target

Plantage [planˈtaːʒə] *f* plantation

Plan(t)schbecken [ˈplan(t)ʃbɛkən] *nt* paddling pool

plan(t)schen [ˈplan(t)ʃən] *vi* to splash

Planung *f* planning

Planwirtschaft *f* planned economy

plappern [ˈplapərn] *vi* to chatter

plärren [ˈplɛrən] *vi (Mensch)* to cry, to whine; *(Radio)* to blare

Plasma [ˈplasma] **(-s, Plasmen)** *nt* plasma

Plastik¹ [ˈplastɪk] *f* sculpture

Plastik² [ˈplastɪk] **(-s)** *nt (Kunststoff)* plastic; **~beutel** *m* plastic bag, carrier bag; **~folie** *f* plastic film

plastisch [ˈplastɪʃ] *adj* plastic; **stell dir das ~ vor!** just picture it!

Platane [plaˈtaːnə] *f* plane (tree)

Platin [ˈplaːtiːn] **(-s)** *nt* platinum

platonisch [plaˈtoːnɪʃ] *adj* platonic

platsch [platʃ] *excl* splash; **~en** *vi* to splash

plätschern [ˈplɛtʃərn] *vi* to babble

platschnass ▲ *adj* drenched

platt [plat] *adj* flat; *(umg: überrascht)* flabbergasted; *(fig: geistlos)* flat, boring; **~deutsch** *adj* low German; **P~e** *f*

(*Speisenplatte, PHOT, TECH*) plate; (*Steinplatte*) flag; (*Kachel*) tile; (*Schallplatte*) record;

P~enspieler *m* record player; **P~enteller** *m* turntable

Platz [plats] (*-es, ¨e*) *m* place; (*Sitzplatz*) seat; (*Raum*) space, room; (*in Stadt*) square; (*Sportplatz*) playing field; **~ nehmen** to take a seat; **jdm ~ machen** to make room for sb; **~angst** *f* claustrophobia;
~anweiser(in) (*-s, -*) *m(f)* usher(ette)

Plätzchen ['plɛtsçən] *nt* spot; (*Gebäck*) biscuit

platzen *vi* to burst; (*Bombe*) to explode; **vor Wut p~en** (*umg*) to be bursting with anger

platzieren ▲ [pla'tsi:rən] *vt* to place ♦ *vr* (*SPORT*) to be placed; (*TENNIS*) to be seeded

Platz- *zW:* **~karte** *f* seat reservation;
~mangel *m* lack of space; **~patrone** *f* blank cartridge; **~regen** *m* downpour;
~reservierung [-rezervi:rʊŋ] *f* seat reservation; **~wunde** *f* cut

Plauderei [plaʊdə'raɪ] *f* chat, conversation; (*RADIO*) talk

plaudern ['plaʊdərn] *vi* to chat, to talk

plausibel [plaʊ'zi:bəl] *adj* plausible

plazieren △ [pla'tsi:rən] *vt, vr siehe* **platzieren**

Pleite ['plaɪtə] *f* bankruptcy; (*umg: Reinfall*) flop; **~ machen** to go bust; **p~** (*umg*) *adj* broke

Plenum ['ple:nʊm] (*-s*) *nt* plenum

Plombe ['plɔmbə] *f* lead seal; (*Zahnplombe*) filling

plombieren [plɔm'bi:rən] *vt* to seal; (*Zahn*) to fill

plötzlich ['plœtslɪç] *adj* sudden ♦ *adv* suddenly

plump [plʊmp] *adj* clumsy; (*Hände*) coarse; (*Körper*) shapeless; **~sen** (*umg*) *vi* to plump down, to fall

Plunder ['plʊndər] (*-s*) *m* rubbish

plündern ['plʏndərn] *vt* to plunder; (*Stadt*) to sack ♦ *vi* to plunder; **Plünderung** *f* plundering, sack, pillage

Plural ['plu:ra:l] (*-s, -e*) *m* plural; **p~istisch** *adj* pluralistic

Plus [plʊs] (*-, -*) *nt* plus; (*FIN*) profit; (*Vorteil*) advantage; **p~** *adv* plus

Plüsch [ply:ʃ] (*-(e)s, -e*) *m* plush

Plus- [plʊs] *zW:* **~pol** *m* (*ELEK*) positive pole;
~punkt *m* point; (*fig*) point in sb's favour

Plutonium [plu'to:niʊm] (*-s*) *nt* plutonium

PLZ *abk* = **Postleitzahl**

Po [po:] (*-s, -s*) (*umg*) *m* bottom, bum

Pöbel ['pø:bəl] (*-s*) *m* mob, rabble; **~ei** *f* vulgarity; **p~haft** *adj* low, vulgar

pochen ['pɔxən] *vi* to knock; (*Herz*) to pound; **auf etw** *akk* **~** (*fig*) to insist on sth

Pocken ['pɔkən] *pl* smallpox *sg*

Podium ['po:diʊm] *nt* podium;
~sdiskussion *f* panel discussion

Poesie [poe'zi:] *f* poetry

Poet [po'e:t] (*-en, -en*) *m* poet; **p~isch** *adj* poetic

Pointe [po'ɛ̃:tə] *f* point

Pokal [po'ka:l] (*-s, -e*) *m* goblet; (*SPORT*) cup; **~spiel** *nt* cup tie

pökeln ['pø:kəln] *vt* to pickle, to salt

Poker ['po:kər] (*-s*) *nt od m* poker

Pol [po:l] (*-s, -e*) *m* pole; **p~ar** *adj* polar;
~arkreis *m* Arctic circle

Pole ['po:lə] (*-n, -n*) *m* Pole

polemisch [po:le:mɪʃ] *adj* polemical

Polen ['po:lən] (*-s*) *nt* Poland

Police [po'li:s(ə)] *f* insurance policy

Polier [po'li:r] (*-s, -e*) *m* foreman

polieren *vt* to polish

Poliklinik [poli'kli:nɪk] *f* outpatients (department) *sg*

Polin *f* Pole

Politik [poli'ti:k] *f* politics *sg*; (*eine bestimmte*) policy; **~er(in)** [poli'ti:kər(ɪn)] (*-s, -*) *m(f)* politician

politisch [po'li:tɪʃ] *adj* political

Politur [poli'tu:r] *f* polish

Polizei [poli'tsaɪ] *f* police; **~beamte(r)** *m* police officer; **p~lich** *adj* police; **sich p~lich melden** to register with the police;
~revier *nt* police station; **~staat** *m* police state; **~streife** *f* police patrol; **~stunde** *f* closing time; **~wache** *f* police station

Polizist(in) [poli'tsɪst(ɪn)] (*-en, -en*) *m(f)* policeman(-woman)

Pollen ['pɔlən] (**-s, -**) *m* pollen; **~flug** *m* pollen count

polnisch ['pɔlnɪʃ] *adj* Polish

Polohemd ['poːlohɛmt] *nt* polo shirt

Polster ['pɔlstər] (**-s, -**) *nt* cushion; (*~ung*) upholstery; (*in Kleidung*) padding; (*fig: Geld*) reserves *pl*; **~er** (**-s, -**) *m* upholsterer; **~möbel** *pl* upholstered furniture *sg*; **p~n** *vt* to upholster; to pad

Polterabend ['pɔltəraːbant] *m* party on eve of wedding

poltern *vi* (*Krach machen*) to crash; (*schimpfen*) to rant

Polyp [po'lyːp] (**-en, -en**) *m* polyp; (*umg*) cop; **~en** *pl* (*MED*) adenoids

Pomade [po'maːdə] *f* pomade

Pommes frites [pɔm'frɪt] *pl* chips, French fried potatoes

Pomp [pɔmp] (**-(e)s**) *m* pomp; **p~ös** [pɔm'pøːs] *adj* (*Auftritt, Fest, Haus*) ostentatious, showy

Pony ['pɔni] (**-s, -s**) *nt* (*Pferd*) pony ♦ *m* (*Frisur*) fringe

Popmusik ['pɔpmuːziːk] *f* pop music

Popo [po'poː] (**-s, -s**) (*umg*) *m* bottom, bum

poppig ['pɔpɪç] *adj* (*Farbe etc*) gaudy

populär [popu'lɛːr] *adj* popular

Popularität [populari'tɛːt] *f* popularity

Pore ['poːrə] *f* pore

Pornografie ▲ [pɔrnogra'fiː] *f* pornography; **pornografisch** ▲ [pɔrno'graːfɪʃ] *adj* pornographic

porös [po'røːs] *adj* porous

Porree ['pɔre] (**-s, -s**) *m* leek

Portefeuille [pɔrt(ə)'føːj] *nt* (*POL, FIN*) portfolio

Portemonnaie [pɔrtmɔ'neː] (**-s, -s**) *nt* purse

Portier [pɔrti'eː] (**-s, -s**) *m* porter

Portion [pɔrtsi'oːn] *f* portion, helping; (*umg: Anteil*) amount

Portmonee ▲ [pɔrtmo'neː] (**-s, -s**) *nt* = Portemonnaie

Porto ['pɔrto] (**-s, -s**) *nt* postage; **p~frei** *adj* post-free, (postage) prepaid

Portrait [pɔr'trɛː] (**-s, -s**) *nt* = Porträt; **p~ieren** *vt* = porträtieren

Porträt [pɔr'trɛː] (**-s, -s**) *nt* portrait; **p~ieren** *vt* to paint, to portray

Portugal ['pɔrtugal] (**-s**) *nt* Portugal; **Portugiese** [pɔrtu'giːzə] (**-n, -n**) *m* Portuguese; **Portu'giesin** *f* Portuguese; **portu'giesisch** *adj* Portuguese

Porzellan [pɔrtsɛ'laːn] (**-s, -e**) *nt* china, porcelain; (*Geschirr*) china

Posaune [po'zaʊnə] *f* trombone

Pose ['poːzə] *f* pose

Position [pozitsi'oːn] *f* position

positiv ['poːzitiːf] *adj* positive; **P~** (**-s, -e**) *nt* (*PHOT*) positive

possessiv ['pɔsɛsiːf] *adj* possessive; **P~pronomen** (**-s, -e**) *nt* possessive pronoun

possierlich [pɔ'siːrlɪç] *adj* funny

Post [pɔst] (**-, -en**) *f* post (office); (*Briefe*) mail; **~amt** *nt* post office; **~anweisung** *f* postal order, money order; **~bote** *m* postman; **~en** (**-s, -**) *m* post, position; (*COMM*) item; (*auf Liste*) entry; (*MIL*) sentry; (*Streikposten*) picket; **~er** (**-s, -(s)**) *nt* poster; **~fach** *nt* post office box; **~karte** *f* postcard; **p~lagernd** *adv* poste restante (*BRIT*), general delivery (*US*); **~leitzahl** *f* postal code; **~scheckkonto** *nt* postal giro account; **~sparbuch** *nt* post office savings book; **~sparkasse** *f* post office savings bank; **~stempel** *m* postmark; **p~wendend** *adv* by return of post; **~wertzeichen** *nt* postage stamp

potent [po'tɛnt] *adj* potent

Potential △ [potɛntsi'aːl] (**-s, -e**) *nt siehe* **Potenzial**

potentiell △ [potɛntsi'ɛl] *adj siehe* **potenziell**

Potenz [po'tɛnts] *f* power; (*eines Mannes*) potency

Potenzial ▲ [potɛn'tsiaːl] (**-s, -e**) *nt* potential

potenziell ▲ [potɛn'tsiɛl] *adj* potential

Pracht [praxt] (**-**) *f* splendour, magnificence

prächtig ['prɛçtɪç] *adj* splendid

Prachtstück *nt* showpiece

prachtvoll *adj* splendid, magnificent

Prädikat [prɛdi'kaːt] (**-(e)s, -e**) *nt* title;

(*GRAM*) predicate; (*Zensur*) distinction

prägen ['prɛːgən] *vt* to stamp; (*Münze*) to mint; (*Ausdruck*) to coin; (*Charakter*) to form

prägnant [prɛ'gnant] *adj* precise, terse

Prägung ['prɛːgʊŋ] *f* minting; forming; (*Eigenart*) character, stamp

prahlen ['praːlən] *vi* to boast, to brag; **Prahle'rei** *f* boasting

Praktik ['praktık] *f* practice; **p~abel** [-'kaːbəl] *adj* practicable; **~ant(in)** [-'kant(ın)] *m(f)* trainee; **~um** (**-s, Praktika** *od* **Praktiken**) *nt* practical training

praktisch ['praktıʃ] *adj* practical, handy; **~er Arzt** general practitioner

praktizieren [prakti'tsiːrən] *vt, vi* to practise

Praline [pra'liːnə] *f* chocolate

prall [pral] *adj* firmly rounded; (*Segel*) taut; (*Arme*) plump; (*Sonne*) blazing; **~en** *vi* to bounce, to rebound; (*Sonne*) to blaze

Prämie ['prɛːmiə] *f* premium; (*Belohnung*) award, prize; **p~ren** *vt* to give an award to

Präparat [prɛpa'raːt] (**-(e)s, -e**) *nt* (*BIOL*) preparation; (*MED*) medicine

Präposition [prɛpozitsi'oːn] *f* preposition

Prärie [prɛ'riː] *f* prairie

Präsens ['prɛːzɛns] (-) *nt* present tense

präsentieren [prɛzɛn'tiːrən] *vt* to present

Präservativ [prɛzɛrva'tiːf] (**-s, -e**) *nt* contraceptive

Präsident(in) [prɛzi'dɛnt(ın)] *m(f)* president; **~schaft** *f* presidency

Präsidium [prɛ'ziːdium] *nt* presidency, chair(manship); (*Polizeipräsidium*) police headquarters *pl*

prasseln ['prasəln] *vi* (*Feuer*) to crackle; (*Hagel*) to drum; (*Wörter*) to rain down

Praxis ['praksıs] (**-, Praxen**) *f* practice; (*Behandlungsraum*) surgery; (*von Anwalt*) office

Präzedenzfall [prɛtse'dɛnts-] *m* precedent

präzis [prɛ'tsiːs] *adj* precise; **P~ion** [prɛtsizi'oːn] *f* precision

predigen ['preːdıgən] *vt, vi* to preach; **Prediger** (**-s, -**) *m* preacher

Predigt ['preːdıçt] (**-, -en**) *f* sermon

Preis [praıs] (**-es, -e**) *m* prize; (*Siegespreis*) prize; **um keinen ~** not at any price;

p~bewusst ▲ *adj* price-conscious

Preiselbeere *f* cranberry

preis- ['praıs] *zW:* **~en** (*unreg*) *vi* to praise; **~geben** (*unreg*) *vt* to abandon; (*opfern*) to sacrifice; (*zeigen*) to expose; **~gekrönt** *adj* prizewinning; **P~gericht** *nt* jury; **~günstig** *adj* inexpensive; **P~lage** *f* price range; **~lich** *adj* (*Lage, Unterschied*) price, in price; **P~liste** *f* price list; **P~richter** *m* judge (*in a competition*); **P~schild** *nt* price tag; **P~träger(in)** *m(f)* prizewinner; **~wert** *adj* inexpensive

Prell- [prɛl] *zW:* **~bock** *m* buffers *pl*; **p~en** *vt* to bump; (*fig*) to cheat, to swindle; **~ung** *f* bruise

Premiere [prəmi'ɛːrə] *f* premiere

Premierminister [prəmi'e:mınıstər] *m* prime minister, premier

Presse ['prɛsə] *f* press; **~agentur** *f* press agency; **~freiheit** *f* freedom of the press; **p~n** *vt* to press

Pressluft ▲ ['prɛslʊft] *f* compressed air; **~bohrer** *m* pneumatic drill

Prestige [prɛs'tiːʒə] (**-s**) *nt* prestige

prickeln ['prıkəln] *vt, vi* to tingle; to tickle

Priester ['priːstər] (**-s, -**) *m* priest

prima *adj inv* first-class, excellent

primär [pri'mɛːr] *adj* primary

Primel ['priːməl] (**-, -n**) *f* primrose

primitiv [primi'tiːf] *adj* primitive

Prinz [prınts] (**-en, -en**) *m* prince; **~essin** *f* princess

Prinzip [prın'tsiːp] (**-s, -ien**) *nt* principle; **p~iell** [-i'ɛl] *adj, adv* on principle; **p~ienlos** *adj* unprincipled

Priorität [priori'tɛːt] *f* priority

Prise ['priːzə] *f* pinch

Prisma ['prısma] (**-s, Prismen**) *nt* prism

privat [pri'vaːt] *adj* private; **P~besitz** *m* private property; **P~fernsehen** *nt* commercial television; **P~patient(in)** *m(f)* private patient; **P~schule** *f* public school

Privileg [privi'leːk] (**-(e)s, -ien**) *nt* privilege

Pro [proː] (-) *nt* pro

pro *präp +akk* per

Probe ['proːbə] *f* test; (*Teststück*) sample; (*THEAT*) rehearsal; **jdn auf die ~ stellen** to put sb to the test; **~exemplar** *nt* specimen copy; **~fahrt** *f* test drive; **p~n** *vt* to try; (*THEAT*) to rehearse; **p~weise** *adv* on approval; **~zeit** *f* probation period

probieren [pro'biːrən] *vt* to try; (*Wein, Speise*) to taste, to sample ♦ *vi* to try; to taste

Problem [pro'bleːm] **(-s, -e)** *nt* problem; **~atik** [-'maːtɪk] *f* problem; **p~atisch** [-'maːtɪʃ] *adj* problematic; **p~los** *adj* problem-free

Produkt [pro'dʊkt] **(-(e)s, -e)** *nt* product; (*AGR*) produce *no pl*; **~ion** [prodʊktsi'oːn] *f* production; output; **p~iv** [-'tiːf] *adj* productive; **~ivi'tät** *f* productivity

Produzent [produ'tsɛnt] *m* manufacturer; (*Film*) producer

produzieren [produ'tsiːrən] *vt* to produce

Professor [pro'fɛsɔr] *m* professor

Profi ['proːfi] **(-s, -s)** *m* (*umg, SPORT*) pro

Profil [pro'fiːl] **(-s, -e)** *nt* profile; (*fig*) image

Profit [pro'fiːt] **(-(e)s, -e)** *m* profit; **p~ieren** *vi*: **p~ieren (von)** to profit (from)

Prognose [pro'gnoːzə] *f* prediction, prognosis

Programm [pro'gram] **(-s, -e)** *nt* programme; (*COMPUT*) program; **p~ieren** [-'miːrən] *vt* to programme; (*COMPUT*) to program; **~ierer(in)** **(-s, -)** *m(f)* programmer

progressiv [progrɛ'siːf] *adj* progressive

Projekt [pro'jɛkt] **(-(e)s, -e)** *nt* project; **~or** [pro'jɛktɔr] *m* projector

proklamieren [prokla'miːrən] *vt* to proclaim

Prokurist(in) [prokuˈrɪst(ɪn)] *m(f)* ≃ company secretary

Prolet [pro'leːt] **(-en, -en)** *m* prole, pleb; **~arier** [-'taːriər] **(-s, -)** *m* proletarian

Prolog [pro'loːk] **(-(e)s, -e)** *m* prologue

Promenade [promə'naːdə] *f* promenade

Promille [pro'milə] **(-(s), -)** *nt* alcohol level

prominent [promi'nɛnt] *adj* prominent

Prominenz [promi'nɛnts] *f* VIPs *pl*

Promotion [promotsi'oːn] *f* doctorate, Ph.D.

promovieren [promo'viːrən] *vi* to do a doctorate *od* Ph.D.

prompt [prɔmpt] *adj* prompt

Pronomen [pro'noːmɛn] **(-s, -)** *nt* pronoun

Propaganda [propa'ganda] **(-)** *f* propaganda

Propeller [pro'pɛlər] **(-s, -)** *m* propeller

Prophet [pro'feːt] **(-en, -en)** *m* prophet

prophezeien [profe'tsaɪən] *vt* to prophesy; **Prophezeiung** *f* prophecy

Proportion [proportsi'oːn] *f* proportion; **p~al** [-'naːl] *adj* proportional

proportioniert [proportsio'niːrt] *adj*: **gut/ schlecht ~** well-/badly-proportioned

Prosa ['proːza] **(-)** *f* prose; **p~isch** [pro'zaːɪʃ] *adj* prosaic

prosit ['proːzɪt] *excl* cheers

Prospekt [pro'spɛkt] **(-(e)s, -e)** *m* leaflet, brochure

prost [proːst] *excl* cheers

Prostituierte [prostitu'iːrtə] *f* prostitute

Prostitution [prostitutsi'oːn] *f* prostitution

Protest [pro'tɛst] **(-(e)s, -e)** *m* protest; **~ant(in)** [protɛs'tant(ɪn)] *m(f)* Protestant; **p~antisch** [protɛs'tantɪʃ] *adj* Protestant; **p~ieren** [protɛs'tiːrən] *vi* to protest

Prothese [pro'teːzə] *f* artificial limb; (*Zahnprothese*) dentures *pl*

Protokoll [proto'kɔl] **(-s, -e)** *nt* register; (*von Sitzung*) minutes *pl*; (*diplomatisch*) protocol; (*Polizeiprotokoll*) statement; **p~ieren** [-'liːrən] *vt* to take down in the minutes

protzen ['prɔtsən] *vi* to show off

Proviant [provi'ant] **(-s, -e)** *m* provisions *pl*, supplies *pl*

Provinz [pro'vɪnts] **(-, -en)** *f* province; **p~i'ell** *adj* provincial

Provision [provizi'oːn] *f* (*COMM*) commission

provisorisch [provi'zoːrɪʃ] *adj* provisional

Provokation [provokatsi'oːn] *f* provocation

provozieren [provo'tsiːrən] *vt* to provoke

Prozedur [protse'duːr] *f* procedure; (*pej*) carry-on

Prozent [pro'tsɛnt] **(-(e)s, -e)** *nt* per cent, percentage; **~satz** *m* percentage; **p~ual** [-u'aːl] *adj* percentage *cpd*; as a percentage

Prozess ▲ [pro'tsɛs] **(-es, -e)** *m* trial, case

Prozession [protsɛsi'oːn] *f* procession

prüde ['pryːdə] *adj* prudish; **P~rie** [-'riː] *f* prudery

Prüf- ['pry:f] zW: **p~en** vt to examine, to test; (nachprüfen) to check; **~er** (-s, -) m examiner; **~ling** m examinee; **~ung** f examination; checking; **~ungsausschuss** ▲ m examining board

Prügel ['pry:gəl] (-s, -) m cudgel ♦ pl (Schläge) beating; **~ei** [-'laı] f fight; **p~n** vt to beat ♦ vr to fight; **~strafe** f corporal punishment

Prunk [prʊŋk] (-(e)s) m pomp, show; **p~voll** adj splendid, magnificent

PS [pe:'ɛs] abk (= Pferdestärke) H.P.

Psych- ['psyç] zW: **~iater** [-i'a:tər] (-s, -) m psychiatrist; **p~iatrisch** adj (MED) psychiatric; **p~isch** adj psychological; **~oanalyse** [-o|ana'ly:zə] f psychoanalysis; **~ologe** (-n, -n) m psychologist; **~olo'gie** f psychology; **p~ologisch** adj psychological; **~otherapeut(in)** (-en, -en) m(f) psychotherapist

Pubertät [puber'tɛ:t] f puberty

Publikum ['pu:blikʊm] (-s) nt audience; (SPORT) crowd

publizieren [publi'tsi:rən] vt to publish, to publicize

Pudding ['pʊdıŋ] (-s, -e od -s) m blancmange

Pudel ['pu:dəl] (-s) m poodle

Puder ['pu:dər] (-s, -) m powder; **~dose** f powder compact; **p~n** vt to powder; **~zucker** m icing sugar

Puff¹ [pʊf] (-s, -e) m (Wäschepuff) linen basket; (Sitzpuff) pouf

Puff² [pʊf] (-s, ²e) (umg) m (Stoß) push

Puff³ [pʊf] (-s, -) (umg) m od nt (Bordell) brothel

Puffer (-s, -) m buffer

Pullover [pʊ'lo:vər] (-s, -) m pullover, jumper

Puls [pʊls] (-es, -e) m pulse; **~ader** f artery; **p~ieren** vi to throb, to pulsate

Pult [pʊlt] (-(e)s, -e) nt desk

Pulver ['pʊlfər] (-s, -) nt powder; **p~ig** adj powdery; **~schnee** m powdery snow

pummelig ['pʊmalıç] adj chubby

Pumpe ['pʊmpə] f pump; **p~n** vt to pump; (umg) to lend; to borrow

Punkt [pʊŋkt] (-(e)s, -e) m point; (bei Muster) dot; (Satzzeichen) full stop; **p~ieren** [-'ti:rən] vt to dot; (MED) to aspirate

pünktlich ['pyŋktlıç] adj punctual; **P~keit** f punctuality

Punktsieg m victory on points

Punktzahl f score

Punsch [pʊnʃ] (-(e)s, -e) m punch

Pupille [pu'pılə] f pupil

Puppe ['pʊpə] f doll; (Marionette) puppet; (Insektenpuppe) pupa, chrysalis

Puppen- zW: **~spieler** m puppeteer; **~stube** f doll's house; **~theater** nt puppet theatre

pur [pu:r] adj pure; (völlig) sheer; (Whisky) neat

Püree [py're:] (-s, -s) nt mashed potatoes pl

Purzelbaum ['pʊrtsəlbaum] m somersault

purzeln ['pʊrtsəln] vi to tumble

Puste ['pu:stə] (-) (umg) f puff; (fig) steam; **p~n** vi to puff, to blow

Pute ['pu:tə] f turkey hen; **~r** (-s, -) m turkey cock

Putsch [pʊtʃ] (-(e)s, -e) m revolt, putsch

Putz [pʊts] (-es) m (Mörtel) plaster, roughcast

putzen vt to clean; (Nase) to wipe, to blow ♦ vr to clean o.s.; to dress o.s. up

Putz- zW: **~frau** f charwoman; **p~ig** adj quaint, funny; **~lappen** m cloth

Puzzle ['pasəl] (-s, -s) nt jigsaw

PVC nt abk PVC

Pyjama [pi'dʒa:ma] (-s, -s) m pyjamas pl

Pyramide [pyra'mi:də] f pyramid

Pyrenäen [pyre'nɛ:ən] pl Pyrenees

Q, q

Quacksalber ['kvakzalbər] (-s, -) m quack (doctor)

Quader ['kva:dər] (-s, -) m square stone; (MATH) cuboid

Quadrat [kva'dra:t] (-(e)s, -e) nt square; **q~isch** adj square; **~meter** m square metre

quaken ['kva:kən] vi to croak; (Ente) to

quack
quäken ['kvɛːkən] *vi* to screech
Qual [kvaːl] (-, -en) *f* pain, agony; *(seelisch)* anguish; **q~en** *vt* to torment ♦ *vr* to struggle; *(geistig)* to torment o.s.; **~erei** *f* torture, torment
Qualifikation [kvalifikatsi'oːn] *f* qualification
qualifizieren [kvalifi'tsiːrən] *vt* to qualify; *(einstufen)* to label ♦ *vr* to qualify
Qualität [kvali'tɛːt] *f* quality; **~sware** *f* article of high quality
Qualle ['kvalə] *f* jellyfish
Qualm [kvalm] (-(e)s) *m* thick smoke; **q~en** *vt, vi* to smoke
qualvoll ['kvaːlfɔl] *adj* excruciating, painful, agonizing
Quant- ['kvant] *zW:* **~ität** [-i'tɛːt] *f* quantity; **q~itativ** [-ita'tiːf] *adj* quantitative; **~um** (-s) *nt* quantity, amount
Quarantäne [karan'tɛːnə] *f* quarantine
Quark [kvark] (-s) *m* curd cheese
Quartal [kvar'taːl] (-s, -e) *nt* quarter (year)
Quartier [kvar'tiːr] (-s, -e) *nt* accommodation; *(MIL)* quarters *pl*; *(Stadtquartier)* district
Quarz [kvaːrts] (-es, -e) *m* quartz
quasseln ['kvasəln] *(umg) vi* to natter
Quatsch [kvatʃ] (-es) *m* rubbish; **q~en** *vi* to chat, to natter
Quecksilber ['kvɛkzilbər] *nt* mercury
Quelle ['kvɛlə] *f* spring; *(eines Flusses)* source; **q~n** *(unreg) vi (hervorquellen)* to pour od gush forth; *(schwellen)* to swell
quer [kveːr] *adv* crossways, diagonally; *(rechtwinklig)* at right angles; **~ auf dem Bett** across the bed; **Q~balken** *m* crossbeam; **Q~flöte** *f* flute; **Q~format** *nt (PHOT)* oblong format; **Q~schnitt** *m* cross-section; **~schnittsgelähmt** *adj* paralysed below the waist; **Q~straße** *f* intersecting road
quetschen ['kvɛtʃən] *vt* to squash, to crush; *(MED)* to bruise
Quetschung *f* bruise, contusion
quieken ['kviːkən] *vi* to squeak
quietschen ['kviːtʃən] *vi* to squeak
Quintessenz ['kvɪntesɛnts] *f* quintessence

Quirl [kvɪrl] (-(e)s, -e) *m* whisk
quitt [kvɪt] *adj* quits, even
Quitte *f* quince
quittieren [kvɪ'tiːrən] *vt* to give a receipt for; *(Dienst)* to leave
Quittung *f* receipt
Quiz [kvɪs] (-, -) *nt* quiz
quoll *etc* [kvɔl] *vb siehe* **quellen**
Quote ['kvoːtə] *f* number, rate

R, r

Rabatt [ra'bat] (-(e)s, -e) *m* discount
Rabattmarke *f* trading stamp
Rabe ['raːbə] (-n, -n) *m* raven
rabiat [rabi'aːt] *adj* furious
Rache ['raxə] (-) *f* revenge, vengeance
Rachen (-s, -) *m* throat
rächen ['rɛçən] *vt* to avenge, to revenge ♦ *vr* to take (one's) revenge; **das wird sich ~** you'll pay for that
Rad [raːt] (-(e)s, ⁼er) *nt* wheel; *(Fahrrad)* bike; **~ fahren** to cycle
Radar ['raːdaːr] (-s) *m od nt* radar; **~falle** *f* speed trap; **~kontrolle** *f* radar-controlled speed trap
Radau [ra'dau] (-s) *(umg) m* row
radeln ['raːdəln] *(umg) vi* to cycle
Radfahr- *zW:* **r~en** △ *(unreg) vi siehe* **Rad**; **~er(in)** *m(f)* cyclist; **~weg** *m* cycle track *od* path
Radier- [ra'diːr] *zW:* **r~en** *vt* to rub out, to erase; *(KUNST)* to etch; **~gummi** *m* rubber, eraser; **~ung** *f* etching
Radieschen [ra'diːsçən] *nt* radish
radikal [radi'kaːl] *adj* radical
Radio ['raːdio] (-s, -s) *nt* radio, wireless; **r~ak'tiv** *adj* radioactive; **~aktivi'tät** *f* radioactivity; **~apparat** *m* radio, wireless set
Radius ['raːdios] (-, **Radien**) *m* radius
Rad- *zW:* **~kappe** *f (AUT)* hub cap; **~ler(in)** *(umg) m(f)* cyclist; **~rennen** *nt* cycle race; cycle racing; **~sport** *m* cycling; **~weg** *m* cycleway
raffen ['rafən] *vt* to snatch, to pick up; *(Stoff)*

to gather (up); (*Geld*) to pile up, to rake in

raffi'niert *adj* crafty, cunning

ragen ['ra:gən] *vi* to tower, to rise

Rahm [ra:m] **(-s)** *m* cream

Rahmen (-s, -) *m* frame(work); **im ~ des Möglichen** within the bounds of possibility; **r~** *vt* to frame

räkeln ['rɛ:kln] *vr* = **rekeln**

Rakete [ra'ke:tə] *f* rocket; **~nstützpunkt** *m* missile base

rammen ['ramən] *vt* to ram

Rampe ['rampə] *f* ramp; **~nlicht** *nt* (THEAT) footlights *pl*

ramponieren [rampo'ni:rən] (*umg*) *vt* to damage

Ramsch [ramʃ] **(-(e)s, -e)** *m* junk

ran [ran] (*umg*) *adv* = **heran**

Rand [rant] **(-(e)s, ᵘer)** *m* edge; (*von Brille, Tasse etc*) rim; (*Hutrand*) brim; (*auf Papier*) margin; (*Schmutzrand, unter Augen*) ring; (*fig*) verge, brink; **außer ~ und Band** wild; **am ~e bemerkt** mentioned in passing

randalieren [randa'li:rən] *vi* to (go on the) rampage

Rang [raŋ] **(-(e)s, ᵘe)** *m* rank; (*Stand*) standing; (*Wert*) quality; (THEAT) circle

Rangier- [rãʒi:r] zW: **r~bahnhof** *m* marshalling yard; **r~en** *vt* (EISENB) to shunt, to switch (US) ♦ *vi* to rank, to be classed; **~gleis** *nt* siding

Ranke ['raŋkə] *f* tendril, shoot

ranzig ['rantsɪç] *adj* rancid

Rappen ['rapən] *m* (FIN) rappen, centime

rar [ra:r] *adj* rare; **sich ~ machen** (*umg*) to keep o.s. to o.s.; **R~i'tät** *f* rarity; (*Sammelobjekt*) curio

rasant [ra'zant] *adj* quick, rapid

rasch [raʃ] *adj* quick

rascheln *vi* to rustle

Rasen ['ra:zən] **(-s, -)** *m* lawn; grass

rasen *vi* to rave; (*schnell*) to race; **~d** *adj* furious; **~de Kopfschmerzen** a splitting headache

Rasenmäher (-s, -) *m* lawnmower

Rasier- [ra'zi:r] zW: **~apparat** *m* shaver; **~creme** *f* shaving cream; **r~en** *vt, vr* to shave; **~klinge** *f* razor blade; **~messer** *nt*

razor; **~pinsel** *m* shaving brush; **~schaum** *m* shaving foam; **~seife** *f* shaving soap *od* stick; **~wasser** *nt* shaving lotion

Rasse ['rasə] *f* race; (*Tierrasse*) breed; **~hund** *m* thoroughbred dog

rasseln ['rasəln] *vi* to clatter

Rassen- zW: **~hass** ▲ *m* race *od* racial hatred; **~trennung** *f* racial segregation

Rassismus [ra'sɪsmʊs] *m* racism

Rast [rast] **(-, -en)** *f* rest; **r~en** *vi* to rest; **~hof** *m* (AUT) service station; **~los** *adj* tireless; (*unruhig*) restless; **~platz** *m* (AUT) layby; **~stätte** *f* (AUT) service station

Rasur [ra'zu:r] *f* shaving

Rat [ra:t] **(-(e)s, -schläge)** *m* advice *no pl*; **ein ~** a piece of advice; **keinen ~ wissen** not to know what to do; *siehe* **zurate**

Rate *f* instalment

raten (*unreg*) *vt, vi* to guess; (*empfehlen*): **jdm ~** to advise sb

Ratenzahlung *f* hire purchase

Ratgeber (-s, -) *m* adviser

Rathaus *nt* town hall

ratifizieren [ratifi'tsi:rən] *vt* to ratify

Ration [ratsi'o:n] *f* ration; **r~al** [-'na:l] *adj* rational; **r~ali'sieren** *vt* to rationalize; **r~ell** [-'nɛl] *adj* efficient; **r~ieren** [-'ni:rən] *vt* to ration

Rat- zW: **r~los** *adj* at a loss, helpless; **r~sam** *adj* advisable; **~schlag** *m* (piece of) advice

Rätsel ['rɛ:tsəl] **(-s, -)** *nt* puzzle; (*Worträtsel*) riddle; **r~haft** *adj* mysterious; **es ist mir r~haft** it's a mystery to me

Ratte ['ratə] *f* rat; **~nfänger (-s, -)** *m* ratcatcher

rattern ['ratərn] *vi* to rattle, to clatter

rau ▲ [rau] *adj* rough, coarse; (*Wetter*) harsh

Raub [raup] **(-(e)s)** *m* robbery; (*Beute*) loot, booty; **~bau** *m* ruthless exploitation; **r~en** ['raubən] *vt* to rob; (*Mensch*) to kidnap, to abduct

Räuber ['rɔybər] **(-s, -)** *m* robber

Raub- zW: **~mord** *m* robbery with murder; **~tier** *nt* predator; **~überfall** *m* robbery with violence; **~vogel** *m* bird of prey

Rauch [raux] **(-(e)s)** *m* smoke; **r~en** *vt, vi* to

smoke; **~er(in)** (**-s, -**) *m(f)* smoker;
~erabteil *nt* (*EISENB*) smoker; **räuchern** *vt*
to smoke, to cure; **~fleisch** *nt* smoked
meat; **r~ig** *adj* smoky

rauf [rauf] (*umg*) *adv* = **herauf; hinauf**

raufen *vt* (*Haare*) to pull out ♦ *vi, vr* to fight;
Raufe'rei *f* brawl, fight

ràuh △ *etc* [rau] *adj siehe* **rau** *etc*

Raum [raum] (**-(e)s, Räume**) *m* space;
(*Zimmer, Platz*) room; (*Gebiet*) area

räumen ['rɔymən] *vt* to clear; (*Wohnung,
Platz*) to vacate; (*wegbringen*) to shift, to
move; (*in Schrank etc*) to put away

Raum- *zW:* **~fähre** *f* space shuttle; **~fahrt** *f*
space travel; **~inhalt** *m* cubic capacity,
volume

räumlich ['rɔymlıç] *adj* spatial; **R~keiten** *pl*
premises

Raum- *zW:* **~pflegerin** *f* cleaner; **~schiff**
nt spaceship; **~schifffahrt** ▲ *f* space
travel

Räumung ['rɔymuŋ] *f* vacating, evacuation;
clearing (away)

Räumungs- *zW:* **~arbeiten** *pl* clearance
operations; **~verkauf** *m* clearance sale; (*bei
Geschäftsaufgabe*) closing down sale

raunen ['raunən] *vt, vi* to whisper

Raupe ['raupə] *f* caterpillar; (*~nkette*)
(caterpillar) track

Raureif ['raurauf] *m* hoarfrost

raus [raus] (*umg*) *adv* = **heraus; hinaus**

Rausch [rauʃ] (**-(e)s, Räusche**) *m*
intoxication

rauschen *vi* (*Wasser*) to rush; (*Baum*) to
rustle; (*Radio etc*) to hiss; (*Mensch*) to
sweep, to sail; **~d** *adj* (*Beifall*) thunderous;
(*Fest*) sumptuous

Rauschgift *nt* drug; **~süchtige(r)** *f(m)*
drug addict

räuspern ['rɔyspərn] *vr* to clear one's throat

Razzia ['ratsia] (**-, Razzien**) *f* raid

Reagenzglas [rea'gɛntsglaːs] *nt* test tube

reagieren [rea'giːrən] *vi:* **~ (auf** +*akk*) to
react (to)

Reakt- *zW:* **~ion** [rɛaktsi'oːn] *f* reaction;
r~io'när *adj* reactionary; **~or** [re'aktɔr] *m*
reactor

real [re'aːl] *adj* real, material

reali'sieren *vt* (*verwirklichen: Pläne*) to carry
out

Realismus [rea'lısmus] *m* realism

rea'listisch *adj* realistic

Realschule *f* secondary school

| **Realschule** |
---

i The Realschule *is one of the secondary
schools a German schoolchild may
attend after the* Grundschule. *On the
successful completion of six years of
schooling in the* Realschule *pupils gain the*
mittlere Reife *and usually go on to
vocational training or further education.*

Rebe ['reːbə] *f* vine

rebellieren [rebe'liːrən] *vi* to rebel;
Rebelli'on *f* rebellion; **re'bellisch** *adj*
rebellious

Rebhuhn ['rɛphuːn] *nt* (*KOCH, ZOOL*)
partridge

Rechen ['rɛçən] (**-s, -**) *m* rake

Rechen- *zW:* **~fehler** *m* miscalculation;
~maschine *f* calculating machine;
~schaft *f* account; **für etw ~schaft
ablegen** to account for sth; **~schieber** *m*
slide rule

Rech- ['rɛç] *zW:* **r~nen** *vt, vi* to calculate;
jdn/etw r~nen zu to count sb/sth among;
r~nen mit to reckon with; **r~nen auf** +*akk*
to count on; **~nen** *nt* arithmetic; **~ner** (**-s,
-**) *m* calculator; (*COMPUT*) computer; **~nung**
f calculation(s); (*COMM*) bill, check (*US*);
jdm/etw ~nung tragen to take sb/sth into
account; **~nungsbetrag** *m* total amount
of a bill/invoice; **~nungsjahr** *nt* financial
year; **~nungsprüfer** *m* auditor

Recht [rɛçt] (**-(e)s, -e**) *nt* right; (*JUR*) law;
mit ~ rightly, justly; **R~ haben** to be right;
jdm R~ geben to agree with sb; **von ~s
wegen** by rights

recht *adj* right ♦ *adv* (*vor Adjektiv*) really,
quite; **das ist mir ~** that suits me; **jetzt
erst ~** now more than ever

Rechte *f* right (hand); (*POL*) Right; **r~(r, s)**
adj right; (*POL*) right-wing; **ein ~r** a right-

winger; **~(s)** nt right thing; **etwas/nichts ~s** something/nothing proper

recht- zW: **~eckig** adj rectangular; **~fertigen** vt insep to justify ♦ vr insep to justify o.s.; **R~fertigung** f justification; **~haberisch** (pej) adj (Mensch) opinionated; **~lich** adj (gesetzlich: Gleichstellung, Anspruch) legal; **~los** adj with no rights; **~mäßig** adj legal, lawful

rechts [reçts] adv on/to the right; **R~anwalt** m lawyer, barrister; **R~anwältin** f lawyer, barrister

Rechtschreibung f spelling

Rechts- zW: **~fall** m (law) case; **~händer** (-s, -) m right-handed person; **r~kräftig** adj valid, legal; **~kurve** f right-hand bend; **r~verbindlich** adj legally binding; **~verkehr** m driving on the right; **r~widrig** adj illegal; **~wissenschaft** f jurisprudence

rechtwinklig adj right-angled

rechtzeitig adj timely ♦ adv in time

Reck [rɛk] (-(e)s, -e) nt horizontal bar; **r~en** vt, vr to stretch

recyceln [riː'saɪkəln] vt to recycle; **Recycling** [riː'saɪklɪŋ] (-s) nt recycling

Redakteur [redak'tøːr] m editor

Redaktion [redaktsi'oːn] f editing; (Leute) editorial staff; (Büro) editorial office(s)

Rede ['reːdə] f speech; (Gespräch) talk; **jdn zur ~ stellen** to take sb to task; **~freiheit** f freedom of speech; **r~gewandt** adj eloquent; **r~n** vi to talk, to speak ♦ vt to say; (Unsinn etc) to talk; **~nsart** f set phrase

redlich ['reːtlɪç] adj honest

Redner (-s, -) m speaker, orator

redselig ['reːtzeːlɪç] adj talkative, loquacious

reduzieren [redu'tsiːrən] vt to reduce

Reede ['reːdə] f protected anchorage; **~r** (-s, -) m shipowner; **~rei** f shipping line od firm

reell [re'ɛl] adj fair, honest; (MATH) real

Refer- zW: **~at** [refe'raːt] (-(e)s, -e) nt report; (Vortrag) paper; (Gebiet) section; **~ent** [refe'rɛnt] m speaker; (Berichterstatter) reporter; (Sachbearbeiter) expert; **r~ieren** [refe'riːrən] vi: **r~ieren über** +akk to speak

od talk on

reflektieren [reflɛk'tiːrən] vt (Licht) to reflect

Reflex [re'flɛks] (-es, -e) m reflex; **r~iv** [-'ksiːf] adj (GRAM) reflexive

Reform [re'fɔrm] (-, -en) f reform; **~ation** f reformation; **~ationstag** m Reformation Day; **~haus** nt health food shop; **r~ieren** [-'miːrən] vt to reform

Regal [re'gaːl] (-s, -e) nt (book)shelves pl, bookcase; stand, rack

rege ['reːgə] adj (lebhaft: Treiben) lively; (wach, lebendig: Geist) keen

Regel ['reːgəl] (-, -n) f rule; (MED) period; **r~mäßig** adj regular; **~mäßigkeit** f regularity; **r~n** vt to regulate, to control; (Angelegenheit) to settle ♦ vr: **sich von selbst r~n** to take care of itself; **r~recht** adj regular, proper, thorough; **~ung** f regulation; settlement; **r~widrig** adj irregular, against the rules

Regen ['reːgən] (-s, -) m rain; **~bogen** m rainbow; **~bogenpresse** f tabloids pl

regenerierbar [regene'riːrbaːr] adj renewable

Regen- zW: **~mantel** m raincoat, mac(kintosh); **~schauer** m shower (of rain); **~schirm** m umbrella; **~wald** m (GEOG) rainforest; **~wurm** m earthworm; **~zeit** f rainy season

Regie [re'ʒiː] f (Film etc) direction; (THEAT) production

Regier- [re'giːr] zW: **r~en** vt, vi to govern, to rule; **~ung** f government; (Monarchie) reign; **~ungssitz** m seat of government; **~ungswechsel** m change of government; **~ungszeit** f period in government; (von König) reign

Regiment [regi'mɛnt] (-s, -er) nt regiment

Region [regi'oːn] f region

Regisseur [reʒɪ'søːr] m director; (THEAT) (stage) producer

Register [re'gɪstər] (-s, -) nt register; (in Buch) table of contents, index

registrieren [regɪs'triːrən] vt to register

Regler ['reːglər] (-s, -) m regulator, governor

reglos ['reːkloːs] adj motionless

regnen ['reːgnən] vi unpers to rain

regnerisch *adj* rainy

regulär [regu'lɛːr] *adj* regular

regulieren [regu'liːrən] *vt* to regulate; (*COMM*) to settle

Regung ['reːɡʊŋ] *f* motion; (*Gefühl*) feeling, impulse; **r~slos** *adj* motionless

Reh [reː] **(-(e)s, -e)** *nt* deer, roe; **~bock** *m* roebuck; **~kitz** *nt* fawn

Reib- ['raɪb] *zW:* **~e** *f* grater; **~eisen** *nt* grater; **r~en** (*unreg*) *vt* to rub; (*KOCH*) to grate; **~fläche** *f* rough surface; **~ung** *f* friction; **r~ungslos** *adj* smooth

Reich **(-(e)s, -e)** *nt* empire, kingdom; (*fig*) realm; **das Dritte R~** the Third Reich

reich [raɪç] *adj* rich

reichen *vi* to reach; (*genügen*) to be enough *od* sufficient ♦ *vt* to hold out; (*geben*) to pass, to hand; (*anbieten*) to offer; **jdm ~** to be enough *od* sufficient for sb

reich- *zW:* **~haltig** *adj* ample, rich; **~lich** *adj* ample, plenty of; **R~tum (-s)** *m* wealth; **R~weite** *f* range

Reif **(-(e)s, -e)** *m* (*Ring*) ring, hoop

reif [raɪf] *adj* ripe; (*Mensch, Urteil*) mature

Reife (-) *f* ripeness; maturity; **r~n** *vi* to mature; to ripen

Reifen **(-s, -)** *m* ring, hoop; (*Fahrzeugreifen*) tyre; **~druck** *m* tyre pressure; **~panne** *f* puncture

Reihe ['raɪə] *f* row; (*von Tagen etc, umg: Anzahl*) series *sg*; **der ~ nach** in turn; **er ist an der ~** it's his turn; **an die ~ kommen** to have one's turn

Reihen- *zW:* **~folge** *f* sequence; **alphabetische ~folge** alphabetical order; **~haus** *nt* terraced house

reihum [raɪ'ʊm] *adv:* **es geht/wir machen das ~** we take turns

Reim [raɪm] **(-(e)s, -e)** *m* rhyme; **r~en** *vt* to rhyme

rein[1] [raɪn] (*umg*) *adv* = **herein; hinein**

rein[2] [raɪn] *adj* pure; (*sauber*) clean ♦ *adv* purely; **etw ins R~e schreiben** to make a fair copy of sth; **etw ins R~e bringen** to clear up sth; **R~fall** (*umg*) *m* let-down; **R~gewinn** *m* net profit; **R~heit** *f* purity; cleanness; **~igen** *vt* to clean; (*Wasser*) to

purify; **R~igung** *f* cleaning; purification; (*Geschäft*) cleaner's; **chemische R~igung** dry cleaning; dry cleaner's; **R~igungsmittel** *nt* cleansing agent; **~rassig** *adj* pedigree; **R~schrift** *f* fair copy

Reis [raɪs] **(-es, -e)** *m* rice

Reise ['raɪzə] *f* journey; (*Schiffsreise*) voyage; **~n** *pl* (*Herumreisen*) travels; **gute ~!** have a good journey; **~apotheke** *f* first-aid kit; **~büro** *nt* travel agency; **r~fertig** *adj* ready to start; **~führer** *m* guide(book); (*Mensch*) travel guide; **~gepäck** *nt* luggage; **~gesellschaft** *f* party of travellers; **~kosten** *pl* travelling expenses; **~leiter** *m* courier; **~lektüre** *f* reading matter for the journey; **r~n** *vi* to travel; **r~n nach** to go to; **~nde(r)** *f(m)* traveller; **~pass** ▲ *m* passport; **~proviant** *m* food and drink for the journey; **~route** *f* route, itinerary; **~ruf** *m* personal message; **~scheck** *m* traveller's cheque; **~veranstalter** *m* tour operator; **~versicherung** *f* travel insurance; **~ziel** *nt* destination

Reißbrett *nt* drawing board

reißen ['raɪsən] (*unreg*) *vt* to tear; (*ziehen*) to pull, to drag; (*Witz*) to crack ♦ *vi* to tear; to pull, to drag; **etw an sich ~** to snatch sth up; (*fig*) to take over sth; **sich um etw ~** to scramble for sth; **~d** *adj* (*Fluss*) raging; (*WIRTS: Verkauf*) rapid

Reiß- *zW:* **~verschluss** ▲ *m* zip(per), zip fastener; **~zwecke** *m* drawing pin (*BRIT*), thumbtack (*US*)

Reit- ['raɪt] *zW:* **r~en** (*unreg*) *vt, vi* to ride; **~er (-s, -)** *m* rider; (*MIL*) cavalryman, trooper; **~erin** *f* rider; **~hose** *f* riding breeches *pl*; **~pferd** *nt* saddle horse; **~stiefel** *m* riding boot; **~weg** *n* bridle path; **~zeug** *nt* riding outfit

Reiz [raɪts] **(-es, -e)** *m* stimulus; (*angenehm*) charm; (*Verlockung*) attraction; **r~bar** *adj* irritable; **~barkeit** *f* irritability; **r~en** *vt* to stimulate; (*unangenehm*) to irritate; (*verlocken*) to appeal to, to attract; **r~end** *adj* charming; **r~voll** *adj* attractive

rekeln ['reːkəln] *vr* to stretch out; (*lümmeln*)

to lounge *od* loll about

Reklamation [reklamatsi'o:n] *f* complaint

Reklame [re'kla:mə] *f* advertising; advertisement; **~ machen für etw** to advertise sth

rekonstruieren [rekɔnstru'i:rən] *vt* to reconstruct

Rekord [re'kɔrt] **(-(e)s, -e)** *m* record; **~leistung** *f* record performance

Rektor ['rɛktɔr] *m* (*UNIV*) rector, vice-chancellor; (*SCH*) headteacher (*BRIT*), principal (*US*); **~at** [-'ra:t] **(-(e)s, -e)** *nt* rectorate, vice-chancellorship; headship; (*Zimmer*) rector's *etc* office

Relais [rə'le:] **(-, -)** *nt* relay

relativ [rela'ti:f] *adj* relative; **R~ität** [relativi'tɛ:t] *f* relativity

relevant [rele'vant] *adj* relevant

Relief [reli'ɛf] **(-s, -s)** *nt* relief

Religion [religi'o:n] *f* religion

religiös [religi'ø:s] *adj* religious

Reling ['re:lɪŋ] **(-, -s)** *f* (*NAUT*) rail

Remoulade [remu'la:də] *f* remoulade

Rendezvous [rãde'vu:] **(-, -)** *nt* rendezvous

Renn- ['rɛn] *zW:* **~bahn** *f* racecourse; (*AUT*) circuit, race track; **r~en** (*unreg*) *vt, vi* to run, to race; **~en (-s, -)** *nt* running; (*Wettbewerb*) race; **~fahrer** *m* racing driver; **~pferd** *nt* racehorse; **~wagen** *m* racing car

renommiert [renɔ'mi:rt] *adj* renowned

renovieren [reno'vi:rən] *vt* to renovate; **Renovierung** *f* renovation

rentabel [rɛn'ta:bəl] *adj* profitable, lucrative

Rentabilität [rɛntabili'tɛ:t] *f* profitability

Rente ['rɛntə] *f* pension

Rentenversicherung *f* pension scheme

rentieren [rɛn'ti:rən] *vr* to pay, to be profitable

Rentner(in) ['rɛntnər(ɪn)] **(-s, -)** *m(f)* pensioner

Reparatur [repara'tu:r] *f* repairing; repair; **~werkstatt** *f* repair shop; (*AUT*) garage

reparieren [repa'ri:rən] *vt* to repair

Reportage [repɔr'ta:ʒə] *f* (on-the-spot) report; (*TV, RADIO*) live commentary *od* coverage

Reporter [re'pɔrtər] **(-s, -)** *m* reporter, commentator

repräsentativ [reprɛzenta'ti:f] *adj* (*stellvertretend, typisch: Menge, Gruppe*) representative; (*beeindruckend: Haus, Auto etc*) impressive

repräsentieren [reprɛzen'ti:rən] *vt* (*Staat, Firma*) to represent; (*darstellen: Wert*) to constitute ♦ *vi* (*gesellschaftlich*) to perform official duties

Repressalie [reprɛ'sa:liə] *f* reprisal

Reprivatisierung [reprivati'zi:rʊŋ] *f* denationalization

Reproduktion [reprodʊktsi'o:n] *f* reproduction

reproduzieren [reprodu'tsi:rən] *vt* to reproduce

Reptil [rɛp'ti:l] **(-s, -ien)** *nt* reptile

Republik [repu'bli:k] *f* republic; **r~anisch** *adj* republican

Reservat [rezɛr'va:t] **(-(e)s, -e)** *nt* reservation

Reserve [re'zɛrvə] *f* reserve; **~rad** *nt* (*AUT*) spare wheel; **~spieler** *m* reserve; **~tank** *m* reserve tank

reservieren [rezɛr'vi:rən] *vt* to reserve

Reservoir [rezɛrvo'a:r] **(-s, -e)** *nt* reservoir

Residenz [rezi'dɛnts] *f* residence, seat

resignieren [rezɪ'gni:rən] *vi* to resign

resolut [rezo'lu:t] *adj* resolute

Resonanz [rezo'nants] *f* resonance; (*fig*) response

Resozialisierung [rezotsiali'zi:rʊŋ] *f* rehabilitation

Respekt [re'spɛkt] **(-(e)s)** *m* respect; **r~ieren** [-'ti:rən] *vt* to respect; **r~los** *adj* disrespectful; **r~voll** *adj* respectful

Ressort [re'so:r] **(-s, -s)** *nt* department

Rest [rɛst] **(-(e)s, -e)** *m* remainder, rest; (*Überrest*) remains *pl*

Restaurant [rɛsto'rã:] **(-s, -s)** *nt* restaurant

restaurieren [rɛstau'ri:rən] *vt* to restore

Rest- *zW:* **~betrag** *m* remainder, outstanding sum; **r~lich** *adj* remaining; **r~los** *adj* complete

Resultat [rezʊl'ta:t] **(-(e)s, -e)** *nt* result

Retorte [re'tɔrtə] *f* retort

Retouren [re'tuːrən] *pl* (COMM) returns

retten ['rɛtən] *vt* to save, to rescue

Retter(in) *m(f)* rescuer

Rettich ['rɛtɪç] **(-s, -e)** *m* radish

Rettung *f* rescue; (Hilfe) help; **seine letzte ~** his last hope

Rettungs- *zW:* **~boot** *nt* lifeboat; **~dienst** *m* rescue service; **r~los** *adj* hopeless; **~ring** *m* lifebelt, life preserver (US); **~wagen** *m* ambulance

retuschieren [retu'ʃiːrən] *vt* (PHOT) to retouch

Reue ['rɔyə] **(-)** *f* remorse; (Bedauern) regret; **r~n** *vt:* **es reut ihn** he regrets (it) *od* is sorry (about it)

Revanche [re'vãːʃə] *f* revenge; (SPORT) return match

revanchieren [revã'ʃiːrən] *vr* (sich rächen) to get one's own back, to have one's revenge; (erwidern) to reciprocate, to return the compliment

Revier [re'viːr] **(-s, -e)** *nt* district; (Jagdrevier) preserve; (Polizeirevier) police station; beat

Revolte [re'vɔltə] *f* revolt

revol'tieren *vi* (gegen jdn/etw) to rebel

Revolution [revolutsi'oːn] *f* revolution; **~är** [-'nɛːr] **(-s, -e)** *m* revolutionary; **r~ieren** [-'niːrən] *vt* to revolutionize

Rezept [re'tsɛpt] **(-(e)s, -e)** *nt* recipe; (MED) prescription; **r~frei** *adj* available without prescription; **~ion** *f* reception; **r~pflichtig** *adj* available only on prescription

R-Gespräch ['ɛrgəʃprɛːç] *nt* reverse charge call (BRIT), collect call (US)

Rhabarber [ra'barbər] **(-s)** *m* rhubarb

Rhein [raɪn] **(-s)** *m* Rhine; **r~isch** *adj* Rhenish

Rheinland-Pfalz *nt* (GEOG) Rheinland-Pfalz, Rhineland-Palatinate

Rhesusfaktor ['reːzusfaktɔr] *m* rhesus factor

rhetorisch [re'toːrɪʃ] *adj* rhetorical

Rheuma ['rɔyma] **(-s)** *nt* rheumatism; **r~tisch** [-'maːtɪʃ] *adj* rheumatic

rhythmisch ['rytmɪʃ] *adj* rhythmical

Rhythmus ['rytmʊs] *m* rhythm

richt- ['rɪçt] *zW:* **~en** *vt* to direct; (Waffe) to aim; (einstellen) to adjust; (instandsetzen) to repair; (zurechtmachen) to prepare; (bestrafen) to pass judgement on ♦ *vr:* **sich ~en nach** to go by; **~en an** +akk to direct at; (fig) to direct to; **~en auf** +akk to aim at; **R~er(in)** **(-s, -)** *m(f)* judge; **~erlich** *adj* judicial; **R~geschwindigkeit** *f* recommended speed

richtig *adj* right, correct; (echt) proper ♦ *adv* (umg: sehr) really; **bin ich hier ~?** am I in the right place?; **der/die R~e** the right one/person; **das R~e** the right thing; **etw ~ stellen** to correct sth; **R~keit** *f* correctness

Richt- *zW:* **~linie** *f* guideline; **~preis** *m* recommended price

Richtung *f* direction; tendency, orientation

rieb *etc* [riːp] *vb siehe* **reiben**

riechen ['riːçən] (unreg) *vt, vi* to smell; **an etw** dat **~** to smell sth; **nach etw ~** to smell of sth; **ich kann das/ihn nicht ~** (umg) I can't stand it/him

rief *etc* [riːf] *vb siehe* **rufen**

Riegel ['riːgəl] **(-s, -)** *m* bolt; (Schokolade usw) bar

Riemen ['riːmən] **(-s, -)** *m* strap; (Gürtel, TECH) belt; (NAUT) oar

Riese ['riːzə] **(-n, -n)** *m* giant

rieseln *vi* to trickle; (Schnee) to fall gently

Riesen- *zW:* **~erfolg** *m* enormous success; **r~groß** *adj* colossal, gigantic, huge; **~rad** *nt* big wheel

riesig ['riːzɪç] *adj* enormous, huge, vast

riet *etc* [riːt] *vb siehe* **raten**

Riff [rɪf] **(-(e)s, -e)** *nt* reef

Rille ['rɪlə] *f* groove

Rind [rɪnt] **(-(e)s, -er)** *nt* ox; cow; cattle *pl*; (KOCH) beef

Rinde ['rɪndə] *f* rind; (Baumrinde) bark; (Brotrinde) crust

Rind- ['rɪnt] *zW:* **~fleisch** *nt* beef; **~vieh** *nt* cattle *pl*; (umg) blockhead, stupid oaf

Ring [rɪŋ] **(-(e)s, -e)** *m* ring; **~buch** *nt* ring binder; **r~en** (unreg) *vi* to wrestle; **~en** **(-s)** *nt* wrestling; **~finger** *m* ring finger; **~kampf** *m* wrestling bout; **~richter** *m* referee; **r~s** *adv:* **r~s um** round; **r~sherum** *adv* round about; **~straße** *f* ring road; **r~sum** adv (rundherum) round about; (überall) all round; **r~sumher** = **ringsum**

Rinn- ['rɪn] zW: **~e** f gutter, drain; **r~en** (unreg) vi to run, to trickle; **~stein** m gutter

Rippchen ['rɪpçən] nt small rib; cutlet

Rippe ['rɪpə] f rib

Risiko ['riːziko] (-s, -s od **Risiken**) nt risk

riskant [rɪs'kant] adj risky, hazardous

riskieren [rɪs'kiːrən] vt to risk

Riss ▲ [rɪs] (-es, -e) m tear; (in Mauer, Tasse etc) crack; (in Haut) scratch; (TECH) design

rissig ['rɪsɪç] adj torn; cracked; scratched

Ritt [rɪt] (-(e)s, -e) m ride

ritt etc vb siehe **reiten**

Ritter (-s, -) m knight; **r~lich** adj chivalrous

Ritze ['rɪtsə] f crack, chink

Rivale [ri'vaːlə] (-n, -n) m rival

Rivalität [rivali'tɛːt] f rivalry

Robbe ['rɔbə] f seal

Roboter ['rɔbɔtər] (-s, -) m robot

robust [ro'bʊst] adj (kräftig: Mensch, Gesundheit) robust

roch etc [rɔx] vb siehe **riechen**

Rock [rɔk] (-(e)s, ᵉe) m skirt; (Jackett) jacket; (Uniformrock) tunic

Rodel ['roːdəl] (-s, -) m toboggan; **~bahn** f toboggan run; **r~n** vi to toboggan

Rogen ['roːgən] (-s, -) m roe, spawn

Roggen ['rɔgən] (-s, -) m rye; **~brot** nt (KOCH) rye bread

roh [roː] adj raw; (Mensch) coarse, crude; **R~bau** m shell of a building; **R~material** nt raw material; **R~öl** nt crude oil

Rohr [roːr] (-(e)s, -e) nt pipe, tube; (BOT) cane; (Schilf) reed; (Gewehrrohr) barrel; **~bruch** m burst pipe

Röhre ['røːrə] f tube, pipe; (RADIO etc) valve; (Backröhre) oven

Rohr- zW: **~leitung** f pipeline; **~zucker** m cane sugar

Rohstoff m raw material

Rokoko ['rɔkoko] (-s) nt rococo

Rolladen △ m siehe **Rollladen**

Rollbahn ['rɔlbaːn] f (AVIAT) runway

Rolle ['rɔlə] f roll; (THEAT, soziologisch) role; (Garnrolle etc) reel, spool; (Walze) roller;

(Wäscherolle) mangle; **keine ~ spielen** not to matter; **eine (wichtige) ~ spielen bei** to play a (major) part od role in; **r~n** vt, vi to roll; (AVIAT) to taxi; **~r (-s, -)** m scooter; (Welle) roller

Roll- zW: **~kragen** m rollneck, polo neck; **~laden** ▲ m shutter; **~mops** m pickled herring; **~schuh** m roller skate; **~stuhl** m wheelchair; **~stuhlfahrer(in)** m(f) wheelchair user; **~treppe** f escalator

Rom [roːm] (-s) nt Rome

Roman [ro'maːn] (-s, -e) m novel; **~tik** f romanticism; **~tiker** [ro'mantɪkər] (-s, -) m romanticist; **r~tisch** [ro'mantɪʃ] adj romantic; **~ze** [ro'mantsə] f romance

Römer ['røːmər] (-s, -) m wineglass; (Mensch) Roman

römisch ['røːmɪʃ] adj Roman; **~-katholisch** adj (REL) Roman Catholic

röntgen ['rœntgən] vt to X-ray; **R~bild** nt X-ray; **R~strahlen** pl X-rays

rosa ['roːza] adj inv pink, rose(-coloured)

Rose ['roːzə] f rose

Rosen- zW: **~kohl** m Brussels sprouts pl; **~kranz** m rosary; **~montag** m Monday before Ash Wednesday

rosig ['roːzɪç] adj rosy

Rosine [ro'ziːnə] f raisin, currant

Ross ▲ [rɔs] (-es, -e) nt horse, steed; **~kastanie** f horse chestnut

Rost [rɔst] (-(e)s, -e) m rust; (Gitter) grill, gridiron; (Bettrost) springs pl; **~braten** m roast(ed) meat, roast; **r~en** vi to rust

rösten ['rœstən] vt to roast; to toast; to grill

Rost- zW: **r~frei** adj rust-free; rustproof; stainless; **r~ig** adj rusty; **~schutz** m rust-proofing

rot [roːt] adj red; **in den ~en Zahlen** in the red

Röte ['røːtə] (-) f redness; **~ln** pl German measles sg; **r~n** vt, vr to redden

rothaarig adj red-haired

rotieren [ro'tiːrən] vi to rotate

Rot- zW: **~kehlchen** nt robin; **~stift** m red pencil; **~wein** m red wine

Rouge [ruːʒ] nt blusher

Roulade [ru'laːdə] f (KOCH) beef olive

Route [ˈruːtə] f route

Routine [ruˈtiːnə] f experience; routine

Rübe [ˈryːbə] f turnip; **Gelbe ~** carrot; **Rote ~** beetroot (*BRIT*), beet (*US*)

rüber [ˈryːbər] (*umg*) *adv* = **herüber; hinüber**

Rubrik [ruˈbriːk] f heading; (*Spalte*) column

Ruck [rʊk] (-(e)s, -e) m jerk, jolt

Rück- [ˈrʏk] *zW*: **~antwort** f reply, answer; **r~bezüglich** *adj* reflexive

Rücken [ˈrʏkən] (-s, -) m back; (*Bergrücken*) ridge

rücken *vt, vi* to move

Rücken- *zW*: **~mark** *nt* spinal cord; **~schwimmen** *nt* backstroke

Rück- *zW*: **~erstattung** f return, restitution; **~fahrkarte** f return (ticket); **~fahrt** f return journey; **~fall** m relapse; **r~fällig** *adj* relapsing; **r~fällig werden** to relapse; **~flug** m return flight; **~frage** f question; **r~fragen** *vi* to check, to inquire (further); **~gabe** f return; **~gaberecht** *nt* right of return; **~gang** m decline, fall; **r~gängig** *adj*: **etw r~gängig machen** to cancel sth; **~grat** (-(e)s, -e) *nt* spine, backbone; **~halt** m (*Unterstützung*) backing, support; **~kehr** (-, -en) f return; **~licht** *nt* back light; **r~lings** *adv* from behind; backwards; **~nahme** f taking back; **~porto** *nt* return postage; **~reise** f return journey; (*NAUT*) home voyage; **~reiseverkehr** m homebound traffic; **~ruf** m recall

Rucksack [ˈrʊkzak] m rucksack; **~tourist(in)** m(f) backpacker

Rück- *zW*: **~schau** f reflection; **~schlag** m (*plötzliche Verschlechterung*) setback; **~schluss** ▲ m conclusion; **~schritt** m retrogression; **r~schrittlich** *adj* reactionary; retrograde; **~seite** f back; (*von Münze etc*) reverse; **~sicht** f consideration; **~sicht nehmen auf** +*akk* to show consideration for; **r~sichtslos** *adj* inconsiderate; (*Fahren*) reckless; (*unbarmherzig*) ruthless; **r~sichtsvoll** *adj* considerate; **~sitz** m back seat; **~spiegel** m (*AUT*) rear-view mirror; **~spiel** *nt* return match; **~sprache** f further discussion *od* talk; **~stand** m arrears *pl*; **r~ständig** *adj* backward, out-of-date; (*Zahlungen*) in arrears; **~strahler** (-s, -) m rear reflector; **~tritt** m resignation; **~trittbremse** f pedal brake; **~vergütung** f repayment; (*COMM*) refund; **~versicherung** f reinsurance; **r~wärtig** *adj* rear; **r~wärts** *adv* backward(s), back; **~wärtsgang** m (*AUT*) reverse gear; **~weg** m return journey, way back; **r~wirkend** *adj* retroactive; **~wirkung** f reaction; retrospective effect; **~zahlung** f repayment; **~zug** m retreat

Rudel [ˈruːdəl] (-s, -) *nt* pack; herd

Ruder [ˈruːdər] (-s, -) *nt* oar; (*Steuer*) rudder; **~boot** *nt* rowing boat; **r~n** *vt, vi* to row

Ruf [ruːf] (-(e)s, -e) m call, cry; (*Ansehen*) reputation; **r~en** (*unreg*) *vt, vi* to call; to cry; **~name** m usual (first) name; **~nummer** f (tele)phone number; **~säule** f (*an Autobahn*) emergency telephone; **~zeichen** *nt* (*RADIO*) call sign; (*TEL*) ringing tone

rügen [ˈryːgən] *vt* to rebuke

Ruhe [ˈruːə] (-) f rest; (*Ungestörtheit*) peace, quiet; (*Gelassenheit, Stille*) calm; (*Schweigen*) silence; **jdn in ~ lassen** to leave sb alone; **sich zur ~ setzen** to retire; **~! be quiet!**, silence!; **r~n** *vi* to rest; **~pause** f break; **~stand** m retirement; **~stätte** f: **letzte ~stätte** final resting place; **~störung** f breach of the peace; **~tag** m (*von Geschäft*) closing day

ruhig [ˈruːɪç] *adj* quiet; (*bewegungslos*) still; (*Hand*) steady; (*gelassen, friedlich*) calm; (*Gewissen*) clear; **kommen Sie ~ herein** just come on in; **tu das ~** feel free to do that

Ruhm [ruːm] (-(e)s) m fame, glory

rühmen [ˈryːmən] *vt* to praise ♦ *vr* to boast

Rühr- [ryːr] *zW*: **~ei** *nt* scrambled egg; **r~en** *vt, vr* (*auch fig*) to move, to stir ♦ *vi*: **r~en von** to come *od* stem from; **r~en an** +*akk* to touch; (*fig*) to touch on; **r~end** *adj* touching, moving; **r~selig** *adj* sentimental, emotional; **~ung** f emotion

Ruin [ruˈiːn] (-s, -e) m ruin; **~e** f ruin; **r~ieren** [-ˈniːrən] *vt* to ruin

rülpsen [ˈrʏlpsən] *vi* to burp, to belch

Rum [rʊm] (-s, -s) m rum

Rumän- [ru'mɛːn] zW: **~ien** (**-s**) nt Ro(u)mania; **r~isch** adj Ro(u)manian

Rummel ['roməl] (**-s**) (umg) m hubbub; (Jahrmarkt) fair; **~platz** m fairground, fair

Rumpf [rompf] (**-(e)s, ⁓e**) m trunk, torso; (AVIAT) fuselage; (NAUT) hull

rümpfen ['rympfən] vt (Nase) to turn up

rund [ront] adj round ♦ adv (etwa) around; **~ um etw** round sth; **R~brief** m circular; **R~e** ['rondə] f round; (in Rennen) lap; (Gesellschaft) circle; **R~fahrt** f (round) trip

Rundfunk ['rontfoŋk] m broadcasting; **im ~** on the radio; **~gerät** nt wireless set; **~sendung** f broadcast, radio programme

Rund- zW: **r~heraus** adv straight out, bluntly; **r~herum** adv round about; all round; **r~lich** adj plump, rounded; **~reise** f round trip; **~schreiben** nt (COMM) circular; **~(wander)weg** m circular path od route

runter ['rontər] (umg) adv = **herunter**; **hinunter**

Runzel ['rontsəl] (**-, -n**) f wrinkle; **r~ig** adj wrinkled; **r~n** vt to wrinkle; **die Stirn r~n** to frown

rupfen ['ropfən] vt to pluck

ruppig ['ropɪç] adj rough, gruff

Rüsche ['ryːʃə] f frill

Ruß [ruːs] (**-es**) m soot

Russe ['rosə] (**-n, -n**) m Russian

Rüssel ['rysəl] (**-s, -**) m snout; (Elefantenrüssel) trunk

rußig ['ruːsɪç] adj sooty

Russin ['rosɪn] f Russian

russisch adj Russian

Russland ▲ ['roslant] (**-s**) nt Russia

rüsten ['rystən] vt to prepare ♦ vi to prepare; (MIL) to arm ♦ vr to prepare (o.s.); to arm o.s.

rüstig ['rystɪç] adj sprightly, vigorous

Rüstung ['rystoŋ] f preparation; arming; (Ritterrüstung) armour; (Waffen etc) armaments pl; **~skontrolle** f arms control

Rute ['ruːtə] f rod

Rutsch [rotʃ] (**-(e)s, -e**) m slide; (Erdrutsch) landslide; **~bahn** f slide; **r~en** vi to slide;

(ausrutschen) to slip; **r~ig** adj slippery

rütteln ['rytəln] vt, vi to shake, to jolt

S, s

S. abk (= Seite) p.; = **Schilling**

s. abk (= siehe) see

Saal [zaːl] (**-(e)s, Säle**) m hall; room

Saarland ['zaːrlant] nt: **das ~** the Saar(land)

Saat [zaːt] (**-, -en**) f seed; (Pflanzen) crop; (Säen) sowing

Säbel ['zɛːbəl] (**-s, -**) m sabre, sword

Sabotage [zabo'taːʒə] f sabotage

Sach- [zax] zW: **~bearbeiter** m specialist; **s~dienlich** adj relevant, helpful; **~e** f thing; (Angelegenheit) affair, business; (Frage) matter; (Pflicht) task; **zur ~e** to the point; **s~kundig** adj expert; **s~lich** adj matter-of-fact; objective; (Irrtum, Angabe) factual

sächlich ['zɛxlɪç] adj neuter

Sachschaden m material damage

Sachsen ['zaksən] (**-s**) nt Saxony

sächsisch ['zɛksɪʃ] adj Saxon

sacht(e) ['zaxt(ə)] adv softly, gently

Sachverständige(r) f(m) expert

Sack [zak] (**-(e)s, ⁓e**) m sack; **~gasse** f cul-de-sac, dead-end street (US)

Sadismus [za'dɪsmʊs] m sadism

Sadist [za'dɪst] m sadist

säen ['zɛːən] vt, vi to sow

Safersex ▲, **Safer Sex** m safe sex

Saft [zaft] (**-(e)s, ⁓e**) m juice; (BOT) sap; **s~ig** adj juicy; **s~los** adj dry

Sage ['zaːgə] f saga

Säge ['zɛːgə] f saw; **~mehl** nt sawdust

sagen ['zaːgən] vt, vi to say; (mitteilen): **jdm ~** to tell sb; **~ Sie ihm, dass ...** tell him ...

sägen vt, vi to saw

sagenhaft adj legendary; (umg) great, smashing

sah etc [zaː] vb siehe **sehen**

Sahne ['zaːnə] (**-**) f cream

Saison [zɛ'zõː] (**-, -s**) f season

Saite ['zaɪtə] f string

Sakko ['zako] **(-s, -s)** *m od nt* jacket
Sakrament [zakra'mɛnt] *nt* sacrament
Sakristei [zakrıs'taı] *f* sacristy
Salat [za'laːt] **(-(e)s, -e)** *m* salad; *(Kopfsalat)* lettuce; **~soße** *f* salad dressing
Salbe ['zalbə] *f* ointment
Salbei ['zalbaı] **(-s** *od* **-)** *m od f* sage
Saldo ['zaldo] **(-s, Salden)** *m* balance
Salmiak [zalmi'ak] **(-s)** *m* sal ammoniac; **~geist** *m* liquid ammonia
Salmonellenvergiftung [zalmo'nɛlən-] *f* salmonella (poisoning)
salopp [za'lɔp] *adj* casual
Salpeter [zal'peːtər] **(-s)** *m* saltpetre; **~säure** *f* nitric acid
Salz [zalts] **(-es, -e)** *nt* salt; **s~en** *(unreg)* *vt* to salt; **s~ig** *adj* salty; **~kartoffeln** *pl* boiled potatoes; **~säure** *f* hydrochloric acid; **~streuer** *m* salt cellar; **~wasser** *nt (Meerwasser)* salt water
Samen ['zaːmən] **(-s, -)** *m* seed; *(ANAT)* sperm
Sammel- ['zaməl] *zW:* **~band** *m* anthology; **~fahrschein** *m* multi-journey ticket; *(für mehrere Personen)* group ticket
sammeln ['zaməln] *vt* to collect ♦ *vr* to assemble, to gather; *(konzentrieren)* to concentrate
Sammlung ['zamlʊŋ] *f* collection; assembly, gathering; concentration
Samstag ['zamstaːk] *m* Saturday; **s~s** *adv* (on) Saturdays
Samt [zamt] **(-(e)s, -e)** *m* velvet; **s~** *präp* +*dat* (along) with, together with; **s~ und sonders** each and every one (of them)
sämtlich ['zɛmtlıç] *adj* all (the), entire
Sand [zant] **(-(e)s, -e)** *m* sand
Sandale [zan'daːlə] *f* sandal
Sand- *zW:* **~bank** *f* sandbank; **s~ig** ['zandıç] *adj* sandy; **~kasten** *m* sandpit; **~kuchen** *m* Madeira cake; **~papier** *nt* sandpaper; **~stein** *m* sandstone; **s~strahlen** *vt, vi insep* to sandblast; **~strand** *m* sandy beach
sandte *etc* ['zantə] *vb siehe* **senden**
sanft [zanft] *adj* soft, gentle; **~mütig** *adj* gentle, meek

sang *etc* [zaŋ] *vb siehe* **singen**
Sänger(in) ['zɛŋər(ın)] **(-s, -)** *m(f)* singer
Sani- *zW:* **s~eren** [za'niːrən] *vt* to redevelop; *(Betrieb)* to make financially sound ♦ *vr* to line one's pockets; to become financially sound; **s~tär** [zani'tɛːr] *adj* sanitary; **s~täre Anlagen** sanitation *sg*; **~täter** [zani'tɛːtər] **(-s, -)** *m* first-aid attendant; *(MIL)* (medical) orderly
sanktionieren [zaŋktsio'niːrən] *vt* to sanction
Sardelle [zar'dɛlə] *f* anchovy
Sardine [zar'diːnə] *f* sardine
Sarg [zark] **(-(e)s, ⁻e)** *m* coffin
Sarkasmus [zar'kasmʊs] *m* sarcasm
saß *etc* [zaːs] *vb siehe* **sitzen**
Satan ['zaːtan] **(-s, -e)** *m* Satan; devil
Satellit [zate'liːt] **(-en, -en)** *m* satellite; **~enfernsehen** *nt* satellite television
Satire [za'tiːrə] *f* satire; **satirisch** *adj* satirical
satt [zat] *adj* full; *(Farbe)* rich, deep; **jdn/etw ~ sein** *od* **haben** to be fed up with sb/sth; **sich ~ hören/sehen an** +*dat* to hear/see enough of; **sich ~ essen** to eat one's fill; **~ machen** to be filling
Sattel ['zatəl] **(-s, ⁻)** *m* saddle; *(Berg)* ridge; **s~n** *vt* to saddle; **~schlepper** *m* articulated lorry
sättigen ['zɛtıgən] *vt* to satisfy; *(CHEM)* to saturate
Satz [zats] **(-es, ⁻e)** *m (GRAM)* sentence; *(Nebensatz, Adverbialsatz)* clause; *(Theorem)* theorem; *(MUS)* movement; *(TENNIS)* set; *(Briefmarken etc)* set; *(Kaffee)* grounds *pl*; *(COMM)* rate; *(Sprung)* jump; **~teil** *m* part of a sentence; **~ung** *f (Statut)* statute, rule; **~zeichen** *nt* punctuation mark
Sau [zau] **(-, Säue)** *f* sow; *(umg)* dirty pig
sauber ['zaubər] *adj* clean; *(ironisch)* fine; **~ halten** to keep clean; **S~keit** *f* cleanness; *(einer Person)* cleanliness
säuberlich ['zɔybərlıç] *adv* neatly
säubern *vt* to clean; *(POL etc)* to purge; **Säuberung** *f* cleaning; purge
Sauce ['zoːsə] *f* sauce, gravy
sauer ['zauər] *adj* sour; *(CHEM)* acid; *(umg)*

cross; **saurer Regen** acid rain; **S~braten** m braised beef marinated in vinegar

Sauerei [zauəˈraɪ] (umg) f rotten state of affairs, scandal; (Schmutz etc) mess; (Unanständigkeit) obscenity

Sauerkraut nt sauerkraut, pickled cabbage

säuerlich [ˈzɔʏərlɪç] adj (Geschmack) sour; (missvergnügt: Gesicht) dour

Sauer- zW: **~milch** f sour milk; **~rahm** m (KOCH) sour cream; **~stoff** m oxygen; **~teig** m leaven

saufen [ˈzaufən] (unreg) (umg) vt, vi to drink, to booze; **Säufer** [ˈzɔʏfər] (-s, -) (umg) m boozer

saugen [ˈzaugən] (unreg) vt, vi to suck

säugen [ˈzɔʏgən] vt to suckle

Sauger [ˈzaugər] (-s, -) m dummy, comforter (US); (auf Flasche) teat

Säugetier [ˈzɔʏgə-] nt mammal

Säugling m infant, baby

Säule [ˈzɔʏlə] f column, pillar

Saum [zaum] (-(e)s, Säume) m hem; (Naht) seam

säumen [ˈzɔʏmən] vt to hem; to seam ♦ vi to delay, to hesitate

Sauna [ˈzauna] (-, -s) f sauna

Säure [ˈzɔʏrə] f acid

sausen [ˈzauzən] vi to blow; (umg: eilen) to rush; (Ohren) to buzz; **etw ~ lassen** (umg) not to bother with sth

Saxofon, Saxophon [zaksoˈfoːn] (-s, -e) nt saxophone

SB abk = **Selbstbedienung**

S-Bahn f abk (= Schnellbahn) high speed railway; (= Stadtbahn) suburban railway

schaben [ˈʃaːbən] vt to scrape

schäbig [ˈʃeːbɪç] adj shabby

Schablone [ʃaˈbloːnə] f stencil; (Muster) pattern; (fig) convention

Schach [ʃax] (-s, -s) nt chess; (Stellung) check; **~brett** nt chessboard; **~figur** f chessman; '**~**'**matt** adj checkmate; **~spiel** nt game of chess

Schacht [ʃaxt] (-(e)s, -e) m shaft

Schachtel [-, -n] f box

schade [ˈʃaːdə] adj a pity od shame ♦ excl: **(wie) ~!** (what a) pity od shame; **sich** dat

zu ~ sein für etw to consider o.s. too good for sth

Schädel [ˈʃeːdəl] (-s, -) m skull; **~bruch** m fractured skull

Schaden [ˈʃaːdən] (-s, -) m damage; (Verletzung) injury; (Nachteil) disadvantage; **s~** vi +dat to hurt; **einer Sache s~** to damage sth; **~ersatz** m compensation, damages pl; **~freude** f malicious glee; **s~froh** adj (Mensch, Lachen) gloating; **~sfall** m: **im ~sfall** in the event of a claim

schadhaft [ˈʃaːthaft] adj faulty, damaged

schäd- [ˈʃeːt] zW: **~igen** [ˈʃeːdɪgən] vt to damage; (Person) to do harm to, to harm; **~lich** adj: **~lich (für)** harmful (to); **S~lichkeit** f harmfulness; **S~ling** m pest

Schadstoff [ˈʃaːtʃtɔf] m harmful substance; **s~arm** adj: **s~arm sein** to contain a low level of harmful substances

Schaf [ʃaːf] (-(e)s, -e) nt sheep

Schäfer [ˈʃeːfər] (-s, -e) m shepherd; **~hund** m Alsatian (dog) (BRIT), German shepherd (dog) (US)

schaffen [ˈʃafən] (-s) nt (creative) activity

schaffen[1] [ˈʃafən] (unreg) vt to create; (Platz) to make

schaffen[2] [ˈʃafən] vt (erreichen) to manage, to do; (erledigen) to finish; (Prüfung) to pass; (transportieren) to take ♦ vi (umg: arbeiten) to work; **sich** dat **etw ~** to get o.s. sth; **sich an etw** dat **zu ~ machen** to busy o.s. with sth

Schaffner(in) [ˈʃafnər(ɪn)] (-s, -) m(f) (Busschaffner) conductor(-tress); (EISENB) guard

Schaft [ʃaft] (-(e)s, -e) m shaft; (von Gewehr) stock; (von Stiefel) leg; (BOT) stalk; tree trunk

Schal [ʃaːl] (-s, -e od -s) m scarf

schal adj flat; (fig) insipid

Schälchen [ˈʃeːlçən] nt cup, bowl

Schale [ˈʃaːlə] f skin; (abgeschält) peel; (Nussschale, Muschelschale, Eischale) shell; (Geschirr) dish, bowl

schälen [ˈʃeːlən] vt to peel; to shell ♦ vr to peel

Schall [ʃal] (-(e)s, -e) m sound; **~dämpfer** (-s, -) m (AUT) silencer; **s~dicht** adj soundproof; **s~en** *vi* to (re)sound; **s~end** *adj* resounding, loud; **~mauer** *f* sound barrier; **~platte** *f* (gramophone) record

Schalt- ['ʃalt] *zW:* **~bild** *nt* circuit diagram; **~brett** *nt* switchboard; **s~en** *vt* to switch, to turn ♦ *vi* (AUT) to change (gear); (*umg:* *begreifen*) to catch on; **~er** (**-s**, **-**) *m* counter; (*an Gerät*) switch; **~erbeamte(r)** *m* counter clerk; **~erstunden** *pl* hours of business; **~hebel** *m* switch; (AUT) gear lever; **~jahr** *nt* leap year; **~ung** *f* switching; (ELEK) circuit; (AUT) gear change

Scham [ʃaːm] (**-**) *f* shame; (*~gefühl*) modesty; (*Organe*) private parts *pl*

schämen ['ʃɛːmən] *vr* to be ashamed

schamlos *adj* shameless

Schande ['ʃandə] (**-**) *f* disgrace

schändlich ['ʃɛntlɪç] *adj* disgraceful, shameful

Schändung ['ʃɛndʊŋ] *f* violation, defilement

Schanze ['ʃantsə] *f* (*Sprungschanze*) ski jump

Schar [ʃaːr] (**-**, **-en**) *f* band, company; (*Vögel*) flock; (*Menge*) crowd; **in ~en** in droves; **s~en** *vr* to assemble, to rally

scharf [ʃarf] *adj* sharp; (*Essen*) hot, spicy; (*Munition*) live; **~ nachdenken** to think hard; **auf etw** *akk* **~ sein** (*umg*) to be keen on sth

Schärfe ['ʃɛrfə] *f* sharpness; (*Strenge*) rigour; **s~n** *vt* to sharpen

Scharf- *zW:* **s~machen** (*umg*) *vt* to stir up; **~richter** *m* executioner; **~schütze** *m* marksman, sharpshooter; **s~sinnig** *adj* astute, shrewd

Scharlach ['ʃarlax] (**-s**, **-e**) *m* (*~fieber*) scarlet fever

Scharnier [ʃar'niːr] (**-s**, **-e**) *nt* hinge

scharren ['ʃarən] *vt, vi* to scrape, to scratch

Schaschlik ['ʃaʃlɪk] (**-s**, **-s**) *m od nt* (shish) kebab

Schatten ['ʃatən] (**-s**, **-**) *m* shadow; **~riss** ▲ *m* silhouette; **~seite** *f* shady side, dark side

schattieren [ʃa'tiːrən] *vt, vi* to shade

schattig ['ʃatɪç] *adj* shady

Schatulle [ʃa'tʊlə] *f* casket; (*Geldschatulle*) coffer

Schatz [ʃats] (**-es**, **⁺e**) *m* treasure; (*Person*) darling

schätz- [ʃɛts] *zW:* **~bar** *adj* assessable; **S~chen** *nt* darling, love; **~en** *vt* (*abschätzen*) to estimate; (*Gegenstand*) to value; (*würdigen*) to value, to esteem; (*vermuten*) to reckon; **S~ung** *f* estimate; estimation; valuation; **nach meiner S~ung ...** I reckon that ...

Schau [ʃau] (**-**) *f* show; (*Ausstellung*) display, exhibition; **etw zur ~ stellen** to make a show of sth, to show sth off; **~bild** *nt* diagram

Schauder ['ʃaudər] (**-s**, **-s**) *m* shudder; (*wegen Kälte*) shiver; **s~haft** *adj* horrible; **s~n** *vi* to shudder; to shiver

schauen ['ʃauən] *vi* to look

Schauer ['ʃauər] (**-s**, **-**) *m* (*Regenschauer*) shower; (*Schreck*) shudder; **~geschichte** *f* horror story; **s~lich** *adj* horrific, spine-chilling

Schaufel ['ʃaufəl] (**-**, **-n**) *f* shovel; (NAUT) paddle; (TECH) scoop; **s~n** *vt* to shovel, to scoop

Schau- *zW:* **~fenster** *nt* shop window; **~fensterbummel** *m* window shopping (expedition); **~kasten** *m* showcase

Schaukel ['ʃaukəl] (**-**, **-n**) *f* swing; **s~n** *vi* to swing, to rock; **~pferd** *nt* rocking horse; **~stuhl** *m* rocking chair

Schaulustige(r) ['ʃaulʊstɪgə(r)] *f(m)* onlooker

Schaum [ʃaum] (**-(e)s**, **Schäume**) *m* foam; (*Seifenschaum*) lather; **~bad** *nt* bubble bath

schäumen ['ʃɔʏmən] *vi* to foam

Schaum- *zW:* **~festiger** (**-s**, **-**) *m* mousse; **~gummi** *m* foam (rubber); **s~ig** *adj* frothy, foamy; **~stoff** *m* foam material; **~wein** *m* sparkling wine

Schauplatz *m* scene

schaurig ['ʃauriç] *adj* horrific, dreadful

Schauspiel *nt* spectacle; (THEAT) play; **~er(in)** *m(f)* actor (actress); **s~ern** *vi insep* to act; **Schauspielhaus** *nt* theatre

Scheck [ʃɛk] (**-s**, **-s**) *m* cheque; **~gebühr** *f* encashment fee; **~heft** *m* cheque book; **~karte** *f* cheque card

scheffeln ['ʃefəln] vt to amass

Scheibe ['ʃaibə] f disc; (Brot etc) slice; (Glasscheibe) pane; (MIL) target

Scheiben- zW: **~bremse** f (AUT) disc brake; **~wischer** m (AUT) windscreen wiper

Scheide ['ʃaidə] f sheath; (Grenze) boundary; (ANAT) vagina; **s~n** (unreg) vt to separate; (Ehe) to dissolve ♦ vi to depart; to part; **sich s~n lassen** to get a divorce

Scheidung f (Ehescheidung) divorce

Schein [ʃain] (-(e)s, -e) m light; (Anschein) appearance; (Geld) (bank)note; (Bescheinigung) certificate; **zum ~** in pretence; **s~bar** adj apparent; **s~en** (unreg) vi to shine; (Anschein haben) to seem; **s~heilig** adj hypocritical; **~werfer** (-s, -) m floodlight; spotlight; (Suchscheinwerfer) searchlight; (AUT) headlamp

Scheiß- [ʃais] (umg) in zW bloody

Scheiße ['ʃaisə] (-) (umg) f shit

Scheitel ['ʃaitəl] (-s, -) m top; (Haarscheitel) parting; **s~n** vt to part

scheitern ['ʃaitərn] vi to fail

Schelle ['ʃelə] f small bell; **s~n** vi to ring

Schellfisch ['ʃelfiʃ] m haddock

Schelm [ʃelm] (-(e)s, -e) m rogue; **s~isch** adj mischievous, roguish

Schelte ['ʃeltə] f scolding; **s~n** (unreg) vt to scold

Schema ['ʃema] (-s, -s od -ta) nt scheme, plan; (Darstellung) schema; **nach ~** quite mechanically; **s~tisch** [ʃe'ma:tiʃ] adj schematic; (pej) mechanical

Schemel ['ʃe:məl] (-s, -) m (foot)stool

Schenkel ['ʃeŋkəl] (-s, -) m thigh

schenken ['ʃeŋkən] vt (auch fig) to give; (Getränk) to pour; **sich dat etw ~** (umg) to skip sth; **das ist geschenkt!** (billig) that's a giveaway!; (nichts wert) that's worthless!

Scherbe ['ʃerbə] f broken piece, fragment; (archäologisch) potsherd

Schere ['ʃe:rə] f scissors pl; (groß) shears pl; **s~n** (unreg) vt to cut; (Schaf) to shear; (kümmern) to bother ♦ vr to care; **scher dich zum Teufel!** get lost!; **~'rei** (umg) f bother, trouble

Scherz [ʃerts] (-es, -e) m joke; fun; **~frage** f conundrum; **s~haft** adj joking, jocular

Scheu [ʃɔy] (-) f shyness; (Angst) fear; (Ehrfurcht) awe; **s~** adj shy; **s~en** vr: **sich s~en vor** +dat to be afraid of; to shrink from ♦ vt to shun ♦ vi (Pferd) to shy

scheuern ['ʃɔyərn] vt to scour, to scrub

Scheune ['ʃɔynə] f barn

Scheusal ['ʃɔyza:l] (-s, -e) nt monster

scheußlich ['ʃɔyslıç] adj dreadful, frightful

Schi [ʃi:] m = **Ski**

Schicht [ʃıçt] (-, -en) f layer; (Klasse) class, level; (in Fabrik etc) shift; **~arbeit** f shift work; **s~en** vt to layer, to stack

schick [ʃık] adj stylish, chic

schicken vt to send ♦ vr: **sich ~ (in** +akk) to resign o.s. (to) ♦ vb unpers (anständig sein) to be fitting

schicklich adj proper, fitting

Schicksal (-s, -e) nt fate; **~sschlag** m great misfortune, blow

Schieb- ['ʃi:b] zW: **~edach** nt (AUT) sun roof; **s~en** (unreg) vt (auch Drogen) to push; (Schuld) to put ♦ vi to push; **~etür** f sliding door; **~ung** f fiddle

Schieds- ['ʃi:ts] zW: **~gericht** nt court of arbitration; **~richter** m referee; umpire; (Schlichter) arbitrator

schief [ʃi:f] adj crooked; (Ebene) sloping; (Turm) leaning; (Winkel) oblique; (Blick) funny; (Vergleich) distorted ♦ adv crooked(ly); (ansehen) askance; **etw ~ stellen** to slope sth; **~ gehen** (umg) to go wrong

Schiefer ['ʃi:fər] (-s, -) m slate

schielen ['ʃi:lən] vi to squint; **nach etw ~** (fig) to eye sth

schien etc [ʃi:n] vb siehe **scheinen**

Schienbein nt shinbone

Schiene ['ʃi:nə] f rail; (MED) splint; **s~n** vt to put in splints

schier [ʃi:r] adj (fig) sheer ♦ adv nearly, almost

Schieß- ['ʃi:s] zW: **~bude** f shooting gallery; **s~en** (unreg) vt to shoot; (Ball) to kick; (Geschoss) to fire ♦ vi to shoot; (Salat etc) to run to seed; **s~en auf** +akk to shoot at; **~e'rei** f shooting incident, shoot-out; **~pulver** nt gunpowder; **~scharte** f embrasure

Schiff [ʃɪf] (-(e)s, -e) nt ship, vessel; (*Kirchenschiff*) nave; **s~bar** adj (*Fluss*) navigable; **~bruch** m shipwreck; **s~brüchig** adj shipwrecked; **~chen** nt small boat; (*Weben*) shuttle; (*Mütze*) forage cap; **~er** (-s, -) m bargeman, boatman; **~fahrt** ▲ f shipping; (*Reise*) voyage

Schikane [ʃiˈkaːnə] f harassment; dirty trick; **mit allen ~n** with all the trimmings

schikanieren [ʃikaˈniːrən] vt to harass, to torment

Schikoree ▲ [ˈʃɪkoreː] (-s) m od f = **Chicorée**

Schild[1] [ʃɪlt] (-(e)s, -e) m shield; **etw im ~e führen** to be up to sth

Schild[2] [ʃɪlt] (-(e)s, -er) nt sign; nameplate; (*Etikett*) label

Schilddrüse f thyroid gland

schildern [ˈʃɪldərn] vt to depict, to portray

Schildkröte f tortoise; (*Wasserschildkröte*) turtle

Schilf [ʃɪlf] (-(e)s, -e) nt (*Pflanze*) reed; (*Material*) reeds pl, rushes pl; **~rohr** nt (*Pflanze*) reed

schillern [ˈʃɪlərn] vi to shimmer; **~d** adj iridescent

Schilling [ˈʃɪlɪŋ] m schilling

Schimmel [ˈʃɪməl] (-s, -) m mould; (*Pferd*) white horse; **s~ig** adj mouldy; **s~n** vi to get mouldy

Schimmer [ˈʃɪmər] (-s) m (*Lichtsein*) glimmer; (*Glanz*) shimmer; **s~n** vi to gleam, to shimmer

Schimpanse [ʃɪmˈpanzə] (-n, -n) m chimpanzee

schimpfen [ˈʃɪmpfən] vt to scold ♦ vi to curse, to complain; to scold

Schimpfwort nt term of abuse

schinden [ˈʃɪndən] (*unreg*) vt to maltreat, to drive too hard ♦ vr: **sich ~ (mit)** to sweat and strain (at), to toil away (at); **Eindruck ~** (*umg*) to create an impression

Schinde'rei f grind, drudgery

Schinken [ˈʃɪŋkən] (-s, -) m ham

Schirm [ʃɪrm] (-(e)s, -e) m (*Regenschirm*) umbrella; (*Sonnenschirm*) parasol, sunshade; (*Wandschirm, Bildschirm*) screen; (*Lampenschirm*) (lamp)shade; (*Mützenschirm*) peak; (*Pilzschirm*) cap; **~mütze** f peaked cap; **~ständer** m umbrella stand

schizophren [ʃitsoˈfreːn] adj schizophrenic

Schlacht [ʃlaxt] (-, -en) f battle; **s~en** vt to slaughter, to kill; **~er** (-s, -) m butcher; **~feld** nt battlefield; **~hof** m slaughterhouse, abattoir; **~schiff** nt battleship; **~vieh** nt animals kept for meat; beef cattle

Schlaf [ʃlaːf] (-(e)s) m sleep; **~anzug** m pyjamas pl

Schläfe f (ANAT) temple

schlafen [ˈʃlaːfən] (*unreg*) vi to sleep; **~ gehen** to go to bed; **S~szeit** f bedtime

schlaff [ʃlaf] adj slack; (*energielos*) limp; (*erschöpft*) exhausted

Schlaf- zW: **~gelegenheit** f sleeping accommodation; **~lied** nt lullaby; **s~los** adj sleepless; **~losigkeit** f sleeplessness, insomnia; **~mittel** nt sleeping pill

schläfrig [ˈʃlɛːfrɪç] adj sleepy

Schlaf- zW: **~saal** m dormitory; **~sack** m sleeping bag; **~tablette** f sleeping pill; **~wagen** m sleeping car, sleeper; **s~wandeln** vi insep to sleepwalk; **~zimmer** nt bedroom

Schlag [ʃlaːk] (-(e)s, ⁺e) m (*auch fig*) blow; (*auch MED*) stroke; (*Pulsschlag, Herzschlag*) beat; (*ELEK*) shock; (*Blitzschlag*) bolt, stroke; (*Autotür*) car door; (*umg: Portion*) helping; (*Art*) kind, type; **Schläge** pl (*Tracht Prügel*) beating sg; **mit einem ~** all at once; **~ auf ~** in rapid succession; **~ader** f artery; **~anfall** m stroke; **s~artig** adj sudden, without warning; **~baum** m barrier

Schlägel [ˈʃlɛːɡəl] (-s, -) m (drum)stick; (*Hammer*) mallet, hammer

schlagen [ˈʃlaːɡən] (*unreg*) vt, vi to strike, to hit; (*wiederholt ~, besiegen*) to beat; (*Glocke*) to ring; (*Stunde*) to strike; (*Sahne*) to whip; (*Schlacht*) to fight ♦ vr to fight; **nach jdm ~** (*fig*) to take after sb; **sich gut ~** (*fig*) to do well; **Schlager** [ˈʃlaːɡər] (-s, -)

m (*auch fig*) hit

Schläger ['ʃlɛːgər] *m* brawler; (*SPORT*) bat; (*TENNIS etc*) racket; (*GOLF*) club; hockey stick; (*Waffe*) rapier; **Schläge'rei** *f* fight, punch-up

Schlagersänger(in) *m(f)* pop singer

Schlag- *zW*: **s~fertig** *adj* quick-witted; **~fertigkeit** *f* ready wit, quickness of repartee; **~loch** *nt* pothole; **~obers** (*ÖSTERR*) *nt* = **Schlagsahne**; **~sahne** *f* (whipped) cream; **~seite** *f* (*NAUT*) list; **~wort** *nt* slogan, catch phrase; **~zeile** *f* headline; **~zeug** *nt* percussion; drums *pl*; **~zeuger** (**-s, -**) *m* drummer

Schlamassel [ʃlaˈmasəl] (**-s, -**) (*umg*) *m* mess

Schlamm [ʃlam] (**-(e)s, -e**) *m* mud; **s~ig** *adj* muddy

Schlamp- ['ʃlamp] *zW*: **~e** (*umg*) *f* slut; **s~en** (*umg*) *vi* to be sloppy; **~e'rei** (*umg*) *f* disorder, untidiness; sloppy work; **s~ig** (*umg*) *adj* (*Mensch, Arbeit*) sloppy, messy

Schlange ['ʃlaŋə] *f* snake; (*Menschenschlange*) queue (*BRIT*), line-up (*US*); **~ stehen** to (form a) queue, to line up

schlängeln ['ʃlɛŋəln] *vr* (*Schlange*) to wind; (*Weg*) to wind, twist; (*Fluss*) to meander

Schlangen- *zW*: **~biss** ▲ *m* snake bite; **~gift** *nt* snake venom; **~linie** *f* wavy line

schlank [ʃlaŋk] *adj* slim, slender; **S~heit** *f* slimness, slenderness; **S~heitskur** *f* diet

schlapp [ʃlap] *adj* limp; (*locker*) slack; **S~e** (*umg*) *f* setback

Schlaraffenland [ʃlaˈrafənlant] *nt* land of milk and honey

schlau [ʃlaʊ] *adj* crafty, cunning

Schlauch [ʃlaʊx] (**-(e)s, Schläuche**) *m* hose; (*in Reifen*) inner tube; (*umg*: *Anstrengung*) grind; **~boot** *nt* rubber dinghy; **s~en** (*umg*) *vt* to tell on, to exhaust

Schläue ['ʃlɔʏə] (**-**) *f* cunning

Schlaufe ['ʃlaʊfə] *f* loop; (*Aufhänger*) hanger

Schlauheit *f* cunning

schlecht [ʃlɛçt] *adj* bad ♦ *adv* badly; **~ gelaunt** in a bad mood; **~ und recht** after

a fashion; **jdm ist ~** sb feels sick *od* bad; **jdm geht es ~** sb is in a bad way; **~ machen** to run down; **S~igkeit** *f* badness; bad deed

schlecken ['ʃlɛkən] *vt, vi* to lick

Schlegel ['ʃleːgəl] (**-s, -**) *m* (*KOCH*) leg; *siehe* **Schlägel**

schleichen ['ʃlaɪçən] (*unreg*) *vi* to creep, to crawl; **~d** *adj* gradual; creeping

Schleichwerbung *f* (*COMM*) plug

Schleier ['ʃlaɪər] (**-s, -**) *m* veil; **s~haft** (*umg*) *adj*: **jdm s~haft sein** to be a mystery to sb

Schleif- ['ʃlaɪf] *zW*: **~e** *f* loop; (*Band*) bow; **s~en¹** *vt, vi* to drag; **s~en²** (*unreg*) *vt* to grind; (*Edelstein*) to cut; **~stein** *m* grindstone

Schleim [ʃlaɪm] (**-(e)s, -e**) *m* slime; (*MED*) mucus; (*KOCH*) gruel; **~haut** *f* (*ANAT*) mucous membrane; **s~ig** *adj* slimy

Schlemm- ['ʃlɛm] *zW*: **s~en** *vi* to feast; **~er** (**-s, -**) *m* gourmet; **~e'rei** *f* gluttony, feasting

schlendern ['ʃlɛndərn] *vi* to stroll

schlenkern ['ʃlɛŋkərn] *vt, vi* to swing, to dangle

Schlepp- ['ʃlɛp] *zW*: **~e** *f* train; **s~en** *vt* to drag; (*Auto, Schiff*) to tow; (*tragen*) to lug; **s~end** *adj* dragging, slow; **~er** (**-s, -**) *m* tractor; (*Schiff*) tug

Schlesien ['ʃleːziən] (**-s**) *nt* Silesia

Schleuder ['ʃlɔʏdər] (**-, -n**) *f* catapult; (*Wäscheschleuder*) spin-drier; (*Butterschleuder etc*) centrifuge; **~gefahr** *f* risk of skidding; „**Achtung „gefahr"** "slippery road ahead"; **s~n** *vt* to hurl; (*Wäsche*) to spin-dry ♦ *vi* (*AUT*) to skid; **~preis** *m* give-away price; **~sitz** *m* (*AVIAT*) ejector seat; (*fig*) hot seat; **~ware** *f* cheap *od* cut-price goods *pl*

schleunigst ['ʃlɔʏnɪçst] *adv* straight away

Schleuse ['ʃlɔʏzə] *f* lock; (**~ntor**) *f* sluice

schlicht [ʃlɪçt] *adj* simple, plain; **~en** *vt* (*glätten*) to smooth, to dress; (*Streit*) to settle; **S~er** (**-s, -**) *m* mediator, arbitrator; **S~ung** *f* settlement; arbitration

Schlick [ʃlɪk] (**-(e)s, -e**) *m* mud; (*Ölschlick*) slick

schlief *etc* [ʃliːf] *vb siehe* **schlafen**

Schließ- [ˈʃliːs] zW: **s~en** (unreg) vt to close, to shut; (beenden) to close; (Freundschaft, Bündnis, Ehe) to enter into; (folgern): **s~en (aus)** to infer (from) ♦ vi, vr to close, to shut; **etw in sich s~en** to include sth; **~fach** nt locker; **s~lich** adv finally; **s~lich doch** after all

Schliff [ʃlɪf] (-(e)s, -e) m cut(ting); (fig) polish

schlimm [ʃlɪm] adj bad; **~er** adj worse; **~ste(r, s)** adj worst; **~stenfalls** adv at (the) worst

Schlinge [ˈʃlɪŋə] f loop; (bes Henkersschlinge) noose; (Falle) snare; (MED) sling; **s~n** (unreg) vt to wind; (essen) to bolt, to gobble ♦ vi (essen) to bolt one's food, to gobble

schlingern vi to roll

Schlips [ʃlɪps] (-és, -e) m tie

Schlitten [ˈʃlɪtən] (-s, -) m sledge, sleigh; **~fahren** (-s) nt tobogganing

schlittern [ˈʃlɪtərn] vi to slide

Schlittschuh [ˈʃlɪtʃuː] m skate; **~ laufen** to skate; **~bahn** f skating rink; **~läufer(in)** m(f) skater

Schlitz [ʃlɪts] (-es, -e) m slit; (für Münze) slot; (Hosenschlitz) flies pl; **s~äugig** adj slant-eyed

Schloss ▲ [ʃlɔs] (-es, ⁺er) nt lock; (an Schmuck etc) clasp; (Bau) castle; chateau

schloss ▲ etc vb siehe **schließen**

Schlosser [ˈʃlɔsər] (-s, -) m (Autoschlosser) fitter; (für Schlüssel etc) locksmith

Schlosserei [-ˈraɪ] f metal (working) shop

Schlot [ʃloːt] (-(e)s, -e) m chimney; (NAUT) funnel

schlottern [ˈʃlɔtərn] vi to shake, to tremble; (Kleidung) to be baggy

Schlucht [ʃlʊxt] (-, -en) f gorge, ravine

schluchzen [ˈʃlʊxtsən] vi to sob

Schluck [ʃlʊk] (-(e)s, -e) m swallow; (Menge) drop; **~auf** (-s, -s) m hiccups pl; **s~en** vt, vi to swallow

schludern [ˈʃluːdərn] vi to skimp, to do sloppy work

schlug etc [ʃluːk] vb siehe **schlagen**

Schlummer [ˈʃlʊmər] (-s) m slumber; **s~n**

vi to slumber

Schlund [ʃlʊnt] (-(e)s, ⁺e) m gullet; (fig) jaw

schlüpfen [ˈʃlʏpfən] vi to slip; (Vogel etc) to hatch (out)

Schlüpfer [ˈʃlʏpfər] (-s, -) m panties pl, knickers pl

schlüpfrig [ˈʃlʏpfrɪç] adj slippery; (fig) lewd; **S~keit** f slipperiness; (fig) lewdness

schlurfen [ˈʃlʊrfən] vi to shuffle

schlürfen [ˈʃlʏrfən] vt, vi to slurp

Schluss ▲ [ʃlʊs] (-es, ⁺e) m end; (~folgerung) conclusion; **am ~** at the end; **~ machen mit** to finish with

Schlüssel [ˈʃlʏsəl] (-s, -) m (auch fig) key; (Schraubenschlüssel) spanner, wrench; (MUS) clef; **~bein** nt collarbone; **~blume** f cowslip, primrose; **~bund** m bunch of keys; **~dienst** m key cutting service; **~loch** nt keyhole; **~position** f key position; **~wort** nt keyword

schlüssig [ˈʃlʏsɪç] adj conclusive

Schluss- ▲ zW: **~licht** nt taillight; (fig) tailender; **~strich** m (fig) final stroke; **~verkauf** m clearance sale

schmächtig [ˈʃmɛçtɪç] adj slight

schmackhaft [ˈʃmakhaft] adj tasty

schmal [ʃmaːl] adj narrow; (Person, Buch etc) slender, slim; (karg) meagre

schmälern [ˈʃmɛːlərn] vt to diminish; (fig) to belittle

Schmalfilm m cine film

Schmalz [ʃmalts] (-es, -e) nt dripping, lard; (fig) sentiment, schmaltz; **s~ig** adj (fig) schmaltzy

schmarotzen [ʃmaˈrɔtsən] vi to sponge; (BOT) to be parasitic; **Schmarotzer** (-s, -) m parasite; sponger

Schmarren [ˈʃmarən] (-s, -) m (ÖSTERR) small piece of pancake; (fig) rubbish, tripe

schmatzen [ˈʃmatsən] vi to smack one's lips; to eat noisily

schmecken [ˈʃmɛkən] vt, vi to taste; **es schmeckt ihm** he likes it

Schmeichel- [ˈʃmaɪçəl] zW: **~ei** [-ˈlaɪ] f flattery; **s~haft** adj flattering; **s~n** vi to flatter

schmeißen [ˈʃmaɪsən] (unreg) (umg) vt to

throw, to chuck

Schmelz [ʃmɛlts] **(-es, -e)** m enamel;
(Glasur) glaze; (von Stimme) melodiousness;
s~en (unreg) vt to melt; (Erz) to smelt ♦ vi
to melt; **~punkt** m melting point;
~wasser nt melted snow

Schmerz [ʃmɛrts] **(-es, -en)** m pain; (Trauer)
grief; **s~empfindlich** adj sensitive to pain;
s~en vt, vi to hurt; **~ensgeld** nt
compensation; **s~haft** adj painful; **s~lich**
adj painful; **s~los** adj painless; **~mittel** nt
painkiller; **~tablette** f painkiller

Schmetterling [ˈʃmɛtərlɪŋ] m butterfly

schmettern [ˈʃmɛtərn] vt (werfen) to hurl;
(TENNIS: Ball) to smash; (singen) to belt out
(inf)

Schmied [ʃmiːt] **(-(e)s, -e)** m blacksmith;
~e [ˈʃmiːdə] f smithy, forge; **~eeisen** nt
wrought iron; **s~en** vt to forge; (Pläne) to
devise, to concoct

schmiegen [ˈʃmiːgən] vt to press, to nestle
♦ vr: **sich ~ (an** +akk) to cuddle up (to), to
nestle (up to)

Schmier- [ˈʃmiːr] zW: **~e** f grease; (THEAT)
greasepaint, make-up; **s~en** vt to smear;
(ölen) to lubricate, to grease; (bestechen) to
bribe; (schreiben) to scrawl ♦ vi (schreiben)
to scrawl; **~fett** nt grease; **~geld** nt bribe;
s~ig adj greasy; **~seife** f soft soap

Schminke [ˈʃmɪŋkə] f make-up; **s~n** vt, vr
to make up

schmirgeln [ˈʃmɪrgəln] vt to sand (down)

Schmirgelpapier nt emery paper

schmollen [ˈʃmɔlən] vi to sulk, to pout

Schmorbraten m stewed od braised meat

schmoren [ˈʃmoːrən] vt to stew, to braise

Schmuck [ʃmʊk] **(-(e)s, -e)** m jewellery;
(Verzierung) decoration

schmücken [ˈʃmʏkən] vt to decorate

Schmuck- zW: **s~los** adj unadorned,
plain; **~sachen** pl jewels, jewellery sg

Schmuggel [ˈʃmʊgəl] **(-s)** m smuggling;
s~n vt, vi to smuggle

Schmuggler **(-s, -)** m smuggler

schmunzeln [ˈʃmʊntsəln] vi to smile
benignly

schmusen [ˈʃmuːzən] (umg) vi (zärtlich sein)

to cuddle, to canoodle (inf)

Schmutz [ʃmʊts] **(-es)** m dirt, filth; **~fink** m
filthy creature; **~fleck** m stain; **s~ig** adj
dirty

Schnabel [ˈʃnaːbəl] **(-s, ̈)** m beak, bill;
(Ausguss) spout

Schnalle [ˈʃnalə] f buckle, clasp; **s~n** vt to
buckle

Schnapp- [ˈʃnap] zW: **s~en** vt to grab, to
catch ♦ vi to snap; **~schloss** ▲ nt spring
lock; **~schuss** ▲ m (PHOT) snapshot

Schnaps [ʃnaps] **(-es, ̈ e)** m spirits pl;
schnapps

schnarchen [ˈʃnarçən] vi to snore

schnattern [ˈʃnatərn] vi (Gänse) to gabble;
(Ente) to quack

schnauben [ˈʃnaubən] vi to snort ♦ vr to
blow one's nose

schnaufen [ˈʃnaufən] vi to puff, to pant

Schnauze f snout, muzzle; (Ausguss) spout;
(umg) gob

schnäuzen ▲ [ˈʃnɔytsən] vr to blow one's
nose

Schnecke [ˈʃnɛkə] f snail; **~nhaus** nt snail's
shell

Schnee [ʃneː] **(-s)** m snow; (Eischnee)
beaten egg white; **~ball** m snowball;
~flocke f snowflake; **s~frei** adj free of
snow; **~gestöber** nt snowstorm;
~glöckchen nt snowdrop; **~grenze** f
snow line; **~kette** f (AUT) snow chain;
~mann m snowman; **~pflug** m
snowplough; **~regen** m sleet; **~schmelze**
f thaw; **~wehe** f snowdrift

Schneide [ˈʃnaidə] f edge; (Klinge) blade;
s~n (unreg) vt to cut; (kreuzen) to cross, to
intersect with ♦ vr to cut o.s.; **s~nd** adj cutting; **~r (-s, -)** m
tailor; **~rei** f (Geschäft) tailor's; **~rin** f
dressmaker; **s~rn** vt to make ♦ vi to be a
tailor; **~zahn** m incisor

schneien [ˈʃnaiən] vi unpers to snow

Schneise [ˈʃnaizə] f clearing

schnell [ʃnɛl] adj quick, fast ♦ adv quick,
quickly, fast; **S~hefter (-s, -)** m loose-leaf
binder; **S~igkeit** f speed; **S~imbiss** ▲ m
(Lokal) snack bar; **S~kochtopf** m

(*Dampfkochtopf*) pressure cooker;
S~reinigung *f* dry cleaner's; **~stens** *adv*
as quickly as possible; **S~straße** *f*
expressway; **S~zug** *m* fast *od* express train
schneuzen △ ['ʃnɔʏtsən] *vr siehe*
schnäuzen
schnippeln ['ʃnɪpəln] (*umg*) *vt*: **~ (an** +*dat*)
to snip (at)
schnippisch ['ʃnɪpɪʃ] *adj* sharp-tongued
Schnitt (-(e)s, -e) *m* cut(ting); (*~punkt*)
intersection; (*Querschnitt*) (cross) section;
(*Durchschnitt*) average; (*~muster*) pattern;
(*an Buch*) edge; (*umg*: *Gewinn*) profit
schnitt *etc vb siehe* **schneiden**
Schnitt- *zW*: **~blumen** *pl* cut flowers; **~e** *f*
slice; (*belegt*) sandwich; **~fläche** *f* section;
~lauch *m* chive; **~punkt** *m* (point of)
intersection; **~stelle** *f* (COMPUT) interface;
~wunde *f* cut
Schnitz- ['ʃnɪts] *zW*: **~arbeit** *f* wood
carving; **~el** (-s, -) *nt* chip; (KOCH)
escalope; **s~en** *vt* to carve; **~er** (-s, -) *m*
carver; (*umg*) blunder; **~erei** *f* carving;
carved woodwork
schnoddrig ['ʃnɔdərɪç] (*umg*) *adj* snotty
Schnorchel ['ʃnɔrçəl] (-s, -) *m* snorkel
Schnörkel ['ʃnœrkəl] (-s, -) *m* flourish;
(ARCHIT) scroll
schnorren ['ʃnɔrən] *vt, vi* to cadge
schnüffeln ['ʃnʏfəln] *vi* to sniff
Schnüffler (-s, -) *m* snooper
Schnuller ['ʃnulər] (-s, -) *m* dummy,
comforter (US)
Schnupfen ['ʃnupfən] (-s, -) *m* cold
schnuppern ['ʃnupərn] *vi* to sniff
Schnur [ʃnuːr] (-, ⁀e) *f* string, cord; (ELEK)
flex
schnüren ['ʃnyːrən] *vt* to tie
schnurgerade *adj* straight (as a die)
Schnurrbart ['ʃnurbaːrt] *m* moustache
schnurren ['ʃnurən] *vi* to purr; (*Kreisel*) to
hum
Schnürschuh *m* lace-up (shoe)
Schnürsenkel *m* shoelace
schnurstracks *adv* straight (away)
Schock [ʃɔk] (-(e)s, -e) *m* shock; **s~ieren**
[ʃɔ'kiːrən] *vt* to shock, to outrage

Schöffe ['ʃœfə] (-n, -n) *m* lay magistrate;
Schöffin *f* lay magistrate
Schokolade [ʃokoˈlaːdə] *f* chocolate
Scholle ['ʃɔlə] *f* clod; (*Eisscholle*) ice floe;
(*Fisch*) plaice

schon [ʃoːn] *adv* **1** (*bereits*) already; **er ist
schon da** he's there already, he's already
there; **ist er schon da?** is he there yet?;
warst du schon einmal da? have you ever
been there?; **ich war schon einmal da** I've
been there before; **das war schon immer
so** that has always been the case; **schon
oft** often; **hast du schon gehört?** have
you heard?
2 (*bestimmt*) all right; **du wirst schon
sehen** you'll see (all right); **das wird
schon noch gut** that'll be OK
3 (*bloß*) just; **allein schon das Gefühl ...**
just the very feeling ...; **schon der
Gedanke** the very thought; **wenn ich das
schon höre** I only have to hear that
4 (*einschränkend*): **ja schon, aber ...** yes
(well), but ...
5: **schon möglich** possible; **schon gut!**
OK!; **du weißt schon** you know; **komm
schon!** come on!

└───────────────────┘

schön [ʃøːn] *adj* beautiful; (*nett*) nice; **~e
Grüße** best wishes; **~e Ferien** have a nice
holiday; **~en Dank** (many) thanks; **sich ~
machen** to make o.s. look nice
schonen ['ʃoːnən] *vr* to look after ♦ *vr* to
take it easy; **~d** *adj* careful, gentle
Schön- *zW*: **~heit** *f* beauty; **~heitsfehler**
m blemish, flaw; **~heitsoperation** *f*
cosmetic surgery
Schonkost (-) *f* light diet; (*Spezialdiät*)
special diet
Schon- *zW*: **~ung** *f* good care; (*Nachsicht*)
consideration; (*Forst*) plantation of young
trees; **s~ungslos** *adj* unsparing, harsh;
~zeit *f* close season
Schöpf- ['ʃœpf] *zW*: **s~en** *vt* to scoop, to
ladle; (*Mut*) to summon up; (*Luft*) to
breathe in; **~er** (-s, -) *m* creator; **s~erisch**

adj creative; **~kelle** *f* ladle; **~ung** *f* creation

Schorf [ʃɔrf] (-(e)s, -e) *m* scab

Schornstein ['ʃɔrnʃtain] *m* chimney; (*NAUT*) funnel; **~feger** (-s, -) *m* chimney sweep

Schoß [ʃoːs] (-es, ⁻e) *m* lap

schoss ▲ *etc vb siehe* **schließen**

Schoßhund *m* pet dog, lapdog

Schote ['ʃoːtə] *f* pod

Schotte ['ʃɔtə] *m* Scot, Scotsman

Schotter ['ʃɔtər] (-s) *m* broken stone, road metal; (*EISENB*) ballast

Schott- [ʃɔt] *zW*: **~in** *f* Scot, Scotswoman; **s~isch** *adj* Scottish, Scots; **~land** *nt* Scotland

schraffieren [ʃraˈfiːrən] *vt* to hatch

schräg [ʃrɛːk] *adj* slanting, not straight; **etw ~ stellen** to put sth at an angle; **~ gegenüber** diagonally opposite; **S~e** ['ʃrɛːgə] *f* slant; **S~strich** *m* oblique stroke

Schramme ['ʃramə] *f* scratch; **s~n** *vt* to scratch

Schrank [ʃraŋk] (-(e)s, ⁻e) *m* cupboard; (*Kleiderschrank*) wardrobe; **~e** *f* barrier; **~koffer** *m* trunk

Schraube ['ʃraubə] *f* screw; **s~n** *vt* to screw; **~nschlüssel** *m* spanner; **~nzieher** (-s, -) *m* screwdriver

Schraubstock ['ʃraupʃtɔk] *m* (*TECH*) vice

Schreck [ʃrɛk] (-(e)s, -e) *m* terror; fright; **~en** (-s, -) *m* terror; fright; **s~en** *vt* to frighten; to scare; **~gespenst** *nt* spectre, nightmare; **s~haft** *adj* jumpy, easily frightened; **s~lich** *adj* terrible, dreadful

Schrei [ʃrai] (-(e)s, -e) *m* scream; (*Ruf*) shout

Schreib- ['ʃraib] *zW*: **~block** *m* writing pad; **s~en** (*unreg*) *vt, vi* to write; (*buchstabieren*) to spell; **~en** (-s, -) *nt* letter, communication; **s~faul** *adj* bad about writing letters; **~kraft** *f* typist; **~maschine** *f* typewriter; **~papier** *nt* notepaper; **~tisch** *m* desk; **~ung** *f* spelling; **~waren** *pl* stationery *sg*; **~weise** *f* spelling; way of writing; **~zentrale** *f* typing pool; **~zeug** *nt* writing materials *pl*

schreien ['ʃraiən] (*unreg*) *vt, vi* to scream; (*rufen*) to shout; **~d** *adj* (*fig*) glaring; (*Farbe*) loud

Schrein [ʃrain] (-(e)s, -e) *m* shrine

Schreiner ['ʃrainər] (-s, -) *m* joiner; (*Zimmermann*) carpenter; (*Möbelschreiner*) cabinetmaker; **~ei** [-ˈrai] *f* joiner's workshop

schreiten ['ʃraitən] (*unreg*) *vi* to stride

schrieb *etc* [ʃriːp] *vb siehe* **schreiben**

Schrift [ʃrift] (-, -en) *f* writing; handwriting; (*~art*) script; (*Gedrucktes*) pamphlet, work; **~deutsch** *nt* written German; **~führer** *m* secretary; **s~lich** *adj* written ♦ *adv* in writing; **~sprache** *f* written language; **~steller(in)** (-s, -) *m(f)* writer; **~stück** *nt* document; **~wechsel** *m* correspondence

schrill [ʃril] *adj* shrill

Schritt [ʃrit] (-(e)s, -e) *m* step; (*Gangart*) walk; (*Tempo*) pace; (*von Hose*) crutch; **~ fahren** to drive at walking pace; **~macher** (-s, -) *m* pacemaker; **~tempo** ▲ *nt*: **im ~tempo** at a walking pace

schroff [ʃrɔf] *adj* steep; (*zackig*) jagged; (*fig*) brusque

schröpfen ['ʃrœpfən] *vt* (*fig*) to fleece

Schrot [ʃroːt] (-(e)s, -e) *m od nt* (*Blei*) (small) shot; (*Getreide*) coarsely ground grain, groats *pl*; **~flinte** *f* shotgun

Schrott [ʃrɔt] (-(e)s, -e) *m* scrap metal; **~haufen** *m* scrap heap; **s~reif** *adj* ready for the scrap heap

schrubben ['ʃrubən] *vt* to scrub

Schrubber (-s, -) *m* scrubbing brush

schrumpfen ['ʃrumpfən] *vi* to shrink; (*Apfel*) to shrivel

Schub- ['ʃuːb] *zW*: **~fach** *nt* drawer; **~karren** *m* wheelbarrow; **~lade** *f* drawer

Schubs [ʃups] (-es, -e) (*umg*) *m* shove (*inf*), push

schüchtern ['ʃʏçtərn] *adj* shy; **S~heit** *f* shyness

Schuft [ʃuft] (-(e)s, -e) *m* scoundrel

schuften (*umg*) *vi* to graft, to slave away

Schuh [ʃuː] (-(e)s, -e) *m* shoe; **~band** *nt* shoelace; **~creme** *f* shoe polish; **~größe** *f* shoe size; **~löffel** *m* shoehorn; **~macher** (-s, -) *m* shoemaker

Schul- *zW*: **~arbeit** *f* homework (*no pl*); **~aufgaben** *pl* homework *sg*; **~besuch** *m*

school attendance; **~buch** nt school book

Schuld [ʃʊlt] (-, **-en**) f guilt; (*FIN*) debt; (*Verschulden*) fault; **~ haben (an** +dat) to be to blame (for); **er hat ~** it's his fault; **jdm ~ geben** to blame sb; *siehe* **zuschulden; s~** adj: **s~ sein (an** +dat) to be to blame (for); **er ist s~** it's his fault; **s~en** ['ʃʊldən] vt to owe; **s~enfrei** adj free from debt; **~gefühl** nt feeling of guilt; **s~ig** adj guilty; (*gebührend*) due; **s~ig an etw** dat **sein** to be guilty of sth; **jdm etw s~ig sein** to owe sb sth; **jdm etw s~ig bleiben** not to provide sb with sth; **s~los** adj innocent, without guilt; **~ner** (-s, -) m debtor; **~schein** m promissory note, IOU

Schule ['ʃuːlə] f school; **s~n** vt to train, to school

Schüler(in) ['ʃyːlər(ɪn)] (-s, -) m(f) pupil; **~austausch** m school od student exchange; **~ausweis** m (school) student card

Schul- zW: **~ferien** pl school holidays; **s~frei** adj: **s~freier Tag** holiday; **s~frei sein** to be a holiday; **~hof** m playground; **~jahr** nt school year; **~kind** nt schoolchild; **s~pflichtig** adj of school age; **~schiff** nt (*NAUT*) training ship; **~stunde** f period, lesson; **~tasche** f school bag

Schulter ['ʃʊltər] (-, -n) f shoulder; **~blatt** nt shoulder blade; **s~n** vt to shoulder

Schulung f education, schooling

Schulzeugnis nt school report

Schund [ʃʊnt] (-(e)s) m trash, garbage

Schuppe ['ʃʊpə] f scale; **~n** pl (*Haarschuppen*) dandruff sg

Schuppen (-s, -) m shed

schuppig ['ʃʊpɪç] adj scaly

Schur [ʃuːr] (-, **-en**) f shearing

schüren ['ʃyːrən] vt to rake; (*fig*) to stir up

schürfen ['ʃʏrfən] vt, vi to scrape, to scratch; (*MIN*) to prospect

Schurke ['ʃʊrkə] (-n, -n) m rogue

Schurwolle f: **„reine ~"** "pure new wool"

Schürze ['ʃʏrtsə] f apron

Schuss ▲ [ʃʊs] (-es, **⁼e**) m shot; (*WEBEN*) woof; **~bereich** m effective range

Schüssel ['ʃʏsəl] (-, -n) f bowl

Schuss- ▲ zW: **~linie** f line of fire; **~verletzung** f bullet wound; **~waffe** f firearm

Schuster ['ʃuːstər] (-s, -) m cobbler, shoemaker

Schutt [ʃʊt] (-(e)s) m rubbish; (*Bauschutt*) rubble

Schüttelfrost m shivering

schütteln ['ʃʏtəln] vt, vr to shake

schütten ['ʃʏtən] vt to pour; (*Zucker, Kies etc*) to tip; (*verschütten*) to spill ♦ vi unpers to pour (down)

Schutthalde f dump

Schutthaufen m heap of rubble

Schutz [ʃʊts] (-es) m protection; (*Unterschlupf*) shelter; **jdn in ~ nehmen** to stand up for sb; **~anzug** m overalls pl; **~blech** nt mudguard

Schütze ['ʃʏtsə] (-n, -n) m gunman; (*Gewehrschütze*) rifleman; (*Scharfschütze, Sportschütze*) marksman; (*ASTROL*) Sagittarius

schützen ['ʃʏtsən] vt to protect; **~ vor** +dat od **gegen** to protect from

Schützenfest nt fair featuring shooting matches

Schutz- zW: **~engel** m guardian angel; **~gebiet** nt protectorate; (*Naturschutzgebiet*) reserve; **~hütte** f shelter, refuge; **~impfung** f immunisation

Schützling ['ʃʏtslɪŋ] m protégé(e); (*bes Kind*) charge

Schutz- zW: **s~los** adj defenceless; **~mann** m policeman; **~patron** m patron saint

Schwaben ['ʃvaːbən] nt Swabia; **schwäbisch** adj Swabian

schwach [ʃvax] adj weak, feeble

Schwäche ['ʃvɛçə] f weakness; **s~n** vt to weaken

Schwachheit f weakness

schwächlich adj weakly, delicate

Schwächling m weakling

Schwach- zW: **~sinn** m imbecility; **s~sinnig** adj mentally deficient; (*Idee*) idiotic; **~strom** m weak current

Schwächung ['ʃvɛçʊŋ] f weakening

Schwager ['ʃvaːgər] (-s, **⁼**) m brother-in-law; **Schwägerin** ['ʃvɛːgərɪn] f sister-in-law

Schwalbe ['ʃvalbə] f swallow

Schwall [ʃval] (-(e)s, -e) m surge; (Worte) flood, torrent

Schwamm [ʃvam] (-(e)s, ̈e) m sponge; (Pilz) fungus

schwamm etc vb siehe **schwimmen**

schwammig adj spongy; (Gesicht) puffy

Schwan [ʃvaːn] (-(e)s, ̈e) m swan

schwanger ['ʃvaŋər] adj pregnant; **S~schaft** f pregnancy

schwanken vi to sway; (taumeln) to stagger, to reel; (Preise, Zahlen) to fluctuate; (zögern) to hesitate, to vacillate

Schwankung f fluctuation

Schwanz [ʃvants] (-es, ̈e) m tail

schwänzen ['ʃventsən] (umg) vt to skip, to cut ♦ vi to play truant

Schwarm [ʃvarm] (-(e)s, ̈e) m swarm; (umg) heart-throb, idol

schwärm- ['ʃverm] zW: **~en** vi to swarm; **~en für** to be mad od wild about; **S~erei** [-ə'raɪ] f enthusiasm; **~erisch** adj impassioned, effusive

Schwarte ['ʃvartə] f hard skin; (Speckschwarte) rind

schwarz [ʃvarts] adj black; **~es Brett** notice board; **ins S~e treffen** (auch fig) to hit the bull's eye; **in den ~en Zahlen** in the black; **~ sehen** (umg) to see the gloomy side of things; **S~arbeit** f illicit work, moonlighting; **S~brot** nt black bread; **S~e(r)** f(m) black (man/woman)

Schwärze ['ʃvertsə] f blackness; (Farbe) blacking; (Druckerschwärze) printer's ink; **s~n** vt to blacken

Schwarz- zW: **s~fahren** (unreg) vi to travel without paying; to drive without a licence; **~handel** m black market (trade); **~markt** m black market; **~wald** m Black Forest; **s~weiß, s~weiß** adj black and white

schwatzen ['ʃvatsən] vi to chatter

schwätzen ['ʃvetsən] vi to chatter

Schwätzer ['ʃvetsər] (-s, -) m gasbag

schwatzhaft adj talkative, gossipy

Schwebe ['ʃveːbə] f: **in der ~** (fig) in abeyance; **~bahn** f overhead railway; **s~n** vi to drift, to float; (hoch) to soar

Schwed- ['ʃveːd] zW: **~e** m Swede; **~en** nt Sweden; **~in** f Swede; **s~isch** adj Swedish

Schwefel ['ʃveːfəl] (-s) m sulphur; **s~ig** adj sulphurous; **~säure** f sulphuric acid

Schweig- ['ʃvaɪg] zW: **~egeld** nt hush money; **~en** (-s) nt silence; **s~en** (unreg) vi to be silent; to stop talking; **~epflicht** f pledge of secrecy; (von Anwalt) requirement of confidentiality; **s~sam** ['ʃvaɪkzaːm] adj silent, taciturn; **~samkeit** f taciturnity, quietness

Schwein [ʃvaɪn] (-(e)s, -e) nt pig; (umg) (good) luck

Schweine- zW: **~fleisch** nt pork; **~'rei** f mess; (Gemeinheit) dirty trick; **~stall** m pigsty

schweinisch adj filthy

Schweinsleder nt pigskin

Schweiß [ʃvaɪs] (-es) m sweat, perspiration; **s~en** vt, vi to weld; **~er** (-s, -) m welder; **~füße** pl sweaty feet; **~naht** f weld

Schweiz [ʃvaɪts] f Switzerland; **~er(in)** m(f) Swiss; **s~erisch** adj Swiss

schwelgen ['ʃvelgən] vi to indulge

Schwelle ['ʃvelə] f (auch fig) threshold; doorstep; (EISENB) sleeper (BRIT), tie (US)

schwellen (unreg) vi to swell

Schwellung f swelling

Schwemme ['ʃvemə] f (WIRTS: Überangebot) surplus

Schwenk- ['ʃveŋk] zW: **s~bar** adj swivel-mounted; **s~en** vt to swing; (Fahne) to wave; (abspülen) to rinse ♦ vi to turn, to swivel; (MIL) to wheel; **~ung** f turn; wheel

schwer [ʃveːr] adj heavy; (schwierig) difficult, hard; (schlimm) serious, bad ♦ adv (sehr) very (much); (verletzt etc) seriously, badly; **~ erziehbar** difficult (to bring up); **jdm ~ fallen** to be difficult for sb; **jdm/sich etw ~ machen** to make sth difficult for sb/o.s.; **~ nehmen** to take to heart; **sich** dat od akk **~ tun** to have difficulties; **~ verdaulich** indigestible, heavy; **~ wiegend** weighty, important; **S~arbeiter** m manual worker, labourer; **S~behinderte(r)** f(m) seriously handicapped person; **S~e** *f* weight, heaviness; (*PHYS*) gravity; **~elos** *adj* weightless; (*Kammer*) zero-G; **~fällig** *adj* ponderous; **S~gewicht** *nt* heavyweight; (*fig*) emphasis; **~hörig** *adj* hard of hearing; **S~industrie** *f* heavy industry; **S~kraft** *f* gravity; **S~kranke(r)** *f(m)* person who is seriously ill; **~lich** *adv* hardly; **~mütig** *adj* melancholy; **S~punkt** *m* centre of gravity; (*fig*) emphasis, crucial point

Schwert [ʃveːrt] **(-(e)s, -er)** *nt* sword; **~lilie** *f* iris

schwer- *zW:* **S~verbrecher(in)** *m(f)* criminal, serious offender; **S~verletzte(r)** *f(m)* serious casualty; (*bei Unfall usw auch*) seriously injured person

Schwester ['ʃvɛstər] **(-, -n)** *f* sister; (*MED*) nurse; **s~lich** *adj* sisterly

Schwieger- ['ʃviːɡər] *zW:* **~eltern** *pl* parents-in-law; **~mutter** *f* mother-in-law; **~sohn** *m* son-in-law; **~tochter** *f* daughter-in-law; **~vater** *m* father-in-law

schwierig ['ʃviːrɪç] *adj* difficult, hard; **S~keit** *f* difficulty

Schwimm- ['ʃvɪm] *zW:* **~bad** *nt* swimming baths *pl*; **~becken** *nt* swimming pool; **s~en** (*unreg*) *vi* to swim; (*treiben, nicht sinken*) to float; (*fig: unsicher sein*) to be all at sea; **~er (-s, -)** *m* swimmer; (*Angeln*) float; **~erin** *f* (female) swimmer; **~lehrer** *m* swimming instructor; **~weste** *f* life jacket

Schwindel ['ʃvɪndəl] **(-s)** *m* giddiness; dizzy spell; (*Betrug*) swindle, fraud; (*Zeug*) stuff; **s~frei** *adj:* **s~frei sein** to have a good head for heights; **s~n** (*umg*) *vi* (*lügen*) to fib; **jdm s~t es** sb feels dizzy

schwinden ['ʃvɪndən] (*unreg*) *vi* to disappear; (*sich verringern*) to decrease; (*Kräfte*) to decline

Schwindler ['ʃvɪndlər] *m* swindler; (*Lügner*) liar

schwindlig *adj* dizzy; **mir ist ~** I feel dizzy

Schwing- ['ʃvɪŋ] *zW:* **s~en** (*unreg*) *vt* to swing; (*Waffe etc*) to brandish ♦ *vi* to swing; (*vibrieren*) to vibrate; (*klingen*) to sound; **~tür** *f* swing door(s); **~ung** *f* vibration;

(*PHYS*) oscillation

Schwips [ʃvɪps] **(-es, -e)** *m:* **einen ~ haben** to be tipsy

schwirren ['ʃvɪrən] *vi* to buzz

schwitzen ['ʃvɪtsən] *vi* to sweat, to perspire

schwören ['ʃvøːrən] (*unreg*) *vt, vi* to swear

schwul [ʃvuːl] (*umg*) *adj* gay, queer

schwül [ʃvyːl] *adj* sultry, close; **S~e (-)** *f* sultriness

Schwule(r) (*umg*) *f(m)* gay (man/woman)

Schwung [ʃvʊŋ] **(-(e)s, ᵉe)** *m* swing; (*Triebkraft*) momentum; (*fig: Energie*) verve, energy; (*umg: Menge*) batch; **s~haft** *adj* brisk, lively; **s~voll** *adj* vigorous

Schwur [ʃvuːr] **(-(e)s, ᵉe)** *m* oath; **~gericht** *nt* court with a jury

sechs [zɛks] *num* six; **~hundert** *num* six hundred; **~te(r, s)** *adj* sixth; **S~tel (-s, -)** *nt* sixth

sechzehn ['zɛçtseːn] *num* sixteen

sechzig ['zɛçtsɪç] *num* sixty

See¹ [zeː] **(-, -n)** *f* sea

See² [zeː] **(-s, -n)** *m* lake

See- [zeː] *zW:* **~bad** *nt* seaside resort; **~hund** *m* seal; **~igel** ['zeːliːɡəl] *m* sea urchin; **s~krank** *adj* seasick; **~krankheit** *f* seasickness; **~lachs** *m* rock salmon

Seele ['zeːlə] *f* soul; **s~nruhig** *adv* calmly

Seeleute ['zeːlɔʏtə] *pl* seamen

Seel- *zW:* **s~isch** *adj* mental; **~sorge** *f* pastoral duties *pl*; **~sorger (-s, -)** *m* clergyman

See- *zW:* **~macht** *f* naval power; **~mann** (*pl* **-leute**) *m* seaman, sailor; **~meile** *f* nautical mile; **~möwe** *f* (*ZOOL*) seagull; **~not** *f* distress; **~räuber** *m* pirate; **~rose** *f* water lily; **~stern** *m* starfish; **s~tüchtig** *adj* seaworthy; **~weg** *m* sea route; **auf dem ~weg** by sea; **~zunge** *f* sole

Segel ['zeːɡəl] **(-s, -)** *nt* sail; **~boot** *nt* yacht; **~fliegen (-s)** *nt* gliding; **~flieger** *m* glider pilot; **~flugzeug** *nt* glider; **s~n** *vt, vi* to sail; **~schiff** *nt* sailing vessel; **~sport** *m* sailing; **~tuch** *nt* canvas

Segen ['zeːɡən] **(-s, -)** *m* blessing

Segler ['zeːɡlər] **(-s, -)** *m* sailor, yachtsman

segnen ['zeːɡnən] *vt* to bless

Seh- ['zeː] zW: **s~behindert** adj partially sighted; **s~en** (unreg) vt, vi to see; (in bestimmte Richtung) to look; **mal s~en(, ob ...)** let's see (if ...); **siehe Seite 5** see page 5; **s~enswert** adj worth seeing; **~enswürdigkeiten** pl sights (of a town); **~fehler** m sight defect

Sehne ['zeːnə] f sinew; (an Bogen) string

sehnen vr: **sich ~ nach** to long od yearn for

sehnig adj sinewy

Sehn- zW: **s~lich** adj ardent; **~sucht** f longing; **s~süchtig** adj longing

sehr [zeːr] adv very; (mit Verben) a lot, (very) much; **zu ~** too much; **~ geehrte(r) ...** dear ...

seicht [zaɪçt] adj (auch fig) shallow

Seide ['zaɪdə] f silk; **s~n** adj silk; **~npapier** nt tissue paper

seidig ['zaɪdɪç] adj silky

Seife ['zaɪfə] f soap

Seifen- zW: **~lauge** f soapsuds pl; **~schale** f soap dish; **~schaum** m lather

seihen ['zaɪən] vt to strain, to filter

Seil [zaɪl] (-(e)s, -e) nt rope; cable; **~bahn** f cable railway; **~hüpfen** (-s) nt skipping; **~springen** (-s) nt skipping; **~tänzer(in)** m(f) tightrope walker

---

sein [zaɪn] (pt **war**, pp **gewesen**) vi **1** to be; **ich bin** I am; **du bist** you are; **er/sie/es ist** he/she/it is; **wir sind/ihr seid/sie sind** we/you/they are; **wir waren** we were; **wir sind gewesen** we have been

2: seien Sie nicht böse don't be angry; **sei so gut und ...** be so kind as to ...; **das wäre gut** that would od that'd be a good thing; **wenn ich Sie wäre** if I were od was you; **das wärs** that's all, that's it; **morgen bin ich in Rom** tomorrow I'll od I will od I shall be in Rome; **waren Sie mal in Rom?** have you ever been to Rome?

3: wie ist das zu verstehen? how is that to be understood?; **er ist nicht zu ersetzen** he cannot be replaced; **mit ihr ist nicht zu reden** you can't talk to her

4: mir ist kalt I'm cold; **was ist?** what's the matter?, what is it?; **ist was?** is something the matter?; **es sei denn, dass ...** unless ...; **wie dem auch sei** be that as it may; **wie wäre es mit ...?** how od what about ...?; **lass das sein!** stop that!

---

sein(e) ['zaɪn(ə)] adj his; its; **~e(r, s)** pron his; its; **~er** (gen von **er**) pron of him; **~erseits** adv for his part; **~erzeit** adv in those days, formerly; **~esgleichen** pron people like him; **~etwegen** adv (für ihn) for his sake; (wegen ihm) on his account; (von ihm aus) as far as he is concerned; **~etwillen** adv: **um ~etwillen = seinetwegen**; **~ige** pron: **der/die/das ~ige** od **S~ige** his

seit [zaɪt] präp +dat since ♦ konj since; **er ist ~ einer Woche hier** he has been here for a week; **~ langem** for a long time; **~dem** [zaɪt'deːm] adv, konj since

Seite ['zaɪtə] f side; (Buch~) page; (MIL) flank

Seiten- zW: **~airbag** m side-impact airbag; **~ansicht** f side view; **~hieb** m (fig) passing shot, dig; **s~s** präp +gen on the part of; **~schiff** nt aisle; **~sprung** m extramarital escapade; **~stechen** nt (a) stitch; **~straße** f side road; **~streifen** m verge; (der Autobahn) hard shoulder

seither [zaɪt'heːr] adv, konj since (then)

seit- zW: **~lich** adj on one od the side; side cpd; **~wärts** adv sidewards

Sekretär [zekre'tɛːr] m secretary; (Möbel) bureau

Sekretariat [zekretari'aːt] (-(e)s, -e) nt secretary's office, secretariat

Sekretärin f secretary

Sekt [zɛkt] (-(e)s, -e) m champagne

Sekte ['zɛktə] f sect

Sekunde [ze'kʊndə] f second

selber ['zɛlbər] = **selbst**

Selbst [zɛlpst] (-) nt self

---

selbst [zɛlpst] pron **1**: **ich/er/wir selbst** I myself/he himself/we ourselves; **sie ist die Tugend selbst** she's virtue itself; **er braut**

---

sein Bier selbst he brews his own beer; **wie gehts? - gut, und selbst?** how are things? - fine, and yourself? **2** (*ohne Hilfe*) alone, on my/his/one's *etc* own; **von selbst** by itself; **er kam von selbst** he came of his own accord; **selbst gemacht** home-made
♦ *adv* even; **selbst wenn** even if; **selbst Gott** even God (himself)

selbständig *etc* ['zɛlpʃtɛndɪç] = **selbstständig** *etc*

Selbst- *zW*: ~**auslöser** *m* (*PHOT*) delayed-action shutter release; ~**bedienung** *f* self-service; ~**befriedigung** *f* masturbation; ~**beherrschung** *f* self-control; ~**bestimmung** *f* (*POL*) self-determination; ~**beteiligung** *f* (*VERSICHERUNG: bei Kosten*) (voluntary) excess; **s~bewusst** ▲ *adj* (self-)confident; ~**bewusstsein** ▲ *nt* self-confidence; ~**erhaltung** *f* self-preservation; ~**erkenntnis** *f* self-knowledge; **s~gefällig** *adj* smug, self-satisfied; ~**gespräch** *nt* conversation with o.s.; ~**kostenpreis** *m* cost price; **s~los** *adj* unselfish, selfless; ~**mord** *m* suicide; ~**mörder(in)** *m(f)* suicide; **s~mörderisch** *adj* suicidal; **s~sicher** *adj* self-assured; **s~ständig** ▲ *adj* independent; ~**ständigkeit** ▲ *f* independence; **s~süchtig** *adj* (*Mensch*) selfish; ~**versorger** (**-s, -**) *m* (*im Urlaub etc*) self-caterer; **s~verständlich** ['zɛlpstfɛrʃtɛntlɪç] *adj* obvious ♦ *adv* naturally; **ich halte das für s~verständlich** I take that for granted; ~**verteidigung** *f* self-defence; ~**vertrauen** *nt* self-confidence; ~**verwaltung** *f* autonomy, self-government

selig ['ze:lɪç] *adj* happy, blissful; (*REL*) blessed; (*tot*) late; **S~keit** *f* bliss

Sellerie ['zɛləri:] (**-s, -(s)** *od* **-, -**) *m od f* celery

selten ['zɛltən] *adj* rare ♦ *adv* seldom, rarely; **S~heit** *f* rarity

Selterswasser ['zɛltərsvasər] *nt* soda water

seltsam ['zɛltza:m] *adj* strange, curious; **S~keit** *f* strangeness

Semester [ze'mɛstər] (**-s, -**) *nt* semester; ~**ferien** *pl* vacation *sg*

Semi- [zemi] *in zW* semi-; ~**kolon** [-'ko:lɔn] (**-s, -s**) *nt* semicolon

Seminar [zemi'na:r] (**-s, -e**) *nt* seminary; (*Kurs*) seminar; (*UNIV: Ort*) department building

Semmel ['zɛməl] (**-, -n**) *f* roll

Senat [ze'na:t] (**-(e)s, -e**) *m* senate, council

Sende- ['zɛndə] *zW*: ~**bereich** *m* transmission range; ~**folge** *f* (*Serie*) series; **s~n** (*unreg*) *vt* to send; (*RADIO, TV*) to transmit, to broadcast ♦ *vi* to transmit, to broadcast; ~**r** (**-s, -**) *m* station; (*Anlage*) transmitter; ~**reihe** *f* series (of broadcasts)

Sendung ['zɛndʊŋ] *f* consignment; (*Aufgabe*) mission; (*RADIO, TV*) transmission; (*Programm*) programme

Senf [zɛnf] (**-(e)s, -e**) *m* mustard

senil [ze'ni:l] (*pej*) *adj* senile

Senior(in) ['ze:niɔr(ɪn)] (**-s, -en**) *m(f)* (*Mensch im Rentenalter*) (old age) pensioner

Seniorenheim [zeni'o:rənhaɪm] *nt* old people's home

Senk- ['zɛŋk] *zW*: ~**blei** *nt* plumb; ~**e** *f* depression; **s~en** *vt* to lower ♦ *vr* to sink, to drop gradually; **s~recht** *adj* vertical, perpendicular; ~**rechte** *f* perpendicular; ~**rechtstarter** *m* (*AVIAT*) vertical take-off plane; (*fig*) high-flyer

Sensation [zɛnzatsi'o:n] *f* sensation; **s~ell** [-'nɛl] *adj* sensational

sensibel [zɛn'zi:bəl] *adj* sensitive

sentimental [zɛntimɛn'ta:l] *adj* sentimental; **S~i'tät** *f* sentimentality

separat [zepa'ra:t] *adj* separate

September [zɛp'tɛmbər] (**-(s), -**) *m* September

Serie ['ze:riə] *f* series

serien- *zW*: ~**mäßig** *adj* standard; **S~mörder(in)** *m(f)* serial killer; ~**weise** *adv* in series

seriös [zeri'ø:s] *adj* serious, bona fide

Service¹ [zɛr'vi:s] (**-(s), -**) *nt* (*Geschirr*) set, service

Service² (**-, -s**) *m* service

servieren [zɛr'vi:rən] *vt, vi* to serve

Serviererin [zɛr'viːrərɪn] f waitress

Serviette [zɛrvi'ɛtə] f napkin, serviette

Servo- ['zɛrvo] zW: **~bremse** f (AUT) servo(-assisted) brake; **~lenkung** f (AUT) power steering

Sessel ['zɛsəl] (**-s, -**) m armchair; **~lift** m chairlift

sesshaft ▲ ['zɛshaft] adj settled; (ansässig) resident

setzen ['zɛtsən] vt to put, to set; (Baum etc) to plant; (Segel, TYP) to set ♦ vr to settle; (Person) to sit down ♦ vi (springen) to leap; (wetten) to bet

Setz- ['zɛts] zW: **~er** (**-s, -**) m (TYP) compositor; **~ling** m young plant

Seuche ['zɔʏçə] f epidemic; **~ngebiet** nt infected area

seufzen ['zɔʏftsən] vt, vi to sigh

Seufzer ['zɔʏftsɐ] (**-s, -**) m sigh

Sex [zɛks] (**-(es)**) m sex; **~ualität** [-uali'tɛt] f sex, sexuality; **~ualkunde** [zɛksu'aːl-] f (SCH) sex education; **s~uell** [-u'ɛl] adj sexual

Shampoo [ʃam'puː] (**-s, -s**) nt shampoo

Sibirien [zi'biːriən] nt Siberia

SCHLÜSSELWORT

sich [zɪç] pron 1 (akk): **er/sie/es ... sich** he/she/it ... himself/herself/itself; **sie pl / man ... sich** ... themselves/oneself; **Sie ... sich** you ... yourself/ yourselves pl; **sich wiederholen** to repeat oneself/itself

2 (dat): **er/sie/es ... sich** he/she/it ... to himself/herself/itself; **sie pl / man ... sich** they/one ... to themselves/oneself; **Sie ... sich** you ... to yourself/yourselves pl; **sie hat sich einen Pullover gekauft** she bought herself a jumper; **sich die Haare waschen** to wash one's hair

3 (mit Präposition): **haben Sie Ihren Ausweis bei sich?** do you have your pass on you?; **er hat nichts bei sich** he's got nothing on him; **sie bleiben gern unter sich** they keep themselves to themselves

4 (einander) each other, one another; **sie bekämpfen sich** they fight each other od

one another

5: **dieses Auto fährt sich gut** this car drives well; **hier sitzt es sich gut** it's good to sit here

---

Sichel ['zɪçəl] (**-, -n**) f sickle; (Mondsichel) crescent

sicher ['zɪçɐ] adj safe; (gewiss) certain; (zuverlässig) secure, reliable; (selbstsicher) confident; **vor jdm/etw ~ sein** to be safe from sb/sth; **ich bin nicht ~** I'm not sure od certain; **~ nicht** surely not; **aber ~!** of course!; **~gehen** (unreg) vi to make sure

Sicherheit ['zɪçɐhaɪt] f safety; (auch FIN) security; (Gewissheit) certainty; (Selbstsicherheit) confidence

Sicherheits- zW: **~abstand** m safe distance; **~glas** nt safety glass; **~gurt** m safety belt; **s~halber** adv for safety; to be on the safe side; **~nadel** f safety pin; **~schloss** ▲ nt safety lock; **~vorkehrung** f safety precaution

sicher- zW: **~lich** adv certainly, surely; **~n** vt to secure; (schützen) to protect; (Waffe) to put the safety catch on; **jdm etw ~n** to secure sth for sb; **sich dat etw ~n** to secure sth (for o.s.); **~stellen** vt to impound; (COMPUT) to save; **S~ung** f (S~n) securing; (Vorrichtung) safety device; (an Waffen) safety catch; (ELEK) fuse; **S~ungskopie** f back-up copy

Sicht [zɪçt] (**-**) f sight; (Aussicht) view; **auf** od **nach ~** (FIN) at sight; **auf lange ~** on a long-term basis; **s~bar** adj visible; **s~en** vt to sight; (auswählen) to sort out; **s~lich** adj evident, obvious; **~verhältnisse** pl visibility sg; **~vermerk** m visa; **~weite** f visibility

sickern ['zɪkɐn] vi to trickle, to seep

Sie [ziː] (nom, akk) pron you

sie [ziː] pron (sg: nom) she, it; (: akk) her, it; (pl: nom) they; (: akk) them

Sieb [ziːp] (**-(e)s, -e**) nt sieve; (KOCH) strainer; **s~en**[1] ['ziːbən] vt to sift; (Flüssigkeit) to strain

sieben[2] num seven; **~hundert** num seven hundred; **S~sachen** pl belongings

---

siebte(r, s) ['zi:ptə(r, s)] *adj* seventh; **S~l (-s, -)** *nt* seventh

siebzehn ['zi:ptse:n] *num* seventeen

siebzig ['zi:ptsɪç] *num* seventy

siedeln ['zi:dəln] *vi* to settle

sieden ['zi:dən] *vt, vi* to boil, to simmer

Siedepunkt *m* boiling point

Siedler (-s, -) *m* settler

Siedlung *f* settlement; (*Häusersiedlung*) housing estate

Sieg [zi:k] **(-(e)s, -e)** *m* victory

Siegel ['zi:gəl] **(-s, -)** *nt* seal; **~ring** *m* signet ring

Sieg- *zW:* **s~en** *vi* to be victorious; (*SPORT*) to win; **~er (-s, -)** *m* victor; (*SPORT etc*) winner; **s~reich** *adj* victorious

siehe *etc* ['zi:ə] *vb siehe* **sehen**

siezen ['zi:tsən] *vt* to address as "Sie"

Signal [zɪ'gna:l] **(-s, -e)** *nt* signal

Silbe ['zɪlbə] *f* syllable

Silber ['zɪlbər] **(-s)** *nt* silver; **~hochzeit** *f* silver wedding (anniversary); **s~n** *adj* silver; **~papier** *nt* silver paper

Silhouette [zilu'ɛtə] *f* silhouette

Silvester [zɪl'vɛstər] **(-s, -)** *nt* New Year's Eve, Hogmanay (*SCOTTISH*); **~abend** *m* = **Silvester**

Silvester

ⓘ *Silvester is the German word for New Year's Eve. Although not an official holiday most businesses close early and shops shut at midday. Most Germans celebrate in the evening, and at midnight they let off fireworks and rockets; the revelry usually lasts until the early hours of the morning.*

---

simpel ['zɪmpəl] *adj* simple

Sims [zɪms] **(-es, -e)** *nt od m* (*Kaminsims*) mantelpiece; (*Fenstersims*) (window)sill

simulieren [zimu'li:rən] *vt* to simulate; (*vortäuschen*) to feign ♦ *vi* to feign illness

simultan [zimʊl'ta:n] *adj* simultaneous

Sinfonie [zɪnfo'ni:] *f* symphony

singen ['zɪŋən] *vt, vi* to sing

Singular ['zɪŋgula:r] *m* singular

Singvogel ['zɪŋfo:gəl] *m* songbird

sinken ['zɪŋkən] (*unreg*) *vi* to sink; (*Preise etc*) to fall, to go down

Sinn [zɪn] **(-(e)s, -e)** *m* mind; (*Wahrnehmungssinn*) sense; (*Bedeutung*) sense, meaning; **~ für etw** sense of sth; **von ~en sein** to be out of one's mind; **es hat keinen ~** there's no point; **~bild** *nt* symbol; **s~en** (*unreg*) *vi* to ponder; **auf etw** *akk* **s~en** to contemplate sth; **~estäuschung** *f* illusion; **s~gemäß** *adj* faithful; (*Wiedergabe*) in one's own words; **s~ig** *adj* clever; **s~lich** *adj* sensual, sensuous; (*Wahrnehmung*) sensory; **~lichkeit** *f* sensuality; **s~los** *adj* senseless; meaningless; **~losigkeit** *f* senselessness; meaninglessness; **s~voll** *adj* meaningful; (*vernünftig*) sensible

Sintflut ['zɪntflu:t] *f* Flood

Sippe ['zɪpə] *f* clan, kin

Sippschaft ['zɪpʃaft] (*pej*) *f* relations *pl*, tribe; (*Bande*) gang

Sirene [zi're:nə] *f* siren

Sirup ['zi:rʊp] **(-s, -e)** *m* syrup

Sitt- ['zɪt] *zW:* **~e** *f* custom; **~en** *pl* (*~lichkeit*) morals; **~enpolizei** *f* vice squad; **s~sam** *adj* modest, demure

Situation [zituatsi'o:n] *f* situation

Sitz [zɪts] **(-es, -e)** *m* seat; **der Anzug hat einen guten ~** the suit is a good fit; **s~en** (*unreg*) *vi* to sit; (*Bemerkung, Schlag*) to strike home, to tell; (*Gelerntes*) to have sunk in; **s~en bleiben** to remain seated; (*SCH*) to have to repeat a year; **auf etw** *dat* **s~en bleiben** to be lumbered with sth; **s~en lassen** (*SCH*) to make (sb) repeat a year; (*Mädchen*) to jilt; (*Wartenden*) to stand up; **etw auf sich** *dat* **s~en lassen** to take sth lying down; **s~end** *adj* (*Tätigkeit*) sedentary; **~gelegenheit** *f* place to sit down; **~platz** *m* seat; **~streik** *m* sit-down strike; **~ung** *f* meeting

Sizilien [zi'tsi:liən] *nt* Sicily

Skala ['ska:la] **(-, Skalen)** *f* scale

Skalpell [skal'pɛl] **(-s, -e)** *nt* scalpel

Skandal [skan'da:l] **(-s, -e)** *m* scandal; **s~ös** [-'lø:s] *adj* scandalous

---

Skandinav- [skandi'na:v] *zW:* **~ien** *nt*
Scandinavia; **~ier(in)** *m(f)* Scandinavian;
s~isch *adj* Scandinavian

Skelett [ske'let] **(-(e)s, -e)** *nt* skeleton

Skepsis ['skepsɪs] **(-)** *f* scepticism

skeptisch ['skeptɪʃ] *adj* sceptical

Ski [ʃi:] **(-s, -er)** *m* ski; **~ laufen** *od* **fahren** to
ski; **~fahrer** *m* skier; **~gebiet** *nt* ski(ing)
area; **~läufer** *m* skier; **~lehrer** *m* ski
instructor; **~lift** *m* ski-lift; **~springen** *nt*
ski-jumping; **~stock** *m* ski-pole

Skizze ['skɪtsə] *f* sketch

skizzieren [skɪ'tsi:rən] *vt, vi* to sketch

Sklave ['skla:və] **(-n, -n)** *m* slave; **~'rei** *f*
slavery; **Sklavin** *f* slave

Skonto ['skɔnto] **(-s, -s)** *m od nt* discount

Skorpion [skɔrpi'o:n] **(-s, -e)** *m* scorpion;
(*ASTROL*) Scorpio

Skrupel ['skru:pəl] **(-s, -)** *m* scruple; **s~los**
adj unscrupulous

Skulptur [skʊlp'tu:r] *f* (*Gegenstand*) sculpture

S-Kurve ['eskʊrvə] *f* S-bend

Slip [slɪp] **(-s, -s)** *m* (under)pants; **~einlage**
f panty liner

Slowakei [slova'kaɪ] *f:* **die ~** Slovakia

Slowenien [slo've:niən] *nt* Slovenia

Smaragd [sma'rakt] **(-(e)s, -e)** *m* emerald

Smoking ['smo:kɪŋ] **(-s, -s)** *m* dinner jacket

SCHLÜSSELWORT

so [zo:] *adv* **1** (*so sehr*) so; **so groß/schön**
etc so big/nice *etc*; **so groß/schön wie ...**
as big/nice as ...; **so viel (wie)** as much as;
rede nicht so viel don't talk so much; **so**
weit sein to be ready; **so weit wie** *od* **als**
möglich as far as possible; **ich bin so weit**
zufrieden by and large I'm quite satisfied;
so wenig (wie) as little (as); **das hat ihn**
so geärgert, dass ... that annoyed him so
much that ...; **so einer wie ich** somebody
like me; **na so was!** well, well!

2 (*auf diese Weise*) like this; **mach es nicht**
so don't do it like that; **so oder so** in one
way or the other; **und so weiter** and so
on; **... oder so was** ... or something like
that; **das ist gut so** that's fine; **so genannt**
so-called

3 (*umg: umsonst*): **ich habe es so**
bekommen I got it for nothing
♦ *konj:* **so dass, sodass** so that; **so wie es**
jetzt ist as things are at the moment
♦ *excl:* **so?** really?; **so, das wärs** so, that's
it then

---

s. o. *abk* = **siehe oben**

Söckchen ['zœkçən] *nt* ankle socks

Socke ['zɔkə] *f* sock

Sockel ['zɔkəl] **(-s, -)** *m* pedestal, base

sodass ▲ [zo'das] *konj* so that

Sodawasser ['zo:davasər] *nt* soda water

Sodbrennen ['zo:tbrenən] **(-s, -)** *nt*
heartburn

soeben [zo'|e:bən] *adv* just (now)

Sofa ['zo:fa] **(-s, -s)** *nt* sofa

sofern [zo'fern] *konj* if, provided (that)

sofort [zo'fɔrt] *adv* immediately, at once;
~ig *adj* immediate

Sog [zo:k] **(-(e)s, -e)** *m* (*Strömung*) undertow

sogar [zo'ga:r] *adv* even

sogleich [zo'glaɪç] *adv* straight away, at
once

Sohle ['zo:lə] *f* sole; (*Talsohle etc*) bottom;
(*MIN*) level

Sohn [zo:n] **(-(e)s, ▪e)** *m* son

Solar- [zo'la:r] *in zW* solar; **~zelle** *f* solar
cell

solch [zɔlç] *pron* such; **ein ~e(r, s) ...** such
a ...

Soldat [zɔl'da:t] **(-en, -en)** *m* soldier

Söldner ['zœldnər] **(-s, -)** *m* mercenary

solidarisch [zoli'da:rɪʃ] *adj in od* with
solidarity; **sich ~ erklären** to declare one's
solidarity

Solidari'tät *f* solidarity

solid(e) [zo'li:d(ə)] *adj* solid; (*Leben, Person*)
respectable

Solist(in) [zo'lɪst(ɪn)] *m(f)* soloist

Soll [zɔl] **(-(s), -(s))** *nt* (*FIN*) debit (side);
(*Arbeitsmenge*) quota, target

SCHLÜSSELWORT

sollen ['zɔlən] (*pt* **sollte**, *pp* **gesollt** *od* (*als*
Hilfsverb) **sollen**) *Hilfsverb* **1** (*Pflicht, Befehl*)
to be supposed to; **du hättest nicht gehen**

Spelling Reform: ▲ *new spelling* △ *old spelling (to be phased out)*

sollen you shouldn't have gone, you oughtn't to have gone; **soll ich?** shall I?; **soll ich dir helfen?** shall I help you?; **sag ihm, er soll warten** tell him he's to wait; **was soll ich machen?** what should I do? **2** (*Vermutung*): **sie soll verheiratet sein** she's said to be married; **was soll das heißen?** what's that supposed to mean?; **man sollte glauben, dass ...** you would think that ...; **sollte das passieren, ...** if that should happen ...
♦ *vt, vi*: **was soll das?** what's all this?; **das sollst du nicht** you shouldn't do that; **was solls?** what the hell!

Solo ['zo:lo] (**-s, -s** *od* **Soli**) *nt* solo
somit [zo'mɪt] *konj* and so, therefore
Sommer ['zɔmər] (**-s, -**) *m* summer; **s~lich** *adj* summery; summer; **~reifen** *m* normal tyre; **~schlussverkauf** ▲ *m* summer sale; **~sprossen** *pl* freckles
Sonde ['zɔndə] *f* probe
Sonder- ['zɔndər] *in zW* special; **~angebot** *nt* special offer; **s~bar** *adj* strange, odd; **~fahrt** *f* special trip; **~fall** *m* special case; **s~lich** *adj* particular; (*außergewöhnlich*) remarkable; (*eigenartig*) peculiar; **~marke** *f* special issue stamp; **s~n** *konj* but ♦ *vt* to separate; **nicht nur ..., s~n auch** not only ..., but also; **~preis** *m* special reduced price; **~zug** *m* special train
Sonnabend ['zɔn a:bənt] *m* Saturday
Sonne ['zɔnə] *f* sun; **s~n** *vr* to sun o.s.
Sonnen- *in zW*: **~aufgang** *m* sunrise; **s~baden** *vi* to sunbathe; **~brand** *m* sunburn; **~brille** *f* sunglasses *pl*; **~creme** *f* suntan lotion; **~energie** *f* solar energy, solar power; **~finsternis** *f* solar eclipse; **~kollektor** *m* solar panel; **~schein** *m* sunshine; **~schirm** *m* parasol, sunshade; **~schutzfaktor** *m* protection factor; **~stich** *m* sunstroke; **~uhr** *f* sundial; **~untergang** *m* sunset; **~wende** *f* solstice
sonnig ['zɔnɪç] *adj* sunny
Sonntag ['zɔnta:k] *m* Sunday
sonst [zɔnst] *adv* otherwise; (*mit pron, in Fragen*) else; (*zu anderer Zeit*) at other times,

normally ♦ *konj* otherwise; **~ noch etwas?** anything else?; **~ nichts** nothing else; **~ jemand** anybody (at all); **~ wo** somewhere else; **~ woher** from somewhere else; **~ wohin** somewhere else; **~ig** *adj* other
sooft [zo'ɔft] *konj* whenever
Sopran [zo'pra:n] (**-s, -e**) *m* soprano
Sorge ['zɔrgə] *f* care, worry
sorgen *vi*: **für jdn ~** to look after sb ♦ *vr*: **sich ~ (um)** to worry (about); **für etw ~** to take care of *od* see to sth; **~frei** *adj* carefree; **~voll** *adj* troubled, worried
Sorgerecht *nt* custody (of a child)
Sorg- [zɔrk] *zW*: **~falt** (**-**) *f* care(fulness); **s~fältig** *adj* careful; **s~los** *adj* careless; (*ohne ~en*) carefree; **s~sam** *adj* careful
Sorte ['zɔrtə] *f* sort; (*Warensorte*) brand; **~n** *pl* (*FIN*) foreign currency *sg*
sortieren [zɔr'ti:rən] *vt* to sort (out)
Sortiment [zɔrti'mɛnt] *nt* assortment
sosehr [zo'ze:r] *konj* as much as
Soße ['zo:sə] *f* sauce; (*Bratensoße*) gravy
soufflieren [zu'fli:rən] *vt, vi* to prompt
Souterrain [zutɛ'rɛ̃:] (**-s, -s**) *nt* basement
souverän [zuvə're:n] *adj* sovereign; (*überlegen*) superior
so- *zW*: **~viel** [zo'fi:l] *konj*: **~viel ich weiß** as far as I know; *siehe* **so**; **~weit** [zo'vait] *konj* as far as; *siehe* **so**; **~wenig** [zo'vɛ:nɪç] *konj* little as; *siehe* **so**; **~wie** [zo'vi:] *konj* (*~bald*) as soon as; (*ebenso*) as well as; **~wieso** [zovi'zo:] *adv* anyway
sowjetisch [zɔ'vjetɪʃ] *adj* Soviet
Sowjetunion *f* Soviet Union
sowohl [zo'vo:l] *konj*: **~ ... als** *od* **wie auch** both ... and
sozial [zotsi'a:l] *adj* social; **S~abgaben** *pl* national insurance contributions; **S~arbeiter(in)** *m(f)* social worker; **S~demokrat** *m* social democrat; **~demokratisch** *adj* social democratic; **S~hilfe** *f* income support (*BRIT*), welfare (aid) (*US*); **~i'sieren** *vt* to socialize; **S~ismus** [-'lɪsmʊs] *m* socialism; **S~ist** [-'lɪst] *m* socialist; **~istisch** *adj* socialist; **S~politik** *f* social welfare policy; **S~produkt** *nt* (net) national product;

S~staat *m* welfare state;
S~versicherung *f* national insurance
(*BRIT*), social security (*US*); **S~wohnung** *f*
council flat
soziologisch [zotsio'lo:gɪʃ] *adj* sociological
sozusagen [zotsu'za:gən] *adv* so to speak
Spachtel ['ʃpaxtəl] **(-s, -)** *m* spatula
spähen ['ʃpɛːən] *vi* to peep, to peek
Spalier [ʃpa'liːr] **(-s, -e)** *nt* (*Gerüst*) trellis;
(*Leute*) guard of honour
Spalt [ʃpalt] **(-(e)s, -e)** *m* crack; (*Türspalt*)
chink; (*fig: Kluft*) split; **~e** *f* crack, fissure;
(*Gletscherspalte*) crevasse; (*in Text*) column;
s~en *vt, vr* (*auch fig*) to split; **~ung** *f*
splitting
Span [ʃpaːn] **(-(e)s, ꞁe)** *m* shaving
Spanferkel *nt* sucking pig
Spange ['ʃpaŋə] *f* clasp; (*Haarspange*) hair
slide; (*Schnalle*) buckle
Spanien ['ʃpaːniən] *nt* Spain; **Spanier(in)**
m(f) Spaniard; **spanisch** *adj* Spanish
Spann- ['ʃpan] *zW:* **~beton** *m* prestressed
concrete; **~betttuch** ▲ *nt* fitted sheet; **~e**
f (*Zeitspanne*) space; (*Differenz*) gap; **s~en**
vt (*straffen*) to tighten, to tauten;
(*befestigen*) to brace ♦ *vi* to be tight;
s~end *adj* exciting, gripping; **~ung** *f*
tension; (*ELEK*) voltage; (*fig*) suspense;
(*unangenehm*) tension
Spar- ['ʃpaːr] *zW:* **~buch** *nt* savings book;
~büchse *f* money box; **s~en** *vt, vi* to
save; **sich** *dat* **etw s~en** to save o.s. sth;
(*Bemerkung*) to keep sth to o.s.; **mit etw**
s~en to be sparing with sth; **an etw** *dat*
s~en to economize on sth; **~er** **(-s, -)** *m*
saver
Spargel ['ʃpargəl] **(-s, -)** *m* asparagus
Sparkasse *f* savings bank
Sparkonto *nt* savings account
spärlich ['ʃpɛːrlɪç] *adj* meagre; (*Bekleidung*)
scanty
Spar- *zW:* **~preis** *m* economy price;
s~sam *adj* economical, thrifty; **~samkeit**
f thrift, economizing; **~schwein** *nt* piggy
bank
Sparte ['ʃpartə] *f* field; line of business;
(*PRESSE*) column

Spaß [ʃpaːs] **(-es, ꞁe)** *m* joke; (*Freude*) fun;
jdm ~ machen to be fun (for sb); **viel ~!**
have fun!; **s~en** *vi* to joke; **mit ihm ist**
nicht zu s~en you can't take liberties with
him; **s~haft** *adj* funny, droll; **s~ig** *adj*
funny, droll
spät [ʃpɛːt] *adj, adv* late; **wie ~ ist es?**
what's the time?
Spaten ['ʃpaːtən] **(-s, -)** *m* spade
später *adj, adv* later
spätestens *adv* at the latest
Spätvorstellung *f* late show
Spatz [ʃpats] **(-en, -en)** *m* sparrow
spazier- [ʃpa'tsiːr] *zW:* **~en** *vi* to stroll, to
walk; **~en fahren** to go for a drive; **~en**
gehen to go for a walk; **S~gang** *m* walk;
S~stock *m* walking stick; **S~weg** *m* path,
walk
Specht [ʃpɛçt] **(-(e)s, -e)** *m* woodpecker
Speck [ʃpɛk] **(-(e)s, -e)** *m* bacon
Spediteur [ʃpedi'tøːr] *m* carrier;
(*Möbelspediteur*) furniture remover
Spedition [ʃpedi'tsio:n] *f* carriage; (*~sfirma*)
road haulage contractor; removal firm
Speer [ʃpeːr] **(-(e)s, -e)** *m* spear; (*SPORT*)
javelin
Speiche ['ʃpaɪçə] *f* spoke
Speichel ['ʃpaɪçəl] **(-s)** *m* saliva, spit(tle)
Speicher ['ʃpaɪçər] **(-s, -)** *m* storehouse;
(*Dachspeicher*) attic, loft; (*Kornspeicher*)
granary; (*Wasserspeicher*) tank; (*TECH*) store;
(*COMPUT*) memory; **s~n** *vt* to store;
(*COMPUT*) to save
speien ['ʃpaɪən] (*unreg*) *vt, vi* to spit;
(*erbrechen*) to vomit; (*Vulkan*) to spew
Speise ['ʃpaɪzə] *f* food; **~eis** [-laɪs] *nt* ice-
cream; **~kammer** *f* larder, pantry; **~karte**
f menu; **s~n** *vt* to feed; to eat ♦ *vi* to dine;
~röhre *f* gullet, oesophagus; **~saal** *m*
dining room; **~wagen** *m* dining car
Speku- [ʃpeku] *zW:* **~lant** *m* speculator;
~lation [-latsi'o:n] *f* speculation; **s~lieren**
[-'liːrən] *vi* (*fig*) to speculate; **auf etw** *akk*
s~lieren to have hopes of sth
Spelunke [ʃpe'lʊŋkə] *f* dive
Spende ['ʃpɛndə] *f* donation; **s~n** *vt* to
donate, to give; **~r** **(-s, -)** *m* donor.

donator

spendieren [ʃpɛnˈdiːrən] *vt* to pay for, to buy; **jdm etw ~** to treat sb to sth, to stand sb sth

Sperling [ˈʃpɛrlɪŋ] *m* sparrow

Sperma [ˈspɛrma] (**-s, Spermen**) *nt* sperm

Sperr- [ˈʃpɛr] *zW:* **~e** *f* barrier; (*Verbot*) ban; **s~en** *vt* to block; (*SPORT*) to suspend, to bar; (*vom Ball*) to obstruct; (*einschließen*) to lock; (*verbieten*) to ban ♦ *vr* to baulk, to jib(e); **~gebiet** *nt* prohibited area; **~holz** *nt* plywood; **s~ig** *adj* bulky; **~müll** *m* bulky refuse; **~sitz** *m* (*THEAT*) stalls *pl*; **~stunde** *f* closing time

Spesen [ˈʃpeːzən] *pl* expenses

Spezial- [ʃpɛtsiˈaːl] *in zW* special; **~gebiet** *nt* specialist field; **s~iˈsieren** *vr* to specialize; **~iˈsierung** *f* specialization; **~ist** [-ˈlɪst] *m* specialist; **~iˈtät** *f* speciality

speziell [ʃpɛtsiˈɛl] *adj* special

spezifisch [ʃpeˈtsiːfɪʃ] *adj* specific

Sphäre [ˈsfɛːrə] *f* sphere

Spiegel [ˈʃpiːɡəl] (**-s, -**) *m* mirror; (*Wasserspiegel*) level; (*MIL*) tab; **~bild** *nt* reflection; **s~bildlich** *adj* reversed; **~ei** *nt* fried egg; **s~n** *vt* to mirror, to reflect ♦ *vr* to be reflected ♦ *vi* to gleam; (*widerspiegeln*) to be reflective; **~ung** *f* reflection

Spiel [ʃpiːl] (**-(e)s, -e**) *nt* game; (*Schauspiel*) play; (*Tätigkeit*) play(ing); (*KARTEN*) deck; (*TECH*) (free) play; **s~en** *vt, vi* to play; (*um Geld*) to gamble; (*THEAT*) to perform, to act; **s~end** *adv* easily; **~er** (**-s, -**) *m* player; (*um Geld*) gambler; **~erei** *f* trifling pastime; **~feld** *nt* pitch, field; **~film** *m* feature film; **~kasino** *nt* casino; **~plan** *m* (*THEAT*) programme; **~platz** *m* playground; **~raum** *m* room to manoeuvre, scope; **~regel** *f* rule; **~sachen** *pl* toys; **~uhr** *f* musical box; **~verderber** (**-s, -**) *m* spoilsport; **~waren** *pl* toys; **~zeug** *nt* toy(s)

Spieß [ʃpiːs] (**-es, -e**) *m* spear; (*Bratspieß*) spit; **~bürger** *m* bourgeois; **~er** (**-s, -**) (*umg*) *m* bourgeois; **s~ig** (*pej*) *adj* (petit) bourgeois

Spinat [ʃpiˈnaːt] (**-(e)s, -e**) *m* spinach

Spind [ʃpɪnt] (**-(e)s, -e**) *m od nt* locker

Spinn- [ˈʃpɪn] *zW:* **~e** *f* spider; **s~en** (*unreg*) *vt, vi* to spin; (*umg*) to talk rubbish; (*verrückt sein*) to be crazy *od* mad; **~eˈrei** *f* spinning mill; **~rad** *nt* spinning wheel; **~webe** *f* cobweb

Spion [ʃpiˈoːn] (**-s, -e**) *m* spy; (*in Tür*) spyhole; **~age** [ʃpioˈnaːʒə] *f* espionage; **s~ieren** [ʃpioˈniːrən] *vi* to spy; **~in** *f* (female) spy

Spirale [ʃpiˈraːlə] *f* spiral

Spirituosen [ʃpirituˈoːzən] *pl* spirits

Spiritus [ˈʃpiːritus] (**-, -se**) *m* (methylated) spirit

Spital [ʃpiˈtaːl] (**-s, ⁻er**) *nt* hospital

spitz [ʃpɪts] *adj* pointed; (*Winkel*) acute; (*fig: Zunge*) sharp; (*: Bemerkung*) caustic

Spitze *f* point, tip; (*Bergspitze*) peak; (*Bemerkung*) taunt, dig; (*erster Platz*) lead, top; (*meist pl: Gewebe*) lace

Spitzel (**-s, -**) *m* police informer

spitzen *vt* to sharpen

Spitzenmarke *f* brand leader

spitzfindig *adj* (over)subtle

Spitzname *m* nickname

Splitter [ˈʃplɪtər] (**-s, -**) *m* splinter

sponsern [ˈʃpɔnzərn] *vt* to sponsor

spontan [ʃpɔnˈtaːn] *adj* spontaneous

Sport [ʃpɔrt] (**-(e)s, -e**) *m* sport; (*fig*) hobby; **~lehrer(in)** *m(f)* games *od* P.E. teacher; **~ler(in)** (**-s, -**) *m(f)* sportsman(-woman); **s~lich** *adj* sporting; (*Mensch*) sporty; **~platz** *m* playing *od* sports field; **~schuh** *m* (*Turnschuh*) training shoe, trainer; **~stadion** *nt* sports stadium; **~verein** *m* sports club; **~wagen** *m* sports car

Spott [ʃpɔt] (**-(e)s**) *m* mockery, ridicule; **s~billig** *adj* dirt-cheap; **s~en** *vi* to mock; **s~en** (*über +akk*) to mock (at), to ridicule

spöttisch [ˈʃpœtɪʃ] *adj* mocking

sprach *etc* [ʃpraːx] *vb siehe* **sprechen**

Sprach- *zW:* **s~begabt** *adj* good at languages; **~e** *f* language; **~enschule** *f* language school; **~fehler** *m* speech defect; **~führer** *m* phrasebook; **~gefühl** *nt* feeling for language; **~kenntnisse** *pl* linguistic proficiency *sg*; **~kurs** *m* language course; **~labor** *nt* language laboratory; **s~lich** *adj* linguistic; **s~los** *adj* speechless

sprang *etc* [ʃpraŋ] *vb siehe* **springen**

Spray [spreː] (**-s, -s**) *m od nt* spray

Sprech- [ˈʃprɛç] *zW:* **~anlage** *f* intercom; **s~en** (*unreg*) *vi* to speak, to talk ♦ *vt* to say; (*Sprache*) to speak; (*Person*) to speak to; **mit jdm s~en** to speak to sb; **das spricht für ihn** that's a point in his favour; **~er(in)** (**-s, -**) *m(f)* speaker; (*für Gruppe*) spokesman/woman; (*RADIO, TV*) announcer; **~stunde** *f* consultation (hour); (*doctor's*) surgery; **~stundenhilfe** *f* (*doctor's*) receptionist; **~zimmer** *nt* consulting room, surgery, office (*US*)

spreizen [ˈʃpraɪtsən] *vt* (*Beine*) to open, to spread; (*Finger, Flügel*) to spread

Spreng- [ˈʃprɛŋ] *zW:* **s~en** *vt* to sprinkle; (*mit ~stoff*) to blow up; (*Gestein*) to blast; (*Versammlung*) to break up; **~stoff** *m* explosive(s)

sprichst *etc* [ʃprɪçst] *vb siehe* **sprechen**

Sprichwort *nt* proverb; **sprichwörtlich** *adj* proverbial

Spring- [ˈʃprɪŋ] *zW:* **~brunnen** *m* fountain; **s~en** (*unreg*) *vi* to jump; (*Glas*) to crack; (*mit Kopfsprung*) to dive; **~er** (**-s, -**) *m* jumper; (*Schach*) knight

Sprit [ʃprɪt] (**-(e)s, -e**) (*umg*) *m* juice, gas

Spritz- [ˈʃprɪts] *zW:* **~e** *f* syringe; injection; (*an Schlauch*) nozzle; **s~en** *vt* to spray; (*MED*) to inject ♦ *vi* to splash; (*herausspritzen*) to spurt; (*MED*) to give injections; **~pistole** *f* spray gun; **~tour** *f* (*umg*) spin

spröde [ˈʃprøːdə] *adj* brittle; (*Person*) reserved, coy

Sprosse [ˈʃprɔsə] *f* rung

Sprössling ▲ [ˈʃprœslɪŋ] (*umg*) *m* (*Kind*) offspring (*pl inv*)

Spruch [ʃprʊx] (**-(e)s, ⁻e**) *m* saying, maxim; (*JUR*) judgement

Sprudel [ˈʃpruːdəl] (**-s, -**) *m* mineral water; lemonade; **s~n** *vi* to bubble; **~wasser** *nt* (*KOCH*) sparkling *od* fizzy mineral water

Sprüh- [ˈʃpryː] *zW:* **~dose** *f* aerosol (can); **s~en** *vi* to spray; (*fig*) to sparkle ♦ *vt* to spray; **~regen** *m* drizzle

Sprung [ʃprʊŋ] (**-(e)s, ⁻e**) *m* jump; (*Riss*) crack; **~brett** *nt* springboard; **s~haft** *adj* erratic; (*Aufstieg*) rapid; **~schanze** *f* ski jump

Spucke [ˈʃpʊkə] (**-**) *f* spit; **s~n** *vt, vi* to spit

Spuk [ʃpuːk] (**-(e)s, -e**) *m* haunting; (*fig*) nightmare; **s~en** *vi* (*Geist*) to walk; **hier s~t es** this place is haunted

Spülbecken [ˈʃpyːlbɛkən] *nt* (*in Küche*) sink

Spule [ˈʃpuːlə] *f* spool; (*ELEK*) coil

Spül- [ˈʃpyːl] *zW:* **~e** *f* (kitchen) sink; **s~en** *vt, vi* to rinse; (*Geschirr*) to wash up; (*Toilette*) to flush; **~maschine** *f* dishwasher; **~mittel** *nt* washing-up liquid; **~stein** *m* sink; **~ung** *f* rinsing; flush; (*MED*) irrigation

Spur [ʃpuːr] (**-, -en**) *f* trace; (*Fußspur, Radspur, Tonbandspur*) track; (*Fährte*) trail; (*Fahrspur*) lane

spürbar *adj* noticeable, perceptible

spüren [ˈʃpyːrən] *vt* to feel

spurlos *adv* without (a) trace

Spurt [ʃpʊrt] (**-(e)s, -s** *od* **-e**) *m* spurt; **s~en** *vi* to spurt

sputen [ˈʃpuːtən] *vr* to make haste

St. *abk* = **Stück**; (= *Sankt*) St.

Staat [ʃtaːt] (**-(e)s, -en**) *m* state; (*Prunk*) show; (*Kleidung*) finery; **s~enlos** *adj* stateless; **s~lich** *adj* state(-); state-run

Staats- *zW:* **~angehörige(r)** *f(m)* national; **~angehörigkeit** *f* nationality; **~anwalt** *m* public prosecutor; **~bürger** *m* citizen; **~dienst** *m* civil service; **~examen** *nt* (*UNIV*) state exam(ination); **s~feindlich** *adj* subversive; **~mann** (*pl* **-männer**) *m* statesman; **~oberhaupt** *nt* head of state

Stab [ʃtaːp] (**-(e)s, ⁻e**) *m* rod; (*Gitterstab*) bar; (*Menschen*) staff; **~hochsprung** *m* pole vault

stabil [ʃtaˈbiːl] *adj* stable; (*Möbel*) sturdy; **~i'sieren** *vt* to stabilize

Stachel [ˈʃtaxəl] (**-s, -n**) *m* spike; (*von Tier*) spine; (*von Insekten*) sting; **~beere** *f* gooseberry; **~draht** *m* barbed wire; **s~ig** *adj* prickly; **~schwein** *nt* porcupine

Stadion [ˈʃtaːdiɔn] (**-s, Stadien**) *nt* stadium

Stadium [ˈʃtaːdiʊm] *nt* stage, phase

Stadt [ʃtat] (-, ⸚e) f town; **~autobahn** f
urban motorway; **~bahn** f suburban
railway; **~bücherei** f municipal library
Städt- ['ʃtɛːt] zW: **~ebau** m town planning;
~epartnerschaft f town twinning;
~er(in) (-s, -) m(f) town dweller; **s~isch**
adj municipal; *(nicht ländlich)* urban
Stadt- zW: **~kern** m town centre, city
centre; **~mauer** f city wall(s); **~mitte** f
town centre; **~plan** m street map; **~rand**
m outskirts pl; **~rat** m *(Behörde)* town
council, city council; **~rundfahrt** f tour of
a/the city; **~teil** m district, part of town;
~zentrum nt town centre
Staffel ['ʃtafəl] (-, -n) f rung; *(SPORT)* relay
(team); *(AVIAT)* squadron; **~lauf** m *(SPORT)*
relay (race); **s~n** vt to graduate
Stahl [ʃtaːl] (-(e)s, ⸚e) m steel
stahl etc vb siehe **stehlen**
stak etc [staːk] vb siehe **stecken**
Stall [ʃtal] (-(e)s, ⸚e) m stable;
(Kaninchenstall) hutch; *(Schweinestall)* sty;
(Hühnerstall) henhouse
Stamm [ʃtam] (-(e)s, ⸚e) m *(Baumstamm)*
trunk; *(Menschenstamm)* tribe; *(GRAM)* stem;
~baum m family tree; *(von Tier)* pedigree;
s~eln vt, vi to stammer; **s~en** vi: **s~en
von** od **aus** to come from; **~gast** m regular
(customer)
stämmig ['ʃtɛmɪç] adj sturdy; *(Mensch)*
stocky
Stammtisch ['ʃtamtɪʃ] m table for the
regulars
stampfen ['ʃtampfən] vt, vi to stamp;
(stapfen) to tramp; *(mit Werkzeug)* to pound
Stand [ʃtant] (-(e)s, ⸚e) m position;
(Wasserstand, Benzinstand etc) level; *(Stehen)*
standing position; *(Zustand)* state;
(Spielstand) score; *(Messestand etc)* stand;
(Klasse) class; *(Beruf)* profession; siehe
imstande, zustande
stand etc vb siehe **stehen**
Standard ['ʃtandart] (-s, -s) m standard
Ständer- ['ʃtɛndər] (-s, -) m stand
Standes- ['ʃtandəs] zW: **~amt** nt registry
office; **~beamte(r)** m registrar; **s~gemäß**
adj, adv according to one's social position;

~unterschied m social difference
Stand- zW: **s~haft** adj steadfast; **s~halten**
(unreg) vi: **(jdm/etw) s~halten** to stand
firm (against sb/sth), to resist (sb/sth)
ständig ['ʃtɛndɪç] adj permanent;
(ununterbrochen) constant, continual
Stand- zW: **~licht** nt sidelights pl, parking
lights pl *(US)*; **~ort** m location; *(MIL)*
garrison; **~punkt** m standpoint; **~spur** f
hard shoulder
Stange ['ʃtaŋə] f stick; *(Stab)* pole, bar; rod;
(Zigaretten) carton; **von der ~** *(COMM)* off
the peg; **eine ~ Geld** *(umg)* quite a packet
Stängel ▲ ['ʃtɛŋəl] (-s, -) m stalk
Stapel ['ʃtaːpəl] (-s, -) m pile; *(NAUT)* stocks
pl; **~lauf** m launch; **s~n** vt to pile (up)
Star¹ [ʃtaːr] (-(e)s, -e) m starling; *(MED)*
cataract
Star² [ʃtaːr] (-s, -s) m *(Filmstar etc)* star
starb etc [ʃtarp] vb siehe **sterben**
stark [ʃtark] adj strong; *(heftig, groß)* heavy;
(Maßangabe) thick
Stärke ['ʃtɛrkə] f strength; heaviness;
thickness; *(KOCH: Wäschestärke)* starch; **s~n**
vt to strengthen; *(Wäsche)* to starch
Starkstrom m heavy current
Stärkung ['ʃtɛrkʊŋ] f strengthening; *(Essen)*
refreshment
starr [ʃtar] adj stiff; *(unnachgiebig)* rigid;
(Blick) staring; **~en** vi to stare; **~en vor** od
von to be covered in; *(Waffen)* to be
bristling with; **S~heit** f rigidity; **~köpfig**
adj stubborn; **S~sinn** m obstinacy
Start [ʃtart] (-(e)s, -e) m start; *(AVIAT)*
takeoff; **~automatik** f *(AUT)* automatic
choke; **~bahn** f runway; **s~en** vt to start
♦ vi to start; to take off; **~er** (-s, -) m
starter; **~erlaubnis** f takeoff clearance;
~hilfekabel nt jump leads pl
Station [ʃtatsiˈoːn] f station; hospital ward;
s~är [ʃtatsioˈnɛːr] adj *(MED)* in-patient attr;
s~ieren [-ˈniːrən] vt to station
Statist [ʃtaˈtɪst] m extra, supernumerary
Statistik f statistics sg; **~er** (-s, -) m
statistician
statistisch adj statistical
Stativ [ʃtaˈtiːf] (-s, -e) nt tripod

statt [ʃtat] *konj* instead of ♦ *präp* (+*gen od dat*) instead of

Stätte ['ʃtɛtə] *f* place

statt- *zW:* **~finden** (*unreg*) *vi* to take place; **~haft** *adj* admissible; **~lich** *adj* imposing, handsome

Statue ['ʃtaːtuə] *f* statue

Status ['ʃtaːtʊs] (**-**, **-**) *m* status

Stau [ʃtaʊ] (**-(e)s**, **-e**) *m* blockage; (*Verkehrsstau*) (traffic) jam

Staub [ʃtaʊp] (**-(e)s**) *m* dust; **~ saugen** to vacuum, to hoover®; **s~en** ['ʃtaʊbən] *vi* to be dusty; **s~ig** *adj* dusty; **s~saugen** *vi* to vacuum, to hoover®; **~sauger** *m* vacuum cleaner; **~tuch** *nt* duster

Staudamm *m* dam

Staude ['ʃtaʊdə] *f* shrub

stauen ['ʃtaʊən] *vt* (*Wasser*) to dam up; (*Blut*) to stop the flow of ♦ *vr* (*Wasser*) to become dammed up; (*MED: Verkehr*) to become congested; (*Menschen*) to collect; (*Gefühle*) to build up

staunen ['ʃtaʊnən] *vi* to be astonished; **S~** (**-s**) *nt* amazement

Stausee ['ʃtaʊzeː] (**-s**, **-n**) *m* reservoir, man-made lake

Stauung ['ʃtaʊʊŋ] *f* (*von Wasser*) damming-up; (*von Blut, Verkehr*) congestion

Std. *abk* (= *Stunde*) hr.

Steak [ʃteːk] *nt* steak

Stech- ['ʃtɛç] *zW:* **s~en** (*unreg*) *vt* (*mit Nadel etc*) to prick; (*mit Messer*) to stab; (*mit Finger*) to poke; (*Biene etc*) to sting; (*Mücke*) to bite; (*Sonne*) to burn; (*KARTEN*) to take; (*ART*) to engrave; (*Torf, Spargel*) to cut; **in See s~en** to put to sea; **~en** (**-s**, **-**) *nt* (*SPORT*) play-off; jump-off; **s~end** *adj* piercing, stabbing; (*Geruch*) pungent; **~palme** *f* holly; **~uhr** *f* time clock

Steck- ['ʃtɛk] *zW:* **~brief** *m* "wanted" poster; **~dose** *f* (wall) socket; **s~en** *vt* to put, to insert; (*Nadel*) to stick; (*Pflanzen*) to plant; (*beim Nähen*) to pin ♦ *vi* (*auch unreg*) to be; (*festsitzen*) to be stuck; (*Nadeln*) to stick; **s~en bleiben** to get stuck; **s~en lassen** to leave in; **~enpferd** *nt* hobby-horse; **~er** (**-s**, **-**) *m* plug; **~nadel** *f* pin

Steg [ʃteːk] (**-(e)s**, **-e**) *m* small bridge; (*Anlegesteg*) landing stage; **~reif** *m*: **aus dem ~reif** just like that

stehen ['ʃteːən] (*unreg*) *vi* to stand; (*sich befinden*) to be; (*in Zeitung*) to say; (*stillstehen*) to have stopped ♦ *vi unpers*: **es steht schlecht um jdn/etw** things are bad for sb/sth; **zu jdm/etw ~** to stand by sb/sth; **jdm ~** to suit sb; **wie stehts?** how are things?; (*SPORT*) what's the score?; **~ bleiben** to remain standing; (*Uhr*) to stop; (*Fehler*) to stay as it is; **~ lassen** to leave; (*Bart*) to grow

Stehlampe ['ʃteːlampə] *f* standard lamp

stehlen ['ʃteːlən] (*unreg*) *vt* to steal

Stehplatz ['ʃteːplats] *m* standing place

steif [ʃtaɪf] *adj* stiff; **S~heit** *f* stiffness

Steig- ['ʃtaɪk] *zW:* **~bügel** *m* stirrup; **s~en** ['ʃtaɪgən] (*unreg*) *vi* to rise; (*klettern*) to climb; **s~en in** +*akk*/**auf** +*akk* to get in/on; **s~ern** *vt* to raise; (*GRAM*) to compare ♦ *vi* (*Auktion*) to bid ♦ *vr* to increase; **~erung** *f* raising; (*GRAM*) comparison; **~ung** *f* incline, gradient, rise

steil [ʃtaɪl] *adj* steep; **S~küste** *f* steep coast; (*Klippen*) cliffs *pl*

Stein [ʃtaɪn] (**-(e)s**, **-e**) *m* stone; (*in Uhr*) jewel; **~bock** *m* (*ASTROL*) Capricorn; **~bruch** *m* quarry; **s~ern** *adj* (made of) stone; (*fig*) stony; **~gut** *nt* stoneware; **s~ig** ['ʃtaɪnɪç] *adj* stony; **s~igen** *vt* to stone; **~kohle** *f* mineral coal; **~zeit** *f* Stone Age

Stelle ['ʃtɛlə] *f* place; (*Arbeit*) post, job; (*Amt*) office; **an Ihrer/meiner ~** in your/my place; *siehe* **anstelle**

stellen *vt* to put; (*Uhr etc*) to set; (*zur Verfügung ~*) to supply; (*fassen: Dieb*) to apprehend ♦ *vr* (*sich aufstellen*) to stand; (*sich einfinden*) to present o.s.; (*bei Polizei*) to give o.s. up; (*vorgeben*) to pretend (to be); **sich zu etw ~** to have an opinion of sth

Stellen- *zW:* **~angebot** *nt* offer of a post; (*in Zeitung*) "vacancies"; **~anzeige** *f* job advertisement; **~gesuch** *nt* application for a post; **~vermittlung** *f* employment agency

Stell- zW: **~ung** f position; (MIL) line; **~ung nehmen zu** to comment on; **~ungnahme** f comment; **s~vertretend** adj deputy, acting; **~vertreter** m deputy

Stelze ['ʃtɛltsə] f stilt

stemmen ['ʃtɛman] vt to lift (up); (drücken) to press; **sich ~ gegen** (fig) to resist, to oppose

Stempel ['ʃtɛmpəl] (**-s, -**) m stamp; (BOT) pistil; **~kissen** nt ink pad; **s~n** vt to stamp; (Briefmarke) to cancel; **s~n gehen** (umg) to be od go on the dole

Stengel △ ['ʃtɛŋəl] (**-s, -**) m = **Stängel**

Steno- [ʃteno] zW: **~gramm** [-'gram] nt shorthand report; **~grafie** ▲ [-gra'fiː] f shorthand; **s~grafieren** ▲ [-gra'fiːrən] vt, vi to write (in) shorthand; **~typist(in)** [-tyˈpɪst(ɪn)] m(f) shorthand typist

Stepp- ['ʃtɛp] zW: **~decke** f quilt; **~e** f prairie; steppe; **s~en** vt to stitch ♦ vi to tap-dance

Sterb- ['ʃtɛrb] zW: **~efall** m death; **~ehilfe** f euthanasia; **s~en** (unreg) vi to die; **s~lich** ['ʃtɛrplɪç] adj mortal; **~lichkeit** f mortality; **~lichkeitsziffer** f death rate

stereo- ['ʃtɛːreo] in zW stereo(-); **S~anlage** f stereo (system); **~typ** [ʃtɛːreoˈtyːp] adj stereotype

steril [ʃteˈriːl] adj sterile; **~isieren** vt to sterilize; **S~isierung** f sterilization

Stern [ʃtɛrn] (**-(e)s, -e**) m star; **~bild** nt constellation; **~schnuppe** f meteor, falling star; **~stunde** f historic moment; **~zeichen** nt sign of the zodiac

stet [ʃteːt] adj steady; **~ig** adj constant, continual; **~s** adv continually, always

Steuer¹ ['ʃtɔ͜yər] (**-s, -**) nt (NAUT) helm; (~ruder) rudder; (AUT) steering wheel

Steuer² ['ʃtɔ͜yər] (**-, -n**) f tax; **~berater(in)** m(f) tax consultant

Steuerbord nt (NAUT, AVIAT) starboard

Steuer- ['ʃtɔ͜yər] zW: **~erklärung** f tax return; **s~frei** adj tax-free; **~freibetrag** m tax allowance; **~klasse** f tax group; **~knüppel** m control column; (AVIAT, COMPUT) joystick; **~mann** (pl **-männer** od **-leute**) m helmsman; **s~n** vt, vi to steer;

(Flugzeug) to pilot; (Entwicklung, Tonstärke) to control; **s~pflichtig** [-pflɪçtɪç] adj taxable; **~rad** nt steering wheel; **~ung** f (auch AUT) steering; piloting; control; (Vorrichtung) controls pl; **~zahler** (**-s, -**) m taxpayer

Steward ['stjuːart] (**-s, -s**) m steward; **~ess** ▲ ['stjuːardɛs] (**-, -en**) f stewardess; air hostess

Stich [ʃtɪç] (**-(e)s, -e**) m (Insektenstich) sting; (Messerstich) stab; (beim Nähen) stitch; (Färbung) tinge; trick; (ART) engraving; **jdn im ~ lassen** to leave sb in the lurch; **s~eln** vi (fig) to jibe; **s~haltig** adj sound, tenable; **~probe** f spot check; **~straße** f cul-de-sac; **~wahl** f final ballot; **~wort** nt cue; (in Wörterbuch) headword; (für Vortrag) note

sticken ['ʃtɪkən] vt, vi to embroider

Sticke'rei f embroidery

stickig adj stuffy, close

Stickstoff m nitrogen

Stief- ['ʃtiːf] in zW step

Stiefel ['ʃtiːfəl] (**-s, -**) m boot

Stief- zW: **~kind** nt stepchild; (fig) Cinderella; **~mutter** f stepmother; **~mütterchen** nt pansy; **s~mütterlich** adj (fig): **jdn/etw s~mütterlich behandeln** to pay little attention to sb/sth; **~vater** m stepfather

stiehlst etc [ʃtiːlst] vb siehe **stehlen**

Stiel [ʃtiːl] (**-(e)s, -e**) m handle; (BOT) stalk

Stier (**-(e)s, -e**) m bull; (ASTROL) Taurus

stieren vi to stare

Stierkampf m bullfight

Stierkämpfer m bullfighter

Stift [ʃtɪft] (**-(e)s, -e**) m peg; (Nagel) tack; (Farbstift) crayon; (Bleistift) pencil ♦ nt (charitable) foundation; (ECCL) religious institution; **s~en** vt to found; (Unruhe) to cause; (spenden) to contribute; **~er(in)** (**-s, -**) m(f) founder; **~ung** f donation; (Organisation) foundation; **~zahn** m post crown

Stil [ʃtiːl] (**-(e)s, -e**) m style

still [ʃtɪl] adj quiet; (unbewegt) still; (heimlich) secret; **S~er Ozean** Pacific; **~ halten** to keep still; **~ stehen** to stand still; **S~e** f

stillness, quietness; **in aller S~e** quietly;
~en vt to stop; (*befriedigen*) to satisfy;
(*Säugling*) to breast-feed; **~legen** ▲ vt to
close down; **~schweigen** (*unreg*) vi to be
silent; **S~schweigen** nt silence;
~schweigend adj silent; (*Einverständnis*)
tacit ♦ adv silently; tacitly; **S~stand** m
standstill

Stimm- ['ʃtɪm] zW: **~bänder** pl vocal cords;
s~berechtigt adj entitled to vote; **~e** f
voice; (*Wahlstimme*) vote; **s~en** vt (MUS) to
tune ♦ vi to be right; **das s~te ihn traurig**
that made him feel sad; **s~en für/gegen**
to vote for/against; **s~t so!** that's right;
~enmehrheit f majority (of votes);
~enthaltung f abstention; **~gabel** f
tuning fork; **~recht** nt right to vote; **~ung**
f mood; atmosphere; **s~ungsvoll** adj
enjoyable; full of atmosphere; **~zettel** m
ballot paper

stinken ['ʃtɪŋkən] (*unreg*) vi to stink
Stipendium ['ʃtiˈpɛndiʊm] nt grant
stirbst etc [ʃtɪrpst] vb siehe **sterben**
Stirn [ʃtɪrn] (-, -en) f forehead, brow;
(*Frechheit*) impudence; **~band** nt
headband; **~höhle** f sinus
stöbern ['ʃtøːbərn] vi to rummage
stochern ['ʃtɔxərn] vi to poke (about)
Stock[1] [ʃtɔk] (-(e)s, ⁺e) m stick; (BOT) stock
Stock[2] [ʃtɔk] (-(e)s, - od **Stockwerke**) m
storey
stocken vi to stop, to pause; **~d** adj halting
Stockung f stoppage
Stockwerk nt storey, floor
Stoff [ʃtɔf] (-(e)s, -e) m (*Gewebe*) material,
cloth; (*Materie*) matter; (*von Buch etc*)
subject (matter); **~lich** adj material; **~tier**
nt soft toy; **~wechsel** m metabolism
stöhnen ['ʃtøːnən] vi to groan
Stollen ['ʃtɔlən] (-s, -) m (MIN) gallery;
(KOCH) cake eaten at Christmas; (*von
Schuhen*) stud
stolpern ['ʃtɔlpərn] vi to stumble, to trip
Stolz [ʃtɔlts] (-es) m pride; **s~** adj proud;
s~ieren [ʃtɔlˈtsiːrən] vi to strut
stopfen ['ʃtɔpfən] vt (*hineinstopfen*) to stuff;
(*voll stopfen*) to fill (up); (*nähen*) to darn ♦ vi

(MED) to cause constipation
Stopfgarn nt darning thread
Stoppel ['ʃtɔpəl] (-, -n) f stubble
Stopp- ['ʃtɔp] zW: **s~en** vt to stop; (*mit Uhr*)
to time ♦ vi to stop; **~schild** nt stop sign;
~uhr f stopwatch
Stöpsel ['ʃtœpsəl] (-s, -) m plug; (*für
Flaschen*) stopper
Storch [ʃtɔrç] (-(e)s, ⁺e) m stork
Stör- [ʃtøːr] zW: **s~en** vt to disturb;
(*behindern*, RADIO) to interfere with ♦ vr:
sich an etw dat **s~en** to let sth bother
one; **s~end** adj disturbing, annoying;
~enfried (-(e)s, -e) m troublemaker
stornieren [ʃtɔrˈniːrən] vt (*Auftrag*) to
cancel; (*Buchung*) to reverse
Stornogebühr ['ʃtɔrno-] f cancellation fee
störrisch ['ʃtœrɪʃ] adj stubborn, perverse
Störung f disturbance; interference
Stoß [ʃtoːs] (-es, ⁺e) m (*Schub*) push; (*Schlag*)
blow; knock; (*mit Schwert*) thrust; (*mit Fuß*)
kick; (*Erdstoß*) shock; (*Haufen*) pile;
~dämpfer (-s, -) m shock absorber; **s~en**
(*unreg*) vt (*mit Druck*) to shove, to push; (*mit
Schlag*) to knock, to bump; (*mit Fuß*) to
kick; (*Schwert etc*) to thrust; (*anstoßen: Kopf
etc*) to bump ♦ vr to get a knock ♦ vi: **s~en
an** od **auf** +akk to bump into; (*finden*) to
come across; (*angrenzen*) to be next to;
sich an etw an +dat (*fig*) to take exception
to; **~stange** f (AUT) bumper
stottern ['ʃtɔtərn] vt, vi to stutter
Str. abk (= *Straße*) St.
Straf- ['ʃtraːf] zW: **~anstalt** f penal
institution; **~arbeit** f (SCH) punishment;
lines pl; **s~bar** adj punishable; **~e** f
punishment; (JUR) penalty; (*Gefängnisstrafe*)
sentence; (*Geldstrafe*) fine; **s~en** vt to
punish
straff [ʃtraf] adj tight; (*streng*) strict; (*Stil etc*)
concise; (*Haltung*) erect; **~en** vt to tighten,
to tauten
Strafgefangene(r) f(m) prisoner, convict
Strafgesetzbuch nt penal code
sträflich ['ʃtrɛːflɪç] adj criminal
Sträfling m convict
Straf- zW: **~porto** nt excess postage

(charge); **~predigt** f telling-off; **~raum** m (SPORT) penalty area; **~recht** nt criminal law; **~stoß** m (SPORT) penalty (kick); **~tat** f punishable act; **~zettel** m ticket

Strahl [ʃtraːl] (**-s, -en**) m ray, beam; (*Wasserstrahl*) jet; **s~en** vi to radiate; (*fig*) to beam; **~ung** f radiation

Strähne [ˈʃtrɛːnə] f strand

stramm [ʃtram] adj tight; (*Haltung*) erect; (*Mensch*) robust

strampeln [ˈʃtrampəln] vi to kick (about), to fidget

Strand [ʃtrant] (**-(e)s, ᵘe**) m shore; (*mit Sand*) beach; **~bad** nt open-air swimming pool, lido; **s~en** [ˈʃtrandən] vi to run aground; (*fig: Mensch*) to fail; **~gut** nt flotsam; **~korb** m beach chair

Strang [ʃtraŋ] (**-(e)s, ᵘe**) m cord, rope; (*Bündel*) skein

Strapaz- zW: **~e** [ʃtraˈpaːtsə] f strain, exertion; **s~ieren** [ʃtrapaˈtsiːrən] vt (*Material*) to treat roughly, to punish; (*Mensch, Kräfte*) to wear out, to exhaust; **s~ierfähig** adj hard-wearing; **s~iös** [ʃtrapatsiˈøːs] adj exhausting, tough

Straße [ˈʃtraːsə] f street, road

Straßen- zW: **~bahn** f tram, streetcar (US); **~glätte** f slippery road surface; **~karte** f road map; **~kehrer** (**-s, -**) m roadsweeper; **~sperre** f roadblock; **~verkehr** m (road) traffic; **~verkehrsordnung** f highway code

Strateg- [ʃtraˈteːg] zW: **~e** (**-n, -n**) m strategist; **~ie** [ʃtrateˈgiː] f strategy; **s~isch** adj strategic

sträuben [ˈʃtrɔybən] vt to ruffle ♦ vr to bristle; (*Mensch*): **sich (gegen etw) ~** to resist (sth)

Strauch [ʃtraux] (**-(e)s, Sträucher**) m bush, shrub

Strauß¹ [ʃtraʊs] (**-es, Sträuße**) m bunch; bouquet

Strauß² [ʃtraʊs] (**-es, -e**) m ostrich

Streb- [ˈʃtreːb] zW: **s~en** vi to strive, to endeavour; **s~en nach** to strive for; **~er** (**-s, -**) m (*pej*) m pusher, climber; (*SCH*) swot (*BRIT*)

Strecke [ˈʃtrɛkə] f stretch; (*Entfernung*) distance; (*EISENB, MATH*) line; **s~n** vt to stretch; (*Waffen*) to lay down; (*KOCH*) to eke out ♦ vr to stretch (o.s.)

Streich [ʃtraiç] (**-(e)s, -e**) m trick, prank; (*Hieb*) blow; **s~eln** vt to stroke; **s~en** (*unreg*) vt (*berühren*) to stroke; (*auftragen*) to spread; (*anmalen*) to paint; (*durchstreichen*) to delete; (*nicht genehmigen*) to cancel ♦ vi (*berühren*) to brush; (*schleichen*) to prowl; **~holz** nt match; **~instrument** nt string instrument

Streif- [ˈʃtraif] zW: **~e** f patrol; **s~en** vt (*leicht berühren*) to brush against, to graze; (*Blick*) to skim over; (*Thema, Problem*) to touch on; (*abstreifen*) to take off ♦ vi (*gehen*) to roam; **~en** (**-s, -**) m (*Linie*) stripe; (*Stück*) strip; (*Film*) film; **~enwagen** m patrol car; **~schuss** ▲ m graze, grazing shot; **~zug** m scouting trip

Streik [ʃtraik] (**-(e)s, -s**) m strike; **~brecher** (**-s, -**) m blackleg, strikebreaker; **s~en** vi to strike; **~posten** m (strike) picket

Streit [ʃtrait] (**-(e)s, -e**) m argument; dispute; **s~en** (*unreg*) vi, vr to argue; to dispute; **~frage** f point at issue; **s~ig** adj: **jdm etw s~ig machen** to dispute sb's right to sth; **~igkeiten** pl quarrel sg, dispute sg; **~kräfte** pl (*MIL*) armed forces

streng [ʃtrɛŋ] adj severe; (*Lehrer, Maßnahme*) strict; (*Geruch etc*) sharp; **~ genommen** strictly speaking; **S~e** (**-**) f severity, strictness, sharpness; **~gläubig** adj orthodox, strict; **~stens** adv strictly

Stress ▲ [ʃtrɛs] (**-es, -e**) m stress

stressen vt to put under stress

streuen [ˈʃtrɔyən] vt to strew, to scatter, to spread

Strich [ʃtriç] (**-(e)s, -e**) m (*Linie*) line; (*Federstrich, Pinselstrich*) stroke; (*von Geweben*) nap; (*von Fell*) pile; **auf den ~ gehen** (*umg*) to walk the streets; **jdm gegen den ~ gehen** to rub sb up the wrong way; **einen ~ machen durch** to cross out; (*fig*) to foil; **~kode** m (*auf Waren*) bar code; **~mädchen** nt streetwalker; **s~weise** adv here and there

Strick [ʃtrɪk] (-(e)s, -e) m rope; **s~en** vt, vi to knit; **~jacke** f cardigan; **~leiter** f rope ladder; **~nadel** f knitting needle; **~waren** pl knitwear sg

strikt [strɪkt] adj strict

strittig ['ʃtrɪtɪç] adj disputed, in dispute

Stroh [ʃtroː] (-(e)s, -e) nt straw; **~blume** f everlasting flower; **~dach** nt thatched roof; **~halm** m (drinking) straw

Strom [ʃtroːm] (-(e)s, ⁼e) m river; (fig) stream; (ELEK) current; **s~abwärts** adv downstream; **s~aufwärts** adv upstream; **~ausfall** m power failure

strömen ['ʃtrøːmən] vi to stream, to pour

Strom- zW: **~kreis** m circuit; **s~linienförmig** adj streamlined; **~sperre** f power cut

Strömung ['ʃtrøːmʊŋ] f current

Strophe ['ʃtroːfə] f verse

strotzen ['ʃtrɔtsən] vi: **~ vor** od **von** to abound in, to be full of

Strudel ['ʃtruːdəl] (-s, -) m whirlpool, vortex; (KOCH) strudel

Struktur [ʃtrʊk'tuːr] f structure

Strumpf [ʃtrʊmpf] (-(e)s, ⁼e) m stocking; **~band** nt garter; **~hose** f (pair of) tights

Stube ['ʃtuːbə] f room

Stuben- zW: **~arrest** m confinement to one's room; (MIL) confinement to quarters; **~hocker** (umg) m stay-at-home; **s~rein** adj house-trained

Stuck [ʃtʊk] (-(e)s) m stucco

Stück [ʃtʏk] (-(e)s, -e) nt piece; (etwas) bit; (THEAT) play; **~chen** nt little piece; **~lohn** m piecework wages pl; **s~weise** adv bit by bit, piecemeal; (COMM) individually

Student(in) [ʃtu'dɛnt(ɪn)] m(f) student; **s~isch** adj student, academic

Studie ['ʃtuːdiə] f study

Studienfahrt f study trip

studieren [ʃtu'diːrən] vt, vi to study

Studio ['ʃtuːdio] (-s, -s) nt studio

Studium ['ʃtuːdiʊm] nt studies pl

Stufe ['ʃtuːfə] f step; (Entwicklungsstufe) stage; **s~nweise** adv gradually

Stuhl [ʃtuːl] (-(e)s, ⁼e) m chair; **~gang** m bowel movement

stülpen ['ʃtʏlpən] vt (umdrehen) to turn upside down; (bedecken) to put

stumm [ʃtʊm] adj silent; (MED) dumb

Stummel ['ʃtʊməl] (-s, -) m stump; (Zigarettenstummel) stub

Stummfilm m silent film

Stümper ['ʃtʏmpər] (-s, -) m incompetent, duffer; **s~haft** adj bungling, incompetent; **s~n** vi to bungle

Stumpf [ʃtʊmpf] (-(e)s, ⁼e) m stump; **s~** adj blunt; (teilnahmslos, glanzlos) dull; (Winkel) obtuse; **~sinn** m tediousness; **s~sinnig** adj dull

Stunde ['ʃtʊndə] f hour; (SCH) lesson

stunden vt: **jdm etw ~** to give sb time to pay sth; **S~geschwindigkeit** f average speed per hour; **S~kilometer** pl kilometres per hour; **~lang** adj for hours; **S~lohn** m hourly wage; **S~plan** m timetable; **~weise** adj by the hour; every hour

stündlich ['ʃtʏntlɪç] adj hourly

Stups [ʃtʊps] (-es, -e) (umg) m push; **~nase** f snub nose

stur [ʃtuːr] adj obstinate, pigheaded

Sturm [ʃtʊrm] (-(e)s, ⁼e) m storm, gale; (MIL etc) attack, assault

stürm- [ʃtʏrm] zW: **~en** vi (Wind) to blow hard, to rage; (rennen) to storm ♦ vt (MIL, fig) to storm ♦ vb unpers: **es ~t** there's a gale blowing; **S~er** (-s, -) m (SPORT) forward, striker; **~isch** adj stormy

Sturmwarnung f gale warning

Sturz [ʃtʊrts] (-es, ⁼e) m fall; (POL) overthrow

stürzen ['ʃtʏrtsən] vt (werfen) to hurl; (POL) to overthrow; (umkehren) to overturn ♦ vr to rush; (hineinstürzen) to plunge ♦ vi to fall; (AVIAT) to dive; (rennen) to dash

Sturzflug m nose dive

Sturzhelm m crash helmet

Stute ['ʃtuːtə] f mare

Stützbalken m brace, joist

Stütze ['ʃtʏtsə] f support; help

stutzen ['ʃtʊtsən] vt to trim; (Ohr, Schwanz) to dock; (Flügel) to clip ♦ vi to hesitate; to become suspicious

stützen vt (auch fig) to support; (Ellbogen

etc) to prop up

stutzig *adj* perplexed, puzzled; (*misstrauisch*) suspicious

Stützpunkt *m* point of support; (*von Hebel*) fulcrum; (*MIL, fig*) base

Styropor [ʃtyro'poːr] (®; **-s**) *nt* polystyrene

s. u. *abk* = **siehe unten**

Subjekt [zʊp'jɛkt] (**-(e)s, -e**) *nt* subject; **s~iv** [-'tiːf] *adj* subjective; **~ivi'tät** *f* subjectivity

Subsidiarität *f* subsidiarity

Substantiv [zʊpstan'tiːf] (**-s, -e**) *nt* noun

Substanz [zʊp'stants] *f* substance

subtil [zʊp'tiːl] *adj* subtle

subtrahieren [zʊptra'hiːrən] *vt* to subtract

subtropisch ['zʊptro:pɪʃ] *adj* subtropical

Subvention [zʊpvɛntsi'oːn] *f* subsidy; **s~ieren** *vt* to subsidize

Such- ['zuːx] *zW*: **~aktion** *f* search; **~ef** search; **s~en** *vt* to look (for), to seek; (*versuchen*) to try ♦ *vi* to seek, to search; **~er(-s, -)** *m* seeker, searcher; (*PHOT*) viewfinder; **~maschine** *f* (*COMPUT*) search engine

Sucht [zʊxt] (**-, ⁻e**) *f* mania; (*MED*) addiction, craving

süchtig ['zʏçtɪç] *adj* addicted; **S~e(r)** *f(m)* addict

Süd- ['zyːt] *zW*: **~en** ['zyːdən] (**-s**) *m* south; **~früchte** *pl* Mediterranean fruit *sg*; **s~lich** *adj* southern; **s~lich von** (to the) south of; **~pol** *m* South Pole; **s~wärts** *adv* southwards

süffig ['zʏfɪç] *adj* (*Wein*) pleasant to the taste

süffisant [zʏfi'zant] *adj* smug

suggerieren [zʊge'riːrən] *vt* to suggest

Sühne ['zyːnə] *f* atonement, expiation; **s~n** *vt* to atone for, to expiate

Sultan ['zʊltan] (**-s, -e**) *m* sultan; **~ine** [zʊlta'niːnə] *f* sultana

Sülze ['zʏltsə] *f* brawn

Summe ['zʊmə] *f* sum, total

summen *vt, vi* to buzz; (*Lied*) to hum

Sumpf [zʊmpf] (**-(e)s, ⁻e**) *m* swamp, marsh; **s~ig** *adj* marshy

Sünde ['zʏndə] *f* sin; **~nbock** (*umg*) *m* scapegoat; **~r(in)(-s, -)** *m(f)* sinner; **sündigen** *vi* to sin

Super ['zuːpər] (**-s**) *nt* (*Benzin*) four star (petrol) (*BRIT*), premium (*US*); **~lativ** [-lati:f] (**-s, -e**) *m* superlative; **~macht** *f* superpower; **~markt** *m* supermarket

Suppe ['zʊpə] *f* soup; **~nteller** *m* soup plate

süß [zyːs] *adj* sweet; **S~e(-)** *f* sweetness; **~en** *vt* to sweeten; **S~igkeit** *f* sweetness; (*Bonbon etc*) sweet (*BRIT*), candy (*US*); **~lich** *adj* sweetish; (*fig*) sugary; **~sauer** *adj* (*Gurke*) pickled; (*Sauce etc*) sweet-and-sour; **S~speise** *f* pudding, sweet; **S~stoff** *m* sweetener; **S~waren** *pl* confectionery (*sing*); **S~wasser** *nt* fresh water

Symbol [zʏm'boːl] (**-s, -e**) *nt* symbol; **s~isch** *adj* symbolic(al)

Symmetrie [zʏme'triː] *f* symmetry

symmetrisch [zʏ'meːtrɪʃ] *adj* symmetrical

Sympathie [zʏmpa'tiː] *f* liking, sympathy; **sympathisch** [zʏm'paːtɪʃ] *adj* likeable; **er ist mir sympathisch** I like him; **sympathi'sieren** *vi* to sympathize

Symphonie [zʏmfo'niː] *f* (*MUS*) symphony

Symptom [zʏmp'toːm] (**-s, -e**) *nt* symptom; **s~atisch** [zʏmpto'maːtɪʃ] *adj* symptomatic

Synagoge [zʏna'goːgə] *f* synagogue

synchron [zʏn'kroːn] *adj* synchronous; **~i'sieren** *vt* to synchronize; (*Film*) to dub

Synonym [zʏno'nyːm] (**-s, -e**) *nt* synonym; **s~** *adj* synonymous

Synthese [zʏn'teːzə] *f* synthesis

synthetisch *adj* synthetic

System [zʏs'teːm] (**-s, -e**) *nt* system; **s~atisch** *adj* systematic; **s~ati'sieren** *vt* to systematize

Szene ['stseːnə] *f* scene; **~rie** [stsenə'riː] *f* scenery

T, t

t *abk* (= **Tonne**) t

Tabak ['taːbak] (**-s, -e**) *m* tobacco

Tabell- [ta'bɛl] *zW*: **t~arisch** [tabɛ'laːrɪʃ] *adj* tabular; **~ef** table

Tablett [ta'blɛt] *nt* tray; **~ef** tablet, pill

Tabu [ta'buː] *nt* taboo; **t~** *adj* taboo

Tachometer [taxo'meːtər] (**-s, -**) *m* (*AUT*)

₅peedometer

Tadel ['ta:dəl] **(-s, -)** m censure; scolding; (Fehler) fault, blemish; **t~los** adj faultless, irreproachable; **t~n** vt to scold

Tafel ['ta:fəl] **(-, -n)** f (auch MATH) table; (Anschlag~) board; (Wand~) blackboard; (Schiefer~) slate; (Gedenk~) plaque; (Illustration) plate; (Schalt~) panel; (Schokolade etc) bar

Tag [ta:k] **(-(e)s, -e)** m day; daylight; **unter/über ~e** (MIN) underground/on the surface; **an den ~ kommen** to come to light; **guten ~!** good morning/afternoon!; siehe zutage; **t~aus** adv: **t~aus, ~ein** day in, day out; **~dienst** m day duty

Tage- ['ta:gə] zW: **~buch** ['ta:gəbu:x] nt diary, journal; **~geld** nt daily allowance; **t~lang** adv for days; **t~n** vi to sit, to meet ♦ vb unpers: **es tagt** dawn is breaking

Tages- zW: **~ablauf** m course of the day; **~anbruch** m dawn; **~fahrt** f day trip; **~karte** f menu of the day; (Fahrkarte) day ticket; **~licht** nt daylight; **~ordnung** f agenda; **~zeit** f time of day; **~zeitung** f daily (paper)

täglich ['tɛ:klɪç] adj, adv daily

tagsüber ['ta:ksy:bər] adv during the day

Tagung f conference

Taille ['taljə] f waist

Takt [takt] **(-(e)s, -e)** m tact; (MUS) time; **~gefühl** nt tact

Taktik f tactics pl; **taktisch** adj tactical

Takt- zW: **t~los** adj tactless; **~losigkeit** f tactlessness; **~stock** m (conductor's) baton; **t~voll** adj tactful

Tal [ta:l] **(-(e)s, -̈er)** nt valley

Talent [ta'lɛnt] **(-(e)s, -e)** nt talent; **t~iert** [talɛn'ti:rt] adj talented, gifted

Talisman ['ta:lɪsman] **(-s, -e)** m talisman

Talsohle f bottom of a valley

Talsperre f dam

Tampon ['tampɔn] **(-s, -s)** m tampon

Tandem ['tandɛm] **(-s, -s)** nt tandem

Tang [taŋ] **(-(e)s, -e)** m seaweed

Tank [taŋk] **(-s, -s)** m tank; **~anzeige** f fuel gauge; **t~en** vi to fill up with petrol (BRIT) od gas (US); (AVIAT) to (re)fuel; **~er (-s, -)** m tanker; **~schiff** nt tanker; **~stelle** f petrol

(BRIT) od gas (US) station; **~wart** m petrol pump (BRIT) od gas station (US) attendant

Tanne ['tanə] f fir

Tannen- zW: **~baum** m fir tree; **~zapfen** m fir cone

Tante ['tantə] f aunt

Tanz [tants] **(-es, -̈e)** m dance; **t~en** vt, vi to dance

Tänzer(in) ['tɛntsər(ɪn)] **(-s, -)** m(f) dancer

Tanzfläche f (dance) floor

Tanzschule f dancing school

Tapete [ta'pe:tə] f wallpaper; **~nwechsel** m (fig) change of scenery

tapezieren [tape'tsi:rən] vt to (wall)paper; **Tapezierer** [tape'tsi:rər] **(-s, -)** m (interior) decorator

tapfer ['tapfər] adj brave; **T~keit** f courage, bravery

Tarif [ta'ri:f] **(-s, -e)** m tariff, (scale of) fares od charges; **~lohn** m standard wage rate; **~verhandlungen** pl wage negotiations; **~zone** f fare zone

Tarn- ['tarn] zW: **t~en** vt to camouflage; (Person, Absicht) to disguise; **~ung** f camouflaging; disguising

Tasche ['taʃə] f pocket; handbag

Taschen- in zW pocket; **~buch** nt paperback; **~dieb** m pickpocket; **~geld** nt pocket money; **~lampe** f (electric) torch, flashlight (US); **~messer** nt penknife; **~tuch** nt handkerchief

Tasse ['tasə] f cup

Tastatur [tasta'tu:r] f keyboard

Taste ['tastə] f push-button control; (an Schreibmaschine) key; **t~n** vt to feel, to touch ♦ vi to feel, to grope ♦ vr to feel one's way

Tat [ta:t] **(-, -en)** f act, deed, action; **in der ~** indeed, as a matter of fact; **t~** etc vb siehe **tun**; **~bestand** m facts pl of the case; **t~enlos** adj inactive

Tät- ['tɛ:t] zW: **~er(in) (-s, -)** m(f) perpetrator, culprit; **t~ig** adj active; **in einer Firma t~ig sein** to work for a firm; **~igkeit** f activity; (Beruf) occupation; **t~lich** adj violent; **~lichkeit** f violence; **~lichkeiten** pl (Schläge) blows

tätowieren [tɛto'viːrən] *vt* to tattoo

Tatsache *f* fact

tatsächlich *adj* actual ♦ *adv* really

Tau¹ [tau] (-(e)s, -e) *nt* rope

Tau² [tau] (-(e)s) *m* dew

taub [taup] *adj* deaf; (*Nuss*) hollow

Taube ['taubə] *f* dove; pigeon; **~nschlag** *m* dovecote; **hier geht es zu wie in einem ~nschlag** it's a hive of activity here

taub- *zW:* **T~heit** *f* deafness; **~stumm** *adj* deaf-and-dumb

Tauch- ['taux] *zW:* **t~en** *vt* to dip ♦ *vi* to dive; (*NAUT*) to submerge; **~er (-s, -)** *m* diver; **~eranzug** *m* diving suit; **~erbrille** *f* diving goggles *pl;* **~sieder (-s, -)** *m* immersion coil (*for boiling water*)

tauen ['tauən] *vt, vi* to thaw ♦ *vb unpers:* **es taut** it's thawing

Tauf- ['tauf] *zW:* **~becken** *nt* font; **~e** *f* baptism; **t~en** *vt* to christen, to baptize; **~pate** *m* godfather; **~patin** *f* godmother; **~schein** *m* certificate of baptism

taug- ['taug] *zW:* **~en** *vi* to be of use; **~en für** to do for, to be good for; **nicht ~en** to be no good *od* useless; **T~enichts (-es, -e)** *m* good-for-nothing; **~lich** ['tauklıç] *adj* suitable; (*MIL*) fit (*for service*)

Taumel ['tauməl] (-s) *m* dizziness; (*fig*) frenzy; **t~n** *vi* to reel, to stagger

Tausch [tauʃ] (-(e)s, -e) *m* exchange; **t~en** *vt* to exchange, to swap

täuschen ['tɔyʃən] *vt* to deceive ♦ *vi* to be deceptive ♦ *vr* to be wrong; **~d** *adj* deceptive

Tauschhandel *m* barter

Täuschung *f* deception; (*optisch*) illusion

tausend ['tauzənt] *num* (a) thousand

Tauwetter *nt* thaw

Taxi ['taksi] (-(s), -(s)) *nt* taxi; **~fahrer** *m* taxi driver; **~stand** *m* taxi rank

Tech- ['tɛç] *zW:* **~nik** *f* technology; (*Methode, Kunstfertigkeit*) technique; **~niker (-s, -)** *m* technician; **t~nisch** *adj* technical; **~nolo'gie** *f* technology; **t~no'logisch** *adj* technological

Tee [teː] (-s, -s) *m* tea; **~beutel** *m* tea bag; **~kanne** *f* teapot; **~löffel** *m* teaspoon

Teer [teːr] (-(e)s, -e) *m* tar; **t~en** *vt* to tar

Teesieb *nt* tea strainer

Teich [taıç] (-(e)s, -e) *m* pond

Teig [taık] (-(e)s, -e) *m* dough; **t~ig** ['taıgıç] *adj* doughy; **~waren** *pl* pasta *sg*

Teil [taıl] (-(e)s, -e) *m od nt* part; (*Anteil*) share; (*Bestandteil*) component; **zum ~** partly; **t~bar** *adj* divisible; **~betrag** *m* instalment; **~chen** *nt* (atomic) particle; **t~en** *vt, vr* to divide; (*mit jdm*) to share; **t~haben** (*unreg*) *vi:* **t~haben an** +*dat* to share in; **t~haber (-s, -)** *m* partner; **~kaskoversicherung** *f* third party, fire and theft insurance; **t~möbliert** *adj* partially furnished; **~nahme** *f* participation; (*Mitleid*) sympathy; **t~nahmslos** *adj* disinterested, apathetic; **t~nehmen** (*unreg*) *vi:* **t~nehmen an** +*dat* to take part in; **~nehmer (-s, -)** *m* participant; **t~s** *adv* partly; **~ung** *f* division; **t~weise** *adv* partially, in part; **~zahlung** *f* payment by instalments; **~zeitarbeit** *f* part-time work

Teint [tɛː] (-s, -s) *m* complexion

Telearbeit ['teːleʔarbaıt] *f* teleworking

Telefax ['teːlefaks] *nt* fax

Telefon [tele'foːn] (-s, -e) *nt* telephone; **~anruf** *m* (tele)phone call; **~at** [telefo'naːt] (-(e)s, -e) *nt* (tele)phone call; **~buch** *nt* telephone directory; **~hörer** *m* (telephone) receiver; **t~ieren** *vi* to telephone; **t~isch** [-ıʃ] *adj* telephone; (*Benachrichtigung*) by telephone; **~ist(in)** [telefo'nıst(ın)] *m(f)* telephonist; **~karte** *f* phonecard; **~nummer** *f* (tele)phone number; **~zelle** *f* telephone kiosk, callbox; **~zentrale** *f* telephone exchange

Telegraf [tele'graːf] (-en, -en) *m* telegraph; **~enmast** *m* telegraph pole; **~ie** [-'fiː] *f* telegraphy; **t~ieren** [-'fiːrən] *vt, vi* to telegraph, to wire

Telegramm [tele'gram] (-s, -e) *nt* telegram, cable; **~adresse** *f* telegraphic address

Tele- *zW:* **~objektiv** ['teːleʔɔpjɛktiːf] *nt* telephoto lens; **t~pathisch** [tele'paːtıʃ] *adj* telepathic; **~skop** [tele'skoːp] (-s, -e) *nt* telescope

Teller ['tɛlər] (-s, -) *m* plate; **~gericht** *nt* (*KOCH*) one-course meal

Tempel ['tɛmpəl] (-s, -) *m* temple

Temperament [tɛmpera'mɛnt] *nt* temperament; (*Schwung*) vivacity, liveliness; **t~voll** *adj* high-spirited, lively

Temperatur [tɛmpera'tu:r] *f* temperature

Tempo¹ ['tɛmpo] (-s, **Tempi**) *nt* (*MUS*) tempo

Tempo² ['tɛmpo] (-s, -s) *nt* speed, pace; **~!** get a move on!; **~limit** [-lɪmɪt] (-s, -s) *nt* speed limit; **~taschentuch** ⓇR *nt* tissue

Tendenz [tɛn'dɛnts] *f* tendency; (*Absicht*) intention; **t~iös** [-i'ø:s] *adj* biased, tendentious

tendieren [tɛn'di:rən] *vi*: **~ zu** to show a tendency to, to incline towards

Tennis ['tɛnɪs] (-) *nt* tennis; **~ball** *m* tennis ball; **~platz** *m* tennis court; **~schläger** *m* tennis racket; **~schuh** *m* tennis shoe; **~spieler(in)** *m(f)* tennis player

Tenor [te'no:r] (-s, ᵉe) *m* tenor

Teppich ['tɛpɪç] (-s, -e) *m* carpet; **~boden** *m* wall-to-wall carpeting

Termin [tɛr'mi:n] (-s, -e) *m* (*Zeitpunkt*) date; (*Frist*) time limit, deadline; (*Arzttermin etc*) appointment; **~kalender** *m* diary, appointments book; **~planer** *m* personal organizer

Terrasse [tɛ'rasə] *f* terrace

Terrine [tɛ'ri:nə] *f* tureen

territorial [tɛritori'a:l] *adj* territorial

Territorium [tɛri'to:riʊm] *nt* territory

Terror ['tɛrɔr] (-s) *m* terror; reign of terror; **t~isieren** [tɛrori'zi:rən] *vt* to terrorize; **~ismus** [-'rɪsmʊs] *m* terrorism; **~ist** [-'rɪst] *m* terrorist

Tesafilm ['te:zafɪlm] ⓇR *m* Sellotape ⓇR (*BRIT*), Scotch tape ⓇR (*US*)

Tessin [tɛ'si:n] (-s) *nt*: **das ~** Ticino

Test [tɛst] (-s, -s) *m* test

Testament [tɛsta'mɛnt] *nt* will, testament; (*REL*) Testament; **t~arisch** [-'ta:rɪʃ] *adj* testamentary

Testamentsvollstrecker *m* executor (of a will)

testen *vt* to test

Tetanus ['te:tanʊs] (-) *m* tetanus; **~impfung** *f* (anti-)tetanus injection

teuer ['tɔyər] *adj* dear, expensive; **T~ung** *f* increase in prices; **T~ungszulage** *f* cost of living bonus

Teufel ['tɔyfəl] (-s, -) *m* devil; **teuflisch** ['tɔyflɪʃ] *adj* fiendish, diabolical

Text [tɛkst] (-(e)s, -e) *m* text; (*Liedertext*) words *pl*; **t~en** *vi* to write the words

textil [tɛks'ti:l] *adj* textile; **T~ien** *pl* textiles; **T~industrie** *f* textile industry; **T~waren** *pl* textiles

Textverarbeitung *f* word processing

Theater [te'a:tər] (-s, -) *nt* theatre; (*umg*) fuss; **~ spielen** (*auch fig*) to playact; **~besucher** *m* playgoer; **~kasse** *f* box office; **~stück** *nt* (stage) play

Theke ['te:kə] *f* (*Schanktisch*) bar; (*Ladentisch*) counter

Thema ['te:ma] (-s, **Themen** *od* **-ta**) *nt* theme, topic, subject

Themse ['tɛmzə] *f* Thames

Theo- [teo] *zW*: **~loge** [-'lo:gə] (-n, -n) *m* theologian; **~logie** [-lo'gi:] *f* theology; **t~logisch** [-'lo:gɪʃ] *adj* theological; **~retiker** [-'re:tikər] (-s, -) *m* theorist; **t~retisch** [-'re:tɪʃ] *adj* theoretical; **~rie** [-'ri:] *f* theory

Thera- [tera] *zW*: **~peut** [-'pɔyt] (-en, -en) *m* therapist; **t~peutisch** [-'pɔytɪʃ] *adj* therapeutic; **~pie** [-'pi:] *f* therapy

Therm- *zW*: **~albad** [tɛr'ma:lba:t] *nt* thermal bath; thermal spa; **~odrucker** [tɛrmo-] *m* thermal printer; **~ometer** [tɛrmo'me:tər] (-s, -) *nt* thermometer; **~osflasche** ['tɛrmɔsflaʃə] ⓇR *f* Thermos ⓇR flask

These ['te:zə] *f* thesis

Thrombose [trɔm'bo:zə] *f* thrombosis

Thron [tro:n] (-(e)s, -e) *m* throne; **t~en** *vi* to sit enthroned; (*fig*) to sit in state; **~folge** *f* succession (to the throne); **~folger(in)** (-s, -) *m(f)* heir to the throne

Thunfisch ['tu:nfɪʃ] *m* tuna

Thüringen ['ty:rɪŋən] (-s) *nt* Thuringia

Thymian ['ty:mia:n] (-s, -e) *m* thyme

Tick [tɪk] (-(e)s, -s) *m* tic; (*Eigenart*) quirk;

(*Fimmel*) craze

ticken *vi* to tick

tief [tiːf] *adj* deep; (*~sinnig*) profound; (*Ausschnitt, Preis, Ton*) low; **~ greifend** far-reaching; **~ schürfend** profound; **T~ (-s, -s)** *nt* (MET) depression; **T~druck** *m* low pressure; **T~e** *f* depth; **T~ebene** *f* plain; **T~enschärfe** *f* (PHOT) depth of focus; **T~garage** *f* underground garage; **~gekühlt** *adj* frozen; **T~kühlfach** *nt* deepfreeze compartment; **T~kühlkost** *f* (deep) frozen food; **T~kühltruhe** *f* deepfreeze, freezer; **T~punkt** *m* low point; (*fig*) low ebb; **T~schlag** *m* (BOXEN, *fig*) blow below the belt; **T~see** *f* deep sea; **~sinnig** *adj* profound; melancholy; **T~stand** *m* low level; **T~stwert** *m* minimum *od* lowest value

Tier [tiːr] **(-(e)s, -e)** *nt* animal; **~arzt** *m* vet(erinary surgeon); **~garten** *m* zoo(logical gardens *pl*); **~heim** *nt* cat/dog home; **t~isch** *adj* animal; (*auch fig*) brutish; (*fig: Ernst etc*) deadly; **~kreis** *m* zodiac; **~kunde** *f* zoology; **t~liebend** *adj* fond of animals; **~park** *m* zoo; **~quälerei** [-kvɛːləˈraɪ] *f* cruelty to animals; **~schutzverein** *m* society for the prevention of cruelty to animals

Tiger(in) [ˈtiːɡər(ɪn)] **(-s, -)** *m(f)* tiger(-gress)

tilgen [ˈtɪlɡən] *vt* to erase; (*Sünden*) to expiate; (*Schulden*) to pay off

Tinte [ˈtɪntə] *f* ink

Tintenfisch *m* cuttlefish

Tipp ▲ [tɪp] *m* tip; **t~en** *vt, vi* to tap, to touch; (*umg: schreiben*) to type; (*im Lotto etc*) to bet (on); **auf jdn t~en** (*umg: raten*) to tip sb, to put one's money on sb (*fig*)

Tipp- [ˈtɪp] *zW*: **~fehler** (*umg*) *m* typing error; **t~topp** (*umg*) *adj* tip-top; **~zettel** *m* (pools) coupon

Tirol [tiˈroːl] *nt* the Tyrol; **~er(in)** *m(f)* Tyrolean; **t~isch** *adj* Tyrolean

Tisch [tɪʃ] **(-(e)s, -e)** *m* table; **bei ~** at table; **vor/nach ~** before/after eating; **unter den ~ fallen** (*fig*) to be dropped; **~decke** *f* tablecloth; **~ler** **(-s, -)** *m* carpenter, joiner; **~leˈrei** *f* joiner's workshop; (*Arbeit*)

carpentry, joinery; **t~lern** *vi* to do carpentry *etc*; **~rede** *f* after-dinner speech; **~tennis** *nt* table tennis; **~tuch** *nt* tablecloth

Titel [ˈtiːtəl] **(-s, -)** *m* title; **~bild** *nt* cover (picture); (*von Buch*) frontispiece; **~rolle** *f* title role; **~seite** *f* cover; (*Buchtitelseite*) title page; **~verteidiger** *m* defending champion, title holder

Toast [toːst] **(-(e)s, -s** *od* **-e)** *m* toast; **~brot** *nt* bread for toasting; **~er (-s, -)** *m* toaster

tob- [ˈtoːb] *zW*: **~en** *vi* to rage; (*Kinder*) to romp about; **~süchtig** *adj* maniacal

Tochter [ˈtɔxtər] **(-, ⁻)** *f* daughter; **~gesellschaft** *f* subsidiary (company)

Tod [toːt] **(-(e)s, -e)** *m* death; **t~ernst** *adj* deadly serious ♦ *adv* in dead earnest

Todes- [ˈtoːdəs] *zW*: **~angst** [-aŋst] *f* mortal fear; **~anzeige** *f* obituary (notice); **~fall** *m* death; **~strafe** *f* death penalty; **~ursache** *f* cause of death; **~urteil** *nt* death sentence; **~verachtung** *f* utter disgust

todkrank *adj* dangerously ill

tödlich [ˈtøːtlɪç] *adj* deadly, fatal

tod- *zW*: **~müde** *adj* dead tired; **~schick** (*umg*) *adj* smart, classy; **~sicher** (*umg*) *adj* absolutely *od* dead certain; **T~sünde** *f* deadly sin

Toilette [toaˈlɛtə] *f* toilet, lavatory; (*Frisiertisch*) dressing table

Toiletten- *zW*: **~artikel** *pl* toiletries, toilet articles; **~papier** *nt* toilet paper; **~tisch** *m* dressing table

toi, toi, toi [ˈtɔyˈtɔyˈtɔy] *excl* touch wood

tolerant [toleˈrant] *adj* tolerant

Toleranz [toleˈrants] *f* tolerance

tolerieren [toleˈriːrən] *vt* to tolerate

toll [tɔl] *adj* mad; (*Treiben*) wild; (*umg*) terrific; **~en** *vi* to romp; **T~kirsche** *f* deadly nightshade; **~kühn** *adj* daring; **T~wut** *f* rabies

Tomate [toˈmaːtə] *f* tomato; **~nmark** *nt* tomato purée

Ton¹ [toːn] **(-(e)s, -e)** *m* (*Erde*) clay

Ton² [toːn] **(-(e)s, ⁻e)** *m* (*Laut*) sound; (*MUS*) note; (*Redeweise*) tone; (*Farbton, Nuance*) shade; (*Betonung*) stress;

t~**angebend** adj leading; ~**art** f (musical) key; ~**band** nt tape; ~**bandgerät** nt tape recorder

tönen ['tøːnən] vi to sound ♦ vt to shade; (Haare) to tint

tönern ['tøːnərn] adj clay

Ton- zW: ~**fall** m intonation; ~**film** m sound film; ~**leiter** f (MUS) scale; t~**los** adj soundless

Tonne ['tɔnə] f barrel; (Maß) ton

Ton- zW: ~**taube** f clay pigeon; ~**waren** pl pottery sg, earthenware sg

Topf [tɔpf] (-(e)s, ⸚e) m pot; ~**blume** f pot plant

Töpfer ['tœpfər] (-s, -) m potter; ~**ei** [-'raɪ] f piece of pottery; potter's workshop; ~**scheibe** f potter's wheel

topografisch ▲ [topo'graːfɪʃ] adj topographic

Tor¹ [toːr] (-en, -en) m fool

Tor² [toːr] (-(e)s, -e) nt gate; (SPORT) goal; ~**bogen** m archway

Torf [tɔrf] (-(e)s) m peat

Torheit f foolishness; foolish deed

töricht ['tøːrɪçt] adj foolish

torkeln ['tɔrkəln] vi to stagger, to reel

Torte ['tɔrtə] f cake; (Obsttorte) flan, tart

Tortur [tɔr'tuːr] f ordeal

Torwart (-(e)s, -e) m goalkeeper

tosen ['toːzən] vi to roar

tot [toːt] adj dead; ~ **geboren** stillborn; **sich ~ stellen** to pretend to be dead

total [to'taːl] adj total; ~**itär** [totali'tɛːr] adj totalitarian; **T~schaden** m (AUT) complete write-off

Tote(r) f(m) dead person

töten ['tøːtən] vt, vi to kill

Toten- zW: ~**bett** nt death bed; t~**blass** ▲ adj deathly pale, white as a sheet; ~**kopf** m skull; ~**schein** m death certificate; ~**stille** f deathly silence

tot- zW: ~**fahren** (unreg) vt to run over; ~**geboren** △ adj siehe **tot**; ~**lachen** (umg) vr to laugh one's head off

Toto ['toːto] (-s, -s) m od nt pools pl; ~**schein** m pools coupon

tot- zW: **T~schlag** m manslaughter;

~**schlagen** (unreg) vt (auch fig) to kill; ~**schweigen** (unreg) vt to hush up; ~**stellen** △ vr siehe **tot**

Tötung ['tøːtʊŋ] f killing

Toupet [tu'pe] (-s, -s) nt toupee

toupieren [tu'piːrən] vt to backcomb

Tour [tuːr] (-, -en) f tour, trip; (Umdrehung) revolution; (Verhaltensart) way; **in einer ~** incessantly; ~**enzähler** m rev counter; ~**ismus** [tu'rɪsmus] m tourism; ~**ist** [tu'rɪst] m tourist; ~**istenklasse** f tourist class; ~**nee** [tur'neː] (-, -n) f (THEAT etc) tour; **auf ~nee gehen** to go on tour

Trab [traːp] (-(e)s) m trot

Trabantenstadt f satellite town

traben ['traːbən] vi to trot

Tracht [traxt] (-, -en) f (Kleidung) costume, dress; **eine ~ Prügel** a sound thrashing; t~**en** vi: t~**en (nach)** to strive (for); **jdm nach dem Leben t~en** to seek to kill sb; **danach t~en, etw zu tun** to strive od endeavour to do sth

trächtig ['trɛçtɪç] adj (Tier) pregnant

Tradition [traditsi'oːn] f tradition; t~**ell** [-'nɛl] adj traditional

traf etc [traːf] vb siehe **treffen**

Tragbahre f stretcher

tragbar adj (Gerät) portable; (Kleidung) wearable; (erträglich) bearable

träge ['trɛːgə] adj sluggish, slow; (PHYS) inert

tragen ['traːgən] (unreg) vt to carry; (Kleidung, Brille) to wear; (Namen, Früchte) to bear; (erdulden) to endure ♦ vi (schwanger sein) to be pregnant; (Eis) to hold; **sich mit einem Gedanken ~** to have an idea in mind; **zum T~ kommen** to have an effect

Träger ['trɛːgər] (-s, -) m carrier; wearer; bearer; (Ordensträger) holder; (an Kleidung) (shoulder) strap; (Körperschaft etc) sponsor

Tragetasche f carrier bag

Tragfläche f (AVIAT) wing

Tragflügelboot nt hydrofoil

Trägheit ['trɛːkhaɪt] f laziness; (PHYS) inertia

Tragik ['traːgɪk] f tragedy; **tragisch** adj tragic

Tragödie [tra'gøːdiə] f tragedy

Tragweite f range; (fig) scope

Train- ['trɛːn] *zW:* **~er (-s, -)** *m* (*SPORT*) trainer, coach; (*Fußball*) manager; **t~ieren** [trɛ'niːrən] *vt, vi* to train; (*Mensch*) to train, to coach; (*Übung*) to practise; **~ing (-s, -s)** *nt* training; **~ingsanzug** *m* track suit

Traktor ['traktɔr] *m* tractor; (*von Drucker*) tractor feed

trällern ['trɛlərn] *vt, vi* to trill, to sing

Tram [tram] **(-, -s)** *f* tram

trampeln ['trampəln] *vt, vi* to trample, to stamp

trampen ['trɛmpən] *vi* to hitch-hike

Tramper(in) [trɛmpər(ɪn)] **(-s, -)** *m(f)* hitch-hiker

Tran [traːn] **(-(e)s, -e)** *m* train oil, blubber

tranchieren [trãˈʃiːrən] *vt* to carve

Träne ['trɛːnə] *f* tear; **t~n** *vi* to water; **~ngas** *nt* teargas

trank *etc* [traŋk] *vb siehe* **trinken**

tränken ['trɛŋkən] *vt* (*Tiere*) to water

transchieren ▲ [tranˈʃiːrən] *vt* to carve

Trans- *zW:* **~formator** [transfɔrˈmaːtɔr] *m* transformer; **~istor** [tranˈzɪstɔr] *m* transistor; **~itverkehr** [tranˈziːtfɛrkeːr] *m* transit traffic; **~itvisum** *nt* transit visa; **t~parent** *adj* transparent; **~parent (-(e)s, -e)** *nt* (*Bild*) transparency; (*Spruchband*) banner; **~plantation** [transplantatsiˈoːn] *f* transplantation; (*Hauttransplantation*) graft(ing)

Transport [transˈpɔrt] **(-(e)s, -e)** *m* transport; **t~ieren** [transpɔrˈtiːrən] *vt* to transport; **~kosten** *pl* transport charges, carriage *sg*; **~mittel** *nt* means *sg* of transportation; **~unternehmen** *nt* carrier

Traube ['traubə] *f* grape; bunch (of grapes); **~nzucker** *m* glucose

trauen ['trauən] *vi*: **jdm/etw ~** to trust sb/ sth ♦ *vr* to dare ♦ *vt* to marry

Trauer ['trauər] **(-)** *f* sorrow; (*für Verstorbenen*) mourning; **~fall** *m* death, bereavement; **~feier** *f* funeral service; **~kleidung** *f* mourning; **t~n** *vi* to mourn; **um jdn t~n** to mourn (for) sb; **~rand** *m* black border; **~spiel** *nt* tragedy

traulich ['traulɪç] *adj* cosy, intimate

Traum [traum] **(-(e)s, Träume)** *m* dream

Trauma (-s, -men) *nt* trauma

träum- ['trɔym] *zW:* **~en** *vt, vi* to dream; **T~er (-s, -)** *m* dreamer; **T~e'rei** *f* dreaming; **~erisch** *adj* dreamy

traumhaft *adj* dreamlike; (*fig*) wonderful

traurig ['traurɪç] *adj* sad; **T~keit** *f* sadness

Trau- ['trau] *zW:* **~ring** *m* wedding ring; **~schein** *m* marriage certificate; **~ung** *f* wedding ceremony; **~zeuge** *m* witness (to a marriage); **~zeugin** *f* witness (to a marriage)

treffen ['trɛfən] (*unreg*) *vt* to strike, to hit; (*Bemerkung*) to hurt; (*begegnen*) to meet; (*Entscheidung etc*) to make; (*Maßnahmen*) to take ♦ *vi* to hit ♦ *vr* to meet; **er hat es gut getroffen** he did well; **~ auf** +*akk* to come across, to meet with; **es traf sich, dass ...** it so happened that ...; **es trifft sich gut** it's convenient; **wie es so trifft** as these things happen; **T~ (-s, -)** *nt* meeting; **~d** *adj* pertinent, apposite

Treffer (-s, -) *m* hit; (*Tor*) goal; (*Los*) winner

Treffpunkt *m* meeting place

Treib- ['traib] *zW:* **~eis** *nt* drift ice; **t~en** (*unreg*) *vt* to drive; (*Studien etc*) to pursue; (*Sport*) to do, to go in for ♦ *vi* (*Schiff etc*) to drift; (*Pflanzen*) to sprout; (*KOCH: aufgehen*) to rise; (*Tee, Kaffee*) to be diuretic; **~haus** *nt* greenhouse; **~hauseffekt** *m* greenhouse effect; **~hausgas** *nt* greenhouse gas; **~stoff** *m* fuel

trenn- ['trɛn] *zW:* **~bar** *adj* separable; **~en** *vt* to separate; (*teilen*) to divide ♦ *vr* to separate; **sich ~en von** to part with; **T~ung** *f* separation; **T~wand** *f* partition (wall)

Trepp- ['trɛp] *zW:* **t~ab** *adv* downstairs; **t~auf** *adv* upstairs; **~e** *f* stair(case); **~engeländer** *nt* banister; **~enhaus** *nt* staircase

Tresor [treˈzoːr] **(-s, -e)** *m* safe

Tretboot *nt* pedalo, pedal boat

treten ['treːtən] (*unreg*) *vi* to step; (*Tränen, Schweiß*) to appear ♦ *vt* (*mit Fußtritt*) to kick; (*niedertreten*) to tread, to trample; **~ nach** to kick at; **~ in** +*akk* to step in(to); **in Verbindung ~** to get in contact; **in**

Erscheinung ~ to appear
treu [trɔʏ] *adj* faithful, true; **T~e** (-) *f* loyalty, faithfulness; **T~händer** (**-s,** -) *m* trustee; **T~handanstalt** *f* trustee organization; **T~handgesellschaft** *f* trust company; **~herzig** *adj* innocent; **~los** *adj* faithless

---

┌─────────────────────────┐
│ **Treuhandanstalt** │
└─────────────────────────┘

𝒊 The **Treuhandanstalt** was the organization set up in 1990 to take over the nationally-owned companies of the former **DDR**, break them down into smaller units and privatize them. It was based in Berlin and had nine branches. Many companies were closed down by the **Treuhandanstalt** because of their outdated equipment and inability to compete with Western firms which resulted in rising unemployment. Having completed its initial task, the **Treuhandanstalt** was closed down in 1995.

Tribüne [tri'byːnə] *f* grandstand; (*Rednertribüne*) platform
Trichter ['trɪçtər] (**-s,** -) *m* funnel; (*in Boden*) crater
Trick [trɪk] (**-s, -e** *od* **-s**) *m* trick; **~film** *m* cartoon
Trieb [triːp] (**-(e)s, -e**) *m* urge, drive; (*Neigung*) inclination; (*an Baum etc*) shoot; **t~** *etc vb siehe* **treiben**; **~kraft** *f* (*fig*) drive; **~täter** *m* sex offender; **~werk** *nt* engine
triefen ['triːfən] *vi* to drip
triffst *etc* [trɪfst] *vb siehe* **treffen**
triftig ['trɪftɪç] *adj* good, convincing
Trikot [tri'koː] (**-s, -s**) *nt* vest; (*SPORT*) shirt
Trimester [tri'mɛstər] (**-s,** -) *nt* term
trimmen ['trɪmən] *vr* to do keep fit exercises
trink- ['trɪŋk] *zW:* **~bar** *adj* drinkable; **~en** (*unreg*) *vt, vi* to drink; **T~er** (**-s,** -) *m* drinker; **T~geld** *nt* tip; **T~halle** *f* refreshment kiosk; **T~wasser** *nt* drinking water
Tripper ['trɪpər] (**-s,** -) *m* gonorrhoea
Tritt [trɪt] (**-(e)s, -e**) *m* step; (*Fußtritt*) kick; **~brett** *nt* (*EISENB*) step; (*AUT*) running board

Triumph [tri'ʊmf] (**-(e)s, -e**) *m* triumph; **~bogen** *m* triumphal arch; **t~ieren** [triʊm'fiːrən] *vi* to triumph; (*jubeln*) to exult
trocken ['trɔkən] *adj* dry; **T~element** *nt* dry cell; **T~haube** *f* hair dryer; **T~heit** *f* dryness; **~legen** *vt* (*Sumpf*) to drain; (*Kind*) to put a clean nappy on; **T~milch** *f* dried milk; **T~rasur** *f* dry shave, electric shave
trocknen ['trɔknən] *vt, vi* to dry
Trödel ['trøːdəl] (**-s**) (*umg*) *m* junk; **~markt** *m* flea market; **t~n** (*umg*) *vi* to dawdle
Trommel ['trɔməl] (**-, -n**) *f* drum; **~fell** *nt* eardrum; **t~n** *vt, vi* to drum
Trompete [trɔm'peːtə] *f* trumpet; **~r** (**-s,** -) *m* trumpeter
Tropen ['troːpən] *pl* tropics; **~helm** *m* sun helmet
tröpfeln ['trœpfəln] *vi* to drop, to trickle
Tropfen ['trɔpfən] (**-s,** -) *m* drop; **t~** *vt, vi* to drip **♦** *vb unpers:* **es tropft** a few raindrops are falling; **t~weise** *adv* in drops
Tropfsteinhöhle *f* stalactite cave
tropisch ['troːpɪʃ] *adj* tropical
Trost [troːst] (**-es**) *m* consolation, comfort
trösten ['trøːstən] *vt* to console, to comfort
trost- *zW:* **~los** *adj* bleak; (*Verhältnisse*) wretched; **T~preis** *m* consolation prize; **~reich** *adj* comforting
Trott [trɔt] (**-(e)s, -e**) *m* trot; (*Routine*) routine; **~el** (**-s,** -) (*umg*) *m* fool, dope; **t~en** *vi* to trot
Trotz [trɔts] (**-es**) *m* pigheadedness; **etw aus ~ tun** to do sth just to show them; **jdm zum ~** in defiance of sb; **t~** *präp* (+*gen od dat*) in spite of; **t~dem** *adv* nevertheless, all the same **♦** *konj* although; **t~en** *vi* (+*dat*) to defy; (*der Kälte, Klima etc*) to withstand; (*der Gefahr*) to brave; (*t~ig sein*) to be awkward; **t~ig** *adj* defiant, pig-headed; **~kopf** *m* obstinate child
trüb [tryːp] *adj* dull; (*Flüssigkeit, Glas*) cloudy; (*fig*) gloomy
Trubel ['truːbəl] (**-s**) *m* hurly-burly
trüb- *zW:* **~en** ['tryːbən] *vt* to cloud **♦** *vr* to become clouded; **T~heit** *f* dullness; cloudiness; gloom; **T~sal** (**-, -e**) *f* distress; **~selig** *adj* sad, melancholy; **T~sinn** *m*

depression; **~sinnig** *adj* depressed, gloomy

Trüffel ['trʏfəl] (-, -n) *f* truffle

trug *etc* [truːk] *vb siehe* **tragen**

trügen ['tryːgən] (*unreg*) *vt* to deceive ♦ *vi* to be deceptive

trügerisch *adj* deceptive

Trugschluss ▲ ['truːgʃlʊs] *m* false conclusion

Truhe ['truːə] *f* chest

Trümmer ['trʏmər] *pl* wreckage *sg*; (*Bautrümmer*) ruins; **~haufen** *m* heap of rubble

Trumpf [trʊmpf] (-(e)s, ⁻e) *m* (*auch fig*) trump; **t~en** *vt, vi* to trump

Trunk [trʊŋk] (-(e)s, ⁻e) *m* drink; **t~en** *adj* intoxicated; **~enheit** *f* intoxication; **~enheit am Steuer** drunken driving; **~sucht** *f* alcoholism

Trupp [trʊp] (-s, -s) *m* troop; **~e** *f* troop; (*Waffengattung*) force; (*Schauspieltruppe*) troupe; **~en** *pl* (*MIL*) troops; **~enübungsplatz** *m* training area

Truthahn ['truːthaːn] *m* turkey

Tschech- ['tʃɛç] *zW*: **~e** *m* Czech; **~ien** (-s) *nt* the Czech Republic; **~in** *f* Czech; **t~isch** *adj* Czech; **~oslowakei** [-oslova'kaɪ] *f*: **die ~oslowakei** Czechoslovakia; **t~oslowakisch** [-oslo'va:kɪʃ] *adj* Czechoslovak(ian)

tschüs(s) [tʃʏs] *excl* cheerio

T-Shirt ['tiːʃɔːt] *nt* T-shirt

Tube ['tuːbə] *f* tube

Tuberkulose [tuberku'lo:zə] *f* tuberculosis

Tuch [tuːx] (-(e)s, ⁻er) *nt* cloth; (*Halstuch*) scarf; (*Kopftuch*) headscarf; (*Handtuch*) towel

tüchtig ['tʏçtɪç] *adj* efficient, (cap)able; (*umg: kräftig*) good, sound; **T~keit** *f* efficiency, ability

Tücke ['tʏkə] *f* (*Arglist*) malice; (*Trick*) trick; (*Schwierigkeit*) difficulty, problem

tückisch ['tʏkɪʃ] *adj* treacherous; (*böswillig*) malicious

Tugend ['tuːgənt] (-, -en) *f* virtue; **t~haft** *adj* virtuous

Tülle *f* spout

Tulpe ['tʊlpə] *f* tulip

Tumor ['tuːmɔr] (-s, -e) *m* tumour

Tümpel ['tʏmpəl] (-s, -) *m* pool, pond

Tumult [tu'mʊlt] (-(e)s, -e) *m* tumult

tun [tuːn] (*unreg*) *vt* (*machen*) to do; (*legen*) to put ♦ *vi* to act ♦ *vr*: **es tut sich etwas/ viel** something/a lot is happening; **jdm etw ~** (*antun*) to do sth to sb; **etw tut es auch** sth will do; **das tut nichts** that doesn't matter; **das tut nichts zur Sache** that's neither here nor there; **so ~ als ob** to act as if

tünchen ['tʏnçən] *vt* to whitewash

Tunfisch ▲ ['tuːnfɪʃ] *m* = **Thunfisch**

Tunke ['tʊŋkə] *f* sauce; **t~n** *vt* to dip, to dunk

tunlichst ['tuːnlɪçst] *adv* if at all possible; **~ bald** as soon as possible

Tunnel ['tʊnəl] (-s, -s *od* -) *m* tunnel

Tupfen ['tʊpfən] (-s, -) *m* dot, spot; **t~** *vt, vi* to dab; (*mit Farbe*) to dot

Tür [tyːr] (-, -en) *f* door

Turbine [tʊr'biːnə] *f* turbine

Türk- [tʏrk] *zW*: **~e** *m* Turk; **~ei** [tʏr'kaɪ] *f*: **die ~ei** Turkey; **~in** *f* Turk

Türkis [tʏr'kiːs] (-es, -e) *m* turquoise; **t~** *adj* turquoise

türkisch ['tʏrkɪʃ] *adj* Turkish

Türklinke *f* doorknob, door handle

Turm [tʊrm] (-(e)s, ⁻e) *m* tower; (*Kirchturm*) steeple; (*Sprungturm*) diving platform; (*SCHACH*) castle, rook

türmen ['tʏrmən] *vr* to tower up ♦ *vt* to heap up ♦ *vi* (*umg*) to scarper, to bolt

Turn- ['tʊrn] *zW*: **t~en** *vi* to do gymnastic exercises ♦ *vt* to perform; **~en** (-s) *nt* gymnastics; (*SCH*) physical education, P.E.; **~er(in)** (-s, -) *m(f)* gymnast; **~halle** *f* gym(nasium); **~hose** *f* gym shorts *pl*

Turnier [tʊr'niːr] (-s, -e) *nt* tournament

Turn- *zW*: **~schuh** *m* gym shoe; **~verein** *m* gymnastics club; **~zeug** *nt* gym things *pl*

Tusche ['tʊʃə] *f* Indian ink

tuscheln ['tʊʃəln] *vt, vi* to whisper

Tuschkasten *m* paintbox

Tüte ['tyːtə] *f* bag

tuten ['tuːtən] *vi* (*AUT*) to hoot (*BRIT*), to honk (*US*)

TÜV [tʏf] (**-s, -s**) *m abk* (= *Technischer Überwachungs-Verein*) ≃ MOT

Typ [ty:p] (**-s, -en**) *m* type; **~e** *f* (*TYP*) type

Typhus ['ty:fʊs] (**-**) *m* typhoid (fever)

typisch ['ty:pɪʃ] *adj*: **~** (**für**) typical (of)

Tyrann [ty'ran] (**-en, -en**) *m* tyrant; **~ei** [-'naɪ] *f* tyranny; **t~isch** *adj* tyrannical; **t~isieren** *vt* to tyrannize

U, u

u. a. *abk* = **unter anderem**

U-Bahn ['u:ba:n] *f* underground, tube

übel ['y:bəl] *adj* bad; (*moralisch*) bad, wicked; **jdm ist ~** sb feels sick; **~ gelaunt** bad-tempered; **jdm eine Bemerkung** *etc* **~ nehmen** to be offended at sb's remark *etc*; **Ü~** (**-s, -**) *nt* evil; (*Krankheit*) disease; **Ü~keit** *f* nausea

üben ['y:bən] *vt, vi* to exercise, to practise

SCHLÜSSELWORT

über ['y:bər] *präp* +*dat* **1** (*räumlich*) over, above; **zwei Grad über null** two degrees above zero

2 (*zeitlich*) over; **über der Arbeit einschlafen** to fall asleep over one's work

♦ *präp* +*akk* **1** (*räumlich*) over; (*hoch über auch*) above; (*quer über auch*) across

2 (*zeitlich*) over; **über Weihnachten** over Christmas; **über kurz oder lang** sooner or later

3 (*mit Zahlen*): **Kinder über 12 Jahren** children over *od* above 12 years of age; **ein Scheck über 200 Mark** a cheque for 200 marks

4 (*auf dem Wege*) via; **nach Köln über Aachen** to Cologne via Aachen; **ich habe es über die Auskunft erfahren** I found out from information

5 (*betreffend*) about; **ein Buch über ...** a book about *od* on ...; **über jdn/etw lachen** to laugh about *od* at sb/sth

6: Macht über jdn haben to have power over sb; **sie liebt ihn über alles** she loves him more than everything

♦ *adv* over; **über und über** over and over; **den ganzen Tag über** all day long; **jdm in etw** *dat* **über sein** to be superior to sb in sth

überall [y:bər'|al] *adv* everywhere; **~'hin** *adv* everywhere

überanstrengen [y:bər'|anʃtrɛŋən] *vt insep* to overexert ♦ *vr insep* to overexert o.s.

überarbeiten [y:bər'|arbaɪtən] *vt insep* to revise, to rework ♦ *vr insep* to overwork (o.s.)

überaus ['y:bər|aʊs] *adv* exceedingly

überbelichten ['y:bərbəlɪçtən] *vt* (*PHOT*) to overexpose

über'bieten (*unreg*) *vt insep* to outbid; (*übertreffen*) to surpass; (*Rekord*) to break

Überbleibsel ['y:bərblaɪpsəl] (**-s, -**) *nt* residue, remainder

Überblick ['y:bərblɪk] *m* view; (*fig: Darstellung*) survey, overview; (*Fähigkeit*): **~** (**über** +*akk*) grasp (of), overall view (of); **ü~en** [-'blɪkən] *vt insep* to survey

überbring- [y:bər'brɪŋ] *zW*: **~en** (*unreg*) *vt insep* to deliver, to hand over; **Ü~er** (**-s, -**) *m* bearer

überbrücken [y:bər'brʏkən] *vt insep* to bridge (over)

überbuchen ['y:bərbu:xən] *vt insep* to overbook

über'dauern *vt insep* to outlast

über'denken (*unreg*) *vt insep* to think over

überdies [y:bər'di:s] *adv* besides

überdimensional ['y:bərdimenziona:l] *adj* oversize

Überdruss ▲ ['y:bərdrʊs] (**-es**) *m* weariness; **bis zum ~** ad nauseam

überdurchschnittlich ['y:bərdʊrçʃnɪtlɪç] *adj* above-average ♦ *adv* exceptionally

übereifrig ['y:bər|aɪfrɪç] *adj* over-keen

übereilt [y:bər'|aɪlt] *adj* (over)hasty, premature

überein- [y:bər'|aɪn] *zW*: **~ander** [y:bər|aɪ'nandər] *adv* one upon the other; (*sprechen*) about each other; **~kommen** (*unreg*) *vi* to agree; **Ü~kunft** (**-, -künfte**) *f* agreement; **~stimmen** *vi* to agree;

Ü~stimmung *f* agreement

überempfindlich ['y:bər|ɛmpfɪntlɪç] *adj* hypersensitive

überfahren [y:bər'fa:rən] (*unreg*) *vt insep* (*AUT*) to run over; (*fig*) to walk all over

Überfahrt ['y:bərfa:rt] *f* crossing

Überfall ['y:bərfal] *m* (*Banküberfall, MIL*) raid; (*auf jdn*) assault; **ü~en** [-'falən] (*unreg*) *vt insep* to attack; (*Bank*) to raid; (*besuchen*) to drop in on, to descend on

überfällig ['y:bərfɛlɪç] *adj* overdue

über'fliegen (*unreg*) *vt insep* to fly over, to overfly; (*Buch*) to skim through

Überfluss ▲ ['y:bərflʊs] *m*: ~ (**an** +*dat*) (super)abundance (of), excess (of)

überflüssig ['y:bərflʏsɪç] *adj* superfluous

über'fordern *vt insep* to demand too much of; (*Kräfte etc*) to overtax

über'führen *vt insep* (*Leiche etc*) to transport; (*Täter*) to have convicted

Über'führung *f* transport; conviction; (*Brücke*) bridge, overpass

über'füllt *adj* (*Schulen, Straßen*) overcrowded; (*Kurs*) oversubscribed

Übergabe ['y:bərga:bə] *f* handing over; (*MIL*) surrender

Übergang ['y:bərgaŋ] *m* crossing; (*Wandel, Überleitung*) transition

Übergangs- *zW*: **~lösung** *f* provisional solution, stopgap; **~zeit** *f* transitional period

über'geben (*unreg*) *vt insep* to hand over; (*MIL*) to surrender ♦ *vr insep* to be sick

übergehen ['y:bərge:ən] (*unreg*) *vi* (*Besitz*) to pass; (*zum Feind etc*) to go over, to defect; ~ **in** +*akk* to turn into; **über'gehen** (*unreg*) *vt insep* to pass over, to omit

Übergewicht ['y:bərgəvɪçt] *nt* excess weight; (*fig*) preponderance

überglücklich ['y:bərglʏklɪç] *adj* overjoyed

Übergröße ['y:bərgrø:sə] *f* oversize

überhaupt [y:bər'haʊpt] *adv* at all; (*im Allgemeinen*) in general; (*besonders*) especially; ~ **nicht/keine** not/none at all

überheblich [y:bər'he:plɪç] *adj* arrogant; **Ü~keit** *f* arrogance

über'holen *vt insep* to overtake; (*TECH*) to

overhaul

über'holt *adj* out-of-date, obsolete

Überholverbot [y:bər'ho:lfɛrboːt] *nt* restriction on overtaking

über'hören *vt insep* not to hear; (*absichtlich*) to ignore

überirdisch ['y:bər|ɪrdɪʃ] *adj* supernatural, unearthly

über'laden (*unreg*) *vt insep* to overload ♦ *adj* (*fig*) cluttered

über'lassen (*unreg*) *vt insep*: **jdm etw** ~ to leave sth to sb ♦ *vr insep*: **sich einer Sache** *dat* ~ to give o.s. over to sth

über'lasten *vt insep* to overload; (*Mensch*) to overtax

überlaufen ['y:bərlaʊfən] (*unreg*) *vi* (*Flüssigkeit*) to flow over; (*zum Feind etc*) to go over, to defect; ~ **sein** to be inundated *od* besieged; **über'laufen** (*unreg*) *vt insep* (*Schauer etc*) to come over

über'leben *vt insep* to survive; **Über'lebende(r)** *f(m)* survivor

über'legen *vt insep* to consider ♦ *adj* superior; **ich muss es mir** ~ I'll have to think about it; **Über'legenheit** *f* superiority

Über'legung *f* consideration, deliberation

über'liefern *vt insep* to hand down, to transmit

Überlieferung *f* tradition

überlisten [y:bər'lɪstən] *vt insep* to outwit

überm ['y:bərm] = **über dem**

Übermacht ['y:bərmaxt] *f* superior force, superiority; **übermächtig** ['y:bərmɛçtɪç] *adj* superior (in strength); (*Gefühl etc*) overwhelming

übermäßig ['y:bərmɛ:sɪç] *adj* excessive

Übermensch ['y:bərmɛnʃ] *m* superman; **ü~lich** *adj* superhuman

übermitteln [y:bər'mɪtəln] *vt insep* to convey

übermorgen ['y:bərmɔrgən] *adv* the day after tomorrow

Übermüdung [y:bər'my:dʊŋ] *f* fatigue, overtiredness

Übermut ['y:bərmuːt] *m* exuberance

übermütig ['y:bərmy:tɪç] *adj* exuberant,

high-spirited; ~ **werden** to get overconfident

übernächste(r, s) ['yːbɐrnɛːçstə(r, s)] *adj* (*Jahr*) next but one

übernacht- [yːbɐr'naxt] *zW*: ~**en** *vi insep*: (**bei jdm**) ~**en** to spend the night (at sb's place); **Ü~ung** *f* overnight stay; **Ü~ung mit Frühstück** bed and breakfast; **Ü~ungsmöglichkeit** *f* overnight accommodation *no pl*

Übernahme ['yːbɐrnaːmə] *f* taking over *od* on, acceptance

über'nehmen (*unreg*) *vt insep* to take on, to accept; (*Amt, Geschäft*) to take over ♦ *vr insep* to take on too much

über'prüfen *vt insep* to examine, to check

überqueren [yːbɐr'kveːrən] *vt insep* to cross

überragen [yːbɐr'raːgən] *vt insep* to tower above; (*fig*) to surpass

überraschen [yːbɐr'raʃən] *vt insep* to surprise

Überraschung *f* surprise

überreden [yːbɐr'reːdən] *vt insep* to persuade

überreichen [yːbɐr'raiçən] *vt insep* to present, to hand over

'Überrest *m* remains, remnants

überrumpeln [yːbɐr'rumpəln] *vt insep* to take by surprise

überrunden [yːbɐr'rundən] *vt insep* to lap

übers ['yːbɐrs] = **über das**

Überschall- ['yːbɐrʃal] *zW*: ~**flugzeug** *nt* supersonic jet; ~**geschwindigkeit** *f* supersonic speed

über'schätzen *vt insep* to overestimate

'überschäumen *vi* (*Bier*) to foam over, bubble over; (*Temperament*) to boil over

Überschlag ['yːbɐrʃlaːk] *m* (*FIN*) estimate; (*SPORT*) somersault; **ü~en** [-'ʃlaːgən] (*unreg*) *vt insep* (*berechnen*) to estimate; (*auslassen: Seite*) to omit ♦ *vr insep* to somersault; (*Stimme*) to crack; (*AVIAT*) to loop the loop; **'überschlagen** (*unreg*) *vt* (*Beine*) to cross ♦ *vi* (*Wellen*) to break; (*Funken*) to flash

überschnappen [yːbɐrʃnapən] *vi* (*Stimme*) to crack; (*umg: Mensch*) to flip one's lid

über'schneiden (*unreg*) *vr insep* (*auch fig*) to overlap; (*Linien*) to intersect

über'schreiben (*unreg*) *vt insep* to provide with a heading; **jdm etw** ~ to transfer *od* make over sth to sb

über'schreiten (*unreg*) *vt insep* to cross over; (*fig*) to exceed; (*verletzen*) to transgress

Überschrift ['yːbɐrʃrɪft] *f* heading, title

Überschuss ▲ ['yːbɐrʃʊs] *m*: ~ (**an** +*dat*) surplus (of); **überschüssig** ['yːbɐrʃʏsɪç] *adj* surplus, excess

über'schütten *vt insep*: **jdn/etw mit etw** ~ to pour sth over sb/sth; **jdn mit etw** ~ (*fig*) to shower sb with sth

überschwänglich ▲ ['yːbɐrʃvɛŋlɪç] *adj* effusive

überschwemmen [yːbɐr'ʃvɛmən] *vt insep* to flood

Überschwemmung *f* flood

Übersee ['yːbɐrzeː] *f*: **nach/in** ~ overseas; **ü~isch** *adj* overseas

über'sehen (*unreg*) *vt insep* to look (out) over; (*fig: Folgen*) to see, to get an overall view of; (: *nicht beachten*) to overlook

über'senden (*unreg*) *vt insep* to send, to forward

übersetz- *zW*: ~**en** [yːbɐr'zɛtsən] *vt insep* to translate; **'übersetzen** *vi* to cross; **Ü~er(in)** [-'zɛtsɐ(ɪn)] (**-s, -**) *m(f)* translator; **Ü~ung** [-'zɛtsʊŋ] *f* translation; (*TECH*) gear ratio

Übersicht ['yːbɐrzɪçt] *f* overall view; (*Darstellung*) survey; **ü~lich** *adj* clear; (*Gelände*) open; ~**lichkeit** *f* clarity, lucidity

übersiedeln [yːbɐrzi:dəln] *vi sep* to move; **über'siedeln** *vi* to move

über'spannt *adj* eccentric; (*Idee*) wild, crazy

überspitzt [yːbɐr'ʃpɪtst] *adj* exaggerated

über'springen (*unreg*) *vt insep* to jump over; (*fig*) to skip

überstehen [yːbɐr'ʃteːən] (*unreg*) *vt insep* to overcome, to get over; (*Winter etc*) to survive, to get through; **'überstehen** (*unreg*) *vi* to project

über'steigen (*unreg*) *vt insep* to climb over; (*fig*) to exceed

über'stimmen *vt insep* to outvote

Überstunden ['y:bərʃtʊndən] *pl* overtime *sg*

über'stürzen *vt insep* to rush ♦ *vr insep* to follow (one another) in rapid succession

überstürzt *adj* (over)hasty

Übertrag ['y:bərtra:k] **(-(e)s, -träge)** *m* (COMM) amount brought forward; **ü~bar** [-'tra:kba:r] *adj* transferable; (MED) infectious; **ü~en** [-'tra:gən] (unreg) *vt insep* to transfer; (RADIO) to broadcast; (übersetzen) to render; (Krankheit) to transmit ♦ *vr insep* to spread ♦ *adj* figurative; **ü~en auf** +akk to transfer to; **jdm etw ü~en** to assign sth to sb; **sich ü~en auf** +akk to spread to; **~ung** [-'tra:gʊŋ] *f* transfer(ence); (RADIO) broadcast; rendering; transmission

über'treffen (unreg) *vt insep* to surpass

über'treiben (unreg) *vt insep* to exaggerate; **Übertreibung** *f* exaggeration

übertreten [y:bər'tre:tən] (unreg) *vt insep* to cross; (Gebot etc) to break; **'übertreten** (unreg) *vi* (über Linie, Gebiet) to step (over); (SPORT) to overstep; (zu anderem Glauben) to be converted; **'übertreten (in** +akk) (POL) to go over (to)

Über'tretung *f* violation, transgression

übertrieben [y:bər'tri:bən] *adj* exaggerated, excessive

übervölkert [y:bər'fœlkərt] *adj* overpopulated

übervoll ['y:bərfɔl] *adj* overfull

übervorteilen [y:bər'fɔrtaɪlən] *vt insep* to dupe, to cheat

über'wachen *vt insep* to supervise; (Verdächtigen) to keep under surveillance; **Überwachung** *f* supervision; surveillance

überwältigen [y:bər'vɛltɪgən] *vt insep* to overpower; **~d** *adj* overwhelming

überweisen [y:bər'vaɪzən] (unreg) *vt insep* to transfer

Überweisung *f* transfer; **~sauftrag** *m* (credit) transfer order

über'wiegen (unreg) *vi insep* to predominate; **~d** *adj* predominant

über'winden (unreg) *vt insep* to overcome ♦ *vr insep* to make an effort, to bring o.s. (to do sth)

Überwindung *f* effort, strength of mind

Überzahl ['y:bərtsa:l] *f* superiority, superior numbers *pl*; **in der ~ sein** to be numerically superior

überzählig ['y:bərtsɛ:lɪç] *adj* surplus

über'zeugen *vt insep* to convince; **~d** *adj* convincing

Überzeugung *f* conviction

überziehen ['y:bərtsi:ən] (unreg) *vt* to put on; **über'ziehen** (unreg) *vt insep* to cover; (Konto) to overdraw

Überziehungskredit *m* overdraft provision

Überzug ['y:bərtsu:k] *m* cover; (Belag) coating

üblich ['y:plɪç] *adj* usual

U-Boot ['u:bo:t] *nt* submarine

übrig ['y:brɪç] *adj* remaining; **für jdn etwas ~ haben** (umg) to be fond of sb; **die Ü~en** the others; **das Ü~e** the rest; **im Ü~en** besides; **~ bleiben** to remain, to be left (over); **~ lassen** to leave (over); **~ens** ['y:brɪgəns] *adv* besides; (nebenbei bemerkt) by the way

Übung ['y:bʊŋ] *f* practice; (Turnübung, Aufgabe etc) exercise; **~ macht den Meister** practice makes perfect

Ufer ['u:fər] **(-s, -)** *nt* bank; (Meeresufer) shore

Uhr [u:r] **(-, -en)** *f* clock; (Armbanduhr) watch; **wie viel ~ ist es?** what time is it?; **1 ~ 1** o'clock; **20 ~ 8** o'clock, 20.00 (twenty hundred) hours; **~(arm)band** *nt* watch strap; **~band** *nt* watch strap; **~macher (-s, -)** *m* watchmaker; **~werk** *nt* clockwork; works of a watch; **~zeiger** *m* hand; **~zeigersinn** *m*: **im ~zeigersinn** clockwise; **entgegen dem ~zeigersinn** anticlockwise; **~zeit** *f* time (of day)

Uhu ['u:hu] **(-s, -s)** *m* eagle owl

UKW [u:ka:'ve:] *abk* (= Ultrakurzwelle) VHF

ulkig ['ʊlkɪç] *adj* funny

Ulme ['ʊlmə] *f* elm

Ultimatum [ʊlti'ma:tʊm] **(-s, Ultimaten)** *nt* ultimatum

Ultra- ['ʊltra] *zW*: **~schall** *m* (PHYS) ultrasound; **u~violett** *adj* ultraviolet

um [ʊm] *präp +akk* **1** (*um herum*) (a)round; **um Weihnachten** around Christmas; **er schlug um sich** he hit about him **2** (*mit Zeitangabe*) at; **um acht (Uhr)** at eight (o'clock) **3** (*mit Größenangabe*) by; **etw um 4 cm kürzen** to shorten sth by 4 cm; **um 10% teurer** 10% more expensive; **um vieles besser** better by far; **um nichts besser** not in the least bit better **4**: **der Kampf um den Titel** the battle for the title; **um Geld spielen** to play for money; **Stunde um Stunde** hour after hour; **Auge um Auge** an eye for an eye
♦ *präp +gen*: **um … willen** for the sake of …; **um Gottes willen** for goodness' *od* (*stärker*) God's sake
♦ *konj*: **um … zu** (in order) to …; **zu klug, um zu …** too clever to …; *siehe* **umso**
♦ *adv* **1** (*ungefähr*) about; **um (die) 30 Leute** about *od* around 30 people **2** (*vorbei*): **die 2 Stunden sind um** the two hours are up

umändern ['ʊmʔɛndərn] *vt* to alter
Umänderung *f* alteration
umarbeiten ['ʊmʔarbaɪtən] *vt* to remodel; (*Buch etc*) to revise, to rework
umarmen [ʊmʔarmən] *vt insep* to embrace
Umbau ['ʊmbaʊ] (**-(e)s, -e** *od* **-ten**) *m* reconstruction, alteration(s); **u~en** *vt* to rebuild, to reconstruct
umbilden ['ʊmbɪldən] *vt* to reorganize; (*POL: Kabinett*) to reshuffle
umbinden ['ʊmbɪndən] (*unreg*) *vt* (*Krawatte etc*) to put on
umblättern ['ʊmblɛtərn] *vt* to turn over
umblicken ['ʊmblɪkən] *vr* to look around
umbringen ['ʊmbrɪŋən] (*unreg*) *vt* to kill
umbuchen ['ʊmbuːxən] *vi* to change one's reservation/flight *etc* ♦ *vt* to change
umdenken ['ʊmdɛŋkən] (*unreg*) *vi* to adjust one's views
umdrehen ['ʊmdreːən] *vt* to turn (round); (*Hals*) to wring ♦ *vr* to turn (round)

Um'drehung *f* revolution; rotation
umeinander [ʊmʔaɪ'nandər] *adv* round one another; (*füreinander*) for one another
umfahren ['ʊmfaːrən] (*unreg*) *vt* to run over; **um'fahren** (*unreg*) *vt insep* to drive round; to sail round
umfallen ['ʊmfalən] (*unreg*) *vi* to fall down *od* over
Umfang ['ʊmfaŋ] *m* extent; (*von Buch*) size; (*Reichweite*) range; (*Fläche*) area; (*MATH*) circumference; **u~reich** *adj* extensive; (*Buch etc*) voluminous
um'fassen *vt insep* to embrace; (*umgeben*) to surround; (*enthalten*) to include; **um'fassend** *adj* comprehensive, extensive
umformen ['ʊmfɔrmən] *vt* to transform
Umfrage ['ʊmfraːgə] *f* poll
umfüllen ['ʊmfʏlən] *vt* to transfer; (*Wein*) to decant
umfunktionieren ['ʊmfʊŋktsioniːrən] *vt* to convert, to transform
Umgang ['ʊmgaŋ] *m* company; (*mit jdm*) dealings *pl*; (*Behandlung*) way of behaving
umgänglich ['ʊmgɛŋlɪç] *adj* sociable
Umgangs- *zW*: **~formen** *pl* manners; **~sprache** *f* colloquial language
umgeben [ʊm'geːbən] (*unreg*) *vt insep* to surround
Umgebung *f* surroundings *pl*; (*Milieu*) environment; (*Personen*) people in one's circle
umgehen ['ʊmgeːən] (*unreg*) *vi* to go (a)round; **im Schlosse ~** to haunt the castle; **mit jdm grob etc ~** to treat sb roughly *etc*; **mit Geld sparsam ~** to be careful with one's money; **um'gehen** *vt insep* to bypass; (*MIL*) to outflank; (*Gesetz etc*) to circumvent; (*vermeiden*) to avoid; **'umgehend** *adj* immediate
Um'gehung *f* bypassing; outflanking; circumvention; avoidance; **~sstraße** *f* bypass
umgekehrt ['ʊmgəkeːrt] *adj* reverse(d); (*gegenteilig*) opposite ♦ *adv* the other way around; **und ~** and vice versa
umgraben ['ʊmgraːbən] (*unreg*) *vt* to dig up
Umhang ['ʊmhaŋ] *m* wrap, cape

umhauen ['ʊmhaʊən] vt to fell; (fig) to bowl over

umher [ʊm'heːr] adv about, around; **~gehen** (unreg) vi to walk about; **~ziehen** (unreg) vi to wander from place to place

umhinkönnen [ʊm'hɪnkœnən] (unreg) vi: **ich kann nicht umhin, das zu tun** I can't help doing it

umhören ['ʊmhøːrən] vr to ask around

Umkehr ['ʊmkeːr] (-) f turning back; (Änderung) change; **u~en** vi to turn back ♦ vt to turn round, to reverse; (Tasche etc) to turn inside out; (Gefäß etc) to turn upside down

umkippen ['ʊmkɪpən] vt to tip over ♦ vi to overturn; (umg: Mensch) to keel over; (fig: Meinung ändern) to change one's mind

Umkleide- ['ʊmklaɪdə] zW: **~kabine** f (im Schwimmbad) (changing) cubicle; **~raum** m changing od dressing room

umkommen ['ʊmkɔmən] (unreg) vi to die, to perish; (Lebensmittel) to go bad

Umkreis ['ʊmkraɪs] m neighbourhood; **im ~ von** within a radius of

Umlage ['ʊmlaːgə] f share of the costs

Umlauf ['ʊmlaʊf] m (Geldumlauf) circulation; (von Gestirn) revolution; **~bahn** f orbit

Umlaut ['ʊmlaʊt] m umlaut

umlegen ['ʊmleːgən] vt to put on; (verlegen) to move, to shift; (Kosten) to share out; (umkippen) to tip over; (umg: töten) to bump off

umleiten ['ʊmlaɪtən] vt to divert

Umleitung f diversion

umliegend ['ʊmliːgənt] adj surrounding

um'randen vt insep to border, to edge

umrechnen ['ʊmrɛçnən] vt to convert

Umrechnung f conversion; **~skurs** m rate of exchange

um'reißen (unreg) vt insep to outline, to sketch

Umriss ▲ ['ʊmrɪs] m outline

umrühren ['ʊmryːrən] vt, vi to stir

ums [ʊms] = **um das**

Umsatz ['ʊmzats] m turnover; **~steuer** f sales tax

umschalten ['ʊmʃaltən] vt to switch

umschauen vr to look round

Umschlag ['ʊmʃlaːk] m cover; (Buchumschlag auch) jacket; (MED) compress; (Briefumschlag) envelope; (Wechsel) change; (von Hose) turn-up; **u~en** [-gən] (unreg) vi to change; (NAUT) to capsize ♦ vt to knock over; (Ärmel) to turn up; (Seite) to turn over; (Waren) to transfer; **~platz** m (COMM) distribution centre

umschreiben ['ʊmʃraɪbən] (unreg) vt (neu schreiben) to rewrite; (übertragen) to transfer; **~ +akk to** transfer to; **um'schreiben** (unreg) vt insep to paraphrase; (abgrenzen) to define

umschulen ['ʊmʃuːlən] vt to retrain; (Kind) to send to another school

Umschweife ['ʊmʃvaɪfə] pl: **ohne ~** without beating about the bush, straight out

Umschwung ['ʊmʃvʊŋ] m change (around), revolution

umsehen ['ʊmzeːən] (unreg) vr to look around od about; (suchen): **sich ~ (nach)** to look out (for)

umseitig ['ʊmzaɪtɪç] adv overleaf

umsichtig ['ʊmzɪçtɪç] adj cautious, prudent

umso ▲ ['ʊmzo] konj: **~ besser/schlimmer** so much the better/worse

umsonst [ʊm'zɔnst] adv in vain; (gratis) for nothing

umspringen ['ʊmʃprɪŋən] (unreg) vi to change; (Wind auch) to veer; **mit jdm ~** to treat sb badly

Umstand ['ʊmʃtant] m circumstance; **Umstände** pl (fig: Schwierigkeiten) fuss; **in anderen Umständen sein** to be pregnant; **Umstände machen** to go to a lot of trouble; **unter Umständen** possibly

umständlich ['ʊmʃtɛntlɪç] adj (Methode) cumbersome, complicated; (Ausdrucksweise, Erklärung) long-winded; (Mensch) ponderous

Umstandskleid nt maternity dress

Umstehende(n) ['ʊmʃteːəndə(n)] pl bystanders

umsteigen ['ʊmʃtaɪgən] (unreg) vi (EISENB) to change

umstellen ['ʊmʃtɛlən] vt (an anderen Ort) to

change round, to rearrange; (TECH) to
convert ♦ vr to adapt (o.s.); **sich auf etw**
akk ~ to adapt to sth; **um'stellen** vt insep
to surround

Umstellung ['ʊmʃtɛlʊŋ] f change;
(Umgewöhnung) adjustment; (TECH)
conversion

umstimmen ['ʊmʃtɪmən] vt (MUS) to
retune; **jdn** ~ to make sb change his mind

umstoßen ['ʊmʃtoːsən] (unreg) vt to
overturn; (Plan etc) to change, to upset

umstritten ['ʊmʃtrɪtən] adj disputed

Umsturz ['ʊmʃtʊrts] m overthrow

umstürzen ['ʊmʃtʏrtsən] vt (umwerfen) to
overturn ♦ vi to collapse, to fall down;
(Wagen) to overturn

Umtausch ['ʊmtaʊʃ] m exchange; **u~en** vt
to exchange

Umverpackung ['ʊmfɛrpakʊŋ] f packaging

umwandeln ['ʊmvandəln] vt to change, to
convert; (ELEK) to transform

umwechseln ['ʊmvɛksəln] vt to change

Umweg ['ʊmveːk] m detour, roundabout
way

Umwelt ['ʊmvɛlt] f environment;
u~freundlich adj not harmful to the
environment, environment-friendly;
u~schädlich adj ecologically harmful;
~schutz m environmental protection;
~schützer m environmentalist;
~verschmutzung f environmental
pollution

umwenden ['ʊmvɛndən] (unreg) vt, vr to
turn (round)

umwerfen ['ʊmvɛrfən] (unreg) vt to upset,
to overturn; (fig: erschüttern) to upset, to
throw; **~d** (umg) adj fantastic

umziehen ['ʊmtsiːən] (unreg) vt, vr to
change ♦ vi to move

Umzug ['ʊmtsuːk] m procession;
(Wohnungsumzug) move, removal

unab- ['ʊnʔap] zW: **~änderlich** adj
irreversible, unalterable; **~hängig** adj
independent; **U~hängigkeit** f
independence; **~kömmlich** adj
indispensable; **zur Zeit ~kömmlich** not free
at the moment; **~lässig** adj incessant,

constant; **~sehbar** adj immeasurable;
(Folgen) unforeseeable; (Kosten) incalculable;
~sichtlich adj unintentional; **~'wendbar**
adj inevitable

unachtsam ['ʊn|axtzaːm] adj careless;
U~keit f carelessness

unan- ['ʊn|an] zW: **~'fechtbar** adj
indisputable; **~gebracht** adj uncalled-for;
~gemessen adj inadequate; **~genehm**
adj unpleasant; **U~nehmlichkeit** f
inconvenience; **U~nehmlichkeiten** pl
(Ärger) trouble sg; **~sehnlich** adj unsightly;
~ständig adj indecent, improper

unappetitlich ['ʊnʔapetiːtlɪç] adj unsavoury

Unart ['ʊn|aːrt] f bad manners pl;
(Angewohnheit) bad habit; **u~ig** adj
naughty, badly behaved

unauf- ['ʊn|aʊf] zW: **~fällig** adj unobtrusive;
(Kleidung) inconspicuous; **~'findbar** adj not
to be found; **~gefordert** adj unasked
♦ adv spontaneously; **~haltsam** adj
irresistible; **~'hörlich** adj incessant,
continuous; **~merksam** adj inattentive;
~richtig adj insincere

unaus- ['ʊn|aʊs] zW: **~geglichen** adj
unbalanced; **~'sprechlich** adj
inexpressible; **~'stehlich** adj intolerable

unbarmherzig ['ʊnbarmhɛrtsɪç] adj pitiless,
merciless

unbeabsichtigt ['ʊnbəʔapzɪçtɪçt] adj
unintentional

unbeachtet ['ʊnbə|axtət] adj unnoticed,
ignored

unbedenklich ['ʊnbədɛŋklɪç] adj (Plan)
unobjectionable

unbedeutend ['ʊnbədɔʏtənt] adj
insignificant, unimportant; (Fehler) slight

unbedingt ['ʊnbədɪŋt] adj unconditional
♦ adv absolutely; **musst du ~ gehen?** do
you really have to go?

unbefangen ['ʊnbəfaŋən] adj impartial,
unprejudiced; (ohne Hemmungen)
uninhibited; **U~heit** f impartiality;
uninhibitedness

unbefriedigend ['ʊnbəfriːdɪgənt] adj
unsatisfactory

unbefriedigt ['ʊnbəfriːdɪçt] adj unsatisfied,

dissatisfied

unbefugt ['ʊnbəfuːkt] *adj* unauthorized

unbegreiflich [ʊnbə'graiflɪç] *adj* inconceivable

unbegrenzt ['ʊnbəgrɛntst] *adj* unlimited

unbegründet ['ʊnbəgrʏndət] *adj* unfounded

Unbehagen ['ʊnbəhaːgən] *nt* discomfort; **unbehaglich** ['ʊnbəhaːklɪç] *adj* uncomfortable; (*Gefühl*) uneasy

unbeholfen ['ʊnbəhɔlfən] *adj* awkward, clumsy

unbekannt ['ʊnbəkant] *adj* unknown

unbekümmert ['ʊnbəkʏmərt] *adj* unconcerned

unbeliebt ['ʊnbəliːpt] *adj* unpopular

unbequem ['ʊnbəkveːm] *adj* (*Stuhl*) uncomfortable; (*Mensch*) bothersome; (*Regelung*) inconvenient

unberechenbar [ʊnbə'rɛçənbaːr] *adj* incalculable; (*Mensch, Verhalten*) unpredictable

unberechtigt ['ʊnbərɛçtɪçt] *adj* unjustified; (*nicht erlaubt*) unauthorized

unberührt ['ʊnbərʏrt] *adj* untouched, intact; **sie ist noch ~** she is still a virgin

unbescheiden ['ʊnbəʃaidən] *adj* presumptuous

unbeschreiblich [ʊnbə'ʃraiplɪç] *adj* indescribable

unbeständig ['ʊnbəʃtɛndɪç] *adj* (*Mensch*) inconstant; (*Wetter*) unsettled; (*Lage*) unstable

unbestechlich [ʊnbə'ʃtɛçlɪç] *adj* incorruptible

unbestimmt ['ʊnbəʃtɪmt] *adj* indefinite; (*Zukunft auch*) uncertain

unbeteiligt [ʊnbə'tailɪçt] *adj* unconcerned, indifferent

unbeweglich ['ʊnbəveːklɪç] *adj* immovable

unbewohnt ['ʊnbəvoːnt] *adj* uninhabited; (*Wohnung*) unoccupied

unbewusst ▲ ['ʊnbəvʊst] *adj* unconscious

unbezahlt ['ʊnbətsaːlt] *adj* (*Rechnung*) outstanding, unsettled; (*Urlaub*) unpaid

unbrauchbar ['ʊnbrauxbaːr] *adj* (*Arbeit*) useless; (*Gerät auch*) unusable

und [ʊnt] *konj* and; **~ so weiter** and so on

Undank ['ʊndaŋk] *m* ingratitude; **u~bar** *adj* ungrateful

undefinierbar [ʊndefi'niːrbaːr] *adj* indefinable

undenkbar [ʊn'dɛŋkbaːr] *adj* inconceivable

undeutlich ['ʊndɔʏtlɪç] *adj* indistinct

undicht ['ʊndɪçt] *adj* leaky

Unding ['ʊndɪŋ] *nt* absurdity

undurch- ['ʊndʊrç] *zW*: **~führbar** [-'fyːrbaːr] *adj* impracticable; **~lässig** [-'lɛsɪç] *adj* waterproof, impermeable; **~sichtig** [-'zɪçtɪç] *adj* opaque; (*fig*) obscure

uneben ['ʊn|eːbən] *adj* uneven

unecht ['ʊn|ɛçt] *adj* (*Schmuck*) fake; (*vorgetäuscht: Freundlichkeit*) false

unehelich ['ʊn|eːəlɪç] *adj* illegitimate

uneinig ['ʊn|ainɪç] *adj* divided; **~ sein** to disagree; **U~keit** *f* discord, dissension

uneins ['ʊn|ains] *adj* at variance, at odds

unempfindlich ['ʊn|ɛmpfɪntlɪç] *adj* insensitive; (*Stoff*) practical

unendlich [ʊn'|ɛntlɪç] *adj* infinite

unent- ['ʊn|ɛnt] *zW*: **~behrlich** [-'beːrlɪç] *adj* indispensable; **~geltlich** [-gɛltlɪç] *adj* free (of charge); **~schieden** [-ʃiːdən] *adj* undecided; **~schieden enden** (*SPORT*) to end in a draw; **~schlossen** [-ʃlɔsən] *adj* undecided; irresolute; **~wegt** [-'veːkt] *adj* unswerving; (*unaufhörlich*) incessant

uner- ['ʊn|ɛr] *zW*: **~bittlich** [-'bɪtlɪç] *adj* unyielding, inexorable; **~fahren** [-faːrən] *adj* inexperienced; **~freulich** [-frɔʏlɪç] *adj* unpleasant; **~gründlich** *adj* unfathomable; **~hört** [-høːrt] *adj* unheard-of; (*Bitte*) outrageous; **~lässlich** ▲ [-'lɛslɪç] *adj* indispensable; **~laubt** *adj* unauthorized; **~messlich** ▲ *adj* immeasurable, immense; **~reichbar** *adj* (*Ziel*) unattainable; (*Ort*) inaccessible; (*telefonisch*) unobtainable; **~schöpflich** [-'ʃœpflɪç] *adj* inexhaustible; **~schwinglich** [-'ʃvɪŋlɪç] *adj* (*Preis*) exorbitant; too expensive; **~träglich** [-'trɛːklɪç] *adj* unbearable; (*Frechheit*) insufferable; **~wartet** *adj* unexpected; **~wünscht** *adj* undesirable, unwelcome

unfähig ['ʊnfɛːɪç] *adj* incapable, incompetent; **zu etw ~ sein** to be incapable of sth; **U~keit** f incapacity; incompetence

unfair ['ʊnfɛːr] adj unfair

Unfall ['ʊnfal] m accident; **~flucht** f hit-and-run (driving); **~schaden** m damages pl; **~station** f emergency ward; **~stelle** f scene of the accident; **~versicherung** f accident insurance

unfassbar ▲ [ʊn'fasbaːr] adj inconceivable

unfehlbar [ʊn'feːlbaːr] adj infallible ♦ adv inevitably; **U~keit** f infallibility

unförmig ['ʊnfœrmɪç] adj (formlos) shapeless

unfrei ['ʊnfraɪ] adj not free, unfree; (Paket) unfranked; **~willig** adj involuntary, against one's will

unfreundlich ['ʊnfrɔʏntlɪç] adj unfriendly; **U~keit** f unfriendliness

Unfriede(n) ['ʊnfriːdə(n)] m dissension, strife

unfruchtbar ['ʊnfrʊxtbaːr] adj infertile; (Gespräche) unfruitful; **U~keit** f infertility; unfruitfulness

Unfug ['ʊnfuːk] (-s) m (Benehmen) mischief; (Unsinn) nonsense; **grober ~** (JUR) gross misconduct; malicious damage

Ungar(in) ['ʊngar(ɪn)] m(f) Hungarian; **u~isch** adj Hungarian; **~n** nt Hungary

ungeachtet ['ʊngə|axtət] präp +gen notwithstanding

ungeahnt ['ʊngə|aːnt] adj unsuspected, undreamt-of

ungebeten ['ʊngəbeːtən] adj uninvited

ungebildet ['ʊngəbɪldət] adj uneducated; uncultured

ungedeckt ['ʊngədɛkt] adj (Scheck) uncovered

Ungeduld ['ʊngədʊlt] f impatience; **u~ig** [-dɪç] adj impatient

ungeeignet ['ʊngə|aɪgnət] adj unsuitable

ungefähr ['ʊngəfɛːr] adj rough, approximate; **das kommt nicht von ~** that's hardly surprising

ungefährlich ['ʊngəfɛːrlɪç] adj not dangerous, harmless

ungehalten ['ʊngəhaltən] adj indignant

ungeheuer ['ʊngəhɔʏər] adj huge ♦ adv (umg) enormously; **U~** (-s, -) nt monster;

~lich [-'hɔʏərlɪç] adj monstrous

ungehörig ['ʊngəhøːrɪç] adj impertinent, improper

ungehorsam ['ʊngəhoːrzaːm] adj disobedient; **U~** m disobedience

ungeklärt ['ʊngəklɛːrt] adj not cleared up; (Rätsel) unsolved

ungeladen ['ʊngəlaːdən] adj not loaded; (Gast) uninvited

ungelegen ['ʊngəleːgən] adj inconvenient

ungelernt ['ʊngəlɛrnt] adj unskilled

ungelogen ['ʊngəloːgən] adv really, honestly

ungemein ['ʊngəmaɪn] adj uncommon

ungemütlich ['ʊngəmyːtlɪç] adj uncomfortable; (Person) disagreeable

ungenau ['ʊngənaʊ] adj inaccurate; **U~igkeit** f inaccuracy

ungenießbar ['ʊngəniːsbaːr] adj inedible; undrinkable; (umg) unbearable

ungenügend ['ʊngənyːgənt] adj insufficient, inadequate

ungepflegt ['ʊngəpfleːkt] adj (Garten etc) untended; (Person) unkempt; (Hände) neglected

ungerade ['ʊngəraːdə] adj uneven, odd

ungerecht ['ʊngərɛçt] adj unjust; **~fertigt** adj unjustified; **U~igkeit** f injustice, unfairness

ungern ['ʊngɛrn] adv unwillingly, reluctantly

ungeschehen ['ʊngəʃeːən] adj: **~ machen** to undo

Ungeschicklichkeit ['ʊngəʃɪklɪçkaɪt] f clumsiness

ungeschickt adj awkward, clumsy

ungeschminkt ['ʊngəʃmɪŋkt] adj without make-up; (fig) unvarnished

ungesetzlich ['ʊngəzɛtslɪç] adj illegal

ungestört ['ʊngəʃtøːrt] adj undisturbed

ungestraft ['ʊngəʃtraːft] adv with impunity

ungestüm ['ʊngəʃtyːm] adj impetuous; tempestuous

ungesund ['ʊngəzʊnt] adj unhealthy

ungetrübt ['ʊngətryːpt] adj clear; (fig) untroubled; (Freude) unalloyed

Ungetüm ['ʊngətyːm] (-(e)s, -e) nt monster

ungewiss ▲ ['ʊngəvɪs] adj uncertain;

U~heit *f* uncertainty
ungewöhnlich ['ʊngəvøːnlɪç] *adj* unusual
ungewohnt ['ʊngəvoːnt] *adj* unaccustomed
Ungeziefer ['ʊngətsiːfər] **(-s)** *nt* vermin
ungezogen ['ʊngətsoːgən] *adj* rude,
impertinent; **U~heit** *f* rudeness,
impertinence
ungezwungen ['ʊngətsvʊŋən] *adj* natural,
unconstrained
unglaublich [ʊn'glaʊplɪç] *adj* incredible
ungleich ['ʊnglaɪç] *adj* dissimilar; unequal
♦ *adv* incomparably; **~artig** *adj* different;
U~heit *f* dissimilarity; inequality; **~mäßig**
adj irregular, uneven
Unglück ['ʊnglʏk] **(-(e)s, -e)** *nt* misfortune;
(*Pech*) bad luck; (*~sfall*) calamity, disaster;
(*Verkehrsunglück*) accident; **u~lich** *adj*
unhappy; (*erfolglos*) unlucky; (*unerfreulich*)
unfortunate; **u~licherweise** [-'vaɪzə] *adv*
unfortunately; **~sfall** *m* accident, calamity
ungültig ['ʊngʏltɪç] *adj* invalid; **U~keit** *f*
invalidity
ungünstig ['ʊngʏnstɪç] *adj* unfavourable
ungut ['ʊnguːt] *adj* (*Gefühl*) uneasy; **nichts**
für ~ no offence
unhaltbar ['ʊnhaltbaːr] *adj* untenable
Unheil ['ʊnhaɪl] *nt* evil; (*Unglück*) misfortune;
~ anrichten to cause mischief; **u~bar** *adj*
incurable
unheimlich ['ʊnhaɪmlɪç] *adj* weird, uncanny
♦ *adv* (*umg*) tremendously
unhöflich ['ʊnhøːflɪç] *adj* impolite; **U~keit** *f*
impoliteness
unhygienisch ['ʊnhygieːnɪʃ] *adj* unhygienic
Uni ['ʊni] **(-, -s)** (*umg*) *f* university
Uniform [uni'fɔrm] *f* uniform; **u~iert**
[-'miːrt] *adj* uniformed
uninteressant ['ʊn|ɪnteresant] *adj*
uninteresting
Uni- *zW:* **~versität** [univerzi'tɛːt] *f* university;
~versum [uni'verzʊm] **(-s)** *nt* universe
unkenntlich ['ʊnkɛntlɪç] *adj* unrecognizable
Unkenntnis ['ʊnkɛntnɪs] *f* ignorance
unklar ['ʊnklaːr] *adj* unclear; **im U~en sein**
über +*akk* to be in the dark about; **U~heit**
f unclarity; (*Unentschiedenheit*) uncertainty
unklug ['ʊnkluːk] *adj* unwise

Unkosten ['ʊnkɔstən] *pl* expense(s);
~beitrag *m* contribution to costs *od*
expenses
Unkraut ['ʊnkraʊt] *nt* weed; weeds *pl*
unkündbar ['ʊnkʏntbaːr] *adj* (*Stelle*)
permanent; (*Vertrag*) binding
unlauter ['ʊnlaʊtər] *adj* unfair
unleserlich ['ʊnleːzərlɪç] *adj* illegible
unlogisch ['ʊnloːgɪʃ] *adj* illogical
unlösbar [ʊn'løːsbar] *adj* insoluble
Unlust ['ʊnlʊst] *f* lack of enthusiasm
Unmenge ['ʊnmeŋə] *f* tremendous number,
hundreds *pl*
Unmensch ['ʊnmenʃ] *m* ogre, brute;
u~lich *adj* inhuman, brutal; (*ungeheuer*)
awful
unmerklich [ʊn'merklɪç] *adj* imperceptible
unmissverständlich ▲ ['ʊnmɪsfersjtentlɪç]
adj unmistakable
unmittelbar ['ʊnmɪtəlbaːr] *adj* immediate
unmodern ['ʊnmodern] *adj* old-fashioned
unmöglich ['ʊnmøːklɪç] *adj* impossible;
U~keit *f* impossibility
unmoralisch ['ʊnmoraːlɪʃ] *adj* immoral
Unmut ['ʊnmuːt] *m* ill humour
unnachgiebig ['ʊnnaːxgiːbɪç] *adj* unyielding
unnahbar [ʊn'naːbaːr] *adj* unapproachable
unnötig ['ʊnnøːtɪç] *adj* unnecessary
unnütz ['ʊnnʏts] *adj* useless
unordentlich ['ʊn|ɔrdəntlɪç] *adj* untidy
Unordnung ['ʊn|ɔrdnʊŋ] *f* disorder
unparteiisch ['ʊnpartaɪʃ] *adj* impartial;
U~e(r) *f(m)* umpire; (*FUSSBALL*) referee
unpassend ['ʊnpasənt] *adj* inappropriate;
(*Zeit*) inopportune
unpässlich ▲ ['ʊnpeslɪç] *adj* unwell
unpersönlich ['ʊnperzøːnlɪç] *adj* impersonal
unpolitisch ['ʊnpoliːtɪʃ] *adj* apolitical
unpraktisch ['ʊnpraktɪʃ] *adj* unpractical
unpünktlich ['ʊnpʏŋktlɪç] *adj* unpunctual
unrationell ['ʊnratsionel] *adj* inefficient
unrealistisch ['ʊnrealɪstɪʃ] *adj* unrealistic
unrecht ['ʊnreçt] *adj* wrong; **U~** *nt* wrong;
zu U~ wrongly; **U~ haben** to be wrong;
~mäßig *adj* unlawful, illegal
unregelmäßig ['ʊnreːgəlmeːsɪç] *adj*
irregular; **U~keit** *f* irregularity

unreif ['ʊnraɪf] *adj* (*Obst*) unripe; (*fig*) immature

unrentabel ['ʊnrɛntaːbəl] *adj* unprofitable

unrichtig ['ʊnrɪçtɪç] *adj* incorrect, wrong

Unruhe ['ʊnruːə] *f* unrest; **~stifter** *m* troublemaker

unruhig ['ʊnruːɪç] *adj* restless

uns [ʊns] (*akk, dat von* **wir**) *pron* us; ourselves

unsachlich ['ʊnzaxlɪç] *adj* not to the point, irrelevant

unsagbar [ʊn'zaːkbaːr] *adj* indescribable

unsanft ['ʊnzanft] *adj* rough

unsauber ['ʊnzaʊbər] *adj* unclean, dirty; (*fig*) crooked; (*MUS*) fuzzy

unschädlich ['ʊnʃɛːtlɪç] *adj* harmless; **jdn/ etw ~ machen** to render sb/sth harmless

unscharf ['ʊnʃarf] *adj* indistinct; (*Bild etc*) out of focus, blurred

unscheinbar ['ʊnʃaɪnbaːr] *adj* insignificant; (*Aussehen, Haus etc*) unprepossessing

unschlagbar [ʊn'ʃlaːkbaːr] *adj* invincible

unschön ['ʊnʃøːn] *adj* (*hässlich: Anblick*) ugly, unattractive; (*unfreundlich: Benehmen*) unpleasant, ugly

Unschuld ['ʊnʃʊlt] *f* innocence; **u~ig** [-dɪç] *adj* innocent

unselbst(st)ändig ['ʊnzɛlpʃtɛndɪç] *adj* dependent, over-reliant on others

unser(e) ['ʊnzər(ə)] *adj* our; **~e(r, s)** *pron* ours; **~einer** *pron* people like us; **~eins** *pron* = **unsereiner**; **~erseits** *adv* on our part; **~twegen** *adv* (*für uns*) for our sake; (*wegen uns*) on our account; **~twillen** *adv*: **um ~twillen** = **unsertwegen**

unsicher ['ʊnzɪçər] *adj* uncertain; (*Mensch*) insecure; **U~heit** *f* uncertainty; insecurity

unsichtbar ['ʊnzɪçtbaːr] *adj* invisible

Unsinn ['ʊnzɪn] *m* nonsense; **u~ig** *adj* nonsensical

Unsitte ['ʊnzɪtə] *f* deplorable habit

unsozial ['ʊnzotsiaːl] *adj* (*Verhalten*) antisocial

unsportlich ['ʊnʃpɔrtlɪç] *adj* not sporty; unfit; (*Verhalten*) unsporting

unsre ['ʊnzrə] = **unsere**

unsterblich ['ʊnʃtɛrplɪç] *adj* immortal

Unstimmigkeit ['ʊnʃtɪmɪçkaɪt] *f* inconsistency; (*Streit*) disagreement

unsympathisch ['ʊnzʏmpaːtɪʃ] *adj* unpleasant; **er ist mir ~** I don't like him

untätig ['ʊntɛːtɪç] *adj* idle

untauglich ['ʊntaʊklɪç] *adj* unsuitable; (*MIL*) unfit

unteilbar [ʊn'taɪlbaːr] *adj* indivisible

unten ['ʊntən] *adv* below; (*im Haus*) downstairs; (*an der Treppe etc*) at the bottom; **nach ~** down; **~ am Berg** *etc* at the bottom of the mountain *etc*; **ich bin bei ihm ~ durch** (*umg*) he's through with me

---

SCHLÜSSELWORT

unter ['ʊntər] *präp +dat* **1** (*räumlich, mit Zahlen*) under; (*drunter*) underneath, below; **unter 18 Jahren** under 18 years

2 (*zwischen*) among(st); **sie waren unter sich** they were by themselves; **einer unter ihnen** one of them; **unter anderem** among other things

♦ *präp +akk* under, below

Unterarm ['ʊntər|arm] *m* forearm

unter- *zW*: **~belichten** *vt* (*PHOT*) to underexpose; **U~bewusstsein** ▲ *nt* subconscious; **~bezahlt** *adj* underpaid

unterbieten [ʊntər'biːtən] (*unreg*) *vt insep* (*COMM*) to undercut; (*Rekord*) to lower

unterbrechen [ʊntər'brɛçən] (*unreg*) *vt insep* to interrupt

Unterbrechung *f* interruption

unterbringen ['ʊntərbrɪŋən] (*unreg*) *vt* (*in Koffer*) to stow; (*in Zeitung*) to place; (*Person: in Hotel etc*) to accommodate, to put up

unterdessen [ʊntər'dɛsən] *adv* meanwhile

Unterdruck ['ʊntərdrʊk] *m* low pressure

unterdrücken [ʊntər'drʏkən] *vt insep* to suppress; (*Leute*) to oppress

untere(r, s) ['ʊntərə(r, s)] *adj* lower

untereinander [ʊntər|aɪ'nandər] *adv* with each other; among themselves *etc*

unterentwickelt ['ʊntər|ɛntvɪkəlt] *adj* underdeveloped

unterernährt ['untər|ɛrnɛːrt] *adj*
undernourished, underfed

Unterernährung *f* malnutrition

Unter'führung *f* subway, underpass

Untergang ['untərgaŋ] *m* (down)fall,
decline; (*NAUT*) sinking; (*von Gestirn*) setting

unter'geben *adj* subordinate

untergehen ['untərgeːən] (*unreg*) *vi* to go
down; (*Sonne auch*) to set; (*Staat*) to fall;
(*Volk*) to perish; (*Welt*) to come to an end;
(*im Lärm*) to be drowned

Untergeschoss ▲ ['untərgəʃɔs] *nt*
basement

'Untergewicht *nt* underweight

unter'gliedern *vt insep* to subdivide

Untergrund ['untərgrunt] *m* foundation;
(*POL*) underground; **~bahn** *f* underground,
tube, subway (*US*)

unterhalb ['untərhalp] *präp +gen* below
♦ *adv* below; **~ von** below

Unterhalt ['untərhalt] *m* maintenance;
u~en (*unreg*) *vt insep* to maintain;
(*belustigen*) to entertain ♦ *vr insep* to talk;
(*sich belustigen*) to enjoy o.s.; **u~sam** *adj*
(*Abend, Person*) entertaining, amusing;
~ung *f* maintenance; (*Belustigung*)
entertainment, amusement; (*Gespräch*) talk

Unterhändler ['untərhɛntlər] *m* negotiator

Unter- *zW:* **~hemd** *nt* vest, undershirt (*US*);
~hose *f* underpants *pl*; **~kiefer** *m* lower
jaw

unterkommen ['untərkɔmən] (*unreg*) *vi* to
find shelter; to find work; **das ist mir noch
nie untergekommen** I've never met with
that

unterkühlt [untər'kyːlt] *adj* (*Körper*) affected
by hypothermia

Unterkunft ['untərkunft] (**-, -künfte**) *f*
accommodation

Unterlage ['untərlaːgə] *f* foundation; (*Beleg*)
document; (*Schreibunterlage etc*) pad

unter'lassen (*unreg*) *vt insep* (*versäumen*) to
fail to do; (*sich enthalten*) to refrain from

unterlaufen [untər'laufən] (*unreg*) *vi insep* to
happen ♦ *adj:* **mit Blut ~** suffused with
blood; (*Augen*) bloodshot

unterlegen ['untərleːgən] *vt* to lay *od* put

unter'legen *adj* inferior; (*besiegt*)
defeated

Unterleib ['untərlaip] *m* abdomen

unter'liegen (*unreg*) *vi insep* (*+dat*) to be
defeated *od* overcome (by); (*unterworfen
sein*) to be subject (to)

Untermiete ['untərmiːtə] *f:* **zur ~ wohnen**
to be a subtenant *od* lodger; **~r(in)** *m(f)*
subtenant, lodger

unter'nehmen (*unreg*) *vt insep* to
undertake; **Unter'nehmen** (**-s, -**) *nt*
undertaking, enterprise (*auch COMM*)

Unternehmer [untər'neːmər] (**-s, -**) *m*
entrepreneur, businessman

'unterordnen ['untərɔrdnən] *vr +dat* to
submit o.s. (to), to give o.s. second place
to

Unterredung [untər'reːduŋ] *f* discussion,
talk

Unterricht ['untərrɪçt] (**-(e)s, -e**) *m*
instruction, lessons *pl;* **u~en** [untər'rɪçtən] *vt*
insep to instruct; (*SCH*) to teach ♦ *vr insep:*
sich u~en (über *+akk*) to inform o.s.
(about), to obtain information (about);
~sfach *nt* subject (on school *etc*
curriculum)

Unterrock ['untərrɔk] *m* petticoat, slip

unter'sagen *vt insep* to forbid; **jdm etw ~**
to forbid sb to do sth

Untersatz ['untərzats] *m* coaster, saucer

unter'schätzen *vt insep* to underestimate

unter'scheiden (*unreg*) *vt insep* to
distinguish ♦ *vr insep* to differ

Unter'scheidung *f* (*Unterschied*)
distinction; (*Unterscheiden*) differentiation

Unterschied ['untərʃiːt] (**-(e)s, -e**) *m*
difference, distinction; **im ~ zu** as distinct
from; **u~lich** *adj* varying, differing;
(*diskriminierend*) discriminatory

unterschiedslos *adv* indiscriminately

unter'schlagen (*unreg*) *vt insep* to
embezzle; (*verheimlichen*) to suppress

Unter'schlagung *f* embezzlement

Unterschlupf ['untərʃlupf] (**-(e)s,
-schlüpfe**) *m* refuge

unter'schreiben (*unreg*) *vt insep* to sign

Unterschrift ['untərʃrɪft] *f* signature

Unterseeboot ['ʊntərzeːboːt] nt submarine

Untersetzer ['ʊntərzɛtsər] m tablemat; (für Gläser) coaster

untersetzt [ʊntərˈzɛtst] adj stocky

unterste(r, s) ['ʊntərstə(r, s)] adj lowest, bottom

unterstehen [ʊntərˈʃteːən] (unreg) vi insep (+dat) to be under ♦ vr insep to dare; '**unterstehen** (unreg) vi to shelter

unterstellen [ʊntərˈʃtɛlən] vt insep to subordinate; (fig) to impute ♦ vt (Auto) to garage, to park ♦ vr to take shelter

unter'streichen (unreg) vt insep (auch fig) to underline

Unterstufe ['ʊntərʃtuːfə] f lower grade

unter'stützen vt insep to support

Unter'stützung f support, assistance

unter'suchen vt insep (MED) to examine; (Polizei) to investigate

Unter'suchung f examination; investigation, inquiry; **~sausschuss** ▲ m committee of inquiry; **~shaft** f imprisonment on remand

Untertasse ['ʊntərtasə] f saucer

untertauchen ['ʊntərtauxən] vi to dive; (fig) to disappear, to go underground

Unterteil ['ʊntərtail] nt od m lower part, bottom; **u~en** [ʊntərˈtailən] vt insep to divide up

Untertitel ['ʊntərtiːtəl] m subtitle

Unterwäsche ['ʊntərvɛʃə] f underwear

unterwegs [ʊntərˈveːks] adv on the way

unter'werfen (unreg) vt insep to subject; (Volk) to subjugate ♦ vr insep (+dat) to submit (to)

unter'zeichnen vt insep to sign

unter'ziehen (unreg) vt insep to subject ♦ vr insep (+dat) to undergo; (einer Prüfung) to take

untragbar [ʊnˈtraːkbaːr] adj unbearable, intolerable

untreu ['ʊntrɔy] adj unfaithful; **U~e** f unfaithfulness

untröstlich [ʊnˈtrøːstlɪç] adj inconsolable

unüberlegt ['ʊnlyːbərleːkt] adj ill-considered ♦ adv without thinking

unübersichtlich adj (Gelände) broken;

(Kurve) blind

unumgänglich [ʊn|ʊmˈɡɛŋlɪç] adj indispensable, vital; absolutely necessary

ununterbrochen ['ʊn|ʊntərbrɔxən] adj uninterrupted

unver- ['ʊnfɛr] zW: **~änderlich** [-'ɛndərlɪç] adj unchangeable; **~antwortlich** [-'antvɔrtlɪç] adj irresponsible; (unentschuldbar) inexcusable; **~besserlich** adj incorrigible; **~bindlich** adj not binding; (Antwort) curt ♦ adv (COMM) without obligation; **~bleit** adj (Benzin usw) unleaded; **ich fahre ~bleit** I use unleaded; **~blümt** [-'blyːmt] adj plain, blunt ♦ adv plainly, bluntly; **~daulich** adj indigestible; **~einbar** adj incompatible; **~fänglich** [-'fɛŋlɪç] adj harmless; **~froren** adj impudent; **~gesslich** ▲ adj (Tag, Erlebnis) unforgettable; **~hofft** [-'hɔft] adj unexpected; **~meidlich** [-'maitlɪç] adj unavoidable; **~mutet** adj unexpected; **~nünftig** [-'nʏnftɪç] adj foolish; **~schämt** adj impudent; **U~schämtheit** f impudence, insolence; **~sehrt** adj uninjured; **~söhnlich** [-'zøːnlɪç] adj irreconcilable; **~ständlich** [-'ʃtɛntlɪç] adj unintelligible; **~träglich** adj quarrelsome; (Meinungen, MED) incompatible; **~zeihlich** adj unpardonable; **~züglich** [-'tsyːklɪç] adj immediate

unvollkommen ['ʊnfɔlkɔmən] adj imperfect

unvollständig adj incomplete

unvor- ['ʊnfoːr] zW: **~bereitet** adj unprepared; **~eingenommen** adj unbiased; **~hergesehen** [-heːrgeːzeːən] adj unforeseen; **~sichtig** [-zɪçtɪç] adj careless, imprudent; **~stellbar** [-'ʃtɛlbaːr] adj inconceivable; **~teilhaft** adj disadvantageous

unwahr ['ʊnvaːr] adj untrue; **~scheinlich** adj improbable, unlikely ♦ adv (umg) incredibly

unweigerlich [ʊnˈvaigərlɪç] adj unquestioning ♦ adv without fail

Unwesen ['ʊnveːzən] nt nuisance; (Unfug) mischief; **sein ~ treiben** to wreak havoc

unwesentlich adj inessential, unimportant; **~ besser** marginally better

Unwetter ['ʊnvɛtər] *nt* thunderstorm
unwichtig ['ʊnvɪçtɪç] *adj* unimportant
unwider- ['ʊnviːdər] *zW:* **~legbar** *adj* irrefutable; **~ruflich** *adj* irrevocable; **~stehlich** *adj* irresistible
unwill- ['ʊnvɪl] *zW:* **U~e(n)** *m* indignation; **~ig** *adj* indignant; (*widerwillig*) reluctant; **~kürlich** [-kyːrlɪç] *adj* involuntary ♦ *adv* instinctively; (*lachen*) involuntarily
unwirklich ['ʊnvɪrklɪç] *adj* unreal
unwirksam ['ʊnvɪrkzaːm] *adj* (*Mittel, Methode*) ineffective
unwirtschaftlich ['ʊnvɪrtʃaftlɪç] *adj* uneconomical
unwissen- ['ʊnvɪsən] *zW:* **~d** *adj* ignorant; **U~heit** *f* ignorance; **~tlich** *adv* unknowingly, unwittingly
unwohl ['ʊnvoːl] *adj* unwell, ill; **U~sein** (**-s**) *nt* indisposition
unwürdig ['ʊnvʏrdɪç] *adj* unworthy
unzählig [ʊn'tsɛːlɪç] *adj* innumerable, countless
unzer- [ʊntsɛr] *zW:* **~brechlich** *adj* unbreakable; **~störbar** *adj* indestructible; **~trennlich** *adj* inseparable
Unzucht ['ʊntsʊxt] *f* sexual offence
unzüchtig ['ʊntsʏçtɪç] *adj* immoral; lewd
unzu- ['ʊntsu] *zW:* **~frieden** *adj* dissatisfied; **U~friedenheit** *f* discontent; **~länglich** *adj* inadequate; **~lässig** *adj* inadmissible; **~rechnungsfähig** *adj* irresponsible; **~treffend** *adj* incorrect; **~verlässig** *adj* unreliable
unzweideutig ['ʊntsvaɪdɔytɪç] *adj* unambiguous
üppig ['ʏpɪç] *adj* (*Frau*) curvaceous; (*Busen*) full, ample; (*Essen*) sumptuous; (*Vegetation*) luxuriant, lush
Ur- ['uːr] *in zW* original
uralt ['uːr|alt] *adj* ancient, very old
Uran [u'raːn] (**-s**) *nt* uranium
Ur- *zW:* **~aufführung** *f* first performance; **~einwohner** *m* original inhabitant; **~eltern** *pl* ancestors; **~enkel(in)** *m(f)* great-grandchild, great-grandson (-daughter); **~großeltern** *pl* great-grandparents; **~heber** (**-s**, **-**) *m* originator;

(*Autor*) author; **~heberrecht** *nt* copyright
Urin [u'riːn] (**-s**, **-e**) *m* urine
Urkunde ['uːrkʊndə] *f* document, deed
Urlaub ['uːrlaʊp] (**-(e)s**, **-e**) *m* holiday(s *pl*) (*BRIT*), vacation (*US*); (*MIL etc*) leave; **~er** [-'laʊbər] (**-s**, **-**) *m* holiday-maker (*BRIT*), vacationer (*US*); **~sort** *m* holiday resort; **~szeit** *f* holiday season
Urne ['ʊrnə] *f* urn
Ursache ['uːrzaxə] *f* cause; **keine ~** that's all right
Ursprung ['uːrʃprʊŋ] *m* origin, source; (*von Fluss*) source
ursprünglich ['uːrʃprʏŋlɪç] *adj* original ♦ *adv* originally
Ursprungsland *nt* country of origin
Urteil ['ʊrtaɪl] (**-s**, **-e**) *nt* opinion; (*JUR*) sentence, judgement; **u~en** *vi* to judge; **~sspruch** *m* sentence, verdict
Urwald *m* jungle
Urzeit *f* prehistoric times *pl*
USA [uː'ɛs'aː] *pl abk* (= *Vereinigte Staaten von Amerika*) USA
usw. *abk* (= *und so weiter*) etc
Utensilien [uten'ziːliən] *pl* utensils
Utopie [uto'piː] *f* pipe dream
utopisch [u'toːpɪʃ] *adj* utopian

V, v

vag(e) [vaːk, 'vaːgə] *adj* vague
Vagina [va'giːna] (**-**, **Vaginen**) *f* vagina
Vakuum ['vaːkuʊm] (**-s**, **Vakua** *od* **Vakuen**) *nt* vacuum
Vampir [vam'piːr] (**-s**, **-e**) *m* vampire
Vanille [va'nɪljə] (**-**) *f* vanilla
Variation [variatsi'oːn] *f* variation
variieren [vari'iːrən] *vt, vi* to vary
Vase ['vaːzə] *f* vase
Vater ['faːtər] (**-s**, **ⁿ**) *m* father; **~land** *nt* native country; Fatherland
väterlich ['fɛːtərlɪç] *adj* fatherly
Vaterschaft *f* paternity
Vaterunser (**-s**, **-**) *nt* Lord's prayer
Vati ['faːti] *m* daddy
v. Chr. *abk* (= *vor Christus*) B.C.

Vegetarier(in) [vege'ta:riər(ɪn)] **(-s, -)** *m(f)*
vegetarian

vegetarisch [vege'ta:rɪʃ] *adj* vegetarian

Veilchen ['failçən] *nt* violet

Vene ['ve:nə] *f* vein

Ventil [vɛn'ti:l] **(-s, -e)** *nt* valve

Ventilator [vɛntila'to:r] *m* ventilator

verab- [fɛr'ap] *zW:* **~reden** *vt* to agree, to
arrange ♦ *vr:* **sich mit jdm ~reden** to
arrange to meet sb; **mit jdm ~redet sein**
to have arranged to meet sb; **V~redung** *f*
arrangement; (*Treffen*) appointment;
~scheuen *vt* to detest, to abhor;
~schieden *vt* (*Gäste*) to say goodbye to;
(*entlassen*) to discharge; (*Gesetz*) to pass
♦ *vr* to take one's leave; **V~schiedung** *f*
leave-taking; discharge; passing

ver- [fɛr] *zW:* **~achten** *vt* to despise;
~ächtlich [-'lɛçtlɪç] *adj* contemptuous;
(*~achtenswert*) contemptible; **jdn ~ächtlich
machen** to run sb down; **V~achtung** *f*
contempt

verallgemeinern [fɛralgə'mainərn] *vt* to
generalize; **Verallgemeinerung** *f*
generalization

veralten [fɛr'altən] *vi* to become obsolete
od out-of-date

Veranda [ve'randa] **(-, Veranden)** *f* veranda

veränder- [fɛr'ɛndər] *zW:* **~lich** *adj*
changeable; **~n** *vt, vr* to change, to alter;
V~ung *f* change, alteration

veran- [fɛr'an] *zW:* **~lagt** *adj* with a ...
nature; **V~lagung** *f* disposition; **~lassen**
vt to cause; **Maßnahmen ~lassen** to take
measures; **sich ~lasst sehen** to feel
prompted; **~schaulichen** *vt* to illustrate;
~schlagen *vt* to estimate; **~stalten** *vt* to
organize, to arrange; **V~stalter (-s, -)** *m*
organizer; **V~staltung** *f* (*V~stalten*)
organizing; (*Konzert etc*) event, function

verantwort- [fɛr'antvort] *zW:* **~en** *vt* to
answer for ♦ *vr* to justify o.s.; **~lich** *adj*
responsible; **V~ung** *f* responsibility;
~ungsbewusst ▲ *adj* responsible;
~ungslos *adj* irresponsible

erarbeiten [fɛr'arbaitən] *vt* to process;
(*geistig*) to assimilate; **etw zu etw ~** to

make sth into sth; **Verarbeitung** *f*
processing; assimilation

verärgern [fɛr'ɛrgərn] *vt* to annoy

verausgaben [fɛr'ausga:bən] *vr* to run out
of money; (*fig*) to exhaust o.s.

Verb [verp] **(-s, -en)** *nt* verb

Verband [fɛr'bant] **(-(e)s, e)** *m* (*MED*)
bandage, dressing; (*Bund*) association,
society; (*MIL*) unit; **~kasten** *m* medicine
chest, first-aid box; **~zeug** *nt* bandage

verbannen [fɛr'banən] *vt* to banish

verbergen [fɛr'bergən] (*unreg*) *vt, vr:* **(sich)
~ (vor +*dat*)** to hide (from)

verbessern [fɛr'besərn] *vt, vr* to improve;
(*berichtigen*) to correct (o.s.)

Verbesserung *f* improvement; correction

verbeugen [fɛr'bɔygən] *vr* to bow

Verbeugung *f* bow

ver'biegen (*unreg*) *vi* to bend

ver'bieten (*unreg*) *vt* to forbid; **jdm etw ~**
to forbid sb to do sth

verbilligen [fɛr'bɪlɪgən] *vt* to reduce the
cost of; (*Preis*) to reduce

ver'binden (*unreg*) *vt* to connect;
(*kombinieren*) to combine; (*MED*) to
bandage ♦ *vr* (*auch CHEM*) to combine, to
join; **jdm die Augen ~** to blindfold sb

verbindlich [fɛr'bɪntlɪç] *adj* binding;
(*freundlich*) friendly

Ver'bindung *f* connection;
(*Zusammensetzung*) combination; (*CHEM*)
compound; (*UNIV*) club

verbissen [fɛr'bɪsən] *adj* (*Kampf*) bitter;
(*Gesichtsausdruck*) grim

ver'bitten (*unreg*) *vt:* **sich** *dat* **etw ~** not to
tolerate sth, not to stand for sth

Verbleib [fɛr'blaip] **(-(e)s)** *m* whereabouts;
v~en (*unreg*) *vi* to remain

verbleit [fɛr'blait] *adj* (*Benzin*) leaded

verblüffen [fɛr'blyfən] *vt* to stagger, to
amaze; **Verblüffung** *f* stupefaction

ver'blühen *vi* to wither, to fade

ver'bluten *vi* to bleed to death

verborgen [fɛr'bɔrgən] *adj* hidden

Verbot [fɛr'bo:t] **(-(e)s, -e)** *nt* prohibition,
ban; **v~en** *adj* forbidden; **Rauchen v~en!**
no smoking; **~sschild** *nt* prohibitory sign

Verbrauch [fɛr'braux] (-(e)s) *m*
consumption; **v~en** *vt* to use up; **~er** (-s,
-) *m* consumer; **v~t** *adj* used up, finished;
(*Luft*) stale; (*Mensch*) worn-out

Verbrechen [fɛr'brɛçən] (-s, -) *nt* crime

Verbrecher [fɛr'brɛçər] (-s, -) *m* criminal;
v~isch *adj* criminal

ver'breiten *vt*, *vr* to spread; **sich über etw**
akk ~ to expound on sth

verbreitern [fɛr'braɪtərn] *vt* to broaden

Verbreitung *f* spread(ing), propagation

verbrenn- [fɛr'brɛn] *zW:* **~bar** *adj*
combustible; **~en** (*unreg*) *vt* to burn;
(*Leiche*) to cremate; **V~ung** *f* burning; (*in
Motor*) combustion; (*von Leiche*) cremation;
V~ungsmotor *m* internal combustion
engine

verbringen [fɛr'brɪŋən] (*unreg*) *vt* to spend

verbrühen [fɛr'bryːən] *vt* to scald

verbuchen [fɛr'buːxən] *vt* (*FIN*) to register;
(*Erfolg*) to enjoy; (*Misserfolg*) to suffer

verbunden [fɛr'bundən] *adj* connected; **jdm
~ sein** to be obliged *od* indebted to sb;
„**falsch ~**" (*TEL*) "wrong number"

verbünden [fɛr'byndən] *vr* to ally o.s.;
Verbündete(r) *f(m)* ally

ver'bürgen *vr:* **sich ~ für** to vouch for

ver'büßen *vt:* **eine Strafe ~** to serve a
sentence

Verdacht [fɛr'daxt] (-(e)s) *m* suspicion

verdächtig [fɛr'dɛçtɪç] *adj* suspicious,
suspect; **~en** [fɛr'dɛçtɪgən] *vt* to suspect

verdammen [fɛr'damən] *vt* to damn, to
condemn; **verdammt!** damn!

verdammt (*umg*) *adj, adv* damned; **~ noch
mal!** damn!, dammit!

ver'dampfen *vi* to vaporize, to evaporate

ver'danken *vt:* **jdm etw ~** to owe sb sth

verdau- [fɛr'dau] *zW:* **~en** *vt* (*auch fig*) to
digest; **~lich** *adj* digestible; **das ist schwer
~lich** that is hard to digest; **V~ung** *f*
digestion

Verdeck [fɛr'dɛk] (-(e)s, -e) *nt* (*AUT*) hood;
(*NAUT*) deck; **v~en** *vt* to cover (up);
(*verbergen*) to hide

Verderb- [fɛr'dɛrp] *zW:* **~en** [-'dɛrbən] (-s)
nt ruin; **v~en** (*unreg*) *vt* to spoil; (*schädigen*)

to ruin; (*moralisch*) to corrupt ♦ *vi* (*Essen*) to
spoil, to rot; (*Mensch*) to go to the bad; **es
mit jdm v~en** to get into sb's bad books;
v~lich *adj* (*Einfluss*) pernicious;
(*Lebensmittel*) perishable

verdeutlichen [fɛr'dɔʏtlɪçən] *vt* to make
clear

ver'dichten *vt*, *vr* to condense

ver'dienen *vt* to earn; (*moralisch*) to
deserve

Ver'dienst (-(e)s, -e) *m* earnings *pl* ♦ *nt*
merit; (*Leistung*) ~ (**um**) service (to)

verdient [fɛr'diːnt] *adj* well-earned; (*Person*)
deserving of esteem; **sich um etw ~
machen** to do a lot for sth

verdoppeln [fɛr'dɔpəln] *vt* to double

verdorben [fɛr'dɔrbən] *adj* spoilt;
(*geschädigt*) ruined; (*moralisch*) corrupt

verdrängen [fɛr'drɛŋən] *vt* to oust, to
displace (*auch PHYS*); (*PSYCH*) to repress

ver'drehen *vt* (*auch fig*) to twist; (*Augen*) to
roll; **jdm den Kopf ~** (*fig*) to turn sb's
head

verdrießlich [fɛr'driːslɪç] *adj* peevish,
annoyed

Verdruss ▲ [fɛr'drʊs] (-es, -e) *m*
annoyance, worry

verdummen [fɛr'dumən] *vt* to make stupid
♦ *vi* to grow stupid

verdunkeln [fɛr'dunkəln] *vt* to darken; (*fig*)
to obscure ♦ *vr* to darken

Verdunk(e)lung *f* blackout; (*fig*) obscuring

verdünnen [fɛr'dynən] *vt* to dilute

verdunsten [fɛr'dunstən] *vi* to evaporate

verdursten [fɛr'durstən] *vi* to die of thirst

verdutzt [fɛr'dutst] *adj* nonplussed, taken
aback

verehr- [fɛr'|eːr] *zW:* **~en** *vt* to venerate, to
worship (*auch REL*); **jdm etw ~en** to present
sb with sth; **V~er(in)** (-s, -) *m(f)* admirer,
worshipper (*auch REL*); **~t** *adj* esteemed;
V~ung *f* respect; (*REL*) worship

Verein [fɛr'|aɪn] (-(e)s, -e) *m* club,
association; **v~bar** *adj* compatible;
v~baren *vt* to agree upon; **~barung** *f*
agreement; **v~en** *vt* (*Menschen, Länder*) to
unite; (*Prinzipien*) to reconcile; **mit v~ten**

Kräften having pooled resources, having joined forces; **~te Nationen** United Nations; **v~fachen** *vt* to simplify; **v~heitlichen** [-haɪtlɪçən] *vt* to standardize; **v~igen** *vt, vr* to unite; **~igung** *f* union; (*Verein*) association; **v~t** *adj* united; **v~zelt** *adj* isolated

ver'eitern *vi* to suppurate, to fester

verengen [fɛrˈʔɛŋən] *vr* to narrow

vererb- [fɛrˈʔɛrb] *zW:* **~en** *vt* to bequeath; (*BIOL*) to transmit ♦ *vr* to be hereditary; **V~ung** *f* bequeathing; (*BIOL*) transmission; (*Lehre*) heredity

verewigen [fɛrˈʔeːvɪgən] *vt* to immortalize ♦ *vr* (*umg*) to immortalize o.s.

ver'fahren (*unreg*) *vi* to act ♦ *vr* to get lost ♦ *adj* tangled; **~ mit** to deal with; **Ver'fahren (-s, -)** *nt* procedure; (*TECH*) process; (*JUR*) proceedings *pl*

Verfall [fɛrˈfal] (-(e)s) *m* decline; (*von Haus*) dilapidation; (*FIN*) expiry; **v~en** (*unreg*) *vi* to decline; (*Haus*) to be falling down; (*FIN*) to lapse; **v~en in** +*akk* to lapse into; **v~en auf** +*akk* to hit upon; **einem Laster v~en sein** to be addicted to a vice; **~sdatum** *nt* expiry date; (*der Haltbarkeit*) sell-by date

ver'färben *vr* to change colour

verfassen [fɛrˈfasən] *vt* to prepare, work out

Verfasser(in) [fɛrˈfasər(ɪn)] (-s, -) *m(f)* author, writer

Verfassung *f* (*auch POL*) constitution

Verfassungs- *zW:* **~gericht** *nt* constitutional court; **v~widrig** *adj* unconstitutional

ver'faulen *vi* to rot

ver'fehlen *vt* to miss; **etw für verfehlt halten** to regard sth as mistaken

verfeinern [fɛrˈfaɪnərn] *vt* to refine

ver'filmen *vt* to film

verflixt [fɛrˈflɪkst] (*umg*) *adj* damned, damn

ver'fluchen *vt* to curse

verfolg- [fɛrˈfɔlg] *zW:* **~en** *vt* to pursue; (*gerichtlich*) to prosecute; (*grausam, bes POL*) to persecute; **V~er (-s, -)** *m* pursuer; **V~ung** *f* pursuit; prosecution; persecution

verfrüht [fɛrˈfryːt] *adj* premature

verfüg- [fɛrˈfyːg] *zW:* **~bar** *adj* available; **~en** *vt* to direct, to order ♦ *vr* to proceed ♦ *vi:* **~en über** +*akk* to have at one's disposal; **V~ung** *f* direction, order; **zur V~ung** at one's disposal; **jdm zur V~ung stehen** to be available to sb

verführ- [fɛrˈfyːr] *zW:* **~en** *vt* to tempt; (*sexuell*) to seduce; **V~er** *m* tempter; seducer; **~erisch** *adj* seductive; **V~ung** *f* seduction; (*Versuchung*) temptation

ver'gammeln (*umg*) *vi* to go to seed; (*Nahrung*) to go off

vergangen [fɛrˈgaŋən] *adj* past; **V~heit** *f* past

vergänglich [fɛrˈgɛŋlɪç] *adj* transitory

vergasen [fɛrˈgaːzən] *vt* (*töten*) to gas

Vergaser (-s, -) *m* (*AUT*) carburettor

vergaß *etc* [fɛrˈgaːs] *vb siehe* **vergessen**

vergeb- [fɛrˈgeːb] *zW:* **~en** (*unreg*) *vt* (*verzeihen*) to forgive; (*weggeben*) to give away; **jdm etw ~en** to forgive sb (for) sth; **~ens** *adv* in vain; **~lich** [fɛrˈgeːplɪç] *adv* in vain ♦ *adj* vain, futile; **V~ung** *f* forgiveness

ver'gehen (*unreg*) *vi* to pass by *od* away ♦ *vr* to commit an offence; **jdm vergeht etw** sb loses sth; **sich an jdm ~** to (sexually) assault sb; **Ver'gehen (-s, -)** *nt* offence

ver'gelten (*unreg*) *vt:* **jdm etw ~** to pay sb back for sth, to repay sb for sth

Ver'geltung *f* retaliation, reprisal

vergessen [fɛrˈgɛsən] (*unreg*) *vt* to forget; **V~heit** *f* oblivion

vergesslich ▲ [fɛrˈgɛslɪç] *adj* forgetful; **V~keit** *f* forgetfulness

vergeuden [fɛrˈgɔydən] *vt* to squander, to waste

vergewaltigen [fɛrgəˈvaltɪgən] *vt* to rape; (*fig*) to violate

Vergewaltigung *f* rape

vergewissern [fɛrgəˈvɪsərn] *vr* to make sure

ver'gießen (*unreg*) *vt* to shed

vergiften [fɛrˈgɪftən] *vt* to poison

Vergiftung *f* poisoning

Vergissmeinnicht ▲ [fɛrˈgɪsmaɪnnɪçt] (-(e)s, -e) *nt* forget-me-not

vergisst ▲ *etc* [fɛrˈgɪst] *vb siehe* **vergessen**

Vergleich [fɛrˈglaɪç] (-(e)s, -e) *m*
comparison; (*JUR*) settlement; **im ~ mit** *od*
zu compared with *od* to; **v~bar** *adj*
comparable; **v~en** (*unreg*) *vt* to compare
♦ *vr* to reach a settlement

vergnügen [fɛrˈgnyːgən] *vr* to enjoy *od*
amuse o.s.; **V~ (-s, -)** *nt* pleasure; **viel V~!**
enjoy yourself!

vergnügt [fɛrˈgnyːkt] *adj* cheerful

Vergnügung *f* pleasure, amusement;
~spark *m* amusement park

vergolden [fɛrˈgɔldən] *vt* to gild

ver'graben *vt* to bury

ver'greifen (*unreg*) *vr*: **sich an jdm ~** to lay
hands on sb; **sich an etw ~** to
misappropriate sth; **sich im Ton ~** to say
the wrong thing

vergriffen [fɛrˈgrɪfən] *adj* (*Buch*) out of print;
(*Ware*) out of stock

vergrößern [fɛrˈgrøːsərn] *vt* to enlarge;
(*mengenmäßig*) to increase; (*Lupe*) to
magnify

Vergrößerung *f* enlargement; increase;
magnification; **~sglas** *nt* magnifying glass

Vergünstigung [fɛrˈgynstɪgʊŋ] *f*
concession, privilege

Vergütung *f* compensation

verhaften [fɛrˈhaftən] *vt* to arrest

Verhaftung *f* arrest

ver'halten (*unreg*) *vr* to be, to stand; (*sich
benehmen*) to behave ♦ *vt* to hold *od* keep
back; (*Schritt*) to check; **sich ~ (zu)** (*MATH*)
to be in proportion (to); **Ver'halten (-s)** *nt*
behaviour

Verhältnis [fɛrˈhɛltnɪs] (-ses, -se) *nt*
relationship; (*MATH*) proportion, ratio; **~se**
pl (*Umstände*) conditions; **über seine ~se
leben** to live beyond one's means;
v~mäßig *adj* relative, comparative ♦ *adv*
relatively, comparatively

verhandeln [fɛrˈhandəln] *vi* to negotiate;
(*JUR*) to hold proceedings ♦ *vt* to discuss;
(*JUR*) to hear; **über etw** *akk* **~** to negotiate
sth *od* about sth

Verhandlung *f* negotiation; (*JUR*)
proceedings *pl*; **~sbasis** *f* (*FIN*) basis for
negotiations

ver'hängen *vt* (*fig*) to impose, to inflict

Verhängnis [fɛrˈhɛŋnɪs] (-ses, -se) *nt* fate,
doom; **jdm zum ~ werden** to be sb's
undoing; **v~voll** *adj* fatal, disastrous

verharmlosen [fɛrˈharmloːzən] *vt* to make
light of, to play down

verhärten [fɛrˈhɛrtən] *vr* to harden

verhasst ▲ [fɛrˈhast] *adj* odious, hateful

verhauen [fɛrˈhaʊən] (*unreg*; *umg*) *vt*
(*verprügeln*) to beat up

verheerend [fɛrˈheːrənt] *adj* disastrous,
devastating

verheimlichen [fɛrˈhaɪmlɪçən] *vt*: **jdm etw
~** to keep sth secret from sb

verheiratet [fɛrˈhaɪraːtət] *adj* married

ver'helfen (*unreg*) *vi*: **jdm ~ zu** to help sb
to get

ver'hindern *vt* to prevent; **verhindert sein**
to be unable to make it

verhöhnen [fɛrˈhøːnən] *vt* to mock, to
sneer at

Verhör [fɛrˈhøːr] (-(e)s, -e) *nt* interrogation;
(*gerichtlich*) (cross-)examination; **v~en** *vt* to
interrogate; to (cross-)examine ♦ *vr* to
misunderstand, to mishear

ver'hungern *vi* to starve, to die of hunger

ver'hüten *vt* to prevent, to avert

Ver'hütung *f* prevention; **~smittel** *nt*
contraceptive

verirren [fɛrˈ|ɪrən] *vr* to go astray

ver'jagen *vt* to drive away *od* out

verkalken [fɛrˈkalkən] *vi* to calcify; (*umg*) to
become senile

Verkauf [fɛrˈkaʊf] *m* sale; **v~en** *vt* to sell

Verkäufer(in) [fɛrˈkɔyfər(ɪn)] (-s, -) *m(f)*
seller; salesman(-woman); (*in Laden*) shop
assistant

verkaufsoffen *adj*: **~er Samstag** *Saturday
when the shops stay open all day*

Verkehr [fɛrˈkeːr] (-s, -e) *m* traffic; (*Umgang,
bes sexuell*) intercourse; (*Umlauf*) circulation;
v~en *vi* (*Fahrzeug*) to ply, to run ♦ *vt*, *vr* to
turn, to transform; **v~en mit** to associate
with; **bei jdm v~en** (*besuchen*) to visit sb
regularly

Verkehrs- *zW*: **~ampel** *f* traffic lights *pl*;
~aufkommen *nt* volume of traffic;

~beruhigung f traffic calming; **~delikt** nt traffic offence; **~funk** m radio traffic service; **v~günstig** adj convenient; **~mittel** nt means of transport; **~schild** nt road sign; **~stau** m traffic jam, stoppage; **~unfall** m traffic accident; **~verein** m tourist information office; **~zeichen** nt traffic sign

verkehrt adj wrong; (umgekehrt) the wrong way round

ver'kennen (unreg) vt to misjudge, not to appreciate

ver'klagen vt to take to court

verkleiden [fer'klaɪdən] vr to disguise (o.s.); (sich kostümieren) to get dressed up ♦ vt (Wand) to cover

Verkleidung f disguise; (ARCHIT) wainscoting

verkleinern [fer'klaɪnərn] vt to make smaller, to reduce in size

ver'kneifen (umg) vt: **sich** dat **etw ~** (Lachen) to stifle sth; (Schmerz) to hide sth; (sich versagen) to do without sth

verknüpfen [fer'knypfən] vt to tie (up), to knot; (fig) to connect

ver'kommen (unreg) vi to deteriorate, to decay; (Mensch) to go downhill, to come down in the world ♦ adj (moralisch) dissolute, depraved

ver'körpern [fer'kœrpərn] vt to embody, to personify

ver'kraften [fer'kraftən] vt to cope with

ver'kriechen (unreg) vr to creep away, to creep into a corner

verkrüppelt [fer'krypəlt] adj crippled

ver'kühlen vr to get a chill

ver'kümmern vi to waste away

verkünden [fer'kyndən] vt to proclaim; (Urteil) to pronounce

verkürzen [fer'kyrtsən] vt to shorten; (Wort) to abbreviate; **sich** dat **die Zeit ~** to while away the time

Verkürzung f shortening; abbreviation

verladen [fer'laːdən] (unreg) vt (Waren, Vieh) to load; (Truppen: auf Schiff) to embark, (auf Zug) to entrain, (auf Flugzeug) to enplane

Verlag [fer'laːk] (-(e)s, -e) m publishing firm

verlangen [fer'laŋən] vt to demand; to desire ♦ vi: **~ nach** to ask for, to desire; **~ Sie Herrn X** ask for Mr X; **V~** (-s, -) nt: **V~ (nach)** desire (for); **auf jds V~ (hin)** at sb's request

verlängern [fer'lɛŋərn] vt to extend; (länger machen) to lengthen

Verlängerung f extension; (SPORT) extra time; **~sschnur** f extension cable

verlangsamen [fer'laŋzaːmən] vt, vr to decelerate, to slow down

Verlass ▲ [fer'las] m: **auf ihn/das ist kein ~** he/it cannot be relied upon

ver'lassen (unreg) vt to leave ♦ vr: **sich ~ auf** +akk to depend on ♦ adj desolate; (Mensch) abandoned

verlässlich ▲ [fer'lɛslɪç] adj reliable

Verlauf [fer'lauf] m course; **v~en** (unreg) vi (zeitlich) to pass; (Farben) to run ♦ vr to get lost; (Menschenmenge) to disperse

ver'lauten vi: **etw ~ lassen** to disclose sth; **wie verlautet** as reported

ver'legen vt to move; (verlieren) to mislay; (Buch) to publish ♦ vr: **sich auf etw** akk **~** to take up od to sth ♦ adj embarrassed; **nicht ~ um** never at a loss for; **Verlegenheit** f embarrassment; (Situation) difficulty, scrape

Verleger [fer'leːgər] (-s, -) m publisher

Verleih [fer'laɪ] (-(e)s, -e) m hire service; **v~en** (unreg) vt to lend; (Kraft, Anschein) to confer, to bestow; (Preis, Medaille) to award; **~ung** f lending; bestowal; award

ver'leiten vt to lead astray; **~ zu** to talk into, to tempt into

ver'lernen vt to forget, to unlearn

ver'lesen (unreg) vt to read out; (aussondern) to sort out ♦ vr to make a mistake in reading

verletz- [fer'lets] zW: **~en** vt (auch fig) to injure, to hurt; (Gesetz etc) to violate; **~end** adj (fig: Worte) hurtful; **~lich** adj vulnerable, sensitive; **V~te(r)** f(m) injured person; **V~ung** f injury; (Verstoß) violation, infringement

verleugnen [fer'lɔygnən] vt (Herkunft, Glauben) to belie; (Menschen) to disown

verleumden [fɛrˈlɔymdən] *vt* to slander;
Verleumdung *f* slander, libel
ver'lieben *vr:* **sich ~ (in** +*akk*) to fall in love
(with)
verliebt [fɛrˈliːpt] *adj* in love
verlieren [fɛrˈliːrən] (*unreg*) *vt, vi* to lose ♦ *vr*
to get lost
Verlierer *m* loser
verlob- [fɛrˈloːb] *zW:* **~en** *vr:* **sich ~en (mit)**
to get engaged (to); **V~te(r)** [fɛrˈloːptə(r)]
f(m) fiancé *m*, fiancée *f*; **V~ung** *f*
engagement
ver'locken *vt* to entice, to lure
Ver'lockung *f* temptation, attraction
verlogen [fɛrˈloːgən] *adj* untruthful
verlor *etc vb siehe* **verlieren**
verloren [fɛrˈloːrən] *adj* lost; (*Eier*) poached
♦ *vb siehe* **verlieren**; **etw ~ geben** to give
sth up for lost; **~ gehen** to get lost
verlosen [fɛrˈloːzən] *vt* to raffle, to draw lots
for; **Verlosung** *f* raffle, lottery
Verlust [fɛrˈlʊst] **(-(e)s, -e)** *m* loss; (*MIL*)
casualty
ver'machen *vt* to bequeath, to leave
Vermächtnis [fɛrˈmɛçtnɪs] **(-ses, -se)** *nt*
legacy
Vermählung [fɛrˈmɛːlʊŋ] *f* wedding,
marriage
vermarkten [fɛrˈmarktən] *vt* (*COMM: Artikel*)
to market
vermehren [fɛrˈmeːrən] *vt, vr* to multiply;
(*Menge*) to increase
Vermehrung *f* multiplying; increase
ver'meiden (*unreg*) *vt* to avoid
vermeintlich [fɛrˈmaɪntlɪç] *adj* supposed
Vermerk [fɛrˈmɛrk] **(-(e)s, -e)** *m* note; (*in
Ausweis*) endorsement; **v~en** *vt* to note
ver'messen (*unreg*) *vt* to survey ♦ *adj*
presumptuous, bold; **Ver'messenheit** *f*
presumptuousness; recklessness
Ver'messung *f* survey(ing)
vermiet- [fɛrˈmiːt] *zW:* **ver'mieten** *vt* to
let, to rent (out); (*Auto*) to hire out, to rent;
Ver'mieter(in) **(-s, -)** *m(f)* landlord(-lady);
Ver'mietung *f* letting, renting (out); (*von
Autos*) hiring (out)
vermindern [fɛrˈmɪndərn] *vt, vr* to lessen, to

decrease; (*Preise*) to reduce
Verminderung *f* reduction
ver'mischen *vt, vr* to mix, to blend
vermissen [fɛrˈmɪsən] *vt* to miss
vermitt- [fɛrˈmɪt] *zW:* **~eln** *vi* to mediate
♦ *vt* (*Gespräch*) to connect; **jdm etw ~eln** t
help sb to obtain sth; **V~ler (-s, -)** *m*
(*Schlichter*) agent, mediator; **V~lung** *f*
procurement; (*Stellenvermittlung*) agency;
(*TEL*) exchange; (*Schlichtung*) mediation;
V~lungsgebühr *f* commission
ver'mögen (*unreg*) *vt* to be capable of; **~
zu** to be able to; **Ver'mögen (-s, -)** *nt*
wealth; (*Fähigkeit*) ability; **ein V~ kosten** to
cost a fortune; **ver'mögend** *adj* wealthy
vermuten [fɛrˈmuːtən] *vt* to suppose, to
guess; (*argwöhnen*) to suspect
vermutlich *adj* supposed, presumed ♦ *adv*
probably
Vermutung *f* supposition; suspicion
vernachlässigen [fɛrˈnaːxlɛsɪgən] *vt* to
neglect
ver'nehmen (*unreg*) *vt* to perceive, to hear
(*erfahren*) to learn; (*JUR*) to (cross-)examine;
dem V~ nach from what I/we *etc* hear
Vernehmung *f* (cross-)examination
verneigen [fɛrˈnaɪgən] *vr* to bow
verneinen [fɛrˈnaɪnən] *vt* (*Frage*) to answer
in the negative; (*ablehnen*) to deny; (*GRAM*)
to negate; **~d** *adj* negative
Verneinung *f* negation
vernichten [fɛrˈnɪçtən] *vt* to annihilate, to
destroy; **~d** *adj* (*fig*) crushing; (*Blick*)
withering; (*Kritik*) scathing
Vernunft [fɛrˈnʊnft] **(-)** *f* reason,
understanding
vernünftig [fɛrˈnʏnftɪç] *adj* sensible,
reasonable
veröffentlichen [fɛrˈʔœfəntlɪçən] *vt* to
publish; **Veröffentlichung** *f* publication
verordnen [fɛrˈʔɔrdnən] *vt* (*MED*) to
prescribe
Verordnung *f* order, decree; (*MED*)
prescription
ver'pachten *vt* to lease (out)
ver'packen *vt* to pack
Ver'packung *f* packing, wrapping;

~smaterial *nt* packing, wrapping
ver'passen *vt* to miss; **jdm eine Ohrfeige ~** (*umg*) to give sb a clip round the ear
verpfänden [fɛrˈpfɛndən] *vt* (*Besitz*) to mortgage
ver'pflanzen *vt* to transplant
ver'pflegen *vt* to feed, to cater for
Ver'pflegung *f* feeding, catering; (*Kost*) food; (*in Hotel*) board
verpflichten [fɛrˈpflɪçtən] *vt* to oblige, to bind; (*anstellen*) to engage ♦ *vr* to undertake; (*MIL*) to sign on ♦ *vi* to carry obligations; **jdm zu Dank verpflichtet sein** to be obliged to sb
Verpflichtung *f* obligation, duty
verpönt [fɛrˈpøːnt] *adj* disapproved (of), taboo
ver'prügeln (*umg*) *vt* to beat up, to do over
Verputz [fɛrˈpʊts] *m* plaster, roughcast; **v~en** *vt* to plaster; (*umg: Essen*) to put away
Verrat [fɛrˈraːt] **(-(e)s)** *m* treachery; (*POL*) treason; **v~en** (*unreg*) *vt* to betray; (*Geheimnis*) to divulge ♦ *vr* to give o.s. away
Verräter [fɛrˈrɛːtər] **(-s, -)** *m* traitor(-tress); **v~isch** *adj* treacherous
ver'rechnen *vt*: **~ mit** to set off against ♦ *vr* to miscalculate
Verrechnungsscheck [fɛrˈrɛçnʊŋsʃɛk] *m* crossed cheque
verregnet [fɛrˈreːgnət] *adj* spoilt by rain, rainy
ver'reisen *vi* to go away (on a journey)
verrenken [fɛrˈrɛŋkən] *vt* to contort; (*MED*) to dislocate; **sich** *dat* **den Knöchel ~** to sprain one's ankle
ver'richten *vt* to do, to perform
verriegeln [fɛrˈriːgəln] *vt* to bolt up, to lock
verringern [fɛrˈrɪŋərn] *vt* to reduce ♦ *vr* to diminish
Verringerung *f* reduction; lessening
ver'rinnen (*unreg*) *vi* to run out *od* away; (*Zeit*) to elapse
ver'rosten *vi* to rust
ver'rotten [fɛrˈrɔtən] *vi* to rot

ver'rücken *vt* to move, to shift
verrückt [fɛrˈrʏkt] *adj* crazy, mad; **V~e(r)** *f(m)* lunatic; **V~heit** *f* madness, lunacy
Verruf [fɛrˈruːf] *m*: **in ~ geraten/bringen** to fall/bring into disrepute; **v~en** *adj* notorious, disreputable
Vers [fɛrs] **(-es, -e)** *m* verse
ver'sagen *vt*: **jdm/sich etw ~** to deny sb/ o.s. sth ♦ *vi* to fail; **Ver'sagen (-s)** *nt* failure
ver'salzen (*unreg*) *vt* to put too much salt in; (*fig*) to spoil
ver'sammeln *vt, vr* to assemble, to gather
Ver'sammlung *f* meeting, gathering
Versand [fɛrˈzant] **(-(e)s)** *m* forwarding; dispatch; (*~abteilung*) dispatch department; **~haus** *nt* mail-order firm
versäumen [fɛrˈzɔymən] *vt* to miss; (*unterlassen*) to neglect, to fail
ver'schaffen *vt*: **jdm/sich etw ~** to get *od* procure sth for sb/o.s.
verschämt [fɛrˈʃɛːmt] *adj* bashful
verschandeln [fɛrˈʃandəln] (*umg*) *vt* to spoil
verschärfen [fɛrˈʃɛrfən] *vt* to intensify; (*Lage*) to aggravate ♦ *vr* to intensify; to become aggravated
ver'schätzen *vr* to be out in one's reckoning
ver'schenken *vt* to give away
verscheuchen [fɛrˈʃɔyçən] *vt* (*Tiere*) to chase off *od* away
ver'schicken *vt* to send off
ver'schieben (*unreg*) *vt* to shift; (*EISENB*) to shunt; (*Termin*) to postpone
verschieden [fɛrˈʃiːdən] *adj* different; (*pl: mehrere*) various; **sie sind ~ groß** they are of different sizes; **~tlich** *adv* several times
verschimmeln *vi* (*Nahrungsmittel*) to go mouldy
verschlafen [fɛrˈʃlaːfən] (*unreg*) *vt* to sleep through; (*fig: versäumen*) to miss ♦ *vi, vr* to oversleep ♦ *adj* sleepy
Verschlag [fɛrˈʃlaːk] *m* shed; **v~en** [-gən] (*unreg*) *vt* to board up ♦ *adj* cunning; **jdm den Atem v~en** to take sb's breath away; **an einen Ort v~en werden** to wind up in a place

Spelling Reform: ▲ *new spelling* △ *old spelling (to be phased out)*

verschlechtern [fɛrˈʃlɛçtərn] vt to make worse ♦ vr to deteriorate, to get worse; **Verschlechterung** f deterioration

Verschleiß [fɛrˈʃlaɪs] (**-es, -e**) m wear and tear; **v~en** (*unreg*) vt to wear out

ver'schleppen vt to carry off, to abduct; (*Krankheit*) to protract; (*zeitlich*) to drag out

ver'schleudern vt to squander; (*COMM*) to sell dirt-cheap

verschließbar adj lockable

verschließen [fɛrˈʃliːsən] (*unreg*) vt to close; to lock ♦ vr: **sich einer Sache** dat **~** to close one's mind to sth

verschlimmern [fɛrˈʃlɪmərn] vt to make worse, to aggravate ♦ vr to get worse, to deteriorate

verschlingen [fɛrˈʃlɪŋən] (*unreg*) vt to devour, to swallow up; (*Fäden*) to twist

verschlossen [fɛrˈʃlɔsən] adj locked; (*fig*) reserved; **V~heit** f reserve

ver'schlucken vt to swallow ♦ vr to choke

Verschluss ▲ [fɛrˈʃlʊs] m lock; (*von Kleid etc*) fastener; (*PHOT*) shutter; (*Stöpsel*) plug

verschlüsseln [fɛrˈʃlʏsəln] vt to encode

verschmieren [fɛrˈʃmiːrən] vt (*verstreichen: Gips, Mörtel*) to apply, spread on; (*schmutzig machen: Wand etc*) to smear

verschmutzen [fɛrˈʃmʊtsən] vt to soil; (*Umwelt*) to pollute

verschneit [fɛrˈʃnaɪt] adj snowed up, covered in snow

verschollen [fɛrˈʃɔlən] adj lost, missing

ver'schonen vt: **jdn mit etw ~** to spare sb sth

verschönern [fɛrˈʃøːnərn] vt to decorate; (*verbessern*) to improve

ver'schreiben (*unreg*) vt (*MED*) to prescribe ♦ vr to make a mistake (in writing); **sich einer Sache** dat **~** to devote o.s. to sth

verschreibungspflichtig adj (*Medikament*) available on prescription only

verschrotten [fɛrˈʃrɔtən] vt to scrap

verschuld- [fɛrˈʃʊld] zW: **~en** vt to be guilty of; **V~en** (**-s**) nt fault, guilt; **~et** adj in debt; **V~ung** f fault; (*Geld*) debts pl

ver'schütten vt to spill; (*zuschütten*) to fill; (*unter Trümmer*) to bury

ver'schweigen (*unreg*) vt to keep secret; **jdm etw ~** to keep sth from sb

verschwend- [fɛrˈʃvɛnd] zW: **~en** vt to squander; **V~er** (**-s, -**) m spendthrift; **~erisch** adj wasteful, extravagant; **V~ung** f waste; extravagance

verschwiegen [fɛrˈʃviːɡən] adj discreet; (*Ort*) secluded; **V~heit** f discretion; seclusion

ver'schwimmen (*unreg*) vi to grow hazy, to become blurred

ver'schwinden (*unreg*) vi to disappear, to vanish; **Ver'schwinden** (**-s**) nt disappearance

verschwitzt [fɛrˈʃvɪtst] adj (*Mensch*) sweaty

verschwommen [fɛrˈʃvɔmən] adj hazy, vague

verschwör- [fɛrˈʃvøːr] zW: **~en** (*unreg*) vr to plot, to conspire; **V~ung** f conspiracy, plot

ver'sehen (*unreg*) vt to supply, to provide; (*Pflicht*) to carry out; (*Amt*) to fill; (*Haushalt*) to keep ♦ vr (*fig*) to make a mistake; **ehe er (es) sich ~ hatte ...** before he knew it ...; **Ver'sehen** (**-s, -**) nt oversight; **aus V~** by mistake; **~tlich** adv by mistake

Versehrte(r) [fɛrˈzeːrtə(r)] f(m) disabled person

ver'senden (*unreg*) vt to forward, to dispatch

ver'senken vt to sink ♦ vr: **sich ~ in** +akk to become engrossed in

versessen [fɛrˈzɛsən] adj: **~ auf** +akk mad about

ver'setzen vt to transfer; (*verpfänden*) to pawn; (*umg*) to stand up ♦ vr: **sich in jdn** od **in jds Lage ~** to put o.s. in sb's place; **jdm einen Tritt/Schlag ~** to kick/hit sb; **etw mit etw ~** to mix sth with sth; **jdn in gute Laune ~** to put sb in a good mood

Ver'setzung f transfer

verseuchen [fɛrˈzɔyçən] vt to contaminate

versichern [fɛrˈzɪçərn] vt to assure; (*mit Geld*) to insure

Versicherung f assurance; insurance

Versicherungs- zW: **~gesellschaft** f insurance company; **~karte** f insurance card; **die grüne ~karte** the green card;

~police *f* insurance policy
ver'sinken (*unreg*) *vi* to sink
versöhnen [fɛr'zøːnən] *vt* to reconcile ♦ *vr* to become reconciled
Versöhnung *f* reconciliation
ver'sorgen *vt* to provide, to supply; (*Familie etc*) to look after
Ver'sorgung *f* provision; (*Unterhalt*) maintenance; (*Altersversorgung etc*) benefit, assistance
verspäten [fɛr'ʃpɛːtən] *vr* to be late
verspätet *adj* (*Zug, Abflug, Ankunft*) late; (*Glückwünsche*) belated
Verspätung *f* delay; **~ haben** to be late
ver'sperren *vt* to bar, to obstruct
verspielt [fɛr'ʃpiːlt] *adj* (*Kind, Tier*) playful
ver'spotten *vt* to ridicule, to scoff at
ver'sprechen (*unreg*) *vt* to promise; **sich** *dat* **etw von etw ~** to expect sth from sth; **Ver'sprechen** (**-s, -**) *nt* promise
verstaatlichen [fɛr'ʃtaːtlɪçən] *vt* to nationalize
Verstand [fɛr'ʃtant] *m* intelligence; mind; **den ~ verlieren** to go out of one's mind; **über jds ~ gehen** to go beyond sb
verständig [fɛr'ʃtɛndɪç] *adj* sensible; **~en** [fɛr'ʃtɛndɪgən] *vt* to inform ♦ *vr* to communicate; (*sich einigen*) to come to an understanding; **V~ung** *f* communication; (*Benachrichtigung*) informing; (*Einigung*) agreement
verständ- [fɛr'ʃtɛnt] *zW*: **~lich** *adj* understandable, comprehensible; **V~lichkeit** *f* clarity, intelligibility; **V~nis** (**-ses, -se**) *nt* understanding; **~nislos** *adj* uncomprehending; **~nisvoll** *adj* understanding, sympathetic
verstärk- [fɛr'ʃtɛrk] *zW*: **~en** *vt* to strengthen; (*Ton*) to amplify; (*erhöhen*) to intensify ♦ *vr* to intensify; **V~er** (**-s, -**) *m* amplifier; **V~ung** *f* strengthening; (*Hilfe*) reinforcements *pl*; (*von Ton*) amplification
verstauchen [fɛr'ʃtauxən] *vt* to sprain
verstauen [fɛr'ʃtauən] *vt* to stow away
Versteck [fɛr'ʃtɛk] (**-(e)s, -e**) *nt* hiding (place); **v~en** *vt*, *vr* to hide; **v~t** *adj* hidden
ver'stehen (*unreg*) *vt* to understand ♦ *vr* to

get on; **das versteht sich (von selbst)** that goes without saying
versteigern [fɛr'ʃtaɪgərn] *vt* to auction; **Versteigerung** *f* auction
verstell- [fɛr'ʃtɛl] *zW*: **~bar** *adj* adjustable, variable; **~en** *vt* to move, to shift; (*Uhr*) to adjust; (*versperren*) to block; (*fig*) to disguise ♦ *vr* to pretend, to put on an act; **V~ung** *f* pretence
versteuern [fɛr'ʃtɔʏərn] *vt* to pay tax on
verstimmt [fɛr'ʃtɪmt] *adj* out of tune; (*fig*) cross, put out; (*Magen*) upset
ver'stopfen *vt* to block, to stop up; (*MED*) to constipate
Ver'stopfung *f* obstruction; (*MED*) constipation
verstorben [fɛr'ʃtɔrbən] *adj* deceased, late
verstört [fɛr'ʃtøːrt] *adj* (*Mensch*) distraught
Verstoß [fɛr'ʃtoːs] *m*: **~ (gegen)** infringement (of), violation (of); **v~en** (*unreg*) *vt* to disown, to reject ♦ *vi*: **v~en gegen** to offend against
ver'streichen (*unreg*) *vt* to spread ♦ *vi* to elapse
ver'streuen *vt* to scatter (about)
verstümmeln [fɛr'ʃtʏməln] *vt* to maim, to mutilate (*auch fig*)
verstummen [fɛr'ʃtumən] *vi* to go silent; (*Lärm*) to die away
Versuch [fɛr'zuːx] (**-(e)s, -e**) *m* attempt; (*SCI*) experiment; **v~en** *vt* to try; (*verlocken*) to tempt ♦ *vr*: **sich an etw** *dat* **v~en** to try one's hand at sth; **~skaninchen** *nt* (*fig*) guinea-pig; **~ung** *f* temptation
vertagen [fɛr'taːgən] *vt*, *vi* to adjourn
ver'tauschen *vt* to exchange; (*versehentlich*) to mix up
verteidig- [fɛr'taɪdɪç] *zW*: **~en** *vt* to defend; **V~er** (**-s, -**) *m* defender; (*JUR*) defence counsel; **V~ung** *f* defence
ver'teilen *vt* to distribute; (*Rollen*) to assign; (*Salbe*) to spread
Verteilung *f* distribution, allotment
vertiefen [fɛr'tiːfən] *vt* to deepen ♦ *vr*: **sich in etw** *akk* **~** to become engrossed *od* absorbed in sth
Vertiefung *f* depression

vertikal [vɛrti'kaːl] *adj* vertical

vertilgen [fɛr'tɪlgən] *vt* to exterminate; (*umg*) to eat up, to consume

vertonen [fɛr'toːnən] *vt* to set to music

Vertrag [fɛr'traːk] (-(e)s, ⁽e) *m* contract, agreement; (*POL*) treaty; **v~en** [-gən] (*unreg*) *vt* to tolerate, to stand ♦ *vr* to get along; (*sich aussöhnen*) to become reconciled; **v~lich** *adj* contractual

verträglich [fɛr'trɛːklɪç] *adj* good-natured, sociable; (*Speisen*) easily digested; (*MED*) easily tolerated; **V~keit** *f* sociability; good nature; digestibility

Vertrags- *zW:* **~bruch** *m* breach of contract; **~händler** *m* appointed retailer; **~partner** *m* party to a contract; **~werkstatt** *f* appointed repair shop; **v~widrig** *adj* contrary to contract

vertrauen [fɛr'trauən] *vi:* **jdm ~** to trust sb; **~ auf** +*akk* to rely on; **V~ (-s)** *nt* confidence; **V~ erweckend** inspiring trust; **~svoll** *adj* trustful; **~swürdig** *adj* trustworthy

vertraulich [fɛr'traulɪç] *adj* familiar; (*geheim*) confidential

vertraut [fɛr'traut] *adj* familiar; **V~heit** *f* familiarity

ver'treiben (*unreg*) *vt* to drive away; (*aus Land*) to expel; (*COMM*) to sell; (*Zeit*) to pass

vertret- [fɛr'treːt] *zW:* **~en** (*unreg*) *vt* to represent; (*Ansicht*) to hold, to advocate; **sich** *dat* **die Beine ~en** to stretch one's legs; **V~er (-s, -)** *m* representative; (*Verfechter*) advocate; **V~ung** *f* representation; advocacy

Vertrieb [fɛr'triːp] (-(e)s, -e) *m* marketing (department)

ver'trocknen *vi* to dry up

ver'trösten *vt* to put off

vertun [fɛr'tuːn] (*unreg*) *vt* to waste ♦ *vr* (*umg*) to make a mistake

vertuschen [fɛr'tuʃən] *vt* to hush *od* cover up

verübeln [fɛr'yːbəln] *vt:* **jdm etw ~** to be cross *od* offended with sb on account of sth

verüben [fɛr'yːbən] *vt* to commit

verun- [fɛr'ʊn] *zW:* **~glimpfen** *vt* to disparage; **~glücken** *vi* to have an accident; **tödlich ~glücken** to be killed in an accident; **~reinigen** *vt* to soil; (*Umwelt*) to pollute; **~sichern** *vt* to rattle; **~treuen** [-trɔyən] *vt* to embezzle

verur- [fɛr'uːr] *zW:* **~sachen** *vt* to cause; **~teilen** [-taɪlən] *vt* to condemn; **V~teilung** *f* condemnation; (*JUR*) sentence

verviel- [fɛr'fiːl] *zW:* **~fachen** *vt* to multiply; **~fältigen** [-fɛltɪgən] *vt* to duplicate, to copy; **V~fältigung** *f* duplication, copying

vervollkommnen [fɛr'fɔlkɔmnən] *vt* to perfect

vervollständigen [fɛr'fɔlʃtɛndɪgən] *vt* to complete

ver'wackeln *vt* (*Foto*) to blur

ver'wählen *vr* (*TEL*) to dial the wrong number

verwahren [fɛr'vaːrən] *vt* to keep, to lock away ♦ *vr* to protest

verwalt- [fɛr'valt] *zW:* **~en** *vt* to manage; to administer; **V~er (-s, -)** *m* manager; (*Vermögensverwalter*) trustee; **V~ung** *f* administration; management

ver'wandeln *vt* to change, to transform ♦ *vr* to change; to be transformed; **Ver'wandlung** *f* change, transformation

verwandt [fɛr'vant] *adj:* **~ (mit)** related (to); **V~e(r)** *f(m)* relative, relation; **V~schaft** *f* relationship; (*Menschen*) relations *pl*

ver'warnen *vt* to caution

Ver'warnung *f* caution

ver'wechseln *vt:* **~ mit** to confuse with; to mistake for; **zum V~ ähnlich** as like as two peas

Ver'wechslung *f* confusion, mixing up

Verwehung [fɛr'veːʊŋ] *f* snowdrift; sand drift

verweichlicht [fɛr'vaɪçlɪçt] *adj* effeminate, soft

ver'weigern *vt:* **jdm etw ~** to refuse sb sth; **den Gehorsam/die Aussage ~** to refuse to obey/testify

Ver'weigerung *f* refusal

Verweis [fɛr'vaɪs] (-es, -e) *m* reprimand,

rebuke; (Hinweis) reference; **v~en** (unreg) vt to refer; **jdn von der Schule v~en** to expel sb (from school); **jdn des Landes v~en** to deport od expel sb

ver'welken vi to fade

verwend- [fɛr'vɛnd] zW: **~bar** [-'vɛntba:r] adj usable; **ver'wenden** (unreg) vt to use; (Mühe, Zeit, Arbeit) to spend ♦ vr to intercede; **Ver'wendung** f use

ver'werfen (unreg) vt to reject

verwerflich [fɛr'vɛrflɪç] adj reprehensible

ver'werten vt to utilize

Ver'wertung f utilization

verwesen [fɛr've:zən] vi to decay

ver'wickeln vt to tangle (up); (fig) to involve ♦ vr to get tangled (up); **jdn in etw** akk ~ to involve sb in sth; **sich in etw** akk ~ to get involved in sth

verwickelt [fɛr'vɪkəlt] adj (Situation, Fall) difficult, complicated

verwildern [fɛr'vɪldərn] vi to run wild

verwirklichen [fɛr'vɪrklɪçən] vt to realize, to put into effect

Verwirklichung f realization

verwirren [fɛr'vɪrən] vt to tangle (up); (fig) to confuse

Verwirrung f confusion

verwittern [fɛr'vɪtərn] vi to weather

verwitwet [fɛr'vɪtvət] adj widowed

verwöhnen [fɛr'vø:nən] vt to spoil

verworren [fɛr'vɔrən] adj confused

verwundbar [fɛr'vʊntba:r] adj vulnerable

verwunden [fɛr'vʊndən] vt to wound

verwunder- [fɛr'vʊndər] zW: **~lich** adj surprising; **V~ung** f astonishment

Verwundete(r) f(m) injured person

Verwundung f wound, injury

ver'wünschen vt to curse

verwüsten [fɛr'vy:stən] vt to devastate

verzagen [fɛr'tsa:gən] vi to despair

ver'zählen vr to miscount

verzehren [fɛr'tse:rən] vt to consume

ver'zeichnen vt to list; (Niederlage, Verlust) to register

Verzeichnis [fɛr'tsaɪçnɪs] (-ses, -se) nt list, catalogue; (in Buch) index

verzeih- [fɛr'tsaɪ] zW: **~en** (unreg) vt, vi to forgive; **jdm etw ~en** to forgive sb for sth; **~lich** adj pardonable; **V~ung** f forgiveness, pardon; **V~ung!** sorry!, excuse me!

verzichten [fɛr'tsɪçtən] vi: ~ **auf** +akk to forgo, to give up

ver'ziehen (unreg) vi to move ♦ vt to put out of shape; (Kind) to spoil; (Pflanzen) to thin out ♦ vr to go out of shape; (Gesicht) to contort; (verschwinden) to disappear; **das Gesicht ~** to pull a face

verzieren [fɛr'tsi:rən] vt to decorate, to ornament

Verzierung f decoration

verzinsen [fɛr'tsɪnzən] vt to pay interest on

ver'zögern vt to delay

Ver'zögerung f delay, time lag; **~staktik** f delaying tactics pl

verzollen [fɛr'tsɔlən] vt to pay duty on

Verzug [fɛr'tsu:k] m delay

verzweif- [fɛr'tsvaɪf] zW: **~eln** vi to despair; **~elt** adj desperate; **V~lung** f despair

Veto ['ve:to] (-s, -s) nt veto

Vetter ['fɛtər] (-s, -n) m cousin

vgl. abk (= vergleiche) cf.

v. H. abk (= vom Hundert) p.c.

vibrieren [vi'bri:rən] vi to vibrate

Video ['vi:deo] nt video; **~gerät** nt video recorder; **~rekorder** m video recorder

Vieh [fi:] (-(e)s) nt cattle pl; **v~isch** adj bestial

viel [fi:l] adj a lot of, much ♦ adv a lot, much; ~ **sagend** significant; ~ **versprechend** promising; **~e** pron pl a lot of, many; ~ **zu wenig** much too little; **~erlei** adj a great variety of; **~es** pron a lot; **~fach** adj, adv many times; **auf ~fachen Wunsch** at the request of many people; **V~falt** (-) f variety; **~fältig** adj varied, many-sided

vielleicht [fi'laɪçt] adv perhaps

viel- zW: **~mal(s)** adv many times; **danke ~mals** many thanks; **~mehr** adv rather, on the contrary; **~seitig** adj many-sided

vier [fi:r] num four; **V~eck** (-(e)s, -e) nt four-sided figure; (gleichseitig) square; **~eckig** adj four-sided; square; **V~takt-motor** m four-stroke engine; **~te(r, s)**

['fi:rtə(r, s)] *adj* fourth; **V~tel** ['fɪrtəl] **(-s, -)**
nt quarter; **V~teljahr** *nt* quarter;
~teljährlich *adj* quarterly; **~teln** *vt* to
divide into four; (*Kuchen usw*) to divide into
quarters; **V~telstunde** *f* quarter of an
hour; **~zehn** ['fɪrtse:n] *num* fourteen; **in
~zehn Tagen** in a fortnight; **~zehntägig**
adj fortnightly; **~zig** ['fɪrtsɪç] *num* forty

Villa ['vɪla] **(-, Villen)** *f* villa

violett [vio'lɛt] *adj* violet

Violin- [vio'li:n] *zW:* **~e** *f* violin;
~schlüssel *m* treble clef

virtuell [vɪrtu'ɛl] *adj* (*COMPUT*) virtual; **~e
Realität** virtual reality

Virus ['vi:rʊs] **(-, Viren)** *m od nt* (*auch
COMPUT*) virus

Visa ['vi:za] *pl von* **Visum**

vis-a-vis ▲, **vis-à-vis** [viza'vi:] *adv* opposite

Visen ['vi:zən] *pl von* **Visum**

Visier [vi'zi:r] **(-s, -e)** *nt* gunsight; (*am Helm*)
visor

Visite [vi'zi:tə] *f* (*MED*) visit; **~nkarte** *f*
visiting card

Visum ['vi:zʊm] **(-s, Visa od Visen)** *nt* visa

vital [vi'ta:l] *adj* lively, full of life, vital

Vitamin [vita'mi:n] **(-s, -e)** *nt* vitamin

Vogel ['fo:gəl] **(-s, ⸚)** *m* bird; **einen ~ haben**
(*umg*) to have bats in the belfry; **jdm den ~
zeigen** (*umg*) to tap one's forehead
(*meaning that one thinks sb stupid*); **~bauer**
nt birdcage; **~perspektive** *f* bird's-eye
view; **~scheuche** *f* scarecrow

Vokabel [vo'ka:bəl] **(-, -n)** *f* word

Vokabular [vokabu'la:r] **(-s, -e)** *nt*
vocabulary

Vokal [vo'ka:l] **(-s, -e)** *m* vowel

Volk [fɔlk] **(-(e)s, ⸚er)** *nt* people; nation

Völker- ['fœlkər] *zW:* **~recht** *nt*
international law; **v~rechtlich** *adj*
according to international law;
~verständigung *f* international
understanding

Volkshochschule

ⓘ   The **Volkshochschule** (*VHS*) is an
institution which offers Adult Education
classes. No set qualifications are necessary

to attend. For a small fee adults can attend
both vocational and non-vocational classes
in the day-time or evening.

Volks- *zW:* **~entscheid** *m* referendum;
~fest *nt* fair; **~hochschule** *f* adult
education classes *pl*; **~lied** *nt* folksong;
~republik *f* people's republic; **~schule** *f*
elementary school; **~tanz** *m* folk dance;
~vertreter(in) *m(f)* people's
representative; **~wirtschaft** *f* economics *sg*

voll [fɔl] *adj* full; **etw ~ machen** to fill sth
up; **~ tanken** to fill up; **~ und ganz**
completely; **jdn für ~ nehmen** (*umg*) to
take sb seriously; **~auf** *adv* amply; **V~bart**
m full beard; **V~beschäftigung** *f* full
employment; **~'bringen** (*unreg*) *vt insep* to
accomplish; **~'enden** *vt insep* to finish, to
complete; **~endet** *adj* (*~kommen*)
completed; **~ends** ['fɔlɛnts] *adv*
completely; **V~'endung** *f* completion

Volleyball ['vɔliba l] *m* volleyball

Vollgas *nt:* **mit ~** at full throttle; **~ geben**
to step on it

völlig ['fœlɪç] *adj* complete ♦ *adv* completely

voll- *zW:* **~jährig** *adj* of age;
V~kaskoversicherung ['fɔlkaskofɛrzɪçərʊŋ]
f fully comprehensive insurance;
~'kommen *adj* perfect; **V~'kommenheit**
f perfection; **V~kornbrot** *nt* wholemeal
bread; **V~macht** **(-, -en)** *f* authority, full
powers *pl*; **V~milch** *f* (*KOCH*) full-cream
milk; **V~mond** *m* full moon; **V~pension** *f*
full board; **~ständig** ['fɔlʃtɛndɪç] *adj*
complete; **~'strecken** *vt insep* to execute;
~tanken △ *vt*, *vi siehe* **voll**;
V~waschmittel *nt* detergent;
V~wertkost *f* wholefood; **~zählig**
['fɔlsɛ:lɪç] *adj* complete; in full number;
~'ziehen (*unreg*) *vt insep* to carry out ♦ *vr
insep* to happen; **V~'zug** *m* execution

Volumen [vo'lu:mən] **(-s, -od Volumina)** *nt*
volume

vom [fɔm] = **von dem**

SCHLÜSSELWORT

von [fɔn] *präp +dat* **1** (*Ausgangspunkt*) from;

---

von from ... to; **von morgens bis abends** from morning till night; **von ... nach ...** from ... to ...; **von ... an** from ...; **von ... aus** from ...; **von dort aus** from there; **etw von sich aus tun** to do sth of one's own accord; **von mir aus** (*umg*) if you like, I don't mind; **von wo/wann ...?** where/ when ... from?

2 (*Ursache, im Passiv*) by; **ein Gedicht von Schiller** a poem by Schiller; **von etw müde** tired from sth

3 (*als Genitiv*) of; **ein Freund von mir** a friend of mine; **nett von dir** nice of you; **jeweils zwei von zehn** two out of every ten

4 (*über*) about; **er erzählte vom Urlaub** he talked about his holiday

5: von wegen! (*umg*) no way!

voneinander *adv* from each other

⌐ *SCHLÜSSELWORT* ⌐

vor [foːr] *präp +dat* **1** (*räumlich*) in front of; **vor der Kirche links abbiegen** turn left before the church

2 (*zeitlich*) before; **ich war vor ihm da** I was there before him; **vor 2 Tagen** 2 days ago; **5 (Minuten) vor 4** 5 (minutes) to 4; **vor kurzem** a little while ago

3 (*Ursache*) with; **vor Wut/Liebe** with rage/love; **vor Hunger sterben** to die of hunger; **vor lauter Arbeit** because of work

4: vor allem, vor allen Dingen most of all
♦ *präp +akk* (*räumlich*) in front of
♦ *adv*: **vor und zurück** backwards and forwards

Vorabend ['foːrˌaːbənt] *m* evening before, eve

voran [foˈran] *adv* before, ahead; **mach ~!** get on with it!; **~gehen** (*unreg*) *vi* to go ahead; **einer Sache** *dat* **~gehen** to precede sth; **~kommen** (*unreg*) *vi* to come along, to make progress

Voranschlag ['foːrˌanʃlaːk] *m* estimate

Vorarbeiter ['foːrˌarbaɪtər] *m* foreman

voraus [foˈraʊs] *adv* ahead; (*zeitlich*) in advance; **jdm ~ sein** to be ahead of sb; **im V~** in advance; **~gehen** (*unreg*) *vi* to go (on) ahead; (*fig*) to precede; **~haben** (*unreg*) *vt*: **jdm etw ~haben** to have the edge on sb in sth; **V~sage** *f* prediction; **~sagen** *vt* to predict; **~sehen** (*unreg*) *vt* to foresee; **~setzen** *vt* to assume; **~gesetzt, dass ...** provided that ...; **V~setzung** *f* requirement, prerequisite; **V~sicht** *f* foresight; **aller V~sicht nach** in all probability; **~sichtlich** *adv* probably

Vorbehalt ['foːrbəhalt] (-(e)s, -e) *m* reservation, proviso; **v~en** (*unreg*) *vt*: **sich/jdm etw v~en** to reserve sth (for o.s.)/for sb; **v~los** *adj* unconditional ♦ *adv* unconditionally

vorbei [foːrˈbaɪ] *adv* by, past; **das ist ~** that's over; **~gehen** (*unreg*) *vi* to pass by, to go past; **~kommen** (*unreg*) *vi*: **bei jdm ~kommen** to drop in *od* call in on sb

vor- *zW*: **~belastet** ['foːrbəlastət] *adj* (*fig*) handicapped; **~bereiten** *vt* to prepare; **V~bereitung** *f* preparation; **V~bestellung** *f* advance order; (*von Platz, Tisch etc*) advance booking; **~bestraft** ['foːrbəʃtraːft] *adj* previously convicted, with a record

vorbeugen ['foːrbɔʏɡən] *vt, vr* to lean forward ♦ *vi +dat* to prevent; **~d** *adj* preventive

Vorbeugung *f* prevention; **zur ~ gegen** for the prevention of

Vorbild ['foːrbɪlt] *nt* model; **sich** *dat* **jdn zum ~ nehmen** to model o.s. on sb; **v~lich** *adj* model, ideal

vorbringen ['foːrbrɪŋən] (*unreg*) *vt* to advance, to state

Vorder- ['fɔrdər] *zW*: **~achse** *f* front axle; **v~e(r, s)** *adj* front; **~grund** *m* foreground; **~mann** (*pl* **-männer**) *m* man in front; **jdn auf ~mann bringen** (*umg*) to get sb to shape up; **~seite** *f* front (side); **v~ste(r, s)** *adj* front

vordrängen ['foːrdrɛŋən] *vr* to push to the front

voreilig ['foːraɪlɪç] *adj* hasty, rash

voreinander [foːraɪˈnandər] *adv* (*räumlich*)

Spelling Reform: ▲ *new spelling* △ *old spelling (to be phased out)*

in front of each other

voreingenommen ['fo:r|aɪngənɔmən] *adj*
biased; **V~heit** *f* bias

vorenthalten ['fo:r|ɛnthaltən] (*unreg*) *vt*:
jdm etw ~ to withhold sth from sb

vorerst ['fo:r|e:rst] *adv* for the moment *od*
present

Vorfahr ['fo:rfa:r] (**-en, -en**) *m* ancestor

vorfahren (*unreg*) *vi* to drive (on) ahead;
(*vors Haus etc*) to drive up

Vorfahrt *f* (*AUT*) right of way; **~ achten!**
give way!

Vorfahrts- *zW*: **~regel** *f* right of way;
~schild *nt* give way sign; **~straße** *f* major
road

Vorfall ['fo:rfal] *m* incident; **v~en** (*unreg*) *vi*
to occur

vorfinden ['fo:rfɪndən] (*unreg*) *vt* to find

Vorfreude ['fo:rfrɔydə] *f* (joyful) anticipation

vorführen ['fo:rfy:rən] *vt* to show, to
display; **dem Gericht ~** to bring before the
court

Vorgabe ['fo:rga:bə] *f* (*SPORT*) start,
handicap ♦ *in zW* (*COMPUT*) default

Vorgang ['fo:rgaŋ] *m* course of events; (*bes
SCI*) process

Vorgänger(in) ['fo:rgɛŋər(ɪn)] (**-s, -**) *m(f)*
predecessor

vorgeben ['fo:rge:bən] (*unreg*) *vt* to pretend,
to use as a pretext; (*SPORT*) to give an
advantage *od* a start of

vorgefertigt ['fo:rgəfertɪçt] *adj* prefabricated

vorgehen ['fo:rge:ən] (*unreg*) *vi* (*voraus*) to
go (on) ahead; (*nach vorn*) to go up front;
(*handeln*) to act, to proceed; (*Uhr*) to be
fast; (*Vorrang haben*) to take precedence;
(*passieren*) to go on

Vorgehen (-s) *nt* action

Vorgeschichte ['fo:rgəʃɪçtə] *f* past history

Vorgeschmack ['fo:rgəʃmak] *m* foretaste

Vorgesetzte(r) ['fo:rgəzɛtstə(r)] *f(m)*
superior

vorgestern ['fo:rgɛstərn] *adv* the day before
yesterday

vorhaben ['fo:rha:bən] (*unreg*) *vt* to intend;
hast du schon was vor? have you got
anything on?; **V~ (-s, -)** *nt* intention

vorhalten ['fo:rhaltən] (*unreg*) *vt* to hold *od*
put up ♦ *vi* to last; **jdm etw ~** (*fig*) to
reproach sb for sth

vorhanden [fo:r'handən] *adj* existing;
(*erhältlich*) available

Vorhang ['fo:rhaŋ] *m* curtain

Vorhängeschloss ▲ ['fo:rhɛŋəʃlɔs] *nt*
padlock

vorher [fo:r'he:r] *adv* before(hand);
~bestimmen *vt* (*Schicksal*) to preordain;
~gehen (*unreg*) *vi* to precede; **~ig** *adj*
previous

Vorherrschaft ['fo:rhɛrʃaft] *f*
predominance, supremacy

vorherrschen ['fo:rhɛrʃən] *vi* to
predominate

vorher- [fo:r'he:r] *zW*: **V~sage** *f* forecast;
~sagen *vt* to forecast, to predict;
~sehbar *adj* predictable; **~sehen** (*unreg*)
vt to foresee

vorhin [fo:r'hɪn] *adv* not long ago, just now;
V~ein ▲ *adv*: **im V~ein** beforehand

vorig ['fo:rɪç] *adj* previous, last

Vorkämpfer(in) ['fo:rkempfər(ɪn)] *m(f)*
pioneer

Vorkaufsrecht ['fo:rkaufsrɛçt] *nt* option to
buy

Vorkehrung ['fo:rke:rʊŋ] *f* precaution

vorkommen ['fo:rkɔmən] (*unreg*) *vi* to come
forward; (*geschehen, sich finden*) to occur;
(*scheinen*) to seem (to be); **sich** *dat* **dumm
etc ~** to feel stupid *etc*; **V~ (-s, -)** *nt*
occurrence

Vorkriegs- [fo:r'kri:ks] *in zW* prewar

Vorladung ['fo:rla:dʊŋ] *f* summons *sg*

Vorlage ['fo:rla:gə] *f* model, pattern;
(*Gesetzesvorlage*) bill; (*SPORT*) pass

vorlassen ['fo:rlasən] (*unreg*) *vt* to admit;
(*vorgehen lassen*) to allow to go in front

vorläufig ['fo:rlɔyfɪç] *adj* temporary,
provisional

vorlaut ['fo:rlaut] *adj* impertinent, cheeky

vorlesen ['fo:rle:zən] (*unreg*) *vt* to read (out)

Vorlesung *f* (*UNIV*) lecture

vorletzte(r, s) ['fo:rletstə(r, s)] *adj* last but
one

vorlieb [fo:r'li:p] *adv*: **~ nehmen mit** to

make do with

Vorliebe ['foːrliːbə] f preference, partiality

vorliegen ['foːrliːgən] (unreg) vi to be (here); **etw liegt jdm vor** sb has sth; **~d** adj present, at issue

vormachen ['foːrmaxən] vt: **jdm etw ~** to show sb how to do sth; (fig) to fool sb; to have sb on

Vormachtstellung ['foːrmaxtʃtɛlʊŋ] f supremacy, hegemony

Vormarsch ['foːrmarʃ] m advance

vormerken ['foːrmɛrkən] vt to book

Vormittag ['foːrmɪtaːk] m morning; **v~s** adv in the morning, before noon

vorn [fɔrn] adv in front; **von ~ anfangen** to start at the beginning; **nach ~** to the front

Vorname ['foːrnaːmə] m first name, Christian name

vorne ['fɔrnə] adv = vorn

vornehm ['foːrneːm] adj distinguished; refined; elegant

vornehmen (unreg) vt (fig) to carry out; **sich** dat **etw ~** to start on sth; (beschließen) to decide to do sth; **sich** dat **jdn ~** to tell sb off

vornherein ['fɔrnheraɪn] adv: **von ~** from the start

Vorort ['foːrʔɔrt] m suburb

Vorrang ['foːrraŋ] m precedence, priority; **v~ig** adj of prime importance, primary

Vorrat ['foːrraːt] m stock, supply

vorrätig ['foːrrɛːtɪç] adj in stock

Vorratskammer f pantry

Vorrecht ['foːrreçt] nt privilege

Vorrichtung ['foːrrɪçtʊŋ] f device, contrivance

vorrücken ['foːrrʏkən] vi to advance ♦ vt to move forward

Vorsaison ['foːrzɛzõ] f early season

Vorsatz ['foːrzats] m intention; (JUR) intent; **einen ~ fassen** to make a resolution

vorsätzlich ['foːrzɛtslɪç] adj intentional; (JUR) premeditated ♦ adv intentionally

Vorschau ['foːrʃaʊ] f (RADIO, TV) (programme) preview; (Film) trailer

Vorschlag ['foːrʃlaːk] m suggestion, proposal; **v~en** (unreg) vt to suggest, to propose

vorschreiben ['foːrʃraɪbən] (unreg) vt to prescribe, to specify

Vorschrift ['foːrʃrɪft] f regulation(s); rule(s); (Anweisungen) instruction(s); **Dienst nach ~** work-to-rule; **v~smäßig** adj as per regulations/instructions

Vorschuss ▲ ['foːrʃʊs] m advance

vorsehen ['foːrzeːən] (unreg) vt to provide for, to plan ♦ vr to take care, to be careful ♦ vi to be visible

Vorsehung f providence

Vorsicht ['foːrzɪçt] f caution, care; **~!** look out!, take care!; (auf Schildern) caution!, danger!; **~, Stufe!** mind the step!; **v~ig** adj cautious, careful; **v~shalber** adv just in case

Vorsilbe ['foːrzɪlbə] f prefix

vorsingen ['foːrzɪŋən] vt (vor Zuhörern) to sing (to); (in Prüfung, für Theater etc) to audition (for) ♦ vi to sing

Vorsitz ['foːrzɪts] m chair(manship); **~ende(r)** f(m) chairman(-woman)

Vorsorge ['foːrzɔrgə] f precaution(s), provision(s); **v~n** vi: **v~n für** to make provision(s) for; **~untersuchung** f check-up

vorsorglich ['foːrzɔrklɪç] adv as a precaution

Vorspeise ['foːrʃpaɪzə] f hors d'oeuvre, appetizer

Vorspiel ['foːrʃpiːl] nt prelude

vorspielen vt: **jdm etw ~** (MUS) to play sth for od to sb ♦ vi (zur Prüfung etc) to play for od to sb

vorsprechen ['foːrʃprɛçən] (unreg) vt to say out loud, to recite ♦ vi: **bei jdm ~** to call on sb

Vorsprung ['foːrʃprʊŋ] m projection, ledge; (fig) advantage, start

Vorstadt ['foːrʃtat] f suburbs pl

Vorstand ['foːrʃtant] m executive committee; (COMM) board (of directors); (Person) director, head

vorstehen ['foːrʃteːən] (unreg) vi to project; **einer Sache** dat **~** (fig) to be the head of sth

vorstell- ['foːrʃtɛl] zW: **~bar** adj

conceivable; **~en** *vt* to put forward;
(*bekannt machen*) to introduce; (*darstellen*)
to represent; **~en vor** +*akk* to put in front
of; **sich** *dat* **etw ~en** to imagine sth;
V~ung *f* (*Bekanntmachen*) introduction;
(*THEAT etc*) performance; (*Gedanke*) idea,
thought

vorstoßen ['fo:rʃtoːsən] (*unreg*) *vi* (*ins
Unbekannte*) to venture (forth)

Vorstrafe ['fo:rʃtraːfə] *f* previous conviction

Vortag ['fo:rtak] *m*: **am ~ einer Sache** *gen*
on the day before sth

vortäuschen ['fo:rtɔʏʃən] *vt* to feign, to
pretend

Vorteil ['fo:rtail] (**-s, -e**) *m*: **~ (gegenüber)**
advantage (over); **im ~ sein** to have the
advantage; **v~haft** *adj* advantageous

Vortrag ['fo:rtraːk] (**-(e)s, Vorträge**) *m* talk,
lecture; **v~en** [-gən] (*unreg*) *vt* to carry
forward; (*fig*) to recite; (*Rede*) to deliver;
(*Lied*) to perform; (*Meinung etc*) to express

vortreten ['fo:rtreːtən] (*unreg*) *vi* to step
forward; (*Augen etc*) to protrude

vorüber [fo'ryːbər] *adv* past, over; **~gehen**
(*unreg*) *vi* to pass (by); **~gehen an** +*dat* (*fig*)
to pass over; **~gehend** *adj* temporary,
passing

Vorurteil ['fo:rʔʊrtail] *nt* prejudice

Vorverkauf ['fo:rferkauf] *m* advance
booking

Vorwahl ['fo:rvaːl] *f* preliminary election;
(*TEL*) dialling code

Vorwand ['fo:rvant] (**-(e)s, Vorwände**) *m*
pretext

vorwärts ['fo:rverts] *adv* forward; **~ gehen**
to progress; **V~gang** *m* (*AUT etc*) forward
gear; **~ kommen** to get on, to make
progress

Vorwäsche *f* prewash

vorweg [fo'r'vek] *adv* in advance; **~nehmen**
(*unreg*) *vt* to anticipate

vorweisen ['fo:rvaizən] (*unreg*) *vt* to show,
to produce

vorwerfen ['fo:rverfən] (*unreg*) *vt*: **jdm etw
~** to reproach sb for sth, to accuse sb of
sth; **sich** *dat* **nichts vorzuwerfen haben** to
have nothing to reproach o.s. with

vorwiegend ['fo:rviːgənt] *adj* predominant
♦ *adv* predominantly

vorwitzig ['fo:rvɪtsɪç] *adj* (*Mensch,
Bemerkung*) cheeky

Vorwort ['fo:rvɔrt] (**-(e)s, -e**) *nt* preface

Vorwurf ['fo:rvʊrf] *m* reproach; **jdm/sich
Vorwürfe machen** to reproach sb/o.s.;
v~svoll *adj* reproachful

vorzeigen ['fo:rtsaigən] *vt* to show, to
produce

vorzeitig ['fo:rtsaitɪç] *adj* premature

vorziehen ['fo:rtsiːən] (*unreg*) *vt* to pull
forward; (*Gardinen*) to draw; (*lieber haben*)
to prefer

Vorzimmer ['fo:rtsɪmər] *nt* (*Büro*) outer
office

Vorzug ['fo:rtsuːk] *m* preference; (*gute
Eigenschaft*) merit, good quality; (*Vorteil*)
advantage

vorzüglich [fo:r'tsyːklɪç] *adj* excellent

Vorzugspreis *m* special discount price

vulgär [vʊl'geːr] *adj* vulgar

Vulkan [vʊl'kaːn] (**-s, -e**) *m* volcano

W, w

Waage ['vaːgə] *f* scales *pl*; (*ASTROL*) Libra;
w~recht *adj* horizontal

Wabe ['vaːbə] *f* honeycomb

wach [vax] *adj* awake; (*fig*) alert; **W~e** *f*
guard, watch; **W~e halten** to keep watch;
W~e stehen to stand guard; **~en** *vi* to be
awake; (*Wache halten*) to guard

Wachs [vaks] (**-es, -e**) *nt* wax

wachsam ['vaxzaːm] *adj* watchful, vigilant,
alert

wachsen (*unreg*) *vi* to grow

Wachstuch ['vakstuːx] *nt* oilcloth

Wachstum ['vakstuːm] (**-s**) *nt* growth

Wächter ['veçtər] (**-s, -**) *m* guard, warden,
keeper; (*Parkplatzwächter*) attendant

wackel- ['vakəl] *zW*: **~ig** *adj* shaky, wobbly;
W~kontakt *m* loose connection; **~n** *vi* to
shake; (*fig: Position*) to be shaky

wacker ['vakər] *adj* valiant, stout ♦ *adv* well,
bravely

Wade ['vaːdə] f (*ANAT*) calf

Waffe ['vafə] f weapon

Waffel ['vafəl] (-, -n) f waffle; wafer

Waffen- *zW:* **~schein** m gun licence; **~stillstand** m armistice, truce

Wagemut ['vaːgəmuːt] m daring

wagen ['vaːgən] vt to venture, to dare

Wagen ['vaːgən] (-s, -) m vehicle; (*Auto*) car; (*EISENB*) carriage; (*Pferdewagen*) cart; **~heber** (-s, -) m jack

Waggon [va'gõː] (-s, -s) m carriage; (*Güterwaggon*) goods van, freight truck (*US*)

Wagnis ['vaːknɪs] (-ses, -se) nt risk

Wagon ▲ [va'gõː, va'goːn] (-s, -s) m = **Waggon**

Wahl [vaːl] (-, -en) f choice; (*POL*) election; **zweite ~** (*COMM*) seconds pl

wähl- ['veːl] *zW:* **~bar** adj eligible; **~en** vt, vi to choose; (*POL*) to elect, to vote (for); (*TEL*) to dial; **W~er(in)** (-s, -) m(f) voter; **~erisch** adj fastidious, particular

Wahl- *zW:* **~fach** nt optional subject; **~gang** m ballot; **~kabine** f polling booth; **~kampf** m election campaign; **~kreis** m constituency; **~lokal** nt polling station; **w~los** adv at random; **~recht** nt franchise; **~spruch** m motto; **~urne** f ballot box

Wahn [vaːn] (-(e)s) m delusion; folly; **~sinn** m madness; **w~sinnig** adj insane, mad ♦ adv (*umg*) incredibly

wahr [vaːr] adj true

wahren vt to maintain, to keep

während ['veːrant] präp +gen during ♦ konj while; **~dessen** adv meanwhile

wahr- *zW:* **~haben** (*unreg*) vt: **etw nicht ~haben wollen** to refuse to admit sth; **~haft** adv (*tatsächlich*) truly; **~haftig** [vaːr'haftɪç] adj true, real ♦ adv really; **W~heit** f truth; **~nehmen** (*unreg*) vt to perceive, to observe; **W~nehmung** f perception; **~sagen** vi to prophesy, to tell fortunes; **W~sager(in)** (-s, -) m(f) fortune teller; **~scheinlich** [vaːr'faɪnlɪç] adj probable ♦ adv probably; **W~'scheinlichkeit** f probability; **aller W~scheinlichkeit nach** in all probability

Währung ['veːrʊŋ] f currency

Wahrzeichen nt symbol

Waise ['vaɪzə] f orphan; **~nhaus** nt orphanage

Wald [valt] (-(e)s, ⁻er) m wood(s); (*groß*) forest; **~brand** m forest fire; **~sterben** nt trees dying due to pollution

Wales [weɪlz] (-) nt Wales

Wal(fisch) ['vaːl(fɪʃ)] (-(e)s, -e) m whale

Waliser [va'liːzər] (-s, -) m Welshman; **Waliserin** [va'liːzərɪn] f Welshwoman; **walisisch** [va'liːzɪʃ] adj Welsh

Walkman ['wɔːkman] (®) -s, **Walkmen**) m Walkman ®, personal stereo

Wall [val] (-(e)s, ⁻e) m embankment; (*Bollwerk*) rampart

Wallfahr- *zW:* **~er(in)** m(f) pilgrim; **~t** f pilgrimage

Walnuss ▲ ['valnʊs] f walnut

Walross ▲ ['valrɔs] nt walrus

Walze ['valtsə] f (*Gerät*) cylinder; (*Fahrzeug*) roller; **w~n** vt to roll (out)

wälzen ['vɛltsən] vt to roll (over); (*Bücher*) to hunt through; (*Probleme*) to deliberate on ♦ vr to wallow; (*vor Schmerzen*) to roll about; (*im Bett*) to toss and turn

Walzer ['valtsər] (-s, -) m waltz

Wand [vant] (-, ⁻e) f wall; (*Trennwand*) partition; (*Bergwand*) precipice

Wandel ['vandəl] (-s) m change; **w~bar** adj changeable, variable; **w~n** vt, vr to change ♦ vi (*gehen*) to walk

Wander- ['vandər] *zW:* **~er** (-s, -) m hiker, rambler; **~karte** f map of country walks; **w~n** vi to hike; (*Blick*) to wander; (*Gedanken*) to stray; **~schaft** f travelling; **~ung** f walk, hike; **~weg** m trail, walk

Wandlung f change, transformation

Wange ['vaŋə] f cheek

wanken ['vaŋkən] vi to stagger; (*fig*) to waver

wann [van] adv when

Wanne ['vanə] f tub

Wanze ['vantsə] f bug

Wappen ['vapən] (-s, -) nt coat of arms, crest; **~kunde** f heraldry

war etc [vaːr] vb siehe **sein**

Ware ['vaːrə] f ware

Waren- *zW:* **~haus** *nt* department store;
~lager *nt* stock, store; **~muster** *nt* trade
sample; **~probe** *f* sample; **~sendung** *f*
trade sample (*sent by post*); **~zeichen** *nt*:
(eingetragenes) ~zeichen (registered)
trademark

warf *etc* [va:rf] *vb siehe* **werfen**

warm [varm] *adj* warm; (*Essen*) hot

Wärm- ['vɛrm] *zW:* **~e** *f* warmth; **w~en** *vt,*
vr to warm (up), to heat (up); **~flasche** *f*
hot-water bottle

Warn- ['varn] *zW:* **~blinkanlage** *f* (*AUT*)
hazard warning lights *pl;* **~dreieck** *nt*
warning triangle; **w~en** *vt* to warn; **~ung** *f*
warning

warten ['vartən] *vi:* **~ (auf** +*akk*) to wait
(for); **auf sich ~ lassen** to take a long time

Wärter(in) ['vɛrtər(ɪn)] (**-s, -**) *m(f)* attendant

Warte- ['vartə] *zW:* **~saal** *m* (*EISENB*) waiting
room; **~zimmer** *nt* waiting room

Wartung *f* servicing; service; **~ und
Instandhaltung** maintenance

warum [va'rʊm] *adv* why

Warze ['vartsə] *f* wart

was [vas] *pron* what; (*umg: etwas*)
something; **~ für (ein) ...** what sort of ...

waschbar *adj* washable

Waschbecken *nt* washbasin

Wäsche ['vɛʃə] *f* wash(ing); (*Bettwäsche*)
linen; (*Unterwäsche*) underclothing

waschecht *adj* colourfast; (*fig*) genuine

Wäsche- *zW:* **~klammer** *f* clothes peg
(*BRIT*), clothespin (*US*); **~leine** *f* washing
line (*BRIT*)

waschen ['vaʃən] (*unreg*) *vt, vi* to wash ♦ *vr*
to (have a) wash; **sich** *dat* **die Hände ~**
to wash one's hands

Wäsche'rei *f* laundry

Wasch- *zW:* **~gelegenheit** *f* washing
facilities; **~küche** *f* laundry room;
~lappen *m* face flannel, washcloth (*US*);
(*umg*) sissy; **~maschine** *f* washing
machine; **~mittel** *nt* detergent, washing
powder; **~pulver** *nt* detergent, washing
powder; **~raum** *m* washroom; **~salon** *m*
Launderette ®

Wasser ['vasər] (**-s, -**) *nt* water; **~ball** *m*

water polo; **w~dicht** *adj* waterproof; **~fall**
m waterfall; **~farbe** *f* watercolour; **~hahn**
m tap, faucet (*US*); **~kraftwerk** *nt*
hydroelectric power station; **~leitung** *f*
water pipe; **~mann** *n* (*ASTROL*) Aquarius

wässern ['vɛsərn] *vt, vi* to water

Wasser- *zW:* **w~scheu** *adj* afraid of (the)
water; **~ski** ['vasərʃiː] *nt* water-skiing;
~stoff *m* hydrogen; **~waage** *f* spirit level;
~zeichen *nt* watermark

wässrig ▲ ['vɛsrɪç] *adj* watery

Watt [vat] (**-(e)s, -en**) *nt* mud flats *pl*

Watte *f* cotton wool, absorbent cotton (*US*)

WC ['veːˈtseː] (**-s, -s**) *nt abk* W.C.

Web [vɛb] (**-s**) *nt* (*COMPUT*) **das ~** the Web

Web- ['veːb] *zW:* **w~en** (*unreg*) *vt* to weave;
~er (**-s, -**) *m* weaver; **~e'rei** *f* (*Betrieb*)
weaving mill

Website ['vɛbsaɪt] *f* (*COMPUT*) website

Webstuhl ['veːpʃtuːl] *m* loom

Wechsel ['vɛksəl] (**-s, -**) *m* change; (*COMM*)
bill of exchange; **~geld** *nt* change; **w~haft**
adj (*Wetter*) variable; **~jahre** *pl* change of
life *sg;* **~kurs** *m* rate of exchange; **w~n** *vt*
to change; (*Blicke*) to exchange ♦ *vi* to
change; to vary; (*Geldwechseln*) to have
change; **~strom** *m* alternating current;
~stube *f* bureau de change; **~wirkung** *f*
interaction

Weck- ['vɛk] *zW:* **~dienst** *m* alarm call
service; **w~en** *vt* to wake (up); to call; **~er**
(**-s, -**) *m* alarm clock

wedeln ['veːdəln] *vi* (*mit Schwanz*) to wag;
(*mit Fächer etc*) to wave

weder ['veːdər] *konj* neither; **~ ... noch ...**
neither ... nor ...

Weg [veːk] (**-(e)s, -e**) *m* way; (*Pfad*) path;
(*Route*) route; **sich auf den ~ machen** to
be on one's way; **jdm aus dem ~ gehen**
to keep out of sb's way; *siehe* **zuwege**

weg [vɛk] *adv* away, off; **über etw** *akk* **~
sein** to be over sth; **er war schon ~** he
had already left; **Finger ~!** hands off!

wegbleiben (*unreg*) *vi* to stay away

wegen ['veːgən] *präp* +*gen* (*umg:* +*dat*)
because of

weg- ['vɛk] *zW:* **~fallen** (*unreg*) *vi* to be left

out; (*Ferien, Bezahlung*) to be cancelled; (*aufhören*) to cease; **~gehen** (*unreg*) *vi* to go away; to leave; **~lassen** (*unreg*) *vt* to leave out; **~laufen** (*unreg*) *vi* to run away *od* off; **~legen** *vt* to put aside; **~machen** (*umg*) *vt* to get rid of; **~müssen** (*unreg*; *umg*) *vi* to have to go; **~nehmen** (*unreg*) *vt* to take away; **~tun** (*unreg*) *vt* to put away; **W~weiser (-s, -)** *m* road sign, signpost; **~werfen** (*unreg*) *vt* to throw away

weh [ve:] *adj* sore; **~(e)** *excl*: **~(e), wenn du ...** woe betide you if ...; **o ~!** oh dear!; **~e!** just you dare!

wehen *vt, vi* to blow; (*Fahnen*) to flutter

weh- *zW*: **~leidig** *adj* whiny, whining; **~mütig** *adj* melancholy

Wehr [ve:r] **(-, -en)** *f*: **sich zur ~ setzen** to defend o.s.; **~dienst** *m* military service; **~dienstverweigerer** *m* ≃ conscientious objector; **w~en** *vr* to defend o.s.; **w~los** *adj* defenceless; **~pflicht** *f* compulsory military service; **w~pflichtig** *adj* liable for military service

---
Wehrdienst

ⓘ **Wehrdienst** *is military service which is still compulsory in Germany. All young men receive their call-up papers at 18 and all those pronounced physically fit are required to spend 10 months in the Bundeswehr. Conscientious objectors are allowed to do Zivildienst as an alternative, after presenting their case.*

---

wehtun ▲ ['ve:tu:n] (*unreg*) *vt* to hurt, to be sore; **jdm/sich ~** to hurt sb/o.s.

Weib [vaip] **(-(e)s, -er)** *nt* woman, female; wife; **~chen** *nt* female; **w~lich** *adj* feminine

weich [vaiç] *adj* soft; **W~e** *f* points *pl*; **~en** (*unreg*) *vi* to yield, to give way; **W~heit** *f* softness; **~lich** *adj* soft, namby-pamby

Weide ['vaidə] *f* (*Baum*) willow; (*Gras*) pasture; **w~n** *vi* to graze ♦ *vr*: **sich an etw** *dat* **w~n** to delight in sth

weigern ['vaigərn] *vr* to refuse

Weigerung ['vaigəruŋ] *f* refusal

Weihe ['vaiə] *f* consecration; (*Priesterweihe*) ordination; **w~n** *vt* to consecrate; to ordain

Weihnacht- *zW*: **~en (-)** *nt* Christmas; **w~lich** *adj* Christmas *cpd*

Weihnachts- *zW*: **~abend** *m* Christmas Eve; **~lied** *nt* Christmas carol; **~mann** *m* Father Christmas, Santa Claus; **~markt** *m* Christmas fair; **~tag** *m* Christmas Day; **zweiter ~tag** Boxing Day

---
Weihnachtsmarkt

ⓘ *The* **Weihnachtsmarkt** *is a market held in most large towns in Germany in the weeks prior to Christmas. People visit it to buy presents, toys and Christmas decorations, and to enjoy the festive atmosphere. Traditional Christmas food and drink can also be consumed there, for example,* Lebkuchen *and* Glühwein.

Weihwasser *nt* holy water

weil [vail] *konj* because

Weile ['vailə] **(-)** *f* while, short time

Wein [vain] **(-(e)s, -e)** *m* wine; (*Pflanze*) vine; **~bau** *m* cultivation of vines; **~berg** *m* vineyard; **~bergschnecke** *f* snail; **~brand** *m* brandy

weinen *vt, vi* to cry; **das ist zum W~** it's enough to make you cry *od* weep

Wein- *zW*: **~glas** *nt* wine glass; **~karte** *f* wine list; **~lese** *f* vintage; **~probe** *f* wine-tasting; **~rebe** *f* vine; **w~rot** *adj* burgundy, claret, wine-red; **~stock** *m* vine; **~stube** *f* wine bar; **~traube** *f* grape

weise ['vaizə] *adj* wise

Weise *f* manner, way; (*Lied*) tune; **auf diese ~** in this way

weisen (*unreg*) *vt* to show

Weisheit ['vaishait] *f* wisdom; **~szahn** *m* wisdom tooth

weiß [vais] *adj* white ♦ *vb siehe* **wissen**; **W~bier** *nt* weissbier (*light, fizzy beer made using top-fermentation yeast*); **W~brot** *nt* white bread; **~en** *vt* to whitewash; **W~glut** *f* (*TECH*) incandescence; **jdn bis zur W~glut bringen** (*fig*) to make sb see red; **W~kohl**

m (white) cabbage; **W~wein** *m* white wine; **W~wurst** *f* veal sausage

weit [vaɪt] *adj* wide; (*Begriff*) broad; (*Reise, Wurf*) long ♦ *adv* far; **wie ~ ist es ...?** how far is it ...?; **in ~er Ferne** in the far distance; **~ blickend** far-seeing; **~ reichend** long-range; (*fig*) far-reaching; **~ verbreitet** widespread; **das geht zu ~** that's going too far; **~aus** *adv* by far; **~blickend** *adj* far-seeing; **W~e** *f* width; (*Raum*) space; (*von Entfernung*) distance; **~en** *vt, vr* to widen

weiter ['vaɪtər] *adj* wider; broader; farther (away); (*zusätzlich*) further ♦ *adv* further; **ohne ~es** without further ado; just like that; **~ nichts/niemand** nothing/nobody else; **~arbeiten** *vi* to go on working; **~bilden** *vr* to continue one's education; **~empfehlen** (*unreg*) *vt* to recommend (to others); **W~fahrt** *f* continuation of the journey; **~führen** *vi* (*Straße*) to lead on (to) ♦ *vt* (*fortsetzen*) to continue, carry on; **~gehen** (*unreg*) *vi* to go on; **~hin** *adv*: **etw ~hin tun** to go on doing sth; **~kommen** (*unreg*) *vi* (*fig: mit Arbeit*) to make progress; **~leiten** *vt* to pass on; **~machen** *vt, vi* to continue

weit- *zW*: **~gehend** *adj* considerable ♦ *adv* largely; **~läufig** *adj* (*Gebäude*) spacious; (*Erklärung*) lengthy; (*Verwandter*) distant; **~reichend** *adj* long-range; (*fig*) far-reaching; **~schweifig** *adj* long-winded; **~sichtig** *adj* (*MED*) long-sighted; (*fig*) far-sighted; **W~sprung** *m* long jump; **~verbreitet** *adj* widespread

Weizen ['vaɪtsən] (*-s, -*) *m* wheat

welche(r, s) *interrogativ pron* which; **welcher von beiden?** which (one) of the two?; **welchen hast du genommen?** which (one) did you take?; **welche eine ...!** what a ...!; **welche Freude!** what joy!
♦ *indef pron* some; (*in Fragen*) any; **ich habe welche** I have some; **haben Sie welche?** do you have any?
♦ *relativ pron* (*bei Menschen*) who; (*bei*

Sachen) which, that; **welche(r, s) auch immer** whoever/whichever/whatever

welk [vɛlk] *adj* withered; **~en** *vi* to wither

Welle ['vɛlə] *f* wave; (*TECH*) shaft

Wellen- *zW*: **~bereich** *m* waveband; **~länge** *f* (*auch fig*) wavelength; **~linie** *f* wavy line; **~sittich** *m* budgerigar

Welt [vɛlt] (*-, -en*) *f* world; **~all** *nt* universe; **~anschauung** *f* philosophy of life; **w~berühmt** *adj* world-famous; **~krieg** *m* world war; **w~lich** *adj* worldly; (*nicht kirchlich*) secular; **~macht** *f* world power; **~meister** *m* world champion; **~raum** *m* space; **~reise** *f* trip round the world; **~stadt** *f* metropolis; **w~weit** *adj* world-wide

wem [ve:m] (*dat von wer*) *pron* to whom

wen [ve:n] (*akk von wer*) *pron* whom

Wende ['vɛndə] *f* turn; (*Veränderung*) change; **~kreis** *m* (*GEOG*) tropic; (*AUT*) turning circle; **~ltreppe** *f* spiral staircase; **w~n** (*unreg*) *vt, vi, vr* to turn; **sich an jdn w~n** to go/come to sb

wendig ['vɛndɪç] *adj* (*Auto etc*) manœuvrable; (*fig*) agile

Wendung *f* turn; (*Redewendung*) idiom

wenig ['ve:nɪç] *adj, adv* little; **~e** *pron pl* few *pl*; **~er** *adj* less; (*mit pl*) fewer ♦ *adv* less; **~ste(r, s)** *adj* least; **am ~sten** least; **~stens** *adv* at least

wenn [vɛn] *konj* **1** (*falls, bei Wünschen*) if; **wenn auch ..., selbst wenn ...** even if ...; **wenn ich doch ...** if only I ...

2 (*zeitlich*) when; **immer wenn** whenever

wennschon ['vɛnʃoːn] *adv*: **na ~** so what?; **~, dennschon!** in for a penny, in for a pound

wer [ve:r] *pron* who

Werbe- ['vɛrbə] *zW*: **~fernsehen** *nt* commercial television; **~geschenk** *nt* gift (*from company*); (*zu Gekauftem*) free gift; **w~n** (*unreg*) *vt* to win; (*Mitglied*) to recruit ♦ *vi* to advertise; **um jdn/etw w~n** to try to win sb/sth; **für jdn/etw w~n** to promote sb/sth

Werbung f advertising; (von Mitgliedern) recruitment; **~ um jdn/etw** promotion of sb/sth

Werdegang ['vɛːrdəgan] m (Laufbahn) development; (beruflich) career

SCHLÜSSELWORT

werden ['vɛːrdən] (pt **wurde**, pp **geworden** od (bei Passiv) **worden**) vi to become; **was ist aus ihm/aus der Sache geworden?** what became of him/it?; **es ist nichts/gut geworden** it came to nothing/turned out well; **es wird Nacht/Tag** it's getting dark/light; **mir wird kalt** I'm getting cold; **mir wird schlecht** I feel ill; **Erster werden** to come od be first; **das muss anders werden** that'll have to change; **rot/zu Eis werden** to turn red/to ice; **was willst du (mal) werden?** what do you want to be?; **die Fotos sind gut geworden** the photos have come out nicely

♦ als Hilfsverb **1** (bei Futur): **er wird es tun** he will od he'll do it; **er wird das nicht tun** he will not od he won't do it; **es wird gleich regnen** it's going to rain

2 (bei Konjunktiv): **ich würde ...** I would ...; **er würde gern ...** he would od he'd like to ...; **ich würde lieber ...** I would od I'd rather ...

3 (bei Vermutung): **sie wird in der Küche sein** she will be in the kitchen

4 (bei Passiv): **gebraucht werden** to be used; **er ist erschossen worden** he has od he's been shot; **mir wurde gesagt, dass ...** I was told that ...

werfen ['vɛrfən] (unreg) vt to throw

Werft [vɛrft] (-, -en) f shipyard, dockyard

Werk [vɛrk] (-(e)s, -e) nt work; (Tätigkeit) job; (Fabrik, Mechanismus) works pl; **ans ~ gehen** to set to work; **~statt** (-, -stätten) f workshop; (AUT) garage; **~tag** m working day; **w~tags** adv on working days; **w~tätig** adj working; **~zeug** nt tool

Wermut ['vɛːrmuːt] (-(e)s) m wormwood;

(Wein) vermouth

Wert [veːrt] (-(e)s, -e) m worth; (FIN) value; **~ legen auf** +akk to attach importance to; **es hat doch keinen ~** it's useless; **w~** adj worth; (geschätzt) dear; worthy; **das ist nichts/viel w~** it's not worth anything/it's worth a lot; **das ist es/er mir w~** it's/he's worth that to me; **~angabe** f declaration of value; **~brief** m registered letter (containing sth of value); **w~en** vt to rate; **~gegenstände** mpl valuables; **w~los** adj worthless; **~papier** nt security; **w~voll** adj valuable

Wesen ['veːzən] (-s, -) nt (Geschöpf) being; (Natur, Charakter) nature; **w~tlich** adj significant; (beträchtlich) considerable

weshalb [vɛs'halp] adv why

Wespe ['vɛspə] f wasp

wessen ['vɛsən] (gen von **wer**) pron whose

Weste ['vɛstə] f waistcoat, vest (US); (Wollweste) cardigan

West- zW: **~en** (-s) m west; **~europa** nt Western Europe; **w~lich** adj western ♦ adv to the west

weswegen [vɛs've:gən] adv why

wett [vɛt] adj even; **W~bewerb** m competition; **W~e** f bet, wager; **~en** vt, vi to bet

Wetter ['vɛtər] (-s, -) nt weather; **~bericht** m weather report; **~dienst** m meteorological service; **~lage** f (weather) situation; **~vorhersage** f weather forecast; **~warte** f weather station

Wett- zW: **~kampf** m contest; **~lauf** m race; **w~machen** vt to make good

wichtig ['vɪçtɪç] adj important; **W~keit** f importance

wickeln ['vɪkəln] vt to wind; (Haare) to set; (Kind) to change; **jdn/etw in etw** akk **~ to** wrap sb/sth in sth

Wickelraum m mothers' (and babies') room

Widder ['vɪdər] (-s, -) m ram; (ASTROL) Aries

wider ['vi:dər] präp +akk against; **~'fahren** (unreg) vi to happen; **~'legen** vt to refute

widerlich ['vi:dərlıç] adj disgusting, repulsive

wider- ['viːdər] *zW:* **~rechtlich** *adj*
unlawful; **W~rede** *f* contradiction; **~'rufen**
(*unreg*) *vt insep* to retract; (*Anordnung*) to
revoke; (*Befehl*) to countermand; **~'setzen**
vr insep: **sich jdm/etw ~setzen** to oppose
sb/sth

widerspenstig ['viːdərʃpɛnstɪç] *adj* wilful

wider- ['viːdər] *zW:* **~spiegeln** *vt*
(*Entwicklung, Erscheinung*) to mirror, reflect
♦ *vr* to be reflected; **~'sprechen** (*unreg*) *vi*
insep: **jdm ~sprechen** to contradict sb

Widerspruch ['viːdərʃprʊx] *m*
contradiction; **w~slos** *adv* without arguing

Widerstand ['viːdərʃtant] *m* resistance

Widerstands- *zW:* **~bewegung** *f*
resistance (movement); **~fähig** *adj*
resistant, tough; **w~los** *adj* unresisting

wider'stehen (*unreg*) *vi insep:* **jdm/etw ~**
to withstand sb/sth

wider- ['viːdər] *zW:* **~wärtig** *adj* nasty,
horrid; **W~wille** *m:* **W~wille (gegen)**
aversion (to); **~willig** *adj* unwilling,
reluctant

widmen ['vɪtmən] *vt* to dedicate; to devote
♦ *vr* to devote o.s.

widrig ['viːdrɪç] *adj* (*Umstände*) adverse

| SCHLÜSSELWORT |
---

wie [viː] *adv* how; **wie groß/schnell?** how
big/fast?; **wie wärs?** how about it?; **wie ist
er?** what's he like?; **wie gut du das
kannst!** you're very good at it; **wie bitte?**
pardon?; (*entrüstet*) I beg your pardon!;
und wie! and how!; **wie viel** how much;
wie viel Menschen how many people;
wie weit to what extent

♦ *konj* **1** (*bei Vergleichen*): **so schön wie ...**
as beautiful as ...; **wie ich schon sagte** as I
said; **wie du** like you; **singen wie ein ...** to
sing like a ...; **wie (zum Beispiel)** such as
(for example)

2 (*zeitlich*): **wie er das hörte, ging er**
when he heard that he left; **er hörte, wie
der Regen fiel** he heard the rain falling

wieder ['viːdər] *adv* again; **~ da sein** to be
back (again); **~ aufbereiten** to recycle; **~**

aufnehmen to resume; **~ erkennen** to
recognize; **~ gutmachen** to make up for;
(*Fehler*) to put right; **~ herstellen** (*Ruhe,
Frieden etc*) to restore; **~ vereinigen** to
reunite; (*POL*) to reunify; **~ verwerten** to
recycle; **gehst du schon ~?** are you off
again?; **~ ein(e) ...** another ...; **W~aufbau**
m rebuilding; **~bekommen** (*unreg*) *vt* to
get back; **W~gabe** *f* reproduction;
~geben (*unreg*) *vt* (*zurückgeben*) to return;
(*Erzählung etc*) to repeat; (*Gefühle etc*) to
convey; **W~'gutmachung** *f* reparation;
~'herstellen *vt* (*Gesundheit, Gebäude*) to
restore; **~'holen** *vt insep* to repeat;
W~'holung *f* repetition; **W~hören** *nt:* **auf
W~hören** (*TEL*) goodbye; **W~kehr** (-) *f*
return; (*von Vorfall*) repetition, recurrence;
~sehen (*unreg*) *vt* to see again; **auf
W~sehen** goodbye; **~um** *adv* again;
(*andererseits*) on the other hand;
W~vereinigung *f* (*POL*) reunification;
W~wahl *f* re-election

Wiege ['viːgə] *f* cradle; **w~n**[1] *vt* (*schaukeln*)
to rock

wiegen[2] (*unreg*) *vt, vi* (*Gewicht*) to weigh

Wien [viːn] *nt* Vienna

Wiese ['viːzə] *f* meadow

Wiesel ['viːzəl] (**-s, -**) *nt* weasel

wieso [viˈzoː] *adv* why

wieviel △ [viːˈfiːl] *adj siehe* **wie**

wievielmal [viːˈfiːlmaːl] *adv* how often

wievielte(r, s) *adj:* **zum ~n Mal?** how
many times?; **den W~n haben wir?** what's
the date?; **an ~r Stelle?** in what place?;
der ~ Besucher war er? how many
visitors were there before him?

wild [vɪlt] *adj* wild; **W~ (-(e)s)** *nt* game;
W~e(r) ['vɪldə(r)] *f(m)* savage; **~ern** *vi* to
poach; **~'fremd** (*umg*) *adj* quite strange *od*
unknown; **W~heit** *f* wildness; **W~leder** *nt*
suede; **W~nis** (-, **-se**) *f* wilderness;
W~schwein *nt* (wild) boar .

will *etc* [vɪl] *vb siehe* **wollen**

Wille ['vɪlə] (**-ns, -n**) *m* will; **w~n** *präp +gen:*
um ... w~n for the sake of ...; **w~nsstark**
adj strong-willed

will- *zW:* **~ig** *adj* willing; **W~kommen**

[vɪl'kɔmən] **(-s, -)** *nt* welcome; **~kommen** *adj* welcome; **jdn ~kommen heißen** to welcome sb; **~kürlich** *adj* arbitrary; *(Bewegung)* voluntary

wimmeln ['vɪməln] *vi*: **~ (von)** to swarm (with)

wimmern ['vɪmərn] *vi* to whimper

Wimper ['vɪmpər] **(-, -n)** *f* eyelash

Wimperntusche *f* mascara

Wind [vɪnt] **(-(e)s, -e)** *m* wind; **~beutel** *m* cream puff; *(fig)* rake; **~e** *f (TECH)* winch, windlass; *(BOT)* bindweed; **~el** ['vɪndəl] **(-, -n)** *f* nappy, diaper *(US)*; **w~en** *vi unpers* to be windy ♦ *vt (unreg)* to wind; *(Kranz)* to weave; *(entwinden)* to twist ♦ *vr (unreg)* to wind; *(Person)* to writhe; **~energie** *f* wind energy; **w~ig** ['vɪndɪç] *adj* windy; *(fig)* dubious; **~jacke** *f* windcheater; **~mühle** *f* windmill; **~pocken** *pl* chickenpox *sg*; **~schutzscheibe** *f (AUT)* windscreen *(BRIT)*, windshield *(US)*; **~stärke** *f* wind force; **w~still** *adj (Tag)* still, windless; *(Platz)* sheltered; **~stille** *f* calm; **~stoß** *m* gust of wind

Wink [vɪŋk] **(-(e)s, -e)** *m (mit Hand)* wave; *(mit Kopf)* nod; *(Hinweis)* hint

Winkel ['vɪŋkəl] **(-s, -)** *m (MATH)* angle; *(Gerät)* set square; *(in Raum)* corner

winken ['vɪŋkən] *vt, vi* to wave

winseln ['vɪnzəln] *vi* to whine

Winter ['vɪntər] **(-s, -)** *m* winter; **w~fest** *adj (Pflanze)* hardy; **~garten** *m* conservatory; **w~lich** *adj* wintry; **~reifen** *m* winter tyre; **~sport** *m* winter sports *pl*

Winzer ['vɪntsər] **(-s, -)** *m* vine grower

winzig ['vɪntsɪç] *adj* tiny

Wipfel ['vɪpfəl] **(-s, -)** *m* treetop

wir [viːr] *pron* we; **~ alle** all of us, we all

Wirbel ['vɪrbəl] **(-s, -)** *m* whirl, swirl; *(Trubel)* hurly-burly; *(Aufsehen)* fuss; *(ANAT)* vertebra; **w~n** *vi* to whirl, to swirl; **~säule** *f* spine

wird [vɪrt] *vb siehe* **werden**

wirfst *etc* [vɪrfst] *vb siehe* **werfen**

wirken ['vɪrkən] *vi* to have an effect; *(erfolgreich sein)* to work; *(scheinen)* to seem ♦ *vt (Wunder)* to work

wirklich ['vɪrklɪç] *adj* real ♦ *adv* really;

W~keit *f* reality

wirksam ['vɪrkzaːm] *adj* effective

Wirkstoff *m (biologisch, chemisch, pflanzlich)* active substance

Wirkung ['vɪrkʊŋ] *f* effect; **w~slos** *adj* ineffective; **w~slos bleiben** to have no effect; **w~svoll** *adj* effective

wirr [vɪr] *adj* confused, wild; **W~warr (-s)** *m* disorder, chaos

wirst [vɪrst] *vb siehe* **werden**

Wirt(in) [vɪrt(ɪn)] **(-(e)s, -e)** *m(f)* landlord(lady); **~schaft** *f (Gaststätte)* pub; *(Haushalt)* housekeeping; *(eines Landes)* economy; *(umg: Durcheinander)* mess; **w~schaftlich** *adj* economical; *(POL)* economic

Wirtschafts- *zW*: **~krise** *f* economic crisis; **~politik** *f* economic policy; **~prüfer** *m* chartered accountant; **~wunder** *nt* economic miracle

Wirtshaus *nt* inn

wischen ['vɪʃən] *vt* to wipe

Wischer (-s, -) *m (AUT)* wiper

Wissbegier(de) ▲ ['vɪsbəgiːr(də)] *f* thirst for knowledge; **wissbegierig** ▲ *adj* inquisitive, eager for knowledge

wissen ['vɪsən] **(unreg)** *vt* to know; **was weiß ich!** I don't know!; **W~ (-s)** *nt* knowledge; **W~schaft** *f* science; **W~schaftler(in) (-s, -)** *m(f)* scientist; **~schaftlich** *adj* scientific; **~swert** *adj* worth knowing

wittern ['vɪtərn] *vt* to scent; *(fig)* to suspect

Witterung *f* weather; *(Geruch)* scent

Witwe ['vɪtvə] *f* widow; **~r (-s, -)** *m* widower

Witz [vɪts] **(-(e)s, -e)** *m* joke; **~bold (-(e)s, -e)** *m* joker, wit; **w~ig** *adj* funny

wo [voː] *adv* where; *(umg: irgendwo)* somewhere; **im Augenblick, ~ ...** the moment (that) ...; **die Zeit, ~ ...** the time when ...; **~anders** [voː|andərs] *adv* elsewhere; **~bei** [-'baɪ] *adv (relativ)* by/with which; *(interrogativ)* what ... in/by/with

Woche ['vɔxə] *f* week

Wochen- **~ende** *nt* weekend; **w~lang** *adj, adv* for weeks; **~markt** *m* weekly market; **~schau** *f* newsreel

wöchentlich ['vœçəntlıç] *adj, adv* weekly
wodurch [vo'dʊrç] *adv* (*relativ*) through
which; (*interrogativ*) what ... through
wofür [vo'fy:r] *adv* (*relativ*) for which;
(*interrogativ*) what ... for
wog *etc* [vo:k] *vb siehe* **wiegen**
wo- [vo:] *zW:* **~'gegen** *adv* (*relativ*) against
which; (*interrogativ*) what ... against; **~her**
[-'he:r] *adv* where ... from; **~hin** [-'hın] *adv*
where ... to

wohl [vo:l] *adv* **1**: **sich wohl fühlen**
(*zufrieden*) to feel happy; (*gesundheitlich*) to
feel well; **jdm wohl tun** to do sb good;
wohl oder übel whether one likes it or not
2 (*wahrscheinlich*) probably; (*gewiss*)
certainly; (*vielleicht*) perhaps; **sie ist wohl
zu Hause** she's probably at home; **das ist
doch wohl nicht dein Ernst!** surely you're
not serious!; **das mag wohl sein** that may
well be; **ob das wohl stimmt?** I wonder if
that's true; **er weiß das sehr wohl** he
knows that perfectly well

Wohl [vo:l] **(-(e)s)** *nt* welfare; **zum ~!**
cheers!; **w~auf** *adv* well; **~behagen** *nt*
comfort; **~fahrt** *f* welfare; **~fahrtsstaat** *m*
welfare state; **w~habend** *adj* wealthy;
w~ig *adj* contented, comfortable;
w~schmeckend *adj* delicious; **~stand** *m*
prosperity; **~standsgesellschaft** *f*
affluent society; **~tat** *f* relief; act of charity;
~täter(in) *m(f)* benefactor; **w~tätig** *adj*
charitable; **~tätigkeits-** *zW* charity,
charitable; **w~tun** (*unreg*) *vi* △ *siehe* **wohl**;
w~verdient *adj* well-earned, well-
deserved; **w~weislich** *adv* prudently;
~wollen (-s) *nt* good will; **w~wollend** *adj*
benevolent
wohn- ['vo:n] *zW:* **~en** *vi* to live;
W~gemeinschaft *f* (*Menschen*) people
sharing a flat; **~haft** *adj* resident; **W~heim**
nt (*für Studenten*) hall of residence; (*für
Senioren*) home; (*bes für Arbeiter*) hostel;
~lich *adj* comfortable; **W~mobil (-s, -e)**
nt camper; **W~ort** *m* domicile; **W~sitz** *m*

place of residence; **W~ung** *f* house;
(*Etagenwohnung*) flat, apartment (*US*);
W~wagen *m* caravan; **W~zimmer** *nt*
living room
wölben ['vœlbən] *vt, vr* to curve
Wolf [vɔlf] **(-(e)s, ²e)** *m* wolf
Wolke ['vɔlkə] *f* cloud; **~nkratzer** *m*
skyscraper; **wolkig** ['vɔlkıç] *adj* cloudy
Wolle ['vɔlə] *f* wool; **w~n¹** *adj* woollen

wollen² ['vɔlən] (*pt* **wollte**, *pp* **gewollt** *od*
(*als Hilfsverb*) **wollen**) *vt, vi* to want; **ich
will nach Hause** I want to go home; **er
will nicht** he doesn't want to; **er wollte
das nicht** he didn't want it; **wenn du
willst** if you like; **ich will, dass du mir
zuhörst** I want you to listen to me
♦ *Hilfsverb*: **er will ein Haus kaufen** he
wants to buy a house; **ich wollte, ich wäre
...** I wish I were ...; **etw gerade tun wollen**
to be going to do sth

wollüstig ['vɔlʏstıç] *adj* lusty, sensual
wo- *zW:* **~mit** *adv* (*relativ*) with which;
(*interrogativ*) what ... with; **~möglich** *adv*
probably, I suppose; **~nach** *adv* (*relativ*)
after/for which; (*interrogativ*) what ... for/
after; **~ran** *adv* (*relativ*) on/at which;
(*interrogativ*) what ... on/at; **~rauf** *adv*
(*relativ*) on which; (*interrogativ*) what ... on;
~raus *adv* (*relativ*) from/out of which;
(*interrogativ*) what ... from/out of; **~rin** *adv*
(*relativ*) in which; (*interrogativ*) what ... in
Wort [vɔrt] **(-(e)s, ²er** *od* **-e)** *nt* word; **jdn
beim ~ nehmen** to take sb at his word;
mit anderen ~en in other words;
w~brüchig *adj* not true to one's word
Wörterbuch ['vœrtərbu:x] *nt* dictionary
Wort- *zW:* **~führer** *m* spokesman; **w~karg**
adj taciturn; **~laut** *m* wording
wörtlich ['vœrtlıç] *adj* literal
Wort- *zW:* **w~los** *adj* mute; **w~reich** *adj*
wordy, verbose; **~schatz** *m* vocabulary;
~spiel *nt* play on words, pun
wo- *zW:* **~rüber** *adv* (*relativ*) over/about
which; (*interrogativ*) what ... over/about;

~rum adv (relativ) about/round which; (interrogativ) what ... about/round; **~runter** adv (relativ) under which; (interrogativ) what ... under; **~von** adv (relativ) from which; (interrogativ) what ... from; **~vor** adv (relativ) in front of/before which; (interrogativ) in front of/before what; of what; **~zu** adv (relativ) to/for which; (interrogativ) what ... for/to; (warum) why

Wrack [vrak] (-(e)s, -s) nt wreck

Wucher ['vu:xər] (-s) m profiteering; **~er** (-s, -) m profiteer; **w~isch** adj profiteering; **w~n** vi (Pflanzen) to grow wild; **~ung** f (MED) growth, tumour

Wuchs [vu:ks] (-es) m (Wachstum) growth; (Statur) build

Wucht [vʊxt] (-) f force

wühlen ['vy:lən] vi to scrabble; (Tier) to root; (Maulwurf) to burrow; (umg: arbeiten) to slave away ♦ vt to dig

Wulst [vʊlst] (-es, ⁻e) m bulge; (an Wunde) swelling

wund [vʊnt] adj sore, raw; **W~e** f wound

Wunder ['vʊndər] (-s, -) nt miracle; **es ist kein ~** it's no wonder; **w~bar** adj wonderful, marvellous; **~kerze** f sparkler; **~kind** nt infant prodigy; **w~lich** adj odd, peculiar; **w~n** vr to be surprised ♦ vt to surprise; **sich w~n über** +akk to be surprised at; **w~schön** adj beautiful; **w~voll** adj wonderful

Wundstarrkrampf ['vʊntʃtarkrampf] m tetanus, lockjaw

Wunsch [vʊnʃ] (-(e)s, ⁻e) m wish

wünschen ['vʏnʃən] vt to wish; **sich** dat **etw ~** to want sth, to wish for sth; **~swert** adj desirable

wurde etc ['vʊrdə] vb siehe **werden**

Würde ['vʏrdə] f dignity; (Stellung) honour; **w~voll** adj dignified

würdig ['vʏrdɪç] adj worthy; (würdevoll) dignified; **~en** vt to appreciate

Wurf [vʊrf] (-s, ⁻e) m throw; (Junge) litter

Würfel ['vʏrfəl] (-s, -) m dice; (MATH) cube; **~becher** m (dice) cup; **w~n** vi to play dice ♦ vt to dice; **~zucker** m lump sugar

würgen ['vʏrgən] vt, vi to choke

Wurm [vʊrm] (-(e)s, ⁻er) m worm; **w~stichig** adj worm-ridden

Wurst [vʊrst] (-, ⁻e) f sausage; **das ist mir ~** (umg) I don't care, I don't give a damn

Würstchen ['vʏrstçən] nt sausage

Würze ['vʏrtsə] f seasoning, spice

Wurzel ['vʊrtsəl] (-, -n) f root

würzen ['vʏrtsən] vt to season, to spice

würzig adj spicy

wusch etc [vʊʃ] vb siehe **waschen**

wusste ▲ etc ['vʊstə] vb siehe **wissen**

wüst [vy:st] adj untidy, messy; (ausschweifend) wild; (öde) waste; (umg: heftig) terrible; **W~e** f desert

Wut [vu:t] (-) f rage, fury; **~anfall** m fit of rage

wüten ['vy:tən] vi to rage; **~d** adj furious, mad

X, x

X-Beine ['ɪksbaɪnə] pl knock-knees

x-beliebig [ɪksbə'li:bɪç] adj any (whatever)

xerokopieren [kseroko'pi:rən] vt to xerox, to photocopy

x-mal ['ɪksma:l] adv any number of times, n times

Xylofon ▲, **Xylophon** [ksylo'fo:n] (-s, -e) nt xylophone

Y, y

Yacht (-, -en) f siehe **Jacht**

Ypsilon ['ʏpsilɔn] (-(s), -s) nt the letter Y

Z, z

Zacke ['tsakə] f point; (Bergzacke) jagged peak; (Gabelzacke) prong; (Kammzacke) tooth

zackig ['tsakɪç] adj jagged; (umg) smart; (Tempo) brisk

zaghaft ['tsa:khaft] adj timid

zäh [tsɛ:] adj tough; (Mensch) tenacious;

(*Flüssigkeit*) thick; (*schleppend*) sluggish;
Z~igkeit *f* toughness; tenacity
Zahl [tsa:l] (**-, -en**) *f* number; **z~bar** *adj*
payable; **z~en** *vt, vi* to pay; **z~en bitte!** the
bill please!
zählen ['tsε:lən] *vt, vi* to count; **~ auf** +*akk*
to count on; **~ zu** to be numbered among
Zahlenschloss ▲ *nt* combination lock
Zähler ['tsε:lər] (**-s, -**) *m* (*TECH*) meter;
(*MATH*) numerator
Zahl- *zW:* **z~los** *adj* countless; **z~reich** *adj*
numerous; **~tag** *m* payday; **~ung** *f*
payment; **~ungsanweisung** *f* giro
transfer order; **z~ungsfähig** *adj* solvent;
~wort *nt* numeral
zahm [tsa:m] *adj* tame
zähmen ['tsε:mən] *vt* to tame; (*fig*) to curb
Zahn [tsa:n] (**-(e)s, ⁻e**) *m* tooth; **~arzt** *m*
dentist; **~ärztin** *f* (female) dentist;
~bürste *f* toothbrush; **~fleisch** *nt* gums
pl; **~pasta** *f* toothpaste; **~rad** *nt*
cog(wheel); **~schmerzen** *pl* toothache *sg*;
~stein *m* tartar; **~stocher** (**-s, -**) *m*
toothpick
Zange ['tsaŋə] *f* pliers *pl*; (*Zuckerzange etc*)
tongs *pl*; (*Beißzange, ZOOL*) pincers *pl*; (*MED*)
forceps *pl*
zanken ['tsaŋkən] *vi, vr* to quarrel
zänkisch ['tsεŋkɪʃ] *adj* quarrelsome
Zäpfchen ['tsεpfçən] *nt* (*ANAT*) uvula; (*MED*)
suppository
Zapfen ['tsapfən] (**-s, -**) *m* plug; (*BOT*) cone;
(*Eiszapfen*) icicle
zappeln ['tsapəln] *vi* to wriggle; to fidget
zart [tsa:rt] *adj* (*weich, leise*) soft; (*Fleisch*)
tender; (*fein, schwächlich*) delicate; **Z~heit** *f*
softness; tenderness; delicacy
zärtlich ['tsε:rtlɪç] *adj* tender, affectionate
Zauber ['tsaubər] (**-s, -**) *m* magic; (*~bann*)
spell; **~ei** [-'rai] *f* magic; **~er** (**-s, -**) *m*
magician; conjuror; **z~haft** *adj* magical,
enchanting; **~künstler** *m* conjuror;
~kunststück *nt* conjuring trick; **z~n** *vi* to
conjure, to practise magic
zaudern ['tsaudərn] *vi* to hesitate
Zaum [tsaum] (**-(e)s, Zäume**) *m* bridle; *etw*
im ~ halten to keep sth in check

Zaun [tsaun] (**-(e)s, Zäune**) *m* fence
z. B. *abk* (= *zum Beispiel*) e.g.
Zebra ['tse:bra] *nt* zebra; **~streifen** *m* zebra
crossing
Zeche ['tsεçə] *f* (*Rechnung*) bill; (*Bergbau*)
mine
Zeh [tse:] (**-s, -en**) *m* toe
Zehe ['tse:ə] *f* toe; (*Knoblauchzehe*) clove
zehn [tse:n] *num* ten; **~te(r, s)** *adj* tenth;
Z~tel (**-s, -**) *nt* tenth (part)
Zeich- ['tsaiç] *zW:* **~en** (**-s, -**) *nt* sign;
z~nen *vt* to draw; (*kennzeichnen*) to mark;
(*unterzeichnen*) to sign ♦ *vi* to draw; to sign;
~ner (**-s, -**) *m* artist; **technischer ~ner**
draughtsman; **~nung** *f* drawing;
(*Markierung*) markings *pl*
Zeige- ['tsaigə] *zW:* **~finger** *m* index finger;
z~n *vt* to show ♦ *vi* to point ♦ *vr* to show
o.s.; **z~n auf** +*akk* to point to; to point at;
es wird sich z~n time will tell; **es zeigte**
sich, dass ... it turned out that ...; **~r** (**-s,**
-) *m* pointer; (*Uhrzeiger*) hand
Zeile ['tsailə] *f* line; (*Häuserzeile*) row
Zeit [tsait] (**-, -en**) *f* time; (*GRAM*) tense; *sich*
dat **~ lassen** to take one's time; **von ~ zu**
from time to time; *siehe* **zurzeit**; **~alter** *nt*
age; **~ansage** *f* (*TEL*) speaking clock;
~arbeit *f* (*COMM*) temporary job;
z~gemäß *adj* in keeping with the times;
~genosse *m* contemporary; **z~ig** *adj*
early; **z~lich** *adj* temporal; **~lupe** *f* slow
motion; **z~raubend** *adj* time-consuming;
~raum *m* period; **~rechnung** *f* time, era;
nach/vor unserer ~rechnung A.D./B.C.;
~schrift *f* periodical; **~ung** *f* newspaper;
~vertreib *m* pastime, diversion; **z~weilig**
adj temporary; **z~weise** *adv* for a time;
~wort *nt* verb
Zelle ['tsεlə] *f* cell; (*Telefonzelle*) callbox
Zellstoff *m* cellulose
Zelt [tsεlt] (**-(e)s, -e**) *nt* tent; **z~en** *vi* to
camp; **~platz** *m* camp site
Zement [tse'mεnt] (**-(e)s, -e**) *m* cement;
z~ieren *vt* to cement
zensieren [tsεn'zi:rən] *vt* to censor; (*SCH*) to
mark
Zensur [tsεn'zu:r] *f* censorship; (*SCH*) mark

Zentimeter [tsɛntiˈmeːtər] *m od nt* centimetre

Zentner [ˈtsɛntnər] **(-s, -)** *m* hundredweight

zentral [tsɛnˈtraːl] *adj* central; **Z~e** *f* central office; (*TEL*) exchange; **Z~heizung** *f* central heating

Zentrum [ˈtsɛntrʊm] **(-s, Zentren)** *nt* centre

zerbrechen [tsɛrˈbrɛçən] (*unreg*) *vt, vi* to break

zerbrechlich *adj* fragile

zer'drücken *vt* to squash, to crush; (*Kartoffeln*) to mash

Zeremonie [tseremoˈniː] *f* ceremony

Zerfall [tsɛrˈfal] *m* decay; **z~en** (*unreg*) *vi* to disintegrate, to decay; (*sich gliedern*): **z~en (in** +*akk*) to fall (into)

zer'gehen (*unreg*) *vi* to melt, to dissolve

zerkleinern [tsɛrˈklaɪnərn] *vt* to reduce to small pieces

zerlegbar [tsɛrˈleːkbaːr] *adj* able to be dismantled

zerlegen [tsɛrˈleːgən] *vt* to take to pieces; (*Fleisch*) to carve; (*Satz*) to analyse

zermürben [tsɛrˈmʏrbən] *vt* to wear down

zerquetschen [tsɛrˈkvɛtʃən] *vt* to squash

zer'reißen (*unreg*) *vt* to tear to pieces ♦ *vi* to tear, to rip

zerren [ˈtsɛrən] *vt* to drag ♦ *vi:* **~ (an** +*dat*) to tug (at)

zer'rinnen (*unreg*) *vi* to melt away

zerrissen [tsɛrˈrɪsən] *adj* torn, tattered; **Z~heit** *f* tattered state; (*POL*) disunion, discord; (*innere Z~heit*) disintegration

Zerrung *f* (*MED*): **eine ~** pulled muscle

zerrütten [tsɛrˈrʏtən] *vt* to wreck, to destroy

zer'schlagen (*unreg*) *vt* to shatter, to smash ♦ *vr* to fall through

zer'schneiden (*unreg*) *vt* to cut up

zer'setzen *vt, vr* to decompose, to dissolve

zer'springen (*unreg*) *vi* to shatter, to burst

Zerstäuber [tsɛrˈʃtɔʏbər] **(-s, -)** *m* atomizer

zerstören [tsɛrˈʃtøːrən] *vt* to destroy

Zerstörung *f* destruction

zerstreu- [tsɛrˈʃtrɔʏ] *zW:* **~en** *vt* to disperse, to scatter; (*unterhalten*) to divert; (*Zweifel etc*) to dispel ♦ *vr* to disperse, to scatter; to be dispelled; **~t** *adj* scattered; (*Mensch*)

absent-minded; **Z~theit** *f* absent-mindedness; **Z~ung** *f* dispersion; (*Ablenkung*) diversion

zerstückeln [tsɛrˈʃtʏkəln] *vt* to cut into pieces

zer'teilen *vt* to divide into parts

Zertifikat [tsɛrtifiˈkaːt] **(-(e)s, -e)** *nt* certificate

zer'treten (*unreg*) *vt* to crush underfoot

zertrümmern [tsɛrˈtrʏmərn] *vt* to shatter; (*Gebäude etc*) to demolish

Zettel [ˈtsɛtəl] **(-s, -)** *m* piece of paper, slip; (*Notizzettel*) note; (*Formular*) form

Zeug [tsɔʏk] **(-(e)s, -e)** (*umg*) *nt* stuff; (*Ausrüstung*) gear; **dummes ~** ▲ (*stupid*) nonsense; **das ~ haben zu** to have the makings of; **sich ins ~ legen** to put one's shoulder to the wheel

Zeuge [ˈtsɔʏgə] **(-n, -n)** *m* witness; **z~n** *vi* to bear witness, to testify ♦ *vt* (*Kind*) to father; **es zeugt von ...** it testifies to ...; **~naussage** *f* evidence; **Zeugin** [ˈtsɔʏgɪn] *f* witness

Zeugnis [ˈtsɔʏgnɪs] **(-ses, -se)** *nt* certificate; (*SCH*) report; (*Referenz*) reference; (*Aussage*) evidence, testimony; **~ geben von** to be evidence of, to testify to

z. H(d). *abk* (= *zu Händen*) attn.

Zickzack [ˈtsɪktsak] **(-(e)s, -e)** *m* zigzag

Ziege [ˈtsiːgə] *f* goat

Ziegel [ˈtsiːgəl] **(-s, -)** *m* brick; (*Dachziegel*) tile

ziehen [ˈtsiːən] (*unreg*) *vt* to draw; (*zerren*) to pull; (*SCHACH etc*) to move; (*züchten*) to rear ♦ *vi* to draw; (*umziehen, wandern*) to move; (*Rauch, Wolke etc*) to drift; (*reißen*) to pull ♦ *vb unpers:* **es zieht** there is a draught, it's draughty ♦ *vr* (*Gummi*) to stretch; (*Grenze etc*) to run; (*Gespräche*) to be drawn out; **etw nach sich ~** to lead to sth, to entail sth

Ziehung [ˈtsiːʊŋ] *f* (*Losziehung*) drawing

Ziel [tsiːl] **(-(e)s, -e)** *nt* (*einer Reise*) destination; (*SPORT*) finish; (*MIL*) target; (*Absicht*) goal; **z~bewusst** ▲ *adj* decisive; **z~en** *vi:* **z~en (auf** +*akk*) to aim (at); **z~los** *adj* aimless; **~scheibe** *f* target; **z~strebig**

adj purposeful

ziemlich ['tsiːmlıç] *adj* quite a; fair ♦ *adv* rather; quite a bit

zieren ['tsiːrən] *vr* to act coy

zierlich ['tsiːrlıç] *adj* dainty

Ziffer ['tsıfər] (-, -n) *f* figure, digit; **~blatt** *nt* dial, clock-face

zig [tsık] (*umg*) *adj* umpteen

Zigarette [tsiga'rɛtə] *f* cigarette

Zigaretten- *zW:* **~automat** *m* cigarette machine; **~schachtel** *f* cigarette packet; **~spitze** *f* cigarette holder

Zigarre [tsi'garə] *f* cigar

Zigeuner(in) [tsi'gɔynər(ın)] (-s, -) *m(f)* gipsy

Zimmer ['tsımər] (-s, -) *nt* room; **~lautstärke** *f* reasonable volume; **~mädchen** *nt* chambermaid; **~mann** *m* carpenter; **z~n** *vt* to make (from wood); **~nachweis** *m* accommodation office; **~pflanze** *f* indoor plant; **~service** *m* room service

zimperlich ['tsımpərlıç] *adj* squeamish; (*pingelig*) fussy, finicky

Zimt [tsımt] (-(e)s, -e) *m* cinnamon

Zink [tsıŋk] (-(e)s) *nt* zinc

Zinn [tsın] (-(e)s) *nt* (*Element*) tin; (*in ~waren*) pewter; **~soldat** *m* tin soldier

Zins [tsıns] (-es, -en) *m* interest; **~eszins** *m* compound interest; **~fuß** *m* rate of interest; **z~los** *adj* interest-free; **~satz** *m* rate of interest

Zipfel ['tsıpfəl] (-s, -) *m* corner; (*spitz*) tip; (*Hemdzipfel*) tail; (*Wurstzipfel*) end

zirka ['tsırka] *adv* (round) about

Zirkel ['tsırkəl] (-s, -) *m* circle; (*MATH*) pair of compasses

Zirkus ['tsırkus] (-, -se) *m* circus

zischen ['tsıʃən] *vi* to hiss

Zitat [tsi'taːt] (-(e)s, -e) *nt* quotation, quote

zitieren [tsi'tiːrən] *vt* to quote

Zitrone [tsi'troːnə] *f* lemon; **~nlimonade** *f* lemonade; **~nsaft** *m* lemon juice

zittern ['tsıtərn] *vi* to tremble

zivil [tsi'viːl] *adj* civil; (*Preis*) moderate; **Z~** (-s) *nt* plain clothes *pl*; (*MIL*) civilian clothing; **Z~courage** *f* courage of one's convictions;

Z~dienst *m* community service; **Z~isation** [tsivilizatsi'oːn] *f* civilization; **Z~isationskrankheit** *f* disease peculiar to civilization; **~i'sieren** *vt* to civilize

---
Zivildienst

ⓘ A young German has to complete his 13 months' **Zivildienst** or service to the community if he has opted out of military service as a conscientious objector. This is usually done in a hospital or old people's home. About 18% of young Germans choose to do this as an alternative to the **Wehrdienst**.

Zivilist [tsivi'lıst] *m* civilian

zögern ['tsøːgərn] *vi* to hesitate

Zoll [tsɔl] (-(e)s, ⁻e) *m* customs *pl*; (*Abgabe*) duty; **~abfertigung** *f* customs clearance; **~amt** *nt* customs office; **~beamte(r)** *m* customs official; **~erklärung** *f* customs declaration; **z~frei** *adj* duty-free; **~kontrolle** *f* customs check; **z~pflichtig** *adj* liable to duty, dutiable

Zone ['tsoːnə] *f* zone

Zoo [tsoː] (-s, -s) *m* zoo; **~loge** [tsoo'loːgə] (-n, -n) *m* zoologist; **~lo'gie** *f* zoology; **z~'logisch** *adj* zoological

Zopf [tsɔpf] (-(e)s, ⁻e) *m* plait; pigtail; **alter ~** antiquated custom

Zorn [tsɔrn] (-(e)s) *m* anger; **z~ig** *adj* angry

zottig ['tsɔtıç] *adj* shaggy

z. T. *abk* = **zum Teil**

SCHLÜSSELWORT

zu [tsuː] *präp +dat* **1** (*örtlich*) to; **zum Bahnhof/Arzt gehen** to go to the station/ doctor; **zur Schule/Kirche gehen** to go to school/church; **sollen wir zu euch gehen?** shall we go to your place?; **sie sah zu ihm hin** she looked towards him; **zum Fenster herein** through the window; **zu meiner Linken** to *od* on my left

2 (*zeitlich*) at; **zu Ostern** at Easter; **bis zum 1. Mai** until May 1st; (*nicht später als*) by May 1st; **zu meiner Zeit** in my time

3 (*Zusatz*) with; **Wein zum Essen trinken**

---

to drink wine with one's meal; **sich zu jdm setzen** to sit down beside sb; **setz dich doch zu uns** (come and) sit with us; **Anmerkungen zu etw** notes on sth **4** (*Zweck*) for; **Wasser zum Waschen** water for washing; **Papier zum Schreiben** paper to write on; **etw zum Geburtstag bekommen** to get sth for one's birthday **5** (*Veränderung*) into; **zu etw werden** to turn into sth; **jdn zu etw machen** to make sb (into) sth; **zu Asche verbrennen** to burn to ashes **6** (*mit Zahlen*): **3 zu 2** (*SPORT*) 3-2; **das Stück zu 2 Mark** at 2 marks each; **zum ersten Mal** for the first time **7**: **zu meiner Freude** *etc* to my joy *etc*; **zum Glück** luckily; **zu Fuß** on foot; **es ist zum Weinen** it's enough to make you cry ♦ *konj* to; **etw zu essen** sth to eat; **um besser sehen zu können** in order to see better; **ohne es zu wissen** without knowing it; **noch zu bezahlende Rechnungen** bills that are still to be paid ♦ *adv* **1** (*allzu*) too; **zu sehr** too much; **zu viel** too much; **zu wenig** too little **2** (*örtlich*) toward(s); **er kam auf mich zu** he came up to me **3** (*geschlossen*) shut, closed; **die Geschäfte haben zu** the shops are closed; **„auf/zu"** (*Wasserhahn etc*) "on/off" **4** (*umg: los*): **nur zu!** just keep on!; **mach zu!** hurry up!

zualler- [tsuˈalər] *zW:* **~erst** [-ˈǀeːrst] *adv* first of all; **~letzt** [-ˈletst] *adv* last of all
Zubehör [ˈtsuːbəhøːr] (**-(e)s, -e**) *nt* accessories *pl*
zubereiten [ˈtsuːbəraɪtən] *vt* to prepare
zubilligen [ˈtsuːbɪlɪgən] *vt* to grant
zubinden [ˈtsuːbɪndən] (*unreg*) *vt* to tie up
zubringen [ˈtsuːbrɪŋən] (*unreg*) *vt* (*Zeit*) to spend
Zubringer (**-s, -**) *m* (*Straße*) approach *od* slip road
Zucchini [tsuˈkiːni] *pl* (*BOT, KOCH*) courgette (*BRIT*), zucchini (*US*)
Zucht [tsʊxt] (**-, -en**) *f* (*von Tieren*) breeding;

(*von Pflanzen*) cultivation; (*Rasse*) breed; (*Erziehung*) raising; (*Disziplin*) discipline
züchten [ˈtsʏçtən] *vt* (*Tiere*) to breed; (*Pflanzen*) to cultivate, to grow; **Züchter** (**-s, -**) *m* breeder; grower
Zuchthaus *nt* prison, penitentiary (*US*)
züchtigen [ˈtsʏçtɪgən] *vt* to chastise
Züchtung *f* (*Zuchtart, Sorte: von Tier*) breed; (*: von Pflanze*) variety
zucken [ˈtsʊkən] *vi* to jerk, to twitch; (*Strahl etc*) to flicker ♦ *vt* (*Schultern*) to shrug
Zucker [ˈtsʊkər] (**-s, -**) *m* sugar; (*MED*) diabetes; **~guss** ▲ *m* icing; **z~krank** *adj* diabetic; **~krankheit** *f* (*MED*) diabetes; **z~n** *vt* to sugar; **~rohr** *nt* sugar cane; **~rübe** *f* sugar beet
Zuckung [ˈtsʊkʊŋ] *f* convulsion, spasm; (*leicht*) twitch
zudecken [ˈtsuːdɛkən] *vt* to cover (up)
zudem [tsuˈdeːm] *adv* in addition (to this)
zudringlich [ˈtsuːdrɪŋlɪç] *adj* forward, pushing, obtrusive
zudrücken [ˈtsuːdrʏkən] *vt* to close; **ein Auge ~** to turn a blind eye
zueinander [tsuʔaɪˈnandər] *adv* to one other; (*in Verbindung*) together
zuerkennen [ˈtsuːʔɛrkɛnən] (*unreg*) *vt* to award; **jdm etw ~** to award sth to sb, to award sb sth
zuerst [tsuˈʔeːrst] *adv* first; (*zu Anfang*) at first; **~ einmal** first of all
Zufahrt [ˈtsuːfaːrt] *f* approach; **~sstraße** *f* approach road; (*von Autobahn etc*) slip road
Zufall [ˈtsuːfal] *m* chance; (*Ereignis*) coincidence; **durch ~** by accident; **so ein ~** what a coincidence; **z~en** (*unreg*) *vi* to close, to shut; (*Anteil, Aufgabe*) to fall
zufällig [ˈtsuːfɛlɪç] *adj* chance ♦ *adv* by chance; (*in Frage*) by any chance
Zuflucht [ˈtsuːflʊxt] *f* recourse; (*Ort*) refuge
zufolge [tsuˈfɔlgə] *präp* (+*dat od gen*) judging by; (*laut*) according to
zufrieden [tsuˈfriːdən] *adj* content(ed), satisfied; **~ geben** to be content *od* satisfied (with); **~ stellen** to satisfy
zufrieren [ˈtsuːfriːrən] (*unreg*) *vi* to freeze up *od* over

zufügen ['tsuːfyːgən] *vt* to add; (*Leid etc*): **(jdm) etw ~** to cause (sb) sth

Zufuhr ['tsuːfuːr] (-, -en) *f* (*Herbeibringen*) supplying; (*MET*) influx

Zug [tsuːk] (-(e)s, ⁼e) *m* (*EISENB*) train; (*Luftzug*) draught; (*Ziehen*) pull(ing); (*Gesichtszug*) feature; (*SCHACH etc*) move; (*Schriftzug*) stroke; (*Atemzug*) breath; (*Charakterzug*) trait; (*an Zigarette*) puff, pull, drag; (*Schluck*) gulp; (*Menschengruppe*) procession; (*von Vögeln*) flight; (*MIL*) platoon; **etw in vollen Zügen genießen** to enjoy sth to the full

Zu- ['tsuː] *zW:* **~gabe** *f* extra; (*in Konzert etc*) encore; **~gang** *m* access, approach; **z~gänglich** *adj* accessible; (*Mensch*) approachable

zugeben ['tsuːgeːbən] (*unreg*) *vt* (*beifügen*) to add, to throw in; (*zugestehen*) to admit; (*erlauben*) to permit

zugehen ['tsuːgeːən] (*unreg*) *vi* (*schließen*) to shut; **es geht dort seltsam zu** there are strange goings-on there; **auf jdn/etw ~** to walk towards sb/sth; **dem Ende ~** to be finishing

Zugehörigkeit ['tsuːgəhøːrɪçkaɪt] *f:* **~ (zu)** membership (of), belonging (to)

Zügel ['tsyːgəl] (-s, -) *m* rein(s); (*fig*) curb; **z~n** *vt* to curb; (*Pferd*) to rein in

zuge- ['tsuːgə] *zW:* **Z~ständnis (-ses, -se)** *nt* concession; **~stehen** (*unreg*) *vt* to admit; (*Rechte*) to concede

Zugführer *m* (*EISENB*) guard

zugig ['tsuːgɪç] *adj* draughty

zügig ['tsyːgɪç] *adj* speedy, swift

zugreifen ['tsuːgraɪfən] (*unreg*) *vi* to seize *od* grab at; (*helfen*) to help; (*beim Essen*) to help o.s.

Zugrestaurant *nt* dining car

zugrunde, zu Grunde [tsuːˈgrundə] *adv:* **~ gehen** to collapse; (*Mensch*) to perish; **einer Sache** *dat* **etw ~ legen** to base sth on sth; **einer Sache** *dat* **~ liegen** to be based on sth; **~ richten** to ruin, to destroy

zugunsten, zu Gunsten [tsuːˈgunstən] *präp* (+*gen od dat*) in favour of

zugute [tsuːˈguːtə] *adv:* **jdm etw ~ halten** to concede sth to sb; **jdm ~ kommen** to be of assistance to sb

Zugvogel *m* migratory bird

zuhalten ['tsuːhaltən] (*unreg*) *vt* to keep closed ♦ *vi:* **auf jdn/etw ~** to make a beeline for sb/sth

Zuhälter ['tsuːhɛltər] (-s, -) *m* pimp

Zuhause [tsuːˈhauzə] (-) *nt* home

zuhause [tsuːˈhauzə] *adv* (*österreichisch, schweizerisch*) at home

zuhören ['tsuːhøːrən] *vi* to listen

Zuhörer (-s, -) *m* listener

zukleben ['tsuːkleːbən] *vt* to paste up

zukommen ['tsuːkɔmən] (*unreg*) *vi* to come up; **auf jdn ~** to come up to sb; **jdm etw ~ lassen** to give sb sth; **etw auf sich ~ lassen** to wait and see; **jdm ~** (*sich gehören*) to be fitting for sb

Zukunft ['tsuːkunft] (-, Zukünfte) *f* future; **zukünftig** ['tsuːkynftɪç] *adj* future ♦ *adv* in future; **mein zukünftiger Mann** my husband to be

Zulage ['tsuːlaːgə] *f* bonus

zulassen ['tsuːlasən] (*unreg*) *vt* (*hereinlassen*) to admit; (*erlauben*) to permit; (*Auto*) to license; (*umg: nicht öffnen*) to (keep) shut

zulässig ['tsuːlɛsɪç] *adj* permissible, permitted

Zulassung *f* (*amtlich*) authorization; (*von Kfz*) licensing

zulaufen ['tsuːlaufən] (*unreg*) *vi* (*subj: Mensch*): **~ auf jdn/etw** to run up to sb/sth; (: *Straße*): **~ auf** to lead towards

zuleide, zu Leide [tsuːˈlaɪdə] *adv:* **jdm etw ~ tun** to hurt *od* harm sb

zuletzt [tsuːˈlɛtst] *adv* finally, at last

zuliebe [tsuːˈliːbə] *adv:* **jdm ~** to please sb

zum [tsum] = **zu dem**; **~ dritten Mal** for the third time; **~ Scherz** as a joke; **~ Trinken** for drinking

zumachen ['tsuːmaxən] *vt* to shut; (*Kleidung*) to do up, to fasten ♦ *vi* to shut; (*umg*) to hurry up

zu- *zW:* **~mal** [tsuːˈmaːl] *konj* especially (as); **~meist** [tsuːˈmaɪst] *adv* mostly; **~mindest** [tsuːˈmɪndəst] *adv* at least

zumutbar ['tsu:mu:tba:r] *adj* reasonable

zumute, zu Mute [tsu'mu:tə] *adv:* **wie ist ihm ~?** how does he feel?

zumuten ['tsu:mu:tən] *vt:* **(jdm) etw ~** to expect *od* ask sth (of sb)

Zumutung ['tsu:mu:tʊŋ] *f* unreasonable expectation *od* demand, impertinence

zunächst [tsu'nɛ:çst] *adv* first of all; **~ einmal** to start with

Zunahme ['tsu:na:mə] *f* increase

Zuname ['tsu:na:mə] *m* surname

Zünd- [tsynd] *zW:* **z~en** *vi* (*Feuer*) to light, to ignite; (*Motor*) to fire; (*begeistern*): **bei jdm z~en** to fire sb (with enthusiasm); **z~end** *adj* fiery; **~er (-s, -)** *m* fuse; (*MIL*) detonator; **~holz** ['tsynt-] *nt* match; **~kerze** *f* (*AUT*) spark(ing) plug; **~schloss** ▲ *nt* ignition lock; **~schlüssel** *m* ignition key; **~schnur** *f* fuse wire; **~stoff** *m* (*fig*) inflammatory stuff; **~ung** *f* ignition

zunehmen ['tsu:ne:mən] (*unreg*) *vi* to increase, to grow; (*Mensch*) to put on weight

Zuneigung ['tsu:naigʊŋ] *f* affection

Zunft [tsʊnft] (-, ⸚e) *f* guild

zünftig ['tsynftiç] *adj* proper, real; (*Handwerk*) decent

Zunge ['tsʊŋə] *f* tongue

zunichte [tsu'niçtə] *adv:* **~ machen** to ruin, to destroy; **~ werden** to come to nothing

zunutze, zu Nutze [tsu'nʊtsə] *adv:* **sich** *dat* **etw ~ machen** to make use of sth

zuoberst [tsu'lo:bərst] *adv* at the top

zupfen ['tsʊpfən] *vt* to pull, to pick, to pluck; (*Gitarre*) to pluck

zur [tsu:r] = **zu der**

zurate, zu Rate [tsu'ra:tə] *adv:* **jdn ~ ziehen** to consult sb

zurechnungsfähig ['tsu:reçnʊŋsfe:iç] *adj* responsible, accountable

zurecht- [tsu'rɛçt] *zW:* **~finden** (*unreg*) *vr* to find one's way (about); **~kommen** (*unreg*) *vi* to (be able to) cope, to manage; **~legen** *vt* to get ready; (*Ausrede etc*) to have ready; **~machen** *vt* to prepare ♦ *vr* to get ready; **~weisen** (*unreg*) *vt* to reprimand

zureden ['tsu:re:dən] *vi:* **jdm ~** to persuade *od* urge sb

zurück [tsu'rʏk] *adv* back; **~behalten** (*unreg*) *vt* to keep back; **~bekommen** (*unreg*) *vt* to get back; **~bleiben** (*unreg*) *vi* (*Mensch*) to remain behind; (*nicht nachkommen*) to fall behind, to lag; (*Schaden*) to remain; **~bringen** (*unreg*) *vt* to bring back; **~fahren** (*unreg*) *vi* to travel back; (*vor Schreck*) to recoil, to start ♦ *vt* to drive back; **~finden** (*unreg*) *vi* to find one's way back; **~fordern** *vt* to demand back; **~führen** *vt* to lead back; **etw auf etw** *akk* **~führen** to trace sth back to sth; **~geben** (*unreg*) *vt* to give back; (*antworten*) to retort with; **~geblieben** *adj* retarded; **~gehen** (*unreg*) *vi* to go back; (*fallen*) to go down, to fall; (*zeitlich*): **~gehen (auf** +*akk*) to date back (to); **~gezogen** *adj* retired, withdrawn; **~halten** (*unreg*) *vt* to hold back; (*Mensch*) to restrain; (*hindern*) to prevent ♦ *vr* (*reserviert sein*) to be reserved; (*im Essen*) to hold back; **~haltend** *adj* reserved; **Z~haltung** *f* reserve; **~kehren** *vi* to return; **~kommen** (*unreg*) *vi* to come back; **auf etw** *akk* **~kommen** to return to sth; **~lassen** (*unreg*) *vt* to leave behind; **~legen** *vt* to put back; (*Geld*) to put by; (*reservieren*) to keep back; (*Strecke*) to cover; **~nehmen** (*unreg*) *vt* to take back; **~stellen** *vt* to put back, to replace; (*aufschieben*) to put off, to postpone; (*Interessen*) to defer; (*Ware*) to keep; **~treten** (*unreg*) *vi* to step back; (*vom Amt*) to retire; **gegenüber etw** *od* **hinter etw** *dat* **~treten** to diminish in importance in view of sth; **~weisen** (*unreg*) *vt* to turn down; (*Mensch*) to reject; **~zahlen** *vt* to repay, to pay back; **~ziehen** (*unreg*) *vt* to pull back; (*Angebot*) to withdraw ♦ *vr* to retire

Zuruf ['tsu:ru:f] *m* shout, cry

zurzeit [tsʊr'tsait] *adv* at the moment

Zusage ['tsu:za:gə] *f* promise; (*Annahme*) consent; **z~n** *vt* to promise ♦ *vi* to accept; **jdm z~n** (*gefallen*) to agree with *od* please sb

zusammen [tsu'zamən] *adv* together;

Z~**arbeit** f cooperation; ~**arbeiten** vi to cooperate; ~**beißen** (unreg) vt (Zähne) to clench; ~**brechen** (unreg) vi to collapse; (Mensch auch) to break down; ~**bringen** (unreg) vt to bring od get together; (Geld) to get; (Sätze) to put together; Z~**bruch** m collapse; ~**fassen** vt to summarize; (vereinigen) to unite; Z~**fassung** f summary, résumé; ~**fügen** vt to join (together), to unite; ~**halten** (unreg) vi to stick together; Z~**hang** m connection; **im/aus dem Z~hang** in/out of context; ~**hängen** (unreg) vi to be connected od linked; ~**kommen** (unreg) vi to meet, to assemble; (sich ereignen) to occur at once od together; ~**legen** vt to put together; (stapeln) to pile up; (falten) to fold; (verbinden) to combine, to unite; (Termine, Fest) to amalgamate; (Geld) to collect; ~**nehmen** (unreg) vt to summon up ♦ vr to pull o.s. together; **alles ~genommen** all in all; ~**passen** vi to go well together, to match; ~**schließen** (unreg) vt, vr to join (together); Z~**schluss** ▲ m amalgamation; ~**schreiben** (unreg) vt to write as one word; (Bericht) to put together; Z~**sein** (-s) nt get-together; ~**setzen** vt to put together ♦ vr (Stoff) to be composed of; (Menschen) to get together; Z~**setzung** f composition; ~**stellen** vt to put together; to compile; Z~**stoß** m collision; ~**stoßen** (unreg) vi to collide; ~**treffen** (unreg) vi to coincide; (Menschen) to meet; Z~**treffen** nt coincidence; meeting; ~**zählen** vt to add up; ~**ziehen** (unreg) vt (verengern) to draw together; (vereinigen) to bring together; (addieren) to add up ♦ vr to shrink; (sich bilden) to form, to develop

zusätzlich ['tsu:zɛtslɪç] adj additional ♦ adv in addition

zuschauen ['tsu:ʃaʊən] vi to watch, to look on; **Zuschauer(in)** (-s, -) m(f) spectator ♦ pl (THEAT) audience sg

zuschicken ['tsu:ʃɪkən] vt: **(jdm etw)** ~ to send od to forward (sth to sb)

Zuschlag ['tsu:ʃla:k] m extra charge,

surcharge; **z~en** (unreg) vt (Tür) to slam; (Ball) to hit; (bei Auktion) to knock down; (Steine etc) to knock into shape ♦ vi (Fenster, Tür) to shut; (Mensch) to hit, to punch; ~**karte** f (EISENB) surcharge ticket; **z~pflichtig** adj subject to surcharge

zuschneiden ['tsu:ʃnaɪdən] (unreg) vt to cut out; to cut to size

zuschrauben ['tsu:ʃraʊbən] vt to screw down od up

zuschreiben ['tsu:ʃraɪbən] (unreg) vt (fig) to ascribe, to attribute; (COMM) to credit

Zuschrift ['tsu:ʃrɪft] f letter, reply

zuschulden, zu Schulden [tsu'ʃuldən] adv: **sich** dat **etw ~ kommen lassen** to make o.s. guilty of sth

Zuschuss ▲ ['tsu:ʃʊs] m subsidy, allowance

zusehen ['tsu:ze:ən] (unreg) vi to watch; (dafür sorgen) to take care; **jdm/etw ~** to watch sb/sth; ~**ds** adv visibly

zusenden ['tsu:zɛndən] (unreg) vt to forward, to send on

zusichern ['tsu:zɪçərn] vt: **jdm etw ~** to assure sb of sth

zuspielen ['tsu:ʃpi:lən] vt, vi to pass

zuspitzen ['tsu:ʃpɪtsən] vt to sharpen ♦ vr (Lage) to become critical

zusprechen ['tsu:ʃprɛçən] (unreg) vt (zuerkennen) to award ♦ vi to speak; **jdm etw ~** to award sb sth od sth to sb; **jdm Trost ~** to comfort sb; **dem Essen/ Alkohol ~** to eat/drink a lot

Zustand ['tsu:ʃtant] m state, condition

zustande, zu Stande [tsu'ʃtandə] adv: ~ **bringen** to bring about; ~ **kommen** to come about

zuständig ['tsu:ʃtɛndɪç] adj responsible; Z~**keit** f competence, responsibility

zustehen ['tsu:ʃte:ən] (unreg) vi: **jdm ~** to be sb's right

zustellen ['tsu:ʃtɛlən] vt (verstellen) to block; (Post etc) to send

Zustellung f delivery

zustimmen ['tsu:ʃtɪmən] vi to agree

Zustimmung f agreement, consent

zustoßen ['tsu:ʃto:sən] (unreg) vi (fig) to happen

zutage, zu Tage [tsuˈtaːgə] *adv*: ~ **bringen** to bring to light; ~ **treten** to come to light

Zutaten [ˈtsuːtaːtən] *pl* ingredients

zuteilen [ˈtsuːtaɪlən] *vt* (*Arbeit, Rolle*) to designate, assign; (*Aktien, Wohnung*) to allocate

zutiefst [tsuˈtiːfst] *adv* deeply

zutragen [ˈtsuːtraːgən] (*unreg*) *vt* to bring; (*Klatsch*) to tell ♦ *vr* to happen

zutrau- [ˈtsuːtraʊ] *zW*: **Z~en (-s)** *nt*: **Z~en (zu)** trust (in); **~en** *vt*: **jdm etw ~en** to credit sb with sth; **~lich** *adj* trusting, friendly

zutreffen [ˈtsuːtrɛfən] (*unreg*) *vi* to be correct; to apply; **~d** *adj* (*richtig*) accurate; **Z~des bitte unterstreichen** please underline where applicable

Zutritt [ˈtsuːtrɪt] *m* access, admittance

Zutun [ˈtsuːtuːn] (-s) *nt* assistance

zuverlässig [ˈtsuːfɛrlɛsɪç] *adj* reliable; **Z~keit** *f* reliability

zuversichtlich [ˈtsuːfɛrzɪçtlɪç] *adj* confident

zuvor [tsuˈfoːr] *adv* before, previously; **~kommen** (*unreg*) *vi* +*dat* to anticipate; **jdm ~kommen** to beat sb to it; **~kommend** *adj* obliging, courteous

Zuwachs [ˈtsuːvaks] (-es) *m* increase, growth; (*umg*) addition; **z~en** (*unreg*) *vi* to become overgrown; (*Wunde*) to heal (up)

zuwege, zu Wege [tsuˈveːgə] *adv*: **etw ~ bringen** to accomplish sth

zuweilen [tsuˈvaɪlən] *adv* at times, now and then

zuweisen [ˈtsuːvaɪzən] (*unreg*) *vt* to assign, to allocate

zuwenden [ˈtsuːvɛndən] (*unreg*) *vt* (+*dat*) to turn (towards) ♦ *vr*: **sich jdm/etw ~** to devote o.s. to sb/sth; to turn to sb/sth

zuwider [tsuˈviːdər] *adv*: **etw ist jdm ~** sb loathes sth, sb finds sth repugnant; **~handeln** *vi*: **einer Sache** *dat* **~handeln** to act contrary to sth; **einem Gesetz ~handeln** to contravene a law

zuziehen [ˈtsuːtsiːən] (*unreg*) *vt* (*schließen*: *Vorhang*) to draw, to close; (*herbeirufen*: *Experten*) to call in ♦ *vi* to move in, to

come; **sich** *dat* **etw ~** (*Krankheit*) to catch sth; (*Zorn*) to incur sth

zuzüglich [ˈtsuːtsyːklɪç] *präp* +*gen* plus, with the addition of

Zwang [tsvaŋ] (**-(e)s, ⁀e**) *m* compulsion, coercion

zwängen [ˈtsvɛŋən] *vt, vr* to squeeze

zwanglos *adj* informal

Zwangs- *zW*: **~arbeit** *f* forced labour; (*Strafe*) hard labour; **~lage** *f* predicament, tight corner; **z~läufig** *adj* necessary, inevitable

zwanzig [ˈtsvantsɪç] *num* twenty

zwar [tsvaːr] *adv* to be sure, indeed; **das ist ~ ..., aber ...** that may be ... but ...; **und ~ am Sonntag** on Sunday to be precise; **und ~ so schnell, dass ...** in fact so quickly that ...

Zweck [tsvɛk] (**-(e)s, -e**) *m* purpose, aim; **es hat keinen ~** there's no point; **z~dienlich** *adj* practical; expedient

Zwecke *f* hobnail; (*Heftzwecke*) drawing pin, thumbtack (*US*)

Zweck- *zW*: **z~los** *adj* pointless; **z~mäßig** *adj* suitable, appropriate; **z~s** *präp* +*gen* for the purpose of

zwei [tsvaɪ] *num* two; **Z~bettzimmer** *nt* twin room; **~deutig** *adj* ambiguous; (*unanständig*) suggestive; **~erlei** *adj*: **~erlei Stoff** two different kinds of material; **~erlei Meinung** of differing opinions; **~fach** *adj* double

Zweifel [ˈtsvaɪfəl] (**-s, -**) *m* doubt; **z~haft** *adj* doubtful, dubious; **z~los** *adj* doubtless; **z~n** *vi*: **(an etw** *dat***) z~n** to doubt (sth)

Zweig [tsvaɪk] (**-(e)s, -e**) *m* branch; **~stelle** *f* branch (office)

zwei- *zW*: **~hundert** *num* two hundred; **~mal** *adv* twice; **~sprachig** *adj* bilingual; **~spurig** *adj* (*AUT*) two-lane; **~stimmig** *adj* for two voices

zweit [tsvaɪt] *adv*: **zu ~** together; (*bei mehreren Paaren*) in twos

zweitbeste(r, s) *adj* second best

zweite(r, s) *adj* second

zweiteilig [ˈtsvaɪtaɪlɪç] *adj* (*Gruppe*) two-piece; (*Fernsehfilm*) two-part; (*Kleidung*) two-piece

zweit- *zW:* **~ens** *adv* secondly; **~größte(r, s)** *adj* second largest; **~klassig** *adj* second-class; **~letzte(r, s)** *adj* last but one, penultimate; **~rangig** *adj* second-rate

Zwerchfell ['tsverçfel] *nt* diaphragm

Zwerg [tsverk] (-(e)s, -e) *m* dwarf

Zwetsch(g)e ['tsvetʃ(g)ə] *f* plum

Zwieback ['tsvi:bak] (-(e)s, -e) *m* rusk

Zwiebel ['tsvi:bəl] (-, -n) *f* onion; (*Blumenzwiebel*) bulb

Zwie- ['tsvi:] *zW:* **z~lichtig** *adj* shady, dubious; **z~spältig** *adj* (*Gefühle*) conflicting; (*Charakter*) contradictory; **~tracht** *f* discord, dissension

Zwilling ['tsvilɪŋ] (-s, -e) *m* twin; **~e** *pl* (*ASTROL*) Gemini

zwingen ['tsvɪŋən] (*unreg*) *vt* to force; **~d** *adj* (*Grund etc*) compelling

zwinkern ['tsvɪŋkərn] *vi* to blink; (*absichtlich*) to wink

Zwirn [tsvɪrn] (-(e)s, -e) *m* thread

zwischen ['tsvɪʃən] *präp* (+*akk od dat*)

between; **Z~bemerkung** *f* (incidental) remark; **Z~ding** *nt* cross; **~durch** *adv* in between; (*räumlich*) here and there; **Z~ergebnis** *nt* intermediate result; **Z~fall** *m* incident; **Z~frage** *f* question; **Z~handel** *m* middlemen *pl*; middleman's trade; **Z~landung** *f* (*AVIAT*) stopover; **~menschlich** *adj* interpersonal; **Z~raum** *m* space; **Z~ruf** *m* interjection; **Z~stecker** *m* adaptor (plug); **Z~zeit** *f* interval; **in der Z~zeit** in the interim, meanwhile

zwitschern ['tsvɪtʃərn] *vt, vi* to twitter, to chirp

zwo [tsvo:] *num* two

zwölf [tsvœlf] *num* twelve

Zyklus ['tsy:klus] (-, Zyklen) *m* cycle

Zylinder [tsi'lɪndər] (-s, -) *m* cylinder; (*Hut*) top hat

Zyniker ['tsy:nikər] (-s, -) *m* cynic

zynisch ['tsy:nɪʃ] *adj* cynical

Zypern ['tsy:pərn] *nt* Cyprus

Zyste ['tsystə] *f* cyst

zz., zzt. *abk* = **zurzeit**

PUZZLES AND WORDGAMES

PUZZLES AND WORDGAMES

Introduction

We are delighted that you have decided to invest in this Collins Pocket Dictionary! Whether you intend to use it in school, at home, on holiday or at work, we are sure that you will find it very useful.

In the pages which follow you will find explanations and wordgames (not too difficult!) designed to give you practice in exploring the dictionary's contents and in retrieving information for a variety of purposes. Answers are provided at the end. If you spend a little time on these pages you should be able to use your dictionary more efficiently and effectively. Have fun!

Supplement by
Roy Simon
reproduced by kind permission of
Tayside Region Education Department

HOW INFORMATION IS PRESENTED IN YOUR DICTIONARY

A great deal of information is packed into your Collins Pocket Dictionary using colour, various typefaces, sizes of type, symbols, abbreviations and brackets. The purpose of this section is to acquaint you with the conventions used in presenting information.

Headwords

A headword is the word you look up in a dictionary. Headwords are listed in alphabetical order throughout the dictionary. They are printed in colour so that they stand out clearly from all the other words on the dictionary page.

Note that at the top of each page a headword appears. This is a guide to the alphabetical order of words on the page. It is there to help you scan through the dictionary more quickly to find the word you want.

The German alphabet consists of the same 26 letters as the English alphabet, plus the letter ß. Although certain letters in the German alphabet take umlaut (ä, ö, ü), this does not affect the order of words in the German-English section of the dictionary.

A Dictionary Entry

An entry is made up of a headword and all the information about that headword. Entries will be short or long depending on how frequently a word is used in either English or German and how many meanings it has. Inevitably, the fuller the dictionary entry the more care is needed in sifting through it to find the information you require.

Meanings

The translations of a headword are given in ordinary type. Where there is more than one meaning or usage, a semi-colon separates one from the other.

abladen ['apla:dən] (*unreg*) *vt* to unload
Ablage ['apla:gə] *f* (*für Akten*) tray; (*für Kleider*) cloakroom
ablassen ['aplasən] (*unreg*) *vt* (*Wasser, Dampf*) to let off; (*vom Preis*) to knock off
♦ *vi*: **von etw ~** to give sth up, to abandon sth

brünett [bry'nɛt] *adj* brunette, dark-haired
Brunnen ['brʊnən] (**-s, -**) *m* fountain; (*tief*)

Bude ['bu:də] *f* booth, stall; (*umg*) digs *pl* (*BRIT*)

Ohnmacht ['o:nmaxt] *f* faint; (*fig*) impotence; **in ~ fallen** to faint
ohnmächtig ['o:nmɛçtɪç] *adj* in a faint, unconscious; (*fig*) weak, impotent; **sie ist ~** she has fainted
Ohr [o:r] (**-(e)s, -en**) *nt* ear
Öhr [ø:r] (**-(e)s, -e**) *nt* eye

Gurt [gʊrt] (**-(e)s, -e**) *m* belt

klar- *zW*: **~legen** *vt* to clear up, to explain; **~machen** *vt* (*Schiff*) to get ready for sea; **jdm etw ~machen** to make sth clear to sb; **~sehen** △ (*unreg*) *vi siehe* **klar; K~sichtfolie** *f* transparent film; **~stellen** *vt* to clarify

Zug [tsu:k] (**-(e)s, ⁻e**) *m* (*EISENB*) train; (*Luftzug*) draught; (*Ziehen*) pull(ing); (*Gesichtszug*) feature; (*SCHACH etc*) move; (*Schriftzug*) stroke; (*Atemzug*) breath; (*Charakterzug*) trait; (*an Zigarette*) puff, pull, drag; (*Schluck*) gulp; (*Menschengruppe*) procession; (*von Vögeln*) flight; (*MIL*) platoon; **etw in vollen Zügen genießen** to enjoy sth to the full

In addition, you will often find other words appearing in *italics* in brackets before the translations. These either give some notion of the contexts in which the headword might appear (as with 'scharf' opposite – 'scharfes Essen', 'scharfe Munition', etc.) or else they provide synonyms (as with 'fremd' opposite – 'unvertraut', 'ausländisch', etc.).

Phonetic Spellings

In square brackets immediately after most headwords you will find the phonetic spelling of the word – i.e. its pronunciation. The phonetic transcription of German and English vowels and consonants is given on page xii near the front of your dictionary.

Additional Information About Headwords

Information about the usage or form of certain headwords is given in brackets between the phonetics and the translation or translations. Have a look at the entries for 'KG', 'Filiale', 'löschen' and 'Bruch' opposite.

This information is usually given in abbreviated form. A helpful list of abbreviations is given on pages viii to x at the front of your dictionary.

You should be particularly careful with colloquial words or phrases. Words labelled '(*umg*)' would not normally be used in formal speech, while those labelled '(*umg!*)' would be considered offensive.

Careful consideration of such style labels will provide indications as to the degree of formality and appropriateness of a word and could help you avoid many an embarrassing situation when using German!

Expressions in which the Headword Appears

An entry will often feature certain common expressions in which the headword appears. These expressions are in **bold** black type. A swung dash (-) is used instead of repeating a headword in an entry. 'Schikane' and 'man' opposite illustrate this point.

Related Words

In the Pocket Dictionary words related to certain headwords are sometimes given at the end of an entry, as with 'Lohn' and 'accept' opposite. These are easily picked out as they are also in colour. To help you find these words, they are placed in alphabetical order after the headword to which they belong – see 'acceptable', 'acceptance' etc opposite.

scharf [ʃarf] *adj* sharp; (*Essen*) hot, spicy; (*Munition*) live; ~ **nachdenken** to think hard; **auf etw** *akk* ~ **sein** (*umg*) to be keen on sth

fremd [fremt] *adj* (*unvertraut*) strange; (*ausländisch*) foreign; (*nicht eigen*) someone else's; **etw ist jdm** ~ sth is foreign to sb; **~artig** *adj* strange; **F~enführer** ['frɛmdən-]

gänzlich ['gɛntslɪç] *adj* complete, entire ♦ *adv* completely, entirely

KG [kaːˈgeː] (-, -s) *f abk* (= *Kommanditgesellschaft*) limited partnership

Filiale [filiˈaːlə] *f* (*COMM*) branch

Teufel ['tɔʏfəl] (-s, -) *m* devil; **teuflisch** ['tɔʏflɪʃ] *adj* fiendish, diabolical

löschen ['lœʃən] *vt* (*Feuer, Licht*) to put out, to extinguish; (*Durst*) to quench; (*COMM*) to cancel; (*COMPUT*) to delete; (*Tonband*) to erase; (*Fracht*) to unload ♦ *vi* (*Feuerwehr*) to put out a fire; (*Tinte*) to blot

Bruch [brʊx] (-(e)s, ⁼e) *m* breakage; (*zerbrochene Stelle*) break; (*fig*) split, breach; (*MED: Eingeweidebruch*) rupture, hernia; (*Beinbruch etc*) fracture; (*MATH*) fraction

schenken ['ʃɛŋkən] *vt* (*auch fig*) to give; (*Getränk*) to pour; **sich** *dat* **etw** ~ (*umg*) to skip sth; **das ist geschenkt!** (*billig*) that's a giveaway!; (*nichts wert*) that's worthless!

Bombenerfolg (*umg*) *m* smash hit

Arsch [arʃ] (-es, ⁼e) (*umg!*) *m* arse (*BRIT!*), ass (*US!*)

Schikane [ʃiˈkaːnə] *f* harassment; dirty trick; **mit allen ~n** with all the trimmings

man [man] *pron* one, you; ~ **sagt, ...** they *od* people say ...; **wie schreibt** ~ **das?** how do you write it?, how is it written?

Lohn [loːn] (-(e)s, ⁼e) *m* reward; (*Arbeitslohn*) pay, wages *pl*; **~büro** *nt* wages office; **~empfänger** *m* wage earner

accept [əkˈsɛpt] *vt* (*take*) annehmen; (*agree to*) akzeptieren; **~able** *adj* annehmbar; **~ance** *n* Annahme *f*

'Key' Words

Your Collins Pocket Dictionary gives special status to certain German and English words which can be looked on as 'key' words in each language. These are words which have many different usages. 'werden', 'alle(r, s)' and 'sich' opposite are typical examples in German. You are likely to become familiar with them in your day-to-day language studies.

There will be occasions, however, when you want to check on a particular usage. Your dictionary can be very helpful here. Note how different parts of speech and different usages are clearly indicated by a combination of lozenges (♦) and numbers. In addition, further guides to usage are given in italics in brackets in the language of the user who needs them.

werden [ˈveːrdən] (*pt* **wurde**, *pp* **geworden** *od* (*bei Passiv*) **worden**) *vi* to become; **was ist aus ihm/aus der Sache geworden?** what became of him/it?; **es ist nichts/gut geworden** it came to nothing/turned out well; **es wird Nacht/Tag** it's getting dark/light; **mir wird kalt** I'm getting cold; **mir wird schlecht** I feel ill; **Erster werden** to come *od* be first; **das muss anders werden** that'll have to change; **rot/zu Eis werden** to turn red/to ice; **was willst du (mal) werden?** what do you want to be?; **die Fotos sind gut geworden** the photos have come out nicely

♦ *als Hilfsverb* **1** (*bei Futur*): **er wird es tun** he will *od* he'll do it; **er wird das nicht tun** he will not *od* he won't do it; **es wird gleich regnen** it's going to rain

2 (*bei Konjunktiv*): **ich würde ...** I would ...; **er würde gern ...** he would *od* he'd like to ...; **ich würde lieber ...** I would *od* I'd rather ...

3 (*bei Vermutung*): **sie wird in der Küche sein** she will be in the kitchen

4 (*bei Passiv*): **gebraucht werden** to be used; **er ist erschossen worden** he has *od* he's been shot; **mir wurde gesagt, dass ...** I was told that ...

alle(r, s) [ˈalə(r,s)] *adj* **1** (*sämtliche*) all; **wir alle** all of us; **alle Kinder waren da** all the children were there; **alle Kinder mögen ...** all children like ...; **alle beide** both of us/them; **sie kamen alle** they all came; **alles Gute** all the best; **alles in allem** all in all

2 (*mit Zeit- oder Maßangaben*) every; **alle vier Jahre** every four years; **alle fünf Meter** every five metres

♦ *pron* everything; **alles was er sagt** everything he says, all that he says

♦ *adv* (*zu Ende, aufgebraucht*) finished; **die Milch ist alle** the milk's all gone, there's no milk left; **etw alle machen** to finish sth up

sich [zɪç] *pron* **1** (*akk*): **er/sie/es ... sich** he/she/it ... himself/herself/itself; **sie** *pl/* **man ... sich** they/one ... themselves/oneself; **Sie ... sich** you ... yourself/yourselves *pl*; **sich wiederholen** to repeat oneself/itself

2 (*dat*): **er/sie/es ... sich** he/she/it ... to himself/herself/itself; **sie** *pl/***man ... sich** they/one ... to themselves/oneself; **Sie ... sich** you ... to yourself/yourselves *pl*; **sie hat sich einen Pullover gekauft** she bought herself a jumper; **sich die Haare waschen** to wash one's hair

3 (*mit Präposition*): **haben Sie Ihren Ausweis bei sich?** do you have your pass on you?; **er hat nichts bei sich** he's got nothing on him; **sie bleiben gern unter sich** they keep themselves to themselves

4 (*einander*) each other, one another; **sie bekämpfen sich** they fight each other *od* one another

5: **dieses Auto fährt sich gut** this car drives well; **hier sitzt es sich gut** it's good to sit here

WORDGAME 1

HEADWORDS

Study the following sentences. In each sentence a wrong word spelt very similarly to the correct word has deliberately been put in and the sentence doesn't make sense. This word is shaded each time. Write out the correct word, which you will find in your dictionary near the wrong word.

Example   Raufen verboten

['Raufen' (= 'to pull out') is the wrong word and should be replaced by 'rauchen' (= 'to smoke')]

1. Hast du das Buch schon gekonnt?

2. Ich habe ein paar VW-Akten gekauft.

3. Wir waren gestern im Kilo.

4. Sollen wir die Theaterkarten schon kauen?

5. Unser Nachbar hat einen kleinen schwarzen Puder.

6. Ich zähle heute die Rechnung.

7. Der Student muss sich für den Kurs einschreiten.

8. Das neue Restaurant ist gar nicht über.

9. Gans viele Leute standen am Unfallort.

10. Ich habe meiner Tanne einen Brief geschrieben.

WORDGAME 2
DICTIONARY ENTRIES

Complete the crossword below by looking up the English words in the list and finding the correct German translations. There is a slight catch, however! All the English words can be translated several ways into German, but only one translation will fit correctly into each part of the crossword. So look carefully through the entries in the English-German section of your dictionary.

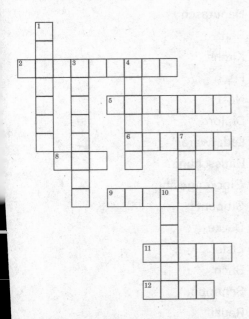

1. FAIR

2. CATCH

3. LEARN

4. FALL

5. HIT

6. HARD

7. CALF

8. PLACE

9. HOLD

10. PLACE

11. TRACK

12. HOME

WORDGAME 3
FINDING MEANINGS

In this list there are eight pairs of words that have some sort of connection with each other. For example, 'Diplom' (= 'diploma') and 'Student' (='student') are linked. Find the other pairs by looking up the words in your dictionary.

1. Morgenrock
2. Handtasche
3. Bett
4. Kirche
5. Fisch
6. Nest
7. Diplom
8. Lederwaren
9. Hausschuhe
10. Glockengeläut
11. Student
12. Decke
13. Elster
14. Buch
15. Schuppe
16. Regal

WORDGAME 4
SYNONYMS

Complete the crossword by supplying synonyms of the words below. You will sometimes find the words you are looking for in italics in brackets in the entries for the words in the list. Sometimes you will have to turn to the English-German section for help.

1. Art
2. probieren
3. Feuer
4. sich ereignen
5. Arroganz

6. namhaft
7. Ladung
8. Plan
9. begegnen
10. Neigung

287

WORDGAME 5
SPELLING

You will often use your dictionary to check spellings. The person who has compiled this list of ten German words has made <u>three</u> spelling mistakes. Find the three words which have been misspelt and write them out correctly.

1. nachsehen
2. nacht
3. Nagetier
4. Name
5. Nature
6. neuriech
7. Nickerchen
8. Nimmersatt
9. nördlich
10. nötig

WORDGAME 6

ANTONYMS

Complete the crossword by supplying ANTONYMS (i.e. opposites) in German of the words below. Use your dictionary to help.

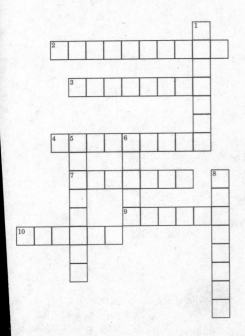

1. gestehen
2. enthüllen
3. unschuldig
4. kaufen
5. verbieten
6. Reichtum
7. ruhig
8. ankommen
9. ängstlich
10. schmutzig

WORDGAME 7
PHONETIC SPELLINGS

The phonetic transcriptions of ten German words are given below. If you study page xii near the front of your dictionary you should be able to work out what the words are.

1. frika'dɛlə
2. ʃpuːr
3. faɪn
4. 'lyːgə
5. 'ʃtaxəl
6. 'naʊtɪʃ
7. gə'vœlbə
8. 'kɔyçən
9. 'møːgən
10. 'glaʊbvʏrdɪç

WORDGAME 8

EXPRESSIONS IN WHICH THE HEADWORD APPEARS

If you look up the headword 'Satz' in the German-English section of your dictionary you will find that the word can have many meanings. Study the entry carefully and translate the following sentences into English.

1. Der Satz ist viel zu lang.

2. Unterstreicht jeden Satz, der mit einer Konjunktion beginnt.

3. Den Satz von Pythagoras kennt jeder.

4. Das Orchester hat den letzten Satz ganz ausgezeichnet gespielt.

5. Steffi Graf hat in der Meisterschaft keinen Satz verloren.

6. Der ganze Satz war in der Tasse.

7. Bei Lieferungen ins Ausland gilt ein anderer Satz.

8. Sie hat vor lauter Begeisterung einen großen Satz gemacht.

WORDGAME 9

RELATED WORDS

Fill in the blanks in the pairs of sentences below. The missing words are related to the headwords on the left. Choose the correct "relative" each time. You will find it in your dictionary near the headword provided.

HEADWORD	RELATED WORDS
Stellung	1. Ich habe die Uhr auf halb sechs _____. 2. Das Auto steht an der gleichen _____.
Hoffnung	3. _____ bleibt das Wetter so. 4. Sie _____, dass sie bald wieder gesund ist.
Betrug	5. Von ihm lassen wir uns nicht mehr _____. 6. Er ist als _____ bekannt.
sprechen	7. Hat er schon mit seiner Mutter _____? 8. Das Buch wurde in fünf _____ übersetzt.
Student	9. Er hat letztes Semester mit dem _____ begonnen. 10. Sie _____ Medizin.
kurz	11. Ich habe _____ noch mit ihm gesprochen. 12. Der Rock muss _____ werden.

WORDGAME 10
'KEY' WORDS

Study carefully the entry 'machen' in your dictionary and find translations for the following:

1. what are you doing (there)?

2. it's the cold that does that

3. that doesn't matter

4. I don't mind the cold

5. 3 and 5 are 8

6. to have the car done

7. how's the work going?

8. hurry up!

9. to set about sth

10. to turn the radio down

THE DICTIONARY AND GRAMMAR

While it is true that a dictionary can never be a substitute for a detailed grammar book, it nevertheless provides a great deal of grammatical information. If you know how to extract this information you will be able to use German more accurately both in speech and in writing.

The Collins Pocket Dictionary presents grammatical information as follows.

Parts of Speech

Parts of speech are given in italics immediately after the phonetic spellings of headwords. Abbreviated forms are used. Abbreviations can be checked on pages viii to x.

Changes in parts of speech within an entry – for example, from adjective to pronoun to adverb, or from noun to intransitive verb to transitive verb – are indicated by means of lozenges (♦), as with the German 'alle(r, s)' and the English 'fast' opposite.

German Nouns

The gender of each noun in the German-English section of the dictionary is indicated in the following way:

> m = Maskulinum
> f = Femininum
> nt = Neutrum

You will occasionally see 'm od nt' or 'm od f' beside an entry. This indicates that the noun can be either masculine or neuter (see 'Knäuel' opposite or masculine or feminine (see 'Sellerie' opposite).

Feminine forms of nouns are shown, as with 'Schaffner(in)' opposite. This is marked $m(f)$ to show that the feminine form has the ending '-in'. Nouns which have the ending '-(r)', like 'Angeklagte(r)' opposite, are formed from adjectives and are marked $f(m)$ to show that they can be either masculine or feminine. Their spelling changes in the same way as adjectives, depending on their article and position in the sentence.

prosit ['proːzɪt] *excl* cheers

leiten ['laɪtən] *vt* to lead; (*Firma*) to manage; (*in eine Richtung*) to direct; (*ELEK*) to conduct

alle(r, s) ['alə(r,s)] *adj* **1** (*sämtliche*) all; **wir alle** all of us; **alle Kinder waren da** all the children were there; **alle Kinder mögen ...** all children like ...; **alle beide** both of us/ them; **sie kamen alle** they all came; **alles Gute** all the best; **alles in allem** all in all **2** (*mit Zeit- oder Maßangaben*) every; **alle vier Jahre** every four years; **alle fünf Meter** every five metres
♦ *pron* everything; **alles was er sagt** everything he says, all that he says
♦ *adv* (*zu Ende, aufgebraucht*) finished; **die Milch ist alle** the milk's all gone, there's no milk left; **etw alle machen** to finish sth up

fast [faːst] *adj* schnell; (*firm*) fest ♦ *adv* schnell; fest ♦ *n* Fasten *nt* ♦ *vi* fasten; **to be ~** (*clock*) vorgehen

Knäuel ['knɔyəl] (**-s, -**) *m od nt* (*Wollknäuel*) ball; (*Menschenknäuel*) knot

Sellerie ['zɛləriː] (**-s, -(s)** *od* **-, -**) *m od f* celery

Schaffner(in) ['ʃafnər(ɪn)] (**-s, -**) *m(f)* (*Busschaffner*) conductor(-tress); (*EISENB*) guard

Angeklagte(r) ['angəklaːktə(r)] *f(m)* accused

So many things depend on you knowing the correct gender of a German noun – whether you use 'er', 'sie' or 'es' to translate 'it'; whether you use 'er' or 'es' to translate 'he', 'sie' or 'es' to translate 'she'; the spelling of adjectives etc. If you are in any doubt as to the gender of a noun, it is always best to check it in your dictionary.

Genitive singular and nominative plural forms of many nouns are also given (see 'Bube' and 'Scheitel' opposite). A list of regular noun endings is given on page xi and nouns which have these forms will not show genitive singular and nominative plural at the headword (see 'Rasur' and 'Forelle' opposite). Nouns formed from two or more words do not have genitive singular and nominative plural shown if the last element appears in the dictionary as a headword. For example, if you want to know how to decline 'Backenzahn', you will find the necessary information at 'Zahn'.

Adjectives

Adjectives are given in the form used when they come after a verb. If the adjective comes before a noun, the spelling changes, depending on the gender of the noun and on the article (if any), which comes before the adjective. Compare 'der Hund ist schwarz' with 'der schwarze Hund'. If you find an unfamiliar adjective in a text and want to look it up in the dictionary, you will have to decide what spelling changes have been made before you can know how it will appear in the dictionary.

Some adjectives are never used after a verb. In these cases, the dictionary shows all the possible nominative singular endings.

Adverbs

German adverbs come in three main types.

Some are just adjectives in their after-verb form, used as adverbs. Sometimes the meaning is similar to the meaning of the adjective (see 'laut'), sometimes it is rather different (see 'richtig').

Some adverbs are formed by adding '-weise', '-sweise' or '-erweise' to the adjective.

Other adverbs are not considered to be derived from particular adjectives.

In your dictionary, adjective-adverbs may be shown by a change of part of speech or by the mention 'adj, adv' at the beginning of the entry.

Fuß [fuːs] (**-es**, **-̈e**) *m* foot; (*von Glas, Säule etc*) base; (*von Möbel*) leg; **zu ~** on foot;

Stube [ˈʃtuːbə] *f* room

Mädchen [ˈmɛːtçən] *nt* girl; **m~haft** *adj* girlish; **~name** *m* maiden name

Rasur [raˈzuːr] *f* shaving

Forelle [foˈrɛlə] *f* trout

schwarz [ʃvarts] *adj* black; **~es Brett** notice board; **ins S~e treffen** (*auch fig*) to hit the bull's eye; **in den ~en Zahlen** in the black; **~ sehen** (*umg*) to see the gloomy side of things; **S~arbeit** *f* illicit work, moonlighting; **S~brot** *nt* black bread; **S~e(r)** *f(m)* black (man/woman)

laut [laut] *adj* loud ♦ *adv* loudly; (*lesen*) aloud ♦ *präp* (*+gen od dat*) according to; **L~** (**-(e)s**, **-e**) *m* sound

richtig *adj* right, correct; (*echt*) proper ♦ *adv* (*umg: sehr*) really; **bin ich hier ~?** am I in the right place?; **der/die R~e** the right one/person; **das R~e** the right thing; **etw ~ stellen** to correct sth; **R~keit** *f* correctness

leider [ˈlaidər] *adv* unfortunately; **ja, ~** yes, I'm afraid so; **~ nicht** I'm afraid not

oben [ˈoːbən] *adv* above; (*in Haus*) upstairs; **~ erwähnt**, **~ genannt** above-mentioned; **nach ~** up; **von ~** down; **~ ohne** topless;

Bube [ˈbuːbə] (**-n**, **-n**) *m* (*Schurke*) rogue; (*KARTEN*) jack

Scheitel [ˈʃaitəl] (**-s**, **-**) *m* top; (*Haarscheitel*) parting; **s~n** *vt* to part

Backenzahn *m* molar

Zahn [tsaːn] (**-(e)s**, **-̈e**) *m* tooth; **~arzt** *m* dentist; **~ärztin** *f* (female) dentist; **~bürste** *f* toothbrush; **~fleisch** *nt* gums *pl*; **~pasta** *f* toothpaste; **~rad** *nt* cog(wheel); **~schmerzen** *pl* toothache *sg*; **~stein** *m* tartar; **~stocher** (**-s**, **-**) *m* toothpick

besondere(r, s) [bəˈzɔndərə(r, s)] *adj* special; (*eigen*) particular; (*gesondert*) separate; (*eigentümlich*) peculiar

letzte(r, s) [ˈlɛtstə(r, s)] *adj* last; (*neueste*) latest; **zum ~n Mal** for the last time; **~ns** *adv* lately; **~re(r, s)** *adj* latter

nett [nɛt] *adj* nice; (*freundlich*) nice, kind; **~erweise** *adv* kindly

glück- zW: **~lich** *adj* fortunate; (*froh*) happy; **~licherweise** *adv* fortunately; **~ˈselig** *adj* blissful

Adjective-plus-ending adverbs will usually appear as subentries.

Adverbs like 'oben' and 'leider' will usually appear as separate headwords.

Where a word in your text seems to be an adverb but does not appear in the dictionary, you should be able to work out a translation from the word it is related to, once you have found that in the dictionary.

Information about Verbs

A major problem facing language learners is that the form of a verb will change according to the subject and/or the tense being used. A typical German verb can take on many different forms – too many to list in a dictionary entry.

Yet, although verbs are listed in your dictionary in their infinitive forms only, this does not mean that the dictionary is of limited value when it comes to handling the verb system of the German language. On the contrary, it contains much valuable information.

First of all, your dictionary will help you with the meanings of unfamiliar verbs. If you came across the word 'füllt' in a text and looked it up in your dictionary you wouldn't find it. What you must do is assume that it is part of a verb and look for the infinitive form. Thus you will deduce that 'füllt' is a form of the verb 'füllen'. You now have the basic meaning of the word you are concerned with – something to do with English verb 'fill' – and this should be enough to help you understand the text you are reading.

It is usually an easy task to make the connection between the form of a verb and the infinitive. For example, 'füllten', 'füllst', 'füllte' and 'gefüllt' are all recognizable as parts of the infinitive 'füllen'. However, sometimes it is less obvious – for example, 'hilft', 'halfen' and 'geholfen' are all parts of 'helfen'. The only real solution to this problem is to learn the various forms of the main German irregular verbs.

And this is the second source of help offered by your dictionary as far as verbs are concerned. The irregular verb lists on pages 609 to 613 at the back of the Collins Pocket Dictionary provide the main forms of the main tenses of the basic irregular verbs. (Verbs which consist of a basic verb with prefix usually follow the rules for the basic verb.) Consider the verb 'sehen' below where the following information is given:

infinitive	present indicative (2nd, 3rd sg)	imperfect	past participle
sehen	siehst, sieht	sah	gesehen

In order to make maximum use of the information contained in these pages, a good working knowledge of the various rules affecting German verbs is required. You will acquire this in the course of your German studies and your Collins dictionary will serve as a useful 'aide-mémoire'. If you happen to forget how to form the second person singular form of the Past Tense of 'sehen' (i.e. how to translate 'You saw'), there will be no need to panic – your dictionary contains the information!

In addition, the main parts of the most common irregular verbs are listed in the body of the dictionary.

WORDGAME 11

PARTS OF SPEECH

In each sentence below a word has been shaded. Put a tick in the appropriate box to indicate the **part of speech** each time.

SENTENCE	Noun	Adj	Adv	Verb
1. Das Essen ist fertig.				
2. Er hat kein Recht dazu.				
3. Warum fahren wir nicht in die Stadt zum Essen?				
4. Ich gehe nicht mit essen.				
5. Rauchen ist strengstens verboten.				
6. Gehen Sie geradeaus und dann die erste Straße links.				
7. Das war aber ein interessanter Vortrag.				
8. Die Schauspielerin trug ein herrliches Kleid.				
9. Hast du schon von deiner Freundin gehört?				
10. Es ist immer noch recht sommerlich.				

WORDGAME 12

MEANING CHANGING WITH GENDER

Some German nouns change meaning according to their gender. Look at the pairs of sentences below and fill in the blanks with either 'ein, einen, eine' or 'der, den, die, das'.

1. Ist das _____ erste Band der Schillerausgabe?

   _____ Band ist nicht lang genug.

2. _____ Mark ist in letzter Zeit wieder gestiegen.

   Der Metzger löst _____ Mark aus den Knochen.

3. Was kostet _____ Bund Petersilie?

   _____ Bund an der Hose ist zu weit.

4. _____ Tau lag noch auf den Wiesen.

   Der Mann konnte _____ Tau nicht heben.

5. Wie steht mir _____ Hut?

   Wir müssen wirklich auf _____ Hut sein.

6. Hinter dem Haus steht _____ Kiefer.

   Er hat sich _____ Kiefer gebrochen.

WORDGAME 13

ADJECTIVES

Try to work out how the adjectives in the following phrases will appear in
the dictionary. Write your answer beside the phrase, then check in the
dictionary.

1. ein englisches Buch

2. der rote Traktor

3. letzte Nacht

4. mein kleiner Bruder

5. eine lange Reise

6. guter Käse

7. das alte Trikot

8. schwarzes Brot

9. die große Kommode

10. ein heftiger Schlag

11. der siebte Sohn

12. die neuen Nachbarn

WORDGAME 14

VERB TENSES

Use your dictionary to help you fill in the blanks in the table below.
(Remember the important pages at the back of your dictionary.)

INFINITIVE	PRESENT TENSE	IMPERFECT	PERFECT TENSE
sehen		ich	
schlafen	du		
sein			ich
schlagen		ich	
anrufen			ich
abfahren	er		
studieren			ich
haben		ich	
anfangen	du		
waschen	er		
werden		ich	
nehmen			ich

WORDGAME 15

PAST PARTICIPLES

Use your dictionary to find the past participle of these verbs.

INFINITIVE	PAST PARTICIPLE
singen	
beißen	
bringen	
frieren	
reiben	
gewinnen	
helfen	
geschehen	
liegen	
lügen	
schneiden	
kennen	
mögen	
wissen	
können	

WORDGAME 16

IDENTIFYING INFINITIVES

In the sentences below you will see various German verbs shaded. Use your dictionary to help you find the INFINITIVE form of each verb.

1. Leider habe ich Ihren Namen vergessen.

2. Bitte ruf mich doch morgen früh mal an.

3. Er ist um 16 Uhr angekommen.

4. Sie hielt an ihrem Argument fest.

5. Wir waren im Sommer in Italien.

6. Ich würde gerne kommen, wenn ich nur könnte.

7. Die Maschine flog über den Nordpol.

8. Ich würde es ja machen, aber ich habe keine Zeit.

9. Wohin fährst du diesen Winter zum Skilaufen?

10. Wen habt ihr sonst noch eingeladen?

11. Er hat deinen Brief erst gestern bekommen.

12. Liest du das Buch nicht zu Ende?

13. Meine Mutter ist letztes Jahr gestorben.

14. Er hat den Zettel aus Versehen weggeworfen.

15. Ich nahm ihn jeden Tag mit nach Hause.

MORE ABOUT MEANING

In this section we will consider some of the problems associated with using a bilingual dictionary.

Overdependence on your dictionary

That the dictionary is an invaluable tool for the language learner is beyond dispute. Nevertheless, it is possible to become overdependent on your dictionary, turning to it in an almost automatic fashion every time you come up against a new German word or phrase. Tackling an unfamiliar text in this way will turn reading in German into an extremely tedious activity. If you stop to look up every new word you may actually be *hindering* your ability to read in German – you are so concerned with the individual words that you pay no attention to the text as a whole and to the context which gives them meaning. It is therefore important to develop appropriate reading skills – using clues such as titles, headlines, illustrations, etc., understanding relations within a sentence, etc. to predict or infer what a text is about.

A detailed study of the development of reading skills is not within the scope of this supplement; we are concerned with knowing how to use a dictionary, which is only one of several important skills involved in reading. Nevertheless, it may be instructive to look at one example. You see the following text in a German newspaper and are interested in working out what it is about.

Contextual clues here include the word in large type which you would probably recognize as a German name, something that looks like a date below, and the name and address at the bottom. Some 'form' words such as 'wir', 'sind', 'und' and 'Tochter' will be familiar to you from your general studies in German. Given that we are dealing with

> *Wir sind glücklich*
> *über die Geburt*
> *unserer Tochter*
>
> ## Julia
>
> am 5. Juni 1999
>
> *Christine und Artur Landgraf*
> *Vacher Straße 50 B, Köln*

a newspaper, you will probably have worked out by now that this could be an announcement placed in the 'Personal Column'.

So you have used a series of cultural, contextual and word-formation clues to get you to the point where you have understood that Christine and Artur Landgraf have placed this notice in the 'Personal Column' of the newspaper and that something happened to Julia on 5 November 1997. And you have reached this point *without* opening your dictionary once. Common sense and your knowledge of newspaper contents in this country might suggest that this must be an announcement of someone's birth or death. Thus 'glücklich' ('happy') and 'Geburt' ('birth') become the only words that you might have to look up in order to confirm that this is indeed a birth announcement.

When learning German we are helped by the fact that some German and English words look and sound alike and have exactly the same meaning. Such words are called 'COGNATES' i.e. words derived from the same root. Many words come from a common Latin root. Other words are the same or nearly the same in both languages because the German language has borrowed a word from English or vice versa. The dictionary should not be necessary where cognates are concerned – provided you know the English word that the German word resembles!

Words With More Than One Meaning

The need to examine with care *all* the information contained in a dictionary entry must be stressed. This is particularly important with the many German words which have more than one meaning. For example, the German 'Zeit' can mean 'grammatical tense' as well as 'time'. How you translated the word would depend on the context in which you found it.

Similarly, if you were trying to translate a phrase such as 'sich vor etwas drücken', you would have to look through the whole entry for 'drücken' to get the right translation. If you restricted your search to the first couple of lines of the entry and saw that the first meaning given is 'press', you might be tempted to assume that the idiom meant 'to press o.s. in front of sth'. But if you examined the entry closely you would see that 'sich vor etwas drücken' means 'to get out of (doing) sth', as in the sentence 'Sie drückt sich immer vor dem Abwasch'.

The same need for care applies when you are using the English-German section of your dictionary to translate a word from English into German. Watch out in particular for the lozenges indicating changes in parts of speech.

If you want to translate 'You can't fool me', the capital letters at 'Narr' and 'Närrin' will remind you that these words are nouns. But watch what you are doing with the verbs or you could end up with a mistranslation like 'Sie können mich nicht herumalbern'!

Phrasal Verbs

Another potential source of difficulty is English phrasal verbs. These consist of a common verb ('go', 'make', etc.) plus an adverb and/or a preposition to give English expressions such as 'to take after', 'to make out', etc. Entries for such verbs tend to be fairly full; therefore close examination of the contents is required.

fool [fuːl] n Narr m, Närrin f ♦ vt (deceive) hereinlegen ♦ vi (also: ~ around) (herum)albern; **~hardy** adj tollkühn; **~ish** adj albern; **~proof** adj idiotensicher

make [meɪk] (pt, pp **made**) vt machen; (appoint) ernennen (zu); (cause to do sth) veranlassen; (reach) erreichen; (in time) schaffen; (earn) verdienen ♦ n Marke f; **to ~ sth happen** etw geschehen lassen; **to ~ it** es schaffen; **what time do you ~ it?** wie spät hast du es?; **to ~ do with** auskommen mit; **~ for** vi gehen/fahren nach; **~ out** vt (write out) ausstellen; (understand) verstehen; **~ up** vt machen; (face) schminken; (quarrel) beilegen; (story etc) erfinden ♦ vi sich versöhnen; **~ up for** vt wieder gutmachen; (COMM) vergüten; **~believe** n Fantasie f; **~r** n (COMM) Hersteller m; **~shift** adj behelfsmäßig, Not-; **~up** n Schminke f, Make-up nt; **~up remover** n Make-up-Entferner m; **making** n: **in the making** im Entstehen; **to have the makings of** das Zeug haben zu

False Friends

Some German and English words have similar forms *and* meanings. There are, however, German words which *look* like English words but have a completely *different* meaning. For example, 'blank' in German means 'bright'; 'Probe' means 'rehearsal'; 'bilden' means 'to educate'. This can easily lead to serious mistranslations.

Sometimes the meaning of the German word is close to the English. For example, 'die Chips' are 'potato crisps' rather than 'chips'; 'der Hund' means a dog of any sort, not just a 'hound'. But some German words have two meanings, one the same as the English, the other completely different! 'Golf' can mean 'gulf' as well as 'golf'; 'senden' can mean 'to send' but can also mean 'to transmit/broadcast'.

Such words are often referred to as 'false friends'. You will have to look at the context in which they appear in order to arrive at the correct meaning. If they seem to fit with the sense of the passage as a whole, it will probably not be necessary to look them up. If they don't make sense, however, you may be dealing with 'false friends'.

WORDGAME 17
WORDS IN CONTEXT

Study the sentences below. Translations of the underlined words are given at the bottom. Match the number of the sentence and the letter of the translation correctly each time.

1. Sprich bitte lauter, ich kann dich nicht hören.

2. Er hört den ganzen Tag Radio.

3. Kannst du das Licht ausmachen, wenn du ins Bett gehst?

4. Können wir heute schon einen Termin ausmachen?

5. Seine Frau saß am Steuer, als der Unfall passierte.

6. Ich muss dieses Jahr viel Steuern nachzahlen.

7. Die Nachfrage nach japanischen Autos ist groß.

8. Aufgrund meiner Nachfrage konnte ich dann doch etwas erfahren.

9. Das Haus wird auf meinen Namen umgeschrieben.

10. Das Referat musst du völlig umschreiben.

11. Sind die Äpfel schon reif?

12. Für ihr Alter wirkt sie schon ziemlich reif.

a. demand	e. ripe	i. steering wheel
b. transferred	f. inquiry	j. listens to
c. turn off	g. mature	k. agree
d. hear	h. rewrite	l. tax

WORDGAME 18

FALSE FRIENDS

Look at the advertisements below. The words which have been shaded resemble English words but have different meanings here. Find a correct translation for each word in the context.

1

Reformhaus
Neustr. 23
Sonderangebot:
Vollkornbrot 2, 78 DM

2

Hotel Olympia

Alle Zimmer mit Dusche/WC
Gemütliche Atmosphäre
Bitte Prospekt anfordern

Heinrichstraße 51 –
7000 STUTTGART 25
Tel. 0711/21 56 93

3

KP- Chef Italiens fliegt
morgen nach New York

4

W. Meinzer   Lebensmittel

Heute Chips
im
Sonderangebot

5

Der Mann
im
Smoking

6

Clinton
will wieder
Präsident der
USA werden

7

Nach der
Jahrtausendwende
erst mit 65 in
Rente

8

Europaparlament
Fraktions-Flanke abdecken

9

Reise sorgenfrei
mit diesen Drei

Reisescheck
Devisen
Sparkassenbuch

BEZIRKSSPARKASSE HAUSACH
Hauptstr. 14

WORDGAME 19

WORDS WITH MORE THAN ONE MEANING

Look at the advertisements and headlines below. The words which have been shaded can have more than one meaning. Use your dictionary to help you work out the correct translation in the context.

1

Landespräsident
tritt
zurück

2

Vermögen:

Vom kleinen zum
großen Geld

3

Ich weiß, wie ich
Schmerzen schnell los werde

Parazetamol
Aus Ihrer Apotheke

4

Heinrich Wohnmobile
GmbH

Spezialisten bieten
günstige Preise

5

Hotel Restaurant
Seeberger

Alle Preise inklusive
Bedienung

Marktplatz 12
Loßurg   Telefon (07165) 33 14

6

Müsli – Riegel

von Cadbury
– gibt Kraft und Energie!

7

Hotel – Pension Miramar

Behagliche Atmosphäre
Günstige Nachsaisonpreise

Strandstr. 6,
24340 Eckernförde
Telefon (04269) 29 51

8

Das Blatt
Finanz- und
Wirtschaftszeitung

313

HAVE FUN WITH YOUR DICTIONARY

Here are some word games for you to try. You will find your dictionary helpful as you attempt the activities.

WORDGAME 20

CODED WORDS

In the boxes below the letters of eight German words have been replaced by numbers. A number represents the same letter each time.

Try to crack the code and find the eight words. If you need help, use your dictionary.

Here is a clue: all the words you are looking for have something to do with TRANSPORT.

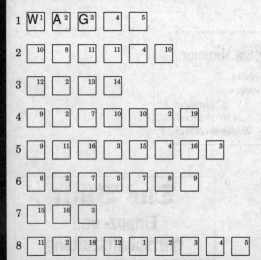

1 | W¹ | A² | G³ | 4 | 5 |

2 | 10 | 8 | 11 | 11 | 4 | 10 |

3 | 12 | 2 | 13 | 14 |

4 | 9 | 2 | 7 | 10 | 10 | 2 | 19 |

5 | 9 | 11 | 16 | 3 | 15 | 4 | 16 | 3 |

6 | 6 | 2 | 7 | 5 | 7 | 8 | 9 |

7 | 15 | 16 | 3 |

8 | 11 | 2 | 18 | 12 | 1 | 2 | 3 | 4 | 5 |

WORDGAME 21

BEHEADED WORDS

If you 'behead' certain German words, i.e. take away their first letter, you are left with another German word. For example, if you behead 'Kleider' (= 'clothes'), you get 'leider' (= 'unfortunately'), and 'dort' (= 'there') gives 'Ort' (= 'place').

The following words have their heads chopped off, i.e. the first letter has been removed. Use your dictionary to help you form a new German word by adding one letter to the start of each word below. Write down the new German word and its meaning.

1. ragen (= to tower)

2. tollen (= to romp)

3. nie (= never)

4. Rand (= edge)

5. oben (= above)

6. ich (= I)

7. Rad (= wheel)

8. innen (= inside)

9. raten (= to guess)

10. indisch (= Indian)

11. eigen (=own)

12. eben (= level)

13. Ohr (= ear)

14. pur (= pure)

WORDGAME 22

CROSSWORD

Complete this crossword by looking up the words listed below in the English-German section of your dictionary. Remember to read through the entry carefully to find the word that will fit.

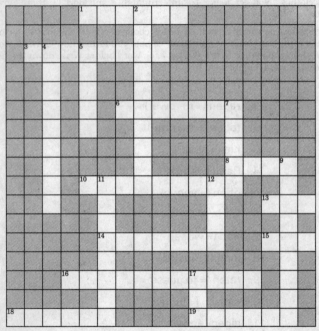

1. Heavily	6. Sad	11. To start up (a car)	15. Clock
2. Tearful	7. Smooth	12. Tap	16. To dirty
3. Meal	8. Deaf	13. Place	17. Day
4. To record	9. To reassure	14. To withdraw	18. To fold
5. Mood	10. (A piece of) news		19. Profit

WORDGAME 23

There are twelve German words hidden in the grid below. Each word is made up of five letters but has been split into two parts.

Find the German words. Each group of letters can only be used once.

Use your dictionary to help you.

Re	ten	cke	er	Lad	Na
rbe	Sch	tr	Sip	eh	wei
unt	en	He	am	ank	pe
ren	be	ne	cht	se	ben

WORDGAME 24

Here is a list of German words for things you will find in the kitchen. Unfortunately, they have all been jumbled up. Try to work out what each word is and put the word in the boxes on the right. You will see that there are six shaded boxes below. With the six letters in the shaded boxes make up <u>another</u> German word for an object you can find in the kitchen.

1. CSIHT

Die Kinder decken den____

2. DERH

Die Kasserolle steht auf dem

____

3. RSNAHKC

Ist die Kaffeekanne in diesem ____ ?

4. SAETS

Sie gießt den Tee in die____

5. SRIGHCRE

Das____ liegt im Spülbecken

6. HKRÜHNSKCLA

Hol die Milch aus dem ____ heraus

The word you are looking for is:

318

WORDGAME 25

Take the four letters given each time and put them in the four empty boxes in the centre of each grid. Arrange them in such a way that you form four six-letter words. Use your dictionary to check the words.

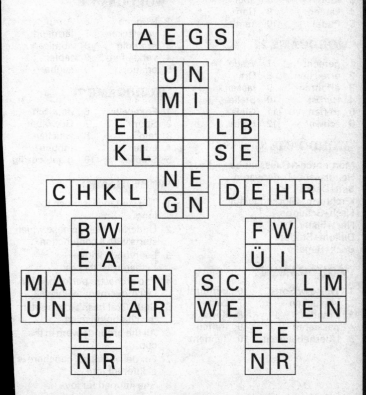

319

ANSWERS

WORDGAME 1

1	gekannt	6	zahle
2	Aktien	7	einschreiben
3	Kino	8	übel
4	kaufen	9	Ganz
5	Pudel	10	Tante

WORDGAME 2

1	gerecht	7	Wade
2	erreichen	8	Ort
3	erfahren	9	fassen
4	Herbst	10	Stelle
5	treffen	11	Gleis
6	schwer	12	Heim

WORDGAME 3

Morgenrock+Hausschuhe
Handtasche+Lederwaren
Bett+Decke
Kirchturm+Glockengeläut
Fisch+Schuppe
Nest+Elster
Diplom+Student
Buch+Regal

WORDGAME 4

1	Weise or Sorte	6	berühmt
2	versuchen	7	Last
3	Brand	8	Karte
4	passieren	9	treffen
5	Überheblichkeit	10	Tendenz

WORDGAME 5

2 Nacht	5 Natur	6 neureich

WORDGAME 6

1	leugnen	6	Armut
2	verstecken	7	lärmend
3	schuldig	8	abreisen
4	verkaufen	9	tapfer
5	erlauben	10	sauber

WORDGAME 7

1	Frikadelle	6	nautisch
2	Spur	7	Gewölbe
3	fein	8	keuchen
4	Lüge	9	mögen
5	Stachel	10	glaubwürdi

WORDGAME 8

1 The sentence is much too long.

2 Underline every clause which starts with a conjunction.

3 Everybody knows Pythagoras' theorem.

4 The orchestra performed the last movement really well.

5 Steffi Graf hasn't lost a set in the championships.

6 All the grounds were in the cup.

7 For deliveries abroad there is a different rate.

8 She jumped for joy.

WORDGAME 9

1	gestellt	7	gesprochen
2	Stelle	8	Sprachen
3	hoffentlich	9	Studium
4	hofft	10	studiert
5	betrügen	11	kürzlich
6	Betrüger	12	gekürzt

WORDGAME 11

1	adj	6	adv
2	noun	7	adj
3	noun	8	verb
4	verb	9	verb
5	adv	10	adj

WORDGAME 12

1 der/das
2 die/das
3 das (or ein)/der
4 der/das
5 der/der
6 eine/den

WORDGAME 13

1	englisch	7	alt
2	rot	8	schwarz
3	letzte(r, s)	9	groß
4	klein	10	heftig
5	lang	11	siebte(r, s)
6	gut	12	neu

WORDGAME 14

ich sah
du schläfst
ich bin gewesen
ich schlug
ich habe angerufen
er fährt ab
ich habe studiert
ich hatte
du fängst an
er wäscht
ich wurde
ich habe genommen

WORDGAME 15

gesungen	gelegen
gebissen	gelogen
gebracht	geschnitten
gefroren	gekannt
gerieben	gemocht
gewonnen	gewusst
geholfen	gekonnt
geschehen	

WORDGAME 16

1	vergessen	9	fahren
2	anrufen	10	einladen
3	ankommen	11	bekommen
4	festhalten	12	lesen
5	sein	13	sterben
6	können	14	wegwerfen
7	fliegen	15	mitnehmen
8	werden		

WORDGAME 17

1	d	5	i	9	b
2	j	6	l	10	h
3	c	7	a	11	e
4	k	8	f	12	g

WORDGAME 18

1. health food shop
2. brochure
3. boss
4. crisps
5. dinner jacket
6. wants
7. pension
8. parliamentary party
9. foreign currency

WORDGAME 19

1. resigns
2. wealth
3. know
4. offer
5. service
6. bar
7. guesthouse
8. newspaper

WORDGAME 20

1. Wagen
2. Roller
3. Taxi
4. Fahrrad
5. Flugzeug
6. Bahnhof
7. Zug
8. Lastwagen

WORDGAME 21

1. tragen (= to carry); fragen (= to ask)
2. Stollen (= gallery)
3. Knie (= knee)
4. Brand (= fire)
5. loben (= to praise)
6. dich (= you); sich (= oneself); mich (= me)
7. Grad (= degree)
8. sinnen (= to ponder); rinnen (= to trickle)
9. braten (= to roast)
10. kindisch (= childish)
11. zeigen (= to show); neigen (= to incline)
12. geben (= to give); leben (= to live); neben (= next to); beben (= to tremble); heben (= to raise); weben (= to weave)
13. Rohr (= pipe, tube)
14. Spur (= race)

WORDGAME 22

1. schwer
2. weinerlich
3. Mahlzeit
4. aufnehmen
5. Laune
6. traurig
7. glatt
8. taub
9. beruhigen
10. Nachricht
11. anlassen
12. Hahn
13. Ort
14. abheben
15. Uhr
16. beschmutzen
17. Tag
18. falten
19. Gewinn

WORDGAME 23

1	Recht	7	neben
2	Laden	8	Sippe
3	Hecke	9	unter
4	ehren	10	Scham
5	beten	11	weise
6	Narbe	12	trank

WORDGAME 24

1	Tisch	4	Tasse
2	Herd	5	Geschirr
3	Schrank	6	Kühlschrank

Hidden word – KESSEL

WORDGAME 25

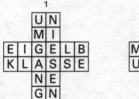

ENGLISH – GERMAN
ENGLISCH – DEUTSCH

A, a

A [eɪ] n (MUS) A nt; ~ **road**
Hauptverkehrsstraße f

KEYWORD
---

a [eɪ, ə] (before vowel or silent h: an) indef art **1**
ein; eine; **a woman** eine Frau; **a book** ein
Buch; **an eagle** ein Adler; **she's a doctor**
sie ist Ärztin

2 (instead of the number "one") ein, eine; **a
year ago** vor einem Jahr; **a hundred/
thousand** etc **pounds** (ein) hundert/(ein)
tausend etc Pfund

3 (in expressing ratios, prices etc) pro; **3 a
day/week** 3 pro Tag/Woche, 3 am Tag/in
der Woche; **10 km an hour** 10 km pro
Stunde/in der Stunde

A.A. n abbr = **Alcoholics Anonymous**;
(BRIT) = **Automobile Association**

A.A.A. (US) n abbr = **American Automobile
Association**

aback [ə'bæk] adv: **to be taken ~** verblüfft
sein

abandon [ə'bændən] vt (give up) aufgeben;
(desert) verlassen ♦ n Hingabe f

abate [ə'beɪt] vi nachlassen, sich legen

abattoir ['æbətwɑ:ʳ] (BRIT) n Schlachthaus nt

abbey ['æbɪ] n Abtei f

abbot ['æbət] n Abt m

abbreviate [ə'bri:vɪeɪt] vt abkürzen;
abbreviation [əbri:vɪ'eɪʃən] n Abkürzung f

abdicate ['æbdɪkeɪt] vt aufgeben ♦ vi
abdanken

abdomen ['æbdəmen] n Unterleib m

abduct [æb'dʌkt] vt entführen

aberration [æbə'reɪʃən] n (geistige)
Verwirrung f

abet [ə'bet] vt see **aid**

abeyance [ə'beɪəns] n: **in ~** in der Schwebe;
(disuse) außer Kraft

abide [ə'baɪd] vt vertragen; leiden; **~ by** vt
sich halten an +acc

ability [ə'bɪlɪtɪ] n (power) Fähigkeit f; (skill)
Geschicklichkeit f

abject ['æbdʒekt] adj (liar) übel; (poverty)
größte(r, s); (apology) zerknirscht

ablaze [ə'bleɪz] adj in Flammen

able ['eɪbl] adj geschickt, fähig; **to be ~ to
do sth** etw tun können; **~-bodied**
['eɪbl'bɔdɪd] adj kräftig; (seaman) Voll-; **ably**
['eɪblɪ] adv geschickt

abnormal [æb'nɔ:məl] adj regelwidrig,
abnorm

aboard [ə'bɔ:d] adv, prep an Bord +gen

abode [ə'bəud] n: **of no fixed ~** ohne festen
Wohnsitz

abolish [ə'bɔlɪʃ] vt abschaffen; **abolition**
[æbə'lɪʃən] n Abschaffung f

abominable [ə'bɔmɪnəbl] adj scheußlich

aborigine [æbə'rɪdʒɪnɪ] n Ureinwohner m

abort [ə'bɔ:t] vt abtreiben; fehlgebären; **~ion**
[ə'bɔ:ʃən] n Abtreibung f; (miscarriage)
Fehlgeburt f; **~ive** adj misslungen

abound [ə'baund] vi im Überfluss vorhanden
sein; **to ~ in** Überfluss haben an +dat

KEYWORD
---

about [ə'baut] adv **1** (approximately) etwa,
ungefähr; **about a hundred/thousand** etc
etwa hundert/tausend etc; **at about 2
o'clock** etwa um 2 Uhr; **I've just about
finished** ich bin gerade fertig

2 (referring to place) herum, umher; **to
leave things lying about** Sachen
herumliegen lassen; **to run/walk** etc **about**
herumrennen/gehen etc

3: to be about to do sth im Begriff sein,
etw zu tun; **he was about to go to bed** er
wollte gerade ins Bett gehen

♦ prep **1** (relating to) über +acc; **a book**

about London ein Buch über London; **what is it about?** worum geht es?; (*book etc*) wovon handelt es?; **we talked about it** wir haben darüber geredet; **what** *or* **how about doing this?** wollen wir das machen? **2** (*referring to place*) um (... herum); **to walk about the town** in der Stadt herumgehen; **her clothes were scattered about the room** ihre Kleider waren über das ganze Zimmer verstreut

about-turn [ə'baut'tə:n] *n* Kehrtwendung *f*
above [ə'bʌv] *adv* oben ♦ *prep* über; ~ **all** vor allem; ~ **board** *adj* offen, ehrlich
abrasive [ə'breɪzɪv] *adj* Abschleif-; (*personality*) zermürbend, aufreibend
abreast [ə'brest] *adv* nebeneinander; **to keep ~ of** Schritt halten mit
abroad [ə'brɔːd] *adv* (*be*) im Ausland; (*go*) ins Ausland
abrupt [ə'brʌpt] *adj* (*sudden*) abrupt, jäh; (*curt*) schroff; ~**ly** *adv* abrupt
abscess ['æbsɪs] *n* Geschwür *nt*
abscond [əb'skɒnd] *vi* flüchten, sich davonmachen
abseil ['æbseɪl] *vi* (*also:* ~ **down**) sich abseilen
absence ['æbsəns] *n* Abwesenheit *f*
absent ['æbsənt] *adj* abwesend, nicht da; (*lost in thought*) geistesabwesend; ~**-minded** *adj* zerstreut
absolute ['æbsəluːt] *adj* absolut; (*power*) unumschränkt; (*rubbish*) vollkommen, rein; ~**ly** [æbsə'luːtlɪ] *adv* absolut, vollkommen; ~**ly!** ganz bestimmt!
absolve [əb'zɒlv] *vt* entbinden; freisprechen
absorb [əb'zɔːb] *vt* aufsaugen, absorbieren; (*fig*) ganz in Anspruch nehmen, fesseln; **to be ~ed in a book** in ein Buch vertieft sein; ~**ent cotton** (*US*) *n* Verbandwatte *f*; ~**ing** *adj* aufsaugend; (*fig*) packend; **absorption** [əb'sɔːpʃən] *n* Aufsaugung *f*, Absorption *f*; .(*fig*) Versunkenheit *f*
abstain [əb'steɪn] *vi* (*in vote*) sich enthalten; **to ~ from** (*keep from*) sich enthalten +*gen*
abstemious [əb'stiːmɪəs] *adj* enthaltsam
abstinence ['æbstɪnəns] *n* Enthaltsamkeit *f*

abstract ['æbstrækt] *adj* abstrakt
absurd [əb'sɜːd] *adj* absurd
abundance [ə'bʌndəns] *n*: ~ **(of)** Überfluss *m* (an +*dat*); **abundant** [ə'bʌndənt] *adj* reichlich
abuse [*n* ə'bjuːs, *vb* ə'bjuːz] *n* (*rude language*) Beschimpfung *f*; (*ill usage*) Missbrauch *m*; (*bad practice*) (Amts)missbrauch *m* ♦ *vt* (*misuse*) missbrauchen; **abusive** [ə'bjuːsɪv] *adj* beleidigend, Schimpf-
abysmal [ə'bɪzməl] *adj* scheußlich; (*ignorance*) bodenlos
abyss [ə'bɪs] *n* Abgrund *m*
AC *abbr* (= *alternating current*) Wechselstrom *m*
academic [ækə'demɪk] *adj* akademisch; (*theoretical*) theoretisch ♦ *n* Akademiker(in) *m(f)*
academy [ə'kædəmɪ] *n* (*school*) Hochschule *f*; (*society*) Akademie *f*
accelerate [æk'seləreɪt] *vi* schneller werden; (*AUT*) Gas geben ♦ *vt* beschleunigen; **acceleration** [æksɛlə'reɪʃən] *n* Beschleunigung *f*; **accelerator** [æk'seləreɪtəʳ] *n* Gas(pedal) *nt*
accent ['æksənt] *n* Akzent *m*, Tonfall *m*; (*mark*) Akzent *m*; (*stress*) Betonung *f*
accept [æk'sept] *vt* (*take*) annehmen; (*agree to*) akzeptieren; ~**able** *adj* annehmbar; ~**ance** *n* Annahme *f*
access ['ækses] *n* Zugang *m*; ~**ible** [æk'sesəbl] *adj* (*easy to approach*) zugänglich; (*within reach*) (leicht) erreichbar
accessory [æk'sesərɪ] *n* Zubehörteil *nt*; **toilet accessories** Toilettenartikel *pl*
accident ['æksɪdənt] *n* Unfall *m*; (*coincidence*) Zufall *m*; **by** ~ zufällig; ~**al** [æksɪ'dentl] *adj* unbeabsichtigt; ~**ally** [æksɪ'dentəlɪ] *adv* zufällig; ~ **insurance** *n* Unfallversicherung *f*; ~**-prone** *adj*: **to be** ~**-prone** zu Unfällen neigen
acclaim [ə'kleɪm] *vt* zujubeln +*dat* ♦ *n* Beifall *m*
acclimatize [ə'klaɪmətaɪz] *vt*: **to become** ~**d (to)** sich gewöhnen (an +*acc*), sich akklimatisieren (in +*dat*)
accommodate [ə'kɒmədeɪt] *vt*

unterbringen; (hold) Platz haben für; (oblige) (aus)helfen +dat

accommodating [ə'kɔmədeɪtɪŋ] adj entgegenkommend

accommodation [əkɔmə'deɪʃən] (US **accommodations**) n Unterkunft f

accompany [ə'kʌmpənɪ] vt begleiten

accomplice [ə'kʌmplɪs] n Helfershelfer m, Komplize m

accomplish [ə'kʌmplɪʃ] vt (fulfil) durchführen; (finish) vollenden; (aim) erreichen; **~ed** adj vollendet, ausgezeichnet; **~ment** n (skill) Fähigkeit f; (completion) Vollendung f; (feat) Leistung f

accord [ə'kɔːd] n Übereinstimmung f ♦ vt gewähren; **of one's own ~** freiwillig; **~ing to** nach, laut +gen; **~ance** n: **in ~ance with** in Übereinstimmung mit; **~ingly** adv danach, dementsprechend

accordion [ə'kɔːdɪən] n Akkordeon nt

accost [ə'kɔst] vt ansprechen

account [ə'kaunt] n (bill) Rechnung f; (narrative) Bericht m; (report) Rechenschaftsbericht m; (in bank) Konto nt; (importance) Geltung f; **~s** npl (FIN) Bücher pl; **on ~** auf Rechnung; **on no ~** keinesfalls; **on ~ of** wegen; **to take into ~** berücksichtigen; **~ for** vt fus (expenditure) Rechenschaft ablegen für; **how do you ~ for that?** wie erklären Sie (sich) das?; **~able** adj verantwortlich; **~ancy** [ə'kauntənsɪ] n Buchhaltung f; **~ant** [ə'kauntənt] n Wirtschaftsprüfer(in) m(f); **~ number** n Kontonummer f

accumulate [ə'kjuːmjuleɪt] vt ansammeln ♦ vi sich ansammeln

accuracy ['ækjurəsɪ] n Genauigkeit f

accurate ['ækjurɪt] adj genau; **~ly** adv genau, richtig

accusation [ækju'zeɪʃən] n Anklage f, Beschuldigung f

accuse [ə'kjuːz] vt anklagen, beschuldigen; **~d** n Angeklagte(r) f(m)

accustom [ə'kʌstəm] vt: **to ~ sb (to sth)** jdn (an etw acc) gewöhnen; **~ed** adj gewohnt

ace [eɪs] n Ass nt; (inf) Ass nt, Kanone f

ache [eɪk] n Schmerz m ♦ vi (be sore) schmerzen, wehtun

achieve [ə'tʃiːv] vt zustande or zu Stande bringen; (aim) erreichen; **~ment** n Leistung f; (act) Erreichen nt

acid ['æsɪd] n Säure f ♦ adj sauer, scharf; **~ rain** n saure(r) Regen m

acknowledge [ək'nɔlɪdʒ] vt (receipt) bestätigen; (admit) zugeben; **~ment** n Anerkennung f; (letter) Empfangsbestätigung f

acne ['æknɪ] n Akne f

acorn ['eɪkɔːn] n Eichel f

acoustic [ə'kuːstɪk] adj akustisch; **~s** npl Akustik f

acquaint [ə'kweɪnt] vt vertraut machen; **to be ~ed with sb** mit jdm bekannt sein; **~ance** n (person) Bekannte(r) f(m); (knowledge) Kenntnis f

acquire [ə'kwaɪəʳ] vt erwerben; **acquisition** [ækwɪ'zɪʃən] n Errungenschaft f; (act) Erwerb m

acquit [ə'kwɪt] vt (free) freisprechen; **to ~ o.s. well** sich bewähren; **~tal** n Freispruch m

acre ['eɪkəʳ] n Morgen m

acrid ['ækrɪd] adj (smell, taste) bitter; (smoke) beißend

acrobat ['ækrəbæt] n Akrobat m

across [ə'krɔs] prep über +acc ♦ adv hinüber, herüber; **he lives ~ the river** er wohnt auf der anderen Seite des Flusses; **ten metres ~** zehn Meter breit; **he lives ~ from us** er wohnt uns gegenüber; **to run/swim ~** hinüberlaufen/schwimmen

acrylic [ə'krɪlɪk] adj Acryl-

act [ækt] n (deed) Tat f; (JUR) Gesetz nt; (THEAT) Akt m; (: turn) Nummer f ♦ vi (take ~ion) handeln; (behave) sich verhalten; (pretend) vorgeben; (THEAT) spielen ♦ vt (in play) spielen; **to ~ as** fungieren als; **~ing** adj stellvertretend ♦ n Schauspielkunst f; (performance) Aufführung f

action ['ækʃən] n (deed) Tat f; Handlung f; (motion) Bewegung f; (way of working) Funktionieren nt; (battle) Einsatz m, Gefecht nt; (lawsuit) Klage f, Prozess m; **out of ~**

(*person*) nicht einsatzfähig; (*thing*) außer Betrieb; **to take ~** etwas unternehmen; **~ replay** n (*TV*) Wiederholung f

activate ['æktıveıt] vt (*mechanism*) betätigen; (*CHEM, PHYS*) aktivieren

active ['æktıv] adj (*brisk*) rege, tatkräftig; (*working*) aktiv; (*GRAM*) aktiv, Tätigkeits-; **~ly** adv aktiv; (*dislike*) offen

activity [æk'tıvıtı] n Aktivität f; (*doings*) Unternehmungen pl; (*occupation*) Tätigkeit f; **~ holiday** n Aktivurlaub m

actor ['æktər] n Schauspieler m

actress ['æktrıs] n Schauspielerin f

actual ['æktjuəl] adj wirklich; **~ly** adv tatsächlich; **~ly no** eigentlich nicht

acumen ['ækjumən] n Scharfsinn m

acute [ə'kju:t] adj (*severe*) heftig, akut; (*keen*) scharfsinnig

ad [æd] n abbr = **advertisement**

A.D. adv abbr (= *Anno Domini*) n. Chr.

adamant ['ædəmənt] adj eisern; hartnäckig

adapt [ə'dæpt] vt anpassen ♦ vi: **to ~ (to)** sich anpassen (an +*acc*); **~able** adj anpassungsfähig; **~ation** [ædæp'teıʃən] n (*THEAT etc*) Bearbeitung f; (*adjustment*) Anpassung f; **~er, ~or** n (*ELEC*) Zwischenstecker m

add [æd] vt (*join*) hinzufügen; (*numbers: also:* **~ up**) addieren; **~ up** vi (*make sense*) stimmen; **~ up to** vt fus ausmachen

adder ['ædər] n Kreuzotter f, Natter f

addict ['ædıkt] n Süchtige(r) f(m); **~ed** [ə'dıktıd] adj: **~ed to** -süchtig; **~ion** [ə'dıkʃən] n Sucht f; **~ive** [ə'dıktıv] adj: **to be ~ive** süchtig machen

addition [ə'dıʃən] n Anhang m, Addition f; (*MATH*) Addition f, Zusammenzählen nt; **in ~** zusätzlich, außerdem; **~al** adj zusätzlich, weiter

additive ['ædıtıv] n Zusatz m

address [ə'dres] n Adresse f; (*speech*) Ansprache f ♦ vt (*letter*) adressieren; (*speak to*) ansprechen; (*make speech to*) eine Ansprache halten an +*acc*

adept ['ædept] adj geschickt; **to be ~ at** gut sein in +*dat*

adequate ['ædıkwıt] adj angemessen

adhere [əd'hıər] vi: **to ~ to** haften an +*dat*; (*fig*) festhalten an +*dat*

adhesive [əd'hi:zıv] adj klebend; Kleb(e)- ♦ n Klebstoff m; **~ tape** n (*BRIT*) Klebestreifen m; (*US*) Heftpflaster nt

ad hoc [æd'hɔk] adj (*decision, committee*) Ad-hoc- ♦ adv ad hoc

adjacent [ə'dʒeısənt] adj benachbart; **~ to** angrenzend an +*acc*

adjective ['ædʒektıv] n Adjektiv nt, Eigenschaftswort nt

adjoining [ə'dʒɔınıŋ] adj benachbart, Neben-

adjourn [ə'dʒə:n] vt vertagen ♦ vi abbrechen

adjudicate [ə'dʒu:dıkeıt] vi entscheiden, ein Urteil fällen

adjust [ə'dʒʌst] vt (*alter*) anpassen; (*put right*) regulieren, richtig stellen ♦ vi sich anpassen; **~able** adj verstellbar

ad-lib [æd'lıb] vt, vi improvisieren ♦ adv: **ad lib** aus dem Stegreif

administer [əd'mınıstər] vt (*manage*) verwalten; (*dispense*) ausüben; (*justice*) sprechen; (*medicine*) geben; **administration** [ədmınıs'treıʃən] n Verwaltung f; (*POL*) Regierung f; **administrative** [əd'mınıstrətıv] adj Verwaltungs-; **administrator** [əd'mınıstreıtər] n Verwaltungsbeamte(r) f(m)

Admiralty ['ædmərəltı] (*BRIT*) n Admiralität f

admiration [ædmə'reıʃən] n Bewunderung f

admire [əd'maıər] vt (*respect*) bewundern; (*love*) verehren; **~r** n Bewunderer m

admission [əd'mıʃən] n (*entrance*) Einlass m; (*fee*) Eintritt(spreis m) m; (*confession*) Geständnis nt; **~ charge** n Eintritt(spreis m

admit [əd'mıt] vt (*let in*) einlassen; (*confess*) gestehen; (*accept*) anerkennen; **~tance** n Zulassung f; **~tedly** adv zugegebenermaßen

admonish [əd'mɔnıʃ] vt ermahnen

ad nauseam [æd'nɔ:sıæm] adv (*repeat, talk*) endlos

ado [ə'du:] n: **without more ~** ohne weitere Umstände

adolescence [ædəʊ'lesns] n Jugendalter nt;
adolescent [ædəʊ'lesnt] adj jugendlich ♦ n
Jugendliche(r) f(m)

adopt [ə'dɒpt] vt (child) adoptieren; (idea)
übernehmen; **~ion** [ə'dɒpʃən] n Adoption f;
Übernahme f

adore [ə'dɔːr] vt anbeten; verehren

adorn [ə'dɔːn] vt schmücken

Adriatic [eɪdrɪ'ætɪk] n: **the ~ (Sea)** die Adria

adrift [ə'drɪft] adv Wind und Wellen
preisgegeben

adult ['ædʌlt] n Erwachsene(r) f(m)

adultery [ə'dʌltərɪ] n Ehebruch m

advance [əd'vɑːns] n (progress) Vorrücken
nt; (money) Vorschuss m ♦ vt (move forward)
vorrücken; (money) vorschießen; (argument)
vorbringen ♦ vi vorwärts gehen; **in ~** im
Voraus, **~ booking** n Vorverkauf m; **~d** adj
(ahead) vorgerückt; (modern)
fortgeschritten; (study) für Fortgeschrittene

advantage [əd'vɑːntɪdʒ] n Vorteil m; **to
have an ~ over sb** jdm gegenüber im
Vorteil sein; **to take ~ of** (misuse)
ausnutzen; (profit from) Nutzen ziehen aus;
~ous [ædvən'teɪdʒəs] adj vorteilhaft

advent ['ædvənt] n Ankunft f; **A~** Advent m

adventure [əd'ventʃər] n Abenteuer nt;
adventurous abenteuerlich, waghalsig

adverb ['ædvɜːb] n Adverb nt,
Umstandswort nt

adversary ['ædvəsərɪ] n Gegner m

adverse ['ædvɜːs] adj widrig; **adversity**
[əd'vɜːsɪtɪ] n Widrigkeit f, Missgeschick nt

advert ['ædvɜːt] n Anzeige f; **~ise** ['ædvətaɪz]
vt werben für ♦ vi annoncieren; **to ~ise for
sth** etw (per Anzeige) suchen; **~isement**
[əd'vɜːtɪsmənt] n Anzeige f, Inserat nt; **~iser**
n (in newspaper etc) Inserent m; **~ising**
Werbung f

advice [əd'vaɪs] n Rat(schlag) m

advisable [əd'vaɪzəbl] adj ratsam

advise [əd'vaɪz] vt: **to ~ (sb)** (jdm) raten;
~dly [əd'vaɪzɪdlɪ] adv (deliberately) bewusst;
~r n Berater m; **advisory** [əd'vaɪzərɪ] adj
beratend, Beratungs-

advocate [vb 'ædvəkeɪt, n 'ædvəkət] vt
vertreten ♦ n Befürworter(in) m(f)

Aegean [iː'dʒiːən] n: **the ~ (Sea)** die Ägäis

aerial ['eərɪəl] n Antenne f ♦ adj Luft-

aerobics [eə'rəʊbɪks] n Aerobic nt

aerodynamic ['eərəʊdaɪ'næmɪk] adj
aerodynamisch

aeroplane ['eərəpleɪn] n Flugzeug nt

aerosol ['eərəsɒl] n Aerosol nt; Sprühdose f

aesthetic [iːs'θetɪk] adj ästhetisch

afar [ə'fɑːr] adv: **from ~** aus der Ferne

affable ['æfəbl] adj umgänglich

affair [ə'feər] n (concern) Angelegenheit f;
(event) Ereignis nt; (love ~) Verhältnis nt; **~s**
npl (business) Geschäfte pl

affect [ə'fekt] vt (influence) (ein)wirken auf
+acc; (move deeply) bewegen; **this change
doesn't ~ us** diese Änderung betrifft uns
nicht; **~ed** adj affektiert, gekünstelt

affection [ə'fekʃən] n Zuneigung f; **~ate** adj
liebevoll

affiliated [ə'fɪlɪeɪtɪd] adj angeschlossen

affinity [ə'fɪnɪtɪ] n (attraction) gegenseitige
Anziehung f; (relationship) Verwandtschaft f

affirmative [ə'fɜːmətɪv] adj bestätigend

afflict [ə'flɪkt] vt quälen, heimsuchen

affluence ['æfluəns] n (wealth) Wohlstand
m; **affluent** adj wohlhabend, Wohlstands-

afford [ə'fɔːd] vt sich dat leisten; (yield)
bieten, einbringen

afield [ə'fiːld] adv: **far ~** weit fort

afloat [ə'fləʊt] adj: **to be ~** schwimmen

afoot [ə'fʊt] adv im Gang

afraid [ə'freɪd] adj ängstlich; **to be ~ of**
Angst haben vor +dat; **to be ~ to do sth**
sich scheuen, etw zu tun; **I am ~ I have ...**
ich habe leider ...; **I'm ~ so/not** leider/
leider nicht; **I am ~ that ...** ich fürchte(,
dass) ...

afresh [ə'freʃ] adv von neuem

Africa ['æfrɪkə] n Afrika nt; **~n** adj afrikanisch
♦ n Afrikaner(in) m(f)

after ['ɑːftər] prep nach; (following, seeking)
hinter ...dat ... her; (in imitation) nach, im
Stil von ♦ adv: **soon ~** bald danach ♦ conj
nachdem; **what are you ~?** was wollen
Sie?; **~ he left** nachdem er gegangen war;
~ you! nach Ihnen!; **~ all** letzten Endes; **~
having shaved** als er sich rasiert hatte;

~effects *npl* Nachwirkungen *pl*; **~math** *n* Auswirkungen *pl*; **~noon** *n* Nachmittag *m*; **~s** *(inf)* *n (dessert)* Nachtisch *m*; **~-sales service** *(BRIT)* *n* Kundendienst *m*; **~shave (lotion)** *n* Rasierwasser *nt*; **~sun** *n* Aftersunlotion *f*; **~thought** *n* nachträgliche(r) Einfall *m*; **~wards** *adv* danach, nachher

again [ə'gɛn] *adv* wieder, noch einmal; *(besides)* außerdem, ferner; **~ and ~** immer wieder

against [ə'gɛnst] *prep* gegen

age [eɪdʒ] *n (of person)* Alter *nt*; *(in history)* Zeitalter *nt* ♦ *vi* altern, alt werden ♦ *vt* älter machen; **to come of ~** mündig werden; **20 years of ~** 20 Jahre alt; **it's been ~s since** ... es ist ewig her, seit ...

aged¹ [eɪdʒd] *adj* ... Jahre alt, -jährig

aged² [eɪdʒd] *adj (elderly)* betagt ♦ *npl*: **the ~** die Alten *pl*

age group *n* Altersgruppe *f*

age limit *n* Altersgrenze *f*

agency ['eɪdʒənsɪ] *n* Agentur *f*; Vermittlung *f*; *(CHEM)* Wirkung *f*; **through** *or* **by the ~** ... mithilfe *or* mit Hilfe von ...

agenda [ə'dʒɛndə] *n* Tagesordnung *f*

agent ['eɪdʒənt] *n (COMM)* Vertreter *m*; *(spy)* Agent *m*

aggravate ['ægrəveɪt] *vt (make worse)* verschlimmern; *(irritate)* reizen

aggregate ['ægrɪgɪt] *n* Summe *f*

aggression [ə'grɛʃən] *n* Aggression *f*; **aggressive** [ə'grɛsɪv] *adj* aggressiv

aghast [ə'gɑːst] *adj* entsetzt

agile ['ædʒaɪl] *adj* flink, agil; *(mind)* rege

agitate ['ædʒɪteɪt] *vt* rütteln; **to ~ for** sich stark machen für

AGM *n abbr* (= *annual general meeting*) JHV *f*

ago [ə'gəu] *adv*: **two days ~** vor zwei Tagen; **not long ~** vor kurzem; **it's so long ~** es ist schon so lange her

agog [ə'gɒg] *adj* gespannt

agonizing ['ægənaɪzɪŋ] *adj* quälend

agony ['ægənɪ] *n* Qual *f*; **to be in ~** Qualen leiden

agree [ə'griː] *vt (date)* vereinbaren ♦ *vi (have same opinion, correspond)* übereinstimmen;

(consent) zustimmen; *(be in harmony)* sich vertragen; **to ~ to sth** einer Sache *dat* zustimmen; **to ~ that ...** *(admit)* zugeben, dass ...; **to ~ to do sth** sich bereit erklären, etw zu tun; **garlic doesn't ~ with me** Knoblauch vertrage ich nicht; **I ~** einverstanden, ich stimme zu; **to ~ on sth** sich auf etw *acc* einigen; **~able** *adj (pleasing)* liebenswürdig; *(willing to consent)* einverstanden; **~d** *adj* vereinbart; **~ment** *n* (*~ing*) Übereinstimmung *f*; *(contract)* Vereinbarung *f*, Vertrag *m*; **to be in ~ment** übereinstimmen

agricultural [ægrɪ'kʌltʃərəl] *adj* landwirtschaftlich, Landwirtschafts-

agriculture ['ægrɪkʌltʃər] *n* Landwirtschaft *f*

aground [ə'graund] *adv*: **to run ~** auf Grund laufen

ahead [ə'hɛd] *adv* vorwärts; **to be ~** voraus sein; **~ of time** der Zeit voraus; **go right** *or* **straight ~** gehen Sie geradeaus; fahren Sie geradeaus

aid [eɪd] *n (assistance)* Hilfe *f*, Unterstützung *f*; *(person)* Hilfe *f*; *(thing)* Hilfsmittel *nt* ♦ *vt* unterstützen, helfen +*dat*; **in ~ of** zugunsten *or* zu Gunsten +*gen*; **to ~ and abet sb** jdm Beihilfe leisten

aide [eɪd] *n (person)* Gehilfe *m*; *(MIL)* Adjutant *m*

AIDS [eɪdz] *n abbr* (= *acquired immune deficiency syndrome*) Aids *nt*; **AIDS-related** aidsbedingt

ailing ['eɪlɪŋ] *adj* kränkelnd

ailment ['eɪlmənt] *n* Leiden *nt*

aim [eɪm] *vt (gun, camera)* richten ♦ *vi (with gun: also:* **take ~**) zielen; *(intend)* beabsichtigen ♦ *n (intention)* Absicht *f*, Ziel *nt*; *(pointing)* Zielen *nt*, Richten *nt*; **to ~ at sth** auf etw *dat* richten; *(fig)* etw anstreben; **to ~ to do sth** vorhaben, etw zu tun; **~less** *adj* ziellos; **~lessly** *adv* ziellos

ain't [eɪnt] *(inf)* = **am not**; **are not**; **is not**; **has not**; **have not**

air [ɛər] *n* Luft *f*; *(manner)* Miene *f*, Anschein *m*; *(MUS)* Melodie *f* ♦ *vt* lüften; *(fig)* an die Öffentlichkeit bringen ♦ *cpd* Luft-; **by ~** *(travel)* auf dem Luftweg; **to be on the ~**

(*RADIO, TV: programme*) gesendet werden; **~bed** (*BRIT*) *n* Luftmatratze *f*; **~-conditioned** *adj* mit Klimaanlage; **~-conditioning** *n* Klimaanlage *f*; **~craft** *n* Flugzeug *nt*, Maschine *f*; **~craft carrier** *n* Flugzeugträger *m*; **~field** *n* Flugplatz *m*; **~ force** *n* Luftwaffe *f*; **~ freshener** *n* Raumspray *nt*; **~gun** *n* Luftgewehr *nt*; **~ hostess** (*BRIT*) *n* Stewardess *f*; **letter** (*BRIT*) *n* Luftpostbrief *m*; **~lift** *n* Luftbrücke *f*; **~line** *n* Luftverkehrsgesellschaft *f*; **~liner** *n* Verkehrsflugzeug *nt*; **~lock** *n* Luftblase *f*; **~mail** *n*: **by ~mail** mit Luftpost; **~ miles** *npl* ≃ Flugkilometer *m*; **~plane** (*US*) *n* Flugzeug *nt*; **~port** *n* Flughafen *m*, Flugplatz *m*; **~ raid** *n* Luftangriff *m*; **~sick** *adj* luftkrank; **~space** *n* Luftraum *m*; **~strip** *n* Landestreifen *m*; **~ terminal** *n* Terminal *m*; **~tight** *adj* luftdicht; **~ traffic controller** *n* Fluglotse *m*; **~y** *adj* luftig; (*manner*) leichtfertig

aisle [aɪl] *n* Gang *m*; **~ seat** *n* Sitz *m* am Gang

ajar [ə'dʒɑːʳ] *adv* angelehnt; einen Spalt offen

alarm [ə'lɑːm] *n* (*warning*) Alarm *m*; (*bell etc*) Alarmanlage *f*; (*anxiety*) Sorge *f* ♦ *vt* erschrecken; **~ call** *n* (*in hotel etc*) Weckruf *m*; **~ clock** *n* Wecker *m*

Albania [æl'beɪnɪə] *n* Albanien *nt*

albeit [ɔːl'biːɪt] *conj* obgleich

album [ˈælbəm] *n* Album *nt*

alcohol [ˈælkəhɒl] *n* Alkohol *m*; **~-free** *adj* alkoholfrei; **~ic** [ælkəˈhɒlɪk] *adj* (*drink*) alkoholisch ♦ *n* Alkoholiker(in) *m(f)*; **~ism** *n* Alkoholismus *m*

alert [ə'lɜːt] *adj* wachsam ♦ *n* Alarm *m* ♦ *vt* alarmieren; **to be on the ~** wachsam sein

Algeria [ælˈdʒɪərɪə] *n* Algerien *nt*

alias [ˈeɪlɪəs] *adv* alias ♦ *n* Deckname *m*

alibi [ˈælɪbaɪ] *n* Alibi *nt*

alien [ˈeɪlɪən] *n* Ausländer *m* ♦ *adj* (*foreign*) ausländisch; (*strange*) fremd; **~ to** fremd +*dat*; **~ate** *vt* entfremden

alight [ə'laɪt] *adj* brennend; (*of building*) in Flammen ♦ *vi* (*descend*) aussteigen; (*bird*) sich setzen

align [ə'laɪn] *vt* ausrichten

alike [ə'laɪk] *adj* gleich, ähnlich ♦ *adv* gleich, ebenso; **to look ~** sich *dat* ähnlich sehen

alimony [ˈælɪmənɪ] *n* Unterhalt *m*, Alimente *pl*

alive [ə'laɪv] *adj* (*living*) lebend; (*lively*) lebendig, aufgeweckt; **~ (with)** (*full of*) voll (von), wimmelnd (von)

KEYWORD

---

all [ɔːl] *adj* alle(r, s); **all day/night** den ganzen Tag/die ganze Nacht; **all men are equal** alle Menschen sind gleich; **all five came** alle fünf kamen; **all the books/food** die ganzen Bücher/das ganze Essen; **all the time** die ganze Zeit (über); **all his life** sein ganzes Leben (lang)

♦ *pron* **1** alles; **I ate it all, I ate all of it** ich habe alles gegessen; **all of us/the boys went** wir alle gingen/alle Jungen gingen; **we all sat down** wir setzten uns alle

2 (*in phrases*): **above all** vor allem; **after all** schließlich; **at all: not at all** (*in answer to question*) überhaupt nicht; (*in answer to thanks*) gern geschehen; **I'm not at all tired** ich bin überhaupt nicht müde; **anything at all will do** es ist egal, welche(r, s); **all in all** alles in allem

♦ *adv* ganz; **all alone** ganz allein; **it's not as hard as all that** so schwer ist es nun auch wieder nicht; **all the more/better** umso mehr/besser; **all but** fast; **the score is 2 all** es steht 2 zu 2

---

allay [ə'leɪ] *vt* (*fears*) beschwichtigen

all clear *n* Entwarnung *f*

allegation [ælɪ'geɪʃən] *n* Behauptung *f*

allege [ə'ledʒ] *vt* (*declare*) behaupten; (*falsely*) vorgeben; **~dly** *adv* angeblich

allegiance [ə'liːdʒəns] *n* Treue *f*

allergic [ə'lɜːdʒɪk] *adj*: **~ (to)** allergisch (gegen)

allergy [ˈælədʒɪ] *n* Allergie *f*

alleviate [ə'liːvɪeɪt] *vt* lindern

alley [ˈælɪ] *n* Gasse *f*, Durchgang *m*

alliance [ə'laɪəns] *n* Bund *m*, Allianz *f*

allied [ˈælaɪd] *adj* vereinigt; (*powers*) alliiert; **~ (to)** verwandt (mit)

all: **~-in** (BRIT) *adj, adv* (*charge*) alles inbegriffen, Gesamt-; **~-in wrestling** *n* Freistilringen *nt*; **~-night** *adj* (*café, cinema*) die ganze Nacht geöffnet, Nacht-

allocate ['æləkeɪt] *vt* zuteilen

allot [ə'lɔt] *vt* zuteilen; **~ment** *n* (*share*) Anteil *m*; (*plot*) Schrebergarten *m*

all-out ['ɔːlaut] *adj* total; **all out** *adv* mit voller Kraft

allow [ə'lau] *vt* (*permit*) erlauben, gestatten; (*grant*) bewilligen; (*deduct*) abziehen; (*concede*): **to ~ that ...** annehmen, dass ...; **to ~ sb sth** jdm etw erlauben, jdm etw gestatten; **to ~ sb to do sth** jdm erlauben *or* gestatten, etw zu tun; **~ for** *vt fus* berücksichtigen, einplanen; **~ance** *n* Beihilfe *f*; **to make ~ances for** berücksichtigen

alloy ['ælɔɪ] *n* Metalllegierung *f*

all: **~ right** *adv* (*well*) gut; (*correct*) richtig; (*as answer*) okay; **~-round** *adj* (*sportsman*) allseitig, Allround-; (*view*) Rundum-; **~-time** *adj* (*record, high*) ... aller Zeiten, Höchst-

allude [ə'luːd] *vi*: **to ~ to** hinweisen auf +*acc*, anspielen auf +*acc*

alluring [ə'ljuərɪŋ] *adj* verlockend

ally [*n* 'ælaɪ, *vb* ə'laɪ] *n* Verbündete(r) *f(m)*; (POL) Alliierte(r) *f(m)* ♦ *vr*: **to ~ o.s. with** sich verbünden mit

almighty [ɔːl'maɪtɪ] *adj* allmächtig

almond ['ɑːmənd] *n* Mandel *f*

almost ['ɔːlməust] *adv* fast, beinahe

alms [ɑːmz] *npl* Almosen *nt*

alone [ə'ləun] *adj, adv* allein; **to leave sth ~** etw sein lassen; **let ~ ...** geschweige denn ...

along [ə'lɔŋ] *prep* entlang, längs ♦ *adv* (*onward*) vorwärts, weiter; **~ with** zusammen mit; **he was limping ~** er humpelte einher; **all ~** (*all the time*) die ganze Zeit; **~side** *adv* (*walk*) nebenher; (*come*) nebendran; (*be*) daneben ♦ *prep* (*walk, compared with*) neben +*dat*; (*come*) neben +*acc*; (*be*) entlang, neben +*dat*; (*of ship*) längsseits +*gen*

aloof [ə'luːf] *adj* zurückhaltend ♦ *adv* fern; **to stand ~** abseits stehen

aloud [ə'laud] *adv* laut

alphabet ['ælfəbet] *n* Alphabet *nt*; **~ical** [ælfə'betɪkl] *adj* alphabetisch

alpine ['ælpaɪn] *adj* alpin, Alpen-

Alps [ælps] *npl*: **the ~** die Alpen *pl*

already [ɔːl'redɪ] *adv* schon, bereits

alright ['ɔːl'raɪt] (BRIT) *adv* = **all right**

Alsatian [æl'seɪʃən] *n* (*dog*) Schäferhund *m*

also ['ɔːlsəu] *adv* auch, außerdem

altar ['ɔːltə] *n* Altar *m*

alter ['ɔːltə] *vt* ändern; (*dress*) umändern; **~ation** [ɔːltə'reɪʃən] *n* Änderung *f*; Umänderung *f*; (*to building*) Umbau *m*

alternate [*adj* ɔl'tɜːnɪt, *vb* 'ɔltə:neɪt] *adj* abwechselnd ♦ *vi* abwechseln; **on ~ days** jeden zweiten Tag

alternating ['ɔltə:neɪtɪŋ] *adj*: **~ current** Wechselstrom *m*; **alternative** [ɔl'tɜːnətɪv] *adj* andere(r, s) ♦ *n* Alternative *f*; **alternative medicine** Alternativmedizin *f*; **alternatively** *adv* im anderen Falle; **alternatively one could ...** oder man könnte ...; **alternator** ['ɔltə:neɪtə] *n* (AUT) Lichtmaschine *f*

although [ɔːl'ðəu] *conj* obwohl

altitude ['æltɪtjuːd] *n* Höhe *f*

alto ['æltəu] *n* Alt *m*

altogether [ɔːltə'geðə] *adv* (*on the whole*) im Ganzen genommen; (*entirely*) ganz und gar

aluminium [ælju'mɪnɪəm] (BRIT) *n* Aluminium *nt*

aluminum [ə'luːmɪnəm] (US) *n* Aluminium *nt*

always ['ɔːlweɪz] *adv* immer

Alzheimer's (disease) ['æltshaɪməz-] *n* (MED) Alzheimerkrankheit *f*

AM *n abbr* (= *Assembly Member*) Mitglied *nt* der walisischen Versammlung

am [æm] *see* **be**

a.m. *adv abbr* (= *ante meridiem*) vormittags

amalgamate [ə'mælgəmeɪt] *vi* (*combine*) sich vereinigen ♦ *vt* (*mix*) amalgamieren

amass [ə'mæs] *vt* anhäufen

amateur ['æmətə] *n* Amateur *m*; (*pej*) Amateur *m*, Stümper *m*; **~ish** (*pej*) *adj* dilettantisch, stümperhaft

amaze [ə'meɪz] *vt* erstaunen; **to be ~d (at)** erstaunt sein (über); **~ment** *n* höchste(s)

Erstaunen nt; **amazing** adj höchst erstaunlich

Amazon ['æməzən] n (GEOG) Amazonas m

ambassador [æm'bæsədəʳ] n Botschafter m

amber ['æmbəʳ] n Bernstein m; **at ~** (BRIT: AUT) auf Gelb, gelb

ambiguous [æm'bɪgjuəs] adj zweideutig; (not clear) unklar

ambition [æm'bɪʃən] n Ehrgeiz m; **ambitious** adj ehrgeizig

amble ['æmbl] vi (usu: ~ along) schlendern

ambulance ['æmbjuləns] n Krankenwagen m; **~ man** (irreg) n Sanitäter m

ambush ['æmbuʃ] n Hinterhalt m ♦ vt (aus dem Hinterhalt) überfallen

amenable [ə'mi:nəbl] adj gefügig; **~ (to)** (reason) zugänglich (+dat); (flattery) empfänglich (für)

amend [ə'mend] vt (law etc) abändern, ergänzen; **to make ~s** etw wieder gutmachen; **~ment** n Abänderung f

amenities [ə'mi:nɪtɪz] npl Einrichtungen pl

America [ə'merɪkə] n Amerika nt; **~n** adj amerikanisch ♦ n Amerikaner(in) m(f)

amiable ['eɪmɪəbl] adj liebenswürdig

amicable ['æmɪkəbl] adj freundschaftlich; (settlement) gütlich

amid(st) [ə'mɪd(st)] prep mitten in or unter +dat

amiss [ə'mɪs] adv: **to take sth ~** etw übel nehmen; **there's something ~** da stimmt irgendetwas nicht

ammonia [ə'məunɪə] n Ammoniak nt

ammunition [æmju'nɪʃən] n Munition f

amnesia [æm'ni:zɪə] n Gedächtnisverlust m

amnesty ['æmnɪstɪ] n Amnestie f

amok [ə'mɔk] adv: **to run ~** Amok laufen

among(st) [ə'mʌŋ(st)] prep unter

amoral [æ'mɔrəl] adj unmoralisch

amorous ['æmərəs] adj verliebt

amount [ə'maunt] n (of money) Betrag m; (of water, sand) Menge f ♦ vi: **to ~ to** (total) sich belaufen auf +acc; **a great ~ of time/ energy** ein großer Aufwand an Zeit/ Energie (dat); **this ~s to treachery** das kommt Verrat gleich; **he won't ~ to much** aus ihm wird nie was

amp(ere) [æmp(ɛəʳ)] n Ampere nt

amphibian [æm'fɪbɪən] n Amphibie f

ample ['æmpl] adj (portion) reichlich; (dress) weit, groß; **~ time** genügend Zeit

amplifier ['æmplɪfaɪəʳ] n Verstärker m

amuse [ə'mju:z] vt (entertain) unterhalten; (make smile) belustigen; **~ment** n (feeling) Unterhaltung f; (recreation) Zeitvertreib m; **~ment arcade** n Spielhalle f; **~ment park** n Vergnügungspark m

an [æn, ən] see **a**

anaemia [ə'ni:mɪə] n Anämie f; **anaemic** adj blutarm

anaesthetic [ænɪs'θetɪk] n Betäubungsmittel nt; **under ~** unter Narkose; **anaesthetist** [æ'ni:sθɪtɪst] n Anästhesist(in) m(f)

analgesic [ænæl'dʒi:sɪk] n schmerzlindernde(s) Mittel nt

analog(ue) ['ænəlɔg] adj Analog-

analogy [ə'nælədʒɪ] n Analogie f

analyse ['ænəlaɪz] (BRIT) vt analysieren

analyses [ə'næləsi:z] (BRIT) npl of **analysis**

analysis [ə'næləsɪs] (pl **analyses**) n Analyse f

analyst ['ænəlɪst] n Analytiker(in) m(f)

analytic(al) [ænə'lɪtɪk(l)] adj analytisch

analyze ['ænəlaɪz] (US) vt = **analyse**

anarchy ['ænəkɪ] n Anarchie f

anatomy [ə'nætəmɪ] n (structure) anato- mische(r) Aufbau m; (study) Anatomie f

ancestor ['ænsɪstəʳ] n Vorfahr m

anchor ['æŋkəʳ] n Anker m ♦ vi (also: **to drop ~**) ankern, vor Anker gehen ♦ vt verankern; **to weigh ~** den Anker lichten

anchovy ['æntʃəvɪ] n Sardelle f

ancient ['eɪnʃənt] adj alt; (car etc) uralt

ancillary [æn'sɪlərɪ] adj Hilfs-

and [ænd] conj und; **~ so on** und so weiter; **try ~ come** versuche zu kommen; **better ~ better** immer besser

Andes ['ændi:z] npl: **the ~** die Anden pl

anemia etc [ə'ni:mɪə] (US) n = **anaemia** etc

anesthetic etc [ænɪs'θetɪk] (US) n = **anaesthetic** etc

anew [ə'nju:] adv von neuem

angel ['eɪndʒəl] n Engel m

anger ['æŋgəʳ] n Zorn m ♦ vt ärgern

angina [æn'dʒaɪnə] *n* Angina *f*

angle ['æŋgl] *n* Winkel *m*; (*point of view*) Standpunkt *m*

angler ['æŋglə'] *n* Angler *m*

Anglican ['æŋglɪkən] *adj* anglikanisch ♦ *n* Anglikaner(in) *m(f)*

angling ['æŋglɪŋ] *n* Angeln *nt*

angrily ['æŋgrɪlɪ] *adv* ärgerlich, böse

angry ['æŋgrɪ] *adj* ärgerlich, ungehalten, böse; (*wound*) entzündet; **to be ~ with sb** auf jdn böse sein; **to be ~ at sth** über etw *acc* verärgert sein

anguish ['æŋgwɪʃ] *n* Qual *f*

angular ['æŋgjulə'] *adj* eckig, winkelförmig; (*face*) kantig

animal ['ænɪməl] *n* Tier *nt*; (*living creature*) Lebewesen *nt* ♦ *adj* tierisch

animate [*vb* 'ænɪmeɪt, *adj* 'ænɪmɪt] *vt* beleben ♦ *adj* lebhaft; **~d** *adj* lebendig; (*film*) Zeichentrick-

animosity [ænɪ'mɔsɪtɪ] *n* Feindseligkeit *f*, Abneigung *f*

aniseed ['ænɪsiːd] *n* Anis *m*

ankle ['æŋkl] *n* (Fuß)knöchel *m*; **~ sock** *n* Söckchen *nt*

annex [*n* 'æneks, *vb* ə'neks] *n* (*BRIT: also:* **~e**) Anbau *m* ♦ *vt* anfügen; (*POL*) annektieren, angliedern

annihilate [ə'naɪəleɪt] *vt* vernichten

anniversary [ænɪ'vəːsərɪ] *n* Jahrestag *m*

announce [ə'nauns] *vt* ankündigen, anzeigen; **~ment** *n* Ankündigung *f*; (*official*) Bekanntmachung *f*; **~r** *n* Ansager(in) *m(f)*

annoy [ə'nɔɪ] *vt* ärgern; **don't get ~ed!** reg dich nicht auf!; **~ance** *n* Ärgernis *nt*, Störung *f*; **~ing** *adj* ärgerlich; (*person*) lästig

annual ['ænjuəl] *adj* jährlich; (*salary*) Jahres- ♦ *n* (*plant*) einjährige Pflanze *f*; (*book*) Jahrbuch *nt*; **~ly** *adv* jährlich

annul [ə'nʌl] *vt* aufheben, annullieren

annum ['ænəm] *n see* **per**

anonymous [ə'nɔnɪməs] *adj* anonym

anorak ['ænəræk] *n* Anorak *m*, Windjacke *f*

anorexia [ænə'reksɪə] *n* (*MED*) Magersucht *f*

another [ə'nʌðə'] *adj, pron* (*different*) ein(e) andere(r, s); (*additional*) noch eine(r, s); *see*

also **one**

answer ['ɑːnsə'] *n* Antwort *f* ♦ *vi* antworten; (*on phone*) sich melden ♦ *vt* (*person*) antworten +*dat*; (*letter, question*) beantworten; (*telephone*) gehen an +*acc*, abnehmen; (*door*) öffnen; **in ~ to your letter** in Beantwortung Ihres Schreibens; **to ~ the phone** ans Telefon gehen; **to ~ the bell** *or* **the door** aufmachen; **~ back** *vi* frech sein; **~ for** *vt fus:* **to ~ for sth** für etw verantwortlich sein; **~able** *adj:* **to be ~able to sb for sth** jdm gegenüber für etw verantwortlich sein; **~ing machine** *n* Anrufbeantworter *m*

ant [ænt] *n* Ameise *f*

antagonism [æn'tægənɪzəm] *n* Antagonismus *m*

antagonize [æn'tægənaɪz] *vt* reizen

Antarctic [ænt'ɑːktɪk] *adj* antarktisch ♦ *n*: **the ~** die Antarktis

antelope ['æntɪləup] *n* Antilope *f*

antenatal ['æntɪ'neɪtl] *adj* vor der Geburt; **~ clinic** *n* Sprechstunde *f* für werdende Mütter

antenna [æn'tenə] *n* (*BIOL*) Fühler *m*; (*RAD*) Antenne *f*

antennae [æn'teniː] *npl of* **antenna**

anthem ['ænθəm] *n* Hymne *f*; **national ~** Nationalhymne *f*

anthology [æn'θɔlədʒɪ] *n* Gedichtsammlung *f*, Anthologie *f*

anti- ['æntɪ] *prefix* Gegen-, Anti-

anti-aircraft ['æntɪ'ɛəkrɑːft] *adj* Flugabwehr-

antibiotic ['æntɪbaɪ'ɔtɪk] *n* Antibiotikum *nt*

antibody ['æntɪbɔdɪ] *n* Antikörper *m*

anticipate [æn'tɪsɪpeɪt] *vt* (*expect: trouble, question*) erwarten, rechnen mit; (*look forward to*) sich freuen auf +*acc*; (*do first*) vorwegnehmen; (*foresee*) ahnen, vorhersehen; **anticipation** [æntɪsɪ'peɪʃən] *n* Erwartung *f*; (*foreshadowing*) Vorwegnahme *f*

anticlimax ['æntɪ'klaɪmæks] *n* Ernüchterung *f*

anticlockwise ['æntɪ'klɔkwaɪz] *adv* entgegen dem Uhrzeigersinn

antics ['æntɪks] *npl* Possen *pl*

anti: ~**cyclone** n Hoch nt, Hochdruckgebiet nt; ~**depressant** n Antidepressivum nt; ~**dote** n Gegenmittel nt; ~**freeze** n Frostschutzmittel nt; ~**histamine** n Antihistamin nt

antiquated ['æntɪkweɪtd] adj antiquiert

antique [æn'tiːk] n Antiquität f ♦ adj antik; (old-fashioned) altmodisch; ~ **shop** n Antiquitätenladen m; **antiquity** [æn'tɪkwɪtɪ] n Altertum nt

antiseptic [æntɪ'septɪk] n Antiseptikum nt ♦ adj antiseptisch

antisocial ['æntɪ'səʊfəl] adj (person) ungesellig; (law) unsozial

antlers ['æntləz] npl Geweih nt

anus ['eɪnəs] n After m

anvil ['ænvɪl] n Amboss m

anxiety [æŋ'zaɪətɪ] n Angst f; (worry) Sorge f; **anxious** ['æŋkʃəs] adj ängstlich; (worried) besorgt; **to be anxious to do sth** etw unbedingt tun wollen

KEYWORD

any ['enɪ] adj 1 (in questions etc): **have you any butter?** haben Sie (etwas) Butter?; **have you any children?** haben Sie Kinder?; **if there are any tickets left** falls noch Karten da sind

2 (with negative): **I haven't any money/ books** ich habe kein Geld/keine Bücher 3 (no matter which) jede(r, s) (beliebige); **any colour (at all)** jede beliebige Farbe; **choose any book you like** nehmen Sie ein beliebiges Buch

4 (in phrases): **in any case** in jedem Fall; **any day now** jeden Tag; **at any moment** jeden Moment; **at any rate** auf jeden Fall ♦ pron 1 (in questions etc): **have you got any?** haben Sie welche?; **can any of you sing?** kann (irgend)einer von euch singen? 2 (with negative): **I haven't any (of them)** ich habe keinen/keines (davon) 3 (no matter which one(s)): **take any of those books (you like)** nehmen Sie irgendeines dieser Bücher ♦ adv 1 (in questions etc): **do you want any more soup/sandwiches?** möchten Sie

noch Suppe/Brote?; **are you feeling any better?** fühlen Sie sich etwas besser? 2 (with negative): **I can't hear him any more** ich kann ihn nicht mehr hören

anybody ['enɪbɒdɪ] pron (no matter who) jede(r); (in questions etc) (irgend)jemand, (irgend)eine(r); (with negative): **I can't see** ~ ich kann niemanden sehen

anyhow ['enɪhaʊ] adv (at any rate): **I shall go** ~ ich gehe sowieso; (haphazardly): **do it** ~ machen Sie es, wie Sie wollen

anyone ['enɪwʌn] pron = **anybody**

KEYWORD

anything ['enɪθɪŋ] pron 1 (in questions etc) (irgend)etwas; **can you see anything?** können Sie etwas sehen?

2 (with negative): **I can't see anything** ich kann nichts sehen

3 (no matter what): **you can say anything you like** Sie können sagen, was Sie wollen; **anything will do** irgendetwas (wird genügen), irgendeine(r, s) (wird genügen); **he'll eat anything** er isst alles

anyway ['enɪweɪ] adv (at any rate) auf jeden Fall; (besides): ~, **I couldn't come even if I wanted to** jedenfalls könnte ich nicht kommen, selbst wenn ich wollte; **why are you phoning,** ~? warum rufst du überhaupt an?

anywhere ['enɪwɛəʳ] adv (in questions etc) irgendwo; (: with direction) irgendwohin; (no matter where) überall; (: with direction) überallhin; (with negative): **I can't see him** ~ ich kann ihn nirgendwo or nirgends sehen; **can you see him** ~? siehst du ihn irgendwo?; **put the books down** ~ leg die Bücher irgendwohin

apart [ə'pɑːt] adv (parted) auseinander; (away) beiseite, abseits; **10 miles** ~ 10 Meilen auseinander; **to take** ~ auseinander nehmen; ~ **from** prep außer

apartheid [ə'pɑːteɪt] n Apartheid f

apartment [ə'pɑːtmənt] (US) n Wohnung f; ~ **building** (US) n Wohnhaus nt

apathy ['æpəθɪ] n Teilnahmslosigkeit f,

Apathie *f*

ape [eɪp] *n* (Menschen)affe *m* ♦ *vt* nachahmen

aperitif [əˈperɪtiːf] *n* Aperitif *m*

aperture [ˈæpətʃjuər] *n* Öffnung *f*; (*PHOT*) Blende *f*

APEX [ˈeɪpeks] *n abbr* (*AVIAT*: = *advance purchase excursion*) APEX (*im Voraus reservierte(r) Fahrkarte/Flugschein zu reduzierten Preisen*)

apex [ˈeɪpeks] *n* Spitze *f*

apiece [əˈpiːs] *adv* pro Stück; (*per person*) pro Kopf

apologetic [əpɒləˈdʒetɪk] *adj* entschuldigend; **to be ~** sich sehr entschuldigen

apologize [əˈpɒlədʒaɪz] *vi*: **to ~ (for sth to sb)** sich (für etw bei jdm) entschuldigen; **apology** *n* Entschuldigung *f*

apostle [əˈpɒsl] *n* Apostel *m*

apostrophe [əˈpɒstrəfɪ] *n* Apostroph *m*

appal [əˈpɔːl] *vt* erschrecken; **~ling** *adj* schrecklich

apparatus [æpəˈreɪtəs] *n* Gerät *nt*

apparel [əˈpærəl] (*US*) *n* Kleidung *f*

apparent [əˈpærənt] *adj* offenbar; **~ly** *adv* anscheinend

apparition [æpəˈrɪʃən] *n* (*ghost*) Erscheinung *f*, Geist *m*

appeal [əˈpiːl] *vi* dringend ersuchen; (*JUR*) Berufung einlegen ♦ *n* Aufruf *m*; (*JUR*) Berufung *f*; **to ~ for** dringend bitten um; **to ~ to** sich wenden an +*acc*; (*to public*) appellieren an +*acc*; **it doesn't ~ to me** es gefällt mir nicht; **~ing** *adj* ansprechend

appear [əˈpɪər] *vi* (*come into sight*) erscheinen; (*be seen*) auftauchen; (*seem*) scheinen; **it would ~ that ...** anscheinend ...; **~ance** *n* (*coming into sight*) Erscheinen *nt*; (*outward show*) Äußere(s) *nt*

appease [əˈpiːz] *vt* beschwichtigen

appendices [əˈpendɪsiːz] *npl of* **appendix**

appendicitis [əpendɪˈsaɪtɪs] *n* Blinddarmentzündung *f*

appendix [əˈpendɪks] (*pl* **appendices**) *n* (*in book*) Anhang *m*; (*MED*) Blinddarm *m*

appetite [ˈæpɪtaɪt] *n* Appetit *m*; (*fig*) Lust *f*

appetizer [ˈæpɪtaɪzər] *n* Appetitanreger *m*; **appetizing** [ˈæpɪtaɪzɪŋ] *adj* appetitanregend

applaud [əˈplɔːd] *vi* Beifall klatschen, applaudieren ♦ *vt* Beifall klatschen +*dat*; **applause** [əˈplɔːz] *n* Beifall *m*, Applaus *m*

apple [ˈæpl] *n* Apfel *m*; **~ tree** *n* Apfelbaum *m*

appliance [əˈplaɪəns] *n* Gerät *nt*

applicable [əˈplɪkəbl] *adj* anwendbar; (*in forms*) zutreffend

applicant [ˈæplɪkənt] *n* Bewerber(in) *m(f)*

application [æplɪˈkeɪʃən] *n* (*request*) Antrag *m*; (*for job*) Bewerbung *f*; (*putting into practice*) Anwendung *f*; (*hard work*) Fleiß *m*; **~ form** *n* Bewerbungsformular *nt*

applied [əˈplaɪd] *adj* angewandt

apply [əˈplaɪ] *vi* (*be suitable*) zutreffen; (*ask*): **to ~ (to)** sich wenden an (+*acc*); (*request*): **to ~ for** sich melden für +*acc* ♦ *vt* (*place on*) auflegen; (*cream*) auftragen; (*put into practice*) anwenden; **to ~ for sth** sich um etw bewerben; **to ~ o.s. to sth** sich bei etw anstrengen

appoint [əˈpɔɪnt] *vt* (*to office*) ernennen, berufen; (*settle*) festsetzen; **~ment** *n* (*meeting*) Verabredung *f*; (*at hairdresser etc*) Bestellung *f*; (*in business*) Termin *m*; (*choice for a position*) Ernennung *f*; (*UNIV*) Berufung *f*

appraisal [əˈpreɪzl] *n* Beurteilung *f*

appreciable [əˈpriːʃəbl] *adj* (*perceptible*) merklich; (*able to be estimated*) abschätzbar

appreciate [əˈpriːʃɪeɪt] *vt* (*value*) zu schätzen wissen; (*understand*) einsehen ♦ *vi* (*increase in value*) im Wert steigen; **appreciation** [əpriːʃɪˈeɪʃən] *n* Wertschätzung *f*; (*COMM*) Wertzuwachs *m*; **appreciative** [əˈpriːʃɪətɪv] *adj* (*showing thanks*) dankbar; (*showing liking*) anerkennend

apprehend [æprɪˈhend] *vt* (*arrest*) festnehmen; (*understand*) erfassen

apprehension [æprɪˈhenʃən] *n* Angst *f*

apprehensive [æprɪˈhensɪv] *adj* furchtsam

apprentice [əˈprentɪs] *n* Lehrling *m*; **~ship** *n* Lehrzeit *f*

approach [əˈprəutʃ] *vi* sich nähern ♦ *vt* herantreten an +*acc*; (*problem*) herangehen an +*acc* ♦ *n* Annäherung *f*; (*to problem*) Ansatz *m*; (*path*) Zugang *m*, Zufahrt *f*; ~**able** *adj* zugänglich

appropriate [*adj* ə'prəuprɪɪt, *vb* ə'prəuprɪeɪt] *adj* angemessen; (*remark*) angebracht ♦ *vt* (*take for o.s.*) sich aneignen; (*set apart*) bereitstellen

approval [ə'pruːvəl] *n* (*show of satisfaction*) Beifall *m*; (*permission*) Billigung *f*; **on ~** (COMM) bei Gefallen

approve [ə'pruːv] *vt*, *vi* billigen; **I don't ~ of it/him** ich halte nichts davon/von ihm; ~**d school** (BRIT) *n* Erziehungsheim *nt*

approximate [*adj* ə'prɔksɪmɪt, *vb* ə'prɔksɪmeɪt] *adj* annähernd, ungefähr ♦ *vt* nahe kommen +*dat*; ~**ly** *adv* rund, ungefähr

apricot ['eɪprɪkɔt] *n* Aprikose *f*

April ['eɪprəl] *n* April *m*; ~ **Fools' Day** *n* der erste April

apron ['eɪprən] *n* Schürze *f*

apt [æpt] *adj* (*suitable*) passend; (*able*) begabt; (*likely*): **to be ~ to do sth** dazu neigen, etw zu tun

aptitude ['æptɪtjuːd] *n* Begabung *f*

aqualung ['ækwəlʌŋ] *n* Unterwasseratmungsgerät *nt*

aquarium [ə'kwɛərɪəm] *n* Aquarium *nt*

Aquarius [ə'kwɛərɪəs] *n* Wassermann *m*

aquatic [ə'kwætɪk] *adj* Wasser-

Arab ['ærəb] *n* Araber(in) *m(f)*

Arabia [ə'reɪbɪə] *n* Arabien *nt*; ~**n** *adj* arabisch

Arabic ['ærəbɪk] *adj* arabisch ♦ *n* Arabisch *nt*

arable ['ærəbl] *adj* bebaubar, Kultur-

arbitrary ['ɑːbɪtrərɪ] *adj* willkürlich

arbitration [ɑːbɪ'treɪʃən] *n* Schlichtung *f*

arc [ɑːk] *n* Bogen *m*

arcade [ɑː'keɪd] *n* Säulengang *m*; (*with video games*) Spielhalle *f*

arch [ɑːtʃ] *n* Bogen *m* ♦ *vt* überwölben; (*back*) krumm machen

archaeologist [ɑːkɪ'ɔlədʒɪst] *n* Archäologe *m*

archaeology [ɑːkɪ'ɔlədʒɪ] *n* Archäologie *f*

archaic [ɑː'keɪɪk] *adj* altertümlich

archbishop [ɑːtʃ'bɪʃəp] *n* Erzbischof *m*

archenemy ['ɑːtʃ'enəmɪ] *n* Erzfeind *m*

archeology *etc* [ɑːkɪ'ɔlədʒɪ] (US) = **archaeology** *etc*

archery ['ɑːtʃərɪ] *n* Bogenschießen *nt*

architect ['ɑːkɪtekt] *n* Architekt(in) *m(f)*; ~**ural** [ɑːkɪ'tektʃərəl] *adj* architektonisch; ~**ure** *n* Architektur *f*

archives ['ɑːkaɪvz] *npl* Archiv *nt*

archway ['ɑːtʃweɪ] *n* Bogen *m*

Arctic ['ɑːktɪk] *adj* arktisch ♦ *n*: **the ~** die Arktis

ardent ['ɑːdənt] *adj* glühend

arduous ['ɑːdjuəs] *adj* mühsam

are [ɑːʳ] *see* **be**

area ['ɛərɪə] *n* Fläche *f*; (*of land*) Gebiet *nt*; (*part of sth*) Teil *m*, Abschnitt *m*

arena [ə'riːnə] *n* Arena *f*

aren't [ɑːnt] = **are not**

Argentina [ɑːdʒən'tiːnə] *n* Argentinien *nt*; **Argentinian** [ɑːdʒən'tɪnɪən] *adj* argentinisch ♦ *n* Argentinier(in) *m(f)*

arguably ['ɑːgjuəblɪ] *adv* wohl

argue ['ɑːgjuː] *vi* diskutieren; (*angrily*) streiten; **argument** *n* (*theory*) Argument *nt*; (*reasoning*) Argumentation *f*; (*row*) Auseinandersetzung *f*, Streit *m*; **to have an argument** sich streiten; **argumentative** [ɑːgju'mentətɪv] *adj* streitlustig

aria ['ɑːrɪə] *n* Arie *f*

Aries ['ɛərɪz] *n* Widder *m*

arise [ə'raɪz] (*pt* **arose**, *pp* **arisen**) *vi* aufsteigen; (*get up*) aufstehen; (*difficulties etc*) entstehen; (*case*) vorkommen; **to ~ from sth** herrühren von etw; ~**n** [ə'rɪzn] *pp* of **arise**

aristocracy [ærɪs'tɔkrəsɪ] *n* Adel *m*, Aristokratie *f*; **aristocrat** ['ærɪstəkræt] *n* Adlige(r) *f(m)*, Aristokrat(in) *m(f)*

arithmetic [ə'rɪθmətɪk] *n* Rechnen *nt*, Arithmetik *f*

arm [ɑːm] *n* Arm *m*; (*branch of military service*) Zweig *m* ♦ *vt* bewaffnen; ~**s** *npl* (*weapons*) Waffen *pl*

armaments ['ɑːməmənts] *npl* Ausrüstung *f*

armchair ['ɑːmtʃɛəʳ] *n* Lehnstuhl *m*

armed [ɑːmd] *adj* (*forces*) Streit-, bewaffnet; ~ **robbery** *n* bewaffnete(r) Raubüberfall *m*

armistice ['ɑːmɪstɪs] n Waffenstillstand m

armour ['ɑːmə˧] (US **armor**) n (knight's) Rüstung f; (MIL) Panzerplatte f; **~ed car** n Panzerwagen m

armpit ['ɑːmpɪt] n Achselhöhle f

armrest ['ɑːmrest] n Armlehne f

army ['ɑːmɪ] n Armee f, Heer nt; (host) Heer nt

aroma [ə'rəumə] n Duft m, Aroma nt; **~therapy** [ərəumə'θerəpɪ] n Aromatherapie f; **~tic** [ærə'mætɪk] adj aromatisch, würzig

arose [ə'rəuz] pt of **arise**

around [ə'raund] adv ringsherum; (almost) ungefähr ♦ prep um ... herum; **is he ~?** ist er hier?

arrange [ə'reɪndʒ] vt (time, meeting) festsetzen; (holidays) festlegen; (flowers, hair, objects) anordnen; **I ~d to meet him** ich habe mit ihm ausgemacht, ihn zu treffen; **it's all ~d** es ist alles arrangiert; **~ment** n (order) Reihenfolge f; (agreement) Vereinbarung f; **~ments** npl (plans) Pläne pl

array [ə'reɪ] n (collection) Ansammlung f

arrears [ə'rɪəz] npl (of debts) Rückstand m; (of work) Unerledigte(s) nt; **in ~** im Rückstand

arrest [ə'rest] vt (person) verhaften; (stop) aufhalten ♦ n Verhaftung f; **under ~** in Haft

arrival [ə'raɪvl] n Ankunft f

arrive [ə'raɪv] vi ankommen; **to ~ at** ankommen in +dat, ankommen bei

arrogance ['ærəgəns] n Überheblichkeit f, Arroganz f; **arrogant** ['ærəgənt] adj überheblich, arrogant

arrow ['ærəu] n Pfeil m

arse [ɑːs] (inf!) n Arsch m (!)

arsenal ['ɑːsɪnl] n Waffenlager nt, Zeughaus nt

arsenic ['ɑːsnɪk] n Arsen nt

arson ['ɑːsn] n Brandstiftung f

art [ɑːt] n Kunst f; **A~s** npl (UNIV) Geisteswissenschaften pl

artery ['ɑːtərɪ] n Schlagader f, Arterie f

art gallery n Kunstgalerie f

arthritis [ɑː'θraɪtɪs] n Arthritis f

artichoke ['ɑːtɪtʃəuk] n Artischocke f;

Jerusalem ~ Erdartischocke f

article ['ɑːtɪkl] n (PRESS, GRAM) Artikel m; (thing) Gegenstand m, Artikel m; (clause) Abschnitt m, Paragraf m; **~ of clothing** Kleidungsstück nt

articulate [adj ɑː'tɪkjulɪt, vb ɑː'tɪkjuleɪt] adj (able to express o.s.) redegewandt; (speaking clearly) deutlich, verständlich ♦ vt (connect) zusammenfügen, gliedern; **to be ~** sich gut ausdrücken können; **~d vehicle** n Sattelschlepper m

artificial [ɑːtɪ'fɪʃəl] adj künstlich, Kunst-; **~ respiration** n künstliche Atmung f

artisan ['ɑːtɪzæn] n gelernte(r) Handwerker m

artist ['ɑːtɪst] n Künstler(in) m(f); **~ic** [ɑː'tɪstɪk] adj künstlerisch; **~ry** n künstlerische(s) Können nt

art school n Kunsthochschule f

KEYWORD

as [æz] conj **1** (referring to time) als; **as the years went by** mit den Jahren; **he came in as I was leaving** als er hereinkam, ging ich gerade; **as from tomorrow** ab morgen

2 (in comparisons): **as big as** so groß wie; **twice as big as** zweimal so groß wie; **as much/many as** so viel/so viele wie; **as soon as** sobald

3 (since, because) da; **he left early as he had to be home by 10** er ging früher, da er um 10 zu Hause sein musste

4 (referring to manner, way) wie; **do as you wish** mach was du willst; **as she said** wie sie sagte

5 (concerning): **as for** or **to that** was das betrifft or angeht

6: **as if** or **though** als ob

♦ prep als; see also **long; he works as a driver** er arbeitet als Fahrer; see also **such; he gave it to me as a present** er hat es mir als Geschenk gegeben; see also **well**

---

a.s.a.p. abbr = **as soon as possible**

asbestos [æz'bestəs] n Asbest m

ascend [ə'send] vi aufsteigen ♦ vt besteigen; **ascent** n Aufstieg m; Besteigung f

ascertain [æsə'teɪn] vt feststellen

ascribe [ə'skraɪb] vt: **to ~ sth to sth /sth to sb** etw einer Sache/jdm etw zuschreiben

ash [æʃ] n Asche f; (tree) Esche f

ashamed [ə'ʃeɪmd] adj beschämt; **to be ~ of sth** sich für etw schämen

ashen ['æʃən] adj (pale) aschfahl

ashore [ə'ʃɔː] adv an Land

ashtray ['æʃtreɪ] n Aschenbecher m

Ash Wednesday n Aschermittwoch m

Asia ['eɪʃə] n Asien nt; **~n** adj asiatisch ♦ n Asiat(in) m(f)

aside [ə'saɪd] adv beiseite

ask [ɑːsk] vt fragen; (permission) bitten um; **~ him his name** frage ihn nach seinem Namen; **he ~ed to see you** er wollte dich sehen; **to ~ sb to do sth** jdn bitten, etw zu tun; **to ~ sb about sth** jdn nach etw fragen; **to ~ (sb) a question** (jdn) etwas fragen; **to ~ sb out to dinner** jdn zum Essen einladen; **~ after** vt fus fragen nach; **~ for** vt fus bitten um

askance [ə'skɑːns] adv: **to look ~ at sb** jdn schief ansehen

asking price ['ɑːskɪŋ-] n Verkaufspreis m

asleep [ə'sliːp] adj: **to be ~** schlafen; **to fall ~** einschlafen

asparagus [əs'pærəgəs] n Spargel m

aspect ['æspekt] n Aspekt m

aspersions [əs'pɜːʃənz] npl: **to cast ~ on sb/sth** sich abfällig über jdn/etw äußern

asphyxiation [æsfɪksɪ'eɪʃən] n Erstickung f

aspirations [æspə'reɪʃənz] npl: **to have ~ towards sth** etw anstreben

aspire [əs'paɪə] vi: **~ to** streben nach

aspirin ['æsprɪn] n Aspirin nt

ass [æs] n (also fig) Esel m; (US: inf!) Arsch m (!)

assailant [ə'seɪlənt] n Angreifer m

assassin [ə'sæsɪn] n Attentäter(in) m(f); **~ate** vt ermorden; **~ation** [əsæsɪ'neɪʃən] n (geglückte(s)) Attentat nt

assault [ə'sɔːlt] n Angriff m ♦ vt überfallen; (woman) herfallen über +acc

assemble [ə'sembl] vt versammeln; (parts) zusammensetzen ♦ vi sich versammeln; **assembly** n (meeting) Versammlung f; (construction) Zusammensetzung f, Montage f; **assembly line** n Fließband nt

assent [ə'sent] n Zustimmung f

assert [ə'sɜːt] vt erklären; **~ion** n Behauptung f

assess [ə'ses] vt schätzen; **~ment** n Bewertung f, Einschätzung f; **~or** n Steuerberater m

asset ['æset] n Vorteil m, Wert m; **~s** npl (FIN) Vermögen nt; (estate) Nachlass m

assign [ə'saɪn] vt zuweisen; **~ment** n Aufgabe f, Auftrag m

assimilate [ə'sɪmɪleɪt] vt sich aneignen, aufnehmen

assist [ə'sɪst] vt beistehen +dat; **~ance** n Unterstützung f, Hilfe f; **~ant** n Assistent(in) m(f), Mitarbeiter(in) m(f); (BRIT: also: **shop ~ant**) Verkäufer(in) m(f)

associate [n ə'səʊʃɪt, vb ə'səʊʃɪeɪt] n (partner) Kollege m, Teilhaber m; (member) außerordentliche(s) Mitglied nt ♦ vt verbinden ♦ vi (keep company) verkehren; **association** [əsəʊsɪ'eɪʃən] n Verband m, Verein m; (PSYCH) Assoziation f; (link) Verbindung f

assorted [ə'sɔːtɪd] adj gemischt

assortment [ə'sɔːtmənt] n Sammlung f; (COMM): **~ (of)** Sortiment nt (von), Auswahl f (an +dat)

assume [ə'sjuːm] vt (take for granted) annehmen; (put on) annehmen, sich geben; **~d name** n Deckname m

assumption [ə'sʌmpʃən] n Annahme f

assurance [ə'ʃʊərəns] n (firm statement) Versicherung f; (confidence) Selbstsicherheit f; (insurance) (Lebens)versicherung f

assure [ə'ʃʊə] vt (make sure) sicherstellen; (convince) versichern +dat; (life) versichern

asterisk ['æstərɪsk] n Sternchen nt

asthma ['æsmə] n Asthma nt

astonish [ə'stɒnɪʃ] vt erstaunen; **~ment** n Erstaunen nt

astound [ə'staʊnd] vt verblüffen

astray [ə'streɪ] adv in die Irre; auf Abwege; **to go ~** (go wrong) sich vertun; **to lead ~** irreführen

astride [ə'straɪd] adv rittlings ♦ prep rittlings

auf

astrologer [əsˈtrɒlədʒəʳ] *n* Astrologe *m*,
Astrologin *f*; **astrology** *n* Astrologie *f*

astronaut [ˈæstrənɔːt] *n* Astronaut(in) *m(f)*

astronomer [əsˈtrɒnəməʳ] *n* Astronom *m*

astronomical [æstrəˈnɒmɪkl] *adj*
astronomisch; (*success*) riesig

astronomy [əsˈtrɒnəmɪ] *n* Astronomie *f*

astute [əsˈtjuːt] *adj* scharfsinnig; schlau,
gerissen

asylum [əˈsaɪləm] *n* (*home*) Heim *nt*; (*refuge*)
Asyl *nt*

KEYWORD

at [æt] *prep* 1 (*referring to position, direction*) an
+*dat*; to +*dat*; (*with place*) in +*dat*; **at the
top** an der Spitze; **at home/school** zu
Hause/in der Schule; **at the baker's** beim
Bäcker; **to look at sth** auf etw *acc* blicken;
to throw sth at sb etw nach jdm werfen
2 (*referring to time*): **at 4 o'clock** um 4 Uhr;
at night bei Nacht; **at Christmas** zu
Weihnachten; **at times** manchmal
3 (*referring to rates, speed etc*): **at £1 a kilo**
zu £1 pro Kilo; **two at a time** zwei auf
einmal; **at 50 km/h** mit 50 km/h
4 (*referring to manner*): **at a stroke** mit
einem Schlag; **at peace** in Frieden
5 (*referring to activity*): **to be at work** bei
der Arbeit sein; **to play at cowboys**
Cowboy spielen; **to be good at sth** gut in
etw *dat* sein
6 (*referring to cause*): **shocked/surprised/
annoyed at sth** schockiert/überrascht/
verärgert über etw *acc*; **I went at his
suggestion** ich ging auf seinen Vorschlag
hin

---

ate [eɪt] *pt of* **eat**

atheist [ˈeɪθɪɪst] *n* Atheist(in) *m(f)*

Athens [ˈæθɪnz] *n* Athen *nt*

athlete [ˈæθliːt] *n* Athlet *m*, Sportler *m*

athletic [æθˈletɪk] *adj* sportlich, athletisch;
~s *n* Leichtathletik *f*

Atlantic [ətˈlæntɪk] *adj* atlantisch ♦ *n*: **the ~
(Ocean)** der Atlantik

atlas [ˈætləs] *n* Atlas *m*

ATM *abbr* (= *automated teller machine*)
Geldautomat *m*

atmosphere [ˈætməsfɪəʳ] *n* Atmosphäre *f*

atom [ˈætəm] *n* Atom *nt*; (*fig*) bisschen *nt*;
~ic [əˈtɒmɪk] *adj* atomar, Atom-; **~(ic)
bomb** *n* Atombombe *f*

atomizer [ˈætəmaɪzəʳ] *n* Zerstäuber *m*

atone [əˈtəun] *vi* sühnen; **to ~ for sth** etw
sühnen

atrocious [əˈtrəuʃəs] *adj* grässlich

atrocity [əˈtrɒsɪtɪ] *n* Scheußlichkeit *f*; (*deed*)
Gräueltat *f*

attach [əˈtætʃ] *vt* (*fasten*) befestigen; **to be
~ed to sb/sth** an jdm/etw hängen; **to ~
importance** *etc* **to sth** Wichtigkeit *etc* auf
etw *acc* legen, einer Sache *dat* Wichtigkeit
etc beimessen

attaché case [əˈtæʃeɪ] *n* Aktenkoffer *m*

attachment [əˈtætʃmənt] *n* (*tool*)
Zubehörteil *nt*; (*love*): **~ (to sb)** Zuneigung
f (zu jdm)

attack [əˈtæk] *vt* angreifen ♦ *n* Angriff *m*;
(*MED*) Anfall *m*; **~er** *n* Angreifer(in) *m(f)*

attain [əˈteɪn] *vt* erreichen; **~ments** *npl*
Kenntnisse *pl*

attempt [əˈtempt] *n* Versuch *m* ♦ *vt*
versuchen; **~ed murder** Mordversuch *m*

attend [əˈtend] *vt* (*go to*) teilnehmen (an
+*dat*); (*lectures*) besuchen; **to ~ to** (*needs*)
nachkommen +*dat*; (*person*) sich kümmern
um; **~ance** *n* (*presence*) Anwesenheit *f*;
(*people present*) Besucherzahl *f*; **good ~ance**
gute Teilnahme; **~ant** *n* (*companion*)
Begleiter(in) *m(f)*; Gesellschafter(in) *m(f)*; (*in
car park etc*) Wächter(in) *m(f)*; (*servant*)
Bedienstete(r) *mf* ♦ *adj* begleitend; (*fig*)
damit verbunden

attention [əˈtenʃən] *n* Aufmerksamkeit *f*;
(*care*) Fürsorge *f*; (*for machine etc*) Pflege *f*
♦ *excl* (*MIL*) Achtung!; **for the ~ of ...** zu
Händen (von) ...

attentive [əˈtentɪv] *adj* aufmerksam

attic [ˈætɪk] *n* Dachstube *f*, Mansarde *f*

attitude [ˈætɪtjuːd] *n* (*mental*) Einstellung *f*

attorney [əˈtɜːnɪ] *n* (*solicitor*) Rechtsanwalt
m; **A~ General** *n* Justizminister *m*

attract [əˈtrækt] *vt* anziehen; (*attention*)

erregen; **~ion** n Anziehungskraft f; (thing)
Attraktion f; **~ive** adj attraktiv

attribute [n 'ætrɪbjuːt, vb ə'trɪbjuːt] n
Eigenschaft f, Attribut nt ♦ vt zuschreiben

attrition [ə'trɪʃən] n: **war of ~**
Zermürbungskrieg m

aubergine ['əubəʒiːn] n Aubergine f

auburn ['ɔːbən] adj kastanienbraun

auction ['ɔːkʃən] n (also: **sale by ~**)
Versteigerung f, Auktion f ♦ vt versteigern;
~eer [ɔːkʃə'nɪə] n Versteigerer m

audacity [ɔː'dæsɪtɪ] n (boldness) Wagemut m;
(impudence) Unverfrorenheit f

audible ['ɔːdɪbl] adj hörbar

audience ['ɔːdɪəns] n Zuhörer pl, Zuschauer
pl; (with queen) Audienz f

audiotypist ['ɔːdɪəu'taɪpɪst] n Phonotypistin
f, Fonotypistin f

audiovisual ['ɔːdɪəu'vɪzjuəl] adj audiovisuell

audit ['ɔːdɪt] vt prüfen

audition [ɔː'dɪʃən] n Probe f

auditor ['ɔːdɪtə] n (accountant)
Rechnungsprüfer(in) m(f), Buchprüfer m

auditorium [ɔːdɪ'tɔːrɪəm] n Zuschauerraum
m

augment [ɔːg'mɛnt] vt vermehren

augur ['ɔːgə] vi bedeuten, voraussagen; **this
~s well** das ist ein gutes Omen

August ['ɔːgəst] n August m

aunt [ɑːnt] n Tante f; **~ie** n Tantchen nt; **~y**
n = **auntie**

au pair ['əu'pɛə] n (also: **~ girl**)
Aupairmädchen nt, Au-pair-Mädchen nt

aura ['ɔːrə] n Nimbus m

auspicious [ɔːs'pɪʃəs] adj günstig;
verheißungsvoll

austere [ɔs'tɪə] adj streng; (room) nüchtern;
austerity [ɔs'tɛrɪtɪ] n Strenge f; (POL)
wirtschaftliche Einschränkung f

Australia [ɔs'treɪlɪə] n Australien nt; **~n** adj
australisch ♦ n Australier(in) m(f)

Austria ['ɔstrɪə] n Österreich nt; **~n** adj
österreichisch ♦ n Österreicher(in) m(f)

authentic [ɔː'θɛntɪk] adj echt, authentisch

author ['ɔːθə] n Autor m, Schriftsteller m;
(beginner) Urheber m, Schöpfer m

authoritarian [ɔːθɔrɪ'tɛərɪən] adj autoritär

authoritative [ɔː'θɔrɪtətɪv] adj (account)
maßgeblich; (manner) herrisch

authority [ɔː'θɔrɪtɪ] n (power) Autorität f;
(expert) Autorität f, Fachmann m; **the
authorities** npl (ruling body) die Behörden
pl

authorize ['ɔːθəraɪz] vt bevollmächtigen;
(permit) genehmigen

auto ['ɔːtəu] (US) n Auto nt, Wagen m

autobiography [ɔːtəbaɪ'ɔgrəfɪ] n
Autobiografie f

autograph ['ɔːtəgrɑːf] n (of celebrity)
Autogramm nt ♦ vt mit Autogramm
versehen

automatic [ɔːtə'mætɪk] adj automatisch ♦ n
(gun) Selbstladepistole f; (car) Automatik m;
~ally adv automatisch

automation [ɔːtə'meɪʃən] n Automatisierung
f

automobile ['ɔːtəməbiːl] (US) n Auto(mobil)
nt

autonomous [ɔː'tɔnəməs] adj autonom;
autonomy n Autonomie f

autumn ['ɔːtəm] n Herbst m

auxiliary [ɔːg'zɪlɪərɪ] adj Hilfs-

Av. abbr = **avenue**

avail [ə'veɪl] vt: **to ~ o.s. of sth** sich einer
Sache gen bedienen ♦ n: **to no ~** nutzlos

availability [əveɪlə'bɪlɪtɪ] n Erhältlichkeit f,
Vorhandensein nt

available [ə'veɪləbl] adj erhältlich; zur
Verfügung stehend; (person) erreichbar,
abkömmlich

avalanche ['ævəlɑːnʃ] n Lawine f

Ave. abbr = **avenue**

avenge [ə'vɛndʒ] vt rächen, sühnen

avenue ['ævənjuː] n Allee f

average ['ævərɪdʒ] n Durchschnitt m ♦ adj
durchschnittlich, Durchschnitts- ♦ vt
(figures) den Durchschnitt nehmen von;
(perform) durchschnittlich leisten; (in car etc)
im Schnitt fahren; **on ~** durchschnittlich,
im Durchschnitt; **~ out** vi: **to ~ out at** im
Durchschnitt betragen

averse [ə'vɜːs] adj: **to be ~ to doing sth**
eine Abneigung dagegen haben, etw zu
tun

avert [ə'vɜːt] vt (turn away) abkehren; (prevent) abwehren

aviary ['eɪvɪərɪ] n Vogelhaus nt

aviation [eɪvɪ'eɪʃən] n Luftfahrt f, Flugwesen nt

avid ['ævɪd] adj: ~ (for) gierig (auf +acc)

avocado [ævə'kɑːdəʊ] n (BRIT: also: ~ pear) Avocado(birne) f

avoid [ə'vɔɪd] vt vermeiden

await [ə'weɪt] vt erwarten, entgegensehen +dat

awake [ə'weɪk] (pt **awoke**, pp **awoken** or **awaked**) adj wach ♦ vt (auf)wecken ♦ vi aufwachen; **to be ~** wach sein; **~ning** n Erwachen nt

award [ə'wɔːd] n (prize) Preis m ♦ vt: **to ~ (sb sth)** (jdm etw) zuerkennen

aware [ə'weər] adj bewusst; **to be ~** sich bewusst sein; **~ness** n Bewusstsein nt

awash [ə'wɒʃ] adj überflutet

away [ə'weɪ] adv weg, fort; **two hours ~ by car** zwei Autostunden entfernt; **the holiday was two weeks ~** es war noch zwei Wochen bis zum Urlaub; **two kilometres ~** zwei Kilometer entfernt; **~ match** n (SPORT) Auswärtsspiel nt

awe [ɔː] n Ehrfurcht f; **~-inspiring** adj Ehrfurcht gebietend; **~some** adj Ehrfurcht gebietend

awful ['ɔːfəl] adj (very bad) furchtbar; **~ly** adv furchtbar, sehr

awhile [ə'waɪl] adv eine Weile

awkward ['ɔːkwəd] adj (clumsy) ungeschickt, linkisch; (embarrassing) peinlich

awning ['ɔːnɪŋ] n Markise f

awoke [ə'wəʊk] pt of **awake**; **~n** pp of **awake**

awry [ə'raɪ] adv schief; (plans) schief gehen

axe [æks] (US **ax**) n Axt f, Beil nt ♦ vt (end suddenly) streichen

axes¹ ['æksɪz] npl of **axe**

axes² ['æksiːz] npl of **axis**

axis ['æksɪs] (pl **axes**) n Achse f

axle ['æksl] n Achse f

ay(e) [aɪ] excl (yes) ja

azalea [ə'zeɪlɪə] n Azalee f

B, b

B [biː] n (MUS) H nt; **~ road** (BRIT) Landstraße f

B.A. n abbr = **Bachelor of Arts**

babble ['bæbl] vi schwätzen

baby ['beɪbɪ] n Baby nt; **~ carriage** (US) n Kinderwagen m; **~ food** n Babynahrung f; **~-sit** vi Kinder hüten, babysitten; **~-sitter** n Babysitter m; **~sitting** n Babysitten nt, Babysitting nt; **~ wipe** n Ölpflegetuch nt

bachelor ['bætʃələr] n Junggeselle m; **B~ of Arts** Bakkalaureus m der philosophischen Fakultät; **B~ of Science** Bakkalaureus m der Naturwissenschaften

back [bæk] n (of person, horse) Rücken m; (of house) Rückseite f; (of train) Ende nt; (FOOTBALL) Verteidiger m ♦ vt (support) unterstützen; (wager) wetten auf +acc; (car) rückwärts fahren ♦ vi (go ~wards) rückwärts gehen or fahren ♦ adj hintere(r, s) ♦ adv zurück; (to the rear) nach hinten; **~ down** vi zurückstecken; **~ out** vi sich zurückziehen; (inf) kneifen; **~ up** vt (support) unterstützen; (car) zurücksetzen; (COMPUT) eine Sicherungskopie machen von; **~ache** n Rückenschmerzen pl; **~bencher** (BRIT) n Parlamentarier(in) m(f); **~bone** n Rückgrat nt; (support) Rückhalt m; **~cloth** n Hintergrund m; **~date** vt rückdatieren; **~drop** n (THEAT) = **backcloth**; (~ground) Hintergrund m; **~fire** vi (plan) fehlschlagen; (TECH) fehlzünden; **~ground** n Hintergrund m; (person's education) Vorbildung f; **family ~ground** Familienverhältnisse pl; **~hand** n (TENNIS: also: **~hand stroke**) Rückhand f; **~hander** (BRIT) n (bribe) Schmiergeld nt; **~ing** n (support) Unterstützung f; **~lash** n (fig) Gegenschlag m; **~log** n (of work) Rückstand m; **~ number** n (PRESS) alte Nummer f; **~pack** n Rucksack m; **~packer** n Rucksacktourist(in) m(f); **~ pain** n Rückenschmerzen pl; **~ pay** n (Gehalts- or Lohn)nachzahlung f; **~ payments** npl

Zahlungsrückstände pl; ~ **seat** n (AUT)
Rücksitz m; **~side** (inf) n Hintern m;
~stage adv hinter den Kulissen; **~stroke** n
Rückenschwimmen nt; **~up** adj (COMPUT)
Sicherungs- ♦ n (COMPUT) Sicherungskopie
f; **~ward** adj (less developed)
zurückgeblieben; (primitive) rückständig;
~wards adv rückwärts; **~water** n (fig) Kaff
nt; **~yard** n Hinterhof m

bacon ['beɪkən] n Schinkenspeck m

bacteria [bæk'tɪərɪə] npl Bakterien pl

bad [bæd] adj schlecht, schlimm; **to go ~**
schlecht werden

bade [bæd] pt of **bid**

badge [bædʒ] n Abzeichen nt

badger ['bædʒər] n Dachs m

badly ['bædlɪ] adv schlecht, schlimm; **~
wounded** schwer verwundet; **he needs it
~** er braucht es dringend; **to be ~ off (for
money)** dringend Geld nötig haben

badminton ['bædmɪntən] n Federball m,
Badminton nt

bad-tempered ['bæd'tempəd] adj schlecht
gelaunt

baffle ['bæfl] vt (puzzle) verblüffen

bag [bæg] n (sack) Beutel m; (paper) Tüte f;
(handbag) Tasche f; (suitcase) Koffer m; (inf:
old woman) alte Schachtel f ♦ vt (put in sack)
in einen Sack stecken; (hunting) erlegen; **~s
of** (inf: lots of) eine Menge +acc; **~gage**
['bægɪdʒ] n Gepäck nt; **~ allowance** n
Freigepäck nt; **~ reclaim** n
Gepäckausgabe f; **~gy** ['bægɪ] adj bauschig,
sackartig

bagpipes ['bægpaɪps] npl Dudelsack m

bail [beɪl] n (money) Kaution f ♦ vt (prisoner:
usu: grant ~ to) gegen Kaution freilassen;
(boat: also: ~ **out**) ausschöpfen; **on ~**
(prisoner) gegen Kaution freigelassen; **to ~
sb out** die Kaution für jdn stellen; see also
bale

bailiff ['beɪlɪf] n Gerichtsvollzieher(in) m(f)

bait [beɪt] n Köder m ♦ vt mit einem Köder
versehen; (fig) ködern

bake [beɪk] vt, vi backen; **~d beans**
gebackene Bohnen pl; **~d potatoes** npl in
der Schale gebackene Kartoffeln pl; **~r** n

Bäcker m; **~ry** n Bäckerei f; **baking** n
Backen nt; **baking powder** n Backpulver
nt

balance ['bæləns] n (scales) Waage f;
(equilibrium) Gleichgewicht nt; (FIN: state of
account) Saldo m; (difference) Bilanz f;
(amount remaining) Restbetrag m ♦ vt
(weigh) wägen; (make equal) ausgleichen; **~
of trade/payments** Handels-/
Zahlungsbilanz f; **~d** adj ausgeglichen; **~
sheet** n Bilanz f, Rechnungsabschluss m

balcony ['bælkənɪ] n Balkon m

bald [bɔːld] adj kahl; (statement) knapp

bale [beɪl] n Ballen m; **bale out** vi (from a
plane) abspringen

ball [bɔːl] n Ball m; **~ bearing** n Kugellager
nt

ballet ['bæleɪ] n Ballett nt; **~ dancer** n
Balletttänzer(in) m(f); **~ shoe** n
Ballettschuh m

balloon [bə'luːn] n (Luft)ballon m

ballot ['bælət] n (geheime) Abstimmung f

ballpoint (pen) ['bɔːlpɔɪnt-] n
Kugelschreiber m

ballroom ['bɔːlrum] n Tanzsaal m

Baltic ['bɔːltɪk] n: **the ~ (Sea)** die Ostsee

bamboo [bæm'buː] n Bambus m

ban [bæn] n Verbot nt ♦ vt verbieten

banana [bə'nɑːnə] n Banane f

band [bænd] n Band nt; (group) Gruppe f; (of
criminals) Bande f; (MUS) Kapelle f, Band f;
~ together vi sich zusammentun

bandage ['bændɪdʒ] n Verband m; (elastic)
Bandage f ♦ vt (cut) verbinden; (broken
limb) bandagieren

Bandaid ['bændeɪd] (® US) n Heftpflaster nt

bandit ['bændɪt] n Bandit m, Räuber m

bandwagon ['bændwægən] n: **to jump on
the ~** (fig) auf den fahrenden Zug
aufspringen

bandy ['bændɪ] vt wechseln; **~-legged** adj
o-beinig, O-beinig

bang [bæŋ] n (explosion) Knall m; (blow) Hieb
m ♦ vt, vi knallen

Bangladesh [bæŋglə'deʃ] n Bangladesch nt

bangle ['bæŋgl] n Armspange f

bangs [bæŋz] (US) npl (fringe) Pony m

banish ['bænɪʃ] *vt* verbannen

banister(s) ['bænɪstə(z)] *n(pl)* (Treppen)geländer *nt*

bank [bæŋk] *n (raised ground)* Erdwall *m; (of lake etc)* Ufer *nt; (FIN)* Bank *f ♦ vt (tilt: AVIAT)* in die Kurve bringen; *(money)* einzahlen; **~ on** *vt fus*: **to ~ on sth** mit etw rechnen; **~ account** *n* Bankkonto *nt;* **~ card** *n* Scheckkarte *f;* **~er** *n* Bankier *m;* **~er's card** *(BRIT) n* = **bank card;** **B~ holiday** *(BRIT) n* gesetzliche(r) Feiertag *m;* **~ing** *n* Bankwesen *nt;* **~note** *n* Banknote *f;* **~ rate** *n* Banksatz *m*

| bank holiday |

ⓘ Als **bank holiday** wird in Großbritannien ein gesetzlicher Feiertag bezeichnet, an dem die Banken geschlossen sind. Die meisten dieser Feiertage, abgesehen von Weihnachten und Ostern, fallen auf Montage im Mai und August. An diesen langen Wochenenden (bank holiday weekends) fahren viele Briten in Urlaub, so dass dann auf den Straßen, Flughäfen und bei der Bahn sehr viel Betrieb ist.

bankrupt ['bæŋkrʌpt] *adj*: **to be ~** bankrott sein; **to go ~** Bankrott machen; **~cy** *n* Bankrott *m*

bank statement *n* Kontoauszug *m*

banned [bænd] *adj*: **he was ~ from driving** *(BRIT)* ihm wurde Fahrverbot erteilt

banner ['bænə'] *n* Banner *nt*

banns [bænz] *npl* Aufgebot *nt*

baptism ['bæptɪzəm] *n* Taufe *f*

baptize [bæp'taɪz] *vt* taufen

bar [bɑ:'] *n (rod)* Stange *f; (obstacle)* Hindernis *nt; (of chocolate)* Tafel *f; (of soap)* Stück *nt; (for food, drink)* Buffet *nt*, Bar *f; (pub)* Wirtschaft *f; (MUS)* Takt(strich) *m ♦ vt (fasten)* verriegeln; *(hinder)* versperren; *(exclude)* ausschließen; **behind ~s** hinter Gittern; **the B~:** **to be called to the B~** als Anwalt zugelassen werden; **~ none** ohne Ausnahme

barbaric [bɑ:'bærɪk] *adj* primitiv, unkultiviert

barbecue ['bɑ:bɪkju:] *n* Barbecue *nt*

barbed wire ['bɑ:bd-] *n* Stacheldraht *m*

barber ['bɑ:bə'] *n* Herrenfriseur *m*

bar code *n (COMM)* Registrierkode *f*

bare [beə'] *adj* nackt; *(trees, country)* kahl; *(mere)* bloß *♦ vt* entblößen; **~back** *adv* ungesattelt; **~faced** *adj* unverfroren; **~foot** *adj, adv* barfuß; **~ly** *adv* kaum, knapp

bargain ['bɑ:gɪn] *n (sth cheap)* günstiger Kauf; *(agreement: written)* Kaufvertrag *m;* *(: oral)* Geschäft *nt;* **into the ~** obendrein; **~ for** *vt*: **he got more than he ~ed for** er erlebte sein blaues Wunder

barge [bɑ:dʒ] *n* Lastkahn *m;* **~ in** *vi* hereinplatzen; **~ into** *vt* rennen gegen

bark [bɑ:k] *n (of tree)* Rinde *f; (of dog)* Bellen *nt ♦ vi (dog)* bellen

barley ['bɑ:lɪ] *n* Gerste *f;* **~ sugar** *n* Malzbonbon *nt*

bar: **~maid** *n* Bardame *f;* **~man** *(irreg) n* Barkellner *m;* **~ meal** *n* einfaches Essen in einem Pub

barn [bɑ:n] *n* Scheune *f*

barometer [bə'rɒmɪtə'] *n* Barometer *nt*

baron ['bærən] *n* Baron *m;* **~ess** *n* Baronin *f*

barracks ['bærəks] *npl* Kaserne *f*

barrage ['bærɑ:ʒ] *n (gunfire)* Sperrfeuer *nt; (dam)* Staudamm *m;* Talsperre *f*

barrel ['bærəl] *n* Fass *nt; (of gun)* Lauf *m*

barren ['bærən] *adj* unfruchtbar

barricade [bærɪ'keɪd] *n* Barrikade *f ♦ vt* verbarrikadieren

barrier ['bærɪə'] *n (obstruction)* Hindernis *nt; (fence)* Schranke *f*

barring ['bɑ:rɪŋ] *prep* außer im Falle +*gen*

barrister ['bærɪstə'] *(BRIT) n* Rechtsanwalt *m*

barrow ['bærəu] *n (cart)* Schubkarren *m*

bartender ['bɑ:tendə'] *(US) n* Barmann *or* -kellner *m*

barter ['bɑ:tə'] *vt* handeln

base [beɪs] *n (bottom)* Boden *m*, Basis *f; (MIL)* Stützpunkt *m ♦ vt* gründen; *(opinion, theory)*: **to be ~d on** basieren auf +*dat ♦ adj (low)* gemein; **I'm ~d in London** ich wohne in London; **~ball** ['beɪsbɔ:l] *n* Baseball *m;* **~ment** ['beɪsmənt] *n* Kellergeschoss *nt*

bases¹ ['beɪsɪz] *npl of* **base**

bases² ['beɪsi:z] *npl of* **basis**

bash [bæʃ] (inf) vt (heftig) schlagen
bashful ['bæʃful] adj schüchtern
basic ['beɪsɪk] adj grundlegend; **~s** npl: **the ~s** das Wesentliche sg; **~ally** adv im Grunde
basil ['bæzl] n Basilikum nt
basin ['beɪsn] n (dish) Schüssel f; (for washing, also valley) Becken nt; (dock) (Trocken)becken nt
basis ['beɪsɪs] (pl **bases**) n Basis f, Grundlage f
bask [bɑːsk] vi: **to ~ in the sun** sich sonnen
basket ['bɑːskɪt] n Korb m; **~ball** n Basketball m
bass [beɪs] n (MUS, also instrument) Bass m; (voice) Bassstimme f; **~ drum** n große Trommel
bassoon [bə'suːn] n Fagott nt
bastard ['bɑːstəd] n Bastard m; (inf!) Arschloch nt (!)
bat [bæt] n (SPORT) Schlagholz nt; Schläger m; (ZOOL) Fledermaus f ♦ vt: **he didn't ~ an eyelid** er hat nicht mit der Wimper gezuckt
batch [bætʃ] n (of letters) Stoß m; (of samples) Satz m
bated ['beɪtɪd] adj: **with ~ breath** mit angehaltenem Atem
bath [bɑːθ] n Bad nt; (~ tub) Badewanne f ♦ vt baden; **to have a ~** baden; see also **baths**
bathe [beɪð] vt, vi baden; **~r** n Badende(r) f(m)
bathing ['beɪðɪŋ] n Baden nt; **~ cap** n Badekappe f; **~ costume** n Badeanzug m; **~ suit** (US) n Badeanzug m; **~ trunks** (BRIT) npl Badehose f
bath: **~robe** n Bademantel m; **~room** n Bad(ezimmer nt) nt; **~s** npl (Schwimm)bad nt; **~ towel** n Badetuch nt
baton ['bætən] n (of police) Gummiknüppel m; (MUS) Taktstock m
batter ['bætə*] vt verprügeln ♦ n Schlagteig m; (for cake) Biskuitteig m; **~ed** adj (hat, pan) verbeult
battery ['bætərɪ] n (ELEC) Batterie f; (MIL) Geschützbatterie f
battery farming n (Hühner- etc)

batterien pl
battle ['bætl] n Schlacht f; (small) Gefecht nt ♦ vi kämpfen; **~field** n Schlachtfeld nt; **~ship** n Schlachtschiff nt
Bavaria [bə'veərɪə] n Bayern nt; **~n** adj bay(e)risch ♦ n (person) Bayer(in) m(f)
bawdy ['bɔːdɪ] adj unflätig
bawl [bɔːl] vi brüllen
bay [beɪ] n (of sea) Bucht f ♦ vi bellen; **to keep at ~** unter Kontrolle halten; **~ window** n Erkerfenster nt
bazaar [bə'zɑː*] n Basar m
B. & B. abbr = **bed and breakfast**
BBC n abbr (= British Broadcasting Corporation) BBC f or m
B.C. adv abbr (= before Christ) v. Chr.

KEYWORD

be [biː] (pt **was, were**, pp **been**) aux vb
1 (with present participle: forming continuous tenses): **what are you doing?** was machst du (gerade)?; **it is raining** es regnet; **I've been waiting for you for hours** ich warte schon seit Stunden auf dich
2 (with pp: forming passives): **to be killed** getötet werden; **the thief was nowhere to be seen** der Dieb war nirgendwo zu sehen
3 (in tag questions): **it was fun, wasn't it?** es hat Spaß gemacht, nicht wahr?
4 (+to +infin): **the house is to be sold** das Haus soll verkauft werden; **he's not to open it** er darf es nicht öffnen
♦ vb +complement **1** (usu) sein; **I'm tired** ich bin müde; **I'm hot/cold** mir ist heiß/kalt; **he's a doctor** er ist Arzt; **2 and 2 are 4** 2 und 2 ist or sind 4; **she's tall/pretty** sie ist groß/hübsch; **be careful/quiet** sei vorsichtig/ruhig
2 (of health): **how are you?** wie geht es dir?; **he's very ill** er ist sehr krank; **I'm fine now** jetzt geht es mir gut
3 (of age): **how old are you?** wie alt bist du?; **I'm sixteen (years old)** ich bin sechzehn (Jahre alt)
4 (cost): **how much was the meal?** was or wie viel hat das Essen gekostet?; **that'll be £5.75, please** das macht £5.75, bitte

♦ *vi* **1** (*exist, occur etc*) sein; **is there a God?** gibt es einen Gott?; **be that as it may** wie dem auch sei; **so be it** also gut **2** (*referring to place*) sein; **I won't be here tomorrow** iche werde morgen nicht hier sein

3 (*referring to movement*): **where have you been?** wo bist du gewesen?; **I've been in the garden** ich war im Garten

♦ *impers vb* **1** (*referring to time, distance, weather*) sein; **it's 5 o'clock** es ist 5 Uhr; **it's 10 km to the village** es sind 10 km bis zum Dorf; **it's too hot/cold** es ist zu heiß/kalt

2 (*emphatic*): **it's me** ich bins; **it's the postman** es ist der Briefträger

beach [biːtʃ] *n* Strand *m* ♦ *vt* (*ship*) auf den Strand setzen

beacon ['biːkən] *n* (*signal*) Leuchtfeuer *nt*; (*traffic ~*) Bake *f*

bead [biːd] *n* Perle *f*; (*drop*) Tropfen *m*

beak [biːk] *n* Schnabel *m*

beaker ['biːkər] *n* Becher *m*

beam [biːm] *n* (*of wood*) Balken *m*; (*of light*) Strahl *m*; (*smile*) strahlende(s) Lächeln *nt* ♦ *vi* strahlen

bean [biːn] *n* Bohne *f*; (*also:* **baked ~s**) gebackene Bohnen *pl*; **~ sprouts** *npl* Sojasprossen *pl*

bear [beər] (*pt* **bore**, *pp* **borne**) *n* Bär *m* ♦ *vt* (*weight, crops*) tragen; (*tolerate*) ertragen; (*young*) gebären ♦ *vi*: **to ~ right/left** sich rechts/links halten; **~ out** *vt* (*suspicions etc*) bestätigen; **~ up** *vi* sich halten

beard [biəd] *n* Bart *m*; **~ed** *adj* bärtig

bearer ['bɛərər] *n* Träger *m*

bearing ['bɛərɪŋ] *n* (*posture*) Haltung *f*; (*relevance*) Relevanz *f*; (*relation*) Bedeutung *f*; (*TECH*) Kugellager *nt*; **~s** *npl* (*direction*) Orientierung *f*; (*also:* **ball ~s**) (Kugel)lager *nt*

beast [biːst] *n* Tier *nt*, Vieh *nt*; (*person*) Biest *nt*

beat [biːt] (*pt* **beat**, *pp* **beaten**) *n* (*stroke*) Schlag *m*; (*pulsation*) (Herz)schlag *m*; (*police round*) Runde *f*; Revier *nt*; (*MUS*) Takt *m*;

Beat *m* ♦ *vt, vi* schlagen; **to ~ it** abhauen; **off the ~en track** abgelegen; **~ off** *vt* abschlagen; **~ up** *vt* zusammenschlagen; **~en** *pp* of **beat**; **~ing** *n* Prügel *pl*

beautiful ['bjuːtɪful] *adj* schön; **~ly** *adv* ausgezeichnet

beauty ['bjuːtɪ] *n* Schönheit *f*; **~ salon** *n* Schönheitssalon *m*; **~ spot** *n* Schönheitsfleck *m*; (*BRIT: TOURISM*) (besonders) schöne(r) Ort *m*

beaver ['biːvər] *n* Biber *m*

became [bɪ'keɪm] *pt* of **become**

because [bɪ'kɒz] *conj* weil ♦ *prep*: **~ of** wegen +*gen*, wegen +*dat* (*inf*)

beck [bek] *n*: **to be at the ~ and call of sb** nach jds Pfeife tanzen

beckon ['bekən] *vt, vi*: **to ~ to sb** jdm ein Zeichen geben

become [bɪ'kʌm] (*irreg: like* **come**) *vi* werden ♦ *vt* werden; (*clothes*) stehen +*dat*

becoming [bɪ'kʌmɪŋ] *adj* (*suitable*) schicklich; (*clothes*) kleidsam

bed [bed] *n* Bett *nt*; (*of river*) Flussbett *nt*; (*foundation*) Schicht *f*; (*in garden*) Beet *nt*; **to go to ~** zu Bett gehen; **~ and breakfast** *n* Übernachtung *f* mit Frühstück; **~clothes** *npl* Bettwäsche *f*; **~ding** *n* Bettzeug *nt*

Bed and Breakfast

i **Bed and Breakfast** *bedeutet "Übernachtung mit Frühstück", wobei sich dies in Großbritannien nicht auf Hotels, sondern auf kleinere Pensionen, Privathäuser und Bauernhöfe bezieht, wo man wesentlich preisgünstiger übernachten kann als in Hotels. Oft wird für Bed and Breakfast, auch B & B genannt, durch ein entsprechendes Schild im Garten oder an der Einfahrt geworben.*

---

bedlam ['bedləm] *n* (*uproar*) tolle(s) Durcheinander *nt*

bed linen *n* Bettwäsche *f*

bedraggled [bɪ'dræɡld] *adj* ramponiert

bed: **~ridden** *adj* bettlägerig; **~room** *n* Schlafzimmer *nt*; **~side** *n*: **at the ~side** am Bett; **~sit(ter)** (*BRIT*) *n* Einzimmerwohnung f, möblierte(s) Zimmer nt; ~**spread** n Tagesdecke f; ~**time** n Schlafenszeit f

bee [biː] n Biene f

beech [biːtʃ] n Buche f

beef [biːf] n Rindfleisch nt; **roast** ~ Roastbeef nt; ~**burger** n Hamburger m

beehive ['biːhaɪv] n Bienenstock m

beeline ['biːlaɪn] n: **to make a** ~ **for** schnurstracks zugehen auf +acc

been [biːn] pp of **be**

beer [bɪəʳ] n Bier nt

beet [biːt] n (vegetable) Rübe f; (US: also: **red** ~) Rote Bete f or Rübe f

beetle ['biːtl] n Käfer m

beetroot ['biːtruːt] (BRIT) n Rote Bete f

before [bɪ'fɔːʳ] prep vor ♦ conj bevor ♦ adv (of time) zuvor; früher; **the week** ~ die Woche zuvor or vorher; **I've done it** ~ das hab ich schon mal getan; ~ **going** bevor er/sie etc geht/ging; ~ **she goes** bevor sie geht; ~**hand** adv im Voraus

beg [beg] vt, vi (implore) dringend bitten; (alms) betteln

began [bɪ'gæn] pt of **begin**

beggar ['begəʳ] n Bettler(in) m(f)

begin [bɪ'gɪn] (pt **began**, pp **begun**) vt, vi anfangen, beginnen; (found) gründen; **to ~ doing** or **to do sth** anfangen or beginnen, etw zu tun; **to ~ with** zunächst (einmal); ~**ner** n Anfänger m; ~**ning** n Anfang m

begun [bɪ'gʌn] pp of **begin**

behalf [bɪ'hɑːf] n: **on** ~ **of** im Namen +gen; **on my** ~ für mich

behave [bɪ'heɪv] vi sich benehmen; **behaviour** [bɪ'heɪvjəʳ] (US **behavior**) n Benehmen nt

beheld [bɪ'held] pt, pp of **behold**

behind [bɪ'haɪnd] prep hinter ♦ adv (late) im Rückstand; (in the rear) hinten ♦ n (inf) Hinterteil nt; ~ **the scenes** (fig) hinter den Kulissen

behold [bɪ'həʊld] (irreg: like **hold**) vt erblicken

beige [beɪʒ] adj beige

Beijing ['beɪ'dʒɪŋ] n Peking nt

being ['biːɪŋ] n (existence) (Da)sein nt; (person) Wesen nt; **to come into** ~

entstehen

Belarus [belə'rus] n Weißrussland nt

belated [bɪ'leɪtɪd] adj verspätet

belch [beltʃ] vi rülpsen ♦ vt (smoke) ausspeien

belfry ['belfrɪ] n Glockenturm m

Belgian ['beldʒən] adj belgisch ♦ n Belgier(in) m(f)

Belgium ['beldʒəm] n Belgien nt

belie [bɪ'laɪ] vt Lügen strafen +acc

belief [bɪ'liːf] n Glaube m; (conviction) Überzeugung f; ~ **in sb/sth** Glaube an jdn/etw

believe [bɪ'liːv] vt glauben +dat; (think) glauben, meinen, denken ♦ vi (have faith) glauben; **to ~ in sth** an etw acc glauben; ~**r** n Gläubige(r) f(m)

belittle [bɪ'lɪtl] vt herabsetzen

bell [bel] n Glocke f

belligerent [bɪ'lɪdʒərənt] adj (person) streitsüchtig; (country) Krieg führend

bellow ['beləʊ] vt, vi brüllen

bellows ['beləʊz] npl (TECH) Gebläse nt; (for fire) Blasebalg m

belly ['belɪ] n Bauch m

belong [bɪ'lɔŋ] vi gehören; **to ~ to sb** jdm gehören; **to ~ to a club** etc einem Klub etc angehören; ~**ings** npl Habe f

beloved [bɪ'lʌvɪd] adj innig geliebt ♦ n Geliebte(r) f(m)

below [bɪ'ləʊ] prep unter ♦ adv unten

belt [belt] n (band) Riemen m; (round waist) Gürtel m ♦ vt (fasten) mit Riemen befestigen; (inf: beat) schlagen; ~**way** (US) n (AUT: ring road) Umgehungsstraße f

bemused [bɪ'mjuːzd] adj verwirrt

bench [bentʃ] n (seat) Bank f; (workshop) Werkbank f; (judge's seat) Richterbank f; (judges) Richter pl

bend [bend] (pt, pp **bent**) vt (curve) biegen; (stoop) beugen ♦ vi sich biegen; sich beugen ♦ n Biegung f; (BRIT: in road) Kurve f; ~ **down** or **over** vi sich bücken

beneath [bɪ'niːθ] prep unter ♦ adv darunter

benefactor ['benɪfæktəʳ] n Wohltäter(in) m(f)

beneficial [benɪ'fɪʃəl] adj vorteilhaft; (to

health) heilsam

benefit ['benɪfɪt] *n (advantage)* Nutzen *m* ♦ *vt* fördern ♦ *vi:* **to ~ (from)** Nutzen ziehen (aus)

Benelux ['benɪlʌks] *n* Beneluxstaaten *pl*

benevolent [bɪ'nevələnt] *adj* wohlwollend

benign [bɪ'naɪn] *adj (person)* gütig; *(climate)* mild

bent [bent] *pt, pp of* **bend** ♦ *n (inclination)* Neigung *f* ♦ *adj (inf: dishonest)* unehrlich; **to be ~ on** versessen sein auf *+acc*

bequest [bɪ'kwest] *n* Vermächtnis *nt*

bereaved [bɪ'riːvd] *npl:* **the ~** die Hinterbliebenen *pl*

beret ['bereɪ] *n* Baskenmütze *f*

Berlin [bə:'lɪn] *n* Berlin *nt*

berm [bə:m] *(US) n (AUT)* Seitenstreifen *m*

berry ['berɪ] *n* Beere *f*

berserk [bə'sə:k] *adj:* **to go ~** wild werden

berth [bə:θ] *n (for ship)* Ankerplatz *m; (in ship)* Koje *f; (in train)* Bett *nt* ♦ *vt* am Kai festmachen ♦ *vi* anlegen

beseech [bɪ'siːtʃ] *(pt, pp* **besought)** *vt* anflehen

beset [bɪ'set] *(pt, pp* **beset)** *vt* bedrängen

beside [bɪ'saɪd] *prep* neben, bei; *(except)* außer; **to be ~ o.s. (with)** außer sich sein (vor *+dat);* **that's ~ the point** das tut nichts zur Sache

besides [bɪ'saɪdz] *prep* außer, neben ♦ *adv* außerdem

besiege [bɪ'siːdʒ] *vt (MIL)* belagern; *(surround)* umlagern, bedrängen

besought [bɪ'sɔːt] *pt, pp of* **beseech**

best [best] *adj* beste(r, s) ♦ *adv* am besten; **the ~ part of** *(quantity)* das meiste *+gen;* **at ~** höchstens; **to make the ~ of it** das Beste daraus machen; **to do one's ~** sein Bestes tun; **to the ~ of my knowledge** meines Wissens; **to the ~ of my ability** so gut ich kann; **for the ~** zum Besten; **~-before date** *n* Mindesthaltbarkeitsdatum *nt;* **~ man** *n* Trauzeuge *m*

bestow [bɪ'stəʊ] *vt* verleihen

bet [bet] *(pt, pp* **bet** *or* **betted)** *n* Wette *f* ♦ *vt, vi* wetten

betray [bɪ'treɪ] *vt* verraten

better ['betər] *adj, adv* besser ♦ *vt* verbessern ♦ *n:* **to get the ~ of sb** jdn überwinden; **he thought ~ of it** er hat sich eines Besseren besonnen; **you had ~ leave** Sie gehen jetzt wohl besser; **to get ~** *(MED)* gesund werden; **~ off** *adj (richer)* wohlhabender

betting ['betɪŋ] *n* Wetten *nt;* **~ shop** *(BRIT) n* Wettbüro *nt*

between [bɪ'twiːn] *prep* zwischen; *(among)* unter ♦ *adv* dazwischen

beverage ['bevərɪdʒ] *n* Getränk *nt*

bevy ['bevɪ] *n* Schar *f*

beware [bɪ'weər] *vt, vi* sich hüten vor *+dat;* **"~ of the dog"** „Vorsicht, bissiger Hund!"

bewildered [bɪ'wɪldəd] *adj* verwirrt

beyond [bɪ'jɔnd] *prep (place)* jenseits *+gen; (time)* über ... hinaus; *(out of reach)* außerhalb *+gen* ♦ *adv* darüber hinaus; **~ doubt** ohne Zweifel; **~ repair** nicht mehr zu reparieren

bias ['baɪəs] *n (slant)* Neigung *f; (prejudice)* Vorurteil *nt;* **~(s)ed** *adj* voreingenommen

bib [bɪb] *n* Latz *m*

Bible ['baɪbl] *n* Bibel *f*

bicarbonate of soda [baɪ'kɑːbənɪt-] *n* Natron *nt*

bicker ['bɪkər] *vi* zanken

bicycle ['baɪsɪkl] *n* Fahrrad *nt*

bid [bɪd] *(pt* **bade** *or* **bid,** *pp* **bid(den))** *n (offer)* Gebot *nt; (attempt)* Versuch *m* ♦ *vt, vi (offer)* bieten; **to ~ farewell** Lebewohl sagen; **~der** *n (person)* Steigerer *m;* **the highest ~der** der Meistbietende; **~ding** *n (command)* Geheiß *nt*

bide [baɪd] *vt:* **to ~ one's time** abwarten

bifocals [baɪ'fəʊklz] *npl* Bifokalbrille *f*

big [bɪg] *adj* groß; **~ dipper** [-'dɪpər] *n* Achterbahn *f;* **~-headed** ['bɪg'hedɪd] *adj* eingebildet

bigot ['bɪgət] *n* Frömmler *m;* **~ed** *adj* bigott; **~ry** *n* Bigotterie *f*

big top *n* Zirkuszelt *nt*

bike [baɪk] *n* Rad *nt*

bikini [bɪ'kiːnɪ] *n* Bikini *m*

bile [baɪl] *n (BIOL)* Galle *f*

bilingual [baɪ'lɪŋgwəl] *adj* zweisprachig

bill [bɪl] *n (account)* Rechnung *f; (POL)*

Gesetzentwurf m; (US: FIN) Geldschein m; to
fit or fill the ~ (fig) der/die/das Richtige
sein; "post no ~s" „Plakate ankleben
verboten"; ~board ['bɪlbɔːd] n
Reklameschild nt

billet ['bɪlɪt] n Quartier nt

billfold ['bɪlfəʊld] (US) n Geldscheintasche f

billiards ['bɪljədz] n Billard nt

billion ['bɪljən] n (BRIT) Billion f; (US)
Milliarde f

bimbo ['bɪmbəʊ] (inf: pej) n Puppe f,
Häschen nt

bin [bɪn] n Kasten m; (dustbin) (Abfall)eimer
m

bind [baɪnd] (pt, pp bound) vt (tie) binden;
(tie together) zusammenbinden; (oblige)
verpflichten; ~ing n (Buch)einband m ♦ adj
verbindlich

binge [bɪndʒ] (inf) n Sauferei f

bingo ['bɪŋgəʊ] n Bingo nt

binoculars [bɪ'nɒkjʊləz] npl Fernglas nt

bio... [baɪəʊ] prefix: ~chemistry n
Biochemie f; ~degradable adj biologisch
abbaubar; ~graphy n Biografie f; ~logical
[baɪə'lɒdʒɪkl] adj biologisch; ~logy
[baɪ'ɒlədʒɪ] n Biologie f

birch [bɜːtʃ] n Birke f

bird [bɜːd] n Vogel m; (BRIT: inf: girl)
Mädchen nt; ~'s-eye view n Vogelschau
f; ~ watcher n Vogelbeobachter(in) m(f);
~ watching n Vogelbeobachten nt

Biro ['baɪərəʊ] ® n Kugelschreiber m

birth [bɜːθ] n Geburt f; to give ~ to zur Welt
bringen; ~ certificate n Geburtsurkunde f;
~ control n Geburtenkontrolle f; ~day n
Geburtstag m; ~day card n
Geburtstagskarte f; ~place n Geburtsort
m; ~ rate n Geburtenrate f

biscuit ['bɪskɪt] n Keks m

bisect [baɪ'sekt] vt halbieren

bishop ['bɪʃəp] n Bischof m

bit [bɪt] pt of bite ♦ n bisschen, Stückchen nt;
(horse's) Gebiss nt; (COMPUT) Bit nt; a ~
tired etwas müde

bitch [bɪtʃ] n (dog) Hündin f; (unpleasant
woman) Weibsstück nt

bite [baɪt] (pt bit, pp bitten) vt, vi beißen ♦ n

Biss m; (mouthful) Bissen m; to ~ one's
nails Nägel kauen; let's have a ~ to eat
lass uns etwas essen

bitten ['bɪtn] pp of bite

bitter ['bɪtə'] adj bitter; (memory etc)
schmerzlich; (person) verbittert ♦ n (BRIT:
beer) dunkle(s) Bier nt; ~ness n Bitterkeit f

blab [blæb] vi klatschen ♦ vt (also: ~ out)
ausplaudern

black [blæk] adj schwarz; (night) finster ♦ vt
schwärzen; (shoes) wichsen; (eye) blau
schlagen; (BRIT: INDUSTRY) boykottieren; to
give sb a ~ eye jdm ein blaues Auge
schlagen; in the ~ (bank account) in den
schwarzen Zahlen; ~ and blue adj grün
und blau; ~berry n Brombeere f; ~bird n
Amsel f; ~board n (Wand)tafel f; ~ coffee
n schwarze(r) Kaffee m; ~currant n
schwarze Johannisbeere f; ~en vt
schwärzen; (fig) verunglimpfen; B~ Forest
n Schwarzwald m; ~ ice n Glatteis nt; ~leg
(BRIT) n Streikbrecher(in) m(f); ~list n
schwarze Liste f; ~mail n Erpressung f ♦ vt
erpressen; ~ market n Schwarzmarkt m;
~out n Verdunklung f; (MED): to have a
~out bewusstlos werden; ~ pudding n ≈
Blutwurst f; B~ Sea n: the B~ Sea das
Schwarze Meer; ~ sheep n schwarze(s)
Schaf nt; ~smith n Schmied m; ~ spot n
(AUT) Gefahrenstelle f; (for unemployment
etc) schwer betroffene(s) Gebiet nt

bladder ['blædə'] n Blase f

blade [bleɪd] n (of weapon) Klinge f; (of grass)
Halm m; (of oar) Ruderblatt nt

blame [bleɪm] n Tadel m, Schuld f ♦ vt
Vorwürfe machen +dat; to ~ sb for sth jdm
die Schuld an etw dat geben; he is to ~ er
ist daran schuld

bland [blænd] adj mild

blank [blæŋk] adj leer, unbeschrieben; (look)
verdutzt; (verse) Blank- ♦ n (space) Lücke f;
Zwischenraum m; (cartridge) Platzpatrone f;
~ cheque n Blankoscheck m; (fig) Freibrief
m

blanket ['blæŋkɪt] n (Woll)decke f

blare [bleə'] vi (radio) plärren; (horn) tuten;
(MUS) schmettern

blasé ['blɑːzeɪ] *adj* blasiert

blast [blɑːst] *n* Explosion *f*; *(of wind)* Windstoß *m* ♦ *vt (blow up)* sprengen; **~!** *(inf)* verflixt!; **~off** *n (SPACE)* (Raketen)abschuss *m*

blatant ['bleɪtənt] *adj* offenkundig

blaze [bleɪz] *n (fire)* lodernde(s) Feuer *nt* ♦ *vi* lodern ♦ *vt:* **to ~ a trail** Bahn brechen

blazer ['bleɪzə'] *n* Blazer *m*

bleach [bliːtʃ] *n (also:* **household ~)** Bleichmittel *nt* ♦ *vt* bleichen; **~ed** *adj* gebleicht

bleachers ['bliːtʃəz] *(US) npl (SPORT)* unüberdachte Tribüne *f*

bleak [bliːk] *adj* kahl, rau; *(future)* trostlos

bleary-eyed ['blɪərˈaɪd] *adj* triefäugig; *(on waking up)* mit verschlafenen Augen

bleat [bliːt] *vi* blöken; *(fig: complain)* meckern

bled [bled] *pt, pp of* **bleed**

bleed [bliːd] *(pt, pp* **bled***) vi* bluten ♦ *vt (draw blood)* zur Ader lassen; **to ~ to death** verbluten

bleeper ['bliːpə'] *n (of doctor etc)* Funkrufempfänger *m*

blemish ['blemɪʃ] *n* Makel *m* ♦ *vt* verunstalten

blend [blend] *n* Mischung *f* ♦ *vt* mischen ♦ *vi* sich mischen; **~er** *n* Mixer *m*, Mixgerät *nt*

bless [bles] *(pt, pp* **blessed***) vt* segnen; *(give thanks)* preisen; *(make happy)* glücklich machen; **~ you!** Gesundheit!; **~ing** *n* Segen *m*; *(at table)* Tischgebet *nt*; *(happiness)* Wohltat *f*; Segen *m*; *(good wish)* Glück *nt*

blew [bluː] *pt of* **blow**

blimey ['blaɪmɪ] *(BRIT: inf) excl* verflucht

blind [blaɪnd] *adj* blind; *(corner)* unübersichtlich ♦ *n (for window)* Rouleau *nt* ♦ *vt* blenden; **~ alley** *n* Sackgasse *f*; **~fold** *n* Augenbinde *f* ♦ *adj, adv* mit verbundenen Augen ♦ *vt:* **to ~fold sb** jdm die Augen verbinden; **~ly** *adv* blind; *(fig)* blindlings; **~ness** *n* Blindheit *f*; **~ spot** *n (AUT)* tote(r) Winkel *m*; *(fig)* schwache(r) Punkt *m*

blink [blɪŋk] *vi* blinzeln; **~ers** *npl* Scheuklappen *pl*

bliss [blɪs] *n* (Glück)seligkeit *f*

blister ['blɪstə'] *n* Blase *f* ♦ *vi* Blasen werfen

blitz [blɪts] *n* Luftkrieg *m*

blizzard ['blɪzəd] *n* Schneesturm *m*

bloated ['bləʊtɪd] *adj* aufgedunsen; *(inf: full)* nudelsatt

blob [blɔb] *n* Klümpchen *nt*

bloc [blɔk] *n (POL)* Block *m*

block [blɔk] *n (of wood)* Block *m*, Klotz *m*; *(of houses)* Häuserblock *m* ♦ *vt* hemmen; **~ade** [blɔ'keɪd] *n* Blockade *f* ♦ *vt* blockieren; **~age** *n* Verstopfung *f*; **~buster** *n* Knüller *m*; **~ letters** *npl* Blockbuchstaben *pl*; **~ of flats** *(BRIT) n* Häuserblock *m*

bloke [bləʊk] *(BRIT: inf) n* Kerl *m*, Typ *m*

blond(e) [blɔnd] *adj* blond ♦ *n* Blondine *f*

blood [blʌd] *n* Blut *nt*; **~ donor** *n* Blutspender *m*; **~ group** *n* Blutgruppe *f*; **~ poisoning** *n* Blutvergiftung *f*; **~ pressure** *n* Blutdruck *m*; **~shed** *n* Blutvergießen *nt*; **~shot** *adj* blutunterlaufen; **~ sports** *npl* Jagdsport, Hahnenkampf *etc*; **~stained** *adj* blutbefleckt; **~stream** *n* Blut *nt*, Blutkreislauf *m*; **~ test** *n* Blutprobe *f*; **~thirsty** *adj* blutrünstig; **~ vessel** *n* Blutgefäß *nt*; **~y** *adj* blutig; *(BRIT: inf)* verdammt; **~y-minded** *(BRIT: inf) adj* stur

bloom [bluːm] *n* Blüte *f*; *(freshness)* Glanz *m* ♦ *vi* blühen

blossom ['blɔsəm] *n* Blüte *f* ♦ *vi* blühen

blot [blɔt] *n* Klecks *m* ♦ *vt* beklecksen; *(ink)* (ab)löschen; **~ out** *vt* auslöschen

blotchy ['blɔtʃɪ] *adj* fleckig

blotting paper ['blɔtɪŋ-] *n* Löschpapier *nt*

blouse [blauz] *n* Bluse *f*

blow [bləʊ] *(pt* **blew***, pp* **blown***) n* Schlag *m* ♦ *vt* blasen ♦ *vi (wind)* wehen; **to ~ one's nose** sich *dat* die Nase putzen; **~ away** *vt* wegblasen; **~ down** *vt* umwehen; **~ off** *vt* wegwehen ♦ *vi* wegfliegen; **~ out** *vi* ausgehen; **~ over** *vi* vorübergehen; **~ up** *vi* explodieren ♦ *vt* sprengen; **~-dry** *n:* **to have a ~-dry** sich föhnen lassen ♦ *vt* föhnen; **~lamp** *(BRIT) n* Lötlampe *f*; **~n** *pp of* **blow**; **~-out** *n (AUT)* geplatzte(r) Reifen *m*; **~torch** *n* = **blowlamp**

blue [bluː] *adj* blau; *(inf: unhappy)* niedergeschlagen; *(obscene)* pornografisch;

(joke) anzüglich ♦ n: **out of the ~** *(fig)* aus heiterem Himmel; **to have the ~s** traurig sein; **~bell** n Glockenblume f; **~bottle** n Schmeißfliege f; **~ film** n Pornofilm m; **~print** n *(fig)* Entwurf m

bluff [blʌf] vi bluffen, täuschen ♦ n *(deception)* Bluff m; **to call sb's ~** es darauf ankommen lassen

blunder ['blʌndəʳ] n grobe(r) Fehler m, Schnitzer m ♦ vi einen groben Fehler machen

blunt [blʌnt] adj *(knife)* stumpf; *(talk)* unverblümt ♦ vt abstumpfen

blur [blɜːʳ] n Fleck m ♦ vt verschwommen machen

blurb [blɜːb] n Waschzettel m

blush [blʌʃ] vi erröten

blustery ['blʌstəri] adj stürmisch

boar [bɔːʳ] n Keiler m, Eber m

board [bɔːd] n *(of wood)* Brett nt; *(of card)* Pappe f; *(committee)* Ausschuss m; *(of firm)* Aufsichtsrat m; *(SCH)* Direktorium nt ♦ vt *(train)* einsteigen in +acc; *(ship)* an Bord gehen +gen; **on ~** *(AVIAT, NAUT)* an Bord; **~ and lodging** Unterkunft f und Verpflegung; **full/half ~** *(BRIT)* Voll-/Halbpension f; **to go by the ~** flachfallen, über Bord gehen; **~ up** vt mit Brettern vernageln; **~er** n Kostgänger m; *(SCH)* Internatsschüler(in) m(f); **~ game** n Brettspiel nt; **~ing card** n *(AVIAT, NAUT)* Bordkarte f; **~ing house** n Pension f; **~ing school** n Internat nt; **~ room** n Sitzungszimmer nt

boast [bəʊst] vi prahlen ♦ vt sich rühmen +gen ♦ n Großtuerei f; Prahlerei f; **to ~ about** or **of sth** mit etw prahlen

boat [bəʊt] n Boot nt; *(ship)* Schiff nt; **~er** n *(hat)* Kreissäge f; **~swain** n = bosun; **~ train** n Zug m mit Fährenanschluss

bob [bɒb] vi sich auf und nieder bewegen; **~ up** vi auftauchen

bobbin ['bɒbɪn] n Spule f

bobby ['bɒbɪ] n *(BRIT: inf)* Bobby m

bobsleigh ['bɒbsleɪ] n Bob m

bode [bəʊd] vi: **to ~ well/ill** ein gutes/ schlechtes Zeichen sein

bodily ['bɒdɪlɪ] adj, adv körperlich

body ['bɒdɪ] n Körper m; *(dead)* Leiche f; *(group)* Mannschaft f; *(AUT)* Karosserie f; *(trunk)* Rumpf m; **~ building** n Bodybuilding nt; **~guard** n Leibwache f; **~work** n Karosserie f

bog [bɒg] n Sumpf m ♦ vt: **to get ~ged down** sich festfahren

boggle ['bɒgl] vi stutzen; **the mind ~s** es ist kaum auszumalen

bog-standard adj stinknormal *(inf)*

bogus ['bəʊgəs] adj unecht, Schein-

boil [bɔɪl] vt, vi kochen ♦ n *(MED)* Geschwür nt; **to come to the** *(BRIT)* or a *(US)* **~** zu kochen anfangen; **to ~ down to** *(fig)* hinauslaufen auf +acc; **~ over** vi überkochen; **~ed egg** n *(weich)* gekochte(s) Ei nt; **~ed potatoes** npl Salzkartoffeln pl; **~er** n Boiler m; **~er suit** n *(BRIT)* Arbeitsanzug m; **~ing point** n Siedepunkt m

boisterous ['bɔɪstərəs] adj ungestüm

bold [bəʊld] adj *(fearless)* unerschrocken; *(handwriting)* fest und klar

bollard ['bɒləd] n *(NAUT)* Poller m; *(BRIT: AUT)* Pfosten m

bolt [bəʊlt] n Bolzen m; *(lock)* Riegel m ♦ adv: **~ upright** kerzengerade ♦ vt verriegeln; *(swallow)* verschlingen ♦ vi *(horse)* durchgehen

bomb [bɒm] n Bombe f ♦ vt bombardieren; **~ard** [bɒmˈbɑːd] vt bombardieren; **~ardment** [bɒmˈbɑːdmənt] n Beschießung f; **~ disposal** n: **~ disposal unit** Bombenräumkommando nt; **~er** n Bomber m; *(terrorist)* Bombenattentäter(in) m(f); **~ing** n Bomben nt; **~shell** n *(fig)* Bombe f

bona fide ['bəʊnə'faɪdɪ] adj echt

bond [bɒnd] n *(link)* Band nt; *(FIN)* Schuldverschreibung f

bondage ['bɒndɪdʒ] n Sklaverei f

bone [bəʊn] n Knochen m; *(of fish)* Gräte f; *(piece of ~)* Knochensplitter m ♦ vt die Knochen herausnehmen +dat; *(fish)* entgräten; **~ dry** adj *(inf)* knochentrocken; **~ idle** adj stinkfaul; **~ marrow** n *(ANAT)* Knochenmark nt

bonfire ['bɒnfaɪəʳ] n Feuer nt im Freien

bonnet ['bɒnɪt] *n* Haube *f*; (*for baby*) Häubchen *nt*; (*BRIT: AUT*) Motorhaube *f*

bonus ['bəʊnəs] *n* Bonus *m*; (*annual ~*) Prämie *f*

bony ['bəʊnɪ] *adj* knochig, knochendürr

boo [buː] *vt* auspfeifen

booby trap ['buːbɪ-] *n* Falle *f*

book [bʊk] *n* Buch *nt* ♦ *vt* (*ticket etc*) vorbestellen; (*person*) verwarnen; **~s** *npl* (*COMM*) Bücher *pl*; **~case** *n* Bücherregal *nt*, Bücherschrank *m*; **~ing office** (*BRIT*) *n* (*RAIL*) Fahrkartenschalter *m*; (*THEAT*) Vorverkaufsstelle *f*; **~-keeping** *n* Buchhaltung *f*; **~let** *n* Broschüre *f*; **~maker** *n* Buchmacher *m*; **~seller** *n* Buchhändler *m*; **~shelf** *n* Bücherbord *nt*; **~shop** ['bʊkʃɒp], **~store** *n* Buchhandlung *f*

boom [buːm] *n* (*noise*) Dröhnen *nt*; (*busy period*) Hochkonjunktur *f* ♦ *vi* dröhnen

boon [buːn] *n* Wohltat *f*, Segen *m*

boost [buːst] *n* Auftrieb *m*; (*fig*) Reklame *f* ♦ *vt* Auftrieb geben; **~er** *n* (*MED*) Wiederholungsimpfung *f*

boot [buːt] *n* Stiefel *m*; (*BRIT: AUT*) Kofferraum *m* ♦ *vt* (*kick*) einen Fußtritt geben; (*COMPUT*) laden; **to ~** (*in addition*) obendrein

booth [buːð] *n* (*at fair*) Bude *f*; (*telephone ~*) Zelle *f*; (*voting ~*) Kabine *f*

booze [buːz] (*inf*) *n* Alkohol *m*, Schnaps *m* ♦ *vi* saufen

border ['bɔːdəʳ] *n* Grenze *f*; (*edge*) Kante *f*; (*in garden*) (Blumen)rabatte *f* ♦ *adj* Grenz-; **the B~s** *Grenzregion zwischen England und Schottland*; **~ on** *vt* grenzen an +*acc*; **~line** *n* Grenze *f*; **~line case** *n* Grenzfall *m*

bore [bɔːʳ] *pt of* **bear** ♦ *vt* bohren; (*weary*) langweilen ♦ *n* (*person*) Langweiler *m*; (*thing*) langweilige Sache *f*; (*of gun*) Kaliber *nt*; **I am ~d** ich langweile mich; **~dom** *n* Langeweile *f*

boring ['bɔːrɪŋ] *adj* langweilig

born [bɔːn] *adj*: **to be ~** geboren werden

borne [bɔːn] *pp of* **bear**

borough ['bʌrə] *n* Stadt(gemeinde) *f*, Stadtbezirk *m*

borrow ['bɒrəʊ] *vt* borgen

Bosnia (and) Herzegovina ['bɒznɪə (ənd) hɑːtsəgəʊ'viːnə] *n* Bosnien und Herzegowina *nt*; **~n** *n* Bosnier(in) *m(f)* ♦ *adj* bosnisch

bosom ['buzəm] *n* Busen *m*

boss [bɒs] *n* Chef *m*, Boss *m* ♦ *vt*: **to ~ around** *or* **about** herumkommandieren; **~y** *adj* herrisch

bosun ['bəʊsn] *n* Bootsmann *m*

botany ['bɒtənɪ] *n* Botanik *f*

botch [bɒtʃ] *vt* (*also*: **~ up**) verpfuschen

both [bəʊθ] *adj* beide(s) ♦ *pron* beide(s) ♦ *adv*: **~ X and Y** sowohl X wie *or* als auch Y; **~ (of) the books** beide Bücher; **~ of us went, we ~ went** wir gingen beide

bother ['bɒðəʳ] *vt* (*pester*) quälen ♦ *vi* (*fuss*) sich aufregen ♦ *n* Mühe *f*, Umstand *m*; **to ~ doing sth** sich *dat* die Mühe machen, etw zu tun; **what a ~!** wie ärgerlich!

bottle ['bɒtl] *n* Flasche *f* ♦ *vt* (*in Flaschen*) abfüllen; **~ up** *vt* aufstauen; **~ bank** *n* Altglascontainer *m*; **~d beer** *n* Flaschenbier *nt*; **~d water** *n* in Flaschen abgefülltes Wasser; **~neck** *n* (*also fig*) Engpass *m*; **~ opener** *n* Flaschenöffner *m*

bottom ['bɒtəm] *n* Boden *m*; (*of person*) Hintern *m*; (*riverbed*) Flussbett *nt* ♦ *adj* unterste(r, s)

bough [baʊ] *n* Zweig *m*, Ast *m*

bought [bɔːt] *pt, pp of* **buy**

boulder ['bəʊldəʳ] *n* Felsbrocken *m*

bounce [baʊns] *vi* (*person*) herumhüpfen; (*ball*) hochspringen; (*cheque*) platzen ♦ *vt* (*auf*)springen lassen ♦ *n* (*rebound*) Aufprall *m*; **~r** *n* Rausschmeißer *m*

bound [baʊnd] *pt, pp of* **bind** ♦ *n* Grenze *f*; (*leap*) Sprung *m* ♦ *vi* (*spring, leap*) (*auf*)springen ♦ *adj* (*obliged*) gebunden, verpflichtet; **out of ~s** Zutritt verboten; **to be ~ to do sth** verpflichtet sein, etw zu tun; **it's ~ to happen** es muss so kommen; **to be ~ for ...** nach ... fahren

boundary ['baʊndrɪ] *n* Grenze *f*

bouquet ['bʊkeɪ] *n* Strauß *m*; (*of wine*) Blume *f*

bourgeois ['bʊəʒwɑː] *adj* kleinbürgerlich, bourgeois ♦ *n* Spießbürger(in) *m(f)*

bout [baʊt] *n* (*of illness*) Anfall *m*; (*of contest*)

Kampf m

bow¹ [bəu] n (ribbon) Schleife f; (weapon, MUS) Bogen m

bow² [bau] n (with head, body) Verbeugung f; (of ship) Bug m ♦ vi sich verbeugen; (submit): **to ~ to** sich beugen +dat

bowels ['bauəlz] npl (ANAT) Darm m

bowl [bəul] n (basin) Schüssel f; (of pipe) (Pfeifen)kopf m; (wooden ball) (Holz)kugel f ♦ vt, vi (die Kugel) rollen

bow-legged ['bəu'legɪd] adj o-beinig, O-beinig

bowler ['bəulə'] n Werfer m; (BRIT: also: ~ **hat**) Melone f

bowling ['bəulɪŋ] n Kegeln nt; ~ **alley** n Kegelbahn f; ~ **green** n Rasen m zum Bowlingspiel

bowls n (game) Bowlsspiel nt

bow tie [bəu-] n Fliege f

box [bɒks] n (also: **cardboard ~**) Schachtel f; (bigger) Kasten m; (THEAT) Loge f ♦ vt einpacken ♦ vi boxen; ~**er** n Boxer m; ~**er shorts** (SPORT) npl Boxershorts pl; ~**ing** n (SPORT) Boxen nt; **B~ing Day** (BRIT) n zweite(r) Weihnachtsfeiertag m; ~**ing gloves** npl Boxhandschuhe pl; ~**ing ring** n Boxring m; ~ **office** n (Theater)kasse f; ~**room** n Rumpelkammer f

boy [bɔɪ] n Junge m

boycott ['bɔɪkɔt] n Boykott m ♦ vt boykottieren

boyfriend ['bɔɪfrend] n Freund m

boyish ['bɔɪʃ] adj jungenhaft

B.R. n abbr = **British Rail**

bra [brɑː] n BH m

brace [breɪs] n (TECH) Stütze f; (MED)

Klammer f ♦ vt stützen; ~**s** npl (BRIT) Hosenträger pl; **to ~ o.s. for sth** (fig) sich auf etw acc gefasst machen

bracelet ['breɪslɪt] n Armband nt

bracing ['breɪsɪŋ] adj kräftigend

bracken ['brækən] n Farnkraut nt

bracket ['brækɪt] n Halter m, Klammer f; (in punctuation) Klammer f; (group) Gruppe f ♦ vt einklammern; (fig) in dieselbe Gruppe einordnen

brag [bræg] vi sich rühmen

braid [breɪd] n (hair) Flechte f; (trim) Borte f

Braille [breɪl] n Blindenschrift f

brain [breɪn] n (ANAT) Gehirn nt; (intellect) Intelligenz f, Verstand m; (person) kluge(r) Kopf m; ~**s** npl (intelligence) Verstand m; ~**child** n Erfindung f; ~**wash** vt eine Gehirnwäsche vornehmen bei; ~**wave** n Geistesblitz m; ~**y** adj gescheit

braise [breɪz] vt schmoren

brake [breɪk] n Bremse f ♦ vt, vi bremsen; ~ **fluid** n Bremsflüssigkeit f; ~ **light** n Bremslicht nt

bramble ['bræmbl] n Brombeere f

bran [bræn] n Kleie f; (food) Frühstücksflocken pl

branch [brɑːntʃ] n Ast m; (division) Zweig m ♦ vi (also: ~ **out**: road) sich verzweigen

brand [brænd] n (COMM) Marke f, Sorte f; (on cattle) Brandmal nt ♦ vt brandmarken; (COMM) ein Warenzeichen geben +dat

brandish ['brændɪʃ] vt (drohend) schwingen

brand-new ['brænd'njuː] adj funkelnagelneu

brandy ['brændɪ] n Weinbrand m, Kognak m

brash [bræʃ] adj unverschämt

brass [brɑːs] n Messing nt; **the ~** (MUS) das Blech; ~ **band** n Blaskapelle f

brassière ['bræsɪə'] n Büstenhalter m

brat [bræt] n Gör nt

bravado [brə'vɑːdəu] n Tollkühnheit f

brave [breɪv] adj tapfer ♦ vt die Stirn bieten +dat; ~**ry** n Tapferkeit f

brawl [brɔːl] n Rauferei f

brawn [brɔːn] n (ANAT) Muskeln pl; (strength) Muskelkraft f

bray [breɪ] vi schreien

brazen ['breɪzn] adj (shameless) unverschämt

♦ *vt*: **to ~ it out** sich mit Lügen und Betrügen durchsetzen

brazier ['breɪzɪəʳ] *n* (*of workmen*) offene(r) Kohlenofen *m*

Brazil [brə'zɪl] *n* Brasilien *nt*; **~ian** *adj* brasilianisch ♦ *n* Brasilianer(in) *m(f)*

breach [briːtʃ] *n* (*gap*) Lücke *f*; (MIL) Durchbruch *m*; (*of discipline*) Verstoß *m* (gegen die Disziplin); (*of faith*) Vertrauensbruch *m* ♦ *vt* durchbrechen; **~ of contract** Vertragsbruch *m*; **~ of the peace** öffentliche Ruhestörung *f*

bread [bred] *n* Brot *nt*; **~ and butter** Butterbrot *nt*; **~bin** *n* Brotkasten *m*; **~ box** (US) *n* Brotkasten *m*; **~crumbs** *npl* Brotkrumen *pl*; (COOK) Paniermehl *nt*; **~line** *n*: **to be on the ~line** sich gerade so durchschlagen

breadth [bretθ] *n* Breite *f*

breadwinner ['bredwɪnəʳ] *n* Ernährer *m*

break [breɪk] (*pt* **broke**, *pp* **broken**) *vt* (*destroy*) (*ab- or zer*)brechen; (*promise*) brechen, nicht einhalten ♦ *vi* (*fall apart*) auseinander brechen; (*collapse*) zusammenbrechen; (*dawn*) anbrechen ♦ *n* (*gap*) Lücke *f*; (*chance*) Chance *f*, Gelegenheit *f*; (*fracture*) Bruch *m*; (*rest*) Pause *f*; **~ down** *vt* (*figures, data*) aufschlüsseln; (*undermine*) überwinden ♦ *vi* (*car*) eine Panne haben; (*person*) zusammenbrechen; **~ even** *vi* die Kosten decken; **~ free** *vi* sich losreißen; **~ in** *vt* (*horse*) zureiten ♦ *vi* (*burglar*) einbrechen; **~ into** *vt fus* (*house*) einbrechen in +*acc*; **~ loose** *vi* sich losreißen; **~ off** *vi* abbrechen; **~ open** *vt* (*door etc*) aufbrechen; **~ out** *vi* ausbrechen; **to ~ out in spots** Pickel bekommen; **~ up** *vi* zerbrechen; (*fig*) sich zerstreuen; (BRIT: SCH) in die Ferien gehen ♦ *vt* brechen; **~age** *n* Bruch *m*, Beschädigung *f*; **~down** *n* (TECH) Panne *f*; (MED: *also*: **nervous ~down**) Zusammenbruch *m*; **~down van** (BRIT) *n* Abschleppwagen *m*; **~er** *n* Brecher *m*

breakfast ['brekfəst] *n* Frühstück *nt*

break: **~-in** *n* Einbruch *m*; **~ing** *n*: **~ing and entering** (JUR) Einbruch *m*; **~through**

n Durchbruch *m*; **~water** *n* Wellenbrecher *m*

breast [brest] *n* Brust *f*; **~-feed** (*irreg: like* **feed**) *vt, vi* stillen; **~-stroke** *n* Brustschwimmen *nt*

breath [breθ] *n* Atem *m*; **out of ~** außer Atem; **under one's ~** flüsternd

Breathalyzer ['breθəlaɪzəʳ] ® *n* Röhrchen *nt*

breathe [briːð] *vt, vi* atmen; **~ in** *vt, vi* einatmen; **~ out** *vt, vi* ausatmen; **~r** *n* Verschnaufpause *f*; **breathing** *n* Atmung *f*

breathless ['breθlɪs] *adj* atemlos

breathtaking ['breθteɪkɪŋ] *adj* atemberaubend

bred [bred] *pt, pp of* **breed**

breed [briːd] (*pt, pp* **bred**) *vi* sich vermehren ♦ *vt* züchten ♦ *n* (*race*) Rasse *f*, Zucht *f*; **~ing** *n* Züchtung *f*; (*upbringing*) Erziehung *f*

breeze [briːz] *n* Brise *f*; **breezy** *adj* windig; (*manner*) munter

brevity ['brevɪtɪ] *n* Kürze *f*

brew [bruː] *vt* (*beer*) brauen ♦ *vi* (*storm*) sich zusammenziehen; **~ery** *n* Brauerei *f*

bribe [braɪb] *n* Bestechungsgeld *nt*, Bestechungsgeschenk *nt* ♦ *vt* bestechen; **~ry** ['braɪbərɪ] *n* Bestechung *f*

bric-a-brac ['brɪkəbræk] *n* Nippes *pl*

brick [brɪk] *n* Backstein *m*; **~layer** *n* Maurer *m*; **~works** *n* Ziegelei *f*

bridal ['braɪdl] *adj* Braut-

bride [braɪd] *n* Braut *f*; **~groom** *n* Bräutigam *m*; **~smaid** *n* Brautjungfer *f*

bridge [brɪdʒ] *n* Brücke *f*; (NAUT) Kommandobrücke *f*; (CARDS) Bridge *nt*; (ANAT) Nasenrücken *m* ♦ *vt* eine Brücke schlagen über +*acc*; (*fig*) überbrücken

bridle ['braɪdl] *n* Zaum *m* ♦ *vt* (*fig*) zügeln; (*horse*) aufzäumen; **~ path** *n* Reitweg *m*

brief [briːf] *adj* kurz ♦ *n* (JUR) Akten *pl* ♦ *vt* instruieren; **~s** *npl* (*underwear*) Schlüpfer *m*, Slip *m*; **~case** *n* Aktentasche *f*; **~ing** *n* (*genaue*) Anweisung *f*; **~ly** *adv* kurz

brigadier [brɪgə'dɪəʳ] *n* Brigadegeneral *m*

bright [braɪt] *adj* hell; (*cheerful*) heiter; (*idea*) klug; **~en (up)** ['braɪtn-] *vt* aufhellen; (*person*) aufheitern ♦ *vi* sich aufheitern

brilliance ['brɪljəns] *n* Glanz *m*; (*of person*)

Scharfsinn m

brilliant ['brɪljənt] *adj* glänzend

brim [brɪm] *n* Rand m

brine [braɪn] *n* Salzwasser nt

bring [brɪŋ] (*pt, pp* **brought**) *vt* bringen; **~ about** *vt* zustande *or* zu Stande bringen; **~ back** *vt* zurückbringen; **~ down** *vt* (*price*) senken; **~ forward** *vt* (*meeting*) vorverlegen; (*COMM*) übertragen; **~ in** *vt* hereinbringen; (*harvest*) einbringen; **~ off** *vt* davontragen; (*success*) erzielen; **~ out** *vt* (*object*) herausbringen; **~ round** *or* **to** *vt* wieder zu sich bringen; **~ up** *vt* aufziehen; (*question*) zur Sprache bringen

brink [brɪŋk] *n* Rand m

brisk [brɪsk] *adj* lebhaft

bristle ['brɪsl] *n* Borste f ♦ *vi* sich sträuben; **bristling with** strotzend vor +*dat*

Britain ['brɪtən] *n* (*also:* **Great ~**) Großbritannien nt

British ['brɪtɪʃ] *adj* britisch ♦ *npl*: **the ~** die Briten pl; **~ Isles** *npl*: **the ~ Isles** die Britischen Inseln pl; **~ Rail** *n* die Britischen Eisenbahnen

Briton ['brɪtən] *n* Brite m, Britin f

Brittany ['brɪtənɪ] *n* die Bretagne

brittle ['brɪtl] *adj* spröde

broach [brəutʃ] *vt* (*subject*) anschneiden

broad [brɔːd] *adj* breit; (*hint*) deutlich; (*general*) allgemein; (*accent*) stark; **in ~ daylight** am helllichten Tag; **~cast** (*pt, pp* **broadcast**) *n* Rundfunkübertragung f ♦ *vt, vi* übertragen, senden; **~en** *vt* erweitern ♦ *vi* sich erweitern; **~ly** *adv* allgemein gesagt; **~-minded** *adj* tolerant

broccoli ['brɒkəlɪ] *n* Brokkoli pl

brochure ['brəʊʃʊə'] *n* Broschüre f

broil [brɔɪl] *vt* (*grill*) grillen

broke [brəʊk] *pt of* **break** ♦ *adj* (*inf*) pleite

broken ['brəʊkn] *pp of* **break** ♦ *adj*: **~ leg** gebrochenes Bein; **in ~ English** in gebrochenem Englisch; **~-hearted** *adj* untröstlich

broker ['brəʊkə'] *n* Makler m

brolly ['brɒlɪ] *n* (*BRIT: inf*) Schirm m

bronchitis [brɒŋ'kaɪtɪs] *n* Bronchitis f

bronze [brɒnz] *n* Bronze f

brooch [brəutʃ] *n* Brosche f

brood [bruːd] *n* Brut f ♦ *vi* brüten

brook [brʊk] *n* Bach m

broom [brʊm] *n* Besen m

Bros. *abbr* = **Brothers**

broth [brɒθ] *n* Suppe f, Fleischbrühe f

brothel ['brɒθl] *n* Bordell nt

brother ['brʌðə'] *n* Bruder m; **~-in-law** *n* Schwager m

brought [brɔːt] *pt, pp of* **bring**

brow [brau] *n* (*eyebrow*) (Augen)braue f; (*forehead*) Stirn f; (*of hill*) Bergkuppe f

brown [braun] *adj* braun ♦ *n* Braun nt ♦ *vt* bräunen; **~ bread** *n* Mischbrot nt; **B~ie** *n* Wichtel m; **~ paper** *n* Packpapier nt; **~ sugar** *n* braune(r) Zucker m

browse [brauz] *vi* (*in books*) blättern; (*in shop*) schmökern, herumschauen; **~r** *n* (*COMPUT*) Browser m

bruise [bruːz] *n* Bluterguss m, blaue(r) Fleck m ♦ *vt* einen blauen Fleck geben ♦ *vi* einen blauen Fleck bekommen

brunt [brʌnt] *n* volle Wucht f

brush [brʌʃ] *n* Bürste f; (*for sweeping*) Handbesen m; (*for painting*) Pinsel m; (*fight*) kurze(r) Kampf m; (*MIL*) Scharmützel nt; (*fig*) Auseinandersetzung f ♦ *vt* (*clean*) bürsten; (*sweep*) fegen; (*usu:* **~ past,** **~ against**) streifen; **~ aside** *vt* abtun; **~ up** *vt* (*knowledge*) auffrischen; **~wood** *n* Gestrüpp nt

brusque [bruːsk] *adj* schroff

Brussels ['brʌslz] *n* Brüssel nt; **~ sprout** *n* Rosenkohl m

brutal ['bruːtl] *adj* brutal

brute [bruːt] *n* (*person*) Scheusal nt ♦ *adj*: **by ~ force** mit roher Kraft

B.Sc. *n abbr* = **Bachelor of Science**

BSE *n abbr* (= *bovine spongiform encephalopathy*) BSE f

bubble ['bʌbl] *n* (Luft)blase f ♦ *vi* sprudeln; (*with joy*) überprudeln; **~ bath** *n* Schaumbad nt; **~ gum** *n* Kaugummi m *or* nt

buck [bʌk] *n* Bock m; (*US: inf*) Dollar m ♦ *vi* bocken; **to pass the ~ (to sb)** die Verantwortung (auf jdn) abschieben; **~ up** (*inf*) *vi* sich zusammenreißen

bucket ['bʌkɪt] *n* Eimer *m*

Buckingham Palace

ⓘ **Buckingham Palace** *ist die offizielle Londoner Residenz der britischen Monarchen und liegt am St James Park. Der Palast wurde 1703 für den Herzog von Buckingham erbaut, 1762 von George III. 'gekauft, zwischen 1821 und 1836 von John Nash umgebaut, und Anfang des 20. Jahrhunderts teilweise neu gestaltet. Teile des Buckingham Palace sind heute der Öffentlichkeit zugänglich.*

---

buckle ['bʌkl] *n* Schnalle *f* ♦ *vt* (an- or zusammen)schnallen ♦ *vi* (bend) sich verziehen

bud [bʌd] *n* Knospe *f* ♦ *vi* knospen, keimen

Buddhism ['budɪzəm] *n* Buddhismus *m*; **Buddhist** *adj* buddhistisch ♦ *n* Buddhist(in) *m(f)*

budding ['bʌdɪŋ] *adj* angehend

buddy ['bʌdɪ] (*inf*) *n* Kumpel *m*

budge [bʌdʒ] *vt, vi* (sich) von der Stelle rühren

budgerigar ['bʌdʒərɪgɑː'] *n* Wellensittich *m*

budget ['bʌdʒɪt] *n* Budget *nt*; (*POL*) Haushalt *m* ♦ *vi*: **to ~ for sth** ètw einplanen

budgie ['bʌdʒɪ] *n* = **budgerigar**

buff [bʌf] *adj* (*colour*) lederfarben ♦ *n* (*enthusiast*) Fan *m*

buffalo ['bʌfələu] (*pl ~ or ~es*) *n* (*BRIT*) Büffel *m*; (*US: bison*) Bison *m*

buffer ['bʌfə'] *n* Puffer *m*; (*COMPUT*) Pufferspeicher *m*; **~ zone** *n* Pufferzone *f*

buffet¹ ['bʌfɪt] *n* (*blow*) Schlag *m* ♦ *vt* (herum)stossen

buffet² ['bufeɪ] (*BRIT*) *n* (*bar*) Imbissraum *m*, Erfrischungsraum *m*; (*food*) (kaltes) Büfett *nt*; **~ car** (*BRIT*) *n* Speisewagen *m*

bug [bʌg] *n* (*also fig*) Wanze *f* ♦ *vt* verwanzen; **the room is bugged** das Zimmer ist verwanzt

bugle ['bjuːgl] *n* Jagdhorn *nt*; (*MIL: MUS*) Bügelhorn *nt*

build [bɪld] (*pt, pp* **built**) *vt* bauen ♦ *n* Körperbau *m*; **~ up** *vt* aufbauen; **~er** *n*

Bauunternehmer *m*; **~ing** *n* Gebäude *nt*; **~ing society** (*BRIT*) *n* Bausparkasse *f*

built [bɪlt] *pt, pp of* **build**; **~-in** *adj* (*cupboard*) eingebaut; **~-up area** *n* Wohngebiet *nt*

bulb [bʌlb] *n* (*BOT*) (Blumen)zwiebel *f*; (*ELEC*) Glühlampe *f*, Birne *f*

Bulgaria [bʌl'geərɪə] *n* Bulgarien *nt*; **~n** *adj* bulgarisch ♦ *n* Bulgare *m*, Bulgarin *f*; (*LING*) Bulgarisch *nt*

bulge [bʌldʒ] *n* Wölbung *f* ♦ *vi* sich wölben

bulk [bʌlk] *n* Größe *f*, Masse *f*; (*greater part*) Großteil *m*; **in ~** (*COMM*) en gros; **the ~ of** der größte Teil +*gen*; **~head** *n* Schott *nt*; **~y** *adj* (sehr) umfangreich; (*goods*) sperrig

bull [bul] *n* Bulle *m*; (*cattle*) Stier *m*; **~dog** *n* Bulldogge *f*

bulldozer ['buldəuzə'] *n* Planierraupe *f*

bullet ['bulɪt] *n* Kugel *f*

bulletin ['bulɪtɪn] *n* Bulletin *nt*, Bekanntmachung *f*

bulletproof ['bulɪtpruːf] *adj* kugelsicher

bullfight ['bulfaɪt] *n* Stierkampf *m*; **~er** *n* Stierkämpfer *m*; **~ing** *n* Stierkamp *m*

bullion ['buljən] *n* Barren *m*

bullock ['bulək] *n* Ochse *m*

bullring ['bulrɪŋ] *n* Stierkampfarena *f*

bull's-eye ['bulzaɪ] *n* Zentrum *nt*

bully ['bulɪ] *n* Raufbold *m* ♦ *vt* einschüchtern

bum [bʌm] *n* (*inf: backside*) Hintern *m*; (*tramp*) Landstreicher *m*

bumblebee ['bʌmblbiː] *n* Hummel *f*

bump [bʌmp] *n* (*blow*) Stoß *m*; (*swelling*) Beule *f* ♦ *vt, vi* stoßen, prallen; **~ into** *vt fus* stoßen gegen ♦ *vt* (*person*) treffen; **~er** *n* (*AUT*) Stoßstange *f* ♦ *adj* (*edition*) dick; (*harvest*) Rekord-

bumpy ['bʌmpɪ] *adj* holprig

bun [bʌn] *n* Korinthenbrötchen *nt*

bunch [bʌntʃ] *n* (*of flowers*) Strauß *m*; (*of keys*) Bund *m*; (*of people*) Haufen *m*; **~es** *npl* (*in hair*) Zöpfe *pl*

bundle ['bʌndl] *n* Bündel *nt* ♦ *vt* (*also: ~ up*) bündeln

bungalow ['bʌŋgələu] *n* einstöckige(s) Haus *nt*, Bungalow *m*

bungle ['bʌŋgl] *vt* verpfuschen

bunion ['bʌnjən] *n* entzündete(r) Fußballen m

bunk [bʌŋk] n Schlafkoje f; **~ beds** npl Etagenbett nt

bunker ['bʌŋkə'] n (coal store) Kohlenbunker m; (GOLF) Sandloch nt

bunny ['bʌnɪ] n (also: ~ **rabbit**) Häschen nt

bunting ['bʌntɪŋ] n Fahnentuch nt

buoy [bɔɪ] n Boje f; (lifebuoy) Rettungsboje f; **~ant** adj (floating) schwimmend; (fig) heiter

burden ['bə:dn] n (weight) Ladung f, Last f; (fig) Bürde f ♦ vt belasten

bureau ['bjuərəu] (pl **~x**) n (BRIT: writing desk) Sekretär m; (US: chest of drawers) Kommode f; (for information etc) Büro nt

bureaucracy [bjuə'rɔkrəsɪ] n Bürokratie f

bureaucrat ['bjuərəkræt] n Bürokrat(in) m(f)

bureaux ['bjuərəuz] npl of **bureau**

burglar ['bə:glə'] n Einbrecher m; **~ alarm** n Einbruchssicherung f; **~y** n Einbruch m

burial ['berɪəl] n Beerdigung f

burly ['bə:lɪ] adj stämmig

Burma ['bə:mə] n Birma nt

burn [bə:n] (pt, pp **burned** or **burnt**) vt verbrennen ♦ vi brennen ♦ n Brandwunde f; **~ down** vt, vi abbrennen; **~er** n Brenner m; **~ing** adj brennend; **~t** [bə:nt] pt, pp of **burn**

burrow ['bʌrəu] n (of fox) Bau m; (of rabbit) Höhle f ♦ vt eingraben

bursar ['bə:sə'] n Kassenverwalter m, Quästor m; **~y** (BRIT) n Stipendium nt

burst [bə:st] (pt, pp **burst**) vt zerbrechen ♦ vi platzen ♦ n Explosion f; (outbreak) Ausbruch m; (in pipe) Bruch(stelle f) m; **to ~ into flames** in Flammen aufgehen; **to ~ into tears** in Tränen ausbrechen; **to ~ out laughing** in Gelächter ausbrechen; **~ into** vt fus (room etc) platzen in +acc; **~ open** vi aufbrechen

bury ['berɪ] vt vergraben; (in grave) beerdigen

bus [bʌs] n (Auto)bus m, Omnibus m

bush [buʃ] n Busch m; **to beat about the ~** wie die Katze um den heißen Brei herumgehen; **~y** [buʃɪ] adj buschig

busily ['bɪzɪlɪ] adv geschäftig

business ['bɪznɪs] n Geschäft nt; (concern)

Angelegenheit f; **it's none of your ~** es geht dich nichts an; **to mean ~** es ernst meinen; **to be away on ~** geschäftlich verreist sein; **it's my ~ to ...** es ist meine Sache, zu ...; **~like** adj geschäftsmäßig; **~man** (irreg) n Geschäftsmann m; **~ trip** n Geschäftsreise f; **~woman** (irreg) n Geschäftsfrau f

busker ['bʌskə'] (BRIT) n Straßenmusikant m

bus: **~ shelter** n Wartehäuschen nt; **~ station** n Busbahnhof m; **~ stop** n Bushaltestelle f

bust [bʌst] n Büste f ♦ adj (broken) kaputt(gegangen); (business) pleite; **to go ~** Pleite machen

bustle ['bʌsl] n Getriebe nt ♦ vi hasten

bustling ['bʌslɪŋ] adj geschäftig

busy ['bɪzɪ] adj beschäftigt; (road) belebt ♦ vt: **to ~ o.s.** sich beschäftigen; **~body** n Übereifrige(r) mf; **~ signal** (US) n (TEL) Besetztzeichen nt

---

KEYWORD

---

but [bʌt] conj **1** (yet) aber; **not X but Y** nicht X sondern Y

2 (however): **I'd love to come, but I'm busy** ich würde gern kommen, bin aber beschäftigt

3 (showing disagreement, surprise etc): **but that's fantastic!** (aber) das ist ja fantastisch!

♦ prep (apart from, except): **nothing but trouble** nichts als Ärger; **no-one but him can do it** niemand außer ihn kann es machen; **but for you/your help** ohne dich/deine Hilfe; **anything but that** alles, nur das nicht

♦ adv (just, only): **she's but a child** sie ist noch ein Kind; **had I but known** wenn ich es nur gewusst hätte; **I can but try** ich kann es immerhin versuchen; **all but finished** so gut wie fertig

---

butcher ['butʃə'] n Metzger m; (murderer) Schlächter m ♦ vt schlachten; (kill) abschlachten; **~'s (shop)** n Metzgerei f

butler ['bʌtlə'] n Butler m

butt [bʌt] n (*cask*) große(s) Fass *nt*; (*BRIT: fig: target*) Zielscheibe *f*; (*of gun*) Kolben *m*; (*of cigarette*) Stummel *m* ♦ *vt* (mit dem Kopf) stoßen; **~ in** *vi* sich einmischen

butter ['bʌtə'] n Butter *f* ♦ *vt* buttern; **~ bean** n Wachsbohne *f*; **~cup** n Butterblume *f*

butterfly ['bʌtəflaɪ] n Schmetterling *m*; (*SWIMMING: also:* **~ stroke**) Butterflystil *m*

buttocks ['bʌtəks] *npl* Gesäß *nt*

button ['bʌtn] n Knopf *m* ♦ *vt, vi* (*also:* **~ up**) zuknöpfen

buttress ['bʌtrɪs] n Strebepfeiler *m*; Stützbogen *m*

buxom ['bʌksəm] *adj* drall

buy [baɪ] (*pt, pp* bought) *vt* kaufen ♦ n Kauf *m*; **to ~ sb a drink** jdm einen Drink spendieren; **~er** n Käufer(in) *m(f)*

buzz [bʌz] n Summen *nt* ♦ *vi* summen; **~er** ['bʌzə'] n Summer *m*; **~ word** n Modewort *nt*

by [baɪ] *prep* **1** (*referring to cause, agent*) of, durch; **killed by lightning** vom Blitz getötet; **a painting by Picasso** ein Gemälde von Picasso

2 (*referring to method, manner*): **by bus/car/train** mit dem Bus/Auto/Zug; **to pay by cheque** per Scheck bezahlen; **by moonlight** bei Mondschein; **by saving hard, he ...** indem er eisern sparte, ... er ...

3 (*via, through*) über +*acc*; **he came in by the back door** er kam durch die Hintertür herein

4 (*close to, past*) bei, an +*dat*; **a holiday by the sea** ein Urlaub am Meer; **she rushed by me** sie eilte an mir vorbei

5 (*not later than*): **by 4 o'clock** bis 4 Uhr; **by this time tomorrow** morgen um diese Zeit; **by the time I got here it was too late** als ich hier ankam, war es zu spät

6 (*during*): **by day** bei Tag

7 (*amount*): **by the kilo/metre** kiloweise/meterweise; **paid by the hour** stundenweise bezahlt

8 (*MATH, measure*): **to divide by 3** durch 3

teilen; **to multiply by 3** mit 3 malnehmen; **a room 3 metres by 4** ein Zimmer 3 mal 4 Meter; **it's broader by a metre** es ist (um) einem Meter breiter

9 (*according to*) nach; **it's all right by me** von mir aus gern

10: (all) by oneself *etc* ganz allein

11: by the way übrigens

♦ *adv* **1** *see* go; **pass** *etc*

2: by and by irgendwann; (*with past tenses*) nach einiger Zeit; **by and large** (*on the whole*) im Großen und Ganzen

bye(-bye) ['baɪ('baɪ)] *excl* (auf) Wiedersehen

by(e)-law ['baɪlɔː] n Verordnung *f*

by-election ['baɪlekʃən] (*BRIT*) n Nachwahl *f*

bygone ['baɪgɒn] *adj* vergangen ♦ n: **let ~s be ~s** lass(t) das Vergangene vergangen sein

bypass ['baɪpɑːs] n Umgehungsstraße *f* ♦ *vt* umgehen

by-product ['baɪprɒdʌkt] n Nebenprodukt *nt*

bystander ['baɪstændə'] n Zuschauer *m*

byte [baɪt] n (*COMPUT*) Byte *nt*

byword ['baɪwəːd] n Inbegriff *m*

C, c

C [siː] n (*MUS*) C *nt*

C. *abbr* (= *centigrade*) C

C.A. *abbr* = **chartered accountant**

cab [kæb] n Taxi *nt*; (*of train*) Führerstand *m*; (*of truck*) Führersitz *m*

cabaret ['kæbəreɪ] n Kabarett *nt*

cabbage ['kæbɪdʒ] n Kohl(kopf) *m*

cabin ['kæbɪn] n Hütte *f*; (*NAUT*) Kajüte *f*; (*AVIAT*) Kabine *f*; **~ crew** n (*AVIAT*) Flugbegleitpersonal *nt*; **~ cruiser** n Motorjacht *f*

cabinet ['kæbɪnɪt] n Schrank *m*; (*for china*) Vitrine *f*; (*POL*) Kabinett *nt*; **~-maker** n Kunsttischler *m*

cable ['keɪbl] n Drahtseil *nt*, Tau *nt*; (*TEL*) (Leitungs)kabel *nt*; (*telegram*) Kabel *nt* ♦ *vt* kabeln, telegrafieren; **~ car** n Seilbahn *f*; **~ television** n Kabelfernsehen *nt*

cache [kæʃ] *n* geheime(s) (Waffen)lager *nt*; geheime(s) (Proviant)lager *nt*

cackle ['kækl] *vi* gackern

cacti ['kæktaɪ] *npl of* **cactus**

cactus ['kæktəs] (*pl* **cacti**) *n* Kaktus *m*, Kaktee *f*

caddie ['kædɪ] *n* (*GOLF*) Golfjunge *m*; **caddy** ['kædɪ] *n* = **caddie**

cadet [kə'dɛt] *n* Kadett *m*

cadge [kædʒ] *vt* schmarotzen

Caesarean [sɪ'zɛərɪən] *adj:* ~ **(section)** Kaiserschnitt *m*

café ['kæfeɪ] *n* Café *nt*, Restaurant *nt*

cafeteria [kæfɪ'tɪərɪə] *n* Selbstbedienungsrestaurant *nt*

caffein(e) ['kæfiːn] *n* Koffein *nt*

cage [keɪdʒ] *n* Käfig *m* ♦ *vt* einsperren

cagey ['keɪdʒɪ] *adj* geheimnistuerisch, zurückhaltend

cagoule [kə'guːl] *n* Windhemd *nt*

Cairo ['kaɪərəu] *n* Kairo *nt*

cajole [kə'dʒəul] *vt* überreden

cake [keɪk] *n* Kuchen *m*; (*of soap*) Stück *nt*; ~**d** *adj* verkrustet

calamity [kə'læmɪtɪ] *n* Unglück *nt*, (Schicksals)schlag *m*

calcium ['kælsɪəm] *n* Kalzium *nt*

calculate ['kælkjuleɪt] *vt* berechnen, kalkulieren; **calculating** *adj* berechnend; **calculation** [kælkju'leɪʃən] *n* Berechnung *f*; **calculator** *n* Rechner *m*

calendar ['kæləndə'] *n* Kalender *m*; ~ **month** *n* Kalendermonat *m*

calf [kɑːf] (*pl* **calves**) *n* Kalb *nt*; (*also:* ~**skin**) Kalbsleder *nt*; (*ANAT*) Wade *f*

calibre ['kælɪbə'] (*US* **caliber**) *n* Kaliber *nt*

call [kɔːl] *vt* rufen; (*name*) nennen; (*meeting*) einberufen; (*awaken*) wecken; (*TEL*) anrufen ♦ *vi* (*shout*) rufen; (*visit: also:* ~ **in**, ~ **round**) vorbeikommen ♦ *n* (*shout*) Ruf *m*; (*TEL*) Anruf *m*; **to be ~ed** heißen; **on** ~ **in** Bereitschaft; ~ **back** *vi* (*return*) wiederkommen; (*TEL*) zurückrufen; ~ **for** *vt fus* (*demand*) erfordern, verlangen; (*fetch*) abholen; ~ **off** *vt* (*cancel*) absagen; ~ **on** *vt fus* (*visit*) besuchen; (*turn to*) bitten; ~ **out** *vi* rufen; ~ **up** *vt* (*MIL*) einberufen;

~**box** (*BRIT*) *n* Telefonzelle *f*; ~ **centre** *n* Telefoncenter *nt*, Callcenter *nt*; ~**er** *n* Besucher(in) *m(f)*; (*TEL*) Anrufer *m*; ~ **girl** *n* Callgirl *nt*; ~**in** (*US*) *n* (*phone-in*) Phone-in *nt*; ~**ing** *n* (*vocation*) Berufung *f*; ~**ing card** (*US*) *n* Visitenkarte *f*

callous ['kæləs] *adj* herzlos

calm [kɑːm] *n* Ruhe *f*; (*NAUT*) Flaute *f* ♦ *vt* beruhigen ♦ *adj* ruhig; (*person*) gelassen; ~ **down** *vi* sich beruhigen ♦ *vt* beruhigen

Calor gas ['kælə'-] ® *n* Propangas *nt*

calorie ['kælərɪ] *n* Kalorie *f*

calves [kɑːvz] *npl of* **calf**

Cambodia [kæm'bəudɪə] *n* Kambodscha *nt*

camcorder ['kæmkɔːdə'] *n* Camcorder *m*

came [keɪm] *pt of* **come**

cameo ['kæmɪəu] *n* Kamee *f*

camera ['kæmərə] *n* Fotoapparat *m*; (*CINE, TV*) Kamera *f*; **in** ~ unter Ausschluss der Öffentlichkeit; ~**man** (*irreg*) *n* Kameramann *m*

camouflage ['kæməflɑːʒ] *n* Tarnung *f* ♦ *vt* tarnen

camp [kæmp] *n* Lager *nt* ♦ *vi* zelten, campen ♦ *adj* affektiert

campaign [kæm'peɪn] *n* Kampagne *f*; (*MIL*) Feldzug *m* ♦ *vi* (*MIL*) Krieg führen; (*fig*) werben, Propaganda machen; (*POL*) den Wahlkampf führen

camp: ~ **bed** (*BRIT*) *n* Campingbett *nt*; ~**er** ['kæmpə'] *n* Camper(in) *m(f)*; (*vehicle*) Campingwagen *m*; ~**ing** ['kæmpɪŋ] *n*: **to go** ~**ing** zelten, Camping machen; ~**ing gas** (*US*) *n* Campinggas *nt*; ~**site** ['kæmpsaɪt] *n* Campingplatz *m*

campus ['kæmpəs] *n* Universitätsgelände *nt*, Campus *m*

can¹ [kæn] *n* Büchse *f*, Dose *f*; (*for water*) Kanne *f* ♦ *vt* konservieren, in Büchsen einmachen

KEYWORD

can² [kæn] (*negative* **cannot**, **can't**, *conditional* **could**) *aux vb* **1** (*be able to, know how to*) können; **I can see you tomorrow, if you like** ich könnte Sie morgen sehen, wenn Sie wollen; **I can swim** ich kann schwimmen; **can you speak German?** sprechen Sie Deutsch?

2 (*may*) können, dürfen; **could I have a word with you?** könnte ich Sie kurz sprechen?

Canada ['kænədə] *n* Kanada *nt*; **Canadian** [kə'neɪdɪən] *adj* kanadisch ♦ *n* Kanadier(in) *m(f)*

canal [kə'næl] *n* Kanal *m*

canapé ['kænəpeɪ] *n* Cocktail- *or* Appetithappen *m*

canary [kə'neərɪ] *n* Kanarienvogel *m*

cancel ['kænsəl] *vt* absagen; (*delete*) durchstreichen; (*train*) streichen; **~lation** [kænsə'leɪʃən] *n* Absage *f*; Streichung *f*

cancer ['kænsə*r*] *n* (*ASTROL*: *C~*) Krebs *m*

candid ['kændɪd] *adj* offen, ehrlich

candidate ['kændɪdeɪt] *n* Kandidat(in) *m(f)*

candle ['kændl] *n* Kerze *f*; **~light** *n* Kerzenlicht *nt*; **~stick** *n* (*also*: **~ holder**) Kerzenhalter *m*

candour ['kændə*r*] (*US* **candor**) *n* Offenheit *f*

candy ['kændɪ] *n* Kandis(zucker) *m*; (*US*) Bonbons *pl*; **~floss** (*BRIT*) *n* Zuckerwatte *f*

cane [keɪn] *n* (*BOT*) Rohr *nt*; (*stick*) Stock *m* ♦ *vt* (*BRIT*: *beat*) schlagen

canine ['keɪnaɪn] *adj* Hunde-

canister ['kænɪstə*r*] *n* Blechdose *f*

cannabis ['kænəbɪs] *n* Hanf *m*, Haschisch *nt*

canned [kænd] *adj* Büchsen-, eingemacht

cannon ['kænən] (*pl* **~** *or* **~s**) *n* Kanone *f*

cannot ['kænɒt] = **can not**

canny ['kænɪ] *adj* schlau

canoe [kə'nuː] *n* Kanu *nt*; **~ing** *n* Kanusport *m*, Kanufahren *nt*

canon ['kænən] *n* (*clergyman*) Domherr *m*; (*standard*) Grundsatz *m*

can-opener ['kænəʊpnə*r*] *n* Büchsenöffner *m*

canopy ['kænəpɪ] *n* Baldachin *m*

can't [kænt] = **can not**

cantankerous [kæn'tæŋkərəs] *adj* zänkisch, mürrisch

canteen [kæn'tiːn] *n* Kantine *f*; (*BRIT*: *of cutlery*) Besteckkasten *m*

canter ['kæntə*r*] *n* Kanter *m* ♦ *vi* in kurzem Galopp reiten

canvas ['kænvəs] *n* Segeltuch *nt*; (*sail*) Segel *nt*; (*for painting*) Leinwand *f*; **under ~** (*camping*) in Zelten

canvass ['kænvəs] *vi* um Stimmen werben; **~ing** *n* Wahlwerbung *f*

canyon ['kænjən] *n* Felsenschlucht *f*

cap [kæp] *n* Mütze *f*; (*of pen*) Kappe *f*; (*of bottle*) Deckel *m* ♦ *vt* (*surpass*) übertreffen; (*SPORT*) aufstellen; (*put limit on*) einen Höchstsatz festlegen für

capability [keɪpə'bɪlɪtɪ] *n* Fähigkeit *f*

capable ['keɪpəbl] *adj* fähig

capacity [kə'pæsɪtɪ] *n* Fassungsvermögen *nt*; (*ability*) Fähigkeit *f*; (*position*) Eigenschaft *f*

cape [keɪp] *n* (*garment*) Cape *nt*, Umhang *m*; (*GEOG*) Kap *nt*

caper ['keɪpə*r*] *n* (*COOK*: *usu*: **~s**) Kaper *f*; (*prank*) Kapriole *f*

capital ['kæpɪtl] *n* (**~** *city*) Hauptstadt *f*; (*FIN*) Kapital *nt*; (**~** *letter*) Großbuchstabe *m*; **~ gains tax** *n* Kapitalertragssteuer *f*; **~ism** *n* Kapitalismus *m*; **~ist** *adj* kapitalistisch ♦ *n* Kapitalist(in) *m(f)*; **~ize** *vi*: **to ~ize on** Kapital schlagen aus; **~ punishment** *n* Todesstrafe *f*

Capitol

ⓘ **Capitol** *ist das Gebäude in Washington auf dem Capitol Hill, in dem der Kongress der USA zusammentritt. Die Bezeichnung wird in vielen amerikanischen Bundesstaaten auch für das Parlamentsgebäude des jeweiligen Staates verwendet.*

Capricorn ['kæprɪkɔːn] *n* Steinbock *m*

capsize [kæp'saɪz] *vt*, *vi* kentern

capsule ['kæpsjuːl] *n* Kapsel *f*

captain ['kæptɪn] *n* Kapitän *m*; (*MIL*) Hauptmann *m* ♦ *vt* anführen

caption ['kæpʃən] *n* (*heading*) Überschrift *f*; (*to picture*) Unterschrift *f*

captivate ['kæptɪveɪt] *vt* fesseln

captive ['kæptɪv] *n* Gefangene(r) *f(m)* ♦ *adj* gefangen (gehalten); **captivity** [kæp'tɪvɪtɪ] *n* Gefangenschaft *f*

capture ['kæptʃəʳ] *vt* gefangen nehmen; (*place*) erobern; (*attention*) erregen ♦ *n* Gefangennahme *f*; (*data ~*) Erfassung *f*

car [kɑːʳ] *n* Auto *nt*, Wagen *m*; (*RAIL*) Wagen *m*

caramel ['kærəməl] *n* Karamelle *f*, Karamellbonbon *m or nt*; (*burnt sugar*) Karamell *m*

carat ['kærət] *n* Karat *nt*

caravan ['kærəvæn] *n* (*BRIT*) Wohnwagen *m*; (*in desert*) Karawane *f*; **~ning** *n* Caravaning *nt*, Urlaub *m* im Wohnwagen; **~ site** (*BRIT*) *n* Campingplatz *m* für Wohnwagen

carbohydrate [kɑːbəʊˈhaɪdreɪt] *n* Kohlenhydrat *nt*

carbon ['kɑːbən] *n* Kohlenstoff *m*; **~ copy** *n* Durchschlag *m*; **~ dioxide** *n* Kohlendioxyd *nt*; **~ monoxide** *n* Kohlenmonoxyd *nt*; **~ paper** *n* Kohlepapier *nt*

car boot sale *n* auf einem Parkplatz stattfindender Flohmarkt mit dem Kofferraum als Auslage

carburettor [kɑːbjuˈretəʳ] (*US* **carburetor**) *n* Vergaser *m*

carcass ['kɑːkəs] *n* Kadaver *m*

card [kɑːd] *n* Karte *f*; **~board** *n* Pappe *f*; **~ game** *n* Kartenspiel *nt*

cardiac ['kɑːdiæk] *adj* Herz-

cardigan ['kɑːdɪgən] *n* Strickjacke *f*

cardinal ['kɑːdɪnl] *adj*: **~ number** Kardinalzahl *f* ♦ *n* (*REL*) Kardinal *m*

card index *n* Kartei *f*; (*in library*) Katalog *m*

cardphone ['kɑːdfəʊn] *n* Kartentelefon *nt*

care [kɛəʳ] *n* (*of teeth, car etc*) Pflege *f*; (*of children*) Fürsorge *f*; (*~fulness*) Sorgfalt *f*; (*worry*) Sorge *f* ♦ *vi*: **to ~ about** sich kümmern um; **~ of** bei; **in sb's ~** in jds Obhut; **I don't ~** das ist mir egal; **I couldn't ~ less** es ist mir doch völlig egal; **to take ~** aufpassen; **to take ~ of** sorgen für; **to take ~ to do sth** sich bemühen, etw zu tun; **~ for** *vt* sorgen für; (*like*) mögen

career [kəˈrɪəʳ] *n* Karriere *f*, Laufbahn *f* ♦ *vi* (*also*: **~ along**) rasen; **~ woman** (*irreg*) *n* Karrierefrau *f*

care: **~free** *adj* sorgenfrei; **~ful** *adj*

sorgfältig; **(be) ~ful!** pass auf!; **~fully** *adv* vorsichtig; (*methodically*) sorgfältig; **~less** *adj* nachlässig; **~lessness** *n* Nachlässigkeit *f*; **~r** *n* (*MED*) Betreuer(in) *m(f)*

caress [kəˈres] *n* Liebkosung *f* ♦ *vt* liebkosen

caretaker ['kɛəteɪkəʳ] *n* Hausmeister *m*

car ferry *n* Autofähre *f*

cargo ['kɑːgəʊ] (*pl* **~es**) *n* Schiffsladung *f*

car hire *n* Autovermietung *f*

Caribbean [kærɪˈbiːən] *n*: **the ~ (Sea)** die Karibik

caricature ['kærɪkətjʊəʳ] *n* Karikatur *f*

caring ['kɛərɪŋ] *adj* (*society, organization*) sozial eingestellt; (*person*) liebevoll

carnage ['kɑːnɪdʒ] *n* Blutbad *nt*

carnation [kɑːˈneɪʃən] *n* Nelke *f*

carnival ['kɑːnɪvl] *n* Karneval *m*, Fasching *m*; (*US: fun fair*) Kirmes *f*

carnivorous [kɑːˈnɪvərəs] *adj* Fleisch fressend

carol ['kærəl] *n*: **(Christmas) ~** (Weihnachts)lied *nt*

carp [kɑːp] *n* (*fish*) Karpfen *m*

car park (*BRIT*) *n* Parkplatz *m*; (*covered*) Parkhaus *nt*

carpenter ['kɑːpɪntəʳ] *n* Zimmermann *m*; **carpentry** ['kɑːpɪntrɪ] *n* Zimmerei *f*

carpet ['kɑːpɪt] *n* Teppich *m* ♦ *vt* mit einem Teppich auslegen; **~ bombing** *n* Flächenbombardierung *f*; **~ slippers** *npl* Pantoffeln *pl*; **~ sweeper** ['kɑːpɪtswiːpəʳ] *n* Teppichkehrer *m*

car phone *n* (*TEL*) Autotelefon *nt*

car rental (*US*) *n* Autovermietung *f*

carriage ['kærɪdʒ] *n* Kutsche *f*; (*RAIL, of typewriter*) Wagen *m*; (*of goods*) Beförderung *f*; (*bearing*) Haltung *f*; **~ return** *n* (*on typewriter*) Rücklauftaste *f*; **~way** (*BRIT*) *n* (*part of road*) Fahrbahn *f*

carrier ['kærɪəʳ] *n* Träger(in) *m(f)*; (*COMM*) Spediteur *m*; **~ bag** (*BRIT*) *n* Tragetasche *f*

carrot ['kærət] *n* Möhre *f*, Karotte *f*

carry ['kærɪ] *vt, vi* tragen; **to get carried away** (*fig*) sich nicht mehr bremsen können; **~ on** *vi* (*continue*) weitermachen; (*inf: complain*) Theater machen; **~ out** *vt* (*orders*) ausführen; (*investigation*) durchführen;~**cot** (*BRIT*) *n* Babytragetasche *f*;~**on** (*inf*) *n* (*fuss*) Theater *nt*

cart [kɑːt] *n* Wagen *m*, Karren *m* ♦ *vt* schleppen

cartilage [ˈkɑːtɪlɪdʒ] *n* Knorpel *m*

carton [ˈkɑːtən] *n* Karton *m*; (*of milk*) Tüte *f*

cartoon [kɑːˈtuːn] *n* (*PRESS*) Karikatur *f*; (*comic strip*) Comics *pl*; (*CINE*) (Zeichen)trickfilm *m*

cartridge [ˈkɑːtrɪdʒ] *n* Patrone *f*

carve [kɑːv] *vt* (*wood*) schnitzen; (*stone*) meißeln; (*meat*) (vor)schneiden;~ **up** *vt* aufschneiden; **carving** [ˈkɑːvɪŋ] *n* Schnitzerei *f*; **carving knife** *n* Tran(s)chiermesser *nt*

car wash *n* Autowäsche *f*

cascade [kæsˈkeɪd] *n* Wasserfall *m* ♦ *vi* kaskadenartig herabfallen

case [keɪs] *n* (*box*) Kasten *m*; (*BRIT*: *also*: **suitcase**) Koffer *m*; (*JUR*, *matter*) Fall *m*; **in ~** falls, im Falle; **in any ~** jedenfalls, auf jeden Fall

cash [kæʃ] *n* (Bar)geld *nt* ♦ *vt* einlösen; **~ on delivery** per Nachnahme; **~ book** *n* Kassenbuch *nt*; **~ card** *n* Scheckkarte *f*; **~ desk** (*BRIT*) *n* Kasse *f*; **~ dispenser** *n* Geldautomat *m*

cashew [kæˈʃuː] *n* (*also*: **~ nut**) Cashewnuss *f*

cash flow *n* Cashflow *m*

cashier [kæˈʃɪəʳ] *n* Kassierer(in) *m(f)*

cashmere [ˈkæʃmɪəʳ] *n* Kaschmirwolle *f*

cash register *n* Registrierkasse *f*

casing [ˈkeɪsɪŋ] *n* Gehäuse *nt*

casino [kəˈsiːnəu] *n* Kasino *nt*

casket [ˈkɑːskɪt] *n* Kästchen *nt*; (*US*: *coffin*) Sarg *m*

casserole [ˈkæsərəul] *n* Kasserolle *f*; (*food*) Auflauf *m*

cassette [kæˈset] *n* Kassette *f*; **~ player** *n* Kassettengerät *nt*

cast [kɑːst] (*pt*, *pp* **cast**) *vt* werfen; (*horns*) verlieren; (*metal*) gießen; (*THEAT*) besetzen; (*vote*) abgeben ♦ *n* (*THEAT*) Besetzung *f*; (*also*: **plaster ~**) Gipsverband *m*; **~ off** *vi* (*NAUT*) losmachen

castaway [ˈkɑːstəweɪ] *n* Schiffbrüchige(r)

f(m)

caste [kɑːst] *n* Kaste *f*

caster sugar [ˈkɑːstə-] (*BRIT*) *n* Raffinade *f*

casting vote [ˈkɑːstɪŋ-] (*BRIT*) *n* entscheidende Stimme *f*

cast iron *n* Gusseisen *nt*

castle [ˈkɑːsl] *n* Burg *f*; Schloss *nt*; (*CHESS*) Turm *m*

castor [ˈkɑːstəʳ] *n* (*wheel*) Laufrolle *f*

castor oil *n* Rizinusöl *nt*

castrate [kæsˈtreɪt] *vt* kastrieren

casual [ˈkæʒjul] *adj* (*attitude*) nachlässig; (*dress*) leger; (*meeting*) zufällig; (*work*) Gelegenheits-;~**ly** *adv* (*dress*) zwanglos, leger; (*remark*) beiläufig

casualty [ˈkæʒjultɪ] *n* Verletzte(r) *f(m)*; (*dead*) Tote(r) *f(m)*; (*also*: **~ department**) Unfallstation *f*

cat [kæt] *n* Katze *f*

catalogue [ˈkætələg] (*US* **catalog**) *n* Katalog *m* ♦ *vt* katalogisieren

catalyst [ˈkætəlɪst] *n* Katalysator *m*

catalytic converter [kætəˈlɪtɪk kənˈvəːtəʳ] *n* Katalysator *m*

catapult [ˈkætəpʌlt] *n* Schleuder *f*

cataract [ˈkætərækt] *n* (*MED*) graue(r) Star *m*

catarrh [kəˈtɑːʳ] *n* Katarr(h) *m*

catastrophe [kəˈtæstrəfɪ] *n* Katastrophe *f*

catch [kætʃ] (*pt*, *pp* **caught**) *vt* fangen; (*arrest*) fassen; (*train*) erreichen; (*person*: *by surprise*) ertappen; (*also*: **~ up**) einholen ♦ *vi* (*fire*) in Gang kommen; (*in branches etc*) hängen bleiben ♦ *n* (*fish etc*) Fang *m*; (*trick*) Haken *m*; (*of lock*) Sperrhaken *m*; **to ~ an illness** sich *dat* eine Krankheit holen; **to ~ fire** Feuer fangen; **~ on** *vi* (*understand*) begreifen; (*grow popular*) ankommen; **~ up** *vi* (*fig*) aufholen; **~ing** [ˈkætʃɪŋ] *adj* ansteckend; **~ment area** [ˈkætʃmənt-] (*BRIT*) *n* Einzugsgebiet *nt*; **~ phrase** *n* Slogan *m*; **~y** [ˈkætʃɪ] *adj* (*tune*) eingängig

categoric(al) [kætɪˈgɔrɪk(l)] *adj* kategorisch

category [ˈkætɪgərɪ] *n* Kategorie *f*

cater [ˈkeɪtəʳ] *vi* versorgen; **~ for** (*BRIT*) *vt fus* (*party*) ausrichten; (*needs*) eingestellt sein auf +*acc*; **~er** *n* Lieferant(in) *m(f)* von Speisen und Getränken; **~ing** *n*

Gastronomie f

caterpillar ['kætəpɪlə'] n Raupe f; ~ **track** ® n Gleiskette f

cathedral [kə'θiːdrəl] n Kathedrale f, Dom m

Catholic ['kæθəlɪk] adj (REL) katholisch ♦ n Katholik(in) m(f); **c~** adj (tastes etc) vielseitig

CAT scan [kæt-] n Computertomografie f

Catseye ['kæts'aɪ] (BRIT: ®) n (AUT) Katzenauge nt

cattle ['kætl] npl Vieh nt

catty ['kætɪ] adj gehässig

caucus ['kɔːkəs] n (POL) Gremium nt; (US: meeting) Sitzung f

caught [kɔːt] pt, pp of **catch**

cauliflower ['kɔlɪflauə'] n Blumenkohl m

cause [kɔːz] n Ursache f; (purpose) Sache f ♦ vt verursachen

causeway ['kɔːzweɪ] n Damm m

caustic ['kɔːstɪk] adj ätzend; (fig) bissig

caution ['kɔːʃən] n Vorsicht f; (warning) Verwarnung f ♦ vt verwarnen; **cautious** ['kɔːʃəs] adj vorsichtig

cavalry ['kævəlrɪ] n Kavallerie f

cave [keɪv] n Höhle f; **~ in** vi einstürzen; **~man** (irreg) n Höhlenmensch m

cavern ['kævən] n Höhle f

caviar(e) ['kævɪɑː'] n Kaviar m

cavity ['kævɪtɪ] n Loch nt

cavort [kə'vɔːt] vi umherspringen

C.B. n abbr (= Citizens' Band (Radio)) CB

C.B.I. n abbr (= Confederation of British Industry) ≈ BDI f

cc n abbr = **carbon copy**; **cubic centimetres**

CCTV n abbr (= closed-circuit television) Videoüberwachung f

CD n abbr (= compact disc) CD f

CDI n abbr (= Compact Disk Interactive) CD-I f

CD player n CD-Spieler m

CD-ROM n abbr (= compact disc read-only memory) CD-Rom f

cease [siːs] vi aufhören ♦ vt beenden; **~fire** n Feuereinstellung f; **~less** adj unaufhörlich

cedar ['siːdə'] n Zeder f

ceiling ['siːlɪŋ] n Decke f; (fig) Höchstgrenze f

celebrate ['selɪbreɪt] vt, vi feiern; **~d** adj gefeiert; **celebration** [selɪ'breɪʃən] n Feier f

celebrity [sɪ'lebrɪtɪ] n gefeierte Persönlichkeit f

celery ['selərɪ] n Sellerie m or f

celibacy ['selɪbəsɪ] n Zölibat nt or m

cell [sel] n Zelle f; (ELEC) Element nt

cellar ['selə'] n Keller m

cello ['tʃeləu] n Cello nt

Cellophane ['seləfeɪn] ® n Cellophan nt ®

cellphone ['selfəun] n Funktelefon nt

cellular ['seljulə'] adj zellular

cellulose ['seljuləus] n Zellulose f

Celt [kelt, selt] n Kelte m, Keltin f; **~ic** ['keltɪk, 'seltɪk] adj keltisch

cement [sə'ment] n Zement m ♦ vt zementieren; **~ mixer** n Betonmischmaschine f

cemetery ['semɪtrɪ] n Friedhof m

censor ['sensə'] n Zensor m ♦ vt zensieren; **~ship** n Zensur f

censure ['senʃə'] vt rügen

census ['sensəs] n Volkszählung f

cent [sent] n (coin) Cent m; see also **per cent**

centenary [sen'tiːnərɪ] n Jahrhundertfeier f

center ['sentə'] (US) n = **centre**

centigrade ['sentɪgreɪd] adj Celsius

centimetre ['sentɪmiːtə'] (US **centimeter**) n Zentimeter nt

centipede ['sentɪpiːd] n Tausendfüßler m

central ['sentrəl] adj zentral; **C~ America** n Mittelamerika nt; **~ heating** n Zentralheizung f; **~ize** vt zentralisieren; **~ reservation** (BRIT) n (AUT) Mittelstreifen m

centre ['sentə'] (US **center**) n Zentrum nt ♦ vt zentrieren; **~-forward** n (SPORT) Mittelstürmer m; **~-half** n (SPORT) Stopper m

century ['sentjurɪ] n Jahrhundert nt

ceramic [sɪ'ræmɪk] adj keramisch; **~s** npl Keramiken pl

cereal ['siːrɪəl] n (grain) Getreide nt; (at breakfast) Getreideflocken pl

cerebral ['serɪbrəl] adj zerebral; (intellectual) geistig

ceremony ['serɪmənɪ] n Zeremonie f; **to**

stand on ~ förmlich sein

certain ['sɜːtən] *adj* sicher; (*particular*) gewiss; **for** ~ ganz bestimmt; **~ly** *adv* sicher, bestimmt; **~ty** *n* Gewissheit *f*

certificate [sə'tɪfɪkɪt] *n* Bescheinigung *f*; (*SCH etc*) Zeugnis *nt*

certified mail ['sɜːtɪfaɪd-l (*US*) *n* Einschreiben *nt*

certified public accountant ['sɜːtɪfaɪd-] (*US*) *n* geprüfte(r) Buchhalter *m*

certify ['sɜːtɪfaɪ] *vt* bescheinigen

cervical ['sɜːvɪkl] *adj* (*smear, cancer*) Gebärmutterhals-

cervix ['sɜːvɪks] *n* Gebärmutterhals *m*

cf. *abbr* (= *compare*) vgl.

CFC *n abbr* (= *chlorofluorocarbon*) FCKW *m*

ch. *abbr* (= *chapter*) Kap.

chafe [tʃeɪf] *vt* scheuern

chaffinch ['tʃæfɪntʃ] *n* Buchfink *m*

chain [tʃeɪn] *n* Kette *f* ♦ *vt* (*also:* ~ **up**) anketten; ~ **reaction** *n* Kettenreaktion *f*; **~-smoke** *vi* kettenrauchen; ~ **store** *n* Kettenladen *m*

chair [tʃeəʳ] *n* Stuhl *m*; (*armchair*) Sessel *m*; (*UNIV*) Lehrstuhl *m* ♦ *vt* (*meeting*) den Vorsitz führen bei; **~lift** *n* Sessellift *m*; **~man** (*irreg*) *n* Vorsitzende(r) *m*

chalet ['ʃæleɪ] *n* Chalet *nt*

chalk [tʃɔːk] *n* Kreide *f*

challenge ['tʃælɪndʒ] *n* Herausforderung *f* ♦ *vt* herausfordern; (*contest*) bestreiten; **challenging** *adj* (*tone*) herausfordernd; (*work*) anspruchsvoll

chamber ['tʃeɪmbəʳ] *n* Kammer *f*; ~ **of commerce** Handelskammer *f*; **~maid** *n* Zimmermädchen *nt*; ~ **music** *n* Kammermusik *f*

chamois ['ʃæmwɑː] *n* Gämse *f*

champagne [ʃæm'peɪn] *n* Champagner *m*, Sekt *m*

champion ['tʃæmpɪən] *n* (*SPORT*) Meister(in) *m(f)*; (*of cause*) Verfechter(in) *m(f)*; **~ship** *n* Meisterschaft *f*

chance [tʃɑːns] *n* (*luck*) Zufall *m*; (*possibility*) Möglichkeit *f*; (*opportunity*) Gelegenheit *f*, Chance *f*; (*risk*) Risiko *nt* ♦ *adj* zufällig ♦ *vt*: **to** ~ **it** es darauf ankommen lassen; **by** ~

zufällig; **to take a** ~ ein Risiko eingehen

chancellor ['tʃɑːnsələʳ] *n* Kanzler *m*; **C~ of the Exchequer** (*BRIT*) *n* Schatzkanzler *m*

chandelier [ʃændə'lɪəʳ] *n* Kronleuchter *m*

change [tʃeɪndʒ] *vt* ändern; (*replace, COMM: money*) wechseln; (*exchange*) umtauschen; (*transform*) verwandeln ♦ *vi* sich ändern; (~ *trains*) umsteigen; (~ *clothes*) sich umziehen ♦ *n* Veränderung *f*; (*money returned*) Wechselgeld *nt*; (*coins*) Kleingeld *nt*; **to** ~ **one's mind** es sich *dat* anders überlegen; **to** ~ **into sth** (*be transformed*) sich in etw *acc* verwandeln; **for a** ~ zur Abwechslung; **~able** *adj* (*weather*) wechselhaft; ~ **machine** *n* Geldwechselautomat *m*; **~over** *n* Umstellung *f*

changing ['tʃeɪndʒɪŋ] *adj* veränderlich; ~ **room** (*BRIT*) *n* Umkleideraum *m*

channel ['tʃænl] *n* (*stream*) Bachbett *nt*; (*NAUT*) Straße *f*; (*TV*) Kanal *m*; (*fig*) Weg *m* ♦ *vt* (*efforts*) lenken; **the (English) C~** der Ärmelkanal; **~-hopping** *n* (*TV*) ständiges Umschalten; **C~ Islands** *npl*: **the C~ Islands** die Kanalinseln *pl*; **C~ Tunnel** *n*: **the C~ Tunnel** der Kanaltunnel

chant [tʃɑːnt] *n* Gesang *m*; (*of fans*) Sprechchor *m* ♦ *vt* intonieren

chaos ['keɪɒs] *n* Chaos *nt*

chap [tʃæp] (*inf*) *n* Kerl *m*

chapel ['tʃæpl] *n* Kapelle *f*

chaperon ['ʃæpərəʊn] *n* Anstandsdame *f*

chaplain ['tʃæplɪn] *n* Kaplan *m*

chapped [tʃæpt] *adj* (*skin, lips*) spröde

chapter ['tʃæptəʳ] *n* Kapitel *nt*

char [tʃɑːʳ] *vt* (*burn*) verkohlen

character ['kærɪktəʳ] *n* Charakter *m*, Wesen *nt*; (*in novel, film*) Figur *f*; **~istic** [kærɪktə'rɪstɪk] *adj*: **~istic (of sb/sth)** (für jdn/etw) charakteristisch ♦ *n* Kennzeichen *nt*; **~ize** *vt* charakterisieren, kennzeichnen

charade [ʃə'rɑːd] *n* Scharade *f*

charcoal ['tʃɑːkəʊl] *n* Holzkohle *f*

charge [tʃɑːdʒ] *n* (*cost*) Preis *m*; (*JUR*) Anklage *f*; (*explosive*) Ladung *f*; (*attack*) Angriff *m* ♦ *vt* (*gun, battery*) laden; (*price*) verlangen; (*JUR*) anklagen; (*MIL*) angreifen ♦ *vi* (*rush*) (an)stürmen; **bank ~s**

Bankgebühren *pl*; **free of ~** kostenlos; **to reverse the ~s** (*TEL*) ein R-Gespräch führen; **to be in ~ of** verantwortlich sein für; **to take ~** (die Verantwortung) übernehmen; **to ~ sth (up) to sb's account** jdm etw in Rechnung stellen; **~ card** *n* Kundenkarte *f*

charitable ['tʃærɪtəbl] *adj* wohltätig; (*lenient*) nachsichtig

charity ['tʃærɪtɪ] *n* (*institution*) Hilfswerk *nt*; (*attitude*) Nächstenliebe *f*

charm [tʃɑːm] *n* Charme *m*; (*spell*) Bann *m*; (*object*) Talisman *m* ♦ *vt* bezaubern; **~ing** *adj* reizend

chart [tʃɑːt] *n* Tabelle *f*; (*NAUT*) Seekarte *f* ♦ *vt* (*course*) abstecken

charter ['tʃɑːtəʳ] *vt* chartern ♦ *n* Schutzbrief *m*; **~ed accountant** *n* Wirtschafts- prüfer(in) *m(f)*; **~ flight** *n* Charter- flug *m*

chase [tʃeɪs] *vt* jagen, verfolgen ♦ *n* Jagd *f*

chasm ['kæzəm] *n* Kluft *f*

chassis ['ʃæsɪ] *n* Fahrgestell *nt*

chat [tʃæt] *vi* (*also:* **have a ~**) plaudern ♦ *n* Plauderei *f*; **~ show** (*BRIT*) *n* Talkshow *f*

chatter ['tʃætəʳ] *vi* schwatzen; (*teeth*) klappern ♦ *n* Geschwätz *nt*; **~box** *n* Quasselstrippe *f*

chatty ['tʃætɪ] *adj* geschwätzig

chauffeur ['ʃəʊfəʳ] *n* Chauffeur *m*

chauvinist ['ʃəʊvɪnɪst] *n* (*male ~*) Chauvi *m* (*inf*)

cheap [tʃiːp] *adj, adv* billig; **~ day return** *n* Tagesrückfahrkarte *f* (*zu einem günstigeren Tarif*); **~ly** *adv* billig

cheat [tʃiːt] *vt, vi* betrügen; (*SCH*) mogeln ♦ *n* Betrüger(in) *m(f)*

check [tʃek] *vt* (*examine*) prüfen; (*make sure*) nachsehen; (*control*) kontrollieren; (*restrain*) zügeln; (*stop*) anhalten ♦ *n* (*examination, restraint*) Kontrolle *f*; (*bill*) Rechnung *f*; (*pattern*) Karo(muster) *nt*; (*US*) = **cheque** ♦ *adj* (*pattern, cloth*) kariert; **~ in** *vi* (*in hotel, airport*) einchecken ♦ *vt* (*luggage*) abfertigen lassen; **~ out** *vi* (*of hotel*) abreisen; **~ up** *vi* nachschauen; **~ up on** *vt* kontrollieren; **~ered** (*US*) *adj* =

chequered; **~ers** (*US*) *n* (*draughts*) Damespiel *nt*; **~-in (desk)** *n* Abfertigung *f*; **~ing account** (*US*) *n* (*current account*) Girokonto *nt*; **~mate** *n* Schachmatt *nt*; **~out** *n* Kasse *f*; **~point** *n* Kontrollpunkt *m*; **~ room** (*US*) *n* (*left-luggage office*) Gepäckaufbewahrung *f*; **~up** *n* (*Nach*)prüfung *f*; (*MED*) (ärztliche) Untersuchung *f*

cheek [tʃiːk] *n* Backe *f*; (*fig*) Frechheit *f*; **~bone** *n* Backenknochen *m*; **~y** *adj* frech

cheep [tʃiːp] *vi* piepsen

cheer [tʃɪəʳ] *n* (*usu pl*) Hurra- *or* Beifallsruf *m* ♦ *vt* zujubeln; (*encourage*) aufmuntern ♦ *vi* jauchzen; **~s!** Prost!; **~ up** *vi* bessere Laune bekommen ♦ *vt* aufmuntern; **~ up!** nun lach doch mal!; **~ful** *adj* fröhlich

cheerio [tʃɪərɪ'əʊ] (*BRIT*) *excl* tschüss!

cheese [tʃiːz] *n* Käse *m*; **~board** *n* (gemischte) Käseplatte *f*

cheetah ['tʃiːtə] *n* Gepard *m*

chef [ʃef] *n* Küchenchef *m*

chemical ['kemɪkl] *adj* chemisch ♦ *n* Chemikalie *f*

chemist ['kemɪst] *n* (*BRIT: pharmacist*) Apotheker *m*, Drogist *m*; (*scientist*) Chemiker *m*; **~ry** *n* Chemie *f*; **~'s (shop)** (*BRIT*) *n* Apotheke *f*, Drogerie *f*

cheque [tʃek] (*BRIT*) *n* Scheck *m*; **~book** *n* Scheckbuch *nt*; **~ card** *n* Scheckkarte *f*

chequered ['tʃekəd] *adj* (*fig*) bewegt

cherish ['tʃerɪʃ] *vt* (*person*) lieben; (*hope*) hegen

cherry ['tʃerɪ] *n* Kirsche *f*

chess [tʃes] *n* Schach *nt*; **~board** *n* Schachbrett *nt*; **~man** (*irreg*) *n* Schachfigur *f*

chest [tʃest] *n* (*ANAT*) Brust *f*; (*box*) Kiste *f*; **~ of drawers** Kommode *f*

chestnut ['tʃesnʌt] *n* Kastanie *f*

chew [tʃuː] *vt, vi* kauen; **~ing gum** *n* Kaugummi *m*

chic [ʃiːk] *adj* schick, elegant

chick [tʃɪk] *n* Küken *nt*; (*US: inf: girl*) Biene *f*

chicken ['tʃɪkɪn] *n* Huhn *nt*; (*food*) Hähnchen *nt*; **~ out** (*inf*) *vi* kneifen

chickenpox ['tʃɪkɪnpɔks] *n* Windpocken *pl*

chicory ['tʃɪkərɪ] n (in coffee) Zichorie f;
(plant) Chicorée f, Schikoree f

chief [tʃiːf] n (of tribe) Häuptling m; (COMM)
Chef m ♦ adj Haupt-; ~ **executive** n
Geschäftsführer(in) m(f); **~ly** adv
hauptsächlich

chilblain ['tʃɪlbleɪn] n Frostbeule f

child [tʃaɪld] (pl **~ren**) n Kind nt; **~birth** n
Entbindung f; **~hood** n Kindheit f; **~ish**
adj kindisch; **~like** adj kindlich; ~ **minder**
(BRIT) n Tagesmutter f; **~ren** ['tʃɪldrən] npl
of **child**; ~ **seat** n Kindersitz m

Chile ['tʃɪlɪ] n Chile nt; **~an** adj chilenisch

chill [tʃɪl] n Kühle f; (MED) Erkältung f ♦ vt
(CULIN) kühlen

chilli ['tʃɪlɪ] n Peperoni pl; (meal, spice) Chili
m

chilly ['tʃɪlɪ] adj kühl, frostig

chime [tʃaɪm] n Geläut nt ♦ vi ertönen

chimney ['tʃɪmnɪ] n Schornstein m; ~
sweep n Schornsteinfeger(in) m(f)

chimpanzee [tʃɪmpæn'ziː] n Schimpanse m

chin [tʃɪn] n Kinn nt

China ['tʃaɪnə] n China nt

china ['tʃaɪnə] n Porzellan nt

Chinese [tʃaɪ'niːz] adj chinesisch ♦ n (inv)
Chinese m, Chinesin f; (LING) Chinesisch nt

chink [tʃɪŋk] n (opening) Ritze f; (noise)
Klirren nt

chip [tʃɪp] n (of wood etc) Splitter m; (in poker
etc; US: crisp) Chip m ♦ vt absplittern; **~s** npl
(BRIT: COOK) Pommes frites pl; ~ **in** vi
Zwischenbemerkungen machen

Chip shop

ⓘ Chip shop, auch fish-and-chip shop, ist
die traditionelle britische Imbissbude, in
der vor allem fritierte Fischfilets und
Pommes frites, aber auch andere einfache
Mahlzeiten angeboten werden. Früher wurde
das Essen zum Mitnehmen in
Zeitungspapier verpackt. Manche chip shops
haben auch einen Essraum.

---

chiropodist [kɪ'rɒpədɪst] (BRIT) n
Fußpfleger(in) m(f)

chirp [tʃəːp] vi zwitschern

chisel ['tʃɪzl] n Meißel m

chit [tʃɪt] n Notiz f

chivalrous ['ʃɪvəlrəs] adj ritterlich; **chivalry**
['ʃɪvəlrɪ] n Ritterlichkeit f

chives [tʃaɪvz] npl Schnittlauch m

chlorine ['klɔːriːn] n Chlor nt

chock-a-block ['tʃɒkə'blɒk] adj voll
gepfropft

chock-full [tʃɒk'ful] adj voll gepfropft

chocolate ['tʃɒklɪt] n Schokolade f

choice [tʃɔɪs] n Wahl f; (of goods) Auswahl f
♦ adj Qualitäts-

choir ['kwaɪər] n Chor m; **~boy** n Chorknabe
m

choke [tʃəuk] vi ersticken ♦ vt erdrosseln;
(block) (ab)drosseln ♦ n (AUT) Starterklappe
f

cholera ['kɒlərə] n Cholera f

cholesterol [kə'lestərɒl] n Cholesterin nt

choose [tʃuːz] (pt **chose**, pp **chosen**) vt
wählen; **choosy** ['tʃuːzɪ] adj wählerisch

chop [tʃɒp] vt (wood) spalten; (COOK: also: ~
up) (zer)hacken ♦ n Hieb m; (COOK)
Kotelett nt; **~s** npl (jaws) Lefzen pl

chopper ['tʃɒpər] n (helicopter) Hubschrauber
m

choppy ['tʃɒpɪ] adj (sea) bewegt

chopsticks ['tʃɒpstɪks] npl (Ess)stäbchen pl

choral ['kɔːrəl] adj Chor-

chord [kɔːd] n Akkord m

chore [tʃɔː] n Pflicht f; **~s** npl (housework)
Hausarbeit f

choreographer [kɒrɪ'ɒɡrəfər] n
Choreograf(in) m(f)

chorister ['kɒrɪstər] n Chorsänger(in) m(f)

chortle ['tʃɔːtl] vi glucksen

chorus ['kɔːrəs] n Chor m; (in song) Refrain
m

chose [tʃəuz] pt of **choose**

chosen ['tʃəuzn] pp of **choose**

chowder ['tʃaudər] (US) n sämige Fischsuppe
f

Christ [kraɪst] n Christus m

christen ['krɪsn] vt taufen; **~ing** n Taufe f

Christian ['krɪstɪən] adj christlich ♦ n
Christ(in) m(f); **~ity** [krɪstɪ'ænɪtɪ] n
Christentum nt; ~ **name** n Vorname m

Christmas ['krɪsməs] n Weihnachten pl;
  Happy or **Merry ~!** frohe or fröhliche
  Weihnachten!; **~ card** n Weihnachtskarte f;
  ~ Day n der erste Weihnachtstag; **~ Eve** n
  Heiligabend m; **~ tree** n Weihnachtsbaum
  m

chrome [krəʊm] n Verchromung f

chromium ['krəʊmɪəm] n Chrom nt

chronic ['krɒnɪk] adj chronisch

chronicle ['krɒnɪkl] n Chronik f

chronological [krɒnə'lɒdʒɪkl] adj
  chronologisch

chubby ['tʃʌbɪ] adj rundlich

chuck [tʃʌk] vt werfen; (BRIT: also: **~ up**)
  hinwerfen; **~ out** vt (person) rauswerfen;
  (old clothes etc) wegwerfen

chuckle ['tʃʌkl] vi in sich hineinlachen

chug [tʃʌg] vi tuckern

chunk [tʃʌŋk] n Klumpen m; (of food)
  Brocken m

church [tʃɜːtʃ] n Kirche f; **~yard** n Kirchhof
  m

churn [tʃɜːn] n (for butter) Butterfass nt; (for
  milk) Milchkanne f; **~ out** (inf) vt
  produzieren

chute [ʃuːt] n Rutsche f; (rubbish ~)
  Müllschlucker m

chutney ['tʃʌtnɪ] n Chutney nt

CIA (US) n abbr (= Central Intelligence Agency)
  CIA f

CID (BRIT) n abbr (= Criminal Investigation
  Department) ≈ Kripo f

cider ['saɪdə'] n Apfelwein m

cigar [sɪ'gɑː'] n Zigarre f

cigarette [sɪgə'ret] n Zigarette f; **~ case** n
  Zigarettenetui nt; **~ end** n
  Zigarettenstummel m

Cinderella [sɪndə'relə] n Aschenbrödel nt

cinders ['sɪndəz] npl Asche f

cine camera ['sɪnɪ-] (BRIT) n Filmkamera f

cine film (BRIT) n Schmalfilm m

cinema ['sɪnəmə] n Kino nt

cinnamon ['sɪnəmən] n Zimt m

circle ['sɜːkl] n Kreis m; (in cinema etc) Rang
  m ♦ vi kreisen ♦ vt (surround) umgeben;
  (move round) kreisen um

circuit ['sɜːkɪt] n (track) Rennbahn f; (lap)

Runde f; (ELEC) Stromkreis m

circular ['sɜːkjʊlə'] adj rund ♦ n
  Rundschreiben nt

circulate ['sɜːkjʊleɪt] vi zirkulieren ♦ vt in
  Umlauf setzen; **circulation** [sɜːkjʊ'leɪʃən] n
  (of blood) Kreislauf m; (of newspaper) Auflage
  f; (of money) Umlauf m

circumcise ['sɜːkəmsaɪz] vt beschneiden

circumference [sə'kʌmfərəns] n
  (Kreis)umfang m

circumspect ['sɜːkəmspekt] adj umsichtig

circumstances ['sɜːkəmstənsɪz] npl
  Umstände pl; (financial) Verhältnisse pl

circumvent [sɜːkəm'vent] vt umgehen

circus ['sɜːkəs] n Zirkus m

CIS n abbr (= Commonwealth of Independent
  States) GUS f

cistern ['sɪstən] n Zisterne f; (of W.C.)
  Spülkasten m

cite [saɪt] vt zitieren, anführen

citizen ['sɪtɪzn] n Bürger(in) m(f); **~ship** n
  Staatsbürgerschaft f

citrus fruit ['sɪtrəs-] n Zitrusfrucht f

city ['sɪtɪ] n Großstadt f; **the C~** die City, das
  Finanzzentrum Londons

city technology college n ≈ Technische
  Fachschule f

civic ['sɪvɪk] adj (of town) städtisch; (of citizen)
  Bürger-; **~ centre** (BRIT) n Stadtverwaltung
  f

civil ['sɪvɪl] adj bürgerlich; (not military) zivil;
  (polite) höflich; **~ engineer** n Bauingenieur
  m; **~ian** [sɪ'vɪlɪən] n Zivilperson f ♦ adj zivil,
  Zivil-

civilization [sɪvɪlaɪ'zeɪʃən] n Zivilisation f

civilized ['sɪvɪlaɪzd] adj zivilisiert

civil: ~ law n Zivilrecht nt; **~ servant** n
  Staatsbeamte(r) m; **C~ Service** n
  Staatsdienst m; **~ war** n Bürgerkrieg m

clad [klæd] adj: **~ in** gehüllt in +acc

claim [kleɪm] vt beanspruchen; (have opinion)
  behaupten ♦ vi (for insurance) Ansprüche
  geltend machen ♦ n (demand) Forderung f;
  (right) Anspruch m; (pretension) Behauptung
  f; **~ant** n Antragsteller(in) m(f)

clairvoyant [kleə'vɔɪənt] n Hellseher(in) m(f)

clam [klæm] n Venusmuschel f

clamber ['klæmbə'] *vi* kraxeln

clammy ['klæmɪ] *adj* klamm

clamour ['klæmə'] *vi*: **to ~ for sth** nach etw verlangen

clamp [klæmp] *n* Schraubzwinge *f* ♦ *vt* einspannen; (*AUT: wheel*) krallen; **~ down on** *vt fus* Maßnahmen ergreifen gegen

clan [klæn] *n* Clan *m*

clandestine [klæn'destɪn] *adj* geheim

clang [klæŋ] *vi* scheppern

clap [klæp] *vi* klatschen ♦ *vt* Beifall klatschen +*dat* ♦ *n* (*of hands*) Klatschen *nt*; (*of thunder*) Donnerschlag *m*; **~ping** *n* Klatschen *nt*

claret ['klærət] *n* rote(r) Bordeaux(wein) *m*

clarify ['klærɪfaɪ] *vt* klären, erklären

clarinet [klærɪ'net] *n* Klarinette *f*

clarity ['klærɪtɪ] *n* Klarheit *f*

clash [klæʃ] *n* (*fig*) Konflikt *m* ♦ *vi* zusammenprallen; (*colours*) sich beißen; (*argue*) sich streiten

clasp [klɑːsp] *n* Griff *m*; (*on jewels, bag*) Verschluss *m* ♦ *vt* umklammern

class [klɑːs] *n* Klasse *f* ♦ *vt* einordnen; **~-conscious** *adj* klassenbewusst

classic ['klæsɪk] *n* Klassiker *m* ♦ *adj* klassisch; **~al** *adj* klassisch

classified ['klæsɪfaɪd] *adj* (*information*) Geheim-; **~ advertisement** *n* Kleinanzeige *f*

classify ['klæsɪfaɪ] *vt* klassifizieren

classmate ['klɑːsmeɪt] *n* Klassenkamerad(in) *m(f)*

classroom ['klɑːsrum] *n* Klassenzimmer *nt*

clatter ['klætə'] *vi* klappern; (*feet*) trappeln

clause [klɔːz] *n* (*JUR*) Klausel *f*; (*GRAM*) Satz *m*

claustrophobia [klɔːstrə'fəubɪə] *n* Platzangst *f*

claw [klɔː] *n* Kralle *f* ♦ *vt* (zer)kratzen

clay [kleɪ] *n* Lehm *m*; (*for pots*) Ton *m*

clean [kliːn] *adj* sauber ♦ *vt* putzen; (*clothes*) reinigen; **~ out** *vt* gründlich putzen; **~ up** *vt* aufräumen; **~-cut** *adj* (*person*) adrett; (*clear*) klar; **~er** *n* (*person*) Putzfrau *f*; **~er's** *n* (*also*: **dry ~er's**) Reinigung *f*; **~ing** *n* Putzen *nt*; (*clothes*) Reinigung *f*; **~liness** ['klenlɪnɪs] *n* Reinlichkeit *f*

cleanse [klenz] *vt* reinigen; **~r** *n* (*for face*) Reinigungsmilch *f*

clean-shaven [kliːn'ʃeɪvn] *adj* glatt rasiert

cleansing department ['klenzɪŋ-] (*BRIT*) *n* Stadtreinigung *f*

clear [klɪə'] *adj* klar; (*road*) frei ♦ *vt* (*road etc*) freimachen; (*obstacle*) beseitigen; (*JUR: suspect*) freisprechen ♦ *vi* klar werden; (*fog*) sich lichten ♦ *adv*: **~ of** von ... entfernt; **to ~ the table** den Tisch abräumen; **~ up** *vt* aufräumen; (*solve*) aufklären; **~ance** ['klɪərəns] *n* (*removal*) Räumung *f*; (*free space*) Lichtung *f*; (*permission*) Freigabe *f*; **~-cut** *adj* (*case*) eindeutig; **~ing** *n* Lichtung *f*; **~ing bank** (*BRIT*) *n* Clearingbank *f*; **~ly** *adv* klar; (*obviously*) eindeutig; **~way** (*BRIT*) *n* (Straße *f* mit) Halteverbot *nt*

cleaver ['kliːvə'] *n* Hackbeil *nt*

cleft [kleft] *n* (*in rock*) Spalte *f*

clementine ['klemǝntaɪn] *n* (*fruit*) Klementine *f*

clench [klentʃ] *vt* (*teeth*) zusammenbeißen; (*fist*) ballen

clergy ['klɜːdʒɪ] *n* Geistliche(n) *pl*; **~man** (*irreg*) *n* Geistliche(r) *m*

clerical ['klerɪkl] *adj* (*office*) Schreib-, Büro-; (*REL*) geistlich

clerk [klɑːk, (*US*) klɜːrk] *n* (*in office*) Büroangestellte(r) *mf*; (*US: sales person*) Verkäufer(in) *m(f)*

clever ['klevə'] *adj* klug; (*crafty*) schlau

cliché ['kliːʃeɪ] *n* Klischee *nt*

click [klɪk] *vt* (*tongue*) schnalzen mit; (*heels*) zusammenklappen; **~ on** *vt* (*COMPUT*) anklicken

client ['klaɪənt] *n* Klient(in) *m(f)*; **~ele** [kliːɑ̃ːn'tel] *n* Kundschaft *f*

cliff [klɪf] *n* Klippe *f*

climate ['klaɪmɪt] *n* Klima *nt*

climax ['klaɪmæks] *n* Höhepunkt *m*

climb [klaɪm] *vt* besteigen ♦ *vi* steigen, klettern ♦ *n* Aufstieg *m*; **~-down** *n* Abstieg *m*; **~er** *n* Bergsteiger(in) *m(f)*; **~ing** *n* Bergsteigen *nt*

clinch [klɪntʃ] *vt* (*decide*) entscheiden; (*deal*) festmachen

cling [klɪŋ] (*pt, pp* **clung**) *vi* (*clothes*) eng anliegen; **to ~ to** sich festklammern an +*da*

clinic ['klɪnɪk] *n* Klinik *f*; **~al** *adj* klinisch

clink [klɪŋk] vi klimpern

clip [klɪp] n Spange f; (also: **paper ~**) Klammer f ♦ vt (papers) heften; (hair, hedge) stutzen; **~pers** npl (for hedge) Heckenschere f; (for hair) Haarschneidemaschine f; **~ping** n Ausschnitt m

cloak [kləuk] n Umhang m ♦ vt hüllen; **~room** n (for coats) Garderobe f; (BRIT: W.C.) Toilette f

clock [klɔk] n Uhr f; **~ in** or **on** vi stempeln; **~ off** or **out** vi stempeln; **~wise** adv im Uhrzeigersinn; **~work** n Uhrwerk nt ♦ adj zum Aufziehen

clog [klɔg] n Holzschuh m ♦ vt verstopfen

cloister ['klɔɪstə*] n Kreuzgang m

clone [kləun] n Klon m ♦ vt klonen

close¹ [kləus] adj (near) in der Nähe; (friend, connection, print) eng; (relative) nahe; (result) knapp; (examination) eingehend; (weather) schwül; (room) stickig ♦ adv nahe, dicht; **~ by** in der Nähe; **~ at hand** in der Nähe; **to have a ~ shave** (fig) mit knapper Not davonkommen

close² [kləuz] vt (shut) schließen; (end) beenden ♦ vi (shop etc) schließen; (door etc) sich schließen ♦ n Ende nt; **~ down** vi schließen; **~d** adj (shop etc) geschlossen; **~d shop** n Gewerkschaftszwang m

close-knit ['kləus'nɪt] adj eng zusammengewachsen

closely ['kləuslɪ] adv eng; (carefully) genau

closet ['klɔzɪt] n Schrank m

close-up ['kləusʌp] n Nahaufnahme f

closure ['kləuʒə*] n Schließung f

clot [klɔt] n (of blood) Blutgerinnsel nt; (fool) Blödmann m ♦ vi gerinnen

cloth [klɔθ] n (material) Tuch nt; (rag) Lappen m

clothe [kləuð] vt kleiden

clothes [kləuðz] npl Kleider pl; **~ brush** n Kleiderbürste f; **~ line** n Wäscheleine f; **~ peg**, **~ pin** (US) n Wäscheklammer f

clothing ['kləuðɪŋ] n Kleidung f

clotted cream ['klɔtɪd-] (BRIT) n Sahne aus erhitzter Milch

cloud [klaud] n Wolke f; **~burst** n Wolkenbruch m; **~y** adj bewölkt; (liquid) trüb

clout [klaut] vt hauen

clove [kləuv] n Gewürznelke f; **~ of garlic** Knoblauchzehe f

clover ['kləuvə*] n Klee m

clown [klaun] n Clown m ♦ vi (also: **~ about**, **~ around**) kaspern

cloying ['klɔɪɪŋ] adj (taste, smell) übersüß

club [klʌb] n (weapon) Knüppel m; (society) Klub m; (also: **golf ~**) Golfschläger m ♦ vt prügeln ♦ vi: **to ~ together** zusammenlegen; **~s** npl (CARDS) Kreuz nt; **~ car** (US) n (RAIL) Speisewagen m; **~ class** n (AVIAT) Club-Klasse f; **~house** n Klubhaus nt

cluck [klʌk] vi glucken

clue [klu:] n Anhaltspunkt m; (in crosswords) Frage f; **I haven't a ~** (ich hab) keine Ahnung

clump [klʌmp] n Gruppe f

clumsy ['klʌmzɪ] adj (person) unbeholfen; (shape) unförmig

clung [klʌŋ] pt, pp of **cling**

cluster ['klʌstə*] n (of trees etc) Gruppe f ♦ vi sich drängen, sich scharen

clutch [klʌtʃ] n Griff m; (AUT) Kupplung f ♦ vt sich festklammern an +dat

clutter ['klʌtə*] vt voll pfropfen; (desk) übersäen

CND n abbr = **Campaign for Nuclear Disarmament**

Co. abbr = **county; company**

c/o abbr (= care of) c/o

coach [kəutʃ] n (bus) Reisebus m; (horse-drawn) Kutsche f; (RAIL) (Personen)wagen m; (trainer) Trainer m ♦ vt (SCH) Nachhilfeunterricht geben +dat; (SPORT) trainieren; **~ trip** n Busfahrt f

coal [kəul] n Kohle f; **~ face** n Streb m

coalition [kəuə'lɪʃən] n Koalition f

coalman ['kəulmən] (irreg) n Kohlenhändler m

coal mine n Kohlenbergwerk nt

coarse [kɔ:s] adj grob; (fig) ordinär

coast [kəust] n Küste f ♦ vi dahinrollen; (AUT) im Leerlauf fahren; **~al** adj Küsten-;

~guard n Küstenwache f; **~line** n Küste(nlinie) f

coat [kəut] n Mantel m; (on animals) Fell nt; (of paint) Schicht f ♦ vt überstreichen; **~hanger** n Kleiderbügel m; **~ing** n Überzug m; (of paint) Schicht f; **~ of arms** n Wappen nt

coax [kəuks] vt beschwatzen

cob [kɔb] n see **corn**

cobbler ['kɔblər] n Schuster m

cobbles ['kɔblz] npl Pflastersteine pl

cobweb ['kɔbweb] n Spinnennetz nt

cocaine [kə'keɪn] n Kokain nt

cock [kɔk] n Hahn m ♦ vt (gun) entsichern; **~erel** ['kɔkərl] n junge(r) Hahn m; **~eyed** adj (fig) verrückt

cockle ['kɔkl] n Herzmuschel f

cockney ['kɔknɪ] n echte(r) Londoner m

cockpit ['kɔkpɪt] n (AVIAT) Pilotenkanzel f

cockroach ['kɔkrəutʃ] n Küchenschabe f

cocktail ['kɔkteɪl] n Cocktail m; **~ cabinet** n Hausbar f; **~ party** n Cocktailparty f

cocoa ['kəukəu] n Kakao m

coconut ['kəukənʌt] n Kokosnuss f

cocoon [kə'kuːn] n Kokon m

cod [kɔd] n Kabeljau m

C.O.D. abbr = **cash on delivery**

code [kəud] n Kode m; (JUR) Kodex m

cod-liver oil ['kɔdlɪvə-] n Lebertran m

coercion [kəu'əːʃən] n Zwang m

coffee ['kɔfɪ] n Kaffee m; **~ bar** (BRIT) n Café nt; **~ bean** n Kaffeebohne f; **~ break** n Kaffeepause f; **~pot** n Kaffeekanne f; **~ table** n Couchtisch m

coffin ['kɔfɪn] n Sarg m

cog [kɔg] n (Rad)zahn m

cognac ['kɔnjæk] n Kognak m

coherent [kəu'hɪərənt] adj zusammenhängend; (person) verständlich

coil [kɔɪl] n Rolle f; (ELEC) Spule f; (contraceptive) Spirale f ♦ vt aufwickeln

coin [kɔɪn] n Münze f ♦ vt prägen; **~age** ['kɔɪnɪdʒ] n (word) Prägung f; **~ box** (BRIT) n Münzfernsprecher m

coincide [kəuɪn'saɪd] vi (happen together) zusammenfallen; (agree) übereinstimmen; **~nce** [kəu'ɪnsɪdəns] n Zufall m

coinphone ['kɔɪnfəun] n Münzfernsprecher m

Coke [kəuk] ® n (drink) Coca-Cola ® f

coke [kəuk] n Koks m

colander ['kɔləndər] n Durchschlag m

cold [kəuld] adj kalt ♦ n Kälte f; (MED) Erkältung f; **I'm ~** mir ist kalt; **to catch ~** sich erkälten; **in ~ blood** kaltblütig; **to give sb the ~ shoulder** jdm die kalte Schulter zeigen; **~ly** adv kalt; **~-shoulder** vt die kalte Schulter zeigen +dat; **~ sore** n Erkältungsbläschen nt

coleslaw ['kəulslɔː] n Krautsalat m

colic ['kɔlɪk] n Kolik f

collaborate [kə'læbəreɪt] vi zusammenarbeiten

collapse [kə'læps] vi (people) zusammenbrechen; (things) einstürzen ♦ n Zusammenbruch m; Einsturz m; **collapsible** adj zusammenklappbar, Klapp-

collar ['kɔlər] n Kragen m; **~bone** n Schlüsselbein nt

collateral [kə'lætərl] n (zusätzliche) Sicherheit f

colleague ['kɔliːg] n Kollege m, Kollegin f

collect [kə'lekt] vt sammeln; (BRIT: call and pick up) abholen ♦ vi sich sammeln ♦ adv: **to call ~** (US: TEL) ein R-Gespräch führen; **~ion** [kə'lekʃən] n Sammlung f; (REL) Kollekte f; (of post) Leerung f; **~ive** [kə'lektɪv] adj gemeinsam; (POL) kollektiv; **~or** [kə'lektər] n Sammler m; (tax ~or) (Steuer)einnehmer m

college ['kɔlɪdʒ] n (UNIV) College nt; (TECH) Fach-, Berufsschule f

collide [kə'laɪd] vi zusammenstoßen

collie ['kɔlɪ] n Collie m

colliery ['kɔlɪərɪ] n (BRIT) Zeche f

collision [kə'lɪʒən] n Zusammenstoß m

colloquial [kə'ləukwɪəl] adj umgangssprachlich

colon ['kəulən] n Doppelpunkt m; (MED) Dickdarm m

colonel ['kəːnl] n Oberst m

colonial [kə'ləunɪəl] adj Kolonial-

colonize ['kɔlənaɪz] vt kolonisieren

colony ['kɔlənɪ] n Kolonie f

colour ['kʌlər] (US color) n Farbe f ♦ vt (also fig) färben ♦ vi sich verfärben; ~s npl (of club) Fahne f; ~ bar n Rassenschranke f; ~-blind adj farbenblind; ~ed adj farbig; ~ film n Farbfilm m; ~ful adj bunt; (personality) schillernd; ~ing n (complexion) Gesichtsfarbe f; (substance) Farbstoff m; ~ scheme n Farbgebung f; ~ television n Farbfernsehen nt

colt [kəult] n Fohlen nt

column ['kɔləm] n Säule f; (MIL) Kolonne f; (of print) Spalte f; ~ist ['kɔləmnɪst] n Kolumnist m

coma ['kəumə] n Koma nt

comb [kəum] n Kamm m ♦ vt kämmen; (search) durchkämmen

combat ['kɔmbæt] n Kampf m ♦ vt bekämpfen

combination [kɔmbɪ'neɪʃən] n Kombination f

combine [vb kəm'baɪn, n 'kɔmbaɪn] vt verbinden ♦ vi sich vereinigen ♦ n (COMM) Konzern m; ~ (harvester) n Mähdrescher m

combustion [kəm'bʌstʃən] n Verbrennung f

come [kʌm] (pt came, pp come) vi kommen; to ~ undone aufgehen; ~ about vi geschehen; ~ across vt fus (find) stoßen auf +acc; ~ away vi (person) weggehen; (handle etc) abgehen; ~ back vi zurückkommen; ~ by vt fus (find): to ~ by sth zu etw kommen; ~ down vi (price) fallen; ~ forward vi (volunteer) sich melden; ~ from vt fus (result) kommen von; where do you ~ from? wo kommen Sie her?; I ~ from London ich komme aus London; ~ in vi hereinkommen; (train) einfahren; ~ in for vt fus abkriegen; ~ into vt fus (inherit) erben; ~ off vi (handle) abgehen; (succeed) klappen; ~ on vi (progress) vorankommen; ~ on! komm!; (hurry) beeil dich!; ~ out vi herauskommen; ~ round vi (MED) wieder zu sich kommen; ~ to vi (MED) wieder zu sich kommen ♦ vt fus (bill) sich belaufen auf +acc; ~ up vi hochkommen; (sun)

aufgehen; (problem) auftauchen; ~ up against vt fus (resistance, difficulties) stoßen auf +acc; ~ upon vt fus stoßen auf +acc; ~ up with vt fus sich einfallen lassen

comedian [kə'miːdɪən] n Komiker m; comedienne [kəmiːdɪ'ɛn] n Komikerin f

comedown ['kʌmdaun] n Abstieg m

comedy ['kɔmɪdɪ] n Komödie f

comet ['kɔmɪt] n Komet m

comeuppance [kʌm'ʌpəns] n: to get one's ~ seine Quittung bekommen

comfort ['kʌmfət] n Komfort m; (consolation) Trost m ♦ vt trösten; ~able adj bequem; ~ably adv (sit etc) bequem; (live) angenehm; ~ station (US) n öffentliche Toilette f

comic ['kɔmɪk] n Comic(heft) nt; (comedian) Komiker m ♦ adj (also: ~al) komisch; ~ strip n Comicstrip m

coming ['kʌmɪŋ] n Kommen nt; ~(s) and going(s) n(pl) Kommen und Gehen nt

comma ['kɔmə] n Komma nt

command [kə'mɑːnd] n Befehl m; (control) Führung f; (MIL) Kommando nt; (mastery) Beherrschung f ♦ vt befehlen +dat; (MIL) kommandieren; (be able to get) verfügen über +acc; ~eer [kɔmən'dɪər] vt requirieren; ~er n Kommandant m; ~ment n (REL) Gebot nt

commando [kə'mɑːndəu] n Kommandotruppe nt; (person) Mitglied nt einer Kommandotruppe

commemorate [kə'mɛməreɪt] vt gedenken +gen

commence [kə'mɛns] vt, vi beginnen

commend [kə'mɛnd] vt (recommend) empfehlen; (praise) loben

commensurate [kə'mɛnʃərɪt] adj: ~ with sth einer Sache dat entsprechend

comment ['kɔmɛnt] n Bemerkung f ♦ vi: to ~ (on) sich äußern (zu); ~ary n Kommentar m; ~ator n Kommentator m; (TV) Reporter(in) m(f)

commerce ['kɔməːs] n Handel m

commercial [kə'məːʃəl] adj kommerziell, geschäftlich; (training) kaufmännisch ♦ n (TV) Fernsehwerbung f; ~ break n

Werbespot *m*; **~ize** *vt* kommerzialisieren

commiserate [kəˈmɪzəreɪt] *vi*: **to ~ with** Mitleid haben mit

commission [kəˈmɪʃən] *n* (*act*) Auftrag *m*; (*fee*) Provision *f*; (*body*) Kommission *f* ♦ *vt* beauftragen; (*MIL*) zum Offizier ernennen; (*work of art*) in Auftrag geben; **out of ~** außer Betrieb; **~er** *n* (*POLICE*) Polizeipräsident *m*

commit [kəˈmɪt] *vt* (*crime*) begehen; (*entrust*) anvertrauen; **to ~ o.s.** sich festlegen; **~ment** *n* Verpflichtung *f*

committee [kəˈmɪtɪ] *n* Ausschuss *m*

commodity [kəˈmɔdɪtɪ] *n* Ware *f*

common [ˈkɔmən] *adj* (*cause*) gemeinsam; (*pej*) gewöhnlich; (*widespread*) üblich, häufig ♦ *n* Gemeindeland *nt*; **C~s** *npl* (*BRIT*): **the C~s** das Unterhaus; **~er** *n* Bürgerliche(r) *mf*; **~ law** *n* Gewohnheitsrecht *nt*; **~ly** *adv* gewöhnlich; **C~ Market** *n* Gemeinsame(r) Markt *m*; **~place** *adj* alltäglich; **~ room** *n* Gemeinschaftsraum *m*; **~ sense** *n* gesunde(r) Menschenverstand *m*; **C~wealth** *n*: **the C~wealth** das Commonwealth

commotion [kəˈməʊʃən] *n* Aufsehen *nt*

communal [ˈkɔmjuːnl] *adj* Gemeinde-; Gemeinschafts-

commune [*n* ˈkɔmjuːn, *vb* kəˈmjuːn] *n* Kommune *f* ♦ *vi*: **to ~ with** sich mitteilen +*dat*

communicate [kəˈmjuːnɪkeɪt] *vt* (*transmit*) übertragen ♦ *vi* (*be in touch*) in Verbindung stehen; (*make self understood*) sich verständigen; **communication** [kəmjuːnɪˈkeɪʃən] *n* (*message*) Mitteilung *f*; (*making understood*) Kommunikation *f*; **communication cord** (*BRIT*) *n* Notbremse *f*

communion [kəˈmjuːnɪən] *n* (*also*: **Holy C~**) Abendmahl *nt*, Kommunion *f*

communism [ˈkɔmjunɪzəm] *n* Kommunismus *m*; **communist** [ˈkɔmjunɪst] *n* Kommunist(in) *m(f)* ♦ *adj* kommunistisch

community [kəˈmjuːnɪtɪ] *n* Gemeinschaft *f*; **~ centre** *n* Gemeinschaftszentrum *nt*; **~**

chest (*US*) *n* Wohltätigkeitsfonds *m*; **~ home** (*BRIT*) *n* Erziehungsheim *nt*

commutation ticket [kɔmjuˈteɪʃən-] (*US*) *n* Zeitkarte *f*

commute [kəˈmjuːt] *vi* pendeln ♦ *vt* umwandeln; **~r** *n* Pendler *m*

compact [*adj* kəmˈpækt, *n* ˈkɔmpækt] *adj* kompakt ♦ *n* (*for make-up*) Puderdose *f*; **~ disc** *n* Compactdisc *f*, Compact Disc *f*; **~ disc player** *n* CD-Spieler *m*

companion [kəmˈpænjən] *n* Begleiter(in) *m(f)*; **~ship** *n* Gesellschaft *f*

company [ˈkʌmpənɪ] *n* Gesellschaft *f*; (*COMM*) Firma *f*, Gesellschaft *f*; **to keep sb ~** jdm Gesellschaft leisten; **~ secretary** (*BRIT*) *n* ≃ Prokurist(in) *m(f)*

comparable [ˈkɔmpərəbl] *adj* vergleichbar

comparative [kəmˈpærətɪv] *adj* (*relative*) relativ; **~ly** *adv* verhältnismäßig

compare [kəmˈpeəʳ] *vt* vergleichen ♦ *vi* sich vergleichen lassen; **comparison** [kəmˈpærɪsn] *n* Vergleich *m*; **in comparison (with)** im Vergleich (mit or zu)

compartment [kəmˈpɑːtmənt] *n* (*RAIL*) Abteil *nt*; (*in drawer*) Fach *nt*

compass [ˈkʌmpəs] *n* Kompass *m*; **~es** *npl* (*MATH etc*: *also*: **pair of ~es**) Zirkel *m*

compassion [kəmˈpæʃən] *n* Mitleid *nt*; **~ate** *adj* mitfühlend

compatible [kəmˈpætɪbl] *adj* vereinbar; (*COMPUT*) kompatibel

compel [kəmˈpel] *vt* zwingen

compensate [ˈkɔmpənseɪt] *vt* entschädigen ♦ *vi*: **to ~ for** Ersatz leisten für; **compensation** [kɔmpənˈseɪʃən] *n* Entschädigung *f*

compère [ˈkɔmpeəʳ] *n* Conférencier *m*

compete [kəmˈpiːt] *vi* (*take part*) teilnehmen; (*vie with*) konkurrieren

competent [ˈkɔmpɪtənt] *adj* kompetent

competition [kɔmpɪˈtɪʃən] *n* (*contest*) Wettbewerb *m*; (*COMM*, *rivalry*) Konkurrenz *f*; **competitive** [kəmˈpetɪtɪv] *adj* Konkurrenz-; (*COMM*) konkurrenzfähig; **competitor** [kəmˈpetɪtəʳ] *n* (*COMM*) Konkurrent(in) *m(f)*; (*participant*) Teilnehmer(in) *m(f)* compile [kəm'paɪl] vt zusammenstellen

complacency [kəm'pleɪsnsɪ] n Selbstzufriedenheit f

complacent [kəm'pleɪsnt] adj selbstzufrieden

complain [kəm'pleɪn] vi sich beklagen; (formally) sich beschweren; ~t n Klage f; (formal ~t) Beschwerde f; (MED) Leiden nt

complement [n 'kɒmplɪmənt, vb 'kɒmplɪment] n Ergänzung f; (ship's crew etc) Bemannung f ♦ vt ergänzen; ~ary [kɒmplɪ'mentərɪ] adj (sich) ergänzend

complete [kəm'pliːt] adj (full) vollkommen, ganz; (finished) fertig ♦ vt vervollständigen; (finish) beenden; (fill in: form) ausfüllen; ~ly adv ganz; completion [kəm'pliːʃən] n Fertigstellung f; (of contract etc) Abschluss m

complex ['kɒmpleks] adj kompliziert

complexion [kəm'plekʃən] n Gesichtsfarbe f; (fig) Aspekt m

complexity [kəm'pleksɪtɪ] n Kompliziertheit f

compliance [kəm'plaɪəns] n Fügsamkeit f, Einwilligung f; in ~ with sth einer Sache dat gemäß

complicate ['kɒmplɪkeɪt] vt komplizieren; ~d adj kompliziert; complication [kɒmplɪ'keɪʃən] n Komplikation f

compliment [n 'kɒmplɪmənt, vb 'kɒmplɪment] n Kompliment nt ♦ vt ein Kompliment machen +dat; ~s npl (greetings) Grüße pl; to pay sb a ~ jdm ein Kompliment machen; ~ary [kɒmplɪ'mentərɪ] adj schmeichelhaft; (free) Frei-, Gratis-

comply [kəm'plaɪ] vi: to ~ with erfüllen +acc; entsprechen +dat

component [kəm'pəʊnənt] adj Teil- ♦ n Bestandteil m

compose [kəm'pəʊz] vt (music) komponieren; (poetry) verfassen; to ~ o.s. sich sammeln; ~d adj gefasst; ~r n Komponist(in) m(f); composition ['kɒmpə'zɪʃən] n (MUS) Komposition f; (SCH) Aufsatz m; (structure) Zusammensetzung f, Aufbau m

composure [kəm'pəʊʒər] n Fassung f

compound ['kɒmpaʊnd] n (CHEM) Verbindung f; (enclosure) Lager nt; (LING)

Kompositum nt ♦ adj zusammengesetzt; (fracture) kompliziert; ~ interest n Zinseszins m

comprehend [kɒmprɪ'hend] vt begreifen; comprehension n Verständnis nt

comprehensive [kɒmprɪ'hensɪv] adj umfassend ♦ n = comprehensive school; ~ insurance n Vollkasko nt; ~ school (BRIT) n Gesamtschule f

compress [vb kəm'pres, n 'kɒmpres] vt komprimieren ♦ n (MED) Kompresse f

comprise [kəm'praɪz] vt (also: be ~d of) umfassen, bestehen aus

compromise ['kɒmprəmaɪz] n Kompromiss m ♦ vt kompromittieren ♦ vi einen Kompromiss schließen

compulsion [kəm'pʌlʃən] n Zwang m; compulsive [kəm'pʌlsɪv] adj zwanghaft; compulsory [kəm'pʌlsərɪ] adj obligatorisch

computer [kəm'pjuːtəʳ] n Computer m, Rechner m; ~ game n Computerspiel nt; ~-generated adj computergeneriert; ~ize vt (information) computerisieren; (company, accounts) auf Computer umstellen; ~ programmer n Programmierer(in) m(f); ~ programming n Programmieren nt; ~ science n Informatik f; computing [kəm'pjuːtɪŋ] n (science) Informatik f; (work) Computerei f

comrade ['kɒmrɪd] n Kamerad m; (POL) Genosse m

con [kɒn] vt hereinlegen ♦ n Schwindel nt

concave ['kɒnkeɪv] adj konkav

conceal [kən'siːl] vt (secret) verschweigen; (hide) verbergen

concede [kən'siːd] vt (grant) gewähren; (point) zugeben ♦ vi (admit defeat) nachgeben

conceit [kən'siːt] n Einbildung f; ~ed adj eingebildet

conceivable [kən'siːvəbl] adj vorstellbar

conceive [kən'siːv] vt (idea) ausdenken; (imagine) sich vorstellen; (baby) empfangen ♦ vi empfangen

concentrate ['kɒnsəntreɪt] vi sich konzentrieren ♦ vt konzentrieren; to ~ on sth sich auf etw acc konzentrieren;

concentration [kɔnsən'treɪʃən] *n*
Konzentration *f*; **concentration camp** *n*
Konzentrationslager *nt*, KZ *nt*

concept ['kɔnsept] *n* Begriff *m*

conception [kən'sepʃən] *n* (*idea*) Vorstellung
f; (BIOL) Empfängnis *f*

concern [kən'sə:n] *n* (*affair*) Angelegenheit
f; (COMM) Unternehmen *nt*; (*worry*) Sorge *f*
♦ *vt* (*interest*) angehen; (*be about*) handeln
von; (*have connection with*) betreffen; **to be**
~ed (about) sich Sorgen machen (um);
~ing *prep* hinsichtlich +*gen*

concert ['kɔnsət] *n* Konzert *nt*

concerted [kən'sə:tɪd] *adj* gemeinsam

concert hall *n* Konzerthalle *f*

concertina [kɔnsə'ti:nə] *n* Handharmonika *f*

concerto [kən'tʃə:təu] *n* Konzert *nt*

concession [kən'seʃən] *n* (*yielding*)
Zugeständnis *nt*; **tax ~** Steuerkonzession *f*

conciliation [kənsɪlɪ'eɪʃən] *n* Versöhnung *f*;
(*official*) Schlichtung *f*

concise [kən'saɪs] *adj* präzis

conclude [kən'klu:d] *vt* (*end*) beenden;
(*treaty*) (ab)schließen; (*decide*) schließen,
folgern; **conclusion** [kən'klu:ʒən] *n*
(Ab)schluss *m*; (*deduction*) Schluss *m*;
conclusive [kən'klu:sɪv] *adj* schlüssig

concoct [kən'kɔkt] *vt* zusammenbrauen;
~ion [kən'kɔkʃən] *n* Gebräu *nt*

concourse ['kɔŋkɔ:s] *n* (Bahnhofs)halle *f*,
Vorplatz *m*

concrete ['kɔŋkri:t] *n* Beton *m* ♦ *adj* konkret

concur [kən'kə:] *vi* übereinstimmen

concurrently [kən'kʌrntlɪ] *adv* gleichzeitig

concussion [kən'kʌʃən] *n*
(Gehirn)erschütterung *f*

condemn [kən'dem] *vt* (JUR) verurteilen;
(*building*) abbruchreif erklären

condensation [kɔndən'seɪʃən] *n*
Kondensation *f*

condense [kən'dens] *vi* (CHEM)
kondensieren ♦ *vt* (*fig*) zusammendrängen;
~d milk *n* Kondensmilch *f*

condescending [kɔndɪ'sendɪŋ] *adj*
herablassend

condition [kən'dɪʃən] *n* (*state*) Zustand *m*;
(*presupposition*) Bedingung *f* ♦ *vt* (*hair etc*)

behandeln; (*accustom*) gewöhnen; **~s** *npl*
(*circumstances*) Verhältnisse *pl*; **on ~ that ...**
unter der Bedingung, dass ...; **~al** *adj*
bedingt; **~er** *n* (*for hair*) Spülung *f*; (*for*
fabrics) Weichspüler *m*

condolences [kən'dəulənsɪz] *npl* Beileid *nt*

condom ['kɔndəm] *n* Kondom *nt* or *m*

condominium [kɔndə'mɪnɪəm] (US) *n*
Eigentumswohnung *f*; (*block*)
Eigentumsblock *m*

condone [kən'dəun] *vt* gutheißen

conducive [kən'dju:sɪv] *adj*: **~ to** dienlich
+*dat*

conduct [*n* 'kɔndʌkt, *vb* kən'dʌkt] *n*
(*behaviour*) Verhalten *nt*; (*management*)
Führung *f* ♦ *vt* führen; (MUS) dirigieren;
~ed tour *n* Führung *f*; **~or** [kən'dʌktə'] *n*
(*of orchestra*) Dirigent *m*; (*in bus, US: on*
train) Schaffner *m*; (ELEC) Leiter *m*; **~ress**
[kən'dʌktrɪs] *n* (*in bus*) Schaffnerin *f*

cone [kəun] *n* (MATH) Kegel *m*; (*for ice cream*)
(Waffel)tüte *f*; (BOT) Tannenzapfen *m*

confectioner's (shop) [kən'fekʃənəz-] *n*
Konditorei *f*; **~y** [kən'fekʃənrɪ] *n* Süßigkeiten
pl

confederation [kənfedə'reɪʃən] *n* Bund *m*

confer [kən'fə:'] *vt* (*degree*) verleihen ♦ *vi*
(*discuss*) konferieren, verhandeln; **~ence**
['kɔnfərəns] *n* Konferenz *f*

confess [kən'fes] *vt, vi* gestehen; (ECCL)
beichten; **~ion** [kən'feʃən] *n* Geständnis *nt*;
(ECCL) Beichte *f*; **~ional** *n* Beichtstuhl *m*

confide [kən'faɪd] *vi*: **to ~ in** (sich)
anvertrauen +*dat*

confidence ['kɔnfɪdns] *n* Vertrauen *nt*;
(*assurance*) Selbstvertrauen *nt*; (*secret*)
Geheimnis *nt*; **in ~** (*speak, write*) vertraulich;
~ trick *n* Schwindel *m*

confident ['kɔnfɪdənt] *adj* (*sure*) überzeugt;
(*self-assured*) selbstsicher

confidential [kɔnfɪ'denʃəl] *adj* vertraulich

confine [kən'faɪn] *vt* (*limit*) beschränken;
(*lock up*) einsperren; **~d** *adj* (*space*) eng;
~ment *n* (*in prison*) Haft *f*; (MED)
Wochenbett *nt*; **~s** ['kɔnfaɪnz] *npl* Grenzen
pl

confirm [kən'fə:m] *vt* bestätigen; **~ation**

[kɒnfə'meɪʃən] n Bestätigung f; (REL)
Konfirmation f; **~ed** adj unverbesserlich;
(bachelor) eingefleischt

confiscate ['kɒnfɪskeɪt] vt beschlagnahmen

conflict [n 'kɒnflɪkt, vb kən'flɪkt] n Konflikt m
♦ vi im Widerspruch stehen; **~ing**
[kən'flɪktɪŋ] adj widersprüchlich

conform [kən'fɔ:m] vi: **to ~ (to)** (things)
entsprechen +dat; (people) sich anpassen
+dat; (to rules) sich richten (nach)

confound [kən'faund] vt verblüffen;
(confuse) durcheinander bringen

confront [kən'frʌnt] vt (enemy)
entgegentreten +dat; (problems) sich stellen
+dat; **to ~ sb with sth** jdn mit etw
konfrontieren; **~ation** [kɒnfrən'teɪʃən] n
Konfrontation f

confuse [kən'fju:z] vt verwirren; (sth with
sth) verwechseln; **~d** adj verwirrt;
confusing adj verwirrend; **confusion**
[kən'fju:ʒən] n (perplexity) Verwirrung f;
(mixing up) Verwechslung f; (tumult) Aufruhr
m

congeal [kən'dʒi:l] vi (freeze) gefrieren; (clot)
gerinnen

congested [kən'dʒestɪd] adj überfüllt

congestion [kən'dʒestʃən] n Stau m

conglomerate [kən'glɒmərɪt] n (COMM,
GEOL) Konglomerat m

conglomeration [kənglɒmə'reɪʃən] n
Anhäufung f

congratulate [kən'grætjuleɪt] vt: **to ~ sb
(on sth)** jdn (zu etw) beglückwünschen;
congratulations [kəngrætju'leɪʃənz] npl
Glückwünsche pl; **congratulations!**
gratuliere!, herzlichen Glückwunsch!

congregate ['kɒŋgrɪgeɪt] vi sich
versammeln; **congregation** [kɒŋgrɪ'geɪʃən]
n Gemeinde f

congress ['kɒŋgres] n Kongress m; **C~man**
(irreg: US) n Mitglied nt des amerikanischen
Repräsentantenhauses

conifer ['kɒnɪfər] n Nadelbaum m

conjunction [kən'dʒʌŋkʃən] n Verbindung f;
(GRAM) Konjunktion f

conjunctivitis [kəndʒʌŋktɪ'vaɪtɪs] n
Bindehautentzündung f

conjure ['kʌndʒər] vi zaubern; **~ up** vt
heraufbeschwören; **~r** n Zauberkünstler(in)
m(f)

conk out [kɒŋk-] (inf) vi den Geist aufgeben

con man (irreg) n Schwindler m

connect [kə'nekt] vt verbinden; (ELEC)
anschließen; **to be ~ed with** eine
Beziehung haben zu; (be related to)
verwandt sein mit; **~ion** [kə'nekʃən] n
Verbindung f; (relation) Zusammenhang m;
(ELEC, TEL, RAIL) Anschluss m

connive [kə'naɪv] vi: **to ~ at** stillschweigend
dulden

connoisseur [kɒnɪ'sə:r] n Kenner m

conquer ['kɒŋkər] vt (feelings) überwinden;
(enemy) besiegen; (country) erobern; **~or** n
Eroberer m

conquest ['kɒŋkwest] n Eroberung f

cons [kɒnz] npl see **convenience**; **pro**

conscience ['kɒnʃəns] n Gewissen nt

conscientious [kɒnʃɪ'enʃəs] adj
gewissenhaft

conscious ['kɒnʃəs] adj bewusst; (MED) bei
Bewusstsein; **~ness** n Bewusstsein nt

conscript ['kɒnskrɪpt] n Wehrpflichtige(r) m;
~ion [kən'skrɪpʃən] n Wehrpflicht f

consecutive [kən'sekjutɪv] adj aufeinander
folgend

consensus [kən'sensəs] n allgemeine
Übereinstimmung f

consent [kən'sent] n Zustimmung f ♦ vi
zustimmen

consequence ['kɒnsɪkwəns] n (importance)
Bedeutung f; (effect) Folge f

consequently ['kɒnsɪkwəntlɪ] adv folglich

conservation [kɒnsə'veɪʃən] n Erhaltung f;
(nature ~) Umweltschutz m

conservative [kən'sə:vətɪv] adj konservativ;
C~ (BRIT) adj konservativ ♦ n
Konservative(r) mf

conservatory [kən'sə:vətrɪ] n (room)
Wintergarten m

conserve [kən'sə:v] vt erhalten

consider [kən'sɪdər] vt überlegen; (take into
account) in Betracht ziehen; (regard as)
halten für; **to ~ doing sth** daran denken,
etw zu tun; **~able** [kən'sɪdərəbl] adj

beträchtlich; **~ably** *adv* beträchtlich; **~ate** *adj* rücksichtsvoll; **~ation** [kənsɪdə'reɪʃən] *n* Rücksicht(nahme) *f*; (*thought*) Erwägung *f*; **~ing** *prep* in Anbetracht +*gen*

consign [kən'saɪn] *vt* übergeben; **~ment** *n* Sendung *f*

consist [kən'sɪst] *vi*: **to ~ of** bestehen aus

consistency [kən'sɪstənsɪ] *n* (*of material*) Konsistenz *f*; (*of argument, person*) Konsequenz *f*

consistent [kən'sɪstənt] *adj* (*person*) konsequent; (*argument*) folgerichtig

consolation [kɒnsə'leɪʃən] *n* Trost *m*

console¹ [kən'səul] *vt* trösten

console² ['kɒnsəul] *n* Kontroll(pult) *nt*

consolidate [kən'sɒlɪdeɪt] *vt* festigen

consommé [kən'sɒmeɪ] *n* Fleischbrühe *f*

consonant ['kɒnsənənt] *n* Konsonant *m*, Mitlaut *m*

conspicuous [kən'spɪkjuəs] *adj* (*prominent*) auffällig; (*visible*) deutlich sichtbar

conspiracy [kən'spɪrəsɪ] *n* Verschwörung *f*

conspire [kən'spaɪə⁹] *vi* sich verschwören

constable ['kʌnstəbl] (*BRIT*) *n* Polizist(in) *m(f)*; **chief ~** Polizeipräsident *m*; **constabulary** [kən'stæbjulərɪ] *n* Polizei *f*

constant ['kɒnstənt] *adj* (*continuous*) ständig; (*unchanging*) konstant; **~ly** *adv* ständig

constellation [kɒnstə'leɪʃən] *n* Sternbild *nt*

consternation [kɒnstə'neɪʃən] *n* Bestürzung *f*

constipated ['kɒnstɪpeɪtɪd] *adj* verstopft; **constipation** [kɒnstɪ'peɪʃən] *n* Verstopfung *f*

constituency [kən'stɪtjuənsɪ] *n* Wahlkreis *m*

constituent [kən'stɪtjuənt] *n* (*person*) Wähler *m*; (*part*) Bestandteil *m*

constitute ['kɒnstɪtjuːt] *vt* (*make up*) bilden; (*amount to*) darstellen

constitution [kɒnstɪ'tjuːʃən] *n* Verfassung *f*; **~al** *adj* Verfassungs-

constraint [kən'streɪnt] *n* Zwang *m*; (*shyness*) Befangenheit *f*

construct [kən'strʌkt] *vt* bauen; **~ion** [kən'strʌkʃən] *n* Konstruktion *f*; (*building*) Bau *m*; **~ive** *adj* konstruktiv

construe [kən'struː] *vt* deuten

consul ['kɒnsl] *n* Konsul *m*; **~ate** *n* Konsulat *nt*

consult [kən'sʌlt] *vt* um Rat fragen; (*doctor*) konsultieren; (*book*) nachschlagen in +*dat*; **~ant** *n* (*MED*) Facharzt *m*; (*other specialist*) Gutachter *m*; **~ation** [kɒnsəl'teɪʃən] *n* Beratung *f*; (*MED*) Konsultation *f*; **~ing room** *n* Sprechzimmer *nt*

consume [kən'sjuːm] *vt* verbrauchen; (*food*) konsumieren; **~r** *n* Verbraucher *m*; **~r goods** *npl* Konsumgüter *pl*; **~rism** *n* Konsum *m*; **~r society** *n* Konsumgesellschaft *f*

consummate ['kɒnsʌmeɪt] *vt* (*marriage*) vollziehen

consumption [kən'sʌmpʃən] *n* Verbrauch *m*; (*of food*) Konsum *m*

cont. *abbr* (= *continued*) Forts.

contact ['kɒntækt] *n* (*touch*) Berührung *f*; (*connection*) Verbindung *f*; (*person*) Kontakt *m* ♦ *vt* sich in Verbindung setzen mit; **~ lenses** *npl* Kontaktlinsen *pl*

contagious [kən'teɪdʒəs] *adj* ansteckend

contain [kən'teɪn] *vt* enthalten; **to ~ o.s.** sich zügeln; **~er** *n* Behälter *m*; (*transport*) Container *m*

contaminate [kən'tæmɪneɪt] *vt* verunreinigen

cont'd *abbr* (= *continued*) Forts.

contemplate ['kɒntəmpleɪt] *vt* (*look at*) (nachdenklich) betrachten; (*think about*) überdenken; (*plan*) vorhaben

contemporary [kən'tempərərɪ] *adj* zeitgenössisch ♦ *n* Zeitgenosse *m*

contempt [kən'tempt] *n* Verachtung *f*; **~ of court** (*JUR*) Missachtung *f* des Gerichts; **~ible** *adj* verachtenswert; **~uous** *adj* verächtlich

contend [kən'tend] *vt* (*argue*) behaupten ♦ *vi* kämpfen; **~er** *n* (*for post*) Bewerber(in) *m(f)*; (*SPORT*) Wettkämpfer(in) *m(f)*

content [*adj, vb* kən'tent, *n* 'kɒntent] *adj* zufrieden ♦ *vt* befriedigen ♦ *n* (*also*: **~s**) Inhalt *m*; **~ed** *adj* zufrieden

contention [kən'tenʃən] *n* (*dispute*) Streit *m*; (*argument*) Behauptung *f*

contentment [kən'tentmənt] *n* Zufriedenheit f

contest [n 'kɒntest, vb kən'test] n (Wett)kampf m ♦ vt (dispute) bestreiten; (JUR) anfechten; (POL) kandidieren in +dat; **~ant** [kən'testənt] n Bewerber(in) m(f)

context ['kɒntekst] n Zusammenhang m

continent ['kɒntinənt] n Kontinent m; **the C~** (BRIT) das europäische Festland; **~al** [kɒntɪ'nentl] adj kontinental; **~al breakfast** n kleines Frühstück nt; **~al quilt** (BRIT) n Federbett nt

contingency [kən'tɪndʒənsɪ] n Möglichkeit f

contingent [kən'tɪndʒənt] n Kontingent nt

continual [kən'tɪnjuəl] adj (endless) fortwährend; (repeated) immer wiederkehrend; **~ly** adv immer wieder

continuation [kəntɪnju'eɪʃən] n Fortsetzung f

continue [kən'tɪnjuː] vi (person) weitermachen; (thing) weitergehen ♦ vt fortsetzen

continuity [kɒntɪ'njuːɪtɪ] n Kontinuität f

continuous [kən'tɪnjuəs] adj ununterbrochen; **~ stationery** n Endlospapier nt

contort [kən'tɔːt] vt verdrehen; **~ion** [kən'tɔːʃən] n Verzerrung f

contour ['kɒntuəʳ] n Umriss m; (also: **~ line**) Höhenlinie f

contraband ['kɒntrəbænd] n Schmuggelware f

contraception [kɒntrə'sepʃən] n Empfängnisverhütung f

contraceptive [kɒntrə'septɪv] n empfängnisverhütende(s) Mittel nt ♦ adj empfängnisverhütend

contract [n 'kɒntrækt, vb kən'trækt] n Vertrag m ♦ vi (muscle, metal) sich zusammenziehen ♦ vt zusammenziehen; **to ~ to do sth** (COMM) sich vertraglich verpflichten, etw zu tun; **~ion** [kən'trækʃən] n (shortening) Verkürzung f; **~or** [kən'træktəʳ] n Unternehmer m

contradict [kɒntrə'dɪkt] vt widersprechen +dat; **~ion** [kɒntrə'dɪkʃən] n Widerspruch m

contraflow ['kɒntrəfləʊ] n (AUT) Gegenverkehr m

contraption [kən'træpʃən] (inf) n Apparat m

contrary¹ ['kɒntrərɪ] adj (opposite) entgegengesetzt ♦ n Gegenteil nt; **on the ~** im Gegenteil

contrary² [kən'treərɪ] adj (obstinate) widerspenstig

contrast [n 'kɒntrɑːst, vb kən'trɑːst] n Kontrast m ♦ vt entgegensetzen; **~ing** [kən'trɑːstɪŋ] adj Kontrast-

contravene [kɒntrə'viːn] vt verstoßen gegen

contribute [kən'trɪbjuːt] vt, vi: **to ~ to** beitragen zu; **contribution** [kɒntrɪ'bjuːʃən] n Beitrag m; **contributor** [kən'trɪbjutəʳ] n Beitragende(r) f(m)

contrive [kən'traɪv] vt ersinnen ♦ vi: **to ~ to do sth** es schaffen, etw zu tun

control [kən'trəʊl] vt (direct, test) kontrollieren ♦ n Kontrolle f; **~s** npl (of vehicle) Steuerung f; (of engine) Schalttafel f; **to be in ~ of** (business, office) leiten; (group of children) beaufsichtigen; **out of ~** außer Kontrolle; **under ~** unter Kontrolle; **~led substance** n verschreibungspflichtiges Medikament; **~ panel** n Schalttafel f; **~ room** n Kontrollraum m; **~ tower** n (AVIAT) Kontrollturm m

controversial [kɒntrə'vɜːʃl] adj umstritten; **controversy** ['kɒntrəvɜːsɪ] n Kontroverse f

conurbation [kɒnə'beɪʃən] n Ballungsgebiet nt

convalesce [kɒnvə'les] vi genesen; **convalescence** [kɒnvə'lesns] n Genesung f

convector [kən'vektəʳ] n Heizlüfter m

convene [kən'viːn] vt zusammenrufen ♦ vi sich versammeln

convenience [kən'viːnɪəns] n Annehmlichkeit f; **all modern ~s** or (BRIT) **mod cons** mit allem Komfort; **at your ~** wann es Ihnen passt

convenient [kən'viːnɪənt] adj günstig

convent ['kɒnvənt] n Kloster nt

convention [kən'venʃən] n Versammlung f; (custom) Konvention f; **~al** adj konventionell

convent school n Klosterschule f

converge [kən'vɜːdʒ] vi zusammenlaufen

conversant [kən'vɜːsnt] *adj*: **to be ~ with** bewandert sein in +*dat*

conversation [kɔnvə'seɪʃən] *n* Gespräch *nt*; **~al** *adj* Unterhaltungs-

converse [*n* 'kɔnvɜːs; *vb* kən'vɜːs] *n* Gegenteil *nt* ♦ *vi* sich unterhalten

conversion [kən'vɜːʃən] *n* Umwandlung *f*; (*REL*) Bekehrung *f*

convert [*vb* kən'vɜːt, *n* 'kɔnvɜːt] *vt* (*change*) umwandeln; (*REL*) bekehren ♦ *n* Bekehrte(r) *mf*; Konvertit(in) *m(f)*; **~ible** *n* (*AUT*) Kabriolett *nt* ♦ *adj* umwandelbar; (*FIN*) konvertierbar

convex ['kɔnveks] *adj* konvex

convey [kən'veɪ] *vt* (*carry*) befördern; (*feelings*) vermitteln; **~or belt** *n* Fließband *nt*

convict [*vb* kən'vɪkt, *n* 'kɔnvɪkt] *vt* verurteilen ♦ *n* Häftling *m*; **~ion** [kən'vɪkʃən] *n* (*verdict*) Verurteilung *f*; (*belief*) Überzeugung *f*

convince [kən'vɪns] *vt* überzeugen; **~d** *adj*: **~d that** überzeugt davon, dass; **convincing** *adj* überzeugend

convoluted ['kɔnvəluːtɪd] *adj* verwickelt; (*style*) gewunden

convoy ['kɔnvɔɪ] *n* (*of vehicles*) Kolonne *f*; (*protected*) Konvoi *m*

convulse [kən'vʌls] *vt* zusammenzucken lassen; **to be ~d with laughter** sich vor Lachen krümmen; **convulsion** [kən'vʌlʃən] *n* (*esp MED*) Zuckung *f*, Krampf *m*

coo [kuː] *vi* gurren

cook [kuk] *vt, vi* kochen ♦ *n* Koch *m*, Köchin *f*; **~ book** *n* Kochbuch *nt*; **~er** *n* Herd *m*; **~ery** *n* Kochkunst *f*; **~ery book** (*BRIT*) *n* = **cook book**; **~ie** (*US*) *n* Plätzchen *nt*; **~ing** *n* Kochen *nt*

cool [kuːl] *adj* kühl ♦ *vt, vi* (ab)kühlen; **~ down** *vt, vi* (*fig*) (sich) beruhigen; **~ness** *n* Kühle *f*; (*of temperament*) kühle(r) Kopf *m*

coop [kuːp] *n* Hühnerstall *m* ♦ *vt*: **~ up** (*fig*) einpferchen

cooperate [kəu'ɔpəreɪt] *vi* zusammenarbeiten; **cooperation** [kəuɔpə'reɪʃən] *n* Zusammenarbeit *f*

cooperative [kəu'ɔpərətɪv] *adj* hilfsbereit; (*COMM*) genossenschaftlich ♦ *n* (*of farmers*) Genossenschaft *f*; (~ *store*) Konsumladen *m*

coordinate [*vb* kəu'ɔːdɪneɪt, *n* kəu'ɔːdɪnət] *vt* koordinieren ♦ *n* (*MATH*) Koordinate *f*; **~s** *npl* (*clothes*) Kombinationen *pl*; **coordination** [kəuɔːdɪ'neɪʃən] *n* Koordination *f*

cop [kɔp] (*inf*) *n* Polyp *m*, Bulle *m*

cope [kəup] *vi*: **to ~ with** fertig werden mit

copious ['kəupɪəs] *adj* reichhaltig

copper ['kɔpə'] *n* (*metal*) Kupfer *nt*; (*inf: policeman*) Polyp *m*, Bulle *m*; **~s** *npl* (*money*) Kleingeld *nt*

copse [kɔps] *n* Unterholz *nt*

copy ['kɔpɪ] *n* (*imitation*) Kopie *f*; (*of book etc*) Exemplar *nt*; (*of newspaper*) Nummer *f* ♦ *vt* kopieren, abschreiben; **~right** *n* Copyright *nt*

coral ['kɔrəl] *n* Koralle *f*; **~ reef** *n* Korallenriff *nt*

cord [kɔːd] *n* Schnur *f*; (*ELEC*) Kabel *nt*

cordial ['kɔːdɪəl] *adj* herzlich ♦ *n* Fruchtsaft *m*

cordon ['kɔːdn] *n* Absperrkette *f*; **~ off** *vt* abriegeln

corduroy ['kɔːdərɔɪ] *n* Kord(samt) *m*

core [kɔː'] *n* Kern *m* ♦ *vt* entkernen

cork [kɔːk] *n* (*bark*) Korkrinde *f*; (*stopper*) Korken *m*; **~screw** *n* Korkenzieher *m*

corn [kɔːn] *n* (*BRIT: wheat*) Getreide *nt*, Korn *nt*; (*US: maize*) Mais *m*; (*on foot*) Hühnerauge *nt*; **~ on the cob** Maiskolben *m*

corned beef ['kɔːnd-] *n* Cornedbeef *nt*, Corned Beef *nt*

corner ['kɔːnə'] *n* Ecke *f*; (*on road*) Kurve *f* ♦ *vt* in die Enge treiben; (*market*) monopolisieren ♦ *vi* (*AUT*) in die Kurve gehen; **~stone** *n* Eckstein *m*

cornet ['kɔːnɪt] *n* (*MUS*) Kornett *nt*; (*BRIT: of ice cream*) Eistüte *f*

corn: ~flakes ['kɔːnfleɪks] *npl* Cornflakes *pl* ®; **~flour** ['kɔːnflauə'] (*BRIT*) *n* Maizena *nt* ®; **~starch** ['kɔːnstɑːtʃ] (*US*) *n* Maizena *nt* ®

corny ['kɔːnɪ] *adj* (*joke*) blöd(e)

coronary ['kɔrənərɪ] *n* (*also*: ~ **thrombosis**) Herzinfarkt *m*

coronation [kɔrəˈneɪʃən] n Krönung f

coroner [ˈkɔrənə] n Untersuchungsrichter m

corporal [ˈkɔːpərl] n Obergefreite(r) m ♦ adj: ~ **punishment** Prügelstrafe f

corporate [ˈkɔːpərɪt] adj gemeinschaftlich, korporativ

corporation [kɔːpəˈreɪʃən] n (of town) Gemeinde f; (COMM) Körperschaft f, Aktiengesellschaft f

corps [kɔːr] (pl ~) n (Armee)korps nt

corpse [kɔːps] n Leiche f

corral [kəˈrɑːl] n Pferch m, Korral m

correct [kəˈrekt] adj (accurate) richtig; (proper) korrekt ♦ vt korrigieren; ~**ion** [kəˈrekʃən] n Berichtigung f

correlation [kɔrɪˈleɪʃən] n Wechselbeziehung f

correspond [kɔrɪsˈpɔnd] vi (agree) übereinstimmen; (exchange letters) korrespondieren; ~**ence** n (similarity) Entsprechung f; (letters) Briefwechsel m, Korrespondenz f; ~**ence course** n Fernkurs m; ~**ent** n (PRESS) Berichterstatter m

corridor [ˈkɔrɪdɔːr] n Gang m

corroborate [kəˈrɔbəreɪt] vt bestätigen

corrode [kəˈrəud] vt zerfressen ♦ vi rosten

corrosion [kəˈrəuʒən] n Korrosion f

corrugated [ˈkɔrəgeɪtɪd] adj gewellt; ~ **iron** n Wellblech nt

corrupt [kəˈrʌpt] adj korrupt ♦ vt verderben; (bribe) bestechen; ~**ion** [kəˈrʌpʃən] n Verdorbenheit f; (bribery) Bestechung f

corset [ˈkɔːsɪt] n Korsett nt

Corsica [ˈkɔːsɪkə] n Korsika nt

cosmetics [kɔzˈmetɪks] npl Kosmetika pl

cosmic [ˈkɔzmɪk] adj kosmisch

cosmonaut [ˈkɔzmənɔːt] n Kosmonaut(in) m(f)

cosmopolitan [kɔzməˈpɔlɪtn] adj international; (city) Welt-

cosmos [ˈkɔzmɔs] n Kosmos m

cost [kɔst] n (pt, pp **cost**) n Kosten pl, Preis m ♦ vt, vi kosten; ~**s** npl (JUR) Kosten pl; **how much does it ~?** wie viel kostet das?; **at all ~s** um jeden Preis

co-star [ˈkəustɑːr] n zweite(r) or weitere(r) Hauptdarsteller(in) m(f)

cost: ~-**effective** adj rentabel; ~**ly** [ˈkɔstlɪ] adj kostspielig; ~-**of- living** [ˈkɔstəvˈlɪvɪŋ] adj (index) Lebenshaltungskosten-; ~ **price** (BRIT) n Selbstkostenpreis m

costume [ˈkɔstjuːm] n Kostüm nt; (fancy dress) Maskenkostüm nt; (BRIT: also: swimming ~) Badeanzug m; ~ **jewellery** n Modeschmuck m

cosy [ˈkəuzɪ] (BRIT) adj behaglich; (atmosphere) gemütlich

cot [kɔt] n (BRIT: child's) Kinderbett(chen) nt; (US: camp bed) Feldbett nt

cottage [ˈkɔtɪdʒ] n kleine(s) Haus nt; ~ **cheese** n Hüttenkäse m; ~ **industry** n Heimindustrie f; ~ **pie** n Auflauf mit Hackfleisch und Kartoffelbrei

cotton [ˈkɔtn] n Baumwolle f; (thread) Garn nt; ~ **on to** (inf) vt kapieren; ~ **candy** (US) n Zuckerwatte f; ~ **wool** (BRIT) n Watte f

couch [kautʃ] n Couch f

couchette [kuːˈʃet] n (on train, boat) Liegewagenplatz m

cough [kɔf] vi husten ♦ n Husten m; ~ **drop** n Hustenbonbon nt

could [kud] pt of **can²**

couldn't [ˈkudnt] = **could not**

council [ˈkaunsl] n (of town) Stadtrat m; ~ **estate** (BRIT) n Siedlung f des sozialen Wohnungsbaus; ~ **house** (BRIT) n Haus nt des sozialen Wohnungsbaus; ~**lor** [ˈkaunslər] n Stadtrat m/-rätin f

counsel [ˈkaunsl] n (barrister) Anwalt m; (advice) Rat(schlag) m ♦ vt beraten; ~**lor** [ˈkaunslər] n Berater m

count [kaunt] vt, vi zählen ♦ n (reckoning) Abrechnung f; (nobleman) Graf m; ~ **on** vt zählen auf +acc

countenance [ˈkauntɪnəns] n (old) Antlitz nt ♦ vt (tolerate) gutheißen

counter [ˈkauntər] n (in shop) Ladentisch m; (in café) Theke f; (in bank, post office) Schalter m ♦ vt entgegnen

counteract [ˈkauntərˈækt] vt entgegenwirken +dat

counterfeit [ˈkauntəfɪt] n Fälschung f ♦ vt fälschen ♦ adj gefälscht

counterfoil ['kauntəfɔɪl] n
(Kontroll)abschnitt m

counterpart ['kauntəpɑːt] n (object)
Gegenstück nt; (person) Gegenüber nt

counterproductive ['kauntəprə'dʌktɪv] adj
destruktiv

countersign ['kauntəsaɪn] vt gegenzeichnen

countess ['kauntɪs] n Gräfin f

countless ['kauntlɪs] adj zahllos, unzählig

country ['kʌntrɪ] n Land nt; ~ **dancing**
(BRIT) n Volkstanz m; ~ **house** n Landhaus
nt; ~**man** (irreg) n (national) Landsmann m;
(rural) Bauer m; ~**side** n Landschaft f

county ['kauntɪ] n Landkreis m; (BRIT)
Grafschaft f

coup [kuː] n (pl ~s) n Coup m; (also: ~ **d'état**)
Staatsstreich m, Putsch m

couple ['kʌpl] n Paar nt ♦ vt koppeln; **a ~ of**
ein paar

coupon ['kuːpɔn] n Gutschein m

coups [kuːs] npl of **coup**

courage ['kʌrɪdʒ] n Mut m; ~**ous**
[kə'reɪdʒəs] adj mutig

courgette [kuə'ʒet] (BRIT) n Zucchini f or pl

courier ['kurɪər] n (for holiday) Reiseleiter m;
(messenger) Kurier m

course [kɔːs] n (race) Bahn f; (of stream) Lauf
m; (golf ~) Platz m; (NAUT, SCH) Kurs m; (in
meal) Gang m; **of ~** natürlich

court [kɔːt] n (royal) Hof m; (JUR) Gericht nt
♦ vt (woman) gehen mit; (danger)
herausfordern; **to take to ~** vor Gericht
bringen

courteous ['kəːtɪəs] adj höflich

courtesy ['kəːtəsɪ] n Höflichkeit f

courtesy bus, courtesy coach n
gebührenfreier Bus m

court: ~ **house** (US) n Gerichtsgebäude nt;
~**ier** ['kɔːtɪər] n Höfling m; ~ **martial**
['kɔːt'mɑːʃəl] (pl ~**s martial**) n Kriegsgericht
nt ♦ vt vor ein Kriegsgericht stellen; ~**room**
n Gerichtssaal m; ~**s martial** npl of **court
martial**; ~**yard** ['kɔːtjɑːd] n Hof m

cousin ['kʌzn] n Cousin m, Vetter m; Kusine
f

cove [kəuv] n kleine Bucht f

covenant ['kʌvənənt] n (ECCL) Bund m; (JUR)

Verpflichtung f

cover ['kʌvər] vt (spread over) bedecken;
(shield) abschirmen; (include) sich erstrecken
über +acc; (protect) decken; (distance)
zurücklegen; (report on) berichten über +acc
♦ n (lid) Deckel m; (for bed) Decke f; (MIL)
Bedeckung f; (of book) Einband m; (of
magazine) Umschlag m; (insurance)
Versicherung f; **to take ~** (from rain) sich
unterstellen; (MIL) in Deckung gehen;
under ~ (indoors) drinnen; **under ~ of** im
Schutze +gen; **under separate ~** (COMM)
mit getrennter Post; **to ~ up for sb** jdn
decken; ~**age** n (PRESS: reports)
Berichterstattung f; (distribution)
Verbreitung f; ~ **charge** n Bedienungsgeld
nt; ~**ing** n Bedeckung f; ~**ing letter** (US ~
letter) n Begleitbrief m; ~ **note** n
(INSURANCE) vorläufige(r)
Versicherungsschein m

covert ['kʌvət] adj geheim

cover-up ['kʌvərʌp] n Vertuschung f

cow [kau] n Kuh f ♦ vt einschüchtern

coward ['kauəd] n Feigling m; ~**ice**
['kauədɪs] n Feigheit f; ~**ly** adj feige

cower ['kauər] vi kauern

coy [kɔɪ] adj schüchtern

coyote [kɔɪ'əutɪ] n Präriewolf m

cozy ['kəuzɪ] (US) adj = **cosy**

CPA (US) n abbr = **certified public
accountant**

crab [kræb] n Krebs m

crab apple n Holzapfel m

crack [kræk] n Riss m, Sprung m; (noise)
Knall m; (drug) Crack nt ♦ vt (break)
springen lassen; (joke) reißen; (nut, safe)
knacken; (whip) knallen lassen ♦ vi springen
♦ adj erstklassig; (troops) Elite-; ~ **down** vi:
to ~ down (on) hart durchgreifen (bei); ~
up vi (fig) zusammenbrechen

cracked [krækt] adj (glass, plate, ice)
gesprungen; (rib, bone) gebrochen,
angeknackst (umg); (broken) gebrochen;
(surface, walls) rissig; (inf: mad)
übergeschnappt

cracker ['krækər] n (firework) Knallkörper m,
Kracher m; (biscuit) Keks m; (Christmas ~)

Knallbonbon *nt*

crackle ['krækl] *vi* knistern; (*fire*) prasseln

cradle ['kreɪdl] *n* Wiege *f*

craft [krɑːft] *n* (*skill*) (Hand- or Kunst)fertigkeit *f*; (*trade*) Handwerk *nt*; (*NAUT*) Schiff *nt*; **~sman** (*irreg*) *n* Handwerker *m*; **~smanship** *n* (*quality*) handwerkliche Ausführung *f*; (*ability*) handwerkliche(s) Können *nt*

crafty ['krɑːftɪ] *adj* schlau

crag [kræg] *n* Klippe *f*

cram [kræm] *vt* voll stopfen ♦ *vi* (*learn*) pauken; **to ~ sth into sth** etw in etw *acc* stopfen

cramp [kræmp] *n* Krampf *m* ♦ *vt* (*limit*) einengen; (*hinder*) hemmen; **~ed** *adj* (*position*) verkrampft; (*space*) eng

crampon ['kræmpən] *n* Steigeisen *nt*

cranberry ['krænbərɪ] *n* Preiselbeere *f*

crane [kreɪn] *n* (*machine*) Kran *m*; (*bird*) Kranich *m*

crank [kræŋk] *n* (*lever*) Kurbel *f*; (*person*) Spinner *m*; **~shaft** *n* Kurbelwelle *f*

cranny ['krænɪ] *n see* **nook**

crash [kræʃ] *n* (*noise*) Krachen *nt*; (*with cars*) Zusammenstoß *m*; (*with plane*) Absturz *m*; (*COMM*) Zusammenbruch *m* ♦ *vt* (*plane*) abstürzen mit ♦ *vi* (*cars*) zusammenstoßen; (*plane*) abstürzen; (*economy*) zusammenbrechen; (*noise*) knallen; **~ course** *n* Schnellkurs *m*; **~ helmet** *n* Sturzhelm *m*; **~ landing** *n* Bruchlandung *f*

crass [kræs] *adj* krass

crate [kreɪt] *n* (*also fig*) Kiste *f*

crater ['kreɪtə^r] *n* Krater *m*

cravat(e) [krə'væt] *n* Halstuch *nt*

crave [kreɪv] *vt* verlangen nach

crawl [krɔːl] *vi* kriechen; (*baby*) krabbeln ♦ *n* Kriechen *nt*; (*swim*) Kraul *nt*

crayfish ['kreɪfɪʃ] *n inv* (*freshwater*) Krebs *m*; (*saltwater*) Languste *f*

crayon ['kreɪən] *n* Buntstift *m*

craze [kreɪz] *n* Fimmel *m*

crazy ['kreɪzɪ] *adj* verrückt

creak [kriːk] *vi* knarren

cream [kriːm] *n* (*from milk*) Rahm *m*, Sahne *f*; (*polish, cosmetic*) Creme *f*; (*fig: people*) Elite *f* ♦ *adj* cremefarbig; **~ cake** *n* Sahnetorte *f*; **~ cheese** *n* Rahmquark *m*; **~y** *adj* sahnig

crease [kriːs] *n* Falte *f* ♦ *vt* falten; (*wrinkle*) zerknittern ♦ *vi* (*wrinkle up*) knittern; **~d** *adj* zerknittert, faltig

create [kriː'eɪt] *vt* erschaffen; (*cause*) verursachen; **creation** [kriː'eɪʃən] *n* Schöpfung *f*; **creative** *adj* kreativ; **creator** *n* Schöpfer *m*

creature ['kriːtʃə^r] *n* Geschöpf *nt*

crèche [krɛʃ] *n* Krippe *f*

credence ['kriːdns] *n*: **to lend** or **give ~ to sth** etw *dat* Glauben schenken

credentials [krɪ'dɛnʃlz] *npl* Beglaubigungsschreiben *nt*

credibility [krɛdɪ'bɪlɪtɪ] *n* Glaubwürdigkeit *f*

credible ['krɛdɪbl] *adj* (*person*) glaubwürdig; (*story*) glaubhaft

credit ['krɛdɪt] *n* (*also COMM*) Kredit *m* ♦ *vt* Glauben schenken +*dat*; (*COMM*) gutschreiben; **~s** *npl* (*of film*) Mitwirkenden *pl*; **~able** *adj* rühmlich; **~ card** *n* Kreditkarte *f*; **~or** *n* Gläubiger *m*

creed [kriːd] *n* Glaubensbekenntnis *nt*

creek [kriːk] *n* (*inlet*) kleine Bucht *f*; (*US: river*) kleine(r) Wasserlauf *m*

creep [kriːp] (*pt, pp* **crept**) *vi* kriechen; **~er** *n* Kletterpflanze *f*; **~y** *adj* (*frightening*) gruselig

cremate [krɪ'meɪt] *vt* einäschern; **cremation** [krɪ'meɪʃən] *n* Einäscherung *f*; **crematorium** [krɛmə'tɔːrɪəm] *n* Krematorium *nt*

crêpe [kreɪp] *n* Krepp *m*; **~ bandage** (*BRIT*) *n* Elastikbinde *f*

crept [krɛpt] *pt, pp of* **creep**

crescent ['krɛsnt] *n* (*of moon*) Halbmond *m*

cress [krɛs] *n* Kresse *f*

crest [krɛst] *n* (*of cock*) Kamm *m*; (*of wave*) Wellenkamm *m*; (*coat of arms*) Wappen *nt*

crestfallen ['krɛstfɔːlən] *adj* niedergeschlagen

Crete [kriːt] *n* Kreta *nt*

crevice ['krɛvɪs] *n* Riss *m*

crew [kruː] *n* Besatzung *f*, Mannschaft *f*; **~-cut** *n* Bürstenschnitt *m*; **~ neck** *n* runde(r)

Ausschnitt m

crib [krɪb] n (bed) Krippe f ♦ vt (inf) spicken

crick [krɪk] n Muskelkrampf m

cricket ['krɪkɪt] n (insect) Grille f; (game) Kricket nt

crime [kraɪm] n Verbrechen nt

criminal ['krɪmɪnl] n Verbrecher m ♦ adj kriminell; (act) strafbar

crimson ['krɪmzn] adj leuchtend rot

cringe [krɪndʒ] vi sich ducken

crinkle ['krɪŋkl] vt zerknittern

cripple ['krɪpl] n Krüppel m ♦ vt lahm legen; (MED) verkrüppeln

crisis ['kraɪsɪs] (pl **crises**) n Krise f

crisp [krɪsp] adj knusprig; ~s (BRIT) npl Chips pl

crisscross ['krɪskrɔs] adj gekreuzt, Kreuz-

criteria [kraɪ'tɪərɪə] npl of **criterion**

criterion [kraɪ'tɪərɪən] (pl **criteria**) n Kriterium nt

critic ['krɪtɪk] n Kritiker(in) m(f); ~al adj kritisch; ~ally adv kritisch; (ill) gefährlich; ~ism ['krɪtɪsɪzəm] n Kritik f; ~ize ['krɪtɪsaɪz] vt kritisieren

croak [krəuk] vi krächzen; (frog) quaken

Croatia [krəu'eɪʃə] n Kroatien nt

crochet ['krəuʃeɪ] n Häkelei f

crockery ['krɔkərɪ] n Geschirr nt

crocodile ['krɔkədaɪl] n Krokodil nt

crocus ['krəukəs] n Krokus m

croft [krɔft] (BRIT) n kleine(s) Pachtgut nt

crony ['krəunɪ] (inf) n Kumpel m

crook [kruk] n (criminal) Gauner m; (stick) Hirtenstab m

crooked ['krukɪd] adj krumm

crop [krɔp] n (harvest) Ernte f; (riding ~) Reitpeitsche f ♦ vt ernten; ~ **up** vi passieren

croquet ['krəukeɪ] n Krocket nt

croquette [krə'ket] n Krokette f

cross [krɔs] n Kreuz nt ♦ vt (road) überqueren; (legs) übereinander legen; kreuzen ♦ adj (annoyed) böse; ~ **out** vt streichen; ~ **over** vi hinübergehen; ~**bar** n Querstange f; ~**-country** (race) n Geländelauf m; ~**-examine** vt ins Kreuzverhör nehmen; ~**-eyed** adj: to be

~**-eyed** schielen; ~**fire** n Kreuzfeuer nt; ~**ing** n (~roads) (Straßen)kreuzung f; (of ship) Überfahrt f; (for pedestrians) Fußgängerüberweg m; ~**ing guard** (US) n Schülerlotse m; ~ **purposes** npl: to be at ~ **purposes** aneinander vorbeireden; ~**reference** n Querverweis m; ~**roads** n Straßenkreuzung f; (fig) Scheideweg m; ~ **section** n Querschnitt m; ~**walk** (US) n Fußgängerüberweg m; ~**wind** n Seitenwind m; ~**word (puzzle)** n Kreuzworträtsel nt

crotch [krɔtʃ] n Zwickel m; (ANAT) Unterleib nt

crouch [krautʃ] vi hocken

crow [krəu] n (bird) Krähe f; (of cock) Krähen nt ♦ vi krähen

crowbar ['krəubɑ:] n Stemmeisen nt

crowd [kraud] n Menge f ♦ vt (fill) überfüllen ♦ vi drängen; ~**ed** adj überfüllt

crown [kraun] n Krone f; (of head, hat) Kopf m ♦ vt krönen; ~ **jewels** npl Kronjuwelen pl; ~ **prince** n Kronprinz m

crow's-feet ['krəuzfi:t] npl Krähenfüße pl

crucial ['kru:ʃl] adj entscheidend

crucifix ['kru:sɪfɪks] n Kruzifix nt; ~**ion** [kru:sɪ'fɪkʃən] n Kreuzigung f

crude [kru:d] adj (raw) roh; (humour, behaviour) grob; (basic) primitiv; ~ **(oil)** n Rohöl nt

cruel ['kruəl] adj grausam; ~**ty** n Grausamkeit f

cruise [kru:z] n Kreuzfahrt f ♦ vi kreuzen; ~**r** n (MIL) Kreuzer m

crumb [krʌm] n Krume f

crumble ['krʌmbl] vt, vi zerbröckeln; **crumbly** adj krümelig

crumpet ['krʌmpɪt] n Tee(pfann)kuchen m

crumple ['krʌmpl] vt zerknittern

crunch [krʌntʃ] n: the ~ (fig) der Knackpunkt ♦ vt knirschen; ~**y** adj knusprig

crusade [kru:'seɪd] n Kreuzzug m

crush [krʌʃ] n Gedränge nt ♦ vt zerdrücken; (rebellion) unterdrücken

crust [krʌst] n Kruste f

crutch [krʌtʃ] n Krücke f

crux [krʌks] n springende(r) Punkt m

cry [kraɪ] vi (shout) schreien; (weep) weinen ♦ n (call) Schrei m; **~ off** vi (plötzlich) absagen

crypt [krɪpt] n Krypta f

cryptic ['krɪptɪk] adj hintergründig

crystal ['krɪstl] n Kristall m; (glass) Kristallglas nt; (mineral) Bergkristall m; **~-clear** adj kristallklar

crystallize ['krɪstəlaɪz] vt, vi kristallisieren; (fig) klären

CSA n abbr (= Child Support Agency) Amt zur Regelung von Unterhaltszahlungen für Kinder

CTC (BRIT) n abbr = **city technology college**

cub [kʌb] n Junge(s) nt; (also: **C~ scout**) Wölfling m

Cuba ['kju:bə] n Kuba nt; **~n** adj kubanisch ♦ n Kubaner(in) m(f)

cubbyhole ['kʌbɪhəul] n Eckchen nt

cube [kju:b] n Würfel m ♦ vt (MATH) hoch drei nehmen

cubic ['kju:bɪk] adj würfelförmig; (centimetre etc) Kubik-; **~ capacity** n Fassungsvermögen nt

cubicle ['kju:bɪkl] n Kabine f

cuckoo ['kuku:] n Kuckuck m; **~ clock** n Kuckucksuhr f

cucumber ['kju:kʌmbə'] n Gurke f

cuddle ['kʌdl] vt, vi herzen, drücken (inf)

cue [kju:] n (THEAT) Stichwort nt; (snooker ~) Billardstock m

cuff [kʌf] n (BRIT: of shirt, coat etc) Manschette f; Aufschlag m; (US) = **turn-up**; **off the ~** aus dem Handgelenk; **~link** n Manschettenknopf m

cuisine [kwɪ'zi:n] n Kochkunst f, Küche f

cul-de-sac ['kʌldəsæk] n Sackgasse f

culinary ['kʌlɪnərɪ] adj Koch-

cull [kʌl] vt (select) auswählen

culminate ['kʌlmɪneɪt] vi gipfeln; **culmination** [kʌlmɪ'neɪʃən] n Höhepunkt m

culottes [kju:'lɒts] npl Hosenrock m

culpable ['kʌlpəbl] adj schuldig

culprit ['kʌlprɪt] n Täter m

cult [kʌlt] n Kult m

cultivate ['kʌltɪveɪt] vt (AGR) bebauen; (mind) bilden; **cultivation** [kʌltɪ'veɪʃən] n

(AGR) Bebauung f; (of person) Bildung f

cultural ['kʌltʃərəl] adj kulturell, Kultur-

culture ['kʌltʃə'] n Kultur f; **~d** adj gebildet

cumbersome ['kʌmbəsəm] adj (object) sperrig

cumulative ['kju:mjulətɪv] adj gehäuft

cunning ['kʌnɪŋ] n Verschlagenheit f ♦ adj schlau

cup [kʌp] n Tasse f; (prize) Pokal m

cupboard ['kʌbəd] n Schrank m

cup tie (BRIT) n Pokalspiel nt

curate ['kjuərɪt] n (Catholic) Kurat m; (Protestant) Vikar m

curator [kjuə'reɪtə'] n Kustos m

curb [kə:b] vt zügeln ♦ n (on spending etc) Einschränkung f; (US) Bordstein m

curdle ['kə:dl] vi gerinnen

cure [kjuə'] n Heilmittel nt; (process) Heilverfahren nt ♦ vt heilen

curfew ['kə:fju:] n Ausgangssperre f; Sperrstunde f

curio ['kjuərɪəu] n Kuriosität f

curiosity [kjuərɪ'ɔsɪtɪ] n Neugier f

curious ['kjuərɪəs] adj neugierig; (strange) seltsam

curl [kə:l] n Locke f ♦ vt locken ♦ vi sich locken; **~ up** vi sich zusammenrollen; (person) sich ankuscheln; **~er** n Lockenwickler m; **~y** ['kə:lɪ] adj lockig

currant ['kʌrnt] n Korinthe f

currency ['kʌrnsɪ] n Währung f; **to gain ~** an Popularität gewinnen

current ['kʌrnt] n Strömung f ♦ adj (expression) gängig, üblich; (issue) neueste; **~ account** (BRIT) n Girokonto nt; **~ affairs** npl Zeitgeschehen nt; **~ly** adv zurzeit

curricula [kə'rɪkjulə] npl of **curriculum**

curriculum [kə'rɪkjuləm] (pl **~s** or **curricula**) n Lehrplan m; **~ vitae** [-'vi:taɪ] n Lebenslauf m

curry ['kʌrɪ] n Currygericht nt ♦ vt: **to ~ favour with** sich einschmeicheln bei; **~ powder** n Curry(pulver) nt

curse [kə:s] vi (swear): **to ~ (at)** fluchen (auf or über +acc) ♦ vt (insult) verwünschen ♦ n Fluch m

cursor ['kə:sə'] n (COMPUT) Cursor m

cursory ['kə:sərɪ] *adj* flüchtig

curt [kə:t] *adj* schroff

curtail [kə:'teɪl] *vt* abkürzen; (*rights*) einschränken

curtain ['kə:tn] *n* Vorhang *m*

curts(e)y ['kə:tsɪ] *n* Knicks *m* ♦ *vi* knicksen

curve [kə:v] *n* Kurve *f*; (*of body, vase etc*) Rundung *f* ♦ *vi* sich biegen; (*hips, breasts*) sich runden; (*road*) einen Bogen machen

cushion ['kuʃən] *n* Kissen *nt* ♦ *vt* dämpfen

custard ['kʌstəd] *n* Vanillesoße *f*

custodian [kʌs'təudiən] *n* Kustos *m*, Verwalter(in) *m(f)*

custody ['kʌstədɪ] *n* Aufsicht *f*; (*police ~*) Haft *f*; **to take into ~** verhaften

custom ['kʌstəm] *n* (*tradition*) Brauch *m*; (*COMM*) Kundschaft *f*; **~ary** *adj* üblich

customer ['kʌstəmə*] *n* Kunde *m*, Kundin *f*

customized ['kʌstəmaɪzd] *adj* (*car etc*) mit Spezialausrüstung

custom-made ['kʌstəm'meɪd] *adj* speziell angefertigt

customs ['kʌstəmz] *npl* Zoll *m*; **~ duty** *n* Zollabgabe *f*; **~ officer** *n* Zollbeamte(r) *m*, Zollbeamtin *f*

cut [kʌt] (*pt, pp* **cut**) *vt* schneiden; (*wages*) kürzen; (*prices*) heruntersetzen ♦ *vi* schneiden; (*intersect*) sich schneiden ♦ *n* Schnitt *m*; (*wound*) Schnittwunde *f*; (*in income etc*) Kürzung *f*; (*share*) Anteil *m*; **to ~ a tooth** zahnen; **~ down** *vt* (*tree*) fällen; (*reduce*) einschränken; **~ off** *vt* (*also fig*) abschneiden; (*allowance*) sperren; **~ out** *vt* (*shape*) ausschneiden; (*delete*) streichen; **~ up** *vt* (*meat*) aufschneiden; **~back** *n* Kürzung *f*

cute [kju:t] *adj* niedlich

cuticle ['kju:tɪkl] *n* Nagelhaut *f*

cutlery ['kʌtlərɪ] *n* Besteck *nt*

cutlet ['kʌtlɪt] *n* (*pork*) Kotelett *nt*; (*veal*) Schnitzel *nt*

cut: ~out *n* (*cardboard ~out*) Ausschneidemodell *nt*; **~-price, ~-rate** (*US*) *adj* verbilligt; **~throat** *n* Verbrechertyp *m* ♦ *adj* mörderisch

cutting ['kʌtɪŋ] *adj* schneidend ♦ *n* (*BRIT: PRESS*) Ausschnitt *m*; (*: RAIL*) Durchstich *m*

CV *n abbr* = **curriculum vitae**

cwt *abbr* = **hundredweight(s)**

cyanide ['saɪənaɪd] *n* Zyankali *nt*

cybercafé ['saɪbəkæfeɪ] *n* Internet-Café *nt*

cyberspace ['saɪbəspeɪs] *n* Cyberspace *m*

cycle ['saɪkl] *n* Fahrrad *nt*; (*series*) Reihe *f* ♦ *vi* Rad fahren; **~ hire** *n* Fahrradverleih *m*; **~ lane, ~ path** *n* (Fahr)radweg *m*; **cycling** *n* Radfahren *nt*; **cyclist** *n* Radfahrer(in) *m(f)*

cyclone ['saɪkləun] *n* Zyklon *m*

cygnet ['sɪgnɪt] *n* junge(r) Schwan *m*

cylinder ['sɪlɪndə*] *n* Zylinder *m*; (*TECH*) Walze *f*

cymbals ['sɪmblz] *npl* Becken *pl*

cynic ['sɪnɪk] *n* Zyniker(in) *m(f)*; **~al** *adj* zynisch; **~ism** ['sɪnɪsɪzəm] *n* Zynismus *m*

cypress ['saɪprɪs] *n* Zypresse *f*

Cyprus ['saɪprəs] *n* Zypern *nt*

cyst [sɪst] *n* Zyste *f*

cystitis [sɪs'taɪtɪs] *n* Blasenentzündung *f*

czar [za:*] *n* Zar *m*

Czech [tʃek] *adj* tschechisch ♦ *n* Tscheche *m*, Tschechin *f*

Czechoslovakia [tʃekəslə'vækɪə] (*HIST*) *n* die Tschechoslowakei; **~n** *adj* tschechoslowakisch ♦ *n* Tschechoslowake *m*, Tschechoslowakin *f*

D, d

D [di:] *n* (*MUS*) D *nt*

dab [dæb] *vt* (*wound, paint*) betupfen ♦ *n* (*little bit*) bisschen *nt*; (*of paint*) Tupfer *m*

dabble ['dæbl] *vi*: **to ~ in sth** in etw *dat* machen

dad [dæd] *n* Papa *m*, Vati *m*; **~dy** ['dædɪ] *n* Papa *m*, Vati *m*; **~dy-long-legs** *n* Weberknecht *m*

daffodil ['dæfədɪl] *n* Osterglocke *f*

daft [da:ft] (*inf*) *adj* blöd(e), doof

dagger ['dægə*] *n* Dolch *m*

daily ['deɪlɪ] *adj* täglich ♦ *n* (*PRESS*) Tageszeitung *f*; (*BRIT: cleaner*) Haushaltshilfe *f* ♦ *adv* täglich

dainty ['deɪntɪ] *adj* zierlich

dairy ['deərɪ] *n* (*shop*) Milchgeschäft *nt*; (*on*

farm) Molkerei *f* ♦ *adj* Milch-; ~ **farm** *n* Hof *m* mit Milchwirtschaft; ~ **produce** *n* Molkereiprodukte *pl*; ~ **products** *npl* Milchprodukte *pl*, Molkereiprodukte *pl*; ~ **store** (*US*) *n* Milchgeschäft *nt*

dais ['deɪɪs] *n* Podium *nt*

daisy ['deɪzɪ] *n* Gänseblümchen *nt*

dale [deɪl] *n* Tal *nt*

dam [dæm] *n* (Stau)damm *m* ♦ *vt* stauen

damage ['dæmɪdʒ] *n* Schaden *m* ♦ *vt* beschädigen; ~**s** *npl* (*JUR*) Schaden(s)ersatz *m*

damn [dæm] *vt* verdammen ♦ *n* (*inf*): **I don't give a** ~ das ist mir total egal ♦ *adj* (*inf*: *also*: ~**ed**) verdammt; ~ **it!** verflucht!; ~**ing** *adj* vernichtend

damp [dæmp] *adj* feucht ♦ *n* Feuchtigkeit *f* ♦ *vt* (*also*: ~**en**) befeuchten; (*discourage*) dämpfen

damson ['dæmzən] *n* Damaszenerpflaume *f*

dance [dɑ:ns] *n* Tanz *m* ♦ *vi* tanzen; ~ **hall** *n* Tanzlokal *nt*; ~**r** *n* Tänzer(in) *m(f)*; **dancing** *n* Tanzen *nt*

dandelion ['dændɪlaɪən] *n* Löwenzahn *m*

dandruff ['dændrəf] *n* (Kopf)schuppen *pl*

Dane [deɪn] *n* Däne *m*, Dänin *f*

danger ['deɪndʒə*] *n* Gefahr *f*; ~**!** (*sign*) Achtung!; **to be in** ~ **of doing sth** Gefahr laufen, etw zu tun; ~**ous** *adj* gefährlich

dangle ['dæŋgl] *vi* baumeln ♦ *vt* herabhängen lassen

Danish ['deɪnɪʃ] *adj* dänisch ♦ *n* Dänisch *nt*

dare [dɛə*] *vt* herausfordern ♦ *vi*: **to** ~ (**to**) **do sth** es wagen, etw zu tun; **I** ~ **say** ich würde sagen; **daring** ['dɛərɪŋ] *adj* (*audacious*) verwegen; (*bold*) wagemutig; (*dress*) gewagt ♦ *n* Mut *m*

dark [dɑ:k] *adj* dunkel; (*fig*) düster, trübe; (*deep colour*) dunkel- ♦ *n* Dunkelheit *f*; **to be left in the** ~ **about** im Dunkeln sein über +*acc*; **after** ~ nach Anbruch der Dunkelheit; ~**en** *vt*, *vi* verdunkeln; ~ **glasses** *npl* Sonnenbrille *f*; ~**ness** *n* Finsternis *nt*; ~**room** *n* Dunkelkammer *f*

darling ['dɑ:lɪŋ] *n* Liebling *m* ♦ *adj* lieb

darn [dɑ:n] *vt* stopfen

dart [dɑ:t] *n* (*weapon*) Pfeil *m*; (*in sewing*) Abnäher *m* ♦ *vi* sausen; ~**s** *n* (*game*) Pfeilwerfen *nt*; ~**board** *n* Zielscheibe *f*

dash [dæʃ] *n* Sprung *m*; (*mark*) (Gedanken)strich *m*; (*small amount*) bisschen *nt* ♦ *vt* (*hopes*) zunichte machen ♦ *vi* stürzen; ~ **away** *vi* davonstürzen; ~ **off** *vi* davonstürzen

dashboard ['dæʃbɔ:d] *n* Armaturenbrett *nt*

dashing ['dæʃɪŋ] *adj* schneidig

data ['deɪtə] *npl* Einzelheiten *pl*, Daten *pl*; ~**base** *n* Datenbank *f*; ~ **processing** *n* Datenverarbeitung *f*

date [deɪt] *n* Datum *nt*; (*for meeting etc*) Termin *m*; (*with person*) Verabredung *f*; (*fruit*) Dattel *f* ♦ *vt* (*letter etc*) datieren; (*person*) gehen mit; ~ **of birth** Geburtsdatum *nt*; **to** ~ bis heute; **out of** ~ überholt; **up to** ~ (*clothes*) modisch; (*report*) up-to-date; (*with news*) auf dem Laufenden; ~**d** *adj* altmodisch; ~ **rape** *n* Vergewaltigung *f* nach einem Rendezvous

daub [dɔ:b] *vt* beschmieren; (*paint*) schmieren

daughter ['dɔ:tə*] *n* Tochter *f*; ~~**-in-law** *n* Schwiegertochter *f*

daunting ['dɔ:ntɪŋ] *adj* entmutigend

dawdle ['dɔ:dl] *vi* trödeln

dawn [dɔ:n] *n* Morgendämmerung *f* ♦ *vi* dämmern; (*fig*): **it** ~**ed on him that ...** es dämmerte ihm, dass ...

day [deɪ] *n* Tag *m*; **the** ~ **before/after** am Tag zuvor/danach; **the** ~ **after tomorrow** übermorgen; **the** ~ **before yesterday** vorgestern; **by** ~ am Tage; ~**break** *n* Tagesanbruch *m*; ~**dream** *vi* mit offenen Augen träumen; ~**light** *n* Tageslicht *nt*; ~ **return** (*BRIT*) *n* Tagesrückfahrkarte *f*; ~**time** *n* Tageszeit *f*; ~~**to**~~ *adj* alltäglich

daze [deɪz] *vt* betäuben ♦ *n* Betäubung *f*; **in a** ~ benommen

dazzle ['dæzl] *vt* blenden

DC *abbr* (= *direct current*) Gleichstrom *m*

D-day ['di:deɪ] *n* (*HIST*) Tag der Invasion durch die Alliierten (6.6.44); (*fig*) der Tag X

deacon ['di:kən] *n* Diakon *m*

dead [ded] *adj* tot; (*without feeling*) gefühllos ♦ *adv* ganz; (*exactly*) genau; *npl*: **the** ~ die

Toten *pl*; **to shoot sb ~** jdn erschießen; **~ tired** todmüde; **to stop ~** abrupt stehen bleiben; **~en** *vt* (*pain*) abtöten; (*sound*) ersticken; **~ end** *n* Sackgasse *f*; **~ heat** *n* tote(s) Rennen *nt*; **~line** *n* Stichtag *m*; **~lock** *n* Stillstand *m*; **~ loss** (*inf*) *n*: **to be a ~ loss** ein hoffnungsloser Fall sein; **~ly** *adj* tödlich; **~pan** *adj* undurchdringlich; **D~ Sea** *n*: **the D~ Sea** das Tote Meer

deaf [dɛf] *adj* taub; **~en** *vt* taub machen; **~ening** *adj* (*noise*) ohrenbetäubend; (*noise*) lautstark; **~-mute** *n* Taubstumme(r) *mf*; **~ness** *n* Taubheit *f*

deal [diːl] (*pt, pp* **dealt**) *n* Geschäft *nt* ♦ *vt* austeilen; (*CARDS*) geben; **a great ~ of** sehr viel; **~ in** *vt fus* handeln mit; **~ with** *vt fus* (*person*) behandeln; (*subject*) sich befassen mit; (*problem*) in Angriff nehmen; **~er** *n* (*COMM*) Händler *m*; (*CARDS*) Kartengeber *m*; **~ings** *npl* (*FIN*) Geschäfte *pl*; (*relations*) Beziehungen *pl*; **~t** [dɛlt] *pt, pp of* **deal**

dean [diːn] *n* (*Protestant*) Superintendent *m*; (*Catholic*) Dechant *m*; (*UNIV*) Dekan *m*

dear [dɪəʳ] *adj* lieb; (*expensive*) teuer ♦ *excl*: **~ me!** du liebe Zeit!; **D~ Sir** Sehr geehrter Herr!; **D~ John** Lieber John!; **~ly** *adv* (*love*) herzlich; (*pay*) teuer

death [dɛθ] *n* Tod *m*; (*statistic*) Todesfall *m*; **~ certificate** *n* Totenschein *m*; **~ly** *adj* totenähnlich, Toten-; **~ penalty** *n* Todesstrafe *f*; **~ rate** *n* Sterblichkeitsziffer *f*

debar [dɪˈbɑːʳ] *vt* ausschließen

debase [dɪˈbeɪs] *vt* entwerten

debatable [dɪˈbeɪtəbl] *adj* anfechtbar

debate [dɪˈbeɪt] *n* Debatte *f* ♦ *vt* debattieren, diskutieren; (*consider*) überlegen

debilitating [dɪˈbɪlɪteɪtɪŋ] *adj* schwächend

debit [ˈdɛbɪt] *n* Schuldposten *m* ♦ *vt* belasten

debris [ˈdɛbriː] *n* Trümmer *pl*

debt [dɛt] *n* Schuld *f*; **to be in ~** verschuldet sein; **~or** *n* Schuldner *m*

debunk [diːˈbʌŋk] *vt* entlarven

decade [ˈdɛkeɪd] *n* Jahrzehnt *nt*

decadence [ˈdɛkədəns] *n* Dekadenz *f*

decaff [ˈdiːkæf] (*inf*) *n* koffeinfreier Kaffee

decaffeinated [dɪˈkæfɪneɪtɪd] *adj* koffeinfrei

decanter [dɪˈkæntəʳ] *n* Karaffe *f*

decay [dɪˈkeɪ] *n* Verfall *m*; (*tooth ~*) Karies *m* ♦ *vi* verfallen; (*teeth, meat etc*) faulen; (*leaves etc*) verrotten

deceased [dɪˈsiːst] *adj* verstorben

deceit [dɪˈsiːt] *n* Betrug *m*; **~ful** *adj* falsch

deceive [dɪˈsiːv] *vt* täuschen

December [dɪˈsɛmbəʳ] *n* Dezember *m*

decency [ˈdiːsənsɪ] *n* Anstand *m*

decent [ˈdiːsənt] *adj* (*respectable*) anständig; (*pleasant*) annehmbar

deception [dɪˈsɛpʃən] *n* Betrug *m*

deceptive [dɪˈsɛptɪv] *adj* irreführend

decibel [ˈdɛsɪbel] *n* Dezibel *nt*

decide [dɪˈsaɪd] *vt* entscheiden ♦ *vi* sich entscheiden; **to ~ on sth** etw beschließen; **~d** *adj* entschieden; **~dly** [dɪˈsaɪdɪdlɪ] *adv* entschieden

deciduous [dɪˈsɪdjuəs] *adj* Laub-

decimal [ˈdɛsɪməl] *adj* dezimal ♦ *n* Dezimalzahl *f*; **~ point** *n* Komma *nt*

decipher [dɪˈsaɪfəʳ] *vt* entziffern

decision [dɪˈsɪʒən] *n* Entscheidung *f*, Entschluss *m*

decisive [dɪˈsaɪsɪv] *adj* entscheidend; (*person*) entschlossen

deck [dɛk] *n* (*NAUT*) Deck *nt*; (*of cards*) Pack *m*; **~chair** *n* Liegestuhl *m*

declaration [dɛkləˈreɪʃən] *n* Erklärung *f*

declare [dɪˈklɛəʳ] *vt* erklären; (*CUSTOMS*) verzollen

decline [dɪˈklaɪn] *n* (*decay*) Verfall *m*; (*lessening*) Rückgang *m* ♦ *vt* (*invitation*) ablehnen ♦ *vi* (*say no*) ablehnen; (*of strength*) nachlassen

decode [ˈdiːˈkəud] *vt* entschlüsseln; **~r** *n* (*TV*) Decoder *m*

decompose [diːkəmˈpəuz] *vi* (sich) zersetzen

décor [ˈdeɪkɔːʳ] *n* Ausstattung *f*

decorate [ˈdɛkəreɪt] *vt* (*room: paper*) tapezieren; (: *paint*) streichen; (*adorn*) (aus)schmücken; (*cake*) verzieren; (*honour*) auszeichnen; **decoration** [dɛkəˈreɪʃən] *n* (*of house*) (Wand)dekoration *f*; (*medal*) Orden *m*; **decorator** [ˈdɛkəreɪtəʳ] *n* Maler *m*, Anstreicher *m*

decorum [dɪˈkɔːrəm] *n* Anstand *m*

decoy ['di:kɔɪ] n Lockvogel m
decrease [n 'di:kri:s, vb di:'kri:s] n Abnahme f ♦ vt vermindern ♦ vi abnehmen
decree [dɪ'kri:] n Erlass m; ~ **nisi** n vorläufige(s) Scheidungsurteil nt
decrepit [dɪ'krepɪt] adj hinfällig
dedicate ['dedɪkeɪt] vt widmen; ~**d** adj hingebungsvoll, engagiert; (COMPUT) dediziert; **dedication** [dedɪ'keɪʃən] n (devotion) Ergebenheit f; (in book) Widmung f
deduce [dɪ'dju:s] vt: **to ~ sth (from sth)** etw (aus etw) ableiten, etw (aus etw) schließen
deduct [dɪ'dʌkt] vt abziehen; ~**ion** [dɪ'dʌkʃən] n (of money) Abzug m; (conclusion) (Schluss)folgerung f
deed [di:d] n Tat f; (document) Urkunde f
deem [di:m] vt: **to ~ sb/sth (to be) sth** jdn/etw für etw halten
deep [di:p] adj tief ♦ adv: **the spectators stood 20 ~** die Zuschauer standen in 20 Reihen hintereinander; **to be 4m ~** 4 Meter tief sein; ~**en** vt vertiefen ♦ vi (darkness) tiefer werden; ~ **end** n: **the ~ end** (of swimming pool) das Tiefe; ~**freeze** n Tiefkühlung f; ~**fry** vt frittieren; ~**ly** adv tief; ~**sea diving** n Tiefseetauchen nt; ~**seated** adj tief sitzend
deer [dɪər] n Reh nt; ~**skin** n Hirsch-/Rehleder nt
deface [dɪ'feɪs] vt entstellen
defamation [defə'meɪʃən] n Verleumdung f
default [dɪ'fɔ:lt] n Versäumnis nt; (COMPUT) Standardwert m ♦ vi versäumen; **by ~** durch Nichterscheinen
defeat [dɪ'fi:t] n Niederlage f ♦ vt schlagen; ~**ist** adj defätistisch ♦ n Defätist m
defect [n 'di:fekt, vb dɪ'fekt] n Fehler m ♦ vi überlaufen; ~**ive** [dɪ'fektɪv] adj fehlerhaft
defence [dɪ'fens] n Verteidigung f; ~**less** adj wehrlos
defend [dɪ'fend] vt verteidigen; ~**ant** n Angeklagte(r) m; ~**er** n Verteidiger m
defense [dɪ'fens] (US) n = **defence**
defensive [dɪ'fensɪv] adj defensiv ♦ n: **on the ~** in der Defensive
defer [dɪ'fə:ʳ] vt verschieben

deference ['defərəns] n Rücksichtnahme f
defiance [dɪ'faɪəns] n Trotz m, Unnachgiebigkeit f; **in ~ of sth** einer Sache dat zum Trotz
defiant [dɪ'faɪənt] adj trotzig, unnachgiebig
deficiency [dɪ'fɪʃənsɪ] n (lack) Mangel m; (weakness) Schwäche f
deficient [dɪ'fɪʃənt] adj mangelhaft
deficit ['defɪsɪt] n Defizit nt
defile [vb dɪ'faɪl, n 'di:faɪl] vt beschmutzen ♦ n Hohlweg m
define [dɪ'faɪn] vt bestimmen; (explain) definieren
definite ['defɪnɪt] adj (fixed) definitiv; (clear) eindeutig; ~**ly** adv bestimmt
definition [defɪ'nɪʃən] n Definition f
deflate [di:'fleɪt] vt die Luft ablassen aus
deflect [dɪ'flekt] vt ablenken
deformity [dɪ'fɔ:mɪtɪ] n Missbildung f
defraud [dɪ'frɔ:d] vt betrügen
defrost [di:'frɒst] vt (fridge) abtauen; (food) auftauen; ~**er** n (US) n (demister) Gebläse nt
deft [deft] adj geschickt
defunct [dɪ'fʌŋkt] adj verstorben
defuse [di:'fju:z] vt entschärfen
defy [dɪ'faɪ] vt (disobey) sich widersetzen +dat; (orders, death) trotzen +dat; (challenge) herausfordern
degenerate [v dɪ'dʒenəreɪt, adj dɪ'dʒenərɪt] vi degenerieren ♦ adj degeneriert
degrading [dɪ'greɪdɪŋ] adj erniedrigend
degree [dɪ'gri:] n Grad m; (UNIV) Universitätsabschluss m; **by ~s** allmählich; **to some ~** zu einem gewissen Grad
dehydrated [di:haɪ'dreɪtɪd] adj (person) ausgetrocknet
de-ice ['di:'aɪs] vt enteisen
deign [deɪn] vi sich herablassen
deity ['di:ɪtɪ] n Gottheit f
dejected [dɪ'dʒektɪd] adj niedergeschlagen
delay [dɪ'leɪ] vt (hold back) aufschieben ♦ vi (linger) sich aufhalten ♦ n Aufschub m, Verzögerung f; (of train etc) Verspätung f; **to be ~ed** (train) Verspätung haben; **without ~** unverzüglich
delectable [dɪ'lektəbl] adj köstlich; (fig) reizend

delegate [*n* 'dɛlɪgɪt, *vb* 'dɛlɪgeɪt] *n* Delegierte(r) *mf* ♦ *vt* delegieren

delete [dɪ'liːt] *vt* (aus)streichen

deliberate [*adj* dɪ'lɪbərɪt, *vb* dɪ'lɪbəreɪt] *adj* (*intentional*) absichtlich; (*slow*) bedächtig ♦ *vi* (*consider*) überlegen; (*debate*) sich beraten; **~ly** *adv* absichtlich

delicacy ['dɛlɪkəsɪ] *n* Zartheit *f*; (*weakness*) Anfälligkeit *f*; (*food*) Delikatesse *f*

delicate ['dɛlɪkɪt] *adj* (*fine*) fein; (*fragile*) zart; (*situation*) heikel; (*MED*) empfindlich

delicatessen [dɛlɪkə'tɛsn] *n* Feinkostgeschäft *nt*

delicious [dɪ'lɪʃəs] *adj* lecker

delight [dɪ'laɪt] *n* Wonne *f* ♦ *vt* entzücken; **to take ~ in sth** Freude an etw *dat* haben; **~ed** *adj*: **~ed (at** *or* **with sth)** entzückt (über +*acc* etw); **~ed to do sth** etw sehr gern tun; **~ful** *adj* entzückend, herrlich

delinquency [dɪ'lɪŋkwənsɪ] *n* Kriminalität *f*

delinquent [dɪ'lɪŋkwənt] *n* Straffällige(r) *mf* ♦ *adj* straffällig

delirious [dɪ'lɪrɪəs] *adj* im Fieberwahn

deliver [dɪ'lɪvə*] *vt* (*goods*) (ab)liefern; (*letter*) zustellen; (*speech*) halten; **~y** *n* (Ab)lieferung *f*; (*of letter*) Zustellung *f*; (*of speech*) Vortragsweise *f*; (*MED*) Entbindung *f*; **to take ~y of** in Empfang nehmen

delude [dɪ'luːd] *vt* täuschen

deluge ['dɛljuːdʒ] *n* Überschwemmung *f*; (*fig*) Flut *f* ♦ *vt* (*fig*) überfluten

delusion [dɪ'luːʒən] *n* (Selbst)täuschung *f*

de luxe [də'lʌks] *adj* Luxus-

delve [dɛlv] *vi*: **to ~ into** sich vertiefen in +*acc*

demand [dɪ'mɑːnd] *vt* verlangen ♦ *n* (*request*) Verlangen *nt*; (*COMM*) Nachfrage *f*; **in ~** gefragt; **on ~** auf Verlangen; **~ing** *adj* anspruchsvoll

demean [dɪ'miːn] *vt*: **to ~ o.s.** sich erniedrigen

demeanour [dɪ'miːnə*] (*US* **demeanor**) *n* Benehmen *nt*

demented [dɪ'mɛntɪd] *adj* wahnsinnig

demister [diː'mɪstə*] *n* (*AUT*) Gebläse *nt*

demo ['dɛməu] (*inf*) *n abbr* (= **demonstration**) Demo *f*

democracy [dɪ'mɔkrəsɪ] *n* Demokratie *f*

democrat ['dɛməkræt] *n* Demokrat *m*; **democratic** [dɛmə'krætɪk] *adj* demokratisch

demolish [dɪ'mɔlɪʃ] *vt* abreißen; (*fig*) vernichten

demolition [dɛmə'lɪʃən] *n* Abbruch *m*

demon ['diːmən] *n* Dämon *m*

demonstrate ['dɛmənstreɪt] *vt*, *vi* demonstrieren; **demonstration** [dɛmən'streɪʃən] *n* Demonstration *f*; **demonstrator** ['dɛmənstreɪtə*] *n* (*POL*) Demonstrant(in) *m(f)*

demote [dɪ'məut] *vt* degradieren

demure [dɪ'mjuə*] *adj* ernst

den [dɛn] *n* (*of animal*) Höhle *f*; (*study*) Bude *f*

denatured alcohol [diː'neɪtʃəd-] (*US*) *n* ungenießbar gemachte(r) Alkohol *m*

denial [dɪ'naɪəl] *n* Leugnung *f*; **official ~** Dementi *nt*

denim ['dɛnɪm] *adj* Denim-; **~s** *npl* Denimjeans *pl*

Denmark ['dɛnmɑːk] *n* Dänemark *nt*

denomination [dɪnɔmɪ'neɪʃən] *n* (*ECCL*) Bekenntnis *nt*; (*type*) Klasse *f*; (*FIN*) Wert *m*

denote [dɪ'nəut] *vt* bedeuten

denounce [dɪ'nauns] *vt* brandmarken

dense [dɛns] *adj* dicht; (*stupid*) schwer von Begriff; **~ly** *adv* dicht; **density** ['dɛnsɪtɪ] *n* Dichte *f*; **single/double density disk** Diskette *f* mit einfacher/doppelter Dichte

dent [dɛnt] *n* Delle *f* ♦ *vt* (*also*: **make a ~ in**) einbeulen

dental ['dɛntl] *adj* Zahn-; **~ surgeon** *n* = **dentist**

dentist ['dɛntɪst] *n* Zahnarzt(ärztin) *m(f)*

dentures ['dɛntʃəz] *npl* Gebiss *nt*

deny [dɪ'naɪ] *vt* leugnen; (*officially*) dementieren; (*help*) abschlagen

deodorant [diː'əudərənt] *n* Deodorant *nt*

depart [dɪ'pɑːt] *vi* abfahren; **to ~ from** (*fig*: *differ from*) abweichen von

department [dɪ'pɑːtmənt] *n* (*COMM*) Abteilung *f*; (*UNIV*) Seminar *nt*; (*POL*) Ministerium *nt*; **~ store** *n* Warenhaus *nt*

departure [dɪ'pɑːtʃə*] *n* (*of person*) Abreise *f*; (*of train*) Abfahrt *f*; (*of plane*) Abflug *m*; **new**

~ Neuerung f; **~ lounge** n (at airport)
Abflughalle f
depend [dɪ'pɛnd] vi: **to ~ on** abhängen von;
(rely on) angewiesen sein auf +acc; **it ~s** es
kommt darauf an; **~ing on the result ...**
abhängend vom Resultat ...; **~able** adj
zuverlässig; **~ant** n Angehörige(r) f(m);
~ence n Abhängigkeit f; **~ent** adj
abhängig ♦ n = **dependant**; **~ent on**
abhängig von
depict [dɪ'pɪkt] vt schildern
depleted [dɪ'pliːtɪd] adj aufgebracht
deplorable [dɪ'plɔːrəbl] adj bedauerlich
deploy [dɪ'plɔɪ] vt einsetzen
depopulation ['diːpɔpju'leɪʃən] n
Entvölkerung f
deport [dɪ'pɔːt] vt deportieren; **~ation**
[diːpɔː'teɪʃən] n Abschiebung f
deportment [dɪ'pɔːtmənt] n Betragen nt
deposit [dɪ'pɔzɪt] n (in bank) Guthaben nt;
(down payment) Anzahlung f; (security)
Kaution f; (CHEM) Niederschlag m ♦ vt (in
bank) deponieren; (put down) niederlegen;
~ account n Sparkonto nt
depot ['dɛpəʊ] n Depot nt
depraved [dɪ'preɪvd] adj verkommen
depreciate [dɪ'priːʃɪeɪt] vi im Wert sinken;
depreciation [dɪpriːʃɪ'eɪʃən] n
Wertminderung f
depress [dɪ'prɛs] vt (press down)
niederdrücken; (in mood) deprimieren; **~ed**
adj deprimiert; **~ion** [dɪ'prɛʃən] n (mood)
Depression f; (in trade) Wirtschaftskrise f;
(hollow) Vertiefung f; (MET)
Tief(druckgebiet) nt
deprivation [dɛprɪ'veɪʃən] n Not f
deprive [dɪ'praɪv] vt: **to ~ sb of sth** jdn
einer Sache gen berauben; **~d** adj (child)
sozial benachteiligt; (area) unterentwickelt
depth [dɛpθ] n Tiefe f; **in the ~s of despair**
in tiefster Verzweiflung
deputation [dɛpju'teɪʃən] n Abordnung f
deputize ['dɛpjʊtaɪz] vi: **to ~ (for sb)** (jdn)
vertreten
deputy ['dɛpjʊtɪ] adj stellvertretend ♦ n
(Stell)vertreter m; **~ head** (BRIT: SCOL) n
Konrektor(in) m(f)

derail [dɪ'reɪl] vt: **to be ~ed** entgleisen;
~ment n Entgleisung f
deranged [dɪ'reɪndʒd] adj verrückt
derby ['dɑːrbɪ] (US) n Melone f
derelict ['dɛrɪlɪkt] adj verlassen
deride [dɪ'raɪd] vt auslachen
derisory [dɪ'raɪsərɪ] adj spöttisch
derivative [dɪ'rɪvətɪv] n Derivat nt ♦ adj
abgeleitet
derive [dɪ'raɪv] vt (get) gewinnen; (deduce)
ableiten ♦ vi (come from) abstammen
dermatitis [dəːmə'taɪtɪs] n Hautentzündung
f
derogatory [dɪ'rɔgətərɪ] adj geringschätzig
derrick ['dɛrɪk] n Drehkran m
descend [dɪ'sɛnd] vt, vi hinuntersteigen; **to
~ from** abstammen von; **~ant** n
Nachkomme m; **descent** [dɪ'sɛnt] n
(coming down) Abstieg m; (origin)
Abstammung f
describe [dɪs'kraɪb] vt beschreiben
description [dɪs'krɪpʃən] n Beschreibung f;
(sort) Art f
descriptive [dɪs'krɪptɪv] adj beschreibend;
(word) anschaulich
desecrate ['dɛsɪkreɪt] vt schänden
desert [n 'dɛzət, vb dɪ'zɜːt] n Wüste f ♦ vt
verlassen; (temporarily) im Stich lassen ♦ vi
(MIL) desertieren; **~s** npl (what one deserves):
to get one's just ~s seinen gerechten
Lohn bekommen; **~er** n Deserteur m; **~ion**
[dɪ'zɜːʃən] n (of wife) Verlassen nt; (MIL)
Fahnenflucht f; **~ island** n einsame Insel f
deserve [dɪ'zɜːv] vt verdienen; **deserving**
adj verdienstvoll
design [dɪ'zaɪn] n (plan) Entwurf m;
(planning) Design nt ♦ vt entwerfen
designate [vb 'dɛzɪgneɪt, adj 'dɛzɪgnɪt] vt
bestimmen ♦ adj designiert
designer [dɪ'zaɪnəʳ] n Designer(in) m(f);
(TECH) Konstrukteur(in) m(f); (fashion ~)
Modeschöpfer(in) m(f)
desirable [dɪ'zaɪərəbl] adj wünschenswert
desire [dɪ'zaɪəʳ] n Wunsch m, Verlangen nt
♦ vt (lust) begehren; (ask for) wollen
desk [dɛsk] n Schreibtisch m; (BRIT: in shop,
restaurant) Kasse f; **~top publishing** n

Desktop-Publishing *nt*

desolate ['desəlɪt] *adj* öde; *(sad)* trostlos; **desolation** [desə'leɪʃən] *n* Trostlosigkeit *f*

despair [dɪs'peəʳ] *n* Verzweiflung *f ♦ vi:* **to ~ (of)** verzweifeln (an *+dat)*

despatch [dɪs'pætʃ] *n, vt* = **dispatch**

desperate ['despərɪt] *adj* verzweifelt; **~ly** *adv* verzweifelt; **desperation** [despə'reɪʃən] *n* Verzweiflung *f*

despicable [dɪs'pɪkəbl] *adj* abscheulich

despise [dɪs'paɪz] *vt* verachten

despite [dɪs'paɪt] *prep* trotz *+gen*

despondent [dɪs'pɒndənt] *adj* mutlos

dessert [dɪ'zɜːt] *n* Nachtisch *m;* **~spoon** *n* Dessertlöffel *m*

destination [destɪ'neɪʃən] *n (of person)* (Reise)ziel *nt; (of goods)* Bestimmungsort *m*

destiny ['destɪnɪ] *n* Schicksal *nt*

destitute ['destɪtjuːt] *adj* Not leidend

destroy [dɪs'trɔɪ] *vt* zerstören; **~er** *n (NAUT)* Zerstörer *m*

destruction [dɪs'trʌkʃən] *n* Zerstörung *f*

destructive [dɪs'trʌktɪv] *adj* zerstörend

detach [dɪ'tætʃ] *vt* loslösen; **~able** *adj* abtrennbar; **~ed** *adj (attitude)* distanziert; *(house)* Einzel-; **~ment** *n (fig)* Abstand *m; (MIL)* Sonderkommando *nt*

detail ['diːteɪl] *n* Einzelheit *f,* Detail *n ♦ vt (relate)* ausführlich berichten; *(appoint)* abkommandieren; **in ~** im Detail; **~ed** *adj* detailliert

detain [dɪ'teɪn] *vt* aufhalten; *(imprison)* in Haft halten

detect [dɪ'tekt] *vt* entdecken; **~ion** [dɪ'tekʃən] *n* Aufdeckung *f;* **~ive** *n* Detektiv *m;* **~ive story** *n* Kriminalgeschichte *f,* Krimi *m*

détente [deɪ'tɑːnt] *n* Entspannung *f*

detention [dɪ'tenʃən] *n* Haft *f; (SCH)* Nachsitzen *nt*

deter [dɪ'tɜːʳ] *vt* abschrecken

detergent [dɪ'tɜːdʒənt] *n* Waschmittel *nt*

deteriorate [dɪ'tɪərɪəreɪt] *vi* sich verschlechtern; **deterioration** [dɪtɪərɪə'reɪʃən] *n* Verschlechterung *f*

determination [dɪtɜːmɪ'neɪʃən] *n* Entschlossenheit *f*

determine [dɪ'tɜːmɪn] *vt* bestimmen; **~d** *adj*

entschlossen

deterrent [dɪ'terənt] *n* Abschreckungsmittel *nt*

detest [dɪ'test] *vt* verabscheuen

detonate ['detəneɪt] *vt* explodieren lassen ♦ *vi* detonieren

detour ['diːtuəʳ] *n* Umweg *m; (US: AUT: diversion)* Umleitung *f ♦ vt (US: AUT: traffic)* umleiten

detract [dɪ'trækt] *vi:* **to ~ from** schmälern

detriment ['detrɪmənt] *n:* **to the ~ of** zum Schaden *+gen;* **~al** [detrɪ'mentl] *adj* schädlich

devaluation [diːvæljʊ'eɪʃən] *n* Abwertung *f*

devastate ['devəsteɪt] *vt* verwüsten; *(fig: shock):* **to be ~d by** niedergeschmettert sein von; **devastating** *adj* verheerend

develop [dɪ'veləp] *vt* entwickeln; *(resources)* erschließen ♦ *vi* sich entwickeln; **~ing country** *n* Entwicklungsland *nt;* **~ment** *n* Entwicklung *f*

deviate ['diːvɪeɪt] *vi* abweichen

device [dɪ'vaɪs] *n* Gerät *nt*

devil ['devl] *n* Teufel *m*

devious ['diːvɪəs] *adj (means)* krumm; *(person)* verschlagen

devise [dɪ'vaɪz] *vt* entwickeln

devoid [dɪ'vɔɪd] *adj:* **~ of** ohne

devolution [diːvə'luːʃən] *n (POL)* Dezentralisierung *f*

devote [dɪ'vəut] *vt:* **to ~ sth (to sth)** etw (einer Sache *dat)* widmen; **~d** *adj* ergeben; **~e** [devəu'tiː] *n* Anhänger(in) *m(f),* Verehrer(in) *m(f);* **devotion** [dɪ'vəuʃən] *n (piety)* Andacht *f; (loyalty)* Ergebenheit *f,* Hingabe *f*

devour [dɪ'vauəʳ] *vt* verschlingen

devout [dɪ'vaut] *adj* andächtig

dew [djuː] *n* Tau *m*

dexterity [deks'terɪtɪ] *n* Geschicklichkeit *f*

DHSS *(BRIT) n abbr* = **Department of Health and Social Security**

diabetes [daɪə'biːtiːz] *n* Zuckerkrankheit *f*

diabetic [daɪə'betɪk] *adj* zuckerkrank; *(food)* Diabetiker- ♦ *n* Diabetiker *m*

diabolical [daɪə'bɒlɪkl] *(inf) adj (weather, behaviour)* saumäßig

diagnose [daɪəg'nəʊz] vt diagnostizieren

diagnoses [daɪəg'nəʊsi:z] npl of **diagnosis**

diagnosis [daɪəg'nəʊsɪs] n Diagnose f

diagonal [daɪ'ægənl] adj diagonal ♦ n
Diagonale f

diagram ['daɪəgræm] n Diagramm nt,
Schaubild nt

dial ['daɪəl] n (TEL) Wählscheibe f; (of clock)
Zifferblatt nt ♦ vt wählen

dialect ['daɪəlekt] n Dialekt m

dialling code ['daɪəlɪŋ-] n Vorwahl f

dialling tone n Amtszeichen nt

dialogue ['daɪəlɒg] n Dialog m

dial tone (US) n = **dialling tone**

diameter [daɪ'æmɪtəʳ] n Durchmesser m

diamond ['daɪəmənd] n Diamant m; ~s npl
(CARDS) Karo nt

diaper ['daɪəpəʳ] (US) n Windel f

diaphragm ['daɪəfræm] n Zwerchfell nt

diarrhoea [daɪə'ri:ə] (US **diarrhea**) n
Durchfall m

diary ['daɪərɪ] n Taschenkalender m; (account)
Tagebuch nt

dice [daɪs] n Würfel pl ♦ vt in Würfel
schneiden

dictate [dɪk'teɪt] vt diktieren; ~s ['dɪkteɪts]
npl Gebote pl; **dictation** [dɪk'teɪʃən] n
Diktat nt

dictator [dɪk'teɪtəʳ] n Diktator m; ~ship
[dɪk'teɪtəʃɪp] n Diktatur f

dictionary ['dɪkʃənrɪ] n Wörterbuch nt

did [dɪd] pt of **do**

didn't ['dɪdnt] = **did not**

die [daɪ] vi sterben; **to be dying for sth** etw
unbedingt haben wollen; **to be dying to
do sth** darauf brennen, etw zu tun; ~
away vi schwächer werden; ~ **down** vi
nachlassen; ~ **out** vi aussterben

diesel ['di:zl] n (car) Diesel m; ~ **engine** n
Dieselmotor m; ~ **oil** n Dieselkraftstoff m

diet ['daɪət] n Nahrung f; (special food) Diät f;
(slimming) Abmagerungskur f ♦ vi (also: **be
on a ~**) eine Abmagerungskur machen

differ ['dɪfəʳ] vi sich unterscheiden; (disagree)
anderer Meinung sein; ~**ence** n
Unterschied m; ~**ent** adj anders; (two
things) verschieden; ~**entiate** [dɪfə'renʃɪeɪt]

vt, vi unterscheiden; ~**ently** adv anders;
(from one another) unterschiedlich

difficult ['dɪfɪkəlt] adj schwierig; ~**y** n
Schwierigkeit f

diffident ['dɪfɪdənt] adj schüchtern

diffuse [adj dɪ'fju:s, vb dɪ'fju:z] adj langatmig
♦ vt verbreiten

dig [dɪg] (pt, pp **dug**) vt graben ♦ n (prod)
Stoß m; (remark) Spitze f; (archaeological)
Ausgrabung f; ~ **in** vi (MIL) sich eingraben;
~ **into** vt fus (savings) angreifen; ~ **up** vt
ausgraben; (fig) aufgraben

digest [vb daɪ'dʒest, n 'daɪdʒest] vt verdauen
♦ n Auslese f; ~**ion** [dɪ'dʒestʃən] n
Verdauung f

digit ['dɪdʒɪt] n Ziffer f; (ANAT) Finger m; ~**al**
adj digital, Digital-; ~**al camera** n
Digitalkamera f; ~**al TV** n Digitalfernsehen nt

dignified ['dɪgnɪfaɪd] adj würdevoll

dignity ['dɪgnɪtɪ] n Würde f

digress [daɪ'gres] vi abschweifen

digs [dɪgz] (BRIT: inf) npl Bude f

dilapidated [dɪ'læpɪdeɪtɪd] adj baufällig

dilate [daɪ'leɪt] vt weiten ♦ vi sich weiten

dilemma [daɪ'lemə] n Dilemma nt

diligent ['dɪlɪdʒənt] adj fleißig

dilute [daɪ'lu:t] vt verdünnen

dim [dɪm] adj trübe; (stupid) schwer von
Begriff ♦ vt verdunkeln; **to ~ one's
headlights** (esp US) abblenden

dime [daɪm] (US) n Zehncentstück nt

dimension [daɪ'menʃən] n Dimension f

diminish [dɪ'mɪnɪʃ] vt, vi verringern

diminutive [dɪ'mɪnjutɪv] adj winzig ♦ n
Verkleinerungsform f

dimmer ['dɪməʳ] (US) n (AUT)
Abblendschalter m; ~**s** npl Abblendlicht nt;
(sidelights) Begrenzungsleuchten pl

dimple ['dɪmpl] n Grübchen nt

din [dɪn] n Getöse nt

dine [daɪn] vi speisen; ~**r** n Tischgast m;
(RAIL) Speisewagen m

dinghy ['dɪŋgɪ] n Dingi nt; **rubber ~**
Schlauchboot nt

dingy ['dɪndʒɪ] adj armselig

dining car (BRIT) n Speisewagen m

dining room ['daɪnɪŋ-] n Esszimmer nt; (in

hotel) Speisezimmer *nt*

dinner ['dɪnə'] *n* (*lunch*) Mittagessen *nt*; (*evening*) Abendessen *nt*; (*public*) Festessen *nt*; ~ **jacket** *n* Smoking *m*; ~ **party** *n* Tischgesellschaft *f*; ~ **time** *n* Tischzeit *f*

dinosaur ['daɪnɔsɔ:'] *n* Dinosaurier *m*

dint [dɪnt] *n*: **by ~ of** durch

diocese ['daɪəsɪs] *n* Diözese *f*

dip [dɪp] *n* (*hollow*) Senkung *f*; (*bathe*) kurze(s) Baden ♦ *vt* eintauchen; (*BRIT: AUT*) abblenden ♦ *vi* (*slope*) sich senken, abfallen

diploma [dɪ'pləumə] *n* Diplom *nt*

diplomacy [dɪ'pləuməsɪ] *n* Diplomatie *f*

diplomat ['dɪpləmæt] *n* Diplomat(in) *m(f)*; ~**ic** [dɪplə'mætɪk] *adj* diplomatisch

dip stick *n* Ölmessstab *m*

dipswitch ['dɪpswɪtʃ] (*BRIT*) *n* (*AUT*) Abblendschalter *m*

dire [daɪə'] *adj* schrecklich

direct [daɪ'rɛkt] *adj* direkt ♦ *vt* leiten; (*film*) die Regie führen +*gen*; (*aim*) richten; (*order*) anweisen; **can you ~ me to …?** können Sie mir sagen, wo ich zu … komme?; ~ **debit** *n* (*BRIT*) Einzugsauftrag *m*; (*transaction*) automatische Abbuchung *f*

direction [dɪ'rɛkʃən] *n* Richtung *f*; (*CINE*) Regie *f*; Leitung *f*; ~**s** *npl* (*for use*) Gebrauchsanleitung *f*; (*orders*) Anweisungen *pl*; **sense of ~** Orientierungssinn *m*

directly [dɪ'rɛktlɪ] *adv* direkt; (*at once*) sofort

director [dɪ'rɛktə'] *n* Direktor *m*; (*of film*) Regisseur *m*

directory [dɪ'rɛktərɪ] *n* (*TEL*) Telefonbuch *nt*; ~ **enquiries**, ~ **assistance** (*US*) *n* (Fernsprech)auskunft *f*

dirt [də:t] *n* Schmutz *m*, Dreck *m*; ~-**cheap** *adj* spottbillig; ~**y** *adj* schmutzig ♦ *vt* beschmutzen; ~**y trick** *n* gemeine(r) Trick *m*

disability [dɪsə'bɪlɪtɪ] *n* Körperbehinderung *f*

disabled [dɪs'eɪbld] *adj* körperbehindert

disadvantage [dɪsəd'vɑ:ntɪdʒ] *n* Nachteil *m*

disagree [dɪsə'gri:] *vi* nicht übereinstimmen; (*quarrel*) (sich) streiten; (*food*): **to ~ with sb** jdm nicht bekommen; ~**able** *adj*

unangenehm; ~**ment** *n* (*between persons*) Streit *m*; (*between things*) Widerspruch *m*

disallow ['dɪsə'lau] *vt* nicht zulassen

disappear [dɪsə'pɪə'] *vi* verschwinden; ~**ance** *n* Verschwinden *nt*

disappoint [dɪsə'pɔɪnt] *vt* enttäuschen; ~**ed** *adj* enttäuscht; ~**ment** *n* Enttäuschung *f*

disapproval [dɪsə'pru:vəl] *n* Missbilligung *f*

disapprove [dɪsə'pru:v] *vi*: **to ~ of** missbilligen

disarm [dɪs'ɑ:m] *vt* entwaffnen; (*POL*) abrüsten; ~**ament** *n* Abrüstung *f*

disarray [dɪsə'reɪ] *n*: **to be in ~** (*army*) in Auflösung (begriffen) sein; (*clothes*) in unordentlichem Zustand sein

disaster [dɪ'zɑ:stə'] *n* Katastrophe *f*; **disastrous** [dɪ'zɑ:strəs] *adj* verhängnisvoll

disband [dɪs'bænd] *vt* auflösen ♦ *vi* auseinander gehen

disbelief ['dɪsbə'li:f] *n* Ungläubigkeit *f*

disc [dɪsk] *n* Scheibe *f*; (*record*) (Schall)platte *f*; (*COMPUT*) = **disk**

discard [dɪs'kɑ:d] *vt* ablegen

discern [dɪ'sə:n] *vt* erkennen; ~**ing** *adj* scharfsinnig

discharge [*vb* dɪs'tʃɑ:dʒ, *n* 'dɪstʃɑ:dʒ] *vt* (*ship*) entladen; (*duties*) nachkommen +*dat*; (*dismiss*) entlassen; (*gun*) abschießen; (*JUR*) freisprechen ♦ *n* (*of ship, ELEC*) Entladung *f*; (*dismissal*) Entlassung *f*; (*MED*) Ausfluss *m*

disciple [dɪ'saɪpl] *n* Jünger *m*

discipline ['dɪsɪplɪn] *n* Disziplin *f* ♦ *vt* (*train*) schulen; (*punish*) bestrafen

disc jockey *n* Diskjockey *m*

disclaim [dɪs'kleɪm] *vt* nicht anerkennen

disclose [dɪs'kləuz] *vt* enthüllen; **disclosure** [dɪs'kləuʒə'] *n* Enthüllung *f*

disco ['dɪskəu] *n abbr* = discotheque

discoloured [dɪs'kʌləd] (*US* **discolored**) *adj* verfärbt

discomfort [dɪs'kʌmfət] *n* Unbehagen *nt*

disconcert [dɪskən'sə:t] *vt* aus der Fassung bringen

disconnect [dɪskə'nɛkt] *vt* abtrennen

discontent [dɪskən'tɛnt] *n* Unzufriedenheit *f*; ~**ed** *adj* unzufrieden

discontinue [dɪskən'tɪnju:] *vt* einstellen

discord ['dɪskɔːd] n Zwietracht f; (noise)
Dissonanz f

discotheque ['dɪskəutek] n Diskothek f

discount [n 'dɪskaunt, vb dɪs'kaunt] n Rabatt
m ♦ vt außer Acht lassen

discourage [dɪs'kʌrɪdʒ] vt entmutigen;
(prevent) abraten

discourteous [dɪs'kəːtɪəs] adj unhöflich

discover [dɪs'kʌvə'] vt entdecken;**~y** n
Entdeckung f

discredit [dɪs'kredɪt] vt in Verruf bringen

discreet [dɪs'kriːt] adj diskret

discrepancy [dɪs'krepənsɪ] n Diskrepanz f

discriminate [dɪs'krɪmɪneɪt] vi
unterscheiden; **to ~ against** diskriminieren;
discriminating adj anspruchsvoll;
discrimination [dɪskrɪmɪ'neɪʃən] n
Urteilsvermögen nt; (pej) Diskriminierung f

discuss [dɪs'kʌs] vt diskutieren, besprechen;
~ion [dɪs'kʌʃən] n Diskussion f,
Besprechung f

disdain [dɪs'deɪn] n Verachtung f

disease [dɪ'ziːz] n Krankheit f

disembark [dɪsɪm'bɑːk] vi von Bord gehen

disenchanted ['dɪsɪn'tʃɑːntɪd] adj
desillusioniert

disengage [dɪsɪn'geɪdʒ] vt (AUT) auskuppeln

disentangle [dɪsɪn'tæŋgl] vt entwirren

disfigure [dɪs'fɪgə'] vt entstellen

disgrace [dɪs'greɪs] n Schande f ♦ vt
Schande bringen über +acc;**~ful** adj
unerhört

disgruntled [dɪs'grʌntld] adj verärgert

disguise [dɪs'gaɪz] vt verkleiden; (feelings)
verhehlen ♦ n Verkleidung f; **in ~** verkleidet,
maskiert

disgust [dɪs'gʌst] n Abscheu f ♦ vt anwidern;
~ed adj angeekelt; (at sb's behaviour)
empört;**~ing** adj widerlich

dish [dɪʃ] n Schüssel f; (food) Gericht nt; **to
do** or **wash the ~es** abwaschen;**~ up** vt
auftischen;**~ cloth** n Spüllappen m

dishearten [dɪs'hɑːtn] vt entmutigen

dishevelled [dɪ'ʃevəld] adj (hair) zerzaust;
(clothing) ungepflegt

dishonest [dɪs'ɒnɪst] adj unehrlich

dishonour [dɪs'ɒnə'] (US **dishonor**) n
Unehre f;**~able** adj unehrenhaft

dishtowel ['dɪʃtauəl] n Geschirrtuch nt

dishwasher ['dɪʃwɒʃə'] n
Geschirrspülmaschine f

disillusion [dɪsɪ'luːʒən] vt enttäuschen,
desillusionieren

disincentive [dɪsɪn'sentɪv] n Entmutigung f

disinfect [dɪsɪn'fekt] vt desinfizieren;**~ant** n
Desinfektionsmittel nt

disintegrate [dɪs'ɪntɪgreɪt] vi sich auflösen

disinterested [dɪs'ɪntrəstɪd] adj
uneigennützig; (inf) uninteressiert

disjointed [dɪs'dʒɔɪntɪd] adj
unzusammenhängend

disk [dɪsk] n (COMPUT) Diskette f; **single/
double sided ~** einseitige/beidseitige
Diskette;**~ drive** n Diskettenlaufwerk nt;
~ette [dɪs'ket] (US) n = **disk**

dislike [dɪs'laɪk] n Abneigung f ♦ vt nicht
leiden können

dislocate ['dɪsləkeɪt] vt auskugeln

dislodge [dɪs'lɒdʒ] vt verschieben; (MIL) aus
der Stellung werfen

disloyal [dɪs'lɔɪəl] adj treulos

dismal ['dɪzml] adj trostlos, trübe

dismantle [dɪs'mæntl] vt demontieren

dismay [dɪs'meɪ] n Bestürzung f ♦ vt
bestürzen

dismiss [dɪs'mɪs] vt (employee) entlassen;
(idea) von sich weisen; (send away)
wegschicken; (JUR) abweisen;**~al** n
Entlassung f

dismount [dɪs'maunt] vi absteigen

disobedience [dɪsə'biːdɪəns] n Ungehorsam
m;**disobedient** adj ungehorsam

disobey [dɪsə'beɪ] vt nicht gehorchen +dat

disorder [dɪs'ɔːdə'] n (confusion) Verwirrung
f; (commotion) Aufruhr m; (MED) Erkrankung
f

disorderly [dɪs'ɔːdəlɪ] adj (untidy)
unordentlich; (unruly) ordnungswidrig

disorganized [dɪs'ɔːgənaɪzd] adj
unordentlich

disorientated [dɪs'ɔːrɪenteɪtɪd] adj (person:
after journey) verwirrt

disown [dɪs'əun] vt (child) verstoßen

disparaging [dɪs'pærɪdʒɪŋ] adj

geringschätzig

dispassionate [dɪs'pæfənət] *adj* objektiv

dispatch [dɪs'pætʃ] *vt (goods)* abschicken, abfertigen ♦ *n* Absendung *f*; *(esp MIL)* Meldung *f*

dispel [dɪs'pɛl] *vt* zerstreuen

dispensary [dɪs'pɛnsərɪ] *n* Apotheke *f*

dispense [dɪs'pɛns] *vt* verteilen, austeilen; **~ with** *vt fus* verzichten auf +*acc*; **~r** *n (container)* Spender *m*; **dispensing** *adj*: **dispensing chemist** *(BRIT)* Apotheker *m*

dispersal [dɪs'pəːsl] *n* Zerstreuung *f*

disperse [dɪs'pəːs] *vt* zerstreuen ♦ *vi* sich verteilen

dispirited [dɪs'pɪrɪtɪd] *adj* niedergeschlagen

displace [dɪs'pleɪs] *vt* verschieben; **~d person** *n* Verschleppte(r) *mf*

display [dɪs'pleɪ] *n (of goods)* Auslage *f*; *(of feeling)* Zurschaustellung *f* ♦ *vt* zeigen; *(ostentatiously)* vorführen; *(goods)* ausstellen

displease [dɪs'pliːz] *vt* missfallen +*dat*

displeasure [dɪs'plɛʒər] *n* Missfallen *nt*

disposable [dɪs'pəuzəbl] *adj* Wegwerf-; **~ nappy** *n* Papierwindel *f*

disposal [dɪs'pəuzl] *n (of property)* Verkauf *m*; *(throwing away)* Beseitigung *f*; **to be at one's ~** einem zur Verfügung stehen

dispose [dɪs'pəuz] *vi*: **to ~ of** loswerden; **~d** *adj* geneigt

disposition [dɪspə'zɪʃən] *n* Wesen *nt*

disproportionate [dɪsprə'pɔːʃənət] *adj* unverhältnismäßig

disprove [dɪs'pruːv] *vt* widerlegen

dispute [dɪs'pjuːt] *n* Streit *m*; *(also:* **industrial ~)** Arbeitskampf *m* ♦ *vt* bestreiten

disqualify [dɪs'kwɔlɪfaɪ] *vt* disqualifizieren

disquiet [dɪs'kwaɪət] *n* Unruhe *f*

disregard [dɪsrɪ'gɑːd] *vt* nicht (be)achten

disrepair ['dɪsrɪ'pɛər] *n*: **to fall into ~** verfallen

disreputable [dɪs'rɛpjutəbl] *adj* verrufen

disrespectful [dɪsrɪ'spɛktful] *adj* respektlos

disrupt [dɪs'rʌpt] *vt* stören; *(service)* unterbrechen; **~ion** [dɪs'rʌpʃən] *n* Störung *f*; Unterbrechung *f*

dissatisfaction [dɪssætɪs'fækʃən] *n*

Unzufriedenheit *f*; **dissatisfied** [dɪs'sætɪsfaɪd] *adj* unzufrieden

dissect [dɪ'sɛkt] *vt* zerlegen, sezieren

dissent [dɪ'sɛnt] *n* abweichende Meinung *f*

dissertation [dɪsə'teɪʃən] *n* wissenschaftliche Arbeit *f*; *(Ph.D.)* Doktorarbeit *f*

disservice [dɪs'səːvɪs] *n*: **to do sb a ~** einen schlechten Dienst erweisen

dissident ['dɪsɪdnt] *adj* anders denkend ♦ *n* Dissident *m*

dissimilar [dɪ'sɪmɪlər] *adj*: **~ (to sb/sth)** (jdm/etw) unähnlich

dissipate ['dɪsɪpeɪt] *vt (waste)* verschwenden; *(scatter)* zerstreuen

dissociate [dɪ'səufɪeɪt] *vt* trennen

dissolve [dɪ'zɔlv] *vt* auflösen ♦ *vi* sich auflösen

dissuade [dɪ'sweɪd] *vt*: **to ~ sb from doing sth** jdn davon abbringen, etw zu tun

distance ['dɪstns] *n* Entfernung *f*; **in the ~** in der Ferne; **distant** *adj* entfernt, fern; *(with time)* fern

distaste [dɪs'teɪst] *n* Abneigung *f*; **~ful** *adj* widerlich

distended [dɪs'tɛndɪd] *adj (stomach)* aufgebläht

distil [dɪs'tɪl] *vt* destillieren; **~lery** *n* Brennerei *f*

distinct [dɪs'tɪŋkt] *adj (separate)* getrennt; *(clear)* klar, deutlich; **as ~ from** im Unterschied zu; **~ion** [dɪs'tɪŋkʃən] *n* Unterscheidung *f*; *(eminence)* Auszeichnung *f*; **~ive** *adj* bezeichnend

distinguish [dɪs'tɪŋgwɪʃ] *vt* unterscheiden; **~ed** *adj (eminent)* berühmt; **~ing** *adj* bezeichnend

distort [dɪs'tɔːt] *vt* verdrehen; *(misrepresent)* entstellen; **~ion** [dɪs'tɔːʃən] *n* Verzerrung *f*

distract [dɪs'trækt] *vt* ablenken; **~ing** *adj* verwirrend; **~ion** [dɪs'trækʃən] *n (distress)* Raserei *f*; *(diversion)* Zerstreuung *f*

distraught [dɪs'trɔːt] *adj* bestürzt

distress [dɪs'trɛs] *n* Not *f*; *(suffering)* Qual *f* ♦ *vt* quälen; **~ing** *adj* erschütternd; **~ signal** *n* Notsignal *nt*

distribute [dɪs'trɪbjuːt] *vt* verteilen; **distribution** [dɪstrɪ'bjuːʃən] *n* Verteilung *f*;

distributor n Verteiler m

district ['dɪstrɪkt] n (of country) Kreis m; (of town) Bezirk m; **~ attorney** (US) n Oberstaatsanwalt m; **~ nurse** n Kreiskrankenschwester f

distrust [dɪs'trʌst] n Misstrauen nt ♦ vt misstrauen +dat

disturb [dɪs'tɜːb] vt stören; (agitate) erregen; **~ance** n Störung f; **~ed** adj beunruhigt; **emotionally ~ed** emotional gestört; **~ing** adj beunruhigend

disuse [dɪs'juːs] n: **to fall into ~** außer Gebrauch kommen; **~d** [dɪs'juːzd] adj außer Gebrauch; (mine, railway line) stillgelegt

ditch [dɪtʃ] n Graben m ♦ vt (person) loswerden; (plan) fallen lassen

dither ['dɪðəʳ] vi verdattert sein

ditto ['dɪtəʊ] adv dito, ebenfalls

divan [dɪ'væn] n Liegesofa nt

dive [daɪv] n (into water) Kopfsprung m; (AVIAT) Sturzflug m ♦ vi tauchen; **~r** n Taucher m

diverge [daɪ'vɜːdʒ] vi auseinander gehen

diverse [daɪ'vɜːs] adj verschieden

diversion [daɪ'vɜːʃən] n Ablenkung f; (BRIT: AUT) Umleitung f

diversity [daɪ'vɜːsɪtɪ] n Vielfalt f

divert [daɪ'vɜːt] vt ablenken; (traffic) umleiten

divide [dɪ'vaɪd] vt teilen ♦ vi sich teilen; **~d highway** (US) n Schnellstraße f

divine [dɪ'vaɪn] adj göttlich

diving ['daɪvɪŋ] n (SPORT) Turmspringen nt; (underwater ~) Tauchen nt; **~ board** n Sprungbrett nt

divinity [dɪ'vɪnɪtɪ] n Gottheit f; (subject) Religion f

division [dɪ'vɪʒən] n Teilung f; (MIL) Division f; (part) Abteilung f; (in opinion) Uneinigkeit f; (BRIT: POL) (Abstimmung f durch) Hammelsprung f

divorce [dɪ'vɔːs] n (Ehe)scheidung f ♦ vt scheiden; **~d** adj geschieden; **~e** [dɪvɔː'siː] n Geschiedene(r) f(m)

divulge [daɪ'vʌldʒ] vt preisgeben

DIY (BRIT) n abbr = **do-it-yourself**

dizzy ['dɪzɪ] adj schwindlig

DJ n abbr = **disc jockey**

DNA fingerprinting n genetische Fingerabdrücke pl

KEYWORD

---

do [duː] (pt **did**, pp **done**) n (inf: party etc) Fete f

♦ aux vb **1** (in negative constructions and questions): **I don't understand** ich verstehe nicht; **didn't you know?** wusstest du das nicht?; **what do you think?** was meinen Sie?

2 (for emphasis, in polite phrases): **she does seem rather tired** sie scheint wirklich sehr müde zu sein; **do sit down/help yourself** setzen Sie sich doch hin/greifen Sie doch zu

3 (used to avoid repeating vb): **she swims better than I do** sie schwimmt besser als ich; **she lives in Glasgow - so do I** sie wohnt in Glasgow - ich auch

4 (in tag questions): **you like him, don't you?** du magst ihn doch, oder?

♦ vt **1** (carry out, perform etc) tun, machen; **what are you doing tonight?** was machst du heute Abend?; **I've got nothing to do** ich habe nichts zu tun; **to do one's hair/ nails** sich die Haare/Nägel machen

2 (AUT etc) fahren

♦ vi **1** (act, behave): **do as I do** mach es wie ich

2 (get on, fare): **he's doing well/badly at school** er ist gut/schlecht in der Schule; **how do you do?** guten Tag

3 (be suitable) gehen; (be sufficient) reichen; **to make do (with)** auskommen mit

do away with vt (kill) umbringen; (abolish: law etc) abschaffen

do up vt (laces, dress, buttons) zumachen; (room, house) renovieren

do with vt (need) brauchen; (be connected) zu tun haben mit

do without vt, vi auskommen ohne

---

docile ['dəʊsaɪl] adj gefügig

dock [dɔk] n Dock nt; (JUR) Anklagebank f ♦ vi ins Dock gehen; **~er** n Hafenarbeiter m; **~yard** n Werft f

doctor ['dɔktəʳ] *n* Arzt *m*, Ärztin *f*; (*UNIV*) Doktor *m* ♦ *vt* (*fig*) fälschen; (*drink etc*) etw beimischen +*dat*; **D~ of Philosophy** *n* Doktor *m* der Philosophie

document ['dɔkjumənt] *n* Dokument *nt*; **~ary** [dɔkju'mɛntəri] *n* Dokumentarbericht *m*; (*film*) Dokumentarfilm *m* ♦ *adj* dokumentarisch; **~ation** [dɔkjumən'teɪʃən] *n* dokumentarische(r) Nachweis *m*

dodge [dɔdʒ] *n* Kniff *m* ♦ *vt* ausweichen +*dat*

dodgems ['dɔdʒəmz] (*BRIT*) *npl* Autoskooter *m*

doe [dəu] *n* (*roe deer*) Ricke *f*; (*red deer*) Hirschkuh *f*; (*rabbit*) Weibchen *nt*

does [dʌz] *vb see* **do**; **~n't** = **does not**

dog [dɔg] *n* Hund *m*; **~ collar** *n* Hundehalsband *nt*; (*ECCL*) Kragen *m* des Geistlichen; **~-eared** *adj* mit Eselsohren

dogged ['dɔgɪd] *adj* hartnäckig

dogsbody ['dɔgzbɔdi] *n* Mädchen *nt* für alles

doings ['duːɪŋz] *npl* (*activities*) Treiben *nt*

do-it-yourself ['duːɪtjɔː'sɛlf] *n* Do-it-yourself *nt*

doldrums ['dɔldrəmz] *npl*: **to be in the ~** (*business*) Flaute haben; (*person*) deprimiert sein

dole [dəul] (*BRIT*) *n* Stempelgeld *nt*; **to be on the ~** stempeln gehen; **~ out** *vt* ausgeben, austeilen

doleful ['dəulful] *adj* traurig

doll [dɔl] *n* Puppe *f* ♦ *vt*: **to ~ o.s. up** sich aufdonnern

dollar ['dɔləʳ] *n* Dollar *m*

dolphin ['dɔlfɪn] *n* Delfin *m*, Delphin *m*

dome [dəum] *n* Kuppel *f*

domestic [də'mɛstɪk] *adj* häuslich; (*within country*) Innen-, Binnen-; (*animal*) Haus-; **~ated** *adj* (*person*) häuslich; (*animal*) zahm

dominant ['dɔmɪnənt] *adj* vorherrschend

dominate ['dɔmɪneɪt] *vt* beherrschen

domineering [dɔmɪ'nɪərɪŋ] *adj* herrisch

dominion [də'mɪnɪən] *n* (*rule*) Regierungsgewalt *f*; (*land*) Staatsgebiet *nt* mit Selbstverwaltung

domino ['dɔmɪnəu] (*pl* **~es**) *n* Dominostein *m*; **~es** *n* (*game*) Domino(spiel) *nt*

don [dɔn] (*BRIT*) *n* akademische(r) Lehrer *m*

donate [də'neɪt] *vt* (*blood, money*) spenden; (*lot of money*) stiften; **donation** [də'neɪʃən] *n* Spende *f*

done [dʌn] *pp of* **do**

donkey ['dɔŋkɪ] *n* Esel *m*

donor ['dəunəʳ] *n* Spender *m*; **~ card** *n* Organspenderausweis *m*

don't [dəunt] = **do not**

doodle ['duːdl] *vi* kritzeln

doom [duːm] *n* böse(s) Geschick *nt*; (*downfall*) Verderben *nt* ♦ *vt*: **to be ~ed** zum Untergang verurteilt sein; **~sday** *n* der Jüngste Tag

door [dɔːʳ] *n* Tür *f*; **~bell** *n* Türklingel *f*; **~handle** *n* Türklinke *f*; **~man** (*irreg*) *n* Türsteher *m*; **~mat** *n* Fußmatte *f*; **~step** *n* Türstufe *f*; **~way** *n* Türöffnung *f*

dope [dəup] *n* (*drug*) Aufputschmittel *nt* ♦ *vt* (*horse*) dopen

dopey ['dəupɪ] (*inf*) *adj* bekloppt

dormant ['dɔːmənt] *adj* latent

dormitory ['dɔːmɪtrɪ] *n* Schlafsaal *m*

dormouse ['dɔːmaus] (*pl* **-mice**) *n* Haselmaus *f*

DOS [dɔs] *n abbr* (= *disk operating system*) DOS *nt*

dosage ['dəusɪdʒ] *n* Dosierung *f*

dose [dəus] *n* Dosis *f*

dosh [dɔʃ] (*inf*) *n* (*money*) Moos *nt*, Knete *f*

doss house ['dɔs-] (*BRIT*) *n* Bleibe *f*

dot [dɔt] *n* Punkt *m*; **~ted with** übersät mit; **on the ~** pünktlich

dote [dəut] *vi*: **to ~ on** *vt fus* vernarrt sein in +*acc*

dotted line ['dɔtɪd-] *n* punktierte Linie *f*

double ['dʌbl] *adj, adv* doppelt ♦ *n* Doppelgänger *m* ♦ *vt* verdoppeln ♦ *vi* sich verdoppeln; **~s** *npl* (*TENNIS*) Doppel *nt*; **on** *or* **at the ~** im Laufschritt; **~ bass** *n* Kontrabass *m*; **~ bed** *n* Doppelbett *nt*; **~ bend** (*BRIT*) *n* S-Kurve *f*; **~-breasted** *adj* zweireihig; **~-cross** *vt* hintergehen; **~-decker** *n* Doppeldecker *m*; **~ glazing** (*BRIT*) *n* Doppelverglasung *f*; **~ room** *n* Doppelzimmer *nt*

doubly ['dʌblɪ] *adv* doppelt

doubt [daut] n Zweifel m ♦ vt bezweifeln;
~**ful** adj zweifelhaft;~**less** adv ohne
Zweifel

dough [dəu] n Teig m;~**nut** n Berliner m

douse [dauz] vt (drench) mit Wasser
begießen, durchtränken; (extinguish)
ausmachen

dove [dʌv] n Taube f

dovetail ['dʌvteɪl] vi (plans) übereinstimmen

dowdy ['daudɪ] adj unmodern

down [daun] n (fluff) Flaum m; (hill) Hügel m
♦ adv unten; (motion) herunter; hinunter
♦ prep: **to go ~ the street** die Straße
hinuntergehen ♦ vt niederschlagen; ~ **with
X!** nieder mit X!;~**-and-out** n Tramp m;
~**-at-heel** adj schäbig;~**cast** adj
niedergeschlagen;~**fall** n Sturz m;
~**hearted** adj niedergeschlagen;~**hill** adv
bergab;~ **payment** n Anzahlung f;~**pour**
n Platzregen m;~**right** adj ausgesprochen;
~**size** vi (ECON: company) sich verkleinern

Downing Street

ℹ️ **Downing Street** ist die Straße in
London, die von Whitehall zum St
James Park führt und in der sich der
offizielle Wohnsitz des Premierministers
(Nr. 10) und des Finanzministers (Nr. 11)
befindet. Im weiteren Sinne bezieht sich der
Begriff Downing Street auf die britische
Regierung.

Down's syndrome [daunz-] n (MED)
Down-Syndrom nt

down: ~**stairs** adv unten; (motion) nach
unten;~**stream** adv flussabwärts;~**-to-
earth** adj praktisch;~**town** adv in der
Innenstadt; (motion) in die Innenstadt;~
under (BRIT: inf) adv in/nach Australien/
Neuseeland;~**ward** adj Abwärts-, nach
unten ♦ adv abwärts, nach unten;~**wards**
adv abwärts, nach unten

dowry ['daurɪ] n Mitgift f

doz. abbr (= dozen) Dtzd.

doze [dauz] vi dösen;~ **off** vi einnicken

dozen ['dʌzn] n Dutzend nt; **a ~ books** ein
Dutzend Bücher; ~**s of** dutzende or
Dutzende von

Dr. abbr = **doctor; drive**

drab [dræb] adj düster, eintönig

draft [drɑːft] n Entwurf m; (FIN) Wechsel m;
(US: MIL) Einberufung f ♦ vt skizzieren; see
also **draught**

draftsman ['drɑːftsmən] (US: irreg) n =
draughtsman

drag [dræg] vt schleppen; (river) mit einem
Schleppnetz absuchen ♦ vi sich
(dahin)schleppen ♦ n (bore) etwas Blödes;
in ~ als Tunte; **a man in** ~ eine Tunte;~
on vi sich in die Länge ziehen;~ **and
drop** vt (COMPUT) Drag & Drop nt

dragon ['drægn] n Drache m;~**fly**
['drægnflaɪ] n Libelle f

drain [dreɪn] n Abfluss m; (fig: burden)
Belastung f ♦ vt ableiten; (exhaust)
erschöpfen ♦ vi (of water) abfließen;~**age**
n Kanalisation f;~**ing board** (US~**board**)
n Ablaufbrett nt;~**pipe** n Abflussrohr nt

dram [dræm] n Schluck m

drama ['drɑːmə] n Drama nt;~**tic**
[drə'mætɪk] adj dramatisch;~**tist** ['dræmətɪst]
n Dramatiker m;~**tize** ['dræmətaɪz] vt
(events) dramatisieren; (for TV etc)
bearbeiten

drank [dræŋk] pt of **drink**

drape [dreɪp] vt drapieren;~**s** (US) npl
Vorhänge pl

drastic ['dræstɪk] adj drastisch

draught [drɑːft] (US **draft**) n Zug m; (NAUT)
Tiefgang m; ~**s** n Damespiel nt; **on ~** (beer)
vom Fass;~ **beer** n Bier vom Fass;~
board (BRIT) n Zeichenbrett nt

draughtsman ['drɑːftsmən] (irreg) n
technische(r) Zeichner m

draw [drɔː] (pt **drew**, pp **drew**) vt ziehen;
(crowd) anlocken; (picture) zeichnen;
(money) abheben; (water) schöpfen ♦ vi
(SPORT) unentschieden spielen ♦ n (SPORT)
Unentschieden nt; (lottery) Ziehung f;~
near vi näher rücken;~ **out** vi (train)
ausfahren; (lengthen) sich hinziehen;~ **up**
vi (stop) halten ♦ vt (document) aufsetzen

drawback ['drɔːbæk] n Nachteil m

drawbridge ['drɔːbrɪdʒ] n Zugbrücke f

drawer [drɔ:ʳ] *n* Schublade *f*

drawing ['drɔ:ɪŋ] *n* Zeichnung *f*; Zeichnen *nt*; **~ board** *n* Reißbrett *nt*; **~ pin** (*BRIT*) *n* Reißzwecke *f*; **~ room** *n* Salon *m*

drawl [drɔ:l] *n* schleppende Sprechweise *f*

drawn [drɔ:n] *pp of* **draw**

dread [dred] *n* Furcht *f* ♦ *vt* fürchten; **~ful** *adj* furchtbar

dream [dri:m] (*pt, pp* **dreamed** *or* **dreamt**) *n* Traum *m* ♦ *vt* träumen ♦ *vi*: **to ~ (about)** träumen (von); **~er** *n* Träumer *m*; **~t** [dremt] *pt, pp of* **dream**; **~y** *adj* verträumt

dreary ['drɪərɪ] *adj* trostlos, öde

dredge [dredʒ] *vt* ausbaggern

dregs [dregz] *npl* Bodensatz *m*; (*fig*) Abschaum *m*

drench [drentʃ] *vt* durchnässen

dress [dres] *n* Kleidung *f*; (*garment*) Kleid *nt* ♦ *vt* anziehen; (*MED*) verbinden; **to get ~ed** sich anziehen; **~ up** *vi* sich fein machen; **~ circle** (*BRIT*) *n* erste(r) Rang *m*; **~er** *n* (*furniture*) Anrichte *f*; **~ing** *n* (*MED*) Verband *m*; (*COOK*) Soße *f*; **~ing gown** (*BRIT*) *n* Morgenrock *m*; **~ing room** *n* (*THEAT*) Garderobe *f*; (*SPORT*) Umkleideraum *m*; **~ing table** *n* Toilettentisch *m*; **~maker** *n* Schneiderin *f*; **~ rehearsal** *n* Generalprobe *f*

drew [dru:] *pt of* **draw**

dribble ['drɪbl] *vi* sabbern ♦ *vt* (*ball*) dribbeln

dried [draɪd] *adj* getrocknet; (*fruit*) Dörr-, gedörrte(r, s); **~ milk** *n* Milchpulver *nt*

drier ['draɪəʳ] *n* = **dryer**

drift [drɪft] *n* Strömung *f*; (*snowdrift*) Schneewehe *f*; (*fig*) Richtung *f* ♦ *vi* sich treiben lassen; **~wood** *n* Treibholz *nt*

drill [drɪl] *n* Bohrer *m*; (*MIL*) Drill *m* ♦ *vt* bohren; (*MIL*) ausbilden ♦ *vi*: **to ~ (for)** bohren (nach)

drink [drɪŋk] (*pt* **drank**, *pp* **drunk**) *n* Getränk *nt*; (*spirits*) Drink *m* ♦ *vt, vi* trinken; **to have a ~** etwas trinken; **~er** *n* Trinker *m*; **~ing water** *n* Trinkwasser *nt*

drip [drɪp] *n* Tropfen *m* ♦ *vi* tropfen; **~-dry** *adj* bügelfrei; **~ping** *n* Bratenfett *nt*

drive [draɪv] (*pt* **drove**, *pp* **driven**) *n* Fahrt *f*; (*road*) Einfahrt *f*; (*campaign*) Aktion *f*; (*energy*) Schwung *m*; (*SPORT*) Schlag *m*;

(*also*: **disk ~**) Diskettenlaufwerk *nt* ♦ *vt* (*car*) fahren; (*animals, people, objects*) treiben; (*power*) antreiben ♦ *vi* fahren; **left-/right-hand ~** Links-/Rechtssteuerung *f*; **to ~ sb mad** jdn verrückt machen; **~-by shooting** *n* Schusswaffenangriff aus einem vorbeifahrenden Wagen

drivel ['drɪvl] *n* Faselei *f*

driven ['drɪvn] *pp of* **drive**

driver ['draɪvəʳ] *n* Fahrer *m*; **~'s license** (*US*) *n* Führerschein *m*

driveway ['draɪvweɪ] *n* Auffahrt *f*; (*longer*) Zufahrtsstraße *f*

driving ['draɪvɪŋ] *adj* (*rain*) stürmisch; **~ instructor** *n* Fahrlehrer *m*; **~ lesson** *n* Fahrstunde *f*; **~ licence** (*BRIT*) *n* Führerschein *m*; **~ school** *n* Fahrschule *f*; **~ test** *n* Fahrprüfung *f*

drizzle ['drɪzl] *n* Nieselregen *m* ♦ *vi* nieseln

droll [drəul] *adj* drollig

drone [drəun] *n* (*sound*) Brummen *nt*; (*bee*) Drohne *f*

drool [dru:l] *vi* sabbern

droop [dru:p] *vi* (*schlaff*) herabhängen

drop [drɔp] *n* (*of liquid*) Tropfen *m*; (*fall*) Fall *m* ♦ *vt* fallen lassen; (*lower*) senken; (*abandon*) fallen lassen ♦ *vi* (*fall*) herunterfallen; **~s** *npl* (*MED*) Tropfen *pl*; **~ off** *vi* (*sleep*) einschlafen ♦ *vt* (*passenger*) absetzen; **~ out** *vi* (*withdraw*) ausscheiden; **~-out** *n* Aussteiger *m*; **~per** *n* Pipette *f*; **~pings** *npl* Kot *m*

drought [draut] *n* Dürre *f*

drove [drəuv] *pt of* **drive**

drown [draun] *vt* ertränken; (*sound*) übertönen ♦ *vi* ertrinken

drowsy ['drauzɪ] *adj* schläfrig

drudgery ['drʌdʒərɪ] *n* Plackerei *f*

drug [drʌg] *n* (*MED*) Arznei *f*; (*narcotic*) Rauschgift *nt* ♦ *vt* betäuben; **~ addict** *n* Rauschgiftsüchtige(r) *f(m)*; **~gist** (*US*) *n* Drogist(in) *m(f)*; **~store** (*US*) *n* Drogerie *f*

drum [drʌm] *n* Trommel *f* ♦ *vi* trommeln; **~s** *npl* (*MUS*) Schlagzeug *nt*; **~mer** *n* Trommler *m*

drunk [drʌŋk] *pp of* **drink** ♦ *adj* betrunken ♦ *n* (*also*: **~ard**) Trinker(in) *m(f)*; **~en** *adj* betrunken

dry [draɪ] adj trocken ♦ vt (ab)trocknen ♦ vi trocknen; **~ up** vi austrocknen ♦ vt (dishes) abtrocknen; **~ cleaner's** n chemische Reinigung f; **~ cleaning** n chemische Reinigung f; **~er** n Trockner m; (US: spin-dryer) (Wäsche)schleuder f; **~ goods store** (US) n Kurzwarengeschäft nt; **~ness** n Trockenheit f; **~ rot** n Hausschwamm m

DSS (BRIT) n abbr (= Department of Social Security) ≈ Sozialministerium nt

DTP n abbr (= desktop publishing) DTP nt

dual ['djuəl] adj doppelt; **~ carriageway** (BRIT) n zweispurige Fahrbahn f; **~ nationality** n doppelte Staatsangehörigkeit f; **~-purpose** adj Mehrzweck-

dubbed [dʌbd] adj (film) synchronisiert

dubious ['djuːbɪəs] adj zweifelhaft

duchess ['dʌtʃɪs] n Herzogin f

duck [dʌk] n Ente f ♦ vi sich ducken; **~ling** n Entchen nt

duct [dʌkt] n Röhre f

dud [dʌd] n Niete f ♦ adj (cheque) ungedeckt

due [djuː] adj fällig; (fitting) angemessen ♦ n Gebühr f; (right) Recht nt ♦ adv (south etc) genau; **~s** npl (for club) Beitrag m; (NAUT) Gebühren pl; **~ to** wegen +gen

duel ['djuəl] n Duell nt

duet [djuː'et] n Duett nt

duffel ['dʌfl] adj: **~ bag** Matchbeutel m, Matchsack m

dug [dʌg] pt, pp of **dig**

duke [djuːk] n Herzog m

dull [dʌl] adj (colour, weather) trübe; (stupid) schwer von Begriff; (boring) langweilig ♦ vt abstumpfen

duly ['djuːlɪ] adv ordnungsgemäß

dumb [dʌm] adj stumm; (inf: stupid) doof, blöde; **~founded** [dʌm'faʊndɪd] adj verblüfft

dummy ['dʌmɪ] n Schneiderpuppe f; (substitute) Attrappe f; (BRIT: for baby) Schnuller m ♦ adj Schein-

~imp [dʌmp] n Abfallhaufen m; (MIL) Stapelplatz m; (inf: place) Nest nt ♦ vt abladen, auskippen; **~ing** n (COMM) Schleuderexport m; (of rubbish)

Schuttabladen nt

dumpling ['dʌmplɪŋ] n Kloß m, Knödel m

dumpy ['dʌmpɪ] adj pummelig

dunce [dʌns] n Dummkopf m

dune [djuːn] n Düne f

dung [dʌŋ] n Dünger m

dungarees [dʌŋgə'riːz] npl Latzhose f

dungeon ['dʌndʒən] n Kerker m

dupe [djuːp] n Gefoppte(r) m ♦ vt hintergehen, anführen

duplex ['djuːpleks] (US) n zweistöckige Wohnung f

duplicate [n 'djuːplɪkət, vb 'djuːplɪkeɪt] n Duplikat nt ♦ vt verdoppeln; (make copies) kopieren; **in ~** in doppelter Ausführung

duplicity [djuː'plɪsɪtɪ] n Doppelspiel nt

durable ['djuərəbl] adj haltbar

duration [djuə'reɪʃən] n Dauer f

duress [djuə'res] n: **under ~** unter Zwang

during ['djuərɪŋ] prep während +gen

dusk [dʌsk] n Abenddämmerung f

dust [dʌst] n Staub m ♦ vt abstauben; (sprinkle) bestäuben; **~bin** (BRIT) n Mülleimer m; **~er** n Staubtuch nt; **~ jacket** n Schutzumschlag m; **~man** (BRIT: irreg) n Müllmann m; **~y** adj staubig

Dutch [dʌtʃ] adj holländisch, niederländisch ♦ n (LING) Holländisch nt, Niederländisch nt; **the ~** npl (people) die Holländer pl, die Niederländer pl; **to go ~** getrennte Kasse machen; **~man/woman** (irreg) n Holländer(in) m(f), Niederländer(in) m(f)

dutiful ['djuːtɪful] adj pflichtbewusst

duty ['djuːtɪ] n Pflicht f; (job) Aufgabe f; (tax) Einfuhrzoll m; **on ~** im Dienst; **~ chemist's** n Apotheke f im Bereitschaftsdienst; **~-free** adj zollfrei

duvet ['duːveɪ] (BRIT) n Daunendecke f

DVD n abbr (= digital video disc) DVD f

dwarf [dwɔːf] (pl **dwarves**) n Zwerg m ♦ vt überragen

dwell [dwel] (pt, pp **dwelt**) vi wohnen; **~ on** vt fus verweilen bei; **~ing** n Wohnung f

dwelt [dwelt] pt, pp of **dwell**

dwindle ['dwɪndl] vi schwinden

dye [daɪ] n Farbstoff m ♦ vt färben

dying ['daɪɪŋ] adj (person) sterbend;

(*moments*) letzt

dyke [daɪk] (*BRIT*) n (*channel*) Kanal m; (*barrier*) Deich m, Damm m

dynamic [daɪ'næmɪk] *adj* dynamisch

dynamite ['daɪnəmaɪt] n Dynamit nt

dyslexia [dɪs'lɛksɪə] n Legasthenie f

E, e

E [iː] n (*MUS*) E nt

each [iːtʃ] *adj* jeder/jede/jedes ♦ *pron* (ein) jeder/(eine) jede/(ein) jedes; ~ **other** einander, sich; **they have two books** ~ sie haben je zwei Bücher

eager ['iːgər] *adj* eifrig

eagle ['iːgl] n Adler m

ear [ɪər] n Ohr nt; (*of corn*) Ähre f; ~**ache** n Ohrenschmerzen *pl*; ~**drum** n Trommelfell nt

earl [ɜːl] n Graf m

earlier ['ɜːlɪər] *adj, adv* früher; **I can't come any** ~ ich kann nicht früher *or* eher kommen

early ['ɜːlɪ] *adj, adv* früh; ~ **retirement** n vorzeitige Pensionierung

earmark ['ɪəmɑːk] *vt* vorsehen

earn [ɜːn] *vt* verdienen

earnest ['ɜːnɪst] *adj* ernst; **in** ~ im Ernst

earnings ['ɜːnɪŋz] *npl* Verdienst m

ear: ~**phones** ['ɪəfəʊnz] *npl* Kopfhörer *pl*; ~**ring** ['ɪərɪŋ] n Ohrring m; ~**shot** ['ɪəʃɒt] n Hörweite f

earth [ɜːθ] n Erde f; (*BRIT: ELEC*) Erdung f ♦ *vt* erden; ~**enware** n Steingut nt; ~**quake** n Erdbeben nt; ~**y** *adj* roh

earwig ['ɪəwɪg] n Ohrwurm m

ease [iːz] n (*simplicity*) Leichtigkeit f; (*social*) Ungezwungenheit f ♦ *vt* (*pain*) lindern; (*burden*) erleichtern; **at** ~ ungezwungen; (*MIL*) rührt euch!; ~ **off** *or* **up** *vi* nachlassen

easel ['iːzl] n Staffelei f

easily ['iːzɪlɪ] *adv* leicht

east [iːst] n Osten m ♦ *adj* östlich ♦ *adv* nach Osten

Easter ['iːstər] n Ostern nt; ~ **egg** n Osterei

nt

east: ~**erly** *adj* östlich, Ost-; ~**ern** *adj* östlich; ~**ward(s)** *adv* ostwärts

easy ['iːzɪ] *adj* (*task*) einfach; (*life*) bequem; (*manner*) ungezwungen, natürlich ♦ *adv* leicht; ~ **chair** n Sessel m; ~-**going** *adj* gelassen; (*lax*) lässig

eat [iːt] (*pt* **ate**, *pp* **eaten**) *vt* essen; (*animals*) fressen; (*destroy*) (zer)fressen ♦ *vi* essen; fressen; ~ **away** *vt* zerfressen; ~ **into** *vt fus* zerfressen; ~**en** *pp* of **eat**

eau de Cologne ['əʊdəkə'ləʊn] n Kölnischwasser nt

eaves [iːvz] *npl* Dachrand m

eavesdrop ['iːvzdrɒp] *vi* lauschen; **to** ~ **on sb** jdn belauschen

ebb [ɛb] n Ebbe f ♦ *vi* (*fig: also:* ~ **away**) (ab)ebben

ebony ['ɛbənɪ] n Ebenholz nt

EC n *abbr* (= European Community) EG f

ECB n *abbr* (= European Central Bank) EZB f

eccentric [ɪk'sɛntrɪk] *adj* exzentrisch ♦ n Exzentriker(in) m(f)

ecclesiastical [ɪkliːzɪ'æstɪkl] *adj* kirchlich

echo ['ɛkəʊ] (*pl* ~**es**) n Echo nt ♦ *vt* zurückwerfen; (*fig*) nachbeten ♦ *vi* widerhallen

eclipse [ɪ'klɪps] n Finsternis f ♦ *vt* verfinstern

ecology [ɪ'kɒlədʒɪ] n Ökologie f

e-commerce ['iːkɒməːs] n Onlinehandel m

economic [iːkə'nɒmɪk] *adj* wirtschaftlich; ~**al** *adj* wirtschaftlich; (*person*) sparsam; ~ **refugee** n Wirtschaftsflüchtling m; ~**s** n Volkswirtschaft f

economist [ɪ'kɒnəmɪst] n Volkswirt(schaftler) m

economize [ɪ'kɒnəmaɪz] *vi* sparen

economy [ɪ'kɒnəmɪ] n (*thrift*) Sparsamkeit f; (*of country*) Wirtschaft f; ~ **class** n Touristenklasse f

ecstasy ['ɛkstəsɪ] n Ekstase f; (*drug*) Ecstasy nt; **ecstatic** [ɛks'tætɪk] *adj* hingerissen

ECU ['eɪkjuː] n *abbr* (= European Currency Unit) ECU m

eczema ['ɛksɪmə] n Ekzem nt

edge [ɛdʒ] n Rand m; (*of knife*) Schneide f ♦ *vt* (*SEWING*) einfassen; **on** ~ (*fig*) = **edgy**;

to ~ away from langsam abrücken von;
~ways *adv*: **he couldn't get a word in
~ways** er kam überhaupt nicht zu Wort

edgy ['edʒɪ] *adj* nervös

edible ['edɪbl] *adj* essbar

edict ['iːdɪkt] *n* Erlass *m*

edit ['edɪt] *vt* redigieren; **~ion** [ɪ'dɪʃən] *n*
Ausgabe *f*; **~or** *n* (*of newspaper*) Redakteur
m; (*of book*) Lektor *m*; **~orial** [edɪ'tɔːrɪəl] *adj*
Redaktions- ♦ *n* Leitartikel *m*

educate ['edjukeɪt] *vt* erziehen, (aus)bilden;
~d *adj* gebildet; **education** [edju'keɪʃən] *n*
(*teaching*) Unterricht *m*; (*system*)
Schulwesen *nt*; (*schooling*) Erziehung *f*;
Bildung *f*; **educational** *adj* pädagogisch

eel [iːl] *n* Aal *m*

eerie ['ɪərɪ] *adj* unheimlich

effect [ɪ'fekt] *n* Wirkung *f* ♦ *vt* bewirken; **~s**
npl (*sound, visual*) Effekte *pl*; **in ~** in der Tat;
to take ~ (*law*) in Kraft treten; (*drug*)
wirken; **~ive** *adj* wirksam, effektiv; **~ively**
adv wirksam, effektiv

effeminate [ɪ'femɪnɪt] *adj* weibisch

effervescent [efə'vesnt] *adj* (*also fig*)
sprudelnd

efficiency [ɪ'fɪʃənsɪ] *n* Leistungsfähigkeit *f*

efficient [ɪ'fɪʃənt] *adj* tüchtig; (*TECH*)
leistungsfähig; (*method*) wirksam

effigy ['efɪdʒɪ] *n* Abbild *nt*

effort ['efət] *n* Anstrengung *f*; **~less** *adj*
mühelos

effusive [ɪ'fjuːsɪv] *adj* überschwänglich

e.g. *adv abbr* (= *exempli gratia*) z. B.

egalitarian [ɪgælɪ'teərɪən] *adj* Gleichheits-,
egalitär

egg [eg] *n* Ei *nt*; **~ on** *vt* anstacheln; **~cup** *n*
Eierbecher *m*; **~plant** (*esp US*) *n* Aubergine
f; **~shell** *n* Eierschale *f*

ego ['iːgəʊ] *n* Ich *nt*, Selbst *nt*; **~tism**
['egəʊtɪzəm] *n* Ichbezogenheit *f*; **~tist**
['egəʊtɪst] *n* Egozentriker *m*

Egypt ['iːdʒɪpt] *n* Ägypten *nt*; **~ian** [ɪ'dʒɪpʃən]
adj ägyptisch ♦ *n* Ägypter(in) *m(f)*

eiderdown ['aɪdədaʊn] *n* Daunendecke *f*

eight [eɪt] *num* acht; **~een** *num* achtzehn;
~h [eɪtθ] *adj* achte(r, s) ♦ *n* Achtel *nt*; **~y**
num achtzig

Eire ['ɛərə] *n* Irland *nt*

either ['aɪðə*] *conj*: **~ ... or** entweder ... oder
♦ *pron*: **~ of the two** eine(r, s) von beiden
♦ *adj*: **on ~ side** auf beiden Seiten ♦ *adv*: **I
don't ~** ich auch nicht; **I don't want ~** ich
will keins von beiden

eject [ɪ'dʒekt] *vt* ausstoßen, vertreiben

eke [iːk] *vt*: **to ~ out** strecken

elaborate [*adj* ɪ'læbərɪt, *vb* ɪ'læbəreɪt] *adj*
sorgfältig ausgearbeitet, ausführlich ♦ *vt*
sorgfältig ausarbeiten ♦ *vi* ausführlich
darstellen

elapse [ɪ'læps] *vi* vergehen

elastic [ɪ'læstɪk] *n* Gummiband *nt* ♦ *adj*
elastisch; **~ band** (*BRIT*) *n* Gummiband *nt*

elated [ɪ'leɪtɪd] *adj* froh

elation [ɪ'leɪʃən] *n* gehobene Stimmung *f*

elbow ['elbəʊ] *n* Ellbogen *m*

elder ['eldə*] *adj* älter ♦ *n* Ältere(r) *f(m)*; **~ly**
adj ältere(r, s) ♦ *npl*: **the ~ly** die Älteren *pl*;
eldest ['eldɪst] *adj* älteste(r, s) ♦ *n* Älteste(r)
f(m)

elect [ɪ'lekt] *vt* wählen ♦ *adj* zukünftig; **~ion**
[ɪ'lekʃən] *n* Wahl *f*; **~ioneering** [ɪlekʃə'nɪərɪŋ]
n Wahlpropaganda *f*; **~or** *n* Wähler *m*;
~oral *adj* Wahl-; **~orate** *n* Wähler *pl*,
Wählerschaft *f*

electric [ɪ'lektrɪk] *adj* elektrisch, Elektro-; **~al**
adj elektrisch; **~ blanket** *n* Heizdecke *f*; **~
chair** *n* elektrische(r) Stuhl *m*; **~ fire** *n*
elektrische(r) Heizofen *m*

electrician [ɪlek'trɪʃən] *n* Elektriker *m*

electricity [ɪlek'trɪsɪtɪ] *n* Elektrizität *f*

electrify [ɪ'lektrɪfaɪ] *vt* elektrifizieren; (*fig*)
elektrisieren

electrocute [ɪ'lektrəkjuːt] *vt* durch
elektrischen Strom töten

electronic [ɪlek'trɒnɪk] *adj* elektronisch,
Elektronen-; **~ mail** *n* E-Mail *f*; **~s** *n*
Elektronik *f*

elegance ['elɪgəns] *n* Eleganz *f*; **elegant**
['elɪgənt] *adj* elegant

element ['elɪmənt] *n* Element *nt*; **~ary**
[elɪ'mentərɪ] *adj* einfach; (*primary*) Grund-

elephant ['elɪfənt] *n* Elefant *m*

elevate ['elɪveɪt] *vt* emporheben; **elevation**
[elɪ'veɪʃən] *n* (*height*) Erhebung *f*; (*ARCHIT*)

(Quer)schnitt *m*; **elevator** (*US*) *n* Fahrstuhl *m*, Aufzug *m*

eleven [ɪ'lɛvn] *num* elf; **~ses** (*BRIT*) *npl* ≈ zweite(s) Frühstück *nt*; **~th** *adj* elfte(r, s)

elicit [ɪ'lɪsɪt] *vt* herausbekommen

eligible ['ɛlɪdʒəbl] *adj* wählbar; **to be ~ for a pension** pensionsberechtigt sein

eliminate [ɪ'lɪmɪneɪt] *vt* ausschalten

elite [eɪ'liːt] *n* Elite *f*

elm [ɛlm] *n* Ulme *f*

elocution [ɛlə'kjuːʃən] *n* Sprecherziehung *f*

elongated ['iːlɒŋgeɪtɪd] *adj* verlängert

elope [ɪ'ləup] *vi* entlaufen

eloquence ['ɛləkwəns] *n* Beredsamkeit *f*; **eloquent** *adj* redegewandt

else [ɛls] *adv* sonst; **who ~?** wer sonst?; **somebody ~** jemand anders; **or ~** sonst; **~where** *adv* anderswo, woanders

elude [ɪ'luːd] *vt* entgehen +*dat*

elusive [ɪ'luːsɪv] *adj* schwer fassbar

emaciated [ɪ'meɪsɪeɪtɪd] *adj* abgezehrt

e-mail ['iːmeɪl] *n abbr* (= *electronic mail*) E-Mail *f* ♦ *vti* mailen

emancipation [ɪmænsɪ'peɪʃən] *n* Emanzipation *f*; Freilassung *f*

embankment [ɪm'bæŋkmənt] *n* (*of river*) Uferböschung *f*; (*of road*) Straßendamm *m*

embargo [ɪm'bɑːgəu] (*pl* **~es**) *n* Embargo *nt*

embark [ɪm'bɑːk] *vi* sich einschiffen; **~ on** *vt fus* unternehmen; **~ation** [ɛmbɑː'keɪʃən] *n* Einschiffung *f*

embarrass [ɪm'bærəs] *vt* in Verlegenheit bringen; **~ed** *adj* verlegen; **~ing** *adj* peinlich; **~ment** *n* Verlegenheit *f*

embassy ['ɛmbəsɪ] *n* Botschaft *f*

embed [ɪm'bɛd] *vt* einbetten

embellish [ɪm'bɛlɪʃ] *vt* verschönern

embers ['ɛmbəz] *npl* Glut(asche) *f*

embezzle [ɪm'bɛzl] *vt* unterschlagen; **~ment** *n* Unterschlagung *f*

embitter [ɪm'bɪtə'] *vt* verbittern

embody [ɪm'bɒdɪ] *vt* (*ideas*) verkörpern; (*new features*) (in sich) vereinigen

embossed [ɪm'bɒst] *adj* geprägt

embrace [ɪm'breɪs] *vt* umarmen; (*include*) einschließen ♦ *vi* sich umarmen ♦ *n* Umarmung *f*

embroider [ɪm'brɔɪdə'] *vt* (be)sticken; (*story*) ausschmücken; **~y** *n* Stickerei *f*

emerald ['ɛmərəld] *n* Smaragd *m*

emerge [ɪ'mɜːdʒ] *vi* auftauchen; (*truth*) herauskommen; **~nce** *n* Erscheinen *nt*

emergency [ɪ'mɜːdʒənsɪ] *n* Notfall *m*; **~ cord** (*US*) *n* Notbremse *f*; **~ exit** *n* Notausgang *m*; **~ landing** *n* Notlandung *f*; **~ services** *npl* Notdienste *pl*

emery board ['ɛmərɪ-] *n* Papiernagelfeile *f*

emigrant ['ɛmɪgrənt] *n* Auswanderer *m*

emigrate ['ɛmɪgreɪt] *vi* auswandern; **emigration** [ɛmɪ'greɪʃən] *n* Auswanderung *f*

eminence ['ɛmɪnəns] *n* hohe(r) Rang *m*

eminent ['ɛmɪnənt] *adj* bedeutend

emission [ɪ'mɪʃən] *n* Ausströmen *nt*; **~s** *npl* Emissionen *fpl*

emit [ɪ'mɪt] *vt* von sich *dat* geben

emotion [ɪ'məuʃən] *n* Emotion *f*, Gefühl *nt*; **~al** *adj* (*person*) emotional; (*scene*) ergreifend

emotive [ɪ'məutɪv] *adj* gefühlsbetont

emperor ['ɛmpərə'] *n* Kaiser *m*

emphases ['ɛmfəsiːz] *npl of* **emphasis**

emphasis ['ɛmfəsɪs] *n* (*LING*) Betonung *f*; (*fig*) Nachdruck *m*; **emphasize** ['ɛmfəsaɪz] *vt* betonen

emphatic [ɛm'fætɪk] *adj* nachdrücklich; **~ally** *adv* nachdrücklich

empire ['ɛmpaɪə'] *n* Reich *nt*

empirical [ɛm'pɪrɪkl] *adj* empirisch

employ [ɪm'plɔɪ] *vt* (*hire*) anstellen; (*use*) verwenden; **~ee** [ɪmplɔɪ'iː] *n* Angestellte(r) *f(m)*; **~er** *n* Arbeitgeber(in) *m(f)*; **~ment** *n* Beschäftigung *f*; **~ment agency** *n* Stellenvermittlung *f*

empower [ɪm'pauə'] *vt*: **to ~ sb to do sth** jdn ermächtigen, etw zu tun

empress ['ɛmprɪs] *n* Kaiserin *f*

emptiness ['ɛmptɪnɪs] *n* Leere *f*

empty ['ɛmptɪ] *adj* leer ♦ *n* (*bottle*) Leergut *nt* ♦ *vt* (*contents*) leeren; (*container*) ausleeren ♦ *vi* (*water*) abfließen; (*river*) münden; (*house*) sich leeren; **~-handed** *adj* mit leeren Händen

EMU ['iːmjuː] *n abbr* (= *economic and monetary union*) EWU *f*

emulate [ˈɛmjuleɪt] vt nacheifern +dat
emulsion [ɪˈmʌlʃən] n Emulsion f
enable [ɪˈneɪbl] vt: **to ~ sb to do sth** es jdm ermöglichen, etw zu tun
enact [ɪˈnækt] vt (law) erlassen; (play) aufführen; (role) spielen
enamel [ɪˈnæməl] n Email nt; (of teeth) (Zahn)schmelz m
encased [ɪnˈkeɪst] adj: ~ **in** (enclosed) eingeschlossen in +dat; (covered) verkleidet mit
enchant [ɪnˈtʃɑːnt] vt bezaubern; ~**ing** adj entzückend
encircle [ɪnˈsɜːkl] vt umringen
encl. abbr (= enclosed) Anl.
enclose [ɪnˈkləʊz] vt einschließen; **to ~ sth (in** or **with a letter)** etw (einem Brief) beilegen; ~**d** (in letter) beiliegend, anbei;
enclosure [ɪnˈkləʊʒəʳ] n Einfriedung f; (in letter) Anlage f
encompass [ɪnˈkʌmpəs] vt (include) umfassen
encore [ɒŋˈkɔːʳ] n Zugabe f
encounter [ɪnˈkaʊntəʳ] n Begegnung f; (MIL) Zusammenstoß m ♦ vt treffen; (resistance) stoßen auf +acc
encourage [ɪnˈkʌrɪdʒ] vt ermutigen; ~**ment** n Ermutigung f, Förderung f;
encouraging adj ermutigend, viel versprechend
encroach [ɪnˈkrəʊtʃ] vi: **to ~ (up)on** eindringen in +acc; (time) in Anspruch nehmen
encrusted [ɪnˈkrʌstɪd] adj: ~ **with** besetzt mit
encyclop(a)edia [ɛnsaɪkləʊˈpiːdɪə] n Konversationslexikon nt
end [ɛnd] n Ende nt, Schluss m; (purpose) Zweck m ♦ vt (also: **bring to an ~, put an ~ to**) beenden ♦ vi zu Ende gehen; **in the ~** zum Schluss; **on ~** (object) hochkant; **to stand on ~** (hair) zu Berge stehen; **for hours on ~** stundenlang; ~ **up** vi landen
endanger [ɪnˈdeɪndʒəʳ] vt gefährden; ~**ed species** n eine vom Aussterben bedrohte Art
endearing [ɪnˈdɪərɪŋ] adj gewinnend

endeavour [ɪnˈdɛvəʳ] (US **endeavor**) n Bestrebung f ♦ vi sich bemühen
ending [ˈɛndɪŋ] n Ende nt
endless [ˈɛndlɪs] adj endlos
endorse [ɪnˈdɔːs] vt unterzeichnen; (approve) unterstützen; ~**ment** n (AUT) Eintrag m
endow [ɪnˈdaʊ] vt: **to ~ sb with sth** jdm etw verleihen; (with money) jdm etw stiften
endurance [ɪnˈdjʊərəns] n Ausdauer f
endure [ɪnˈdjʊəʳ] vt ertragen ♦ vi (last) (fort)dauern
enemy [ˈɛnəmɪ] n Feind m ♦ adj feindlich
energetic [ɛnəˈdʒɛtɪk] adj tatkräftig
energy [ˈɛnədʒɪ] n Energie f
enforce [ɪnˈfɔːs] vt durchsetzen
engage [ɪnˈɡeɪdʒ] vt (employ) einstellen; (in conversation) verwickeln; (TECH) einschalten ♦ vi (TECH) ineinander greifen; (clutch) fassen; **to ~ in** sich beteiligen an +dat; ~**d** adj verlobt; (BRIT: TEL, toilet) besetzt; (: busy) beschäftigt; **to get ~d** sich verloben; ~**d tone** n (TEL) Besetztzeichen nt; ~**ment** n (appointment) Verabredung f; (to marry) Verlobung f; (MIL) Gefecht nt; ~**ment ring** n Verlobungsring m;
engaging adj gewinnend
engender [ɪnˈdʒɛndəʳ] vt hervorrufen
engine [ˈɛndʒɪn] n (AUT) Motor m; (RAIL) Lokomotive f; ~ **driver** n Lok(omotiv)führer(in) m(f)
engineer [ɛndʒɪˈnɪəʳ] n Ingenieur m; (US: RAIL) Lok(omotiv)führer(in) m(f); ~**ing** [ɛndʒɪˈnɪərɪŋ] n Technik f
England [ˈɪŋɡlənd] n England nt
English [ˈɪŋɡlɪʃ] adj englisch ♦ n (LING) Englisch nt; **the ~** npl (people) die Engländer pl; ~ **Channel** n: **the ~ Channel** der Ärmelkanal m; ~**man/ woman** (irreg) n Engländer(in) m(f)
engraving [ɪnˈɡreɪvɪŋ] n Stich m
engrossed [ɪnˈɡrəʊst] adj vertieft
engulf [ɪnˈɡʌlf] vt verschlingen
enhance [ɪnˈhɑːns] vt steigern, heben
enigma [ɪˈnɪɡmə] n Rätsel nt; ~**tic** [ɛnɪɡˈmætɪk] adj rätselhaft
enjoy [ɪnˈdʒɔɪ] vt genießen; (privilege) besitzen; **to ~ o.s.** sich amüsieren; ~**able**

adj erfreulich; **~ment** *n* Genuss *m*, Freude *f*

enlarge [ɪn'lɑːdʒ] *vt* erweitern; (*PHOT*) vergrößern ♦ *vi*: **to ~ on sth** etw weiter ausführen; **~ment** *n* Vergrößerung *f*

enlighten [ɪn'laɪtn] *vt* aufklären; **~ment** *n*: **the E~ment** (*HIST*) die Aufklärung

enlist [ɪn'lɪst] *vt* gewinnen ♦ *vi* (*MIL*) sich melden

enmity ['enmɪtɪ] *n* Feindschaft *f*

enormity [ɪ'nɔːmɪtɪ] *n* Ungeheuerlichkeit *f*

enormous [ɪ'nɔːməs] *adj* ungeheuer

enough [ɪ'nʌf] *adj, adv* genug; **funnily ~** komischerweise

enquire [ɪn'kwaɪəʳ] *vt, vi* = **inquire**

enrage [ɪn'reɪdʒ] *vt* wütend machen

enrich [ɪn'rɪtʃ] *vt* bereichern

enrol [ɪn'rəul] *vt* einschreiben ♦ *vi* (*register*) sich anmelden; **~ment** *n* (*for course*) Anmeldung *f*

en route [ɔn'ruːt] *adv* unterwegs

ensign ['ensaɪn, 'ensən] *n* (*NAUT*) Flagge *f*; (*MIL*) Fähnrich *m*

enslave [ɪn'sleɪv] *vt* versklaven

ensue [ɪn'sjuː] *vi* folgen, sich ergeben

en suite [ɔnswiːt] *adj*: **room with ~ bathroom** Zimmer *nt* mit eigenem Bad

ensure [ɪn'ʃuəʳ] *vt* garantieren

entail [ɪn'teɪl] *vt* mit sich bringen

entangle [ɪn'tæŋgl] *vt* verwirren, verstricken; **~d** *adj*: **to become ~d (in)** (*in net, rope etc*) sich verfangen (in +*dat*)

enter ['entəʳ] *vt* eintreten in +*dat*, betreten; (*club*) beitreten +*dat*; (*into book*) eintragen ♦ *vi* hereinkommen, hineingehen; **~ for** *vt fus* sich beteiligen an +*dat*; **~ into** *vt fus* (*agreement*) eingehen; (*plans*) eine Rolle spielen bei; **~ (up)on** *vt fus* beginnen

enterprise ['entəpraɪz] *n* (*in person*) Initiative *f*; (*COMM*) Unternehmen *nt*; **enterprising** ['entəpraɪzɪŋ] *adj* unternehmungslustig

entertain [entə'teɪn] *vt* (*guest*) bewirten; (*amuse*) unterhalten; **~er** *n* Unterhaltungskünstler(in) *m(f)*; **~ing** *adj* unterhaltsam; **~ment** *n* Unterhaltung *f*

enthralled [ɪn'θrɔːld] *adj* gefesselt

enthusiasm [ɪn'θuːzɪæzəm] *n* Begeisterung *f*

enthusiast [ɪn'θuːzɪæst] *n* Enthusiast *m*; **~ic** [ɪnθuːzɪ'æstɪk] *adj* begeistert

entice [ɪn'taɪs] *vt* verleiten, locken

entire [ɪn'taɪəʳ] *adj* ganz; **~ly** *adv* ganz, völlig; **~ty** [ɪn'taɪərətɪ] *n*: **in its ~ty** in seiner Gesamtheit

entitle [ɪn'taɪtl] *vt* (*allow*) berechtigen; (*name*) betiteln; **~d** *adj* (*book*) mit dem Titel; **to be ~d to sth** das Recht auf etw *acc* haben; **to be ~d to do sth** das Recht haben, etw zu tun

entity ['entɪtɪ] *n* Ding *nt*, Wesen *nt*

entourage [ɔntu'rɑːʒ] *n* Gefolge *nt*

entrails ['entreɪlz] *npl* Eingeweide *pl*

entrance [*n* 'entrns, *vb* ɪn'trɑːns] *n* Eingang *m*; (*entering*) Eintritt *m* ♦ *vt* hinreißen; **~ examination** *n* Aufnahmeprüfung *f*; **~ fee** *n* Eintrittsgeld *nt*; **~ ramp** (*US*) *n* (*AUT*) Einfahrt *f*

entrant ['entrnt] *n* (*for exam*) Kandidat *m*; (*in race*) Teilnehmer *m*

entreat [en'triːt] *vt* anflehen

entrenched [en'trentʃt] *adj* (*fig*) verwurzelt

entrepreneur ['ɔntrəprə'nɜːʳ] *n* Unternehmer(in) *m(f)*

entrust [ɪn'trʌst] *vt*: **to ~ sb with sth** *or* **sth to sb** jdm etw anvertrauen

entry ['entrɪ] *n* Eingang *m*; (*THEAT*) Auftritt *m*; (*in account*) Eintragung *f*; (*in dictionary*) Eintrag *m*; **"no ~"** "Eintritt verboten"; (*for cars*) "Einfahrt verboten"; **~ form** *n* Anmeldeformular *nt*; **~ phone** *n* Sprechanlage *f*

enumerate [ɪ'njuːməreɪt] *vt* aufzählen

enunciate [ɪ'nʌnsɪeɪt] *vt* aussprechen

envelop [ɪn'veləp] *vt* einhüllen

envelope ['envələup] *n* Umschlag *m*

enviable ['envɪəbl] *adj* beneidenswert

envious ['envɪəs] *adj* neidisch

environment [ɪn'vaɪrnmənt] *n* Umgebung *f*; (*ECOLOGY*) Umwelt *f*; **~al** [ɪnvaɪərn'mentl] *adj* Umwelt-; **~-friendly** *adj* umweltfreundlich

envisage [ɪn'vɪzɪdʒ] *vt* sich *dat* vorstellen

envoy ['envɔɪ] *n* Gesandte(r) *mf*

envy ['envɪ] *n* Neid *m* ♦ *vt*: **to ~ sb sth** jdn um etw beneiden

enzyme ['enzaɪm] *n* Enzym *nt*

epic ['ɛpɪk] n Epos nt ♦ adj episch

epidemic [ɛpɪ'dɛmɪk] n Epidemie f

epilepsy ['ɛpɪlɛpsɪ] n Epilepsie f; **epileptic** [ɛpɪ'lɛptɪk] adj epileptisch ♦ n Epileptiker(in) m(f)

episode ['ɛpɪsəud] n (incident) Vorfall m; (story) Episode f

epitaph ['ɛpɪtɑːf] n Grabinschrift f

epitomize [ɪ'pɪtəmaɪz] vt verkörpern

equable ['ɛkwəbl] adj ausgeglichen

equal ['iːkwl] adj gleich ♦ n Gleichgestellte(r) mf ♦ vt gleichkommen +dat; ~ **to the task** der Aufgabe gewachsen; **equality** [iː'kwɒlɪtɪ] n Gleichheit f; (equal rights) Gleichberechtigung f; ~**ize** vt gleichmachen ♦ vi (SPORT) ausgleichen; ~**izer** n (SPORT) Ausgleich(streffer) m; ~**ly** adv gleich

equanimity [ɛkwə'nɪmɪtɪ] n Gleichmut m

equate [ɪ'kweɪt] vt gleichsetzen

equation [ɪ'kweɪʃən] n Gleichung f

equator [ɪ'kweɪtə] n Äquator m

equestrian [ɪ'kwɛstrɪən] adj Reit-

equilibrium [iːkwɪ'lɪbrɪəm] n Gleichgewicht nt

equinox ['iːkwɪnɒks] n Tagundnachtgleiche f

equip [ɪ'kwɪp] vt ausrüsten; **to be well ~ped** gut ausgerüstet sein; ~**ment** n Ausrüstung f; (TECH) Gerät nt

equitable ['ɛkwɪtəbl] adj gerecht, billig

equities ['ɛkwɪtɪz] (BRIT) npl (FIN) Stammaktien pl

equivalent [ɪ'kwɪvələnt] adj gleichwertig, entsprechend ♦ n Äquivalent nt; (in money) Gegenwert m; ~ **to** gleichwertig +dat, entsprechend +dat

equivocal [ɪ'kwɪvəkl] adj zweideutig

era ['ɪərə] n Epoche f, Ära f

eradicate [ɪ'rædɪkeɪt] vt ausrotten

erase [ɪ'reɪz] vt ausradieren; (tape) löschen; ~ **r** n Radiergummi nt

erect [ɪ'rɛkt] adj aufrecht ♦ vt errichten; ~**ion** [ɪ'rɛkʃən] n Errichtung f; (ANAT) Erektion f

ERM n abbr (= Exchange Rate Mechanism) Wechselkursmechanismus m

erode [ɪ'rəud] vt zerfressen; (land)

auswaschen

erotic [ɪ'rɒtɪk] adj erotisch

err [əː] vi sich irren

errand ['ɛrənd] n Besorgung f

erratic [ɪ'rætɪk] adj unberechenbar

erroneous [ɪ'rəunɪəs] adj irrig

error ['ɛrə] n Fehler m

erupt [ɪ'rʌpt] vi ausbrechen; ~**ion** [ɪ'rʌpʃən] n Ausbruch m

escalate ['ɛskəleɪt] vi sich steigern

escalator ['ɛskəleɪtə] n Rolltreppe f

escape [ɪs'keɪp] n Flucht f; (of gas) Entweichen nt ♦ vi entkommen; (prisoners) fliehen; (leak) entweichen ♦ vt entkommen +dat; **escapism** n Flucht f (vor der Wirklichkeit)

escort [n 'ɛskɔːt, vb ɪs'kɔːt] n (person accompanying) Begleiter m; (guard) Eskorte f ♦ vt (lady) begleiten; (MIL) eskortieren

Eskimo ['ɛskɪməu] n Eskimo(frau) m(f)

especially [ɪs'pɛʃlɪ] adv besonders

espionage ['ɛspɪənɑːʒ] n Spionage f

esplanade [ɛsplə'neɪd] n Promenade f

Esquire [ɪs'kwaɪə] n: **J. Brown ~** Herrn J. Brown

essay ['ɛseɪ] n Aufsatz m; (LITER) Essay m

essence ['ɛsns] n (quality) Wesen nt; (extract) Essenz f

essential [ɪ'sɛnʃl] adj (necessary) unentbehrlich; (basic) wesentlich ♦ n Allernötigste(s) nt; ~**ly** adv eigentlich

establish [ɪs'tæblɪʃ] vt (set up) gründen; (prove) nachweisen; ~**ed** adj anerkannt; (belief, laws etc) herrschend; ~**ment** n (setting up) Einrichtung f

estate [ɪs'teɪt] n Gut nt; (BRIT: housing ~) Siedlung f; (will) Nachlass m; ~ **agent** (BRIT) n Grundstücksmakler m; ~ **car** (BRIT) n Kombiwagen m

esteem [ɪs'tiːm] n Wertschätzung f

esthetic [ɪs'θɛtɪk] (US) adj = **aesthetic**

estimate [n 'ɛstɪmət, vb 'ɛstɪmeɪt] n Schätzung f; (of price) (Kosten)voranschlag m ♦ vt schätzen; **estimation** [ɛstɪ'meɪʃən] n Einschätzung f; (esteem) Achtung f

estranged [ɪs'treɪndʒd] adj entfremdet

estuary ['ɛstjuərɪ] n Mündung f

etc *abbr* (= *et cetera*) usw.

etching ['etʃɪŋ] *n* Kupferstich *m*

eternal [ɪ'tɜːnl] *adj* ewig

eternity [ɪ'tɜːnɪtɪ] *n* Ewigkeit *f*

ether ['iːθəʳ] *n* Äther *m*

ethical ['eθɪkl] *adj* ethisch

ethics ['eθɪks] *n* Ethik *f* ♦ *npl* Moral *f*

Ethiopia [iːθɪ'əʊpɪə] *n* Äthiopien *nt*

ethnic ['eθnɪk] *adj* Volks-, ethnisch; **~ minority** *n* ethnische Minderheit *f*

ethos ['iːθɒs] *n* Gesinnung *f*

etiquette ['etɪket] *n* Etikette *f*

EU *abbr* (= *European Union*) EU *f*

euphemism ['juːfəmɪzəm] *n* Euphemismus *m*

euro ['jʊərəʊ] *n* (*FIN*) Euro *m*

Eurocheque ['jʊərəʊtʃek] *n* Euroscheck *m*

Euroland ['jʊərəʊlænd] *n* Eurozone *f*, Euroland *nt*

Europe ['jʊərəp] *n* Europa *nt*; **~an** [jʊərə'piːən] *adj* europäisch ♦ *n* Europäer(in) *m(f)*; **~an Community** *n*: **the ~an Community** die Europäische Gemeinschaft

Euro-sceptic ['jʊərəʊskeptɪk] *n* Kritiker der Europäischen Gemeinschaft

evacuate [ɪ'vækjʊeɪt] *vt* (*place*) räumen; (*people*) evakuieren; **evacuation** [ɪvækjʊ'eɪʃən] *n* Räumung *f*; Evakuierung *f*

evade [ɪ'veɪd] *vt* (*escape*) entkommen +*dat*; (*avoid*) meiden; (*duty*) sich entziehen +*dat*

evaluate [ɪ'væljʊeɪt] *vt* bewerten; (*information*) auswerten

evaporate [ɪ'væpəreɪt] *vi* verdampfen ♦ *vt* verdampfen lassen; **~d milk** *n* Kondensmilch *f*

evasion [ɪ'veɪʒən] *n* Umgehung *f*

evasive [ɪ'veɪsɪv] *adj* ausweichend

eve [iːv] *n*: **on the ~ of** am Vorabend +*gen*

even ['iːvn] *adj* eben; gleichmäßig; (*score etc*) unentschieden; (*number*) gerade ♦ *adv*: **~ you** sogar du; **to get ~ with sb** jdm heimzahlen; **~ if** selbst wenn; **~ so** dennoch; **~ though** obwohl; **~ more** sogar noch mehr; **~ out** *vi* sich ausgleichen

evening ['iːvnɪŋ] *n* Abend *m*; **in the ~** abends, am Abend; **~ class** *n* Abendschule *f*; **~ dress** *n* (*man's*) Gesellschaftsanzug *m*;

(*woman's*) Abendkleid *nt*

event [ɪ'vent] *n* (*happening*) Ereignis *nt*; (*SPORT*) Disziplin *f*; **in the ~ of** im Falle +*gen*; **~ful** *adj* ereignisreich

eventual [ɪ'ventʃʊəl] *adj* (*final*) schließlich; **~ity** [ɪventʃʊ'ælɪtɪ] *n* Möglichkeit *f*; **~ly** *adv* am Ende; (*given time*) schließlich

ever ['evəʳ] *adv* (*always*) immer; (*at any time*) je(mals) ♦ *conj* seit; **~ since** seitdem; **have you ~ seen it?** haben Sie es je gesehen?; **~green** *n* Immergrün *nt*; **~lasting** *adj* immer während

every ['evrɪ] *adj* jede(r, s); **~ other/third day** jeden zweiten/dritten Tag; **~ one of them** alle; **I have ~ confidence in him** ich habe uneingeschränktes Vertrauen in ihn; **we wish you ~ success** wir wünschen Ihnen viel Erfolg; **he's ~ bit as clever as his brother** er ist genauso klug wie sein Bruder; **~ now and then** ab und zu; **~body** *pron* = **everyone**; **~day** *adj* (*daily*) täglich; (*commonplace*) alltäglich, Alltags-; **~one** *pron* jeder, alle *pl*; **~thing** *pron* alles; **~where** *adv* überall(hin); (*wherever*) wohin; **~where you go** wohin du auch gehst

evict [ɪ'vɪkt] *vt* ausweisen; **~ion** [ɪ'vɪkʃən] *n* Ausweisung *f*

evidence ['evɪdns] *n* (*sign*) Spur *f*; (*proof*) Beweis *m*; (*testimony*) Aussage *f*

evident ['evɪdnt] *adj* augenscheinlich; **~ly** *adv* offensichtlich

evil ['iːvl] *adj* böse ♦ *n* Böse *nt*

evocative [ɪ'vɒkətɪv] *adj*: **to be ~ of sth** an etw *acc* erinnern

evoke [ɪ'vəʊk] *vt* hervorrufen

evolution [iːvə'luːʃən] *n* Entwicklung *f*; (*of life*) Evolution *f*

evolve [ɪ'vɒlv] *vt* entwickeln ♦ *vi* sich entwickeln

ewe [juː] *n* Mutterschaf *nt*

ex- [eks] *prefix* Ex-, Alt-, ehemalig

exacerbate [eks'æsəbeɪt] *vt* verschlimmern

exact [ɪg'zækt] *adj* genau ♦ *vt* (*demand*) verlangen; **~ing** *adj* anspruchsvoll; **~ly** *adv* genau

exaggerate [ɪg'zædʒəreɪt] *vt*, *vi* übertreiben; **exaggeration** [ɪgzædʒə'reɪʃən] *n*

Übertreibung f

exalted [ɪgˈzɔːltɪd] adj (position, style) hoch; (person) exaltiert

exam [ɪgˈzæm] n abbr (SCH) = **examination**

examination [ɪgzæmɪˈneɪʃən] n Untersuchung f; (SCH) Prüfung f, Examen nt; (customs) Kontrolle f

examine [ɪgˈzæmɪn] vt untersuchen; (SCH) prüfen; (consider) erwägen; **~r** n Prüfer m

example [ɪgˈzɑːmpl] n Beispiel nt; **for ~** zum Beispiel

exasperate [ɪgˈzɑːspəreɪt] vt zur Verzweiflung bringen; **exasperating** adj ärgerlich, zum Verzweifeln bringend; **exasperation** [ɪgzɑːspəˈreɪʃən] n Verzweiflung f

excavate [ˈɛkskəveɪt] vt ausgraben; **excavation** [ɛkskəˈveɪʃən] n Ausgrabung f

exceed [ɪkˈsiːd] vt überschreiten; (hopes) übertreffen; **~ingly** adv äußerst

excel [ɪkˈsɛl] vi sich auszeichnen; **~lence** [ˈɛksələns] n Vortrefflichkeit f; **E~lency** [ˈɛksələnsɪ] n: **His E~lency** Seine Exzellenz f; **~lent** [ˈɛksələnt] adj ausgezeichnet

except [ɪkˈsɛpt] prep (also: **~ for, ~ing**) außer +dat ♦ vt ausnehmen; **~ion** [ɪkˈsɛpʃən] n Ausnahme f; **to take ~ion to** Anstoß nehmen an +dat; **~ional** [ɪkˈsɛpʃnl] adj außergewöhnlich

excerpt [ˈɛksɜːpt] n Auszug m

excess [ɪkˈsɛs] n Übermaß nt; **an ~ of** ein Übermaß an +dat; **~ baggage** n Mehrgepäck nt; **~ fare** n Nachlösegebühr f; **~ive** adj übermäßig

exchange [ɪksˈtʃeɪndʒ] n Austausch m; (also: **telephone ~**) Zentrale f ♦ vt (goods) tauschen; (greetings) austauschen; (money, blows) wechseln; **~ rate** n Wechselkurs m

Exchequer [ɪksˈtʃekər] (BRIT) n: **the ~** das Schatzamt

excise [ˈɛksaɪz] n Verbrauchssteuer f

excite [ɪkˈsaɪt] vt erregen; **to get ~d** sich aufregen; **~ment** n Aufregung f; **exciting** adj spannend

exclaim [ɪksˈkleɪm] vi ausrufen

exclamation [ɛkskləˈmeɪʃən] n Ausruf m; **~ mark** n Ausrufezeichen nt

exclude [ɪksˈkluːd] vt ausschließen

exclusion [ɪksˈkluːʒən] n Ausschluss m; **~ zone** n Sperrzone f

exclusive [ɪksˈkluːsɪv] adj (select) exklusiv; (sole) ausschließlich, Allein-; **~ of** exklusive +gen; **~ly** adv nur, ausschließlich

excrement [ˈɛkskrəmənt] n Kot m

excruciating [ɪksˈkruːʃɪeɪtɪŋ] adj qualvoll

excursion [ɪksˈkɜːʃən] n Ausflug m

excusable [ɪksˈkjuːzəbl] adj entschuldbar

excuse [n ɪksˈkjuːs, vb ɪksˈkjuːz] n Entschuldigung f ♦ vt entschuldigen; **~ me!** entschuldigen Sie!

ex-directory [ˈɛksdɪˈrɛktərɪ] (BRIT) adj: **to be ~** nicht im Telefonbuch stehen

execute [ˈɛksɪkjuːt] vt (carry out) ausführen; (kill) hinrichten; **execution** [ɛksɪˈkjuːʃən] n Ausführung f; (killing) Hinrichtung f; **executioner** [ɛksɪˈkjuːʃnər] n Scharfrichter m

executive [ɪgˈzɛkjutɪv] n (COMM) Geschäftsführer m; (POL) Exekutive f ♦ adj Exekutiv-, ausführend

executor [ɪgˈzɛkjutər] n Testamentsvollstrecker m

exemplary [ɪgˈzɛmplərɪ] adj musterhaft

exemplify [ɪgˈzɛmplɪfaɪ] vt veranschaulichen

exempt [ɪgˈzɛmpt] adj befreit ♦ vt befreien; **~ion** [ɪgˈzɛmpʃən] n Befreiung f

exercise [ˈɛksəsaɪz] n Übung f ♦ vt (power) ausüben; (muscle, patience) üben; (dog) ausführen ♦ vi Sport treiben; **~ bike** n Heimtrainer m; **~ book** n (Schul)heft nt

exert [ɪgˈzɜːt] vt (influence) ausüben; **to ~ o.s.** sich anstrengen; **~ion** [ɪgˈzɜːʃən] n Anstrengung f

exhale [ɛksˈheɪl] vt, vi ausatmen

exhaust [ɪgˈzɔːst] n (fumes) Abgase pl; (pipe) Auspuffrohr nt ♦ vt erschöpfen; **~ed** adj erschöpft; **~ion** [ɪgˈzɔːstʃən] n Erschöpfung f; **~ive** adj erschöpfend

exhibit [ɪgˈzɪbɪt] n (JUR) Beweisstück nt; (ART) Ausstellungsstück nt ♦ vt ausstellen; **~ion** [ɛksɪˈbɪʃən] n (ART) Ausstellung f; (of temper etc) Zurschaustellung f; **~ionist** [ɛksɪˈbɪʃənɪst] n Exhibitionist m

exhilarating [ɪgˈzɪləreɪtɪŋ] adj erhebend

ex-husband *n* Ehemann *m*

exile ['eksaɪl] *n* Exil *nt*; *(person)* Verbannte(r) *f(m)* ♦ *vt* verbannen

exist [ɪg'zɪst] *vi* existieren; **~ence** *n* Existenz *f*; **~ing** *adj* bestehend

exit ['eksɪt] *n* Ausgang *m*; *(THEAT)* Abgang *m* ♦ *vi (THEAT)* abtreten; *(COMPUT)* aus einem Programm herausgehen; **~ poll** *n bei Wahlen unmittelbar nach Verlassen der Wahllokale durchgeführte Umfrage*; **~ ramp** *n (US)* Ausfahrt *f*

exodus ['eksədəs] *n* Auszug *m*

exonerate [ɪg'zɒnəreɪt] *vt* entlasten

exorbitant [ɪg'zɔːbɪtnt] *adj* übermäßig; *(price)* Fantasie-

exotic [ɪg'zɒtɪk] *adj* exotisch

expand [ɪks'pænd] *vt* ausdehnen ♦ *vi* sich ausdehnen

expanse [ɪks'pæns] *n* Fläche *f*

expansion [ɪks'pænʃən] *n* Erweiterung *f*

expatriate [eks'pætrɪət] *n* Ausländer(in) *m(f)*

expect [ɪks'pekt] *vt* erwarten; *(suppose)* annehmen ♦ *vi*: **to be ~ing** ein Kind erwarten; **~ancy** *n* Erwartung *f*; **~ant mother** *n* werdende Mutter *f*; **~ation** [ekspek'teɪʃən] *n* Hoffnung *f*

expedient [ɪks'piːdɪənt] *adj* zweckdienlich ♦ *n* (Hilfs)mittel *nt*

expedition [ekspə'dɪʃən] *n* Expedition *f*

expel [ɪks'pel] *vt* ausweisen; *(student)* (ver)weisen

expend [ɪks'pend] *vt (effort)* aufwenden; **~iture** *n* Ausgaben *pl*

expense [ɪks'pens] *n* Kosten *pl*; **~s** *npl* *(COMM)* Spesen *pl*; **at the ~ of** auf Kosten von; **~ account** *n* Spesenkonto *nt*; **expensive** [ɪks'pensɪv] *adj* teuer

experience [ɪks'pɪərɪəns] *n (incident)* Erlebnis *nt*; *(practice)* Erfahrung *f* ♦ *vt* erleben; **~d** *adj* erfahren

experiment [ɪks'perɪmənt] *n* Versuch *m*, Experiment *n* ♦ *vi* experimentieren; **~al** [ɪkspərɪ'mentl] *adj* experimentell

expert ['ekspɜːt] *n* Fachmann *m*; *(official)* Sachverständige(r) *m* ♦ *adj* erfahren; **~ise** [ekspɜː'tiːz] *n* Sachkenntnis *f*

expire [ɪks'paɪər] *vi (end)* ablaufen; *(ticket)*

verfallen; *(die)* sterben; **expiry** *n* Ablauf *m*

explain [ɪks'pleɪn] *vt* erklären

explanation [eksplə'neɪʃən] *n* Erklärung *f*; **explanatory** [ɪks'plænətrɪ] *adj* erklärend

explicit [ɪks'plɪsɪt] *adj* ausdrücklich

explode [ɪks'pləʊd] *vi* explodieren ♦ *vt (bomb)* sprengen

exploit [*n* 'eksplɔɪt, *vb* ɪks'plɔɪt] *n* (Helden)tat *f* ♦ *vt* ausbeuten; **~ation** [eksplɔɪ'teɪʃən] *n* Ausbeutung *f*

exploration [eksplə'reɪʃən] *n* Erforschung *f*

exploratory [ɪks'plɒrətrɪ] *adj* Probe-

explore [ɪks'plɔː] *vt (travel)* erforschen; *(search)* untersuchen; **~r** *n* Erforscher(in) *m(f)*

explosion [ɪks'pləʊʒən] *n* Explosion *f*; *(fig)* Ausbruch *m*

explosive [ɪks'pləʊsɪv] *adj* explosiv, Spreng- ♦ *n* Sprengstoff *m*

export [*vb* eks'pɔːt, *n* 'ekspɔːt] *vt* exportieren ♦ *n* Export *m* ♦ *cpd (trade)* Export-; **~er** [eks'pɔːtər] *n* Exporteur *m*

expose [ɪks'pəʊz] *vt (to danger etc)* aussetzen; *(impostor)* entlarven; **to ~ sb to sth** jdn einer Sache *dat* aussetzen; **~d** *adj (position)* exponiert; **exposure** [ɪks'pəʊʒər] *n (MED)* Unterkühlung *f*; *(PHOT)* Belichtung *f*; **exposure meter** *n* Belichtungsmesser *m*

express [ɪks'pres] *adj* ausdrücklich; *(speedy)* Express-, Eil- ♦ *n (RAIL)* Schnellzug *m* ♦ *adv (send)* per Express ♦ *vt* ausdrücken; **to ~ o.s.** sich ausdrücken; **~ion** [ɪks'preʃən] *n* Ausdruck *m*; **~ive** *adj* ausdrucksvoll; **~ly** *adv* ausdrücklich; **~way** *n (US) (urban motorway)* Schnellstraße *f*

expulsion [ɪks'pʌlʃən] *n* Ausweisung *f*

exquisite [eks'kwɪzɪt] *adj* erlesen

extend [ɪks'tend] *vt (visit etc)* verlängern; *(building)* ausbauen; *(hand)* ausstrecken; *(welcome)* bieten ♦ *vi (land)* sich erstrecken

extension [ɪks'tenʃən] *n* Erweiterung *f*; *(of building)* Anbau *m*; *(TEL)* Apparat *m*

extensive [ɪks'tensɪv] *adj (knowledge)* umfassend; *(use)* weitgehend, weit gehend

extent [ɪks'tent] *n* Ausdehnung *f*; *(fig)* Ausmaß *nt*; **to a certain ~** bis zu einem gewissen Grade; **to such an ~ that ...** dermaßen, dass ...; **to what ~?** inwieweit?

extenuating [ɪks'tenjueɪtɪŋ] *adj* mildernd

exterior [eks'tɪərɪəʳ] *adj* äußere(r, s), Außen- ♦ *n* Äußere(s) *nt*

exterminate [ɪks'tə:mɪneɪt] *vt* ausrotten

external [eks'tə:nl] *adj* äußere(r, s), Außen-

extinct [ɪks'tɪŋkt] *adj* ausgestorben; **~ion** [ɪks'tɪŋkʃən] *n* Aussterben *nt*

extinguish [ɪks'tɪŋgwɪʃ] *vt* (aus)löschen

extort [ɪks'tɔ:t] *vt* erpressen; **~ion** [ɪks'tɔ:ʃən] *n* Erpressung *f*; **~ionate** [ɪks'tɔ:ʃnɪt] *adj* überhöht, erpresserisch

extra ['ekstrə] *adj* zusätzlich ♦ *adv* besonders ♦ *n* (*for car etc*) Extra *nt*; (*charge*) Zuschlag *m*; (*THEAT*) Statist *m* ♦ *prefix* außer...

extract [*v* ɪks'trækt, *n* 'ekstrækt] *vt* (heraus)ziehen ♦ *n* (*from book etc*) Auszug *m*; (*COOK*) Extrakt *m*

extracurricular ['ekstrəkə'rɪkjuləʳ] *adj* außerhalb des Stundenplans

extradite ['ekstrədaɪt] *vt* ausliefern

extramarital ['ekstrə'mærɪtl] *adj* außerehelich

extramural ['ekstrə'mjuərl] *adj* (*course*) Volkshochschul-

extraordinary [ɪks'trɔ:dnrɪ] *adj* außerordentlich; (*amazing*) erstaunlich

extravagance [ɪks'trævəgəns] *n* Verschwendung *f*; (*lack of restraint*) Zügellosigkeit *f*; (*an ~*) Extravaganz *f*

extravagant [ɪks'trævəgənt] *adj* extravagant

extreme [ɪks'tri:m] *adj* (*edge*) äußerste(r, s), hinterste(r, s); (*cold*) äußerste(r, s); (*behaviour*) außergewöhnlich, übertrieben ♦ *n* Extrem *nt*; **~ly** *adv* äußerst, höchst; **extremist** *n* Extremist(in) *m(f)*

extremity [ɪks'tremɪtɪ] *n* (*end*) Spitze *f*, äußerste(s) Ende *nt*; (*hardship*) bitterste Not *f*; (*ANAT*) Hand *f*; Fuß *m*

extricate ['ekstrɪkeɪt] *vt* losmachen, befreien

extrovert ['ekstrəvə:t] *n* extrovertierte(r) Mensch *m*

exuberant [ɪg'zju:bərnt] *adj* ausgelassen

exude [ɪg'zju:d] *vt* absondern

eye [aɪ] *n* Auge *nt*; (*of needle*) Öhr *nt* ♦ *vt* betrachten; (*up and down*) mustern; **to keep an ~ on** aufpassen auf +*acc*; **~ball** *n* Augapfel *m*; **~bath** *n* Augenbad *nt*; **~brow** *n* Augenbraue *f*; **~brow pencil** *n* Augenbrauenstift *m*; **~drops** *npl* Augentropfen *pl*; **~lash** *n* Augenwimper *f*; **~lid** *n* Augenlid *nt*; **~liner** *n* Eyeliner *nt*; **~-opener** *n*: **that was an ~-opener** das hat mir/ihm *etc* die Augen geöffnet; **~shadow** *n* Lidschatten *m*; **~sight** *n* Sehkraft *f*; **~sore** *n* Schandfleck *m*; **~ witness** *n* Augenzeuge *m*

F, f

F [ef] *n* (*MUS*) F *nt*

F. *abbr* (= *Fahrenheit*) F

fable ['feɪbl] *n* Fabel *f*

fabric ['fæbrɪk] *n* Stoff *m*; (*fig*) Gefüge *nt*

fabrication [fæbrɪ'keɪʃən] *n* Erfindung *f*

fabulous ['fæbjuləs] *adj* sagenhaft

face [feɪs] *n* Gesicht *nt*; (*surface*) Oberfläche *f*; (*of clock*) Zifferblatt *nt* ♦ *vt* (*point towards*) liegen nach; (*situation, difficulty*) sich stellen +*dat*; **~ down** (*person*) mit dem Gesicht nach unten; (*card*) mit der Vorderseite nach unten; **to make** *or* **pull a ~** das Gesicht verziehen; **in the ~ of** angesichts +*gen*; **on the ~ of it** so, wie es aussieht; **~ to ~** Auge in Auge; **to ~ up to sth** einer Sache *dat* ins Auge sehen; **~ cloth** (*BRIT*) *n* Waschlappen *m*; **~ cream** *n* Gesichtscreme *f*; **~ lift** *n* Facelifting *nt*; **~ powder** *n* (Gesichts)puder *m*

facet ['fæsɪt] *n* Aspekt *m*; (*of gem*) Facette *f*, Fassette *f*

facetious [fə'si:ʃəs] *adj* witzig

face value *n* Nennwert *m*; **to take sth at (its) ~** (*fig*) etw für bare Münze nehmen

facial ['feɪʃl] *adj* Gesichts-

facile ['fæsaɪl] *adj* (*easy*) leicht

facilitate [fə'sɪlɪteɪt] *vt* erleichtern

facilities [fə'sɪlɪtɪz] *npl* Einrichtungen *pl*; **credit ~** Kreditmöglichkeiten *pl*

facing ['feɪsɪŋ] *adj* zugekehrt ♦ *prep* gegenüber

facsimile [fæk'sɪmɪlɪ] *n* Faksimile *nt*;

(*machine*) Telekopierer *m*

fact [fækt] *n* Tatsache *f*; **in ~** in der Tat

faction ['fækʃən] *n* Splittergruppe *f*

factor ['fæktər] *n* Faktor *m*

factory ['fæktərɪ] *n* Fabrik *f*

factual ['fæktjuəl] *adj* sachlich

faculty ['fækəltɪ] *n* Fähigkeit *f*; (*UNIV*) Fakultät *f*; (*US: teaching staff*) Lehrpersonal *nt*

fad [fæd] *n* Tick *m*; (*fashion*) Masche *f*

fade [feɪd] *vi* (*lose colour*) verblassen; (*dim*) nachlassen; (*sound, memory*) schwächer werden; (*wilt*) verwelken

fag [fæg] (*inf*) *n* (*cigarette*) Kippe *f*

fail [feɪl] *vt* (*exam*) nicht bestehen; (*student*) durchfallen lassen; (*courage*) verlassen; (*memory*) im Stich lassen ♦ *vi* (*supplies*) zu Ende gehen; (*student*) durchfallen; (*eyesight*) nachlassen; (*light*) schwächer werden; (*crop*) fehlschlagen; (*remedy*) nicht wirken; **to ~ to do sth** (*neglect*) es unterlassen, etw zu tun; (*be unable*) es nicht schaffen, etw zu tun; **without ~** unbedingt; **~ing** *n* Schwäche *f* ♦ *prep* mangels +*gen*; **~ure** ['feɪljər] *n* (*person*) Versager *m*; (*act*) Versagen *nt*; (*TECH*) Defekt *m*

faint [feɪnt] *adj* schwach ♦ *n* Ohnmacht *f* ♦ *vi* ohnmächtig werden

fair [feər] *adj* (*just*) gerecht, fair; (*hair*) blond; (*skin*) hell; (*weather*) schön; (*not very good*) mittelmäßig; (*sizeable*) ansehnlich ♦ *adv* (*play*) fair ♦ *n* (*COMM*) Messe *f*; (*BRIT: funfair*) Jahrmarkt *m*; **~ly** *adv* (*honestly*) gerecht, fair; (*rather*) ziemlich; **~ness** *n* Fairness *f*

fairy ['feərɪ] *n* Fee *f*; **~ tale** *n* Märchen *nt*

faith [feɪθ] *n* Glaube *m*; (*trust*) Vertrauen *nt*; (*sect*) Bekenntnis *nt*; **~ful** *adj* treu; **~fully** *adv* treu; **yours ~fully** (*BRIT*) hochachtungsvoll

fake [feɪk] *n* (*thing*) Fälschung *f*; (*person*) Schwindler *m* ♦ *adj* vorgetäuscht ♦ *vt* fälschen

falcon ['fɔːlkən] *n* Falke *m*

fall [fɔːl] (*pt* **fell**, *pp* **fallen**) *n* Fall *m*, Sturz *m*; (*decrease*) Fallen *nt*; (*of snow*) (Schnee)fall *m*; (*US: autumn*) Herbst *m* ♦ *vi* (*also fig*) fallen; (*night*) hereinbrechen; **~s** *npl* (*waterfall*) Fälle *pl*; **to ~ flat** platt hinfallen;

(*joke*) nicht ankommen; **~ back** *vi* zurückweichen; **~ back on** *vt fus* zurückgreifen auf +*acc*; **~ behind** *vi* zurückbleiben; **~ down** *vi* (*person*) hinfallen; (*building*) einstürzen; **~ for** *vt fus* (*trick*) hereinfallen auf +*acc*; (*person*) sich verknallen in +*acc*; **~ in** *vi* (*roof*) einstürzen; **~ off** *vi* herunterfallen; (*diminish*) sich vermindern; **~ out** *vi* sich streiten; (*MIL*) wegtreten; **~ through** *vi* (*plan*) ins Wasser fallen

fallacy ['fæləsɪ] *n* Trugschluss *m*

fallen ['fɔːlən] *pp of* **fall**

fallible ['fæləbl] *adj* fehlbar

fallout ['fɔːlaut] *n* radioaktive(r) Niederschlag *m*; **~ shelter** *n* Atombunker *m*

fallow ['fæləu] *adj* brach(liegend)

false [fɔːls] *adj* falsch; (*artificial*) künstlich; **under ~ pretences** unter Vorspiegelung falscher Tatsachen; **~ alarm** *n* Fehlalarm *m*; **~ teeth** (*BRIT*) *npl* Gebiss *nt*

falter ['fɔːltər] *vi* schwanken; (*in speech*) stocken

fame [feɪm] *n* Ruhm *m*

familiar [fə'mɪlɪər] *adj* bekannt; (*intimate*) familiär; **to be ~ with** vertraut sein mit; **~ize** *vt* vertraut machen

family ['fæmɪlɪ] *n* Familie *f*; (*relations*) Verwandtschaft *f*; **~ business** *n* Familienunternehmen *nt*; **~ doctor** *n* Hausarzt *m*

famine ['fæmɪn] *n* Hungersnot *f*

famished ['fæmɪʃt] *adj* ausgehungert

famous ['feɪməs] *adj* berühmt

fan [fæn] *n* (*folding*) Fächer *m*; (*ELEC*) Ventilator *m*; (*admirer*) Fan *m* ♦ *vt* fächeln; **~ out** *vi* sich (fächerförmig) ausbreiten

fanatic [fə'nætɪk] *n* Fanatiker(in) *m(f)*

fan belt *n* Keilriemen *m*

fanciful ['fænsɪful] *adj* (*odd*) seltsam; (*imaginative*) fantasievoll

fancy ['fænsɪ] *n* (*liking*) Neigung *f*; (*imagination*) Einbildung *f* ♦ *adj* schick ♦ *vt* (*like*) gern haben; wollen; (*imagine*) sich einbilden; **he fancies her** er mag sie; **~ dress** *n* Maskenkostüm *nt*; **~-dress ball** *n* Maskenball *m*

fang [fæŋ] n Fangzahn m; (of snake) Giftzahn m

fantastic [fæn'tæstɪk] adj fantastisch

fantasy ['fæntəsɪ] n Fantasie f

far [fɑː] adj weit ♦ adv weit entfernt; (very much) weitaus; **by ~** bei weitem; **so ~** so weit; bis jetzt; **go as ~ as the station** gehen Sie bis zum Bahnhof; **as ~ as I know** soweit or soviel ich weiß; **~away** adj weit entfernt

farce [fɑːs] n Farce f; **farcical** ['fɑːsɪkl] adj lächerlich

fare [fɛə] n Fahrpreis m; Fahrgeld nt; (food) Kost f; **half/full ~** halber/voller Fahrpreis m

Far East n: **the ~** der Ferne Osten

farewell [fɛə'wɛl] n Abschied(sgruß) m ♦ excl lebe wohl!

farm [fɑːm] n Bauernhof m, Farm f ♦ vt bewirtschaften; **~er** n Bauer m, Landwirt m; **~hand** n Landarbeiter m; **~house** n Bauernhaus nt; **~ing** n Landwirtschaft f; **~land** n Ackerland nt; **~yard** n Hof m

far-reaching ['fɑː'riːtʃɪŋ] adj (reform, effect) weitreichend, weit reichend

fart [fɑːt] (inf!) n Furz m ♦ vi furzen

farther ['fɑːðə] adv weiter; **farthest** ['fɑːðɪst] adv fernste(r, s) ♦ adv am weitesten

fascinate ['fæsɪneɪt] vt faszinieren; **fascinating** adj faszinierend; **fascination** [fæsɪ'neɪʃən] n Faszination f

fascism ['fæʃɪzəm] n Faschismus m

fashion ['fæʃən] n (of clothes) Mode f; (manner) Art f (und Weise f) ♦ vt machen; **in ~** in Mode; **out of ~** unmodisch; **~able** adj (clothes) modisch; (place) elegant; **~ show** n Mode(n)schau f

fast [fɑːst] adj schnell; (firm) fest ♦ adv schnell; fest ♦ n Fasten nt ♦ vi fasten; **to be ~** (clock) vorgehen

fasten ['fɑːsn] vt (attach) befestigen; (with rope) zuschnüren; (seat belt) festmachen; (coat) zumachen ♦ vi sich schließen lassen; **~er** n Verschluss m; **~ing** n Verschluss m

fast food n Fastfood nt, Fast Food nt

fastidious [fæs'tɪdɪəs] adj wählerisch

fat [fæt] adj dick ♦ n Fett nt

fatal ['feɪtl] adj tödlich; (disastrous)

verhängnisvoll; **~ity** [fə'tælɪtɪ] n (road death etc) Todesopfer nt; **~ly** adv tödlich

fate [feɪt] n Schicksal nt; **~ful** adj (prophetic) schicksalsschwer; (important) schicksalhaft

father ['fɑːðə] n Vater m; (REL) Pater m; **~-in-law** n Schwiegervater m; **~ly** adj väterlich

fathom ['fæðəm] n Klafter m ♦ vt ausloten; (fig) ergründen

fatigue [fə'tiːg] n Ermüdung f

fatten ['fætn] vt dick machen; (animals) mästen ♦ vi dick werden

fatty ['fætɪ] adj fettig ♦ n (inf) Dickerchen nt

fatuous ['fætjuəs] adj albern, affig

faucet ['fɔːsɪt] (US) n Wasserhahn m

fault [fɔːlt] n (defect) Defekt m; (ELEC) Störung f; (blame) Schuld f; (GEOG) Verwerfung f; **it's your ~** du bist daran schuld; **to find ~ with (sth/sb)** etwas auszusetzen haben an (etw/jdm); **at ~** im Unrecht; **~less** adj tadellos; **~y** adj fehlerhaft, defekt

fauna ['fɔːnə] n Fauna f

favour ['feɪvə] (US **favor**) n (approval) Wohlwollen nt; (kindness) Gefallen m ♦ vt (prefer) vorziehen; **in ~ of** für; zugunsten or zu Gunsten +gen; **to find ~ with sb** bei jdm Anklang finden; **~able** ['feɪvrəbl] adj günstig; **~ite** ['feɪvrɪt] adj Lieblings- ♦ n (child) Liebling m; (SPORT) Favorit m

fawn [fɔːn] adj rehbraun ♦ n (animal) (Reh)kitz nt ♦ vi: **to ~ (up)on** (fig) katzbuckeln vor +dat

fax [fæks] n (document) Fax nt; (machine) Telefax nt ♦ vt: **to ~ sth to sb** jdm etw faxen

FBI (US) n abbr (= Federal Bureau of Investigation) FBI nt

fear [fɪə] n Furcht f ♦ vt fürchten; **~ful** adj (timid) furchtsam; (terrible) fürchterlich; **~less** adj furchtlos

feasible ['fiːzəbl] adj durchführbar

feast [fiːst] n Festmahl nt; (REL: also: **~ day**) Feiertag m ♦ vi: **to ~ (on)** sich gütlich tun (an +dat)

feat [fiːt] n Leistung f

feather ['fɛðə] n Feder f

feature ['fiːtʃə] n (Gesichts)zug m;

(*important part*) Grundzug m; (*CINE, PRESS*)
Feature nt ♦ vt darstellen; (*advertising etc*)
groß herausbringen ♦ vi vorkommen;
featuring X mit X; ~ **film** n Spielfilm m
February ['februəri] n Februar m
fed [fed] pt, pp of **feed**
federal ['fedərəl] adj Bundes-
federation [fedə'reɪʃən] n (*society*) Verband
m; (*of states*) Staatenbund m
fed up adj: **to be ~ with sth** etw satt
haben; **I'm ~** ich habe die Nase voll
fee [fiː] n Gebühr f
feeble ['fiːbl] adj (*person*) schwach; (*excuse*)
lahm
feed [fiːd] (pt, pp **fed**) n (*for animals*) Futter
nt ♦ vt füttern; (*support*) ernähren; (*data*)
eingeben; **to ~ on** fressen; **~back** n
(*information*) Feed-back nt, Feedback nt;
~ing bottle (*BRIT*) n Flasche f
feel [fiːl] (pt, pp **felt**) n: **it has a soft ~** es
fühlt sich weich an ♦ vt (*sense*) fühlen;
(*touch*) anfassen; (*think*) meinen ♦ vi
(*person*) sich fühlen; (*thing*) sich anfühlen;
to get the ~ of sth sich an etw acc
gewöhnen; **I ~ cold** mir ist kalt; **I ~ like a
cup of tea** ich habe Lust auf eine Tasse
Tee; **~ about or around** vi
herumsuchen; **~er** n Fühler m; **~ing** n
Gefühl nt; (*opinion*) Meinung f
feet [fiːt] npl of **foot**
feign [feɪn] vt vortäuschen
feline ['fiːlaɪn] adj katzenartig
fell [fel] pt of **fall** ♦ vt (*tree*) fällen
fellow ['feləu] n (*man*) Kerl m; ~ **citizen** n
Mitbürger(in) m(f); ~ **countryman** (*irreg*) n
Landsmann m; ~ **men** npl Mitmenschen pl;
~ship n (*group*) Körperschaft f; (*friendliness*)
Kameradschaft f; (*scholarship*)
Forschungsstipendium nt; ~ **student** n
Kommilitone m, Kommilitonin f
felony ['feləni] n schwere(s) Verbrechen nt
felt [felt] pt, pp of **feel** ♦ n Filz m; **~-tip pen**
n Filzstift m
female ['fiːmeɪl] n (*of animals*) Weibchen nt
♦ adj weiblich
feminine ['femɪnɪn] adj (*LING*) weiblich;
(*qualities*) fraulich

feminist ['femɪnɪst] n Feminist(in) m(f)
fence [fens] n Zaun m ♦ vt (*also*: ~ **in**)
einzäunen ♦ vi fechten; **fencing** ['fensɪŋ] n
Zaun m; (*SPORT*) Fechten nt
fend [fend] vi: **to ~ for o.s.** sich (allein)
durchschlagen; ~ **off** vt abwehren
fender ['fendər] n Kaminvorsetzer m; (*US*:
AUT) Kotflügel m
ferment [vb fə'ment, n 'fɜːment] vi (*CHEM*)
gären ♦ n (*unrest*) Unruhe f
fern [fɜːn] n Farn m
ferocious [fə'rəuʃəs] adj wild, grausam
ferret ['ferɪt] n Frettchen nt ♦ vt: **to ~ out**
aufspüren
ferry ['feri] n Fähre f ♦ vt übersetzen
fertile ['fɜːtaɪl] adj fruchtbar
fertilize ['fɜːtɪlaɪz] vt (*AGR*) düngen; (*BIOL*)
befruchten; **~r** n (*Kunst*)dünger m
fervent ['fɜːvənt] adj (*admirer*) glühend;
(*hope*) innig
fervour ['fɜːvər] (*US* **fervor**) n Leidenschaft f
fester ['festər] vi eitern
festival ['festɪvəl] n (*REL etc*) Fest nt; (*ART,
MUS*) Festspiele pl
festive ['festɪv] adj festlich; **the ~ season**
(*Christmas*) die Festzeit; **festivities**
[fes'tɪvɪtɪz] npl Feierlichkeiten pl
festoon [fes'tuːn] vt: **to ~ with** schmücken
mit
fetch [fetʃ] vt holen; (*in sale*) einbringen
fetching ['fetʃɪŋ] adj reizend
fête [feɪt] n Fest nt
fetus ['fiːtəs] (*esp US*) n = **foetus**
feud [fjuːd] n Fehde f
feudal ['fjuːdl] adj Feudal-
fever ['fiːvər] n Fieber nt; **~ish** adj (*MED*)
fiebrig; (*fig*) fieberhaft
few [fjuː] adj wenig; **a ~** einige; **~er** adj
weniger; **~est** adj wenigste(r,s)
fiancé [fɪ'ɑːnseɪ] n Verlobte(r) m; **~e** n
Verlobte f
fib [fɪb] n Flunkerei f ♦ vi flunkern
fibre ['faɪbər] (*US* **fiber**) n Faser f; **~glass** n
Glaswolle f
fickle ['fɪkl] adj unbeständig
fiction ['fɪkʃən] n (*novels*) Romanliteratur f;
(*story*) Erdichtung f; **~al** adj erfunden

fictitious [fɪk'tɪʃəs] *adj* erfunden, fingiert

fiddle ['fɪdl] *n* Geige *f*; (*trick*) Schwindelei *f*
♦ *vt* (*BRIT: accounts*) frisieren; ~ **with** *vt fus*
herumfummeln an +*dat*

fidelity [fɪ'delɪtɪ] *n* Treue *f*

fidget ['fɪdʒɪt] *vi* zappeln

field [fi:ld] *n* Feld *nt*; (*range*) Gebiet *nt*; ~
marshal *n* Feldmarschall *m*; ~**work** *n*
Feldforschung *f*

fiend [fi:nd] *n* Teufel *m*

fierce [fɪəs] *adj* wild

fiery ['faɪərɪ] *adj* (*person*) hitzig

fifteen [fɪf'ti:n] *num* fünfzehn

fifth [fɪfθ] *adj* fünfte(r, s) ♦ *n* Fünftel *nt*

fifty ['fɪftɪ] *num* fünfzig; ~-**fifty** *adj, adv*
halbe-halbe, fifty-fifty (*inf*)

fig [fɪg] *n* Feige *f*

fight [faɪt] (*pt, pp* **fought**) *n* Kampf *m*; (*brawl*)
Schlägerei *f*; (*argument*) Streit *m* ♦ *vt*
kämpfen gegen; sich schlagen mit; (*fig*)
bekämpfen ♦ *vi* kämpfen; sich schlagen;
streiten; ~**er** *n* Kämpfer(in) *m(f)*; (*plane*)
Jagdflugzeug *nt*; ~**ing** *n* Kämpfen *nt*; (*war*)
Kampfhandlungen *pl*

figment ['fɪgmənt] *n*: ~ **of the imagination**
reine Einbildung *f*

figurative ['fɪgjʊrətɪv] *adj* bildlich

figure ['fɪgər] *n* (*of person*) Figur *f*; (*person*)
Gestalt *f*; (*number*) Ziffer *f* ♦ *vt* (*US: imagine*)
glauben ♦ *vi* (*appear*) erscheinen; ~ **out** *vt*
herausbekommen; ~**head** *n* (*NAUT, fig*)
Galionsfigur *f*; ~ **of speech** *n* Redensart *f*

file [faɪl] *n* (*tool*) Feile *f*; (*dossier*) Akte *f*;
(*folder*) Aktenordner *m*; (*COMPUT*) Datei *f*;
(*row*) Reihe *f* ♦ *vt* (*metal, nails*) feilen;
(*papers*) abheften; (*claim*) einreichen ♦ *vi*: **to**
~ **in/out** hintereinander hereinkommen/
hinausgehen; **to** ~ **past** vorbeimarschieren;
filing ['faɪlɪŋ] *n* Ablage *f*; **filing cabinet** *n*
Aktenschrank *m*

fill [fɪl] *vt* füllen; (*occupy*) ausfüllen; (*satisfy*)
sättigen ♦ *n*: **to eat one's** ~ sich richtig
satt essen; ~ **in** *vt* (*hole*) (auf)füllen; (*form*)
ausfüllen; ~ **up** *vt* (*container*) auffüllen;
(*form*) ausfüllen ♦ *vi* (*AUT*) tanken

fillet ['fɪlɪt] *n* Filet *nt*; ~ **steak** *n* Filetsteak *nt*

filling ['fɪlɪŋ] *n* (*COOK*) Füllung *f*; (*for tooth*)

(*Zahn*)plombe *f*; ~ **station** *n* Tankstelle *f*

film [fɪlm] *n* Film *m* ♦ *vt* (*scene*) filmen; ~
star *n* Filmstar *m*

filter ['fɪltər] *n* Filter *m* ♦ *vt* filtern; ~ **lane**
(*BRIT*) *n* Abbiegespur *f*; ~-**tipped** *adj* Filter-

filth [fɪlθ] *n* Dreck *m*; ~**y** *adj* dreckig;
(*weather*) scheußlich

fin [fɪn] *n* Flosse *f*

final ['faɪnl] *adj* letzte(r, s); End-; (*conclusive*)
endgültig ♦ *n* (*FOOTBALL etc*) Endspiel *nt*; ~**s**
npl (*UNIV*) Abschlussexamen *nt*; (*SPORT*)
Schlussrunde *f*

finale [fɪ'nɑ:lɪ] *n* (*MUS*) Finale *nt*

final: ~**ist** *n* (*SPORT*) Schluss-
rundenteilnehmer *m*; ~**ize** *vt* endgültige
Form geben +*dat*; abschließen; ~**ly** *adv*
(*lastly*) zuletzt; (*eventually*) endlich;
(*irrevocably*) endgültig

finance [faɪ'næns] *n* Finanzwesen *nt* ♦ *vt*
finanzieren; ~**s** *npl* (*funds*) Finanzen *pl*;
financial [faɪ'nænʃəl] *adj* Finanz-; finanziell

find [faɪnd] (*pt, pp* **found**) *vt* finden ♦ *n* Fund
m; **to** ~ **sb guilty** jdn für schuldig erklären;
~ **out** *vt* herausfinden; ~**ings** *npl* (*JUR*)
Ermittlungsergebnis *nt*; (*of report*) Befund *m*

fine [faɪn] *adj* fein; (*good*) gut; (*weather*)
schön ♦ *adv* (*well*) gut; (*small*) klein ♦ *n* (*JUR*)
Geldstrafe *f* ♦ *vt* (*JUR*) mit einer Geldstrafe
belegen; ~ **arts** *npl* schöne(n) Künste *pl*

finger ['fɪŋgər] *n* Finger *m* ♦ *vt* befühlen;
~**nail** *n* Fingernagel *m*; ~**print** *n*
Fingerabdruck *m*; ~**tip** *n* Fingerspitze *f*

finicky ['fɪnɪkɪ] *adj* pingelig

finish ['fɪnɪʃ] *n* Ende *nt*; (*SPORT*) Ziel *nt*; (*of
object*) Verarbeitung *f*; (*of paint*)
Oberflächenwirkung *f* ♦ *vt* beenden; (*book*)
zu Ende lesen ♦ *vi* aufhören; (*SPORT*) ans
Ziel kommen; **to be ~ed with sth** fertig
sein mit etw; **to ~ doing sth** mit etw fertig
werden; ~ **off** *vt* (*complete*) fertig machen;
(*kill*) den Gnadenstoß geben +*dat*; (*knock
out*) erledigen (*umg*); ~ **up** *vt* (*food*)
aufessen; (*drink*) austrinken ♦ *vi* (*end up*)
enden; ~**ing line** *n* Ziellinie *f*; ~**ing
school** *n* Mädchenpensionat *nt*

finite ['faɪnaɪt] *adj* endlich, begrenzt

Finland ['fɪnlənd] *n* Finnland *nt*

Finn [fɪn] *n* Finne *m*, Finnin *f*; **~ish** *adj*
finnisch ♦ *n* (*LING*) Finnisch *nt*

fir [fɜːʳ] *n* Tanne *f*

fire [ˈfaɪəʳ] *n* Feuer *nt*; (*in house etc*) Brand *m*
♦ *vt* (*gun*) abfeuern; (*imagination*)
entzünden; (*dismiss*) hinauswerfen ♦ *vi*
(*AUT*) zünden; **to be on ~** brennen; **~
alarm** *n* Feueralarm *m*; **~arm** *n*
Schusswaffe *f*; **~ brigade** (*BRIT*) *n*
Feuerwehr *f*; **~ department** (*US*) *n*
Feuerwehr *f*; **~ engine** *n* Feuerwehrauto
nt; **~ escape** *n* Feuerleiter *f*; **~
extinguisher** *n* Löschgerät *nt*; **~man**
(*irreg*) *n* Feuerwehrmann *m*; **~place** *n*
Kamin *m*; **~side** *n* Kamin *m*; **~ station** *n*
Feuerwehrwache *f*; **~wood** *n* Brennholz *nt*;
~works *npl* Feuerwerk *nt*; **~ squad** *n*
Exekutionskommando *nt*

firm [fɜːm] *adj* fest ♦ *n* Firma *f*; **~ly** [ˈfɜːmlɪ]
adv (*grasp, speak*) fest; (*push, tug*) energisch;
(*decide*) endgültig

first [fɜːst] *adj* erste(r, s) ♦ *adv* zuerst; (*arrive*)
als Erste(r); (*happen*) zum ersten Mal ♦ *n*
(*person: in race*) Erste(r) *mf*; (*UNIV*) Eins *f*;
(*AUT*) erste(r) Gang *m*; **at ~** zuerst; **~ of all**
zuallererst; **~ aid** *n* erste Hilfe *f*; **~-aid kit** *n*
Verbandskasten *m*; **~-class** *adj* erstklassig;
(*travel*) erster Klasse; **~-hand** *adj* aus erster
Hand; **~ lady** (*US*) *n* First Lady *f*; **~ly** *adv*
erstens; **~ name** *n* Vorname *m*; **~-rate** *adj*
erstklassig

fiscal [ˈfɪskl] *adj* Finanz-

fish [fɪʃ] *n inv* Fisch *m* ♦ *vi* fischen; angeln; **to
go ~ing** angeln gehen; (*in sea*) fischen
gehen; **~erman** (*irreg*) *n* Fischer *m*; **~ farm**
n Fischzucht *f*; **~ fingers** (*BRIT*) *npl*
Fischstäbchen *pl*; **~ing boat** *n* Fischerboot
nt; **~ing line** *n* Angelschnur *f*; **~ing rod** *n*
Angel(rute) *f*; **~ing tackle** *n* (*for sport*)
Angelgeräte *pl*; **~monger's (shop)** *n*
Fischhändler *m*; **~ slice** *n*
Fischvorlegemesser *nt*; **~ sticks** (*US*) *npl* =
fish fingers

fishy [ˈfɪʃɪ] (*inf*) *adj* (*suspicious*) faul

fission [ˈfɪʃən] *n* Spaltung *f*

fissure [ˈfɪʃəʳ] *n* Riss *m*

fist [fɪst] *n* Faust *f*

fit [fɪt] *adj* (*MED*) gesund; (*SPORT*) in Form, fit;
(*suitable*) geeignet ♦ *vt* passen +*dat*; (*insert,
attach*) einsetzen ♦ *vi* passen; (*in space, gap*)
hineinpassen ♦ *n* (*of clothes*) Sitz *m*; (*MED, of
anger*) Anfall *m*; (*of laughter*) Krampf *m*; **by
~s and starts** (*move*) ruckweise; (*work*)
unregelmäßig; **~ in** *vi* hineinpassen; (*fig:
person*) passen; **~ out** *vt* (*also:* **~ up**)
ausstatten; **~ful** *adj* (*sleep*) unruhig; **~ment**
n Einrichtungsgegenstand *m*; **~ness** *n*
(*suitability*) Eignung *f*; (*MED*) Gesundheit *f*;
(*SPORT*) Fitness *f*; **~ted carpet** *n*
Teppichboden *m*; **~ted kitchen** *n*
Einbauküche *f*; **~ter** *n* (*TECH*) Monteur *m*;
~ting *adj* passend ♦ *n* (*of dress*) Anprobe *f*;
(*piece of equipment*) (Ersatz)teil *nt*; **~tings**
npl (*equipment*) Zubehör *nt*; **~ting room** *n*
Anproberaum *m*

five [faɪv] *num* fünf; **~r** (*inf*) *n* (*BRIT*)
Fünfpfundnote *f*; (*US*) Fünfdollarnote *f*

fix [fɪks] *vt* befestigen; (*settle*) festsetzen;
(*repair*) reparieren ♦ *n*: **in a ~** in der
Klemme; **~ up** *vt* (*meeting*) arrangieren; **to
~ sb up with sth** jdm etw *acc* verschaffen;
~ation [fɪkˈseɪʃən] *n* Fixierung *f*; **~ed** [fɪkst]
adj fest; **~ture** [ˈfɪkstʃəʳ] *n* Installationsteil *nt*;
(*SPORT*) Spiel *nt*

fizzy [ˈfɪzɪ] *adj* Sprudel-, sprudelnd

flabbergasted [ˈflæbəgɑːstɪd] (*inf*) *adj* platt

flabby [ˈflæbɪ] *adj* wabbelig

flag [flæg] *n* Fahne *f* ♦ *vi* (*strength*)
nachlassen; (*spirit*) erlahmen; **~ down** *vt*
anhalten; **~pole** [ˈflægpəul] *n* Fahnenstange
f

flair [fleəʳ] *n* Talent *nt*

flak [flæk] *n* Flakfeuer *nt*

flake [fleɪk] *n* (*of snow*) Flocke *f*; (*of rust*)
Schuppe *f* ♦ *vi* (*also:* **~ off**) abblättern

flamboyant [flæmˈbɔɪənt] *adj* extravagant

flame [fleɪm] *n* Flamme *f*

flamingo [fləˈmɪŋgəu] *n* Flamingo *m*

flammable [ˈflæməbl] *adj* brennbar

flan [flæn] (*BRIT*) *n* Obsttorte *f*

flank [flæŋk] *n* Flanke *f* ♦ *vt* flankieren

flannel [ˈflænl] *n* Flanell *m*; (*BRIT: also:* **face
~**) Waschlappen *m*; (: *inf*) Geschwafel *nt*;
~s *npl* (*trousers*) Flanellhose *f*

flap [flæp] n Klappe f; (inf: crisis) (helle) Aufregung f ♦ vt (wings) schlagen mit ♦ vi flattern

flare [fleəʳ] n (signal) Leuchtsignal nt; (in skirt etc) Weite f; ~ **up** vi aufflammen; (fig) aufbrausen; (revolt) (plötzlich) ausbrechen

flash [flæʃ] n Blitz m; (also: **news ~**) Kurzmeldung f; (PHOT) Blitzlicht nt ♦ vt aufleuchten lassen ♦ vi aufleuchten; **in a ~** im Nu; ~ **by** or **past** vi vorbeirasen; **~back** n Rückblende f; **~bulb** n Blitzlichtbirne f; ~ **cube** n Blitzwürfel m; **~light** n Blitzlicht nt

flashy ['flæʃɪ] (pej) adj knallig

flask [flɑ:sk] n (CHEM) Kolben m; (also: **vacuum ~**) Thermosflasche f®

flat [flæt] adj flach; (dull) matt; (MUS) erniedrigt; (beer) schal; (tyre) platt ♦ n (BRIT: rooms) Wohnung f; (MUS) b nt; (AUT) Platte(r) m; **to work ~ out** auf Hochtouren arbeiten; **~ly** adv glatt; **~-screen** adj (TV, COMPUT) mit flachem Bildschirm; **~ten** vt (also: **~ten out**) ebnen

flatter ['flætəʳ] vt schmeicheln +dat; **~ing** adj schmeichelhaft; **~y** n Schmeichelei f

flatulence ['flætjʊləns] n Blähungen pl

flaunt [flɔ:nt] vt prunken mit

flavour ['fleɪvəʳ] (US **flavor**) n Geschmack m ♦ vt würzen; **~ed** adj: **strawberry-~ed** mit Erdbeergeschmack; **~ing** n Würze f

flaw [flɔ:] n Fehler m; **~less** adj einwandfrei

flax [flæks] n Flachs m; **~en** adj flachsfarben

flea [fli:] n Floh m

fleck [flek] n (mark) Fleck m; (pattern) Tupfen m

fled [fled] pt, pp of **flee**

flee [fli:] (pt, pp **fled**) vi fliehen ♦ vt fliehen vor +dat; (country) fliehen aus

fleece [fli:s] n Vlies nt ♦ vt (inf) schröpfen

fleet [fli:t] n Flotte f

fleeting ['fli:tɪŋ] adj flüchtig

Flemish ['flemɪʃ] adj flämisch

flesh [fleʃ] n Fleisch nt; ~ **wound** n Fleischwunde f

flew [flu:] pt of **fly**

flex [fleks] n Kabel nt ♦ vt beugen; **~ibility** [fleksɪ'bɪlɪtɪ] n Biegsamkeit f; (fig) Flexibilität

f; **~ible** adj biegsam; (plans) flexibel

flick [flɪk] n leichte(r) Schlag m ♦ vt leicht schlagen; ~ **through** vt fus durchblättern

flicker ['flɪkəʳ] n Flackern nt ♦ vi flackern

flier ['flaɪəʳ] n Flieger m

flight [flaɪt] n Flug m; (fleeing) Flucht f; (also: ~ **of steps**) Treppe f; **to take ~** die Flucht ergreifen; ~ **attendant** (US) n Steward(ess) m(f); ~ **deck** n Flugdeck nt

flimsy ['flɪmzɪ] adj (thin) hauchdünn; (excuse) fadenscheinig

flinch [flɪntʃ] vi: **to ~ (away from)** zurückschrecken (vor +dat)

fling [flɪŋ] (pt, pp **flung**) vt schleudern

flint [flɪnt] n Feuerstein m

flip [flɪp] vt werfen

flippant ['flɪpənt] adj schnippisch

flipper ['flɪpəʳ] n Flosse f

flirt [flɜ:t] vi flirten ♦ n: **he/she is a ~** er/sie flirtet gern

flit [flɪt] vi flitzen

float [fləʊt] n (FISHING) Schwimmer m; (esp in procession) Plattformwagen m ♦ vi schwimmen; (in air) schweben ♦ vt (COMM) gründen; (currency) floaten

flock [flɒk] n (of sheep, REL) Herde f; (of birds) Schwarm m

flog [flɒg] vt prügeln; (inf: sell) verkaufen

flood [flʌd] n Überschwemmung f; (fig) Flut f ♦ vt überschwemmen; **~ing** n Überschwemmung f; **~light** n Flutlicht nt

floor [flɔ:ʳ] n (Fuß)boden m; (storey) Stock m ♦ vt (person) zu Boden schlagen; **ground ~** (BRIT) Erdgeschoss nt; **first ~** (BRIT) erste(r) Stock m; (US) Erdgeschoss nt; **~board** n Diele f; ~ **show** n Kabarettvorstellung f

flop [flɒp] n Plumps m; (failure) Reinfall m ♦ vi (fail) durchfallen

floppy ['flɒpɪ] adj hängend; ~ **(disk)** n (COMPUT) Diskette f

flora ['flɔ:rə] n Flora f; **~l** adj Blumen-

florist ['flɒrɪst] n Blumenhändler(in) m(f); **~'s (shop)** n Blumengeschäft nt

flotation [fləʊ'teɪʃən] n (FIN) Auflegung f

flounce [flaʊns] n Volant m

flounder ['flaʊndəʳ] vi (fig) ins Schleudern kommen ♦ n (ZOOL) Flunder f

flour ['flauə^r] *n* Mehl *nt*

flourish ['flʌrɪʃ] *vi* blühen; gedeihen ♦ *n* (*waving*) Schwingen *nt*; (*of trumpets*) Tusch *m*, Fanfare *f*

flout [flaut] *vt* missachten

flow [fləu] *n* Fließen *nt*; (*of sea*) Flut *f* ♦ *vi* fließen; **~ chart** *n* Flussdiagramm *nt*

flower ['flauə^r] *n* Blume *f* ♦ *vi* blühen; **~ bed** *n* Blumenbeet *nt*; **~pot** *n* Blumentopf *m*; **~y** *adj* (*style*) blumenreich

flown [fləun] *pp of* fly

flu [flu:] *n* Grippe *f*

fluctuate ['flʌktjueɪt] *vi* schwanken; **fluctuation** [flʌktjuˈeɪʃən] *n* Schwankung *f*

fluency ['flu:ənsɪ] *n* Flüssigkeit *f*

fluent ['flu:ənt] *adj* fließend; **~ly** *adv* fließend

fluff [flʌf] *n* Fussel *f*; **~y** *adj* flaumig

fluid ['flu:ɪd] *n* Flüssigkeit *f* ♦ *adj* flüssig; (*fig: plans*) veränderbar

fluke [flu:k] (*inf*) *n* Dusel *m*

flung [flʌŋ] *pt*, *pp of* fling

fluoride ['fluəraɪd] *n* Fluorid *nt*; **~ toothpaste** *n* Fluorzahnpasta *f*

flurry ['flʌrɪ] *n* (*of snow*) Gestöber *nt*; (*of activity*) Aufregung *f*

flush [flʌʃ] *n* Erröten *nt*; (*excited*) Glühen *nt* ♦ *vt* (aus)spülen ♦ *vi* erröten ♦ *adj* glatt; **~ out** *vt* aufstöbern; **~ed** *adj* rot

flustered ['flʌstəd] *adj* verwirrt

flute [flu:t] *n* Querflöte *f*

flutter ['flʌtə^r] *n* Flattern *nt* ♦ *vi* flattern

flux [flʌks] *n*: **in a state of ~** im Fluss

fly [flaɪ] (*pt* flew, *pp* flown) *n* (*insect*) Fliege *f*; (*on trousers: also*: **flies**) (Hosen)schlitz *m* ♦ *vt* fliegen ♦ *vi* fliegen; (*flee*) fliehen; (*flag*) wehen; **~ away** *or* **off** *vi* (*bird, insect*) wegfliegen; **~-drive** *n*: **~-drive holiday** Fly & Drive-Urlaub *m*; **~ing** *n* Fliegen *nt* ♦ *adj*: **with ~ing colours** mit fliegenden Fahnen; **~ing start** gute(r) Start *m*; **~ing visit** Stippvisite *f*; **~ing saucer** *n* fliegende Untertasse *f*; **~over** (*BRIT*) *n* Überführung *f*; **~sheet** *n* (*for tent*) Regendach *nt*

foal [fəul] *n* Fohlen *nt*

foam [fəum] *n* Schaum *m* ♦ *vi* schäumen; **~ rubber** *n* Schaumgummi *m*

fob [fɔb] *vt*: **to ~ sb off with sth** jdm etw

andrehen; (*with promise*) jdn mit etw abspeisen

focal ['fəukl] *adj* Brenn-; **~ point** *n* (*of room, activity*) Mittelpunkt *m*

focus ['fəukəs] (*pl* **~es**) *n* Brennpunkt *m* ♦ *vt* (*attention*) konzentrieren; (*camera*) scharf einstellen ♦ *vi*: **to ~ (on)** sich konzentrieren (auf +*acc*); **in ~** scharf eingestellt; **out of ~** unscharf

fodder ['fɔdə^r] *n* Futter *nt*

foe [fəu] *n* Feind *m*

foetus ['fi:təs] (*US* fetus) *n* Fötus *m*

fog [fɔg] *n* Nebel *m*; **~gy** *adj* neblig; **~ lamp** (*BRIT*), **~ light** (*US*) *n* (*AUT*) Nebelscheinwerfer *m*

foil [fɔɪl] *vt* vereiteln ♦ *n* (*metal, also fig*) Folie *f*; (*FENCING*) Florett *nt*

fold [fəuld] *n* (*bend, crease*) Falte *f*; (*AGR*) Pferch *m* ♦ *vt* falten; **~ up** *vt* (*map etc*) zusammenfalten ♦ *vi* (*business*) eingehen; **~er** *n* Schnellhefter *m*; **~ing** *adj* (*chair etc*) Klapp-

foliage ['fəulɪdʒ] *n* Laubwerk *nt*

folk [fəuk] *npl* Leute *pl* ♦ *adj* Volks-; **~s** *npl* (*family*) Leute *pl*; **~lore** ['fəuklɔ:^r] *n* (*study*) Volkskunde *f*; (*tradition*) Folklore *f*; **~ song** *n* Volkslied *nt*; (*modern*) Folksong *m*

follow ['fɔləu] *vt* folgen +*dat*; (*fashion*) mitmachen ♦ *vi* folgen; **~ up** *vt* verfolgen; **~er** *n* Anhänger(in) *m(f)*; **~ing** *adj* folgend ♦ *n* (*people*) Gefolgschaft *f*; **~-on call** *n* weiteres Gespräch in einer Telefonzelle um Guthaben zu verbrauchen

folly ['fɔlɪ] *n* Torheit *f*

fond [fɔnd] *adj*: **to be ~ of** gern haben

fondle ['fɔndl] *vt* streicheln

font [fɔnt] *n* Taufbecken *nt*

food [fu:d] *n* Essen *nt*; (*fodder*) Futter *nt*; **~ mixer** *n* Küchenmixer *m*; **~ poisoning** *n* Lebensmittelvergiftung *f*; **~ processor** *n* Küchenmaschine *f*; **~stuffs** *npl* Lebensmittel *pl*

fool [fu:l] *n* Narr *m*, Närrin *f* ♦ *vt* (*deceive*) hereinlegen ♦ *vi* (*also*: **~ around**) (herum)albern; **~hardy** *adj* tollkühn; **~ish** *adj* albern; **~proof** *adj* idiotensicher

foot [fut] (*pl* feet) *n* Fuß *m* ♦ *vt* (*bill*)

bezahlen; **on** ~ zu Fuß

footage ['futɪdʒ] n (CINE) Filmmaterial nt

football ['futbɔːl] n Fußball m; (game: BRIT) Fußball m; (: US) Football m; ~ **player** n (BRIT: also: **~er**) Fußballspieler m, Fußballer m; (US) Footballer m

---

Football Pools

i Football Pools, *umgangssprachlich auch* the pools *genannt, ist das in Großbritannien sehr beliebte Fußballtoto, bei dem auf die Ergebnisse der samstäglichen Fußballspiele gewettet wird. Teilnehmer schicken ihren ausgefüllten Totoschein vor den Spielen an die Totogesellschaft und vergleichen nach den Spielen die Ergebnisse mit ihrem Schein. Die Gewinne können sehr hoch sein und gelegentlich Millionen von Pfund betragen.*

---

foot: **~brake** n Fußbremse f; **~bridge** n Fußgängerbrücke f; **~hills** npl Ausläufer pl; **~hold** n Halt m; **~ing** n Halt m; (fig) Verhältnis nt; **~lights** npl Rampenlicht nt; **~man** (irreg) n Bedienstete(r) m; **~note** n Fußnote f; **~path** n Fußweg m; **~print** n Fußabdruck m; **~sore** adj fußkrank; **~step** n Schritt m; **~wear** n Schuhzeug nt

---

KEYWORD

for [fɔːr] prep **1** für; **is this for me?** ist das für mich?; **the train for London** der Zug nach London; **he went for the paper** er ging die Zeitung holen; **give it to me – what for?** gib es mir – warum?

2 (because of) wegen; **for this reason** aus diesem Grunde

3 (referring to distance): **there are roadworks for 5 km** die Baustelle ist 5 km lang; **we walked for miles** wir sind meilenweit gegangen

4 (referring to time) seit; (: with future sense) für; **he was away for 2 years** er war zwei Jahre lang weg

5 (+infin clauses): **it is not for me to decide** das kann ich nicht entscheiden; **for this to be possible ...** damit dies möglich wird/

wurde ...

6 (in spite of) trotz +gen or (inf) dat ; **for all his complaints** obwohl er sich ständig beschwert

♦ conj denn

---

forage ['fɔrɪdʒ] n (Vieh)futter nt

foray ['fɔreɪ] n Raubzug m

forbad(e) [fə'bæd] pt of **forbid**

forbid [fə'bɪd] (pt **forbad(e)**, pp **forbidden**) vt verbieten; **~ding** adj einschüchternd

force [fɔːs] n Kraft f; (compulsion) Zwang m ♦ vt zwingen; (lock) aufbrechen; **the F~s** npl (BRIT) die Streitkräfte; **in** ~ (rule) gültig; (group) in großer Stärke; **~d** adj (smile) gezwungen; (landing) Not-; **~feed** vt zwangsernähren; **~ful** adj (speech) kraftvoll; (personality) resolut

forceps ['fɔːseps] npl Zange f

forcibly ['fɔːsəblɪ] adv zwangsweise

ford [fɔːd] n Furt f ♦ vt durchwaten

fore [fɔːr] n: **to the** ~ in den Vordergrund; **~arm** ['fɔːrɑːm] n Unterarm m; **~boding** [fɔː'bəudɪŋ] n Vorahnung f; **~cast** ['fɔːkɑːst] (irreg: like **cast**) n Vorhersage f ♦ vt voraussagen; **~court** ['fɔːkɔːt] n (of garage) Vorplatz m; **~fathers** ['fɔːfɑːðəz] npl Vorfahren pl; **~finger** ['fɔːfɪŋɡər] n Zeigefinger m; **~front** ['fɔːfrʌnt] n Spitze f

forego [fɔː'ɡəu] (irreg: like **go**) vt verzichten auf +acc

fore: **~gone** ['fɔːɡɔn] adj: **it's a ~gone conclusion** es steht von vornherein fest; **~ground** ['fɔːɡraund] n Vordergrund m; **~head** ['fɔrɪd] n Stirn f

foreign ['fɔrɪn] adj Auslands-; (accent) ausländisch; (trade) Außen-; (body) Fremd-; **~er** n Ausländer(in) m(f); **~ exchange** n Devisen pl; **F~ Office** (BRIT) n Außenministerium nt; **F~ Secretary** (BRIT) n Außenminister m

fore: **~leg** n Vorderbein nt; **~man** (irreg) n Vorarbeiter m; **~most** adj erste(r, s) ♦ adv: **first and ~most** vor allem

forensic [fə'rensɪk] adj gerichtsmedizinisch

fore ['fɔː-]: **~runner** n Vorläufer m; **~see** [fɔː'siː] (irreg: like **see**) vt vorhersehen;

~seeable *adj* absehbar; **~shadow**
[fɔːˈʃædəu] *vt* andeuten; **~sight** [ˈfɔːsaɪt] *n*
Voraussicht *f*

forest [ˈfɒrɪst] *n* Wald *m*

forestall [fɔːˈstɔːl] *vt* zuvorkommen +*dat*

forestry [ˈfɒrɪstrɪ] *n* Forstwirtschaft *f*

foretaste [ˈfɔːteɪst] *n* Vorgeschmack *m*

foretell [fɔːˈtel] (*irreg: like* tell) *vt*
vorhersagen

forever [fəˈrevəʳ] *adv* für immer

foreword [ˈfɔːwəːd] *n* Vorwort *nt*

forfeit [ˈfɔːfɪt] *n* Einbuße *f* ♦ *vt* verwirken

forgave [fəˈgeɪv] *pt of* **forgive**

forge [fɔːdʒ] *n* Schmiede *f* ♦ *vt* fälschen;
(*iron*) schmieden; **~ ahead** *vi* Fortschritte
machen; **~d** *adj* gefälscht; **~d banknotes**
Blüten (*inf*) *pl*; **~r** *n* Fälscher *m*; **~ry** *n*
Fälschung *f*

forget [fəˈget] (*pt* **forgot**, *pp* **forgotten**) *vt, vi*
vergessen; **~ful** *adj* vergesslich; **~-me-not**
n Vergissmeinnicht *nt*

forgive [fəˈgɪv] (*pt* **forgave**, *pp* **forgiven**) *vt*
verzeihen; **to ~ sb (for sth)** jdm (etw)
verzeihen; **~ness** *n* Verzeihung *f*

forgot [fəˈgɒt] *pt of* **forget**; **~ten** *pp of* **forget**

fork [fɔːk] *n* Gabel *f*; (*in road*) Gabelung *f* ♦ *vi*
(*road*) sich gabeln; **~ out** (*inf*) *vt* (*pay*)
blechen; **~-lift truck** *n* Gabelstapler *m*

forlorn [fəˈlɔːn] *adj* (*person*) verlassen; (*hope*)
vergeblich

form [fɔːm] *n* Form *f*; (*type*) Art *f*; (*figure*)
Gestalt *f*; (*SCH*) Klasse *f*; (*bench*) (Schul)bank
f; (*document*) Formular *nt* ♦ *vt* formen; (*be
part of*) bilden

formal [ˈfɔːməl] *adj* formell; (*occasion*)
offiziell; **~ly** *adv* (*ceremoniously*) formell;
(*officially*) offiziell

format [ˈfɔːmæt] *n* Format *nt* ♦ *vt* (*COMPUT*)
formatieren

formation [fɔːˈmeɪʃən] *n* Bildung *f*; (*AVIAT*)
Formation *f*

formative [ˈfɔːmətɪv] *adj* (*years*) formend

former [ˈfɔːməʳ] *adj* früher; (*opposite of latter*)
erstere(r, s); **~ly** *adv* früher

formidable [ˈfɔːmɪdəbl] *adj* furchtbar

formula [ˈfɔːmjulə] (*pl* **~e** *or* **~s**) *n* Formel *f*;
~e [ˈfɔːmjuliː] *npl of* **formula**; **~te**

[ˈfɔːmjuleɪt] *vt* formulieren

fort [fɔːt] *n* Feste *f*, Fort *nt*

forte [ˈfɔːtɪ] *n* Stärke *f*, starke Seite *f*

forth [fɔːθ] *adv*: **and so ~** und so weiter;
~coming *adj* kommend; (*character*)
entgegenkommend; **~right** *adj* offen;
~with *adv* umgehend

fortify [ˈfɔːtɪfaɪ] *vt* (ver)stärken; (*protect*)
befestigen

fortitude [ˈfɔːtɪtjuːd] *n* Seelenstärke *f*

fortnight [ˈfɔːtnaɪt] (*BRIT*) *n* vierzehn Tage *pl*;
~ly (*BRIT*) *adj* zweiwöchentlich ♦ *adv* alle
vierzehn Tage

fortress [ˈfɔːtrɪs] *n* Festung *f*

fortunate [ˈfɔːtʃənɪt] *adj* glücklich; **~ly** *adv*
glücklicherweise, zum Glück

fortune [ˈfɔːtʃən] *n* Glück *nt*; (*money*)
Vermögen *nt*; **~-teller** *n* Wahrsager(in)
m(f)

forty [ˈfɔːtɪ] *num* vierzig

forum [ˈfɔːrəm] *n* Forum *nt*

forward [ˈfɔːwəd] *adj* vordere(r, s);
(*movement*) Vorwärts-; (*person*) vorlaut;
(*planning*) Voraus- ♦ *adv* vorwärts ♦ *n*
(*SPORT*) Stürmer *m* ♦ *vt* (*send*) schicken;
(*help*) fördern; **~s** *adv* vorwärts

fossil [ˈfɒsl] *n* Fossil *nt*, Versteinerung *f*

foster [ˈfɒstəʳ] *vt* (*talent*) fördern; **~ child** *n*
Pflegekind *nt*; **~ mother** *n* Pflegemutter *f*

fought [fɔːt] *pt, pp of* **fight**

foul [faul] *adj* schmutzig; (*language*) gemein;
(*weather*) schlecht ♦ *n* (*SPORT*) Foul *nt* ♦ *vt*
(*mechanism*) blockieren; (*SPORT*) foulen; **~
play** *n* (*SPORT*) Foulspiel *nt*; (*LAW*)
Verbrechen *nt*

found [faund] *pt, pp of* **find** ♦ *vt* gründen;
~ation [faunˈdeɪʃən] *n* (*act*) Gründung *f*;
(*fig*) Fundament *nt*; (*also:* **~ation cream**)
Grundierungscreme *f*; **~ations** *npl* (*of
house*) Fundament *nt*; **~er** *n* Gründer(in)
m(f) ♦ *vi* sinken

foundry [ˈfaundrɪ] *n* Gießerei *f*

fountain [ˈfauntɪn] *n* (Spring)brunnen *m*; **~
pen** *n* Füllfederhalter *m*

four [fɔːʳ] *num* vier; **on all ~s** auf allen
vieren; **~-poster** *n* Himmelbett *nt*; **~some**
n Quartett *nt*; **~teen** *num* vierzehn;

~teenth adj vierzehnte(r, s); **~th** adj
vierte(r, s)

fowl [faul] n Huhn nt; (food) Geflügel nt

fox [fɒks] n Fuchs m ♦ vt täuschen

foyer ['fɔɪeɪ] n Foyer nt, Vorhalle f

fraction ['frækʃən] n (MATH) Bruch m; (part)
Bruchteil m

fracture ['fræktʃəʳ] n (MED) Bruch m ♦ vt
brechen

fragile ['frædʒaɪl] adj zerbrechlich

fragment ['frægmənt] n Bruchstück nt; (small
part) Splitter m

fragrance ['freɪgrəns] n Duft m; **fragrant**
['freɪgrənt] adj duftend

frail [freɪl] adj schwach, gebrechlich

frame [freɪm] n Rahmen m; (of spectacles:
also: **~s**) Gestell nt; (body) Gestalt f ♦ vt
einrahmen; **to ~ sb** (inf: incriminate) jdm
etwas anhängen; **~ of mind** Verfassung f;
~work n Rahmen m; (of society) Gefüge nt

France [frɑːns] n Frankreich nt

franchise ['fræntʃaɪz] n (POL) (aktives)
Wahlrecht nt; (COMM) Lizenz f

frank [fræŋk] adj offen ♦ vt (letter) frankieren;
~ly adv offen gesagt

frantic ['fræntɪk] adj verzweifelt

fraternal [frə'tɜːnl] adj brüderlich

fraternity [frə'tɜːnɪtɪ] n (club) Vereinigung f;
(spirit) Brüderlichkeit f; (US: SCH)
Studentenverbindung f

fraternize ['frætənaɪz] vi fraternisieren

fraud [frɔːd] n (trickery) Betrug m; (person)
Schwindler(in) m(f); **~ulent** ['frɔːdjulənt] adj
betrügerisch

fraught [frɔːt] adj: **~ with** voller +gen

fray [freɪ] vt, vi ausfransen; **tempers were
~ed** die Gemüter waren erhitzt

freak [friːk] n Monstrosität f ♦ cpd (storm etc)
anormal

freckle ['frekl] n Sommersprosse f

free [friː] adj frei; (loose) lose; (liberal)
freigebig ♦ vt (set ~) befreien; (unblock)
freimachen; **~ (of charge)** gratis, umsonst;
for ~ gratis, umsonst; **~dom** ['friːdəm] n
Freiheit f; **F~fone** ® n: **call F~fone 0800
...** rufen Sie gebührenfrei 0800 ... an; **~-
for-all** n (fight) allgemeine(s)

Handgemenge nt; **~ gift** n Geschenk nt; **~
kick** n Freistoß m; **~lance** adj frei; (artist)
freischaffend; **~ly** adv frei; (admit) offen;
F~post ® n ≈ Gebühr zahlt Empfänger;
~-range adj (hen) Farmhof-; (eggs) Land-;
~ trade n Freihandel m; **~way** n (US) n
Autobahn f; **~wheel** vi im Freilauf fahren;
~ will n: **of one's own ~ will** aus freien
Stücken

freeze [friːz] (pt **froze**, pp **frozen**) vi
gefrieren; (feel cold) frieren ♦ vt (also fig)
einfrieren ♦ n (fig, FIN) Stopp m; **~r** n
Tiefkühltruhe f; (in fridge) Gefrierfach nt;

freezing adj eisig; (freezing cold) eiskalt;
freezing point n Gefrierpunkt m

freight [freɪt] n Fracht f; **~ train** n Güterzug
m

French [frentʃ] adj französisch ♦ n (LING)
Französisch nt; **the ~** npl (people) die
Franzosen pl; **~ bean** n grüne Bohne f; **~
fried potatoes** (BRIT) npl Pommes frites pl;
~ fries (US) npl Pommes frites pl; **~ horn** n
(MUS) (Wald)horn nt; **~ kiss** n Zungenkuss
m; **~ loaf** n Baguette f; **~man/woman**
(irreg) n Franzose m/Französin f; **~ window**
n Verandatür f

frenzy ['frenzɪ] n Raserei f

frequency ['friːkwənsɪ] n Häufigkeit f; (PHYS)
Frequenz f

frequent [adj 'friːkwənt, vb frɪ'kwent] adj
häufig ♦ vt (regelmäßig) besuchen; **~ly** adv
(often) häufig, oft

fresh [freʃ] adj frisch; **~en** vi (also: **~en up**)
(sich) auffrischen; (person) sich frisch
machen; **~er** (inf: BRIT) n (UNIV)
Erstsemester nt; **~ly** adv gerade; **~man**
(irreg) (US) n = **fresher**; **~ness** n Frische f;
~water adj (fish) Süßwasser-

fret [fret] vi sich dat Sorgen machen

friar ['fraɪəʳ] n Klosterbruder m

friction ['frɪkʃən] n (also fig) Reibung f

Friday ['fraɪdɪ] n Freitag m

fridge [frɪdʒ] (BRIT) n Kühlschrank m

fried [fraɪd] adj gebraten

friend [frend] n Freund(in) m(f); **~ly** adj
freundlich; (relations) freundschaftlich; **~ly**
fire n Beschuss m durch die eigene Seite;

~ship n Freundschaft f
frieze [friːz] n Fries m
frigate ['frɪgɪt] n Fregatte f
fright [fraɪt] n Schrecken m; **to take ~** es mit
der Angst zu tun bekommen; **~en** vt
erschrecken; **to be ~ened** Angst haben;
~ening adj schrecklich; **~ful** (inf) adj
furchtbar
frigid ['frɪdʒɪd] adj frigide
frill [frɪl] n Rüsche f
fringe [frɪndʒ] n Besatz m; (BRIT: of hair) Pony
m; (fig) Peripherie f; **~ benefits** npl
zusätzliche Leistungen pl
Frisbee ['frɪzbɪ] ® n Frisbee ® nt
frisk [frɪsk] vt durchsuchen
frisky ['frɪskɪ] adj lebendig, ausgelassen
fritter ['frɪtə*] vt: **to ~ away** vergeuden
frivolous ['frɪvələs] adj frivol
frizzy ['frɪzɪ] adj kraus
fro [frəʊ] adv see **to**
frock [frɒk] n Kleid nt
frog [frɒg] n Frosch m; **~man** (irreg) n
Froschmann m
frolic ['frɒlɪk] vi ausgelassen sein

KEYWORD
---

from [frɒm] prep **1** (indicating starting place)
of; (indicating origin etc) aus +dat; **a letter /
telephone call from my sister** ein Brief /
Anruf von meiner Schwester; **where do
you come from?** woher kommen Sie?; **to
drink from the bottle** aus der Flasche
trinken
2 (indicating time) von ... an; (: past) seit;
from one o'clock to or **until** or **till two** von
ein Uhr bis zwei; **from January (on)** ab
Januar
3 (indicating distance) von ... (entfernt)
4 (indicating price, number etc) ab +dat; **from
£10 ab £10; there were from 20 to 30
people there** es waren zwischen 20 und
30 Leute da
5 (indicating difference): **he can't tell red
from green** er kann nicht zwischen Rot
und Grün unterscheiden; **to be different
from sb/sth** anders sein als jd/etw
6 (because of, based on): **from what he**

says aus dem, was er sagt; **weak from
hunger** schwach vor Hunger

front [frʌnt] n Vorderseite f; (of house)
Fassade f; (promenade: also: **sea ~**)
Strandpromenade f; (MIL, POL, MET) Front f;
(fig: appearances) Fassade f ♦ adj (forward)
vordere(r, s), Vorder-; (first) vorderste(r, s);
in ~ vorne; **in ~ of** vor; **~age** ['frʌntɪdʒ] n
Vorderfront f; **~ door** n Haustür f; **~ier**
['frʌntɪə*] n Grenze f; **~ page** n Titelseite f;
~ room (BRIT) n Wohnzimmer nt; **~-wheel
drive** n Vorderradantrieb m
frost [frɒst] n Frost m; (also ~**bite** n Erfrierung f;
~ed (glass) Milch-; **~y** adj frostig
froth [frɒθ] n Schaum m
frown [fraʊn] n Stirnrunzeln n ♦ vi die Stirn
runzeln
froze [frəʊz] pt of **freeze**
frozen ['frəʊzn] pp of **freeze**
frugal ['fruːgl] adj sparsam, bescheiden
fruit [fruːt] n inv (as collective) Obst nt;
(particular) Frucht f; **~ful** adj fruchtbar;
~ion [fruːˈɪʃən] n: **to come to ~ion** in
Erfüllung gehen; **~ juice** n Fruchtsaft m; **~
machine** n (BRIT) Spielautomat m; **~ salad**
n Obstsalat m
frustrate [frʌsˈtreɪt] vt vereiteln; **~d** adj
gehemmt; (PSYCH) frustriert
fry [fraɪ] (pt, pp **fried**) vt braten ♦ npl: **small
~** kleine Fische pl; **~ing pan** n Bratpfanne
f
ft. abbr = **foot; feet**
fuddy-duddy ['fʌdɪdʌdɪ] n altmodische(r)
Kauz m
fudge [fʌdʒ] n Fondant m
fuel ['fjʊəl] n Treibstoff m; (for heating)
Brennstoff m; (for lighter) Benzin nt; **~ oil** n
(diesel fuel) Heizöl m; **~ tank** n Tank m
fugitive ['fjuːdʒɪtɪv] n Flüchtling m
fulfil [fʊlˈfɪl] vt (duty) erfüllen; (promise)
einhalten; **~ment** n Erfüllung f
full [fʊl] adj (box, bottle, price) voll; (person:
satisfied) satt; (member, power, employment)
Voll-; (complete) vollständig, Voll-; (speed)
höchste(r, s); (skirt) weit ♦ adv: **~ well** sehr
wohl; **in ~** vollständig; **a ~ two hours** volle

zwei Stunden; **~-length** adj (*lifesize*) lebensgroß; **a ~-length photograph** eine Ganzaufnahme; **~ moon** n Vollmond m; **~-scale** adj (*drawing*) in Originalgröße; **~ stop** n Punkt m; **~-time** adj (*job*) Ganztags- ♦ adv (*work*) ganztags ♦ n (*SPORT*) Spielschluss nt; **~y** adv völlig; **~y fledged** adj (*also fig*) flügge; **~y licensed** adj (*hotel, restaurant*) mit voller Schankkonzession or -erlaubnis

fumble ['fʌmbl] vi: **to ~ (with)** herumfummeln (an +dat)

fume [fjuːm] vi qualmen; (*fig*) kochen (*inf*); **~s** npl (*of fuel, car*) Abgase pl

fumigate ['fjuːmɪgeɪt] vt ausräuchern

fun [fʌn] n Spaß m; **to make ~ of** sich lustig machen über +acc

function ['fʌŋkʃən] n Funktion f; (*occasion*) Veranstaltung f ♦ vi funktionieren; **~al** adj funktionell

fund [fʌnd] n (*money*) Geldmittel pl, Fonds m; (*store*) Vorrat m; **~s** npl (*resources*) Mittel pl

fundamental [fʌndəˈmentl] adj fundamental, grundlegend

funeral ['fjuːnərəl] n Beerdigung f; **~ parlour** n Leichenhalle f; **~ service** n Trauergottesdienst m

funfair ['fʌnfeəʳ] (*BRIT*) n Jahrmarkt m

fungi ['fʌŋgaɪ] npl of **fungus**

fungus ['fʌŋgəs] n Pilz m

funnel ['fʌnl] n Trichter m; (*NAUT*) Schornstein m

funny ['fʌnɪ] adj komisch

fur [fɜːʳ] n Pelz m; **~ coat** n Pelzmantel m

furious ['fjuərɪəs] adj wütend; (*attempt*) heftig

furlong ['fɜːlɔŋ] n = 201.17 m

furnace ['fɜːnɪs] n (Brenn)ofen m

furnish ['fɜːnɪʃ] vt einrichten; (*supply*) versehen; **~ings** npl Einrichtung f

furniture ['fɜːnɪtʃəʳ] n Möbel pl; **piece of ~** Möbelstück nt

furrow ['fʌrəu] n Furche f

furry ['fɜːrɪ] adj (*tongue*) pelzig; (*animal*) Pelz-

further ['fɜːðəʳ] adj weitere(r, s) ♦ adv weiter ♦ vt fördern; **~ education** n Weiterbildung

f; Erwachsenenbildung f; **~more** adv ferner

furthest ['fɜːðɪst] superl of **far**

furtive ['fɜːtɪv] adj verstohlen

fury ['fjuərɪ] n Wut f, Zorn m

fuse [fjuːz] (*US* **fuze**) n (*ELEC*) Sicherung f; (*of bomb*) Zünder m ♦ vt verschmelzen ♦ vi (*BRIT: ELEC*) durchbrennen; **~ box** n Sicherungskasten m

fuselage ['fjuːzəlɑːʒ] n Flugzeugrumpf m

fusion ['fjuːʒən] n Verschmelzung f

fuss [fʌs] n Theater nt; **~y** adj kleinlich

futile ['fjuːtaɪl] adj zwecklos, sinnlos; **futility** [fjuːˈtɪlɪtɪ] n Zwecklosigkeit f

future ['fjuːtʃəʳ] adj zukünftig ♦ n Zukunft f; **in (the) ~** in Zukunft

fuze [fjuːz] (*US*) = **fuse**

fuzzy ['fʌzɪ] adj (*indistinct*) verschwommen; (*hair*) kraus

G, g

G [dʒiː] n (*MUS*) G nt

G7 n abbr (= Group of Seven) G7 f

gabble ['gæbl] vi plappern

gable ['geɪbl] n Giebel m

gadget ['gædʒɪt] n Vorrichtung f

Gaelic ['geɪlɪk] adj gälisch ♦ n (*LING*) Gälisch nt

gaffe [gæf] n Fauxpas m

gag [gæg] n Knebel m; (*THEAT*) Gag m ♦ vt knebeln

gaiety ['geɪətɪ] n Fröhlichkeit f

gain [geɪn] vt (*obtain*) erhalten; (*win*) gewinnen ♦ vi (*clock*) vorgehen ♦ n Gewinn m; **to ~ in sth** an etw dat gewinnen; **~ on** vt fus einholen

gait [geɪt] n Gang m

gal. abbr = **gallon**

gala ['gɑːlə] n Fest nt

galaxy ['gæləksɪ] n Sternsystem nt

gale [geɪl] n Sturm m

gallant ['gælənt] adj tapfer; (*polite*) galant

gallbladder [gɔːl-] n Gallenblase f

gallery ['gælərɪ] n (*also:* **art ~**) Galerie f

galley ['gælɪ] n (*ship's kitchen*) Kombüse f; (*ship*) Galeere f

gallon ['gæln] *n* Gallone *f*

gallop ['gæləp] *n* Galopp *m* ♦ *vi* galoppieren

gallows ['gæləuz] *n* Galgen *m*

gallstone ['gɔːlstəun] *n* Gallenstein *m*

galore [gə'lɔːʳ] *adv* in Hülle und Fülle

galvanize ['gælvənaɪz] *vt* (*metal*) galvanisieren; (*fig*) elektrisieren

gambit ['gæmbɪt] *n* (*fig*): **opening ~** (einleitende(r)) Schachzug *m*

gamble ['gæmbl] *vi* (um Geld) spielen ♦ *vt* (*risk*) aufs Spiel setzen ♦ *n* Risiko *nt*; **~r** *n* Spieler(in) *m(f)*; **gambling** *n* Glücksspiel *nt*

game [geɪm] *n* Spiel *nt*; (*hunting*) Wild *nt* ♦ *adj*: **~ (for)** bereit (zu); **~keeper** *n* Wildhüter *m*; **~s console** *n* (*COMPUT*) Gameboy *m* ®, Konsole *f*

gammon ['gæmən] *n* geräucherte(r) Schinken *m*

gamut ['gæmət] *n* Tonskala *f*

gang [gæŋ] *n* (*of criminals, youths*) Bande *f*; (*of workmen*) Kolonne *f* ♦ *vi*: **to ~ up on sb** sich gegen jdn verschwören

gangrene ['gæŋgriːn] *n* Brand *m*

gangster ['gæŋstəʳ] *n* Gangster *m*

gangway ['gæŋweɪ] *n* (*NAUT*) Laufplanke *f*; (*aisle*) Gang *m*

gaol [dʒeɪl] (*BRIT*) *n*, *vt* = **jail**

gap [gæp] *n* Lücke *f*

gape [geɪp] *vi* glotzen; **gaping** ['geɪpɪŋ] *adj* (*wound*) klaffend; (*hole*) gähnend

garage ['gærɑːʒ] *n* Garage *f*; (*for repair*) (Auto)reparaturwerkstatt *f*; (*for petrol*) Tankstelle *f*

garbage ['gɑːbɪdʒ] *n* Abfall *m*; **~ can** (*US*) *n* Mülltonne *f*

garbled ['gɑːbld] *adj* (*story*) verdreht

garden ['gɑːdn] *n* Garten *m*; **~s** *npl* (*public park*) Park *m*; (*private*) Gartenanlagen *pl*; **~er** *n* Gärtner(in) *m(f)*; **~ing** *n* Gärtnern *nt*

gargle ['gɑːgl] *vi* gurgeln

gargoyle ['gɑːgɔɪl] *n* Wasserspeier *m*

garish ['gɛərɪʃ] *adj* grell

garland ['gɑːlənd] *n* Girlande *f*

garlic ['gɑːlɪk] *n* Knoblauch *m*

garment ['gɑːmənt] *n* Kleidungsstück *nt*

garnish ['gɑːnɪʃ] *vt* (*food*) garnieren

garrison ['gærɪsn] *n* Garnison *f*

garter ['gɑːtəʳ] *n* Strumpfband *nt*; (*US*) Strumpfhalter *m*

gas [gæs] *n* Gas *nt*; (*esp US: petrol*) Benzin *nt* ♦ *vt* vergasen; **~ cooker** (*BRIT*) *n* Gasherd *m*; **~ cylinder** *n* Gasflasche *f*; **~ fire** *n* Gasofen *m*

gash [gæʃ] *n* klaffende Wunde *f* ♦ *vt* tief verwunden

gasket ['gæskɪt] *n* Dichtungsring *m*

gas mask *n* Gasmaske *f*

gas meter *n* Gaszähler *m*

gasoline ['gæsəliːn] (*US*) *n* Benzin *nt*

gasp [gɑːsp] *vi* keuchen; (*in surprise*) tief Luft holen ♦ *n* Keuchen *nt*

gas: **~ ring** *n* Gasring *m*; **~ station** (*US*) *n* Tankstelle *f*; **~ tap** *n* Gashahn *m*

gastric ['gæstrɪk] *adj* Magen-

gate [geɪt] *n* Tor *nt*; (*barrier*) Schranke *f*

gateau ['gætəu] (*pl* **~x**) *n* Torte *f*

gatecrash ['geɪtkræʃ] (*BRIT*) *vt* (*party*) platzen in +*acc*

gateway ['geɪtweɪ] *n* Toreingang *m*

gather ['gæðəʳ] *vt* (*people*) versammeln; (*things*) sammeln; (*understand*) annehmen ♦ *vi* (*assemble*) sich versammeln; **to ~ speed** schneller werden; **to ~ (from)** schließen (aus); **~ing** *n* Versammlung *f*

gauche [gəuʃ] *adj* linkisch

gaudy ['gɔːdɪ] *adj* schreiend

gauge [geɪdʒ] *n* (*instrument*) Messgerät *nt*; (*RAIL*) Spurweite *f*; (*dial*) Anzeiger *m*; (*measure*) Maß *nt* ♦ *vt* (ab)messen; (*fig*) abschätzen

gaunt [gɔːnt] *adj* hager

gauze [gɔːz] *n* Gaze *f*

gave [geɪv] *pt of* **give**

gay [geɪ] *adj* (*homosexual*) schwul; (*lively*) lustig

gaze [geɪz] *n* Blick *m* ♦ *vi* starren; **to ~ at sth** etw *dat* anstarren

gazelle [gə'zɛl] *n* Gazelle *f*

gazumping [gə'zʌmpɪŋ] (*BRIT*) *n* Hausverkauf an Höherbietenden trotz Zusage an anderen

GB *n abbr* = **Great Britain**

GCE (*BRIT*) *n abbr* = **General Certificate of Education**

GCSE (*BRIT*) *n abbr* = **General Certificate of Secondary Education**

gear [gɪəʳ] *n* Getriebe *nt*; (*equipment*) Ausrüstung *f*; (*AUT*) Gang *m* ♦ *vt* (*fig: adapt*): **to be ~ed to** ausgerichtet sein auf +*acc*; **top ~** höchste(r) Gang *m*; **high ~** (*US*) höchste(r) Gang *m*; **low ~** niedrige(r) Gang *m*; **in ~** eingekuppelt; **~ box** *n* Getriebe(gehäuse) *nt*; **~ lever** *n* Schalthebel *m*; **~ shift** (*US*) *n* Schalthebel *m*

geese [giːs] *npl of* **goose**

gel [dʒɛl] *n* Gel *nt*

gelatin(e) [ˈdʒɛlətiːn] *n* Gelatine *f*

gem [dʒɛm] *n* Edelstein *m*; (*fig*) Juwel *nt*

Gemini [ˈdʒɛmɪnaɪ] *n* Zwillinge *pl*

gender [ˈdʒɛndəʳ] *n* (*GRAM*) Geschlecht *nt*

gene [dʒiːn] *n* Gen *nt*

general [ˈdʒɛnərl] *n* General *m* ♦ *adj* allgemein; **~ delivery** (*US*) *n* Ausgabe(schalter *m*) *f* postlagernder Sendungen; **~ election** *n* allgemeine Wahlen *pl*; **~ize** *vi* verallgemeinern; **~ knowledge** *n* Allgemeinwissen *nt*; **~ly** *adv* allgemein, im Allgemeinen; **~ practitioner** *n* praktische(r) Arzt *m*, praktische Ärztin *f*

generate [ˈdʒɛnəreɪt] *vt* erzeugen

generation [dʒɛnəˈreɪʃən] *n* Generation *f*; (*act*) Erzeugung *f*

generator [ˈdʒɛnəreɪtəʳ] *n* Generator *m*

generosity [dʒɛnəˈrɔsɪtɪ] *n* Großzügigkeit *f*

generous [ˈdʒɛnərəs] *adj* großzügig

genetic [dʒɪˈnɛtɪk] *adj* genetisch; **~ally** *adv* genetisch; **~ally modified** genmanipuliert; **~ engineering** *n* Gentechnik *f*; **~ fingerprinting** [-ˈfɪŋɡəprɪntɪŋ] *n* genetische Fingerabdrücke *pl*

genetics [dʒɪˈnɛtɪks] *n* Genetik *f*

Geneva [dʒɪˈniːvə] *n* Genf *nt*

genial [ˈdʒiːnɪəl] *adj* freundlich, jovial

genitals [ˈdʒɛnɪtlz] *npl* Genitalien *pl*

genius [ˈdʒiːnɪəs] *n* Genie *nt*

genocide [ˈdʒɛnəusaɪd] *n* Völkermord *m*

gent [dʒɛnt] *n abbr* = **gentleman**

genteel [dʒɛnˈtiːl] *adj* (*polite*) wohlanständig; (*affected*) affektiert

gentle [ˈdʒɛntl] *adj* sanft, zart

gentleman [ˈdʒɛntlmən] (*irreg*) *n* Herr *m*;

(*polite*) Gentleman *m*

gentleness [ˈdʒɛntlnɪs] *n* Zartheit *f*, Milde *f*

gently [ˈdʒɛntlɪ] *adv* zart, sanft

gentry [ˈdʒɛntrɪ] *n* Landadel *m*

gents [dʒɛnts] *n*: **G~** (*lavatory*) Herren *pl*

genuine [ˈdʒɛnjuɪn] *adj* echt

geographic(al) [dʒɪəˈɡræfɪk(l)] *adj* geografisch

geography [dʒɪˈɔɡrəfɪ] *n* Geografie *f*

geological [dʒɪəˈlɔdʒɪkl] *adj* geologisch

geology [dʒɪˈɔlədʒɪ] *n* Geologie *f*

geometric(al) [dʒɪəˈmɛtrɪk(l)] *adj* geometrisch

geometry [dʒɪˈɔmətrɪ] *n* Geometrie *f*

geranium [dʒɪˈreɪnɪəm] *n* Geranie *f*

geriatric [dʒɛrɪˈætrɪk] *adj* Alten- ♦ *n* Greis(in) *m(f)*

germ [dʒəːm] *n* Keim *m*; (*MED*) Bazillus *m*

German [ˈdʒəːmən] *adj* deutsch ♦ *n* Deutsche(r) *f(m)*; (*LING*) Deutsch *nt*; **~ measles** *n* Röteln *pl*; **~y** *n* Deutschland *nt*

germination [dʒəːmɪˈneɪʃən] *n* Keimen *nt*

gesticulate [dʒɛsˈtɪkjuleɪt] *vi* gestikulieren

gesture [ˈdʒɛstjəʳ] *n* Geste *f*

KEYWORD
---

get [gɛt] (*pt*, *pp* **got**, *pp* **gotten** (*US*)) *vi* **1** (*become, be*) werden; **to get old/tired** alt/müde werden; **to get married** heiraten

2 (*go*) (an)kommen, gehen

3 (*begin*): **to get to know sb** jdn kennen lernen; **let's get going** *or* **started!** fangen wir an!

4 (*modal aux vb*): **you've got to do it** du musst es tun

♦ *vt* **1**: **to get sth done** (*do*) etw machen; (*have done*) etw machen lassen; **to get sth going** *or* **to go** etw in Gang bringen *or* bekommen; **to get sb to do sth** jdn dazu bringen, etw zu tun

2 (*obtain: money, permission, results*) erhalten; (*find: job, flat*) finden; (*fetch: person, object*) holen; **to get sth for sb** jdm etw besorgen; **get me Mr Jones, please** (*TEL*) verbinden Sie mich bitte mit Mr Jones

3 (*receive: present, letter*) bekommen, kriegen; (*acquire: reputation etc*) erwerben

4 (*catch*) bekommen, kriegen; (*hit: target etc*) treffen, erwischen; **get him!** (*to dog*) fass!

5 (*take, move*) bringen; **to get sth to sb** jdm etw bringen

6 (*understand*) verstehen; (*hear*) mitbekommen; **I've got it!** ich habs!

7 (*have, possess*): **to have got sth** etw haben

get about *vi* herumkommen; (*news*) sich verbreiten

get along *vi* (*people*) (gut) zurechtkommen; (*depart*) sich *acc* auf den Weg machen

get at *vt* (*facts*) herausbekommen; **to get at sb** (*nag*) an jdm herumnörgeln

get away *vi* (*leave*) sich *acc* davonmachen; (*escape*): **to get away from sth** von etw *dat* entkommen; **to get away with sth** mit etw davonkommen

get back *vi* (*return*) zurückkommen ♦ *vt* zurückbekommen

get by *vi* (*pass*) vorbeikommen; (*manage*) zurechtkommen

get down *vi* (her)untergehen ♦ *vt* (*depress*) fertig machen; **to get down to** in Angriff nehmen; (*find time to do*) kommen zu

get in *vi* (*train*) ankommen; (*arrive home*) heimkommen

get into *vt* (*enter*) hinein-/hereinkommen in +*acc*; (*: car, train etc*) einsteigen in +*acc*; (*clothes*) anziehen

get off *vi* (*from train etc*) aussteigen; (*from horse*) absteigen ♦ *vt* aussteigen aus; absteigen von

get on *vi* (*progress*) vorankommen; (*be friends*) auskommen; (*age*) alt werden; (*onto train etc*) einsteigen; (*onto horse*) aufsteigen ♦ *vt* einsteigen in +*acc*; auf etw *acc* aufsteigen

get out *vi* (*of house*) herauskommen; (*of vehicle*) aussteigen ♦ *vt* (*take out*) herausholen

get out of *vt* (*duty etc*) herumkommen um

get over *vt* (*illness*) sich *acc* erholen von;

(*surprise*) verkraften; (*news*) fassen; (*loss*) sich abfinden mit

get round *vt* herumkommen; (*fig: person*) herumkriegen

get through to *vt* (*TEL*) durchkommen zu

get together *vi* zusammenkommen

get up *vi* aufstehen ♦ *vt* hinaufbringen; (*go up*) hinaufgehen; (*organize*) auf die Beine stellen

get up to *vt* (*reach*) erreichen; (*prank etc*) anstellen

getaway ['gɛtəweɪ] *n* Flucht *f*

get-up ['gɛtʌp] (*inf*) *n* Aufzug *m*

geyser ['giːzəʳ] *n* Geiser *m*; (*heater*) Durchlauferhitzer *m*

ghastly ['gɑːstlɪ] *adj* grässlich

gherkin ['gəːkɪn] *n* Gewürzgurke *f*

ghetto ['gɛtəu] *n* G(h)etto *nt*; **~ blaster** *n* (große(r)) Radiorekorder *m*

ghost [gəust] *n* Gespenst *nt*

giant ['dʒaɪənt] *n* Riese *m* ♦ *adj* riesig, Riesen-

gibberish ['dʒɪbərɪʃ] *n* dumme(s) Geschwätz *nt*

gibe [dʒaɪb] *n* spöttische Bemerkung *f*

giblets ['dʒɪblɪts] *npl* Geflügelinnereien *pl*

giddiness ['gɪdɪnɪs] *n* Schwindelgefühl *nt*

giddy ['gɪdɪ] *adj* schwindlig

gift [gɪft] *n* Geschenk *nt*; (*ability*) Begabung *f*; **~ed** *adj* begabt; **~ shop** *n* Geschenkeladen *m*; **~ token**, **~ voucher** *n* Geschenkgutschein *m*

gigantic [dʒaɪˈgæntɪk] *adj* riesenhaft

giggle ['gɪgl] *vi* kichern ♦ *n* Gekicher *nt*

gild [gɪld] *vt* vergolden

gill [dʒɪl] *n* (1/4 *pint*) Viertelpinte *f*

gills [gɪlz] *npl* (*of fish*) Kiemen *pl*

gilt [gɪlt] *n* Vergoldung *f* ♦ *adj* vergoldet; **~-edged** *adj* mündelsicher

gimmick ['gɪmɪk] *n* Gag *m*

gin [dʒɪn] *n* Gin *m*

ginger ['dʒɪndʒəʳ] *n* Ingwer *m*; **~ ale** *n* Ingwerbier *nt*; **~ beer** *n* Ingwerbier *nt*; **~bread** *n* Pfefferkuchen *m*; **~-haired** *adj* rothaarig

gingerly ['dʒɪndʒəlɪ] *adv* behutsam

gipsy ['dʒɪpsɪ] n Zigeuner(in) m(f)

giraffe [dʒɪ'rɑːf] n Giraffe f

girder ['gəːdəʳ] n Eisenträger m

girdle ['gəːdl] n Hüftgürtel m

girl [gəːl] n Mädchen nt; **an English ~** eine (junge) Engländerin; **~friend** n Freundin f; **~ish** adj mädchenhaft

giro ['dʒaɪrəʊ] n (bank ~) Giro nt; (post office ~) Postscheckverkehr m

girth [gəːθ] n (measure) Umfang m; (strap) Sattelgurt m

gist [dʒɪst] n Wesentliche(s) nt

give [gɪv] (pt **gave**, pp **given**) vt geben ♦ vi (break) nachgeben; **~ away** vt verschenken; (betray) verraten; **~ back** vt zurückgeben; **~ in** vi nachgeben ♦ vt (hand in) abgeben; **~ off** vt abgeben; **~ out** vt verteilen; (announce) bekannt geben; **~ up** vt, vi aufgeben; **to ~ o.s. up** sich stellen; (after siege) sich ergeben; **~ way** vi (BRIT: traffic) Vorfahrt lassen; (to feelings): **to ~ way to** nachgeben +dat

glacier ['glæsɪəʳ] n Gletscher m

glad [glæd] adj froh; **~ly** ['glædlɪ] adv gern(e)

glamorous ['glæmərəs] adj reizvoll

glamour ['glæməʳ] n Glanz m

glance [glɑːns] n Blick m ♦ vi: **to ~ (at)** (hin)blicken (auf +acc); **~ off** vt fus (fly off) abprallen von; **glancing** ['glɑːnsɪŋ] adj (blow) Streif-

gland [glænd] n Drüse f

glare [glɛəʳ] n (light) grelle(s) Licht nt; (stare) wilde(r) Blick m ♦ vi grell scheinen; (angrily): **to ~ at** böse ansehen; **glaring** ['glɛərɪŋ] adj (injustice) schreiend; (mistake) krass

glass [glɑːs] n Glas nt; (mirror: also: looking ~) Spiegel m; **~es** npl (spectacles) Brille f; **~house** n Gewächshaus nt; **~ware** n Glaswaren pl; **~y** adj glasig

glaze [gleɪz] vt verglasen; (finish with a ~) glasieren ♦ n Glasur f; **~d** adj (eye) glasig; (pot) glasiert; **glazier** ['gleɪzɪəʳ] n Glaser m

gleam [gliːm] n Schimmer m ♦ vi schimmern

glean [gliːn] vt (fig) ausfindig machen

glen [glɛn] n Bergtal nt

glib [glɪb] adj oberflächlich

glide [glaɪd] vi gleiten; **~r** n (AVIAT) Segelflugzeug nt; **gliding** ['glaɪdɪŋ] n Segelfliegen nt

glimmer ['glɪməʳ] n Schimmer m

glimpse [glɪmps] n flüchtige(r) Blick m ♦ vt flüchtig erblicken

glint [glɪnt] n Glitzern nt ♦ vi glitzern

glisten ['glɪsn] vi glänzen

glitter ['glɪtəʳ] vi funkeln ♦ n Funkeln nt

gloat [gləʊt] vi: **to ~ over** sich weiden an +dat

global ['gləʊbl] adj: **~ warming** globale(r) Temperaturanstieg m

globe [gləʊb] n Erdball m; (sphere) Globus m

gloom [gluːm] n (darkness) Dunkel nt; (depression) düstere Stimmung f; **~y** adj düster

glorify ['glɔːrɪfaɪ] vt verherrlichen

glorious ['glɔːrɪəs] adj glorreich

glory ['glɔːrɪ] n Ruhm m

gloss [glɒs] n (shine) Glanz m; **~ over** vt fus übertünchen

glossary ['glɒsərɪ] n Glossar nt

glossy ['glɒsɪ] adj (surface) glänzend

glove [glʌv] n Handschuh m; **~ compartment** n (AUT) Handschuhfach nt

glow [gləʊ] vi glühen ♦ n Glühen nt

glower ['glaʊəʳ] vi: **to ~ at** finster anblicken

glucose ['gluːkəʊs] n Traubenzucker m

glue [gluː] n Klebstoff m ♦ vt kleben

glum [glʌm] adj bedrückt

glut [glʌt] n Überfluss m

glutton ['glʌtn] n Vielfraß m; **a ~ for work** ein Arbeitstier nt

glycerin(e) ['glɪsəriːn] n Glyzerin nt

GM abbr = **genetically modified**

gnarled [nɑːld] adj knorrig

gnat [næt] n Stechmücke f

gnaw [nɔː] vt nagen an +dat

gnome [nəʊm] n Gnom m

go [gəʊ] (pt **went**, pp **gone**, pl **~es**) vi gehen; (travel) reisen, fahren; (depart: train) (ab)fahren; (be sold) verkauft werden; (work) gehen, funktionieren; (fit, suit) passen; (become) werden; (break etc) nachgeben ♦ n (energy) Schwung m;

(attempt) Versuch *m*; **he's ~ing to do it** er wird es tun; **to ~ for a walk** spazieren gehen; **to ~ dancing** tanzen gehen; **how did it ~?** wie wars?; **to ~ with** *(be suitable)* passen zu; **to have a ~ at sth** etw versuchen; **to be on the ~** auf Trab sein; **whose ~ is it?** wer ist dran?; **~ about** *vi* *(rumour)* umgehen ♦ *vt fus:* **how do I ~ about this?** wie packe ich das an?; **~ after** *vt fus (pursue: person)* nachgehen +*dat*; **~ ahead** *vi (proceed)* weitergehen; **~ along** *vi* dahingehen, dahinfahren ♦ *vt* entlanggehen, entlangfahren; **to ~ along with** *(support)* zustimmen +*dat*; **~ away** *vi (depart)* weggehen; **~ back** *vi (return)* zurückgehen; **~ back on** *vt fus (promise)* nicht halten; **~ by** *vi (years, time)* vergehen ♦ *vt fus* sich richten nach; **~ down** *vi (sun)* untergehen ♦ *vt fus* hinuntergehen, hinunterfahren; **~ for** *vt fus (fetch)* holen (gehen); *(like)* mögen; *(attack)* sich stürzen auf +*acc*; **~ in** *vi* hineingehen; **~ in for** *vt fus (competition)* teilnehmen an; **~ into** *vt fus (enter)* hineingehen in +*acc*; *(study)* sich befassen mit; **~ off** *vi (depart)* weggehen; *(lights)* ausgehen; *(milk etc)* sauer werden; *(explode)* losgehen ♦ *vt fus (dislike)* nicht mehr mögen; **~ on** *vi (continue)* weitergehen; *(inf: complain)* meckern; *(lights)* angehen; **to ~ on with sth** mit etw weitermachen; **~ out** *vi (fire, light)* ausgehen; *(of house)* hinausgehen; **~ over** *vi (ship)* kentern ♦ *vt fus (examine, check)* durchgehen; **~ past** *vi:* **to ~ past sth** an etw *dat* vorbeigehen; **~ round** *vi (visit):* **to ~ round (to sb's)** (bei jdm) vorbeigehen; **~ through** *vt fus (town etc)* durchgehen, durchfahren; **~ up** *vi (price)* steigen; **~ with** *vt fus (suit)* zu etw passen; **~ without** *vt fus* sich behelfen ohne; *(food)* entbehren

goad [gəud] *vt* anstacheln

go-ahead ['gəuəhed] *adj* zielstrebig; *(progressive)* fortschrittlich ♦ *n* grüne(s) Licht *nt*

goal [gəul] *n* Ziel *nt*; *(SPORT)* Tor *nt*; **~keeper** *n* Torwart *m*; **~ post** *n*

Torpfosten *m*

goat [gəut] *n* Ziege *f*

gobble ['gɔbl] *vt (also:* **~ down, ~ up)** hinunterschlingen

go-between ['gəubitwi:n] *n* Mittelsmann *m*

god [gɔd] *n* Gott *m*; **G~** *n* Gott *m*; **~child** *n* Patenkind *nt*; **~daughter** *n* Patentochter *f*; **~dess** *n* Göttin *f*; **~father** *n* Pate *m*; **~forsaken** *adj* gottverlassen; **~mother** *n* Patin *f*; **~send** *n* Geschenk *nt* des Himmels; **~son** *n* Patensohn *m*

goggles ['gɔglz] *npl* Schutzbrille *f*

going ['gəuiŋ] *n (HORSE-RACING)* Bahn *f* ♦ *adj (rate)* gängig; *(concern)* gut gehend; **it's hard ~** es ist schwierig

gold [gəuld] *n* Gold *nt* ♦ *adj* golden; **~en** *adj* golden, Gold-; **~fish** *n* Goldfisch *m*; **~ mine** *n* Goldgrube *f*; **~-plated** *adj* vergoldet; **~smith** *n* Goldschmied(in) *m(f)*

golf [gɔlf] *n* Golf *nt*; **~ ball** *n* Golfball *m*; *(on typewriter)* Kugelkopf *m*; **~ club** *n (society)* Golfklub *m*; *(stick)* Golfschläger *m*; **~ course** *n* Golfplatz *m*; **~er** *n* Golfspieler(in) *m(f)*

gondola ['gɔndələ] *n* Gondel *f*

gone [gɔn] *pp of* **go**

gong [gɔŋ] *n* Gong *m*

good [gud] *n (benefit)* Wohl *nt*; *(moral excellence)* Güte *f* ♦ *adj* gut; **~s** *npl (merchandise etc)* Waren *pl*, Güter *pl*; **a ~ deal (of)** ziemlich viel; **a ~ many** ziemlich viele; **~ morning!** guten Morgen!; **~ afternoon!** guten Tag!; **~ evening!** guten Abend!; **~ night!** gute Nacht!; **would you be ~ enough to ...?** könnten Sie bitte ...?

goodbye [gud'bai] *excl* auf Wiedersehen!

good: G~ Friday *n* Karfreitag *m*; **~-looking** *adj* gut aussehen; **~-natured** *adj* gutmütig; *(joke)* harmlos; **~ness** *n* Güte *f*; *(virtue)* Tugend *f*; **~s train** *n (BRIT)* *n* Güterzug *m*; **~will** *n (favour)* Wohlwollen *nt*; *(COMM)* Firmenansehen *nt*

goose [gu:s] *n (pl* **geese)** *n* Gans *f*

gooseberry ['guzbəri] *n* Stachelbeere *f*

gooseflesh ['gu:sfleʃ] *n* Gänsehaut *f*

goose pimples *npl* Gänsehaut *f*

gore [gɔːr] *vt* aufspießen ♦ *n* Blut *nt*

gorge [gɔːdʒ] n Schlucht f ♦ vt: **to ~ o.s.** (sich voll) fressen

gorgeous ['gɔːdʒəs] adj prächtig

gorilla [gəˈrɪlə] n Gorilla m

gorse [gɔːs] n Stechginster m

gory ['gɔːrɪ] adj blutig

go-slow ['gəuˈsləu] (BRIT) n Bummelstreik m

gospel ['gɔspl] n Evangelium nt

gossip ['gɔsɪp] n Klatsch m; (person) Klatschbase f ♦ vi klatschen

got [gɔt] pt, pp of **get**

gotten ['gɔtn] (US) pp of **get**

gout [gaut] n Gicht f

govern ['gʌvən] vt regieren; verwalten

governess ['gʌvənɪs] n Gouvernante f

government ['gʌvnmənt] n Regierung f

governor ['gʌvənər] n Gouverneur m

gown [gaun] n Gewand nt; (UNIV) Robe f

G.P. n abbr = **general practitioner**

grab [græb] vt packen

grace [greɪs] n Anmut f; (blessing) Gnade f; (prayer) Tischgebet nt ♦ vt (adorn) zieren; (honour) auszeichnen; **5 days' ~** 5 Tage Aufschub; **~ful** adj anmutig

gracious ['greɪʃəs] adj gnädig; (kind) freundlich

grade [greɪd] n Grad m; (slope) Gefälle nt ♦ vt (classify) einstufen; **~ crossing** (US) n Bahnübergang m; **~ school** (US) n Grundschule f

gradient ['greɪdɪənt] n Steigung f; Gefälle nt

gradual ['grædjuəl] adj allmählich; **~ly** adv allmählich

graduate [n 'grædjuɪt, vb 'grædjueɪt] n: **to be a ~** das Staatsexamen haben ♦ vi das Staatsexamen machen; **graduation** [grædjuˈeɪʃən] n Abschlussfeier f

graffiti [grəˈfiːtɪ] npl Graffiti pl

graft [grɑːft] n (hard work) Schufterei f; (MED) Verpflanzung f ♦ vt pfropfen; (fig) aufpfropfen; (MED) verpflanzen

grain [greɪn] n Korn nt; (in wood) Maserung f

gram [græm] n Gramm nt

grammar ['græmər] n Grammatik f; **~ school** (BRIT) n Gymnasium nt; **grammatical** [grəˈmætɪkl] adj grammat(ikal)isch

gramme [græm] n = **gram**

granary ['grænərɪ] n Kornspeicher m

grand [grænd] adj großartig; **~child** (pl **~children**) n Enkelkind nt, Enkel(in) m(f); **~dad** n Opa m; **~daughter** n Enkelin f; **~eur** ['grændjər] n Erhabenheit f; **~father** n Großvater m; **~iose** ['grændɪəus] adj (imposing) großartig; (pompous) schwülstig; **~ma** n Oma f; **~mother** n Großmutter f; **~pa** n = **granddad**; **~parents** npl Großeltern pl; **~ piano** n Flügel m; **~son** n Enkel m; **~stand** n Haupttribüne f

granite ['grænɪt] n Granit m

granny ['grænɪ] n Oma f

grant [grɑːnt] vt gewähren ♦ n Unterstützung f; (UNIV) Stipendium nt; **to take sth for ~ed** etw als selbstverständlich (an)nehmen

granulated sugar ['grænjuleɪtɪd-] n Zuckerraffinade f

granule ['grænjuːl] n Körnchen nt

grape [greɪp] n (Wein)traube f

grapefruit ['greɪpfruːt] n Pampelmuse f, Grapefruit f

graph [grɑːf] n Schaubild nt; **~ic** ['græfɪk] adj (descriptive) anschaulich; (drawing) grafisch; **~ics** npl Grafik f

grapple ['græpl] vi: **to ~ with** kämpfen mit

grasp [grɑːsp] vt ergreifen; (understand) begreifen ♦ n Griff m; (of subject) Beherrschung f; **~ing** adj habgierig

grass [grɑːs] n Gras nt; **~hopper** n Heuschrecke f; **~land** n Weideland nt; **~-roots** adj an der Basis; **~ snake** n Ringelnatter f

grate [greɪt] n Kamin m ♦ vi (sound) knirschen ♦ vt (cheese etc) reiben; **to ~ on the nerves** auf die Nerven gehen

grateful ['greɪtful] adj dankbar

grater ['greɪtər] n Reibe f

gratify ['grætɪfaɪ] vt befriedigen; **~ing** adj erfreulich

grating ['greɪtɪŋ] n (iron bars) Gitter nt ♦ adj (noise) knirschend

gratitude ['grætɪtjuːd] n Dankbarkeit f

gratuity [grəˈtjuːɪtɪ] n Gratifikation f

grave [greɪv] n Grab nt ♦ adj (serious) ernst

gravel ['grævl] n Kies m

gravestone ['greɪvstəʊn] n Grabstein m

graveyard ['greɪvjɑːd] n Friedhof m

gravity ['grævɪtɪ] n Schwerkraft f; (seriousness) Schwere f

gravy ['greɪvɪ] n (Braten)soße f

gray [greɪ] adj = **grey**

graze [greɪz] vi grasen ♦ vt (touch) streifen; (MED) abschürfen ♦ n Abschürfung f

grease [griːs] n (fat) Fett nt; (lubricant) Schmiere f ♦ vt (ab)schmieren; **~proof** (BRIT) adj (paper) Butterbrot-; **greasy** ['griːsɪ] adj fettig

great [greɪt] adj groß; (inf: good) prima; **G~ Britain** n Großbritannien nt; **~grandfather** n Urgroßvater m; **~grandmother** n Urgroßmutter f; **~ly** adv sehr

Greece [griːs] n Griechenland nt

greed [griːd] n (also: **~iness**) Gier f; (meanness) Geiz m; **~(iness) for** Gier nach; **~y** adj gierig

Greek [griːk] adj griechisch ♦ n Grieche m, Griechin f ♦ (LING) Griechisch nt

green [griːn] adj grün ♦ n (village ~) Dorfwiese f; **~ belt** n Grüngürtel m; **~ card** n (AUT) grüne Versicherungskarte f; **~ery** n Grün nt; grüne(s) Laub nt; **~gage** n Reneklode f, Reineclaude f; **~grocer** (BRIT) n Obst- und Gemüsehändler m; **~house** n Gewächshaus nt; **~house effect** n Treibhauseffekt m; **~house gas** n Treibhausgas nt

Greenland ['griːnlənd] n Grönland nt

greet [griːt] vt grüßen; **~ing** n Gruß m; **~ing(s) card** n Glückwunschkarte f

gregarious [grə'geərɪəs] adj gesellig

grenade [grə'neɪd] n Granate f

grew [gruː] pt of **grow**

grey [greɪ] adj grau; **~haired** adj grauhaarig; **~hound** n Windhund m

grid [grɪd] n Gitter nt; (ELEC) Leitungsnetz nt; (on map) Gitternetz nt

gridlock ['grɪdlɒk] n (AUT: traffic jam) totale(r) Stau m; **~ed** adj: **to be ~ed** (roads) total verstopft sein; (talks etc) festgefahren sein

grief [griːf] n Gram m, Kummer m

grievance ['griːvəns] n Beschwerde f

grieve [griːv] vi sich grämen ♦ vt betrüben

grievous ['griːvəs] adj: **~ bodily harm** (JUR) schwere Körperverletzung f

grill [grɪl] n Grill m ♦ vt (BRIT) grillen; (question) in die Mangel nehmen

grille [grɪl] n (AUT) (Kühler)gitter nt

grim [grɪm] adj grimmig; (situation) düster

grimace [grɪ'meɪs] n Grimasse f ♦ vi Grimassen schneiden

grime [graɪm] n Schmutz m; **grimy** ['graɪmɪ] adj schmutzig

grin [grɪn] n Grinsen nt ♦ vi grinsen

grind [graɪnd] (pt, pp **ground**) vt mahlen; (US: meat) durch den Fleischwolf drehen; (sharpen) schleifen; (teeth) knirschen mit ♦ n (bore) Plackerei f

grip [grɪp] n Griff m; (suitcase) Handkoffer m ♦ vt packen; **~ping** adj (exciting) spannend

grisly ['grɪzlɪ] adj grässlich

gristle ['grɪsl] n Knorpel m

grit [grɪt] n Splitt m; (courage) Mut m ♦ vt (teeth) zusammenbeißen; (road) (mit Splitt be)streuen

groan [grəʊn] n Stöhnen nt ♦ vi stöhnen

grocer ['grəʊsəʳ] n Lebensmittelhändler m; **~ies** npl Lebensmittel pl; **~'s (shop)** n Lebensmittelgeschäft nt

groggy ['grɒgɪ] adj benommen

groin [grɔɪn] n Leistengegend f

groom [gruːm] n (also: **bridegroom**) Bräutigam m; (for horses) Pferdeknecht m ♦ vt (horse) striegeln; **(well-)ed** gepflegt

groove [gruːv] n Rille f, Furche f

grope [grəʊp] vi tasten; **~ for** vt fus suchen nach

gross [grəʊs] adj (coarse) dick, plump; (bad) grob, schwer; (COMM) brutto; **~ly** adv höchst

grotesque [grə'tesk] adj grotesk

grotto ['grɒtəʊ] n Grotte f

ground [graʊnd] pt, pp of **grind** ♦ n Boden m; (land) Grundbesitz m; (reason) Grund m; (US: also: **~ wire**) Erdleitung f ♦ vi (run ashore) stranden, auflaufen; **~s** npl (dregs) Bodensatz m; (around house)

(Garten)anlagen pl; **on the ~** am Boden; **to the ~** zu Boden; **to gain/lose ~** Boden gewinnen/verlieren; **~ cloth** (US) n = **groundsheet; ~ing** n (instruction) Anfangsunterricht m; **~less** adj grundlos; **~sheet** (BRIT) n Zeltboden m; **~ staff** n Bodenpersonal nt; **~work** n Grundlage f

group [gru:p] n Gruppe f ♦ vt (also: **~ together**) gruppieren ♦ vi sich gruppieren

grouse [graus] n inv (bird) schottische(s) Moorhuhn nt

grove [grəuv] n Gehölz nt, Hain m

grovel ['grɔvl] vi (fig) kriechen

grow [grəu] (pt grew, pp grown) vi wachsen; (become) werden ♦ vt (raise) anbauen; **~ up** vi aufwachsen; **~er** n Züchter m; **~ing** adj zunehmend

growl [graul] vi knurren

grown [grəun] pp of **grow**; **~-up** n Erwachsene(r) mf

growth [grəuθ] n Wachstum nt; (increase) Zunahme f; (of beard etc) Wuchs m

grub [grʌb] n Made f, Larve f; (inf: food) Futter nt; **~by** ['grʌbɪ] adj schmutzig

grudge [grʌdʒ] n Groll m ♦ vt: **to ~ sb sth** jdm etw missgönnen; **to bear sb a ~** einen Groll gegen jdn hegen

gruelling ['gruəlɪŋ] adj (climb, race) mörderisch

gruesome ['gru:səm] adj grauenhaft

gruff [grʌf] adj barsch

grumble ['grʌmbl] vi murren

grumpy ['grʌmpɪ] adj verdrießlich

grunt [grʌnt] vi grunzen ♦ n Grunzen nt

G-string ['dʒi:strɪŋ] n Minislip m

guarantee [gærən'ti:] n Garantie f ♦ vt garantieren

guard [gɑ:d] n (sentry) Wache f; (BRIT: RAIL) Zugbegleiter m ♦ vt bewachen

guarded ['gɑ:dɪd] adj vorsichtig

guardian ['gɑ:dɪən] n Vormund m; (keeper) Hüter m

guard's van ['gɑ:dz] (BRIT) n (RAIL) Dienstwagen m

guerrilla [gə'rɪlə] n Guerilla(kämpfer) m; **~ warfare** n Guerillakrieg m

guess [ges] vt, vi (er)raten, schätzen ♦ n Vermutung f; **~work** n Raterei f

guest [gest] n Gast m; **~ house** n Pension f; **~ room** n Gastzimmer nt

guffaw [gʌ'fɔ:] vi schallend lachen

guidance ['gaɪdəns] n (control) Leitung f; (advice) Beratung f

guide [gaɪd] n Führer m; (also: **girl ~**) Pfadfinderin f ♦ vt führen; **~book** n Reiseführer m; **~ dog** n Blindenhund m; **~lines** npl Richtlinien pl

guild [gɪld] n (HIST) Gilde f

guillotine ['gɪləti:n] n Guillotine f

guilt [gɪlt] n Schuld f; **~y** adj schuldig

guinea pig ['gɪnɪ-] n Meerschweinchen nt; (fig) Versuchskaninchen nt

guise [gaɪz] n: **in the ~ of** in der Form +gen

guitar [gɪ'tɑ:] n Gitarre f

gulf [gʌlf] n Golf m; (fig) Abgrund m

gull [gʌl] n Möwe f

gullet ['gʌlɪt] n Schlund m

gullible ['gʌlɪbl] adj leichtgläubig

gully ['gʌlɪ] n (Wasser)rinne f

gulp [gʌlp] vt (also: **~ down**) hinunterschlucken ♦ vi (gasp) schlucken

gum [gʌm] n (around teeth) Zahnfleisch nt; (glue) Klebstoff m; (also: **chewing ~**) Kaugummi m ♦ vt gummieren; **~boots** (BRIT) npl Gummistiefel pl

gun [gʌn] n Schusswaffe f; **~boat** n Kanonenboot nt; **~fire** n Geschützfeuer nt; **~man** (irreg) n bewaffnete(r) Verbrecher m; **~point** n: **at ~point** mit Waffengewalt; **~powder** n Schießpulver nt; **~shot** n Schuss m

gurgle ['gə:gl] vi gluckern

gush [gʌʃ] vi (rush out) hervorströmen; (fig) schwärmen

gust [gʌst] n Windstoß m, Bö f

gusto ['gʌstəu] n Genuss m, Lust f

gut [gʌt] n (ANAT) Gedärme pl; (string) Darm m; **~s** npl (fig) Schneid m

gutter ['gʌtər] n Dachrinne f; (in street) Gosse f

guttural ['gʌtərəl] adj guttural, Kehl-

guy [gaɪ] n (also: **~rope**) Halteseil nt; (man) Typ m, Kerl m

---

Guy Fawkes' Night

ⓘ **Guy Fawkes' Night**, *auch bonfire night genannt, erinnert an den Gunpowder Plot, einen Attentatsversuch auf James I. und sein Parlament am 5. November 1605. Einer der Verschwörer, Guy Fawkes, wurde auf frischer Tat ertappt, als er das Parlamentsgebäude in die Luft sprengen wollte. Vor der Guy Fawkes' Night basteln Kinder in Großbritannien eine Puppe des Guy Fawkes, mit der sie Geld für Feuerwerkskörper von Passanten erbetteln, und die dann am 5. November auf einem Lagerfeuer mit Feuerwerk verbrannt wird.*

---

guzzle ['gʌzl] *vt, vi* (*drink*) saufen; (*eat*) fressen

gym [dʒɪm] *n* (*also:* **~nasium**) Turnhalle *f*; (*also:* **~nastics**) Turnen *nt*

gymnast ['dʒɪmnæst] *n* Turner(in) *m(f)*

gymnastics [dʒɪm'næstɪks] *n* Turnen *nt*, Gymnastik *f*

gym shoes *npl* Turnschuhe *pl*

gynaecologist [gaɪnɪ'kɔlədʒɪst] (*US* **gynecologist**) *n* Frauenarzt(-ärztin) *m(f)*

gypsy ['dʒɪpsɪ] *n* = **gipsy**

gyrate [dʒaɪ'reɪt] *vi* kreisen

H, h

haberdashery [hæbə'dæʃərɪ] (*BRIT*) *n* Kurzwaren *pl*

habit ['hæbɪt] *n* (An)gewohnheit *f*; (*monk's*) Habit *nt or m*

habitable ['hæbɪtəbl] *adj* bewohnbar

habitat ['hæbɪtæt] *n* Lebensraum *m*

habitual [hə'bɪtjuəl] *adj* gewohnheitsmäßig; **~ly** *adv* gewöhnlich

hack [hæk] *vt* hacken ♦ *n* Hieb *m*; (*writer*) Schreiberling *m*

hacker ['hækə*r*] *n* (*COMPUT*) Hacker *m*

hackneyed ['hæknɪd] *adj* abgedroschen

had [hæd] *pt, pp of* **have**

haddock ['hædək] (*pl* **~** *or* **~s**) *n* Schellfisch *m*

hadn't ['hædnt] = **had not**

haemorrhage ['hemərɪdʒ] (*US* **hemorrhage**) *n* Blutung *f*

haemorrhoids ['hemərɔɪdz] (*US* **hemorrhoids**) *npl* Hämorr(ho)iden *pl*

haggard ['hægəd] *adj* abgekämpft

haggle ['hægl] *vi* feilschen

Hague [heɪg] *n* (*GEOG*) **The ~** Den Haag *nt*

hail [heɪl] *n* Hagel *m* ♦ *vt* umjubeln ♦ *vi* hageln; **~stone** *n* Hagelkorn *nt*

hair [heə*r*] *n* Haar *nt*, Haare *pl*; (*one* ~) Haar *nt*; **~brush** *n* Haarbürste *f*; **~cut** *n* Haarschnitt *m*; **to get a ~cut** sich *dat* die Haare schneiden lassen; **~do** *n* Frisur *f*; **~dresser** *n* Friseur *m*, Friseuse *f*; **~dresser's** *n* Friseursalon *m*; **~ dryer** *n* Trockenhaube *f*; (*hand-held*) Föhn *m*, Fön *m* ®; **~ gel** *n* Haargel *nt*; **~grip** *n* Klemme *f*; **~net** *n* Haarnetz *nt*; **~pin** *n* Haarnadel *f*; **~pin bend** (*US* **~pin curve**) *n* Haarnadelkurve *f*; **~raising** *adj* haarsträubend; **~ removing cream** *n* Enthaarungscreme *nt*; **~ spray** *n* Haarspray *nt*; **~style** *n* Frisur *f*

hairy ['heərɪ] *adj* haarig

hake [heɪk] *n* Seehecht *m*

half [hɑːf] (*pl* **halves**) *n* Hälfte *f* ♦ *adj* halb ♦ *adv* halb, zur Hälfte; **~ an hour** eine halbe Stunde; **two and a ~** zweieinhalb; **to cut sth in ~** etw halbieren; **~ a dozen** ein halbes Dutzend, sechs; **~ board** *n* Halbpension *f*; **~-caste** *n* Mischling *m*; **~-fare** *n* halbe(r) Fahrpreis *m*; **~-hearted** *adj* lustlos; **~-hour** *n* halbe Stunde *f*; **~-price** *n*: **(at) ~-price** zum halben Preis; **~ term** (*BRIT*) *n* (*SCH*) Ferien *pl* in der Mitte des Trimesters; **~-time** *n* Halbzeit *f*; **~way** *adv* halbwegs, auf halbem Wege

halibut ['hælɪbət] *n inv* Heilbutt *m*

hall [hɔːl] *n* Saal *m*; (*entrance* ~) Hausflur *m*; (*building*) Halle *f*; **~ of residence** (*BRIT*) *n* Studentenwohnheim *nt*

hallmark ['hɔːlmɑːk] *n* Stempel *m*

hallo [hə'ləu] *excl* = **hello**

Hallowe'en ['hæləu'iːn] *n* Tag *m* vor Allerheiligen

Hallowe'en

ⓘ **Hallowe'en** *ist der 31. Oktober, der Vorabend von Allerheiligen und nach altem Glauben der Abend, an dem man Geister und Hexen sehen kann. In Großbritannien und vor allem in den USA feiern die Kinder Hallowe'en, indem sie sich verkleiden und mit selbst gemachten Laternen aus Kürbissen von Tür zu Tür ziehen.*

---

hallucination [həluːsɪ'neɪʃən] *n* Halluzination *f*

hallway ['hɔːlweɪ] *n* Korridor *m*

halo ['heɪləu] *n* Heiligenschein *m*

halt [hɔːlt] *n* Halt *m ♦ vt, vi* anhalten

halve [haːv] *vt* halbieren

halves [haːvz] *pl of* **half**

ham [hæm] *n* Schinken *m*

hamburger ['hæmbəːgəʳ] *n* Hamburger *m*

hamlet ['hæmlɪt] *n* Weiler *m*

hammer ['hæməʳ] *n* Hammer *m ♦ vt, vi* hämmern

hammock ['hæmək] *n* Hängematte *f*

hamper ['hæmpəʳ] *vt* (be)hindern *♦ n* Picknickkorb *m*

hamster ['hæmstəʳ] *n* Hamster *m*

hand [hænd] *n* Hand *f; (of clock)* (Uhr)zeiger *m; (worker)* Arbeiter *m ♦ vt (pass)* geben; **to give sb a ~** jdm helfen; **at ~** nahe; **to ~** zur Hand; **in ~** *(under control)* unter Kontrolle; *(being done)* im Gange; *(extra)* übrig; **on ~** zur Verfügung; **on the one ~ ..., on the other ~ ...** einerseits ..., andererseits ...; **~ in** *vt* abgeben; *(forms)* einreichen; **~ out** *vt* austeilen; **~ over** *vt (deliver)* übergeben; *(surrender)* abgeben; *(: prisoner)* ausliefern; **~bag** *n* Handtasche *f;* **~book** *n* Handbuch *nt;* **~brake** *n* Handbremse *f;* **~cuffs** *npl* Handschellen *pl;* **~ful** *n* Hand *f* voll; *(inf: person)* Plage *f*

handicap ['hændɪkæp] *n* Handikap *nt ♦ vt* benachteiligen; **mentally/physically ~ped** geistig/körperlich behindert

handicraft ['hændɪkrɑːft] *n* Kunsthandwerk *nt*

handiwork ['hændɪwəːk] *n* Arbeit *f; (fig)* Werk *nt*

handkerchief ['hæŋkətʃɪf] *n* Taschentuch *nt*

handle ['hændl] *n (of door etc)* Klinke *f; (of cup etc)* Henkel *m; (for winding)* Kurbel *f ♦ vt (touch)* anfassen; *(deal with: things)* sich befassen mit; *(: people)* umgehen mit; **~bar(s)** *n(pl)* Lenkstange *f*

hand: **~ luggage** *n* Handgepäck *nt;* **~made** *adj* handgefertigt; **~out** *n (distribution)* Verteilung *f; (charity)* Geldzuwendung *f; (leaflet)* Flugblatt *nt;* **~rail** *n* Geländer *nt; (on ship)* Reling *f;* **~set** *n (TEL)* Hörer *m;* **please replace the ~set** bitte legen Sie auf; **~shake** *n* Händedruck *f*

handsome ['hænsəm] *adj* gut aussehend

handwriting ['hændraɪtɪŋ] *n* Handschrift *f*

handy ['hændɪ] *adj* praktisch; *(shops)* leicht erreichbar; **~man** ['hændɪmæn] *(irreg) n* Bastler *m*

hang [hæŋ] *(pt, pp* **hung)** *vt* aufhängen; *(pt, pp* **hanged:** *criminal)* hängen *♦ vi* hängen *♦ n:* **to get the ~ of sth** *(inf)* den richtigen Dreh bei etw herauskriegen; **~ about, ~ around** *vi* sich herumtreiben; **~ on** *vi (wait)* warten; **~ up** *vi (TEL)* auflegen

hangar ['hæŋəʳ] *n* Hangar *m*

hanger ['hæŋəʳ] *n* Kleiderbügel *m*

hanger-on [hæŋər'ɔn] *n* Anhänger(in) *m(f)*

hang ['hæŋ-]: **~-gliding** *n* Drachenfliegen *nt;* **~over** *n* Kater *m;* **~-up** *n* Komplex *m*

hanker ['hæŋkəʳ] *vi:* **to ~ for** *or* **after** sich sehnen nach

hankie ['hæŋkɪ] *n abbr* = **handkerchief**

hanky ['hæŋkɪ] *n abbr* = **handkerchief**

haphazard [hæp'hæzəd] *adj* zufällig

happen ['hæpən] *vi* sich ereignen, passieren; **as it ~s** I'm going there today zufällig(erweise) gehe ich heute (dort)hin; **~ing** *n* Ereignis *nt*

happily ['hæpɪlɪ] *adv* glücklich; *(fortunately)* glücklicherweise

happiness ['hæpɪnɪs] *n* Glück *nt*

happy ['hæpɪ] *adj* glücklich; **~ birthday!** alles Gute zum Geburtstag!; **~-go-lucky** *adj* sorglos; **~ hour** *n* Happy Hour *f*

harass ['hærəs] *vt* plagen; **~ment** *n*
Belästigung *f*

harbour ['hɑːbər] (*US* **harbor**) *n* Hafen *m*
♦ *vt* (*hope etc*) hegen; (*criminal etc*)
Unterschlupf gewähren

hard [hɑːd] *adj* (*firm*) hart; (*difficult*) schwer;
(*harsh*) hart(herzig) ♦ *adv* (*work*) hart; (*try*)
sehr; (*push, hit*) fest; **no ~ feelings!** ich
nehme es dir nicht übel; **~ of hearing**
schwerhörig; **to be ~ done by** übel dran
sein; **~back** *n* kartonierte Ausgabe *f*; **~
cash** *n* Bargeld *nt*; **~ disk** *n* (*COMPUT*)
Festplatte *f*; **~en** *vt* erhärten; (*fig*) verhärten
♦ *vi* hart werden; (*fig*) sich verhärten; **~-
headed** *adj* nüchtern; **~ labour** *n*
Zwangsarbeit *f*

hardly ['hɑːdlɪ] *adv* kaum

hard: **~ship** *n* Not *f*; **~ shoulder** (*BRIT*) *n*
(*AUT*) Seitenstreifen *m*; **~ up** *adj* knapp bei
Kasse; **~ware** *n* Eisenwaren *pl*; (*COMPUT*)
Hardware *f*; **~ware shop** *n*
Eisenwarenhandlung *f*; **~-wearing** *adj*
strapazierfähig; **~-working** *adj* fleißig

hardy ['hɑːdɪ] *adj* widerstandsfähig

hare [heər] *n* Hase *m*; **~-brained** *adj*
schwachsinnig

harm [hɑːm] *n* Schaden *m* ♦ *vt* schaden
+*dat*; **out of ~'s way** in Sicherheit; **~ful** *adj*
schädlich; **~less** *adj* harmlos

harmonica [hɑːˈmɔnɪkə] *n* Mundharmonika
f

harmonious [hɑːˈməʊnɪəs] *adj* harmonisch

harmonize ['hɑːmənaɪz] *vt* abstimmen ♦ *vi*
harmonieren

harmony ['hɑːmənɪ] *n* Harmonie *f*

harness ['hɑːnɪs] *n* Geschirr *nt* ♦ *vt* (*horse*)
anschirren; (*fig*) nutzbar machen

harp [hɑːp] *n* Harfe *f* ♦ *vi*: **to ~ on about sth**
auf etw *dat* herumreiten

harpoon [hɑːˈpuːn] *n* Harpune *f*

harrowing ['hærəʊɪŋ] *adj* nervenaufreibend

harsh [hɑːʃ] *adj* (*rough*) rau; (*severe*) streng;
~ness *n* Härte *f*

harvest ['hɑːvɪst] *n* Ernte *f* ♦ *vt, vi* ernten

has [hæz] *vb see* **have**

hash [hæʃ] *vt* klein hacken ♦ *n* (*mess*)
Kuddelmuddel *m*

hashish ['hæʃɪʃ] *n* Haschisch *nt*

hasn't ['hæznt] = **has not**

hassle ['hæsl] (*inf*) *n* Theater *nt*

haste [heɪst] *n* Eile *f*; **~n** ['heɪsn] *vt*
beschleunigen ♦ *vi* eilen; **hasty** *adj* hastig;
(*rash*) vorschnell

hat [hæt] *n* Hut *m*

hatch [hætʃ] *n* (*NAUT: also:* **~way**) Luke *f*; (*in
house*) Durchreiche *f* ♦ *vi* (*young*)
ausschlüpfen ♦ *vt* (*brood*) ausbrüten; (*plot*)
aushecken; **~back** ['hætʃbæk] *n* (*AUT*) (Auto
nt mit) Heckklappe *f*

hatchet ['hætʃɪt] *n* Beil *nt*

hate [heɪt] *vt* hassen ♦ *n* Hass *m*; **~ful** *adj*
verhasst

hatred ['heɪtrɪd] *n* Hass *m*

haughty ['hɔːtɪ] *adj* hochnäsig, überheblich

haul [hɔːl] *vt* ziehen ♦ *n* (*catch*) Fang *m*;
~age *n* Spedition *f*; **~ier** (*US* **hauler**) *n*
Spediteur *m*

haunch [hɔːntʃ] *n* Lende *f*

haunt [hɔːnt] *vt* (*ghost*) spuken in +*dat*;
(*memory*) verfolgen; (*pub*) häufig besuchen
♦ *n* Lieblingsplatz *m*; **the castle is ~ed** in
dem Schloss spukt es

KEYWORD

have [hæv] (*pt, pp* **had**) *aux vb* **1** haben; (*esp
with vbs of motion*) sein; **to have arrived/
slept** angekommen sein/geschlafen haben;
to have been gewesen sein; **having eaten**
or **when he had eaten, he left** nachdem
er gegessen hatte, ging er
2 (*in tag questions*): **you've done it,
haven't you?** du hast es doch gemacht,
oder nicht?
3 (*in short answers and questions*): **you've
made a mistake – so I have/no I haven't**
du hast einen Fehler gemacht – ja,
stimmt/nein; **we haven't paid – yes we
have!** wir haben nicht bezahlt – doch; **I've
been there before, have you?** ich war
schon einmal da, du auch?
♦ *modal aux vb* (*be obliged*): **to have (got)
to do sth** etw tun müssen; **you haven't to
tell her** du darfst es ihr nicht erzählen
♦ *vt* **1** (*possess*) haben; **he has (got) blue**

eyes er hat blaue Augen; **I have (got) an
idea** ich habe eine Idee
2 (*referring to meals etc*): **to have
breakfast/a cigarette** frühstücken/eine
Zigarette rauchen
3 (*receive, obtain etc*) haben; **may I have
your address?** kann ich Ihre Adresse
haben?; **to have a baby** ein Kind
bekommen
4 (*maintain, allow*): **he will have it that he
is right** er besteht darauf, dass er Recht
hat; **I won't have it** das lasse ich mir nicht
bieten
5: to have sth done etw machen lassen;
to have sb do sth jdn etw machen lassen;
he soon had them all laughing er brachte
sie alle zum Lachen
6 (*experience, suffer*): **she had her bag
stolen** man hat ihr die Tasche gestohlen;
he had his arm broken er hat sich den
Arm gebrochen
7 (*+noun: take, hold etc*): **to have a walk/
rest** spazieren gehen/sich ausruhen; **to
have a meeting/party** eine Besprechung/
Party haben
have out *vt*: **to have it out with sb** (*settle
problem*) etw mit jdm bereden

haven ['heɪvn] *n* Zufluchtsort *m*
haven't ['hævnt] = **have not**
havoc ['hævək] *n* Verwüstung *f*
hawk [hɔːk] *n* Habicht *m*
hay [heɪ] *n* Heu *nt*; **~ fever** *n* Heuschnupfen
m; **~stack** *n* Heuschober *m*
haywire ['heɪwaɪə'] (*inf*) *adj* durcheinander
hazard ['hæzəd] *n* Risiko *nt* ♦ *vt* aufs Spiel
setzen; **~ous** *adj* gefährlich; **~ (warning)
lights** *npl* (*AUT*) Warnblinklicht *nt*
haze [heɪz] *n* Dunst *m*
hazelnut ['heɪzlnʌt] *n* Haselnuss *f*
hazy ['heɪzɪ] *adj* (*misty*) dunstig; (*vague*)
verschwommen
he [hiː] *pron* er
head [hɛd] *n* Kopf *m*; (*leader*) Leiter *m* ♦ *vt*
(an)führen, leiten; (*ball*) köpfen; **~s (or
tails)** Kopf (oder Zahl); **~ first** mit dem
Kopf nach unten; **~ over heels** kopfüber;

~ for *vt fus* zugehen auf *+acc*; **~ache** *n*
Kopfschmerzen *pl*; **~dress** *n* Kopfschmuck
m; **~ing** *n* Überschrift *f*; **~lamp** (*BRIT*) *n*
Scheinwerfer *m*; **~land** *n* Landspitze *f*;
~light *n* Scheinwerfer *m*; **~line** *n*
Schlagzeile *f*; **~long** *adv* kopfüber;
~master *n* (*of primary school*) Rektor *m*; (*of
secondary school*) Direktor *m*; **~mistress** *n*
Rektorin *f*; Direktorin *f*; **~ office** *n* Zentrale
f; **~-on** *adj* Frontal-; **~phones** *npl*
Kopfhörer *pl*; **~quarters** *npl* Zentrale *f*;
(*MIL*) Hauptquartier *nt*; **~rest** *n* Kopfstütze
f; **~room** *n* (*of bridges etc*) lichte Höhe *f*;
~scarf *n* Kopftuch *nt*; **~strong** *adj*
eigenwillig; **~teacher** (*BRIT*) *n*
Schulleiter(in) *m*(*f*); (*of secondary school also*)
Direktor(in) *m*; **~ waiter** *n* Oberkellner *m*;
~way *n* Fortschritte *pl*; **~wind** *n*
Gegenwind *m*; **~y** *adj* berauschend
heal [hiːl] *vt* heilen ♦ *vi* verheilen
health [hɛlθ] *n* Gesundheit *f*; **~ food** *n*
Reformkost *f*; **H~ Service** (*BRIT*) *n*: **the H~
Service** das Gesundheitswesen; **~y** *adj*
gesund
heap [hiːp] *n* Haufen *m* ♦ *vt* häufen
hear [hɪə'] (*pt, pp* **heard**) *vt* hören; (*listen to*)
anhören ♦ *vi* hören; **~d** [hɜːd] *pt, pp of*
hear; **~ing** *n* Gehör *nt*; (*JUR*) Verhandlung
f; **~ing aid** *n* Hörapparat *m*; **~say** *n*
Hörensagen *nt*
hearse [hɜːs] *n* Leichenwagen *m*
heart [hɑːt] *n* Herz *nt*; **~s** *npl* (*CARDS*) Herz
nt; **by ~** auswendig; **~ attack** *n* Herzanfall
m; **~beat** *n* Herzschlag *m*; **~breaking** *adj*
herzzerbrechend; **~broken** *adj* untröstlich;
~burn *n* Sodbrennen *nt*; **~ failure** *n*
Herzschlag *m*; **~felt** *adj* aufrichtig
hearth [hɑːθ] *n* Herd *m*
heartily ['hɑːtɪlɪ] *adv* herzlich; (*eat*) herzhaft
heartless ['hɑːtlɪs] *adj* herzlos
hearty ['hɑːtɪ] *adj* kräftig; (*friendly*) freundlich
heat [hiːt] *n* Hitze *f*; (*of food, water etc*)
Wärme *f*; (*SPORT: also:* **qualifying ~**)
Ausscheidungsrunde *f* ♦ *vt* (*house*) heizen;
(*substance*) heiß machen, erhitzen; **~ up** *vi*
warm werden ♦ *vt* aufwärmen; **~ed** *adj*
erhitzt; (*fig*) hitzig; **~er** *n* (Heiz)ofen *m*

heath [hi:θ] (*BRIT*) n Heide f
heathen ['hi:ðn] n Heide m/Heidin f ♦ adj
heidnisch, Heiden-
heather ['heðə'] n Heidekraut nt
heat: ~ing n Heizung f; ~-seeking adj
Wärme suchend; ~stroke n Hitzschlag m;
~ wave n Hitzewelle f
heave [hi:v] vt hochheben; (*sigh*) ausstoßen
♦ vi wogen; (*breast*) sich heben ♦ n Heben
nt
heaven ['hevn] n Himmel m; ~ly adj
himmlisch
heavily ['hevɪlɪ] adv schwer
heavy ['hevɪ] adj schwer; ~ goods vehicle
n Lastkraftwagen m; ~weight n (*SPORT*)
Schwergewicht nt
Hebrew ['hi:bru:] adj hebräisch ♦ n (*LING*)
Hebräisch nt
Hebrides ['hebrɪdi:z] npl Hebriden pl
heckle ['hekl] vt unterbrechen
hectic ['hektɪk] adj hektisch
he'd [hi:d] = he had; he would
hedge [hedʒ] n Hecke f ♦ vt einzäunen ♦ vi
(*fig*) ausweichen; to ~ one's bets sich
absichern
hedgehog ['hedʒhɔg] n Igel m
heed [hi:d] vt (*also:* take ~ of) beachten ♦ n
Beachtung f; ~less adj achtlos
heel [hi:l] n Ferse f; (*of shoe*) Absatz m ♦ vt
mit Absätzen versehen
hefty ['heftɪ] adj (*person*) stämmig; (*portion*)
reichlich
heifer ['hefə'] n Färse f
height [haɪt] n (*of person*) Größe f; (*of object*)
Höhe f; ~en vt erhöhen
heir [eə'] n Erbe m; ~ess ['eəres] n Erbin f;
~loom n Erbstück nt
held [held] pt, pp of hold
helicopter ['helɪkɔptə'] n Hubschrauber m
heliport ['helɪpɔ:t] n Hubschrauber-
landeplatz m
hell [hel] n Hölle f ♦ excl verdammt!
he'll [hi:l] = he will; he shall
hellish ['helɪʃ] adj höllisch, verteufelt
hello [hə'ləu] excl hallo
helm [helm] n Ruder nt, Steuer nt
helmet ['helmɪt] n Helm m

help [help] n Hilfe f ♦ vt helfen +*dat*; I can't
~ it ich kann nichts dafür; ~ yourself
bedienen Sie sich; ~er n Helfer m; ~ful adj
hilfreich; ~ing n Portion f; ~less adj hilflos
hem [hem] n Saum m ♦ vt säumen; ~ in vt
einengen
hemorrhage ['hemərɪdʒ] (*US*) n =
haemorrhage
hemorrhoids ['hemərɔɪdz] (*US*) npl =
haemorrhoids
hen [hen] n Henne f
hence [hens] adv von jetzt an; (*therefore*)
daher; ~forth adv von nun an; (*from then
on*) von da an
henchman ['hentʃmən] (*irreg*) n
Gefolgsmann m
her [hɜ:'] pron (*acc*) sie; (*dat*) ihr ♦ adj ihr; see
also me; my
herald ['herəld] n (Vor)bote m ♦ vt
verkünden
heraldry ['herəldrɪ] n Wappenkunde f
herb [hɜ:b] n Kraut nt
herd [hɜ:d] n Herde f
here [hɪə'] adv hier; (*to this place*) hierher;
~after [hɪər'ɑ:ftə'] adv hernach, künftig ♦ n
Jenseits nt; ~by [hɪə'baɪ] adv hiermit
hereditary [hɪ'redɪtrɪ] adj erblich
heredity [hɪ'redɪtɪ] n Vererbung f
heritage ['herɪtɪdʒ] n Erbe nt
hermit ['hɜ:mɪt] n Einsiedler m
hernia ['hɜ:nɪə] n Bruch m
hero ['hɪərəu] (*pl* ~es) n Held m; ~ic
[hɪ'rəuɪk] adj heroisch
heroin ['herəuɪn] n Heroin nt
heroine ['herəuɪn] n Heldin f
heroism ['herəuɪzəm] n Heldentum nt
heron ['herən] n Reiher m
herring ['herɪŋ] n Hering m
hers [hɜ:z] pron ihre(r, s); see also mine²
herself [hɜ:'self] pron sich (selbst); (*emphatic*)
selbst; see also oneself
he's [hi:z] = he is; he has
hesitant ['hezɪtənt] adj zögernd
hesitate ['hezɪteɪt] vi zögern; hesitation
[hezɪ'teɪʃən] n Zögern nt
heterosexual ['hetərəu'seksjuəl] adj
heterosexuell ♦ n Heterosexuelle(r) mf

hew [hju:] (pt **hewed**, pp **hewn**) vt hauen, hacken

hexagonal [hɛkˈsægənl] adj sechseckig

heyday [ˈheɪdeɪ] n Blüte f, Höhepunkt m

HGV n abbr = **heavy goods vehicle**

hi [haɪ] excl he, hallo

hibernate [ˈhaɪbəneɪt] vi Winterschlaf m halten; **hibernation** [haɪbəˈneɪʃən] n Winterschlaf m

hiccough [ˈhɪkʌp] vi den Schluckauf haben; **~s** npl Schluckauf m

hiccup [ˈhɪkʌp] = **hiccough**

hid [hɪd] pt of **hide**; **~den** [ˈhɪdn] pp of **hide**

hide [haɪd] (pt **hid**, pp **hidden**) n (skin) Haut f, Fell nt ♦ vt verstecken ♦ vi sich verstecken; **~-and-seek** n Versteckspiel nt; **~away** n Versteck nt

hideous [ˈhɪdɪəs] adj abscheulich

hiding [ˈhaɪdɪŋ] n (beating) Tracht f Prügel; **to be in ~** (concealed) sich versteckt halten; **~ place** n Versteck nt

hi-fi [ˈhaɪfaɪ] n Hi-Fi nt ♦ adj Hi-Fi-

high [haɪ] adj hoch; (wind) stark ♦ adv hoch; **it is 20m ~** es ist 20 Meter hoch; **~brow** adj (betont) intellektuell; **~chair** n Hochstuhl m; **~er education** n Hochschulbildung f; **~-handed** adj eigenmächtig; **~-heeled** adj hochhackig; **~ jump** n (SPORT) Hochsprung m; **H~lands** npl: **the H~lands** das schottische Hochland; **~light** n (fig) Höhepunkt m ♦ vt hervorheben; **~ly** adv höchst; **~ly strung** adj überempfindlich; **~ness** n Höhe f; **Her H~ness** Ihre Hoheit f; **~-pitched** adj hoch; **~-rise block** n Hochhaus nt; **~ school** (US) n Oberschule f; **~ season** (BRIT) n Hochsaison f; **~ street** (BRIT) n Hauptstraße f

highway [ˈhaɪweɪ] n Landstraße f; **H~ Code** (BRIT) n Straßenverkehrsordnung f

hijack [ˈhaɪdʒæk] vt entführen; **~er** n Entführer(in) m(f)

hike [haɪk] vi wandern ♦ n Wanderung f; **~r** n Wanderer m; **hiking** n Wandern nt

hilarious [hɪˈlɛərɪəs] adj lustig

hill [hɪl] n Berg m; **~side** n (Berg)hang m; **~walking** n Bergwandern nt; **~y** adj hügelig

hilt [hɪlt] n Heft nt; **(up) to the ~** ganz und gar

him [hɪm] pron (acc) ihn; (dat) ihm; see also **me**; **~self** pron sich (selbst); (emphatic) selbst; see also **oneself**

hind [haɪnd] adj hinter, Hinter-

hinder [ˈhɪndər] vt (stop) hindern; (delay) behindern; **hindrance** f (delay) Behinderung f; (obstacle) Hindernis nt

hindsight [ˈhaɪndsaɪt] n: **with ~** im nachhinein

Hindu [ˈhɪnduː] n Hindu m

hinge [hɪndʒ] n Scharnier nt; (on door) Türangel f ♦ vi (fig): **to ~ on** abhängen von

hint [hɪnt] n Tipp m; (trace) Anflug m ♦ vt: **to ~ that** andeuten, dass ♦ vi: **to ~ at** andeuten

hip [hɪp] n Hüfte f

hippie [ˈhɪpɪ] n Hippie m

hippo [ˈhɪpəʊ] (inf) n Nilpferd nt

hippopotami [hɪpəˈpɒtəmaɪ] npl of **hippopotamus**

hippopotamus [hɪpəˈpɒtəməs] (pl **~es** or **hippopotami**) n Nilpferd nt

hire [ˈhaɪər] vt (worker) anstellen; (BRIT: car) mieten ♦ n Miete f; **for ~** (taxi) frei; **~(d) car** (BRIT) n Mietwagen m, Leihwagen m; **~ purchase** (BRIT) n Teilzahlungskauf m

his [hɪz] adj sein ♦ pron seine(r, s); see also **my**; **mine²**

hiss [hɪs] vi zischen ♦ n Zischen nt

historian [hɪˈstɔːrɪən] n Historiker m

historic [hɪˈstɒrɪk] adj historisch; **~al** adj historisch, geschichtlich

history [ˈhɪstərɪ] n Geschichte f

hit [hɪt] (pt, pp **hit**) vt schlagen; (injure) treffen ♦ n (blow) Schlag m; (success) Erfolg m; (MUS) Hit m; **to ~ it off with sb** prima mit jdm auskommen; **~-and-run driver** n jemand, der Fahrerflucht begeht

hitch [hɪtʃ] vt festbinden; (also: **~ up**) hochziehen ♦ n (difficulty) Haken m; **to ~ a lift** trampen; **~hike** vi trampen; **~hiker** n Tramper m; **~hiking** n Trampen nt

hi-tech [ˈhaɪˈtek] adj Hightech- ♦ n Spitzentechnologie f

hitherto [hɪðəˈtuː] adv bislang

hit man (*inf*) (*irreg*) *n* Killer *m*

HIV *n abbr*: **HIV-negative/-positive** HIV-negativ/-positiv

hive [haɪv] *n* Bienenkorb *m*

HMS *abbr* = **His/Her Majesty's Ship**

hoard [hɔːd] *n* Schatz *m* ♦ *vt* horten, hamstern

hoarding ['hɔːdɪŋ] *n* Bretterzaun *m*; (*BRIT: for posters*) Reklamewand *f*

hoarse [hɔːs] *adj* heiser, rau

hoax [həʊks] *n* Streich *m*

hob [hɔb] *n* Kochmulde *f*

hobble ['hɔbl] *vi* humpeln

hobby ['hɔbɪ] *n* Hobby *nt*

hobby-horse ['hɔbɪhɔːs] *n* (*fig*) Steckenpferd *nt*

hobo ['həʊbəʊ] (*US*) *n* Tippelbruder *m*

hockey ['hɔkɪ] *n* Hockey *nt*

hoe [həʊ] *n* Hacke *f* ♦ *vt* hacken

hog [hɔg] *n* Schlachtschwein *nt* ♦ *vt* mit Beschlag belegen; **to go the whole ~** aufs Ganze gehen

hoist [hɔɪst] *n* Winde *f* ♦ *vt* hochziehen

hold [həʊld] (*pt, pp* **held**) *vt* halten; (*contain*) enthalten; (*be able to contain*) fassen; (*breath*) anhalten; (*meeting*) abhalten ♦ *vi* (*withstand pressure*) aushalten ♦ *n* (*grasp*) Halt *m*; (*NAUT*) Schiffsraum *m*; **~ the line!** (*TEL*) bleiben Sie am Apparat!; **to ~ one's own** sich behaupten; **~ back** *vt* zurückhalten; **~ down** *vt* niederhalten; (*job*) behalten; **~ off** *vt* (*enemy*) abwehren; **~ on** *vi* sich festhalten; (*resist*) durchhalten; (*wait*) warten; **~ on to** *vt fus* festhalten an +*dat*; (*keep*) behalten; **~ out** *vt* hinhalten ♦ *vi* aushalten; **~ up** *vt* (*delay*) aufhalten; (*rob*) überfallen; **~all** (*BRIT*) *n* Reisetasche *f*; **~er** *n* Behälter *m*; (*share*) (Aktien)anteil *m*; **~up** *n* (*BRIT: in traffic*) Stockung *f*; (*robbery*) Überfall *m*; (*delay*) Verzögerung *f*

hole [həʊl] *n* Loch *nt*; **~ in the wall** (*inf*) *n* (*cash dispenser*) Geldautomat *m*

holiday ['hɔlɪdeɪ] *n* (*day*) Feiertag *m*; freie(r) Tag *m*; (*vacation*) Urlaub *m*; (*SCH*) Ferien *pl*; **~-maker** (*BRIT*) *n* Urlauber(in) *m(f)*; **~ resort** *n* Ferienort *m*

Holland ['hɔlənd] *n* Holland *nt*

hollow ['hɔləʊ] *adj* hohl; (*fig*) leer ♦ *n* Vertiefung *f*; **~ out** *vt* aushöhlen

holly ['hɔlɪ] *n* Stechpalme *f*

holocaust ['hɔləkɔːst] *n* Inferno *nt*

holster ['həʊlstə*] *n* Pistolenhalfter *m*

holy ['həʊlɪ] *adj* heilig; **H~ Ghost** *or* **Spirit** *n*: **the H~ Ghost** *or* **Spirit** der Heilige Geist

homage ['hɔmɪdʒ] *n* Huldigung *f*; **to pay ~ to** huldigen +*dat*

home [həʊm] *n* Zuhause *nt*; (*institution*) Heim *nt*, Anstalt *f* ♦ *adj* einheimisch; (*POL*) inner ♦ *adv* heim, nach Hause; **at ~** zu Hause; **~ address** *n* Heimatadresse *f*; **~coming** *n* Heimkehr *f*; **~land** *n* Heimat(land *nt*) *f*; **~less** *adj* obdachlos; **~ly** *adj* häuslich; (*US: ugly*) unscheinbar; **~-made** *adj* selbst gemacht; **~ match** *adj* Heimspiel *nt*; **H~ Office** (*BRIT*) *n* Innenministerium *nt*; **~ page** *n* (*COMPUT*) Homepage *f*; **~ rule** *n* Selbstverwaltung *f*; **H~ Secretary** (*BRIT*) *n* Innenminister(in) *m(f)*; **~sick** *adj*: **to be ~sick** Heimweh haben; **~ town** *n* Heimatstadt *f*; **~ward** *adj* (*journey*) Heim-; **~work** *n* Hausaufgaben *pl*

homicide ['hɔmɪsaɪd] (*US*) *n* Totschlag *m*

homoeopathic [həʊmɪə'pæθɪk] (*US* **homeopathic**) *adj* homöopathisch; **homoeopathy** [həʊmɪ'ɔpəθɪ] (*US* **homeopathy**) *n* Homöopathie *f*

homogeneous [hɔmə'dʒiːnɪəs] *adj* homogen

homosexual [hɔməu'seksjuəl] *adj* homosexuell ♦ *n* Homosexuelle(r) *mf*

honest ['ɔnɪst] *adj* ehrlich; **~ly** *adv* ehrlich; **~y** *n* Ehrlichkeit *f*

honey ['hʌnɪ] *n* Honig *m*; **~comb** *n* Honigwabe *f*; **~moon** *n* Flitterwochen *pl*, Hochzeitsreise *f*; **~suckle** ['hʌnɪsʌkl] *n* Geißblatt *nt*

honk [hɔŋk] *vi* hupen

honor *etc* ['ɔnə*] (*US*) *vt*, *n* = **honour** *etc*

honorary ['ɔnərərɪ] *adj* Ehren-

honour ['ɔnə*] (*US* **honor**) *vt* ehren; (*cheque*) einlösen ♦ *n* Ehre *f*; **~able** *adj* ehrenwert; (*intention*) ehrenhaft; **~s degree** *n* (*UNIV*) *akademischer Grad mit Prüfung im*

Spezialfach

hood [hud] *n* Kapuze *f*; (*BRIT*: *AUT*) Verdeck *nt*; (*US*: *AUT*) Kühlerhaube *f*

hoof [hu:f] (*pl* **hooves**) *n* Huf *m*

hook [huk] *n* Haken *m* ♦ *vt* einhaken

hooligan ['hu:lɪgən] *n* Rowdy *m*

hoop [hu:p] *n* Reifen *m*

hooray [hu:'reɪ] *excl* = **hurrah**

hoot [hu:t] *vi* (*AUT*) hupen; **~er** *n* (*NAUT*) Dampfpfeife *f*; (*BRIT*: *AUT*) (Auto)hupe *f*

Hoover ['hu:vəʳ] (ℝ; *BRIT*) *n* Staubsauger *m* ♦ *vt*: **to h~** staubsaugen, Staub saugen

hooves [hu:vz] *pl of* **hoof**

hop [hɔp] *vi* hüpfen, hopsen ♦ *n* (*jump*) Hopser *m*

hope [həup] *vt*, *vi* hoffen ♦ *n* Hoffnung *f*; **I ~ so/not** hoffentlich/hoffentlich nicht; **~ful** *adj* hoffnungsvoll; (*promising*) viel versprechend; **~fully** *adv* hoffentlich; **~less** *adj* hoffnungslos

hops [hɔps] *npl* Hopfen *m*

horizon [hə'raɪzn] *n* Horizont *m*; **~tal** [hɔrɪ'zɔntl] *adj* horizontal

hormone ['hɔ:məun] *n* Hormon *nt*

horn [hɔ:n] *n* Horn *nt*; (*AUT*) Hupe *f*

hornet ['hɔ:nɪt] *n* Hornisse *f*

horny [hɔ:nɪ] *adj* schwielig; (*US*: *inf*) scharf

horoscope ['hɔrəskəup] *n* Horoskop *nt*

horrendous [hə'rendəs] *adj* (*crime*) abscheulich; (*error*) schrecklich

horrible ['hɔrɪbl] *adj* fürchterlich

horrid ['hɔrɪd] *adj* scheußlich

horrify ['hɔrɪfaɪ] *vt* entsetzen

horror ['hɔrəʳ] *n* Schrecken *m*; **~ film** *n* Horrorfilm *m*

hors d'oeuvre [ɔ:'də:vrə] *n* Vorspeise *f*

horse [hɔ:s] *n* Pferd *nt*; **~back** *n*: **on ~back** beritten; **~ chestnut** *n* Rosskastanie *f*; **~man/woman** (*irreg*) *n* Reiter(in) *m(f)*; **~power** *n* Pferdestärke *f*; **~-racing** *n* Pferderennen *nt*; **~radish** *n* Meerrettich *m*; **~shoe** *n* Hufeisen *nt*

horticulture ['hɔ:tɪkʌltʃəʳ] *n* Gartenbau *m*

hose [həuz] *n* (*also*: **~pipe**) Schlauch *m*

hosiery ['həuzɪərɪ] *n* Strumpfwaren *pl*

hospitable ['hɔspɪtəbl] *adj* gastfreundlich

hospital ['hɔspɪtl] *n* Krankenhaus *nt*

hospitality [hɔspɪ'tælɪtɪ] *n* Gastfreundschaft *f*

host [həust] *n* Gastgeber *m*; (*innkeeper*) (Gast)wirt *m*; (*large number*) Heerschar *f*; (*ECCL*) Hostie *f*

hostage ['hɔstɪdʒ] *n* Geisel *f*

hostel ['hɔstl] *n* Herberge *f*; (*also*: **youth ~**) Jugendherberge *f*

hostess ['həustɪs] *n* Gastgeberin *f*

hostile ['hɔstaɪl] *adj* feindlich; **hostility** [hɔ'stɪlɪtɪ] *n* Feindschaft *f*; **hostilities** *npl* (*fighting*) Feindseligkeiten *pl*

hot [hɔt] *adj* heiß; (*food, water*) warm; (*spiced*) scharf; **I'm ~** mir ist heiß; **~bed** *n* (*fig*) Nährboden *m*; **~ dog** *n* heiße(s) Würstchen *nt*

hotel [həu'tel] *n* Hotel *nt*; **~ier** [həu'telɪəʳ] *n* Hotelier *m*

hot: ~house *n* Treibhaus *nt*; **~ line** *n* (*POL*) heiße(r) Draht *m*; **~ly** *adv* (*argue*) hitzig; **~plate** *n* Kochplatte *f*; **~pot** ['hɔtpɔt] (*BRIT*) *n* Fleischeintopf *m*; **~-water bottle** *n* Wärmflasche *f*

hound [haund] *n* Jagdhund *m* ♦ *vt* hetzen

hour ['auəʳ] *n* Stunde *f*; (*time of day*) (Tages)zeit *f*; **~ly** *adj*, *adv* stündlich

house [*n* haus, *vb* hauz] *n* Haus *nt* ♦ *vt* unterbringen; **on the ~** auf Kosten des Hauses; **~ arrest** *n* (*POL, MIL*) Hausarrest *m*; **~boat** *n* Hausboot *nt*; **~breaking** *n* Einbruch *m*; **~coat** *n* Morgenmantel *m*; **~hold** *n* Haushalt *m*; **~keeper** *n* Haushälterin *f*; **~keeping** *n* Haushaltung *f*; **~-warming party** *n* Einweihungsparty *f*; **~wife** (*irreg*) *n* Hausfrau *f*; **~work** *n* Hausarbeit *f*

housing ['hauzɪŋ] *n* (*act*) Unterbringung *f*; (*houses*) Wohnungen *pl*; (*POL*) Wohnungsbau *m*; (*covering*) Gehäuse *nt*; **~ estate** (*US* **~ development**) *n* (Wohn)siedlung *f*

hovel ['hɔvl] *n* elende Hütte *f*

hover ['hɔvəʳ] *vi* (*bird*) schweben; (*person*) herumstehen; **~craft** *n* Luftkissenfahrzeug *nt*

how [hau] *adv* wie; **~ are you?** wie geht es Ihnen?; **~ much milk?** wie viel Milch?; **~**

many people? wie viele Leute?

however [hau'ɛvə^r] *adv* (*but*) (je)doch, aber; **~ you phrase it** wie Sie es auch ausdrücken

howl [haul] *n* Heulen *nt* ♦ *vi* heulen

H.P. *abbr* = **hire purchase**

h.p. *abbr* = **horsepower**

H.Q. *abbr* = **headquarters**

HTML *abbr* (= *hypertext markup language*) HTML

hub [hʌb] *n* Radnabe *f*

hubbub ['hʌbʌb] *n* Tumult *m*

hubcap ['hʌbkæp] *n* Radkappe *f*

huddle ['hʌdl] *vi*: **to ~ together** sich zusammendrängen

hue [hju:] *n* Färbung *f*; **~ and cry** *n* Zetergeschrei *nt*

huff [hʌf] *n*: **to go into a ~** einschnappen

hug [hʌg] *vt* umarmen ♦ *n* Umarmung *f*

huge [hju:dʒ] *adj* groß, riesig

hulk [hʌlk] *n* (*ship*) abgetakelte(s) Schiff *nt*; (*person*) Koloss *m*

hull [hʌl] *n* Schiffsrumpf *m*

hullo [hə'ləu] *excl* = **hello**

hum [hʌm] *vt*, *vi* summen

human ['hju:mən] *adj* menschlich ♦ *n* (*also*: **~ being**) Mensch *m*

humane [hju:'meɪn] *adj* human

humanitarian [hju:mænɪ'teərɪən] *adj* humanitär

humanity [hju:'mænɪtɪ] *n* Menschheit *f*; (*kindliness*) Menschlichkeit *f*

humble ['hʌmbl] *adj* demütig; (*modest*) bescheiden ♦ *vt* demütigen

humbug ['hʌmbʌg] *n* Humbug *m*; (*BRIT*: *sweet*) Pfefferminzbonbon *nt*

humdrum ['hʌmdrʌm] *adj* stumpfsinnig

humid ['hju:mɪd] *adj* feucht; **~ity** [hju:'mɪdɪtɪ] *n* Feuchtigkeit *f*

humiliate [hju:'mɪlɪeɪt] *vt* demütigen; **humiliation** [hju:mɪlɪ'eɪʃən] *n* Demütigung *f*

humility [hju:'mɪlɪtɪ] *n* Demut *f*

humor ['hju:mə^r] (*US*) *n*, *vt* = **humour**

humorous ['hju:mərəs] *adj* humorvoll

humour ['hju:mə^r] (*US* **humor**) *n* (*fun*) Humor *m*; (*mood*) Stimmung *f* ♦ *vt* bei Stimmung halten

hump [hʌmp] *n* Buckel *m*

hunch [hʌntʃ] *n* Buckel *m*; (*premonition*) (Vor)ahnung *f*; **~back** *n* Bucklige(r) *mf*; **~ed** *adj* gekrümmt

hundred ['hʌndrəd] *num* hundert; **~weight** *n* Zentner *m* (*BRIT* = 50.8 *kg; US* = 45.3 *kg*)

hung [hʌŋ] *pt*, *pp of* **hang**

Hungarian [hʌŋ'geərɪən] *adj* ungarisch ♦ *n* Ungar(in) *m(f)*; (*LING*) Ungarisch *nt*

Hungary ['hʌŋgərɪ] *n* Ungarn *nt*

hunger ['hʌŋgə^r] *n* Hunger *m* ♦ *vi* hungern

hungry ['hʌŋgrɪ] *adj* hungrig; **to be ~** Hunger haben

hunk [hʌŋk] *n* (*of bread*) Stück *nt*

hunt [hʌnt] *vt*, *vi* jagen ♦ *n* Jagd *f*; **to ~ for** suchen; **~er** *n* Jäger *m*; **~ing** *n* Jagd *f*

hurdle ['hɜ:dl] *n* (*also fig*) Hürde *f*

hurl [hɜ:l] *vt* schleudern

hurrah [hu'rɑ:] *n* Hurra *nt*

hurray [hu'reɪ] *n* Hurra *nt*

hurricane ['hʌrɪkən] *n* Orkan *m*

hurried ['hʌrɪd] *adj* eilig; (*hasty*) hastig; **~ly** *adv* übereilt, hastig

hurry ['hʌrɪ] *n* Eile *f* ♦ *vi* sich beeilen ♦ *vt* (an)treiben; (*job*) übereilen; **to be in a ~** es eilig haben; **~ up** *vi* sich beeilen ♦ *vt* (*person*) zur Eile antreiben; (*work*) vorantreiben

hurt [hɜ:t] (*pt*, *pp* **hurt**) *vt* wehtun +*dat*; (*injure*, *fig*) verletzen ♦ *vi* wehtun; **~ful** *adj* schädlich; (*remark*) verletzend

hurtle ['hɜ:tl] *vi* sausen

husband ['hʌzbənd] *n* (Ehe)mann *m*

hush [hʌʃ] *n* Stille *f* ♦ *vt* zur Ruhe bringen ♦ *excl* pst, still

husky ['hʌskɪ] *adj* (*voice*) rau ♦ *n* Eskimohund *m*

hustle ['hʌsl] *vt* (*push*) stoßen; (*hurry*) antreiben ♦ *n*: **~ and bustle** Geschäftigkeit *f*

hut [hʌt] *n* Hütte *f*

hutch [hʌtʃ] *n* (Kaninchen)stall *m*

hyacinth ['haɪəsɪnθ] *n* Hyazinthe *f*

hydrant ['haɪdrənt] *n* (*also*: **fire ~**) Hydrant *m*

hydraulic [haɪ'drɔ:lɪk] *adj* hydraulisch

hydroelectric ['haɪdrəu'lektrɪk] *adj* (*energy*) durch Wasserkraft erzeugt; **~ power station** *n* Wasserkraftwerk *nt*

hydrofoil ['haɪdrəfɔɪl] *n* Tragflügelboot *nt*

hydrogen ['haɪdrədʒən] n Wasserstoff m
hyena [haɪ'iːnə] n Hyäne f
hygiene ['haɪdʒiːn] n Hygiene f; **hygienic** [haɪ'dʒiːnɪk] adj hygienisch
hymn [hɪm] n Kirchenlied nt
hype [haɪp] (inf) n Publicity f
hypermarket ['haɪpəmaːkɪt] (BRIT) n Hypermarket m
hypertext ['haɪpətekst] n (COMPUT) Hypertext m
hyphen ['haɪfn] n Bindestrich m
hypnosis [hɪp'nəusɪs] n Hypnose f
hypnotize ['hɪpnətaɪz] vt hypnotisieren
hypocrisy [hɪ'pɔkrɪsɪ] n Heuchelei f
hypocrite ['hɪpəkrɪt] n Heuchler m; **hypocritical** [hɪpə'krɪtɪkl] adj scheinheilig, heuchlerisch
hypothermia [haɪpə'θəːmɪə] n Unterkühlung f
hypotheses [haɪ'pɔθɪsiːz] npl of **hypothesis**
hypothesis [haɪ'pɔθɪsɪs] (pl **hypotheses**) n Hypothese f
hypothetic(al) [haɪpəu'θetɪk(l)] adj hypothetisch
hysterical [hɪ'sterɪkl] adj hysterisch
hysterics [hɪ'sterɪks] npl hysterische(r) Anfall m

I, i

I [aɪ] pron ich
ice [aɪs] n Eis nt ♦ vt (COOK) mit Zuckerguss überziehen ♦ vi (also: ~ **up**) vereisen; ~ **axe** n Eispickel m; **~berg** n Eisberg m; **~box** (US) n Kühlschrank m; ~ **cream** n Eis nt; ~ **cube** n Eiswürfel m; **~d** [aɪst] adj (cake) mit Zuckerguss überzogen, glasiert; (tea, coffee) Eis-; ~ **hockey** n Eishockey nt
Iceland ['aɪslənd] n Island nt
ice: ~ **lolly** (BRIT) n Eis am Stiel; ~ **rink** n (Kunst)eisbahn f; ~ **skating** n Schlittschuhlaufen nt
icicle ['aɪsɪkl] n Eiszapfen m
icing ['aɪsɪŋ] n (on cake) Zuckerguss m; (on window) Vereisung f; ~ **sugar** (BRIT) n Puderzucker m

icon ['aɪkɔn] n Ikone f; (COMPUT) Icon nt
icy ['aɪsɪ] adj (slippery) vereist; (cold) eisig
I'd [aɪd] = **I would**; **I had**
idea [aɪ'dɪə] n Idee f
ideal [aɪ'dɪəl] n Ideal nt ♦ adj ideal
identical [aɪ'dentɪkl] adj identisch; (twins) eineiig
identification [aɪdentɪfɪ'keɪʃən] n Identifizierung f; **means of ~** Ausweispapiere pl
identify [aɪ'dentɪfaɪ] vt identifizieren; (regard as the same) gleichsetzen
Identikit [aɪ'dentɪkɪt] ® n: ~ **picture** Phantombild nt
identity [aɪ'dentɪtɪ] n Identität f; ~ **card** n Personalausweis m
ideology [aɪdɪ'ɔlədʒɪ] n Ideologie f
idiom ['ɪdɪəm] n (expression) Redewendung f; (dialect) Idiom nt; **~atic** [ɪdɪə'mætɪk] adj idiomatisch
idiosyncrasy [ɪdɪəu'sɪŋkrəsɪ] n Eigenart f
idiot ['ɪdɪət] n Idiot(in) m(f); **~ic** [ɪdɪ'ɔtɪk] adj idiotisch
idle ['aɪdl] adj (doing nothing) untätig; (lazy) faul; (useless) nutzlos; (machine) still(stehend); (threat, talk) leer ♦ vi (machine) leer laufen ♦ vt: **to ~ away the time** die Zeit vertrödeln; **~ness** n Müßiggang m; Faulheit f
idol ['aɪdl] n Idol nt; **~ize** vt vergöttern
i.e. abbr (= id est) d. h.

KEYWORD

if [ɪf] conj **1** wenn; (in case also) falls; **if I were you** wenn ich Sie wäre
2 (although): **(even) if** (selbst or auch) wenn
3 (whether) ob
4: **if so/not** wenn ja/nicht; **if only ...** wenn ... doch nur ...; **if only I could** wenn ich doch nur könnte; see also **as**

ignite [ɪg'naɪt] vt (an)zünden ♦ vi sich entzünden; **ignition** [ɪg'nɪʃən] n Zündung f; **to switch on/off the ignition** den Motor anlassen/abstellen; **ignition key** n (AUT) Zündschlüssel m

ignorance ['ɪgnərəns] *n* Unwissenheit *f*

ignorant ['ɪgnərənt] *adj* unwissend; **to be ~ of** nicht wissen

ignore [ɪgˈnɔːʳ] *vt* ignorieren

I'll [aɪl] = **I will; I shall**

ill [ɪl] *adj* krank ♦ *n* Übel *nt* ♦ *adv* schlecht; **~-advised** *adj* unklug; **~-at-ease** *adj* unbehaglich

illegal [ɪˈliːgl] *adj* illegal

illegible [ɪˈledʒɪbl] *adj* unleserlich

illegitimate [ɪlɪˈdʒɪtɪmət] *adj* unehelich

ill-fated [ɪlˈfeɪtɪd] *adj* unselig

ill feeling *n* Verstimmung *f*

illicit [ɪˈlɪsɪt] *adj* verboten

illiterate [ɪˈlɪtərət] *adj* ungebildet

ill-mannered [ɪlˈmænəd] *adj* ungehobelt

illness ['ɪlnɪs] *n* Krankheit *f*

illogical [ɪˈlɔdʒɪkl] *adj* unlogisch

ill-treat [ɪlˈtriːt] *vt* misshandeln

illuminate [ɪˈluːmɪneɪt] *vt* beleuchten; **illumination** [ɪluːmɪˈneɪʃən] *n* Beleuchtung *f*; **illuminations** *pl* (*decorative lights*) festliche Beleuchtung *f*

illusion [ɪˈluːʒən] *n* Illusion *f*; **to be under the ~ that ...** sich *dat* einbilden, dass ...

illustrate ['ɪləstreɪt] *vt* (*book*) illustrieren; (*explain*) veranschaulichen; **illustration** [ɪləˈstreɪʃən] *n* Illustration *f*; (*explanation*) Veranschaulichung *f*

illustrious [ɪˈlʌstrɪəs] *adj* berühmt

I'm [aɪm] = **I am**

image ['ɪmɪdʒ] *n* Bild *nt*; (*public ~*) Image *nt*; **~ry** *n* Symbolik *f*

imaginary [ɪˈmædʒɪnərɪ] *adj* eingebildet; (*world*) Fantasie-

imagination [ɪmædʒɪˈneɪʃən] *n* Einbildung *f*; (*creative*) Fantasie *f*

imaginative [ɪˈmædʒɪnətɪv] *adj* fantasiereich, einfallsreich

imagine [ɪˈmædʒɪn] *vt* sich vorstellen; (*wrongly*) sich einbilden

imbalance [ɪmˈbæləns] *n* Unausgeglichenheit *f*

imbecile ['ɪmbəsiːl] *n* Schwachsinnige(r) *mf*

imitate ['ɪmɪteɪt] *vt* imitieren; **imitation** [ɪmɪˈteɪʃən] *n* Imitation *f*

immaculate [ɪˈmækjulət] *adj* makellos;

(*dress*) tadellos; (*ECCL*) unbefleckt

immaterial [ɪməˈtɪərɪəl] *adj* unwesentlich; **it is ~ whether ...** es ist unwichtig, ob ...

immature [ɪməˈtjuəʳ] *adj* unreif

immediate [ɪˈmiːdɪət] *adj* (*instant*) sofortig; (*near*) unmittelbar; (*relatives*) nächste(r, s); (*needs*) dringlich; **~ly** *adv* sofort; **~ly next to** direkt neben

immense [ɪˈmens] *adj* unermesslich

immerse [ɪˈmɜːs] *vt* eintauchen; **to be ~d in** (*fig*) vertieft sein in +*acc*

immersion heater [ɪˈmɜːʃən-] (*BRIT*) *n* Boiler *m*

immigrant ['ɪmɪgrənt] *n* Einwanderer *m*

immigrate ['ɪmɪgreɪt] *vi* einwandern; **immigration** [ɪmɪˈgreɪʃən] *n* Einwanderung *f*

imminent ['ɪmɪnənt] *adj* bevorstehend

immobile [ɪˈməubaɪl] *adj* unbeweglich; **immobilize** [ɪˈməubɪlaɪz] *vt* lähmen

immoral [ɪˈmɔrl] *adj* unmoralisch; **~ity** [ɪmɔˈrælɪtɪ] *n* Unsittlichkeit *f*

immortal [ɪˈmɔːtl] *adj* unsterblich

immune [ɪˈmjuːn] *adj* (*secure*) sicher; (*MED*) immun; **~ from** sicher vor +*dat*; **immunity** *n* (*MED, JUR*) Immunität *f*; (*fig*) Freiheit *f*; **immunize** ['ɪmjunaɪz] *vt* immunisieren

impact ['ɪmpækt] *n* Aufprall *m*; (*fig*) Wirkung *f*

impair [ɪmˈpeəʳ] *vt* beeinträchtigen

impart [ɪmˈpɑːt] *vt* mitteilen; (*knowledge*) vermitteln; (*exude*) abgeben

impartial [ɪmˈpɑːʃl] *adj* unparteiisch

impassable [ɪmˈpɑːsəbl] *adj* unpassierbar

impassive [ɪmˈpæsɪv] *adj* gelassen

impatience [ɪmˈpeɪʃəns] *n* Ungeduld *f*; **impatient** *adj* ungeduldig; **impatiently** *adv* ungeduldig

impeccable [ɪmˈpekəbl] *adj* tadellos

impede [ɪmˈpiːd] *vt* (be)hindern; **impediment** [ɪmˈpedɪmənt] *n* Hindernis *nt*; **speech impediment** Sprachfehler *m*

impending [ɪmˈpendɪŋ] *adj* bevorstehend

impenetrable [ɪmˈpenɪtrəbl] *adj* (*also fig*) undurchdringlich

imperative [ɪmˈperətɪv] *adj* (*necessary*) unbedingt erforderlich

imperceptible [ɪmpə'septɪbl] *adj* nicht wahrnehmbar

imperfect [ɪm'pə:fɪkt] *adj* (*faulty*) fehlerhaft; **~ion** [ɪmpə'fekʃən] *n* Unvollkommenheit *f*; (*fault*) Fehler *m*

imperial [ɪm'pɪərɪəl] *adj* kaiserlich

impersonal [ɪm'pə:sənl] *adj* unpersönlich

impersonate [ɪm'pə:səneɪt] *vt* sich ausgeben als; (*for fun*) imitieren

impertinent [ɪm'pə:tɪnənt] *adj* unverschämt, frech

impervious [ɪm'pə:vɪəs] *adj* (*fig*): **~ (to)** unempfänglich (für)

impetuous [ɪm'petjuəs] *adj* ungestüm

impetus ['ɪmpətəs] *n* Triebkraft *f*; (*fig*) Auftrieb *m*

impinge [ɪm'pɪndʒ]: **~ on** *vt* beeinträchtigen

implacable [ɪm'plækəbl] *adj* unerbittlich

implement [*n* 'ɪmplɪmənt, *vb* 'ɪmplɪment] *n* Werkzeug *nt* ♦ *vt* ausführen

implicate ['ɪmplɪkeɪt] *vt* verwickeln; **implication** [ɪmplɪ'keɪʃən] *n* (*effect*) Auswirkung *f*; (*in crime*) Verwicklung *f*

implicit [ɪm'plɪsɪt] *adj* (*suggested*) unausgesprochen; (*utter*) vorbehaltlos

implore [ɪm'plɔ:r] *vt* anflehen

imply [ɪm'plaɪ] *vt* (*hint*) andeuten; (*be evidence for*) schließen lassen auf +*acc*

impolite [ɪmpə'laɪt] *adj* unhöflich

import [*vb* ɪm'pɔ:t, *n* 'ɪmpɔ:t] *vt* einführen ♦ *n* Einfuhr *f*; (*meaning*) Bedeutung *f*

importance [ɪm'pɔ:tns] *n* Bedeutung *f*

important [ɪm'pɔ:tənt] *adj* wichtig; **it's not ~** es ist unwichtig

importer [ɪm'pɔ:tər] *n* Importeur *m*

impose [ɪm'pəuz] *vt, vi*: **to ~ (on)** auferlegen (+*dat*); (*penalty, sanctions*) verhängen (gegen); **to ~ (o.s.) on sb** sich jdm aufdrängen

imposing [ɪm'pəuzɪŋ] *adj* eindrucksvoll

imposition [ɪmpə'zɪʃən] *n* (*of burden, fine*) Auferlegung *f*; **to be an ~** (*on person*) eine Zumutung sein

impossible [ɪm'pɒsɪbl] *adj* unmöglich

impostor [ɪm'pɒstər] *n* Hochstapler *m*

impotent ['ɪmpətnt] *adj* machtlos; (*sexually*) impotent

impound [ɪm'paund] *vt* beschlagnahmen

impoverished [ɪm'pɒvərɪʃt] *adj* verarmt

impracticable [ɪm'præktɪkəbl] *adj* undurchführbar

impractical [ɪm'præktɪkl] *adj* unpraktisch

imprecise [ɪmprɪ'saɪs] *adj* ungenau

impregnable [ɪm'pregnəbl] *adj* (*castle*) uneinnehmbar

impregnate ['ɪmpregneɪt] *vt* (*saturate*) sättigen; (*fertilize*) befruchten

impress [ɪm'pres] *vt* (*influence*) beeindrucken; (*imprint*) (auf)drücken; **to ~ sth on sb** jdm etw einschärfen; **~ed** *adj* beeindruckt; **~ion** [ɪm'preʃən] *n* Eindruck *m*; (*on wax, footprint*) Abdruck *m*; (*of book*) Auflage *f*; (*take-off*) Nachahmung *f*; **I was under the ~ion** ich hatte den Eindruck; **~ionable** *adj* leicht zu beeindrucken; **~ive** *adj* eindrucksvoll

imprint ['ɪmprɪnt] *n* Abdruck *m*

imprison [ɪm'prɪzn] *vt* ins Gefängnis schicken; **~ment** *n* Inhaftierung *f*

improbable [ɪm'prɒbəbl] *adj* unwahrscheinlich

impromptu [ɪm'prɒmptju:] *adj, adv* aus dem Stegreif, improvisiert

improper [ɪm'prɒpər] *adj* (*indecent*) unanständig; (*unsuitable*) unpassend

improve [ɪm'pru:v] *vt* verbessern ♦ *vi* besser werden; **~ment** *n* (Ver)besserung *f*

improvise ['ɪmprəvaɪz] *vt, vi* improvisieren

imprudent [ɪm'pru:dnt] *adj* unklug

impudent ['ɪmpjudnt] *adj* unverschämt

impulse ['ɪmpʌls] *n* Impuls *m*; **to act on ~** spontan handeln; **impulsive** [ɪm'pʌlsɪv] *adj* impulsiv

impure [ɪm'pjuər] *adj* (*dirty*) verunreinigt; (*bad*) unsauber; **impurity** [ɪm'pjuərɪtɪ] *n* Unreinheit *f*; (*TECH*) Verunreinigung *f*

KEYWORD
---

in [ɪn] *prep* **1** (*indicating place, position*) in +*dat*; (*with motion*) in +*acc*; **in here/there** hier/dort; **in London** in London; **in the United States** in den Vereinigten Staaten **2** (*indicating time: during*) in +*dat*; **in summer** im Sommer; **in 1988** (im Jahre)

1988; **in the afternoon** nachmittags, am Nachmittag
3 (*indicating time: in the space of*) innerhalb von; **I'll see you in 2 weeks** *or* **in 2 weeks' time** ich sehe Sie in zwei Wochen
4 (*indicating manner, circumstances, state etc*) in +*dat*; **in the sun/rain** in der Sonne/im Regen; **in English/French** auf Englisch/Französisch; **in a loud/soft voice** mit lauter/leiser Stimme
5 (*with ratios, numbers*): **1 in 10** jeder Zehnte; **20 pence in the pound** 20 Pence pro Pfund; **they lined up in twos** sie stellten sich in Zweierreihe auf
6 (*referring to people, works*): **the disease is common in children** die Krankheit ist bei Kindern häufig; **in Dickens** bei Dickens; **we have a loyal friend in him** er ist uns ein treuer Freund
7 (*indicating profession etc*): **to be in teaching/the army** Lehrer(in)/beim Militär sein; **to be in publishing** im Verlagswesen arbeiten
8 (*with present participle*): **in saying this, I ...** wenn ich das sage, ... ich; **in accepting this view, he ...** weil er diese Meinung akzeptierte, ... er
♦ *adv*: **to be in** (*person: at home, work*) da sein; (*train, ship, plane*) angekommen sein; (*in fashion*) in sein; **to ask sb in** jdn hereinbitten; **to run/limp** *etc* **in** hereingerannt/gehumpelt *etc* kommen
♦ *n*: **the ins and outs** (*of proposal, situation etc*) die Feinheiten

in. *abbr* = **inch**
inability [ɪnəˈbɪlɪtɪ] *n* Unfähigkeit *f*
inaccessible [ɪnəkˈsesɪbl] *adj* unzugänglich
inaccurate [ɪnˈækjurət] *adj* ungenau; (*wrong*) unrichtig
inactivity [ɪnækˈtɪvɪtɪ] *n* Untätigkeit *f*
inadequate [ɪnˈædɪkwət] *adj* unzulänglich
inadvertently [ɪnədˈvɜːtntlɪ] *adv* unabsichtlich
inadvisable [ɪnədˈvaɪzəbl] *adj* nicht ratsam
inane [ɪˈneɪn] *adj* dumm, albern
inanimate [ɪnˈænɪmət] *adj* leblos

inappropriate [ɪnəˈprəuprɪət] *adj* (*clothing*) ungeeignet; (*remark*) unangebracht
inarticulate [ɪnɑːˈtɪkjulət] *adj* unklar
inasmuch as [ɪnəzˈmʌtʃ-] *adv* da; (*in so far as*) so weit
inaudible [ɪnˈɔːdɪbl] *adj* unhörbar
inauguration [ɪnɔːgjuˈreɪʃən] *n* Eröffnung *f*; (*feierliche*) Amtseinführung *f*
inborn [ɪnˈbɔːn] *adj* angeboren
inbred [ɪnˈbred] *adj* angeboren
Inc. *abbr* = **incorporated**
incalculable [ɪnˈkælkjulabl] *adj* (*consequences*) unabsehbar
incapable [ɪnˈkeɪpəbl] *adj*: **~ (of doing sth)** unfähig(, etw zu tun)
incapacitate [ɪnkəˈpæsɪteɪt] *vt* untauglich machen
incapacity [ɪnkəˈpæsɪtɪ] *n* Unfähigkeit *f*
incarcerate [ɪnˈkɑːsəreɪt] *vt* einkerkern
incarnation [ɪnkɑːˈneɪʃən] *n* (*ECCL*) Menschwerdung *f*; (*fig*) Inbegriff *m*
incendiary [ɪnˈsendɪərɪ] *adj* Brand-
incense [*n* ˈɪnsens, *vb* ɪnˈsens] *n* Weihrauch *m* ♦ *vt* erzürnen
incentive [ɪnˈsentɪv] *n* Anreiz *m*
incessant [ɪnˈsesnt] *adj* unaufhörlich
incest [ˈɪnsest] *n* Inzest *m*
inch [ɪntʃ] *n* Zoll *m* ♦ *vi*: **to ~ forward** sich Stückchen für Stückchen vorwärts bewegen; **to be within an ~ of** kurz davor sein; **he didn't give an ~** er gab keinen Zentimeter nach
incidence [ˈɪnsɪdns] *n* Auftreten *nt*; (*of crime*) Quote *f*
incident [ˈɪnsɪdnt] *n* Vorfall *m*; (*disturbance*) Zwischenfall *m*
incidental [ɪnsɪˈdentl] *adj* (*music*) Begleit-; (*unimportant*) nebensächlich; (*remark*) beiläufig; **~ly** *adv* übrigens
incinerator [ɪnˈsɪnəreɪtəʳ] *n* Verbrennungsofen *m*
incision [ɪnˈsɪʒən] *n* Einschnitt *m*
incisive [ɪnˈsaɪsɪv] *adj* (*style*) treffend; (*person*) scharfsinnig
incite [ɪnˈsaɪt] *vt* anstacheln
inclination [ɪnklɪˈneɪʃən] *n* Neigung *f*
incline [*n* ˈɪnklaɪn, *vb* ɪnˈklaɪn] *n* Abhang *m*

♦ vt neigen; (fig) veranlassen ♦ vi sich neigen; **to be ~d to do sth** dazu neigen, etw zu tun

include [ɪnˈkluːd] vt einschließen; (on list, in group) aufnehmen; **including** prep: **including X** X inbegriffen; **inclusion** [ɪnˈkluːʒən] n Aufnahme f; **inclusive** [ɪnˈkluːsɪv] adj einschließlich; (COMM) inklusive; **inclusive of** einschließlich +gen

incoherent [ɪnkəʊˈhɪərənt] adj zusammenhanglos

income [ˈɪnkʌm] n Einkommen nt; (from business) Einkünfte pl; **~ tax** n Lohnsteuer f; (of self-employed) Einkommenssteuer f

incoming [ˈɪnkʌmɪŋ] adj: **~ flight** eintreffende Maschine f

incomparable [ɪnˈkɒmpərəbl] adj unvergleichlich

incompatible [ɪnkəmˈpætɪbl] adj unvereinbar; (people) unverträglich

incompetence [ɪnˈkɒmpɪtns] n Unfähigkeit f; **incompetent** adj unfähig

incomplete [ɪnkəmˈpliːt] adj unvollständig

incomprehensible [ɪnkɒmprɪˈhensɪbl] adj unverständlich

inconceivable [ɪnkənˈsiːvəbl] adj unvorstellbar

incongruous [ɪnˈkɒŋɡruəs] adj seltsam; (remark) unangebracht

inconsiderate [ɪnkənˈsɪdərət] adj rücksichtslos

inconsistency [ɪnkənˈsɪstənsɪ] n Widersprüchlichkeit f; (state) Unbeständigkeit f

inconsistent [ɪnkənˈsɪstnt] adj (action, speech) widersprüchlich; (person, work) unbeständig; **~ with** nicht übereinstimmend mit

inconspicuous [ɪnkənˈspɪkjuəs] adj unauffällig

incontinent [ɪnˈkɒntɪnənt] adj (MED) nicht fähig, Stuhl und Harn zurückzuhalten

inconvenience [ɪnkənˈviːnjəns] n Unbequemlichkeit f; (trouble to others) Unannehmlichkeiten pl

inconvenient [ɪnkənˈviːnjənt] adj ungelegen; (journey) unbequem

incorporate [ɪnˈkɔːpəreɪt] vt (include) aufnehmen; (contain) enthalten; **~d** adj: **~d company** (US) eingetragene Aktiengesellschaft f

incorrect [ɪnkəˈrekt] adj unrichtig

incorrigible [ɪnˈkɒrɪdʒɪbl] adj unverbesserlich

incorruptible [ɪnkəˈrʌptɪbl] adj unzerstörbar; (person) unbestechlich

increase [n ˈɪnkriːs, vb ɪnˈkriːs] n Zunahme f; (pay ~) Gehaltserhöhung f; (in size) Vergrößerung f ♦ vt erhöhen; (wealth, rage) vermehren; (business) erweitern ♦ vi zunehmen; (prices) steigen; (in size) größer werden; (in number) sich vermehren; **increasing** adj (number) steigend; **increasingly** [ɪnˈkriːsɪŋlɪ] adv zunehmend

incredible [ɪnˈkredɪbl] adj unglaublich

incredulous [ɪnˈkredjuləs] adj ungläubig

increment [ˈɪnkrɪmənt] n Zulage f

incriminate [ɪnˈkrɪmɪneɪt] vt belasten

incubation [ɪnkjuˈbeɪʃən] n Ausbrüten nt

incubator [ˈɪnkjubeɪtə] n Brutkasten m

incumbent [ɪnˈkʌmbənt] n ♦ adj: **it is ~ on him to ...** es obliegt ihm, ...

incur [ɪnˈkɜː] vt sich zuziehen; (debts) machen

incurable [ɪnˈkjuərəbl] adj unheilbar

indebted [ɪnˈdetɪd] adj (obliged): **~ (to sb)** (jdm) verpflichtet

indecent [ɪnˈdiːsnt] adj unanständig; **~ assault** (BRIT) n Notzucht f; **~ exposure** n Exhibitionismus m

indecisive [ɪndɪˈsaɪsɪv] adj (battle) nicht entscheidend; (person) unentschlossen

indeed [ɪnˈdiːd] adv tatsächlich, in der Tat; **yes ~!** allerdings!

indefinite [ɪnˈdefɪnɪt] adj unbestimmt; **~ly** adv auf unbestimmte Zeit; (wait) unbegrenzt lange

indelible [ɪnˈdelɪbl] adj unauslöschlich

indemnity [ɪnˈdemnɪtɪ] n (insurance) Versicherung f; (compensation) Entschädigung f

independence [ɪndɪˈpendns] n Unabhängigkeit f; **independent** adj unabhängig

---

Independence Day

i **Independence Day** *(der 4. Juli)* ist in den USA ein gesetzlicher Feiertag zum Gedenken an die Unabhängigkeitserklärung am 4. Juli 1776, mit der die 13 amerikanischen Kolonien ihre Freiheit und Unabhängigkeit von Großbritannien erklärten.

---

indestructible [ɪndɪs'trʌktəbl] *adj* unzerstörbar

indeterminate [ɪndɪ'tə:mɪnɪt] *adj* unbestimmt

index ['ɪndeks] *(pl* **~es** *or* **indices)** *n* Index *m;* **~ card** *n* Karteikarte *f;* **~ finger** *n* Zeigefinger *m;* **~-linked** *(US* **~ed)** *adj (salaries)* der Inflationsrate *dat* angeglichen; *(pensions)* dynamisch

India ['ɪndɪə] *n* Indien *nt;* **~n** *adj* indisch ♦ *n* Inder(in) *m(f);* **American ~n** Indianer(in) *m(f);* **~n Ocean** *n:* **the ~n Ocean** der Indische Ozean

indicate ['ɪndɪkeɪt] *vt* anzeigen; *(hint)* andeuten; **indication** [ɪndɪ'keɪʃən] *n* Anzeichen *nt; (information)* Angabe *f;* **indicative** [ɪn'dɪkətɪv] *adj:* **indicative of** bezeichnend für; **indicator** *n* (An)zeichen *nt; (AUT)* Richtungsanzeiger *m*

indict [ɪn'daɪt] *vt* anklagen; **~ment** *n* Anklage *f*

indifference [ɪn'dɪfrəns] *n* Gleichgültigkeit *f;* Unwichtigkeit *f;* **indifferent** *adj* gleichgültig; *(mediocre)* mäßig

indigenous [ɪn'dɪdʒɪnəs] *adj* einheimisch

indigestion [ɪndɪ'dʒestʃən] *n* Verdauungsstörung *f*

indignant [ɪn'dɪgnənt] *adj:* **to be ~ about sth** über etw *acc* empört sein

indignation [ɪndɪg'neɪʃən] *n* Entrüstung *f*

indignity [ɪn'dɪgnɪtɪ] *n* Demütigung *f*

indirect [ɪndɪ'rekt] *adj* indirekt

indiscreet [ɪndɪs'kri:t] *adj (insensitive)* taktlos; *(telling secrets)* indiskret; **indiscretion** [ɪndɪs'kreʃən] *n* Taktlosigkeit *f;* Indiskretion *f*

indiscriminate [ɪndɪs'krɪmɪnət] *adj* wahllos;

kritiklos

indispensable [ɪndɪs'pensəbl] *adj* unentbehrlich

indisposed [ɪndɪs'pəuzd] *adj* unpässlich

indisputable [ɪndɪs'pju:təbl] *adj* unbestreitbar; *(evidence)* unanfechtbar

indistinct [ɪndɪs'tɪŋkt] *adj* undeutlich

individual [ɪndɪ'vɪdjuəl] *n* Individuum *nt* ♦ *adj* individuell; *(case)* Einzel-; *(of, for one person)* eigen, individuell; *(characteristic)* eigentümlich; **~ly** *adv* einzeln, individuell

indivisible [ɪndɪ'vɪzɪbl] *adj* unteilbar

indoctrinate [ɪn'dɔktrɪneɪt] *vt* indoktrinieren

Indonesia [ɪndə'ni:zɪə] *n* Indonesien *nt*

indoor ['ɪndɔ:'] *adj* Haus-; Zimmer-; Innen-; *(SPORT)* Hallen-; **~s** [ɪn'dɔ:z] *adv* drinnen, im Haus

induce [ɪn'dju:s] *vt* dazu bewegen; *(reaction)* herbeiführen

induction course [ɪn'dʌkʃən-] *(BRIT) n* Einführungskurs *m*

indulge [ɪn'dʌldʒ] *vt (give way)* nachgeben *+dat; (gratify)* frönen *+dat* ♦ *vi:* **to ~ (in)** frönen *(+dat);* **~nce** *n* Nachsicht *f; (enjoyment)* Genuss *m;* **~nt** *adj* nachsichtig; *(pej)* nachgiebig

industrial [ɪn'dʌstrɪəl] *adj* Industrie-, industriell; *(dispute, injury)* Arbeits-; **~ action** *n* Arbeitskampfmaßnahmen *pl;* **~ estate** *(BRIT) n* Industriegebiet *nt;* **~ist** *n* Industrielle(r) *mf;* **~ize** *vt* industrialisieren; **~ park** *(US) n* Industriegebiet *nt*

industrious [ɪn'dʌstrɪəs] *adj* fleißig

industry ['ɪndəstrɪ] *n* Industrie *f; (diligence)* Fleiß *m*

inebriated [ɪ'ni:brɪeɪtɪd] *adj* betrunken

inedible [ɪn'edɪbl] *adj* ungenießbar

ineffective [ɪnɪ'fektɪv] *adj* unwirksam; *(person)* untauglich

ineffectual [ɪnɪ'fektʃuəl] *adj* = **ineffective**

inefficiency [ɪnɪ'fɪʃənsɪ] *n* Ineffizienz *f*

inefficient [ɪnɪ'fɪʃənt] *adj* ineffizient; *(ineffective)* unwirksam

inept [ɪ'nept] *adj (remark)* unpassend; *(person)* ungeeignet

inequality [ɪnɪ'kwɔlɪtɪ] *n* Ungleichheit *f*

inert [ɪ'nə:t] *adj* träge; *(CHEM)* inaktiv;

(*motionless*) unbeweglich

inescapable [ɪnɪ'skeɪpəbl] *adj* unvermeidbar

inevitable [ɪn'evɪtəbl] *adj* unvermeidlich; **inevitably** *adv* zwangsläufig

inexcusable [ɪnɪks'kju:zəbl] *adj* unverzeihlich

inexhaustible [ɪnɪg'zɔːstɪbl] *adj* unerschöpflich

inexpensive [ɪnɪk'spensɪv] *adj* preiswert

inexperience [ɪnɪk'spɪərɪəns] *n* Unerfahrenheit *f*; **~d** *adj* unerfahren

inexplicable [ɪnɪk'splɪkəbl] *adj* unerklärlich

inextricably [ɪnɪk'strɪkəblɪ] *adv* untrennbar

infallible [ɪn'fælɪbl] *adj* unfehlbar

infamous ['ɪnfəməs] *adj* (*deed*) schändlich; (*person*) niederträchtig

infancy ['ɪnfənsɪ] *n* frühe Kindheit *f*; (*fig*) Anfangsstadium *nt*

infant ['ɪnfənt] *n* kleine(s) Kind *nt*, Säugling *m*; **~ile** [-aɪl] *adj* kindisch, infantil; **~ school** (*BRIT*) *n* Vorschule *f*

infatuated [ɪn'fætjueɪtɪd] *adj* vernarrt; **to become ~ with** sich vernarren in +*acc*; **infatuation** [ɪnfætjʊ'eɪʃən] *n*: **infatuation (with)** Vernarrtheit *f* (in +*acc*)

infect [ɪn'fekt] *vt* anstecken (*also fig*); **~ed with** (*illness*) infiziert mit; **~ion** [ɪn'fekʃən] *n* Infektion *f*; **~ious** [ɪn'fekʃəs] *adj* ansteckend

infer [ɪn'fɜː] *vt* schließen

inferior [ɪn'fɪərɪə] *adj* (*rank*) untergeordnet; (*quality*) minderwertig ♦ *n* Untergebene(r) *m*; **~ity** [ɪnfɪərɪ'ɔrətɪ] *n* Minderwertigkeit *f*; (*in rank*) untergeordnete Stellung *f*; **~ity complex** *n* Minderwertigkeitskomplex *m*

infernal [ɪn'fɜːnl] *adj* höllisch

infertile [ɪn'fɜːtaɪl] *adj* unfruchtbar; **infertility** [ɪnfə'tɪlɪtɪ] *n* Unfruchtbarkeit *f*

infested [ɪn'festɪd] *adj*: **to be ~ with** wimmeln von

infidelity [ɪnfɪ'delɪtɪ] *n* Untreue *f*

infighting ['ɪnfaɪtɪŋ] *n* Nahkampf *m*

infiltrate ['ɪnfɪltreɪt] *vt* infiltrieren; (*spies*) einschleusen ♦ *vi* (*MIL, liquid*) einsickern; (*POL*): **to ~ (into)** unterwandern (+*acc*)

infinite ['ɪnfɪnɪt] *adj* unendlich

infinitive [ɪn'fɪnɪtɪv] *n* Infinitiv *m*

infinity [ɪn'fɪnɪtɪ] *n* Unendlichkeit *f*

infirm [ɪn'fɜːm] *adj* gebrechlich; **~ary** *n* Krankenhaus *nt*

inflamed [ɪn'fleɪmd] *adj* entzündet

inflammable [ɪn'flæməbl] (*BRIT*) *adj* feuergefährlich

inflammation [ɪnflə'meɪʃən] *n* Entzündung *f*

inflatable [ɪn'fleɪtəbl] *adj* aufblasbar

inflate [ɪn'fleɪt] *vt* aufblasen; (*tyre*) aufpumpen; (*prices*) hoch treiben; **inflation** [ɪn'fleɪʃən] *n* Inflation *f*; **inflationary** [ɪn'fleɪʃənrɪ] *adj* (*increase*) inflationistisch; (*situation*) inflationär

inflexible [ɪn'fleksɪbl] *adj* (*person*) nicht flexibel; (*opinion*) starr; (*thing*) unbiegsam

inflict [ɪn'flɪkt] *vt*: **to ~ sth on sb** jdm etw zufügen; (*wound*) jdm etw beibringen

influence ['ɪnflʊəns] *n* Einfluss *m* ♦ *vt* beeinflussen

influential [ɪnflʊ'enʃl] *adj* einflussreich

influenza [ɪnflʊ'enzə] *n* Grippe *f*

influx ['ɪnflʌks] *n* (*of people*) Zustrom *m*; (*of ideas*) Eindringen *nt*

infomercial ['ɪnfəuməːʃl] *n* Werbeinformationssendung *f*

inform [ɪn'fɔːm] *vt* informieren ♦ *vi*: **to ~ on sb** jdn denunzieren; **to keep sb ~ed** jdn auf dem Laufenden halten

informal [ɪn'fɔːml] *adj* zwanglos; **~ity** [ɪnfɔː'mælɪtɪ] *n* Ungezwungenheit *f*

informant [ɪn'fɔːmənt] *n* Informant(in) *m(f)*

information [ɪnfə'meɪʃən] *n* Auskunft *f*, Information *f*; **a piece of ~** eine Auskunft, eine Information; **~ desk** *n* Auskunftsschalter *m*; **~ office** *n* Informationsbüro *nt*

informative [ɪn'fɔːmətɪv] *adj* informativ; (*person*) mitteilsam

informer [ɪn'fɔːmə] *n* Denunziant(in) *m(f)*

infra-red [ɪnfrə'red] *adj* infrarot

infrequent [ɪn'fri:kwənt] *adj* selten

infringe [ɪn'frɪndʒ] *vt* (*law*) verstoßen gegen; **~ upon** *vt* verletzen; **~ment** *n* Verstoß *m*, Verletzung *f*

infuriating [ɪn'fjʊərɪeɪtɪŋ] *adj* ärgerlich

ingenuity [ɪndʒɪ'nju:ɪtɪ] *n* Genialität *f*

ingenuous [ɪn'dʒenjuəs] *adj* aufrichtig; (*naive*) naiv

ingot ['ɪŋgət] *n* Barren *m*

ingrained [ɪn'greɪnd] *adj* tief sitzend

ingratiate [ɪn'greɪʃɪeɪt] *vt*: **to ~ o.s. with sb** sich bei jdm einschmeicheln

ingratitude [ɪn'grætɪtjuːd] *n* Undankbarkeit *f*

ingredient [ɪn'griːdɪənt] *n* Bestandteil *m*; (*COOK*) Zutat *f*

inhabit [ɪn'hæbɪt] *vt* bewohnen; **~ant** *n* Bewohner(in) *m(f)*; (*of island, town*) Einwohner(in) *m(f)*

inhale [ɪn'heɪl] *vt* einatmen; (*MED, cigarettes*) inhalieren

inherent [ɪn'hɪərənt] *adj*: **~ (in)** innewohnend (+*dat*)

inherit [ɪn'herɪt] *vt* erben; **~ance** *n* Erbe *nt*, Erbschaft *f*

inhibit [ɪn'hɪbɪt] *vt* hemmen; **to ~ sb from doing sth** jdn daran hindern, etw zu tun; **~ion** [ɪnhɪ'bɪʃən] *n* Hemmung *f*

inhospitable [ɪnhɔs'pɪtəbl] *adj* (*person*) ungastlich; (*country*) unwirtlich

inhuman [ɪn'hjuːmən] *adj* unmenschlich

initial [ɪ'nɪʃl] *adj* anfänglich, Anfangs- ♦ *n* Initiale *f* ♦ *vt* abzeichnen; (*POL*) paraphieren; **~ly** *adv* anfangs

initiate [ɪ'nɪʃɪeɪt] *vt* einführen; (*negotiations*) einleiten; **to ~ proceedings against sb** (*JUR*) gerichtliche Schritte gegen jdn einleiten; **initiation** [ɪnɪʃɪ'eɪʃən] *n* Einführung *f*; Einleitung *f*

initiative [ɪ'nɪʃɪətɪv] *n* Initiative *f*

inject [ɪn'dʒekt] *vt* einspritzen; (*fig*) einflößen; **~ion** [ɪn'dʒekʃən] *n* Spritze *f*

injunction [ɪn'dʒʌŋkʃən] *n* Verfügung *f*

injure ['ɪndʒə*] *vt* verletzen; **~d** *adj* (*person, arm*) verletzt; **injury** ['ɪndʒərɪ] *n* Verletzung *f*; **to play injury time** (*SPORT*) nachspielen

injustice [ɪn'dʒʌstɪs] *n* Ungerechtigkeit *f*

ink [ɪŋk] *n* Tinte *f*

inkling ['ɪŋklɪŋ] *n* (dunkle) Ahnung *f*

inlaid ['ɪnleɪd] *adj* eingelegt, Einlege-

inland [*adj* 'ɪnlənd, *adv* ɪn'lænd] *adj* Binnen-; (*domestic*) Inlands- ♦ *adv* landeinwärts; **~ revenue** (*BRIT*) *n* Fiskus *m*

in-laws ['ɪnlɔːz] *npl* (*parents-in-law*) Schwiegereltern *pl*; (*others*) angeheiratete Verwandte *pl*

inlet ['ɪnlet] *n* Einlass *m*; (*bay*) kleine Bucht *f*

inmate ['ɪnmeɪt] *n* Insasse *m*

inn [ɪn] *n* Gasthaus *nt*, Wirtshaus *nt*

innate [ɪ'neɪt] *adj* angeboren

inner ['ɪnə*] *adj* inner, Innen-; (*fig*) verborgen; **~ city** *n* Innenstadt *f*; **~ tube** *n* (*of tyre*) Schlauch *m*

innings ['ɪnɪŋz] *n* (*CRICKET*) Innenrunde *f*

innocence ['ɪnəsns] *n* Unschuld *f*; (*ignorance*) Unkenntnis *f*

innocent ['ɪnəsnt] *adj* unschuldig

innocuous [ɪ'nɔkjuəs] *adj* harmlos

innovation [ɪnəu'veɪʃən] *n* Neuerung *f*

innuendo [ɪnju'endəu] *n* (versteckte) Anspielung *f*

innumerable [ɪ'njuːmrəbl] *adj* unzählig

inoculation [ɪnɔkju'leɪʃən] *n* Impfung *f*

inopportune [ɪn'ɔpətjuːn] *adj* (*remark*) unangebracht; (*visit*) ungelegen

inordinately [ɪ'nɔːdɪnətlɪ] *adv* unmäßig

inpatient ['ɪnpeɪʃənt] *n* stationäre(r) Patient *m*/stationäre Patientin *f*

input ['ɪnput] *n* (*COMPUT*) Eingabe *f*; (*power ~*) Energiezufuhr *f*; (*of energy, work*) Aufwand *m*

inquest ['ɪnkwest] *n* gerichtliche Untersuchung *f*

inquire [ɪn'kwaɪə*] *vi* sich erkundigen ♦ *vt* (*price*) sich erkundigen nach; **~ into** *vt* untersuchen; **inquiry** [ɪn'kwaɪərɪ] *n* (*question*) Erkundigung *f*; (*investigation*) Untersuchung *f*; **inquiries** Auskunft *f*; **inquiry office** (*BRIT*) *n* Auskunft(sbüro *nt*) *f*

inquisitive [ɪn'kwɪzɪtɪv] *adj* neugierig

ins. *abbr* = **inches**

insane [ɪn'seɪn] *adj* wahnsinnig; (*MED*) geisteskrank; **insanity** [ɪn'sænɪtɪ] *n* Wahnsinn *m*

insatiable [ɪn'seɪʃəbl] *adj* unersättlich

inscribe [ɪn'skraɪb] *vt* eingravieren; **inscription** [ɪn'skrɪpʃən] *n* (*on stone*) Inschrift *f*; (*in book*) Widmung *f*

insect ['ɪnsekt] *n* Insekt *nt*; **~icide** [ɪn'sektɪsaɪd] *n* Insektenvertilgungsmittel *nt*; **~ repellent** *n* Insektenbekämpfungsmittel *nt*

insecure [ɪnsɪ'kjuə*] *adj* (*person*) unsicher;

(thing) nicht fest *or* sicher; **insecurity**
[ɪnsɪˈkjʊərɪtɪ] *n* Unsicherheit *f*

insemination [ɪnsemɪˈneɪʃən] *n*: **artificial ~**
künstliche Befruchtung *f*

insensible [ɪnˈsensɪbl] *adj (unconscious)*
bewusstlos

insensitive [ɪnˈsensɪtɪv] *adj (to pain)*
unempfindlich; *(unfeeling)* gefühllos

inseparable [ɪnˈseprəbl] *adj (people)*
unzertrennlich; *(word)* untrennbar

insert [*vb* ɪnˈsəːt, *n* ˈɪnsəːt] *vt* einfügen; *(coin)*
einwerfen; *(stick into)* hineinstecken;
(advertisement) aufgeben ♦ *n (in book)*
Einlage *f*; *(in magazine)* Beilage *f*; **~ion**
[ɪnˈsəːʃən] *n* Einfügung *f*; *(PRESS)* Inserat *nt*

in-service [ˈɪnˈsəːvɪs] *adj (training)*
berufsbegleitend

inshore [ˈɪnˈʃɔːʳ] *adj* Küsten- ♦ *adv* an der
Küste

inside [ˈɪnˈsaɪd] *n* Innenseite *f*, Innere(s) *nt*
♦ *adj* innere(r, s), Innen- ♦ *adv (place)*
innen; *(direction)* nach innen, hinein ♦ *prep*
(place) in +*dat*; *(direction)* in +*acc* ♦ *adv*
(time) innerhalb +*gen*; **~s** *npl (inf)*
Eingeweide *nt*; **~ 10 minutes** unter 10
Minuten; **~ information** *n* interne
Informationen *pl*; **~ lane** *n (AUT: in Britain)*
linke Spur; **~ out** *adv* linksherum; *(know)*
in- und auswendig

insider dealing, insider trading
[ɪnˈsaɪdəʳ-] *n (STOCK EXCHANGE)* Insiderhandel
m

insidious [ɪnˈsɪdɪəs] *adj* heimtückisch

insight [ˈɪnsaɪt] *n* Einsicht *f*; **~ into** Einblick
m in +*acc*

insignificant [ɪnsɪgˈnɪfɪknt] *adj*
unbedeutend

insincere [ɪnsɪnˈsɪəʳ] *adj* unaufrichtig

insinuate [ɪnˈsɪnjʊeɪt] *vt (hint)* andeuten

insipid [ɪnˈsɪpɪd] *adj* fad(e)

insist [ɪnˈsɪst] *vi*: **to ~ on** bestehen (auf
+*acc*); **~ence** *n* Bestehen *nt*; **~ent** *adj*
hartnäckig; *(urgent)* dringend

insole [ˈɪnsəʊl] *n* Einlegesohle *f*

insolence [ˈɪnsələns] *n* Frechheit *f*

insolent [ˈɪnsələnt] *adj* frech

insoluble [ɪnˈsɔljubl] *adj* unlösbar; *(CHEM)*

unlöslich

insolvent [ɪnˈsɔlvənt] *adj* zahlungsunfähig

insomnia [ɪnˈsɔmnɪə] *n* Schlaflosigkeit *f*

inspect [ɪnˈspekt] *vt* prüfen; *(officially)*
inspizieren; **~ion** [ɪnˈspekʃən] *n* Inspektion *f*;
~or *n (official)* Inspektor *m*; *(police)*
Polizeikommissar *m*; *(BRIT: on buses, trains)*
Kontrolleur *m*

inspiration [ɪnspəˈreɪʃən] *n* Inspiration *f*

inspire [ɪnˈspaɪəʳ] *vt (person)* inspirieren; **to ~
sth in sb** *(respect)* jdm etw einflößen;
(hope) etw in jdm wecken

instability [ɪnstəˈbɪlɪtɪ] *n* Unbeständigkeit *f*,
Labilität *f*

install [ɪnˈstɔːl] *vt (put in)* installieren;
(telephone) anschließen; *(establish)*
einsetzen; **~ation** [ɪnstəˈleɪʃən] *n (of person)*
(Amts)einsetzung *f*; *(of machinery)*
Installierung *f*; *(machines etc)* Anlage *f*

instalment [ɪnˈstɔːlmənt] *(US* **installment**) *n*
Rate *f*; *(of story)* Fortsetzung *f*; **to pay in ~s**
in Raten zahlen

instance [ˈɪnstəns] *n* Fall *m*; *(example)*
Beispiel *nt*; **for ~** zum Beispiel; **in the first
~** zunächst

instant [ˈɪnstənt] *n* Augenblick *m* ♦ *adj*
augenblicklich, sofortig; **~aneous**
[ɪnstənˈteɪnɪəs] *adj* unmittelbar; **~ coffee** *n*
Pulverkaffee *m*; **~ly** *adv* sofort

instead [ɪnˈsted] *adv* stattdessen; **~ of** *prep*
anstatt +*gen*

instep [ˈɪnstep] *n* Spann *m*; *(of shoe)* Blatt *nt*

instil [ɪnˈstɪl] *vt (fig)*: **to ~ sth in sb** jdm etw
beibringen

instinct [ˈɪnstɪŋkt] *n* Instinkt *m*; **~ive**
[ɪnˈstɪŋktɪv] *adj* instinktiv

institute [ˈɪnstɪtjuːt] *n* Institut *nt* ♦ *vt*
einführen; *(search)* einleiten

institution [ɪnstɪˈtjuːʃən] *n* Institution *f*;
(home) Anstalt *f*

instruct [ɪnˈstrʌkt] *vt* anweisen; *(officially)*
instruieren; **~ion** [ɪnˈstrʌkʃən] *n* Unterricht
m; **~ions** *npl (orders)* Anweisungen *pl*; *(for
use)* Gebrauchsanweisung *f*; **~or** *n* Lehrer
m

instrument [ˈɪnstrumənt] *n* Instrument *nt*;
~al [ɪnstruˈmentl] *adj (MUS)* Instrumental-;

(*helpful*): **~al (in)** behilflich (bei); **~ panel**n Armaturenbrett *nt*

insubordinate [ɪnsə'bɔːdənɪt] *adj* aufsässig, widersetzlich

insufferable [ɪn'sʌfrəbl] *adj* unerträglich

insufficient [ɪnsə'fɪʃənt] *adj* ungenügend

insular ['ɪnsjulə'] *adj* (*fig*) engstirnig

insulate ['ɪnsjuleɪt] *vt* (*ELEC*) isolieren; (*fig*): **to ~ (from)** abschirmen (vor +*dat*); **insulating tape**n Isolierband *nt*; **insulation** [ɪnsju'leɪʃən] *n* Isolierung *f*

insulin ['ɪnsjulɪn] *n* Insulin *nt*

insult [*n* 'ɪnsʌlt, *vb* ɪn'sʌlt] *n* Beleidigung *f* ♦ *vt* beleidigen

insurance [ɪn'ʃuərəns] *n* Versicherung *f*; **fire-/life ~** Feuer-/Lebensversicherung; **~ agent**n Versicherungsvertreter *m*; **~ policy**n Versicherungspolice *f*

insure [ɪn'ʃuə'] *vt* versichern

intact [ɪn'tækt] *adj* unversehrt

intake ['ɪnteɪk] *n* (*place*) Einlassöffnung *f*; (*act*) Aufnahme *f*; (*BRIT: SCH*): **an ~ of 200 a year** ein Neuzugang von 200 im Jahr

intangible [ɪn'tændʒɪbl] *adj* nicht greifbar

integral ['ɪntɪgrəl] *adj* (*essential*) wesentlich; (*complete*) vollständig; (*MATH*) Integral-

integrate ['ɪntɪgreɪt] *vt* integrieren ♦ *vi* sich integrieren

integrity [ɪn'tegrɪtɪ] *n* (*honesty*) Redlichkeit *f*, Integrität *f*

intellect ['ɪntəlekt] *n* Intellekt *m*; **~ual** [ɪntə'lektjuəl] *adj* geistig, intellektuell ♦ *n* Intellektuelle(r) *mf*

intelligence [ɪn'telɪdʒəns] *n* (*understanding*) Intelligenz *f*; (*news*) Information *f*; (*MIL*) Geheimdienst *m*; **~ service**n Nachrichtendienst *m*, Geheimdienst *m*

intelligent [ɪn'telɪdʒənt] *adj* intelligent; **~ly** *adv* klug; (*write, speak*) verständlich

intelligentsia [ɪntelɪ'dʒentsɪə] *n* Intelligenz *f*

intelligible [ɪn'telɪdʒɪbl] *adj* verständlich

intend [ɪn'tend] *vt* beabsichtigen; **that was ~ed for you** das war für dich gedacht

intense [ɪn'tens] *adj* stark, intensiv; (*person*) ernsthaft; **~ly**adv äußerst; (*study*) intensiv

intensify [ɪn'tensɪfaɪ] *vt* verstärken, intensivieren

intensity [ɪn'tensɪtɪ] *n* Intensität *f*

intensive [ɪn'tensɪv] *adj* intensiv; **~ care unit**n Intensivstation *f*

intent [ɪn'tent] *n* Absicht *f* ♦ *adj*: **to be ~ on doing sth** fest entschlossen sein, etw zu tun; **to all ~s and purposes** praktisch

intention [ɪn'tenʃən] *n* Absicht *f*; **~al**adj absichtlich

intently [ɪn'tentlɪ] *adv* konzentriert

interact [ɪntər'ækt] *vi* aufeinander einwirken; **~ion** [ɪntər'ækʃən] *n* Wechselwirkung *f*; **~ive**adj (*COMPUT*) interaktiv

intercept [ɪntə'sept] *vt* abfangen

interchange [*n* 'ɪntətʃeɪndʒ], *vb* ɪntə'tʃeɪndʒ] *n* (*exchange*) Austausch *m*; (*on roads*) Verkehrskreuz *nt* ♦ *vt* austauschen; **~able** [ɪntə'tʃeɪndʒəbl] *adj* austauschbar

intercom ['ɪntəkɔm] *n* (*Gegen*)sprechanlage *f*

intercourse ['ɪntəkɔːs] *n* (*exchange*) Beziehungen *pl*; (*sexual*) Geschlechtsverkehr *m*

interest ['ɪntrɪst] *n* Interesse *nt*; (*FIN*) Zinsen *pl*; (*COMM: share*) Anteil *m*; (*group*) Interessengruppe *f* ♦ *vt* interessieren; **~ed** *adj* (*having claims*) beteiligt; (*attentive*) interessiert; **to be ~ed in** sich interessieren für; **~ing**adj interessant; **~ rate**n Zinssatz *m*

interface ['ɪntəfeɪs] *n* (*COMPUT*) Schnittstelle *f*, Interface *nt*

interfere [ɪntə'fɪə'] *vi*: **to ~ (with)** (*meddle*) sich einmischen (in +*acc*); (*disrupt*) stören +*acc*; **~nce** [ɪntə'fɪərəns] *n* Einmischung *f*; (*TV*) Störung *f*

interim ['ɪntərɪm] *n*: **in the ~** inzwischen

interior [ɪn'tɪərɪə'] *n* Innere(s) *nt* ♦ *adj* innere(r, s), Innen-; **~ designer**n Innenarchitekt(in) *m(f)*

interjection [ɪntə'dʒekʃən] *n* Ausruf *m*

interlock [ɪntə'lɔk] *vi* ineinander greifen

interlude ['ɪntəluːd] *n* Pause *f*

intermediary [ɪntə'miːdɪən] *n* Vermittler *m*

intermediate [ɪntə'miːdɪət] *adj* Zwischen-, Mittel-

interminable [ɪn'təːmɪnəbl] *adj* endlos

intermission [ɪntə'mɪʃən] *n* Pause *f*

intermittent [ɪntə'mɪtnt] *adj* periodisch, stoßweise

intern [*vb* ɪn'tɜːn, *n* 'ɪntɜːn] *vt* internieren ♦ *n* (US) Assistenzarzt *m*/-ärztin *f*

internal [ɪn'tɜːnl] *adj* (*inside*) innere(r, s); (*domestic*) Inlands-; **~ly** *adv* innen; (MED) innerlich; **"not to be taken ~ly"** „nur zur äußerlichen Anwendung"; **Internal Revenue Service** (US) *n* Finanzamt *nt*

international [ɪntə'næʃənl] *adj* international ♦ *n* (SPORT) Nationalspieler(in) *m(f)*; (: *match*) internationale(s) Spiel *nt*

Internet ['ɪntənɛt] *n*: **the ~** das Internet; **~ café** *n* Internet-Café *nt*

interplay ['ɪntəpleɪ] *n* Wechselspiel *nt*

interpret [ɪn'tɜːprɪt] *vt* (*explain*) auslegen, interpretieren; (*translate*) dolmetschen; **~er** *n* Dolmetscher(in) *m(f)*

interrelated [ɪntərɪ'leɪtɪd] *adj* untereinander zusammenhängend

interrogate [ɪn'terəʊgeɪt] *vt* verhören; **interrogation** [ɪnterəʊ'geɪʃən] *n* Verhör *nt*

interrupt [ɪntə'rʌpt] *vt* unterbrechen; **~ion** [ɪntə'rʌpʃən] *n* Unterbrechung *f*

intersect [ɪntə'sekt] *vt* (durch)schneiden ♦ *vi* sich schneiden; **~ion** [ɪntə'sekʃən] *n* (of *roads*) Kreuzung *f*; (of *lines*) Schnittpunkt *m*

intersperse [ɪntə'spɜːs] *vt*: **to ~ sth with sth** etw mit etw durchsetzen

intertwine [ɪntə'twaɪn] *vt* verflechten ♦ *vi* sich verflechten

interval ['ɪntəvl] *n* Abstand *m*; (BRIT: THEAT, SPORT) Pause *f*; **at ~s** in Abständen

intervene [ɪntə'viːn] *vi* dazwischenliegen; (*act*): **to ~ (in)** einschreiten (gegen); **intervention** [ɪntə'venʃən] *n* Eingreifen *nt*, Intervention *f*

interview ['ɪntəvjuː] *n* (PRESS etc) Interview *nt*; (for *job*) Vorstellungsgespräch *nt* ♦ *vt* interviewen; **~er** *n* Interviewer *m*

intestine [ɪn'testɪn] *n*: **large/small ~** Dick-/Dünndarm *m*

intimacy ['ɪntɪməsɪ] *n* Intimität *f*

intimate [*adj* 'ɪntɪmɪt, *vb* 'ɪntɪmeɪt] *adj* (*inmost*) innerste(r, s); (*knowledge*) eingehend; (*familiar*) vertraut; (*friends*) eng ♦ *vt* andeuten

intimidate [ɪn'tɪmɪdeɪt] *vt* einschüchtern

into ['ɪntu] *prep* (*motion*) in +*acc* ... hinein; **5 ~ 25** 25 durch 5

intolerable [ɪn'tɔlərəbl] *adj* unerträglich

intolerant [ɪn'tɔlərnt] *adj*: **~ of** unduldsam gegen(über)

intoxicate [ɪn'tɔksɪkeɪt] *vt* berauschen; **~d** *adj* betrunken; **intoxication** [ɪntɔksɪ'keɪʃən] *n* Rausch *m*

intractable [ɪn'træktəbl] *adj* schwer zu handhaben; (*problem*) schwer lösbar

intranet ['ɪntrənɛt] *n* Intranet *nt*

intransitive [ɪn'trænsɪtɪv] *adj* intransitiv

intravenous [ɪntrə'viːnəs] *adj* intravenös

in-tray ['ɪntreɪ] *n* Eingangskorb *m*

intrepid [ɪn'trepɪd] *adj* unerschrocken

intricate ['ɪntrɪkət] *adj* kompliziert

intrigue [ɪn'triːg] *n* Intrige *f* ♦ *vt* faszinieren ♦ *vi* intrigieren

intrinsic [ɪn'trɪnsɪk] *adj* innere(r, s); (*difference*) wesentlich

introduce [ɪntrə'djuːs] *vt* (*person*) vorstellen; (*sth new*) einführen; (*subject*) anschneiden; **to ~ sb to sb** jdm jdn vorstellen; **to ~ sb to sth** jdn in etw *acc* einführen; **introduction** [ɪntrə'dʌkʃən] *n* Einführung *f*; (to *book*) Einleitung *f*; **introductory** [ɪntrə'dʌktərɪ] *adj* Einführungs-, Vor-

introspective [ɪntrəʊ'spektɪv] *adj* nach innen gekehrt

introvert ['ɪntrəʊvɜːt] *n* Introvertierte(r) *mf* ♦ *adj* introvertiert

intrude [ɪn'truːd] *vi*: **to ~ (on sb/sth)** (jdn/etw) stören; **~r** *n* Eindringling *m*

intrusion [ɪn'truːʒən] *n* Störung *f*

intrusive [ɪn'truːsɪv] *adj* aufdringlich

intuition [ɪntjuː'ɪʃən] *n* Intuition *f*

inundate ['ɪnʌndeɪt] *vt* überschwemmen

invade [ɪn'veɪd] *vt* einfallen in +*acc*; **~r** *n* Eindringling *m*

invalid¹ ['ɪnvəlɪd] *n* (*disabled*) Invalide *m* ♦ *adj* (*ill*) krank; (*disabled*) invalide

invalid² [ɪn'vælɪd] *adj* (*not valid*) ungültig

invaluable [ɪn'væljuəbl] *adj* unschätzbar

invariable [ɪn'veərɪəbl] *adj* unveränderlich; **invariably** *adv* ausnahmslos

invent [ɪn'vent] *vt* erfinden; **~ion** [ɪn'venʃən]

n Erfindung *f;* **~ive** *adj* erfinderisch; **~or** *n* Erfinder *m*

inventory ['ɪnvəntrɪ] *n* Inventar *nt*

inverse [ɪn'vɜːs] *n* Umkehrung *f* ♦ *adj* umgekehrt

invert [ɪn'vɜːt] *vt* umdrehen; **~ed commas** (*BRIT*) *npl* Anführungsstriche *pl*

invest [ɪn'vest] *vt* investieren

investigate [ɪn'vestɪgeɪt] *vt* untersuchen; **investigation** [ɪnvestɪ'geɪʃən] *n* Untersuchung *f;* **investigator** [ɪn'vestɪgeɪtəʳ] *n* Untersuchungsbeamte(r) *m*

investiture [ɪn'vestɪtʃəʳ] *n* Amtseinsetzung *f*

investment [ɪn'vestmənt] *n* Investition *f*

investor [ɪn'vestəʳ] *n* (Geld)anleger *m*

invigilate [ɪn'vɪdʒɪleɪt] *vi* (*in exam*) Aufsicht führen ♦ *vt* Aufsicht führen bei

invigorating [ɪn'vɪgəreɪtɪŋ] *adj* stärkend

invincible [ɪn'vɪnsɪbl] *adj* unbesiegbar

invisible [ɪn'vɪzɪbl] *adj* unsichtbar

invitation [ɪnvɪ'teɪʃən] *n* Einladung *f*

invite [ɪn'vaɪt] *vt* einladen

invoice ['ɪnvɔɪs] *n* Rechnung *f* ♦ *vt* (*goods*): **to ~ sb for sth** jdm etw *acc* in Rechnung stellen

invoke [ɪn'vəuk] *vt* anrufen

involuntary [ɪn'vɔləntrɪ] *adj* unabsichtlich

involve [ɪn'vɔlv] *vt* (*entangle*) verwickeln; (*entail*) mit sich bringen; **~d** *adj* verwickelt; **~ment** *n* Verwicklung *f*

inward ['ɪnwəd] *adj* innere(r, s); (*curve*) Innen- ♦ *adv* nach innen; **~ly** *adv* im Innern; **~s** *adv* nach innen

I/O *abbr* (*COMPUT*) (= *input/output*) I/O

iodine ['aɪəudiːn] *n* Jod *nt*

ioniser ['aɪənaɪzəʳ] *n* Ionisator *m*

iota [aɪ'əutə] *n* (*fig*) bisschen *nt*

IOU *n abbr* (= *I owe you*) Schuldschein *m*

IQ *n abbr* (= *intelligence quotient*) IQ *m*

IRA *n abbr* (= *Irish Republican Army*) IRA *f*

Iran [ɪ'rɑːn] *n* Iran *m;* **~ian** [ɪ'reɪnɪən] *adj* iranisch ♦ *n* Iraner(in) *m(f);* (*LING*) Iranisch *nt*

Iraq [ɪ'rɑːk] *n* Irak *m;* **~i** *adj* irakisch ♦ *n* Iraker(in) *m(f)*

irate [aɪ'reɪt] *adj* zornig

Ireland ['aɪələnd] *n* Irland *nt*

iris ['aɪrɪs] (*pl* **~es**) *n* Iris *f*

Irish ['aɪrɪʃ] *adj* irisch ♦ *npl:* **the ~** die Iren *pl,* die Irländer *pl;* **~man** (*irreg*) *n* Ire *m,* Irländer *m;* **~ Sea** *n:* **the ~ Sea** die Irische See *f;* **~woman** (*irreg*) *n* Irin *f,* Irländerin *f*

irksome ['ɜːksəm] *adj* lästig

iron ['aɪən] *n* Eisen *nt;* (*for ~ing*) Bügeleisen *nt* ♦ *adj* eisern ♦ *vt* bügeln; **~ out** *vt* (*also fig*) ausbügeln; **Iron Curtain** *n* (*HIST*) Eiserne(r) Vorhang *m*

ironic(al) [aɪ'rɔnɪk(l)] *adj* ironisch; (*coincidence etc*) witzig

iron: ~ing *n* Bügeln *nt;* (*laundry*) Bügelwäsche *f;* **~ing board** *n* Bügelbrett *nt;* **~monger's (shop)** *n* Eisen- und Haushaltswarenhandlung *f*

irony ['aɪrənɪ] *n* Ironie *f*

irrational [ɪ'ræʃənl] *adj* irrational

irreconcilable [ɪrekən'saɪləbl] *adj* unvereinbar

irrefutable [ɪrɪ'fjuːtəbl] *adj* unwiderlegbar

irregular [ɪ'regjuləʳ] *adj* unregelmäßig; (*shape*) ungleich(mäßig); (*fig*) unüblich; (*: behaviour*) ungehörig

irrelevant [ɪ'reləvənt] *adj* belanglos, irrelevant

irreparable [ɪ'reprəbl] *adj* nicht wieder gutzumachen

irreplaceable [ɪrɪ'pleɪsəbl] *adj* unersetzlich

irresistible [ɪrɪ'zɪstɪbl] *adj* unwiderstehlich

irrespective [ɪrɪ'spektɪv]: **~ of** *prep* ungeachtet *+gen*

irresponsible [ɪrɪ'spɔnsɪbl] *adj* verantwortungslos

irreverent [ɪ'revərnt] *adj* respektlos

irrevocable [ɪ'revəkəbl] *adj* unwiderrufbar

irrigate ['ɪrɪgeɪt] *vt* bewässern

irritable ['ɪrɪtəbl] *adj* reizbar

irritate ['ɪrɪteɪt] *vt* irritieren, reizen (*also MED*); **irritating** *adj* ärgerlich, irritierend; **he is irritating** er kann einem auf die Nerven gehen; **irritation** [ɪrɪ'teɪʃən] *n* (*anger*) Ärger *m;* (*MED*) Reizung *f*

IRS *n abbr* = **Internal Revenue Service**

is [ɪz] *vb see* **be**

Islam ['ɪzlɑːm] *n* Islam *m;* **~ic** [ɪz'læmɪk] *adj* islamisch

island ['aɪlənd] n Insel f; **~er** n Inselbewohner(in) m(f)

isle [aɪl] n (kleine) Insel f

isn't ['ɪznt] = **is not**

isolate ['aɪsəleɪt] vt isolieren; **~d** adj isoliert; (case) Einzel-; **isolation** [aɪsə'leɪʃən] n Isolierung f

ISP n abbr (= Internet Service Provider) Internet-Anbieter m

Israel ['ɪzreɪl] n Israel nt; **~i** [ɪz'reɪlɪ] adj israelisch ♦ n Israeli mf

issue ['ɪʃjuː] n (matter) Frage f; (outcome) Ausgang m; (of newspaper, shares) Ausgabe f; (offspring) Nachkommenschaft f ♦ vt ausgeben; (warrant) erlassen; (documents) ausstellen; (orders) erteilen; (books) herausgeben; (verdict) aussprechen; **to be at ~** zur Debatte stehen; **to take ~ with sb over sth** jdm in etw dat widersprechen

---

KEYWORD

it [ɪt] pron 1 (specific: subject) er/sie/es; (: direct object) ihn/sie/es; (: indirect object) ihm/ihr/ihm; **about/from/in/of it** darüber/davon/darin/davon

2 (impers) es; **it's raining** es regnet; **it's Friday tomorrow** morgen ist Freitag; **who is it? - it's me** wer ist da? - ich (bins)

Italian [ɪ'tæljən] adj italienisch ♦ n Italiener(in) m(f); (LING) Italienisch nt

italic [ɪ'tælɪk] adj kursiv; **~s** npl Kursivschrift f

Italy ['ɪtəlɪ] n Italien nt

itch [ɪtʃ] n Juckreiz m; (fig) Lust f ♦ vi jucken; **to be ~ing to do sth** darauf brennen, etw zu tun; **~y** adj juckend

it'd ['ɪtd] = **it would; it had**

item ['aɪtəm] n Gegenstand m; (on list) Posten m; (in programme) Nummer f; (in agenda) (Programm)punkt m; (in newspaper) (Zeitungs)notiz f; **~ize** vt verzeichnen

itinerant [ɪ'tɪnərənt] adj umherreisend

itinerary [aɪ'tɪnərərɪ] n Reiseroute f

it'll ['ɪtl] = **it will; it shall**

its [ɪts] adj (masculine, neuter) sein; (feminine) ihr

it's [ɪts] = **it is; it has**

itself [ɪt'sɛlf] pron sich (selbst); (emphatic) selbst

ITV (BRIT) n abbr = **Independent Television**

I.U.D. n abbr (= intra-uterine device) Pessar nt

I've [aɪv] = **I have**

ivory ['aɪvərɪ] n Elfenbein nt

ivy ['aɪvɪ] n Efeu nt

J, j

jab [dʒæb] vt (hinein)stechen ♦ n Stich m, Stoß m; (inf) Spritze f

jack [dʒæk] n (AUT) (Wagen)heber m; (CARDS) Bube m; **~ up** vt aufbocken

jackal ['dʒækl] n (ZOOL) Schakal m

jackdaw ['dʒækdɔː] n Dohle f

jacket ['dʒækɪt] n Jacke f; (of book) Schutzumschlag m; (TECH) Ummantelung f; **~ potatoes** npl in der Schale gebackene Kartoffeln pl

jackknife ['dʒæknaɪf] vi (truck) sich zusammenschieben

jack plug n (ELEC) Buchsenstecker m

jackpot ['dʒækpɒt] n Haupttreffer m

jaded ['dʒeɪdɪd] adj ermattet

jagged ['dʒægɪd] adj zackig

jail [dʒeɪl] n Gefängnis nt ♦ vt einsperren; **~er** n Gefängniswärter m

jam [dʒæm] n Marmelade f; (also: **traffic ~**) (Verkehrs)stau m; (inf: trouble) Klemme f ♦ vt (wedge) einklemmen; (cram) hineinzwängen; (obstruct) blockieren ♦ vi sich verklemmen; **to ~ sth into sth** etw in etw acc hineinstopfen

Jamaica [dʒə'meɪkə] n Jamaika nt

jam jar n Marmeladenglas nt

jammed [dʒæmd] adj: **it's ~** es klemmt

jam-packed [dʒæm'pækt] adj überfüllt, proppenvoll

jangle ['dʒæŋgl] vt, vi klimpern

janitor ['dʒænɪtər] n Hausmeister m

January ['dʒænjuərɪ] n Januar m

Japan [dʒə'pæn] n Japan nt; **~ese** [dʒæpə'niːz] adj japanisch ♦ n inv Japaner(in) m(f); (LING) Japanisch nt

jar [dʒɑːr] n Glas nt ♦ vi kreischen; (colours

etc) nicht harmonieren

jargon ['dʒɑːgən] *n* Fachsprache *f*, Jargon *m*

jaundice ['dʒɔːndɪs] *n* Gelbsucht *f*; **~d** *adj* (*fig*) missgünstig

jaunt [dʒɔːnt] *n* Spritztour *f*

javelin ['dʒævlɪn] *n* Speer *m*

jaw [dʒɔː] *n* Kiefer *m*

jay [dʒeɪ] *n* (*ZOOL*) Eichelhäher *m*

jaywalker ['dʒeɪwɔːkəʳ] *n* unvorsichtige(r) Fußgänger *m*

jazz [dʒæz] *n* Jazz *m*; **~ up** *vt* (*MUS*) verjazzen; (*enliven*) aufpolieren

jealous ['dʒeləs] *adj* (*envious*) missgünstig; (*husband*) eifersüchtig; **~y** *n* Missgunst *f*; Eifersucht *f*

jeans [dʒiːnz] *npl* Jeans *pl*

Jeep [dʒiːp] ® *n* Jeep *m* ®

jeer [dʒɪəʳ] *vi*: **to ~ (at sb)** (über jdn) höhnisch lachen, (jdn) verspotten

Jehovah's Witness [dʒɪ'həʊvəz-] *n* Zeuge *m*/Zeugin *f* Jehovas

jelly ['dʒelɪ] *n* Gelee *nt*; (*dessert*) Grütze *f*; **~fish** *n* Qualle *f*

jeopardize ['dʒepədaɪz] *vt* gefährden

jeopardy ['dʒepədɪ] *n*: **to be in jeopardy** in Gefahr sein

jerk [dʒɜːk] *n* Ruck *m*; (*inf: idiot*) Trottel *m* ♦ *vt* ruckartig bewegen ♦ *vi* sich ruckartig bewegen

jerky ['dʒɜːkɪ] *adj* (*movement*) ruckartig; (*ride*) rüttelnd

jersey ['dʒɜːzɪ] *n* Pullover *m*

jest [dʒest] *n* Scherz *m* ♦ *vi* spaßen; **in ~** im Spaß

Jesus ['dʒiːzəs] *n* Jesus *m*

jet [dʒet] *n* (*stream: of water etc*) Strahl *m*; (*spout*) Düse *f*; (*AVIAT*) Düsenflugzeug *nt*; **~-black** *adj* rabenschwarz; **~ engine** *n* Düsenmotor *m*; **~ lag** *n* Jetlag *m*

jettison ['dʒetɪsn] *vt* über Bord werfen

jetty ['dʒetɪ] *n* Landesteg *m*, Mole *f*

Jew [dʒuː] *n* Jude *m*

jewel ['dʒuːəl] *n* (*also fig*) Juwel *nt*; **~ler** (*US* **jeweler**) *n* Juwelier *m*; **~ler's (shop)** *n* Juwelier *m*; **~lery** (*US* **jewelry**) *n* Schmuck *m*

Jewess ['dʒuːɪs] *n* Jüdin *f*

Jewish ['dʒuːɪʃ] *adj* jüdisch

jibe [dʒaɪb] *n* spöttische Bemerkung *f*

jiffy ['dʒɪfɪ] (*inf*) *n*: **in a ~** sofort

jigsaw ['dʒɪgsɔː] *n* (*also*: **~ puzzle**) Puzzle(spiel) *nt*

jilt [dʒɪlt] *vt* den Laufpass geben +*dat*

jingle ['dʒɪŋgl] *n* (*advertisement*) Werbesong *m* ♦ *vi* klimpern; (*bells*) bimmeln ♦ *vt* klimpern mit; bimmeln lassen

jinx [dʒɪŋks] *n*: **there's a ~ on it** es ist verhext

jitters ['dʒɪtəz] (*inf*) *npl*: **to get the ~** einen Bammel kriegen

job [dʒɔb] *n* (*piece of work*) Arbeit *f*; (*position*) Stellung *f*; (*duty*) Aufgabe *f*; (*difficulty*) Mühe *f*; **it's a good ~ he ...** es ist ein Glück, dass er ...; **just the ~** genau das Richtige; **J~centre** (*BRIT*) *n* Arbeitsamt *nt*; **~less** *adj* arbeitslos

jockey ['dʒɔkɪ] *n* Jockei *m*, Jockey *m* ♦ *vi*: **to ~ for position** sich in eine gute Position drängen

jocular ['dʒɔkjʊləʳ] *adj* scherzhaft

jog [dʒɔg] *vt* (an)stoßen ♦ *vi* (*run*) joggen; **to ~ along** vor sich *acc* hinwursteln; (*work*) seinen Gang gehen; **~ging** *n* Jogging *nt*

join [dʒɔɪn] *vt* (*club*) beitreten +*dat*; (*person*) sich anschließen +*dat*; (*fasten*): **to ~ (sth to sth)** (etw mit etw) verbinden ♦ *vi* (*unite*) sich vereinigen ♦ *n* Verbindungsstelle *f*, Naht *f*; **~ in** *vt*, *vi*: **to ~ in (sth)** (bei etw) mitmachen; **~ up** *vi* (*MIL*) zur Armee gehen

joiner ['dʒɔɪnəʳ] *n* Schreiner *m*; **~y** *n* Schreinerei *f*

joint [dʒɔɪnt] *n* (*TECH*) Fuge *f*; (*of bones*) Gelenk *nt*; (*of meat*) Braten *m*; (*inf: place*) Lokal *nt* ♦ *adj* gemeinsam; **~ account** *n* (*with bank etc*) gemeinsame(s) Konto *nt*; **~ly** *adv* gemeinsam

joke [dʒəʊk] *n* Witz *m* ♦ *vi* Witze machen; **to play a ~ on sb** jdm einen Streich spielen

joker [dʒəʊkəʳ] *n* Witzbold *m*; (*CARDS*) Joker *m*

jolly ['dʒɔlɪ] *adj* lustig ♦ *adv* (*inf*) ganz schön

jolt [dʒəʊlt] *n* (*shock*) Schock *m*; (*jerk*) Stoß *m*

♦ vt (push) stoßen; (shake) durchschütteln; (fig) aufrütteln ♦ vi holpern

Jordan ['dʒɔːdən] n Jordanien nt

jostle ['dʒɔsl] vt anrempeln

jot [dʒɔt] n: **not one ~** kein Jota nt; **~ down** vt notieren; **~ter** (BRIT) n Notizblock m

journal ['dʒɜːnl] n (diary) Tagebuch nt; (magazine) Zeitschrift f; **~ism** n Journalismus m; **~ist** n Journalist(in) m(f)

journey ['dʒɜːnɪ] n Reise f

jovial ['dʒəuvɪəl] adj jovial

joy [dʒɔɪ] n Freude f; **~ful** adj freudig; **~ous** adj freudig; **~ ride** n Schwarzfahrt f; **~rider** n Autodieb, der den Wagen nur für eine Spritztour stiehlt; **~stick** n Steuerknüppel m; (COMPUT) Joystick m

J.P. n abbr = **Justice of the Peace**

Jr abbr = **junior**

jubilant ['dʒuːbɪlnt] adj triumphierend

jubilee ['dʒuːbɪliː] n Jubiläum nt

judge [dʒʌdʒ] n Richter m; (fig) Kenner m ♦ vt (JUR: person) die Verhandlung führen über +acc; (case) verhandeln; (assess) beurteilen; (estimate) einschätzen; **~ment** n (JUR) Urteil nt; (ECCL) Gericht nt; (ability) Urteilsvermögen nt

judicial [dʒuːˈdɪʃl] adj gerichtlich, Justiz-

judiciary [dʒuːˈdɪʃərɪ] n Gerichtsbehörden pl; (judges) Richterstand m

judicious [dʒuːˈdɪʃəs] adj weise

judo ['dʒuːdəu] n Judo nt

jug [dʒʌg] n Krug m

juggernaut ['dʒʌgənɔːt] (BRIT) n (huge truck) Schwertransporter m

juggle ['dʒʌgl] vt, vi jonglieren; **~r** n Jongleur m

Jugoslav etc ['juːgəuˈslɑːv] = **Yugoslav** etc

juice [dʒuːs] n Saft m; **juicy** ['dʒuːsɪ] adj (also fig) saftig

jukebox ['dʒuːkbɔks] n Musikautomat m

July [dʒuːˈlaɪ] n Juli m

jumble ['dʒʌmbl] n Durcheinander nt ♦ vt (also: **~ up**) durcheinander werfen; (facts) durcheinander bringen

jumble sale (BRIT) n Basar m, Flohmarkt m

> **Jumble sale**
>
> ⓘ **Jumble sale** ist ein Wohltätigkeitsbasar, meist in einer Aula oder einem Gemeindehaus abgehalten, bei dem alle möglichen Gebrauchtwaren (vor allem Kleidung, Spielzeug, Bücher, Geschirr und Möbel) verkauft werden. Der Erlös fließt entweder einer Wohltätigkeitsorganisation zu oder wird für örtliche Zwecke verwendet, z.B. die Pfadfinder, die Grundschule, Reparatur der Kirche usw.

---

jumbo (jet) ['dʒʌmbəu-] n Jumbo(jet) m

jump [dʒʌmp] vi springen; (nervously) zusammenzucken ♦ vt überspringen ♦ n Sprung m; **to ~ the queue** (BRIT) sich vordrängeln

jumper ['dʒʌmpəʳ] n (BRIT: pullover) Pullover m; (US: dress) Trägerkleid nt

jump leads BRIT, **jumper cables** US npl Überbrückungskabel nt

jumpy ['dʒʌmpɪ] adj nervös

Jun. abbr = **junior**

junction ['dʒʌŋkʃən] n (BRIT: of roads) (Straßen)kreuzung f; (RAIL) Knotenpunkt m

juncture ['dʒʌŋktʃəʳ] n: **at this ~** in diesem Augenblick

June [dʒuːn] n Juni m

jungle ['dʒʌŋgl] n Dschungel m

junior ['dʒuːnɪəʳ] adj (younger) jünger; (after name) junior; (SPORT) Junioren-; (lower position) untergeordnet; (for young people) Junioren- ♦ n Jüngere(r) mf; **~ school** (BRIT) n Grundschule f

junk [dʒʌŋk] n (rubbish) Plunder m; (ship) Dschunke f; **~ bond** n (COMM) niedrig eingestuftes Wertpapier mit hohen Ertragschancen bei erhöhtem Risiko; **~ food** n Junk food nt; **~ mail** n Reklame, die unangefordert in den Briefkasten gesteckt wird; **~ shop** n Ramschladen m

Junr abbr = **junior**

jurisdiction [dʒuərɪsˈdɪkʃən] n Gerichtsbarkeit f; (range of authority) Zuständigkeit(sbereich m) f

juror [ˈdʒuərəʳ] *n* Geschworene(r) *mf*; (*in competition*) Preisrichter *m*

jury [ˈdʒuərɪ] *n* (*court*) Geschworene *pl*; (*panel*) Jury *f*

just [dʒʌst] *adj* gerecht ♦ *adv* (*recently, now*) gerade, eben; (*barely*) gerade noch; (*exactly*) genau, gerade; (*only*) nur, bloß; (*a small distance*) gleich; (*absolutely*) einfach; ~ **as I arrived** gerade als ich ankam; ~ **as nice** genauso nett; ~ **as well** umso besser; ~ **now** soeben, gerade; ~ **try** versuch es mal; **she's** ~ **left** sie ist gerade *or* (so)eben gegangen; **he's** ~ **done it** er hat es gerade *or* (so)eben getan; ~ **before** gerade *or* kurz bevor; ~ **enough** gerade genug; **he** ~ **missed** er hat fast *or* beinahe getroffen

justice [ˈdʒʌstɪs] *n* (*fairness*) Gerechtigkeit *f*; **J~ of the Peace** *n* Friedensrichter *m*

justifiable [dʒʌstɪˈfaɪəbl] *adj* berechtigt

justification [dʒʌstɪfɪˈkeɪʃən] *n* Rechtfertigung *f*

justify [ˈdʒʌstɪfaɪ] *vt* rechtfertigen; (*text*) justieren

justly [ˈdʒʌstlɪ] *adv* (*say*) mit Recht; (*condemn*) gerecht

jut [dʒʌt] *vi* (*also:* ~ **out**) herausragen, vorstehen

juvenile [ˈdʒuːvənaɪl] *adj* (*young*) jugendlich; (*for the young*) Jugend- ♦ *n* Jugendliche(r) *mf*

juxtapose [ˈdʒʌkstəpəuz] *vt* nebeneinander stellen

K, k

K [keɪ] *abbr* (= *one thousand*) Tsd.; (= *kilobyte*) K

kangaroo [kæŋgəˈruː] *n* Känguru *nt*

karate [kəˈrɑːtɪ] *n* Karate *nt*

kebab [kəˈbæb] *n* Kebab *m*

keel [kiːl] *n* Kiel *m*; **on an even** ~ (*fig*) im Lot

keen [kiːn] *adj* begeistert; (*wind, blade, intelligence*) scharf; (*sight, hearing*) gut; **to be** ~ **to do** *or* **on doing sth** etw unbedingt tun wollen; **to be** ~ **on sth/sb** scharf auf etw/jdn sein

keep [kiːp] (*pt, pp* **kept**) *vt* (*retain*) behalten; (*have*) haben; (*animals, one's word*) halten; (*support*) versorgen; (*maintain in state*) halten; (*preserve*) aufbewahren; (*restrain*) abhalten ♦ *vi* (*continue in direction*) sich halten; (*food*) sich halten; (*remain: quiet etc*) bleiben ♦ *n* Unterhalt *m*; (*tower*) Burgfried *m*; (*inf*): **for** ~**s** für immer; **to** ~ **sth to o.s.** etw für sich behalten; **it** ~**s happening** es passiert immer wieder; ~ **back** *vt* fern halten; (*information*) verschweigen; ~ **on** *vi*: ~ **on doing sth** etw immer weiter tun; ~ **out** *vt* nicht hereinlassen; "~ **out**" „Eintritt verboten!"; ~ **up** *vi* Schritt halten ♦ *vt* aufrechterhalten; (*continue*) weitermachen; **to** ~ **up with** Schritt halten mit; ~**er** *n* Wärter(in) *m(f)*; (*goalkeeper*) Torhüter(in) *m(f)*; ~**-fit** *n* Keep-fit *nt*; ~**ing** *n* (*care*) Obhut *f*; **in** ~**ing with** in Übereinstimmung mit; ~**sake** *n* Andenken *nt*

keg [kɛg] *n* Fass *nt*

kennel [ˈkɛnl] *n* Hundehütte *f*; ~**s** *npl*: **to put a dog in** ~**s** (*for boarding*) einen Hund in Pflege geben

Kenya [ˈkɛnjə] *n* Kenia *nt*; ~**n** *adj* kenianisch ♦ *n* Kenianer(in) *m(f)*

kept [kɛpt] *pt, pp* of **keep**

kerb [kɜːb] *n* (*BRIT*) Bordstein *m*

kernel [ˈkɜːnl] *n* Kern *m*

kerosene [ˈkɛrəsiːn] *n* Kerosin *nt*

kettle [ˈkɛtl] *n* Kessel *m*; ~**drum** *n* Pauke *f*

key [kiː] *n* Schlüssel *m*; (*of piano, typewriter*) Taste *f*; (*MUS*) Tonart *f* ♦ *vt* (*also:* ~ **in**) eingeben; ~**board** *n* Tastatur *f*; ~**ed up** *adj* (*person*) überdreht; ~**hole** *n* Schlüsselloch *nt*; ~**hole surgery** *n* minimal invasive Chirurgie *f*, Schlüssellochchirurgie *f*; ~**note** *n* Grundton *m*; ~ **ring** *n* Schlüsselring *m*

khaki [ˈkɑːkɪ] *n* K(h)aki *nt* ♦ *adj* k(h)aki(farben)

kick [kɪk] *vt* einen Fußtritt geben +*dat*, treten ♦ *vi* treten; (*baby*) strampeln; (*horse*) ausschlagen ♦ *n* (Fuß)tritt *m*; (*thrill*) Spaß *m*; **he does it for** ~**s** er macht das aus Jux;

~ off vi (SPORT) anstoßen; **~-off** n (SPORT) Anstoß m

kid [kɪd] n (inf: child) Kind nt; (goat) Zicklein nt; (leather) Glacéleder nt, Glaceeleder nt ♦ vi (inf) Witze machen

kidnap ['kɪdnæp] vt entführen; **~per** n Entführer m; **~ping** n Entführung f

kidney ['kɪdnɪ] n Niere f

kill [kɪl] vt töten, umbringen ♦ vi töten ♦ n (hunting) (Jagd)beute f; **~er** n Mörder(in) m(f); **~ing** n Mord m; **~joy** n Spaßverderber(in) m(f)

kiln [kɪln] n Brennofen m

kilo ['ki:ləʊ] n Kilo nt; **~byte** n (COMPUT) Kilobyte nt; **~gram(me)** n Kilogramm nt; **~metre** ['kɪləmi:tə'] (US **kilometer**) n Kilometer m; **~watt** n Kilowatt nt

kilt [kɪlt] n Schottenrock m

kind [kaɪnd] adj freundlich ♦ n Art f; **a ~ of** eine Art von; **(two) of a ~** (zwei) von der gleichen Art; **in ~** auf dieselbe Art; (in goods) in Naturalien

kindergarten ['kɪndəgɑːtn] n Kindergarten m

kind-hearted [kaɪnd'hɑːtɪd] adj gutherzig

kindle ['kɪndl] vt (set on fire) anzünden; (rouse) reizen, (er)wecken

kindly ['kaɪndlɪ] adj freundlich ♦ adv liebenswürdig(erweise); **would you ~ ...?** wären Sie so freundlich und ...?

kindness ['kaɪndnɪs] n Freundlichkeit f

kindred ['kɪndrɪd] adj: **~ spirit** Gleichgesinnte(r) mf

king [kɪŋ] n König m; **~dom** n Königreich nt

kingfisher ['kɪŋfɪʃə'] n Eisvogel m

king-size(d) ['kɪŋsaɪz(d)] adj (cigarette) Kingsize

kinky ['kɪŋkɪ] (inf) adj (person, ideas) verrückt; (sexual) abartig

kiosk ['ki:ɔsk] (BRIT) n (TEL) Telefonhäuschen nt

kipper ['kɪpə'] n Räucherhering m

kiss [kɪs] n Kuss m ♦ vt küssen ♦ vi: **they ~ed** sie küssten sich; **~ of life** (BRIT) n: **the ~ of life** Mund-zu-Mund-Beatmung f

kit [kɪt] n Ausrüstung f; (tools) Werkzeug nt

kitchen ['kɪtʃɪn] n Küche f; **~ sink** n Spülbecken nt

kite [kaɪt] n Drachen m

kitten ['kɪtn] n Kätzchen nt

kitty ['kɪtɪ] n (money) Kasse f

km abbr (= kilometre) km

knack [næk] n Dreh m, Trick m

knapsack ['næpsæk] n Rucksack m; (MIL) Tornister m

knead [ni:d] vt kneten

knee [ni:] n Knie nt; **~cap** n Kniescheibe f

kneel [ni:l] (pt, pp **knelt**) vi (also: **~ down**) knien

knelt [nɛlt] pt, pp of **kneel**

knew [nju:] pt of **know**

knickers ['nɪkəz] (BRIT) npl Schlüpfer m

knife [naɪf] (pl **knives**) n Messer nt ♦ vt erstechen

knight [naɪt] n Ritter m; (chess) Springer m; **~hood** n (title): **to get a ~hood** zum Ritter geschlagen werden

knit [nɪt] vt stricken ♦ vi stricken; (bones) zusammenwachsen; **~ting** n (occupation) Stricken nt; (work) Strickzeug nt; **~ting needle** n Stricknadel f; **~wear** n Strickwaren pl

knives [naɪvz] pl of **knife**

knob [nɔb] n Knauf m; (on instrument) Knopf m; (BRIT: of butter etc) kleine(s) Stück nt

knock [nɔk] vt schlagen; (criticize) heruntermachen ♦ vi: **to ~ at** or **on the door** an die Tür klopfen ♦ n Schlag m; (on door) Klopfen nt; **~ down** vt umwerfen; (with car) anfahren; **~ off** vt (do quickly) hinhauen; (inf: steal) klauen ♦ vi (finish) Feierabend machen; **~ out** vt ausschlagen; (BOXING) k. o. schlagen; **~ over** vt (person, object) umwerfen; (with car) anfahren; **~er** n (on door) Türklopfer m; **~out** n K.-o.-Schlag m; (fig) Sensation f

knot [nɔt] n Knoten m ♦ vt (ver)knoten

knotty ['nɔtɪ] adj (fig) kompliziert

know [nəʊ] (pt **knew**, pp **known**) vt, vi wissen; (be able to) können; (be acquainted with) kennen; (recognize) erkennen; **to ~ how to do sth** wissen, wie man etw macht, etw tun können; **to ~ about** or **of sth/sb** etw/jdn kennen; **~-all** n Alleswisser

m; **~-how** *n* Kenntnis *f,* Know-how *nt;*
~ing *adj (look, smile)* wissend; **~ingly** *adv*
wissend; *(intentionally)* wissentlich
knowledge ['nɔlɪdʒ] *n* Wissen *nt,* Kenntnis
f; **~able** *adj* informiert
known [nəʊn] *pp of* **know**
knuckle ['nʌkl] *n* Fingerknöchel *m*
K.O. *n abbr =* **knockout**
Koran [kɔ'rɑːn] *n* Koran *m*
Korea [kə'rɪə] *n* Korea *nt*
kosher ['kəʊfəʳ] *adj* koscher

L, l

L [ɛl] *abbr (BRIT: AUT) (= learner)* am Auto
angebrachtes Kennzeichen für Fahrschüler; =
lake; *(= large)* gr.; *(= left)* l.
l. *abbr =* **litre**
lab [læb] *(inf) n* Labor *nt*
label ['leɪbl] *n* Etikett *nt ♦ vt* etikettieren
labor *etc* ['leɪbəʳ] *(US) =* **labour** *etc*
laboratory [lə'bɔrətərɪ] *n* Laboratorium *nt*
laborious [lə'bɔːrɪəs] *adj* mühsam
labour ['leɪbəʳ] *(US* **labor**) *n* Arbeit *f;*
(workmen) Arbeitskräfte *pl;* (*MED)* Wehen *pl*
♦ vi: **to ~ (at)** sich abmühen (mit) *♦ vt*
breittreten *(inf);* **in ~** (*MED)* in den Wehen;
L~ *(BRIT: also:* **the L~ party**) die Labour
Party; **~ed** *adj (movement)* gequält; *(style)*
schwerfällig; **~er** *n* Arbeiter *m;* **farm ~er**
(Land)arbeiter *m*
lace [leɪs] *n (fabric)* Spitze *f;* (*of shoe)*
Schnürsenkel *m;* (*braid)* Litze *f ♦ vt (also: ~*
up) (zu)schnüren
lack [læk] *n* Mangel *m ♦ vt* nicht haben; **sb**
~s sth jdm fehlt etw *nom;* **to be ~ing**
fehlen; **sb is ~ing in sth** es fehlt jdm an
etw *dat;* **for** *or* **through ~ of** aus Mangel an
+dat
lacquer ['lækəʳ] *n* Lack *m*
lad [læd] *n* Junge *m*
ladder ['lædəʳ] *n* Leiter *f;* (*BRIT: in tights)*
Laufmasche *f ♦ vt (BRIT: tights)* Laufmaschen
bekommen in *+dat*
laden ['leɪdn] *adj* beladen, voll
ladle ['leɪdl] *n* Schöpfkelle *f*

lady ['leɪdɪ] *n* Dame *f;* (*title)* Lady *f;* **young ~**
junge Dame; **the ladies' (room)** die
Damentoilette; **~bird** *(US* **~bug**) *n*
Marienkäfer *m;* **~like** *adj* damenhaft,
vornehm; **~ship** *n:* **your L~ship** Ihre
Ladyschaft
lag [læg] *vi (also: ~* **behind**) zurückbleiben
♦ vt (pipes) verkleiden
lager ['lɑːgəʳ] *n* helle(s) Bier *nt*
lagging ['lægɪŋ] *n* Isolierung *f*
lagoon [lə'guːn] *n* Lagune *f*
laid [leɪd] *pt, pp of* **lay**; **~ back** *(inf) adj* cool
lain [leɪn] *pp of* **lie**
lair [lɛəʳ] *n* Lager *nt*
lake [leɪk] *n* See *m*
lamb [læm] *n* Lamm *nt;* (*meat)* Lammfleisch
nt; **~ chop** *n* Lammkotelett *nt;* **~swool** *n*
Lammwolle *f*
lame [leɪm] *adj* lahm; *(excuse)* faul
lament [lə'mɛnt] *n* Klage *f ♦ vt* beklagen
laminated ['læmɪneɪtɪd] *adj* beschichtet
lamp [læmp] *n* Lampe *f;* (*in street)*
Straßenlaterne *f;* **~post** *n* Laternenpfahl *m;*
~shade *n* Lampenschirm *m*
lance [lɑːns] *n* Lanze *f;* **~ corporal** *(BRIT) n*
Obergefreite(r) *m*
land [lænd] *n* Land *nt ♦ vi (from ship)* an
Land gehen; *(AVIAT, end up)* landen *♦ vt*
(obtain) kriegen; *(passengers)* absetzen;
(goods) abladen; *(troops, space probe)*
landen; **~fill site** ['lændfɪl-] *n* Mülldeponie
f; **~ing** *n* Landung *f;* (*on stairs)*
(Treppen)absatz *m;* **~ing gear** *n*
Fahrgestell *nt;* **~ing stage** *(BRIT) n*
Landesteg *m;* **~ing strip** *n* Landebahn *f;*
~lady *n* (Haus)wirtin *f;* **~locked** *adj*
landumschlossen, Binnen-; **~lord** *n (of*
house) Hauswirt *m,* Besitzer *m;* (*of pub)*
Gastwirt *m;* (*of area)* Grundbesitzer *m;*
~mark *n* Wahrzeichen *nt;* (*fig)* Meilenstein
m; **~owner** *n* Grundbesitzer *m;* **~scape** *n*
Landschaft *f;* **~ gardener** *n*
Landschaftsgärtner(in) *m(f);* **~slide** *n*
(GEOG) Erdrutsch *m;* (*POL)*
überwältigende(r) Sieg *m*
lane [leɪn] *n (in town)* Gasse *f;* (*in country)*
Weg *m;* (*of motorway)* Fahrbahn *f,* Spur *f;*

(SPORT) Bahn f; **"get in ~"** „bitte einordnen"

language ['læŋgwɪdʒ] n Sprache f; **bad ~** unanständige Ausdrücke pl; **~ laboratory** n Sprachlabor nt

languish ['læŋgwɪʃ] vi schmachten

lank [læŋk] adj dürr

lanky ['læŋkɪ] adj schlaksig

lantern ['læntən] n Laterne f

lap [læp] n Schoß m; (SPORT) Runde f ♦ vt (also: ~ **up**) auflecken ♦ vi (water) plätschern

lapel [lə'pɛl] n Revers nt or m

Lapland ['læplænd] n Lappland nt

lapse [læps] n (moral) Fehltritt m ♦ vi (decline) nachlassen; (expire) ablaufen; (claims) erlöschen; **to ~ into bad habits** sich schlechte Gewohnheiten angewöhnen

laptop (computer) ['læptɔp-] n Laptop(-Computer) m

lard [lɑːd] n Schweineschmalz nt

larder ['lɑːdəʳ] n Speisekammer f

large [lɑːdʒ] adj groß; **at ~** auf freiem Fuß; **~ly** adv zum größten Teil; **~-scale** adj groß angelegt, Groß-

lark [lɑːk] n (bird) Lerche f; (joke) Jux m; **~ about** (inf) vi herumalbern

laryngitis [lærɪn'dʒaɪtɪs] n Kehlkopfentzündung f

laser ['leɪzəʳ] n Laser m; **~ printer** n Laserdrucker m

lash [læʃ] n Peitschenhieb m; (eyelash) Wimper f ♦ vt (rain) schlagen gegen; (whip) peitschen; (bind) festbinden; **~ out** vi (with fists) um sich schlagen

lass [læs] n Mädchen nt

lasso [læ'suː] n Lasso nt

last [lɑːst] adj letzte(r, s) ♦ adv zuletzt; (~ time) das letzte Mal ♦ vi (continue) dauern; (remain good) sich halten; (money) ausreichen; **at ~** endlich; **~ night** gestern Abend; **~ week** letzte Woche; **~ but one** vorletzte(r, s); **~-ditch** adj (attempt) in letzter Minute; **~ing** adj dauerhaft; (shame etc) andauernd; **~ly** adv schließlich; **~-minute** adj in letzter Minute

latch [lætʃ] n Riegel m

late [leɪt] adj spät; (dead) verstorben ♦ adv spät; (after proper time) zu spät; **to be ~** zu spät kommen; **of ~** in letzter Zeit; **in ~ May** Ende Mai; **~comer** n Nachzügler(in) m(f); **~ly** adv in letzter Zeit; **later** ['leɪtəʳ] adj (date) später; (version) neuer ♦ adv später

lateral ['lætərəl] adj seitlich

latest ['leɪtɪst] adj (fashion) neueste(r, s) ♦ n (news) Neu(e)ste(s) nt; **at the ~** spätestens

lathe [leɪð] n Drehbank f

lather ['lɑːðəʳ] n (Seifen)schaum m ♦ vt einschäumen ♦ vi schäumen

Latin ['lætɪn] n Latein nt ♦ adj lateinisch; (Roman) römisch; **~ America** n Lateinamerika nt; **~ American** adj lateinamerikanisch

latitude ['lætɪtjuːd] n (GEOG) Breite f; (freedom) Spielraum m

latter ['lætəʳ] adj (second of two) letztere; (coming at end) letzte(r, s), später ♦ n: **the ~** der/die/das letztere, die letzteren; **~ly** adv in letzter Zeit

lattice ['lætɪs] n Gitter nt

laudable ['lɔːdəbl] adj löblich

laugh [lɑːf] n Lachen nt ♦ vi lachen; **~ at** vt lachen über +acc; **~ off** vt lachend abtun; **~able** adj lachhaft; **~ing stock** n Zielscheibe f des Spottes; **~ter** n Gelächter nt

launch [lɔːntʃ] n (of ship) Stapellauf m; (of rocket) Abschuss m; (boat) Barkasse f; (of product) Einführung f ♦ vt (set afloat) vom Stapel lassen; (rocket) (ab)schießen; (product) auf den Markt bringen; **~(ing) pad** n Abschussrampe f

launder ['lɔːndəʳ] vt waschen

Launderette [lɔːn'drɛt] (® BRIT) n Waschsalon m

Laundromat ['lɔːndrəmæt] (® US) n Waschsalon m

laundry ['lɔːndrɪ] n (place) Wäscherei f; (clothes) Wäsche f; **to do the ~** waschen

laureate ['lɔːrɪət] adj see **poet**

laurel ['lɔrl] n Lorbeer m

lava ['lɑːvə] n Lava f

lavatory ['lævətərɪ] n Toilette f

lavender ['lævəndər] n Lavendel m

lavish ['lævɪʃ] adj (extravagant) verschwenderisch; (generous) großzügig ♦ vt (money): **to ~ sth on sth** etw auf etw acc verschwenden; (attention, gifts): **to ~ sth on sb** jdn mit etw überschütten

law [lɔː] n Gesetz nt; (system) Recht nt; (as studies) Jura no art; **~-abiding** adj gesetzestreu; **~ and order** n Recht nt und Ordnung f; **~ court** n Gerichtshof m; **~ful** adj gesetzlich; **~less** adj gesetzlos

lawn [lɔːn] n Rasen m; **~mower** n Rasenmäher m; **~ tennis** n Rasentennis m

law: ~ school n Rechtsakademie f; **~suit** n Prozess m; **~yer** n Rechtsanwalt m, Rechtsanwältin f

lax [læks] adj (behaviour) nachlässig; (standards) lax

laxative ['læksətɪv] n Abführmittel nt

lay [leɪ] (pt, pp laid) pt of **lie** ♦ adj Laien- ♦ vt (place) legen; (table) decken; (egg) legen; (trap) stellen; (money) wetten; **~ aside** vt zurücklegen; **~ by** (set aside) beiseite legen; **~ down** vt hinlegen; (rules) vorschreiben; (arms) strecken; **to ~ down the law** Vorschriften machen; **~ off** vt (workers) (vorübergehend) entlassen; **~ on** vt (water, gas) anschließen; (concert etc) veranstalten; **~ out** vt (her)auslegen; (money) ausgeben; (corpse) aufbahren; **~ up** vt (subj: illness) ans Bett fesseln; **~about** n Faulenzer m; **~-by** (BRIT) n Parkbucht f; (bigger) Rastplatz m

layer ['leɪər] n Schicht f

layman ['leɪmən] (irreg) n Laie m

layout ['leɪaʊt] n Anlage f; (ART) Lay-out nt, Layout nt

laze [leɪz] vi faulenzen

laziness ['leɪzɪnɪs] n Faulheit f

lazy ['leɪzɪ] adj faul; (slow-moving) träge

lb. abbr = pound (weight)

lead¹ [lɛd] n (chemical) Blei nt; (of pencil) (Bleistift)mine f ♦ adj bleiern, Blei-

lead² [liːd] (pt, pp led) n (front position) Führung f; (distance, time ahead) Vorsprung f; (example) Vorbild nt; (clue) Tipp m; (of police) Spur f; (THEAT) Hauptrolle f; (dog's)

Leine f ♦ vt (guide) führen; (group etc) leiten ♦ vi (be first) führen; **in the ~** (SPORT, fig) in Führung; **~ astray** vt irreführen; **~ away** vt wegführen; (prisoner) abführen; **~ back** vi zurückführen; **~ on** vt anführen; **~ on to** vt (induce) dazu bringen; **~ to** vt (street) (hin)führen nach; (result in) führen zu; **~ up to** vt (drive) führen zu; (speaker etc) hinführen auf +acc

leaded petrol ['lɛdɪd-] n verbleites Benzin nt

leaden ['lɛdn] adj (sky, sea) bleiern; (heavy: footsteps) bleischwer

leader ['liːdər] n Führer m, Leiter m; (of party) Vorsitzende(r) m; (PRESS) Leitartikel m; **~ship** n (office) Leitung f; (quality) Führerschaft f

lead-free ['lɛdfriː] adj (petrol) bleifrei

leading ['liːdɪŋ] adj führend; **~ lady** n (THEAT) Hauptdarstellerin f; **~ light** n (person) führende(r) Geist m

lead singer [liːd-] n Leadsänger(in) m(f)

leaf [liːf] (pl leaves) n Blatt nt ♦ vi: **to ~ through** durchblättern; **to turn over a new ~** einen neuen Anfang machen

leaflet ['liːflɪt] n (advertisement) Prospekt m; (pamphlet) Flugblatt nt; (for information) Merkblatt nt

league [liːg] n (union) Bund m; (SPORT) Liga f; **to be in ~ with** unter einer Decke stecken mit

leak [liːk] n undichte Stelle f; (in ship) Leck nt ♦ vt (liquid etc) durchlassen ♦ vi (pipe etc) undicht sein; (liquid etc) auslaufen; **the information was ~ed to the enemy** die Information wurde dem Feind zugespielt; **~ out** vi (liquid etc) auslaufen; (information) durchsickern; **~y** ['liːkɪ] adj undicht

lean [liːn] (pt, pp leaned or leant) adj mager ♦ vi sich neigen ♦ vt (an)lehnen; **to ~ against sth** an etw dat angelehnt sein; sich an etw acc anlehnen; **~ back** vi sich zurücklehnen; **~ forward** vi sich vorbeugen; **~ on** vt fus sich stützen auf +acc; **~ out** vi sich hinauslehnen; **~ over** vi sich hinüberbeugen; **~ing** n Neigung f ♦ adj schief; **~t** [lɛnt] pt, pp of **lean**; **~-to** n

Anbau m

leap [liːp] (pt, pp **leaped** or **leapt**) n Sprung m ♦ vi springen; **~frog** n Bockspringen nt; **~t** [lept] pt, pp of leap; **~ year** n Schaltjahr nt

learn [ləːn] (pt, pp **learned** or **learnt**) vt, vi lernen; (find out) erfahren; **to ~ how to do sth** etw (er)lernen; **~ed** ['ləːnɪd] adj gelehrt; **~er** n Anfänger(in) m(f); (AUT: BRIT: also: **~er driver**) Fahrschüler(in) m(f); **~ing** n Gelehrsamkeit f; **~t** [ləːnt] pt, pp of **learn**

lease [liːs] n (of property) Mietvertrag m ♦ vt pachten

leash [liːʃ] n Leine f

least [liːst] adj geringste(r, s) ♦ adv am wenigsten ♦ n Mindeste(s) nt; **the ~ possible effort** möglichst geringer Aufwand; **at ~** zumindest; **not in the ~!** durchaus nicht!

leather ['lɛðər] n Leder nt

leave [liːv] (pt, pp **left**) vt verlassen; (~ behind) zurücklassen; (forget) vergessen; (allow to remain) lassen; (after death) hinterlassen; (entrust): **to ~ sth to sb** jdm etw überlassen ♦ vi weggehen, wegfahren; (for journey) abreisen; (bus, train) abfahren ♦ n Erlaubnis f; (MIL) Urlaub m; **to be left** (remain) übrig bleiben; **there's some milk left over** es ist noch etwas Milch übrig; **on ~** auf Urlaub; **~ behind** vt (person, object) dalassen; (forget) liegen lassen, stehen lassen; **~ out** vt auslassen; **~ of absence** n Urlaub m

leaves [liːvz] pl of **leaf**

Lebanon ['lɛbənən] n Libanon m

lecherous ['lɛtʃərəs] adj lüstern

lecture ['lɛktʃər] n Vortrag m; (UNIV) Vorlesung f ♦ vi einen Vortrag halten; (UNIV) lesen ♦ vt (scold) abkanzeln; **to give a ~ on sth** einen Vortrag über etw halten; **~r** ['lɛktʃərər] n Vortragende(r) mf; (BRIT: UNIV) Dozent(in) m(f)

led [lɛd] pt, pp of **lead²**

ledge [lɛdʒ] n Leiste f; (window ~) Sims m or nt; (of mountain) (Fels)vorsprung m

ledger ['lɛdʒər] n Hauptbuch nt

leech [liːtʃ] n Blutegel m

leek [liːk] n Lauch m

leer [lɪər] vi: **to ~ (at sb)** (nach jdm) schielen

leeway ['liːweɪ] n (fig): **to have some ~** etwas Spielraum haben

left [lɛft] pt, pp of leave ♦ adj linke(r, s) ♦ n (side) linke Seite f ♦ adv links; **on the ~** links; **to the ~** nach links; **the L~** (POL) die Linke f; **~-hand** adj: **~-hand drive** mit Linkssteuerung; **~-handed** adj linkshändig; **~-hand side** n linke Seite f; **~-luggage locker** n Gepäckschließfach nt; **~-luggage (office)** (BRIT) n Gepäckaufbewahrung f; **~-overs** npl Reste pl; **~-wing** adj linke(r, s)

leg [lɛg] n Bein nt; (of meat) Keule f; (stage) Etappe f; **1st/2nd ~** (SPORT) 1./2. Etappe

legacy ['lɛgəsɪ] n Erbe nt, Erbschaft f

legal ['liːgl] adj gesetzlich; (allowed) legal; **~ holiday** (US) n gesetzliche(r) Feiertag m; **~ize** vt legalisieren; **~ly** adv gesetzlich; legal; **~ tender** n gesetzliche(s) Zahlungsmittel nt

legend ['lɛdʒənd] n Legende f; **~ary** adj legendär

leggings ['lɛgɪnz] npl Leggings pl

legible ['lɛdʒəbl] adj leserlich

legislation [lɛdʒɪs'leɪʃən] n Gesetzgebung f; **legislative** ['lɛdʒɪslətɪv] adj gesetzgebend; **legislature** ['lɛdʒɪslətʃər] n Legislative f

legitimate [lɪ'dʒɪtɪmət] adj rechtmäßig, legitim; (child) ehelich

legroom ['lɛgruːm] n Platz m für die Beine

leisure ['lɛʒər] n Freizeit f; **to be at ~** Zeit haben; **~ centre** n Freizeitzentrum nt; **~ly** adj gemächlich

lemon ['lɛmən] n Zitrone f; (colour) Zitronengelb nt; **~ade** [lɛmə'neɪd] n Limonade f; **~ tea** n Zitronentee m

lend [lɛnd] (pt, pp **lent**) vt leihen; **to ~ sb sth** jdm etw leihen; **~ing library** n Leihbibliothek f

length [lɛŋθ] n Länge f; (of road, pipe etc) Strecke f; (of material) Stück nt; **at ~** (lengthily) ausführlich; (at last) schließlich; **~en** vt verlängern ♦ vi länger werden; **~ways** adv längs; **~y** adj sehr lang, langatmig

lenient ['liːnɪənt] adj nachsichtig

lens [lɛnz] *n* Linse *f*; (*PHOT*) Objektiv *nt*

Lent [lɛnt] *n* Fastenzeit *f*

lent [lɛnt] *pt, pp of* **lend**

lentil ['lɛntɪl] *n* Linse *f*

Leo ['liːəu] *n* Löwe *m*

leotard ['liːətɑːd] *n* Trikot *nt*, Gymnastikanzug *m*

leper ['lɛpəʳ] *n* Leprakranke(r) *f(m)*

leprosy ['lɛprəsɪ] *n* Lepra *f*

lesbian ['lɛzbɪən] *adj* lesbisch ♦ *n* Lesbierin *f*

less [lɛs] *adj, adv* weniger ♦ *n* weniger ♦ *pron* weniger; **~ than half** weniger als die Hälfte; **~ than ever** weniger denn je; **~ and ~** immer weniger; **the ~ he works** je weniger er arbeitet; **~en** ['lɛsn] *vi* abnehmen ♦ *vt* verringern, verkleinern; **~er** ['lɛsəʳ] *adj* kleiner, geringer; **to a ~er extent** in geringerem Maße

lesson ['lɛsn] *n* (*SCH*) Stunde *f*; (*unit of study*) Lektion *f*; (*fig*) Lehre *f*; (*ECCL*) Lesung *f*; **a maths ~** eine Mathestunde

lest [lɛst] *conj*: **~ it happen** damit es nicht passiert

let [lɛt] (*pt, pp* **let**) *vt* lassen; (*BRIT*: *lease*) vermieten; **to ~ sb do sth** jdn etw tun lassen; **to ~ sb know sth** jdn etw wissen lassen; **~'s go!** gehen wir!; **~ him come** soll er doch kommen; **~ down** *vt* hinunterlassen; (*disappoint*) enttäuschen; **~ go** *vi* loslassen ♦ *vt* (*things*) loslassen; (*person*) gehen lassen; **~ in** *vt* hereinlassen; (*water*) durchlassen; **~ off** *vt* (*gun*) abfeuern; (*steam*) ablassen; (*forgive*) laufen lassen; **~ on** *vi* durchblicken lassen; (*pretend*) vorgeben; **~ out** *vt* herauslassen; (*scream*) fahren lassen; **~ up** *vi* nachlassen; (*stop*) aufhören

lethal ['liːθl] *adj* tödlich

lethargic [lɛ'θɑːdʒɪk] *adj* lethargisch

letter ['lɛtəʳ] *n* Brief *m*; (*of alphabet*) Buchstabe *m*; **~ bomb** *n* Briefbombe *f*; **~box** (*BRIT*) *n* Briefkasten *m*; **~ing** *n* Beschriftung *f*; **~ of credit** *n* Akkreditiv *m*

lettuce ['lɛtɪs] *n* (Kopf)salat *m*

let-up ['lɛtʌp] (*inf*) *n* Nachlassen *nt*

leukaemia [luː'kiːmɪə] (*US* **leukemia**) *n* Leukämie *f*

level ['lɛvl] *adj* (*ground*) eben; (*at same height*) auf gleicher Höhe; (*equal*) gleich gut; (*head*) kühl ♦ *adv* auf gleicher Höhe ♦ *n* (*instrument*) Wasserwaage *f*; (*altitude*) Höhe *f*; (*flat place*) ebene Fläche *f*; (*position on scale*) Niveau *nt*; (*amount, degree*) Grad *m* ♦ *vt* (*ground*) einebnen; **to draw ~ with** gleichziehen mit; **to be ~ with** auf einer Höhe sein mit; **A ~s** (*BRIT*) ≃ Abitur *nt*; **O ~s** (*BRIT*) ≃ mittlere Reife *f*; **on the ~** (*fig*: *honest*) ehrlich; **to ~ sth at sb** (*blow*) etw versetzen; (*remark*) etw gegen jdn richten; **~ off** *or* **out** *vi* flach *or* eben werden; (*fig*) sich (*angleichen*; (*plane*) horizontal fliegen ♦ *vt* (*ground*) planieren; (*differences*) ausgleichen; **~ crossing** (*BRIT*) *n* Bahnübergang *m*; **~-headed** *adj* vernünftig

lever ['liːvəʳ] *n* Hebel *m*; (*fig*) Druckmittel *nt* ♦ *vt* (*hoch*)stemmen; **~age** *n* Hebelkraft *f*; (*fig*) Einfluss *m*

levy ['lɛvɪ] *n* (*of taxes*) Erhebung *f*; (*tax*) Abgaben *pl*; (*MIL*) Aushebung *f* ♦ *vt* erheben; (*MIL*) ausheben

lewd [luːd] *adj* unzüchtig, unanständig

liability [laɪə'bɪlətɪ] *n* (*burden*) Belastung *f*; (*duty*) Pflicht *f*; (*debt*) Verpflichtung *f*; (*responsibility*) Haftung *f*; (*proneness*) Anfälligkeit *f*

liable ['laɪəbl] *adj* (*responsible*) haftbar; (*prone*) anfällig; **to be ~ for sth** etw *dat* unterliegen; **it's ~ to happen** es kann leicht vorkommen

liaise [liː'eɪz] *vi*: **to ~ (with sb)** (mit jdm) zusammenarbeiten; **liaison** *n* Verbindung *f*

liar ['laɪəʳ] *n* Lügner *m*

libel ['laɪbl] *n* Verleumdung *f* ♦ *vt* verleumden

liberal ['lɪbərl] *adj* (*generous*) großzügig; (*open-minded*) aufgeschlossen; (*POL*) liberal

liberate ['lɪbəreɪt] *vt* befreien; **liberation** [lɪbə'reɪʃən] *n* Befreiung *f*

liberty ['lɪbətɪ] *n* Freiheit *f*; (*permission*) Erlaubnis *f*; **to be at ~ to do sth** etw tun dürfen; **to take the ~ of doing sth** sich *dat* erlauben, etw zu tun

Libra ['liːbrə] *n* Waage *f*

librarian [laɪˈbrɛərɪən] n Bibliothekar(in) m(f)

library [ˈlaɪbrərɪ] n Bibliothek f; (lending ~) Bücherei f

Libya [ˈlɪbɪə] n Libyen nt; **~n** adj libysch ♦ n Libyer(in) m(f)

lice [laɪs] npl of **louse**

licence [ˈlaɪsns] (US **license**) n (permit) Erlaubnis f; (also: **driving ~**, (US) **driver's ~**) Führerschein m

license [ˈlaɪsns] n (US) = **licence** ♦ vt genehmigen, konzessionieren; **~d** adj (for alcohol) konzessioniert (für den Alkoholausschank); **~ plate** (US) n (AUT) Nummernschild nt

lichen [ˈlaɪkən] n Flechte f

lick [lɪk] vt lecken ♦ n Lecken nt; **a ~ of paint** ein bisschen Farbe

licorice [ˈlɪkərɪs] (US) n = **liquorice**

lid [lɪd] n Deckel m; (eyelid) Lid nt

lie [laɪ] (pt **lay**, pp **lain**) vi (rest, be situated) liegen; (put o.s. in position) sich legen; (pt, pp lied: tell lies) lügen ♦ n Lüge f; **to ~ low** (fig) untertauchen; **~ about** vi (things) herumliegen; (people) faulenzen; **~-down** (BRIT) n: **to have a ~-down** ein Nickerchen machen; **~-in** (BRIT) n: **to have a ~-in** sich ausschlafen

lieu [luː] n: **in ~ of** anstatt +gen

lieutenant [lefˈtɛnənt, (US) luːˈtɛnənt] n Leutnant m

life [laɪf] (pl **lives**) n Leben nt; **~ assurance** (BRIT) n = **life insurance**; **~belt** (BRIT) n Rettungsring m; **~boat** n Rettungsboot nt; **~guard** n Rettungsschwimmer m; **~ insurance** n Lebensversicherung f; **~ jacket** n Schwimmweste f; **~less** adj (dead) leblos; (dull) langweilig; **~like** adj lebenswahr, naturgetreu; **~line** n Rettungsleine f; (fig) Rettungsanker m; **~long** adj lebenslang; **~ preserver** (US) n = **lifebelt**; **~-saver** n Lebensretter(in) m(f); **~-saving** adj lebensrettend, Rettungs-; **~ sentence** n lebenslängliche Freiheitsstrafe f; **~ span** n Lebensspanne f; **~-style** n Lebensstil m; **~ support system** n (MED) Lebenserhaltungssystem nt; **~time** n: **in his ~time** während er lebte; **once in a**

~time einmal im Leben

lift [lɪft] vt hochheben ♦ vi sich heben ♦ n (BRIT: elevator) Aufzug m, Lift m; **to give sb a ~** jdn mitnehmen; **~-off** n Abheben nt (vom Boden)

ligament [ˈlɪgəmənt] n Band nt

light [laɪt] (pt, pp **lighted** or **lit**) n Licht nt; (for cigarette etc): **have you got a ~?** haben Sie Feuer? ♦ vt beleuchten; (lamp) anmachen; (fire, cigarette) anzünden ♦ adj (bright) hell; (pale) hell-; (not heavy, easy) leicht; (punishment) milde; (touch) leicht; **~s** npl (AUT) Beleuchtung f; **~ up** vi (lamp) angehen; (face) aufleuchten ♦ vt (illuminate) beleuchten; (~s) anmachen; **~ bulb** n Glühbirne f; **~en** vi (brighten) hell werden; (~ning) blitzen ♦ vt (give ~ to) erhellen; (hair) aufhellen; (gloom) aufheitern; (make less heavy) leichter machen; (fig) erleichtern; **~er** n Feuerzeug nt; **~-headed** adj (thoughtless) leichtsinnig; (giddy) schwindlig; **~-hearted** adj leichtherzig, fröhlich; **~house** n Leuchtturm m; **~ing** n Beleuchtung f; **~ly** adv leicht; (irresponsibly) leichtfertig; **to get off ~ly** mit einem blauen Auge davonkommen; **~ness** n (of weight) Leichtigkeit f; (of colour) Helle f

lightning [ˈlaɪtnɪŋ] n Blitz m; **~ conductor** (US **~ rod**) n Blitzableiter m

light: **~ pen** n Lichtstift m; **~weight** adj (suit) leicht; **~weight** n (BOXING) Leichtgewichtler m; **~ year** n Lichtjahr nt

like [laɪk] vt mögen, gern haben ♦ prep wie ♦ adj (similar) ähnlich; (equal) gleich ♦ n: **the ~** dergleichen; **I would** or **I'd ~** ich möchte gern; **would you ~ a coffee?** möchten Sie einen Kaffee?; **to be** or **look ~ sb/sth** jdm/etw ähneln; **that's just ~ him** das ist typisch für ihn; **do it ~ this** mach es so; **it is nothing ~ ...** es ist nicht zu vergleichen mit ...; **what does it look ~?** wie sieht es aus?; **what does it sound ~?** wie hört es sich an?; **what does it taste ~?** wie schmeckt es?; **his ~s and dislikes** was er mag und was er nicht mag; **~able** adj sympathisch

likelihood [ˈlaɪklɪhud] n Wahrscheinlichkeit f

likely ['laɪklɪ] *adj* wahrscheinlich; **he's ~ to leave** er geht möglicherweise; **not ~!** wohl kaum!

likeness ['laɪknɪs] *n* Ähnlichkeit *f*; (*portrait*) Bild *nt*

likewise ['laɪkwaɪz] *adv* ebenso

liking ['laɪkɪŋ] *n* Zuneigung *f*; (*taste*) Vorliebe *f*

lilac ['laɪlək] *n* Flieder *m* ♦ *adj* (*colour*) fliederfarben

lily ['lɪlɪ] *n* Lilie *f*; **~ of the valley** *n* Maiglöckchen *nt*

limb [lɪm] *n* Glied *nt*

limber up ['lɪmbər-] *vi* sich auflockern; (*fig*) sich vorbereiten

limbo ['lɪmbəu] *n*: **to be in ~** (*fig*) in der Schwebe sein

lime [laɪm] *n* (*tree*) Linde *f*; (*fruit*) Limone *f*; (*substance*) Kalk *m*

limelight ['laɪmlaɪt] *n*: **to be in the ~** (*fig*) im Rampenlicht stehen

limestone ['laɪmstəun] *n* Kalkstein *m*

limit ['lɪmɪt] *n* Grenze *f*; (*inf*) Höhe *f* ♦ *vt* begrenzen, einschränken; **~ation** [lɪmɪ'teɪʃən] *n* Einschränkung *f*; **~ed** *adj* beschränkt; **to be ~ed to** sich beschränken auf +*acc*; **~ed (liability) company** (*BRIT*) *n* Gesellschaft *f* mit beschränkter Haftung

limousine ['lɪməziːn] *n* Limousine *f*

limp [lɪmp] *n* Hinken *nt* ♦ *vi* hinken ♦ *adj* schlaff

limpet ['lɪmpɪt] *n* (*fig*) Klette *f*

line [laɪn] *n* Linie *f*; (*rope*) Leine *f*; (*on face*) Falte *f*; (*row*) Reihe *f*; (*of hills*) Kette *f*; (*US: queue*) Schlange *f*; (*company*) Linie *f*, Gesellschaft *f*; (*RAIL*) Strecke *f*; (*TEL*) Leitung *f*; (*written*) Zeile *f*; (*direction*) Richtung *f*; (*fig: business*) Branche *f*; (*range of items*) Kollektion *f* ♦ *vt* (*coat*) füttern; (*border*) säumen; **~s** *npl* (*RAIL*) Gleise *pl*; **in ~ with** in Übereinstimmung mit; **~ up** *vi* sich aufstellen ♦ *vt* aufstellen; (*prepare*) sorgen für; (*support*) mobilisieren; (*surprise*) planen; **~ar** ['lɪnɪər] *adj* gerade; (*measure*) Längen-; **~d** *adj* (*face*) faltig; (*paper*) liniert

linen ['lɪnɪn] *n* Leinen *nt*; (*sheets etc*) Wäsche *f*

liner ['laɪnər] *n* Überseedampfer *m*

linesman ['laɪnzmən] (*irreg*) *n* (*SPORT*) Linienrichter *m*

line-up ['laɪnʌp] *n* Aufstellung *f*

linger ['lɪŋgər] *vi* (*remain long*) verweilen; (*taste*) (zurück)bleiben; (*delay*) zögern, verharren

lingerie ['lænʒəriː] *n* Damenunterwäsche *f*

lingering ['lɪŋgərɪŋ] *adj* (*doubt*) zurückbleibend; (*disease*) langwierig; (*taste*) nachhaltend; (*look*) lang

lingo ['lɪŋgəu] (*pl* **~es**) (*inf*) *n* Sprache *f*

linguist ['lɪŋgwɪst] *n* Sprachkundige(r) *mf*; (*UNIV*) Sprachwissenschaftler(in) *m(f)*; **~ic** [lɪŋ'gwɪstɪk] *adj* sprachlich; sprachwissenschaftlich; **~ics** *n* Sprachwissenschaft *f*, Linguistik *f*

lining ['laɪnɪŋ] *n* Futter *nt*

link [lɪŋk] *n* Glied *nt*; (*connection*) Verbindung *f* ♦ *vt* verbinden; **~s** *npl* (*GOLF*) Golfplatz *m*; **~ up** *vt* verbinden ♦ *vi* zusammenkommen; (*companies*) sich zusammenschließen; **~-up** *n* (*TEL*) Verbindung *f*; (*of spaceships*) Kopplung *f*

lino ['laɪnəu] *n* = **linoleum**

linoleum [lɪ'nəuliəm] *n* Linoleum *nt*

linseed oil ['lɪnsiːd-] *n* Leinöl *nt*

lion ['laɪən] *n* Löwe *m*; **~ess** *n* Löwin *f*

lip [lɪp] *n* Lippe *f*; (*of jug*) Schnabel *m*; **to pay ~ service (to)** ein Lippenbekenntnis ablegen (zu)

liposuction ['lɪpəusʌkʃən] *n* Fettabsaugen *nt*

lip: **~read** (*irreg*) *vi* von den Lippen ablesen; **~ salve** *n* Lippenbalsam *m*; **~stick** *n* Lippenstift *m*

liqueur [lɪ'kjuər] *n* Likör *m*

liquid ['lɪkwɪd] *n* Flüssigkeit *f* ♦ *adj* flüssig

liquidate ['lɪkwɪdeɪt] *vt* liquidieren

liquidize ['lɪkwɪdaɪz] *vt* (*COOK*) (im Mixer) pürieren; **~r** ['lɪkwɪdaɪzər] *n* Mixgerät *nt*

liquor ['lɪkər] *n* Alkohol *m*

liquorice ['lɪkərɪs] (*BRIT*) *n* Lakritze *f*

liquor store (*US*) *n* Spirituosengeschäft *nt*

Lisbon ['lɪzbən] *n* Lissabon *f*

lisp [lɪsp] *n* Lispeln *nt* ♦ *vt*, *vi* lispeln

list [lɪst] *n* Liste *f*, Verzeichnis *nt*; (*of ship*) Schlagseite *f* ♦ *vt* (*write down*) eine Liste

machen von; (verbally) aufzählen ♦ vi (ship)
Schlagseite haben

listen ['lɪsn] vi hören; **~ to** vt zuhören +dat;
~er n (Zu)hörer(in) m(f)

listless ['lɪstlɪs] adj lustlos

lit [lɪt] pt, pp of **light**

liter ['liːtə*] (US) n = **litre**

literacy ['lɪtərəsɪ] n Fähigkeit f zu lesen und
zu schreiben

literal ['lɪtərəl] adj buchstäblich; (translation)
wortwörtlich; **~ly** adv wörtlich;
buchstäblich

literary ['lɪtərərɪ] adj literarisch

literate ['lɪtərət] adj des Lesens und
Schreibens kundig

literature ['lɪtrɪtʃə*] n Literatur f

litigation [lɪtɪ'geɪʃən] n Prozess m

litre ['liːtə*] (US **liter**) n Liter m

litter ['lɪtə*] n (rubbish) Abfall m; (of animals)
Wurf m ♦ vt in Unordnung bringen; **to be
~ed with** übersät sein mit; **~ bin** (BRIT) n
Abfalleimer m

little ['lɪtl] adj klein ♦ adv, n wenig; **a ~** ein
bisschen; **~ by ~** nach und nach

live¹ [laɪv] adj lebendig; (MIL) scharf; (ELEC)
geladen; (broadcast) live

live² [lɪv] vi leben; (dwell) wohnen ♦ vt (life)
führen; **~ down** vt: **I'll never ~ it down**
das wird man mir nie vergessen; **~ on** vi
weiterleben ♦ vt fus: **to ~ on sth** von etw
leben; **~ together** vi zusammenleben;
(share a flat) zusammenwohnen; **~ up to**
vt (standards) gerecht werden +dat;
(principles) anstreben; (hopes) entsprechen
+dat

livelihood ['laɪvlɪhud] n Lebensunterhalt m

lively ['laɪvlɪ] adj lebhaft, lebendig

liven up ['laɪvn-] vt beleben

liver ['lɪvə*] n (ANAT) Leber f

lives [laɪvz] pl of **life**

livestock ['laɪvstɔk] n Vieh nt

livid ['lɪvɪd] adj bläulich; (furious)
fuchsteufelswild

living ['lɪvɪŋ] n (Lebens)unterhalt m ♦ adj
lebendig; (language etc) lebend; **to earn** or
make a ~ sich dat seinen Lebensunterhalt
verdienen; **~ conditions** npl

Wohnverhältnisse pl; **~ room** n
Wohnzimmer nt; **~ standards** npl
Lebensstandard m; **~ wage** n
ausreichender Lohn m

lizard ['lɪzəd] n Eidechse f

load [ləud] n (burden) Last f; (amount)
Ladung f ♦ vt (also: **~ up**) (be)laden;
(COMPUT) laden; (camera) Film einlegen in
+acc; (gun) laden; **a ~ of, ~s of** (fig) jede
Menge; **~ed** adj beladen; (dice) präpariert;
(question) Fang-; (inf: rich) steinreich; **~ing
bay** n Ladeplatz m

loaf [ləuf] (pl **loaves**) n Brot nt ♦ vi (also: **~
about, ~ around**) herumlungern, faulenzen

loan [ləun] n (FIN) Darlehen nt
♦ vt leihen; **on ~** geliehen

loath [ləuθ] adj: **to be ~ to do sth** etw
ungern tun

loathe [ləuð] vt verabscheuen

loaves [ləuvz] pl of **loaf**

lobby ['lɔbɪ] n Vorhalle f; (POL) Lobby f ♦ vt
politisch beeinflussen (wollen)

lobster ['lɔbstə*] n Hummer m

local ['ləukl] adj ortsansässig, Orts- ♦ n (pub)
Stammwirtschaft f; **the ~s** npl (people) die
Ortsansässigen pl; **~ anaesthetic** n (MED)
örtliche Betäubung f; **~ authority** n
städtische Behörden pl; **~ call** n (TEL)
Ortsgespräch nt; **~ government** n
Gemeinde-/Kreisverwaltung f; **~ity**
[ləu'kælɪtɪ] n Ort m; **~ly** adv örtlich, am Ort

locate [ləu'keɪt] vt ausfindig machen;
(establish) errichten; **location** [ləu'keɪʃən] n
Platz m, Lage f; **on location** (CINE) auf
Außenaufnahme

loch [lɔx] (SCOTTISH) n See m

lock [lɔk] n Schloss nt; (NAUT) Schleuse f; (of
hair) Locke f ♦ vt (fasten) (ver)schließen ♦ vi
(door etc) sich schließen (lassen); (wheels)
blockieren; **~ up** vt (criminal, mental patient)
einsperren; (house) abschließen

locker ['lɔkə*] n Spind m

locket ['lɔkɪt] n Medaillon nt

lock ['lɔk-]: **~out** n Aussperrung f; **~smith** n
Schlosser(in) m(f); **~up** n (jail) Gefängnis nt;
(garage) Garage f

locum ['ləukəm] n (MED) Vertreter(in) m(f)

lodge [lɔdʒ] *n* (*gatehouse*) Pförtnerhaus *nt*;
(*freemasons'*) Loge *f* ♦ *vi* (*get stuck*) stecken
(bleiben); (*in Untermiete*): **to ~ (with)**
wohnen (bei) ♦ *vt* (*protest*) einreichen; **~r** *n*
(Unter)mieter *m*; **lodgings** *n*
(Miet)wohnung *f*

loft [lɔft] *n* (Dach)boden *m*

lofty ['lɔftɪ] *adj* hoch(ragend); (*proud*)
hochmütig

log [lɔg] *n* Klotz *m*; (*book*) = **logbook**

logbook ['lɔgbʊk] *n* Bordbuch *nt*; (*for lorry*)
Fahrtenschreiber *m*; (*AUT*)
Kraftfahrzeugbrief *m*

loggerheads ['lɔgəhɛdz] *npl*: **to be at ~**
sich in den Haaren liegen

logic ['lɔdʒɪk] *n* Logik *f*; **~al** *adj* logisch

log in *or* **on** *vi* (*COMPUT*) einloggen

log off *or* **out** *vi* (*COMPUT*) ausloggen

logistics [lɔ'dʒɪstɪks] *npl* Logistik *f*

logo ['laʊgəʊ] *n* Firmenzeichen *nt*

loin [lɔɪn] *n* Lende *f*

loiter ['lɔɪtə'] *vi* herumstehen

loll [lɔl] *vi* (*also*: **~ about**) sich rekeln *or*
räkeln

lollipop ['lɔlɪpɔp] *n* (Dauer)lutscher *m*; **~
man/lady** (*irreg*; *BRIT*) *n* ≃ Schülerlotse *m*

> Lollipop man/lady
>
> ⓘ **Lollipop man/lady** *heißen in
> Großbritannien die Männer bzw.
> Frauen, die mit Hilfe eines runden Stopp-
> schildes den Verkehr anhalten, damit Schul-
> kinder die Straße überqueren können. Der
> Name bezieht sich auf die Form des
> Schildes, die an einen Lutscher erinnert.*

lolly ['lɔlɪ] (*inf*) *n* (*sweet*) Lutscher *m*

London ['lʌndən] *n* London *nt*; **~er** *n*
Londoner(in) *m(f)*

lone [ləʊn] *adj* einsam

loneliness ['ləʊnlɪnɪs] *n* Einsamkeit *f*

lonely ['ləʊnlɪ] *adj* einsam

loner ['ləʊnə'] *n* Einzelgänger(in) *m(f)*

long [lɔŋ] *adj* lang; (*distance*) weit ♦ *adv*
lange ♦ *vi*: **to ~ for** sich sehnen nach;
before ♦ *bald*; **as ~ as** solange; **in the ~
run** auf die Dauer; **don't be ~!** beeil dich!;

how ~ is the street? wie lang ist die
Straße?; **how ~ is the lesson?** wie lange
dauert die Stunde?; **6 metres ~** 6 Meter
lang; **6 months ~** 6 Monate lang; **all night
~** die ganze Nacht; **he no ~er comes** er
kommt nicht mehr; **~ ago** vor langer Zeit;
~ before lange vorher; **at ~ last** endlich;
~-distance *adj* Fern-

longevity [lɔn'dʒɛvɪtɪ] *n* Langlebigkeit *f*

long: ~-haired *adj* langhaarig; **~hand** *n*
Langschrift *f*; **~ing** *n* Sehnsucht *f* ♦ *adj*
sehnsüchtig

longitude ['lɔŋgɪtjuːd] *n* Längengrad *m*

long: ~ jump *n* Weitsprung *m*; **~-life** *adj*
(*batteries etc*) mit langer Lebensdauer; **~-
lost** *adj* längst verloren geglaubt; **~-
playing record** *n* Langspielplatte *f*; **~-
range** *adj* Langstrecken-, Fern-; **~-sighted**
adj weitsichtig; **~-standing** *adj* alt, seit
langer Zeit bestehend; **~-suffering** *adj*
schwer geprüft; **~-term** *adj* langfristig; **~
wave** *n* Langwelle *f*; **~-winded** *adj*
langatmig

loo [luː] (*BRIT*: *inf*) *n* Klo *nt*

look [lʊk] *vi* schauen; (*seem*) aussehen;
(*building etc*): **to ~ on to the sea** aufs Meer
gehen ♦ *n* Blick *m*; **~s** *npl* (*appearance*)
Aussehen *nt*; **~ after** *vt* (*care for*) sorgen
für; (*watch*) aufpassen auf +*acc*; **~ at** *vt*
ansehen; (*consider*) sich überlegen; **~ back**
vi sich umsehen; (*fig*) zurückblicken; **~
down on** *vt* (*fig*) herabsehen auf +*acc*; **~
for** *vt* (*seek*) suchen; **~ forward to** *vt* sich
freuen auf +*acc*; (*in letters*): **we ~ forward
to hearing from you** wir hoffen, bald von
Ihnen zu hören; **~ into** *vt* untersuchen; **~
on** *vi* zusehen; **~ out** *vi* hinaussehen; (*take
care*) aufpassen; **~ out for** *vt* Ausschau
halten nach; (*be careful*) Acht geben auf
+*acc*; **~ round** *vi* sich umsehen; **~ to** *vt*
(*take care of*) Acht geben auf +*acc*; (*rely on*)
sich verlassen auf +*acc*; **~ up** *vi* aufblicken;
(*improve*) sich bessern ♦ *vt* (*word*)
nachschlagen; (*person*) besuchen; **~ up to**
vt aufsehen zu; **~out** *n* (*watch*) Ausschau *f*;
(*person*) Wachposten *m*; (*place*) Ausguck *m*;
(*prospect*) Aussichten *pl*; **to be on the ~ out**

for sth nach etw Ausschau halten
loom [luːm] n Webstuhl m ♦ vi sich abzeichnen
loony ['luːnɪ] (inf) n Verrückte(r) mf
loop [luːp] n Schlaufe f; **~hole** n (fig) Hintertürchen nt
loose [luːs] adj lose, locker; (free) frei; (inexact) unpräzise ♦ vt lösen, losbinden; **~ change** n Kleingeld nt; **~ chippings** npl (on road) Rollsplit m; **~ end** n: **to be at a ~ end** (BRIT) or **at ~ ends** (US) nicht wissen, was man tun soll; **~ly** adv locker, lose; **~n** vt lockern, losmachen
loot [luːt] n Beute f ♦ vt plündern
lop off [lɔp-] vt abhacken
lopsided ['lɔp'saɪdɪd] adj schief
lord [lɔːd] n (ruler) Herr m; (BRIT: title) Lord m; **the L~** (God) der Herr; **the (House of) L~s** das Oberhaus; **~ship** n: **Your L~ship** Eure Lordschaft
lorry ['lɔrɪ] (BRIT) n Lastwagen m; **~ driver** (BRIT) n Lastwagenfahrer(in) m(f)
lose [luːz] (pt, pp **lost**) vt verlieren; (chance) verpassen ♦ vi verlieren; **to ~ (time)** (clock) nachgehen; **~r** n Verlierer m
loss [lɔs] n Verlust m; **at a ~** (COMM) mit Verlust; (unable) außerstande, außer Stande
lost [lɔst] pt, pp of **lose** ♦ adj verloren; **~ property** (US ~ **and found**) n Fundsachen pl
lot [lɔt] n (quantity) Menge f; (fate, at auction) Los nt; (inf: people, things) Haufen m; **the ~** alles; (people) alle; **a ~ of** (with sg) viel; (with pl) viele; **~s of** massenhaft, viel(e); **I read a ~** ich lese viel; **to draw ~s for sth** etw verlosen
lotion ['ləuʃən] n Lotion f
lottery ['lɔtərɪ] n Lotterie f
loud [laud] adj laut; (showy) schreiend ♦ adv laut; **~ly** adv laut; **~speaker** n Lautsprecher m
lounge [laundʒ] n (in hotel) Gesellschaftsraum m; (in house) Wohnzimmer nt ♦ vi sich herumlümmeln
louse [laus] (pl **lice**) n Laus f
lousy ['lauzɪ] adj (fig) miserabel
lout [laut] n Lümmel m

louvre ['luːvər] (US **louver**) adj (door, window) Jalousie-
lovable ['lʌvəbl] adj liebenswert
love [lʌv] n Liebe f; (person) Liebling m; (SPORT) null ♦ vt (person) lieben; (activity) gerne mögen; **to be in ~ with sb** in jdn verliebt sein; **to make ~** sich lieben; **for the ~ of** aus Liebe zu; **"15 ~"** (TENNIS) „15 null"; **to ~ to do sth** etw (sehr) gerne tun; **~ affair** n (Liebes)verhältnis nt; **~ letter** n Liebesbrief m; **~ life** n Liebesleben nt
lovely ['lʌvlɪ] adj schön
lover ['lʌvər] n Liebhaber(in) m(f)
loving ['lʌvɪŋ] adj liebend, liebevoll
low [ləu] adj niedrig; (rank) niedere(r, s); (level, note, neckline) tief; (intelligence, density) gering; (vulgar) ordinär; (not loud) leise; (depressed) gedrückt ♦ adv (not high) niedrig; (not loudly) leise ♦ n (~ point) Tiefstand m; (MET) Tief nt; **to feel ~** sich mies fühlen; **to turn (down) ~** leiser stellen; **~ alcohol** adj alkoholarm; **~-calorie** adj kalorienarm; **~-cut** adj (dress) tief ausgeschnitten; **~er** vt herunterlassen; (eyes, gun) senken; (reduce) herabsetzen, senken ♦ vr: **to ~er o.s. to** (fig) sich herablassen zu; **~er sixth** (BRIT) n (SCOL) ≈ zwölfte Klasse; **~-fat** adj fettarm, Mager-; **~lands** npl (GEOG) Flachland nt; **~ly** adj bescheiden; **~-lying** adj tief gelegen
loyal ['lɔɪəl] adj treu; **~ty** n Treue f; **~ty card** n Kundenkarte f
lozenge ['lɔzɪndʒ] n Pastille f
L-plates ['ɛlpleɪts] (BRIT) npl L-Schild nt

L-Plates

ⓘ Als **L-Plates** werden in Großbritannien die weißen Schilder mit einem roten „L" bezeichnet, die an jedem von einem Fahrschüler geführten Fahrzeug befestigt werden müssen. Fahrschüler bekommen einen vorläufigen Führerschein und dürfen damit unter Aufsicht eines erfahrenen Autofahrers auf allen Straßen außer Autobahnen fahren.

Ltd abbr (= limited company) GmbH
lubricant ['luːbrɪkənt] n Schmiermittel nt

lubricate ['lu:brɪkeɪt] *vt* schmieren
lucid ['lu:sɪd] *adj* klar; (*sane*) bei klarem Verstand; (*moment*) licht
luck [lʌk] *n* Glück *nt*; **bad** *or* **hard** *or* **tough ~!** (so ein) Pech!; **good ~!** viel Glück!; **~ily** *adv* glücklicherweise, zum Glück; **~y** *adj* Glücks-; **to be ~y** Glück haben
lucrative ['lu:krətɪv] *adj* einträglich
ludicrous ['lu:dɪkrəs] *adj* grotesk
lug [lʌg] *vt* schleppen
luggage ['lʌgɪdʒ] *n* Gepäck *nt*; **~ rack** *n* Gepäcknetz *nt*
lukewarm ['lu:kwɔ:m] *adj* lauwarm; (*indifferent*) lau
lull [lʌl] *n* Flaute *f* ♦ *vt* einlullen; (*calm*) beruhigen
lullaby ['lʌləbaɪ] *n* Schlaflied *nt*
lumbago [lʌm'beɪgəu] *n* Hexenschuss *m*
lumber ['lʌmbə*r*] *n* Plunder *m*; (*wood*) Holz *nt*; **~jack** *n* Holzfäller *m*
luminous ['lu:mɪnəs] *adj* Leucht-
lump [lʌmp] *n* Klumpen *m*; (*MED*) Schwellung *f*; (*in breast*) Knoten *m*; (*of sugar*) Stück *nt* ♦ *vt* (*also:* **~ together**) zusammentun; (*judge together*) in einen Topf werfen; **~ sum** *n* Pauschalsumme *f*; **~y** *adj* klumpig
lunacy ['lu:nəsɪ] *n* Irrsinn *m*
lunar ['lu:nə*r*] *adj* Mond-
lunatic ['lu:nətɪk] *n* Wahnsinnige(r) *mf* ♦ *adj* wahnsinnig, irr
lunch [lʌntʃ] *n* Mittagessen *nt*; **~eon** ['lʌntʃən] *n* Mittagessen *nt*; **~eon meat** *n* Frühstücksfleisch *nt*; **~eon voucher** (*BRIT*) *n* Essenmarke *f*; **~time** *n* Mittagszeit *f*
lung [lʌŋ] *n* Lunge *f*
lunge [lʌndʒ] *vi* (*also:* **~ forward**) (los)stürzen; **to ~** at sich stürzen auf +*acc*
lurch [lə:tʃ] *vi* taumeln; (*NAUT*) schlingern ♦ *n* Ruck *m*; (*NAUT*) Schlingern *nt*; **to leave sb in the ~** jdn im Stich lassen
lure [luə*r*] *n* Köder *m*; (*fig*) Lockung *f* ♦ *vt* (ver)locken
lurid ['luərɪd] *adj* (*shocking*) grausig, widerlich; (*colour*) grell
lurk [lə:k] *vi* lauern
luscious ['lʌʃəs] *adj* köstlich

lush [lʌʃ] *adj* satt; (*vegetation*) üppig
lust [lʌst] *n* Wollust *f*; (*greed*) Gier *f* ♦ *vi*: **to ~ after** gieren nach
lustre ['lʌstə*r*] (*US* **luster**) *n* Glanz *m*
Luxembourg ['lʌksəmbə:g] *n* Luxemburg *nt*
luxuriant [lʌg'zjuərɪənt] *adj* üppig
luxurious [lʌg'zjuərɪəs] *adj* luxuriös, Luxus-
luxury ['lʌkʃərɪ] *n* Luxus *m* ♦ *cpd* Luxus-
lying ['laɪɪŋ] *n* Lügen *nt* ♦ *adj* verlogen
lynx [lɪŋks] *n* Luchs *m*
lyric ['lɪrɪk] *n* Lyrik *f* ♦ *adj* lyrisch; **~s** *pl* (*words for song*) (Lied)text *m*; **~al** *adj* lyrisch, gefühlvoll

M, m

m *abbr* = **metre**; **mile**; **million**
M.A. *n abbr* = **Master of Arts**
mac [mæk] (*BRIT: inf*) *n* Regenmantel *m*
macaroni [mækə'rəunɪ] *n* Makkaroni *pl*
machine [mə'ʃi:n] *n* Maschine *f* ♦ *vt* (*dress etc*) mit der Maschine nähen; **~ gun** *n* Maschinengewehr *nt*; **~ language** *n* (*COMPUT*) Maschinensprache *f*; **~ry** *n* Maschinerie *f*
macho ['mætʃəu] *adj* macho
mackerel ['mækrl] *n* Makrele *f*
mackintosh ['mækɪntɔʃ] (*BRIT*) *n* Regenmantel *m*
mad [mæd] *adj* verrückt; (*dog*) tollwütig; (*angry*) wütend; **~ about** (*fond of*) verrückt nach, versessen auf +*acc*
madam ['mædəm] *n* gnädige Frau *f*
madden ['mædn] *vt* verrückt machen; (*make angry*) ärgern
made [meɪd] *pt, pp of* **make**
made-to-measure ['meɪdtə'meʒə*r*] (*BRIT*) *adj* Maß-
mad ['mæd-]: **~ly** *adv* wahnsinnig; **~man** (*irreg*) *n* Verrückte(r) *m*, Irre(r) *m*; **~ness** *n* Wahnsinn *m*
magazine [mægə'zi:n] *n* Zeitschrift *f*; (*in gun*) Magazin *nt*
maggot ['mægət] *n* Made *f*
magic ['mædʒɪk] *n* Zauberei *f*, Magie *f*; (*fig*) Zauber *m* ♦ *adj* magisch, Zauber-; **~al** *adj*

magisch; **~ian** [mə'dʒɪʃən] n Zauberer m

magistrate ['mædʒɪstreɪt] n (Friedens)richter m

magnanimous [mæg'nænɪməs] adj großmütig

magnet ['mægnɪt] n Magnet m; **~ic** [mæg'netɪk] adj magnetisch; **~ic tape** n Magnetband nt; **~ism** n Magnetismus m; (fig) Ausstrahlungskraft f

magnificent [mæg'nɪfɪsnt] adj großartig

magnify ['mægnɪfaɪ] vt vergrößern; **~ing glass** n Lupe f

magnitude ['mægnɪtjuːd] n (size) Größe f; (importance) Ausmaß nt

magpie ['mægpaɪ] n Elster f

mahogany [mə'hɒgənɪ] n Mahagoni nt
♦ cpd Mahagoni-

maid [meɪd] n Dienstmädchen nt; **old ~** alte Jungfer f

maiden ['meɪdn] n Maid f ♦ adj (flight, speech) Jungfern-; **~ name** n Mädchenname m

mail [meɪl] n Post f ♦ vt aufgeben; **~ box** (US) n Briefkasten m; **~ing list** n Anschreibeliste f; **~ order** n Bestellung f durch die Post; **~ order firm** n Versandhaus nt

maim [meɪm] vt verstümmeln

main [meɪn] adj hauptsächlich, Haupt- ♦ n (pipe) Hauptleitung f; **the ~s** npl (ELEC) das Stromnetz; **in the ~** im Großen und Ganzen; **~frame** n (COMPUT) Großrechner m; **~land** n Festland nt; **~ly** adv hauptsächlich; **~ road** n Hauptstraße f; **~stay** n (fig) Hauptstütze f; **~stream** n Hauptrichtung f

maintain [meɪn'teɪn] vt (machine, roads) instand or in Stand halten; (support) unterhalten; (keep up) aufrechterhalten; (claim) behaupten; (innocence) beteuern

maintenance ['meɪntənəns] n (TECH) Wartung f; (of family) Unterhalt m

maize [meɪz] n Mais m

majestic [mə'dʒestɪk] adj majestätisch

majesty ['mædʒɪstɪ] n Majestät f

major ['meɪdʒəʳ] n Major m ♦ adj (MUS) Dur; (more important) Haupt-; (bigger) größer

Majorca [mə'jɔːkə] n Mallorca nt

majority [mə'dʒɒrɪtɪ] n Mehrheit f; (JUR) Volljährigkeit f

make [meɪk] (pt, pp made) vt machen; (appoint) ernennen (zu); (cause to do sth) veranlassen; (reach) erreichen; (in time) schaffen; (earn) verdienen ♦ n Marke f; **to ~ sth happen** etw geschehen lassen; **to ~ it** es schaffen; **what time do you ~ it?** wie spät hast du es?; **to ~ do with** auskommen mit; **~ for** vi gehen/fahren nach; **~ out** vt (write out) ausstellen; (understand) verstehen; **~ up** vt machen; (face) schminken; (quarrel) beilegen; (story etc) erfinden ♦ vi sich versöhnen; **~ up for** vt wieder gutmachen; (COMM) vergüten; **~-believe** n Fantasie f; **~r** n (COMM) Hersteller m; **~shift** adj behelfsmäßig, Not-; **~up** n Schminke f, Make-up nt; **~-up remover** n Make-up-Entferner m; **making** n: **in the making** im Entstehen; **to have the makings of** das Zeug haben zu

malaria [mə'leərɪə] n Malaria f

Malaysia [mə'leɪzɪə] n Malaysia nt

male [meɪl] n Mann m; (animal) Männchen nt ♦ adj männlich

malevolent [mə'levələnt] adj übel wollend

malfunction [mæl'fʌŋkʃən] n (MED) Funktionsstörung f; (of machine) Defekt m

malice ['mælɪs] n Bosheit f; **malicious** [mə'lɪʃəs] adj böswillig, gehässig

malign [mə'laɪn] vt verleumden ♦ adj böse

malignant [mə'lɪgnənt] adj bösartig

mall [mɔːl] n (also: **shopping ~**) Einkaufszentrum nt

malleable ['mælɪəbl] adj formbar

mallet ['mælɪt] n Holzhammer m

malnutrition [mælnjuː'trɪʃən] n Unterernährung f

malpractice [mæl'præktɪs] n Amtsvergehen nt

malt [mɔːlt] n Malz nt

Malta ['mɔːltə] n Malta nt; **Maltese** [mɔːl'tiːz] adj inv maltesisch ♦ n inv Malteser(in) m(f)

maltreat [mæl'triːt] vt misshandeln

mammal ['mæml] n Säugetier nt

mammoth ['mæməθ] *n* Mammut *nt* ♦ *adj* Mammut-

man [mæn] (*pl* **men**) *n* Mann *m*; (*human race*) der Mensch, die Menschen *pl* ♦ *vt* bemannen; **an old ~** ein alter Mann, ein Greis *m*; **~ and wife** Mann und Frau

manage ['mænɪdʒ] *vi* zurechtkommen ♦ *vt* (*control*) führen, leiten; (*cope with*) fertig werden mit; **~able** *adj* (*person, animal*) fügsam; (*object*) handlich; **~ment** *n* (*control*) Führung *f*, Leitung *f*; (*directors*) Management *nt*; **~r** *n* Geschäftsführer *m*; **~ress** [mænɪdʒə'res] *n* Geschäftsführerin *f*; **~rial** [mænɪ'dʒɪərɪəl] *adj* (*post*) leitend; (*problem etc*) Management-; **managing** ['mænɪdʒɪŋ] *adj*: **managing director** Betriebsleiter *m*

mandarin ['mændərɪn] *n* (*fruit*) Mandarine *f*

mandatory ['mændətərɪ] *adj* obligatorisch

mane [meɪn] *n* Mähne *f*

maneuver [mə'nu:vər] (*US*) = **manoeuvre**

manfully ['mænfəlɪ] *adv* mannhaft

mangle ['mæŋgl] *vt* verstümmeln ♦ *n* Mangel *f*

mango ['mæŋgəu] (*pl* **~es**) *n* Mango(pflaume) *f*

mangy ['meɪndʒɪ] *adj* (*dog*) räudig

man ['mæn-]: **~handle** *vt* grob behandeln; **~hole** *n* (Straßen)schacht *m*; **~hood** *n* Mannesalter *nt*; (*~liness*) Männlichkeit *f*; **~-hour** *n* Arbeitsstunde *f*; **~hunt** *n* Fahndung *f*

mania ['meɪnɪə] *n* Manie *f*; **~c** ['meɪnɪæk] *n* Wahnsinnige(r) *mf*

manic ['mænɪk] *adj* (*behaviour, activity*) hektisch

manicure ['mænɪkjuər] *n* Maniküre *f*; **~ set** *n* Necessaire *nt*, Nessessär *nt*

manifest ['mænɪfest] *vt* offenbaren ♦ *adj* offenkundig; **~ation** [mænɪfes'teɪʃən] *n* (*sign*) Anzeichen *nt*

manifesto [mænɪ'festəu] *n* Manifest *nt*

manipulate [mə'nɪpjuleɪt] *vt* handhaben; (*fig*) manipulieren

man ['mæn-]: **~kind** *n* Menschheit *f*; **~ly** ['mænlɪ] *adj* männlich; mannhaft; **~-made** *adj* (*fibre*) künstlich

manner ['mænər] *n* Art *f*, Weise *f*; **~s** *npl* (*behaviour*) Manieren *pl*; **in a ~ of speaking** sozusagen; **~ism** *n* (*of person*) Angewohnheit *f*; (*of style*) Manieriertheit *f*

manoeuvre [mə'nu:vər] (*US* **maneuver**) *vt, vi* manövrieren ♦ *n* (*MIL*) Feldzug *m*; (*general*) Manöver *nt*, Schachzug *m*

manor ['mænər] *n* Landgut *nt*

manpower ['mænpauər] *n* Arbeitskräfte *pl*

mansion ['mænʃən] *n* Villa *f*

manslaughter ['mænslɔ:tər] *n* Totschlag *m*

mantelpiece ['mæntlpi:s] *n* Kaminsims *m*

manual ['mænjuəl] *adj* manuell, Hand- ♦ *n* Handbuch *nt*

manufacture [mænju'fæktʃər] *vt* herstellen ♦ *n* Herstellung *f*; **~r** *n* Hersteller *m*

manure [mə'njuər] *n* Dünger *m*

manuscript ['mænjuskrɪpt] *n* Manuskript *nt*

Manx [mæŋks] *adj* der Insel Man

many ['menɪ] *adj, pron* viele; **a great ~** sehr viele; **~ a time** oft

map [mæp] *n* (Land)karte *f*; (*of town*) Stadtplan *m* ♦ *vt* eine Karte machen von; **~ out** *vt* (*fig*) ausarbeiten

maple ['meɪpl] *n* Ahorn *m*

mar [mɑ:r] *vt* verderben

marathon ['mærəθən] *n* (*SPORT*) Marathonlauf *m*; (*fig*) Marathon *m*

marble ['mɑ:bl] *n* Marmor *m*; (*for game*) Murmel *f*

March [mɑ:tʃ] *n* März *m*

march [mɑ:tʃ] *vi* marschieren ♦ *n* Marsch *m*

mare [meər] *n* Stute *f*

margarine [mɑ:dʒə'ri:n] *n* Margarine *f*

margin ['mɑ:dʒɪn] *n* Rand *m*; (*extra amount*) Spielraum *m*; (*COMM*) Spanne *f*; **~al** *adj* (*note*) Rand-; (*difference etc*) geringfügig; **~al (seat)** *n* (*POL*) *Wahlkreis, der nur mit knapper Mehrheit gehalten wird*

marigold ['mærɪgəuld] *n* Ringelblume *f*

marijuana [mærɪ'wɑ:nə] *n* Marihuana *nt*

marina [mə'ri:nə] *n* Jachthafen *m*

marinate ['mærɪneɪt] *vt* marinieren

marine [mə'ri:n] *adj* Meeres-, See- ♦ *n* (*MIL*) Marineinfanterist *m*

marital ['mærɪtl] *adj* ehelich, Ehe-; **~ status** *n* Familienstand *m*

maritime ['mærɪtaɪm] adj See-

mark [mɑːk] n (coin) Mark f; (spot) Fleck m; (scar) Kratzer m; (sign) Zeichen nt; (target) Ziel nt; (SCH) Note f ♦ vt (make ~ on) Flecken/Kratzer machen auf +acc; (indicate) markieren; (exam) korrigieren; **to ~ time** (also fig) auf der Stelle treten; **~ out** vt bestimmen; (area) abstecken; **~ed** adj deutlich; **~er** n (in book) (Lese)zeichen nt; (on road) Schild nt

market ['mɑːkɪt] n Markt m; (stock ~) Börse f ♦ vt (COMM: new product) auf den Markt bringen; (sell) vertreiben; **~ garden** (BRIT) n Handelsgärtnerei f; **~ing** n Marketing nt; **~ research** n Marktforschung f; **~ value** n Marktwert m

marksman ['mɑːksmən] (irreg) n Scharfschütze m

marmalade ['mɑːməleɪd] n Orangenmarmelade f

maroon [mə'ruːn] vt aussetzen ♦ adj (colour) kastanienbraun

marquee [mɑː'kiː] n große(s) Zelt nt

marriage ['mærɪdʒ] n Ehe f; (wedding) Heirat f; **~ bureau** n Heiratsinstitut nt; **~ certificate** n Heiratsurkunde f

married ['mærɪd] adj (person) verheiratet; (couple, life) Ehe-

marrow ['mærəʊ] n (Knochen)mark nt; (BOT) Kürbis m

marry ['mærɪ] vt (join) trauen; (take as husband, wife) heiraten ♦ vi (also: **get married**) heiraten

marsh [mɑːʃ] n Sumpf m

marshal ['mɑːʃl] n (US) Bezirkspolizeichef m ♦ vt (an)ordnen, arrangieren

marshy ['mɑːʃɪ] adj sumpfig

martial law ['mɑːʃl] n Kriegsrecht nt

martyr ['mɑːtə*] n (also fig) Märtyrer(in) m(f) ♦ vt zum Märtyrer machen; **~dom** n Martyrium nt

marvel ['mɑːvl] n Wunder nt ♦ vi: **to ~ (at)** sich wundern (über +acc); **~lous** (US **marvelous**) adj wunderbar

Marxist ['mɑːksɪst] n Marxist(in) m(f)

marzipan ['mɑːzɪpæn] n Marzipan nt

mascara [mæs'kɑːrə] n Wimperntusche f

mascot ['mæskət] n Maskottchen nt

masculine ['mæskjʊlɪn] adj männlich

mash [mæʃ] n Brei m; **~ed potatoes** npl Kartoffelbrei m or -püree nt

mask [mɑːsk] n (also fig) Maske f ♦ vt maskieren, verdecken

mason ['meɪsn] n (stonemason) Steinmetz m; (freemason) Freimaurer m; **~ry** n Mauerwerk nt

masquerade [mæskə'reɪd] n Maskerade f ♦ vi: **to ~ as** sich ausgeben als

mass [mæs] n Masse f; (greater part) Mehrheit f; (REL) Messe f ♦ vi sich sammeln; **the ~es** npl (people) die Masse(n) f(pl)

massacre ['mæsəkə*] n Blutbad nt ♦ vt niedermetzeln, massakrieren

massage ['mæsɑːʒ] n Massage f ♦ vt massieren

massive ['mæsɪv] adj gewaltig, massiv

mass media npl Massenmedien pl

mass production n Massenproduktion f

mast [mɑːst] n Mast m

master ['mɑːstə*] n Herr m; (NAUT) Kapitän m; (teacher) Lehrer m; (artist) Meister m ♦ vt meistern; (language etc) beherrschen; **~ly** adj meisterhaft; **~mind** n Kapazität f ♦ vt geschickt lenken; **M~ of Arts** n Magister m der philosophischen Fakultät; **M~ of Science** n Magister m der naturwissenschaftlichen Fakultät; **~piece** n Meisterwerk nt; **~ plan** n kluge(r) Plan m; **~y** n Können nt

masturbate ['mæstəbeɪt] vi masturbieren, onanieren

mat [mæt] n Matte f; (for table) Untersetzer m ♦ adj = **matt**

match [mætʃ] n Streichholz nt; (sth corresponding) Pendant nt; (SPORT) Wettkampf m; (ball games) Spiel nt ♦ vt (be like, suit) passen zu; (equal) gleichkommen +dat ♦ vi zusammenpassen; **it's a good ~ (for)** es passt gut (zu); **~box** n Streichholzschachtel f; **~ing** adj passend

mate [meɪt] n (companion) Kamerad m; (spouse) Lebensgefährte m; (of animal) Weibchen nt/Männchen nt; (NAUT) Schiffsoffizier m ♦ vi (animals) sich paaren

♦ *vt (animals)* paaren

material [məˈtɪərɪəl] *n* Material *nt; (for book, cloth)* Stoff *m* ♦ *adj (important)* wesentlich; *(damage)* Sach-; *(comforts etc)* materiell; **~s** *npl (for building etc)* Materialien *pl;* **~istic** [mətɪərɪəˈlɪstɪk] *adj* materialistisch; **~ize** *vi* sich verwirklichen, zustande *or* zu Stande kommen

maternal [məˈtəːnl] *adj* mütterlich, Mutter-

maternity [məˈtəːnɪtɪ] *adj (dress)* Umstands-; *(benefit)* Wochen-; **~ hospital** *n* Entbindungsheim *nt*

math [mæθ] *(US) n* = **maths**

mathematical [mæθəˈmætɪkl] *adj* mathematisch; **mathematics** *n* Mathematik *f;* **maths** *(US* **math)** *n* Mathe *f*

matinée [ˈmætɪneɪ] *n* Matinee *f*

matrices [ˈmeɪtrɪsiːz] *npl of* **matrix**

matriculation [mətrɪkjuˈleɪʃən] *n* Immatrikulation *f*

matrimonial [mætrɪˈməunɪəl] *adj* ehelich, Ehe-

matrimony [ˈmætrɪmənɪ] *n* Ehestand *m*

matrix [ˈmeɪtrɪks] *(pl* **matrices)** *n* Matrize *f; (GEOL etc)* Matrix *f*

matron [ˈmeɪtrən] *n (MED)* Oberin *f; (SCH)* Hausmutter *f*

matt [mæt] *adj (paint)* matt

matted [ˈmætɪd] *adj* verfilzt

matter [ˈmætəʳ] *n (substance)* Materie *f; (affair)* Angelegenheit *f* ♦ *vi* darauf ankommen; **no ~ how/what** egal wie/was; **what is the ~?** was ist los?; **as a ~ of course** selbstverständlich; **as a ~ of fact** eigentlich; **it doesn't ~** es macht nichts; **~-of-fact** *adj* sachlich, nüchtern

mattress [ˈmætrɪs] *n* Matratze *f*

mature [məˈtjuəʳ] *adj* reif ♦ *vi* reif werden; **maturity** [məˈtjuərɪtɪ] *n* Reife *f*

maul [mɔːl] *vt* übel zurichten

maxima [ˈmæksɪmə] *npl of* **maximum**

maximum [ˈmæksɪməm] *(pl* **maxima)** *adj* Höchst-, Maximal- ♦ *n* Maximum *nt*

May [meɪ] *n* Mai *m*

may [meɪ] *(conditional* **might)** *vi (be possible)* können; *(have permission)* dürfen; **he ~ come** er kommt vielleicht; **~be** [ˈmeɪbiː]

adv vielleicht

May Day *n* der 1. Mai

mayhem [ˈmeɪhem] *n* Chaos *nt; (US)* Körperverletzung *f*

mayonnaise [meɪəˈneɪz] *n* Majonäse *f,* Mayonnaise *f*

mayor [mɛəʳ] *n* Bürgermeister *m;* **~ess** *n* Bürgermeisterin *f; (wife)* (die) Frau *f* Bürgermeister

maypole [ˈmeɪpəul] *n* Maibaum *m*

maze [meɪz] *n* Irrgarten *m; (fig)* Wirrwarr *nt*

M.D. *abbr* = **Doctor of Medicine**

KEYWORD

me [miː] *pron* **1** *(direct)* mich; **it's me** ich bins

2 *(indirect)* mir; **give them to me** gib sie mir

3 *(after prep: +acc)* mich; *(: +dat)* mir; **with/without me** mit mir/ohne mich

meadow [ˈmedəu] *n* Wiese *f*

meagre [ˈmiːgəʳ] *(US* **meager)** *adj* dürftig, spärlich

meal [miːl] *n* Essen *nt,* Mahlzeit *f; (grain)* Schrotmehl *nt;* **to have a ~** essen (gehen); **~time** *n* Essenszeit *f*

mean [miːn] *(pt, pp* **meant)** *adj (stingy)* geizig; *(spiteful)* gemein; *(average)* durchschnittlich, Durchschnitts- ♦ *vt (signify)* bedeuten; *(intend)* vorhaben, beabsichtigen ♦ *n (average)* Durchschnitt *m;* **~s** *npl (wherewithal)* Mittel *pl; (wealth)* Vermögen *nt;* **do you ~ me?** meinst du mich?; **do you ~ it?** meinst du das ernst?; **what do you ~?** was willst du damit sagen?; **to be ~t for sb/sth** für jdn/etw bestimmt sein; **by ~s of** durch; **by all ~s** selbstverständlich; **by no ~s** keineswegs

meander [mɪˈændəʳ] *vi* sich schlängeln

meaning [ˈmiːnɪŋ] *n* Bedeutung *f; (of life)* Sinn *m;* **~ful** *adj* bedeutungsvoll; *(life)* sinnvoll; **~less** *adj* sinnlos

meanness [ˈmiːnnɪs] *n (stinginess)* Geiz *m; (spitefulness)* Gemeinheit *f*

meant [ment] *pt, pp of* **mean**

meantime [ˈmiːntaɪm] *adv* inzwischen

meanwhile ['mi:nwaıl] *adv* inzwischen

measles ['mi:zlz] *n* Masern *pl*

measly ['mi:zlı] (*inf*) *adj* poplig

measure ['mɛʒəʳ] *vt, vi* messen ♦ *n* Maß *nt*; (*step*) Maßnahme *f*; **~ments** *npl* Maße *pl*

meat [mi:t] *n* Fleisch *nt*; **cold ~** Aufschnitt *m*; **~ ball** *n* Fleischkloß *m*; **~ pie** *n* Fleischpastete *f*; **~y** *adj* fleischig; (*fig*) gehaltvoll

Mecca ['mɛkə] *n* Mekka *nt* (*also fig*)

mechanic [mı'kænık] *n* Mechaniker *m*; **~al** *adj* mechanisch; **~s** *n* Mechanik *f* ♦ *npl* Technik *f*

mechanism ['mɛkənızəm] *n* Mechanismus *m*

mechanize ['mɛkənaız] *vt* mechanisieren

medal ['mɛdl] *n* Medaille *f*; (*decoration*) Orden *m*; **~list** (*US* **medalist**) *n* Medaillengewinner(in) *m(f)*

meddle ['mɛdl] *vi*: **to ~ (in)** sich einmischen (in +*acc*); **to ~ with sth** sich an etw *dat* zu schaffen machen

media ['mi:dıə] *npl* Medien *pl*

mediaeval [mɛdı'i:vl] *adj* = **medieval**

median ['mi:dıən] (*US*) *n* (*also*: **~ strip**) Mittelstreifen *m*

mediate ['mi:dıeıt] *vi* vermitteln; **mediator** *n* Vermittler *m*

Medicaid ['mɛdıkeıd] (® *US*) *n* medizinisches Versorgungsprogramm für sozial Schwache

medical ['mɛdıkl] *adj* medizinisch; Medizin-; ärztlich ♦ *n* (ärztliche) Untersuchung *f*

Medicare ['mɛdıkeəʳ] (*US*) *n* staatliche Krankenversicherung besonders für Ältere

medicated ['mɛdıkeıtıd] *adj* medizinisch

medication [mɛdı'keıʃən] *n* (*drugs etc*) Medikamente *pl*

medicinal [mɛ'dısınl] *adj* medizinisch, Heil-

medicine ['mɛdsın] *n* Medizin *f*; (*drugs*) Arznei *f*

medieval [mɛdı'i:vl] *adj* mittelalterlich

mediocre [mi:dı'əukəʳ] *adj* mittelmäßig

meditate ['mɛdıteıt] *vi* meditieren; **to ~ (on sth)** (über etw *acc*) nachdenken; **meditation** [mɛdı'teıʃən] *n* Nachsinnen *nt*; Meditation *f*

Mediterranean [mɛdıtə'reınıən] *adj*

Mittelmeer-; (*person*) südländisch; **the ~ (Sea)** das Mittelmeer

medium ['mi:dıəm] *adj* mittlere(r, s), Mittel-, mittel- ♦ *n* Mitte *f*; (*means*) Mittel *nt*; (*person*) Medium *nt*; **happy ~** goldener Mittelweg *m*; **~-sized** *adj* mittelgroß; **~ wave** *n* Mittelwelle *f*

medley ['mɛdlı] *n* Gemisch *nt*

meek [mi:k] *adj* sanft(mütig)

meet [mi:t] (*pt, pp* **met**) *vt* (*encounter*) treffen, begegnen +*dat*; (*by arrangement*) sich treffen mit; (*difficulties*) stoßen auf +*acc*; (*get to know*) kennen lernen; (*fetch*) abholen; (*join*) zusammentreffen mit; (*satisfy*) entsprechen +*dat* ♦ *vi* sich treffen; (*become acquainted*) sich kennen lernen; **~ with** *vt* (*problems*) stoßen auf +*acc*; (*US*: *people*) zusammentreffen mit; **~ing** *n* Treffen *nt*; (*business ~ing*) Besprechung *f*; (*of committee*) Sitzung *f*; (*assembly*) Versammlung *f*

mega- ['mɛgə-] (*inf*) *prefix* Mega-; **~byte** *n* (*COMPUT*) Megabyte *nt*; **~phone** *n* Megafon *nt*, Megaphon *nt*

melancholy ['mɛlənkəlı] *adj* (*person*) melancholisch; (*sight, event*) traurig

mellow ['mɛləu] *adj* mild, weich; (*fruit*) reif; (*fig*) gesetzt ♦ *vi* reif werden

melodious [mı'ləudıəs] *adj* wohlklingend

melody ['mɛlədı] *n* Melodie *f*

melon ['mɛlən] *n* Melone *f*

melt [mɛlt] *vi* schmelzen; (*anger*) verfliegen ♦ *vt* schmelzen; **~ away** *vi* dahinschmelzen; **~ down** *vt* einschmelzen; **~down** *n* (*in nuclear reactor*) Kernschmelze *f*; **~ing point** *n* Schmelzpunkt *m*; **~ing pot** *n* (*fig*) Schmelztiegel *m*

member ['mɛmbəʳ] *n* Mitglied *nt*; (*of tribe, species*) Angehörige(r) *f(m)*; (*ANAT*) Glied *nt*; **M~ of Parliament** (*BRIT*) *n* Parlamentsmitglied *nt*; **M~ of the European Parliament** (*BRIT*) *n* Mitglied *nt* des Europäischen Parlaments; **M~ of the Scottish Parliament** *n* Mitglied *nt* des schottischen Parlaments; **~ship** *n* Mitgliedschaft *f*; **to seek ~ship of** einen Antrag auf Mitgliedschaft stellen; **~ship**

card n Mitgliedskarte f
memento [mə'mɛntəu] n Andenken nt
memo ['mɛməu] n Mitteilung f
memoirs ['mɛmwɑːz] npl Memoiren pl
memorable ['mɛmərəbl] adj denkwürdig
memoranda [mɛmə'rændə] npl of
memorandum
memorandum [mɛmə'rændəm] (pl
memoranda) n Mitteilung f
memorial [mɪ'mɔːrɪəl] n Denkmal n ♦ adj
Gedenk-
memorize ['mɛməraɪz] vt sich einprägen
memory ['mɛmərɪ] n Gedächtnis nt; (of
computer) Speicher m; (sth recalled)
Erinnerung f
men [mɛn] pl of **man** ♦ n (human race) die
Menschen pl
menace ['mɛnɪs] n Drohung f; Gefahr f ♦ vt
bedrohen; **menacing** adj drohend
menagerie [mɪ'nædʒərɪ] n Tierschau f
mend [mɛnd] vt reparieren, flicken ♦ vi
(ver)heilen ♦ n ausgebesserte Stelle f; on
the ~ auf dem Wege der Besserung; ~ing
n (articles) Flickarbeit f
menial ['miːnɪəl] adj niedrig
meningitis [mɛnɪn'dʒaɪtɪs] n
Hirnhautentzündung f, Meningitis f
menopause ['mɛnəupɔːz] n Wechseljahre
pl, Menopause f
menstruation [mɛnstru'eɪʃən] n
Menstruation f
mental ['mɛntl] adj geistig, Geistes-;
(arithmetic) Kopf-; (hospital) Nerven-;
(cruelty) seelisch; (inf: abnormal) verrückt;
~ity [mɛn'tælɪtɪ] n Mentalität f
menthol ['mɛnθɔl] n Menthol nt
mention ['mɛnʃən] n Erwähnung f ♦ vt
erwähnen; **don't ~ it!** bitte (sehr), gern
geschehen
mentor ['mɛntɔːr] n Mentor m
menu ['mɛnjuː] n Speisekarte f
MEP n abbr = **Member of the European
Parliament**
mercenary ['mɜːsɪnərɪ] adj (person)
geldgierig ♦ n Söldner m
merchandise ['mɜːtʃəndaɪz] n
(Handels)ware f

merchant ['mɜːtʃənt] n Kaufmann m; ~
bank (BRIT) n Handelsbank f; ~ **navy** (US ~
marine) n Handelsmarine f
merciful ['mɜːsɪful] adj gnädig
merciless ['mɜːsɪlɪs] adj erbarmungslos
mercury ['mɜːkjurɪ] n Quecksilber nt
mercy ['mɜːsɪ] n Erbarmen nt; Gnade f; **at
the ~ of** ausgeliefert +dat
mere [mɪər] adj bloß; ~**ly** adv bloß
merge [mɜːdʒ] vt verbinden; (COMM)
fusionieren ♦ vi verschmelzen; (roads)
zusammenlaufen; (COMM) fusionieren; ~**r** n
(COMM) Fusion f
meringue [mə'ræŋ] n Baiser nt
merit ['mɛrɪt] n Verdienst nt; (advantage)
Vorzug m ♦ vt verdienen
mermaid ['mɜːmeɪd] n Wassernixe f
merry ['mɛrɪ] adj fröhlich; ~~-**go-round** n
Karussell nt
mesh [mɛʃ] n Masche f
mesmerize ['mɛzməraɪz] vt hypnotisieren;
(fig) faszinieren
mess [mɛs] n Unordnung f; (dirt) Schmutz
m; (trouble) Schwierigkeiten pl; (MIL) Messe
f; ~ **about** or **around** vi (play the fool)
herumalbern; (do nothing in particular)
herumgammeln; ~ **about** or **around
with** vt fus (tinker with) herummurksen an
+dat; ~ **up** vt verpfuschen; (make untidy) in
Unordnung bringen
message ['mɛsɪdʒ] n Mitteilung f; **to get
the ~** kapieren
messenger ['mɛsɪndʒər] n Bote m
Messrs ['mɛsəz] abbr (on letters) die Herren
messy ['mɛsɪ] adj schmutzig; (untidy)
unordentlich
met [mɛt] pt, pp of **meet**
metabolism [mɛ'tæbəlɪzəm] n Stoffwechsel
m
metal ['mɛtl] n Metall nt; ~**lic** adj metallisch;
(made of ~) aus Metall
metaphor ['mɛtəfər] n Metapher f
meteorology [miːtɪə'rɔlədʒɪ] n Meteorologie
f
meter ['miːtər] n Zähler m; (US) = **metre**
method ['mɛθəd] n Methode f; ~**ical**
[mɪ'θɔdɪkl] adj methodisch; **M~ist**

['meθədɪst] adj methodistisch ♦ n
Methodist(in) m(f); ~ology [meθə'dɔlədʒɪ] n
Methodik f

meths [meθs] (BRIT) n(pl) = **methylated spirit(s)**

methylated spirit(s) ['meθɪleɪtɪd-] (BRIT) n
(Brenn)spiritus m

meticulous [mɪ'tɪkjuləs] adj (über)genau

metre ['miːtər] (US **meter**) n Meter m or nt

metric ['metrɪk] adj (also: ~al) metrisch

metropolitan [metrə'pɔlɪtn] adj der
Großstadt; **M~ Police** (BRIT) n: **the M~
Police** die Londoner Polizei

mettle ['metl] n Mut m

mew [mjuː] vi (cat) miauen

mews [mjuːz] n: ~ **cottage** ehemaliges
Kutscherhäuschen

Mexican ['meksɪkən] adj mexikanisch ♦ n
Mexikaner(in) m(f)

Mexico ['meksɪkəu] n Mexiko nt

miaow [miːˈau] vi miauen

mice [maɪs] pl of **mouse**

micro ['maɪkrəu] n (also: ~**computer**)
Mikrocomputer m; ~**chip** n Mikrochip m;
~**cosm** ['maɪkrəukɔzəm] n Mikrokosmos m;
~**phone** n Mikrofon nt, Mikrophon nt;
~**scope** n Mikroskop nt; ~**wave** n (also:
~**wave oven**) Mikrowelle(nherd nt) f

mid [mɪd] adj: **in ~ afternoon** am
Nachmittag; **in ~ air** in der Luft; **in ~ May**
Mitte Mai

midday [mɪd'deɪ] n Mittag m

middle ['mɪdl] n Mitte f; (waist) Taille f ♦ adj
mittlere(r, s), Mittel-; **in the ~ of** mitten in
+dat; ~-**aged** adj mittleren Alters; **M~
Ages** npl: **the M~ Ages** das Mittelalter;
~-**class** adj Mittelstands-; **M~ East** n: **the
M~ East** der Nahe Osten; ~**man** (irreg) n
(COMM) Zwischenhändler m; ~ **name** n
zweiter Vorname m; ~ **weight** n (BOXING)
Mittelgewicht nt

middling ['mɪdlɪŋ] adj mittelmäßig

midge [mɪdʒ] n Mücke f

midget ['mɪdʒɪt] n Liliputaner(in) m(f)

midnight ['mɪdnaɪt] n Mitternacht f

midriff ['mɪdrɪf] n Taille f

midst [mɪdst] n: **in the ~ of** (persons) mitten

unter +dat; (things) mitten in +dat

mid [mɪd'-]: ~**summer** n Hochsommer m;
~**way** adv auf halbem Wege ♦ adj Mittel-;
~**week** adv in der Mitte der Woche

midwife ['mɪdwaɪf] (irreg) n Hebamme f; ~**ry**
['mɪdwɪfərɪ] n Geburtshilfe f

midwinter [mɪd'wɪntər] n tiefste(r) Winter m

might [maɪt] vi see **may** ♦ n Macht f, Kraft f;
I ~ come ich komme vielleicht; ~**y** adj, adv
mächtig

migraine ['miːgreɪn] n Migräne f

migrant ['maɪgrənt] adj Wander-; (bird) Zug-

migrate [maɪ'greɪt] vi (ab)wandern; (birds)
(fort)ziehen; **migration** [maɪ'greɪʃən] n
Wanderung f, Zug m

mike [maɪk] n = **microphone**

Milan [mɪ'læn] n Mailand nt

mild [maɪld] adj mild; (medicine, interest)
leicht; (person) sanft ♦ n (beer) leichtes
dunkles Bier

mildew ['mɪldjuː] n (on plants) Mehltau m;
(on food) Schimmel m

mildly ['maɪldlɪ] adv leicht; **to put it ~**
gelinde gesagt

mile [maɪl] n Meile f; ~**age** n Meilenzahl f;
~**ometer** n = **milometer**; ~**stone** n (also
fig) Meilenstein m

militant ['mɪlɪtnt] adj militant ♦ n
Militante(r) mf

military ['mɪlɪtərɪ] adj militärisch, Militär-,
Wehr-

militate ['mɪlɪteɪt] vi: **to ~ against**
entgegenwirken +dat

militia [mɪ'lɪʃə] n Miliz f

milk [mɪlk] n Milch f ♦ vt (also fig) melken; ~
chocolate n Milchschokolade f; ~**man**
(irreg) n Milchmann m; ~ **shake** n
Milchmixgetränk nt; ~**y** adj milchig; **M~y
Way** n Milchstraße f

mill [mɪl] n Mühle f; (factory) Fabrik f ♦ vt
mahlen ♦ vi umherlaufen

millennia [mɪ'lenɪə] npl of **millennium**

millennium [mɪ'lenɪəm] (pl ~**s** or **millennia**)
n Jahrtausend nt; ~ **bug** n (COMPUT)
Jahrtausendfehler m

miller ['mɪlər] n Müller m

milligram(me) ['mɪlɪgræm] n Milligramm nt

millimetre ['mɪlɪmiːtəʳ] (*US* **millimeter**) *n*
Millimeter *m*

million ['mɪljən] *n* Million *f*; **a ~ times**
tausendmal; **~aire** [mɪljə'nɛəʳ] *n*
Millionär(in) *m(f)*

millstone ['mɪlstəun] *n* Mühlstein *m*

milometer [maɪ'lɒmɪtəʳ] *n* ≃ Kilometerzähler
m

mime [maɪm] *n* Pantomime *f* ♦ *vt, vi* mimen

mimic ['mɪmɪk] *n* Mimiker *m* ♦ *vt, vi*
nachahmen; **~ry** *n* Nachahmung *f*; (*BIOL*)
Mimikry *f*

min. *abbr* = **minutes; minimum**

mince [mɪns] *vt* (zer)hacken ♦ *n* (*meat*)
Hackfleisch *nt*; (~meat *n* süße
Pastetenfüllung *f*; **~ pie** *n* gefüllte (süße)
Pastete *f*; **~r** *n* Fleischwolf *m*

mind [maɪnd] *n* Verstand *m*, Geist *m*;
(*opinion*) Meinung *f* ♦ *vt* aufpassen auf +*acc*;
(*object to*) etwas haben gegen; **on my ~** auf
dem Herzen; **to my ~** meiner Meinung
nach; **to be out of one's ~** wahnsinnig
sein; **to bear** *or* **keep in ~** bedenken; **to
change one's ~** es sich *dat* anders
überlegen; **to make up one's ~** sich
entschließen; **I don't ~** das macht mir
nichts aus; **~ you, ...** allerdings ...; **never
~! I** macht nichts!; **"~ the step"** „Vorsicht
Stufe"; **~ your own business** kümmern Sie
sich um Ihre eigenen Angelegenheiten); **~er**
n Aufpasser(in) *m(f)*; **~ful** *adj*: **~ful of**
achtsam auf +*acc*; **~less** *adj* sinnlos

mine¹ [maɪn] *n* (*coalmine*) Bergwerk *nt*;
(*MIL*) Mine *f* ♦ *vt* abbauen; (*MIL*) verminen

mine² [maɪn] *pron* meine(r, s); **that book is
~** das Buch gehört mir; **a friend of ~** ein
Freund von mir

minefield ['maɪnfiːld] *n* Minenfeld *nt*

miner ['maɪnəʳ] *n* Bergarbeiter *m*

mineral ['mɪnərəl] *adj* mineralisch, Mineral-
♦ *n* Mineral *nt*; **~s** *npl* (*BRIT*: *soft drinks*)
alkoholfreie Getränke *pl*; **~ water** *n*
Mineralwasser *nt*

minesweeper ['maɪnswiːpəʳ] *n*
Minensuchboot *nt*

mingle ['mɪŋgl] *vi*: **to ~ (with)** sich mischen
(unter +*acc*)

miniature ['mɪnətʃəʳ] *adj* Miniatur- ♦ *n*
Miniatur *f*

minibus ['mɪnɪbʌs] *n* Kleinbus *m*

Minidisc ['mɪnɪdɪsk] *n* Minidisc ® *f*

minimal ['mɪnɪml] *adj* minimal

minimize ['mɪnɪmaɪz] *vt* auf das
Mindestmaß beschränken

minimum ['mɪnɪməm] (*pl* **minima**) *n*
Minimum *nt* ♦ *adj* Mindest-

mining ['maɪnɪŋ] *n* Bergbau *m* ♦ *adj*
Bergbau-, Berg-

miniskirt ['mɪnɪskɔːt] *n* Minirock *m*

minister ['mɪnɪstəʳ] *n* (*BRIT*: *POL*) Minister *m*;
(*ECCL*) Pfarrer *m* ♦ *vi*: **to ~ to sb/sb's
needs** sich um jdn kümmern; **~ial**
[mɪnɪs'tɪərɪəl] *adj* ministeriell, Minister-

ministry ['mɪnɪstrɪ] *n* (*BRIT*: *POL*) Ministerium
nt; (*ECCL*: *office*) geistliche(s) Amt *nt*

mink [mɪŋk] *n* Nerz *m*

minnow ['mɪnəu] *n* Elritze *f*

minor ['maɪnəʳ] *adj* kleiner; (*operation*) leicht;
(*problem, poet*) unbedeutend; (*MUS*) Moll
♦ *n* (*BRIT*: *under 18*) Minderjährige(r) *mf*

minority [maɪ'nɒrɪtɪ] *n* Minderheit *f*

mint [mɪnt] *n* Minze *f*; (*sweet*)
Pfefferminzbonbon *nt* ♦ *vt* (*coins*) prägen;
the (Royal (*BRIT*) *or* **US** (*US*)) **M~** die
Münzanstalt; **in ~ condition** in tadellosem
Zustand

minus ['maɪnəs] *n* Minuszeichen *nt*; (*amount*)
Minusbetrag *m* ♦ *prep* minus, weniger

minuscule ['mɪnəskjuːl] *adj* winzig

minute¹ [maɪ'njuːt] *adj* winzig; (*detailed*)
minutiös, minuziös

minute² ['mɪnɪt] *n* Minute *f*; (*moment*)
Augenblick *m*; **~s** *npl* (*of meeting etc*)
Protokoll *n*

miracle ['mɪrəkl] *n* Wunder *nt*

miraculous [mɪ'rækjuləs] *adj* wunderbar

mirage ['mɪrɑːʒ] *n* Fata Morgana *f*

mire ['maɪəʳ] *n* Morast *m*

mirror ['mɪrəʳ] *n* Spiegel *m* ♦ *vt*
(wider)spiegeln

mirth [mɜːθ] *n* Heiterkeit *f*

misadventure [mɪsəd'vɛntʃəʳ] *n*
Missgeschick *nt*, Unfall *m*

misanthropist [mɪ'zænθrəpɪst] *n*

Menschenfeind *m*

misapprehension ['mɪsæprɪ'henʃən] *n*
Missverständnis *nt*

misbehave [mɪsbɪ'heɪv] *vi* sich schlecht
benehmen

miscalculate [mɪs'kælkjuleɪt] *vt* falsch
berechnen

miscarriage ['mɪskærɪdʒ] *n* (*MED*)
Fehlgeburt *f*; **~ of justice** Fehlurteil *nt*

miscellaneous [mɪsɪ'leɪnɪəs] *adj*
verschieden

mischief ['mɪstʃɪf] *n* Unfug *m*;
mischievous ['mɪstʃɪvəs] *adj* (*person*)
durchtrieben; (*glance*) verschmitzt; (*rumour*)
bösartig

misconception ['mɪskən'sepʃən] *n*
fälschliche Annahme *f*

misconduct [mɪs'kɔndʌkt] *n* Vergehen *nt*;
professional ~ Berufsvergehen *nt*

misconstrue [mɪskən'struː] *vt*
missverstehen

misdemeanour [mɪsdɪ'miːnəʳ] (*US*
misdemeanor) *n* Vergehen *nt*

miser ['maɪzəʳ] *n* Geizhals *m*

miserable ['mɪzərəbl] *adj* (*unhappy*)
unglücklich; (*headache, weather*)
fürchterlich; (*poor*) elend; (*contemptible*)
erbärmlich

miserly ['maɪzəlɪ] *adj* geizig

misery ['mɪzərɪ] *n* Elend *nt*, Qual *f*

misfire [mɪs'faɪəʳ] *vi* (*gun*) versagen; (*engine*)
fehlzünden; (*plan*) fehlgehen

misfit ['mɪsfɪt] *n* Außenseiter *m*

misfortune [mɪs'fɔːtʃən] *n* Unglück *nt*

misgiving(s) [mɪs'gɪvɪŋ(z)] *n(pl)* Bedenken
pl

misguided [mɪs'gaɪdɪd] *adj* fehlgeleitet;
(*opinions*) irrig

mishandle [mɪs'hændl] *vt* falsch handhaben

mishap ['mɪshæp] *n* Missgeschick *nt*

misinform [mɪsɪn'fɔːm] *vt* falsch
unterrichten

misinterpret [mɪsɪn'təːprɪt] *vt* falsch
auffassen

misjudge [mɪs'dʒʌdʒ] *vt* falsch beurteilen

mislay [mɪs'leɪ] (*irreg: like* **lay**) *vt* verlegen

mislead [mɪs'liːd] (*irreg: like* **lead²**) *vt*
(*deceive*) irreführen; **~ing** *adj* irreführend

mismanage [mɪs'mænɪdʒ] *vt* schlecht
verwalten

misnomer [mɪs'nəuməʳ] *n* falsche
Bezeichnung *f*

misplace [mɪs'pleɪs] *vt* verlegen

misprint ['mɪsprɪnt] *n* Druckfehler *m*

Miss [mɪs] *n* Fräulein *nt*

miss [mɪs] *vt* (*fail to hit, catch*) verfehlen; (*not
notice*) verpassen; (*be too late*) versäumen,
verpassen; (*omit*) auslassen; (*regret the
absence of*) vermissen ♦ *vi* fehlen ♦ *n* (*shot*)
Fehlschuss *m*; (*failure*) Fehlschlag *m*; **I ~ you**
du fehlst mir; **~ out** *vt* auslassen

misshapen [mɪs'ʃeɪpən] *adj* missgestaltet

missile ['mɪsaɪl] *n* Rakete *f*

missing ['mɪsɪŋ] *adj* (*person*) vermisst;
(*thing*) fehlend; **to be ~** fehlen

mission ['mɪʃən] *n* (*work*) Auftrag *m*;
(*people*) Delegation *f*; (*REL*) Mission *f*; **~ary**
n Missionar(in) *m(f)*; **~ statement** *n*
Kurzdarstellung *f* der Firmenphilosophie

misspell ['mɪs'spel] (*irreg: like* **spell**) *vt*
falsch schreiben

misspent ['mɪs'spent] *adj* (*youth*) vergeudet

mist [mɪst] *n* Dunst *m*, Nebel *m* ♦ *vi* (*also: ~
over, ~ up*) sich trüben; (*BRIT: windows*) sich
beschlagen

mistake [mɪs'teɪk] (*irreg: like* **take**) *n* Fehler
m ♦ *vt* (*misunderstand*) missverstehen; (*mix
up*): **to ~ (sth for sth)** (etw mit etw)
verwechseln; **to make a ~** einen Fehler
machen; **by ~** aus Versehen; **to ~ A for B** A
mit B verwechseln; **~n** *pp of* **mistake** ♦ *adj*
(*idea*) falsch; **to be ~n** sich irren

mister ['mɪstəʳ] *n* (*inf*) Herr *m*; *see* **Mr**

mistletoe ['mɪsltəu] *n* Mistel *f*

mistook [mɪs'tuk] *pt of* **mistake**

mistress ['mɪstrɪs] *n* (*teacher*) Lehrerin *f*; (*in
house*) Herrin *f*; (*lover*) Geliebte *f*; *see* **Mrs**

mistrust [mɪs'trʌst] *vt* misstrauen +*dat*

misty ['mɪstɪ] *adj* neblig

misunderstand [mɪsʌndə'stænd] (*irreg: like*
understand) *vt*, *vi* missverstehen, falsch
verstehen; **~ing** *n* Missverständnis *nt*;
(*disagreement*) Meinungsverschiedenheit *f*

misuse [*n* mɪs'juːs, *vb* mɪs'juːz] *n* falsche(r)

Gebrauch *m* ♦ *vt* falsch gebrauchen
mitigate ['mɪtɪgeɪt] *vt* mildern
mitt(en) ['mɪt(n)] *n* Fausthandschuh *m*
mix [mɪks] *vt* (*blend*) (ver)mischen ♦ *vi*
(*liquids*) sich (ver)mischen lassen; (*people:
get on*) sich vertragen; (: *associate*) Kontakt
haben *n* (~*ture*) Mischung *f*; ~ **up** *vt*
zusammenmischen; (*confuse*) verwechseln;
~ed *adj* gemischt; **~ed-up** *adj*
durcheinander; **~er** *n* (*for food*) Mixer *m*;
~ture *n* Mischung *f*; **~-up** *n*
Durcheinander *nt*
mm *abbr* (= *millimetre(s)*) mm
moan [məun] *n* Stöhnen *nt*; (*complaint*)
Klage *f* ♦ *vi* stöhnen; (*complain*) maulen
moat [məut] *n* (Burg)graben *m*
mob [mɔb] *n* Mob *m*; (*the masses*) Pöbel *m*
♦ *vt* herfallen über +*acc*
mobile ['məubaɪl] *adj* beweglich; (*library etc*)
fahrbar ♦ *n* (*decoration*) Mobile *nt*; ~ **home**
n Wohnwagen *m*; ~ **phone** *n* (*TEL*)
Mobiltelefon *nt*; **mobility** [məu'bɪlɪtɪ] *n*
Beweglichkeit *f*; **mobilize** ['məubɪlaɪz] *vt*
mobilisieren
mock [mɔk] *vt* verspotten; (*defy*) trotzen
+*dat* ♦ *adj* Schein-; **~ery** *n* Spott *m*; (*person*)
Gespött *nt*
mod [mɔd] *adj see* **convenience**
mode [məud] *n* (Art *f* und) Weise *f*
model ['mɔdl] *n* Modell *nt*; (*example*) Vorbild
nt; (*in fashion*) Mannequin *nt* ♦ *adj* (*railway*)
Modell-; (*perfect*) Muster-; vorbildlich ♦ *vt*
(*make*) bilden; (*clothes*) vorführen ♦ *vi* als
Mannequin arbeiten
modem ['məudem] *n* (*COMPUT*) Modem *nt*
moderate [*adj, n* 'mɔdərət, *vb* 'mɔdəreɪt] *adj*
gemäßigt ♦ *n* (*POL*) Gemäßigte(r) *mf* ♦ *vi*
sich mäßigen ♦ *vt* mäßigen; **moderation**
[mɔdə'reɪʃən] *n* Mäßigung *f*; **in moderation**
mit Maßen
modern ['mɔdən] *adj* modern; (*history,
languages*) neuere(r, s); **~ize** *vt*
modernisieren
modest ['mɔdɪst] *adj* bescheiden; **~y** *n*
Bescheidenheit *f*
modicum ['mɔdɪkəm] *n* bisschen *nt*
modification [mɔdɪfɪ'keɪʃən] *n*

(Ab)änderung *f*
modify ['mɔdɪfaɪ] *vt* abändern
module ['mɔdjuːl] *n* (*component*)
(Bau)element *nt*; (*SPACE*) (Raum)kapsel *f*
mogul ['məugl] *n* (*fig*) Mogul *m*
mohair ['məuheəʳ] *n* Mohär *m*, Mohair *m*
moist [mɔɪst] *adj* feucht; **~en** ['mɔɪsn] *vt*
befeuchten; **~ure** ['mɔɪstʃəʳ] *n* Feuchtigkeit
f; **~urizer** ['mɔɪstʃəraɪzəʳ] *n*
Feuchtigkeitscreme *f*
molar ['məuləʳ] *n* Backenzahn *m*
molasses [mə'læsɪz] *n* Melasse *f*
mold [məuld] (*US*) = **mould**
mole [məul] *n* (*spot*) Leberfleck *m*; (*animal*)
Maulwurf *m*; (*pier*) Mole *f*
molest [mə'lest] *vt* belästigen
mollycoddle ['mɔlɪkɔdl] *vt* verhätscheln
molt [məult] (*US*) *vi* = **moult**
molten ['məultən] *adj* geschmolzen
mom [mɔm] (*US*) *n* = **mum**
moment ['məumənt] *n* Moment *m*,
Augenblick *m*; (*importance*) Tragweite *f*; **at
the ~** im Augenblick; **~ary** *adj* kurz; **~ous**
[məu'mentəs] *adj* folgenschwer
momentum [məu'mentəm] *n* Schwung *m*;
to gather ~ in Fahrt kommen
mommy ['mɔmɪ] (*US*) *n* = **mummy**
Monaco ['mɔnəkəu] *n* Monaco *nt*
monarch ['mɔnək] *n* Herrscher(in) *m(f)*; **~y**
n Monarchie *f*
monastery ['mɔnəstərɪ] *n* Kloster *nt*
monastic [mə'næstɪk] *adj* klösterlich,
Kloster-
Monday ['mʌndɪ] *n* Montag *m*
monetary ['mʌnɪtərɪ] *adj* Geld-; (*of currency*)
Währungs-
money ['mʌnɪ] *n* Geld *nt*; **to make ~** Geld
verdienen; ~ **belt** *n* Geldgürtel *nt*; **~lender**
n Geldverleiher *m*; ~ **order** *n*
Postanweisung *f*; **~-spinner** (*inf*) *n*
Verkaufsschlager *m*
mongol ['mɔngəl] *n* (*MED*) mongoloide(s)
Kind *nt* ♦ *adj* mongolisch; (*MED*) mongoloid
mongrel ['mʌngrəl] *n* Promenadenmischung
f
monitor ['mɔnɪtəʳ] *n* (*SCH*) Klassenordner *m*;
(*television ~*) Monitor *m* ♦ *vt* (*broadcasts*)

abhören; (control) überwachen

monk [mʌŋk] n Mönch m

monkey ['mʌŋki] n Affe m; ~ **nut** (BRIT) n Erdnuss f; ~ **wrench** n (TECH) Engländer m, Franzose m

monochrome ['mɔnəkrəum] adj schwarzweiß, schwarzweiß

monopolize [mə'nɔpəlaiz] vt beherrschen

monopoly [mə'nɔpəli] n Monopol nt

monosyllable ['mɔnəsiləbl] n einsilbige(s) Wort nt

monotone ['mɔnətəun] n gleich bleibende(r) Ton(fall) m; **to speak in a ~** monoton sprechen; **monotonous** [mə'nɔtənəs] adj eintönig; **monotony** [mə'nɔtəni] n Eintönigkeit f, Monotonie f

monsoon [mɔn'suːn] n Monsun m

monster ['mɔnstə^r] n Ungeheuer nt; (person) Scheusal nt

monstrosity [mɔn'strɔsiti] n Ungeheuerlichkeit f; (thing) Monstrosität f

monstrous ['mɔnstrəs] adj (shocking) grässlich, ungeheuerlich; (huge) riesig

month [mʌnθ] n Monat m; ~**ly** adj monatlich, Monats- ♦ adv einmal im Monat ♦ n (magazine) Monatsschrift f

monument ['mɔnjumənt] n Denkmal nt; ~**al** [mɔnju'mentl] adj (huge) gewaltig; (ignorance) ungeheuer

moo [muː] vi muhen

mood [muːd] n Stimmung f, Laune f; **to be in a good/bad ~** gute/schlechte Laune haben; ~**y** adj launisch

moon [muːn] n Mond m; ~**light** n Mondlicht nt; ~**lighting** n Schwarzarbeit f; ~**lit** adj mondhell

moor [muə^r] n Heide f, Hochmoor nt ♦ vt (ship) festmachen, verankern ♦ vi anlegen; ~**ings** npl Liegeplatz m; ~**land** ['muələnd] n Heidemoor nt

moose [muːs] n Elch m

mop [mɔp] n Mopp m ♦ vt (auf)wischen; ~ **up** vt aufwischen

mope [məup] vi Trübsal blasen

moped ['məuped] n Moped nt

moral ['mɔrl] adj moralisch; (values) sittlich; (virtuous) tugendhaft ♦ n Moral f; ~**s** npl

(ethics) Moral f

morale [mɔ'rɑːl] n Moral f

morality [mə'ræliti] n Sittlichkeit f

morass [mə'ræs] n Sumpf m

morbid ['mɔːbid] adj krankhaft; (jokes) makaber

KEYWORD

---

more [mɔː^r] adj (greater in number etc) mehr; (additional) noch mehr; **do you want (some) more tea?** möchten Sie noch etwas Tee?; **I have no** or **I don't have any more money** ich habe kein Geld mehr
♦ pron (greater amount) mehr; (further or additional amount) noch mehr; **is there any more?** gibt es noch mehr?; (left over) ist noch etwas da?; **there's no more** es ist nichts mehr da
♦ adv mehr; **more dangerous/easily** etc **(than)** gefährlicher/einfacher etc (als); **more and more** immer mehr; **more and more excited** immer aufgeregter; **more or less** mehr oder weniger; **more than ever** mehr denn je; **more beautiful than ever** schöner denn je

---

moreover [mɔː'rəuvə^r] adv überdies

morgue [mɔːg] n Leichenschauhaus nt

Mormon ['mɔːmən] n Mormone m, Mormonin f

morning ['mɔːnɪŋ] n Morgen m; **in the ~** am Morgen; **7 o'clock in the ~** 7 Uhr morgens; ~ **sickness** n (Schwangerschafts)übelkeit f

Morocco [mə'rɔkəu] n Marokko nt

moron ['mɔːrɔn] n Schwachsinnige(r) mf

morose [mə'rəus] adj mürrisch

morphine ['mɔːfiːn] n Morphium nt

Morse [mɔːs] n (also: ~ **code**) Morsealphabet nt

morsel ['mɔːsl] n Bissen m

mortal ['mɔːtl] adj sterblich; (deadly) tödlich; (very great) Todes- ♦ n (human being) Sterbliche(r) mf; ~**ity** [mɔː'tæliti] n Sterblichkeit f; (death rate) Sterblichkeitsziffer f

mortar ['mɔːtə^r] n (for building) Mörtel m;

(MIL) Granatwerfer *m*

mortgage ['mɔːgɪdʒ] *n* Hypothek *f* ♦ *vt* hypothekarisch belasten; **~ company** *(US)* *n* ≃ Bausparkasse *f*

mortify ['mɔːtɪfaɪ] *vt* beschämen

mortuary ['mɔːtjʊərɪ] *n* Leichenhalle *f*

mosaic [məʊ'zeɪɪk] *n* Mosaik *nt*

Moscow ['mɒskəʊ] *n* Moskau *nt*

Moslem ['mɒzləm] = **Muslim**

mosque [mɒsk] *n* Moschee *f*

mosquito [mɒs'kiːtəʊ] *(pl* **~es)** *n* Moskito *m*

moss [mɒs] *n* Moos *nt*

most [məʊst] *adj* meiste(r, s) ♦ *adv* am meisten; *(very)* höchst ♦ *n* das meiste, der größte Teil; *(people)* die meisten; **~ men** die meisten Männer; **at the (very) ~** allerhöchstens; **to make the ~ of** das Beste machen aus; **a ~ interesting book** ein höchstinteressantes Buch; **~ly** *adv* größtenteils

MOT *(BRIT)* *n abbr* (= *Ministry of Transport*): **the MOT (test)** ≃ der TÜV

motel [məʊ'tel] *n* Motel *nt*

moth [mɒθ] *n* Nachtfalter *m*; *(wool-eating)* Motte *f*; **~ball** *n* Mottenkugel *f*

mother ['mʌðə*] *n* Mutter *f* ♦ *vt* bemuttern; **~hood** *n* Mutterschaft *f*; **~-in-law** *n* Schwiegermutter *f*; **~ly** *adj* mütterlich; **~-of-pearl** *n* Perlmut *nt*; **M~'s Day** *(BRIT)* *n* Muttertag *m*; **~-to-be** *n* werdende Mutter *f*; **~ tongue** *n* Muttersprache *f*

motion ['məʊʃən] *n* Bewegung *f*; *(in meeting)* Antrag *m* ♦ *vt, vi:* **to ~ (to) sb** jdm winken, jdm zu verstehen geben; **~less** *adj* regungslos; **~ picture** *n* Film *m*

motivated ['məʊtɪveɪtɪd] *adj* motiviert

motivation [məʊtɪ'veɪʃən] *n* Motivierung *f*

motive ['məʊtɪv] *n* Motiv *nt*, Beweggrund *m* ♦ *adj* treibend

motley ['mɒtlɪ] *adj* bunt

motor ['məʊtə*] *n* Motor *m*; *(BRIT: inf: vehicle)* Auto *nt* ♦ *adj* Motor-; **~bike** *n* Motorrad *nt*; **~boat** *n* Motorboot *nt*; **~car** *(BRIT)* *n* Auto *nt*; **~cycle** *n* Motorrad *nt*; **~cyclist** *n* Motorradfahrer(in) *m(f)*; **~ing** *(BRIT)* *n* Autofahren *nt* ♦ *adj* Auto-; **~ist** *n* Autofahrer(in) *m(f)*; **~ mechanic** *n*

Kraftfahrzeugmechaniker(in) *m(f)*, Kfz-Mechaniker(in) *m(f)*; **~ racing** *(BRIT)* *n* Autorennen *nt*; **~ vehicle** *n* Kraftfahrzeug *nt*; **~way** *(BRIT)* *n* Autobahn *f*

mottled ['mɒtld] *adj* gesprenkelt

mould [məʊld] *(US* **mold)** *n* Form *f*; *(mildew)* Schimmel *m* ♦ *vt (also fig)* formen; **~y** *adj* schimmelig

moult [məʊlt] *(US* **molt)** *vi* sich mausern

mound [maʊnd] *n* (Erd)hügel *m*

mount [maʊnt] *n (liter. hill)* Berg *m*; *(horse)* Pferd *nt*; *(for jewel etc)* Fassung *f* ♦ *vt (horse)* steigen auf +*acc*; *(put in setting)* fassen; *(exhibition)* veranstalten; *(attack)* unternehmen ♦ *vi (also:* **~ up)** sich häufen; *(on horse)* aufsitzen

mountain ['maʊntɪn] *n* Berg *m* ♦ *cpd* Berg-; **~ bike** *n* Mountainbike *nt*; **~eer** *n* Bergsteiger(in) *m(f)*; **~eering** [maʊntɪ'nɪərɪŋ] *n* Bergsteigen *nt*; **~ous** *adj* bergig; **~ rescue team** *n* Bergwacht *f*; **~side** *n* Berg(ab)hang *m*

mourn [mɔːn] *vt* betrauen, beklagen ♦ *vi:* **to ~ (for sb)** (um jdn) trauern; **~er** *n* Trauernde(r) *mf*; **~ful** *adj* traurig; **~ing** *n (grief)* Trauer *f* ♦ *cpd (dress)* Trauer-; **in ~ing** *(period etc)* in Trauer; *(dress)* in Trauerkleidung

mouse [maʊs] *(pl* **mice)** *n* Maus *f*; **~trap** *n* Mausefalle *f*; **~ mat, ~ pad** *(COMPUT)* *n* Mousepad *nt*

mousse [muːs] *n (COOK)* Creme *f*; *(cosmetic)* Schaumfestiger *m*

moustache [məs'tɑːʃ] *n* Schnurrbart *m*

mousy ['maʊsɪ] *adj (colour)* mausgrau; *(person)* schüchtern

mouth [maʊθ] *n* Mund *m*; *(opening)* Öffnung *f*; *(of river)* Mündung *f*; **~ful** *n* Mund *m* voll; **~ organ** *n* Mundharmonika *f*; **~piece** *n* Mundstück *nt*; *(fig)* Sprachrohr *nt*; **~wash** *n* Mundwasser *nt*; **~watering** *adj* lecker, appetitlich

movable ['muːvəbl] *adj* beweglich

move [muːv] *n (~ment)* Bewegung *f*; *(in game)* Zug *m*; *(step)* Schritt *m*; *(of house)* Umzug *m* ♦ *vt* bewegen; *(people)* transportieren; *(in job)* versetzen;

(*emotionally*) bewegen ♦ *vi* sich bewegen; (*vehicle, ship*) fahren; (~ *house*) umziehen; **to get a ~ on** sich beeilen; **to ~ sb to do sth** jdn veranlassen, etw zu tun; **~ about** *or* **around** *vi* sich hin und her bewegen; (*travel*) unterwegs sein; **~ along** *vi* weitergehen; (*cars*) weiterfahren; **~ away** *vi* weggehen; **~ back** *vi* zurückgehen; (*to the rear*) zurückweichen; **~ forward** *vi* vorwärts gehen, sich vorwärts bewegen ♦ *vt* vorschieben; (*time*) vorverlegen; **~ in** *vi* (*to house*) einziehen; (*troops*) einrücken; **~ on** *vi* weitergehen ♦ *vt* weitergehen lassen; **~ out** *vi* (*of house*) ausziehen; (*troops*) abziehen; **~ over** *vi* zur Seite rücken; **~ up** *vi* aufsteigen; (*in job*) befördert werden ♦ *vt* nach oben bewegen; (*in job*) befördern; **~ment** ['muːvmənt] *n* Bewegung *f*

movie ['muːvɪ] *n* Film *m*; **to go to the ~s** ins Kino gehen; **~ camera** *n* Filmkamera *f*

moving ['muːvɪŋ] *adj* beweglich; (*touching*) ergreifend

mow [məu] (*pt* **mowed**, *pp* **mowed** *or* **mown**) *vt* mähen; **~ down** *vt* (*fig*) niedermähen; **~er** *n* (*lawnmower*) Rasenmäher *m*; **~n** *pp of* **mow**

MP *n abbr* = **Member of Parliament**

m.p.h. *abbr* = **miles per hour**

Mr ['mɪstə*] (*US* **Mr.**) *n* Herr *m*

Mrs ['mɪsɪz] (*US* **Mrs.**) *n* Frau *f*

Ms [mɪz] (*US* **Ms.**) *n* (= *Miss or Mrs*) Frau *f*

M.Sc. *n abbr* = **Master of Science**

MSP *n abbr* = **Member of the Scottish Parliament**) Mitglied *nt* des schottischen Parlaments

much [mʌtʃ] *adj* viel ♦ *adv* sehr; viel ♦ *n* viel, eine Menge; **how ~ is it?** wie viel kostet das?; **too ~** zu viel; **it's not ~** es ist nicht viel; **as ~ as** so sehr, so viel; **however ~ he tries** sosehr er es auch versucht

muck [mʌk] *n* Mist *m*; (*fig*) Schmutz *m*; **~ about** *or* **around** (*inf*) *vi*: **to ~ about** *or* **around (with sth)** (an etw *dat*) herumalbern; **~ up** *vt* (*inf*: ruin) vermasseln; (*dirty*) dreckig machen; **~y** *adj* (*dirty*) dreckig

mud [mʌd] *n* Schlamm *m*

muddle ['mʌdl] *n* Durcheinander *nt* ♦ *vt* (*also*: **~ up**) durcheinander bringen; **~ through** *vi* sich durchwursteln

mud ['mʌd-]: **~dy** *adj* schlammig; **~guard** *n* Schutzblech *nt*; **~-slinging** (*inf*) *n* Verleumdung *f*

muesli ['mjuːzlɪ] *n* Müsli *nt*

muffin ['mʌfɪn] *n* süße(s) Teilchen *nt*

muffle ['mʌfl] *vt* (*sound*) dämpfen; (*wrap up*) einhüllen; **~d** *adj* gedämpft; **~r** (*US*) *n* (*AUT*) Schalldämpfer *m*

mug [mʌg] *n* (*cup*) Becher *m*; (*inf*: *face*) Visage *f*; (: *fool*) Trottel *m* ♦ *vt* überfallen und ausrauben; **~ger** *n* Straßenräuber *m*; **~ging** *n* Überfall *m*

muggy ['mʌgɪ] *adj* (*weather*) schwül

mule [mjuːl] *n* Maulesel *m*

mull [mʌl]: **~ over** *vt* nachdenken über +*acc*

multicoloured ['mʌltɪkʌləd] (*US* **multicolored**) *adj* mehrfarbig

multi-level ['mʌltɪlevl] (*US*) *adj* = **multistorey**

multiple ['mʌltɪpl] *n* Vielfache(s) *nt* ♦ *adj* mehrfach; (*many*) mehrere; **~ sclerosis** *n* multiple Sklerose *f*

multiplex cinema ['mʌltɪpleks-] *n* Kinocenter *nt*

multiplication [mʌltɪplɪ'keɪʃən] *n* Multiplikation *f*; (*increase*) Vervielfachung *f*

multiply ['mʌltɪplaɪ] *vt*: **to ~ (by)** multiplizieren (mit) ♦ *vi* (*BIOL*) sich vermehren

multistorey ['mʌltɪ'stɔːrɪ] (*BRIT*) *adj* (*building, car park*) mehrstöckig

multitude ['mʌltɪtjuːd] *n* Menge *f*

mum [mʌm] *n* (*BRIT*: *inf*) Mutti *f* ♦ *adj*: **to keep ~ (about)** den Mund halten (über +*acc*)

mumble ['mʌmbl] *vt*, *vi* murmeln ♦ *n* Gemurmel *nt*

mummy ['mʌmɪ] *n* (*dead body*) Mumie *f*; (*BRIT*: *inf*) Mami *f*

mumps [mʌmps] *n* Mumps *m*

munch [mʌntʃ] *vt*, *vi* mampfen

mundane [mʌn'deɪn] *adj* banal

municipal [mjuː'nɪsɪpl] *adj* städtisch, Stadt-

mural ['mjuərl] *n* Wandgemälde *nt*

murder ['mɜːdə*] *n* Mord *m* ♦ *vt* ermorden; **~er** *n* Mörder *m*; **~ous** *adj* Mord-; (*fig*)

mörderisch
murky ['mɜːkɪ] *adj* finster
murmur ['mɜːməʳ] *n* Murmeln *nt*; (*of water, wind*) Rauschen *nt* ♦ *vt, vi* murmeln
muscle ['mʌsl] *n* Muskel *m*; ~ **in** *vi* mitmischen; **muscular** ['mʌskjʊləʳ] *adj* Muskel-; (*strong*) muskulös
museum [mju:'zɪəm] *n* Museum *nt*
mushroom ['mʌʃrʊm] *n* Champignon *m*; Pilz *m* ♦ *vi* (*fig*) emporschießen
music ['mju:zɪk] *n* Musik *f*; (*printed*) Noten *pl*; **~al** *adj* (*sound*) melodisch; (*person*) musikalisch ♦ *n* (*show*) Musical *nt*; **~al instrument** *n* Musikinstrument *nt*; **~ centre** *n* Stereoanlage *f*; **~ hall** *n* Varietee *nt*, Varieté *nt*; **~ian** [mju:'zɪʃən] *n* Musiker(in) *m(f)*
Muslim ['mʌzlɪm] *adj* moslemisch ♦ *n* Moslem *m*
muslin ['mʌzlɪn] *n* Musselin *m*
mussel ['mʌsl] *n* Miesmuschel *f*
must [mʌst] *vb aux* müssen; (*in negation*) dürfen ♦ *n* Muss *nt*; **the film is a ~** den Film muss man einfach gesehen haben
mustard ['mʌstəd] *n* Senf *m*
muster ['mʌstəʳ] *vt* (*MIL*) antreten lassen; (*courage*) zusammennehmen
mustn't ['mʌsnt] = **must not**
musty ['mʌstɪ] *adj* muffig
mute [mju:t] *adj* stumm ♦ *n* (*person*) Stumme(r) *mf*; (*MUS*) Dämpfer *m*; **~d** *adj* gedämpft
mutilate ['mju:tɪleɪt] *vt* verstümmeln
mutiny ['mju:tɪnɪ] *n* Meuterei *f* ♦ *vi* meutern
mutter ['mʌtəʳ] *vt, vi* murmeln
mutton ['mʌtn] *n* Hammelfleisch *nt*
mutual ['mju:tʃʊəl] *adj* gegenseitig; beiderseitig; **~ly** *adv* gegenseitig; für beide Seiten
muzzle ['mʌzl] *n* (*of animal*) Schnauze *f*; (*for animal*) Maulkorb *m*; (*of gun*) Mündung *f* ♦ *vt* einen Maulkorb anlegen +*dat*
my [maɪ] *adj* mein; **this is ~ car** das ist mein Auto; **I've washed ~ hair** ich habe mir die Haare gewaschen
myself [maɪ'self] *pron* mich *acc*; mir *dat*; (*emphatic*) selbst; *see also* **oneself**

mysterious [mɪs'tɪərɪəs] *adj* geheimnisvoll
mystery ['mɪstərɪ] *n* (*secret*) Geheimnis *nt*; (*sth difficult*) Rätsel *nt*
mystify ['mɪstɪfaɪ] *vt* ein Rätsel *nt* sein +*dat*; verblüffen
mystique [mɪs'ti:k] *n* geheimnisvolle Natur *f*
myth [mɪθ] *n* Mythos *m*; (*fig*) Erfindung *f*; **~ology** [mɪ'θɒlədʒɪ] *n* Mythologie *f*

N, n

n/a *abbr* (= *not applicable*) nicht zutreffend
nab [næb] (*inf*) *vt* schnappen
naff [næf] (*BRIT: inf*) *adj* blöd
nag [næg] *n* (*horse*) Gaul *m*; (*person*) Nörgler(in) *m(f)* ♦ *vt, vi*: **to ~ (at) sb** an jdm herumnörgeln; **~ging** *adj* (*doubt*) nagend ♦ *n* Nörgelei *f*
nail [neɪl] *n* Nagel *m* ♦ *vt* nageln; **to ~ sb down to doing sth** jdn darauf festnageln, etw zu tun; **~brush** *n* Nagelbürste *f*; **~file** *n* Nagelfeile *f*; **~ polish** *n* Nagellack *m*; **~ polish remover** *n* Nagellackentferner *m*; **~ scissors** *npl* Nagelschere *f*; **~ varnish** (*BRIT*) *n* = **nail polish**
naïve [naɪ'i:v] *adj* naiv
naked ['neɪkɪd] *adj* nackt
name [neɪm] *n* Name *m*; (*reputation*) Ruf *m* ♦ *vt* nennen; (*sth new*) benennen; (*appoint*) ernennen; **by ~** mit Namen; **I know him only by ~** ich kenne ihn nur dem Namen nach; **what's your ~?** wie heißen Sie?; **in the ~ of** im Namen +*gen*; (*for the sake of*) um +*gen* ... willen; **~less** *adj* namenlos; **~ly** *adv* nämlich; **~sake** *n* Namensvetter *m*
nanny ['nænɪ] *n* Kindermädchen *nt*
nap [næp] *n* (*sleep*) Nickerchen *nt*; (*on cloth*) Strich *m* ♦ *vi*: **to be caught ~ping** (*fig*) überrumpelt werden
nape [neɪp] *n* Nacken *m*
napkin ['næpkɪn] *n* (*at table*) Serviette *f*; (*BRIT: for baby*) Windel *f*
nappy ['næpɪ] (*BRIT*) *n* (*for baby*) Windel *f*; **~ rash** *n* wunde Stellen *pl*
narcotic [nɑ:'kɒtɪk] *adj* betäubend ♦ *n* Betäubungsmittel *nt*

narrative ['nærətɪv] n Erzählung f ♦ adj erzählend

narrator [nə'reɪtə'] n Erzähler(in) m(f)

narrow ['nærəu] adj eng, schmal; (limited) beschränkt ♦ vi sich verengen; **to have a ~ escape** mit knapper Not davonkommen; **to ~ sth down to sth** etw auf etw acc einschränken; **~ly** adv (miss) knapp; (escape) mit knapper Not; **~-minded** adj engstirnig

nasty ['nɑːstɪ] adj ekelhaft, fies; (business, wound) schlimm

nation ['neɪʃən] n Nation f, Volk nt; **~al** ['næʃənl] adj national, National-, Landes- ♦ n Staatsangehörige(r) mf; **~al anthem** (BRIT) n Nationalhymne f; **~al dress** n Tracht f; **N~al Health Service** (BRIT) n staatliche(r) Gesundheitsdienst m; **N~al Insurance** (BRIT) n Sozialversicherung f; **~alism** ['næʃnəlɪzəm] n Nationalismus m; **~alist** ['næʃnəlɪst] n Nationalist(in) m(f) ♦ adj nationalistisch; **~ality** [næʃə'nælɪtɪ] n Staatsangehörigkeit f; **~alize** ['næʃnəlaɪz] vt verstaatlichen; **~ally** ['næʃnəlɪ] adv national, auf Staatsebene; **~al park** (BRIT) n Nationalpark m; **~wide** ['neɪʃənwaɪd] adj, adv allgemein, landesweit

---

National Trust

ⓘ *Der* **National Trust** *ist ein 1895 gegründeter Natur- und Denkmalschutzverband in Großbritannien, der Gebäude und Gelände von besonderem historischen oder ästhetischen Interesse erhält und der Öffentlichkeit zugänglich macht. Viele Gebäude im Besitz des National Trust sind (z.T. gegen ein Eintrittsgeld) zu besichtigen.*

---

native ['neɪtɪv] n (born in) Einheimische(r) mf; (original inhabitant) Eingeborene(r) mf ♦ adj einheimisch; Eingeborenen-; (belonging by birth) heimatlich, Heimat-; (inborn) angeboren, natürlich; **a ~ of Germany** ein gebürtiger Deutscher; **a ~ speaker of French** ein französischer Muttersprachler; **N~ American** n

Indianer(in) m(f), Ureinwohner(in) m(f) Amerikas; **~ language** n Muttersprache f

Nativity [nə'tɪvɪtɪ] n: **the ~** Christi Geburt no art

NATO ['neɪtəu] n abbr (= North Atlantic Treaty Organization) NATO f

natural ['nætʃrəl] adj natürlich; Natur-; (inborn) (an)geboren; **~ gas** n Erdgas nt; **~ist** n Naturkundler(in) m(f); **~ly** adv natürlich

nature ['neɪtʃə'] n Natur f; **by ~** von Natur (aus)

naught [nɔːt] n = nought

naughty ['nɔːtɪ] adj (child) unartig, ungezogen; (action) ungehörig

nausea ['nɔːsɪə] n (sickness) Übelkeit f; (disgust) Ekel m; **~te** ['nɔːsɪeɪt] vt anekeln

nautical ['nɔːtɪkl] adj nautisch; See-; (expression) seemännisch

naval ['neɪvl] adj Marine-, Flotten-; **~ officer** n Marineoffizier m

nave [neɪv] n Kirchen(haupt)schiff nt

navel ['neɪvl] n Nabel m

navigate ['nævɪgeɪt] vi navigieren; **navigation** [nævɪ'geɪʃən] n Navigation f; **navigator** ['nævɪgeɪtə'] n Steuermann m; (AVIAT) Navigator m; (AUT) Beifahrer(in) m(f)

navvy ['nævɪ] (BRIT) n Straßenarbeiter m

navy ['neɪvɪ] n (Kriegs)marine f ♦ adj (also: **~ blue**) marineblau

Nazi ['nɑːtsɪ] n Nazi m

NB abbr (= nota bene) NB

near [nɪə'] adj nah ♦ adv in der Nähe ♦ prep (also: **~ to**: space) in der Nähe +gen; (: time) um +acc ... herum ♦ vt sich nähern +dat; **a ~ miss** knapp daneben; **~by** adj nahe (gelegen) ♦ adv in der Nähe; **~ly** adv fast; **I ~ly fell** ich wäre fast gefallen; **~side** n (AUT) Beifahrerseite f ♦ adj auf der Beifahrerseite; **~-sighted** adj kurzsichtig

neat [niːt] adj (tidy) ordentlich; (solution) sauber; (pure) pur; **~ly** adv (tidily) ordentlich

necessarily ['nesɪsrɪlɪ] adv unbedingt

necessary ['nesɪsrɪ] adj notwendig, nötig; **he did all that was ~** er erledigte alles, was nötig war; **it is ~ to/that ...** man muss ...

necessitate [nɪ'sesɪteɪt] *vt* erforderlich machen

necessity [nɪ'sesɪtɪ] *n* (*need*) Not *f*; (*compulsion*) Notwendigkeit *f*; **necessities** *npl* (*things needed*) das Notwendigste

neck [nɛk] *n* Hals *m* ♦ *vi* (*inf*) knutschen; **~ and ~** Kopf an Kopf; **~lace** ['nɛklɪs] *n* Halskette *f*; **~line** ['nɛklaɪn] *n* Ausschnitt *m*; **~tie** ['nɛktaɪ] (*US*) *n* Krawatte *f*

née [neɪ] *adj* geborene

need [niːd] *n* Bedürfnis *nt*; (*lack*) Mangel *m*; (*necessity*) Notwendigkeit *f*; (*poverty*) Not *f* ♦ *vt* brauchen; **I ~ to do it** ich muss es tun; **you don't ~ to go** du brauchst nicht zu gehen

needle ['niːdl] *n* Nadel *f* ♦ *vt* (*fig: inf*) ärgern

needless ['niːdlɪs] *adj* unnötig; **~ to say** natürlich

needlework ['niːdlwəːk] *n* Handarbeit *f*

needn't ['niːdnt] = **need not**

needy ['niːdɪ] *adj* bedürftig

negative ['negətɪv] *n* (PHOT) Negativ *nt* ♦ *adj* negativ; (*answer*) abschlägig; **~ equity** *n* Differenz zwischen gefallenem Wert und hypothekarischer Belastung eines Wohneigentums

neglect [nɪ'glɛkt] *vt* vernachlässigen ♦ *n* Vernachlässigung *f*; **~ed** *adj* vernachlässigt

negligee ['neglɪʒeɪ] *n* Negligee *nt*, Negligé *nt*

negligence ['neglɪdʒəns] *n* Nachlässigkeit *f*

negligible ['neglɪdʒɪbl] *adj* unbedeutend, geringfügig

negotiable [nɪ'gəʊʃɪəbl] *adj* (*cheque*) übertragbar, einlösbar

negotiate [nɪ'gəʊʃɪeɪt] *vi* verhandeln ♦ *vt* (*treaty*) abschließen; (*difficulty*) überwinden; (*corner*) nehmen; **negotiation** [nɪgəʊʃɪ'eɪʃən] *n* Verhandlung *f*; **negotiator** *n* Unterhändler *m*

neigh [neɪ] *vi* wiehern

neighbour ['neɪbər] (*US* **neighbor**) *n* Nachbar(in) *m(f)*; **~hood** *n* Nachbarschaft *f*; Umgebung *f*; **~ing** *adj* benachbart, angrenzend; **~ly** *adj* (*person, attitude*) nachbarlich

neither ['naɪðər] *adj, pron* keine(r, s) (von beiden) ♦ *conj*: **he can't do it, and ~ can I** er kann es nicht und ich auch nicht ♦ *adv*: **~ good nor bad** weder gut noch schlecht; **~ story is true** keine der beiden Geschichten stimmt

neon ['niːɔn] *n* Neon *nt*; **~ light** *n* Neonlampe *f*

nephew ['nevjuː] *n* Neffe *m*

nerve [nəːv] *n* Nerv *m*; (*courage*) Mut *m*; (*impudence*) Frechheit *f*; **to have a fit of ~s** in Panik geraten; **~-racking** *adj* nervenaufreibend

nervous ['nəːvəs] *adj* (*of the nerves*) Nerven-; (*timid*) nervös, ängstlich; **~ breakdown** *n* Nervenzusammenbruch *m*; **~ness** *n* Nervosität *f*

nest [nɛst] *n* Nest *nt* ♦ *vi* nisten; **~ egg** *n* (*fig*) Notgroschen *m*

nestle ['nɛsl] *vi* sich kuscheln

Net [nɛt] *n*: **the ~** das Internet

net *n* Netz *nt* ♦ *adj* netto, Netto- ♦ *vt* netto einnehmen; **~ball** *n* Netzball *m*

Netherlands ['neðələndz] *npl*: **the ~** die Niederlande *pl*

nett [nɛt] *adj* = **net**

netting ['nɛtɪŋ] *n* Netz(werk) *nt*

nettle ['nɛtl] *n* Nessel *f*

network ['nɛtwəːk] *n* Netz *nt*

neurotic [njʊə'rɔtɪk] *adj* neurotisch

neuter ['njuːtər] *adj* (BIOL) geschlechtslos; (GRAM) sächlich ♦ *vt* kastrieren

neutral ['njuːtrəl] *adj* neutral ♦ *n* (AUT) Leerlauf *m*; **~ity** [njuː'trælɪtɪ] *n* Neutralität *f*; **~ize** *vt* (*fig*) ausgleichen

never ['nevər] *adv* nie(mals); **I ~ went** ich bin gar nicht gegangen; **~ in my life** nie im Leben; **~-ending** *adj* endlos; **~theless** [nevəðə'lɛs] *adv* trotzdem, dennoch

new [njuː] *adj* neu; **N~ Age** *adj* Newage-, New-Age-; **~born** *adj* neugeboren; **~comer** ['njuːkʌmər] *n* Neuankömmling *m*; **~-fangled** (*pej*) *adj* neumodisch; **~-found** *adj* neu entdeckt; **~ly** *adv* frisch, neu; **~lyweds** *npl* Frischvermählte *pl*; **~ moon** *n* Neumond *m*

news [njuːz] *n* Nachricht *f*; (RAD, TV) Nachrichten *pl*; **a piece of ~** eine

Nachricht; ~ **agency** n
Nachrichtenagentur f; ~**agent** (BRIT) n
Zeitungshändler m; ~**caster** n
Nachrichtensprecher(in) m(f); ~ **flash** n
Kurzmeldung f; ~**letter** n Rundschreiben
nt; ~**paper** n Zeitung f; ~**print** n
Zeitungspapier nt; ~**reader** n =
newscaster; ~**reel** n Wochenschau f; ~
stand n Zeitungsstand m

newt [njuːt] n Wassermolch m

New Year n Neujahr nt; ~'**s Day** n
Neujahrstag m; ~'**s Eve** n Silvester(abend
m) nt

New Zealand [-'ziːlənd] n Neuseeland nt;
~**er** n Neuseeländer(in) m(f)

next [nɛkst] adj nächste(r, s) ♦ adv (after)
dann, darauf; (~ time) das nächste Mal; **the
~ day** am nächsten or folgenden Tag; ~
time das nächste Mal; ~ **year** nächstes
Jahr; ~ **door** adv nebenan ♦ adj (neighbour,
flat) von nebenan; ~ **of kin** n nächste(r)
Verwandte(r) mf; ~ **to** prep neben; ~ **to
nothing** so gut wie nichts

NHS n abbr = **National Health Service**

nib [nɪb] n Spitze f

nibble ['nɪbl] vt knabbern an +dat

nice [naɪs] adj (person) nett; (thing) schön;
(subtle) fein; ~-**looking** adj gut aussehend;
~**ly** adv gut, nett; ~**ties** ['naɪsɪtɪz] npl
Feinheiten pl

nick [nɪk] n Einkerbung f ♦ vt (inf: steal)
klauen; **in the ~ of time** gerade rechtzeitig

nickel ['nɪkl] n Nickel nt; (US) Nickel m (5
cents)

nickname ['nɪkneɪm] n Spitzname m ♦ vt
taufen

nicotine patch ['nɪkətiːn-] n Nikotinpflaster
nt

niece [niːs] n Nichte f

Nigeria [naɪ'dʒɪərɪə] n Nigeria nt

niggling ['nɪglɪŋ] adj pedantisch; (doubt,
worry) quälend

night [naɪt] n Nacht f; (evening) Abend m;
the ~ before last vorletzte Nacht; **at** or **by
~** (before midnight) abends; (after midnight)
nachts; ~**cap** n (drink) Schlummertrunk m;
~**club** n Nachtlokal nt; ~**dress** n

Nachthemd nt; ~**fall** n Einbruch m der
Nacht; ~ **gown** n = **nightdress**; ~**ie** (inf) n
Nachthemd nt

nightingale ['naɪtɪŋgeɪl] n Nachtigall f

night: ~life ['naɪtlaɪf] n Nachtleben nt; ~**ly**
['naɪtlɪ] adj, adv jeden Abend; jede Nacht;
~**mare** ['naɪtmɛəʳ] n Albtraum m; ~ **porter**
n Nachtportier m; ~ **school** n Abendschule
f; ~ **shift** n Nachtschicht f; ~**time** n Nacht
f

nil [nɪl] n Null f

Nile [naɪl] n: **the ~** der Nil

nimble ['nɪmbl] adj beweglich

nine [naɪn] num neun; ~**teen** num
neunzehn; ~**ty** num neunzig

ninth [naɪnθ] adj neunte(r, s)

nip [nɪp] vt kneifen ♦ n Kneifen nt

nipple ['nɪpl] n Brustwarze f

nippy ['nɪpɪ] (inf) adj (person) flink; (BRIT: car)
flott; (: cold) frisch

nitrogen ['naɪtrədʒən] n Stickstoff m

KEYWORD
---

no [nəʊ] (pl **noes**) adv (opposite of yes) nein;
to answer no (to question) mit Nein
antworten; (to request) Nein or nein sagen;
no thank you nein, danke
♦ adj (not any) kein(e); **I have no money/
time** ich habe kein Geld/keine Zeit; **"no
smoking"** „Rauchen verboten"
♦ n Nein nt; (no vote) Neinstimme f

---

nobility [nəʊ'bɪlɪtɪ] n Adel m

noble ['nəʊbl] adj (rank) adlig; (splendid)
nobel, edel

nobody ['nəʊbədɪ] pron niemand, keiner

nocturnal [nɔk'tɜːnl] adj (tour, visit)
nächtlich; (animal) Nacht-

nod [nɔd] vi nicken ♦ vt nicken mit ♦ n
Nicken nt; ~ **off** vi einnicken

noise [nɔɪz] n (sound) Geräusch nt;
(unpleasant, loud) Lärm m; **noisy** ['nɔɪzɪ] adj
laut; (crowd) lärmend

nominal ['nɔmɪnl] adj nominell

nominate ['nɔmɪneɪt] vt (suggest)
vorschlagen; (in election) aufstellen;
(appoint) ernennen; **nomination**

[nɔmɪ'neɪʃən] n (*election*) Nominierung f; (*appointment*) Ernennung f; **nominee** [nɔmɪ'niː] n Kandidat(in) m(f)

non... [nɔn] *prefix* Nicht-, un-; **~-alcoholic** *adj* alkoholfrei

nonchalant ['nɔnʃələnt] *adj* lässig

non-committal [nɔnkə'mɪtl] *adj* (*reserved*) zurückhaltend; (*uncommitted*) unverbindlich

nondescript ['nɔndɪskrɪpt] *adj* mittelmäßig

none [nʌn] *adj, pron* kein(e, er, es) ♦ *adv:* **he's ~ the worse for it** es hat ihm nicht geschadet; **~ of you** keiner von euch; **I've ~ left** ich habe keinen mehr

nonentity [nɔ'nentɪtɪ] n Null f (*inf*)

nonetheless ['nʌnðə'les] *adv* nichtsdestoweniger

non-existent [nɔnɪg'zɪstənt] *adj* nicht vorhanden

non-fiction [nɔn'fɪkʃən] n Sachbücher *pl*

nonplussed [nɔn'plʌst] *adj* verdutzt

nonsense ['nɔnsəns] n Unsinn m

non: **~-smoker** n Nichtraucher(in) m(f); **~-smoking** *adj* Nichtraucher-; **~-stick** *adj* (*pan, surface*) Teflon- ®; **~-stop** *adj* Nonstop-, Non-Stop-

noodles ['nuːdlz] *npl* Nudeln *pl*

nook [nuk] n Winkel m; **~s and crannies** Ecken und Winkel

noon [nuːn] n (12 Uhr) Mittag m

no one ['nəuwʌn] *pron* = **nobody**

noose [nuːs] n Schlinge f

nor [nɔːʳ] *conj* = **neither** ♦ *adv see* **neither**

norm [nɔːm] n (*convention*) Norm f; (*rule, requirement*) Vorschrift f

normal ['nɔːməl] *adj* normal; **~ly** *adv* normal; (*usually*) normalerweise

Normandy ['nɔːməndɪ] n Normandie f

north [nɔːθ] n Norden m ♦ *adj* nördlich, Nord- ♦ *adv* nördlich, nach *or* im Norden; **N~ Africa** n Nordafrika nt; **N~ America** n Nordamerika nt; **~-east** n Nordosten m; **~erly** ['nɔːðəlɪ] *adj* nördlich; **~ern** ['nɔːðən] *adj* nördlich, Nord-; **N~ern Ireland** n Nordirland nt; **N~ Pole** n Nordpol m; **N~ Sea** n Nordsee f; **~ward(s)** ['nɔːθwəd(z)] *adv* nach Norden; **~-west** n Nordwesten m

Norway ['nɔːweɪ] n Norwegen nt

Norwegian [nɔː'wiːdʒən] *adj* norwegisch ♦ n Norweger(in) m(f); (*LING*) Norwegisch nt

nose [nəuz] n Nase f ♦ *vi:* **to ~ about** herumschnüffeln; **~bleed** n Nasenbluten nt; **~ dive** n Sturzflug m; **~y** *adj* = **nosy**

nostalgia [nɔs'tældʒɪə] n Nostalgie f; **nostalgic** *adj* nostalgisch

nostril ['nɔstrɪl] n Nasenloch nt

nosy ['nəuzɪ] (*inf*) *adj* neugierig

not [nɔt] *adv* nicht; **he is ~** *or* **isn't here** er ist nicht hier; **it's too late, isn't it?** es ist zu spät, oder *or* nicht wahr?; **~ yet/now** noch nicht/nicht jetzt; *see also* **all**; **only**

notably ['nəutəblɪ] *adv* (*especially*) besonders; (*noticeably*) bemerkenswert

notary ['nəutərɪ] n Notar(in) m(f)

notch [nɔtʃ] n Kerbe f, Einschnitt m

note [nəut] n (*MUS*) Note f, Ton m; (*short letter*) Nachricht f; (*POL*) Note f; (*comment, attention*) Notiz f; (*of lecture etc*) Aufzeichnung f; (*banknote*) Schein m; (*fame*) Ruf m ♦ *vt* (*observe*) bemerken; (*also:* **~ down**) notieren; **~book** n Notizbuch nt; **~d** *adj* bekannt; **~pad** n Notizblock m; **~paper** n Briefpapier nt

nothing ['nʌθɪŋ] n nichts; **~ new/much** nichts Neues/nicht viel; **for ~** umsonst

notice ['nəutɪs] n (*announcement*) Bekanntmachung f; (*warning*) Ankündigung f; (*dismissal*) Kündigung f ♦ *vt* bemerken; **to take ~ of** beachten; **at short ~** kurzfristig; **until further ~** bis auf weiteres; **to hand in one's ~** kündigen; **~able** *adj* merklich; **~ board** n Anschlagtafel f

notify ['nəutɪfaɪ] *vt* benachrichtigen

notion ['nəuʃən] n Idee f

notorious [nəu'tɔːrɪəs] *adj* berüchtigt

notwithstanding [nɔtwɪθ'stændɪŋ] *adv* trotzdem; **~ this** ungeachtet dessen

nought [nɔːt] n Null f

noun [naun] n Substantiv nt

nourish ['nʌrɪʃ] *vt* nähren; **~ing** *adj* nahrhaft; **~ment** n Nahrung f

novel ['nɔvl] n Roman m ♦ *adj* neu(artig); **~ist** n Schriftsteller(in) m(f); **~ty** n Neuheit f

November [nəu'vembə'] n November m

novice ['nɔvɪs] n Neuling m

now [nau] adv jetzt; **right ~** jetzt, gerade; **by ~** inzwischen; **just ~** gerade; **~ and then, ~ and again** ab und zu, manchmal; **from ~ on** von jetzt an; **~adays** adv heutzutage

nowhere ['nəuweə'] adv nirgends

nozzle ['nɔzl] n Düse f

nuclear ['nju:klɪə'] adj (energy etc) Atom-, Kern-

nuclei ['nju:klɪaɪ] npl of nucleus

nucleus ['nju:klɪəs] n Kern m

nude [nju:d] adj nackt ♦ n (ART) Akt m; **in the ~** nackt

nudge [nʌdʒ] vt leicht anstoßen

nudist ['nju:dɪst] n Nudist(in) m(f)

nudity ['nju:dɪtɪ] n Nacktheit f

nuisance ['nju:sns] n Ärgernis nt; **what a ~!** wie ärgerlich!

nuke [nju:k] (inf) n Kernkraftwerk nt ♦ vt atomar vernichten

null [nʌl] adj: **~ and void** null und nichtig

numb [nʌm] adj taub, gefühllos ♦ vt betäuben

number ['nʌmbə'] n Nummer f; (numeral also) Zahl f; (quantity) (An)zahl f ♦ vt nummerieren; (amount to) sein; **to be ~ed among** gezählt werden zu; **a ~ of** (several) einige; **they were ten in ~** sie waren zehn an der Zahl; **~ plate** (BRIT) n (AUT) Nummernschild nt

numeral ['nju:mərəl] n Ziffer f

numerate ['nju:mərɪt] adj rechenkundig

numerical [nju:'merɪkl] adj (order) zahlenmäßig

numerous ['nju:mərəs] adj zahlreich

nun [nʌn] n Nonne f

nurse [nə:s] n Krankenschwester f; (for children) Kindermädchen nt ♦ vt (patient) pflegen; (doubt etc) hegen

nursery ['nə:sərɪ] n (for children) Kinderzimmer nt; (for plants) Gärtnerei f; (for trees) Baumschule f; **~ rhyme** n Kinderreim m; **~ school** n Kindergarten m; **~ slope** (BRIT) n (SKI) Idiotenhügel m (inf), Anfängerhügel m

nursing ['nə:sɪŋ] n (profession) Krankenpflege f; **~ home** n Privatklinik f

nurture ['nə:tʃə'] vt aufziehen

nut [nʌt] n Nuss f; (TECH) Schraubenmutter f; (inf) Verrückte(r) mf; **he's ~s** er ist verrückt; **~crackers** ['nʌtkrækəz] npl Nussknacker m

nutmeg ['nʌtmeg] n Muskat(nuss f) m

nutrient ['nju:trɪənt] n Nährstoff m

nutrition [nju:'trɪʃən] n Nahrung f; **nutritious** [nju:'trɪʃəs] adj nahrhaft

nutshell ['nʌtʃel] n Nussschale f; **in a ~** (fig) kurz gesagt

nutter ['nʌtə'] (BRIT: inf) n Spinner(in) m(f)

nylon ['naɪlɔn] n Nylon nt ♦ adj Nylon-

O, o

oak [əuk] n Eiche f ♦ adj Eichen(holz)-

O.A.P. abbr = old-age pensioner

oar [ɔ:'] n Ruder nt

oases [əu'eɪsi:z] npl of oasis

oasis [əu'eɪsɪs] n Oase f

oath [əuθ] n (statement) Eid m, Schwur m; (swearword) Fluch m

oatmeal ['əutmi:l] n Haferschrot m

oats [əuts] npl Hafer m

obedience [ə'bi:dɪəns] n Gehorsam m

obedient [ə'bi:dɪənt] adj gehorsam

obesity [əu'bi:sɪtɪ] n Fettleibigkeit f

obey [ə'beɪ] vt, vi: **to ~ (sb)** (jdm) gehorchen

obituary [ə'bɪtjuərɪ] n Nachruf m

object [n 'ɔbdʒɪkt, vb əb'dʒekt] n (thing) Gegenstand m, Objekt nt; (purpose) Ziel nt ♦ vi dagegen sein; **expense is no ~** Ausgaben spielen keine Rolle; **I ~!** ich protestiere!; **to ~ to sth** Einwände gegen etw haben; (morally) Anstoß an etw acc nehmen; **to ~ that** einwenden, dass; **~ion** [əb'dʒekʃən] n (reason against) Einwand m, Einspruch m; (dislike) Abneigung f; **I have no ~ion to ...** ich habe nichts gegen ... einzuwenden; **~ionable** [əb'dʒekʃənəbl] adj nicht einwandfrei; (language) anstößig

objective [əb'dʒektɪv] n Ziel nt ♦ adj objektiv

obligation [ɔblɪ'geɪʃən] n Verpflichtung f; **without ~** unverbindlich; **obligatory**

[ə'blɪgətərɪ] *adj* obligatorisch

oblige [ə'blaɪdʒ] *vt (compel)* zwingen; *(do a favour)* einen Gefallen tun +*dat;* **to be ~d to sb for sth** jdm für etw verbunden sein

obliging [ə'blaɪdʒɪŋ] *adj* entgegenkommend

oblique [ə'bli:k] *adj* schräg, schief ♦ *n* Schrägstrich *m*

obliterate [ə'blɪtəreɪt] *vt* auslöschen

oblivion [ə'blɪvɪən] *n* Vergessenheit *f*

oblivious [ə'blɪvɪəs] *adj* nicht bewusst

oblong [ˈɒblɒŋ] *n* Rechteck *nt* ♦ *adj* länglich

obnoxious [əb'nɒkʃəs] *adj* widerlich

oboe [ˈəʊbəʊ] *n* Oboe *f*

obscene [əb'si:n] *adj* obszön; **obscenity** [əb'senɪtɪ] *n* Obszönität *f;* **obscenities** *npl (oaths)* Zoten *pl*

obscure [əb'skjʊəʳ] *adj* unklar; *(indistinct)* undeutlich; *(unknown)* unbekannt, obskur; *(dark)* düster ♦ *vt* verdunkeln; *(view)* verbergen; *(confuse)* verwirren; **obscurity** [əb'skjʊərɪtɪ] *n* Unklarheit *f; (darkness)* Dunkelheit *f*

observance [əb'zɜ:vəns] *n* Befolgung *f*

observant [əb'zɜ:vənt] *adj* aufmerksam

observation [ɒbzə'veɪʃən] *n (noticing)* Beobachtung *f; (surveillance)* Überwachung *f; (remark)* Bemerkung *f*

observatory [əb'zɜ:vətrɪ] *n* Sternwarte *f,* Observatorium *nt*

observe [əb'zɜ:v] *vt (notice)* bemerken; *(watch)* beobachten; *(customs)* einhalten; **~r** *n* Beobachter(in) *m(f)*

obsess [əb'ses] *vt* verfolgen, quälen; **~ion** [əb'seʃən] *n* Besessenheit *f,* Wahn *m;* **~ive** *adj* krankhaft

obsolete [ˈɒbsəli:t] *adj* überholt, veraltet

obstacle [ˈɒbstəkl] *n* Hindernis *nt;* **~ race** *n* Hindernisrennen *nt*

obstetrics [ɒb'stetrɪks] *n* Geburtshilfe *f*

obstinate [ˈɒbstɪnɪt] *adj* hartnäckig, stur

obstruct [əb'strʌkt] *vt* versperren; *(pipe)* verstopfen; *(hinder)* hemmen; **~ion** [əb'strʌkʃən] *n* Versperrung *f;* Verstopfung *f; (obstacle)* Hindernis *nt*

obtain [əb'teɪn] *vt* erhalten, bekommen; *(result)* erzielen

obtrusive [əb'tru:sɪv] *adj* aufdringlich

obvious [ˈɒbvɪəs] *adj* offenbar, offensichtlich; **~ly** *adv* offensichtlich

occasion [ə'keɪʒən] *n* Gelegenheit *f; (special event)* Ereignis *nt; (reason)* Anlass *m* ♦ *vt* veranlassen; **~al** *adj* gelegentlich; **~ally** *adv* gelegentlich

occupant [ˈɒkjʊpənt] *n* Inhaber(in) *m(f); (of house)* Bewohner(in) *m(f)*

occupation [ɒkjʊ'peɪʃən] *n (employment)* Tätigkeit *f,* Beruf *m; (pastime)* Beschäftigung *f; (of country)* Besetzung *f,* Okkupation *f;* **~al hazard** *n* Berufsrisiko *nt*

occupier [ˈɒkjʊpaɪəʳ] *n* Bewohner(in) *m(f)*

occupy [ˈɒkjʊpaɪ] *vt (take possession of)* besetzen; *(seat)* belegen; *(live in)* bewohnen; *(position, office)* bekleiden; *(position in sb's life)* einnehmen; *(time)* beanspruchen; **to ~ o.s. with sth** sich mit etw beschäftigen; **to ~ o.s. by doing sth** sich damit beschäftigen, etw zu tun

occur [ə'kɜ:ʳ] *vi* vorkommen; **to ~ to sb** jdm einfallen; **~rence** *n (event)* Ereignis *nt; (appearing)* Auftreten *nt*

ocean [ˈəʊʃən] *n* Ozean *m,* Meer *nt;* **~-going** *adj* Hochsee-

o'clock [ə'klɒk] *adv:* **it is 5 ~** es ist 5 Uhr

OCR *n abbr =* **optical character reader**

octagonal [ɒk'tægənl] *adj* achteckig

October [ɒk'təʊbəʳ] *n* Oktober *m*

octopus [ˈɒktəpəs] *n* Krake *f; (small)* Tintenfisch *m*

odd [ɒd] *adj (strange)* sonderbar; *(not even)* ungerade; *(sock etc)* einzeln; *(surplus)* übrig; **60-~** so um die 60; **at ~ times** ab und zu; **to be the ~ one out** *(person)* das fünfte Rad am Wagen sein; *(thing)* nicht dazugehören; **~ity** *n (strangeness)* Merkwürdigkeit *f; (queer person)* seltsame(r) Kauz *m; (thing)* Kuriosität *f;* **~-job man** *(irreg) n* Mädchen *nt* für alles; **~ jobs** *npl* gelegentlich anfallende Arbeiten; **~ly** *adv* seltsam; **~ments** *npl* Reste *pl;* **~s** *npl* Chancen *pl; (betting)* Gewinnchancen *pl;* **it makes no ~s** es spielt keine Rolle; **at ~s** uneinig; **~s and ends** *npl* Krimskrams *m*

odometer [ˈɒdɒmɪtəʳ] *(esp US) n* Tacho(meter) *m*

odour ['əudə'] (*US* **odor**) *n* Geruch *m*

KEYWORD
---

of [ɒv, əv] *prep* **1** von +*dat*; *use of gen*: **the history of Germany** die Geschichte Deutschlands; **a friend of ours** ein Freund von uns; **a boy of 10** ein 10-jähriger Junge; **that was kind of you** das war sehr freundlich von Ihnen

2 (*expressing quantity, amount, dates etc*): **a kilo of flour** ein Kilo Mehl; **how much of this do you need?** wie viel brauchen Sie (davon)?; **there were 3 of them** (*people*) sie waren zu dritt; (*objects*) es gab 3 (davon); **a cup of tea/vase of flowers** eine Tasse Tee/Vase mit Blumen; **the 5th of July** der 5. Juli

3 (*from, out of*) aus; **a bridge made of wood** eine Holzbrücke, eine Brücke aus Holz

---

off [ɒf] *adj, adv* (*absent*) weg, fort; (*switch*) aus(geschaltet), ab(geschaltet); (*BRIT: food: bad*) schlecht; (*cancelled*) abgesagt ♦ *prep* von +*dat*; **to be ~** (*to leave*) gehen; **to be ~ sick** krank sein; **a day ~** ein freier Tag; **to have an ~ day** einen schlechten Tag haben; **he had his coat ~** er hatte seinen Mantel aus; **10% ~** (*COMM*) 10% Rabatt; **5 km ~ (the road)** 5 km (von der Straße) entfernt; **~ the coast** vor der Küste; **I'm ~ meat** (*no longer eat it*) ich esse kein Fleisch mehr; (*no longer like it*) ich mag kein Fleisch mehr; **on the ~ chance** auf gut Glück

offal ['ɒfl] *n* Innereien *pl*

off-colour ['ɒf'kʌlə'] *adj* nicht wohl

offence [ə'fens] (*US* **offense**) *n* (*crime*) Vergehen *nt*, Straftat *f*; (*insult*) Beleidigung *f*; **to take ~ at** gekränkt sein wegen

offend [ə'fend] *vt* beleidigen; **~er** *n* Gesetzesübertreter *m*

offense [ə'fens] (*US*) *n* = **offence**

offensive [ə'fensɪv] *adj* (*unpleasant*) übel, abstoßend; (*weapon*) Kampf-; (*remark*) verletzend ♦ *n* Angriff *m*

offer ['ɒfə'] *n* Angebot *f* ♦ *vt* anbieten; (*opinion*) äußern; (*resistance*) leisten; **on ~**

zum Verkauf angeboten; **~ing** *n* Gabe *f*

offhand [ɒf'hænd] *adj* lässig ♦ *adv* ohne weiteres

office ['ɒfɪs] *n* Büro *nt*; (*position*) Amt *nt*; **doctor's ~** (*US*) Praxis *f*; **to take ~** sein Amt antreten; (*POL*) die Regierung übernehmen; **~ automation** *n* Büroautomatisierung *f*; **~ block** (*US* ~ **building**) *n* Büro(hoch)haus *nt*; **~ hours** *npl* Dienstzeit *f*; (*US: MED*) Sprechstunde *f*

officer ['ɒfɪsə'] *n* (*MIL*) Offizier *m*; (*public* ~) Beamte(r) *m*

official [ə'fɪʃl] *adj* offiziell, amtlich ♦ *n* Beamte(r) *m*; **~dom** *n* Beamtentum *nt*

officiate [ə'fɪʃɪeɪt] *vi* amtieren

officious [ə'fɪʃəs] *adj* aufdringlich

offing ['ɒfɪŋ] *n*: **in the ~** in (Aus)sicht

Off-licence

ⓘ **Off-licence** *ist ein Geschäft (oder eine Theke in einer Gaststätte), wo man alkoholische Getränke kaufen kann, die aber anderswo konsumiert werden müssen. In solchen Geschäften, die oft von landesweiten Ketten betrieben werden, kann man auch andere Getränke, Süßigkeiten, Zigaretten und Knabbereien kaufen.*

---

off: ~-licence (*BRIT*) *n* (*shop*) Wein- und Spirituosenhandlung *f*; **~-line** *adj* (*COMPUT*) Offline- ♦ *adv* (*COMPUT*) offline; **~-peak** *adj* (*charges*) verbilligt; **~-putting** (*BRIT*) *adj* (*person, remark etc*) abstoßend; **~-road vehicle** *n* Geländefahrzeug *nt*; **~-season** *adj* außer Saison; **~-set** (*irreg: like* **set**) *vt* ausgleichen ♦ *n* (*also:* ~-**set printing**) Offset(druck) *m*; **~-shoot** *n* (*fig: of organization*) Zweig *m*; (*: of discussion etc*) Randergebnis *nt*; **~-shore** *adv* in einiger Entfernung von der Küste ♦ *adj* küstennah, Küsten-; **~-side** *adj* (*SPORT*) im Abseits ♦ *adv* abseits ♦ *n* (*AUT*) Fahrerseite *f*; **~-spring** *n* Nachkommenschaft *f*; (*one*) Sprössling *m*; **~-stage** *adv* hinter den Kulissen; **~-the-cuff** *adv* unvorbereitet, aus dem Stegreif; **~-the-peg** (*US* **~-the-rack**) *adv* von der Stange; **~-white** *adj* naturweiß

Oftel [ˈɔftɛl] *n* Überwachungsgremium zum Verbraucherschutz nach Privatisierung der Telekommunikationsindustrie

often [ˈɔfn] *adv* oft

Ofwat [ˈɔfwɔt] *n* Überwachungsgremium zum Verbraucherschutz nach Privatisierung der Wasserindustrie

ogle [ˈəugl] *vt* liebäugeln mit

oil [ɔɪl] *n* Öl *nt* ♦ *vt* ölen; **~can** *n* Ölkännchen *nt*; **~field** *n* Ölfeld *nt*; **~ filter** *n* (AUT) Ölfilter *m*; **~fired** *adj* Öl-; **~ painting** *n* Ölgemälde *nt*; **~ rig** *n* Ölplattform *f*; **~skins** *npl* Ölzeug *nt*; **~ slick** *n* Ölteppich *m*; **~ tanker** *n* (Öl)tanker *m*; **~ well** *n* Ölquelle *f*; **~y** *adj* ölig; (*dirty*) ölbeschmiert

ointment [ˈɔɪntmənt] *n* Salbe *f*

O.K. [ˈəuˈkeɪ] *excl* in Ordnung, O. K., o. k. ♦ *adj* in Ordnung ♦ *vt* genehmigen

okay [ˈəuˈkeɪ] = **O.K.**

old [əuld] *adj* alt; **how ~ are you?** wie alt bist du?; **he's 10 years ~** er ist 10 Jahre alt; **~er brother** ältere(r) Bruder *m*; **~ age** *n* Alter *nt*; **~-age pensioner** (BRIT) *n* Rentner(in) *m(f)*; **~-fashioned** *adj* altmodisch

olive [ˈɔlɪv] *n* (*fruit*) Olive *f*; (*colour*) Olive *nt* ♦ *adj* Oliven-; (*coloured*) olivenfarbig; **~ oil** *n* Olivenöl *nt*

Olympic [əuˈlɪmpɪk] *adj* olympisch; **the ~ Games, the ~s** die Olympischen Spiele

omelet(te) [ˈɔmlɪt] *n* Omelett *nt*

omen [ˈəumən] *n* Omen *nt*

ominous [ˈɔmɪnəs] *adj* bedrohlich

omission [əuˈmɪʃən] *n* Auslassung *f*; (*neglect*) Versäumnis *nt*

omit [əuˈmɪt] *vt* auslassen; (*fail to do*) versäumen

on [ɔn] *prep* **1** (*indicating position*) auf +*dat*; (*with vb of motion*) auf +*acc*; (*on vertical surface, part of body*) an +*dat/acc*; **it's on the table** es ist auf dem Tisch; **she put the book on the table** sie legte das Buch auf den Tisch; **on the left** links
2 (*indicating means, method, condition etc*): **on foot** (*go, be*) zu Fuß; **on the train/**

plane (*go*) mit dem Zug/Flugzeug; (*be*) im Zug/Flugzeug; **on the telephone/television** am Telefon/im Fernsehen; **to be on drugs** Drogen nehmen; **to be on holiday/business** im Urlaub/auf Geschäftsreise sein
3 (*referring to time*): **on Friday** (am) Freitag; **on Fridays** freitags; **on June 20th** am 20. Juni; **a week on Friday** Freitag in einer Woche; **on arrival he ...** als er ankam, ... er ...
4 (*about, concerning*) über +*acc*
♦ *adv* **1** (*referring to dress*) an; **she put her boots/hat on** sie zog ihre Stiefel an/setzte ihren Hut auf
2 (*further, continuously*) weiter; **to walk on** weitergehen
♦ *adj* **1** (*functioning, in operation: machine, TV, light*) an; (: *tap*) aufgedreht; (: *brakes*) angezogen; **is the meeting still on?** findet die Versammlung noch statt?; **there's a good film on** es läuft ein guter Film
2: that's not on! (*inf: of behaviour*) das liegt nicht drin!

once [wʌns] *adv* einmal ♦ *conj* wenn ... einmal; **~ he had left/it was done** nachdem er gegangen war/es fertig war; **at ~** sofort; (*at the same time*) gleichzeitig; **~ a week** einmal in der Woche; **~ more** noch einmal; **~ and for all** ein für alle Mal; **~ upon a time** es war einmal

oncoming [ˈɔnkʌmɪŋ] *adj* (*traffic*) Gegen-, entgegenkommend

one [wʌn] *num* eins; (*with noun, referring back to noun*) ein/eine/ein; **it is one (o'clock)** es ist eins, es ist ein Uhr; **one hundred and fifty** einhundertfünfzig
♦ *adj* **1** (*sole*) einzige(r, s); **the one book which** das einzige Buch, welches
2 (*same*) derselbe/dieselbe/dasselbe; **they came in the one car** sie kamen alle in dem einen Auto
3 (*indef*): **one day I discovered ...** eines Tages bemerkte ich ...

◆ *pron* **1** eine(r, s); **do you have a red one?** haben Sie einen roten/eine rote/ein rotes?; **this one** diese(r, s); **that one** der/die/das; **which one?** welche(r, s)?; **one by one** einzeln
2: one another einander; **do you two ever see one another?** seht ihr beide euch manchmal?
3 (*impers*) man; **one never knows** man kann nie wissen; **to cut one's finger** sich in den Finger schneiden

one: ~-armed bandit *n* einarmiger Bandit *m*; **~-day excursion** (*US*) *n* (*day return*) Tagesrückfahrkarte *f*; **~-man** *adj* Einmann-; **~-man band** *n* Einmannkapelle *f*; (*fig*) Einmannbetrieb *m*; **~-off** (*BRIT: inf*) *n* Einzelfall *m*
oneself [wʌn'self] *pron* (*reflexive: after prep*) sich; (*~ personally*) sich selbst *or* selber; (*emphatic*) (sich) selbst; **to hurt ~** sich verletzen
one: ~-sided *adj* (*argument*) einseitig; **~-to-~** *adj* (*relationship*) eins-zu-eins; **~-upmanship** *n* die Kunst, anderen um eine Nasenlänge voraus zu sein; **~-way** *adj* (*street*) Einbahn-
ongoing ['ɒngəuɪŋ] *adj* momentan; (*progressing*) sich entwickelnd
onion ['ʌnjən] *n* Zwiebel *f*
on-line ['ɒnlaɪn] *adj* (*COMPUT*) Online-
onlooker ['ɒnlukəʳ] *n* Zuschauer(in) *m(f)*
only ['əunlɪ] *adv* nur, bloß ◆ *adj* einzige(r, s) ◆ *conj* nur, bloß; **an ~ child** ein Einzelkind *n*; **not ~ ... but also ...** nicht nur ..., sondern auch ...
onset ['ɒnset] *n* (*start*) Beginn *m*
onshore ['ɒnʃɔːʳ] *adj* (*wind*) See-
onslaught ['ɒnslɔːt] *n* Angriff *m*
onto ['ɒntu] *prep* = **on to**
onus ['əunəs] *n* Last *f*, Pflicht *f*
onward(s) ['ɒnwəd(z)] *adv* (*place*) voran, vorwärts; **from that day ~** von dem Tag an; **from today ~** ab heute
ooze [uːz] *vi* sickern
opaque [əu'peɪk] *adj* undurchsichtig
OPEC ['əupɛk] *n abbr* (= *Organization of Petroleum-Exporting Countries*) OPEC *f*
open ['əupn] *adj* offen; (*public*) öffentlich; (*mind*) aufgeschlossen ◆ *vt* öffnen, aufmachen; (*trial, motorway, account*) eröffnen ◆ *vi* (*begin*) anfangen; (*shop*) aufmachen; (*door, flower*) aufgehen; (*play*) Premiere haben; **in the ~ (air)** im Freien; **~ on to** *vt fus* sich öffnen auf +*acc*; **~ up** *vt* (*route*) erschließen; (*shop, prospects*) eröffnen ◆ *vi* öffnen; **~ing** *n* (*hole*) Öffnung *f*; (*beginning*) Anfang *m*; (*good chance*) Gelegenheit *f*; **~ing hours** *npl* Öffnungszeiten *pl*; **~ learning centre** *n* Weiterbildungseinrichtung auf Teilzeitbasis; **~ly** *adv* offen; (*publicly*) öffentlich; **~-minded** *adj* aufgeschlossen; **~-necked** *adj* offen; **~-plan** *adj* (*office*) Großraum-; (*flat etc*) offen angelegt

---

Open University

i **Open University** ist eine 1969 in Großbritannien gegründete Fernuniversität für Spätstudierende. Der Unterricht findet durch Fernseh- und Radiosendungen statt, schriftliche Arbeiten werden mit der Post verschickt, und der Besuch von Sommerkursen ist Pflicht. Die Studenten müssen eine bestimmte Anzahl von Unterrichtseinheiten in einem bestimmten Zeitraum absolvieren und für die Verleihung eines akademischen Grades eine Mindestzahl von Scheinen machen.

---

opera ['ɒpərə] *n* Oper *f*; **~ house** *n* Opernhaus *nt*
operate ['ɒpəreɪt] *vt* (*machine*) bedienen; (*brakes, light*) betätigen ◆ *vi* (*machine*) laufen, in Betrieb sein; (*person*) arbeiten; (*MED*): **to ~ on** operieren
operatic [ɒpə'rætɪk] *adj* Opern-
operating ['ɒpəreɪtɪŋ] *adj*: **~ table/theatre** Operationstisch *m*/-saal *m*
operation [ɒpə'reɪʃən] *n* (*working*) Betrieb *m*; (*MED*) Operation *f*; (*undertaking*) Unternehmen *nt*; (*MIL*) Einsatz *m*; **to be in ~** (*JUR*) in Kraft sein; (*machine*) in Betrieb sein; **to have an ~** (*MED*) operiert werden;

~al *adj* einsatzbereit

operative ['ɔprətɪv] *adj* wirksam

operator ['ɔpəreɪtə'] *n* (*of machine*) Arbeiter *m*; (*TEL*) Telefonist(in) *m(f)*

opinion [ə'pɪnjən] *n* Meinung *f*; **in my ~** meiner Meinung nach; **~ated** *adj* starrsinnig; **~ poll** *n* Meinungsumfrage *f*

opponent [ə'pəunənt] *n* Gegner *m*

opportunity [ɔpə'tju:nɪtɪ] *n* Gelegenheit *f*, Möglichkeit *f*; **to take the ~ of doing sth** die Gelegenheit ergreifen, etw zu tun

oppose [ə'pəuz] *vt* entgegentreten +*dat*; (*argument, idea*) ablehnen; (*plan*) bekämpfen; **to be ~d to sth** gegen etw sein; **as ~d to** im Gegensatz zu; **opposing** *adj* gegnerisch; (*points of view*) entgegengesetzt

opposite ['ɔpəzɪt] *adj* (*house*) gegenüberliegend; (*direction*) entgegengesetzt ♦ *adv* gegenüber ♦ *prep* gegenüber ♦ *n* Gegenteil *nt*

opposition [ɔpə'zɪʃən] *n* (*resistance*) Widerstand *m*; (*POL*) Opposition *f*; (*contrast*) Gegensatz *m*

oppress [ə'pres] *vt* unterdrücken; (*heat etc*) bedrücken; **~ion** [ə'preʃən] *n* Unterdrückung *f*; **~ive** *adj* (*authority, law*) repressiv; (*burden, thought*) bedrückend; (*heat*) drückend

opt [ɔpt] *vi*: **to ~ for** sich entscheiden für; **to ~ to do sth** sich entscheiden, etw zu tun; **to ~ out of** sich drücken vor +*dat*

optical ['ɔptɪkl] *adj* optisch; **~ character reader** *n* optische(s) Lesegerät *nt*

optician [ɔp'tɪʃən] *n* Optiker *m*

optimist ['ɔptɪmɪst] *n* Optimist *m*; **~ic** [ɔptɪ'mɪstɪk] *adj* optimistisch

optimum ['ɔptɪməm] *adj* optimal

option ['ɔpʃən] *n* Wahl *f*; (*COMM*) Option *f*; **to keep one's ~s open** sich alle Möglichkeiten offen halten; **~al** *adj* freiwillig; (*subject*) wahlfrei; **~al extras** *npl* Extras auf Wunsch

or [ɔ:'] *conj* oder; **he could not read ~ write** er konnte weder lesen noch schreiben; **~ else** sonst

oral ['ɔ:rəl] *adj* mündlich ♦ *n* (*exam*)

mündliche Prüfung *f*

orange ['ɔrɪndʒ] *n* (*fruit*) Apfelsine *f*, Orange *f*; (*colour*) Orange *nt* ♦ *adj* orange

orator ['ɔrətə'] *n* Redner(in) *m(f)*

orbit ['ɔ:bɪt] *n* Umlaufbahn *f*

orbital (motorway) ['ɔ:bɪtəl-] *n* Ringautobahn *f*

orchard ['ɔ:tʃəd] *n* Obstgarten *m*

orchestra ['ɔ:kɪstrə] *n* Orchester *nt*; (*US: seating*) Parkett *nt*; **~l** [ɔ:'kestrəl] *adj* Orchester-, orchestral

orchid ['ɔ:kɪd] *n* Orchidee *f*

ordain [ɔ:'deɪn] *vt* (*ECCL*) weihen

ordeal [ɔ:'di:l] *n* Qual *f*

order ['ɔ:də'] *n* (*sequence*) Reihenfolge *f*; (*good arrangement*) Ordnung *f*; (*command*) Befehl *m*; (*JUR*) Anordnung *f*; (*peace*) Ordnung *f*; (*condition*) Zustand *m*; (*rank*) Klasse *f*; (*COMM*) Bestellung *f*; (*ECCL, honour*) Orden *m* ♦ *vt* (*also*: **put in ~**) ordnen; (*command*) befehlen; (*COMM*) bestellen; **in ~** in der Reihenfolge; **in (working) ~** in gutem Zustand; **in ~ to do sth** um etw zu tun; **on ~** (*COMM*) auf Bestellung; **to ~ sb to do sth** jdm befehlen, etw zu tun; **to ~ sth** (*command*) etw *acc* befehlen; **~ form** *n* Bestellschein *m*; **~ly** *n* (*MIL*) Sanitäter *m*; (*MED*) Pfleger *m* ♦ *adj* (*tidy*) ordentlich; (*well-behaved*) ruhig

ordinary ['ɔ:dnrɪ] *adj* gewöhnlich ♦ *n*: **out of the ~** außergewöhnlich

Ordnance Survey ['ɔ:dnəns-] (*BRIT*) *n* amtliche(r) Kartografiedienst *m*

ore [ɔ:'] *n* Erz *nt*

organ ['ɔ:gən] *n* (*MUS*) Orgel *f*; (*BIOL, fig*) Organ *nt*

organic [ɔ:'gænɪk] *adj* (*food, farming etc*) biodynamisch

organization [ɔ:gənaɪ'zeɪʃən] *n* Organisation *f*; (*make-up*) Struktur *f*

organize ['ɔ:gənaɪz] *vt* organisieren; **~r** *n* Organisator *m*, Veranstalter *m*

orgasm ['ɔ:gæzəm] *n* Orgasmus *m*

orgy ['ɔ:dʒɪ] *n* Orgie *f*

Orient ['ɔ:rɪənt] *n* Orient *m*; **o~al** [ɔ:rɪ'entl] *adj* orientalisch

origin ['ɔrɪdʒɪn] *n* Ursprung *m*; (*of the world*)

Anfang m, Entstehung f; **~al** [əˈrɪdʒɪnl] adj
(first) ursprünglich; (painting) original; (idea)
originell ♦ n Original nt; **~ally** adv
ursprünglich; originell; **~ate** [əˈrɪdʒɪneɪt] vi
entstehen ♦ vt ins Leben rufen; **to ~ate
from** stammen aus

Orkney [ˈɔːknɪ] npl (also: **the ~ Islands**) die
Orkneyinseln pl

ornament [ˈɔːnəmənt] n Schmuck m; (on
mantelpiece) Nippesfigur f; **~al** [ɔːnəˈmɛntl]
adj Zier-

ornate [ɔːˈneɪt] adj reich verziert

orphan [ˈɔːfn] n Waise f, Waisenkind nt ♦ vt:
to be ~ed Waise werden; **~age** n
Waisenhaus nt

orthodox [ˈɔːθədɒks] adj orthodox; **~y** n
Orthodoxie f; (fig) Konventionalität f

orthopaedic [ɔːθəˈpiːdɪk] (US **orthopedic**)
adj orthopädisch

ostentatious [ɒstɛnˈteɪʃəs] adj großtuerisch,
protzig

ostracize [ˈɒstrəsaɪz] vt ausstoßen

ostrich [ˈɒstrɪtʃ] n Strauß m

other [ˈʌðəʳ] adj andere(r, s) ♦ pron andere(r,
s) ♦ adv: **~ than** anders als; **the ~ (one)**
der/die/das andere; **the ~ day** neulich; **~s**
(~ people) andere; **~wise** adv (in a different
way) anders; (or else) sonst

otter [ˈɒtəʳ] n Otter m

ouch [autʃ] excl aua

ought [ɔːt] vb aux sollen; **I ~ to do it** ich
sollte es tun; **this ~ to have been
corrected** das hätte korrigiert werden
sollen

ounce [auns] n Unze f

our [ˈauəʳ] adj unser; see also **my**; **~s** pron
unsere(r, s); see also **mine²**; **~selves** pron
uns (selbst); (emphatic) (wir) selbst; see also
oneself

oust [aust] vt verdrängen

out [aut] adv hinaus/heraus; (not indoors)
draußen; (not alight) aus; (unconscious)
bewusstlos; (results) bekannt gegeben; **to
eat/go ~** auswärts essen/ausgehen; **~
there** da draußen; **he is ~** (absent) er ist
nicht da; **he was ~ in his calculations**
seine Berechnungen waren nicht richtig; **~**

loud laut; **~ of** aus; (away from) außerhalb
+gen; **to be ~ of milk** etc keine Milch etc
mehr haben; **~ of order** außer Betrieb;
~and-~ adj (liar, thief etc) ausgemacht;
~back n Hinterland nt; **~board (motor)** n
Außenbordmotor m; **~break** n Ausbruch
m; **~burst** n Ausbruch m; **~cast** n
Ausgestoßene(r) mf; **~come** n Ergebnis nt;
~crop n (of rock) Felsnase f; **~cry** n Protest
m; **~dated** adj überholt; **~do** (irreg: like
do) vt übertrumpfen; **~door** adj Außen-;
(SPORT) im Freien; **~doors** adv im Freien

outer [ˈautəʳ] adj äußere(r, s); **~ space** n
Weltraum m

outfit [ˈautfɪt] n Kleidung f

out: ~going adj (character) aufgeschlossen;
~goings (BRIT) npl Ausgaben pl; **~grow**
(irreg: like grow) vt (clothes) herauswachsen
aus; (habit) ablegen; **~house** n
Nebengebäude nt

outing [ˈautɪŋ] n Ausflug m

outlandish [autˈlændɪʃ] adj eigenartig

out: ~law n Geächtete(r) f(m) ♦ vt ächten;
(thing) verbieten; **~lay** n Auslage f; **~let** n
Auslass m, Abfluss m; (also: retail **~let**)
Absatzmarkt m; (US: ELEC) Steckdose f; (for
emotions) Ventil nt

outline [ˈautlaɪn] n Umriss m

out: ~live vt überleben; **~look** n (also fig)
Aussicht f; (attitude) Einstellung f; **~lying**
adj entlegen; (district) Außen-; **~moded** adj
veraltet; **~number** vt zahlenmäßig
überlegen sein +dat; **~of-date** adj
(passport) abgelaufen; (clothes etc)
altmodisch; (ideas etc) überholt; **~of-the-
way** adj abgelegen; **~patient** n
ambulante(r) Patient m/ambulante
Patientin f; **~post** n (MIL, fig) Vorposten m;
~put n Leistung f, Produktion f; (COMPUT)
Ausgabe f

outrage [ˈautreɪdʒ] n (cruel deed)
Ausschreitung f; (indecency) Skandal m ♦ vt
(morals) verstoßen gegen; (person)
empören; **~ous** [autˈreɪdʒəs] adj unerhört

outreach worker [ˈautriːtʃ-] n
Streetworker(in) m(f)

outright [adv autˈraɪt, adj ˈautraɪt] adv (at

once) sofort; *(openly)* ohne Umschweife
♦ *adj (denial)* völlig; *(sale)* Total-; *(winner)*
unbestritten

outset ['autset] *n* Beginn *m*

outside [aut'said] *n* Außenseite *f* ♦ *adj*
äußere(r, s), Außen-; *(chance)* gering ♦ *adv*
außen ♦ *prep* außerhalb +gen; **at the ~** *(fig)*
maximal; *(time)* spätestens; **to go ~** nach
draußen gehen; **~ lane** *n (AUT)* äußere
Spur *f*; **~ line** *n (TEL)* Amtsanschluss *m*; **~r**
n Außenseiter(in) *m(f)*

out: ~size *adj* übergroß; **~skirts** *npl*
Stadtrand *m*; **~spoken** *adj* freimütig;
~standing *adj* hervorragend; *(debts etc)*
ausstehend; **~stay** *vt*: **to ~stay one's
welcome** länger bleiben als erwünscht;
~stretched *adj* ausgestreckt; **~strip** *vt*
übertreffen; **~ tray** *n* Ausgangskorb *m*

outward ['autwad] *adj* äußere(r, s); *(journey)*
Hin-; *(freight)* ausgehend ♦ *adv* nach außen;
~ly *adv* äußerlich

outweigh [aut'wei] *vt (fig)* überwiegen

outwit [aut'wit] *vt* überlisten

oval ['əuvl] *adj* oval ♦ *n* Oval *nt*

Oval Office

ⓘ **Oval Office**, *ein großer ovaler Raum im
Weißen Haus, ist das private Büro des
amerikanischen Präsidenten. Im weiteren
Sinne bezieht sich dieser Begriff oft auf die
Präsidentschaft selbst.*

ovary ['əuvəri] *n* Eierstock *m*

ovation [əu'veifən] *n* Beifallssturm *m*

oven ['ʌvn] *n* Backofen *m*; **~proof** *adj*
feuerfest

over ['əuvə'] *adv (across)* hinüber/herüber;
(finished) vorbei; *(left)* übrig; *(again)* wieder,
noch einmal ♦ *prep* über ♦ *prefix (excessively)*
übermäßig; **~ here** hier(hin); **~ there**
dort(hin); **all ~** *(everywhere)* überall;
(finished) vorbei; **~ and ~** immer wieder; **~
and above** darüber hinaus; **to ask sb ~**
jdn einladen; **to bend ~** sich bücken

overall [*adj, n* 'əuvərɔ:l, *adv* əuvər'ɔ:l] *adj*
(situation) allgemein; *(length)* Gesamt- ♦ *n*
(BRIT) Kittel *m* ♦ *adv* insgesamt; **~s** *npl (for*

man) Overall *m*

over: ~awe *vt (frighten)* einschüchtern;
(make impression) überwältigen; **~balance**
vi Übergewicht bekommen; **~bearing** *adj*
aufdringlich; **~board** *adv* über Bord;
~book *vi* überbuchen

overcast ['əuvəkɑ:st] *adj* bedeckt

overcharge [əuvə'tʃɑ:dʒ] *vt*: **to ~ sb** von
jdm zu viel verlangen

overcoat ['əuvəkəut] *n* Mantel *m*

overcome [əuvə'kʌm] *(irreg: like* **come***) vt*
überwinden

over: ~crowded *adj* überfüllt; **~crowding**
n Überfüllung *f*; **~do** *(irreg: like* **do***) vt (cook
too much)* verkochen; *(exaggerate)*
übertreiben; **~done** *adj* übertrieben;
(COOK) verbraten, verkocht; **~dose** *n*
Überdosis *f*; **~draft** *n* (Konto)überziehung
f; **~drawn** *adj (account)* überzogen; **~due**
adj überfällig; **~estimate** *vt* überschätzen;
~excited *adj* überreizt; *(children)* aufgeregt

overflow [əuvə'fləu] *vi* überfließen ♦ *n*
(excess) Überschuss *m*; *(also:* **~ pipe***)*
Überlaufrohr *nt*

overgrown [əuvə'grəun] *adj (garden)*
verwildert

overhaul [*vb* əuvə'hɔ:l, *n* 'əuvəhɔ:l] *vt (car)*
überholen; *(plans)* überprüfen ♦ *n*
Überholung *f*

overhead [*adv* əuvə'hed, *adj, n* 'əuvəhed] *adv*
oben ♦ *adj* Hoch-; *(wire)* oberirdisch;
(lighting) Decken- ♦ *n (US)* = **overheads**; **~s**
npl (costs) allgemeine Unkosten *pl*; **~
projector** *n* Overheadprojektor *m*

over: ~hear *(irreg: like* **hear***) vt* (mit
an)hören; **~heat** *vi (engine)* heiß laufen;
~joyed *adj* überglücklich; **~kill** *n (fig)*
Rundumschlag *m*

overland ['əuvəlænd] *adj* Überland- ♦ *adv*
(travel) über Land

overlap [*vb* əuvə'læp, *n* 'əuvəlæp] *vi* sich
überschneiden; *(objects)* sich teilweise
decken ♦ *n* Überschneidung *f*

over: ~leaf *adv* umseitig; **~load** *vt*
überladen; **~look** *vt (view from above)*
überblicken; *(not notice)* übersehen;
(pardon) hinwegsehen über +acc

overnight [adv əuvə'naɪt, adj 'əuvənaɪt] adv über Nacht ♦ adj (journey) Nacht-; **~ stay** Übernachtung f; **to stay ~** übernachten

overpass ['əuvəpɑːs] n Überführung f

overpower [əuvə'pauə'] vt überwältigen

over: ~rate vt überschätzen; **~ride** (irreg: like **ride**) vt (order, decision) aufheben; (objection) übergehen; **~riding** adj vorherrschend; **~rule** vt verwerfen; **~run** (irreg: like **run**) vt (country) einfallen in; (time limit) überziehen

overseas [əuvə'siːz] adv nach/in Übersee ♦ adj überseeisch, Übersee-

overseer ['əuvəsiːə'] n Aufseher m

overshadow [əuvə'ʃædəu] vt überschatten

overshoot [əuvə'ʃuːt] (irreg: like **shoot**) vt (runway) hinausschießen über +acc

oversight ['əuvəsaɪt] n (mistake) Versehen nt

over: ~sleep (irreg: like **sleep**) vi verschlafen; **~spill** n (Bevölkerungs)überschuss m; **~state** vt übertreiben; **~step** vt: **to ~step the mark** zu weit gehen

overt [əu'vɜːt] adj offen(kundig)

overtake [əuvə'teɪk] (irreg: like **take**) vt, vi überholen

over: ~throw (irreg: like **throw**) vt (POL) stürzen; **~time** n Überstunden pl; **~tone** n (fig) Note f

overture ['əuvətʃuə'] n Ouvertüre f

over: ~turn vt, vi umkippen; **~weight** adj zu dick; **~whelm** vt überwältigen; **~work** n Überarbeitung f ♦ vt überlasten ♦ vi sich überarbeiten; **~wrought** adj überreizt

owe [əu] vt schulden; **to ~ sth to sb** (money) jdm etw schulden; (favour etc) jdm etw verdanken; **owing to** prep wegen +gen

owl [aul] n Eule f

own [əun] vt besitzen ♦ adj eigen; **a room of my ~** mein eigenes Zimmer; **to get one's ~ back** sich rächen; **on one's ~** allein; **~ up** vi: **to ~ up (to sth)** (etw) zugeben; **~er** n Besitzer(in) m(f); **~ership** n Besitz m

ox [ɔks] (pl **~en**) n Ochse m

oxtail ['ɔksteɪl] n: **~ soup** Ochsenschwanzsuppe f

oxygen ['ɔksɪdʒən] n Sauerstoff m; **~ mask**, n Sauerstoffmaske f; **~ tent** n Sauerstoffzelt nt

oyster ['ɔɪstə'] n Auster f

oz. abbr = **ounce(s)**

ozone ['əuzəun] n Ozon nt; **~-friendly** adj (aerosol) ohne Treibgas; (fridge) FCKW-frei; **~ hole** n Ozonloch nt; **~ layer** n Ozonschicht f

P, p

p abbr = **penny**; **pence**

pa [pɑː] (inf) n Papa m

P.A. n abbr = **personal assistant**; **public address system**

p.a. abbr = **per annum**

pace [peɪs] n Schritt m; (speed) Tempo nt ♦ vi schreiten; **to keep ~ with** Schritt halten mit; **~maker** n Schrittmacher m

pacific [pə'sɪfɪk] adj pazifisch ♦ n: **the P~ (Ocean)** der Pazifik

pacifist ['pæsɪfɪst] n Pazifist m

pacify ['pæsɪfaɪ] vt befrieden; (calm) beruhigen

pack [pæk] n (of goods) Packung f; (of hounds) Meute f; (of cards) Spiel nt; (gang) Bande f ♦ vt (case) packen; (clothes) einpacken ♦ vi packen; **to ~ sb off to ...** jdn nach ... schicken; **~ it in!** lass es gut sein!

package ['pækɪdʒ] n Paket nt; **~ tour** n Pauschalreise f

packed [pækt] adj abgepackt; **~ lunch** n Lunchpaket nt

packet ['pækɪt] n Päckchen nt

packing ['pækɪŋ] n (action) Packen nt; (material) Verpackung f; **~ case** n (Pack)kiste f

pact [pækt] n Pakt m, Vertrag m

pad [pæd] n (of paper) (Schreib)block m; (stuffing) Polster nt ♦ vt polstern; **~ding** n Polsterung f

paddle ['pædl] n Paddel nt; (US: SPORT) Schläger m ♦ vt (boat) paddeln ♦ vi (in sea) plan(t)schen; **~ steamer** n Raddampfer m

paddling pool ['pædlɪŋ-] (BRIT) n

Plan(t)schbecken *nt*

paddock ['pædək] *n* Koppel *f*

paddy field ['pædɪ-] *n* Reisfeld *nt*

padlock ['pædlɔk] *n* Vorhängeschloss *nt* ♦ *vt* verschließen

paediatrics [piːdɪ'ætrɪks] (*US* **pediatrics**) *n* Kinderheilkunde *f*

pagan ['peɪgən] *adj* heidnisch ♦ *n* Heide *m*, Heidin *f*

page [peɪdʒ] *n* Seite *f*; (*person*) Page *m* ♦ *vt* (*in hotel*) ausrufen lassen

pageant ['pædʒənt] *n* Festzug *m*; **~ry** *n* Gepränge *nt*

pager ['peɪdʒə*r*] *n* (*TEL*) Funkrufempfänger *m*, Piepser *m* (*inf*)

paging device ['peɪdʒɪŋ-] *n* (*TEL*) = **pager**

paid [peɪd] *pt*, *pp of* **pay** ♦ *adj* bezahlt; **to put ~ to** (*BRIT*) zunichte machen

pail [peɪl] *n* Eimer *m*

pain [peɪn] *n* Schmerz *m*; **to be in ~** Schmerzen haben; **on ~ of death** bei Todesstrafe; **to take ~s to do sth** sich *dat* Mühe geben, etw zu tun; **~ed** *adj* (*expression*) gequält; **~ful** *adj* (*physically*) schmerzhaft; (*embarrassing*) peinlich; (*difficult*) mühsam; **~fully** *adv* (*fig: very*) schrecklich; **~killer** *n* Schmerzmittel *nt*; **~less** *adj* schmerzlos; **~staking** ['zteɪkɪŋ] *adj* gewissenhaft

paint [peɪnt] *n* Farbe *f* ♦ *vt* anstreichen; (*picture*) malen; **to ~ the door blue** die Tür blau streichen; **~brush** *n* Pinsel *m*; **~er** *n* Maler *m*; **~ing** *n* Malerei *f*; (*picture*) Gemälde *nt*; **~work** *n* Anstrich *m*; (*of car*) Lack *m*

pair [peə*r*] *n* Paar *nt*; **~ of scissors** Schere *f*; **~ of trousers** Hose *f*

pajamas [pə'dʒɑːməz] (*US*) *npl* Schlafanzug *m*

Pakistan [pɑːkɪ'stɑːn] *n* Pakistan *nt*; **~i** *adj* pakistanisch ♦ *n* Pakistani *mf*

pal [pæl] (*inf*) *n* Kumpel *m*

palace ['pæləs] *n* Palast *m*, Schloss *nt*

palatable ['pælɪtəbl] *adj* schmackhaft

palate ['pælɪt] *n* Gaumen *m*

palatial [pə'leɪʃəl] *adj* palastartig

pale [peɪl] *adj* blass, bleich ♦ *n*: **to be**

beyond the ~ die Grenzen überschreiten

Palestine ['pælɪstaɪn] *n* Palästina *nt*; **Palestinian** [pælɪs'tɪnɪən] *adj* palästinensisch ♦ *n* Palästinenser(in) *m(f)*

palette ['pælɪt] *n* Palette *f*

paling ['peɪlɪŋ] *n* (*stake*) Zaunpfahl *m*; (*fence*) Lattenzaun *m*

pall [pɔːl] *vi* jeden Reiz verlieren, verblassen

pallet ['pælɪt] *n* (*for goods*) Palette *f*

pallid ['pælɪd] *adj* blass, bleich

pallor ['pælə*r*] *n* Blässe *f*

palm [pɑːm] *n* (*of hand*) Handfläche *f*; (*also:* **~ tree**) Palme *f* ♦ *vt*: **to ~ sth off on sb** jdm etw andrehen; **P~ Sunday** *n* Palmsonntag *m*

palpable ['pælpəbl] *adj* (*also fig*) greifbar

palpitation [pælpɪ'teɪʃən] *n* Herzklopfen *nt*

paltry ['pɔːltrɪ] *adj* armselig

pamper ['pæmpə*r*] *vt* verhätscheln

pamphlet ['pæmflət] *n* Broschüre *f*

pan [pæn] *n* Pfanne *f* ♦ *vi* (*CINE*) schwenken

panache [pə'næʃ] *n* Schwung *m*

pancake ['pænkeɪk] *n* Pfannkuchen *m*

pancreas ['pæŋkrɪəs] *n* Bauchspeicheldrüse *f*

panda ['pændə] *n* Panda *m*; **~ car** (*BRIT*) *n* (*Funk*)streifenwagen *m*

pandemonium [pændɪ'məʊnɪəm] *n* Hölle *f*; (*noise*) Höllenlärm *m*

pander ['pændə*r*] *vi*: **to ~ to** sich richten nach

pane [peɪn] *n* (*Fenster*)scheibe *f*

panel ['pænl] *n* (*of wood*) Tafel *f*; (*TV*) Diskussionsrunde *f*; **~ling** (*US* **paneling**) *n* Täfelung *f*

pang [pæŋ] *n*: **~s of hunger** quälende(r) Hunger *m*; **~s of conscience** Gewissensbisse *pl*

panic ['pænɪk] *n* Panik *f* ♦ *vi* in Panik geraten; **don't ~** (*nur*) keine Panik; **~ky** *adj* (*person*) überängstlich; **~-stricken** *adj* von panischem Schrecken erfasst; (*look*) panisch

pansy ['pænzɪ] *n* Stiefmütterchen *nt*; (*inf*) Schwule(r) *m*

pant [pænt] *vi* keuchen; (*dog*) hecheln

panther ['pænθə*r*] *n* Pant(h)er *m*

panties ['pæntɪz] npl (Damen)slip m

pantihose ['pæntɪhəʊz] (US) n Strumpfhose f

pantomime ['pæntəmaɪm] (BRIT) n Märchenkomödie f um Weihnachten

---
Pantomime

ℹ **Pantomime** oder umgangssprachlich **panto** ist in Großbritannien ein zur Weihnachtszeit aufgeführtes Märchenspiel mit possenhaften Elementen, Musik, Standardrollen (ein als Frau verkleideter Mann, ein Junge, ein Bösewicht) und aktuellen Witzen. Publikumsbeteiligung wird gern gesehen (z.B. warnen die Kinder den Helden mit dem Ruf „He's behind you" vor einer drohenden Gefahr), und viele der Witze sprechen vor allem Erwachsene an, so dass pantomimes Unterhaltung für die ganze Familie bieten.

---

pantry ['pæntrɪ] n Vorratskammer f

pants [pænts] npl (BRIT: woman's) Schlüpfer m; (: man's) Unterhose f; (US: trousers) Hose f

papal ['peɪpəl] adj päpstlich

paper ['peɪpə*] n Papier nt; (newspaper) Zeitung f; (essay) Referat n ♦ adj Papier-, aus Papier ♦ vt (wall) tapezieren; **~s** npl (identity ~s) Ausweis(papiere pl) m; **~back** n Taschenbuch nt; **~ bag** n Tüte f; **~ clip** n Büroklammer f; **~ hankie** n Tempotaschentuch nt ®; **~weight** n Briefbeschwerer m; **~work** n Schreibarbeit f

par [pɑ:*] n (COMM) Nennwert m; (GOLF) Par nt; **on a ~ with** ebenbürtig +dat

parable ['pærəbl] n (REL) Gleichnis nt

parachute ['pærəʃu:t] n Fallschirm m ♦ vi (mit dem Fallschirm) abspringen

parade [pə'reɪd] n Parade f ♦ vt aufmarschieren lassen; (fig) zur Schau stellen ♦ vi paradieren, vorbeimarschieren

paradise ['pærədaɪs] n Paradies nt

paradox ['pærədɔks] n Paradox nt; **~ically** [pærə'dɔksɪklɪ] adv paradoxerweise

paraffin ['pærəfɪn] (BRIT) n Paraffin nt

paragraph ['pærəgrɑ:f] n Absatz m

parallel ['pærəlel] adj parallel ♦ n Parallele f

paralyse ['pærəlaɪz] (US **paralyze**) vt (MED) lähmen, paralysieren; (fig: organization, production etc) lahm legen; **~d** adj gelähmt; **paralysis** [pə'rælɪsɪs] n Lähmung f

paralyze ['pærəlaɪz] (US) = **paralyse** vt

parameter [pə'ræmɪtə*] n Parameter m; **~s** npl (framework, limits) Rahmen m

paramount ['pærəmaʊnt] adj höchste(r, s), oberste(r, s)

paranoid ['pærənɔɪd] adj (person) an Verfolgungswahn leidend, paranoid; (feeling) krankhaft

parapet ['pærəpɪt] n Brüstung f

paraphernalia [pærəfə'neɪlɪə] n Zubehör nt, Utensilien pl

paraphrase ['pærəfreɪz] vt umschreiben

paraplegic [pærə'pli:dʒɪk] n Querschnittsgelähmte(r) f(m)

parasite ['pærəsaɪt] n (also fig) Schmarotzer m, Parasit m

parasol ['pærəsɔl] n Sonnenschirm m

paratrooper ['pærətru:pə*] n Fallschirmjäger m

parcel ['pɑ:sl] n Paket nt ♦ vt (also: ~ up) einpacken

parch [pɑ:tʃ] vt (aus)dörren; **~ed** adj ausgetrocknet; (person) am Verdursten

parchment ['pɑ:tʃmənt] n Pergament nt

pardon ['pɑ:dn] n Verzeihung f ♦ vt (JUR) begnadigen; **~ me!, I beg your ~!** verzeihen Sie bitte!; **~ me?** (US) wie bitte?; **(I beg your) ~?** wie bitte?

parent ['pɛərənt] n Elternteil m; **~s** npl (mother and father) Eltern pl; **~al** [pə'rentl] adj elterlich, Eltern-

parentheses [pə'renθɪsi:z] npl of **parenthesis**

parenthesis [pə'renθɪsɪs] n Klammer f; (sentence) Parenthese f

Paris ['pærɪs] n Paris nt

parish ['pærɪʃ] n Gemeinde f

park [pɑ:k] n Park m ♦ vt, vi parken

parking ['pɑ:kɪŋ] n Parken nt; **"no ~"** „Parken verboten"; **~ lot** (US) n Parkplatz m; **~ meter** n Parkuhr f; **~ ticket** n

Strafzettel *m*

parlance ['pɑːləns] *n* Sprachgebrauch *m*

parliament ['pɑːləmənt] *n* Parlament *nt*; **~ary** [pɑːlə'mentəri] *adj* parlamentarisch, Parlaments-

parlour ['pɑːləʳ] (*US* **parlor**) *n* Salon *m*

parochial [pə'rəukɪəl] *adj* (*narrow-minded*) eng(stirnig)

parole [pə'rəul] *n*: **on ~** (*prisoner*) auf Bewährung

parrot ['pærət] *n* Papagei *m*

parry ['pærɪ] *vt* parieren, abwehren

parsley ['pɑːslɪ] *n* Petersilie *m*

parsnip ['pɑːsnɪp] *n* Pastinake *f*

parson ['pɑːsn] *n* Pfarrer *m*

part [pɑːt] *n* (*piece*) Teil *m*; (*THEAT*) Rolle *f*; (*of machine*) Teil *nt* ♦ *adv* = **partly**; ♦ *vt* trennen; (*hair*) scheiteln ♦ *vi* (*people*) sich trennen; **to take ~ in** teilnehmen an +*dat*; **to take sth in good ~** etw nicht übel nehmen; **to take sb's ~** sich auf jds Seite *acc* stellen; **for my ~** ich für meinen Teil; **for the most ~** meistens, größtenteils; **in ~ exchange** (*BRIT*) in Zahlung; **~ with** *vt fus* hergeben; (*renounce*) aufgeben; **~ial** ['pɑːʃl] *adj* (*incomplete*) teilweise; (*biased*) parteiisch; **to be ~ial to** eine (besondere) Vorliebe haben für

participant [pɑː'tɪsɪpənt] *n* Teilnehmer(in) *m(f)*

participate [pɑː'tɪsɪpeɪt] *vi*: **to ~ (in)** teilnehmen (an +*dat*); **participation** [pɑːtɪsɪ'peɪʃən] *n* Teilnahme *f*; (*sharing*) Beteiligung *f*

participle ['pɑːtɪsɪpl] *n* Partizip *nt*

particle ['pɑːtɪkl] *n* Teilchen *nt*

particular [pə'tɪkjuləʳ] *adj* bestimmt; (*exact*) genau; (*fussy*) eigen; **in ~** besonders; **~ly** *adv* besonders

particulars *npl* (*details*) Einzelheiten *pl*; (*of person*) Personalien *pl*

parting ['pɑːtɪŋ] *n* (*separation*) Abschied *m*; (*BRIT: of hair*) Scheitel *m* ♦ *adj* Abschieds-

partition [pɑː'tɪʃən] *n* (*wall*) Trennwand *f*; (*division*) Teilung *f* ♦ *vt* aufteilen

partly ['pɑːtlɪ] *adv* zum Teil, teilweise

partner ['pɑːtnəʳ] *n* Partner *m* ♦ *vt* der

Partner sein von; **~ship** *n* Partnerschaft *f*; (*COMM*) Teilhaberschaft *f*

partridge ['pɑːtrɪdʒ] *n* Rebhuhn *nt*

part-time ['pɑːt'taɪm] *adj* Teilzeit- ♦ *adv* stundenweise

party ['pɑːtɪ] *n* (*POL, JUR*) Partei *f*; (*group*) Gesellschaft *f*; (*celebration*) Party *f* ♦ *adj* (*dress*) Party-; (*politics*) Partei-; **~ line** *n* (*TEL*) Gemeinschaftsanschluss *m*

pass [pɑːs] *vt* (*on foot*) vorbeigehen an +*dat*; (*driving*) vorbeifahren an +*dat*; (*surpass*) übersteigen; (*hand on*) weitergeben; (*approve*) genehmigen; (*time*) verbringen; (*exam*) bestehen ♦ *vi* (*go by*) vorbeigehen; vorbeifahren; (*years*) vergehen; (*be successful*) bestehen ♦ *n* (*in mountains, SPORT*) Pass *m*; (*permission*) Passierschein *m*; (*in exam*): **to get a ~** bestehen; **to ~ sth through sth** etw durch etw führen; **to make a ~ at sb** (*inf*) bei jdm Annäherungsversuche machen; **~ away** *vi* (*euph*) verscheiden; **~ by** *vi* vorbeigehen; vorbeifahren; (*years*) vergehen; **~ on** *vt* weitergeben; **~ out** *vi* (*faint*) ohnmächtig werden; **~ up** *vt* vorbeigehen lassen; **~able** *adj* (*road*) passierbar; (*fairly good*) passabel

passage ['pæsɪdʒ] *n* (*corridor*) Gang *m*; (*in book*) (Text)stelle *f*; (*voyage*) Überfahrt *f*; **~way** *n* Durchgang *m*

passbook ['pɑːsbuk] *n* Sparbuch *nt*

passenger ['pæsɪndʒəʳ] *n* Passagier *m*; (*on bus*) Fahrgast *m*

passer-by [pɑːsə'baɪ] *n* Passant(in) *m(f)*

passing ['pɑːsɪŋ] *adj* (*car*) vorbeifahrend; (*thought, affair*) momentan ♦ *n*: **in ~** beiläufig; **~ place** *n* (*AUT*) Ausweichstelle *f*

passion ['pæʃən] *n* Leidenschaft *f*; **~ate** *adj* leidenschaftlich

passive ['pæsɪv] *adj* passiv; (*LING*) passivisch; **~ smoking** *n* Passivrauchen *nt*

Passover ['pɑːsəuvəʳ] *n* Passahfest *nt*

passport ['pɑːspɔːt] *n* (Reise)pass *m*; **~ control** *n* Passkontrolle *f*; **~ office** *n* Passamt *nt*

password ['pɑːswɜːd] *n* Parole *f*, Kennwort *nt*, Losung *f*

past [pɑːst] prep (motion) an +dat ... vorbei; (position) hinter +dat; (later than) nach ♦ adj (years) vergangen; (president etc) ehemalig ♦ n Vergangenheit f; **he's ~ forty** er ist über vierzig; **for the ~ few/3 days** in den letzten paar/3 Tagen; **to run ~** vorbeilaufen; **ten/quarter ~ eight** zehn/Viertel nach acht

pasta ['pæstə] n Teigwaren pl

paste [peɪst] n (fish ~ etc) Paste f; (glue) Kleister m ♦ vt kleben

pasteurized ['pæstʃəraɪzd] adj pasteurisiert

pastime ['pɑːstaɪm] n Zeitvertreib m

pastor ['pɑːstə*] n Pfarrer m

pastry ['peɪstrɪ] n Blätterteig m; **pastries** npl (tarts etc) Stückchen pl

pasture ['pɑːstʃə*] n Weide f

pasty [n 'pæstɪ, adj 'peɪstɪ] n (Fleisch)pastete f ♦ adj blässlich, käsig

pat [pæt] n leichte(r) Schlag m, Klaps m ♦ vt tätscheln

patch [pætʃ] n Fleck m ♦ vt flicken; **(to go through) a bad ~** eine Pechsträhne (haben); **~ up** vt flicken; (quarrel) beilegen; **~ed** adj geflickt; **~y** adj (irregular) ungleichmäßig

pâté ['pæteɪ] n Pastete f

patent ['peɪtnt] n Patent nt ♦ vt patentieren lassen; (by authorities) patentieren ♦ adj offenkundig; **~ leather** n Lackleder nt

paternal [pə'tɜːnl] adj väterlich

paternity [pə'tɜːnɪtɪ] n Vaterschaft f

path [pɑːθ] n Pfad m; Weg m

pathetic [pə'θetɪk] adj (very bad) kläglich

pathological [pæθə'lɒdʒɪkl] adj pathologisch

pathology [pə'θɒlədʒɪ] n Pathologie f

pathos ['peɪθɒs] n Rührseligkeit f

pathway ['pɑːθweɪ] n Weg m

patience ['peɪʃns] n Geduld f; (BRIT: CARDS) Patience f

patient ['peɪʃnt] n Patient(in) m(f), Kranke(r) mf ♦ adj geduldig

patio ['pætɪəʊ] n Terrasse f

patriotic [pætrɪ'ɒtɪk] adj patriotisch

patrol [pə'trəʊl] n Patrouille f; (police) Streife f ♦ vt patrouillieren in +dat ♦ vi (police) die Runde machen; (MIL) patrouillieren; **~ car** n Streifenwagen m; **~man** (US) (irreg) n (Streifen)polizist m

patron ['peɪtrən] n (in shop) (Stamm)kunde m; (in hotel) (Stamm)gast m; (supporter) Förderer m; **~ of the arts** Mäzen m; **~age** ['pætrənɪdʒ] n Schirmherrschaft f; **~ize** ['pætrənaɪz] vt (support) unterstützen; (shop) besuchen; (treat condescendingly) von oben herab behandeln; **~ saint** n Schutzpatron(in) m(f)

patter ['pætə*] n (sound: of feet) Trappeln nt; (: of rain) Prasseln nt; (sales talk) Gerede nt ♦ vi (feet) trappeln; (rain) prasseln

pattern ['pætən] n Muster nt; (SEWING) Schnittmuster nt; (KNITTING) Strickanleitung f

pauper ['pɔːpə*] n Arme(r) mf

pause [pɔːz] n Pause f ♦ vi innehalten

pave [peɪv] vt pflastern; **to ~ the way for** den Weg bahnen für

pavement ['peɪvmənt] (BRIT) n Bürgersteig m

pavilion [pə'vɪlɪən] n Pavillon m; (SPORT) Klubhaus nt

paving ['peɪvɪŋ] n Straßenpflaster nt; **~ stone** n Pflasterstein m

paw [pɔː] n Pfote f; (of big cats) Tatze f, Pranke f ♦ vt (scrape) scharren; (handle) betatschen

pawn [pɔːn] n Pfand nt; (chess) Bauer m ♦ vt verpfänden; **~broker** n Pfandleiher m; **~shop** n Pfandhaus nt

pay [peɪ] (pt, pp paid) n Bezahlung f, Lohn m ♦ vt bezahlen ♦ vi zahlen; (be profitable) sich bezahlt machen; **to ~ attention (to)** Acht geben (auf +acc); **to ~ sb a visit** jdn besuchen; **~ back** vt zurückzahlen; **~ for** vt fus bezahlen; **~ in** vt einzahlen; **~ off** vt abzahlen ♦ vi (scheme, decision) sich bezahlt machen; **~ up** vt zahlen; **~able** adj zahlbar, fällig; **~ee** n Zahlungsempfänger m; **~ envelope** (US) n Lohntüte f; **~ment** n Bezahlung f; **advance ~ment** Vorauszahlung f; **monthly ~ment** monatliche Rate f; **~ packet** (BRIT) n Lohntüte f; **~phone** n Münzfernsprecher

m; **~roll** *n* Lohnliste *f*; **~ slip** *n* Lohn-/
Gehaltsstreifen *m*; **~ television** *n*
Abonnenten-Fernsehen *nt*
PC *n abbr* = **personal computer**
p.c. *abbr* = **per cent**
pea [piː] *n* Erbse *f*
peace [piːs] *n* Friede(n) *m*; **~able** *adj*
friedlich; **~ful** *adj* friedlich, ruhig;
~keeping *adj* Friedens-
peach [piːtʃ] *n* Pfirsich *m*
peacock ['piːkɔk] *n* Pfau *m*
peak [piːk] *n* Spitze *f*; (*of mountain*) Gipfel *m*;
(*fig*) Höhepunkt *m*; **~ hours** *npl* (*traffic*)
Hauptverkehrszeit *f*; (*telephone, electricity*)
Hauptbelastungszeit *f*; **~ period** *n* Stoßzeit
f, Hauptzeit *f*
peal [piːl] *n* (Glocken)läuten *nt*; **~s of**
laughter schallende(s) Gelächter *nt*
peanut ['piːnʌt] *n* Erdnuss *f*; **~ butter** *n*
Erdnussbutter *f*
pear [pɛəʳ] *n* Birne *f*
pearl [pəːl] *n* Perle *f*
peasant ['pɛznt] *n* Bauer *m*
peat [piːt] *n* Torf *m*
pebble ['pɛbl] *n* Kiesel *m*
peck [pɛk] *vt, vi* picken **~** *n* (*with beak*)
Schnabelhieb *m*; (*kiss*) flüchtige(r) Kuss *m*;
~ing order *n* Hackordnung *f*; **~ish** (*BRIT:*
inf) *adj* ein bisschen hungrig
peculiar [pɪ'kjuːlɪəʳ] *adj* (*odd*) seltsam; **~ to**
charakteristisch für; **~ity** [pɪkjuːlɪ'ærɪtɪ] *n*
(*singular quality*) Besonderheit *f*;
(*strangeness*) Eigenartigkeit *f*
pedal ['pɛdl] *n* Pedal *nt* **~** *vt, vi* (*cycle*) fahren,
Rad fahren
pedantic [pɪ'dæntɪk] *adj* pedantisch
peddler ['pɛdləʳ] *n* Hausierer(in) *m(f)*; (*of*
drugs) Drogenhändler(in) *m(f)*
pedestal ['pɛdəstl] *n* Sockel *m*
pedestrian [pɪ'dɛstrɪən] *n* Fußgänger *m*
~ *adj* Fußgänger-; (*humdrum*) langweilig; **~**
crossing (*BRIT*) *n* Fußgängerüberweg *m*;
~ized *n* in eine Fußgängerzone
umgewandelt; **~ precinct** (*BRIT*), **~ zone**
(*US*) *n* Fußgängerzone *f*
pediatrics [piːdɪ'ætrɪks] (*US*) *n* = **paediatrics**
pedigree ['pɛdɪgriː] *n* Stammbaum *m* **~** *cpd*

(*animal*) reinrassig, Zucht-
pee [piː] (*inf*) *vi* pissen, pinkeln
peek [piːk] *vi* gucken
peel [piːl] *n* Schale *f* **~** *vt* schälen **~** *vi* (*paint*
etc) abblättern; (*skin*) sich schälen
peep [piːp] *n* (*BRIT: look*) kurze(r) Blick *m*;
(*sound*) Piepsen *nt* **~** *vi* (*BRIT: look*) gucken;
~ out *vi* herausgucken; **~hole** *n* Guckloch
nt
peer [pɪəʳ] *vi* starren; (*peep*) gucken **~** *n*
(*nobleman*) Peer *m*; (*equal*) Ebenbürtige(r)
m; **~age** *n* Peerswürde *f*
peeved [piːvd] *adj* (*person*) sauer
peg [pɛg] *n* (*stake*) Pflock *m*; (*BRIT: also:*
clothes ~) Wäscheklammer *f*
Pekinese [piːkɪ'niːz] *n* (*dog*) Pekinese *m*
pelican ['pɛlɪkən] *n* Pelikan *m*; **~ crossing**
(*BRIT*) *n* (*AUT*) Ampelüberweg *m*
pellet ['pɛlɪt] *n* Kügelchen *nt*
pelmet ['pɛlmɪt] *n* Blende *f*
pelt [pɛlt] *vt* bewerfen **~** *vi* (*rain*) schütten
~ *n* Pelz *m*, Fell *nt*
pelvis ['pɛlvɪs] *n* Becken *nt*
pen [pɛn] *n* (*fountain ~*) Federhalter *m*; (*ball-*
point ~) Kuli *m*; (*for sheep*) Pferch *m*
penal ['piːnl] *adj* Straf-; **~ize** *vt* (*punish*)
bestrafen; (*disadvantage*) benachteiligen
penalty ['pɛnltɪ] *n* Strafe *f*; (*FOOTBALL*)
Elfmeter *m*; **~ (kick)** *n* Elfmeter *m*
penance ['pɛnəns] *n* Buße *f*
pence [pɛns] (*BRIT*) *npl of* **penny**
pencil ['pɛnsl] *n* Bleistift *m*; **~ case** *n*
Federmäppchen *nt*; **~ sharpener** *n*
Bleistiftspitzer *m*
pendant ['pɛndnt] *n* Anhänger *m*
pending ['pɛndɪŋ] *prep* bis (zu) **~** *adj*
unentschieden, noch offen
pendulum ['pɛndjuləm] *n* Pendel *nt*
penetrate ['pɛnɪtreɪt] *vt* durchdringen;
(*enter into*) eindringen in *+acc*;
penetration [pɛnɪ'treɪʃən] *n* Durchdringen
nt; Eindringen *nt*
penfriend ['pɛnfrɛnd] (*BRIT*) *n* Brieffreund(in)
m(f)
penguin ['pɛŋgwɪn] *n* Pinguin *m*
penicillin [pɛnɪ'sɪlɪn] *n* Penizillin *nt*
peninsula [pə'nɪnsjulə] *n* Halbinsel *f*

penis ['piːnɪs] n Penis m

penitentiary [penɪ'tenʃərɪ] (US) n Zuchthaus nt

penknife ['pennaɪf] n Federmesser nt

pen name n Pseudonym nt

penniless ['penɪlɪs] adj mittellos

penny ['penɪ] (pl **pennies** or (BRIT) **pence**) n Penny m; (US) Centstück nt

penpal ['penpæl] n Brieffreund(in) m(f)

pension ['penʃən] n Rente f; **~er** (BRIT) n Rentner(in) m(f); **~ fund** n Rentenfonds m; **~ plan** n Rentenversicherung f

pensive ['pensɪv] adj nachdenklich

Pentagon ['pentəgɒn]

i Pentagon *heißt das fünfeckige Gebäude in Arlington, Virginia, in dem das amerikanische Verteidigungsministerium untergebracht ist. Im weiteren Sinne bezieht sich dieses Wort auf die amerikanische Militärführung.*

---

pentathlon [pen'tæθlən] n Fünfkampf m

Pentecost ['pentɪkɒst] n Pfingsten pl or nt

penthouse ['penthaus] n Dach-terrassenwohnung f

pent-up ['pentʌp] adj (feelings) angestaut

penultimate [pe'nʌltɪmət] adj vorletzte(r, s)

people ['piːpl] n (nation) Volk nt ♦ npl (persons) Leute pl; (inhabitants) Bevölkerung f ♦ vt besiedeln; **several ~ came** mehrere Leute kamen; **~ say that ...** man sagt, dass ...

pepper ['pepə'] n Pfeffer m; (vegetable) Paprika m ♦ vt (pelt) bombardieren; **~ mill** n Pfeffermühle f; **~mint** n (plant) Pfefferminze f; (sweet) Pfefferminz m

pep talk [pep-] (inf) n Anstachelung f

per [pəː'] prep pro; **~ day/person** pro Tag/Person; **~ annum** adv pro Jahr; **~ capita** adj (income) Pro-Kopf- ♦ adv pro Kopf

perceive [pə'siːv] vt (realize) wahrnehmen; (understand) verstehen

per cent n Prozent nt; **percentage** [pə'sentɪdʒ] n Prozentsatz m

perception [pə'sepʃən] n Wahrnehmung f; (insight) Einsicht f

perceptive [pə'septɪv] adj (person) aufmerksam; (analysis) tief gehend

perch [pəːtʃ] n Stange f; (fish) Flussbarsch m ♦ vi sitzen, hocken

percolator ['pəːkəleɪtə'] n Kaffeemaschine f

percussion [pə'kʌʃən] n (MUS) Schlagzeug nt

perennial [pə'renɪəl] adj wiederkehrend; (everlasting) unvergänglich

perfect [adj, n 'pəːfɪkt, vb pə'fekt] adj vollkommen; (crime, solution) perfekt ♦ n (GRAM) Perfekt nt ♦ vt vervollkommnen; **~ion** n Vollkommenheit f; **~ly** adv vollkommen, perfekt; (quite) ganz, einfach

perforate ['pəːfəreɪt] vt durchlöchern; **~d** adj (eardrum) perforiert

perforation [pəːfə'reɪʃən] n Perforieren nt; (line of holes) Perforation f

perform [pə'fɔːm] vt (carry out) durch- or ausführen; (task) verrichten; (THEAT) spielen, geben ♦ vi (THEAT) auftreten; **~ance** n Durchführung f; (efficiency) Leistung f; (show) Vorstellung f; **~er** n Künstler(in) m(f)

perfume ['pəːfjuːm] n Duft m; (lady's) Parfüm nt

perhaps [pə'hæps] adv vielleicht

peril ['perɪl] n Gefahr f

perimeter [pə'rɪmɪtə'] n Peripherie f; (of circle etc) Umfang m

period ['pɪərɪəd] n Periode f; (GRAM) Punkt m; (MED) Periode f ♦ adj (costume) historisch; **~ic** [pɪərɪ'ɔdɪk] adj periodisch; **~ical** [pɪərɪ'ɔdɪkl] n Zeitschrift f; **~ically** [pɪərɪ'ɔdɪklɪ] adv periodisch

peripheral [pə'rɪfərəl] adj Rand-, peripher ♦ n (COMPUT) Peripheriegerät nt

perish ['perɪʃ] vi umkommen; (fruit) verderben; **~able** adj leicht verderblich

perjury ['pəːdʒərɪ] n Meineid m

perk [pəːk] (inf) n (fringe benefit) Vergünstigung f; **~ up** vi munter werden; **~y** adj keck

perm [pəːm] n Dauerwelle f

permanent ['pəːmənənt] adj dauernd, ständig

permeate ['pəːmɪeɪt] vt, vi durchdringen

permissible [pə'mɪsɪbl] adj zulässig

permission [pə'mɪʃən] n Erlaubnis f

permissive [pə'mɪsɪv] *adj* nachgiebig; **the ~ society** die permissive Gesellschaft

permit [*n* 'pə:mɪt, *vb* pə'mɪt] *n* Zulassung *f* ♦ *vt* erlauben, zulassen

perpendicular [pə:pən'dɪkjulər] *adj* senkrecht

perpetrate ['pə:pɪtreɪt] *vt* begehen

perpetual [pə'petjuəl] *adj* dauernd, ständig

perpetuate [pə'petjueɪt] *vt* verewigen, bewahren

perplex [pə'pleks] *vt* verblüffen

persecute ['pə:sɪkju:t] *vt* verfolgen; **persecution** [pə:sɪ'kju:ʃən] *n* Verfolgung *f*

perseverance [pə:sɪ'vɪərns] *n* Ausdauer *f*

persevere [pə:sɪ'vɪəʳ] *vi* durchhalten

Persian ['pə:ʃən] *adj* persisch ♦ *n* Perser(in) *m(f)*; **the (Persian) Gulf** der Persische Golf

persist [pə'sɪst] *vi* (*in belief etc*) bleiben; (*rain, smell*) andauern; (*continue*) nicht aufhören; **to ~ in** bleiben bei; **~ence** *n* Beharrlichkeit *f*; **~ent** *adj* beharrlich; (*unending*) ständig

person ['pə:sn] *n* Person *f*; **in ~** persönlich; **~able** *adj* gut aussehend; **~al** *adj* persönlich; (*private*) privat; (*of body*) körperlich, Körper-; **~al assistant** *n* Assistent(in) *m(f)*; **~al column** *n* private Kleinanzeigen *pl*; **~al computer** *n* Personalcomputer *m*; **~ality** [pə:sə'nælɪtɪ] *n* Persönlichkeit *f*; **~ally** *adv* persönlich; **~al organizer** *n* Terminplaner *m*, Zeitplaner *m*; (*electronic*) elektronisches Notizbuch *nt*; **~al stereo** *n* Walkman *m* ®; **~ify** [pə:'sɔnɪfaɪ] *vt* verkörpern

personnel [pə:sə'nel] *n* Personal *nt*

perspective [pə'spektɪv] *n* Perspektive *f*

Perspex ['pə:speks] ® *n* Acrylglas *nt*, Akrylglas *nt*

perspiration [pə:spɪ'reɪʃən] *n* Transpiration *f*

perspire [pə'spaɪəʳ] *vi* transpirieren

persuade [pə'sweɪd] *vt* überreden; (*convince*) überzeugen

persuasion [pə'sweɪʒən] *n* Überredung *f*; Überzeugung *f*

persuasive [pə'sweɪsɪv] *adj* überzeugend

pert [pə:t] *adj* keck

pertaining [pə:'teɪnɪŋ]: **~ to** *prep* betreffend +*acc*

pertinent ['pə:tɪnənt] *adj* relevant

perturb [pə'tə:b] *vt* beunruhigen

pervade [pə'veɪd] *vt* erfüllen

perverse [pə'və:s] *adj* pervers; (*obstinate*) eigensinnig

pervert [*n* 'pə:və:t, *vb* pə'və:t] *n* perverse(r) Mensch *m* ♦ *vt* verdrehen; (*morally*) verderben

pessimist ['pesɪmɪst] *n* Pessimist *m*; **~ic** *adj* pessimistisch

pest [pest] *n* (*insect*) Schädling *m*; (*fig: person*) Nervensäge *f*; (: *thing*) Plage *f*; **~er** ['pestəʳ] *vt* plagen; **~icide** ['pestɪsaɪd] *n* Insektenvertilgungsmittel *nt*

pet [pet] *n* (*animal*) Haustier *nt* ♦ *vt* liebkosen, streicheln

petal ['petl] *n* Blütenblatt *nt*

peter out ['pi:tə-] *vi* allmählich zu Ende gehen

petite [pə'ti:t] *adj* zierlich

petition [pə'tɪʃn] *n* Bittschrift *f*

petrified ['petrɪfaɪd] *adj* versteinert; (*person*) starr (vor Schreck)

petrify ['petrɪfaɪ] *vt* versteinern; (*person*) erstarren lassen

petrol ['petrəl] (*BRIT*) *n* Benzin *nt*, Kraftstoff *m*; **two-/four-star ~** ≈ Normal-/ Superbenzin *nt*; **~ can** *n* Benzinkanister *m*

petroleum [pə'trəulɪəm] *n* Petroleum *nt*

petrol: ~ pump (*BRIT*) *n* (*in car*) Benzinpumpe *f*; (*at garage*) Zapfsäule *f*; **~ station** (*BRIT*) *n* Tankstelle *f*; **~ tank** (*BRIT*) *n* Benzintank *m*

petticoat ['petɪkəut] *n* Unterrock *m*

petty ['petɪ] *adj* (*unimportant*) unbedeutend; (*mean*) kleinlich; **~ cash** *n* Portokasse *f*; **~ officer** *n* Maat *m*

pew [pju:] *n* Kirchenbank *f*

pewter ['pju:təʳ] *n* Zinn *nt*

phantom ['fæntəm] *n* Phantom *nt*

pharmacist ['fɑ:məsɪst] *n* Pharmazeut *m*; (*druggist*) Apotheker *m*

pharmacy ['fɑ:məsɪ] *n* Pharmazie *f*; (*shop*) Apotheke *f*

phase [feɪz] *n* Phase *f* ♦ *vt*: **to ~ sth in** etw allmählich einführen; **to ~ sth out** etw auslaufen lassen

Ph.D. n abbr = **Doctor of Philosophy**
pheasant ['feznt] n Fasan m
phenomena [fə'nɔmɪnə] npl of
phenomenon
phenomenon [fə'nɔmɪnən] n Phänomen nt
philanthropist [fɪ'lænθrəpɪst] n Philanthrop
m, Menschenfreund m
Philippines ['fɪlɪpi:nz] npl: **the ~** die
Philippinen pl
philosopher [fɪ'lɔsəfəʳ] n Philosoph m;
philosophical [fɪlə'sɔfɪkl] adj
philosophisch; **philosophy** [fɪ'lɔsəfɪ] n
Philosophie f
phlegm [flɛm] n (MED) Schleim m
phobia ['fəubjə] n (irrational fear: of insects,
flying, water etc) Phobie f
phone [fəun] n Telefon nt ♦ vt, vi
telefonieren, anrufen; **to be on the ~**
telefonieren; **~ back** vt, vi zurückrufen;**~
up** vt, vi anrufen; **~ bill** n Telefonrechnung
f; **~ book** n Telefonbuch nt; **~ booth** n
Telefonzelle f; **~ box** n Telefonzelle f; **~
call** n Telefonanruf m; **~ card** n (TEL)
Telefonkarte f; **~-in** n (RAD, TV) Phone-in nt;
~ number n Telefonnummer f
phonetics [fə'nɛtɪks] n Phonetik f
phoney ['fəunɪ] (inf) adj unecht ♦ n (person)
Schwindler m; (thing) Fälschung f;
(banknote) Blüte f
phony ['fəunɪ] adj, n = **phoney**
photo ['fəutəu] n Foto nt; **~copier**
['fəutəukɔpɪəʳ] n Kopiergerät nt; **~copy**
['fəutəukɔpɪ] n Fotokopie f ♦ vt fotokopieren;
~genic [fəutəu'dʒenɪk] adj fotogen; **~graph**
n Fotografie f, Aufnahme f ♦ vt
fotografieren; **~grapher** ['fəutəgræf] n
Fotograf m; **~graphic** [fəutə'græfɪk] adj
fotografisch; **~graphy** [fə'tɔgrəfɪ] n
Fotografie f
phrase [freɪz] n Satz m; (expression)
Ausdruck m ♦ vt ausdrücken, formulieren; **~
book** n Sprachführer m
physical ['fɪzɪkl] adj physikalisch; (bodily)
körperlich, physisch; **~ education** n
Turnen nt; **~ly** adv physikalisch
physician [fɪ'zɪʃən] n Arzt m
physicist ['fɪzɪsɪst] n Physiker(in) m(f)

physics ['fɪzɪks] n Physik f
physiotherapist [fɪzɪəu'θerəpɪst] n
Physiotherapeut(in) m(f)
physiotherapy [fɪzɪəu'θerəpɪ] n
Heilgymnastik f, Physiotherapie f
physique [fɪ'zi:k] n Körperbau m
pianist ['pi:ənɪst] n Pianist(in) m(f)
piano [pɪ'ænəu] n Klavier nt
pick [pɪk] n (tool) Pickel m; (choice) Auswahl f
♦ vt (fruit) pflücken; (choose) aussuchen;
take your ~ such dir etwas aus; **to ~ sb's
pocket** jdn bestehlen; **~ on** vt fus (person)
herumhacken auf +dat; **~ out** vt
auswählen; **~ up** vi (improve) sich erholen
♦ vt (lift up) aufheben; (learn) (schnell)
mitbekommen; (collect) abholen; (girl) (sich
dat) anlachen; (AUT: passenger) mitnehmen;
(speed) gewinnen an +dat; **to ~ o.s. up**
aufstehen
picket ['pɪkɪt] n (striker) Streikposten m ♦ vt
(factory) (Streik)posten aufstellen vor +dat
♦ vi (Streik)posten stehen
pickle ['pɪkl] n (salty mixture) Pökel m; (inf)
Klemme f ♦ vt (in Essig) einlegen; einpökeln
pickpocket ['pɪkpɔkɪt] n Taschendieb m
pick-up ['pɪkʌp] n (BRIT: on record player)
Tonabnehmer m; (small truck) Lieferwagen
m
picnic ['pɪknɪk] n Picknick nt ♦ vi picknicken;
~ area n Rastplatz m
pictorial [pɪk'tɔ:rɪəl] adj in Bildern
picture ['pɪktʃəʳ] n Bild nt ♦ vt (visualize) sich
dat vorstellen; **the ~s** npl (BRIT) das Kino; **~
book** n Bilderbuch nt
picturesque [pɪktʃə'rɛsk] adj malerisch
pie [paɪ] n (meat) Pastete f; (fruit) Torte f
piece [pi:s] n Stück nt ♦ vt: **to ~ together**
zusammenstückeln; (fig) sich dat
zusammenreimen; **to take to ~s** in
Einzelteile zerlegen; **~meal** adv stückweise,
Stück für Stück; **~work** n Akkordarbeit f
pie chart n Kreisdiagramm nt
pier [pɪəʳ] n Pier m, Mole f
pierce [pɪəs] vt durchstechen, durchbohren
(also look); **~d** adj durchgestochen;
piercing ['pɪəsɪŋ] adj (cry) durchdringend
pig [pɪg] n Schwein nt

pigeon ['pɪdʒən] n Taube f; **~hole** n (compartment) Ablegefach nt

piggy bank ['pɪgɪ-] n Sparschwein nt

pig: **~headed** ['pɪg'hɛdɪd] adj dickköpfig; **~let** ['pɪglɪt] n Ferkel nt; **~skin** ['pɪgskɪn] n Schweinsleder nt; **~sty** ['pɪgstaɪ] n Schweinestall m; **~tail** ['pɪgteɪl] n Zopf m

pike [paɪk] n Pike f; (fish) Hecht m

pilchard ['pɪltʃəd] n Sardine f

pile [paɪl] n Haufen m; (of books, wood) Stapel m; (in ground) Pfahl m; (on carpet) Flausch m ♦ vt (also: ~ up) anhäufen ♦ vi (also: ~ up) sich anhäufen

piles [paɪlz] npl Hämorr(ho)iden pl

pile-up ['paɪlʌp] n (AUT) Massenzusammenstoß m

pilfering ['pɪlfərɪŋ] n Diebstahl m

pilgrim ['pɪlgrɪm] n Pilger(in) m(f); **~age** n Wallfahrt f

pill [pɪl] n Tablette f, Pille f; **the ~** die (Antibaby)pille

pillage ['pɪlɪdʒ] vt plündern

pillar ['pɪlə'] n Pfeiler m, Säule f (also fig); **~box** (BRIT) n Briefkasten m

pillion ['pɪljən] n Soziussitz m

pillow ['pɪləʊ] n Kissen nt; **~case** n Kissenbezug m

pilot ['paɪlət] n Pilot m; (NAUT) Lotse m ♦ adj (scheme etc) Versuchs- ♦ vt führen; (ship) lotsen; **~ light** n Zündflamme f

pimp [pɪmp] n Zuhälter m

pimple ['pɪmpl] n Pickel m

PIN n abbr (= personal identification number) PIN f

pin [pɪn] n Nadel f; (for sewing) Stecknadel f; (TECH) Stift m, Bolzen m ♦ vt stecken; (keep in one position) pressen, drücken; **to ~ sth to sth** etw an etw acc heften; **to ~ sth on sb** (fig) jdm etw anhängen; **~s and needles** Kribbeln nt; **~ down** vt (fig: person): **to ~ sb down (to sth)** jdn (auf etw acc) festnageln

pinafore ['pɪnəfɔː'] n Schürze f; **~ dress** n Kleiderrock m

pinball ['pɪnbɔːl] n Flipper m

pincers ['pɪnsəz] npl Kneif- or Beißzange f; (MED) Pinzette f

pinch [pɪntʃ] n Zwicken nt, Kneifen nt; (of salt) Prise f ♦ vt zwicken, kneifen; (inf: steal) klauen ♦ vi (shoe) drücken; **at a ~** notfalls, zur Not

pincushion ['pɪnkʊʃən] n Nadelkissen nt

pine [paɪn] n (also: ~ tree) Kiefer f ♦ vi: **to ~ for** sich sehnen nach; **~ away** vi sich zu Tode sehnen

pineapple ['paɪnæpl] n Ananas f

ping [pɪŋ] n Klingeln nt; **~-pong** ® n Pingpong nt

pink [pɪŋk] adj rosa inv ♦ n Rosa nt; (BOT) Nelke f

pinnacle ['pɪnəkl] n Spitze f

PIN (number) n Geheimnummer f

pinpoint ['pɪnpɔɪnt] vt festlegen

pinstripe ['pɪnstraɪp] n Nadelstreifen m

pint [paɪnt] n Pint nt; (BRIT: inf: of beer) große(s) Bier nt

pioneer [paɪə'nɪə'] n Pionier m; (fig also) Bahnbrecher m

pious ['paɪəs] adj fromm

pip [pɪp] n Kern m; **the ~s** npl (BRIT: RAD) das Zeitzeichen

pipe [paɪp] n (smoking) Pfeife f; (tube) Rohr nt; (in house) (Rohr)leitung f ♦ vt (durch Rohre) leiten; (MUS) blasen; **~s** npl (also: bagpipes) Dudelsack m; **~ down** vi (be quiet) die Luft anhalten; **~ cleaner** n Pfeifenreiniger m; **~ dream** n Luftschloss nt; **~line** n (for oil) Pipeline f; **~r** n Pfeifer m; (bagpipes) Dudelsackbläser m

piping ['paɪpɪŋ] adv: **~ hot** siedend heiß

pique ['piːk] n gekränkte(r) Stolz m

pirate ['paɪərət] n Pirat m, Seeräuber m; **~d** adj: **~d version** Raubkopie f; **~ radio** (BRIT) n Piratensender m

Pisces ['paɪsiːz] n Fische pl

piss [pɪs] (inf) vi pissen; **~ed** (inf) adj (drunk) voll

pistol ['pɪstl] n Pistole f

piston ['pɪstən] n Kolben m

pit [pɪt] n Grube f; (THEAT) Parterre nt; (orchestra ~) Orchestergraben m ♦ vt (mark with scars) zerfressen; (compare): **to ~ sth against sb** jdn an jdm messen; **the ~s** npl (MOTOR RACING) die Boxen pl

pitch [pɪtʃ] n Wurf m; (of trader) Stand m; (SPORT) (Spiel)feld nt; (MUS) Tonlage f; (substance) Pech m ♦ vt werfen; (set up) aufschlagen ♦ vi (NAUT) rollen; **to ~ a tent** ein Zelt aufbauen; **~-black** adj pechschwarz; **~ed battle** n offene Schlacht f

piteous ['pɪtɪəs] adj kläglich, erbärmlich

pitfall ['pɪtfɔːl] n (fig) Falle f

pith [pɪθ] n Mark nt

pithy ['pɪθɪ] adj prägnant

pitiful ['pɪtɪful] adj (deserving pity) bedauernswert; (contemptible) jämmerlich

pitiless ['pɪtɪlɪs] adj erbarmungslos

pittance ['pɪtns] n Hungerlohn m

pity ['pɪtɪ] n (sympathy) Mitleid nt ♦ vt Mitleid haben mit; **what a ~!** wie schade!

pivot ['pɪvət] n Drehpunkt m ♦ vi: **to ~ (on)** sich drehen (um)

pizza ['piːtsə] n Pizza f

placard ['plækɑːd] n Plakat nt, Anschlag m

placate [plə'keɪt] vt beschwichtigen

place [pleɪs] n Platz m; (spot) Stelle f; (town etc) Ort m ♦ vt setzen, stellen, legen; (order) aufgeben; (SPORT) platzieren; (identify) unterbringen; **to take ~** stattfinden; **out of ~** nicht am rechten Platz; (fig: remark) unangebracht; **in the first ~** erstens; **to change ~s with sb** mit jdm den Platz tauschen; **to be ~d third** (in race, exam) auf dem dritten Platz liegen

placid ['plæsɪd] adj gelassen, ruhig

plagiarism ['pleɪdʒjərɪzəm] n Plagiat nt

plague [pleɪg] n Pest f; (fig) Plage f ♦ vt plagen

plaice [pleɪs] n Scholle f

plaid [plæd] n Plaid nt

plain [pleɪn] adj (clear) klar, deutlich; (simple) einfach, schlicht; (not beautiful) alltäglich ♦ n Ebene f; **in ~ clothes** (police) in Zivil(kleidung); **~ chocolate** n Bitterschokolade f

plaintiff ['pleɪntɪf] n Kläger m

plaintive ['pleɪntɪv] adj wehleidig

plait [plæt] n Zopf m ♦ vt flechten

plan [plæn] n Plan m ♦ vt, vi planen; **according to ~** planmäßig; **to ~ to do sth**

vorhaben, etw zu tun

plane [pleɪn] n Ebene f; (AVIAT) Flugzeug nt; (tool) Hobel m; (tree) Platane f

planet ['plænɪt] n Planet m

plank [plæŋk] n Brett nt

planning ['plænɪŋ] n Planung f; **family ~** Familienplanung f; **~ permission** n Baugenehmigung f

plant [plɑːnt] n Pflanze f; (TECH) (Maschinen)anlage f; (factory) Fabrik f, Werk nt ♦ vt pflanzen; (set firmly) stellen; **~ation** [plæn'teɪʃən] n Plantage f

plaque [plæk] n Gedenktafel f; (on teeth) (Zahn)belag m

plaster ['plɑːstə*] n Gips m; (in house) Verputz m; (BRIT: also: **sticking ~**) Pflaster nt; (for fracture: **~ of Paris**) Gipsverband m ♦ vt gipsen; (hole) zugipsen; (ceiling) verputzen; (fig: with pictures etc) bekleben, verkleben; **~ed** (inf) adj besoffen; **~er** n Gipser m

plastic ['plæstɪk] n Plastik nt or f ♦ adj (made of ~) Plastik-; (ART) plastisch, bildend; **~ bag** n Plastiktüte f

plasticine ['plæstɪsiːn] ® n Plastilin nt

plastic surgery n plastische Chirurgie f

plate [pleɪt] n Teller m; (gold/silver ~) vergoldete(s)/versilberte(s) Tafelgeschirr nt; (in book) (Bild)tafel f

plateau ['plætəu] (pl **~s** or **~x**) n (GEOG) Plateau nt, Hochebene f

plateaux ['plætəuz] npl of **plateau**

plate glass n Tafelglas nt

platform ['plætfɔːm] n (at meeting) Plattform f, Podium nt; (RAIL) Bahnsteig m; (POL) Parteiprogramm nt; **~ ticket** n Bahnsteigkarte f

platinum ['plætɪnəm] n Platin nt

platoon [plə'tuːn] n (MIL) Zug m

platter ['plætə*] n Platte f

plausible ['plɔːzɪbl] adj (theory, excuse, statement) plausibel; (person) überzeugend

play [pleɪ] n (also TECH) Spiel nt; (THEAT) (Theater)stück nt ♦ vt spielen; (another team) spielen gegen ♦ vi spielen; **to ~ safe** auf Nummer sicher or Sicher gehen; **~ down** vt herunterspielen; **~ up** vi (cause *trouble)* frech werden; *(bad leg etc)* wehtun ♦ *vt (person)* plagen; **to ~ up to sb** jdm flattieren; **~-acting** *n* Schauspielerei *f*; **~er** *n* Spieler(in) *m(f)*; **~ful** *adj* spielerisch; **~ground** *n* Spielplatz *m*; **~group** *n* Kindergarten *m*; **~ing card** *n* Spielkarte *f*; **~ing field** *n* Sportplatz *m*; **~mate** *n* Spielkamerad *m*; **~-off** *n (SPORT)* Entscheidungsspiel *nt*; **~pen** *n* Laufstall *m*; **~school** *n* = **playgroup**; **~thing** *n* Spielzeug *nt*; **~time** *n (kleine)* Pause *f*; **~wright** *n* Theaterschriftsteller *m*

plc *abbr (= public limited company)* AG

plea [pliː] *n* Bitte *f*; *(general appeal)* Appell *m*; *(JUR)* Plädoyer *nt*; **~ bargaining** *n (LAW) Aushandeln der Strafe zwischen Staatsanwaltschaft und Verteidigung*

plead [pliːd] *vt (poverty)* zur Entschuldigung anführen; *(JUR: sb's case)* vertreten ♦ *vi (beg)* dringend bitten; *(JUR)* plädieren; **to ~ with sb** jdn dringend bitten

pleasant ['plɛznt] *adj* angenehm; **~ries** *npl (polite remarks)* Nettigkeiten *pl*

please [pliːz] *vt, vi (be agreeable to)* gefallen *+dat*; **~!** bitte!; **~ yourself!** wie du willst!; **~d** *adj* zufrieden; *(glad)*: **~d (about sth)** erfreut *(über etw acc)*; **~d to meet you** angenehm; **pleasing** ['pliːzɪŋ] *adj* erfreulich

pleasure ['plɛʒər] *n* Freude *f* ♦ *cpd* Vergnügungs-; **"it's a ~"** „gern geschehen"

pleat [pliːt] *n* Falte *f*

plectrum ['plɛktrəm] *n* Plektron *nt*

pledge [plɛdʒ] *n* Pfand *nt*; *(promise)* Versprechen *nt* ♦ *vt* verpfänden; *(promise)* geloben, versprechen

plentiful ['plɛntɪfʊl] *adj* reichlich

plenty ['plɛntɪ] *n* Fülle *f*, Überfluss *m*; **~ of** eine Menge, viel

pleurisy ['plʊərɪsɪ] *n* Rippenfellentzündung *f*

pliable ['plaɪəbl] *adj* biegsam; *(person)* beeinflussbar

pliers ['plaɪəz] *npl* (Kneif)zange *f*

plight [plaɪt] *n* (Not)lage *f*

plimsolls ['plɪmsəlz] *(BRIT) npl* Turnschuhe *pl*

plinth [plɪnθ] *n* Sockel *m*

P.L.O. *n abbr (= Palestine Liberation Organization)* PLO *f*

plod [plɒd] *vi (work)* sich abplagen; *(walk)* trotten

plonk [plɒŋk] *n (BRIT: inf: wine)* billige(r) Wein *m* ♦ *vt*: **to ~ sth down** etw hinknallen

plot [plɒt] *n* Komplott *nt*; *(story)* Handlung *f*; *(of land)* Grundstück *nt* ♦ *vt* markieren; *(curve)* zeichnen; *(movements)* nachzeichnen ♦ *vi (plan secretly)* sich verschwören

plough [plaʊ] *(US* **plow***) n* Pflug *m* ♦ *vt* pflügen; **~ back** *vt (COMM)* wieder in das Geschäft stecken; **~ through** *vt fus (water)* durchpflügen; *(book)* sich kämpfen durch

plow [plaʊ] *(US)* = **plough**

ploy [plɔɪ] *n* Masche *f*

pluck [plʌk] *vt (fruit)* pflücken; *(guitar)* zupfen; *(goose etc)* rupfen ♦ *n* Mut *m*; **to ~ up courage** all seinen Mut zusammennehmen

plug [plʌg] *n* Stöpsel *m*; *(ELEC)* Stecker *m*; *(inf: publicity)* Schleichwerbung *f*; *(AUT)* Zündkerze *f* ♦ *vt* (zu)stopfen; *(inf: advertise)* Reklame machen für; **~ in** *vt (ELEC)* anschließen

plum [plʌm] *n* Pflaume *f*, Zwetsch(g)e *f*

plumage ['pluːmɪdʒ] *n* Gefieder *nt*

plumber ['plʌmər] *n* Klempner *m*, Installateur *m*; **plumbing** ['plʌmɪŋ] *n (craft)* Installieren *nt*; *(fittings)* Leitungen *pl*

plummet ['plʌmɪt] *vi* (ab)stürzen

plump [plʌmp] *adj* rundlich, füllig ♦ *vt* plumpsen lassen; **to ~ for** *(inf: choose)* sich entscheiden für

plunder ['plʌndər] *n* Plünderung *f*; *(loot)* Beute *f* ♦ *vt* plündern

plunge [plʌndʒ] *n* Sturz *m* ♦ *vt* stoßen ♦ *vi* (sich) stürzen; **to take the ~** den Sprung wagen; **plunging** ['plʌndʒɪŋ] *adj (neckline)* offenherzig

plural ['plʊərəl] *n* Plural *m*, Mehrzahl *f*

plus [plʌs] *n (also:* **~ sign***)* Plus(zeichen) *nt* ♦ *prep* plus, und; **ten/twenty ~** mehr als zehn/zwanzig

plush [plʌʃ] *adj (also:* **~y***: inf)* feudal

ply [plaɪ] *vt (trade)* (be)treiben; *(with questions)* zusetzen *+dat*; *(ship, taxi)* befahren ♦ *vi (ship, taxi)* verkehren ♦ *n*:

three-~ (*wool*) Dreifach-; **to ~ sb with drink** jdn zum Trinken animieren; **~wood** n Sperrholz nt

P.M. n abbr = **prime minister**

p.m. adv abbr (= post meridiem) nachmittags

pneumatic drill n Presslufthammer m

pneumonia [nju:ˈməʊnɪə] n Lungenentzündung f

poach [pəʊtʃ] vt (COOK) pochieren; (*game*) stehlen ♦ vi (*steal*) wildern; **~ed** adj (*egg*) verloren; **~er** n Wilddieb m

P.O. Box n abbr = **Post Office Box**

pocket [ˈpɒkɪt] n Tasche f; (*of resistance*) (Widerstands)nest nt ♦ vt einstecken; **to be out of ~** (BRIT) draufzahlen; **~book** n Taschenbuch nt; **~ calculator** n Taschenrechner m; **~ knife** n Taschenmesser nt; **~ money** n Taschengeld nt

pod [pɒd] n Hülse f; (*of peas also*) Schote f

podgy [ˈpɒdʒɪ] adj pummelig

podiatrist [pɒˈdiːətrɪst] (US) n Fußpfleger(in) m(f)

poem [ˈpəʊɪm] n Gedicht nt

poet [ˈpəʊɪt] n Dichter m, Poet m; **~ic** [pəʊˈetɪk] adj poetisch, dichterisch; **~ laureate** n Hofdichter m; **~ry** n Poesie f; (*poems*) Gedichte pl

poignant [ˈpɔɪnjənt] adj (*touching*) ergreifend

point [pɔɪnt] n (*also in discussion, scoring*) Punkt m; (*spot*) Punkt m, Stelle f; (*sharpened tip*) Spitze f; (*moment*) (Zeit)punkt m; (*purpose*) Zweck m; (*idea*) Argument nt; (*decimal*) Dezimalstelle f; (*personal characteristic*) Seite f ♦ vt zeigen mit; (*gun*) richten ♦ vi zeigen; **~s** npl (RAIL) Weichen pl; **to be on the ~ of doing sth** drauf und dran sein, etw zu tun; **to make a ~ of** Wert darauf legen; **to get the ~** verstehen, worum es geht; **to come to the ~** zur Sache kommen; **there's no ~ (in doing sth)** es hat keinen Sinn(, etw zu tun); **~ out** vt hinweisen auf +acc; **~ to** vt fus zeigen auf +acc; **~-blank** adv (*at close range*) aus nächster Entfernung; (*bluntly*) unverblümt; **~ed** adj (*also fig*) spitz, scharf;

~edly adv (*fig*) spitz; **~er** n Zeigestock m; (*on dial*) Zeiger m; **~less** adj sinnlos; **~ of view** n Stand- or Gesichtspunkt m

poise [pɔɪz] n Haltung f; (*fig*) Gelassenheit f

poison [ˈpɔɪzn] n (*also fig*) Gift nt ♦ vt vergiften; **~ing** n Vergiftung f; **~ous** adj giftig, Gift-

poke [pəʊk] vt stoßen; (*put*) stecken; (*fire*) schüren; (*hole*) bohren; **~ about** vi herumstochern; (*nose around*) herumwühlen

poker [ˈpəʊkə*] n Schürhaken m; (CARDS) Poker nt

poky [ˈpəʊkɪ] adj eng

Poland [ˈpəʊlənd] n Polen nt

polar [ˈpəʊlə*] adj Polar-, polar; **~ bear** n Eisbär m

Pole [pəʊl] n Pole m, Polin f

pole [pəʊl] n Stange f, Pfosten m; (*flagpole, telegraph ~*) Stange f, Mast m; (ELEC, GEOG) Pol m; (SPORT: *vaulting ~*) Stab m; (*ski ~*) Stock m; **~ bean** (US) n (*runner bean*) Stangenbohne f; **~ vault** n Stabhochsprung m

police [pəˈliːs] n Polizei f ♦ vt kontrollieren; **~ car** n Polizeiwagen m; **~man** (*irreg*) n Polizist m; **~ state** n Polizeistaat m; **~ station** n (Polizei)revier nt, Wache f; **~woman** (*irreg*) n Polizistin f

policy [ˈpɒlɪsɪ] n Politik f; (*insurance*) (Versicherungs)police f

polio [ˈpəʊlɪəʊ] n (*spinale*) Kinderlähmung f, Polio f

Polish [ˈpəʊlɪʃ] adj polnisch ♦ n (LING) Polnisch nt

polish [ˈpɒlɪʃ] n Politur f; (*for floor*) Wachs nt; (*for shoes*) Creme f; (*for nails*) Lack m; (*shine*) Glanz m; (*of furniture*) Politur f; (*fig*) Schliff m ♦ vt polieren; (*shoes*) putzen; (*fig*) den letzten Schliff geben +dat; **~ off** vt (*inf: food*) wegputzen; (: *drink*) hinunterschütten; **~ed** adj glänzend; (*manners*) verfeinert

polite [pəˈlaɪt] adj höflich; **~ly** adv höflich; **~ness** n Höflichkeit f

politic-: ~al [pəˈlɪtɪkl] adj politisch; **~ally** [pəˈlɪtɪklɪ] adv politisch; **~ally correct**

politisch korrekt; **~ian** [pɒlɪ'tɪʃən] *n* Politiker *m*; **~s** *npl* Politik *f*

polka dot ['pɒlkə-] *n* Tupfen *m*

poll [pəʊl] *n* Abstimmung *f*; (*in election*) Wahl *f*; (*votes cast*) Wahlbeteiligung *f*; (*opinion ~*) Umfrage *f* ♦ *vt* (*votes*) erhalten

pollen ['pɒlən] *n* (*BOT*) Blütenstaub *m*, Pollen *m*

polling ['pəʊlɪŋ-]: **~ booth** (*BRIT*) *n* Wahlkabine *f*; **~ day** (*BRIT*) *n* Wahltag *m*; **~ station** (*BRIT*) *n* Wahllokal *nt*

pollute [pə'luːt] *vt* verschmutzen, verunreinigen; **~d** *adj* verschmutzt; **pollution** [pə'luːʃən] *n* Verschmutzung *f*

polo ['pəʊləʊ] *n* Polo *nt*; **~ neck** *n* (*also:* **~-necked sweater**) Rollkragen *m*; Rollkragenpullover *m*; **~ shirt** *n* Polohemd *nt*

polystyrene [pɒlɪ'staɪriːn] *n* Styropor *nt*

polytechnic [pɒlɪ'teknɪk] *n* technische Hochschule *f*

polythene ['pɒlɪθiːn] *n* Plastik *nt*; **~ bag** *n* Plastiktüte *f*

pomegranate ['pɒmɪɡrænɪt] *n* Granatapfel *m*

pompom ['pɒmpɒm] *n* Troddel *f*, Pompon *m*

pompous ['pɒmpəs] *adj* aufgeblasen; (*language*) geschwollen

pond [pɒnd] *n* Teich *m*, Weiher *m*

ponder ['pɒndəʳ] *vt* nachdenken über +*acc*; **~ous** *adj* schwerfällig

pong [pɒŋ] (*BRIT*: *inf*) *n* Mief *m*

pontiff ['pɒntɪf] *n* Pontifex *m*

pontoon [pɒn'tuːn] *n* Ponton *m*; (*CARDS*) 17-und-4 *nt*

pony ['pəʊnɪ] *n* Pony *nt*; **~tail** *n* Pferdeschwanz *m*; **~ trekking** (*BRIT*) *n* Ponyreiten *nt*

poodle ['puːdl] *n* Pudel *m*

pool [puːl] *n* (*swimming ~*) Schwimmbad *nt*; (: *private*) Swimmingpool *m*; (*of liquid, blood*) Lache *f*; (*fund*) (gemeinsame) Kasse *f*; (*billiards*) Poolspiel *nt* ♦ *vt* (*money etc*) zusammenlegen; (*football*) **~s** Toto *nt*

poor [pʊəʳ] *adj* arm; (*not good*) schlecht ♦ *npl*: **the ~** die Armen *pl*; **~ in** (*resources*)

arm an +*dat*; **~ly** *adv* schlecht; (*dressed*) ärmlich ♦ *adj* schlecht

pop [pɒp] *n* Knall *m*; (*music*) Popmusik *f*; (*drink*) Limo(nade) *f*; (*US*: *inf*) Pa *m* ♦ *vt* (*put*) stecken; (*balloon*) platzen lassen ♦ *vi* knallen; **~ in** *vi* kurz vorbeigehen *or* vorbeikommen; **~ out** *vi* (*person*) kurz rausgehen; (*thing*) herausspringen; **~ up** *vi* auftauchen; **~corn** *n* Puffmais *m*

pope [pəʊp] *n* Papst *m*

poplar ['pɒpləʳ] *n* Pappel *f*

poppy ['pɒpɪ] *n* Mohn *m*

Popsicle ['pɒpsɪkl] ® *US*) *n* (*ice lolly*) Eis *nt* am Stiel

populace ['pɒpjʊləs] *n* Volk *nt*

popular ['pɒpjʊləʳ] *adj* beliebt, populär; (*of the people*) volkstümlich; (*widespread*) allgemein; **~ity** [pɒpjʊ'lærɪtɪ] *n* Beliebtheit *f*, Popularität *f*; **~ly** *adv* allgemein, überall

population [pɒpjʊ'leɪʃən] *n* Bevölkerung *f*; (*of town*) Einwohner *pl*

populous ['pɒpjʊləs] *adj* dicht besiedelt

porcelain ['pɔːslɪn] *n* Porzellan *nt*

porch [pɔːtʃ] *n* Vorbau *m*, Veranda *f*

porcupine ['pɔːkjʊpaɪn] *n* Stachelschwein *nt*

pore [pɔːʳ] *n* Pore *f* ♦ *vi*: **to ~ over** brüten über +*dat*

pork [pɔːk] *n* Schweinefleisch *nt*

porn [pɔːn] *n* Porno *m*; **~ographic** [pɔːnə'ɡræfɪk] *adj* pornografisch; **~ography** [pɔː'nɒɡrəfɪ] *n* Pornografie *f*

porous ['pɔːrəs] *adj* porös; (*skin*) porig

porpoise ['pɔːpəs] *n* Tümmler *m*

porridge ['pɒrɪdʒ] *n* Haferbrei *m*

port [pɔːt] *n* Hafen *m*; (*town*) Hafenstadt *f*; (*NAUT*: *left side*) Backbord *nt*; (*wine*) Portwein *m*; **~ of call** Anlaufhafen *m*

portable ['pɔːtəbl] *adj* tragbar

porter ['pɔːtəʳ] *n* Pförtner(in) *m(f)*; (*for luggage*) (Gepäck)träger *m*

portfolio [pɔːt'fəʊlɪəʊ] *n* (*case*) Mappe *f*; (*POL*) Geschäftsbereich *m*; (*FIN*) Portefeuille *nt*; (*of artist*) Kollektion *f*

porthole ['pɔːthəʊl] *n* Bullauge *nt*

portion ['pɔːʃən] *n* Teil *m*, Stück *nt*; (*of food*) Portion *f*

portrait ['pɔːtreɪt] *n* Porträt *nt*

portray [pɔː'treɪ] vt darstellen; **~al** n
Darstellung f

Portugal [ˈpɔːtjʊgl] n Portugal nt

Portuguese [pɔːtjuˈgiːz] adj portugiesisch
♦ n inv Portugiese m, Portugiesin f; (LING)
Portugiesisch nt

pose [pəʊz] n Stellung f, Pose f; (affectation)
Pose f ♦ vi posieren ♦ vt stellen

posh [pɔʃ] (inf) adj (piek)fein

position [pəˈzɪʃən] n Stellung f; (place) Lage
f; (job) Stelle f; (attitude) Standpunkt m ♦ vt
aufstellen

positive [ˈpɒzɪtɪv] adj positiv; (convinced)
sicher; (definite) eindeutig

posse [ˈpɒsɪ] n (US) Aufgebot nt

possess [pəˈzes] vt besitzen; **~ion** [pəˈzeʃən]
n Besitz m; **~ive** adj besitzergreifend,
eigensüchtig

possibility [pɒsɪˈbɪlɪtɪ] n Möglichkeit f

possible [ˈpɒsɪbl] adj möglich; **as big as ~**
so groß wie möglich, möglichst groß;
possibly adv möglicherweise, vielleicht; **I
cannot possibly come** ich kann
unmöglich kommen

post [pəʊst] n (BRIT: letters, delivery) Post f;
(pole) Pfosten m, Pfahl m; (place of duty)
Posten m; (job) Stelle f ♦ vt (notice)
anschlagen; (BRIT: letters) aufgeben;
(: appoint) versetzen; (soldiers) aufstellen;
~age n Postgebühr f, Porto nt; **~al** adj
Post-; **~al order** n Postanweisung f; **~box**
(BRIT) n Briefkasten m; **~card** n Postkarte f;
~code (BRIT) n Postleitzahl f

postdate [ˈpəʊstˈdeɪt] vt (cheque)
nachdatieren

poster [ˈpəʊstəʳ] n Plakat nt, Poster nt

poste restante [pəʊstˈrestãːnt] n
Aufbewahrungsstelle f für postlagernde
Sendungen

posterior [pɒsˈtɪərɪəʳ] (inf) n Hintern m

posterity [pɒsˈterɪtɪ] n Nachwelt f

postgraduate [ˈpəʊstˈgrædjuət] n
Weiterstudierende(r) mf

posthumous [ˈpɒstjuməs] adj post(h)um

postman [ˈpəʊstmən] (irreg) n Briefträger m

postmark [ˈpəʊstmɑːk] n Poststempel m

post-mortem [pəʊstˈmɔːtəm] n Autopsie f

post office n Postamt nt, Post f;
(organization) Post f; **Post Office Box** n
Postfach nt

postpone [pəʊsˈpəʊn] vt verschieben

postscript [ˈpəʊstskrɪpt] n Postskript nt; (to
affair) Nachspiel nt

posture [ˈpɒstʃəʳ] n Haltung f ♦ vi posieren

postwar [pəʊstˈwɔːʳ] adj Nachkriegs-

postwoman [ˈpəʊstwʊmən] (irreg) n
Briefträgerin f

posy [ˈpəʊzɪ] n Blumenstrauß m

pot [pɒt] n Topf m; (teapot) Kanne f; (inf:
marijuana) Hasch m ♦ vt (plant) eintopfen;
to go to ~ (inf: work) auf den Hund
kommen

potato [pəˈteɪtəʊ] (pl **~es**) n Kartoffel f; **~
peeler** n Kartoffelschäler m

potent [ˈpəʊtnt] adj stark; (argument)
zwingend

potential [pəˈtenʃl] adj potenziell, potentiell
♦ n Potenzial nt, Potential nt; **~ly** adv
potenziell, potentiell

pothole [ˈpɒthəʊl] n (in road) Schlagloch nt;
(BRIT: underground) Höhle f; **potholing**
(BRIT) n: **to go potholing** Höhlen erforschen

potion [ˈpəʊʃən] n Trank m

potluck [pɒtˈlʌk] n: **to take ~ with sth** etw
auf gut Glück nehmen

pot plant n Topfpflanze f

potter [ˈpɒtəʳ] n Töpfer m ♦ vi
herumhantieren; **~y** n Töpferwaren pl;
(place) Töpferei f

potty [ˈpɒtɪ] adj (inf: mad) verrückt ♦ n
Töpfchen nt

pouch [paʊtʃ] n Beutel m

pouf(fe) [puːf] n Sitzkissen nt

poultry [ˈpəʊltrɪ] n Geflügel nt

pounce [paʊns] vi sich stürzen ♦ n Sprung
m, Satz m; **to ~ on** sich stürzen auf +acc

pound [paʊnd] n (FIN, weight) Pfund nt; (for
cars, animals) Auslösestelle f ♦ vt
(zer)stampfen ♦ vi klopfen, hämmern; **~
sterling** n Pfund Sterling nt

pour [pɔːʳ] vt gießen, schütten ♦ vi gießen;
(crowds etc) strömen; **~ away** vt abgießen;
~ in vi (people) hereinströmen; **~ off** vt
abgießen; **~ out** vi (people) herausströmen

♦ *vt* (*drink*) einschenken; **~ing** *adj*: **~ing rain** strömende(r) Regen *m*

pout [paʊt] *vi* schmollen

poverty ['pɒvətɪ] *n* Armut *f*; **~-stricken** *adj* verarmt, sehr arm

powder ['paʊdəʳ] *n* Pulver *nt*; (*cosmetic*) Puder *m* ♦ *vt* pulverisieren; **to ~ one's nose** sich *dat* die Nase pudern; **~ compact** *n* Puderdose *f*; **~ed milk** *n* Milchpulver *nt*; **~ room** *n* Damentoilette *f*; **~y** *adj* pulverig

power ['paʊəʳ] *n* (*also POL*) Macht *f*; (*ability*) Fähigkeit *f*; (*strength*) Stärke *f*; (*MATH*) Potenz *f*; (*ELEC*) Strom *m* ♦ *vt* betreiben, antreiben; **to be in ~** (*POL etc*) an der Macht sein; **~ cut** *n* Stromausfall *m*; **~ed** *adj*: **~ed by** betrieben mit; **~ failure** (*US*) *n* Stromausfall *m*; **~ful** *adj* (*person*) mächtig; (*engine, government*) stark; **~less** *adj* machtlos; **~ point** (*BRIT*) *n* elektrische(r) Anschluss *m*; **~ station** *n* Elektrizitätswerk *nt*; **~ struggle** *n* Machtkampf *m*

p.p. *abbr* (= *per procurationem*): **p.p. J. Smith** i. A. J. Smith

PR *n abbr* = **public relations**

practicable ['præktɪkəbl] *adj* durchführbar

practical ['præktɪkl] *adj* praktisch; **~ity** [præktɪ'kælɪtɪ] *n* (*of person*) praktische Veranlagung *f*; (*of situation etc*) Durchführbarkeit *f*; **~ joke** *n* Streich *m*; **~ly** *adv* praktisch

practice ['præktɪs] *n* Übung *f*; (*reality, also of doctor, lawyer*) Praxis *f*; (*custom*) Brauch *m*; (*in business*) Usus *m* ♦ *vt, vi* (*US*) = **practise**; **in ~** (*in reality*) in der Praxis; **out of ~** außer Übung; **practicing** (*US*) *adj* = **practising**

practise ['præktɪs] (*US* **practice**) *vt* üben; (*profession*) ausüben ♦ *vi* (sich) üben; (*doctor, lawyer*) praktizieren; **practising** (*US* **practicing**) *adj* praktizierend; (*Christian etc*) aktiv

practitioner [præk'tɪʃənəʳ] *n* praktische(r) Arzt *m*, praktische Ärztin *f*

pragmatic [præg'mætɪk] *adj* pragmatisch

prairie ['preərɪ] *n* Prärie *f*, Steppe *f*

praise [preɪz] *n* Lob *nt* ♦ *vt* loben; **~worthy** *adj* lobenswert

pram [præm] (*BRIT*) *n* Kinderwagen *m*

prance [prɑːns] *vi* (*horse*) tänzeln; (*person*) stolzieren

prank [præŋk] *n* Streich *m*

prawn [prɔːn] *n* Garnele *f*; Krabbe *f*; **~ cocktail** *n* Krabbencocktail *m*

pray [preɪ] *vi* beten; **~er** [prɛəʳ] *n* Gebet *nt*

preach [priːtʃ] *vi* predigen; **~er** *n* Prediger *m*

preamble [prɪ'æmbl] *n* Einleitung *f*

precarious [prɪ'kɛərɪəs] *adj* prekär, unsicher

precaution [prɪ'kɔːʃən] *n* (Vorsichts)maßnahme *f*

precede [prɪ'siːd] *vi* vorausgehen ♦ *vt* vorausgehen +*dat*; **~nce** ['presɪdəns] *n* Vorrang *m*; **~nt** ['presɪdənt] *n* Präzedenzfall *m*; **preceding** [prɪ'siːdɪŋ] *adj* vorhergehend

precinct ['priːsɪŋkt] *n* (*US: district*) Bezirk *m*; **~s** *npl* (*round building*) Gelände *nt*; (*area, environs*) Umgebung *f*; **pedestrian ~** Fußgängerzone *f*; **shopping ~** Geschäftsviertel *nt*

precious ['preʃəs] *adj* kostbar, wertvoll; (*affected*) pretiös, preziös, geziert

precipice ['presɪpɪs] *n* Abgrund *m*

precipitate [*adj* prɪ'sɪpɪtɪt, *vb* prɪ'sɪpɪteɪt] *adj* überstürzt, übereilt ♦ *vt* hinunterstürzen; (*events*) heraufbeschwören

precise [prɪ'saɪs] *adj* genau, präzis; **~ly** *adv* genau, präzis

precision [prɪ'sɪʒən] *n* Präzision *f*

preclude [prɪ'kluːd] *vt* ausschließen

precocious [prɪ'kəʊʃəs] *adj* frühreif

preconceived [priːkən'siːvd] *adj* (*idea*) vorgefasst

precondition ['priːkən'dɪʃən] *n* Vorbedingung *f*, Voraussetzung *f*

precursor [priː'kɜːsəʳ] *n* Vorläufer *m*

predator ['predətəʳ] *n* Raubtier *nt*

predecessor ['priːdɪsesəʳ] *n* Vorgänger *m*

predicament [prɪ'dɪkəmənt] *n* missliche Lage *f*

predict [prɪ'dɪkt] *vt* voraussagen; **~able** *adj* vorhersagbar; **~ion** [prɪ'dɪkʃən] *n* Voraussage *f*

predominantly [prɪ'dɒmɪnəntlɪ] *adv*

überwiegend, hauptsächlich

predominate [prɪ'dɔmɪneɪt] vi
vorherrschen; (fig) vorherrschen,
überwiegen

pre-eminent [pri:'emɪnənt] adj
hervorragend, herausragend

pre-empt [prɪ'emt] vt (action, decision)
vorwegnehmen

preen [pri:n] vt putzen; **to ~ o.s.** (person)
sich brüsten

prefab ['pri:fæb] n Fertighaus nt

preface ['prefəs] n Vorwort nt

prefect ['pri:fekt] n Präfekt m; (SCH)
Aufsichtsschüler(in) m(f)

prefer [prɪ'fɜ:ʳ] vt vorziehen, lieber mögen;
to ~ to do sth etw lieber tun; **~ably**
['prefrəblɪ] adv vorzugsweise, am liebsten;
~ence ['prefrəns] n Präferenz f, Vorzug m;
~ential [prefə'renʃəl] adj bevorzugt,
Vorzugs-

prefix ['pri:fɪks] n Vorsilbe f, Präfix nt

pregnancy ['pregnənsɪ] n Schwangerschaft f

pregnant ['pregnənt] adj schwanger

prehistoric ['pri:hɪs'tɔrɪk] adj prähistorisch,
vorgeschichtlich

prejudice ['predʒudɪs] n (bias)
Voreingenommenheit f; (opinion) Vorurteil
nt; (harm) Schaden m ♦ vt beeinträchtigen;
~d adj (person) voreingenommen

preliminary [prɪ'lɪmɪnərɪ] adj einleitend,
Vor-

prelude ['prelju:d] n Vorspiel nt; (fig) Auftakt
m

premarital ['pri:'mærɪtl] adj vorehelich

premature ['premətʃuəʳ] adj vorzeitig,
verfrüht; (birth) Früh-

premeditated [pri:'medɪteɪtɪd] adj geplant;
(murder) vorsätzlich

premenstrual syndrome [pri:'menstruəl-]
n prämenstruelles Syndrom nt

premier ['premɪəʳ] adj erste(r, s) ♦ n Premier
m

première ['premɪeəʳ] n Premiere f;
Uraufführung f

Premier League [-li:g] n ≃ 1. Bundesliga
(höchste Spielklasse im Fußball)

premise ['premɪs] n Voraussetzung f,

Prämisse f; **~s** npl (shop) Räumlichkeiten pl;
(grounds) Gelände nt; **on the ~s** im Hause

premium ['pri:mɪəm] n Prämie f; **to be at a
~** über pari stehen; **~ bond** (BRIT) n
Prämienanleihe f

premonition [premə'nɪʃən] n Vorahnung f

preoccupation [pri:ɔkju'peɪʃən] n Sorge f

preoccupied [pri:'ɔkjupaɪd] adj (look)
geistesabwesend

prep [prep] n (SCH) Hausaufgabe f

prepaid [pri:'peɪd] adj vorausbezahlt; (letter)
frankiert

preparation [prepə'reɪʃən] n Vorbereitung f

preparatory [prɪ'pærətərɪ] adj
Vor(bereitungs)-; **~ school** n (BRIT) private
Vorbereitungsschule für die Public School;
(US) private Vorbereitungsschule für die
Hochschule

prepare [prɪ'peəʳ] vt vorbereiten ♦ vi sich
vorbereiten; **to ~ for/prepare sth for**
sich/etw vorbereiten auf +acc; **to be ~d to
...** bereit sein zu ...

preponderance [prɪ'pɔndərns] n
Übergewicht nt

preposition [prepə'zɪʃən] n Präposition f,
Verhältniswort nt

preposterous [prɪ'pɔstərəs] adj absurd

prep school n = **preparatory school**

prerequisite [pri:'rekwɪzɪt] n (unerlässliche)
Voraussetzung f

prerogative [prɪ'rɔgətɪv] n Vorrecht nt

Presbyterian [prezbɪ'tɪərɪən] adj
presbyterianisch ♦ n Presbyterianer(in) m(f)

preschool ['pri:'sku:l] adj Vorschul-

prescribe [prɪ'skraɪb] vt vorschreiben; (MED)
verschreiben

prescription [prɪ'skrɪpʃən] n (MED) Rezept nt

presence ['prezns] n Gegenwart f; **~ of
mind** Geistesgegenwart f

present [adj, n 'preznt, vb prɪ'zent] adj (here)
anwesend; (current) gegenwärtig ♦ n
Gegenwart f; (gift) Geschenk nt ♦ vt
vorlegen; (introduce) vorstellen; (show)
zeigen; (give): **to ~ sb with sth** jdm etw
überreichen; **at ~** im Augenblick; **to give
sb a ~** jdm ein Geschenk machen; **~able**
[prɪ'zentəbl] adj präsentabel; **~ation**

[prezn'teıʃən] *n* Überreichung *f*; **~-day** *adj* heutig; **~er** [prı'zentə'] *n* (*RAD, TV*) Moderator(in) *m(f)*; **~ly** *adv* bald; (*at ~*) im Augenblick

preservation [prezə'veıʃən] *n* Erhaltung *f*

preservative [prı'zə:vətıv] *n* Konservierungsmittel *nt*

preserve [prı'zə:v] *vt* erhalten; (*food*) einmachen ♦ *n* (*jam*) Eingemachte(s) *nt*; (*reserve*) Schutzgebiet *nt*

preside [prı'zaıd] *vi* den Vorsitz haben

president ['prezıdənt] *n* Präsident *m*; **~ial** [prezı'denʃl] *adj* Präsidenten-; (*election*) Präsidentschafts-; (*system*) Präsidial-

press [pres] *n* Presse *f*; (*printing house*) Druckerei *f* ♦ *vt* drücken; (*iron*) bügeln; (*urge*) (be)drängen ♦ *vi* (*push*) drücken; **to be ~ed for time** unter Zeitdruck stehen; **to ~ for sth** drängen auf etw *acc*; **~ on** *vi* vorwärts drängen; **~ agency** *n* Presseagentur *f*; **~ conference** *n* Pressekonferenz *f*; **~ed** *adj* (*clothes*) gebügelt; **~ing** *adj* dringend; **~ stud** (*BRIT*) *n* Druckknopf *m*; **~-up** (*BRIT*) *n* Liegestütz *m*

pressure ['preʃə'] *n* Druck *m*; **~ cooker** *n* Schnellkochtopf *m*; **~ gauge** *n* Druckmesser *m*

pressurized ['preʃəraızd] *adj* Druck-

prestige [pres'ti:ʒ] *n* Prestige *nt*;

prestigious [pres'tıdʒəs] *adj* Prestige-

presumably [prı'zju:məblı] *adv* vermutlich

presume [prı'zju:m] *vt, vi* annehmen; **to ~ to do sth** sich erlauben, etw zu tun; **presumption** [prı'zʌmpʃən] *n* Annahme *f*; **presumptuous** [prı'zʌmpʃəs] *adj* anmaßend

pretence [prı'tens] (*US* **pretense**) *n* Vorgabe *f*, Vortäuschung *f*; (*false claim*) Vorwand *m*

pretend [prı'tend] *vt* vorgeben, so tun als ob ... ♦ *vi* so tun; **to ~ to sth** Anspruch erheben auf etw *acc*

pretense [prı'tens] (*US*) *n* = **pretence**

pretension [prı'tenʃən] *n* Anspruch *m*; (*impudent claim*) Anmaßung *f*

pretentious [prı'tenʃəs] *adj* angeberisch

pretext ['pri:tekst] *n* Vorwand *m*

pretty ['prıtı] *adj* hübsch ♦ *adv* (*inf*) ganz schön

prevail [prı'veıl] *vi* siegen; (*custom*) vorherrschen; **to ~ against** *or* **over** siegen über +*acc*; **to ~ (up)on sb to do sth** jdn dazu bewegen, etw zu tun; **~ing** *adj* vorherrschend

prevalent ['prevələnt] *adj* vorherrschend

prevent [prı'vent] *vt* (*stop*) verhindern, verhüten; **to ~ sb from doing sth** jdn (daran) hindern, etw zu tun; **~ative** *n* Vorbeugungsmittel *nt*; **~ion** [prı'venʃən] *n* Verhütung *f*; **~ive** *adj* vorbeugend, Schutz-

preview ['pri:vju:] *n* private Voraufführung *f*; (*trailer*) Vorschau *f*

previous ['pri:vıəs] *adj* früher, vorherig; **~ly** *adv* früher

prewar [pri:'wɔ:'] *adj* Vorkriegs-

prey [preı] *n* Beute *f*; **~ on** *vt fus* Jagd machen auf +*acc*; **it was ~ing on his mind** es quälte sein Gewissen

price [praıs] *n* Preis *m*; (*value*) Wert *m* ♦ *vt* (*label*) auszeichnen; **~less** *adj* (*also fig*) unbezahlbar; **~ list** *n* Preisliste *f*

prick [prık] *n* Stich *m* ♦ *vt, vi* stechen; **to ~ up one's ears** die Ohren spitzen

prickle ['prıkl] *n* Stachel *m*, Dorn *m*

prickly ['prıklı] *adj* stachelig; (*fig: person*) reizbar; **~ heat** *n* Hitzebläschen *pl*

pride [praıd] *n* Stolz *m*; (*arrogance*) Hochmut *m* ♦ *vt*: **to ~ o.s. on sth** auf etw *acc* stolz sein

priest [pri:st] *n* Priester *m*; **~hood** *n* Priesteramt *nt*

prim [prım] *adj* prüde

primarily ['praımərılı] *adv* vorwiegend

primary ['praımərı] *adj* (*main*) Haupt-; (*SCH*) Grund-; **~ school** (*BRIT*) *n* Grundschule *f*

prime [praım] *adj* erste(r, s); (*excellent*) erstklassig ♦ *vt* vorbereiten; (*gun*) laden; **in the ~ of life** in der Blüte der Jahre; **~ minister** *n* Premierminister *m*, Ministerpräsident *m*; **~r** ['praımə'] *n* Fibel *f*

primeval [praı'mi:vl] *adj* vorzeitlich; (*forests*) Ur-

primitive ['prımıtıv] *adj* primitiv

primrose ['prımrəuz] *n* (gelbe) Primel *f*

primus (stove) ['praıməs-] (® *BRIT*) *n*

Primuskocher m

prince [prɪns] n Prinz m; (*ruler*) Fürst m;
princess [prɪnˈses] n Prinzessin f; Fürstin f

principal [ˈprɪnsɪpl] adj Haupt- ♦ n (SCH)
(Schul)direktor m, Rektor m; (*money*)
(Grund)kapital nt

principle [ˈprɪnsɪpl] n Grundsatz m, Prinzip
nt; **in ~** im Prinzip; **on ~** aus Prinzip,
prinzipiell

print [prɪnt] n Druck m; (*made by feet, fingers*)
Abdruck m; (PHOT) Abzug m ♦ vt drucken;
(*name*) in Druckbuchstaben schreiben;
(PHOT) abziehen; **out of ~** vergriffen; **~ed
matter** n Drucksache f; **~er** n Drucker m;
~ing n Drucken nt; (*of photos*) Abziehen nt;
~out n (COMPUT) Ausdruck m

prior [ˈpraɪəʳ] adj früher ♦ n Prior m; **~ to sth**
vor etw dat; **~ to going abroad, she had
...** bevor sie ins Ausland ging, hatte sie ...

priority [praɪˈɒrɪtɪ] n Vorrang m; Priorität f

prise [praɪz] vt: **to ~ open** aufbrechen

prison [ˈprɪzn] n Gefängnis nt ♦ adj
Gefängnis-; (*system etc*) Strafvollzugs-; **~er**
n Gefangene(r) mf

pristine [ˈprɪstiːn] adj makellos

privacy [ˈprɪvəsɪ] n Ungestörtheit f, Ruhe f;
Privatleben nt

private [ˈpraɪvɪt] adj privat, Privat-; (*secret*)
vertraulich, geheim ♦ n einfache(r) Soldat
m; **"~"** (*on envelope*) „persönlich"; (*on door*)
„Privat"; **in ~** privat, unter vier Augen; **~
enterprise** n Privatunternehmen nt; **~
eye** n Privatdetektiv m; **~ property** n
Privatbesitz m; **~ school** n Privatschule f;
privatize vt privatisieren

privet [ˈprɪvɪt] n Liguster m

privilege [ˈprɪvɪlɪdʒ] n Privileg nt; **~d** adj
bevorzugt, privilegiert

privy [ˈprɪvɪ] adj geheim, privat; **P~ Council**
n Geheime(r) Staatsrat m

prize [praɪz] n Preis m ♦ adj (*example*)
erstklassig; (*idiot*) Voll- ♦ vt (hoch) schätzen;
~-giving n Preisverteilung f; **~winner** n
Preisträger(in) m(f)

pro [prəʊ] n (*professional*) Profi m; **the ~s and
cons** das Für und Wider

probability [prɒbəˈbɪlɪtɪ] n

Wahrscheinlichkeit f

probable [ˈprɒbəbl] adj wahrscheinlich;
probably adv wahrscheinlich

probation [prəˈbeɪʃən] n Probe(zeit) f; (JUR)
Bewährung f; **on ~** auf Probe; auf
Bewährung

probe [prəʊb] n Sonde f; (*enquiry*)
Untersuchung f ♦ vt, vi erforschen

problem [ˈprɒbləm] n Problem nt; **~atic**
[prɒbləˈmætɪk] adj problematisch

procedure [prəˈsiːdʒəʳ] n Verfahren nt

proceed [prəˈsiːd] vi (*advance*) vorrücken;
(*start*) anfangen; (*carry on*) fortfahren; (*set
about*) vorgehen; **~ings** npl Verfahren nt

proceeds [ˈprəʊsiːdz] npl Erlös m

process [ˈprəʊses] n Prozess m; (*method*)
Verfahren nt ♦ vt bearbeiten; (*food*)
verarbeiten; (*film*) entwickeln; **~ing** n
(PHOT) Entwickeln nt

procession [prəˈseʃən] n Prozession f,
Umzug m; **funeral ~** Trauerprozession f

pro-choice [prəʊˈtʃɔɪs] adj (*movement*) Pro-
Abtreibungs-; **~ campaigner**
Abtreibungsbefürworter(in) m(f)

proclaim [prəˈkleɪm] vt verkünden

procrastinate [prəʊˈkræstɪneɪt] vi zaudern

procure [prəˈkjʊəʳ] vt beschaffen

prod [prɒd] vt stoßen ♦ n Stoß m

prodigal [ˈprɒdɪgl] adj: **~ (with** or **of)**
verschwenderisch (mit)

prodigy [ˈprɒdɪdʒɪ] n Wunder nt

produce [n ˈprɒdjuːs, vb prəˈdjuːs] n (AGR)
(Boden)produkte pl, (Natur)erzeugnis nt
♦ vt herstellen, produzieren; (*cause*)
hervorrufen; (*farmer*) erzeugen; (*yield*)
liefern, bringen; (*play*) inszenieren; **~r** n
Hersteller m, Produzent m (also CINE);
Erzeuger m

product [ˈprɒdʌkt] n Produkt nt, Erzeugnis
nt; **~ion** [prəˈdʌkʃən] n Produktion f,
Herstellung f; (*thing*) Erzeugnis nt, Produkt
nt; (THEAT) Inszenierung f; **~ion line** n
Fließband nt; **~ive** [prəˈdʌktɪv] adj
produktiv; (*fertile*) ertragreich, fruchtbar

productivity [prɒdʌkˈtɪvɪtɪ] n Produktivität f

profane [prəˈfeɪn] adj weltlich, profan;
(*language etc*) gotteslästerlich

profess [prə'fes] *vt* bekennen; (*show*) zeigen; (*claim to be*) vorgeben

profession [prə'feʃən] *n* Beruf *m*; (*declaration*) Bekenntnis *nt*; **~al** *n* Fachmann *m*; (*SPORT*) Berufsspieler(in) *m(f)* ♦ *adj* Berufs-; (*expert*) fachlich; (*player*) professionell; **~ally** *adv* beruflich, fachmännisch

professor [prə'fesə'] *n* Professor *m*

proficiency [prə'fɪʃənsɪ] *n* Können *nt*

proficient [prə'fɪʃənt] *adj* fähig

profile ['prəʊfaɪl] *n* Profil *nt*; (*fig: report*) Kurzbiografie *f*

profit ['prɒfɪt] *n* Gewinn *m* ♦ *vi*: **to ~ (by** *or* **from)** profitieren (von); **~ability** [prɒfɪtə'bɪlɪtɪ] *n* Rentabilität *f*; **~able** *adj* einträglich, rentabel; **~eering** [prɒfɪ'tɪərɪŋ] *n* Profitmacherei *f*

profound [prə'faʊnd] *adj* tief

profuse [prə'fjuːs] *adj* überreich; **~ly** [prə'fjuːslɪ] *adv* überschwänglich; (*sweat*) reichlich; **profusion** [prə'fjuːʒən] *n*: **profusion (of)** Überfülle *f* (von), Überfluss *m* (an +*dat*)

• **program** ['prəʊgræm] *n* (*COMPUT*) Programm *nt* ♦ *vt* (*machine*) programmieren; **~me** (*US* **program**) *n* Programm *nt* ♦ *vt* planen; (*computer*) programmieren; **~mer** (*US* **programer**) *n* Programmierer(in) *m(f)*

progress [*n* 'prəʊgres, *vb* prə'gres] *n* Fortschritt *m* ♦ *vi* fortschreiten, weitergehen; **in ~** im Gang; **~ion** [prə'greʃən] *n* Folge *f*; **~ive** [prə'gresɪv] *adj* fortschrittlich, progressiv

prohibit [prə'hɪbɪt] *vt* verbieten; **to ~ sb from doing sth** jdm untersagen, etw zu tun; **~ion** [prəʊɪ'bɪʃən] *n* Verbot *nt*; (*US*) Alkoholverbot *nt*, Prohibition *f*; **~ive** *adj* unerschwinglich

project [*n* 'prɒdʒekt, *vb* prə'dʒekt] *n* Projekt *nt* ♦ *vt* vorausplanen; (*film etc*) projizieren; (*personality, voice*) zum Tragen bringen ♦ *vi* (*stick out*) hervorragen, (her)vorstehen

projectile [prə'dʒektaɪl] *n* Geschoss *nt*

projection [prə'dʒekʃən] *n* Projektion *f*; (*sth prominent*) Vorsprung *m*

projector [prə'dʒektə'] *n* Projektor *m*

proletariat [prəʊlɪ'teərɪət] *n* Proletariat *nt*

pro-life [prəʊ'laɪf] *adj* (*movement*) Anti-Abtreibungs-; **~ campaigner** Abtreibungsgegner(in) *m(f)*

prolific [prə'lɪfɪk] *adj* fruchtbar; (*author etc*) produktiv

prologue ['prəʊlɒg] *n* Prolog *m*; (*event*) Vorspiel *nt*

prolong [prə'lɒŋ] *vt* verlängern

prom [prɒm] *n abbr* = **promenade; promenade concert**

Prom

ℹ️ **Prom** (*promenade concert*) ist in Großbritannien ein Konzert, bei dem ein Teil der Zuhörer steht (ursprünglich spazieren ging). Die seit 1895 alljährlich stattfindenden Proms (seit 1941 immer in der Londoner Royal Albert Hall) zählen zu den bedeutendsten Musikereignissen in England. Der letzte Abend der Proms steht ganz im Zeichen des Patriotismus und gipfelt im Singen des Lieds „Land of Hope and Glory". In den USA und Kanada steht das Wort für **promenade**, *ein Ball an einer* **High School** *oder einem* **College**.

---

promenade [prɒmə'nɑːd] *n* Promenade *f*; **~ concert** *n* Promenadenkonzert *nt*

prominence ['prɒmɪnəns] *n* (große) Bedeutung *f*

prominent ['prɒmɪnənt] *adj* bedeutend; (*politician*) prominent; (*easily seen*) herausragend, auffallend

promiscuous [prə'mɪskjuəs] *adj* lose

promise ['prɒmɪs] *n* Versprechen *nt*; (*hope: ~ of sth*) Aussicht *f* auf etw *acc* ♦ *vt, vi* versprechen; **promising** *adj* viel versprechend

promontory ['prɒməntrɪ] *n* Vorsprung *m*

promote [prə'məʊt] *vt* befördern; (*help on*) fördern, unterstützen; **~r** *n* (*in entertainment, sport*) Veranstalter *m*; (*for charity etc*) Organisator *m*; **promotion** [prə'məʊʃən] *n* (*in rank*) Beförderung *f*; (*furtherance*) Förderung *f*; (*COMM*): **promotion (of)** Werbung *f* (für)

prompt [prɒmpt] adj prompt, schnell ♦ adv (punctually) genau ♦ n (COMPUT) Meldung f ♦ vt veranlassen; (THEAT) soufflieren +dat; **to ~ sb to do sth** jdn dazu veranlassen, etw zu tun; **~ly** adv sofort

prone [prəun] adj hingestreckt; **to be ~ to sth** zu etw neigen

prong [prɒŋ] n Zinke f

pronoun ['prəunaun] n Fürwort nt

pronounce [prə'nauns] vt aussprechen; (JUR) verkünden ♦ vi: **to ~ (on)** sich äußern (zu)

pronunciation [prənʌnsɪ'eɪʃən] n Aussprache f

proof [pru:f] n Beweis m; (PRINT) Korrekturfahne f; (of alcohol) Alkoholgehalt m ♦ adj sicher

prop [prɒp] n (also fig) Stütze f; (THEAT) Requisit nt ♦ vt (also: ~ up) (ab)stützen

propaganda [prɒpə'gændə] n Propaganda f

propel [prə'pel] vt (an)treiben; **~ler** n Propeller m; **~ling pencil** (BRIT) n Drehbleistift m

propensity [prə'pensɪtɪ] n Tendenz f

proper ['prɒpər] adj richtig; (seemly) schicklich; **~ly** adv richtig; **~ noun** n Eigenname m

property ['prɒpətɪ] n Eigentum nt; (quality) Eigenschaft f; (land) Grundbesitz m; **~ owner** n Grundbesitzer m

prophecy ['prɒfɪsɪ] n Prophezeiung f

prophesy ['prɒfɪsaɪ] vt prophezeien

prophet ['prɒfɪt] n Prophet m

proportion [prə'pɔ:ʃən] n Verhältnis nt; (share) Teil m ♦ vt: **to ~ (to)** abstimmen (auf +acc); **~al** adj proportional; **~ate** adj verhältnismäßig

proposal [prə'pəuzl] n Vorschlag m; (of marriage) Heiratsantrag m

propose [prə'pəuz] vt vorschlagen; (toast) ausbringen ♦ vi (offer marriage) einen Heiratsantrag machen; **to ~ to do sth** beabsichtigen, etw zu tun

proposition [prɒpə'zɪʃən] n Angebot nt; (statement) Satz m

proprietor [prə'praɪətə] n Besitzer m, Eigentümer m

propriety [prə'praɪətɪ] n Anstand m

pro rata [prəu'rɑ:tə] adv anteilmäßig

prose [prəuz] n Prosa f

prosecute ['prɒsɪkju:t] vt (strafrechtlich) verfolgen; **prosecution** [prɒsɪ'kju:ʃən] n (JUR) strafrechtliche Verfolgung f; (party) Anklage f; **prosecutor** n Vertreter m der Anklage; **Public Prosecutor** Staatsanwalt m

prospect [n 'prɒspekt, vb prə'spekt] n Aussicht f ♦ vt auf Bodenschätze hin untersuchen ♦ vi: **to ~ (for)** suchen (nach); **~ing** ['prɒspektɪŋ] n (for minerals) Suche f; **~ive** [prə'spektɪv] adj (son-in-law etc) zukünftig; (customer, candidate) voraussichtlich

prospectus [prə'spektəs] n (Werbe)prospekt m

prosper ['prɒspə] vi blühen, gedeihen; (person) erfolgreich sein; **~ity** [prɒ'sperɪtɪ] n Wohlstand m; **~ous** adj wohlhabend, reich

prostitute ['prɒstɪtju:t] n Prostituierte f

prostrate ['prɒstreɪt] adj ausgestreckt (liegend)

protagonist [prə'tægənɪst] n Hauptperson f, Held m

protect [prə'tekt] vt (be)schützen; **~ed species** n geschützte Art; **~ion** [prə'tekʃən] n Schutz m; **~ive** adj Schutz-, (be)schützend

protégé ['prəuteʒeɪ] n Schützling m

protein ['prəuti:n] n Protein nt, Eiweiß nt

protest [n 'prəutest, vb prə'test] n Protest m ♦ vi protestieren ♦ vt (affirm) beteuern

Protestant ['prɒtɪstənt] adj protestantisch ♦ n Protestant(in) m(f)

protester [prə'testə] n (demonstrator) Demonstrant(in) m(f)

protracted [prə'træktɪd] adj sich hinziehend

protrude [prə'tru:d] vi (her)vorstehen

proud [praud] adj: **~ (of)** stolz (auf +acc)

prove [pru:v] vt beweisen ♦ vi: **to ~ (to be) correct** sich als richtig erweisen; **to ~ o.s.** sich bewähren

proverb ['prɒvə:b] n Sprichwort nt; **~ial** [prə'və:bɪəl] adj sprichwörtlich

provide [prə'vaɪd] vt versehen; (supply) besorgen; **to ~ sb with sth** jdn mit etw

versorgen; **~ for** *vt fus* sorgen für;
(*emergency*) Vorkehrungen treffen für; **~d
(that)** *conj* vorausgesetzt(, dass)
providing [prə'vaɪdɪŋ] *conj* vorausgesetzt(,
dass)
province ['prɒvɪns] *n* Provinz *f*; (*division of
work*) Bereich *m*; **provincial** [prə'vɪnʃəl] *adj*
provinziell, Provinz-
provision [prə'vɪʒən] *n* Vorkehrung *f*;
(*condition*) Bestimmung *f*; **~s** *npl* (*food*)
Vorräte *pl*, Proviant *m*; **~al** *adj* provisorisch
proviso [prə'vaɪzəu] *n* Bedingung *f*
provocative [prə'vɒkətɪv] *adj* provozierend
provoke [prə'vəuk] *vt* provozieren; (*cause*)
hervorrufen
prowess ['prauɪs] *n* überragende(s) Können
nt
prowl [praul] *vi* herumstreichen; (*animal*)
schleichen ♦ *n*: **on the ~** umherstreifend;
~er *n* Herumtreiber(in) *m(f)*
proximity [prɒk'sɪmɪtɪ] *n* Nähe *f*
proxy ['prɒksɪ] *n* (Stell)vertreter *m*; (*authority,
document*) Vollmacht *f*; **by ~** durch einen
Stellvertreter
prudent ['pru:dnt] *adj* klug, umsichtig
prudish ['pru:dɪʃ] *adj* prüde
prune [pru:n] *n* Backpflaume *f* ♦ *vt*
ausputzen; (*fig*) zurechtstutzen
pry [praɪ] *vi*: **to ~ (into)** seine Nase stecken
(in +*acc*)
PS *n abbr* (= *postscript*) PS
pseudonym ['sju:dənɪm] *n* Pseudonym *nt*,
Deckname *m*
psychiatric [saɪkɪ'ætrɪk] *adj* psychiatrisch
psychiatrist [saɪ'kaɪətrɪst] *n* Psychiater *m*
psychic ['saɪkɪk] *adj* (*also*: **~al**) übersinnlich;
(*person*) paranormal begabt
psychoanalyse [saɪkəu'ænəlaɪz] (*US*
psychoanalyze) *vt* psychoanalytisch
behandeln; **psychoanalyst** [saɪkəu'ænəlɪst]
n Psychoanalytiker(in) *m(f)*
psychological [saɪkə'lɒdʒɪkl] *adj*
psychologisch; **psychologist** [saɪ'kɒlədʒɪst]
n Psychologe *m*, Psychologin *f*;
psychology [saɪ'kɒlədʒɪ] *n* Psychologie *f*
PTO *abbr* = **please turn over**
pub [pʌb] *n abbr* (= *public house*) Kneipe *f*

Pub

ⓘ **Pub** *ist ein Gasthaus mit einer Lizenz
zum Ausschank von alkoholischen
Getränken. Ein Pub besteht meist aus
verschiedenen gemütlichen (*lounge*, snug)
oder einfacheren Räumen (*public bar*), in
der oft auch Spiele wie Darts, Domino und
Poolbillard zur Verfügung stehen. In Pubs
werden vor allem mittags oft auch
Mahlzeiten angeboten. Pubs sind
normalerweise von 11 bis 23 Uhr geöffnet,
aber manchmal nachmittags geschlossen.*

---

pubic ['pju:bɪk] *adj* Scham-
public ['pʌblɪk] *adj* öffentlich ♦ *n* (*also*:
general ~) Öffentlichkeit *f*; **in ~** in der
Öffentlichkeit; **~ address system** *n*
Lautsprecheranlage *f*
publican ['pʌblɪkən] *n* Wirt *m*
publication [pʌblɪ'keɪʃən] *n*
Veröffentlichung *f*
public: ~ company *n* Aktiengesellschaft *f*;
~ convenience (*BRIT*) *n* öffentliche
Toiletten *pl*; **~ holiday** *n* gesetzliche(r)
Feiertag *m*; **~ house** (*BRIT*) *n* Lokal *nt*,
Kneipe *f*
publicity [pʌb'lɪsɪtɪ] *n* Publicity *f*, Werbung *f*
publicize ['pʌblɪsaɪz] *vt* bekannt machen;
(*advertise*) Publicity machen für
publicly ['pʌblɪklɪ] *adv* öffentlich
public: ~ opinion *n* öffentliche Meinung *f*;
~ relations *npl* Publicrelations *pl*, Public
Relations *pl*; **~ school** *n* (*BRIT*) Privatschule
f; (*US*) staatliche Schule *f*; **~-spirited** *adj*
mit Gemeinschaftssinn; **~ transport** *n*
öffentliche Verkehrsmittel *pl*
publish ['pʌblɪʃ] *vt* veröffentlichen; (*event*)
bekannt geben; **~er** *n* Verleger *m*; **~ing** *n*
(*business*) Verlagswesen *nt*
pub lunch *n* in Pubs servierter Imbiss
pucker ['pʌkə*] *vt* (*face*) verziehen; (*lips*)
kräuseln
pudding ['pudɪŋ] *n* (*BRIT*: *course*) Nachtisch
m; Pudding *m*; **black ~** ≃ Blutwurst *f*
puddle ['pʌdl] *n* Pfütze *f*
puff [pʌf] *n* (*of wind etc*) Stoß *m*; (*cosmetic*)

Puderquaste f ♦ vt blasen, pusten; (*pipe*)
paffen ♦ vi keuchen, schnaufen; (*smoke*)
paffen; **to ~ out smoke** Rauch ausstoßen;
~ pastry (US = **paste**) n Blätterteig m; **~y**
adj aufgedunsen

pull [pʊl] n Ruck m; (*influence*) Beziehung f
♦ vt ziehen; (*trigger*) abdrücken ♦ vi ziehen;
to ~ sb's leg jdn auf den Arm nehmen; **to
~ to pieces** in Stücke reißen; (*fig*)
verreißen; **to ~ one's punches** sich
zurückhalten; **to ~ one's weight** sich in die
Riemen legen; **to ~ o.s. together** sich
zusammenreißen; **~ apart** vt (*break*)
zerreißen; (*dismantle*) auseinander nehmen;
(*separate*) trennen; **~ down** vt (*house*)
abreißen; **~ in** vi hineinfahren; (*stop*)
anhalten; (*RAIL*) einfahren; **~ off** vt (*deal
etc*) abschließen; **~ out** vi (*car*)
herausfahren; (*fig: partner*) aussteigen ♦ vt
herausziehen; **~ over** vi (*AUT*) an die Seite
fahren; **~ through** vi durchkommen; **~
up** vi anhalten ♦ vt (*uproot*) herausreißen;
(*stop*) anhalten

pulley ['pʊlɪ] n Rolle f, Flaschenzug m
pullover ['pʊləʊvər] n Pullover m
pulp [pʌlp] n Brei m; (*of fruit*) Fruchtfleisch nt
pulpit ['pʊlpɪt] n Kanzel f
pulsate [pʌl'seɪt] vi pulsieren
pulse [pʌls] n Puls m; **~s** npl (*BOT*)
Hülsenfrüchte pl
pummel ['pʌml] vt mit den Fäusten
bearbeiten
pump [pʌmp] n Pumpe f; (*shoe*) leichter
(Tanz)schuh m ♦ vt pumpen; **~ up** vt (*tyre*)
aufpumpen
pumpkin ['pʌmpkɪn] n Kürbis m
pun [pʌn] n Wortspiel nt
punch [pʌntʃ] n (*tool*) Locher m; (*blow*)
(Faust)schlag m; (*drink*) Punsch m, Bowle f
♦ vt lochen; (*strike*) schlagen, boxen; **~ line**
n Pointe f; **~-up** (*BRIT: inf*) n Keilerei f
punctual ['pʌŋktjʊəl] adj pünktlich
punctuate ['pʌŋktjʊeɪt] vt mit Satzzeichen
versehen; (*fig*) unterbrechen; **punctuation**
[pʌŋktjʊ'eɪʃən] n Zeichensetzung f,
Interpunktion f
puncture ['pʌŋktʃər] n Loch nt; (*AUT*)

Reifenpanne f ♦ vt durchbohren
pundit ['pʌndɪt] n Gelehrte(r) m
pungent ['pʌndʒənt] adj scharf
punish ['pʌnɪʃ] vt bestrafen; (*in boxing etc*)
übel zurichten; **~ment** n Strafe f; (*action*)
Bestrafung f
punk [pʌŋk] n (*also:* **~ rocker**) Punker(in)
m(f); (*also:* **~ rock**) Punk m; (*US: inf:
hoodlum*) Ganove m
punt [pʌnt] n Stechkahn m
punter ['pʌntər] (*BRIT*) n (*better*) Wetter m
puny ['pjuːnɪ] adj kümmerlich
pup [pʌp] n = **puppy**
pupil ['pjuːpl] n Schüler(in) m(f); (*in eye*)
Pupille f
puppet ['pʌpɪt] n Puppe f; Marionette f
puppy ['pʌpɪ] n junge(r) Hund m
purchase ['pɜːtʃɪs] n Kauf m; (*grip*) Halt m
♦ vt kaufen, erwerben; **~r** n Käufer(in) m(f)
pure [pjʊər] adj (*also fig*) rein; **~ly** ['pjʊəlɪ]
adv rein
purgatory ['pɜːgətərɪ] n Fegefeuer nt
purge [pɜːdʒ] n (*also POL*) Säuberung f ♦ vt
reinigen; (*body*) entschlacken
purify ['pjʊərɪfaɪ] vt reinigen
purity ['pjʊərɪtɪ] n Reinheit f
purple ['pɜːpl] adj violett; (*face*) dunkelrot
purport [pɜː'pɔːt] vi vorgeben
purpose ['pɜːpəs] n Zweck m, Ziel nt; (*of
person*) Absicht f; **on ~** absichtlich; **~ful** adj
zielbewusst, entschlossen
purr [pɜːr] n Schnurren nt ♦ vi schnurren
purse [pɜːs] n Portemonnaie nt, Portmonee
nt, Geldbeutel m ♦ vt (*lips*)
zusammenpressen, schürzen
purser ['pɜːsər] n Zahlmeister m
pursue [pə'sjuː] vt verfolgen; (*study*)
nachgehen +dat; **~r** n Verfolger m; **pursuit**
[pə'sjuːt] n Verfolgung f; (*occupation*)
Beschäftigung f
pus [pʌs] n Eiter m
push [pʊʃ] n Stoß m, Schub m; (*MIL*) Vorstoß
m ♦ vt stoßen, schieben; (*button*) drücken;
(*idea*) durchsetzen ♦ vi stoßen, schieben; **~
aside** vt beiseite schieben; **~ off** (*inf*) vi
abschieben; **~ on** vi weitermachen; **~
through** vt durchdrücken; (*policy*)

durchsetzen; ~ **up** vt (*total*) erhöhen;
(*prices*) hoch treiben; **~chair** (*BRIT*) n
(Kinder)sportwagen m; **~er** n (*drug dealer*)
Pusher m; **~over** (*inf*) n Kinderspiel nt; **~-
up** (*US*) n (*press-up*) Liegestütz m; **~y** (*inf*)
adj aufdringlich

puss [pʊs] n Miece(katze) f; **~y(cat)** n
Miece(katze) f

put [pʊt] (*pt, pp* **put**) vt setzen, stellen, legen;
(*express*) ausdrücken, sagen; (*write*)
schreiben; ~ **about** vi (*turn back*) wenden
♦ vt (*spread*) verbreiten; ~ **across** vt
(*explain*) erklären; ~ **away** vt weglegen;
(*store*) beiseite legen; ~ **back** vt
zurückstellen or -legen; ~ **by** vt
zurücklegen, sparen; ~ **down** vt hinstellen
or -legen; (*rebellion*) niederschlagen;
(*animal*) einschläfern; (*in writing*)
niederschreiben; ~ **forward** vt (*idea*)
vorbringen; (*clock*) vorstellen; ~ **in** vt
(*application, complaint*) einreichen; ~ **off** vt
verschieben; (*discourage*): **to ~ sb off sth**
jdn von etw abbringen; ~ **on** vt (*clothes
etc*) anziehen; (*light etc*) anschalten,
anmachen; (*play etc*) aufführen; (*brake*)
anziehen; ~ **out** vt (*hand etc*)
(her)ausstrecken; (*news, rumour*) verbreiten;
(*light etc*) ausschalten, ausmachen; ~
through vt (*TEL: person*) verbinden; (: *call*)
durchstellen; ~ **up** vt (*tent*) aufstellen;
(*building*) errichten; (*price*) erhöhen; (*person*)
unterbringen; ~ **up with** vt fus sich
abfinden mit

putrid ['pjuːtrɪd] adj faul

putt [pʌt] vt (*golf*) putten ♦ n (*golf*) Putten nt;
~ing green n kleine(r) Golfplatz m nur
zum Putten

putty ['pʌtɪ] n Kitt m; (*fig*) Wachs nt

put-up ['pʊtʌp] adj: ~ **job** abgekartete(s)
Spiel nt

puzzle ['pʌzl] n Rätsel nt; (*toy*) Geduldspiel
nt ♦ vt verwirren ♦ vi sich den Kopf
zerbrechen; **~d** adj verdutzt, verblüfft;
puzzling adj rätselhaft, verwirrend

pyjamas [pə'dʒɑːməz] (*BRIT*) npl Schlafanzug
m, Pyjama m

pylon ['paɪlən] n Mast m

pyramid ['pɪrəmɪd] n Pyramide f

Q, q

quack [kwæk] n Quaken nt; (*doctor*)
Quacksalber m ♦ vi quaken

quad [kwɒd] n abbr = **quadrangle**;
quadruplet

quadrangle ['kwɒdræŋgl] n (*court*) Hof m;
(*MATH*) Viereck nt

quadruple [kwɔ'druːpl] adj ♦ vi sich
vervierfachen ♦ vt vervierfachen

quadruplets [kwɔ'druːplɪts] npl Vierlinge pl

quagmire ['kwægmaɪəʳ] n Morast m

quail [kweɪl] n (*bird*) Wachtel f ♦ vi (*vor
Angst*) zittern

quaint [kweɪnt] adj kurios; malerisch

quake [kweɪk] vi beben, zittern ♦ n abbr =
earthquake

qualification [kwɒlɪfɪ'keɪʃən] n Qualifikation
f; (*sth which limits*) Einschränkung f

qualified ['kwɒlɪfaɪd] adj (*competent*)
qualifiziert; (*limited*) bedingt

qualify ['kwɒlɪfaɪ] vt (*prepare*) befähigen;
(*limit*) einschränken ♦ vi sich qualifizieren;
to ~ as a doctor / lawyer sein
medizinisches/juristisches Staatsexamen
machen

quality ['kwɒlɪtɪ] n Qualität f; (*characteristic*)
Eigenschaft f

> [!NOTE]
> Quality press

ⓘ **Quality press** *bezeichnet die seriösen
Tages- und Wochenzeitungen, im
Gegensatz zu den Massenblättern. Diese
Zeitungen sind fast alle großformatig und
wenden sich an den anspruchsvolleren Leser,
der voll informiert sein möchte und bereit
ist, für die Zeitungslektüre viel Zeit
aufzuwenden. Siehe auch* tabloid press.

quality time n intensiv genutzte Zeit

qualm [kwɑːm] n Bedenken nt

quandary ['kwɒndrɪ] n: **to be in a ~** in
Verlegenheit sein

quantity ['kwɒntɪtɪ] n Menge f; ~ **surveyor**

n Baukostenkalkulator *m*

quarantine ['kwɔrntiːn] *n* Quarantäne *f*

quarrel ['kwɔrl] *n* Streit *m* ♦ *vi* sich streiten; **~some** *adj* streitsüchtig

quarry ['kwɔrɪ] *n* Steinbruch *m*; (*animal*) Wild *nt*; (*fig*) Opfer *nt*

quarter ['kwɔːtəʳ] *n* Viertel *nt*; (*of year*) Quartal *nt* ♦ *vt* (*divide*) vierteln; (*MIL*) einquartieren; **~s** *npl* (*esp MIL*) Quartier *nt*; **~ of an hour** Viertelstunde *f*; **~ final** *n* Viertelfinale *nt*; **~ly** *adj* vierteljährlich

quartet(te) [kwɔːˈtet] *n* Quartett *nt*

quartz [kwɔːts] *n* Quarz *m*

quash [kwɔʃ] *vt* (*verdict*) aufheben

quaver ['kweɪvəʳ] *vi* (*tremble*) zittern

quay [kiː] *n* Kai *m*

queasy ['kwiːzɪ] *adj* übel

queen [kwiːn] *n* Königin *f*; **~ mother** *n* Königinmutter *f*

queer [kwɪəʳ] *adj* seltsam ♦ *n* (*inf: homosexual*) Schwule(r) *m*

quell [kwel] *vt* unterdrücken

quench [kwentʃ] *vt* (*thirst*) löschen

querulous ['kweruləs] *adj* nörglerisch

query ['kwɪərɪ] *n* (*question*) (An)frage *f*; (*question mark*) Fragezeichen *nt* ♦ *vt* in Zweifel ziehen, infrage *or* in Frage stellen

quest [kwest] *n* Suche *f*

question ['kwestʃən] *n* Frage *f* ♦ *vt* (*ask*) (be)fragen; (*suspect*) verhören; (*doubt*) infrage *or* in Frage stellen, bezweifeln; **beyond ~** ohne Frage; **out of the ~** ausgeschlossen; **~able** *adj* zweifelhaft; **~ mark** *n* Fragezeichen *nt*

questionnaire [kwestʃəˈnɛəʳ] *n* Fragebogen *m*

queue [kjuː] *n* (*BRIT*) *n* Schlange *f* ♦ *vi* (*also: ~ up*) Schlange stehen

quibble ['kwɪbl] *vi* kleinlich sein

quick [kwɪk] *adj* schnell ♦ *n* (*of nail*) Nagelhaut *f*; **be ~!** mach schnell!; **cut to the ~** (*fig*) tief getroffen; **~en** *vt* (*hasten*) beschleunigen ♦ *vi* sich beschleunigen; **~ly** *adv* schnell; **~sand** *n* Treibsand *m*; **~-witted** *adj* schlagfertig

quid [kwɪd] (*BRIT: inf*) *n* Pfund *nt*

quiet ['kwaɪət] *adj* (*without noise*) leise;

(*peaceful, calm*) still, ruhig ♦ *n* Stille *f*, Ruhe *f* ♦ *vt*, *vi* (*US*) = **quieten; keep ~!** sei still!; **~en** *vi* (*also: ~en down*) ruhig werden ♦ *vt* beruhigen; **~ly** *adv* leise, ruhig; **~ness** *n* Ruhe *f*, Stille *f*

quilt [kwɪlt] *n* (*continental ~*) Steppdecke *f*

quin [kwɪn] *n abbr* = **quintuplet**

quintuplets [kwɪnˈtjuːplɪts] *npl* Fünflinge *pl*

quip [kwɪp] *n* witzige Bemerkung *f*

quirk [kwɜːk] *n* (*oddity*) Eigenart *f*

quit [kwɪt] (*pt, pp* **quit** *or* **quitted**) *vt* verlassen ♦ *vi* aufhören

quite [kwaɪt] *adv* (*completely*) ganz, völlig; (*fairly*) ziemlich; **~ a few of them** ziemlich viele von ihnen; **~ (so)!** richtig!

quits [kwɪts] *adj* quitt; **let's call it ~** lassen wirs gut sein

quiver ['kwɪvəʳ] *vi* zittern ♦ *n* (*for arrows*) Köcher *m*

quiz [kwɪz] *n* (*competition*) Quiz *nt* ♦ *vt* prüfen; **~zical** *adj* fragend

quota ['kwəʊtə] *n* Anteil *m*; (*COMM*) Quote *f*

quotation [kwəʊˈteɪʃən] *n* Zitat *nt*; (*price*) Kostenvoranschlag *m*; **~ marks** *npl* Anführungszeichen *pl*

quote [kwəʊt] *n* = **quotation** ♦ *vi* (*from book*) zitieren ♦ *vt* zitieren; (*price*) angeben

R, r

rabbi ['ræbaɪ] *n* Rabbiner *m*; (*title*) Rabbi *m*

rabbit ['ræbɪt] *n* Kaninchen *nt*; **~ hole** *n* Kaninchenbau *m*; **~ hutch** *n* Kaninchenstall *m*

rabble ['ræbl] *n* Pöbel *m*

rabies ['reɪbiːz] *n* Tollwut *f*

RAC (*BRIT*) *n abbr* = **Royal Automobile Club**

raccoon [rəˈkuːn] *n* Waschbär *m*

race [reɪs] *n* (*species*) Rasse *f*; (*competition*) Rennen *nt*; (*on foot*) Rennen *nt*, Wettlauf *m*; (*rush*) Hetze *f* ♦ *vt* um die Wette laufen mit; (*horses*) laufen lassen ♦ *vi* (*run*) rennen; (*in contest*) am Rennen teilnehmen; **~ car** (*US*) *n* = **racing car; ~ car driver** (*US*) *n* = **racing driver; ~course** *n* (*for horses*) Rennbahn *f*; **~horse** *n* Rennpferd *nt*; **~r** *n*

(*person*) Rennfahrer(in) *m(f)*; (*car*)
Rennwagen *m*; **~track** *n* (*for cars etc*)
Rennstrecke *f*

racial ['reɪʃl] *adj* Rassen-

racing ['reɪsɪŋ] *n* Rennen *nt*; **~ car** (*BRIT*) *n*
Rennwagen *m*; **~ driver** (*BRIT*) *n*
Rennfahrer *m*

racism ['reɪsɪzəm] *n* Rassismus *m*; **racist**
['reɪsɪst] *n* Rassist *m* ♦ *adj* rassistisch

rack [ræk] *n* Ständer *m*, Gestell *nt* ♦ *vt*
plagen; **to go to ~ and ruin** verfallen; **to ~
one's brains** sich *dat* den Kopf zerbrechen

racket ['rækɪt] *n* (*din*) Krach *m*; (*scheme*)
(Schwindel)geschäft *nt*; (*TENNIS*)
(Tennis)schläger *m*

racquet ['rækɪt] *n* (Tennis)schläger *m*

racy ['reɪsɪ] *adj* gewagt; (*style*) spritzig

radar ['reɪdɑː] *n* Radar *nt or m*

radial ['reɪdɪəl] *adj* (*also: US:* **~-ply**) radial

radiant ['reɪdɪənt] *adj* strahlend; (*giving out
rays*) Strahlungs-

radiate ['reɪdɪeɪt] *vi* ausstrahlen; (*roads, lines*)
strahlenförmig wegführen ♦ *vt* ausstrahlen;
radiation [reɪdɪ'eɪʃən] *n* (Aus)strahlung *f*

radiator ['reɪdɪeɪtə'] *n* (*for heating*)
Heizkörper *m*; (*AUT*) Kühler *m*

radical ['rædɪkl] *adj* radikal

radii ['reɪdɪaɪ] *npl of* **radius**

radio ['reɪdɪəu] *n* Rundfunk *m*, Radio *nt*; (*set*)
Radio *nt*, Radioapparat *m*; **on the ~** im
Radio; **~active** ['reɪdɪəu'æktɪv] *adj*
radioaktiv; **~ cassette** *n* Radiorekorder *m*;
~-controlled *adj* ferngesteuert; **~logy**
[reɪdɪ'ɔlədʒɪ] *n* Strahlenkunde *f*; **~ station** *n*
Rundfunkstation *f*; **~therapy**
['reɪdɪəu'θerəpɪ] *n* Röntgentherapie *f*

radish ['rædɪʃ] *n* (*big*) Rettich *m*; (*small*)
Radieschen *nt*

radius ['reɪdɪəs] *n* (*pl* **radii**) *n* Radius *m*; (*area*)
Umkreis *m*

RAF *n abbr* = **Royal Air Force**

raffle ['ræfl] *n* Verlosung *f*, Tombola *f* ♦ *vt*
verlosen

raft [rɑːft] *n* Floß *nt*

rafter ['rɑːftə'] *n* Dachsparren *m*

rag [ræg] *n* (*cloth*) Lumpen *m*, Lappen *m*;
(*inf: newspaper*) Käseblatt *nt*; (*UNIV: for*

charity) studentische Sammelaktion *f* ♦ *vt*
(*BRIT*) auf den Arm nehmen; **~s** *npl* (*cloth*)
Lumpen *pl*; **~ doll** *n* Flickenpuppe *f*

rage [reɪdʒ] *n* Wut *f*; (*fashion*) große Mode *f*
♦ *vi* wüten, toben

ragged ['rægɪd] *adj* (*edge*) gezackt; (*clothes*)
zerlumpt

raid [reɪd] *n* Überfall *m*; (*MIL*) Angriff *m*; (*by
police*) Razzia *f* ♦ *vt* überfallen

rail [reɪl] *n* (*also* RAIL) Schiene *f*; (*on stair*)
Geländer *nt*; (*of ship*) Reling *f*; **~s** *npl* (*RAIL*)
Geleise *pl*; **by ~** per Bahn; **~ing(s)** *n(pl)*
Geländer *nt*; **~road** (*US*) *n* Eisenbahn *f*;
~way (*BRIT*) *n* Eisenbahn *f*; **~way line**
(*BRIT*) *n* (Eisen)bahnlinie *f*; (*track*) Gleis *nt*;
~wayman (*irreg; BRIT*) *n* Eisenbahner *m*;
~way station (*BRIT*) *n* Bahnhof *m*

rain [reɪn] *n* Regen *m* ♦ *vt, vi* regnen; **in the
~** im Regen; **it's ~ing** es regnet; **~bow** *n*
Regenbogen *m*; **~coat** *n* Regenmantel *m*;
~drop *n* Regentropfen *m*; **~fall** *n*
Niederschlag *m*; **~forest** *n* Regenwald *m*;
~y *adj* (*region, season*) Regen-; (*day*)
regnerisch, verregnet

raise [reɪz] *n* (*esp US: increase*)
(Gehalts)erhöhung *f* ♦ *vt* (*lift*) (hoch)heben;
(*increase*) erhöhen; (*question*) aufwerfen;
(*doubts*) äußern; (*funds*) beschaffen; (*family*)
großziehen; (*livestock*) züchten; **to ~ one's
voice** die Stimme erheben

raisin ['reɪzn] *n* Rosine *f*

rake [reɪk] *n* Rechen *m*, Harke *f*; (*person*)
Wüstling *m* ♦ *vt* rechen, harken; (*search*)
(durch)suchen

rally ['rælɪ] *n* (*POL etc*) Kundgebung *f*; (*AUT*)
Rallye *f* ♦ *vt* (*MIL*) sammeln ♦ *vi* Kräfte
sammeln; **~ round** *vt fus* (sich) scharen
um; (*help*) zu Hilfe kommen +*dat* ♦ *vi* zu
Hilfe kommen

RAM [ræm] *n abbr* (= *random access memory*)
RAM *m*

ram [ræm] *n* Widder *m* ♦ *vt* (*hit*) rammen;
(*stuff*) (hinein)stopfen

ramble ['ræmbl] *n* Wanderung *f* ♦ *vi* (*talk*)
schwafeln; **~r** *n* Wanderer *m*; **rambling** *adj*
(*speech*) weitschweifig; (*town*) ausgedehnt

ramp [ræmp] *n* Rampe *f*; **on/off ~** (*US: AUT*)

Ein-/Ausfahrt f

rampage [ræm'peɪdʒ] n: **to be on the ~** randalieren ♦ vi randalieren

rampant ['ræmpənt] adj wild wuchernd

rampart ['ræmpɑːt] n (Schutz)wall m

ram raid n Raubüberfall, bei dem eine Geschäftsfront mit einem Fahrzeug gerammt wird

ramshackle ['ræmʃækl] adj baufällig

ran [ræn] pt of **run**

ranch [rɑːntʃ] n Ranch f

rancid ['rænsɪd] adj ranzig

rancour ['ræŋkər] (US **rancor**) n Verbitterung f, Groll m

random ['rændəm] adj ziellos, wahllos ♦ n: **at ~** aufs Geratewohl; **~ access** n (COMPUT) wahlfreie(r) Zugriff m

randy ['rændɪ] (BRIT: inf) adj geil, scharf

rang [ræŋ] pt of **ring**

range [reɪndʒ] n Reihe f; (of mountains) Kette f; (COMM) Sortiment nt; (reach) (Reich)weite f; (of gun) Schussweite f; (for shooting practice) Schießplatz m; (stove) (großer) Herd m ♦ vt (set in row) anordnen, aufstellen; (roam) durchstreifen ♦ vi: **to ~ over** (wander) umherstreifen in +dat; (extend) sich erstrecken auf +acc; **a ~ of** (selection) eine (große) Auswahl an +dat; **prices ranging from £5 to £10** Preise, die sich zwischen £5 und £10 bewegen; **~r** ['reɪndʒər] n Förster m

rank [ræŋk] n (row) Reihe f; (BRIT: also: **taxi ~**) (Taxi)stand m; (MIL) Rang m; (social position) Stand m ♦ vi (have ~): **to ~ among** gehören zu ♦ adj (strong-smelling) stinkend; (extreme) kraß; **the ~ and file** (fig) die breite Masse

rankle ['ræŋkl] vi nagen

ransack ['rænsæk] vt (plunder) plündern; (search) durchwühlen

ransom ['rænsəm] n Lösegeld nt; **to hold sb to ~** jdn gegen Lösegeld festhalten

rant [rænt] vi hochtrabend reden

rap [ræp] n Schlag m; (music) Rap m ♦ vt klopfen

~ape [reɪp] n Vergewaltigung f; (BOT) Raps m ♦ vt vergewaltigen; **~(seed) oil** n Rapsöl nt

rapid ['ræpɪd] adj rasch, schnell; **~ity** [rə'pɪdɪtɪ] n Schnelligkeit f; **~s** npl Stromschnellen pl

rapist ['reɪpɪst] n Vergewaltiger m

rapport [ræ'pɔːr] n gute(s) Verhältnis nt

rapture ['ræptʃər] n Entzücken nt; **rapturous** ['ræptʃərəs] adj (applause) stürmisch; (expression) verzückt

rare [reər] adj selten, rar; (underdone) nicht durchgebraten; **~ly** ['reəlɪ] adv selten

raring ['reərɪŋ] adj: **to be ~ to go** (inf) es kaum erwarten können, bis es losgeht

rarity ['reərɪtɪ] n Seltenheit f

rascal ['rɑːskl] n Schuft m

rash [ræʃ] adj übereilt; (reckless) unbesonnen ♦ n (Haut)ausschlag m

rasher ['ræʃər] n Speckscheibe f

raspberry ['rɑːzbərɪ] n Himbeere f

rasping ['rɑːspɪŋ] adj (noise) kratzend; (voice) krächzend

rat [ræt] n (animal) Ratte f; (person) Halunke m

rate [reɪt] n (proportion) Rate f; (price) Tarif m; (speed) Tempo nt ♦ vt (ein)schätzen; **~s** npl (BRIT: tax) Grundsteuer f; **to ~ as** für etw halten; **~able value** (BRIT) n Einheitswert m (als Bemessungsgrundlage); **~payer** (BRIT) n Steuerzahler(in) m(f)

rather ['rɑːðər] adv (in preference) lieber, eher; (to some extent) ziemlich; **I would or I'd ~ go** ich würde lieber gehen; **it's ~ expensive** (quite) es ist ziemlich teuer; (too) es ist etwas zu teuer; **there's ~ a lot** es ist ziemlich viel

ratify ['rætɪfaɪ] vt (POL) ratifizieren

rating ['reɪtɪŋ] n Klasse f

ratio ['reɪʃɪəu] n Verhältnis nt; **in the ~ of 100 to 1** im Verhältnis 100 zu 1

ration ['ræʃən] n (usu pl) Ration f ♦ vt rationieren

rational ['ræʃənl] adj rational

rationale [ræʃə'nɑːl] n Grundprinzip nt

rationalize ['ræʃnəlaɪz] vt rationalisieren

rat race n Konkurrenzkampf m

rattle ['rætl] n (sound) Rasseln nt; (toy) Rassel f ♦ vi ratteln, klappern ♦ vt rasseln mit; **~snake** n Klapperschlange f

raucous ['rɔːkəs] *adj* heiser, rau

rave [reɪv] *vi* (*talk wildly*) fantasieren; (*rage*) toben ♦ *n* (BRIT: *inf: party*) Rave *m*, Fete *f*

raven ['reɪvən] *n* Rabe *m*

ravenous ['rævənəs] *adj* heißhungrig

ravine [rə'viːn] *n* Schlucht *f*

raving ['reɪvɪŋ] *adj*: ~ **lunatic** völlig Wahnsinnige(r) *mf*

ravishing ['rævɪʃɪŋ] *adj* atemberaubend

raw [rɔː] *adj* roh; (*tender*) wund (gerieben); (*inexperienced*) unerfahren; **to get a ~ deal** (*inf*) schlecht wegkommen; ~ **material** *n* Rohmaterial *nt*

ray [reɪ] *n* (*of light*) Strahl *m*; ~ **of hope** Hoffnungsschimmer *m*

raze [reɪz] *vt* (*also*: ~ **to the ground**) dem Erdboden gleichmachen

razor ['reɪzə'] *n* Rasierapparat *m*; ~ **blade** *n* Rasierklinge *f*

Rd *abbr* = **road**

RE (BRIT: SCH) *abbr* (= *religious education*) Religionsunterricht *m*

re [riː] *prep* (COMM) betreffs +*gen*

reach [riːtʃ] *n* Reichweite *f*; (*of river*) Strecke *f* ♦ *vt* (*arrive at*) erreichen; (*give*) reichen ♦ *vi* (*stretch*) sich erstrecken; **within ~** (*shops etc*) in erreichbarer Weite *or* Entfernung; **out of ~** außer Reichweite; **to ~ for** (*try to get*) langen nach; ~ **out** *vi* die Hand ausstrecken; **to ~ out for sth** nach etw greifen

react [riː'ækt] *vi* reagieren; ~**ion** [riː'ækʃən] *n* Reaktion *f*; ~**or** [riː'æktə'] *n* Reaktor *m*

read¹ [red] *pt, pp of* **read²**

read² [riːd] (*pt, pp* **read**) *vt, vi* lesen; (*aloud*) vorlesen; ~ **out** *vt* vorlesen; ~**able** *adj* leserlich; (*worth ~ing*) lesenswert; ~**er** *n* (*person*) Leser(in) *m(f)*; ~**ership** *n* Leserschaft *f*

readily ['redɪlɪ] *adv* (*willingly*) bereitwillig; (*easily*) prompt

readiness ['redɪnɪs] *n* (*willingness*) Bereitwilligkeit *f*; (*being ready*) Bereitschaft *f*; **in ~** (*prepared*) bereit

reading ['riːdɪŋ] *n* Lesen *nt*

readjust [riːə'dʒʌst] *vt* neu einstellen ♦ *vi* (*person*): **to ~ to** sich wieder anpassen an

+*acc*

ready ['redɪ] *adj* (*prepared, willing*) bereit ♦ *adv*: ~-**cooked** vorgekocht ♦ *n*: **at the ~** bereit; ~-**made** *adj* gebrauchsfertig, Fertig-; (*clothes*) Konfektions-; ~ **money** *n* Bargeld *nt*; ~ **reckoner** *n* Rechentabelle *f*; ~-**to-wear** *adj* Konfektions-

real [rɪəl] *adj* wirklich; (*actual*) eigentlich; (*not fake*) echt; **in ~ terms** effektiv; ~ **estate** *n* Grundbesitz *m*; ~**istic** [rɪə'lɪstɪk] *adj* realistisch

reality [riː'ælɪtɪ] *n* Wirklichkeit *f*, Realität *f*; **in ~** in Wirklichkeit

realization [rɪəlaɪ'zeɪʃən] *n* (*understanding*) Erkenntnis *f*; (*fulfilment*) Verwirklichung *f*

realize ['rɪəlaɪz] *vt* (*understand*) begreifen; (*make real*) verwirklichen; **I didn't ~ ...** ich wusste nicht, ...

really ['rɪəlɪ] *adv* wirklich; ~? (*indicating interest*) tatsächlich?; (*expressing surprise*) wirklich?

realm [relm] *n* Reich *nt*

realtor ['rɪəltɔː'] (US) *n* Grundstücks-makler(in) *m(f)*

reap [riːp] *vt* ernten

reappear [riːə'pɪə'] *vi* wieder erscheinen

rear [rɪə'] *adj* hintere(r, s), Rück- ♦ *n* Rückseite *f*; (*last part*) Schluss *m* ♦ *vt* (*bring up*) aufziehen ♦ *vi* (*horse*) sich aufbäumen; ~**guard** *n* Nachhut *f*

rearmament [riː'ɑːməmənt] *n* Wiederaufrüstung *f*

rearrange [riːə'reɪndʒ] *vt* umordnen

rear-view mirror ['rɪəvjuː-] *n* Rückspiegel *m*

reason ['riːzn] *n* (*cause*) Grund *m*; (*ability to think*) Verstand *m*; (*sensible thoughts*) Vernunft *f* ♦ *vi* (*think*) denken; (*use arguments*) argumentieren; **it stands to ~ that** es ist logisch, dass; **to ~ with sb** mit jdm diskutieren; ~**able** *adj* vernünftig; ~**ably** *adv* vernünftig; (*fairly*) ziemlich; ~**ed** *adj* (*argument*) durchdacht; ~**ing** *n* Urteilen *nt*; (*argumentation*) Beweisführung *f*

reassurance [riːə'ʃuərəns] *n* Beruhigung *f*; (*confirmation*) Bestätigung *f*; **reassure** [riːə'ʃuə'] *vt* beruhigen; **to reassure sb of**

sth jdm etw versichern

rebate ['ri:beɪt] n Rückzahlung f

rebel [n 'rebl, vb rɪ'bel] n Rebell m ♦ vi rebellieren; **~lion** [rɪ'beljən] n Rebellion f, Aufstand m; **~lious** [rɪ'beljəs] adj rebellisch

rebirth [ri:'bə:θ] n Wiedergeburt f

rebound [vb rɪ'baʊnd, n 'ri:baʊnd] vi zurückprallen ♦ n Rückprall m

rebuff [rɪ'bʌf] n Abfuhr f ♦ vt abblitzen lassen

rebuild [ri:'bɪld] (irreg) vt wieder aufbauen; (fig) wieder herstellen

rebuke [rɪ'bju:k] n Tadel m ♦ vt tadeln, rügen

rebut [rɪ'bʌt] vt widerlegen

recall [vb rɪ'kɔ:l, n 'ri:kɔl] vt (call back) zurückrufen; (remember) sich erinnern an +acc ♦ n Rückruf m

recap ['ri:kæp] vt, vi wiederholen

rec'd abbr (= received) Eing.

recede [rɪ'si:d] vi zurückweichen; **receding** adj: **receding hairline** Stirnglatze f

receipt [rɪ'si:t] n (document) Quittung f; (receiving) Empfang m; **~s** npl (ECON) Einnahmen pl

receive [rɪ'si:v] vt erhalten; (visitors etc) empfangen; **~r** n (TEL) Hörer m

recent ['ri:snt] adj vor kurzem (geschehen), neuerlich; (modern) neu; **~ly** adv kürzlich, neulich

receptacle [rɪ'septɪkl] n Behälter m

reception [rɪ'sepʃən] n Empfang m; **~ desk** n Empfang m; (in hotel) Rezeption f; **~ist** n (in hotel) Empfangschef m, Empfangsdame f; (MED) Sprechstundenhilfe f

receptive [rɪ'septɪv] adj aufnahmebereit

recess [rɪ'ses] n (break) Ferien pl; (hollow) Nische f

recession [rɪ'seʃən] n Rezession f

recharge [ri:'tʃɑ:dʒ] vt (battery) aufladen

recipe ['resɪpɪ] n Rezept nt

recipient [rɪ'sɪpɪənt] n Empfänger m

reciprocal [rɪ'sɪprəkl] adj gegenseitig; (mutual) wechselseitig

recital [rɪ'saɪtl] n Vortrag m

recite [rɪ'saɪt] vt vortragen, aufsagen

reckless ['rekləs] adj leichtsinnig; (driving)

fahrlässig

reckon ['rekən] vt (count) rechnen, berechnen, errechnen; (estimate) schätzen; (think): **I ~ that ...** ich nehme an, dass ...; **~ on** vt fus rechnen mit; **~ing** n (calculation) Rechnen nt

reclaim [rɪ'kleɪm] vt (expenses) zurückverlangen; (land): **to ~ (from sth)** (etw dat) gewinnen; **reclamation** [reklə'meɪʃən] n (of land) Gewinnung f

recline [rɪ'klaɪn] vi sich zurücklehnen; **reclining** adj Liege-

recluse [rɪ'klu:s] n Einsiedler m

recognition [rekəg'nɪʃən] n (recognizing) Erkennen nt; (acknowledgement) Anerkennung f; **transformed beyond ~** völlig verändert

recognizable ['rekəgnaɪzəbl] adj erkennbar

recognize ['rekəgnaɪz] vt erkennen; (POL, approve) anerkennen; **to ~ as** anerkennen als; **to ~ by** erkennen an +dat

recoil [rɪ'kɔɪl] vi (in horror) zurückschrecken; (rebound) zurückprallen; (person): **to ~ from doing sth** davor zurückschrecken, etw zu tun

recollect [rekə'lekt] vt sich erinnern an +acc; **~ion** [rekə'lekʃən] n Erinnerung f

recommend [rekə'mend] vt empfehlen; **~ation** [rekəmen'deɪʃən] n Empfehlung f

recompense ['rekəmpens] n (compensation) Entschädigung f; (reward) Belohnung f ♦ vt entschädigen; belohnen

reconcile ['rekənsaɪl] vt (facts) vereinbaren; (people) versöhnen; **to ~ o.s. to sth** sich mit etw abfinden; **reconciliation** [rekənsɪlɪ'eɪʃən] n Versöhnung f

recondition [ri:kən'dɪʃən] vt (machine) generalüberholen

reconnoitre [rekə'nɔɪtə*] (US **reconnoiter**) vt erkunden ♦ vi aufklären

reconsider [ri:kən'sɪdə*] vt von neuem erwägen, noch einmal überdenken ♦ vi es noch einmal überdenken

reconstruct [ri:kən'strʌkt] vt wieder aufbauen; (crime) rekonstruieren

record [n 'rekɔ:d, vb rɪ'kɔ:d] n Aufzeichnung f; (MUS) Schallplatte f; (best performance)

Rekord *m* ♦ *vt* aufzeichnen; *(music etc)* aufnehmen; **off the ~** vertraulich, im Vertrauen; **in ~ time** in Rekordzeit; **~ card** *n (in file)* Karteikarte *f*; **~ed delivery** *(BRIT)* *n (POST)* Einschreiben *nt*; **~er** *n (TECH)* Registriergerät *nt*; *(MUS)* Blockflöte *f*; **~ holder** *n (SPORT)* Rekordinhaber *m*; **~ing** *n (MUS)* Aufnahme *f*; **~ player** *n* Plattenspieler *m*

recount [rɪˈkaunt] *vt (tell)* berichten

re-count [ˈriːkaunt] *n* Nachzählung *f*

recoup [rɪˈkuːp] *vt*: **to ~ one's losses** seinen Verlust wieder gutmachen

recourse [rɪˈkɔːs] *n*: **to have ~ to** Zuflucht nehmen zu *or* bei

recover [rɪˈkʌvəʳ] *vt (get back)* zurückerhalten ♦ *vi* sich erholen

re-cover [rɪˈkʌvəʳ] *vt (quilt etc)* neu überziehen

recovery [rɪˈkʌvərɪ] *n* Wiedererlangung *f*; *(of health)* Erholung *f*

recreate [riːkrɪˈeɪt] *vt* wieder herstellen

recreation [rekrɪˈeɪʃən] *n* Erholung *f*; **~al** *adj* Erholungs-; **~al drug** *n* Freizeitdroge *f*

recrimination [rɪkrɪmɪˈneɪʃən] *n* Gegenbeschuldigung *f*

recruit [rɪˈkruːt] *n* Rekrut *m* ♦ *vt* rekrutieren; **~ment** *n* Rekrutierung *f*

rectangle [ˈrektæŋgl] *n* Rechteck *nt*; **rectangular** [rekˈtæŋgjuləʳ] *adj* rechteckig, rechtwinklig

rectify [ˈrektɪfaɪ] *vt* berichtigen

rector [ˈrektəʳ] *n (REL)* Pfarrer *m*; *(SCH)* Direktor(in) *m(f)*; **~y** [ˈrektərɪ] *n* Pfarrhaus *nt*

recuperate [rɪˈkjuːpəreɪt] *vi* sich erholen

recur [rɪˈkɜːʳ] *vi* sich wiederholen; **~rence** *n* Wiederholung *f*; **~rent** *adj* wiederkehrend

recycle [riːˈsaɪkl] *vt* wieder verwerten, wieder aufbereiten; **recycling** *n* Recycling *nt*

red [red] *n* Rot *nt*; *(POL)* Rote(r) *m* ♦ *adj* rot; **in the ~** in den roten Zahlen; **~ carpet treatment** *n* Sonderbehandlung *f*, große(r) Bahnhof *m*; **R~ Cross** *n* Rote(s) Kreuz *nt*; **~currant** *n* rote Johannisbeere *f*; **~den** *vi* sich röten; *(blush)* erröten ♦ *vt* röten; **~dish** *adj* rötlich

redecorate [riːˈdekəreɪt] *vt* neu tapezieren, neu streichen

redeem [rɪˈdiːm] *vt (COMM)* einlösen; *(save)* retten; **~ing** *adj*: **~ing feature** versöhnende(s) Moment *nt*

redeploy [riːdɪˈplɔɪ] *vt (resources)* umverteilen

red: **~-haired** [redˈhɛəd] *adj* rothaarig; **~-handed** [redˈhændɪd] *adv*: **to be caught ~-handed** auf frischer Tat ertappt werden; **~head** [ˈredhed] *n* Rothaarige(r) *mf*; **~herring** *n* Ablenkungsmanöver *nt*; **~-hot** [redˈhɔt] *adj* rot glühend

redirect [riːdaɪˈrekt] *vt* umleiten

red light *n*: **to go through a ~** *(AUT)* bei Rot über die Ampel fahren; **red-light district** *n* Strichviertel *nt*

redo [riːˈduː] *(irreg: like* **do**) *vt* nochmals machen

redolent [ˈredələnt] *adj*: **~ of** *(fig)* erinnernd an +*acc*

redouble [riːˈdʌbl] *vt*: **to ~ one's efforts** seine Anstrengungen verdoppeln

redress [rɪˈdres] *vt* wieder gutmachen

red: **R~ Sea** *n*: **the R~ Sea** das Rote Meer; **~skin** [ˈredskɪn] *n* Rothaut *f*; **~ tape** *n* Bürokratismus *m*

reduce [rɪˈdjuːs] *vt (speed, temperature)* vermindern; *(photo)* verkleinern; **"~ speed now"** *(AUT)* ≃ **"langsam"**; **to ~ the price (to)** den Preis herabsetzen (auf +*acc*); **at a ~d price** zum ermäßigten Preis

reduction [rɪˈdʌkʃən] *n* Verminderung *f*; Verkleinerung *f*; Herabsetzung *f*; *(amount of money)* Nachlass *m*

redundancy [rɪˈdʌndənsɪ] *n* Überflüssigkeit *f*; *(of workers)* Entlassung *f*

redundant [rɪˈdʌndnt] *adj* überflüssig; *(workers)* ohne Arbeitsplatz; **to be made ~** arbeitslos werden

reed [riːd] *n* Schilf *nt*; *(MUS)* Rohrblatt *nt*

reef [riːf] *n* Riff *nt*

reek [riːk] *vi*: **to ~ (of)** stinken (nach)

reel [riːl] *n* Spule *f*, Rolle *f* ♦ *vt (also:* **~ in)** wickeln, spulen ♦ *vi (stagger)* taumeln

ref [ref] *(inf)* *n abbr* (= *referee*) Schiri *m*

refectory [rɪˈfektərɪ] *n (UNIV)* Mensa *f*; *(SCH)*

Speisesaal m; (ECCL) Refektorium nt

refer [rɪ'fɜːʳ] vt: **to ~ sb to sb/sth** jdn an jdn/etw verweisen ♦ vi: **to ~ to** (to book) nachschlagen in +dat; (mention) sich beziehen auf +acc

referee [refə'riː] n Schiedsrichter m; (BRIT: for job) Referenz f ♦ vt schiedsrichtern

reference ['refrəns] n (for job) Referenz f; (in book) Verweis m; (number, code) Aktenzeichen nt; (allusion): ~ **(to)** Anspielung (auf +acc); **with ~ to** in Bezug auf +acc; ~ **book** n Nachschlagewerk nt; ~ **number** n Aktenzeichen nt

referenda [refə'rendə] npl of **referendum**

referendum [refə'rendəm] (pl **-da**) n Volksabstimmung f

refill [vb riː'fɪl, n 'riːfɪl] vt nachfüllen ♦ n (for pen) Ersatzmine f

refine [rɪ'faɪn] vt (purify) raffinieren; ~**d** adj kultiviert; ~**ment** n Kultiviertheit f; ~**ry** n Raffinerie f

reflect [rɪ'flekt] vt (light) reflektieren; (fig) (wider)spiegeln ♦ vi (meditate): **to ~ (on)** nachdenken (über +acc); **it ~s badly/well on him** das stellt ihn in ein schlechtes/ gutes Licht; ~**ion** [rɪ'flekʃən] n Reflexion f; (image) Spiegelbild nt; (thought) Überlegung f; **on ~ion** wenn man sich dat das recht überlegt

reflex ['riːfleks] adj Reflex- ♦ n Reflex m; ~**ive** [rɪ'fleksɪv] adj reflexiv

reform [rɪ'fɔːm] n Reform f ♦ vt (person) bessern; ~**atory** (US) n Besserungsanstalt f

refrain [rɪ'freɪn] vi: **to ~ from** unterlassen ♦ n Refrain m

refresh [rɪ'freʃ] vt erfrischen; ~**er course** (BRIT) n Wiederholungskurs m; ~**ing** adj erfrischend; ~**ments** npl Erfrischungen pl

refrigeration [rɪfrɪdʒə'reɪʃən] n Kühlung f

refrigerator [rɪ'frɪdʒəreɪtəʳ] n Kühlschrank m

refuel [riː'fjuːl] vt, vi auftanken

refuge ['refjuːdʒ] n Zuflucht f; **to take ~ in** sich flüchten in +acc; ~**e** [refjuˈdʒiː] n Flüchtling m

refund [n 'riːfʌnd, vb rɪ'fʌnd] n Rückvergütung f ♦ vt zurückerstatten

refurbish [riː'fɜːbɪʃ] vt aufpolieren

refusal [rɪ'fjuːzəl] n (Ver)weigerung f; **first ~** Vorkaufsrecht nt

refuse¹ [rɪ'fjuːz] vt abschlagen ♦ vi sich weigern

refuse² ['refjuːs] n Abfall m, Müll m; ~ **collection** n Müllabfuhr f

refute [rɪ'fjuːt] vt widerlegen

regain [rɪ'geɪn] vt wiedergewinnen; (consciousness) wiedererlangen

regal ['riːgl] adj königlich

regalia [rɪ'geɪlɪə] npl Insignien pl

regard [rɪ'gɑːd] n Achtung f ♦ vt ansehen; **to send one's ~s to sb** jdn grüßen lassen; **"with kindest ~s"** „mit freundlichen Grüßen"; ~**ing** or **as ~s** or **with ~ to** bezüglich +gen, in Bezug auf +acc; ~**less** adj: ~**less of** ohne Rücksicht auf +acc ♦ adv trotzdem

regenerate [rɪ'dʒenəreɪt] vt erneuern

régime [reɪ'ʒiːm] n Regime nt

regiment [n 'redʒɪmənt, vb 'redʒɪment] n Regiment nt ♦ vt (fig) reglementieren; ~**al** [redʒɪ'mentl] adj Regiments-

region ['riːdʒən] n Region f; **in the ~ of** (fig) so um; ~**al** adj örtlich, regional

register ['redʒɪstəʳ] n Register nt ♦ vt (list) registrieren; (emotion) zeigen; (write down) eintragen ♦ vi (at hotel) sich eintragen; (with police) sich melden; (make impression) wirken, ankommen; ~**ed** (BRIT) adj (letter) Einschreibe-, eingeschrieben; ~**ed trademark** n eingetragene(s) Warenzeichen nt

registrar ['redʒɪstrɑːʳ] n Standesbeamte(r) m

registration [redʒɪs'treɪʃən] n (act) Registrierung f; (AUT: also: ~ **number**) polizeiliche(s) Kennzeichen nt

registry ['redʒɪstrɪ] n Sekretariat nt; ~ **office** (BRIT) n Standesamt nt; **to get married in a ~ office** standesamtlich heiraten

regret [rɪ'gret] n Bedauern nt ♦ vt bedauern; ~**fully** adv mit Bedauern, ungern; ~**table** adj bedauerlich

regroup [riː'gruːp] vt umgruppieren ♦ vi sich umgruppieren

regular ['regjuləʳ] adj regelmäßig; (usual) üblich; (inf) regelrecht ♦ n (client etc)

Stammkunde *m*; **~ity** [regju'lærɪtɪ] *n*
Regelmäßigkeit *f*; **~ly** *adv* regelmäßig
regulate ['regjuleɪt] *vt* regeln, regulieren;
regulation [regju'leɪʃən] *n* (*rule*) Vorschrift *f*;
(*control*) Regulierung *f*
rehabilitation ['riːəbɪlɪ'teɪʃən] *n* (*of criminal*)
Resozialisierung *f*
rehearsal [rɪ'hɜːsəl] *n* Probe *f*
rehearse [rɪ'hɜːs] *vt* proben
reign [reɪn] *n* Herrschaft *f* ♦ *vi* herrschen
reimburse [riːɪm'bɜːs] *vt*: **to ~ sb for sth**
jdn für etw entschädigen, jdm etw
zurückzahlen
rein [reɪn] *n* Zügel *m*
reincarnation [riːɪnkɑː'neɪʃən] *n*
Wiedergeburt *f*
reindeer ['reɪndɪə*] *n* Ren *nt*
reinforce [riːɪn'fɔːs] *vt* verstärken; **~d
concrete** *n* Stahlbeton *m*; **~ment** *n*
Verstärkung *f*; **~ments** *npl* (*MIL*)
Verstärkungstruppen *pl*
reinstate [riːɪn'steɪt] *vt* wieder einsetzen
reissue [riː'ɪʃjuː] *vt* neu herausgeben
reiterate [riː'ɪtəreɪt] *vt* wiederholen
reject [*n* 'riːdʒekt, *vb* rɪ'dʒekt] *n* (*COMM*)
Ausschuss(artikel) *m* ♦ *vt* ablehnen; **~ion**
[rɪ'dʒekʃən] *n* Zurückweisung *f*
rejoice [rɪ'dʒɔɪs] *vi*: **to ~ at** *or* **over** sich
freuen über +*acc*
rejuvenate [rɪ'dʒuːvəneɪt] *vt* verjüngen
rekindle [riː'kɪndl] *vt* wieder anfachen
relapse [rɪ'læps] *n* Rückfall *m*
relate [rɪ'leɪt] *vt* (*tell*) erzählen; (*connect*)
verbinden ♦ *vi*: **to ~ to** zusammenhängen
mit; (*form relationship*) eine Beziehung
aufbauen zu; **~d** *adj*: **~d (to)** verwandt
(mit); **relating** *prep*: **relating to** bezüglich
+*gen*; **relation** [rɪ'leɪʃən] *n* Verwandte(r) *mf*;
(*connection*) Beziehung *f*; **relationship** *n*
Verhältnis *nt*, Beziehung *f*
relative ['relətɪv] *n* Verwandte(r) *mf* ♦ *adj*
relativ; **~ly** *adv* verhältnismäßig
relax [rɪ'læks] *vi* (*slacken*) sich lockern;
(*muscles, person*) sich entspannen ♦ *vt* (*ease*)
lockern, entspannen; **~ation** [riːlæk'seɪʃən] *n*
Entspannung *f*; **~ed** *adj* entspannt, locker;
~ing *adj* entspannend

relay [*n* 'riːleɪ, *vb* rɪ'leɪ] *n* (*SPORT*) Staffel *f* ♦ *vt*
(*message*) weiterleiten; (*RAD, TV*) übertragen
release [rɪ'liːs] *n* (*freedom*) Entlassung *f*;
(*TECH*) Auslöser *m* ♦ *vt* befreien; (*prisoner*)
entlassen; (*report, news*) verlautbaren,
bekannt geben
relegate ['relɪgeɪt] *vt* (*SPORT*): **to be ~d**
absteigen
relent [rɪ'lent] *vi* nachgeben; **~less** *adj*
unnachgiebig
relevant ['reləvənt] *adj* wichtig, relevant; **~
to** relevant für
reliability [rɪlaɪə'bɪlɪtɪ] *n* Zuverlässigkeit *f*
reliable [rɪ'laɪəbl] *adj* zuverlässig; **reliably**
adv zuverlässig; **to be reliably informed
that ...** aus zuverlässiger Quelle wissen,
dass ...
reliance [rɪ'laɪəns] *n*: **~ (on)** Abhängigkeit *f*
(von)
relic ['relɪk] *n* (*from past*) Überbleibsel *nt*;
(*REL*) Reliquie *f*
relief [rɪ'liːf] *n* Erleichterung *f*; (*help*) Hilfe *f*;
(*person*) Ablösung *f*
relieve [rɪ'liːv] *vt* (*ease*) erleichtern; (*help*)
entlasten; (*person*) ablösen; **to ~ sb of sth**
jdm etw abnehmen; **to ~ o.s.** (*euph*) sich
erleichtern (*euph*); **~d** *adj* erleichtert
religion [rɪ'lɪdʒən] *n* Religion *f*; **religious**
[rɪ'lɪdʒəs] *adj* religiös
relinquish [rɪ'lɪŋkwɪʃ] *vt* aufgeben
relish ['relɪʃ] *n* Würze *f* ♦ *vt* genießen; **to ~
doing** gern tun
relocate [riːləu'keɪt] *vt* verlegen ♦ *vi*
umziehen
reluctance [rɪ'lʌktəns] *n* Widerstreben *nt*,
Abneigung *f*
reluctant [rɪ'lʌktənt] *adj* widerwillig; **~ly** *adv*
ungern
rely [rɪ'laɪ] *vt fus*: **to ~ on** sich verlassen auf
+*acc*
remain [rɪ'meɪn] *vi* (*be left*) übrig bleiben;
(*stay*) bleiben; **~der** *n* Rest *m*; **~ing** *adj*
übrig (geblieben); **~s** *npl* Überreste *pl*
remake ['riːmeɪk] *n* (*CINE*) Neuverfilmung *f*
remand [rɪ'mɑːnd] *n*: **on ~** in
Untersuchungshaft ♦ *vt*: **to ~ in custody** in
Untersuchungshaft schicken; **~ home**

(BRIT) n Untersuchungsgefängnis nt für Jugendliche

remark [rɪˈmɑːk] n Bemerkung f ♦ vt bemerken; **~able** adj bemerkenswert; **remarkably** adv außergewöhnlich

remarry [riːˈmærɪ] vi sich wieder verheiraten

remedial [rɪˈmiːdɪəl] adj Heil-; (teaching) Hilfsschul-

remedy [ˈremədɪ] n Mittel nt ♦ vt (pain) abhelfen +dat; (trouble) in Ordnung bringen

remember [rɪˈmembəʳ] vt sich erinnern an +acc; **remembrance** [rɪˈmembrəns] n Erinnerung f; (official) Gedenken nt; **R~ Day** n ≈ Volkstrauertag m

---
Remembrance Day
---

i Remembrance Day oder
Remembrance Sunday ist der
britische Gedenktag für die Gefallenen der
beiden Weltkriege und anderer Konflikte. Er
fällt auf einen Sonntag vor oder nach dem
11. November (am 11. November 1918
endete der erste Weltkrieg) und wird mit
einer Schweigeminute, Kranzniederlegungen
an Kriegerdenkmälern und dem Tragen von
Ansteckknadeln in Form einer Mohnblume
begangen.

---

remind [rɪˈmaɪnd] vt: **to ~ sb to do sth** jdn daran erinnern, etw zu tun; **to ~ sb of sth** jdn an etw acc erinnern; **she ~s me of her mother** sie erinnert mich an ihre Mutter; **~er** n Mahnung f

reminisce [remɪˈnɪs] vi in Erinnerungen schwelgen; **~nt** [remɪˈnɪsnt] adj: **to be ~nt of sth** an etw acc erinnern

remiss [rɪˈmɪs] adj nachlässig

remission [rɪˈmɪʃən] n Nachlass m; (of debt, sentence) Erlass m

remit [rɪˈmɪt] vt (money): **to ~ (to)** überweisen (an +acc); **~tance** n Geldanweisung f

remnant [ˈremnənt] n Rest m; **~s** npl (COMM) Einzelstücke pl

remorse [rɪˈmɔːs] n Gewissensbisse pl; **~ful** adj reumütig; **~less** adj unbarmherzig

remote [rɪˈməʊt] adj abgelegen; (slight)

gering; **~ control** n Fernsteuerung f; **~ly** adv entfernt

remould [ˈriːməʊld] (BRIT) n runderneuerte(r) Reifen m

removable [rɪˈmuːvəbl] adj entfernbar

removal [rɪˈmuːvəl] n Beseitigung f; (of furniture) Umzug m; (from office) Entlassung f; **~ van** (BRIT) n Möbelwagen m

remove [rɪˈmuːv] vt beseitigen, entfernen; **~rs** npl Möbelspedition f

remuneration [rɪmjuːnəˈreɪʃən] n Vergütung f, Honorar nt

render [ˈrendəʳ] vt machen; (translate) übersetzen; **~ing** n (MUS) Wiedergabe f

rendezvous [ˈrɒndɪvuː] n (meeting) Rendezvous nt; (place) Treffpunkt m ♦ vi sich treffen

renew [rɪˈnjuː] vt erneuern; (contract, licence) verlängern; (replace) ersetzen; **~able** adj regenerierbar; **~al** n Erneuerung f; Verlängerung f

renounce [rɪˈnaʊns] vt (give up) verzichten auf +acc; (disown) verstoßen

renovate [ˈrenəveɪt] vt renovieren; (building) restaurieren

renown [rɪˈnaʊn] n Ruf m; **~ed** adj namhaft

rent [rent] n Miete f; (for land) Pacht f ♦ vt (hold as tenant) mieten; pachten; (let) vermieten; verpachten; (car etc) mieten; (firm) vermieten; **~al** n Miete f

renunciation [rɪnʌnsɪˈeɪʃən] n: **~ (of)** Verzicht m (auf +acc)

reorganize [riːˈɔːɡənaɪz] vt umgestalten, reorganisieren

rep [rep] n abbr (COMM) = **representative**; (THEAT) = **repertory**

repair [rɪˈpɛəʳ] n Reparatur f ♦ vt reparieren; (damage) wieder gutmachen; **in good/bad ~** in gutem/schlechtem Zustand; **~ kit** n Werkzeugkasten m

repartee [repɑːˈtiː] n Witzeleien pl

repatriate [riːˈpætrɪeɪt] vt in die Heimat zurückschicken

repay [riːˈpeɪ] (irreg) vt zurückzahlen; (reward) vergelten; **~ment** n Rückzahlung f; (fig) Vergeltung f

repeal [rɪˈpiːl] vt aufheben

repeat [rɪ'piːt] *n* (*RAD, TV*)
Wiederholung(ssendung) *f* ♦ *vt*
wiederholen; **~edly** *adv* wiederholt

repel [rɪ'pel] *vt* (*drive back*) zurückschlagen;
(*disgust*) abstoßen; **~lent** *adj* abstoßend
♦ *n*: **insect ~lent** Insektenmittel *nt*

repent [rɪ'pent] *vt, vi*: **to ~ (of)** bereuen;
~ance *n* Reue *f*

repercussion [riːpə'kʌʃən] *n* Auswirkung *f*;
to have ~s ein Nachspiel haben

repertory ['repətərɪ] *n* Repertoire *nt*

repetition [repɪ'tɪʃən] *n* Wiederholung *f*

repetitive [rɪ'petɪtɪv] *adj* sich wiederholend

replace [rɪ'pleɪs] *vt* ersetzen; (*put back*)
zurückstellen; **~ment** *n* Ersatz *m*

replay ['riːpleɪ] *n* (*of match*)
Wiederholungsspiel *nt*; (*of tape, film*)
Wiederholung *f*

replenish [rɪ'plenɪʃ] *vt* ergänzen

replica ['replɪkə] *n* Kopie *f*

reply [rɪ'plaɪ] *n* Antwort *f* ♦ *vi* antworten; **~
coupon** *n* Antwortschein *m*

report [rɪ'pɔːt] *n* Bericht *m*; (*BRIT: SCH*)
Zeugnis *nt* ♦ *vt* (*tell*) berichten; (*give
information against*) melden; (*to police*)
anzeigen ♦ *vi* (*make ~*) Bericht erstatten;
(*present o.s.*): **to ~ (to sb)** sich (bei jdm)
melden; **~ card** (*US, SCOTTISH*) *n* Zeugnis
nt; **~edly** *adv* wie verlautet; **~er** *n* Reporter
m

reprehensible [reprɪ'hensɪbl] *adj*
tadelnswert

represent [reprɪ'zent] *vt* darstellen; (*speak
for*) vertreten; **~ation** [reprɪzen'teɪʃən] *n*
Darstellung *f*; (*being ~ed*) Vertretung *f*;
~ations *npl* (*protest*) Vorhaltungen *pl*;
~ative *n* (*person*) Vertreter *m*; (*US: POL*)
Abgeordnete(r) *mf* ♦ *adj* repräsentativ

repress [rɪ'pres] *vt* unterdrücken; **~ion**
[rɪ'preʃən] *n* Unterdrückung *f*

reprieve [rɪ'priːv] *n* (*JUR*) Begnadigung *f*;
(*fig*) Gnadenfrist *f* ♦ *vt* (*JUR*) begnadigen

reprimand ['reprɪmɑːnd] *n* Verweis *m* ♦ *vt*
einen Verweis erteilen +*dat*

reprint [*n* 'riːprɪnt, *vb* riː'prɪnt] *n* Neudruck *m*
♦ *vt* wieder abdrucken

reprisal [rɪ'praɪzl] *n* Vergeltung *f*

reproach [rɪ'prəʊtʃ] *n* Vorwurf *m* ♦ *vt*
Vorwürfe machen +*dat*; **to ~ sb with sth**
jdm etw vorwerfen; **~ful** *adj* vorwurfsvoll

reproduce [riːprə'djuːs] *vt* reproduzieren
♦ *vi* (*have offspring*) sich vermehren;
reproduction [riːprə'dʌkʃən] *n* (*ART, PHOT*)
Reproduktion *f*; (*breeding*) Fortpflanzung *f*;
reproductive [riːprə'dʌktɪv] *adj*
reproduktiv; (*breeding*) Fortpflanzungs-

reprove [rɪ'pruːv] *vt* tadeln

reptile ['reptaɪl] *n* Reptil *nt*

republic [rɪ'pʌblɪk] *n* Republik *f*

repudiate [rɪ'pjuːdɪeɪt] *vt* zurückweisen

repugnant [rɪ'pʌgnənt] *adj* widerlich

repulse [rɪ'pʌls] *vt* (*drive back*)
zurückschlagen; (*reject*) abweisen

repulsive [rɪ'pʌlsɪv] *adj* abstoßend

reputable ['repjutəbl] *adj* angesehen

reputation [repju'teɪʃən] *n* Ruf *m*

reputed [rɪ'pjuːtɪd] *adj* angeblich; **~ly**
[rɪ'pjuːtɪdlɪ] *adv* angeblich

request [rɪ'kwest] *n* Bitte *f* ♦ *vt* (*thing*)
erbitten; **to ~ sth of** *or* **from sb** jdn um etw
bitten; (*formally*) jdn um etw ersuchen; **~
stop** (*BRIT*) *n* Bedarfshaltestelle *f*

require [rɪ'kwaɪə*] *vt* (*need*) brauchen;
(*demand*) erfordern; **~ment** *n* (*condition*)
Anforderung *f*; (*need*) Bedarf *m*

requisite ['rekwɪzɪt] *adj* erforderlich

requisition [rekwɪ'zɪʃən] *n* Anforderung *f*
♦ *vt* beschlagnahmen

rescue ['reskjuː] *n* Rettung *f* ♦ *vt* retten; **~
party** *n* Rettungsmannschaft *f*; **~r** *n* Retter
m

research [rɪ'sɜːtʃ] *n* Forschung *f* ♦ *vi*
forschen ♦ *vt* erforschen; **~er** *n* Forscher *m*

resemblance [rɪ'zembləns] *n* Ähnlichkeit *f*

resemble [rɪ'zembl] *vt* ähneln +*dat*

resent [rɪ'zent] *vt* übel nehmen; **~ful** *adj*
nachtragend, empfindlich; **~ment** *n*
Verstimmung *f*, Unwille *m*

reservation [rezə'veɪʃən] *n* (*booking*)
Reservierung *f*; (*THEAT*) Vorbestellung *f*;
(*doubt*) Vorbehalt *m*; (*land*) Reservat *nt*

reserve [rɪ'zɜːv] *n* (*store*) Vorrat *m*, Reserve
f; (*manner*) Zurückhaltung *f*; (*game ~*)
Naturschutzgebiet *nt*; (*SPORT*)

Ersatzspieler(in) *m(f)* ♦ *vt* reservieren; (*judgement*) sich *dat* vorbehalten; **~s** *npl* (*MIL*) Reserve *f*; **in ~** in Reserve; **~d** *adj* reserviert

reshuffle [riːˈʃʌfl] *n* (*POL*): **cabinet ~** Kabinettsumbildung *f* ♦ *vt* (*POL*) umbilden

reside [rɪˈzaɪd] *vi* wohnen, ansässig sein

residence [ˈrezɪdəns] *n* (*house*) Wohnsitz *m*; (*living*) Aufenthalt *m*; **~ permit** (*BRIT*) *n* Aufenthaltserlaubnis *f*

resident [ˈrezɪdənt] *n* (*in house*) Bewohner *m*; (*in area*) Einwohner *m* ♦ *adj* wohnhaft, ansässig; **~ial** [rezɪˈdenʃəl] *adj* Wohn-

residue [ˈrezɪdjuː] *n* Rest *m*; (*CHEM*) Rückstand *m*; (*fig*) Bodensatz *m*

resign [rɪˈzaɪn] *vt* (*office*) aufgeben, zurücktreten von ♦ *vi* (*from office*) zurücktreten; (*employee*) kündigen; **to be ~ed to sth, to ~ o.s. to sth** sich mit etw abfinden; **~ation** [rezɪgˈneɪʃən] *n* (*from job*) Kündigung *f*; (*POL*) Rücktritt *m*; (*submission*) Resignation *f*; **~ed** *adj* resigniert

resilience [rɪˈzɪlɪəns] *n* Spannkraft *f*; (*of person*) Unverwüstlichkeit *f*; **resilient** [rɪˈzɪlɪənt] *adj* unverwüstlich

resin [ˈrezɪn] *n* Harz *nt*

resist [rɪˈzɪst] *vt* widerstehen +*dat*; **~ance** *n* Widerstand *m*

resit [*vb* riːˈsɪt, *n* ˈriːsɪt] *vt* (*exam*) wiederholen ♦ *n* Wiederholung(sprüfung) *f*

resolute [ˈrezəluːt] *adj* entschlossen, resolut; **resolution** [rezəˈluːʃən] *n* (*firmness*) Entschlossenheit *f*; (*intention*) Vorsatz *m*; (*decision*) Beschluss *m*

resolve [rɪˈzɒlv] *n* Entschlossenheit *f* ♦ *vt* (*decide*) beschließen ♦ *vi* sich lösen; **~d** *adj* (*fest*) entschlossen

resonant [ˈrezənənt] *adj* voll

resort [rɪˈzɔːt] *n* (*holiday place*) Erholungsort *m*; (*help*) Zuflucht *f* ♦ *vi*: **to ~ to** Zuflucht nehmen zu; **as a last ~** als letzter Ausweg

resound [rɪˈzaund] *vi*: **to ~ (with)** widerhallen (von); **~ing** *adj* nachhallend; (*success*) groß

resource [rɪˈsɔːs] *n* Findigkeit *f*; **~s** *npl* (*financial*) Geldmittel *pl*; (*natural*) Bodenschätze *pl*; **~ful** *adj* findig

respect [rɪsˈpekt] *n* Respekt *m* ♦ *vt* achten, respektieren; **~s** *npl* (*regards*) Grüße *pl*; **with ~ to** in Bezug auf +*acc*, hinsichtlich +*gen*; **in this ~** in dieser Hinsicht; **~able** *adj* anständig; (*not bad*) leidlich; **~ful** *adj* höflich

respective [rɪsˈpektɪv] *adj* jeweilig; **~ly** *adv* beziehungsweise

respiration [respɪˈreɪʃən] *n* Atmung *f*

respite [ˈrespaɪt] *n* Ruhepause *f*

resplendent [rɪsˈplendənt] *adj* strahlend

respond [rɪsˈpɒnd] *vi* antworten; (*react*): **to ~ (to)** reagieren (auf +*acc*); **response** [rɪsˈpɒns] *n* Antwort *f*; Reaktion *f*; (*to advert*) Resonanz *f*

responsibility [rɪspɒnsɪˈbɪlɪtɪ] *n* Verantwortung *f*

responsible [rɪsˈpɒnsɪbl] *adj* verantwortlich; (*reliable*) verantwortungsvoll

responsive [rɪsˈpɒnsɪv] *adj* empfänglich

rest [rest] *n* Ruhe *f*; (*break*) Pause *f*; (*remainder*) Rest *m* ♦ *vi* sich ausruhen; (*be supported*) (auf)liegen ♦ *vt* (*lean*): **to ~ sth on/against sth** etw gegen etw *acc* lehnen; **the ~ of them** die Übrigen; **it ~s with him to ...** es liegt bei ihm, zu ...

restaurant [ˈrestərɒn] *n* Restaurant *nt*; **~ car** (*BRIT*) *n* Speisewagen *m*

restful [ˈrestful] *adj* erholsam, ruhig

rest home *n* Erholungsheim *nt*

restive [ˈrestɪv] *adj* unruhig

restless [ˈrestlɪs] *adj* unruhig

restoration [restəˈreɪʃən] *n* Rückgabe *f*; (*of building etc*) Rückerstattung *f*

restore [rɪˈstɔː] *vt* (*order*) wieder herstellen; (*customs*) wieder einführen; (*person to position*) wieder einsetzen; (*give back*) zurückgeben; (*renovate*) restaurieren

restrain [rɪsˈtreɪn] *vt* zurückhalten; (*curiosity etc*) beherrschen; (*person*): **to ~ sb from doing sth** jdn davon abhalten, etw zu tun; **~ed** *adj* (*style etc*) gedämpft, verhalten; **~t** *n* (*self-control*) Zurückhaltung *f*

restrict [rɪsˈtrɪkt] *vt* einschränken; **~ion** [rɪsˈtrɪkʃən] *n* Einschränkung *f*; **~ive** *adj* einschränkend

rest room (*US*) *n* Toilette *f*

restructure [riː'strʌktʃəʳ] *vt* umstrukturieren

result [rɪ'zʌlt] *n* Resultat *nt*, Folge *f*; (*of exam, game*) Ergebnis *nt* ♦ *vi*: **to ~ in sth** etw zur Folge haben; **as a ~ of** als Folge +*gen*

resume [rɪ'zjuːm] *vt* fortsetzen; (*occupy again*) wieder einnehmen ♦ *vi* (*work etc*) wieder beginnen

résumé ['reɪzjuːmeɪ] *n* Zusammenfassung *f*

resumption [rɪ'zʌmpʃən] *n* Wiederaufnahme *f*

resurgence [rɪ'səːdʒəns] *n* Wiedererwachen *nt*

resurrection [rezə'rekʃən] *n* Auferstehung *f*

resuscitate [rɪ'sʌsɪteɪt] *vt* wieder beleben; **resuscitation** [rɪsʌsɪ'teɪʃən] *n* Wiederbelebung *f*

retail [*n, adj* 'riːteɪl, *vb* 'riː'teɪl] *n* Einzelhandel *m* ♦ *adj* Einzelhandels- ♦ *vt* im Kleinen verkaufen ♦ *vi* im Einzelhandel kosten; **~er** ['riːteɪləʳ] *n* Einzelhändler *m*, Kleinhändler *m*; **~ price** *n* Ladenpreis *m*

retain [rɪ'teɪn] *vt* (*keep*) (zurück)behalten; **~er** *n* (*fee*) (Honorar)vorschuss *m*

retaliate [rɪ'tælɪeɪt] *vi* zum Vergeltungsschlag ausholen; **retaliation** [rɪtælɪ'eɪʃən] *n* Vergeltung *f*

retarded [rɪ'taːdɪd] *adj* zurückgeblieben

retch [retʃ] *vi* würgen

retentive [rɪ'tentɪv] *adj* (*memory*) gut

reticent ['retɪsnt] *adj* schweigsam

retina ['retɪnə] *n* Netzhaut *f*

retire [rɪ'taɪəʳ] *vi* (*from work*) in den Ruhestand treten; (*withdraw*) sich zurückziehen; (*go to bed*) schlafen gehen; **~d** *adj* (*person*) pensioniert, im Ruhestand; **~ment** *n* Ruhestand *m*

retiring [rɪ'taɪərɪŋ] *adj* zurückhaltend

retort [rɪ'tɔːt] *n* (*reply*) Erwiderung *f* ♦ *vi* (*scharf*) erwidern

retrace [riː'treɪs] *vt* zurückverfolgen; **to ~ one's steps** denselben Weg zurückgehen

retract [rɪ'trækt] *vt* (*statement*) zurücknehmen; (*claws*) einziehen ♦ *vi* einen Rückzieher machen; **~able** *adj* (*aerial*) ausziehbar

retrain [riː'treɪn] *vt* umschulen

retread ['riːtred] *n* (*tyre*) Reifen *m* mit

erneuerter Lauffläche

retreat [rɪ'triːt] *n* Rückzug *m*; (*place*) Zufluchtsort *m* ♦ *vi* sich zurückziehen

retribution [retrɪ'bjuːʃən] *n* Strafe *f*

retrieval [rɪ'triːvəl] *n* Wiedergewinnung *f*

retrieve [rɪ'triːv] *vt* wiederbekommen; (*rescue*) retten; **~r** *n* Apportierhund *m*

retrograde ['retrəgreɪd] *adj* (*step*) Rück-; (*policy*) rückschrittlich

retrospect ['retrəspekt] *n*: **in ~** im Rückblick, rückblickend; **~ive** [retrə'spektɪv] *adj* (*action*) rückwirkend; (*look*) rückblickend

return [rɪ'təːn] *n* Rückkehr *f*; (*profits*) Ertrag *m*; (*BRIT: rail ticket etc*) Rückfahrkarte *f*; (*: plane ticket*) Rückflugkarte *f* ♦ *adj* (*journey, match*) Rück- ♦ *vi* zurückkehren, zurückkommen ♦ *vt* zurückgeben, zurücksenden; (*pay back*) zurückzahlen; (*elect*) wählen; (*verdict*) aussprechen; **~s** *npl* (*COMM*) Gewinn *m*; (*receipts*) Einkünfte *pl*; **in ~** dafür; **by ~ of post** postwendend; **many happy ~s!** herzlichen Glückwunsch zum Geburtstag!

reunion [riː'juːnɪən] *n* Wiedervereinigung *f*; (*SCH etc*) Treffen *nt*

reunite [riːjuː'naɪt] *vt* wieder vereinigen

reuse [riː'juːz] *vt* wieder verwenden, wieder verwerten

rev [rev] *n abbr* (*AUT: = revolution*) Drehzahl *f*

revamp [riː'væmp] *vt* aufpolieren

reveal [rɪ'viːl] *vt* enthüllen; **~ing** *adj* aufschlussreich

revel ['revl] *vi*: **to ~ in sth/in doing sth** seine Freude an etw *dat* haben/daran haben, etw zu tun

revelation [revə'leɪʃən] *n* Offenbarung *f*

revelry ['revlrɪ] *n* Rummel *m*

revenge [rɪ'vendʒ] *n* Rache *f*; **to take ~ on** sich rächen an +*dat*

revenue ['revənjuː] *n* Einnahmen *pl*

reverberate [rɪ'vəːbəreɪt] *vi* widerhallen

revere [rɪ'vɪəʳ] *vt* (ver)ehren; **~nce** ['revərəns] *n* Ehrfurcht *f*

Reverend ['revərənd] *adj*: **the ~ Robert Martin** ≈ Pfarrer Robert Martin

reversal [rɪ'vəːsl] *n* Umkehrung *f*

reverse [rɪ'vəːs] *n* Rückseite *f*; (*AUT: gear*)

Rückwärtsgang *m* ♦ *adj* (*order, direction*) entgegengesetzt ♦ *vt* umkehren ♦ *vi* (BRIT: AUT) rückwärts fahren; **~-charge call** (BRIT) *n* R-Gespräch *nt*; **reversing lights** *npl* (AUT) Rückfahrscheinwerfer *pl*

revert [rɪ'vɜːt] *vi:* **to ~ to** zurückkehren zu; (*to bad state*) zurückfallen in +*acc*

review [rɪ'vjuː] *n* (*of book*) Rezension *f*; (*magazine*) Zeitschrift *f* ♦ *vt* Rückschau halten auf +*acc*; (MIL) mustern; (*book*) rezensieren; (*reexamine*) von neuem untersuchen; **~er** *n* (*critic*) Rezensent *m*

revise [rɪ'vaɪz] *vt* (*book*) überarbeiten; (*reconsider*) ändern, revidieren; **revision** [rɪ'vɪʒən] *n* Prüfung *f*; (COMM) Revision *f*; (SCH) Wiederholung *f*

revitalize [riː'vaɪtəlaɪz] *vt* neu beleben

revival [rɪ'vaɪvəl] *n* Wiederbelebung *f*; (REL) Erweckung *f*; (THEAT) Wiederaufnahme *f*

revive [rɪ'vaɪv] *vt* wieder beleben; (*fig*) wieder auffrischen ♦ *vi* wieder erwachen; (*fig*) wieder aufleben

revoke [rɪ'vəuk] *vt* aufheben

revolt [rɪ'vəult] *n* Aufstand *m*, Revolte *f* ♦ *vi* sich auflehnen ♦ *vt* entsetzen; **~ing** *adj* widerlich

revolution [revə'luːʃən] *n* (*turn*) Umdrehung *f*; (POL) Revolution *f*; **~ary** *adj* revolutionär ♦ *n* Revolutionär *m*; **~ize** *vt* revolutionieren

revolve [rɪ'vɒlv] *vi* kreisen; (*on own axis*) sich drehen

revolver [rɪ'vɒlvə*] *n* Revolver *m*

revolving door [rɪ'vɒlvɪŋ-] *n* Drehtür *f*

revulsion [rɪ'vʌlʃən] *n* Ekel *m*

reward [rɪ'wɔːd] *n* Belohnung *f* ♦ *vt* belohnen; **~ing** *adj* lohnend

rewind [riː'waɪnd] (*irreg: like* wind) *vt* (*tape etc*) zurückspulen

rewire [riː'waɪə*] *vt* (*house*) neu verkabeln

reword [riː'wɜːd] *vt* anders formulieren

rewrite [riː'raɪt] (*irreg: like* write) *vt* umarbeiten, neu schreiben

rheumatism ['ruːmətɪzəm] *n* Rheumatismus *m*, Rheuma *nt*

Rhine [raɪn] *n:* **the ~** der Rhein

rhinoceros [raɪ'nɒsərəs] *n* Nashorn *nt*

Rhone [rəun] *n:* **the ~** die Rhone

rhubarb ['ruːbɑːb] *n* Rhabarber *m*

rhyme [raɪm] *n* Reim *m*

rhythm ['rɪðm] *n* Rhythmus *m*

rib [rɪb] *n* Rippe *f* ♦ *vt* (*mock*) hänseln, aufziehen

ribbon ['rɪbən] *n* Band *nt*; **in ~s** (*torn*) in Fetzen

rice [raɪs] *n* Reis *m*; **~ pudding** *n* Milchreis *m*

rich [rɪtʃ] *adj* reich; (*food*) reichhaltig ♦ *npl:* **the ~** die Reichen *pl*; **~es** *npl* Reichtum *m*; **~ly** *adv* reich; (*deserve*) völlig

rickets ['rɪkɪts] *n* Rachitis *f*

rickety ['rɪkɪtɪ] *adj* wack(e)lig

rickshaw ['rɪkʃɔː] *n* Rikscha *f*

ricochet ['rɪkəʃeɪ] *n* Abprallen *nt*; (*shot*) Querschläger *m* ♦ *vi* abprallen

rid [rɪd] (*pt, pp* rid) *vt* befreien; **to get ~ of** loswerden

riddle ['rɪdl] *n* Rätsel *nt* ♦ *vt:* **to be ~d with** völlig durchlöchert sein von

ride [raɪd] (*pt* rode, *pp* ridden) *n* (*in vehicle*) Fahrt *f*; (*on horse*) Ritt *m* ♦ *vt* (*horse*) reiten; (*bicycle*) fahren ♦ *vi* fahren, reiten; **to take sb for a ~** mit jdm eine Fahrt *etc* machen; (*fig*) jdn aufs Glatteis führen; **~r** *n* Reiter *m*

ridge [rɪdʒ] *n* Kamm *m*; (*of roof*) First *m*

ridicule ['rɪdɪkjuːl] *n* Spott *m* ♦ *vt* lächerlich machen

ridiculous [rɪ'dɪkjuləs] *adj* lächerlich

riding ['raɪdɪŋ] *n* Reiten *nt*; **~ school** *n* Reitschule *f*

rife [raɪf] *adj* weit verbreitet; **to be ~** grassieren; **to be ~ with** voll sein von

riffraff ['rɪfræf] *n* Pöbel *m*

rifle ['raɪfl] *n* Gewehr *nt* ♦ *vt* berauben; **~ range** *n* Schießstand *m*

rift [rɪft] *n* Spalte *f*; (*fig*) Bruch *m*

rig [rɪg] *n* (*oil ~*) Bohrinsel *f* ♦ *vt* (*election etc*) manipulieren; **~ out** (BRIT) *vt* ausstatten; **~ up** *vt* zusammenbasteln; **~ging** *n* Takelage *f*

right [raɪt] *adj* (*correct, just*) richtig, recht; (*~ side*) rechte(r, s) ♦ *n* Recht *nt*; (*not left,* POL) Rechte *f* ♦ *adv* (*on the ~*) rechts; (*to the ~*) nach rechts; (*look, work*) richtig, recht; (*directly*) gerade; (*exactly*) genau ♦ *vt* in

Ordnung bringen, korrigieren ♦ *excl* gut;
on the ~ rechts; **to be in the ~** im Recht
sein; **by ~s** von Rechts wegen; **to be ~**
Recht haben; **~ away** sofort; **~ now** in
diesem Augenblick, eben; **~ in the middle**
genau in der Mitte; **~ angle** *n* rechte(r)
Winkel *m*; **~eous** ['raɪtʃəs] *adj*
rechtschaffen; **~ful** *adj* rechtmäßig; **~-
hand** *adj*: **~-hand drive** mit
Rechtssteuerung; **~-handed** *adj*
rechtshändig; **~-hand man** (*irreg*) *n* rechte
Hand *f*; **~-hand side** *n* rechte Seite *f*; **~ly**
adv mit Recht; **~ of way** *n* Vorfahrt *f*; **~-
wing** *adj* rechtsorientiert

rigid ['rɪdʒɪd] *adj* (*stiff*) starr, steif; (*strict*)
streng; **~ity** [rɪ'dʒɪdɪtɪ] *n* Starrheit *f*; Strenge
f

rigmarole ['rɪgmərəʊl] *n* Gewäsch *nt*

rigor ['rɪgəʳ] (*US*) *n* = **rigour**

rigorous ['rɪgərəs] *adj* streng

rigour ['rɪgəʳ] (*US* **rigor**) *n* Strenge *f*, Härte *f*

rile [raɪl] *vt* ärgern

rim [rɪm] *n* (*edge*) Rand *m*; (*of wheel*) Felge *f*

rind [raɪnd] *n* Rinde *f*

ring [rɪŋ] (*pt* **rang**, *pp* **rung**) *n* Ring *m*; (*of
people*) Kreis *m*; (*arena*) Manege *f*; (*of
telephone*) Klingeln *nt* ♦ *vt*, *vi* (*bell*) läuten;
(*BRIT*) anrufen; **~ back** (*BRIT*) *vt*, *vi*
zurückrufen; **~ off** (*BRIT*) *vi* aufhängen; **~
up** (*BRIT*) *vt* anrufen; **~ binder** *n* Ringbuch
nt; **~er** *n* Klingeln *nt*; (*of large bell*) Läuten
nt; (*in ears*) Klingen *nt*; **~ing tone** *n* (*TEL*)
Rufzeichen *nt*

ringleader ['rɪŋliːdəʳ] *n* Anführer *m*,
Rädelsführer *m*

ringlets ['rɪŋlɪts] *npl* Ringellocken *pl*

ring road (*BRIT*) *n* Umgehungsstraße *f*.

rink [rɪŋk] *n* (*ice* ~) Eisbahn *f*

rinse [rɪns] *n* Spülen *nt* ♦ *vt* spülen

riot ['raɪət] *n* Aufruhr *m* ♦ *vi* randalieren; **to
run ~** (*people*) randalieren; (*vegetation*)
wuchern; **~er** *n* Aufrührer *m*; **~ous** *adj*
aufrührerisch; (*noisy*) lärmend

rip [rɪp] *n* Schlitz *m*, Riss *m* ♦ *vt*, *vi*
(zer)reißen; **~cord** *n* Reißleine *f*

ripe [raɪp] *adj* reif; **~n** *vi* reifen ♦ *vt* reifen
lassen

rip-off ['rɪpɒf] (*inf*) *n*: **it's a ~~~!** das ist
Wucher!

ripple ['rɪpl] *n* kleine Welle *f* ♦ *vt* kräuseln
♦ *vi* sich kräuseln

rise [raɪz] (*pt* **rose**, *pp* **risen**) *n* (*slope*)
Steigung *f*; (*esp in wages: BRIT*) Erhöhung *f*;
(*growth*) Aufstieg *m* ♦ *vi* (*sun*) aufgehen;
(*smoke*) aufsteigen; (*mountain*) sich
erheben; (*ground*) ansteigen; (*prices*)
steigen; (*in revolt*) sich erheben; **to give ~
to** Anlass geben zu; **to ~ to the occasion**
sich der Lage gewachsen zeigen; **~n** [rɪzn]
pp of **rise**; **~r** ['raɪzəʳ] *n*: **to be an early ~r**
ein(e) Frühaufsteher(in) *m(f)* sein; **rising**
['raɪzɪŋ] *adj* (*tide, prices*) steigend; (*sun,
moon*) aufgehend ♦ *n* (*uprising*) Aufstand *m*

risk [rɪsk] *n* Gefahr *f*, Risiko *nt* ♦ *vt* (*venture*)
wagen; (*chance loss of*) riskieren, aufs Spiel
setzen; **to take or run the ~ of doing sth**
das Risiko eingehen, etw zu tun; **at ~** in
Gefahr; **at one's own ~** auf eigene Gefahr;
~y *adj* riskant

risqué ['riːskeɪ] *adj* gewagt

rissole ['rɪsəʊl] *n* Fleischklößchen *nt*

rite [raɪt] *n* Ritus *m*; **last ~s** Letzte Ölung *f*

ritual ['rɪtjuəl] *n* Ritual *nt* ♦ *adj* ritual, Ritual-;
(*fig*) rituell

rival ['raɪvl] *n* Rivale *m*, Konkurrent *m* ♦ *adj*
rivalisierend ♦ *vt* rivalisieren mit; (*COMM*)
konkurrieren mit; **~ry** *n* Rivalität *f*;
Konkurrenz *f*

river ['rɪvəʳ] *n* Fluss *m*, Strom *m* ♦ *cpd* (*port,
traffic*) Fluss-; **up/down ~** flussaufwärts/
-abwärts; **~bank** *n* Flussufer *nt*; **~bed** *n*
Flussbett *nt*

rivet ['rɪvɪt] *n* Niete *f* ♦ *vt* (*fasten*) (ver)nieten

Riviera [rɪvɪ'ɛərə] *n*: **the ~** die Riviera

road [rəʊd] *n* Straße *f* ♦ *cpd* Straßen-;
major/minor ~ Haupt-/Nebenstraße *f*; **~
accident** *n* Verkehrsunfall *m*; **~block** *n*
Straßensperre *f*; **~hog** *n* Verkehrsrowdy *m*;
~ map *n* Straßenkarte *f*; **~ rage** *n*
Aggressivität *f* im Straßenverkehr; **~ safety**
n Verkehrssicherheit *f*; **~side** *n* Straßenrand
m ♦ *adj* an der Landstraße (gelegen); **~
sign** *n* Straßenschild *nt*; **~ user** *n*
Verkehrsteilnehmer *m*; **~way** *n* Fahrbahn *f*

~ **works** *npl* Straßenbauarbeiten *pl*;
~**worthy** *adj* verkehrssicher

roam [rəum] *vi* (umher)streifen ♦ *vt* durchstreifen

roar [rɔːʳ] *n* Brüllen *nt*, Gebrüll *nt* ♦ *vi* brüllen; **to ~ with laughter** vor Lachen brüllen; **to do a ~ing trade** ein Riesengeschäft machen

roast [rəust] *n* Braten *m* ♦ *vt* braten, schmoren; ~ **beef** *n* Roastbeef *nt*

rob [rɔb] *vt* bestehlen, berauben; (*bank*) ausrauben; **to ~ sb of sth** jdm etw rauben; ~**ber** *n* Räuber *m*; ~**bery** *n* Raub *m*

robe [rəub] *n* (*dress*) Gewand *nt*; (*US*) Hauskleid *nt*; (*judge's*) Robe *f*

robin [ˈrɔbɪn] *n* Rotkehlchen *nt*

robot [ˈrəubɔt] *n* Roboter *m*

robust [rəuˈbʌst] *adj* (*person*) robust; (*appetite, economy*) gesund

rock [rɔk] *n* Felsen *m*; (*BRIT: sweet*) Zuckerstange *f* ♦ *vt, vi* wiegen, schaukeln; **on the ~s** (*drink*) mit Eis(würfeln); (*marriage*) gescheitert; (*ship*) aufgelaufen; ~ **and roll** *n* Rock and Roll *m*; ~-**bottom** *n* (*fig*) Tiefpunkt *m*; ~**ery** *n* Steingarten *m*

rocket [ˈrɔkɪt] *n* Rakete *f*

rocking chair [ˈrɔkɪŋ-] *n* Schaukelstuhl *m*

rocking horse *n* Schaukelpferd *nt*

rocky [ˈrɔkɪ] *adj* felsig

rod [rɔd] *n* (*bar*) Stange *f*; (*stick*) Rute *f*

rode [rəud] *pt of* **ride**

rodent [ˈrəudnt] *n* Nagetier *nt*

roe [rəu] *n* (*also:* ~ **deer**) Reh *nt*; (*of fish: also:* **hard** ~) Rogen *m*; (**soft** ~) Milch *f*

rogue [rəug] *n* Schurke *m*

role [rəul] *n* Rolle *f*; ~ **play** *n* Rollenspiel *nt*

roll [rəul] *n* Rolle *f*; (*bread*) Brötchen *nt*; (*list*) (Namens)liste *f*; (*of drum*) Wirbel *m* ♦ *vt* (*turn*) rollen, (herum)wälzen; (*grass etc*) walzen ♦ *vi* (*swing*) schlingern; (*sound*) rollen, grollen; ~ **about** *or* **around** *vi* herumkugeln; (*ship*) schlingern; (*dog etc*) sich wälzen; ~ **by** *vi* (*time*) verfließen; ~ **over** *vi* sich (herum)drehen; ~ **up** *vi* (*arrive*) kommen, auftauchen ♦ *vt* (*carpet*) aufrollen; ~ **call** *n* Namensaufruf *m*; ~**er** *n* Rolle *f*, Walze *f*; (*road ~er*) Straßenwalze *f*;

R~**erblade** ® *n* Rollerblade *m*; ~**er coaster** *n* Achterbahn *f*; ~**er skates** *npl* Rollschuhe *pl*; ~-**skating** *n* Rollschuhlaufen *nt*

rolling [ˈrəulɪŋ] *adj* (*landscape*) wellig; ~ **pin** *n* Nudel- *or* Wellholz *nt*; ~ **stock** *n* Wagenmaterial *nt*

ROM [rɔm] *n abbr* (= *read only memory*) ROM *m*

Roman [ˈrəumən] *adj* römisch ♦ *n* Römer(in) *m(f)*; ~ **Catholic** *adj* römisch-katholisch ♦ *n* Katholik(in) *m(f)*

romance [rəˈmæns] *n* Romanze *f*; (*story*) (Liebes)roman *m*

Romania [rəuˈmeɪnɪə] *n* = **Rumania**; ~**n** *n* = **Rumanian**

Roman numeral *n* römische Ziffer

romantic [rəˈmæntɪk] *adj* romantisch; ~**ism** [rəˈmæntɪsɪzəm] *n* Romantik *f*

Rome [rəum] *n* Rom *nt*

romp [rɔmp] *n* Tollen *nt* ♦ *vi* (*also:* ~ **about**) herumtollen

rompers [ˈrɔmpəz] *npl* Spielanzug *m*

roof [ruːf] (*pl* ~**s**) *n* Dach *nt*; (*of mouth*) Gaumen *m* ♦ *vt* überdachen, überdecken; ~**ing** *n* Deckmaterial *nt*; ~ **rack** *n* (*AUT*) Dachgepäckträger *m*

rook [ruk] *n* (*bird*) Saatkrähe *f*; (*chess*) Turm *m*

room [ruːm] *n* Zimmer *nt*, Raum *m*; (*space*) Platz *m*; (*fig*) Spielraum *m*; ~**s** *npl* (*accommodation*) Wohnung *f*; "~**s to let** (*BRIT*) *or* **for rent** (*US*)" „Zimmer zu vermieten"; **single/double** ~ Einzel-/ Doppelzimmer *nt*; ~**ing house** (*US*) *n* Mietshaus *nt* (*mit möblierten Wohnungen*); ~**mate** *n* Mitbewohner(in) *m(f)*; ~ **service** *n* Zimmerbedienung *f*; ~**y** *adj* geräumig

roost [ruːst] *n* Hühnerstange *f* ♦ *vi* auf der Stange hocken

rooster [ˈruːstəʳ] *n* Hahn *m*

root [ruːt] *n* (*also fig*) Wurzel *f* ♦ *vi* wurzeln; ~ **about** *vi* (*fig*) herumwühlen; ~ **for** *vt fus* Stimmung machen für; ~ **out** *vt* ausjäten; (*fig*) ausrotten

rope [rəup] *n* Seil *nt* ♦ *vt* (*tie*) festschnüren; **to know the ~s** sich auskennen; **to ~ sb in** jdn gewinnen; ~ **off** *vt* absperren;

~ ladder *n* Strickleiter *f*
rosary ['rəʊzərɪ] *n* Rosenkranz *m*
rose [rəʊz] *pt of* **rise** ♦ *n* Rose *f* ♦ *adj* Rosen-,
rosenrot
rosé ['rəʊzeɪ] *n* Rosé *m*
rosebud ['rəʊzbʌd] *n* Rosenknospe *f*
rosebush ['rəʊzbʊʃ] *n* Rosenstock *m*
rosemary ['rəʊzmərɪ] *n* Rosmarin *m*
rosette [rəʊ'zɛt] *n* Rosette *f*
roster ['rɒstəʳ] *n* Dienstplan *m*
rostrum ['rɒstrəm] *n* Rednerbühne *f*
rosy ['rəʊzɪ] *adj* rosig
rot [rɒt] *n* Fäulnis *f*; (*nonsense*) Quatsch *m*
♦ *vi* verfaulen ♦ *vt* verfaulen lassen
rota ['rəʊtə] *n* Dienstliste *f*
rotary ['rəʊtərɪ] *adj* rotierend
rotate [rəʊ'teɪt] *vt* rotieren lassen; (*take turns*)
turnusmäßig wechseln ♦ *vi* rotieren;
rotating *adj* rotierend; **rotation** [rəʊ'teɪʃən]
n Umdrehung *f*
rote [rəʊt] *n*: **by ~** auswendig
rotten ['rɒtn] *adj* faul; (*fig*) schlecht, gemein;
to feel ~ (*ill*) sich elend fühlen
rotund [rəʊ'tʌnd] *adj* rundlich
rouble ['ru:bl] (*US* **ruble**) *n* Rubel *m*
rough [rʌf] *adj* (*not smooth*) rau; (*path*)
uneben; (*violent*) roh, grob; (*crossing*)
stürmisch; (*without comforts*) hart,
unbequem; (*unfinished, makeshift*) grob;
(*approximate*) ungefähr ♦ *n* (*BRIT: person*)
Rowdy *m*, Rohling *m*; (*GOLF*): **in the ~** im
Rau ♦ *vt*: **to ~ it** primitiv leben; **to sleep ~**
im Freien schlafen; **~age** *n* Ballaststoffe *pl*;
~-and-ready *adj* provisorisch; (*work*)
zusammengehauen; **~ copy** *n* Entwurf *m*;
~ draft *n* Entwurf *m*; **~ly** *adv* grob; (*about*)
ungefähr; **~ness** *n* Rauheit *f*; (*of manner*)
Ungeschliffenheit *f*
roulette [ru:'lɛt] *n* Roulett(e) *nt*
Roumania [ru:'meɪnɪə] *n* = **Rumania**
round [raʊnd] *adj* rund; (*figures*) aufgerundet
♦ *adv* (*in a circle*) rundherum ♦ *prep* um ...
herum ♦ *n* Runde *f*; (*of ammunition*)
Magazin *nt* ♦ *vt* (*corner*) biegen um; **all ~**
überall; **the long way ~** der Umweg; **all
the year ~** das ganze Jahr über; **it's just ~
the corner** (*fig*) es ist gerade um die Ecke;

~ the clock rund um die Uhr; **to go ~ to
sb's (house)** jdn besuchen; **to go ~ the
back** hintenherum gehen; **enough to go ~**
genug für alle; **to go the ~s** (*story*) die
Runde machen; **a ~ of applause** ein Beifall
m; **a ~ of drinks** eine Runde Drinks; **a ~ of
sandwiches** ein Sandwich *nt or m*, ein
belegtes Brot; **~ off** *vt* abrunden; **~ up** *vt*
(*end*) abschließen; (*figures*) aufrunden;
(*criminals*) hochnehmen; **~about** *n* (*BRIT:
traffic*) Kreisverkehr *m*; (: *merry-go-*)
Karussell *nt* ♦ *adj* auf Umwegen; **~ers** *npl*
(*game*) ≃ Schlagball *m*; **~ly** *adv* (*fig*)
gründlich; **~-shouldered** *adj* mit
abfallenden Schultern; **~ trip** *n* Rundreise *f*;
~up *n* Zusammentreiben *nt*, Sammeln *nt*
rouse [raʊz] *vt* (*waken*) (auf)wecken; (*stir up*)
erregen; **rousing** *adj* (*welcome*) stürmisch;
(*speech*) zündend
route [ru:t] *n* Weg *m*, Route *f*; **~ map** (*BRIT*)
n (*for journey*) Streckenkarte *f*
routine [ru:'ti:n] *n* Routine *f* ♦ *adj* Routine-
row¹ [raʊ] *n* (*noise*) Lärm *m*; (*dispute*) Streit
m ♦ *vi* sich streiten
row² [rəʊ] *n* (*line*) Reihe *f* ♦ *vt, vi* (*boat*)
rudern; **in a ~** (*fig*) hintereinander; **~boat**
['rəʊbəʊt] (*US*) *n* Ruderboot *nt*
rowdy ['raʊdɪ] *adj* rüpelhaft ♦ *n* (*person*)
Rowdy *m*
rowing ['rəʊɪŋ] *n* Rudern *nt*; (*SPORT*)
Rudersport *m*; **~ boat** (*BRIT*) *n* Ruderboot *nt*
royal ['rɔɪəl] *adj* königlich, Königs-; **R~ Air
Force** *n* Königliche Luftwaffe *f*; **~ty** ['rɔɪəltɪ]
n (*family*) königliche Familie *f*; (*for novel etc*)
Tantieme *f*
rpm *abbr* (= *revs per minute*) U/min
R.S.V.P. *abbr* (= *répondez s'il vous plaît*) u.
A. w. g.
Rt. Hon. (*BRIT*) *abbr* (= *Right Honourable*)
Abgeordnete(r) *mf*
rub [rʌb] *n* (*with cloth*) Polieren *nt*; (*on person*)
Reiben *nt* ♦ *vt* reiben; **to ~ sb up** (*BRIT*) *or*
to ~ sb (*US*) **the wrong way** jdn aufreizen;
~ off *vi* (*also fig*): **to ~ off (on)** abfärben
(auf +*acc*); **~ out** *vt* herausreiben; (*with
eraser*) ausradieren
rubber ['rʌbəʳ] *n* Gummi *m*; (*BRIT*)

Radiergummi *m*; **~ band** *n* Gummiband *nt*; **~ plant** *n* Gummibaum *m*

rubbish ['rʌbɪʃ] *n* (*waste*) Abfall *m*; (*nonsense*) Blödsinn *m*, Quatsch *m*; **~ bin** (*BRIT*) *n* Mülleimer *m*; **~ dump** *n* Müllabladeplatz *m*

rubble ['rʌbl] *n* (*Stein*)schutt *m*

ruby ['ruːbɪ] *n* Rubin *m* ♦ *adj* rubinrot

rucksack ['rʌksæk] *n* Rucksack *m*

rudder ['rʌdəʳ] *n* Steuerruder *nt*

ruddy ['rʌdɪ] *adj* (*colour*) rötlich; (*inf: bloody*) verdammt

rude [ruːd] *adj* unverschämt; (*shock*) hart; (*awakening*) unsanft; (*unrefined, rough*) grob; **~ness** *n* Unverschämtheit *f*; Grobheit *f*

rudiment ['ruːdɪmənt] *n* Grundlage *f*

rueful ['ruːful] *adj* reuevoll

ruffian ['rʌfɪən] *n* Rohling *m*

ruffle ['rʌfl] *vt* kräuseln

rug [rʌg] *n* Brücke *f*; (*in bedroom*) Bettvorleger *m*; (*BRIT: for knees*) (Reise)decke *f*

rugby ['rʌgbɪ] *n* (*also: ~ football*) Rugby *nt*

rugged ['rʌgɪd] *adj* (*coastline*) zerklüftet; (*features*) markig

rugger ['rʌgəʳ] (*BRIT: inf*) *n* = **rugby**

ruin ['ruːɪn] *n* Ruine *f*; (*downfall*) Ruin *m* ♦ *vt* ruinieren; **~s** *npl* (*fig*) Trümmer *pl*; **~ous** *adj* ruinierend

rule [ruːl] *n* Regel *f*; (*government*) Regierung *f*; (*for measuring*) Lineal *nt* ♦ *vt* (*govern*) herrschen über +*acc*, regieren; (*decide*) anordnen, entscheiden; (*make lines on*) linieren ♦ *vi* herrschen, regieren; entscheiden; **as a ~** in der Regel; **~ out** *vt* ausschließen; **~d** *adj* (*paper*) liniert; **~r** *n* Lineal *nt*; Herrscher *m*; **ruling** ['ruːlɪŋ] *adj* (*party*) Regierungs-; (*class*) herrschend ♦ *n* (*JUR*) Entscheid *m*

rum [rʌm] *n* Rum *m*

Rumania [ruːˈmeɪnɪə] *n* Rumänien *nt*; **~n** *adj* rumänisch ♦ *n* Rumäne *m*, Rumänin *f*; (*LING*) Rumänisch *nt*

rumble ['rʌmbl] *n* Rumpeln *nt*; (*of thunder*) Grollen *nt* ♦ *vi* rumpeln; grollen

rummage ['rʌmɪdʒ] *vi* durchstöbern

rumour ['ruːməʳ] (*US* **rumor**) *n* Gerücht *nt*

♦ *vt*: **it is ~ed that** man sagt *or* man munkelt, dass

rump [rʌmp] *n* Hinterteil *nt*; **~ steak** *n* Rumpsteak *nt*

rumpus ['rʌmpəs] *n* Spektakel *m*

run [rʌn] (*pt* ran, *pp* run) *n* Lauf *m*; (*in car*) (Spazier)fahrt *f*; (*series*) Serie *f*, Reihe *f*; (*ski ~*) (Ski)abfahrt *f*; (*in stocking*) Laufmasche *f* ♦ *vt* (*cause to ~*) laufen lassen; (*car, train, bus*) fahren; (*race, distance*) laufen, rennen; (*manage*) leiten; (*COMPUT*) laufen lassen; (*pass: hand, eye*) gleiten lassen ♦ *vi* laufen; (*move quickly*) laufen, rennen; (*bus, train*) fahren; (*flow*) fließen, laufen; (*colours*) (ab)färben; **there was a ~ on** (*meat, tickets*) es gab einen Ansturm auf +*acc*; **on the ~** auf der Flucht; **in the long ~** auf die Dauer; **I'll ~ you to the station** ich fahre dich zum Bahnhof; **to ~ a risk** ein Risiko eingehen; **~ about** *or* **around** *vi* (*children*) umherspringen; **~ across** *vt fus* (*find*) stoßen auf +*acc*; **~ away** *vi* weglaufen; **~ down** *vi* (*clock*) ablaufen ♦ *vt* (*production, factory*) allmählich auflösen; (*with car*) überfahren; (*talk against*) heruntermachen; **to be ~ down** erschöpft *or* abgespannt sein; **~ in** (*BRIT*) *vt* (*car*) einfahren; **~ into** *vt fus* (*meet: person*) zufällig treffen; (*trouble*) bekommen; (*collide with*) rennen gegen; fahren gegen; **~ off** *vi* fortlaufen; **~ out** *vi* (*person*) hinauslaufen; (*liquid*) auslaufen; (*lease*) ablaufen; (*money*) ausgehen; **he ran out of money/petrol** ihm ging das Geld/ Benzin aus; **~ over** *vt* (*in accident*) überfahren; **~ through** *vt* (*instructions*) durchgehen; **~ up** *vt* (*debt, bill*) machen; **~ up against** *vt fus* (*difficulties*) stoßen auf +*acc*; **~away** *adj* (*horse*) ausgebrochen; (*person*) flüchtig

rung [rʌŋ] *pp* of **ring** ♦ *n* Sprosse *f*

runner ['rʌnəʳ] *n* Läufer(in) *m(f)*; (*for sleigh*) Kufe *f*; (*BRIT*) Stangenbohne *f*; **~-up** *n* Zweite(r) *mf*

running ['rʌnɪŋ] *n* (*of business*) Leitung *f*; (*of machine*) Betrieb *m* ♦ *adj* (*water*) fließend; (*commentary*) laufend; **to be in/out of the ~ for sth** im/aus dem Rennen für etw sein;

3 days ~ 3 Tage lang *or* hintereinander; **~ costs** *npl (of car, machine)* Unterhaltungskosten *pl*

runny ['rʌnɪ] *adj* dünn; *(nose)* laufend

run-of-the-mill ['rʌnəvðə'mɪl] *adj* gewöhnlich, alltäglich

runt [rʌnt] *n (animal)* Kümmerer *m*

run-up ['rʌnʌp] *n*: **the ~~~ to** *(election etc)* die Endphase vor *+dat*

runway ['rʌnweɪ] *n* Startbahn *f*

rupture ['rʌptʃə'] *n (MED)* Bruch *m*

rural ['ruərl] *adj* ländlich, Land-

ruse [ruːz] *n* Kniff *m*, List *f*

rush [rʌʃ] *n* Eile *f*, Hetze *f*; *(FIN)* starke Nachfrage *f* ♦ *vt (carry along)* auf dem schnellsten Wege schaffen *or* transportieren; *(attack)* losstürmen auf *+acc* ♦ *vi (hurry)* eilen, stürzen; **don't ~ me** dräng mich nicht; **~ hour** *n* Hauptverkehrszeit *f*

rusk [rʌsk] *n* Zwieback *m*

Russia ['rʌʃə] *n* Russland *nt*; **~n** *adj* russisch ♦ *n* Russe *m*, Russin *f*; *(LING)* Russisch *nt*

rust [rʌst] *n* Rost *m* ♦ *vi* rosten

rustic ['rʌstɪk] *adj* bäuerlich, ländlich

rustle ['rʌsl] *vi* rauschen, rascheln ♦ *vt* rascheln lassen

rustproof ['rʌstpruːf] *adj* rostfrei

rusty ['rʌstɪ] *adj* rostig

rut [rʌt] *n (in track)* Radspur *f*; **to be in a ~** im Trott stecken

ruthless ['ruːθlɪs] *adj* rücksichtslos

rye [raɪ] *n* Roggen *m*; **~ bread** *n* Roggenbrot *nt*

S, s

sabbath ['sæbəθ] *n* Sabbat *m*

sabotage ['sæbətɑːʒ] *n* Sabotage *f* ♦ *vt* sabotieren

saccharin ['sækərɪn] *n* Sa(c)charin *nt*

sachet ['sæʃeɪ] *n (of shampoo etc)* Briefchen *nt*, Kissen *nt*

sack [sæk] *n* Sack *m* ♦ *vt (inf)* hinauswerfen; *(pillage)* plündern; **to get the ~** rausfliegen; **~ing** *n (material)* Sackleinen *nt*; *(inf)*

Rausschmiss *m*

sacrament ['sækrəmənt] *n* Sakrament *nt*

sacred ['seɪkrɪd] *adj* heilig

sacrifice ['sækrɪfaɪs] *n* Opfer *nt* ♦ *vt (also fig)* opfern

sacrilege ['sækrɪlɪdʒ] *n* Schändung *f*

sad [sæd] *adj* traurig; **~den** *vt* traurig machen, betrüben

saddle ['sædl] *n* Sattel *m* ♦ *vt (burden)*: **to ~ sb with sth** jdm etw aufhalsen; **~bag** *n* Satteltasche *f*

sadistic [sə'dɪstɪk] *adj* sadistisch

sadly ['sædlɪ] *adv* traurig; *(unfortunately)* leider

sadness ['sædnɪs] *n* Traurigkeit *f*

s.a.e. *abbr (= stamped addressed envelope)* adressierte(r) Rückumschlag *m*

safe [seɪf] *adj (careful)* vorsichtig ♦ *n* Safe *m*; **~ and sound** gesund und wohl; **(just) to be on the ~ side** um ganz sicherzugehen; **~ from** *(attack)* sicher vor *+dat*; **~-conduct** *n* freie(s) Geleit *nt*; **~-deposit** *n (vault)* Tresorraum *m*; *(box)* Banksafe *m*; **~guard** *n* Sicherung *f* ♦ *vt* sichern, schützen; **~keeping** *n* sichere Verwahrung *f*; **~ly** *adv* sicher; *(arrive)* wohlbehalten; **~ sex** *n* geschützter Sex *m*

safety ['seɪftɪ] *n* Sicherheit *f*; **~ belt** *n* Sicherheitsgurt *m*; **~ pin** *n* Sicherheitsnadel *f*; **~ valve** *n* Sicherheitsventil *nt*

sag [sæg] *vi* (durch)sacken

sage [seɪdʒ] *n (herb)* Salbei *m*; *(person)* Weise(r) *mf*

Sagittarius [sædʒɪ'teərɪəs] *n* Schütze *m*

Sahara [sə'hɑːrə] *n*: **the ~ (Desert)** die (Wüste) Sahara

said [sɛd] *pt, pp of* **say**

sail [seɪl] *n* Segel *nt*; *(trip)* Fahrt *f* ♦ *vt* segeln ♦ *vi* segeln; *(begin voyage: person)* abfahren; *(: ship)* auslaufen; *(fig: cloud etc)* dahinsegeln; **to go for a ~** segeln gehen; **they ~ed into Copenhagen** sie liefen in Kopenhagen ein; **~ through** *vt fus, vi (fig)* (es) spielend schaffen; **~boat** *(US) n* Segelboot *nt*; **~ing** *n* Segeln *nt*; **~ing ship** *n* Segelschiff *nt*; **~or** *n* Matrose *m*, Seemann *m*

saint [seɪnt] n Heilige(r) mf; **~ly** adj heilig, fromm

sake [seɪk] n: **for the ~ of** um +gen willen

salad ['sæləd] n Salat m; **~ bowl** n Salatschüssel f; **~ cream** (BRIT) n Salatmayonnaise f, Salatmajonäse f; **~ dressing** n Salatsoße f

salary ['sæləri] n Gehalt nt

sale [seɪl] n Verkauf m; (reduced prices) Schlussverkauf m; **"for ~"** „zu verkaufen"; **on ~** zu verkaufen; **~room** n Verkaufsraum m; **~s assistant** n Verkäufer(in) m(f); **~s clerk** (US) n Verkäufer(in) m(f); **~sman** (irreg) n Verkäufer m; (representative) Vertreter m; **~s rep** n (COMM) Vertreter(in) m(f); **~swoman** (irreg) n Verkäuferin f

salient ['seɪlɪənt] adj bemerkenswert

saliva [sə'laɪvə] n Speichel m

sallow ['sæləʊ] adj fahl; (face) bleich

salmon ['sæmən] n Lachs m

salon ['sælɒn] n Salon m

saloon [sə'luːn] n (BRIT: AUT) Limousine f; (ship's lounge) Salon m; **~ car** (BRIT) n Limousine f

salt [sɔːlt] n Salz nt ♦ vt (cure) einsalzen; (flavour) salzen; **~cellar** n Salzfass nt; **~water** adj Salzwasser-; **~y** adj salzig

salute [sə'luːt] n (MIL) Gruß m; (with guns) Salutschüsse pl ♦ vt (MIL) salutieren

salvage ['sælvɪdʒ] n (from ship) Bergung f; (property) Rettung f ♦ vt bergen; retten

salvation [sæl'veɪʃən] n Rettung f; **S~ Army** n Heilsarmee f

same [seɪm] adj, pron (similar) gleiche(r, s); (identical) derselbe/dieselbe/dasselbe; **the ~ book as** das gleiche Buch wie; **at the ~ time** zur gleichen Zeit, gleichzeitig; (however) zugleich, andererseits; **all or just the ~** trotzdem; **the ~ to you!** gleichfalls!; **to do the ~ (as sb)** das Gleiche tun (wie jd)

sample ['sɑːmpl] n Probe f ♦ vt probieren

sanctify ['sæŋktɪfaɪ] vt weihen

sanctimonious [sæŋktɪ'məʊnɪəs] adj scheinheilig

sanction ['sæŋkʃən] n Sanktion f

sanctity ['sæŋktɪtɪ] n Heiligkeit f; (fig) Unverletzlichkeit f

sanctuary ['sæŋktjuərɪ] n (for fugitive) Asyl nt; (refuge) Zufluchtsort m; (for animals) Schutzgebiet nt

sand [sænd] n Sand m ♦ vt (furniture) schmirgeln

sandal ['sændl] n Sandale f

sand: ~box (US) n = **sandpit; ~castle** n Sandburg f; **~ dune** n (Sand)düne f; **~paper** n Sandpapier nt; **~pit** n Sandkasten m; **~stone** n Sandstein m

sandwich ['sændwɪtʃ] n Sandwich m or nt ♦ vt (also: **~ in**) einklemmen; **cheese/ham ~** Käse-/Schinkenbrot; **~ed between** eingeklemmt zwischen; **~ board** n Reklametafel f; **~ course** (BRIT) n Theorie und Praxis abwechselnde(r) Ausbildungsgang m

sandy ['sændɪ] adj sandig; (hair) rotblond

sane [seɪn] adj geistig gesund or normal; (sensible) vernünftig, gescheit

sang [sæŋ] pt of **sing**

sanitary ['sænɪtərɪ] adj hygienisch; **~ towel** n (Monats)binde f

sanitation [sænɪ'teɪʃən] n sanitäre Einrichtungen pl; **~ department** (US) n Stadtreinigung f

sanity ['sænɪtɪ] n geistige Gesundheit f; (sense) Vernunft f

sank [sæŋk] pt of **sink**

Santa Claus [sæntə'klɔːz] n Nikolaus m, Weihnachtsmann m

sap [sæp] n (of plants) Saft m ♦ vt (strength) schwächen

sapling ['sæplɪŋ] n junge(r) Baum m

sapphire ['sæfaɪə] n Saphir m

sarcasm ['sɑːkæzm] n Sarkasmus m

sarcastic [sɑː'kæstɪk] adj sarkastisch

sardine [sɑː'diːn] n Sardine f

Sardinia [sɑː'dɪnɪə] n Sardinien nt

sardonic [sɑː'dɒnɪk] adj zynisch

sash [sæʃ] n Schärpe f

sat [sæt] pt, pp of **sit**

Satan ['seɪtn] n Satan m

satchel ['sætʃl] n (for school) Schulmappe f

satellite ['sætəlaɪt] n Satellit m; **~ dish** n (TECH) Parabolantenne f, Satellitenantenne *f;* **~ television** *n* Satellitenfernsehen *nt*

satisfaction [sætɪsˈfækʃən] *n* Befriedigung *f,* Genugtuung *f;* **satisfactory** [sætɪsˈfæktərɪ] *adj* zufrieden stellend, befriedigend; **satisfied** *adj* befriedigt

satisfy [ˈsætɪsfaɪ] *vt* befriedigen, zufrieden stellen; (*convince*) überzeugen; (*conditions*) erfüllen; **~ing** *adj* befriedigend; (*meal*) sättigend

saturate [ˈsætʃəreɪt] *vt* (durch)tränken

Saturday [ˈsætədɪ] *n* Samstag *m,* Sonnabend *m*

sauce [sɔːs] *n* Soße *f,* Sauce *f;* **~pan** *n* Kasserolle *f*

saucer [ˈsɔːsəʳ] *n* Untertasse *f*

saucy [ˈsɔːsɪ] *adj* frech, keck

Saudi [ˈsaudɪ]: **~ Arabia** *n* Saudi-Arabien *nt;* **~ (Arabian)** *adj* saudi-arabisch ♦ *n* Saudi-Araber(in) *m(f)*

sauna [ˈsɔːnə] *n* Sauna *f*

saunter [ˈsɔːntəʳ] *vi* schlendern

sausage [ˈsɔsɪdʒ] *n* Wurst *f;* **~ roll** *n* Wurst *f* im Schlafrock, Wurstpastete *f*

sauté [ˈsəuteɪ] *adj* Röst-

savage [ˈsævɪdʒ] *adj* wild ♦ *n* Wilde(r) *mf* ♦ *vt* (*animals*) zerfleischen

save [seɪv] *vt* retten; (*money, electricity etc*) sparen; (*strength etc*) aufsparen; (*COMPUT*) speichern ♦ *vi* (*also:* **~ up**) sparen ♦ *n* (*SPORT*) (Ball)abwehr *f* ♦ *prep, conj* außer, ausgenommen

saving [ˈseɪvɪŋ] *adj:* **the ~ grace of** das Versöhnende an +*dat* ♦ *n* Sparen *nt,* Ersparnis *f;* **~s** *npl* (*money*) Ersparnisse *pl;* **~s account** *n* Sparkonto *nt;* **~s bank** *n* Sparkasse *f*

saviour [ˈseɪvjəʳ] (*US* **savior**) *n* (*REL*) Erlöser *m*

savour [ˈseɪvəʳ] (*US* **savor**) *vt* (*taste*) schmecken; (*fig*) genießen; **~y** *adj* pikant, würzig

saw [sɔː] (*pt* **sawed**, *pp* **sawed** *or* **sawn**) *pt of* **see** ♦ *n* (*tool*) Säge *f* ♦ *vt, vi* sägen; **~dust** *n* Sägemehl *nt;* **~mill** *n* Sägewerk *nt;* **~n** *pp of* **saw;** **~n-off shotgun** *n* Gewehr *nt* mit abgesägtem Lauf

sax [sæks] (*inf*) *n* Saxon *nt,* Saxophon *nt*

saxophone [ˈsæksəfəun] *n* Saxofon *nt,*

Saxophon *nt*

say [seɪ] (*pt, pp* **said**) *n:* **to have a/no ~ in sth** Mitspracherecht/kein Mitspracherecht bei etw haben ♦ *vt, vi* sagen; **let him have his ~** lass ihn doch reden; **to ~ yes/no** Ja/Nein *or* ja/nein sagen; **that goes without ~ing** das versteht sich von selbst; **that is to ~** das heißt; **~ing** *n* Sprichwort *nt*

scab [skæb] *n* Schorf *m;* (*pej*) Streikbrecher *m*

scaffold [ˈskæfəld] *n* (*for execution*) Schafott *nt;* **~ing** *n* (Bau)gerüst *nt*

scald [skɔːld] *n* Verbrühung *f* ♦ *vt* (*burn*) verbrühen

scale [skeɪl] *n* (*of fish*) Schuppe *f;* (*MUS*) Tonleiter *f;* (*on map, size*) Maßstab *m;* (*gradation*) Skala *f* ♦ *vt* (*climb*) erklimmen; **~s** *npl* (*balance*) Waage *f;* **on a large ~** (*fig*) im Großen, in großem Umfang; **~ of charges** Gebührenordnung *f;* **~ down** *vt* verkleinern; **~ model** *n* maßstabgetreue(s) Modell *nt*

scallop [ˈskɔləp] *n* Kammmuschel *f*

scalp [skælp] *n* Kopfhaut *f*

scamper [ˈskæmpəʳ] *vi:* **to ~ away** *or* **off** sich davonmachen

scampi [ˈskæmpɪ] *npl* Scampi *pl*

scan [skæn] *vt* (*examine*) genau prüfen; (*quickly*) überfliegen; (*horizon*) absuchen

scandal [ˈskændl] *n* Skandal *m;* (*piece of gossip*) Skandalgeschichte *f*

Scandinavia [skændɪˈneɪvɪə] *n* Skandinavien *nt;* **~n** *adj* skandinavisch ♦ *n* Skandinavier(in) *m(f)*

scant [skænt] *adj* knapp; **~ily** *adv* knapp, dürftig; **~y** *adj* knapp, unzureichend

scapegoat [ˈskeɪpgəut] *n* Sündenbock *m*

scar [skɑːʳ] *n* Narbe *f* ♦ *vt* durch Narben entstellen

scarce [skeəs] *adj* selten, rar; (*goods*) knapp; **~ly** *adv* kaum; **scarcity** *n* Mangel *m*

scare [skeəʳ] *n* Schrecken *m* ♦ *vt* erschrecken; **bomb ~** Bombendrohung *f;* **to ~ sb stiff** jdn zu Tode erschrecken; **to be ~d** Angst haben; **~ away** *vt* (*animal*) verscheuchen; **~ off** *vt* = **scare away;**

~crow n Vogelscheuche f
scarf [skɑːf] (pl **scarves**) n Schal m;
(headscarf) Kopftuch nt
scarlet ['skɑːlɪt] adj scharlachrot ♦ n
Scharlachrot nt; **~ fever** n Scharlach m
scarves [skɑːvz] npl of **scarf**
scary ['skɛərɪ] (inf) adj schaurig
scathing ['skeɪðɪŋ] adj scharf, vernichtend
scatter ['skætər] vt (sprinkle) (ver)streuen;
(disperse) zerstreuen ♦ vi sich zerstreuen;
~brained adj flatterhaft, schusselig
scavenger ['skævəndʒər] n (animal)
Aasfresser m
scenario [sɪ'nɑːrɪəʊ] n (THEAT, CINE)
Szenarium nt; (fig) Szenario nt
scene [siːn] n (of happening) Ort m; (of play,
incident) Szene f; (view) Anblick m;
(argument) Szene f, Auftritt m; **~ry**
n (THEAT) Bühnenbild nt; (landscape)
Landschaft f
scenic ['siːnɪk] adj landschaftlich
scent [sent] n Parfüm nt; (smell) Duft m ♦ vt
parfümieren
sceptical ['skeptɪkl] (US **skeptical**) adj
skeptisch
schedule ['ʃedjuːl, (US) 'skedjuːl] n (list) Liste
f; (plan) Programm nt; (of work) Zeitplan m
♦ vt planen; **on ~** pünktlich; **to be ahead
of/behind ~** dem Zeitplan voraus/im
Rückstand sein; **~d flight** n (not charter)
Linienflug m
scheme [skiːm] n Schema nt; (dishonest)
Intrige f; (plan of action) Plan m ♦ vi
intrigieren ♦ vt planen; **scheming**
['skiːmɪŋ] adj intrigierend
scholar ['skɒlər] n Gelehrte(r) m; (holding
~ship) Stipendiat m; **~ly** adj gelehrt; **~ship**
n Gelehrsamkeit f; (grant) Stipendium nt
school [skuːl] n Schule f; (UNIV) Fakultät f
♦ vt schulen; **~ age** n schulpflichtige(s)
Alter nt; **~book** n Schulbuch nt; **~boy** n
Schüler m; **~children** npl Schüler pl,
Schulkinder pl; **~days** npl (alte) Schulzeit f;
~girl n Schülerin f; **~ing** n Schulung f,
Ausbildung f; **~master** n Lehrer m;
~mistress n Lehrerin f; **~teacher** n
Lehrer(in) m(f)

sciatica [saɪ'ætɪkə] n Ischias m or nt
science ['saɪəns] n Wissenschaft f; (natural
~) Naturwissenschaft f; **~ fiction** n
Sciencefiction f; **scientific** [saɪən'tɪfɪk] adj
wissenschaftlich; (natural ~s)
naturwissenschaftlich; **scientist** ['saɪəntɪst]
n Wissenschaftler(in) m(f)
scintillating ['sɪntɪleɪtɪŋ] adj sprühend
scissors ['sɪzəz] npl Schere f; **a pair of ~**
eine Schere
scoff [skɒf] vt (BRIT: inf: eat) fressen ♦ vi
(mock): **to ~ (at)** spotten (über +acc)
scold [skəʊld] vt schimpfen
scone [skɒn] n weiche(s) Teegebäck nt
scoop [skuːp] n Schaufel f; (news)
sensationelle Erstmeldung f; **~ out** vt
herausschaufeln; **~ up** vt aufschaufeln;
(liquid) aufschöpfen
scooter ['skuːtər] n Motorroller m; (child's)
Roller m
scope [skəʊp] n Ausmaß nt; (opportunity)
(Spiel)raum m
scorch [skɔːtʃ] n Brandstelle f ♦ vt
versengen; **~ing** adj brennend
score [skɔːr] n (in game) Punktzahl f; (final ~)
(Spiel)ergebnis nt; (MUS) Partitur f; (line)
Kratzer m; (twenty) zwanzig, zwanzig Stück
♦ vt (goal) schießen; (points) machen;
(mark) einritzen ♦ vi (keep record) Punkte
zählen; **on that ~** in dieser Hinsicht;
what's the ~? wie stehts?; **to ~ 6 out of
10** 6 von 10 Punkten erzielen; **~ out** vt
ausstreichen; **~board** n Anschreibetafel f;
~r n Torschütze m; (recorder) (Auf)schreiber
m
scorn [skɔːn] n Verachtung f ♦ vt verhöhnen;
~ful adj verächtlich
Scorpio ['skɔːpɪəʊ] n Skorpion m
Scot [skɒt] n Schotte m, Schottin f
Scotch [skɒtʃ] n Scotch m
scotch [skɒtʃ] vt (end) unterbinden
scot-free ['skɒt'friː] adv: **to get off ~~~**
(unpunished) ungeschoren davonkommen
Scotland ['skɒtlənd] n Schottland nt
Scots [skɒts] adj schottisch; **~man/woman**
(irreg) n Schotte m/Schottin f
Scottish ['skɒtɪʃ] adj schottisch

scoundrel ['skaundrl] *n* Schuft *m*

scour ['skauəʳ] *vt* (*search*) absuchen; (*clean*) schrubben

scourge [skə:dʒ] *n* (*whip*) Geißel *f*; (*plague*) Qual *f*

scout [skaut] *n* (*MIL*) Späher *m*; (*also:* **boy ~**) Pfadfinder *m*; **~ around** *vi:* **to ~ around (for)** sich umsehen (nach)

scowl [skaul] *n* finstere(r) Blick *m* ♦ *vi* finster blicken

scrabble ['skræbl] *vi* (*also:* **~ around**: *search*) (herum)tasten; (*claw*): **to ~ (at)** kratzen (an +*dat*) ♦ *n:* **S~** ® Scrabble *nt* ®

scraggy ['skrægi] *adj* dürr, hager

scram [skræm] (*inf*) *vi* abhauen

scramble ['skræmbl] *n* (*climb*) Kletterei *f*; (*struggle*) Kampf *m* ♦ *vi* klettern; (*fight*) sich schlagen; **to ~ out/through** krabbeln aus/ durch; **to ~ for sth** sich um etw raufen; **~d eggs** *npl* Rührei *nt*

scrap [skræp] *n* (*bit*) Stückchen *nt*; (*fight*) Keilerei *f*; (*also:* **~ iron**) Schrott *m* ♦ *vt* verwerfen ♦ *vi* (*fight*) streiten, sich prügeln; **~s** *npl* (*leftovers*) Reste *pl*; (*waste*) Abfall *m*; **~book** *n* Einklebealbum *nt*; **~ dealer** *n* Schrotthändler(in) *m(f)*

scrape [skreip] *n* Kratzen *nt*; (*trouble*) Klemme *f* ♦ *vt* kratzen; (*car*) zerkratzen; (*clean*) abkratzen ♦ *vi* (*make harsh noise*) kratzen; **to ~ through** gerade noch durchkommen; **~r** *n* Kratzer *m*

scrap: **~ heap** *n* Schrotthaufen *m*; **on the ~ heap** (*fig*) beim alten Eisen; **~ iron** *n* Schrott *m*; **~ merchant** (*BRIT*) *n* Altwarenhändler(in) *m(f)*; **~ paper** *n* Schmierpapier *nt*

scrappy ['skræpi] *adj* zusammengestoppelt

scratch [skrætʃ] *n* (*wound*) Kratzer *m*, Schramme *f* ♦ *adj:* **~ team** zusammengewürfelte Mannschaft ♦ *vt* kratzen; (*car*) zerkratzen ♦ *vi* (*sich*) kratzen; **to start from ~** ganz von vorne anfangen; **to be up to ~** den Anforderungen entsprechen

scrawl [skrɔ:l] *n* Gekritzel *nt* ♦ *vt*, *vi* kritzeln

scrawny ['skrɔ:ni] *adj* (*person, neck*) dürr

scream [skri:m] *n* Schrei *m* ♦ *vi* schreien

scree [skri:] *n* Geröll(halde *f*) *nt*

screech [skri:tʃ] *n* Schrei *m* ♦ *vi* kreischen

screen [skri:n] *n* (*protective*) Schutzschirm *m*; (*CINE*) Leinwand *f*; (*TV*) Bildschirm *m* ♦ *vt* (*shelter*) (be)schirmen; (*film*) zeigen, vorführen; **~ing** *n* (*MED*) Untersuchung *f*; **~play** *n* Drehbuch *nt*; **~ saver** *n* (*COMPUT*) Bildschirmschoner *m*

screw [skru:] *n* Schraube *f* ♦ *vt* (*fasten*) schrauben; (*vulgar*) bumsen; **~ up** *vt* (*paper etc*) zerknüllen; (*inf: ruin*) vermasseln (*inf*); **~driver** *n* Schraubenzieher *m*

scribble ['skribl] *n* Gekritzel *nt* ♦ *vt* kritzeln

script [skript] *n* (*handwriting*) Handschrift *f*; (*for film*) Drehbuch *nt*; (*THEAT*) Manuskript *nt*, Text *m*

Scripture ['skriptʃəʳ] *n* Heilige Schrift *f*

scroll [skrəul] *n* Schriftrolle *f*

scrounge [skraundʒ] (*inf*) *vt:* **to ~ sth off or from sb** etw bei jdm abstauben ♦ *n:* **on the ~** beim Schnorren

scrub [skrʌb] *n* (*clean*) Schrubben *nt*; (*in countryside*) Gestrüpp *nt* ♦ *vt* (*clean*) schrubben

scruff [skrʌf] *n:* **by the ~ of the neck** am Genick

scruffy ['skrʌfi] *adj* unordentlich, vergammelt

scrum(mage) ['skrʌm(idʒ)] *n* Getümmel *nt*

scruple ['skru:pl] *n* Skrupel *m*, Bedenken *nt*

scrupulous ['skru:pjuləs] *adj* peinlich genau, gewissenhaft

scrutinize ['skru:tinaiz] *vt* genau prüfen; **scrutiny** ['skru:tini] *n* genaue Untersuchung *f*

scuff [skʌf] *vt* (*shoes*) abstoßen

scuffle ['skʌfl] *n* Handgemenge *nt*

sculptor ['skʌlptəʳ] *n* Bildhauer(in) *m(f)*

sculpture ['skʌlptʃəʳ] *n* (*ART*) Bildhauerei *f*; (*statue*) Skulptur *f*

scum [skʌm] *n* (*also fig*) Abschaum *m*

scurry ['skʌri] *vi* huschen

scuttle ['skʌtl] *n* (*also:* **coal ~**) Kohleneimer *m* ♦ *vt* (*ship*) versenken ♦ *vi* (*scamper*): **to ~ away** *or* **off** sich davonmachen

scythe [saið] *n* Sense *f*

SDP (*BRIT*) *n abbr* = **Social Democratic**

Party

sea [siː] n Meer nt, See f; (fig) Meer nt ♦ adj Meeres-, See-; **by ~** (travel) auf dem Seeweg; **on the ~** (boat) auf dem Meer; (town) am Meer; **out to ~** aufs Meer hinaus; **out at ~** aufs Meer; **~board** n Küste f; **~food** n Meeresfrüchte pl; **~ front** n Strandpromenade f; **~going** adj seetüchtig, Hochsee-; **~gull** n Möwe f

seal [siːl] n (animal) Robbe f, Seehund m; (stamp, impression) Siegel nt ♦ vt versiegeln; **~ off** vt (place) abriegeln

sea level n Meeresspiegel m

sea lion n Seelöwe m

seam [siːm] n Saum m; (edges joining) Naht f; (of coal) Flöz nt

seaman [ˈsiːmən] (irreg) n Seemann m

seaplane [ˈsiːpleɪn] n Wasserflugzeug nt

seaport [ˈsiːpɔːt] n Seehafen m

search [sɜːtʃ] n (for person, thing) Suche f; (of drawer, pockets, house) Durchsuchung f ♦ vi suchen ♦ vt durchsuchen; **in ~ of** auf der Suche nach; **to ~ for** suchen nach; **~ through** vt durchsuchen; **~ engine** n (COMPUT) Suchmaschine f; **~ing** adj (look) forschend; **~light** n Scheinwerfer m; **~ party** n Suchmannschaft f; **~ warrant** n Durchsuchungsbefehl m

sea: ~shore [ˈsiːʃɔːʳ] n Meeresküste f; **~sick** [ˈsiːsɪk] adj seekrank; **~side** [ˈsiːsaɪd] n Küste f; **~side resort** n Badeort m

season [ˈsiːzn] n Jahreszeit f; (Christmas etc) Zeit f, Saison f ♦ vt (flavour) würzen; **~al** adj Saison-; **~ed** adj (fig) erfahren; **~ing** n Gewürz nt, Würze f; **~ ticket** n (RAIL) Zeitkarte f; (THEAT) Abonnement nt

seat [siːt] n Sitz m, Platz m; (in Parliament) Sitz m; (part of body) Gesäß nt; (of trousers) Hosenboden m ♦ vt (place) setzen; (have space for) Sitzplätze bieten für; **to be ~ed** sitzen; **~ belt** n Sicherheitsgurt m

sea: ~ water n Meerwasser nt; **~weed** [ˈsiːwiːd] n (See)tang m; **~worthy** [ˈsiːwəːðɪ] adj seetüchtig

sec. abbr (= second(s)) Sek.

secluded [sɪˈkluːdɪd] adj abgelegen

seclusion [sɪˈkluːʒən] n Zurückgezogenheit f

second [ˈsekənd] adj zweite(r,s) ♦ adv (in ~ position) an zweiter Stelle ♦ n Sekunde f; (person) Zweite(r) mf; (COMM: imperfect) zweite Wahl f; (SPORT) Sekundant m; (AUT: also: ~ gear) zweite(r) Gang m; (BRIT: UNIV: degree) mittlere Note bei Abschlussprüfungen ♦ vt (support) unterstützen; **~ary** adj zweitrangig; **~ary school** n höhere Schule f, Mittelschule f; **~-class** adj zweiter Klasse; **~hand** adj aus zweiter Hand; (car etc) gebraucht; **~ hand** n (on clock) Sekundenzeiger m; **~ly** adv zweitens

secondment [sɪˈkɒndmənt] (BRIT) n Abordnung f

second-rate [ˈsekəndˈreɪt] adj mittelmäßig

second thoughts npl: **to have ~** es sich dat anders überlegen; **on ~** (BRIT) or **thought** (US) oder lieber (nicht)

secrecy [ˈsiːkrəsɪ] n Geheimhaltung f

secret [ˈsiːkrɪt] n Geheimnis nt ♦ adj geheim, Geheim-; **in ~** geheim

secretarial [sekrɪˈtɛərɪəl] adj Sekretärinnen-

secretary [ˈsekrətərɪ] n Sekretär(in) m(f); **S~ of State** (BRIT) n (POL): **S~ of State (for)** Minister(in) m(f) (für)

secretion [sɪˈkriːʃən] n Absonderung f

secretive [ˈsiːkrətɪv] adj geheimtuerisch

secretly [ˈsiːkrɪtlɪ] adv geheim

sectarian [sekˈtɛərɪən] adj (riots etc) Konfessions-, zwischen den Konfessionen

section [ˈsekʃən] n Teil m; (department) Abteilung f; (of document) Abschnitt m

sector [ˈsektəʳ] n Sektor m

secular [ˈsekjʊləʳ] adj weltlich, profan

secure [sɪˈkjʊəʳ] adj (safe) sicher; (firmly fixed) fest ♦ vt (make firm) befestigen, sichern; (obtain) sichern; **security** [sɪˈkjʊərɪtɪ] n Sicherheit f; (pledge) Pfand nt; (document) Wertpapier nt; (national security) Staatssicherheit f; **security guard** n Sicherheitsbeamte(r) m, Wächter m, Wache f

sedan [səˈdæn] (US) n (AUT) Limousine f

sedate [sɪˈdeɪt] adj gesetzt ♦ vt (MED) ein Beruhigungsmittel geben +dat; **sedation** [sɪˈdeɪʃən] n (MED) Einfluss m von Beruhigungsmitteln; **sedative** [ˈsedɪtɪv] n

Beruhigungsmittel *nt* ♦ *adj* beruhigend, einschläfernd

sediment ['sedɪmənt] *n* (Boden)satz *m*

seduce [sɪ'djuːs] *vt* verführen; **seductive** [sɪ'dʌktɪv] *adj* verführerisch

see [siː] (*pt* saw, *pp* seen) *vt* sehen; (*understand*) (ein)sehen, erkennen; (*visit*) besuchen ♦ *vi* (*be aware*) sehen; (*find out*) nachsehen ♦ *n* (*ECCL: R.C.*) Bistum *nt*; (: *Protestant*) Kirchenkreis *m*; **to ~ sb to the door** jdn hinausbegleiten; **to ~ that** (*ensure*) dafür sorgen, dass; **~ you soon!** bis bald!; **~ about** *vt fus* sich kümmern um; **~ off** *vt*: **to ~ sb off** jdn zum Zug *etc* begleiten; **~ through** *vt*: **to ~ sth through** etw durchfechten; **to ~ through sb/sth** jdn/etw durchschauen; **to ~ it** *vt fus*: **to ~ to it** dafür sorgen

seed [siːd] *n* Samen *m* ♦ *vt* (*TENNIS*) platzieren; **to go to ~** (*plant*) schießen; (*fig*) herunterkommen; **~ling** *n* Setzling *m*; **~y** *adj* (*café*) übel; (*person*) zweifelhaft

seeing ['siːɪŋ] *conj*: **~ (that)** da

seek [siːk] (*pt, pp* sought) *vt* suchen

seem [siːm] *vi* scheinen; **it ~s that ...** es scheint, dass ...; **~ingly** *adv* anscheinend

seen [siːn] *pp* of **see**

seep [siːp] *vi* sickern

seesaw ['siːsɔː] *n* Wippe *f*

seethe [siːð] *vi*: **to ~ with anger** vor Wut kochen

see-through ['siːθruː] *adj* (*dress etc*) durchsichtig

segment ['segmənt] *n* Teil *m*; (*of circle*) Ausschnitt *m*

segregate ['segrɪgeɪt] *vt* trennen

seize [siːz] *vt* (*grasp*) (er)greifen, packen; (*power*) ergreifen; (*take legally*) beschlagnahmen; **~ (up)on** *vt fus* sich stürzen auf *+acc*; **~ up** *vi* (*TECH*) sich festfressen; **seizure** ['siːʒə'] *n* (*illness*) Anfall *m*

seldom ['seldəm] *adv* selten

select [sɪ'lekt] *adj* ausgewählt ♦ *vt* auswählen; **~ion** [sɪ'lekʃən] *n* Auswahl *f*; **~ive** *adj* (*person*) wählerisch

self [self] (*pl* selves) *pron* selbst ♦ *n* Selbst

nt, Ich *nt*; **the ~** das Ich; **~-assured** *adj* selbstbewusst; **~-catering** (*BRIT*) *adj* für Selbstversorger; **~-centred** (*US* self-centered) *adj* egozentrisch; **~-coloured** (*US* self-colored) *adj* (*of one colour*) einfarbig, uni; **~-confidence** *n* Selbstvertrauen *nt*, Selbstbewusstsein *nt*; **~-conscious** *adj* gehemmt, befangen; **~-contained** *adj* (*complete*) (in sich) geschlossen; (*person*) verschlossen; (*BRIT*: *flat*) separat; **~-control** *n* Selbstbeherrschung *f*; **~-defence** (*US* self-defense) *n* Selbstverteidigung *f*; (*JUR*) Notwehr *f*; **~-discipline** *n* Selbstdisziplin *f*; **~-employed** *adj* frei(schaffend) *nt*; **~-evident** *adj* offensichtlich; **~-governing** *adj* selbst verwaltet; **~-indulgent** *adj* zügellos; **~-interest** *n* Eigennutz *m*

selfish ['selfɪʃ] *adj* egoistisch, selbstsüchtig; **~ness** *n* Egoismus *m*, Selbstsucht *f*

self: **~lessly** *adv* selbstlos; **~-made** *adj*: **~-made man** Selfmademan *m*; **~-pity** *n* Selbstmitleid *nt*; **~-portrait** *n* Selbstbildnis *nt*; **~-possessed** *adj* selbstbeherrscht; **~-preservation** *n* Selbsterhaltung *f*; **~-reliant** *adj* unabhängig; **~-respect** *n* Selbstachtung *f*; **~-righteous** *adj* selbstgerecht; **~-sacrifice** *n* Selbstaufopferung *f*; **~-satisfied** *adj* selbstzufrieden; **~-service** *adj* Selbstbedienungs-; **~-sufficient** *adj* selbstgenügsam; **~-taught** *adj* selbst erlernt; **~-taught person** Autodidakt *m*

sell [sel] (*pt, pp* sold) *vt* verkaufen ♦ *vi* verkaufen; (*goods*) sich verkaufen; **to ~ at** *or* **for £10** für £10 verkaufen; **~ off** *vt* verkaufen; **~ out** *vi* alles verkaufen; **~-by date** *n* Verfalldatum *nt*; **~er** *n* Verkäufer *m*; **~ing price** *n* Verkaufspreis *m*

Sellotape ['seləuteɪp] (®) *BRIT*) *n* Tesafilm *m* ®

sellout ['selaut] *n* (*of tickets*): **it was a ~** es war ausverkauft

selves [selvz] *npl* of **self**

semaphore ['seməfɔː'] *n* Winkzeichen *pl*

semblance ['sembləns] *n* Anschein *m*

semen ['siːmən] *n* Sperma *nt*

semester [sɪˈmestəʳ] (*US*) *n* Semester *nt*

semi [ˈsemɪ] *n* = **semidetached house**;
~circle *n* Halbkreis *m*; **~colon** *n*
Semikolon *nt*; **~conductor** *n* Halbleiter *m*;
~detached house (*BRIT*) *n* halbe(s)
Doppelhaus *nt*; **~final** *n* Halbfinale *nt*

seminary [ˈsemɪnərɪ] *n* (*REL*) Priesterseminar
nt

semiskilled [semɪˈskɪld] *adj* angelernt

semi-skimmed [semɪˈskɪmd] *adj* (*milk*)
teilentrahmt, Halbfett-

senate [ˈsenɪt] *n* Senat *m*; **senator** *n*
Senator *m*

send [send] (*pt*, *pp* **sent**) *vt* senden,
schicken; (*inf: inspire*) hinreißen; **~ away**
vt wegschicken; **~ away for** *vt fus*
anfordern; **~ back** *vt* zurückschicken; **~
for** *vt fus* holen lassen; **~ off** *vt* (*goods*)
abschicken; (*BRIT: SPORT: player*) vom Feld
schicken; **~ out** *vt* (*invitation*) aussenden; **~
up** *vt* hinaufsenden; (*BRIT: parody*) verulken;
~er *n* Absender *m*; **~-off** *n*: **to give sb a
good ~-off** jdn (ganz) groß verabschieden

senior [ˈsiːnɪəʳ] *adj* (*older*) älter; (*higher rank*)
Ober- ♦ *n* (*older person*) Ältere(r) *mf*; (*higher
ranking*) Rangälteste(r) *mf*; **~ citizen** *n*
ältere(r) Mitbürger(in) *m(f)*; **~ity** [siːnɪˈɔrɪtɪ]
n (*of age*) höhere(s) Alter *nt*; (*in rank*)
höhere(r) Dienstgrad *m*

sensation [senˈseɪʃən] *n* Gefühl *nt*;
(*excitement*) Sensation *f*, Aufsehen *nt*; **~al**
adj (*wonderful*) wunderbar; (*result*)
sensationell; (*headlines etc*) reißerisch

sense [sens] *n* Sinn *m*; (*understanding*)
Verstand *m*, Vernunft *f*; (*feeling*) Gefühl *nt*
♦ *vt* fühlen, spüren; **~ of humour** Humor
m; **to make ~** Sinn ergeben; **~less** *adj*
sinnlos; (*unconscious*) besinnungslos

sensibility [sensɪˈbɪlɪtɪ] *n* Empfindsamkeit *f*;
(*feeling*) Empfindlichkeit *f*; **sensibilities**
npl (*feelings*) Zartgefühl *nt*

sensible [ˈsensɪbl] *adj* vernünftig

sensitive [ˈsensɪtɪv] *adj*: **~ (to)** empfindlich
(gegen); **sensitivity** [sensɪˈtɪvɪtɪ] *n*
Empfindlichkeit *f*; (*artistic*) Feingefühl *nt*;
(*tact*) Feinfühligkeit *f*

sensual [ˈsensjuəl] *adj* sinnlich

sensuous [ˈsensjuəs] *adj* sinnlich

sent [sent] *pt*, *pp* of **send**

sentence [ˈsentns] *n* Satz *m*; (*JUR*) Strafe *f*;
Urteil *nt* ♦ *vt*: **to ~ sb to death/to 5 years**
jdn zum Tode/zu 5 Jahren verurteilen

sentiment [ˈsentɪmənt] *n* Gefühl *nt*;
(*thought*) Gedanke *m*; **~al** [sentɪˈmentl] *adj*
sentimental; (*of feelings rather than reason*)
gefühlsmäßig

sentry [ˈsentrɪ] *n* (Schild)wache *f*

separate [*adj* ˈseprɪt, *vb* ˈsepəreɪt] *adj*
getrennt, separat ♦ *vt* trennen ♦ *vi* sich
trennen; **~ly** *adv* getrennt; **~s** *npl* (*clothes*)
Röcke, Pullover *etc*; **separation** [sepəˈreɪʃən]
n Trennung *f*

September [sepˈtembəʳ] *n* September *m*

septic [ˈseptɪk] *adj* vereitert, septisch; **~ tank**
n Klärbehälter *m*

sequel [ˈsiːkwl] *n* Folge *f*

sequence [ˈsiːkwəns] *n* (Reihen)folge *f*

sequin [ˈsiːkwɪn] *n* Paillette *f*

Serbia [ˈsəːbɪə] *n* Serbien *nt*

serene [sɪˈriːn] *adj* heiter

sergeant [ˈsɑːdʒənt] *n* Feldwebel *m*; (*POLICE*)
(Polizei)wachtmeister *m*

serial [ˈsɪərɪəl] *n* Fortsetzungsroman *m*; (*TV*)
Fernsehserie *f* ♦ *adj* (*number*) (fort)laufend;
~ize *vt* in Fortsetzungen veröffentlichen; in
Fortsetzungen senden

series [ˈsɪərɪz] *n inv* Serie *f*, Reihe *f*

serious [ˈsɪərɪəs] *adj* ernst; (*injury*) schwer;
~ly *adv* ernst(haft); (*hurt*) schwer; **~ness** *n*
Ernst *m*, Ernsthaftigkeit *f*

sermon [ˈsəːmən] *n* Predigt *f*

serrated [sɪˈreɪtɪd] *adj* gezackt

servant [ˈsəːvənt] *n* Diener(in) *m(f)*

serve [səːv] *vt* dienen +*dat*; (*guest, customer*)
bedienen; (*food*) servieren ♦ *vi* dienen,
nützen; (*at table*) servieren; (*TENNIS*) geben,
aufschlagen; **it ~s him right** das geschieht
ihm recht; **that'll ~ as a table** das geht als
Tisch; **to ~ a summons (on sb)** (jdn) vor
Gericht laden; **~ out** *or* **up** *vt* (*food*)
auftragen, servieren

service [ˈsəːvɪs] *n* (*help*) Dienst *m*; (*trains etc*)
Verbindung *f*; (*hotel*) Service *m*, Bedienung
f; (*set of dishes*) Service *nt*; (*REL*)

Gottesdienst *m*; (*car*) Inspektion *f*; (*for TVs etc*) Kundendienst *m*; (*TENNIS*) Aufschlag *m* ♦ *vt* (*AUT, TECH*) warten, überholen; **the S~s** *npl* (*armed forces*) die Streitkräfte *pl*; **to be of ~ to sb** jdm einen großen Dienst erweisen; **~ included/not included** Bedienung inbegriffen/nicht inbegriffen; **~able** *adj* brauchbar; **~ area** *n* (*on motorway*) Raststätte *f*; **~ charge** (*BRIT*) *n* Bedienung *f*; **~man** (*irreg*) *n* (*soldier etc*) Soldat *m*; **~ station** *n* (*Groß*)tankstelle *f*

serviette [sə:vɪ'et] *n* Serviette *f*

servile ['sə:vaɪl] *adj* unterwürfig

session ['seʃən] *n* Sitzung *f*; (*POL*) Sitzungsperiode *f*; **to be in ~** tagen

set [set] (*pt, pp* **set**) *n* (*collection of things*) Satz *m*, Set *nt*; (*RAD, TV*) Apparat *m*; (*TENNIS*) Satz *m*; (*group of people*) Kreis *m*; (*CINE*) Szene *f*; (*THEAT*) Bühnenbild *nt* ♦ *adj* festgelegt; (*ready*) bereit ♦ *vt* (*place*) setzen, stellen, legen; (*arrange*) (an)ordnen; (*table*) decken; (*time, price*) festsetzen; (*alarm, watch, task*) stellen; (*jewels*) (ein)fassen; (*exam*) ausarbeiten ♦ *vi* (*sun*) untergehen; (*become hard*) fest werden; (*bone*) zusammenwachsen; **to be ~ on doing sth** etw unbedingt tun wollen; **to ~ to music** vertonen; **to ~ on fire** anstecken; **to ~ free** freilassen; **to ~ sth going** etw in Gang bringen; **to ~ sail** losfahren; **~ about** *vt fus* (*task*) anpacken; **~ aside** *vt* beiseite legen; **~ back** *vt*: **to ~ back (by)** zurückwerfen (um); **~ off** *vi* aufbrechen ♦ *vt* (*explode*) sprengen; (*alarm*) losgehen lassen; (*show up well*) hervorheben; **~ out** *vi*: **to ~ out to do sth** vorhaben, etw zu tun ♦ *vt* (*arrange*) anlegen, arrangieren; (*state*) darlegen; **~ up** *vt* (*organization*) aufziehen; (*record*) aufstellen; (*monument*) erstellen; **~back** *n* Rückschlag *m*; **~ meal** *n* Menü *nt*; **~ menu** *n* Tageskarte *f*

settee [se'ti:] *n* Sofa *nt*

setting ['setɪŋ] *n* Hintergrund *m*

settle ['setl] *vt* beruhigen; (*pay*) begleichen, bezahlen; (*agree*) regeln ♦ *vi* sich einleben; (*come to rest*) sich niederlassen; (*sink*) sich setzen; (*calm down*) sich beruhigen; **to ~ for**

sth sich mit etw zufrieden geben; **to ~ on** sth sich für etw entscheiden; **to ~ up with** sb mit jdm abrechnen; **~ down** *vi* (*feel at home*) sich einleben; (*calm down*) sich beruhigen; **~ in** *vi* sich eingewöhnen; **~ment** *n* Regelung *f*; (*payment*) Begleichung *f*; (*colony*) Siedlung *f*; **~r** *n* Siedler *m*

setup ['setʌp] *n* (*situation*) Lage *f*

seven ['sevn] *num* sieben; **~teen** *num* siebzehn; **~th** *adj* siebte(r, s) ♦ *n* Siebtel *nt*; **~ty** *num* siebzig

sever ['sevər] *vt* abtrennen

several ['sevrəl] *adj* mehrere, verschiedene ♦ *pron* mehrere; **~ of us** einige von uns

severance ['sevərəns] *n*: **~ pay** Abfindung *f*

severe [sɪ'vɪər] *adj* (*strict*) streng; (*serious*) schwer; (*climate*) rau; **severity** [sɪ'verɪtɪ] *n* Strenge *f*; Schwere *f*; Rauheit *f*

sew [səu] (*pt* **sewed**, *pp* **sewn**) *vt, vi* nähen; **~ up** *vt* zunähen

sewage ['su:ɪdʒ] *n* Abwässer *pl*

sewer ['su:ər] *n* (*Abwasser*)kanal *m*

sewing ['səuɪŋ] *n* Näharbeit *f*; **~ machine** *n* Nähmaschine *f*

sewn [səun] *pp* of **sew**

sex [seks] *n* Sex *m*; (*gender*) Geschlecht *nt*; **to have ~ with sb** mit jdm Geschlechtsverkehr haben; **~ism** *n* Sexismus *m*; **~ist** *adj* sexistisch ♦ *n* Sexist(in) *m(f)*; **~ual** ['seksjual] *adj* sexuell, geschlechtlich, Geschlechts-; **~uality** [seksju'ælɪtɪ] *n* Sexualität *f*; **~y** *adj* sexy

shabby ['ʃæbɪ] *adj* (*also fig*) schäbig

shack [ʃæk] *n* Hütte *f*

shackles ['ʃæklz] *npl* (*also fig*) Fesseln *pl*, Ketten *pl*

shade [ʃeɪd] *n* Schatten *m*; (*for lamp*) Lampenschirm *m*; (*colour*) Farbton *m* ♦ *vt* abschirmen; **in the ~** im Schatten; **a ~ smaller** ein bisschen kleiner

shadow ['ʃædəu] *n* Schatten *m* ♦ *vt* (*follow*) beschatten ♦ *adj*: **~ cabinet** (*BRIT: POL*) Schattenkabinett *nt*; **~y** *adj* schattig

shady ['ʃeɪdɪ] *adj* schattig; (*fig*) zwielichtig

shaft [ʃɑ:ft] *n* (*of spear etc*) Schaft *m*; (*in mine*) Schacht *m*; (*TECH*) Welle *f*; (*of light*)

Strahl m

shaggy ['ʃægɪ] *adj* struppig

shake [ʃeɪk] (*pt* **shook**, *pp* **shaken**) *vt* schütteln, rütteln; (*shock*) erschüttern ♦ *vi* (*move*) schwanken; (*tremble*) zittern, beben ♦ *n* (*jerk*) Schütteln *nt*, Rütteln *nt*; **to ~ hands with** die Hand geben +*dat*; **to ~ one's head** den Kopf schütteln; **~ off** *vt* abschütteln; **~ up** *vt* aufschütteln; (*fig*) aufrütteln; **~n** ['ʃeɪkn] *pp of* **shake**; **shaky** ['ʃeɪkɪ] *adj* zittrig; (*weak*) unsicher

shall [ʃæl] *vb aux*: **I ~ go** ich werde gehen; **~ I open the door?** soll ich die Tür öffnen?; **I'll buy some cake, ~ I?** soll ich Kuchen kaufen?, ich kaufe Kuchen, oder?

shallow ['ʃæləʊ] *adj* seicht

sham [ʃæm] *n* Schein *m* ♦ *adj* unecht, falsch

shambles ['ʃæmblz] *n* Durcheinander *nt*

shame [ʃeɪm] *n* Scham *f*; (*disgrace, pity*) Schande *f* ♦ *vt* beschämen; **it is a ~ that** es ist schade, dass; **it is a ~ to do ...** es ist eine Schande, ... zu tun; **what a ~!** wie schade!; **~-faced** *adj* beschämt; **~ful** *adj* schändlich; **~less** *adj* schamlos

shampoo [ʃæm'puː] *n* Shampoo(n) *nt* ♦ *vt* (*hair*) waschen; **~ and set** *n* Waschen *nt* und Legen

shamrock ['ʃæmrɔk] *n* Kleeblatt *nt*

shandy ['ʃændɪ] *n* Bier *nt* mit Limonade

shan't [ʃɑːnt] = **shall not**

shantytown ['ʃæntɪtaʊn] *n* Bidonville *f*

shape [ʃeɪp] *n* Form *f* ♦ *vt* formen, gestalten ♦ *vi* (*also*: **~ up**) sich entwickeln; **to take ~** Gestalt annehmen; **~~d** *suffix*: **heart-~d** herzförmig; **~less** *adj* formlos; **~ly** *adj* wohlproportioniert

share [ʃeə¹] *n* (An)teil *m*; (*FIN*) Aktie *f* ♦ *vt* teilen; **to ~ out (among/between)** verteilen (unter/zwischen); **~holder** *n* Aktionär(in) *m(f)*

shark [ʃɑːk] *n* Hai(fisch) *m*; (*swindler*) Gauner *m*

sharp [ʃɑːp] *adj* scharf; (*pin*) spitz; (*person*) clever; (*MUS*) erhöht ♦ *n* Kreuz *nt* ♦ *adv* zu hoch; **nine o'clock ~** Punkt neun; **~en** *vt* schärfen; (*pencil*) spitzen; **~ener** *n* (*also*: **pencil ~ener**) Anspitzer *m*; **~~eyed** *adj*

scharfsichtig; **~ly** *adv* (*turn, stop*) plötzlich; (*stand out, contrast*) deutlich; (*criticize, retort*) scharf

shatter ['ʃætə¹] *vt* zerschmettern; (*fig*) zerstören ♦ *vi* zerspringen

shave [ʃeɪv] *n* Rasur *f* ♦ *vt* rasieren ♦ *vi* sich rasieren; **to have a ~** sich rasieren (lassen); **~r** *n* (*also*: **electric ~r**) Rasierapparat *m*

shaving ['ʃeɪvɪŋ] *n* (*action*) Rasieren *nt*; **~s** *npl* (*of wood etc*) Späne *pl*; **~ brush** *n* Rasierpinsel *m*; **~ cream** *n* Rasiercreme *f*; **~ foam** *n* Rasierschaum *m*

shawl [ʃɔːl] *n* Schal *m*, Umhang *m*

she [ʃiː] *pron* sie ♦ *adj* weiblich

sheaf [ʃiːf] (*pl* **sheaves**) *n* Garbe *f*

shear [ʃɪə¹] (*pt* **sheared**, *pp* **sheared** or **shorn**) *vt* scheren; **~ off** *vi* abbrechen; **~s** *npl* Heckenschere *f*

sheath [ʃiːθ] *n* Scheide *f*; (*condom*) Kondom *m* or *nt*

sheaves [ʃiːvz] *npl of* **sheaf**

shed [ʃed] (*pt, pp* **shed**) *n* Schuppen *m*; (*for animals*) Stall *m* ♦ *vt* (*leaves etc*) verlieren; (*tears*) vergießen

she'd [ʃiːd] = **she had**; **she would**

sheen [ʃiːn] *n* Glanz *m*

sheep [ʃiːp] *n inv* Schaf *nt*; **~dog** *n* Schäferhund *m*; **~ish** *adj* verlegen; **~skin** *n* Schaffell *nt*

sheer [ʃɪə¹] *adj* bloß, rein; (*steep*) steil; (*transparent*) (hauch)dünn ♦ *adv* (*directly*) direkt

sheet [ʃiːt] *n* Betttuch *nt*, Bettlaken *nt*; (*of paper*) Blatt *nt*; (*of metal etc*) Platte *f*; (*of ice*) Fläche *f*

sheik(h) [ʃeɪk] *n* Scheich *m*

shelf [ʃelf] (*pl* **shelves**) *n* Bord *nt*, Regal *nt*

shell [ʃel] *n* Schale *f*; (*seashell*) Muschel *f*; (*explosive*) Granate *f* ♦ *vt* (*peas*) schälen; (*fire on*) beschießen

she'll [ʃiːl] = **she will**; **she shall**

shellfish ['ʃelfɪʃ] *n* Schalentier *nt*; (*as food*) Meeresfrüchte *pl*

shell suit *n* Ballonseidenanzug *m*

shelter ['ʃeltə¹] *n* Schutz *m*; (*air-raid ~*) Bunker *m* ♦ *vt* schützen, bedecken; (*refugees*) aufnehmen ♦ *vi* sich unterstellen;

~ed adj (life) behütet; (spot) geschützt; **~ housing** n (for old people) Altenwohnungen pl; (for handicapped people) Behindertenwohnungen pl

shelve [ʃɛlv] vt aufschieben ♦ vi abfallen

shelves [ʃɛlvz] npl of **shelf**

shepherd [ˈʃɛpəd] n Schäfer m ♦ vt treiben, führen; **~'s pie** n Auflauf aus Hackfleisch und Kartoffelbrei

sheriff [ˈʃerɪf] n Sheriff m; (SCOTTISH) Friedensrichter m

she's [ʃiːz] = **she is; she has**

Shetland [ˈʃetlənd] n (also: **the ~s, the ~ Isles**) die Shetlandinseln pl

shield [ʃiːld] n Schild m; (fig) Schirm m ♦ vt (be)schirmen; (TECH) abschirmen

shift [ʃɪft] n Verschiebung f; (work) Schicht f ♦ vt (ver)rücken, verschieben; (arm) wegnehmen ♦ vi sich verschieben; **~less** adj (person) träge; **~ work** n Schichtarbeit f; **~y** adj verschlagen

shilly-shally [ˈʃɪlɪʃælɪ] vi zögern

shin [ʃɪn] n Schienbein nt

shine [ʃaɪn] (pt, pp **shone**) n Glanz m, Schein m ♦ vt polieren ♦ vi scheinen; (fig) glänzen; **to ~ a torch on sb** jdn (mit einer Lampe) anleuchten

shingle [ˈʃɪŋgl] n Strandkies m; **~s** npl (MED) Gürtelrose f

shiny [ˈʃaɪnɪ] adj glänzend

ship [ʃɪp] n Schiff nt ♦ vt verschiffen; **~building** n Schiffbau m; **~ment** n Schiffsladung f; **~per** n Verschiffer m; **~ping** n (act) Verschiffung f; (~s) Schifffahrt f; **~wreck** n Schiffbruch m; (destroyed ~) Wrack nt ♦ vt: **to be ~wrecked** Schiffbruch erleiden; **~yard** n Werft f

shire [ˈʃaɪə] (BRIT) n Grafschaft f

shirk [ʃəːk] vt ausweichen +dat

shirt [ʃəːt] n (Ober)hemd nt; **in ~ sleeves** in Hemdsärmeln

shit [ʃɪt] (inf!) excl Scheiße (!)

shiver [ˈʃɪvə] n Schauer m ♦ vi frösteln, zittern

shoal [ʃəʊl] n (Fisch)schwarm m

shock [ʃɔk] n Erschütterung f; (mental)

Schock m; (ELEC) Schlag m ♦ vt erschüttern; (offend) schockieren; **~ absorber** n Stoßdämpfer m; **~ed** adj geschockt, schockiert, erschüttert; **~ing** adj unerhört

shod [ʃɔd] pt, pp of **shoe**

shoddy [ˈʃɔdɪ] adj schäbig

shoe [ʃuː] (pt, pp **shod**) n Schuh m; (of horse) Hufeisen nt ♦ vt (horse) beschlagen; **~brush** n Schuhbürste f; **~horn** n Schuhlöffel m; **~lace** n Schnürsenkel m; **~ polish** n Schuhcreme f; **~ shop** n Schuhgeschäft nt; **~string** n (fig): **on a ~string** mit sehr wenig Geld

shone [ʃɔn] pt, pp of **shine**

shoo [ʃuː] excl sch; (to dog etc) pfui

shook [ʃʊk] pt of **shake**

shoot [ʃuːt] (pt, pp **shot**) n (branch) Schössling m ♦ vt (gun) abfeuern; (goal, arrow) schießen; (person) anschießen; (kill) erschießen; (film) drehen ♦ vi (move quickly) schießen; **to ~ (at)** schießen (auf +acc); **~ down** vt abschießen; **~ in** vi hineinschießen; **~ out** vi hinausschießen; **~ up** vi (fig) aus dem Boden schießen; **~ing** n Schießerei f; **~ing star** n Sternschnuppe f

shop [ʃɔp] n (esp BRIT) Geschäft nt, Laden m; (workshop) Werkstatt f ♦ vi (also: **go ~ping**) einkaufen gehen; **~ assistant** (BRIT) n Verkäufer(in) m(f); **~ floor** (BRIT) n Werkstatt f; **~keeper** n Geschäftsinhaber m; **~lifting** n Ladendiebstahl m; **~per** n Käufer(in) m(f); **~ping** n Einkaufen nt, Einkauf m; **~ping bag** n Einkaufstasche f; **~ping centre** (US **shopping center**) n Einkaufszentrum nt; **~-soiled** adj angeschmutzt; **~ steward** (BRIT) n (INDUSTRY) Betriebsrat m; **~ window** n Schaufenster nt

shore [ʃɔː] n Ufer nt; (of sea) Strand m ♦ vt: **to ~ up** abstützen

shorn [ʃɔːn] pp of **shear**

short [ʃɔːt] adj kurz; (person) klein; (curt) kurz angebunden; (measure) zu knapp ♦ n (also: **~ film**) Kurzfilm m ♦ adv (suddenly) plötzlich ♦ vi (ELEC) einen Kurzschluss haben; **~s** npl (clothes) Shorts pl; **to be ~ of sth** nicht genug von etw haben; **in ~** kurz gesagt; **~ of doing sth** ohne so weit zu gehen, etw zu tun; **everything ~ of ...** alles außer ...; **it is ~ for** das ist die Kurzform von; **to cut ~** abkürzen; **to fall ~ of sth** etw nicht erreichen; **to stop ~** plötzlich anhalten; **to stop ~ of** Halt machen vor; **~age** n Knappheit f, Mangel m; **~bread** n Mürbegebäck nt; **~change** vt: **to ~change sb** jdm zu wenig herausgeben; **~circuit** n Kurzschluss m ♦ vi einen Kurzschluss haben ♦ vt kurzschließen; **~coming** n Mangel m; **~(crust) pastry** (BRIT) n Mürbeteig m; **~ cut** n Abkürzung f; **~en** vt (ab)kürzen; (clothes) kürzer machen; **~fall** n Defizit nt; **~hand** (BRIT) n Stenografie f; **~hand typist** (BRIT) n Stenotypistin f; **~ list** (BRIT) n (for job) engere Wahl f; **~lived** adj kurzlebig; **~ly** adv bald; **~ notice** n: **at ~ notice** kurzfristig; **~sighted** (BRIT) adj (also fig) kurzsichtig; **~staffed** adj: **to be ~staffed** zu wenig Personal haben; **~stay** n (car park) Kurzparken nt; **~ story** n Kurzgeschichte f; **~tempered** adj leicht aufbrausend; **~term** adj (effect) kurzfristig; **~ wave** n (RAD) Kurzwelle f

shot [ʃɒt] pt, pp of **shoot** ♦ n (from gun) Schuss m; (person) Schütze m; (try) Versuch m; (injection) Spritze f; (PHOT) Aufnahme f; **like a ~** wie der Blitz; **~gun** n Schrotflinte f

should [ʃʊd] vb aux: **I ~ go now** ich sollte jetzt gehen; **he ~ be there now** er sollte eigentlich schon da sein; **I ~ go if I were you** ich würde gehen, wenn ich du wäre; **I ~ like to** ich möchte gerne

shoulder [ˈʃəʊldəʳ] n Schulter f; (BRIT: of road): **hard ~** Seitenstreifen m ♦ vt (rifle) schultern; (fig) auf sich nehmen; **~ bag** n Umhängetasche f; **~ blade** n Schulterblatt nt; **~ strap** n (of dress etc) Träger m

shouldn't [ˈʃʊdnt] = **should not**

shout [ʃaʊt] n Schrei m; (call) Ruf m ♦ vt rufen ♦ vi schreien; **~ down** vt niederbrüllen; **~ing** n Geschrei nt

shove [ʃʌv] n Schubs m, Stoß m ♦ vt

schieben, stoßen, schubsen; (inf: put): **to ~ sth in(to) sth** etw in etw acc hineinschieben; **~ off** vi (NAUT) abstoßen; (fig: inf) abhauen

shovel [ˈʃʌvl] n Schaufel f ♦ vt schaufeln

show [ʃəʊ] (pt showed, pp shown) n (display) Schau f; (exhibition) Ausstellung f; (CINE, THEAT) Vorstellung f, Show f ♦ vt zeigen; (kindness) erweisen ♦ vi zu sehen sein; **to be on ~** (exhibits etc) ausgestellt sein; **to ~ sb in** jdn hereinführen; **to ~ sb out** jdn hinausbegleiten; **~ off** vi (pej) angeben ♦ vt (display) ausstellen; **~ up** vi (stand out) sich abheben; (arrive) erscheinen ♦ vt aufzeigen; (unmask) bloßstellen; **~ business** n Showbusiness nt; **~down** n Kraftprobe f

shower [ˈʃaʊəʳ] n Schauer m; (of stones) (Stein)hagel m; (~ bath) Dusche f ♦ vi duschen ♦ vt: **to ~ sb with sth** jdn mit etw überschütten; **~proof** adj Wasser abstoßend

showing [ˈʃəʊɪŋ] n Vorführung f

show jumping n Turnierreiten nt

shown [ʃəʊn] pp of **show**

show: ~-off [ˈʃəʊɒf] n Angeber(in) m(f); **~piece** [ˈʃəʊpiːs] n Paradestück nt; **~room** [ˈʃəʊrʊm] n Ausstellungsraum m

shrank [ʃræŋk] pt of **shrink**

shred [ʃred] n Fetzen m ♦ vt zerfetzen; (COOK) raspeln; **~der** n (COOK) Gemüseschneider m; (for documents) Reißwolf m

shrewd [ʃruːd] adj clever

shriek [ʃriːk] n Schrei m ♦ vt, vi kreischen, schreien

shrill [ʃrɪl] adj schrill

shrimp [ʃrɪmp] n Krabbe f, Garnele f

shrine [ʃraɪn] n Schrein m; (fig) Gedenkstätte f

shrink [ʃrɪŋk] (pt shrank, pp shrunk) vi schrumpfen, eingehen ♦ vt einschrumpfen lassen; **to ~ from doing sth** davor zurückschrecken, etw zu tun; **~age** n Schrumpfung f; **~-wrap** vt einschweißen

shrivel [ˈʃrɪvl] vt, vi (also: ~ up) schrumpfen, schrumpeln

shroud [ʃraud] n Leichentuch nt ♦ vt: ~ed in mystery mit einem Geheimnis umgeben

Shrove Tuesday [ʃrəuv-] n Fastnachtsdienstag m

shrub [ʃrʌb] n Busch m, Strauch m; ~bery n Gebüsch nt

shrug [ʃrʌg] n Achselzucken nt ♦ vt, vi: to ~ (one's shoulders) die Achseln zucken; ~ off vt auf die leichte Schulter nehmen

shrunk [ʃrʌŋk] pp of shrink

shudder [ʃʌdə'] n Schauder m ♦ vi schaudern

shuffle [ʃʌfl] vt (cards) mischen; to ~ (one's feet) schlurfen

shun [ʃʌn] vt scheuen, (ver)meiden

shunt [ʃʌnt] vt rangieren

shut [ʃʌt] (pt, pp shut) vt schließen, zumachen ♦ vi sich schließen (lassen); ~ down vt, vi schließen; ~ off vt (supply) abdrehen; ~ up vi (keep quiet) den Mund halten ♦ vt (close) zuschließen; ~ter n Fensterladen m; (PHOT) Verschluss m

shuttle [ʃʌtl] n (plane, train etc) Pendelflugzeug nt/-zug m etc; (space ~) Raumtransporter m; (also: ~ service) Pendelverkehr m; ~cock [ʃʌtlkɔk] n Federball m; ~ diplomacy n Pendeldiplomatie f

shy [ʃaɪ] adj schüchtern; ~ness n Schüchternheit f

Siamese [saɪə'miːz] adj: ~ cat Siamkatze f

Siberia [saɪ'bɪərɪə] n Sibirien nt

sibling [sɪblɪŋ] n Geschwister nt

Sicily [sɪsɪlɪ] n Sizilien nt

sick [sɪk] adj krank; (joke) makaber; I feel ~ mir ist schlecht; I was ~ ich habe gebrochen; to be ~ of sb/sth jdn/etw satt haben; ~ bay n (Schiffs)lazarett nt; ~en vt (disgust) krank machen ♦ vi krank werden; ~ening adj (annoying) zum Weinen

sickle [sɪkl] n Sichel f

sick: ~ leave n: to be on ~ leave krankgeschrieben sein; ~ly adj kränklich, blass; (causing nausea) widerlich; ~ness n Krankheit f; (vomiting) Übelkeit f, Erbrechen nt; ~ note n Arbeitsunfähigkeits- bescheinigung f; ~ pay n Krankengeld

nt

side [saɪd] n Seite f ♦ adj (door, entrance) Seiten-, Neben- ♦ vi: to ~ with sb jds Partei ergreifen; by the ~ of neben; ~ by ~ nebeneinander; on all ~s von allen Seiten; to take ~s (with) Partei nehmen (für); from all ~s von allen Seiten; ~board n Sideboard nt; ~boards (BRIT) npl Koteletten pl; ~burns npl Koteletten pl; ~car n Beiwagen m; ~ drum n (MUS) kleine Trommel; ~ effect n Nebenwirkung f; ~light n (AUT) Parkleuchte f; ~line n (SPORT) Seitenlinie f; (fig: hobby) Nebenbeschäftigung f; ~long adj Seiten-; ~ order n Beilage f; ~saddle adv im Damensattel; ~ show n Nebenausstellung f; ~step vt (fig) ausweichen; ~ street n Seitenstraße f; ~track vt (fig) ablenken; ~walk (US) n Bürgersteig m; ~ways adv seitwärts

siding [saɪdɪŋ] n Nebengleis nt

sidle [saɪdl] vi: to ~ up (to) sich heranmachen (an +acc)

siege [siːdʒ] n Belagerung f

sieve [sɪv] n Sieb nt ♦ vt sieben

sift [sɪft] vt sieben; (fig) sichten

sigh [saɪ] n Seufzer m ♦ vi seufzen

sight [saɪt] n (power of seeing) Sehvermögen nt; (look) Blick m; (fact of seeing) Anblick m; (of gun) Visier nt ♦ vt sichten; in ~ in Sicht; out of ~ außer Sicht; ~seeing n Besuch m von Sehenswürdigkeiten; to go ~seeing Sehenswürdigkeiten besichtigen

sign [saɪn] n Zeichen nt; (notice, road ~ etc) Schild nt ♦ vt unterschreiben; to ~ sth over to sb jdm etw überschreiben; ~ on vi (as unemployed) sich (arbeitslos) melden ♦ vt (employee) anstellen; ~ up vi (MIL) sich verpflichten ♦ vt verpflichten

signal [sɪgnl] n Signal nt ♦ vt ein Zeichen geben +dat; ~man (irreg) n (RAIL) Stellwerkswärter m

signature [sɪgnətʃə'] n Unterschrift f; ~ tune n Erkennungsmelodie f

signet ring [sɪgnət-] n Siegelring m

significance [sɪg'nɪfɪkəns] n Bedeutung f

significant [sɪg'nɪfɪkənt] adj (meaning sth)

bedeutsam; (*important*) bedeutend

signify ['sɪgnɪfaɪ] *vt* bedeuten; (*show*) andeuten, zu verstehen geben

sign language *n* Zeichensprache *f*, Fingersprache *f*

signpost ['saɪnpəust] *n* Wegweiser *m*

silence ['saɪləns] *n* Stille *f*; (*of person*) Schweigen *nt* ♦ *vt* zum Schweigen bringen; **~r** *n* (*on gun*) Schalldämpfer *m*; (*BRIT: AUT*) Auspufftopf *m*

silent ['saɪlənt] *adj* still; (*person*) schweigsam; **to remain ~** schweigen; **~ partner** *n* (*COMM*) stille(r) Teilhaber *m*

silicon chip ['sɪlɪkən-] *n* Siliciumchip *m*, Siliziumchip *m*

silk [sɪlk] *n* Seide *f* ♦ *adj* seiden, Seiden-; **~y** *adj* seidig

silly ['sɪlɪ] *adj* dumm, albern

silt [sɪlt] *n* Schlamm *m*, Schlick *m*

silver ['sɪlvəʳ] *n* Silber *nt* ♦ *adj* silbern, Silber-; **~ paper** (*BRIT*) *n* Silberpapier *nt*; **~-plated** *adj* versilbert; **~smith** *n* Silberschmied *m*; **~ware** *n* Silber *nt*; **~y** *adj* silbern

similar ['sɪmɪləʳ] *adj*: **~ (to)** ähnlich (+*dat*); **~ity** [sɪmɪˈlærɪtɪ] *n* Ähnlichkeit *f*; **~ly** *adv* in ähnlicher Weise

simmer ['sɪməʳ] *vi* sieden ♦ *vt* sieden lassen

simple ['sɪmpl] *adj* einfach; **~(-minded)** *adj* einfältig

simplicity [sɪmˈplɪsɪtɪ] *n* Einfachheit *f*; (*of person*) Einfältigkeit *f*

simplify ['sɪmplɪfaɪ] *vt* vereinfachen

simply ['sɪmplɪ] *adv* einfach

simulate ['sɪmjuleɪt] *vt* simulieren

simultaneous [sɪməlˈteɪnɪəs] *adj* gleichzeitig

sin [sɪn] *n* Sünde *f* ♦ *vi* sündigen

since [sɪns] *adv* seither ♦ *prep* seit, seitdem ♦ *conj* (*time*) seit; (*because*) da, weil; **~ then** seitdem

sincere [sɪnˈsɪəʳ] *adj* aufrichtig; **~ly** *adv*: **yours ~ly** mit freundlichen Grüßen; **sincerity** [sɪnˈserɪtɪ] *n* Aufrichtigkeit *f*

sinew ['sɪnjuː] *n* Sehne *f*

sinful ['sɪnful] *adj* sündig, sündhaft

sing [sɪŋ] (*pt* **sang**, *pp* **sung**) *vt*, *vi* singen

Singapore [sɪŋgəˈpɔːʳ] *n* Singapur *nt*

singe [sɪndʒ] *vt* versengen

singer ['sɪŋəʳ] *n* Sänger(in) *m(f)*

singing ['sɪŋɪŋ] *n* Singen *nt*, Gesang *m*

single ['sɪŋgl] *adj* (*one only*) einzig; (*bed, room*) Einzel-, einzeln; (*unmarried*) ledig; (*BRIT: ticket*) einfach; (*having one part only*) einzeln ♦ *n* (*BRIT: also:* **~ ticket**) einfache Fahrkarte *f*; **in ~ file** hintereinander; **~ out** *vt* aussuchen, auswählen; **~ bed** *n* Einzelbett *nt*; **~-breasted** *adj* einreihig; **~-handed** *adj* allein; **~-minded** *adj* zielstrebig; **~ parent** *n* Alleinerziehende(r) *f(m)*; **~ room** *n* Einzelzimmer *nt*; **~s** *n* (*TENNIS*) Einzel *nt*; **~-track road** *n* einspurige Straße (mit Ausweichstellen); **singly** *adv* einzeln, allein

singular ['sɪŋgjuləʳ] *adj* (*odd*) merkwürdig, seltsam ♦ *n* (*GRAM*) Einzahl *f*, Singular *m*

sinister ['sɪnɪstəʳ] *adj* (*evil*) böse; (*ghostly*) unheimlich

sink [sɪŋk] (*pt* **sank**, *pp* **sunk**) *n* Spülbecken *nt* ♦ *vt* (*ship*) versenken ♦ *vi* sinken; **to ~ sth into** (*teeth, claws*) etw schlagen in +*acc*; **~ in** *vi* (*news etc*) eingehen

sinner ['sɪnəʳ] *n* Sünder(in) *m(f)*

sinus ['saɪnəs] *n* (*ANAT*) Sinus *m*

sip [sɪp] *n* Schlückchen *nt* ♦ *vt* nippen an +*dat*

siphon ['saɪfən] *n* Siphon(flasche *f*) *m*; **~ off** *vt* absaugen; (*fig*) abschöpfen

sir [səʳ] *n* (*respect*) Herr *m*; (*knight*) Sir *m*; **S~ John Smith** Sir John Smith; **yes ~** ja(wohl, mein Herr)

siren ['saɪərən] *n* Sirene *f*

sirloin ['səːlɔɪn] *n* Lendenstück *nt*

sissy ['sɪsɪ] (*inf*) *n* Waschlappen *m*

sister ['sɪstəʳ] *n* Schwester *f*; (*BRIT: nurse*) Oberschwester *f*; (*nun*) Ordensschwester *f*; **~-in-law** *n* Schwägerin *f*

sit [sɪt] (*pt*, *pp* **sat**) *vi* sitzen; (*hold session*) tagen ♦ *vt* (*exam*) machen; **~ down** *vi* sich hinsetzen; **~ in on** *vt fus* dabei sein bei; **~ up** *vi* (*after lying*) sich aufsetzen; (*straight*) sich gerade setzen; (*at night*) aufbleiben

sitcom ['sɪtkɔm] *n abbr* (= *situation comedy*) Situationskomödie *f*

site [saɪt] *n* Platz *m*; (*also:* **building ~**)

Baustelle f ♦ vt legen
sitting ['sɪtɪŋ] n (meeting) Sitzung f; **~ room** n Wohnzimmer nt
situated ['sɪtjueɪtɪd] adj: **to be ~** liegen
situation [sɪtju'eɪʃən] n Situation f, Lage f; (place) Lage f; (employment) Stelle f; **"~s vacant"** (BRIT) „Stellenangebote" pl
six [sɪks] num sechs; **~teen** num sechzehn; **~th** adj sechste(r, s) ♦ n Sechstel nt; **~ty** num sechzig
size [saɪz] n Größe f; (of project) Umfang m; **~ up** v (assess) abschätzen, einschätzen; **~able** adj ziemlich groß, ansehnlich
sizzle ['sɪzl] vi zischen; (COOK) brutzeln
skate [skeɪt] n Schlittschuh m; (fish: pl inv) Rochen m ♦ vi Schlittschuh laufen; **~board** n Skateboard nt; **~boarding** n Skateboardfahren nt; **~r** n Schlittschuhläufer(in) m(f); **skating** ['skeɪtɪŋ] n Eislauf m; **to go skating** Eis laufen gehen; **skating rink** n Eisbahn f
skeleton ['skɛlɪtn] n Skelett nt; (fig) Gerüst nt; **~ key** n Dietrich m; **~ staff** n Notbesetzung f
skeptical ['skɛptɪkl] (US) adj = **sceptical**
sketch [skɛtʃ] n Skizze f; (THEAT) Sketch m ♦ vt skizzieren; **~book** n Skizzenbuch nt; **~y** adj skizzenhaft
skewer ['skjuːəʳ] n Fleischspieß m
ski [skiː] n Ski m, Schi m ♦ vi Ski or Schi laufen; **~ boot** n Skistiefel m
skid [skɪd] n (AUT) Schleudern nt ♦ vi rutschen; (AUT) schleudern
ski: ~er ['skiːəʳ] n Skiläufer(in) m(f); **~ing** ['skiːɪŋ] n: **to go ~ing** Ski laufen gehen; **~-jump** n Sprungschanze f ♦ vi Ski springen
skilful ['skɪlful] adj geschickt
ski-lift n Skilift m
skill [skɪl] n Können nt; **~ed** adj geschickt; (worker) Fach-, gelernt
skim [skɪm] vt (liquid) abschöpfen; (glide over) gleiten über +acc ♦ vi: **~ through** (book) überfliegen; **~med milk** n Magermilch f
skimp [skɪmp] vt (do carelessly) oberflächlich tun; **~y** adj (dress) knapp
skin [skɪn] n Haut f; (peel) Schale f ♦ vt

abhäuten; schälen; **~ cancer** n Hautkrebs m; **~-deep** adj oberflächlich; **~ diving** n Schwimmtauchen nt; **~head** n Skinhead m; **~ny** adj dünn; **~tight** adj (dress etc) hauteng
skip [skɪp] n Sprung m ♦ vi hüpfen; (with rope) Seil springen ♦ vt (pass over) übergehen
ski: ~ pants npl Skihosen pl; **~ pass** n Skipass nt; **~ pole** n Skistock m
skipper ['skɪpəʳ] n Kapitän m ♦ vt führen
skipping rope ['skɪpɪŋ-] (BRIT) n Hüpfseil nt
skirmish ['skɜːmɪʃ] n Scharmützel nt
skirt [skɜːt] n Rock m ♦ vt herumgehen um; (fig) umgehen; **~ing board** (BRIT) n Fußleiste f
ski suit n Skianzug m
skit [skɪt] n Parodie f
ski tow n Schlepplift m
skittle ['skɪtl] n Kegel m; **~s** n (game) Kegeln nt
skive [skaɪv] (BRIT: inf) vi schwänzen
skulk [skʌlk] vi sich herumdrücken
skull [skʌl] n Schädel m
skunk [skʌŋk] n Stinktier nt
sky [skaɪ] n Himmel m; **~light** n Oberlicht nt; **~scraper** n Wolkenkratzer m
slab [slæb] n (of stone) Platte f
slack [slæk] adj (loose) locker; (business) flau; (careless) nachlässig, lasch ♦ vi nachlässig sein ♦ n: **to take up the ~** straff ziehen; **~s** npl (trousers) Hose(n pl) f; **~en** vi (also: **~en off**) locker werden; (: slow down) stocken, nachlassen ♦ vt (: loosen) lockern
slag [slæg] (BRIT) vt: **~ off** (criticize) (he)runtermachen
slag heap [slæg-] n Halde f
slain [sleɪn] pp of **slay**
slam [slæm] n Knall m ♦ vt (door) zuschlagen; (throw down) knallen ♦ vi zuschlagen
slander ['slɑːndəʳ] n Verleumdung f ♦ vt verleumden
slang [slæŋ] n Slang m; (jargon) Jargon m
slant [slɑːnt] n Schräge f; (fig) Tendenz f ♦ vt schräg legen ♦ vi schräg liegen; **~ed** adj schräg; **~ing** adj schräg

slap [slæp] n Klaps m ♦ vt einen Klaps geben +dat ♦ adv (directly) geradewegs; ~**dash** adj salopp; ~**stick** n (comedy) Klamauk m; ~-**up** [BRIT] adj (meal) erstklassig, prima

slash [slæʃ] n Schnittwunde f ♦ vt (auf)schlitzen

slat [slæt] n Leiste f

slate [sleɪt] n (stone) Schiefer m; (roofing) Dachziegel m ♦ vt (criticize) verreißen

slaughter ['slɔːtə*] n (of animals) Schlachten nt; (of people) Gemetzel nt ♦ vt schlachten; (people) niedermetzeln; ~**house** n Schlachthof m

Slav [slɑːv] adj slawisch

slave [sleɪv] n Sklave m, Sklavin f ♦ vi schuften, sich schinden; ~**ry** n Sklaverei f

slay [sleɪ] (pt slew, pp slain) vt ermorden

sleazy ['sliːzɪ] adj (place) schmierig

sledge [slɛdʒ] n Schlitten m

sledgehammer ['slɛdʒhæmə*] n Schmiedehammer m

sledging n Schlittenfahren nt

sleek [sliːk] adj glatt; (shape) rassig

sleep [sliːp] (pt, pp slept) n Schlaf m ♦ vi schlafen; **to go to** ~ einschlafen; ~ **in** vi ausschlafen; (oversleep) verschlafen; ~**er** n (person) Schläfer m; [BRIT: RAIL] Schlafwagen m; (: beam) Schwelle f; ~**ing bag** n Schlafsack m; ~**ing car** n Schlafwagen m; ~**ing partner** n = **silent partner**; ~**ing pill** n Schlaftablette f; ~**less** adj (night) schlaflos; ~**walker** n Schlafwandler(in) m(f); ~**y** adj schläfrig

sleet [sliːt] n Schneeregen m

sleeve [sliːv] n Ärmel m; (of record) Umschlag m; ~**less** adj ärmellos

sleigh [sleɪ] n Pferdeschlitten m

sleight [slaɪt] n: ~ **of hand** Fingerfertigkeit f

slender ['slɛndə*] adj schlank; (fig) gering

slept [slɛpt] pt, pp of **sleep**

slew [sluː] vi (veer) (herum)schwenken ♦ pt of **slay**

slice [slaɪs] n Scheibe f ♦ vt in Scheiben schneiden

slick [slɪk] adj (clever) raffiniert, aalglatt ♦ n Ölteppich m

slid [slɪd] pt, pp of **slide**

slide [slaɪd] (pt, pp slid) n Rutschbahn f; [PHOT] Dia(positiv) nt; (BRIT: for hair) (Haar)spange f ♦ vt schieben ♦ vi (slip) gleiten, rutschen; **sliding** adj (door) Schiebe-; **sliding scale** n gleitende Skala f

slight [slaɪt] adj zierlich; (trivial) geringfügig; (small) gering ♦ n Kränkung f ♦ vt (offend) kränken; **not in the** ~**est** nicht im Geringsten; ~**ly** adv etwas, ein bisschen

slim [slɪm] adj schlank; (book) dünn; (chance) gering ♦ vi eine Schlankheitskur machen

slime [slaɪm] n Schleim m

slimming ['slɪmɪŋ] n Schlankheitskur f

slimy ['slaɪmɪ] adj glitschig; (dirty) schlammig; (person) schmierig

sling [slɪŋ] (pt, pp slung) n Schlinge f; (weapon) Schleuder f ♦ vt schleudern

slip [slɪp] n (mistake) Flüchtigkeitsfehler m; (petticoat) Unterrock m; (of paper) Zettel m ♦ vt (put) stecken, schieben ♦ vi (lose balance) ausrutschen; (move) gleiten, rutschen; (decline) nachlassen; (move smoothly): **to** ~ **in/out** (person) hinein-/ hinausschlüpfen; **to give sb the** ~ jdm entwischen; ~ **of the tongue** Versprecher m; **it** ~**ped my mind** das ist mir entfallen; **to** ~ **sth on/off** etw über-/abstreifen; ~ **away** vi sich wegstehlen; ~ **in** vt hineingleiten lassen ♦ vi (errors) sich einschleichen; ~**ped disc** n Bandscheibenschaden m

slipper ['slɪpə*] n Hausschuh m

slippery ['slɪpərɪ] adj glatt

slip: ~ **road** (BRIT) n Auffahrt f/Ausfahrt f; ~**shod** adj schlampig; ~-**up** n Panne f; ~**way** n Auslaufbahn f

slit [slɪt] (pt, pp slit) n Schlitz m ♦ vt aufschlitzen

slither ['slɪðə*] vi schlittern; (snake) sich schlängeln

sliver ['slɪvə*] n (of glass, wood) Splitter m; (of cheese) Scheibchen nt

slob [slɔb] (inf) n Klotz m

slog [slɔg] vi (work hard) schuften ♦ n: **it was a** ~ es war eine Plackerei

slogan ['sləʊgən] n Schlagwort nt; (COMM)

Werbespruch *m*

slop [slɔp] *vi* (*also:* ~ **over**) überschwappen ♦ *vt* verschütten

slope [sləup] *n* Neigung *f*; (*of mountains*) (Ab)hang *m* ♦ *vi*: **to** ~ **down** sich senken; **to** ~ **up** ansteigen; **sloping** ['sləupɪŋ] *adj* schräg

sloppy ['slɔpɪ] *adj* schlampig

slot [slɔt] *n* Schlitz *m* ♦ *vt*: **to** ~ **sth in** etw einlegen

sloth [sləuθ] *n* (*laziness*) Faulheit *f*

slot machine *n* (*BRIT*) Automat *m*; (*for gambling*) Spielautomat *m*

slouch [slautʃ] *vi*: **to** ~ **about** (*laze*) herumhängen (*inf*)

slovenly ['slʌvənlɪ] *adj* schlampig; (*speech*) salopp

slow [sləu] *adj* langsam ♦ *adv* langsam; **to be** ~ (*clock*) nachgehen; (*stupid*) begriffsstutzig sein; **"~"** (*road sign*) „Langsam"; **in** ~ **motion** in Zeitlupe; ~ **down** *vi* langsamer werden ♦ *vt* verlangsamen; ~ **up** *vi* sich verlangsamen, sich verzögern ♦ *vt* aufhalten, langsamer machen; **~ly** *adv* langsam

sludge [slʌdʒ] *n* Schlamm *m*

slug [slʌg] *n* Nacktschnecke *f*; (*inf: bullet*) Kugel *f*

sluggish ['slʌgɪʃ] *adj* träge; (*COMM*) schleppend

sluice [sluːs] *n* Schleuse *f*

slum [slʌm] *n* (*house*) Elendsquartier *nt*

slump [slʌmp] *n* Rückgang *m* ♦ *vi* fallen, stürzen

slung [slʌŋ] *pt, pp of* **sling**

slur [slɜːʳ] *n* Undeutlichkeit *f*; (*insult*) Verleumdung *f*; **~red** [slɜːd] *adj* (*pronunciation*) undeutlich

slush [slʌʃ] *n* (*snow*) Schneematsch *m*; ~ **fund** *n* Schmiergeldfonds *m*

slut [slʌt] *n* Schlampe *f*

sly [slaɪ] *adj* schlau

smack [smæk] *n* Klaps *m* ♦ *vt* einen Klaps geben +*dat* ♦ *vi*: **to** ~ **of** riechen nach; **to** ~ **one's lips** schmatzen, sich *dat* die Lippen lecken

small [smɔːl] *adj* klein; **in the** ~ **hours** in den

frühen Morgenstunden; ~ **ads** (*BRIT*) *npl* Kleinanzeigen *pl*; ~ **change** *n* Kleingeld *nt*; **~holder** (*BRIT*) *n* Kleinbauer *m*; **~pox** *n* Pocken *pl*; ~ **talk** *n* Geplauder *nt*

smart [smɑːt] *adj* (*fashionable*) elegant, schick; (*neat*) adrett; (*clever*) clever; (*quick*) scharf ♦ *vi* brennen, schmerzen; ~ **card** *n* Chipkarte *f*; **~en up** *vi* sich in Schale werfen ♦ *vt* herausputzen

smash [smæʃ] *n* Zusammenstoß *m*; (*TENNIS*) Schmetterball *m* ♦ *vt* (*break*) zerschmettern; (*destroy*) vernichten ♦ *vi* (*break*) zersplittern, zerspringen; **~ing** (*inf*) *adj* toll

smattering ['smætərɪŋ] *n* oberflächliche Kenntnis *f*

smear [smɪəʳ] *n* Fleck *m* ♦ *vt* beschmieren

smell [smɛl] (*pt, pp* **smelt** *or* **smelled**) *n* Geruch *m*; (*sense*) Geruchssinn *m* ♦ *vt* riechen ♦ *vi*: **to** ~ (**of**) riechen (nach); (*fragrantly*) duften (nach); **~y** *adj* übel riechend

smile [smaɪl] *n* Lächeln *nt* ♦ *vi* lächeln

smiling ['smaɪlɪŋ] *adj* lächelnd

smirk [smɜːk] *n* blöde(s) Grinsen *nt*

smock [smɔk] *n* Kittel *m*

smoke [sməuk] *n* Rauch *m* ♦ *vt* rauchen; (*food*) räuchern ♦ *vi* rauchen; **~d** *adj* (*bacon*) geräuchert; (*glass*) Rauch-; **~r** *n* Raucher(in) *m(f)*; (*RAIL*) Raucherabteil *nt*; ~ **screen** *n* Rauchwand *f*

smoking ['sməukɪŋ] *n*: **"no** ~" „Rauchen verboten"; ~ **compartment** (*BRIT*), ~ **car** (*US*) *n* Raucherabteil *nt*

smoky ['sməukɪ] *adj* rauchig; (*room*) verraucht; (*taste*) geräuchert

smolder ['sməuldəʳ] (*US*) *vi* = **smoulder**

smooth [smuːð] *adj* glatt ♦ *vt* (*also:* ~ **out**) glätten, glatt streichen

smother ['smʌðəʳ] *vt* ersticken

smoulder ['sməuldəʳ] (*US* **smolder**) *vi* schwelen

smudge [smʌdʒ] *n* Schmutzfleck *m* ♦ *vt* beschmieren

smug [smʌg] *adj* selbstgefällig

smuggle ['smʌgl] *vt* schmuggeln; **~r** *n* Schmuggler *m*

smuggling ['smʌglɪŋ] *n* Schmuggel *m*

smutty ['smʌtɪ] adj schmutzig

snack [snæk] n Imbiss m; **~ bar** n Imbissstube f

snag [snæg] n Haken m

snail [sneɪl] n Schnecke f

snake [sneɪk] n Schlange f

snap [snæp] n Schnappen nt; (photograph) Schnappschuss m ♦ adj (decision) schnell ♦ vt (break) zerbrechen; (PHOT) knipsen ♦ vi (break) brechen; (speak) anfauchen; **to ~ shut** zuschnappen; **~ at** vt fus schnappen nach; **~ off** vt (break) abbrechen **~ up** vt aufschnappen; **~shot** n Schnappschuss m

snare [snɛəʳ] n Schlinge f ♦ vt mit einer Schlinge fangen

snarl [snɑːl] n Zähnefletschen nt ♦ vi (dog) knurren

snatch [snætʃ] n (small amount) Bruchteil m ♦ vt schnappen, packen

sneak [sniːk] vi schleichen ♦ n (inf) Petze/f mf; **~ers** ['sniːkəz] (US) npl Freizeitschuhe pl; **~y** ['sniːkɪ] adj raffiniert

sneer [snɪəʳ] n Hohnlächeln nt ♦ vi spötteln

sneeze [sniːz] n Niesen nt ♦ vi niesen

sniff [snɪf] n Schnüffeln nt ♦ vi schnieben; (smell) schnüffeln ♦ vt schnuppern

snigger ['snɪgəʳ] n Kichern nt ♦ vi hämisch kichern

snip [snɪp] n Schnippel m, Schnipsel m ♦ vt schnippeln

sniper ['snaɪpəʳ] n Heckenschütze m

snippet ['snɪpɪt] n Schnipsel m; (of conversation) Fetzen m

snivelling ['snɪvlɪŋ] adj weinerlich

snob [snɒb] n Snob m

snooker ['snuːkəʳ] n Snooker nt

snoop [snuːp] vi: **to ~ about** herumschnüffeln

snooze [snuːz] n Nickerchen nt ♦ vi ein Nickerchen machen, dösen

snore [snɔːʳ] vi schnarchen ♦ n Schnarchen nt

snorkel ['snɔːkl] n Schnorchel m

snort [snɔːt] n Schnauben nt ♦ vi schnauben

snout [snaut] n Schnauze f

snow [snəu] n Schnee m ♦ vi schneien; **~ball** n Schneeball m ♦ vi eskalieren;

~bound adj eingeschneit; **~drift** n Schneewehe f; **~drop** n Schneeglöckchen nt; **~fall** n Schneefall m; **~flake** n Schneeflocke f; **~man** (irreg) n Schneemann m; **~plough** (US **snowplow**) n Schneepflug m; **~ shoe** n Schneeschuh m; **~storm** n Schneesturm m

snub [snʌb] vt schroff abfertigen ♦ n Verweis m; **~-nosed** adj stupsnasig

snuff [snʌf] n Schnupftabak m

snug [snʌg] adj gemütlich, behaglich

snuggle ['snʌgl] vi: **to ~ up to sb** sich an jdn kuscheln

KEYWORD

---

so [səu] adv **1** (thus) so; (likewise) auch; **so saying he walked away** indem er das sagte, ging er; **if so** wenn ja; **I didn't do it – you did so!** ich hab das nicht gemacht – hast du wohl!; **so do I, so am I** etc ich auch; **so it is!** tatsächlich!; **I hope/think so** hoffentlich/ich glaube schon; **so far** bis jetzt

2 (in comparisons etc: to such a degree) so; **so quickly/big (that)** so schnell/groß, dass; **I'm so glad to see you** ich freue mich so, dich zu sehen

3: **so many** so viele; **so much work** so viel Arbeit; **I love you so much** ich liebe dich so sehr

4 (phrases): **10 or so** etwa 10; **so long!** (inf: goodbye) tschüss!

♦ conj **1** (expressing purpose): **so as to** um ... zu; **so (that)** damit

2 (expressing result) also; **so I was right after all** ich hatte also doch Recht; **so you see ...** wie du siehst ...

---

soak [səuk] vt durchnässen; (leave in liquid) einweichen ♦ vi (ein)weichen; **~ in** vi einsickern; **~ up** vt aufsaugen; **~ed** adj völlig durchnässt; **~ing** adj klitschnass, patschnass

so-and-so ['səuənsəu] n (somebody) Soundso m

soap [səup] n Seife f; **~flakes** npl Seifenflocken pl; **~ opera** n Familienserie f *(im Fernsehen, Radio)*; **~ powder** n Waschpulver nt; **~y** adj seifig, Seifen-

soar [sɔːr] vi aufsteigen; *(prices)* in die Höhe schnellen

sob [sɔb] n Schluchzen nt ♦ vi schluchzen

sober ['səubər] adj *(also fig)* nüchtern; **~ up** vi nüchtern werden

so-called ['səu'kɔːld] adj so genannt

soccer ['sɔkər] n Fußball m

sociable ['səufəbl] adj gesellig

social ['səufəl] adj sozial; *(friendly, living with others)* gesellig ♦ n gesellige(r) Abend m; **~ club** n Verein m *(für Freizeitgestaltung)*; **~ism** n Sozialismus m; **~ist** n Sozialist(in) m(f) ♦ adj sozialistisch; **~ize** vi: **to ~ize (with)** gesellschaftlich verkehren (mit); **~ly** adv gesellschaftlich, privat; **~ security** n Sozialversicherung f; **~ work** n Sozialarbeit f; **~ worker** n Sozialarbeiter(in) m(f)

society [sə'saɪətɪ] n Gesellschaft f; *(fashionable world)* die große Welt

sociology [səusɪ'ɔlədʒɪ] n Soziologie f

sock [sɔk] n Socke f

socket ['sɔkɪt] n *(ELEC)* Steckdose f; *(of eye)* Augenhöhle f

sod [sɔd] n Rasenstück nt; *(inf!)* Saukerl m *(!)*

soda ['səudə] n Soda f; *(also: ~ water)* Soda(wasser) nt; *(US: also: ~ pop)* Limonade f

sodden ['sɔdn] adj durchweicht

sodium ['səudɪəm] n Natrium nt

sofa ['səufə] n Sofa nt

soft [sɔft] adj weich; *(not loud)* leise; *(weak)* nachgiebig; **~ drink** n alkoholfreie(s) Getränk nt; **~en** ['sɔfn] vt weich machen; *(blow)* abschwächen, mildern ♦ vi weich werden; **~ly** adv sanft; leise; **~ness** n Weichheit f; *(fig)* Sanftheit f

software ['sɔftwεər] n *(COMPUT)* Software f

soggy ['sɔgɪ] adj *(ground)* sumpfig; *(bread)* aufgeweicht

soil [sɔɪl] n Erde f ♦ vt beschmutzen

solace ['sɔlɪs] n Trost m

solar ['səulər] adj Sonnen-; **~ cell** n Solarzelle f; **~ energy** n Sonnenenergie f; **~ panel** n Sonnenkollektor m; **~ power** n Sonnenenergie f

sold [səuld] pt, pp of **sell**; **~ out** *(COMM)* ausverkauft

solder ['səuldər] vt löten

soldier ['səuldʒər] n Soldat m

sole [səul] n Sohle f; *(fish)* Seezunge f ♦ adj alleinig, Allein-; **~ly** adv ausschließlich

solemn ['sɔləm] adj feierlich

sole trader n *(COMM)* Einzelunternehmen nt

solicit [sə'lɪsɪt] vt *(request)* bitten um ♦ vi *(prostitute)* Kunden anwerben

solicitor [sə'lɪsɪtər] n Rechtsanwalt m/-anwältin f

solid ['sɔlɪd] adj *(hard)* fest; *(of same material, not hollow)* massiv; *(without break)* voll, ganz; *(reliable, sensible)* solide ♦ n Festkörper m; **~arity** [sɔlɪ'dærɪtɪ] n Solidarität f; **~ify** [sə'lɪdɪfaɪ] vi fest werden

solitary ['sɔlɪtərɪ] adj einsam, einzeln; **~ confinement** n Einzelhaft f

solitude ['sɔlɪtjuːd] n Einsamkeit f

solo ['səuləu] n Solo nt; **~ist** ['səuləuɪst] n Solist(in) m(f)

soluble ['sɔljubl] adj *(substance)* löslich; *(problem)* (auf)lösbar

solution [sə'luːfən] n *(also fig)* Lösung f; *(of mystery)* Erklärung f

solve [sɔlv] vt (auf)lösen

solvent ['sɔlvənt] adj *(FIN)* zahlungsfähig ♦ n *(CHEM)* Lösungsmittel nt

sombre ['sɔmbər] *(US* **somber***)* adj düster

┌─────────────────┐
│ KEYWORD │
└─────────────────┘

some [sʌm] adj **1** *(a certain amount or number of)* einige; *(a few)* ein paar; *(with singular nouns)* etwas; **some tea/biscuits** etwas Tee/ein paar Plätzchen; **I've got some money, but not much** ich habe ein bisschen Geld, aber nicht viel

2 *(certain: in contrasts)* manche(r, s); **some people say that ...** manche Leute sagen, dass ...

3 *(unspecified)* irgendein(e); **some woman was asking for you** da hat eine Frau nach Ihnen gefragt; **some day** eines Tages; **some day next week** irgendwann nächste Woche

◆ *pron* **1** (*a certain number*) einige; **have you got some?** haben Sie welche? **2** (*a certain amount*) etwas; **I've read some of the book** ich habe das Buch teilweise gelesen
◆ *adv*: **some 10 people** etwa 10 Leute

somebody ['sʌmbədɪ] *pron* = **someone**
somehow ['sʌmhaʊ] *adv* (*in some way, for some reason*) irgendwie
someone ['sʌmwʌn] *pron* jemand; (*direct obj*) jemand(en); (*indirect obj*) jemandem
someplace ['sʌmpleɪs] (*US*) *adv* = **somewhere**
somersault ['sʌməsɔ:lt] *n* Salto *m* ◆ *vi* einen Salto machen
something ['sʌmθɪŋ] *pron* etwas
sometime ['sʌmtaɪm] *adv* (irgend)einmal
sometimes ['sʌmtaɪmz] *adv* manchmal
somewhat ['sʌmwɔt] *adv* etwas
somewhere ['sʌmweəʳ] *adv* irgendwo; (*to a place*) irgendwohin; **~ else** irgendwo anders
son [sʌn] *n* Sohn *m*
sonar ['səʊnɑːʳ] *n* Echolot *nt*
song [sɒŋ] *n* Lied *nt*
sonic boom ['sɒnɪk-] *n* Überschallknall *m*
son-in-law ['sʌnɪnlɔ:] *n* Schwiegersohn *m*
soon [su:n] *adv* bald; **~ afterwards** kurz danach; **~er** *adv* (*time*) früher; (*for preference*) lieber; **~er or later** früher oder später
soot [sʊt] *n* Ruß *m*
soothe [su:ð] *vt* (*person*) beruhigen; (*pain*) lindern
sophisticated [sə'fɪstɪkeɪtɪd] *adj* (*person*) kultiviert; (*machinery*) hoch entwickelt
sophomore ['sɒfəmɔːʳ] (*US*) *n* College-student *m* im 2. Jahr
soporific [sɒpə'rɪfɪk] *adj* einschläfernd
sopping ['sɒpɪŋ] *adj* patschnass
soppy ['sɒpɪ] (*inf*) *adj* schmalzig
soprano [sə'prɑːnəʊ] *n* Sopran *m*
sorcerer ['sɔːsərəʳ] *n* Hexenmeister *m*
sordid ['sɔːdɪd] *adj* erbärmlich
sore [sɔːʳ] *adj* schmerzend; (*point*) wund ◆ *n* Wunde *f*; **~ly** *adv* (*tempted*) stark, sehr

sorrow ['sɒrəʊ] *n* Kummer *m*, Leid *nt*; **~ful** *adj* sorgenvoll
sorry ['sɒrɪ] *adj* traurig, erbärmlich; **~!** Entschuldigung!; **to feel ~ for sb** jdn bemitleiden; **I feel ~ for him** er tut mir Leid; **~?** (*pardon*) wie bitte?
sort [sɔːt] *n* Art *f*, Sorte *f* ◆ *vt* (*also*: **~ out**: *papers*) sortieren; (: *problems*) sichten, in Ordnung bringen; **~ing office** *n* Sortierstelle *f*
SOS *n* SOS *nt*
so-so ['səʊsəʊ] *adv* so(so) lala
sought [sɔːt] *pt, pp of* **seek**
soul [səʊl] *n* Seele *f*; (*music*) Soul *m*; **~-destroying** *adj* trostlos; **~ful** *adj* seelenvoll
sound [saʊnd] *adj* (*healthy*) gesund; (*safe*) sicher; (*sensible*) vernünftig; (*theory*) stichhaltig; (*thorough*) tüchtig, gehörig
◆ *adv*: **to be ~ asleep** fest schlafen ◆ *n* (*noise*) Geräusch *nt*, Laut *m*; (*GEOG*) Sund *m*
◆ *vt* erschallen lassen; (*alarm*) (Alarm) schlagen ◆ *vi* (*make a ~*) schallen, tönen; (*seem*) klingen; **to ~ like** sich anhören wie; **~ out** *vt* erforschen; (*person*) auf den Zahn fühlen +*dat*; **~ barrier** *n* Schallmauer *f*; **~ bite** *n* (*RAD, TV*) prägnante(s) Zitat *nt*; **~ effects** *npl* Toneffekte *pl*; **~ly** *adv* (*sleep*) fest; (*beat*) tüchtig; **~proof** *adj* (*room*) schalldicht; **~ track** *n* Tonstreifen *m*; (*music*) Filmmusik *f*
soup [su:p] *n* Suppe *f*; **~ plate** *n* Suppenteller *m*; **~spoon** *n* Suppenlöffel *m*
sour ['saʊəʳ] *adj* (*also fig*) sauer; **it's ~ grapes** (*fig*) die Trauben hängen zu hoch
source [sɔːs] *n* (*also fig*) Quelle *f*
south [saʊθ] *n* Süden *m* ◆ *adj* Süd-, südlich ◆ *adv* nach Süden, südwärts; **S~ Africa** *n* Südafrika *nt*; **S~ African** *adj* südafrikanisch ◆ *n* Südafrikaner(in) *m(f)*; **S~ America** *n* Südamerika *nt*; **S~ American** *adj* südamerikanisch ◆ *n* Südamerikaner(in) *m(f)*; **~-east** *n* Südosten *m*; **~erly** ['sʌðəlɪ] *adj* südlich; **~ern** ['sʌðən] *adj* südlich, Süd-; **S~ Pole** *n* Südpol *m*; **S~ Wales** *n* Südwales *nt*; **~ward(s)** *adv* südwärts, nach Süden; **~-west** *n* Südwesten *m*
souvenir [su:və'nɪəʳ] *n* Souvenir *nt*

sovereign ['sɔvrɪn] *n* (*ruler*) Herrscher(in) *m(f)* ♦ *adj* (*independent*) souverän

soviet ['sauvɪət] *adj* sowjetisch; **the S~ Union** die Sowjetunion

sow[1] [sau] *n* Sau *f*

sow[2] [səu] (*pt* **sowed**, *pp* **sown**) *vt* (*also fig*) säen

soya ['sɔɪə] (*US* **soy**) *n*: **~ bean** Sojabohne *f*; **~ sauce** Sojasauce *f*

spa [spɑ:] *n* (*place*) Kurort *m*

space [speɪs] *n* Platz *m*, Raum *m*; (*universe*) Weltraum *m*, All *nt*; (*length of time*) Abstand *m* ♦ *vt* (*also*: ~ **out**) verteilen; **~craft** *n* Raumschiff *nt*; **~man** (*irreg*) *n* Raumfahrer *m*; **~ ship** *n* Raumschiff *nt*

spacing ['speɪsɪŋ] *n* Abstand *m*; (*also*: ~ **out**) Verteilung *f*

spacious ['speɪʃəs] *adj* geräumig, weit

spade [speɪd] *n* Spaten *m*; **~s** *npl* (*CARDS*) Pik *nt*

Spain [speɪn] *n* Spanien *nt*

span [spæn] *n* Spanne *f*; (*of bridge etc*) Spannweite *f* ♦ *vt* überspannen

Spaniard ['spænjəd] *n* Spanier(in) *m(f)*

spaniel ['spænjəl] *n* Spaniel *m*

Spanish ['spænɪʃ] *adj* spanisch ♦ *n* (*LING*) Spanisch *nt*; **the ~** *npl* (*people*) die Spanier *pl*

spank [spæŋk] *vt* verhauen, versohlen

spanner ['spænə*] (*BRIT*) *n* Schraubenschlüssel *m*

spar [spɑ:*] *n* (*NAUT*) Sparren *m* ♦ *vi* (*BOXING*) einen Sparring machen

spare [speə*] *adj* Ersatz- ♦ *n* = **spare part** ♦ *vt* (*lives, feelings*) verschonen; (*trouble*) ersparen; **to ~** (*surplus*) übrig; **~ part** *n* Ersatzteil *nt*; **~ time** *n* Freizeit *f*; **~ wheel** *n* (*AUT*) Reservereifen *m*

sparing ['speərɪŋ] *adj*: **to be ~ with** geizen mit; **~ly** *adv* sparsam; (*eat, spend etc*) in Maßen

spark [spɑ:k] *n* Funken *m*; **~(ing) plug** *n* Zündkerze *f*

sparkle ['spɑ:kl] *n* Funkeln *nt*; (*gaiety*) Schwung *m* ♦ *vi* funkeln; **sparkling** *adj* funkelnd; (*wine*) Schaum-; (*mineral water*) mit Kohlensäure; (*conversation*) spritzig,

geistreich

sparrow ['spærəu] *n* Spatz *m*

sparse [spɑ:s] *adj* spärlich

spasm ['spæzəm] *n* (*MED*) Krampf *m*; (*fig*) Anfall *m*; **~odic** [spæz'mɔdɪk] *adj* (*fig*) sprunghaft

spastic ['spæstɪk] (*old*) *n* Spastiker(in) *m(f)* ♦ *adj* spastisch

spat [spæt] *pt, pp of* **spit**

spate [speɪt] *n* (*fig*) Flut *f*, Schwall *m*; **in ~** (*river*) angeschwollen

spatter ['spætə*] *vt* bespritzen, verspritzen

spatula ['spætjulə] *n* Spatel *m*

spawn [spɔ:n] *vi* laichen ♦ *n* Laich *m*

speak [spi:k] (*pt* **spoke**, *pp* **spoken**) *vt* sprechen, reden; (*truth*) sagen; (*language*) sprechen ♦ *vi*: **to ~ (to)** sprechen (mit *or* zu); **to ~ to sb of** *or* **about sth** mit jdm über etw *acc* sprechen; **~ up!** sprich lauter!; **~er** *n* Sprecher(in) *m(f)*, Redner(in) *m(f)*; (*loudspeaker*) Lautsprecher *m*; (*POL*): **the S~er** der Vorsitzende des Parlaments (*BRIT*) *or* des Kongresses (*US*)

spear [spɪə*] *n* Speer *m* ♦ *vt* aufspießen; **~head** *vt* (*attack etc*) anführen

spec [spek] (*inf*) *n*: **on ~** auf gut Glück

special ['speʃl] *adj* besondere(r, s); **~ist** *n* (*TECH*) Fachmann *m*; (*MED*) Facharzt *m*/ Fachärztin *f*; **~ity** [speʃɪ'ælɪtɪ] *n* Spezialität *f*; (*study*) Spezialgebiet *nt*; **~ize** *vi*: **to ~ize (in)** sich spezialisieren (auf +*acc*); **~ly** *adv* besonders; (*explicitly*) extra; **~ needs** *adj*: **~ needs children** behinderte Kinder *pl*; **~ty** (*esp US*) *n* = **speciality**

species ['spi:ʃi:z] *n* Art *f*

specific [spə'sɪfɪk] *adj* spezifisch; **~ally** *adv* spezifisch

specification [spesɪfɪ'keɪʃən] *n* Angabe *f*; (*stipulation*) Bedingung *f*; **~s** *npl* (*TECH*) technische Daten *pl*

specify ['spesɪfaɪ] *vt* genau angeben

specimen ['spesɪmən] *n* Probe *f*

speck [spek] *n* Fleckchen *nt*

speckled ['spekld] *adj* gesprenkelt

specs [speks] (*inf*) *npl* Brille *f*

spectacle ['spektəkl] *n* Schauspiel *nt*; **~s** *npl* (*glasses*) Brille *f*

spectacular [spek'tækjʊlə'] *adj* sensationell; (*success etc*) spektakulär

spectator [spek'teɪtə'] *n* Zuschauer(in) *m(f)*

spectre ['spektə'] (*US* **specter**) *n* Geist *m*, Gespenst *nt*

speculate ['spekjʊleɪt] *vi* spekulieren

speech [spiːtʃ] *n* Sprache *f*; (*address*) Rede *f*; (*way one speaks*) Sprechweise *f*; **~less** *adj* sprachlos

speed [spiːd] *n* Geschwindigkeit *f*; (*gear*) Gang *m* ♦ *vi* (*JUR*) (zu) schnell fahren; **at full** *or* **top ~** mit Höchstgeschwindigkeit; **~ up** *vt* beschleunigen ♦ *vi* schneller werden; schneller fahren; **~boat** *n* Schnellboot *nt*; **~ily** *adv* schleunigst; **~ing** *n* Geschwindigkeitsüberschreitung *f*; **~ limit** *n* Geschwindigkeitsbegrenzung *f*; **~ometer** [spɪ'dɔmɪtə'] *n* Tachometer *m*; **~way** *n* (*bike racing*) Motorradrennstrecke *f*; **~y** *adj* schnell

spell [spel] (*pt, pp* **spelt** (*BRIT*) *or* **spelled**) *n* (*magic*) Bann *m*; (*period of time*) (eine) Zeit lang ♦ *vt* buchstabieren; (*imply*) bedeuten; **to cast a ~ on sb** jdn verzaubern; **~bound** *adj* (wie) gebannt; **~ing** *n* Rechtschreibung *f*

spelt [spelt] (*BRIT*) *pt, pp of* **spell**

spend [spend] (*pt, pp* **spend**) *vt* (*money*) ausgeben; (*time*) verbringen; **~thrift** *n* Verschwender(in) *m(f)*

spent [spent] *pt, pp of* **spend**

sperm [spəːm] *n* (*BIOL*) Samenflüssigkeit *f*

spew [spjuː] *vt* (er)brechen

sphere [sfɪə'] *n* (*globe*) Kugel *f*; (*fig*) Sphäre *f*, Gebiet *nt*; **spherical** ['sferɪkl] *adj* kugelförmig

spice [spaɪs] *n* Gewürz *nt* ♦ *vt* würzen

spick-and-span ['spɪkən'spæn] *adj* blitzblank

spicy ['spaɪsɪ] *adj* (*food*) stark gewürzt; (*fig*) pikant

spider ['spaɪdə'] *n* Spinne *f*

spike [spaɪk] *n* Dorn *m*, Spitze *f*

spill [spɪl] (*pt, pp* **spilt** *or* **spilled**) *vt* verschütten ♦ *vi* sich ergießen; **~ over** *vi* überlaufen; (*fig*) sich ausbreiten

spilt [spɪlt] *pt, pp of* **spill**

spin [spɪn] (*pt, pp* **spun**) *n* (*trip in car*) Spazierfahrt *f*; (*AVIAT*) (Ab)trudeln *nt*; (*on ball*) Drall *m* ♦ *vt* (*thread*) spinnen; (*like top*) (herum)wirbeln ♦ *vi* sich drehen; **~ out** *vt* in die Länge ziehen

spinach ['spɪnɪtʃ] *n* Spinat *m*

spinal ['spaɪnl] *adj* Rückgrat-; **~ cord** *n* Rückenmark *nt*

spindly ['spɪndlɪ] *adj* spindeldürr

spin doctor *n* PR-Fachmann *m*, PR-Fachfrau *f*

spin-dryer [spɪn'draɪə'] (*BRIT*) *n* Wäscheschleuder *f*

spine [spaɪn] *n* Rückgrat *nt*; (*thorn*) Stachel *m*; **~less** *adj* (*also fig*) rückgratlos

spinning ['spɪnɪŋ] *n* Spinnen *nt*; **~ top** *n* Kreisel *m*; **~ wheel** *n* Spinnrad *nt*

spin-off ['spɪnɔf] *n* Nebenprodukt *nt*

spinster ['spɪnstə'] *n* unverheiratete Frau *f*; (*pej*) alte Jungfer *f*

spiral ['spaɪərl] *n* Spirale *f* ♦ *adj* spiralförmig; (*movement etc*) in Spiralen ♦ *vi* sich (hoch)winden; **~ staircase** *n* Wendeltreppe *f*

spire ['spaɪə'] *n* Turm *m*

spirit ['spɪrɪt] *n* Geist *m*; (*humour, mood*) Stimmung *f*; (*courage*) Mut *m*; (*verve*) Elan *m*; (*alcohol*) Alkohol *m*; **~s** *npl* (*drink*) Spirituosen *pl*; **in good ~s** gut aufgelegt; **~ed** *adj* beherzt; **~ level** *n* Wasserwaage *f*

spiritual ['spɪrɪtjʊəl] *adj* geistig, seelisch; (*REL*) geistlich ♦ *n* Spiritual *nt*

spit [spɪt] (*pt, pp* **spat**) *n* (*for roasting*) (Brat)spieß *m*; (*saliva*) Spucke *f* ♦ *vi* spucken; (*rain*) sprühen; (*make a sound*) zischen; (*cat*) fauchen

spite [spaɪt] *n* Gehässigkeit *f* ♦ *vt* kränken; **in ~ of** trotz; **~ful** *adj* gehässig

spittle ['spɪtl] *n* Speichel *m*, Spucke *f*

splash [splæʃ] *n* Spritzer *m*; (*of colour*) (Farb)fleck *m* ♦ *vt* bespritzen ♦ *vi* spritzen

spleen [spliːn] *n* (*ANAT*) Milz *f*

splendid ['splendɪd] *adj* glänzend

splendour ['splendə'] (*US* **splendor**) *n* Pracht *f*

splint [splɪnt] *n* Schiene *f*

splinter ['splɪntə'] *n* Splitter *m* ♦ *vi* (zer)splittern

split [splɪt] (*pt, pp* **split**) *n* Spalte *f*; (*fig*)
Spaltung *f*; (*division*) Trennung *f* ♦ *vt*
spalten *vi* ♦ *vi* (*divide*) reißen *vi*; ~ **up** *vi* sich
trennen

splutter ['splʌtəʳ] *vi* stottern

spoil [spɔɪl] (*pt, pp* **spoilt** *or* **spoiled**) *vt* (*ruin*)
verderben; (*child*) verwöhnen; ~**s** *npl* Beute
f; ~**sport** *n* Spielverderber *m*; ~**t** *pt, pp of*
spoil

spoke [spəuk] *pt of* **speak** ♦ *n* Speiche *f*; ~**n**
pp of **speak**

spokesman ['spəuksmən] (*irreg*) *n* Sprecher
m; **spokeswoman** ['spəukswumən] (*irreg*) *n*
Sprecherin *f*

sponge [spʌndʒ] *n* Schwamm *m* ♦ *vt*
abwaschen ♦ *vi*: **to ~ on** auf Kosten +*gen*
leben; ~ **bag** (*BRIT*) *n* Kulturbeutel *m*; ~
cake *n* Rührkuchen *m*

sponsor ['spɔnsəʳ] *n* Sponsor *m* ♦ *vt* fördern;
~**ship** *n* Finanzierung *f*; (*public*)
Schirmherrschaft *f*

spontaneous [spɔn'teɪnɪəs] *adj* spontan

spooky ['spu:kɪ] (*inf*) *adj* gespenstisch

spool [spu:l] *n* Spule *f*, Rolle *f*

spoon [spu:n] *n* Löffel *m*; ~**-feed** (*irreg*) *vt*
mit dem Löffel füttern; (*fig*) hochpäppeln;
~**ful** *n* Löffel *m* (voll)

sport [spɔ:t] *n* Sport *m*; (*person*) feine(r) Kerl
m; ~**ing** *adj* (*fair*) sportlich, fair; **to give sb
a ~ing chance** jdm eine faire Chance
geben; ~ **jacket** (*US*) *n* = **sports jacket**; ~**s
car** *n* Sportwagen *m*; ~**s jacket** *n*
Sportjackett *nt*; ~**sman** (*irreg*) *n* Sportler *m*;
~**smanship** *n* Sportlichkeit *f*; ~**swear** *n*
Sportkleidung *f*; ~**swoman** (*irreg*) *n*
Sportlerin *f*; ~**y** *adj* sportlich

spot [spɔt] *n* Punkt *m*; (*dirty*) Fleck(en) *m*;
(*place*) Stelle *f*; (*MED*) Pickel *m* ♦ *vt*
erspähen; (*mistake*) bemerken; **on the ~** an
Ort und Stelle; (*at once*) auf der Stelle; ~
check *n* Stichprobe *f*; ~**less** *adj* fleckenlos;
~**light** *n* Scheinwerferlicht *nt*; (*lamp*)
Scheinwerfer *m*; ~**ted** *adj* gefleckt; ~**ty** *adj*
(*face*) pickelig

spouse [spaus] *n* Gatte *m*/Gattin *f*

spout [spaut] *n* (*of pot*) Tülle *f*; (*jet*)
Wasserstrahl *m* ♦ *vi* speien

sprain [spreɪn] *n* Verrenkung *f* ♦ *vt*
verrenken

sprang [spræŋ] *pt of* **spring**

sprawl [sprɔ:l] *vi* sich strecken

spray [spreɪ] *n* Spray *nt*; (*off sea*) Gischt *f*; (*of
flowers*) Zweig *m* ♦ *vt* besprühen, sprayen

spread [spred] (*pt, pp* **spread**) *n* (*extent*)
Verbreitung *f*; (*inf: meal*) Schmaus *m*; (*for
bread*) Aufstrich *m* ♦ *vt* ausbreiten; (*scatter*)
verbreiten; (*butter*) streichen ♦ *vi* sich
ausbreiten; ~ **out** *vi* (*move apart*) sich
verteilen; ~**-eagled** ['spredi:gld] *adj*: **to be
~-eagled** alle viere von sich strecken;
~**sheet** *n* Tabellenkalkulation *f*

spree [spri:] *n* (*shopping*) Einkaufsbummel
m; **to go on a ~** einen draufmachen

sprightly ['spraɪtlɪ] *adj* munter, lebhaft

spring [sprɪŋ] (*pt* **sprang**, *pp* **sprung**) *n*
(*leap*) Sprung *m*; (*TECH*) Feder *f*; (*season*)
Frühling *m*; (*water*) Quelle *f* ♦ *vi* (*leap*)
springen; ~ **up** *vi* (*problem*) auftauchen;
~**board** *n* Sprungbrett *nt*; ~**-clean** *n* (*also:
~-cleaning*) Frühjahrsputz *m*; ~**time** *n*
Frühling *m*; ~**y** *adj* federnd, elastisch

sprinkle ['sprɪŋkl] *vt* (*salt*) streuen; (*liquid*)
sprenkeln; **to ~ water on, to ~ with water**
mit Wasser besprengen; ~**r** ['sprɪŋkləʳ] *n* (*for
lawn*) Sprenger *m*; (*for fire fighting*) Sprinkler
m

sprint [sprɪnt] *n* (*race*) Sprint *m* ♦ *vi* (*run fast*)
rennen; (*SPORT*) sprinten; ~**er** *n* Sprinter(in)
m(f)

sprout [spraut] *vi* sprießen

sprouts [sprauts] *npl* (*also:* **Brussels ~**)
Rosenkohl *m*

spruce [spru:s] *n* Fichte *f* ♦ *adj* schmuck,
adrett

sprung [sprʌŋ] *pp of* **spring**

spry [spraɪ] *adj* flink, rege

spun [spʌn] *pt, pp of* **spin**

spur [spə:ʳ] *n* Sporn *m*; (*fig*) Ansporn *m* ♦ *vt*
(*also:* ~ **on:** *fig*) ansporenen; **on the ~ of the
moment** spontan

spurious ['spjuərɪəs] *adj* falsch

spurn [spə:n] *vt* verschmähen

spurt [spə:t] *n* (*jet*) Strahl *m*; (*acceleration*)
Spurt *m* ♦ *vi* (*liquid*) schießen

spy [spaɪ] n Spion(in) m(f) ♦ vi spionieren ♦ vt erspähen; **~ing** n Spionage f

sq. abbr = **square**

squabble ['skwɒbl] n Zank m ♦ vi sich zanken

squad [skwɒd] n (MIL) Abteilung f; (POLICE) Kommando nt

squadron ['skwɒdrn] n (cavalry) Schwadron f; (NAUT) Geschwader nt; (air force) Staffel f

squalid ['skwɒlɪd] adj verkommen

squall [skwɔ:l] n Bö(e) f, Windstoß m

squalor ['skwɒlər] n Verwahrlosung f

squander ['skwɒndər] vt verschwenden

square [skweər] n Quadrat nt; (open space) Platz m; (instrument) Winkel m; (inf: person) Spießer m ♦ adj viereckig; (inf: ideas, tastes) spießig ♦ vt (arrange) ausmachen; (MATH) ins Quadrat erheben ♦ vi (agree) übereinstimmen; **all ~** quitt; **á ~ meal** eine ordentliche Mahlzeit; **2 metres ~** 2 Meter im Quadrat; **1 ~ metre** 1 Quadratmeter; **~ly** adv fest, gerade

squash [skwɒʃ] n (BRIT: drink) Saft m; (game) Squash nt ♦ vt zerquetschen

squat [skwɒt] adj untersetzt ♦ vi hocken; **~ter** n Hausbesetzer m

squawk [skwɔ:k] vi kreischen

squeak [skwi:k] vi quiek(s)en; (spring, door etc) quietschen

squeal [skwi:l] vi schrill schreien

squeamish ['skwi:mɪʃ] adj empfindlich

squeeze [skwi:z] vt pressen, drücken; (orange) auspressen; **~ out** vt ausquetschen

squelch [skweltʃ] vi platschen

squib [skwɪb] n Knallfrosch m

squid [skwɪd] n Tintenfisch m

squiggle ['skwɪgl] n Schnörkel m

squint [skwɪnt] vi schielen ♦ n: **to have a ~** schielen; **to ~ at sb/sth** nach jdm/etw schielen

squirm [skwə:m] vi sich winden

squirrel ['skwɪrəl] n Eichhörnchen nt

squirt [skwə:t] vt, vi spritzen

Sr abbr (= senior) sen.

St abbr (= saint) hl., St.; (= street) Str.

stab [stæb] n (blow) Stich m; (inf: try) Versuch m ♦ vt erstechen

stabilize ['steɪbəlaɪz] vt stabilisieren ♦ vi sich stabilisieren

stable ['steɪbl] adj stabil ♦ n Stall m

stack [stæk] n Stapel m ♦ vt stapeln

stadium ['steɪdɪəm] n Stadion nt

staff [stɑ:f] n (stick, MIL) Stab m; (personnel) Personal nt; (BRIT: SCH) Lehrkräfte pl ♦ vt besetzen

stag [stæg] n Hirsch m

stage [steɪdʒ] n Bühne f; (of journey) Etappe f; (degree) Stufe f; (point) Stadium nt ♦ vt (put on) aufführen; (simulate) inszenieren; (demonstration) veranstalten; **in ~s** etappenweise; **~coach** n Postkutsche f; **~ door** n Bühneneingang m; **~ manager** n Intendant m

stagger ['stægər] vi wanken, taumeln ♦ vt (amaze) verblüffen; (hours) staffeln; **~ing** adj unglaublich

stagnant ['stægnənt] adj stagnierend; (water) stehend; **stagnate** [stæg'neɪt] vi stagnieren

stag party n Männerabend m (vom Bräutigam vor der Hochzeit gegeben)

staid [steɪd] adj gesetzt

stain [steɪn] n Fleck m ♦ vt beflecken; **~ed glass window** buntes Glasfenster nt; **~less** adj (steel) rostfrei; **~ remover** n Fleckentferner m

stair [steər] n (Treppen)stufe f; **~s** npl (flight of steps) Treppe f; **~case** n Treppenhaus nt, Treppe f; **~way** n Treppenaufgang m

stake [steɪk] n (post) Pfahl m; (money) Einsatz m ♦ vt (bet: money) setzen; **to be at ~** auf dem Spiel stehen

stale [steɪl] adj alt; (bread) altbacken

stalemate ['steɪlmeɪt] n (CHESS) Patt nt; (fig) Stillstand m

stalk [stɔ:k] n Stängel m, Stiel m ♦ vt (game) jagen; **~ off** vi abstolzieren

stall [stɔ:l] n (in stable) Stand m, Box f; (in market) (Verkaufs)stand m ♦ vt (AUT) abwürgen ♦ vi (AUT) stehen bleiben; (fig) Ausflüchte machen; **~s** npl (BRIT: THEAT) Parkett nt

stallion ['stæljən] n Zuchthengst m

stalwart ['stɔːlwət] *n* treue(r) Anhänger *m*

stamina ['stæminə] *n* Durchhaltevermögen *nt*, Zähigkeit *f*

stammer ['stæmə'] *n* Stottern *nt ♦ vt, vi* stottern, stammeln

stamp [stæmp] *n* Briefmarke *f*; (*for document*) Stempel *m ♦ vi* stampfen *♦ vt* (*mark*) stempeln; (*mail*) frankieren; (*foot*) stampfen mit; ~ **album** *n* Briefmarkenalbum *nt*; ~ **collecting** *n* Briefmarkensammeln *nt*

stampede [stæm'piːd] *n* panische Flucht *f*

stance [stæns] *n* Haltung *f*

stand [stænd] (*pt, pp* **stood**) *n* (*for objects*) Gestell *nt*; (*seats*) Tribüne *f ♦ vi* stehen; (*rise*) aufstehen; (*decision*) feststehen *♦ vt* setzen, stellen; (*endure*) aushalten; (*person*) ausstehen; (*nonsense*) dulden; **to make a ~** Widerstand leisten; **to ~ for parliament** (*BRIT*) für das Parlament kandidieren; ~ **by** *vi* (*be ready*) bereitstehen *♦ vt fus* (*opinion*) treu bleiben +*dat*; ~ **down** *vi* (*withdraw*) zurücktreten; ~ **for** *vt fus* (*signify*) stehen für; (*permit, tolerate*) hinnehmen; ~ **in for** *vt fus* einspringen für; ~ **out** *vi* (*be prominent*) hervorstechen; ~ **up** *vi* (*rise*) aufstehen; ~ **up for** *vt fus* sich einsetzen für; ~ **up to** *vt fus*: **to ~ up to sth** einer Sache *dat* gewachsen sein; **to ~ up to sb** sich jdm gegenüber behaupten

standard ['stændəd] *n* (*measure*) Norm *f*; (*flag*) Fahne *f ♦ adj* (*size etc*) Normal-; ~**s** *npl* (*morals*) Maßstäbe *pl*; ~**ize** *vt* vereinheitlichen; ~ **lamp** (*BRIT*) *n* Stehlampe *f*; ~ **of living** *n* Lebensstandard *m*

stand: ~**-by** *n* Reserve *f*; **to be on ~-by** in Bereitschaft sein; ~**-by ticket** *n* (*AVIAT*) Standbyticket *nt*; ~**-in** [stændin] *n* Ersatz *m*

standing ['stændin] *adj* (*erect*) stehend; (*permanent*) ständig; (*invitation*) offen *♦ n* (*duration*) Dauer *f*; (*reputation*) Ansehen *nt*; **of many years'** ~ langjährig; ~ **order** (*BRIT*) *n* (*at bank*) Dauerauftrag *m*; ~ **room** *n* Stehplatz *m*

stand: ~**-offish** [stænd'ɔfiʃ] *adj* zurückhaltend, sehr reserviert; ~**point** ['stændpɔint] *n* Standpunkt *m*; ~**still**

['stændstil] *n*: **to be at a ~still** stillstehen; **to come to a ~still** zum Stillstand kommen

stank [stæŋk] *pt of* **stink**

staple ['steipl] *n* (*in paper*) Heftklammer *f*; (*article*) Haupterzeugnis *nt ♦ adj* Grund-, Haupt- *♦ vt* (*fest*)klammern; ~**r** *n* Heftmaschine *f*

star [stɑː'] *n* Stern *m*; (*person*) Star *m ♦ vi* die Hauptrolle spielen *♦ vt*: ~**ring ...** in der Hauptrolle/den Hauptrollen ...

starboard ['stɑːbəːd] *n* Steuerbord *nt*

starch [stɑːtʃ] *n* Stärke *f*

stardom ['stɑːdəm] *n* Berühmtheit *f*

stare [steə'] *n* starre(r) Blick *m ♦ vi*: **to ~ at** starren auf +*acc*, anstarren

starfish ['stɑːfiʃ] *n* Seestern *m*

stark [stɑːk] *adj* öde *♦ adv*: ~ **naked** splitternackt

starling ['stɑːliŋ] *n* Star *m*

starry ['stɑːri] *adj* Sternen-; ~**-eyed** *adj* (*innocent*) blauäugig

start [stɑːt] *n* Anfang *m*; (*SPORT*) Start *m*; (*lead*) Vorsprung *m ♦ vt* in Gang setzen; (*car*) anlassen *♦ vi* anfangen; (*car*) anspringen; (*on journey*) aufbrechen; (*SPORT*) starten; (*with fright*) zusammenfahren; **to ~ doing** *or* **to do sth** anfangen, etw zu tun; ~ **off** *vi* anfangen; (*begin moving*) losgehen; losfahren; ~ **up** *vi* anfangen *♦ vt* beginnen; (*car*) anlassen; (*engine*) starten; ~**er** *n* (*AUT*) Anlasser *m*; (*for race*) Starter *m*; (*BRIT: COOK*) Vorspeise *f*; ~**ing point** *n* Ausgangspunkt *m*

startle ['stɑːtl] *vt* erschrecken; **startling** *adj* erschreckend

starvation [stɑː'veiʃən] *n* Verhungern *nt*

starve [stɑːv] *vi* verhungern *♦ vt* verhungern lassen; **I'm starving** ich sterbe vor Hunger

state [steit] *n* (*condition*) Zustand *m*; (*POL*) Staat *m ♦ vt* erklären; (*facts*) angeben; **the S~s** (*USA*) die Staaten; **to be in a ~** durchdrehen; ~**ly** *adj* würdevoll; ~**ly home** *n* herrschaftliches Anwesen *nt*, Schloss *nt*; ~**ment** *n* Aussage *f*; (*POL*) Erklärung *f*; ~**sman** (*irreg*) *n* Staatsmann *m*

static ['stætik] *n* (*also*: ~ **electricity**) Reibungselektrizität *f*

station ['steɪʃən] n (RAIL etc) Bahnhof m; (police etc) Wache f; (in society) Stand m ♦ vt stationieren

stationary ['steɪʃnərɪ] adj stillstehend; (car) parkend

stationer's n (shop) Schreibwarengeschäft nt; **~y** n Schreibwaren pl

station master n Bahnhofsvorsteher m

station wagon n Kombiwagen m

statistics [stə'tɪstɪks] n Statistik f

statue ['stætjuː] n Statue f

stature ['stætʃəʳ] n Größe f

status ['steɪtəs] n Status m

statute ['stætjuːt] n Gesetz nt; **statutory** ['stætjutrɪ] adj gesetzlich

staunch [stɔːntʃ] adj standhaft

stay [steɪ] n Aufenthalt m ♦ vi bleiben; (reside) wohnen; **to ~ put** an Ort und Stelle bleiben; **to ~ the night** übernachten; **~ behind** vi zurückbleiben; **~ in** vi (at home) zu Hause bleiben; **~ on** vi (continue) länger bleiben; **~ out** vi (of house) wegbleiben; **~ up** vi (at night) aufbleiben; **~ing power** n Durchhaltevermögen nt

stead [sted] n: **in sb's ~** an jds Stelle dat; **to stand sb in good ~** jdm zugute kommen

steadfast ['stedfɑːst] adj standhaft, treu

steadily ['stedɪlɪ] adv stetig, regelmäßig

steady ['stedɪ] adj (firm) fest, stabil; (regular) gleichmäßig; (reliable) beständig; (hand) ruhig; (job, boyfriend) fest ♦ vt festigen; **to ~ o.s. on/against sth** sich stützen auf/ gegen etw acc

steak [steɪk] n Steak nt; (fish) Filet nt

steal [stiːl] (pt **stole**, pp **stolen**) vt stehlen ♦ vi stehlen; (go quietly) sich stehlen

stealth [stelθ] n Heimlichkeit f; **~y** adj verstohlen, heimlich

steam [stiːm] n Dampf m ♦ vt (COOK) im Dampfbad erhitzen ♦ vi dampfen; **~ engine** n Dampfmaschine f; **~er** n Dampfer m; **~roller** n Dampfwalze f; **~ship** n = **steamer**; **~y** adj dampfig

steel [stiːl] n Stahl m ♦ adj Stahl-; (fig) stählern; **~works** n Stahlwerke pl

steep [stiːp] adj steil; (price) gepfeffert ♦ vt einweichen

steeple ['stiːpl] n Kirchturm m; **~chase** n Hindernisrennen nt

steer [stɪəʳ] vt, vi steuern; (car etc) lenken; **~ing** n (AUT) Steuerung f; **~ing wheel** n Steuer- or Lenkrad nt

stem [stem] n Stiel m ♦ vt aufhalten; **~ from** vt fus abstammen von

stench [stentʃ] n Gestank m

stencil ['stensl] n Schablone f ♦ vt (auf)drucken

stenographer [ste'nɔgrəfəʳ] (US) n Stenograf(in) m(f)

step [step] n Schritt m; (stair) Stufe f ♦ vi treten, schreiten; **~s** npl (BRIT) = **stepladder**; **to take ~s** Schritte unternehmen; **in/out of ~ (with)** im/nicht im Gleichklang (mit); **~ down** vi (fig) abtreten; **~ off** vt fus aussteigen aus; **~ up** vt steigern

stepbrother ['stepbrʌðəʳ] n Stiefbruder m

stepdaughter ['stepdɔːtəʳ] n Stieftochter f

stepfather ['stepfɑːðəʳ] n Stiefvater m

stepladder ['steplædəʳ] n Trittleiter f

stepmother ['stepmʌðəʳ] n Stiefmutter f

stepping stone ['stepɪŋ-] n Stein m; (fig) Sprungbrett nt

stepsister ['stepsɪstəʳ] n Stiefschwester f

stepson ['stepsʌn] n Stiefsohn m

stereo ['stɛrɪəu] n Stereoanlage f ♦ adj (also: **~phonic**) stereofonisch, stereophonisch

stereotype ['stɪərɪətaɪp] n (fig) Klischee nt ♦ vt stereotypieren; (fig) stereotyp machen

sterile ['steraɪl] adj steril; (person) unfruchtbar; **sterilize** vt sterilisieren

sterling ['stəːlɪŋ] adj (FIN) Sterling-; (character) gediegen ♦ n (ECON) das Pfund Sterling; **a pound ~** ein Pfund Sterling

stern [stəːn] adj streng ♦ n Heck nt, Achterschiff nt

stew [stjuː] n Eintopf m ♦ vt, vi schmoren

steward ['stjuːəd] n Steward m; **~ess** n Stewardess f

stick [stɪk] (pt, pp **stuck**) n Stock m; (of chalk etc) Stück nt ♦ vt (stab) stechen; (fix) stecken; (put) stellen; (gum) (an)kleben; (inf: tolerate) vertragen ♦ vi (stop) stecken bleiben; (get stuck) klemmen; (hold fast)

kleben, haften; **~ out** *vi* (*project*)
hervorstehen; **~ up** *vi* (*project*) in die Höhe
stehen; **~ up for** *vt fus* (*defend*) eintreten
für; **~er** *n* Aufkleber *m*; **~ing plaster** *n*
Heftpflaster *nt*

stickler ['stɪklər] *n*: **~ (for)** Pedant *m* (in
+*acc*)

stick-up ['stɪkʌp] (*inf*) *n* (Raub)überfall *m*

sticky ['stɪkɪ] *adj* klebrig; (*atmosphere*) stickig

stiff [stɪf] *adj* steif; (*difficult*) hart; (*paste*) dick;
(*drink*) stark; **to have a ~ neck** einen steifen
Hals haben; **~en** *vt* versteifen, (ver)stärken
♦ *vi* sich versteifen

stifle ['staɪfl] *vt* unterdrücken; **stifling** *adj*
drückend

stigma ['stɪgmə] (*pl BOT, MED, REL* **~ta**; *fig* **~s**)
n Stigma *nt*

stigmata ['stɪg'mɑːtə] *npl of* **stigma**

stile [staɪl] *n* Steige *f*

stiletto [stɪ'letəu] (*BRIT*) *n* (*also:* **~ heel**)
Pfennigabsatz *m*

still [stɪl] *adj* still ♦ *adv* (immer) noch;
(*anyhow*) immerhin; **~born** *adj* tot
geboren; **~ life** *n* Stillleben *nt*

stilt [stɪlt] *n* Stelze *f*

stilted ['stɪltɪd] *adj* gestelzt

stimulate ['stɪmjuleɪt] *vt* anregen,
stimulieren

stimuli ['stɪmjulaɪ] *npl of* **stimulus**

stimulus ['stɪmjuləs] (*pl* **-li**) *n* Anregung *f*,
Reiz *m*

sting [stɪŋ] (*pt, pp* **stung**) *n* Stich *m*; (*organ*)
Stachel *m* ♦ *vi* stechen; (*on skin*) brennen
♦ *vt* stechen

stingy ['stɪndʒɪ] *adj* geizig, knauserig

stink [stɪŋk] (*pt* **stank**, *pp* **stunk**) *n* Gestank
m ♦ *vi* stinken; **~ing** *adj* (*fig*) widerlich

stint [stɪnt] *n* (*period*) Betätigung *f*; **to do
one's ~** seine Arbeit tun; (*share*) seinen Teil
beitragen

stipulate ['stɪpjuleɪt] *vt* festsetzen

stir [stəːr] *n* Bewegung *f*; (*COOK*) Rühren *nt*;
(*sensation*) Aufsehen *nt* ♦ *vt* (um)rühren ♦ *vi*
sich rühren; **~ up** *vt* (*mob*) aufhetzen;
(*mixture*) umrühren; (*dust*) aufwirbeln

stirrup ['stɪrəp] *n* Steigbügel *m*

stitch [stɪtʃ] *n* (*with needle*) Stich *m*; (*MED*)

Faden *m*; (*of knitting*) Masche *f*; (*pain*) Stich
m ♦ *vt* nähen

stoat [stəut] *n* Wiesel *nt*

stock [stɔk] *n* Vorrat *m*; (*COMM*)
(Waren)lager *nt*; (*livestock*) Vieh *nt*; (*COOK*)
Brühe *f*; (*FIN*) Grundkapital *nt* ♦ *adj* stets
vorrätig; (*standard*) Normal- ♦ *vt* (*in shop*)
führen; **~s** *npl* (*FIN*) Aktien *pl*; **in/out of ~**
vorrätig/nicht vorrätig; **to take ~ of ~**
Inventur machen von; (*fig*) Bilanz ziehen
aus; **~s and shares** Effekten *pl*; **~ up** *vi*: **to
~ up (with)** Reserven anlegen (von);
~broker ['stɔkbrəukər] *n* Börsenmakler *m*; **~
cube** *n* Brühwürfel *m*; **~ exchange** *n*
Börse *f*

stocking ['stɔkɪŋ] *n* Strumpf *m*

stock: ~ market *n* Börse *f*; **~ phrase** *n*
Standardsatz *m*; **~pile** *n* Vorrat *m* ♦ *vt*
aufstapeln; **~taking** (*BRIT*) *n* (*COMM*)
Inventur *f*, Bestandsaufnahme *f*

stocky ['stɔkɪ] *adj* untersetzt

stodgy ['stɔdʒɪ] *adj* pappig

stoke [stəuk] *vt* schüren

stole [stəul] *pt of* **steal** ♦ *n* Stola *f*

stolen ['stəuln] *pp of* **steal**

stomach ['stʌmək] *n* Bauch *m*, Magen *m*
♦ *vt* vertragen; **~-ache** *n* Magen- or
Bauchschmerzen *pl*

stone [stəun] *n* Stein *m*; (*BRIT: weight*)
Gewichtseinheit = 6.35 kg ♦ *vt* (*olive*)
entkernen; (*kill*) steinigen; **~-cold** *adj*
eiskalt; **~-deaf** *adj* stocktaub; **~work** *n*
Mauerwerk *nt*; **stony** ['stəunɪ] *adj* steinig

stood [stud] *pt, pp of* **stand**

stool [stuːl] *n* Hocker *m*

stoop [stuːp] *vi* sich bücken

stop [stɔp] *n* Halt *m*; (*bus* **~**) Haltestelle *f*;
(*punctuation*) Punkt *m* ♦ *vt* anhalten; (*bring
to an end*) aufhören (mit), sein lassen ♦ *vi*
aufhören; (*clock*) stehen bleiben; (*remain*)
bleiben; **to ~ doing sth** aufhören, etw zu
tun; **to ~ dead** innehalten; **~ off** *vi* kurz
Halt machen; **~ up** *vt* (*hole*) zustopfen,
verstopfen; **~gap** *n* Notlösung *f*; **~lights**
npl (*AUT*) Bremslichter *pl*; **~over** *n* (*on
journey*) Zwischenaufenthalt *m*; **~page**
['stɔpɪdʒ] *n* (An)halten *nt*; (*traffic*)

Verkehrsstockung f; (strike)
Arbeitseinstellung f; ~**per** ['stɒpər] n
Propfen m, Stöpsel m; ~ **press** n letzte
Meldung f; ~**watch** ['stɒpwɒtʃ] n Stoppuhr f

storage ['stɔːrɪdʒ] n Lagerung f; ~ **heater** n
(Nachtstrom)speicherofen m

store [stɔːr] n Vorrat m; (place) Lager nt,
Warenhaus nt; (BRIT: large shop) Kaufhaus
nt; (US) Laden m ♦ vt lagern; ~**s** npl
(supplies) Vorräte pl; ~ **up** vt sich
eindecken mit; ~**room** n Lagerraum m,
Vorratsraum m

storey ['stɔːrɪ] (US **story**) n Stock m

stork [stɔːk] n Storch m

storm [stɔːm] n (also fig) Sturm m ♦ vt, vi
stürmen; ~**y** adj stürmisch

story ['stɔːrɪ] n Geschichte f; (lie) Märchen
nt; (US) = **storey**; ~**book** n
Geschichtenbuch nt; ~**teller** n
Geschichtenerzähler m

stout [staut] adj (bold) tapfer; (fat) beleibt
♦ n Starkbier nt; (also: **sweet** ~) ≈ Malzbier
nt

stove [stəuv] n (Koch)herd m; (for heating)
Ofen m

stow [stəu] vt verstauen; ~**away** n blinde(r)
Passagier m

straddle ['strædl] vt (horse, fence) rittlings
sitzen auf +dat; (fig) überbrücken

straggle ['strægl] vi (people) nachhinken; ~**r**
n Nachzügler m; **straggly** adj (hair) zottig

straight [streɪt] adj gerade; (honest) offen,
ehrlich; (drink) pur ♦ adv (direct) direkt,
geradewegs; **to put** or **get sth** ~ etw in
Ordnung bringen; ~ **away** sofort; ~ **off**
sofort; ~**en** vt (also: ~**en out**) gerade
machen; (fig) klarstellen; ~**-faced** adv ohne
die Miene zu verziehen ♦ adj: **to be** ~-
faced keine Miene verziehen; ~**forward**
adj einfach, unkompliziert

strain [streɪn] n Belastung f; (streak, trace)
Zug m; (of music) Fetzen m ♦ vt
überanstrengen; (stretch) anspannen;
(muscle) zerren; (filter) (durch)seihen ♦ vi
sich anstrengen; ~**ed** adj (laugh)
gezwungen; (relations) gespannt; ~**er** n
Sieb nt

strait [streɪt] n Straße f, Meerenge f;
~**jacket** n Zwangsjacke f; ~-**laced** adj
engherzig, streng

strand [strænd] n (of hair) Strähne f; (also fig)
Faden m

stranded ['strændɪd] adj (also fig) gestrandet

strange [streɪndʒ] adj fremd; (unusual)
seltsam; ~**r** n Fremde(r) mf

strangle ['stræŋgl] vt erwürgen; ~**hold** n
(fig) Umklammerung f

strap [stræp] n Riemen m; (on clothes) Träger
m ♦ vt (fasten) festschnallen

strapping ['stræpɪŋ] adj stramm

strata ['strɑːtə] npl of **stratum**

strategic [strə'tiːdʒɪk] adj strategisch

strategy ['strætɪdʒɪ] n (fig) Strategie f

stratum ['strɑːtəm] (pl -**ta**) n Schicht f

straw [strɔː] n Stroh nt; (single stalk, drinking
~) Strohhalm m; **that's the last** ~! das ist
der Gipfel!

strawberry ['strɔːbərɪ] n Erdbeere f

stray [streɪ] adj (animal) verirrt ♦ vi
herumstreunen

streak [striːk] n Streifen m; (in character)
Einschlag m; (in hair) Strähne f ♦ vt streifen
♦ vi zucken; (move quickly) flitzen; ~ **of bad
luck** Pechsträhne f; ~**y** adj gestreift; (bacon)
durchwachsen

stream [striːm] n (brook) Bach m; (fig) Strom
m ♦ vt (SCH) in (Leistungs)gruppen einteilen
♦ vi strömen; **to** ~ **in/out** (people) hinein-/
hinausströmen

streamer ['striːmər] n (flag) Wimpel m; (of
paper) Luftschlange f

streamlined ['striːmlaɪnd] adj
stromlinienförmig; (effective) rationell

street [striːt] n Straße f ♦ adj Straßen-; ~**car**
(US) n Straßenbahn f; ~ **lamp** n
Straßenlaterne f; ~ **plan** n Stadtplan m;
~**wise** (inf) adj: **to be** ~**wise** wissen, wo es
langgeht

strength [streŋθ] n (also fig) Stärke f; Kraft f;
~**en** vt (ver)stärken

strenuous ['strenjuəs] adj anstrengend

stress [stres] n Druck m; (mental) Stress m;
(GRAM) Betonung f ♦ vt betonen

stretch [stretʃ] n Strecke f ♦ vt ausdehnen,

strecken ♦ *vi* sich erstrecken; (*person*) sich
strecken; ~ **out** *vi* sich ausstrecken ♦ *vt*
ausstrecken

stretcher ['stretʃər] *n* Tragbahre *f*

stretchy ['stretʃɪ] *adj* elastisch, dehnbar

strewn [struːn] *adj*: ~ **with** übersät mit

stricken ['strɪkən] *adj* (*person*) ergriffen; (*city, country*) heimgesucht; ~ **with** (*disease*) leidend unter +*dat*

strict [strɪkt] *adj* (*exact*) genau; (*severe*) streng; ~**ly** *adv* streng, genau

stridden ['strɪdn] *pp* of **stride**

stride [straɪd] (*pt* **strode**, *pp* **stridden**) *n* lange(r) Schritt *m* ♦ *vi* schreiten

strident ['straɪdnt] *adj* schneidend, durchdringend

strife [straɪf] *n* Streit *m*

strike [straɪk] (*pt, pp* **struck**) *n* Streik *m*; (*attack*) Schlag *m* ♦ *vt* (*hit*) schlagen; (*collide*) stoßen gegen; (*come to mind*) einfallen +*dat*; (*stand out*) auffallen +*dat*; (*find*) finden ♦ *vi* (*stop work*) streiken; (*attack*) zuschlagen; (*clock*) schlagen; **on** ~ (*workers*) im Streik; **to ~ a match** ein Streichholz anzünden; ~ **down** *vt* (*lay low*) niederschlagen; ~ **out** *vt* (*cross out*) ausstreichen; ~ **up** *vt* (*music*) anstimmen; (*friendship*) schließen; ~**r** *n* Streikende(r) *mf*; **striking** ['straɪkɪŋ] *adj* auffallend

string [strɪŋ] (*pt, pp* **strung**) *n* Schnur *f*; (*row*) Reihe *f*; (*MUS*) Saite *f* ♦ *vt*: **to ~ together** aneinander reihen ♦ *vi*: **to ~ out** (sich) verteilen; **the ~s** *npl* (*MUS*) die Streichinstrumente *pl*; **to pull ~s** (*fig*) Fäden ziehen; ~ **bean** *n* grüne Bohne *f*; ~**(ed) instrument** *n* (*MUS*) Saiteninstrument *nt*

stringent ['strɪndʒənt] *adj* streng

strip [strɪp] *n* Streifen *m* ♦ *vt* (*uncover*) abstreifen, abziehen; (*clothes*) ausziehen; (*TECH*) auseinander nehmen ♦ *vi* (*undress*) sich ausziehen; ~ **cartoon** *n* Bildserie *f*

stripe [straɪp] *n* Streifen *m*; ~**d** *adj* gestreift

strip lighting *n* Neonlicht *nt*

stripper ['strɪpər] *n* Stripteasetänzerin *f*

strip-search ['strɪpsɜːtʃ] *n* Leibesvisitation *f* (*bei der man sich ausziehen muss*) ♦ *vt*: **to be ~~ed** sich ausziehen müssen und

durchsucht werden

stripy ['straɪpɪ] *adj* gestreift

strive [straɪv] (*pt* **strove**, *pp* **striven**) *vi*: **to ~ (for)** streben (nach)

strode [strəud] *pt* of **stride**

stroke [strəuk] *n* Schlag *m*; (*SWIMMING, ROWING*) Stoß *m*; (*MED*) Schlaganfall *m*; (*caress*) Streicheln *nt* ♦ *vt* streicheln; **at a ~** mit einem Schlag

stroll [strəul] *n* Spaziergang *m* ♦ *vi* schlendern; ~**er** (*US*) *n* (*pushchair*) Sportwagen *m*

strong [strɔŋ] *adj* stark; (*firm*) fest; **they are 50 ~** sie sind 50 Mann stark; ~**box** *n* Kassette *f*; ~**hold** *n* Hochburg *f*; ~**ly** *adv* stark; ~**room** *n* Tresor *m*

strove [strəuv] *pt* of **strive**

struck [strʌk] *pt, pp* of **strike**

structure ['strʌktʃər] *n* Struktur *f*, Aufbau *m*; (*building*) Bau *m*

struggle ['strʌgl] *n* Kampf *m* ♦ *vi* (*fight*) kämpfen

strum [strʌm] *vt* (*guitar*) klimpern auf +*dat*

strung [strʌŋ] *pt, pp* of **string**

strut [strʌt] *n* Strebe *f*, Stütze *f* ♦ *vi* stolzieren

stub [stʌb] *n* Stummel *m*; (*of cigarette*) Kippe *f* ♦ *vt*: **to ~ one's toe** sich *dat* den Zeh anstoßen; ~ **out** *vt* ausdrücken

stubble ['stʌbl] *n* Stoppel *f*

stubborn ['stʌbən] *adj* hartnäckig

stuck [stʌk] *pt, pp* of **stick** ♦ *adj* (*jammed*) klemmend; ~~**up** *adj* hochnäsig

stud [stʌd] *n* (*button*) Kragenknopf *m*; (*place*) Gestüt *nt* ♦ *vt* (*fig*): ~**ded with** übersät mit

student ['stjuːdənt] *n* Student(in) *m(f)*; (*US*) Student(in) *m(f)*, Schüler(in) *m(f)* ♦ *adj* Studenten-; ~ **driver** (*US*) *n* Fahrschüler(in) *m(f)*

studio ['stjuːdɪəu] *n* Studio *nt*; (*for artist*) Atelier *nt*; ~ **apartment** (*US*) *n* Appartement *nt*; ~ **flat** *n* Appartement *nt*

studious ['stjuːdɪəs] *adj* lernbegierig

study ['stʌdɪ] *n* Studium *nt*; (*investigation*) Studium *nt*, Untersuchung *f*; (*room*) Arbeitszimmer *nt*; (*essay etc*) Studie *f* ♦ *vt* studieren; (*face*) erforschen; (*evidence*) prüfen ♦ *vi* studieren

stuff [stʌf] n Stoff m; (inf) Zeug nt ♦ vt stopfen, füllen; (animal) ausstopfen; **~ing** n Füllung f; **~y** adj (room) schwül; (person) spießig

stumble ['stʌmbl] vi stolpern; **to ~ across** (fig) zufällig stoßen auf +acc

stumbling block ['stʌmblɪŋ-] n Hindernis nt

stump [stʌmp] n Stumpf m

stun [stʌn] vt betäuben; (shock) niederschmettern

stung [stʌŋ] pt, pp of **sting**

stunk [stʌŋk] pp of **stink**

stunned adj benommen, fassungslos

stunning ['stʌnɪŋ] adj betäubend; (news) überwältigend, umwerfend

stunt [stʌnt] n Kunststück nt, Trick m

stunted ['stʌntɪd] adj verkümmert

stuntman ['stʌntmæn] (irreg) n Stuntman m

stupefy ['stju:pɪfaɪ] vt betäuben; (by news) bestürzen

stupendous [stju:'pɛndəs] adj erstaunlich, enorm

stupid ['stju:pɪd] adj dumm; **~ity** [stju:'pɪdɪtɪ] n Dummheit f

stupor ['stju:pə'] n Betäubung f

sturdy ['stɜːdɪ] adj kräftig, robust

stutter ['stʌtə'] n Stottern nt ♦ vi stottern

sty [staɪ] n Schweinestall m

stye [staɪ] n Gerstenkorn nt

style [staɪl] n Stil m; (fashion) Mode f; **stylish** ['staɪlɪʃ] adj modisch; **stylist** ['staɪlɪst] n (hair stylist) Friseur m, Friseuse f

stylus ['staɪləs] n (Grammofon)nadel f

suave [swɑːv] adj zuvorkommend

sub... [sʌb] prefix Unter...; **~conscious** adj unterbewusst ♦ n: **the ~conscious** das Unterbewusste; **~contract** vt (vertraglich) untervermitteln; **~divide** vt unterteilen; **~dued** adj (lighting) gedämpft; (person) still

subject [n, adj 'sʌbdʒɪkt, vb səb'dʒɛkt] n (of kingdom) Untertan m; (citizen) Staatsangehörige(r) mf; (topic) Thema nt; (SCH) Fach nt; (GRAM) Subjekt nt ♦ adj: **to be ~** unterworfen sein +dat; (exposed) ausgesetzt sein +dat ♦ vt (subdue) unterwerfen; (expose) aussetzen; **~ive**

[səb'dʒɛktɪv] adj subjektiv; **~ matter** n Thema nt

sublet [sʌb'lɛt] (irreg: like let) vt untervermieten

sublime [sə'blaɪm] adj erhaben

submachine gun ['sʌbmə'ʃiːn-] n Maschinenpistole f

submarine [sʌbmə'riːn] n Unterseeboot nt, U-Boot nt

submerge [səb'mɜːdʒ] vt untertauchen; (flood) überschwemmen ♦ vi untertauchen

submission [səb'mɪʃən] n (obedience) Gehorsam m; (claim) Behauptung f; (of plan) Unterbreitung f; **submissive** [səb'mɪsɪv] adj demütig, unterwürfig (pej)

submit [səb'mɪt] vt behaupten; (plan) unterbreiten ♦ vi sich ergeben

subnormal [sʌb'nɔːml] adj minderbegabt

subordinate [sə'bɔːdɪnət] adj untergeordnet ♦ n Untergebene(r) mf

subpoena [sə'piːnə] n Vorladung f ♦ vt vorladen

subscribe [səb'skraɪb] vi: **to ~ to** (view etc) unterstützen; (newspaper) abonnieren; **~r** n (to periodical) Abonnent m; (TEL) Telefonteilnehmer m

subscription [səb'skrɪpʃən] n Abonnement nt; (money subscribed) (Mitglieds)beitrag m

subsequent ['sʌbsɪkwənt] adj folgend, später; **~ly** adv später

subside [səb'saɪd] vi sich senken; **~nce** [səb'saɪdns] n Senkung f

subsidiarity [səbsɪdɪ'ærɪtɪ] n (POL) Subsidiarität f

subsidiary [səb'sɪdɪərɪ] adj Neben- ♦ n Tochtergesellschaft f

subsidize ['sʌbsɪdaɪz] vt subventionieren

subsidy ['sʌbsɪdɪ] n Subvention f

subsistence [səb'sɪstəns] n Unterhalt m

substance ['sʌbstəns] n Substanz f

substantial [səb'stænʃl] adj (strong) fest, kräftig; (important) wesentlich; **~ly** adv erheblich

substantiate [səb'stænʃɪeɪt] vt begründen, belegen

substitute ['sʌbstɪtjuːt] n Ersatz m ♦ vt ersetzen; **substitution** [sʌbstɪ'tjuːʃən] n

Ersetzung f

subterfuge ['sʌbtəfjuːdʒ] n Vorwand m; (trick) Trick m

subterranean [sʌbtəˈreɪnɪən] adj unterirdisch

subtitle ['sʌbtaɪtl] n Untertitel m; ~**d** adj untertitelt, mit Untertiteln versehen

subtle ['sʌtl] adj fein; ~**ty** n Feinheit f

subtotal [sʌbˈtəʊtl] n Zwischensumme f

subtract [səbˈtrækt] vt abziehen; ~**ion** [səbˈtrækʃən] n Abziehen nt, Subtraktion f

suburb ['sʌbɜːb] n Vorort m; **the ~s** die Außenbezirke pl; ~**an** [səˈbɜːbən] adj Vorort(s)-; ~**ia** [səˈbɜːbɪə] n Vorstadt f

subversive [səbˈvɜːsɪv] adj subversiv

subway ['sʌbweɪ] n (US) U-Bahn f; (BRIT) Unterführung f

succeed [səkˈsiːd] vi (person) erfolgreich sein, Erfolg haben; (plan etc also) gelingen ♦ vt (nach)folgen +dat; **he ~ed in doing it** es gelang ihm, es zu tun; ~**ing** adj (nach)folgend

success [səkˈses] n Erfolg m; ~**ful** adj erfolgreich; **to be ~ful (in doing sth)** Erfolg haben (bei etw); ~**fully** adv erfolgreich

succession [səkˈseʃən] n (Aufeinander)folge f; (to throne) Nachfolge f

successive [səkˈsesɪv] adj aufeinander folgend

successor [səkˈsesəʳ] n Nachfolger(in) m(f)

succinct [səkˈsɪŋkt] adj knapp

succulent ['sʌkjulənt] adj saftig

succumb [səˈkʌm] vi: **to ~ (to)** erliegen (+dat); (yield) nachgeben (+dat)

such [sʌtʃ] adj solche(r, s); ~ **a book** so ein Buch; ~ **books** solche Bücher; ~ **courage** so ein Mut; ~ **a long trip** so eine lange Reise; ~ **a lot of** so viel(e); ~ **as** wie; **a noise** ~ **as to** ein derartiger Lärm, dass; **as** ~ an sich; ~-**and**-~ **a time** die und die Zeit

suck [sʌk] vt saugen; (lollipop etc) lutschen

sucker ['sʌkəʳ] (inf) n Idiot m

suction ['sʌkʃən] n Saugkraft f

sudden ['sʌdn] adj plötzlich; **all of a** ~ auf einmal; ~**ly** adv plötzlich

suds [sʌdz] npl Seifenlauge f; (lather) Seifenschaum m

sue [suː] vt verklagen

suede [sweɪd] n Wildleder nt

suet ['suɪt] n Nierenfett nt

Suez ['suːɪz] n: **the ~ Canal** der Suezkanal

suffer ['sʌfəʳ] vt (er)leiden ♦ vi leiden; ~**er** n Leidende(r) mf; ~**ing** n Leiden nt

suffice [səˈfaɪs] vi genügen

sufficient [səˈfɪʃənt] adj ausreichend; ~**ly** adv ausreichend

suffix ['sʌfɪks] n Nachsilbe f

suffocate ['sʌfəkeɪt] vi, vt ersticken

suffrage ['sʌfrɪdʒ] n Wahlrecht nt

sugar ['ʃugəʳ] n Zucker m ♦ vt zuckern; ~ **beet** n Zuckerrübe f; ~ **cane** n Zuckerrohr nt; ~**y** adj süß

suggest [səˈdʒest] vt vorschlagen; (show) schließen lassen auf +acc; ~**ion** [səˈdʒestʃən] n Vorschlag m; ~**ive** adj anregend; (indecent) zweideutig

suicide ['suɪsaɪd] n Selbstmord m; **to commit** ~ Selbstmord begehen

suit [suːt] n Anzug m; (CARDS) Farbe f ♦ vt passen +dat; (clothes) stehen +dat; **well** ~**ed** (well matched) gut zusammenpassend; ~**able** adj geeignet, passend; ~**ably** adv passend, angemessen

suitcase ['suːtkeɪs] n (Hand)koffer m

suite [swiːt] n (of rooms) Zimmerflucht f; (of furniture) Einrichtung f; (MUS) Suite f

suitor ['suːtəʳ] n (JUR) Kläger(in) m(f)

sulfur ['sʌlfəʳ] (US) n = **sulphur**

sulk [sʌlk] vi schmollen; ~**y** adj schmollend

sullen ['sʌlən] adj mürrisch

sulphur ['sʌlfəʳ] (US **sulfur**) n Schwefel m

sultana [sʌlˈtɑːnə] n (fruit) Sultanine f

sultry ['sʌltrɪ] adj schwül

sum [sʌm] n Summe f; (money) Betrag m, Summe f; (arithmetic) Rechenaufgabe f; ~ **up** vt, vi zusammenfassen

summarize ['sʌməraɪz] vt kurz zusammenfassen

summary ['sʌmərɪ] n Zusammenfassung f ♦ adj (justice) kurzerhand erteilt

summer ['sʌməʳ] n Sommer m ♦ adj Sommer-; ~**house** n (in garden) Gartenhaus nt; ~**time** n Sommerzeit f

summit ['sʌmɪt] n Gipfel m; ~

(conference) n Gipfelkonferenz f

summon ['sʌmən] vt herbeirufen; (JUR) vorladen; (gather up) aufbringen; **~s** (JUR) n Vorladung f ♦ vt vorladen

sump [sʌmp] (BRIT) n (AUT) Ölwanne f

sumptuous ['sʌmptjʊəs] adj prächtig

sun [sʌn] n Sonne f; **~bathe** vi sich sonnen; **~block** n Sonnenschutzcreme f; **~burn** n Sonnenbrand m; **~burnt** adj sonnenverbrannt, sonnengebräunt; **to be ~burnt** (painfully) einen Sonnenbrand haben

Sunday ['sʌndɪ] n Sonntag m; **~ school** n Sonntagsschule f

sundial ['sʌndaɪəl] n Sonnenuhr f

sundown ['sʌndaʊn] n Sonnenuntergang m

sundries ['sʌndrɪz] npl (miscellaneous items) Verschiedene(s) nt

sundry ['sʌndrɪ] adj verschieden; **all and ~** alle

sunflower ['sʌnflaʊəʳ] n Sonnenblume f

sung [sʌŋ] pp of **sing**

sunglasses ['sʌnɡlɑːsɪz] npl Sonnenbrille f

sunk [sʌŋk] pp of **sink**

sun: ~light ['sʌnlaɪt] n Sonnenlicht nt; **~lit** ['sʌnlɪt] adj sonnenbeschienen; **~ny** ['sʌnɪ] adj sonnig; **~rise** n Sonnenaufgang m; **~roof** n (AUT) Schiebedach nt; **~screen** ['sʌnskriːn] n Sonnenschutzcreme f; **~set** ['sʌnset] n Sonnenuntergang m; **~shade** ['sʌnʃeɪd] n Sonnenschirm m; **~shine** ['sʌnʃaɪn] n Sonnenschein m; **~stroke** ['sʌnstrəʊk] n Hitzschlag m; **~tan** ['sʌntæn] n (Sonnen)bräune f; **~tan oil** n Sonnenöl nt

super ['suːpəʳ] (inf) adj prima, klasse

superannuation [suːpərænjuˈeɪʃən] n Pension f

superb [suːˈpəːb] adj ausgezeichnet, hervorragend

supercilious [suːpəˈsɪlɪəs] adj herablassend

superficial [suːpəˈfɪʃəl] adj oberflächlich

superfluous [suːˈpəːflʊəs] adj überflüssig

superhuman [suːpəˈhjuːmən] adj (effort) übermenschlich

superimpose ['suːpərɪmˈpəʊz] vt übereinander legen

superintendent [suːpərɪnˈtendənt] n Polizeichef m

superior [suːˈprɪərɪəʳ] adj überlegen; (better) besser ♦ n Vorgesetzte(r) mf; **~ity** [suːprɪˈɒrɪtɪ] n Überlegenheit f

superlative [suːˈpəːlətɪv] adj überragend

super: ~man ['suːpəmæn] (irreg) n Übermensch m; **~market** ['suːpəmɑːkɪt] n Supermarkt m; **~natural** [suːpəˈnætʃərəl] adj übernatürlich; **~power** ['suːpəpaʊəʳ] n Weltmacht f

supersede [suːpəˈsiːd] vt ersetzen

supersonic ['suːpəˈsɒnɪk] adj Überschall-

superstition [suːpəˈstɪʃən] n Aberglaube m; **superstitious** [suːpəˈstɪʃəs] adj abergläubisch

supervise ['suːpəvaɪz] vt beaufsichtigen, kontrollieren; **supervision** [suːpəˈvɪʒən] n Aufsicht f; **supervisor** ['suːpəvaɪzəʳ] n Aufsichtsperson f; **supervisory** ['suːpəvaɪzərɪ] adj Aufsichts-

supper ['sʌpəʳ] n Abendessen nt

supplant [səˈplɑːnt] vt (person, thing) ersetzen

supple ['sʌpl] adj geschmeidig

supplement [n 'sʌplɪmənt, vb sʌplɪˈment] n Ergänzung f; (in book) Nachtrag m ♦ vt ergänzen; **~ary** [sʌplɪˈmentərɪ] adj ergänzend; **~ary benefit** (BRIT: old) n ≈ Sozialhilfe f

supplier [səˈplaɪəʳ] n Lieferant m

supplies [səˈplaɪz] npl (food) Vorräte pl; (MIL) Nachschub m

supply [səˈplaɪ] vt liefern ♦ n Vorrat m; (~ing) Lieferung f; see also **supplies**; **~ teacher** (BRIT) n Vertretung f

support [səˈpɔːt] n Unterstützung f; (TECH) Stütze f ♦ vt (hold up) stützen, tragen; (provide for) ernähren; (be in favour of) unterstützen; **~er** n Anhänger(in) m(f)

suppose [səˈpəʊz] vt, vi annehmen; **to be ~d to do sth** etw tun sollen; **~dly** [səˈpəʊzɪdlɪ] adv angeblich; **supposing** conj angenommen; **supposition** [sʌpəˈzɪʃən] n Voraussetzung f

suppress [səˈpres] vt unterdrücken

supremacy [suːˈpreməsɪ] n Vorherrschaft f, Oberhoheit f

supreme [su'priːm] *adj* oberste(r, s), höchste(r, s)

surcharge ['səːtʃɑːdʒ] *n* Zuschlag *m*

sure [ʃuəʳ] *adj* sicher, gewiss; **~!** (*of course*) klar!; **to make ~ of sth/that** sich einer Sache *gen* vergewissern/vergewissern, dass; **~ enough** (*with past*) tatsächlich; (*with future*) ganz bestimmt; **~-footed** *adj* sicher (auf den Füßen); **~ly** *adv* (*certainly*) sicherlich, gewiss; **~ly it's wrong** das ist doch wohl falsch

surety ['ʃuərətɪ] *n* Sicherheit *f*

surf [səːf] *n* Brandung *f*

surface ['səːfɪs] *n* Oberfläche *f* ♦ *vt* (*roadway*) teeren ♦ *vi* auftauchen; **~ mail** *n* gewöhnliche Post *f*

surfboard ['səːfbɔːd] *n* Surfbrett *nt*

surfeit ['səːfɪt] *n* Übermaß *nt*

surfing ['səːfɪŋ] *n* Surfen *nt*

surge [səːdʒ] *n* Woge *f* ♦ *vi* wogen

surgeon ['səːdʒən] *n* Chirurg(in) *m(f)*

surgery ['səːdʒərɪ] *n* (*BRIT: place*) Praxis *f*; (*: time*) Sprechstunde *f*; (*treatment*) Operation *f*; **to undergo ~** operiert werden; **~ hours** (*BRIT*) *npl* Sprechstunden *pl*

surgical ['səːdʒɪkl] *adj* chirurgisch; **~ spirit** (*BRIT*) *n* Wundbenzin *nt*

surly ['səːlɪ] *adj* verdrießlich, grob

surmount [səːˈmaunt] *vt* überwinden

surname ['səːneɪm] *n* Zuname *m*

surpass [səːˈpɑːs] *vt* übertreffen

surplus ['səːpləs] *n* Überschuss *m* ♦ *adj* überschüssig, Über(schuss)-

surprise [səˈpraɪz] *n* Überraschung *f* ♦ *vt* überraschen; **~d** *adj* überrascht; **surprising** *adj* überraschend; **surprisingly** *adv* überraschend(erweise)

surrender [səˈrendəʳ] *n* Kapitulation *f* ♦ *vi* sich ergeben

surreptitious [sʌrəpˈtɪʃəs] *adj* heimlich; (*look also*) verstohlen

surrogate ['sʌrəgɪt] *n* Ersatz *m*; **~ mother** *n* Leihmutter *f*

surround [səˈraund] *vt* umgeben; **~ing** *adj* (*countryside*) umliegend; **~ings** *npl* Umgebung *f*; (*environment*) Umwelt *f*

surveillance [səːˈveɪləns] *n* Überwachung *f*

survey [*n* 'səːveɪ, *vb* səːˈveɪ] *n* Übersicht *f* ♦ *vt* überblicken; (*land*) vermessen; **~or** [səˈveɪəʳ] *n* Land(ver)messer(in) *m(f)*

survival [səˈvaɪvl] *n* Überleben *nt*

survive [səˈvaɪv] *vt, vi* überleben; **survivor** [səˈvaɪvəʳ] *n* Überlebende(r) *mf*

susceptible [səˈseptəbl] *adj:* **~ (to)** empfindlich (gegen); (*charms etc*) empfänglich (für)

suspect [*n* 'sʌspekt, *vb* səsˈpekt] *n* Verdächtige(r) *mf* ♦ *adj* verdächtig ♦ *vt* verdächtigen; (*think*) vermuten

suspend [səsˈpend] *vt* verschieben; (*from work*) suspendieren; (*hang up*) aufhängen; (*SPORT*) sperren; **~ed sentence** *n* (*JUR*) zur Bewährung ausgesetzte Strafe; **~er belt** *n* Strumpf(halter)gürtel *m*; **~ers** *npl* (*BRIT*) Strumpfhalter *m*; (*US*) Hosenträger *m*

suspense [səsˈpens] *n* Spannung *f*

suspension [səsˈpenʃən] *n* (*from work*) Suspendierung *f*; (*SPORT*) Sperrung *f*; (*AUT*) Federung *f*; **~ bridge** *n* Hängebrücke *f*

suspicion [səsˈpɪʃən] *n* Misstrauen *nt*; Verdacht *m*; **suspicious** [səsˈpɪʃəs] *adj* misstrauisch; (*causing ~*) verdächtig

sustain [səsˈteɪn] *vt* (*maintain*) aufrechterhalten; (*confirm*) bestätigen; (*injury*) davontragen; **~able** *adj* (*development, growth etc*) aufrechtzuerhalten; **~ed** *adj* (*effort*) anhaltend

sustenance ['sʌstɪnəns] *n* Nahrung *f*

swab [swɒb] *n* (*MED*) Tupfer *m*

swagger ['swægəʳ] *vi* stolzieren

swallow ['swɒləu] *n* (*bird*) Schwalbe *f*; (*of food etc*) Schluck *m* ♦ *vt* (ver)schlucken; **~ up** *vt* verschlingen

swam [swæm] *pt of* **swim**

swamp [swɒmp] *n* Sumpf *m* ♦ *vt* überschwemmen

swan [swɒn] *n* Schwan *m*

swap [swɒp] *n* Tausch *m* ♦ *vt:* **to ~ sth (for sth)** etw (gegen etw) tauschen *or* eintauschen

swarm [swɔːm] *n* Schwarm *m* ♦ *vi:* **to ~** *or* **be ~ing with** wimmeln von

swarthy ['swɔːðɪ] adj dunkel, braun
swastika ['swɒstɪkə] n Hakenkreuz nt
swat [swɒt] vt totschlagen
sway [sweɪ] vi schwanken; (branches) schaukeln, sich wiegen ♦ vt schwenken; (influence) beeinflussen
swear [sweər] (pt swore, pp sworn) vi (promise) schwören; (curse) fluchen; **to ~ to sth** schwören auf etw acc; **~word** n Fluch m
sweat [swet] n Schweiß m ♦ vi schwitzen
sweater ['swetər] n Pullover m
sweatshirt ['swetʃɜːt] n Sweatshirt nt
sweaty ['swetɪ] adj verschwitzt
Swede [swiːd] n Schwede m, Schwedin f
swede [swiːd] (BRIT) n Steckrübe f
Sweden ['swiːdn] n Schweden nt
Swedish ['swiːdɪʃ] adj schwedisch ♦ n (LING) Schwedisch nt
sweep [swiːp] (pt, pp swept) n (chimney ~) Schornsteinfeger m ♦ vt fegen, kehren; **~ away** vt wegfegen; **~ past** vi vorbeisausen; **~ up** vt zusammenkehren; **~ing** adj (gesture) schwungvoll; (statement) verallgemeinernd
sweet [swiːt] n (course) Nachtisch m; (candy) Bonbon nt ♦ adj süß; **~corn** n Zuckermais m; **~en** vt süßen; (fig) versüßen; **~heart** n Liebste(r) mf; **~ness** n Süße f; **~ pea** n Gartenwicke f
swell [swel] (pt swelled, pp swollen or swelled) n Seegang m ♦ adj (inf) todschick ♦ vt (numbers) vermehren ♦ vi (also: ~ up) (an)schwellen; **~ing** n Schwellung f
sweltering ['sweltərɪŋ] adj drückend
swept [swept] pt, pp of **sweep**
swerve [swɜːv] vt, vi ausscheren
swift [swɪft] n Mauersegler m ♦ adj geschwind, schnell, rasch; **~ly** adv geschwind, schnell, rasch
swig [swɪg] n Zug m
swill [swɪl] n (for pigs) Schweinefutter nt ♦ vt spülen
swim [swɪm] (pt swam, pp swum) n: **to go for a ~** schwimmen gehen ♦ vi schwimmen ♦ vt (cross) (durch)schwimmen; **~mer** n Schwimmer(in) m(f); **~ming** n

Schwimmen nt; **~ming cap** n Badehaube f, Badekappe f; **~ming costume** (BRIT) n Badeanzug m; **~ming pool** n Schwimmbecken nt; (private) Swimmingpool m; **~ming trunks** npl Badehose f; **~suit** n Badeanzug m
swindle ['swɪndl] n Schwindel m, Betrug m ♦ vt betrügen
swine [swaɪn] n (also fig) Schwein nt
swing [swɪŋ] (pt, pp swung) n (child's) Schaukel f; (movement) Schwung m ♦ vt schwingen ♦ vi schwingen, schaukeln; (turn quickly) schwenken; **in full ~** in vollem Gange; **~ bridge** n Drehbrücke f; **~ door** (BRIT) n Schwingtür f
swingeing ['swɪndʒɪŋ] (BRIT) adj hart; (taxation, cuts) extrem
swinging door ['swɪŋɪŋ-] (US) n Schwingtür f
swipe [swaɪp] n Hieb m ♦ vt (inf: hit) hart schlagen; (: steal) klauen
swirl [swɜːl] vi wirbeln
swish [swɪʃ] adj (inf: smart) schick ♦ vi zischen; (grass, skirts) rascheln
Swiss [swɪs] adj Schweizer, schweizerisch ♦ n Schweizer(in) m(f); **the ~** npl (people) die Schweizer pl
switch [swɪtʃ] n (ELEC) Schalter m; (change) Wechsel m ♦ vt (ELEC) schalten; (change) wechseln ♦ vi wechseln; **~ off** vt ab- or ausschalten; **~ on** vt an- or einschalten; **~board** n Zentrale f; (board) Schaltbrett nt
Switzerland ['swɪtsələnd] n die Schweiz
swivel ['swɪvl] vt (also: ~ round) drehen ♦ vi (also: ~ round) sich drehen
swollen ['swəʊlən] pp of **swell**
swoon [swuːn] vi (old) in Ohnmacht fallen
swoop [swuːp] n Sturzflug m; (esp by police) Razzia f ♦ vi (also: ~ down) stürzen
swop [swɒp] = **swap**
sword [sɔːd] n Schwert nt; **~fish** n Schwertfisch m
swore [swɔːr] pt of **swear**
sworn [swɔːn] pp of **swear**
swot [swɒt] vt, vi pauken
swum [swʌm] pp of **swim**
swung [swʌŋ] pt, pp of **swing**

sycamore ['sɪkəmɔːʳ] n (US) Platane f; (BRIT) Bergahorn m

syllable ['sɪləbl] n Silbe f

syllabus ['sɪləbəs] n Lehrplan m

symbol ['sɪmbl] n Symbol nt; **~ic(al)** [sɪm'bɒlɪk(l)] adj symbolisch

symmetry ['sɪmɪtrɪ] n Symmetrie f

sympathetic [sɪmpə'θetɪk] adj mitfühlend

sympathize ['sɪmpəθaɪz] vi mitfühlen; **~r** n (POL) Sympathisant(in) m(f)

sympathy ['sɪmpəθɪ] n Mitleid nt, Mitgefühl nt; (condolence) Beileid nt; **with our deepest ~** mit tief empfundenem Beileid

symphony ['sɪmfənɪ] n Sinfonie f

symptom ['sɪmptəm] n Symptom nt; **~atic** [sɪmptə'mætɪk] adj (fig): **~atic of** bezeichnend für

synagogue ['sɪnəgɒg] n Synagoge f

synchronize ['sɪŋkrənaɪz] vt synchronisieren

syndicate ['sɪndɪkɪt] n Konsortium nt

synonym ['sɪnənɪm] n Synonym nt; **~ous** [sɪ'nɒnɪməs] adj gleichbedeutend

synopsis [sɪ'nɒpsɪs] n Zusammenfassung f

synthetic [sɪn'θetɪk] adj synthetisch; **~s** npl (man-made fabrics) Synthetik f

syphon ['saɪfən] = **siphon**

Syria ['sɪrɪə] n Syrien nt

syringe [sɪ'rɪndʒ] n Spritze f

syrup ['sɪrəp] n Sirup m; (of sugar) Melasse f

system ['sɪstəm] n System nt; **~atic** [sɪstə'mætɪk] adj systematisch; **~ disk** n (COMPUT) Systemdiskette f; **~s analyst** n Systemanalytiker(in) m(f)

T, t

ta [tɑː] (BRIT: inf) excl danke!

tab [tæb] n Aufhänger m; (name ~) Schild nt; **to keep ~s on** (fig) genau im Auge behalten

tabby ['tæbɪ] n (also: ~ **cat**) getigerte Katze f

table ['teɪbl] n Tisch m; (list) Tabelle f ♦ vt (PARL: propose) vorlegen, einbringen; **to lay** or **set the ~** den Tisch decken; **~cloth** n Tischtuch m; **~ d'hôte** [tɑːbl'dəut] n Tagesmenü nt; **~ lamp** n Tischlampe f;

~mat n Untersatz m; **~ of contents** n Inhaltsverzeichnis nt; **~spoon** n Esslöffel m; **~spoonful** n Esslöffel m (voll)

tablet ['tæblɪt] n (MED) Tablette f

table tennis n Tischtennis nt

table wine n Tafelwein m

tabloid ['tæblɔɪd] n Zeitung f in kleinem Format; (pej) Boulevardzeitung f

---
tabloid press
---

i *Der Ausdruck* **tabloid press** *bezieht sich auf kleinformatige Zeitungen (ca 30 x 40cm); sie sind in Großbritannien fast ausschließlich Massenblätter. Im Gegensatz zur* **quality press** *verwenden diese Massenblätter viele Fotos und einen knappen, oft reißerischen Stil. Sie kommen den Lesern entgegen, die mehr Wert auf Unterhaltung legen.*

---

tabulate ['tæbjuleɪt] vt tabellarisch ordnen

tacit ['tæsɪt] adj stillschweigend

taciturn ['tæsɪtɜːn] adj wortkarg

tack [tæk] n (small nail) Stift m; (US: thumbtack) Reißzwecke f; (stitch) Heftstich m; (NAUT) Lavieren nt; (course) Kurs m ♦ vt (nail) nageln; (stitch) heften ♦ vi aufkreuzen

tackle ['tækl] n (for lifting) Flaschenzug m; (NAUT) Takelage f; (SPORT) Tackling nt ♦ vt (deal with) anpacken, in Angriff nehmen; (person) festhalten; (player) angehen

tacky ['tækɪ] adj klebrig

tact [tækt] n Takt m; **~ful** adj taktvoll

tactical ['tæktɪkl] adj taktisch

tactics ['tæktɪks] npl Taktik f

tactless ['tæktlɪs] adj taktlos

tadpole ['tædpəul] n Kaulquappe f

taffy ['tæfɪ] (US) n Sahnebonbon nt

tag [tæg] n (label) Schild nt, Anhänger m; (maker's name) Etikett nt; **~ along** vi mitkommen

tail [teɪl] n Schwanz m; (of list) Schluss m ♦ vt folgen +dat; **~ away** or **off** vi abfallen, schwinden; **~back** (BRIT) n (AUT) (Rück)stau m; **~ coat** n Frack m; **~ end** n Schluss m, Ende nt; **~gate** n (AUT) Heckklappe f

tailor ['teɪləʳ] n Schneider m; **~ing** n

Schneidern nt; **~-made** adj
maßgeschneidert; (fig): **~-made for sb** jdm
wie auf den Leib geschnitten
tailwind ['teɪlwɪnd] n Rückenwind m
tainted ['teɪntɪd] adj verdorben
take [teɪk] (pt **took**, pp **taken**) vt nehmen;
(trip, exam, PHOT) machen; (capture: person)
fassen; (: town; also COMM, FIN) einnehmen;
(carry to a place) bringen; (get for o.s.) sich
dat nehmen; (gain, obtain) bekommen; (put
up with) hinnehmen; (respond to)
aufnehmen; (interpret) auffassen; (assume)
annehmen; (contain) Platz haben für;
(GRAM) stehen mit; **to ~ sth from sb** jdm
etw wegnehmen; **to ~ sth from sth** (MATH:
subtract) etw von etw abziehen; (extract,
quotation) etw einer Sache dat entnehmen;
~ after vt fus ähnlich sein +dat; **~ apart**
vt auseinander nehmen; **~ away** vt
(remove) wegnehmen; (carry off)
wegbringen; **~ back** vt (return)
zurückbringen; (retract) zurücknehmen; **~
down** vt (pull down) abreißen; (write down)
aufschreiben; **~ in** vt (deceive) hereinlegen;
(understand) begreifen; (include)
einschließen; **~ off** vi (plane) starten ♦ vt
(remove) wegnehmen; (clothing) ausziehen;
(imitate) nachmachen; **~ on** vt (undertake)
übernehmen; (engage) einstellen;
(opponent) antreten gegen; **~ out** vt (girl,
dog) ausführen; (extract) herausnehmen;
(insurance) abschließen; (licence) sich dat
geben lassen; (book) ausleihen; (remove)
entfernen; **to ~ sth out of sth** (drawer,
pocket etc) etw aus etw herausnehmen; **~
over** vt übernehmen ♦ vi: **to ~ over from
sb** jdn ablösen; **~ to** vt fus (like) mögen;
(adopt as practice) sich dat angewöhnen; **~
up** vt (raise) aufnehmen; (dress etc) kürzer
machen; (occupy) in Anspruch nehmen;
(engage in) sich befassen mit; **~away** adj
zum Mitnehmen; **~-home pay** n
Nettolohn m; **~n** pp of **take**; **~off** n (AVIAT)
Start m; (imitation) Nachahmung f; **~out**
(US) adj = **takeaway**; **~over** n (COMM)
Übernahme f; **takings** ['teɪkɪŋz] npl (COMM)
Einnahmen pl

talc [tælk] n (also: **~um powder**)
Talkumpuder m
tale [teɪl] n Geschichte f, Erzählung f; **to tell
~s** (fig: lie) Geschichten erfinden
talent ['tælnt] n Talent nt; **~ed** adj begabt
talk [tɔːk] n (conversation) Gespräch nt;
(rumour) Gerede nt; (speech) Vortrag m ♦ vi
sprechen, reden; **~s** npl (POL etc) Gespräche
pl; **to ~ about** sprechen von +dat or über
+acc; **to ~ sb into doing sth** jdn
überreden, etw zu tun; **to ~ sb out of
doing sth** jdm ausreden, etw zu tun; **to ~
shop** fachsimpeln; **~ over** vt besprechen;
~ative adj gesprächig
tall [tɔːl] adj groß; (building) hoch; **to be 1 m
80 ~** 1,80 m groß sein; **~boy** (BRIT) n
Kommode f; **~ story** n übertriebene
Geschichte f
tally ['tælɪ] n Abrechnung f ♦ vi
übereinstimmen
talon ['tælən] n Kralle f
tame [teɪm] adj zahm; (fig) fade
tamper ['tæmpər] vi: **to ~ with**
herumpfuschen an +dat
tampon ['tæmpɔn] n Tampon m
tan [tæn] n (Sonnen)bräune f; (colour)
Gelbbraun nt ♦ adj (colour) (gelb)braun ♦ vt
bräunen ♦ vi braun werden
tang [tæŋ] n Schärfe f
tangent ['tændʒənt] n Tangente f; **to go off
at a ~** (fig) vom Thema abkommen
tangerine [tændʒə'riːn] n Mandarine f
tangible ['tændʒəbl] adj greifbar
tangle ['tæŋgl] n Durcheinander nt; (trouble)
Schwierigkeiten pl; **to get in(to) a ~** sich
verheddern
tank [tæŋk] n (container) Tank m, Behälter m;
(MIL) Panzer m; **~er** ['tæŋkər] n (ship) Tanker
m; (vehicle) Tankwagen m
tanned [tænd] adj gebräunt
tantalizing ['tæntəlaɪzɪŋ] adj verlockend;
(annoying) quälend
tantamount ['tæntəmaunt] adj: **~ to**
gleichbedeutend mit
tantrum ['tæntrəm] n Wutanfall m
tap [tæp] n Hahn m; (gentle blow) Klopfen nt
♦ vt (strike) klopfen; (supply) anzapfen;

(*telephone*) abhören; **on ~** (*fig: resources*) zur Hand; **~-dancing** *n* Steppen *nt*

tape [teɪp] *n* Band *nt*; (*magnetic*) (Ton)band *nt*; (*adhesive*) Klebstreifen *m* ♦ *vt* (*record*) aufnehmen; **~ deck** *n* Tapedeck *nt*; **~ measure** *n* Maßband *nt*

taper ['teɪpə'] *vi* spitz zulaufen

tape recorder *n* Tonbandgerät *nt*

tapestry ['tæpɪstrɪ] *n* Wandteppich *m*

tar [tɑ:] *n* Teer *m*

target ['tɑ:gɪt] *n* Ziel *nt*; (*board*) Zielscheibe *f*

tariff ['tærɪf] *n* (*duty paid*) Zoll *m*; (*list*) Tarif *m*

tarmac ['tɑ:mæk] *n* (*AVIAT*) Rollfeld *nt*

tarnish ['tɑ:nɪʃ] *vt* matt machen; (*fig*) beflecken

tarpaulin [tɑ:'pɔ:lɪn] *n* Plane *f*

tarragon ['tærəgən] *n* Estragon *m*

tart [tɑ:t] *n* (*Obst*)torte *f*; (*inf*) Nutte *f* ♦ *adj* scharf; **~ up** (*inf*) *vt* aufmachen; (*person*) auftakeln

tartan ['tɑ:tn] *n* Schottenkaro *nt* ♦ *adj* mit Schottenkaro

tartar ['tɑ:tə'] *n* Zahnstein *m*

tartar(e) sauce ['tɑ:tə-] *n* Remoulade *f*

task [tɑ:sk] *n* Aufgabe *f*; **to take sb to ~** sich *dat* jdn vornehmen; **~ force** *n* Sondertrupp *m*

tassel ['tæsl] *n* Quaste *f*

taste [teɪst] *n* Geschmack *m*; (*sense*) Geschmackssinn *m*; (*small quantity*) Kostprobe *f*; (*liking*) Vorliebe *f* ♦ *vt* schmecken; (*try*) probieren ♦ *vi* schmecken; **can I have a ~ of this wine?** kann ich diesen Wein probieren?; **to have a ~ for sth** etw mögen; **in good / bad ~** geschmackvoll/geschmacklos; **you can ~ the garlic (in it)** man kann den Knoblauch herausschmecken; **to ~ of sth** nach einer Sache schmecken; **~ful** *adj* geschmackvoll; **~less** *adj* (*insipid*) fade; (*in bad ~*) geschmacklos; **tasty** ['teɪstɪ] *adj* schmackhaft

tattered ['tætəd] *adj* = **in tatters**

tatters ['tætəz] *npl*: **in ~** in Fetzen

tattoo [tə'tu:] *n* (*MIL*) Zapfenstreich *m*; (*on skin*) Tätowierung *f* ♦ *vt* tätowieren

tatty ['tætɪ] (*BRIT: inf*) *adj* schäbig

taught [tɔ:t] *pt, pp* of **teach**

taunt [tɔ:nt] *n* höhnische Bemerkung *f* ♦ *vt* verhöhnen

Taurus ['tɔ:rəs] *n* Stier *m*

taut [tɔ:t] *adj* straff

tawdry ['tɔ:drɪ] *adj* (bunt und) billig

tax [tæks] *n* Steuer *f* ♦ *vt* besteuern; (*strain*) strapazieren; (*strength*) angreifen; **~able** *adj* (*income*) steuerpflichtig; **~ation** [tæk'seɪʃən] *n* Besteuerung *f*; **~ avoidance** *n* Steuerumgehung *f*; **~ disc** (*BRIT*) *n* (*AUT*) Kraftfahrzeugsteuerplakette *f*; **~ evasion** *n* Steuerhinterziehung *f*; **~-free** *adj* steuerfrei

taxi ['tæksɪ] *n* Taxi *nt* ♦ *vi* (*plane*) rollen; **~ driver** *n* Taxifahrer *m*; **~ rank** (*BRIT*) *n* Taxistand *m*; **~ stand** *n* Taxistand *m*

tax: ~payer *n* Steuerzahler *m*; **~ relief** *n* Steuerermäßigung *f*; **~ return** *n* Steuererklärung *f*

TB *n abbr* (= *tuberculosis*) Tb *f*, Tbc *f*

tea [ti:] *n* Tee *m*; (*meal*) (frühes) Abendessen *nt*; **high ~** (*BRIT*) Abendessen *nt*; **~ bag** *n* Teebeutel *m*; **~ break** (*BRIT*) *n* Teepause *f*

teach [ti:tʃ] (*pt, pp* **taught**) *vt* lehren; (*SCH*) lehren, unterrichten; (*show*): **to ~ sb sth** jdm etw beibringen ♦ *vi* lehren, unterrichten; **~er** *n* Lehrer(in) *m(f)*; **~er's pet** *n* Lehrers Liebling *m*; **~ing** *n* (*~er's work*) Unterricht *m*; (*doctrine*) Lehre *f*

tea: ~ cloth *n* Geschirrtuch *nt*; **~ cosy** *n* Teewärmer *m*; **~cup** *n* Teetasse *f*; **~ leaves** *npl* Teeblätter *pl*

team [ti:m] *n* (*workers*) Team *nt*; (*SPORT*) Mannschaft *f*; (*animals*) Gespann *nt*; **~work** *n* Gemeinschaftsarbeit *f*, Teamarbeit *f*

teapot ['ti:pɔt] *n* Teekanne *f*

tear¹ [teə'] (*pt* **tore**, *pp* **torn**) *n* Riss *m* ♦ *vt* zerreißen; (*muscle*) zerren ♦ *vi* (zer)reißen; (*rush*) rasen; **~ along** *vi* (*rush*) entlangrasen; **~ up** *vt* (*sheet of paper etc*) zerreißen

tear² [tɪə'] *n* Träne *f*; **~ful** ['tɪəful] *adj* weinend; (*voice*) weinerlich; **~ gas** ['tɪəgæs] *n* Tränengas *nt*

tearoom ['ti:ru:m] *n* Teestube *f*

tease [ti:z] *n* Hänsler *m* ♦ *vt* necken

tea set *n* Teeservice *nt*

teaspoon ['tiːspuːn] n Teelöffel m

teat [tiːt] n Brustwarze f; (of animal) Zitze f; (of bottle) Sauger m

tea time n (in the afternoon) Teestunde f; (mealtime) Abendessen nt

tea towel n Geschirrtuch nt

technical ['teknɪkl] adj technisch; (knowledge, terms) Fach-; ~**ity** [teknɪ'kælɪtɪ] n technische Einzelheit f; (JUR) Formsache f; ~**ly** adv technisch; (speak) spezialisiert; (fig) genau genommen

technician [tek'nɪʃən] n Techniker m

technique [tek'niːk] n Technik f

techno ['teknəu] n Techno m

technological [teknə'lɒdʒɪkl] adj technologisch

technology [tek'nɒlədʒɪ] n Technologie f

teddy (bear) ['tedɪ-] n Teddybär m

tedious ['tiːdɪəs] adj langweilig, ermüdend

tee [tiː] n (GOLF: object) Tee nt

teem [tiːm] vi (swarm): **to ~ (with)** wimmeln (von); **it is ~ing (with rain)** es gießt in Strömen

teenage ['tiːneɪdʒ] adj (fashions etc) Teenager-, jugendlich; ~**r** n Teenager m, Jugendliche(r) mf

teens [tiːnz] npl Teenageralter nt

tee-shirt ['tiːʃəːt] n T-Shirt nt

teeter ['tiːtə*] vi schwanken

teeth [tiːθ] npl of **tooth**

teethe [tiːð] vi zahnen; **teething ring** n Beißring m; **teething troubles** npl (fig) Kinderkrankheiten pl

teetotal ['tiː'təutl] adj abstinent

tele: ~**communications** npl Fernmeldewesen nt; ~**conferencing** n Telefon- or Videokonferenz f; ~**gram** n Telegramm nt; ~**graph** n Telegraf m; ~**graph pole** n Telegrafenmast m

telephone ['telɪfəun] n Telefon nt, Fernsprecher m ♦ vt anrufen; (message) telefonisch mitteilen; **to be on the ~** (talking) telefonieren; (possessing phone) Telefon haben; ~ **booth** n Telefonzelle f; ~ **box** (BRIT) n Telefonzelle f; ~ **call** n Telefongespräch nt, Anruf m; ~ **directory** n Telefonbuch nt; ~ **number** n

Telefonnummer f; **telephonist** [tə'lefənɪst] (BRIT) n Telefonist(in) m(f)

telephoto lens ['telɪ'fəutəu-] n Teleobjektiv nt

telesales ['telɪseɪlz] n Telefonverkauf m

telescope ['telɪskəup] n Teleskop nt, Fernrohr nt ♦ vt ineinander schieben

televise ['telɪvaɪz] vt durch das Fernsehen übertragen

television ['telɪvɪʒən] n Fernsehen nt; **on ~** im Fernsehen; ~ **(set)** n Fernsehapparat m, Fernseher m

teleworking ['telɪwəːkɪŋ] n Telearbeit f

telex ['teleks] n Telex nt ♦ vt per Telex schicken

tell [tel] (pt, pp **told**) vt (story) erzählen; (secret) ausplaudern; (say, make known) sagen; (distinguish) erkennen; (be sure) wissen ♦ vi (talk) sprechen; (be sure) wissen; (divulge) es verraten; (have effect) sich auswirken; **to ~ sb to do sth** jdm sagen, dass er etw tun soll; **to ~ sb sth** or **sth to sb** jdm etw sagen; **to ~ sb by sth** jdn an etw dat erkennen; **to ~ sth from** etw unterscheiden von; **to ~ of sth** von etw sprechen; ~ **off** vt: **to ~ sb off** jdn ausschimpfen

teller ['telə*] n Kassenbeamte(r) mf

telling ['telɪŋ] adj verräterisch; (blow) hart

telltale ['telteɪl] adj verräterisch

telly ['telɪ] (BRIT: inf) n abbr (= television) TV nt

temp [temp] n abbr (= temporary) Aushilfssekretärin f

temper ['tempə*] n (disposition) Temperament nt; (anger) Zorn m ♦ vt (tone down) mildern; (metal) härten; **to be in a (bad) ~** wütend sein; **to lose one's ~** die Beherrschung verlieren

temperament ['temprəmənt] n Temperament nt; ~**al** [temprə'mentl] adj (moody) launisch

temperate ['temprət] adj gemäßigt

temperature ['temprətʃə*] n Temperatur f; (MED: high ~) Fieber nt; **to have** or **run a ~** Fieber haben

template ['templɪt] n Schablone f

temple ['templ] n Tempel m; (ANAT) Schläfe *f*

temporal ['tempərl] *adj (of time)* zeitlich; *(worldly)* irdisch, weltlich

temporarily ['tempərərılı] *adv* zeitweilig, vorübergehend

temporary ['tempərərı] *adj* vorläufig; *(road, building)* provisorisch

tempt [tempt] *vt (persuade)* verleiten; *(attract)* reizen, (ver)locken; **to ~ sb into doing sth** jdn dazu verleiten, etw zu tun; **~ation** [temp'teıʃən] *n* Versuchung *f*; **~ing** *adj (person)* verführerisch; *(object, situation)* verlockend

ten [ten] *num* zehn

tenable ['tenəbl] *adj* haltbar

tenacious [tə'neıʃəs] *adj* zäh, hartnäckig

tenacity [tə'næsıtı] *n* Zähigkeit *f*, Hartnäckigkeit *f*

tenancy ['tenənsı] *n* Mietverhältnis *nt*

tenant ['tenənt] *n* Mieter *m*; *(of larger property)* Pächter *m*

tend [tend] *vt (look after)* sich kümmern um ♦ *vi:* **to ~ to do sth** etw gewöhnlich tun

tendency ['tendənsı] *n* Tendenz *f*; *(of person)* Tendenz *f*, Neigung *f*

tender ['tendə*] *adj* zart; *(loving)* zärtlich ♦ *n (COMM: offer)* Kostenanschlag *m* ♦ *vt* (an)bieten; *(resignation)* einreichen; **~ness** *n* Zartheit *f*; *(being loving)* Zärtlichkeit *f*

tendon ['tendən] *n* Sehne *f*

tenement ['tenəmənt] *n* Mietshaus *nt*

tennis ['tenıs] *n* Tennis *nt*; **~ ball** *n* Tennisball *m*; **~ court** *n* Tennisplatz *m*; **~ player** *n* Tennisspieler(in) *m(f)*; **~ racket** *n* Tennisschläger *m*; **~ shoes** *npl* Tennisschuhe *pl*

tenor ['tenə*] *n* Tenor *m*

tenpin bowling ['tenpın-] *n* Bowling *nt*

tense [tens] *adj* angespannt ♦ *n* Zeitform *f*

tension ['tenʃən] *n* Spannung *f*

tent [tent] *n* Zelt *nt*

tentacle ['tentəkl] *n* Fühler *m*; *(of sea animals)* Fangarm *m*

tentative ['tentətıv] *adj (movement)* unsicher; *(offer)* Probe-; *(arrangement)* vorläufig; *(suggestion)* unverbindlich; **~ly** *adv* versuchsweise; *(try, move)* vorsichtig

tenterhooks ['tentəhuks] *npl:* **to be on ~** auf die Folter gespannt sein

tenth [tenθ] *adj* zehnte(r, s)

tent peg *n* Hering *m*

tent pole *n* Zeltstange *f*

tenuous ['tenjuəs] *adj* schwach

tenure ['tenjuə*] *n (of land)* Besitz *m*; *(of office)* Amtszeit *f*

tepid ['tepıd] *adj* lauwarm

term [tə:m] *n (period of time)* Zeit(raum *m*) *f*; *(limit)* Frist *f*; *(SCH)* Quartal *nt*; *(UNIV)* Trimester *nt*; *(expression)* Ausdruck *m* ♦ *vt* (be)nennen; **~s** *npl (conditions)* Bedingungen *pl*; **in the short/long ~** auf kurze/lange Sicht; **to be on good ~s with sb** gut mit jdm auskommen; **to come to ~s with** *(person)* sich einigen mit; *(problem)* sich abfinden mit

terminal ['tə:mınl] *n (BRIT: also:* **coach ~**) Endstation *f*; *(AVIAT)* Terminal *m*; *(COMPUT)* Terminal *nt or m* ♦ *adj* Schluss-; *(MED)* unheilbar; **~ly** *adj (MED):* **~ly ill** unheilbar krank

terminate ['tə:mıneıt] *vt* beenden ♦ *vi* enden, aufhören

termini ['tə:mınaı] *npl of* **terminus**

terminus ['tə:mınəs] *(pl* **termini**) *n* Endstation *f*

terrace ['terəs] *n (BRIT: row of houses)* Häuserreihe *f*; *(in garden etc)* Terrasse *f*; **the ~s** *npl (BRIT: SPORT)* die Ränge; **~d** *adj (garden)* terrassenförmig angelegt; *(house)* Reihen-

terrain [te'reın] *n* Gelände *nt*

terrible ['terıbl] *adj* schrecklich, entsetzlich, fürchterlich; **terribly** *adv* fürchterlich

terrier ['terıə*] *n* Terrier *m*

terrific [tə'rıfık] *adj* unwahrscheinlich; **~!** klasse!

terrified *adj:* **to be ~ of sth** vor etw schreckliche Angst haben

terrify ['terıfaı] *vt* erschrecken

territorial [terı'tɔ:rıəl] *adj* Gebiets-, territorial

territory ['terıtərı] *n* Gebiet *nt*

terror ['terə*] *n* Schrecken *m*

terrorism ['terərızəm] *n* Terrorismus *m*; **~ist** *n* Terrorist(in) *m(f)*; **~ize** *vt* terrorisieren

terse [tɜːs] adj knapp, kurz, bündig
test [test] n Probe f; (examination) Prüfung f; (PSYCH, TECH) Test m ♦ vt prüfen; (PSYCH) testen
testicle ['testɪkl] n (ANAT) Hoden m
testify ['testɪfaɪ] vi aussagen; **to ~ to sth** etw bezeugen
testimony ['testɪmənɪ] n (JUR) Zeugenaussage f; (fig) Zeugnis nt
test match n (SPORT) Länderkampf m
test tube n Reagenzglas nt
tetanus ['tetənəs] n Wundstarrkrampf m, Tetanus m
tether ['teðər] vt anbinden ♦ n: **at the end of one's ~** völlig am Ende
text [tekst] n Text m; (of document) Wortlaut m; **~book** n Lehrbuch nt
textiles ['tekstaɪlz] npl Textilien pl
texture ['tekstʃər] n Beschaffenheit f
Thai [taɪ] adj thailändisch ♦ n Thailänder(in) m(f); **~land** n Thailand nt
Thames [temz] n: **the ~** die Themse
than [ðæn, ðən] prep (in comparisons) als
thank [θæŋk] vt danken +dat; **you've him to ~ for your success** Sie haben Ihren Erfolg ihm zu verdanken; **~ you (very much)** danke (vielmals), danke schön; **~ful** adj dankbar; **~less** adj undankbar; **~s** npl Dank m ♦ excl danke!; **~s to** dank +gen; **T~sgiving (Day)** (US) n Thanksgiving Day m

Thanksgiving (Day)

ℹ️ **Thanksgiving (Day)** ist ein Feiertag in den USA, der auf den vierten Donnerstag im November fällt. Er soll daran erinnern, wie die Pilgerväter die gute Ernte im Jahre 1621 feierten. In Kanada gibt es einen ähnlichen Erntedanktag (der aber nichts mit dem Pilgervätern zu tun hat) am zweiten Montag im Oktober.

KEYWORD

that [ðæt, ðət] adj (demonstrative: pl those) der/die/das; jene(r, s); **that one** das da ♦ pron **1** (demonstrative: pl those) das;

who's/what's that? wer ist da/was ist das?; **is that you?** bist du das?; **that's what he said** genau das hat er gesagt; **what happened after that?** was passierte danach?; **that is** das heißt
2 (relative: subj) der/die/das, die; (: direct obj) den/die/das, die; (: indirect obj) dem/der/dem, denen; **all (that) I have** alles, was ich habe
3 (relative: of time): **the day (that)** an dem Tag, als; **the winter (that) he came** in dem Winter, in dem er kam
♦ conj dass; **he thought that I was ill** er dachte, dass ich krank sei, er dachte, ich sei krank
♦ adv (demonstrative) so; **I can't work that much** ich kann nicht so viel arbeiten

thatched [θætʃt] adj strohgedeckt; (cottage) mit Strohdach
thaw [θɔː] n Tauwetter nt ♦ vi tauen; (frozen foods, fig: people) auftauen ♦ vt (auf)tauen lassen

KEYWORD

the [ðiː, ðə] def art **1** der/die/das; **to play the piano/violin** Klavier/Geige spielen; **I'm going to the butcher's/the cinema** ich gehe zum Fleischer/ins Kino; **Elizabeth the First** Elisabeth die Erste
2 (+adj to form noun) das, die; **the rich and the poor** die Reichen und die Armen
3 (in comparisons): **the more he works the more he earns** je mehr er arbeitet, desto mehr verdient er

theatre ['θɪətər] (US **theater**) n Theater nt; (for lectures etc) Saal m; (MED) Operationssaal m; **~goer** n Theaterbesucher(in) m(f); **theatrical** [θɪ'ætrɪkl] adj Theater-; (career) Schauspieler-; (showy) theatralisch
theft [θeft] n Diebstahl m
their [ðeər] adj ihr; see also **my**; **~s** pron ihre(r, s); see also **mine**²
them [ðem, ðəm] pron (acc) sie; (dat) ihnen; see also **me**

theme [θi:m] *n* Thema *nt*; (*MUS*) Motiv *nt*; **~ park** *n* (thematisch gestalteter) Freizeitpark *m*; **~ song** *n* Titelmusik *f*

themselves [ðəm'sɛlvz] *pl pron* (*reflexive*) sich (selbst); (*emphatic*) selbst; *see also* **oneself**

then [ðɛn] *adv* (*at that time*) damals; (*next*) dann ♦ *conj* also, folglich; (*furthermore*) ferner ♦ *adj* damalig; **from ~ on** von da an; **by ~** bis dahin; **the ~ president** der damalige Präsident

theology [θɪ'ɔlədʒɪ] *n* Theologie *f*

theoretical [θɪə'rɛtɪkl] *adj* theoretisch; **~ly** *adv* theoretisch

theory ['θɪərɪ] *n* Theorie *f*

therapist ['θɛrəpɪst] *n* Therapeut(in) *m(f)*

therapy ['θɛrəpɪ] *n* Therapie *f*

KEYWORD

there [ðɛər] *adv* **1:** **there is, there are** es *or* da ist/sind; (*there exists/exist also*) es gibt; **there are 3 of them** (*people, things*) es gibt 3 davon; **there has been an accident** da war ein Unfall

2 (*place*) da, dort; (*direction*) dahin, dorthin; **put it in/on there** leg es dahinein/dorthinauf

3: there, there (*esp to child*) na, na

---

there: **~abouts** ['ðɛərə'bauts] *adv* (*place*) dort in der Nähe, dort irgendwo; (*amount*): **20 or ~abouts** ungefähr 20; **~after** [ðɛər'ɑ:ftər] *adv* danach; **~by** ['ðɛəbaɪ] *adv* dadurch, damit

therefore ['ðɛəfɔ:r] *adv* deshalb, daher

there's ['ðɛəz] = **there is; there has**

thermometer [θə'mɔmɪtər] *n* Thermometer *nt*

Thermos ['θə:məs] ® *n* Thermosflasche *f*

thesaurus [θɪ'sɔ:rəs] *n* Synonymwörterbuch *nt*

these [ði:z] *pron, adj* (*pl*) diese

theses ['θi:si:z] *npl of* **thesis**

thesis ['θi:sɪs] (*pl* **theses**) *n* (*for discussion*) These *f*; (*UNIV*) Dissertation *f*, Doktorarbeit *f*

they [ðeɪ] *pl pron* sie; (*people in general*) man; **~ say that ...** (*it is said that*) es wird gesagt,

dass; **~'d** = **they had; they would**; **~=** **they shall; they will; ~=** **they are; ~=** **they have**

thick [θɪk] *adj* dick; (*forest*) dicht; (*liquid*) dickflüssig; (*slow, stupid*) dumm, schwer von Begriff ♦ *n*: **in the ~ of** mitten in +*dat*; **it's 20 cm ~** es ist 20 cm dick *or* stark; **~en** *vi* (*fog*) dichter werden ♦ *vt* (*sauce etc*) verdicken; **~ness** *n* Dicke *f*; Dichte *f*; Dickflüssigkeit *f*; **~set** *adj* untersetzt; **~-skinned** *adj* dickhäutig

thief [θi:f] (*pl* **thieves**) *n* Dieb(in) *m(f)*

thieves [θi:vz] *npl of* **thief**

thieving ['θi:vɪŋ] *n* Stehlen *nt* ♦ *adj* diebisch

thigh [θaɪ] *n* Oberschenkel *m*

thimble ['θɪmbl] *n* Fingerhut *m*

thin [θɪn] *adj* dünn; (*person*) dünn, mager; (*excuse*) schwach ♦ *vt*: **to ~ (down)** (*sauce, paint*) verdünnen

thing [θɪŋ] *n* Ding *nt*; (*affair*) Sache *f*; **my ~s** meine Sachen *pl*; **the best ~ would be to ...** das Beste wäre, ...; **how are ~s?** wie gehts?

think [θɪŋk] (*pt, pp* **thought**) *vt, vi* denken; **what did you ~ of them?** was halten Sie von ihnen?; **to ~ about sth/sb** nachdenken über etw/jdn; **I'll ~ about it** ich überlege es mir; **to ~ of doing sth** vorhaben *or* beabsichtigen, etw zu tun; **I ~ so/not** ich glaube (schon)/glaube nicht; **to ~ well of sb** viel von jdm halten; **~ over** *vt* überdenken; **~ up** *vt* sich *dat* ausdenken

think tank *n* Expertengruppe *f*

thinly ['θɪnlɪ] *adv* dünn; (*disguised*) kaum

third [θə:d] *adj* dritte(r, s) ♦ *n* (*person*) Dritte(r) *mf*; (*part*) Drittel *nt*; **~ly** *adv* drittens; **~ party insurance** (*BRIT*) *n* Haftpflichtversicherung *f*; **~-rate** *adj* minderwertig; **T~ World** *n*: **the T~ World** die Dritte Welt *f*

thirst [θə:st] *n* (*also fig*) Durst *m*; **~y** *adj* (*person*) durstig; (*work*) durstig machend; **to be ~y** Durst haben

thirteen [θə:'ti:n] *num* dreizehn

thirty ['θə:tɪ] *num* dreißig

this [ðɪs] adj (demonstrative: pl these) diese(r, s); **this evening** heute Abend; **this one** diese(r, s) (da)
♦ pron (demonstrative: pl these) dies, das; **who/what is this?** wer/was ist das?; **this is where I live** hier wohne ich; **this is what he said** das hat er gesagt; **this is Mr Brown** dies ist Mr Brown; (on telephone) hier ist Mr Brown
♦ adv (demonstrative): **this high/long** etc so groß/lang etc

thistle ['θɪsl] n Distel f

thorn [θɔ:n] n Dorn m; **~y** adj dornig; (problem) schwierig

thorough ['θʌrə] adj gründlich; **~bred** n Vollblut nt ♦ adj reinrassig, Vollblut-; **~fare** n Straße f; **"no ~fare"** „Durchfahrt verboten"; **~ly** adv gründlich; (extremely) äußerst

those [ðəuz] pl pron die (da), jene ♦ adj die, jene

though [ðəu] conj obwohl ♦ adv trotzdem

thought [θɔ:t] pt, pp of **think** ♦ n (idea) Gedanke m; (thinking) Denken nt, Denkvermögen nt; **~ful** adj (thinking) gedankenvoll, nachdenklich; (kind) rücksichtsvoll, aufmerksam; **~less** adj gedankenlos, unbesonnen; (unkind) rücksichtslos

thousand ['θauzənd] num tausend; **two ~** zweitausend; **~s of** tausende or Tausende (von); **~th** adj tausendste(r, s)

thrash [θræʃ] vt verdreschen; (fig) (vernichtend) schlagen; **~ about** vi um sich schlagen; **~ out** vt ausdiskutieren

thread [θred] n Faden m, Garn nt; (TECH) Gewinde nt; (in story) Faden m ♦ vt (needle) einfädeln; **~bare** adj fadenscheinig

threat [θret] n Drohung f; (danger) Gefahr f; **~en** vt bedrohen ♦ vi drohen; **to ~en sb with sth** jdm etw androhen

three [θri:] num drei; **~-dimensional** adj dreidimensional; **~-piece suite** n dreiteilige Polstergarnitur f; **~-wheeler** n Dreiradwagen m

thresh [θreʃ] vt, vi dreschen

threshold ['θreʃhəuld] n Schwelle f

threw [θru:] pt of **throw**

thrift [θrɪft] n Sparsamkeit f; **~y** adj sparsam

thrill [θrɪl] n Reiz m, Erregung f ♦ vt begeistern, packen; **to be ~ed with** (gift etc) sich unheimlich freuen über +acc; **~er** n Krimi m; **~ing** adj spannend; (news) aufregend

thrive [θraɪv] (pt thrived, pp thrived) vi: **to ~ (on)** gedeihen (bei); **thriving** ['θraɪvɪŋ] adj blühend

throat [θrəut] n Hals m, Kehle f; **to have a sore ~** Halsschmerzen haben

throb [θrɔb] vi klopfen, pochen

throes [θrəuz] npl: **in the ~ of** mitten in +dat

throne [θrəun] n Thron m; **on the ~** auf dem Thron

throng ['θrɔŋ] n (Menschen)schar f ♦ vt sich drängen in +dat

throttle ['θrɔtl] n Gashebel m ♦ vt erdrosseln

through [θru:] prep durch; (time) während +gen; (because of) aus, durch ♦ adv durch ♦ adj (ticket, train) durchgehend; (finished) fertig; **to put sb ~ (to)** jdn verbinden (mit); **to be ~** (TEL) eine Verbindung haben; (have finished) fertig sein; **no ~ way** (BRIT) Sackgasse f; **~out** [θru:'aut] prep (place) überall in +dat; (time) während +gen ♦ adv überall; die ganze Zeit

throw [θrəu] (pt threw, pp thrown) n Wurf m ♦ vt werfen; **to ~ a party** eine Party geben; **~ away** vt wegwerfen; (waste) verschenken; (money) verschwenden; **~ off** vt abwerfen; (pursuer) abschütteln; **~ out** vt hinauswerfen; (rubbish) wegwerfen; (plan) verwerfen; **~ up** vt, vi (vomit) speien; **~away** adj Wegwerf-; **~-in** n Einwurf m; **~n** pp of **throw**

thru [θru:] (US) = **through**

thrush [θrʌʃ] n Drossel f

thrust [θrʌst] (pt, pp thrust) vt, vi (push) stoßen

thud [θʌd] n dumpfe(r) (Auf)schlag m

thug [θʌg] n Schlägertyp m

thumb[θʌm] *n* Daumen *m* ♦ *vt* (*book*) durchblättern; **to ~ a lift** per Anhalter fahren (wollen); **~tack**(US) *n* Reißzwecke *f*

thump[θʌmp] *n* (*blow*) Schlag *m*; (*noise*) Bums *m* ♦ *vi* hämmern, pochen ♦ *vt* schlagen auf +*acc*

thunder[ˈθʌndəʳ] *n* Donner *m* ♦ *vi* donnern; (*train etc*): **to ~ past** vorbeidonnern ♦ *vt* brüllen; **~bolt**n Blitz *m*; **~clap**n Donnerschlag *m*; **~storm**n Gewitter *nt*, Unwetter *nt*; **~y**adj gewitterschwül

Thursday[ˈθəːzdɪ] *n* Donnerstag *m*

thus[ðʌs] *adv* (*in this way*) so; (*therefore*) somit, also, folglich

thwart[θwɔːt] *vt* vereiteln, durchkreuzen; (*person*) hindern

thyme[taɪm] *n* Thymian *m*

thyroid[ˈθaɪrɔɪd] *n* Schilddrüse *f*

tiara[tɪˈɑːrə] *n* Diadem *nt*

tic[tɪk] *n* Tick *m*

tick[tɪk] *n* (*sound*) Ticken *nt*; (*mark*) Häkchen *nt* ♦ *vi* ticken ♦ *vt* abhaken; **in a ~** (*BRIT: inf*) sofort; **~ off**vt abhaken; (*person*) ausschimpfen; **~ over**vi (*engine*) im Leerlauf laufen; (*fig*) auf Sparflamme laufen

ticket[ˈtɪkɪt] *n* (*for travel*) Fahrkarte *f*; (*for entrance*) (Eintritts)karte *f*; (*price ~*) Preisschild *nt*; (*luggage ~*) (Gepäck)schein *m*; (*raffle ~*) Los *nt*; (*parking ~*) Strafzettel *m*; (*in car park*) Parkschein *m*; **~ collector**n Fahrkartenkontrolleur *m*; **~ inspector**n Fahrkartenkontrolleur *m*; **~ office**n (*THEAT etc*) Kasse *f*; (*RAIL etc*) Fahrkartenschalter *m*

tickle[ˈtɪkl] *n* Kitzeln *nt* ♦ *vt* kitzeln; (*amuse*) amüsieren; **ticklish**[ˈtɪklɪʃ] *adj* (*also fig*) kitzlig

tidal[ˈtaɪdl] *adj* Flut-, Tide-; **~ wave**n Flutwelle *f*

tidbit[ˈtɪdbɪt] (*US*) *n* Leckerbissen *m*

tiddlywinks[ˈtɪdlɪwɪŋks] *n* Floh(hüpf)spiel *nt*

tide[taɪd] *n* Gezeiten *pl*; **high/low ~** Flut *f*/ Ebbe *f*

tidy[ˈtaɪdɪ] *adj* ordentlich ♦ *vt* aufräumen, in Ordnung bringen

tie[taɪ] *n* (*BRIT: neck*) Krawatte *f*, Schlips *m*; (*sth connecting*) Band *nt*; (*SPORT*) Unentschieden *nt* ♦ *vt* (*fasten, restrict*) binden ♦ *vi* (*SPORT*) unentschieden spielen; (*in competition*) punktgleich sein; **to ~ in a bow** zur Schleife binden; **to ~ a knot in sth** einen Knoten in etw *acc* machen; **~ down** *vt* festbinden; **to ~ sb down to** jdn binden an +*acc*; **~ up**vt (*dog*) anbinden; (*parcel*) verschnüren; (*boat*) festmachen; (*person*) fesseln; **to be ~d up** (*busy*) beschäftigt sein

tier[tɪəʳ] *n* Rang *m*; (*of cake*) Etage *f*

tiff[tɪf] *n* Krach *m*

tiger[ˈtaɪgəʳ] *n* Tiger *m*

tight[taɪt] *adj* (*close*) eng, knapp; (*schedule*) gedrängt; (*firm*) fest; (*control*) streng; (*stretched*) stramm, (*an*)gespannt; (*inf: drunk*) blau, stramm ♦ *adv* (*squeeze*) fest; **~en**vt anziehen, anspannen; (*restrictions*) verschärfen ♦ *vi* sich spannen; **~fisted**adj knauserig; **~ly**adv eng; fest; (*stretched*) straff; **~rope**n Seil *nt*; **~s**npl (*esp BRIT*) Strumpfhose *f*

tile[taɪl] *n* (*on roof*) Dachziegel *m*; (*on wall or floor*) Fliese *f*; **~d**adj (*roof*) gedeckt, Ziegel-; (*floor, wall*) mit Fliesen belegt

till[tɪl] *n* Kasse *f* ♦ *vt* bestellen ♦ *prep, conj* = **until**

tiller[ˈtɪləʳ] *n* Ruderpinne *f*

tilt[tɪlt] *vt* kippen, neigen ♦ *vi* sich neigen

timber[ˈtɪmbəʳ] *n* (*wood*) Holz *nt*

time[taɪm] *n* Zeit *f*; (*occasion*) Mal *nt*; (*rhythm*) Takt *m* ♦ *vt* zur rechten Zeit tun, zeitlich einrichten; (*SPORT*) stoppen; **in 2 weeks' ~** in 2 Wochen; **a long ~** lange; **for the ~ being** vorläufig; **4 at a ~** zu jeweils 4; **from ~ to ~** gelegentlich; **to have a good ~** sich amüsieren; **in ~** (*soon enough*) rechtzeitig; (*after some ~*) mit der Zeit; (*MUS*) im Takt; **in no ~** im Handumdrehen; **any ~** jederzeit; **on ~** pünktlich, rechtzeitig; **five ~s 5** fünfmal 5; **what ~ is it?** wie viel Uhr ist es?, wie spät ist es?; **at ~s** manchmal; **~ bomb**n Zeitbombe *f*; **~less**adj (*beauty*) zeitlos; **~ limit**n Frist *f*; **~ly**adj rechtzeitig; günstig; **~ off**n freie Zeit *f*; **~r**n (*timer switch: in kitchen*) Schaltuhr *f*; **~ scale**n Zeitspanne *f*; **~-share**adj Timesharing-; **~ switch**

(*BRIT*) n Zeitschalter m; **~table** n Fahrplan m; (*SCH*) Stundenplan m; **~ zone** n Zeitzone f

timid ['tɪmɪd] adj ängstlich, schüchtern

timing ['taɪmɪŋ] n Wahl f des richtigen Zeitpunkts, Timing nt

timpani ['tɪmpənɪ] npl Kesselpauken pl

tin [tɪn] n (metal) Blech nt; (*BRIT*: can) Büchse f, Dose f; **~foil** n Stanniolpapier nt

tinge [tɪndʒ] n (colour) Färbung f; (fig) Anflug m ♦ vt färben; **~d with** mit einer Spur von

tingle ['tɪŋgl] n Prickeln nt ♦ vi prickeln

tinker ['tɪŋkəʳ] n Kesselflicker m; **~ with** vt fus herumpfuschen an +dat

tinkle ['tɪŋkl] vi klingeln

tinned [tɪnd] (*BRIT*) adj (food) Dosen-, Büchsen-

tin opener [-əupnəʳ] (*BRIT*) n Dosen- or Büchsenöffner m

tinsel ['tɪnsl] n Rauschgold nt

tint [tɪnt] n Farbton m; (slight colour) Anflug m; (hair) Tönung f; **~ed** adj getönt

tiny ['taɪnɪ] adj winzig

tip [tɪp] n (pointed end) Spitze f; (money) Trinkgeld nt; (hint) Wink m, Tipp m ♦ vt (slant) kippen; (hat) antippen; (~ over) umkippen; (waiter) ein Trinkgeld geben +dat; **~-off** n Hinweis m, Tipp m; **~ped** (*BRIT*) adj (cigarette) Filter-

tipsy ['tɪpsɪ] adj beschwipst

tiptoe ['tɪptəu] n: **on ~** auf Zehenspitzen

tiptop [tɪp'tɒp] adj: **in ~ condition** tipptopp, erstklassig

tire ['taɪəʳ] n (*US*) = **tyre** ♦ vt, vi ermüden, müde machen/werden; **~d** adj müde; **to be ~d of sth** etw satt haben; **~less** adj unermüdlich; **~some** adj lästig

tiring ['taɪərɪŋ] adj ermüdend

tissue ['tɪʃuː] n Gewebe nt; (paper handkerchief) Papiertaschentuch nt; **~ paper** n Seidenpapier nt

tit [tɪt] n (bird) Meise f; **~ for tat** wie du mir, so ich dir

titbit ['tɪtbɪt] (*US* **tidbit**) n Leckerbissen m

titillate ['tɪtɪleɪt] vt kitzeln

title ['taɪtl] n Titel m; **~ deed** n Eigentumsurkunde f; **~ role** n Hauptrolle f

titter ['tɪtəʳ] vi kichern

titular ['tɪtjuləʳ] adj (in name only) nominell

TM abbr (= trademark) Wz

KEYWORD
---

to [tuː, tə] prep **1** (direction) zu, nach; **I go to France/school** ich gehe nach Frankreich/ zur Schule; **to the left** nach links

2 (as far as) bis

3 (with expressions of time) vor; **a quarter to 5** Viertel vor 5

4 (for, of) für; **secretary to the director** Sekretärin des Directors

5 (expressing indirect object): **to give sth to sb** jdm etw geben; **to talk to sb** mit jdm sprechen; **I sold it to a friend** ich habe es einem Freund verkauft

6 (in relation to) zu; **30 miles to the gallon** 30 Meilen pro Gallone

7 (purpose, result) zu; **to my surprise** zu meiner Überraschung

♦ with vb **1** (infin): **to go/eat** gehen/essen; **to want to do sth** etw tun wollen; **to try/ start to do sth** versuchen/anfangen, etw zu tun; **he has a lot to lose** er hat viel zu verlieren

2 (with vb omitted): **I don't want to** ich will (es) nicht

3 (purpose, result) um; **I did it to help you** ich tat es, um dir zu helfen

4 (after adj etc): **ready to use** gebrauchsfertig; **too old/young to ...** zu alt/jung, um ... zu ...

♦ adv: **push/pull the door to** die Tür zuschieben/zuziehen

---

toad [təud] n Kröte f; **~stool** n Giftpilz m

toast [təust] n (bread) Toast m; (drinking) Trinkspruch m ♦ vt trinken auf +acc; (bread) toasten; (warm) wärmen; **~er** n Toaster m

tobacco [tə'bækəu] n Tabak m; **~nist** [tə'bækənɪst] n Tabakhändler m; **~nist's (shop)** n Tabakladen m

toboggan [tə'bɒgən] n (Rodel)schlitten m; **~ing** n Rodeln nt

today [tə'deɪ] adv heute; (at the present time) heutzutage

toddler [ˈtɒdləʳ] *n* Kleinkind *nt*

toddy [ˈtɒdɪ] *n* (Whisky)grog *m*

to-do [təˈduː] *n* Theater *nt*

toe [təʊ] *n* Zehe *f*; (*of sock, shoe*) Spitze *f*
♦ *vt*: **to ~ the line** (*fig*) sich einfügen; **~nail**
n Zehennagel *m*

toffee [ˈtɒfɪ] *n* Sahnebonbon *nt*; **~ apple**
(*BRIT*) *n* kandierte(r) Apfel *m*

together [təˈgeðəʳ] *adv* zusammen; (*at the
same time*) gleichzeitig; **~ with** zusammen
mit; gleichzeitig mit

toil [tɔɪl] *n* harte Arbeit *f*, Plackerei *f* ♦ *vi* sich
abmühen, sich plagen

toilet [ˈtɔɪlət] *n* Toilette *f* ♦ *cpd* Toiletten-; **~
bag** *n* Waschbeutel *m*; **~ paper** *n*
Toilettenpapier *nt*; **~ries** [ˈtɔɪlətrɪz] *npl*
Toilettenartikel *pl*; **~ roll** *n* Rolle *f*
Toilettenpapier; **~ water** *n* Toilettenwasser
nt

token [ˈtəʊkən] *n* Zeichen *nt*; (*gift ~*)
Gutschein *m*; **book/record ~** (*BRIT*)
Bücher-/Plattengutschein *m*

Tokyo [ˈtəʊkjəʊ] *n* Tokio *f*

told [təʊld] *pt, pp of* **tell**

tolerable [ˈtɒlərəbl] *adj* (*bearable*) erträglich;
(*fairly good*) leidlich

tolerant [ˈtɒlərnt] *adj*: **be ~ (of)** vertragen
+*acc*

tolerate [ˈtɒləreɪt] *vt* dulden; (*noise*) ertragen

toll [təʊl] *n* Gebühr *f* ♦ *vi* (*bell*) läuten

tomato [təˈmɑːtəʊ] *n* (*pl* **~es**) Tomate *f*

tomb [tuːm] *n* Grab(mal) *nt*

tomboy [ˈtɒmbɔɪ] *n* Wildfang *m*

tombstone [ˈtuːmstəʊn] *n* Grabstein *m*

tomcat [ˈtɒmkæt] *n* Kater *m*

tomorrow [təˈmɒrəʊ] *n* Morgen *m* ♦ *adv*
morgen; **the day after ~** übermorgen; **~
morning** morgen früh; **a week ~** morgen
in einer Woche

ton [tʌn] *n* Tonne *f* (*BRIT* = 1016kg; *US*
= 907kg); **~s of** (*inf*) eine Unmenge von

tone [təʊn] *n* Ton *m*; **~ down** *vt* (*criticism,
demands*) mäßigen; (*colours*) abtonen; **~ up**
vt in Form bringen; **~-deaf** *adj* ohne
musikalisches Gehör

tongs [tɒŋz] *npl* Zange *f*; (*curling ~*)
Lockenstab *m*

tongue [tʌŋ] *n* Zunge *f*; (*language*) Sprache
f; **with ~ in cheek** scherzhaft; **~-tied** *adj*
stumm, sprachlos; **~ twister** *n*
Zungenbrecher *m*

tonic [ˈtɒnɪk] *n* (*drink*) Tonic *nt*; (*MED*)
Stärkungsmittel *nt*

tonight [təˈnaɪt] *adv* heute Abend

tonsil [ˈtɒnsl] *n* Mandel *f*; **~litis** [tɒnsɪˈlaɪtɪs] *n*
Mandelentzündung *f*

too [tuː] *adv* zu; (*also*) auch; **~ bad!** Pech!; **~
many** zu viele

took [tʊk] *pt of* **take**

tool [tuːl] *n* (*also fig*) Werkzeug *nt*; **~box** *n*
Werkzeugkasten *m*

toot [tuːt] *n* Hupen *nt* ♦ *vi* tuten; (*AUT*)
hupen

tooth [tuːθ] (*pl* **teeth**) *n* Zahn *m*; **~ache** *n*
Zahnschmerzen *pl*, Zahnweh *nt*; **~brush** *n*
Zahnbürste *f*; **~paste** *n* Zahnpasta *f*;
~pick *n* Zahnstocher *m*

top [tɒp] *n* Spitze *f*; (*of mountain*) Gipfel *m*;
(*of tree*) Wipfel *m*; (*toy*) Kreisel *m*; (*~ gear*)
vierte(r)/fünfte(r) Gang *m* ♦ *adj* oberste(r, s)
♦ *vt* (*list*) an erster Stelle stehen auf +*dat*;
on ~ of oben auf +*dat*; **from ~ to bottom**
von oben bis unten; **~ off** (*US*) *vt* auffüllen;
~ up *vt* auffüllen; **~ floor** *n* oberste(s)
Stockwerk *nt*; **~ hat** *n* Zylinder *m*; **~-
heavy** *adj* kopflastig

topic [ˈtɒpɪk] *n* Thema *nt*,
Gesprächsgegenstand *m*; **~al** *adj* aktuell

top: ~less [ˈtɒplɪs] *adj* (*bather etc*) oben
ohne; **~-level** [ˈtɒplevl] *adj* auf höchster
Ebene; **~most** [ˈtɒpməʊst] *adj* oberste(r, s)

topple [ˈtɒpl] *vt, vi* stürzen, kippen

top-secret [ˈtɒpˈsiːkrɪt] *adj* streng geheim

topsy-turvy [ˈtɒpsɪˈtɜːvɪ] *adv* durcheinander
♦ *adj* auf den Kopf gestellt

torch [tɔːtʃ] *n* (*BRIT: ELEC*) Taschenlampe *f*;
(*with flame*) Fackel *f*

tore [tɔː] *pt of* **tear¹**

torment [*n* ˈtɔːment, *vb* tɔːˈment] *n* Qual *f*
♦ *vt* (*distress*) quälen

torn [tɔːn] *pp of* **tear¹** ♦ *adj* hin- und
hergerissen

torrent [ˈtɒrnt] *n* Sturzbach *m*; **~ial** [tɒˈrenʃl]
adj wolkenbruchartig

torrid ['tɒrɪd] adj heiß

tortoise ['tɔːtəs] n Schildkröte f; **~shell** ['tɔːtəʃel] n Schildpatt m

torture ['tɔːtʃəʳ] n Folter f ♦ vt foltern

Tory ['tɔːrɪ] (BRIT) n (POL) Tory m ♦ adj Tory-, konservativ

toss [tɒs] vt schleudern; **to ~ a coin** or **to ~ up for sth** etw mit einer Münze entscheiden; **to ~ and turn** (in bed) sich hin und her werfen

tot [tɒt] n (small quantity) bisschen nt; (small child) Knirps m

total ['təutl] n Gesamtheit f; (money) Endsumme f ♦ adj Gesamt-, total ♦ vt (add up) zusammenzählen; (amount to) sich belaufen auf

totalitarian [təutælɪ'tɛərɪən] adj totalitär

totally ['təutəlɪ] adv total

totter ['tɒtəʳ] vi wanken, schwanken

touch [tʌtʃ] n Berührung f; (sense of feeling) Tastsinn m ♦ vt (feel) berühren; (come against) leicht anstoßen; (emotionally) rühren; **a ~ of** (fig) eine Spur von; **to get in ~ with sb** sich mit jdm in Verbindung setzen; **to lose ~** (friends) Kontakt verlieren; **~ on** vt fus (topic) berühren, erwähnen; **~ up** vt (paint) auffrischen; **~-and-go** adj riskant, knapp; **~down** n Landen nt, Niedergehen nt; **~ed** adj (moved) gerührt; **~ing** adj rührend; **~line** n Seitenlinie f; **~sensitive screen** n (COMPUT) berührungsempfindlicher Bildschirm m; **~y** adj empfindlich, reizbar

tough [tʌf] adj zäh; (difficult) schwierig ♦ n Schläger(typ) m; **~en** vt zäh machen; (make strong) abhärten

toupee ['tuːpeɪ] n Toupet nt

tour ['tuəʳ] n Tour f ♦ vi umherreisen; (THEAT) auf Tour sein; auf Tour gehen; **~ guide** n Reiseleiter(in) m(f)

tourism ['tuərɪzm] n Fremdenverkehr m, Tourismus m

tourist ['tuərɪst] n Tourist(in) m(f) ♦ cpd (class) Touristen-; **~ office** n Verkehrsamt nt

tournament ['tuənəmənt] n Turnier nt

tousled ['tauzld] adj zerzaust

tout [taut] vi: **to ~ for** auf Kundenfang gehen für ♦ n: **ticket ~** Kundenschlepper(in) m(f)

tow [təu] vt (ab)schleppen; **on** (BRIT) or **in** (US) **~** (AUT) im Schlepp

toward(s) [tə'wɔːd(z)] prep (with time) gegen; (in direction of) nach

towel ['tauəl] n Handtuch nt; **~ling** n (fabric) Frottee nt or m; **~ rack** (US) n Handtuchstange f; **~ rail** n Handtuchstange f

tower ['tauəʳ] n Turm m; **~ block** (BRIT) n Hochhaus nt; **~ing** adj hochragend

town [taun] n Stadt f; **to go to ~** (fig) sich ins Zeug legen; **~ centre** n Stadtzentrum nt; **~ clerk** n Stadtdirektor m; **~ council** n Stadtrat m; **~ hall** n Rathaus nt; **~ plan** n Stadtplan m; **~ planning** n Stadtplanung f

towrope ['təurəup] n Abschlepptau nt

tow truck (US) n Abschleppwagen m

toxic ['tɒksɪk] adj giftig, Gift-

toy [tɔɪ] n Spielzeug nt; **~ with** vt fus spielen mit; **~shop** n Spielwarengeschäft nt

trace [treɪs] n Spur f ♦ vt (follow a course) nachspüren +dat; (find out) aufspüren; (copy) durchpausen; **tracing paper** n Pauspapier nt

track [træk] n (mark) Spur f; (path) Weg m; (racetrack) Rennbahn f; (RAIL) Gleis nt ♦ vt verfolgen; **to keep ~ of sb** jdn im Auge behalten; **~ down** vt aufspüren; **~suit** n Trainingsanzug m.

tract [trækt] n (of land) Gebiet nt

traction ['trækʃən] n (power) Zugkraft f; (AUT: grip) Bodenhaftung f; (MED): **in ~** im Streckverband

tractor ['træktəʳ] n Traktor m

trade [treɪd] n (commerce) Handel m; (business) Geschäft nt, Gewerbe nt; (people) Geschäftsleute pl; (skilled manual work) Handwerk nt ♦ vi: **to ~ (in)** handeln (mit) ♦ vt tauschen; **~ in** vt in Zahlung geben; **~ fair** n Messe nt; **~-in price** n Preis, zu dem etw in Zahlung genommen wird; **~mark** n Warenzeichen nt; **~ name** n Handelsbezeichnung f; **~r** n Händler m; **~sman** (irreg) n (shopkeeper) Geschäftsmann m; (workman) Handwerker *m*; (*delivery man*) Lieferant *m*; ~ **union** *n* Gewerkschaft *f*; ~ **unionist** *n* Gewerkschaftler(in) *m(f)*

trading ['treɪdɪŋ] *n* Handel *m*; ~ **estate** (*BRIT*) *n* Industriegelände *nt*

tradition [trə'dɪʃən] *n* Tradition *f*; ~**al** *adj* traditionell, herkömmlich

traffic ['træfɪk] *n* Verkehr *m*; (*esp in drugs*): ~ **(in)** Handel *m* (mit) ♦ *vi*: **to ~ in** (*esp drugs*) handeln mit; ~ **calming** *n* Verkehrsberuhigung *f*; ~ **circle** (*US*) *n* Kreisverkehr *m*; ~ **jam** *n* Verkehrsstauung *f*; ~ **lights** *npl* Verkehrsampel *f*; ~ **warden** *n* ≃ Verkehrspolizist *m* (*ohne amtliche Befugnisse*), Politesse *f* (*ohne amtliche Befugnisse*)

tragedy ['trædʒədɪ] *n* Tragödie *f*

tragic ['trædʒɪk] *adj* tragisch

trail [treɪl] *n* (*track*) Spur *f*; (*of smoke*) Rauchfahne *f*; (*of dust*) Staubwolke *f*; (*road*) Pfad *m*, Weg *m* ♦ *vt* (*animal*) verfolgen; (*person*) folgen +*dat*; (*drag*) schleppen ♦ *vi* (*hang loosely*) schleifen; (*plants*) sich ranken; (*be behind*) hinterherhinken; (*SPORT*) weit zurückliegen; (*walk*) zuckeln; ~ **behind** *vi* zurückbleiben; ~**er** *n* Anhänger *m*; (*US*: *caravan*) Wohnwagen *m*; (*for film*) Vorschau *f*; ~**er truck** (*US*) *n* Sattelschlepper *m*

train [treɪn] *n* Zug *m*; (*of dress*) Schleppe *f*; (*series*) Folge *f* ♦ *vt* (*teach*: *person*) ausbilden; (: *animal*) abrichten; (: *mind*) schulen; (*SPORT*) trainieren; (*aim*) richten ♦ *vi* (*exercise*) trainieren; (*study*) ausgebildet werden; ~ **of thought** Gedankengang *m*; **to ~ sth on** (*aim*) etw richten auf +*acc*; ~**ed** *adj* (*eye*) geschult; (*person, voice*) ausgebildet; ~**ee** *n* Lehrling *m*; Praktikant(in) *m(f)*; ~**er** *n* (*SPORT*) Trainer *m*; Ausbilder *m*; ~**ers** *npl* Turnschuhe *pl*; ~**ing** *n* (*for occupation*) Ausbildung *f*; (*SPORT*) Training *nt*; **in ~ing** im Training; ~**ing college** *n* pädagogische Hochschule *f*, Lehrerseminar *nt*; ~**ing shoes** *npl* Turnschuhe *pl*

traipse [treɪps] *vi* latschen

trait [treɪt] *n* Zug *m*, Merkmal *nt*

traitor ['treɪtə'] *n* Verräter *m*

trajectory [trə'dʒɛktərɪ] *n* Flugbahn *f*

tram [træm] (*BRIT*) *n* (*also*: ~**car**) Straßenbahn *f*

tramp [træmp] *n* Landstreicher *m* ♦ *vi* (*trudge*) stampfen, stapfen

trample ['træmpl] *vt* (nieder)trampeln ♦ *vi* (*herum*)trampeln; **to ~ (underfoot)** herumtrampeln auf +*dat*

trampoline ['træmpəli:n] *n* Trampolin *m*

tranquil ['træŋkwɪl] *adj* ruhig, friedlich; ~**lity** [træŋ'kwɪlɪtɪ] (*US* **tranquility**) *n* Ruhe *f*; ~**lizer** (*US* **tranquilizer**) *n* Beruhigungsmittel *nt*

transact [træn'zækt] *vt* abwickeln; ~**ion** [træn'zækʃən] *n* Abwicklung *f*; (*piece of business*) Geschäft *nt*, Transaktion *f*

transcend [træn'sɛnd] *vt* übersteigen

transcription [træn'skrɪpʃən] *n* Transkription *f*; (*product*) Abschrift *f*

transfer [*n* 'trænsfə', *vb* træns'fə:'] *n* (~*ring*) Übertragung *f*; (*of business*) Umzug *m*; (*being ~red*) Versetzung *f*; (*design*) Abziehbild *nt*; (*SPORT*) Transfer *m* ♦ *vt* (*business*) verlegen; (*person*) versetzen; (*prisoner*) überführen; (*drawing*) übertragen; (*money*) überweisen; **to ~ the charges** (*BRIT*: *TEL*) ein R-Gespräch führen; ~ **desk** *n* (*AVIAT*) Transitschalter *m*

transform [træns'fɔ:m] *vt* umwandeln; ~**ation** [trænsfə'meɪʃən] *n* Umwandlung *f*, Verwandlung *f*

transfusion [træns'fju:ʒən] *n* Blutübertragung *f*, Transfusion *f*

transient ['trænzɪənt] *adj* kurz(lebig)

transistor [træn'zɪstə'] *n* (*ELEC*) Transistor *m*; (*RAD*) Transistorradio *nt*

transit ['trænzɪt] *n*: **in ~** unterwegs

transition [træn'zɪʃən] *n* Übergang *m*; ~**al** *adj* Übergangs-

transit lounge *n* Warteraum *m*

translate [trænz'leɪt] *vt*, *vi* übersetzen; **translation** [trænz'leɪʃən] *n* Übersetzung *f*; **translator** [trænz'leɪtə'] *n* Übersetzer(in) *m(f)*

transmission [trænz'mɪʃən] *n* (*of information*) Übermittlung *f*; (*ELEC, MED, TV*) Übertragung *f*; (*AUT*) Getriebe *nt*

transmit [trænz'mɪt] vt (message) übermitteln; (ELEC, MED, TV) übertragen; **~ter** n Sender m

transparency [træns'pɛərnsɪ] n Durchsichtigkeit f; (BRIT: PHOT) Dia(positiv) nt

transparent [træns'pærnt] adj durchsichtig; (fig) offenkundig

transpire [træns'paɪər] vi (turn out) sich herausstellen; (happen) passieren

transplant [vb træns'plɑːnt, n 'trænsplɑːnt] vt umpflanzen; (MED, also fig: person) verpflanzen ♦ n (MED) Transplantation f; (organ) Transplantat nt

transport [n 'trænspɔːt, vb træns'pɔːt] n Transport m, Beförderung f ♦ vt befördern; transportieren; **means of ~** Transportmittel nt; **~ation** ['trænspɔː'teɪʃən] n Transport m, Beförderung f; (means) Beförderungsmittel nt; (cost) Transportkosten pl; **~ café** (BRIT) n Fernfahrerlokal nt

trap [træp] n Falle f; (carriage) zweirädrige(r) Einspänner m; (inf: mouth) Klappe f ♦ vt fangen; (person) in eine Falle locken; **~door** n Falltür f

trappings ['træpɪŋz] npl Aufmachung f

trash [træʃ] n (rubbish) Plunder m; (nonsense) Mist m; **~ can** (US) n Mülleimer m; **~y** (inf) adj minderwertig, wertlos; (novel) Schund-

traumatic [trɔː'mætɪk] adj traumatisch

travel ['trævl] n Reisen nt ♦ vi reisen ♦ vt (distance) zurücklegen; (country) bereisen; **~s** npl (journeys) Reisen pl; **~ agency** n Reisebüro nt; **~ agent** n Reisebürokaufmann(-frau) m(f); **~ler** (US **traveler**) n Reisende(r) mf; (salesman) Handlungsreisende(r) m; **~ler's cheque** (US **traveler's check**) n Reisescheck m; **~ling** (US **traveling**) n Reisen nt; **~sick** adj reisekrank; **~ sickness** n Reisekrankheit f

trawler ['trɔːlər] n (NAUT, FISHING) Fischdampfer m, Trawler m

tray [treɪ] n (tea ~) Tablett nt; (for mail) Ablage f

treacherous ['tretʃərəs] adj verräterisch; (road) tückisch

treachery ['tretʃərɪ] n Verrat m

treacle ['triːkl] n Sirup m, Melasse f

tread [tred] (pt **trod**, pp **trodden**) n Schritt m, Tritt m; (of stair) Stufe f; (on tyre) Profil nt ♦ vi treten; **~ on** vt fus treten auf +acc

treason ['triːzn] n Verrat m

treasure ['treʒər] n Schatz m ♦ vt schätzen

treasurer ['treʒərər] n Kassenverwalter m, Schatzmeister m

treasury ['treʒərɪ] n (POL) Finanzministerium nt

treat [triːt] n besondere Freude f ♦ vt (deal with) behandeln; **to ~ sb to sth** jdm etw spendieren

treatise ['triːtɪz] n Abhandlung f

treatment ['triːtmənt] n Behandlung f

treaty ['triːtɪ] n Vertrag m

treble ['trebl] adj dreifach ♦ vt verdreifachen; **~ clef** n Violinschlüssel m

tree [triː] n Baum m; **~ trunk** n Baumstamm m

trek [trek] n Treck m, Zug m; (inf) anstrengende(r) Weg m ♦ vi trecken

trellis ['trelɪs] n Gitter nt; (for gardening) Spalier nt

tremble ['trembl] vi zittern; (ground) beben

tremendous [trɪ'mendəs] adj gewaltig, kolossal; (inf: good) prima

tremor ['tremər] n Zittern nt; (of earth) Beben nt

trench [trentʃ] n Graben m; (MIL) Schützengraben m

trend [trend] n Tendenz f; **~y** (inf) adj modisch

trepidation [trepɪ'deɪʃən] n Beklommenheit f

trespass ['trespəs] vi: **to ~ on** widerrechtlich betreten; **"no ~ing"** „Betreten verboten"

trestle ['tresl] n Bock m; **~ table** n Klapptisch m

trial ['traɪəl] n (JUR) Prozess m; (test) Versuch m, Probe f; (hardship) Prüfung f; **by ~ and error** durch Ausprobieren; **~ period** n Probezeit f

triangle ['traɪæŋgl] n Dreieck nt; (MUS) Triangel f; **triangular** [traɪ'æŋgjulər] adj dreieckig

tribal ['traɪbl] adj Stammes-

tribe [traɪb] n Stamm m; **~sman** (irreg) n

Stammesangehörige(r) *m*

tribulation [trɪbjuˈleɪʃən] *n* Not *f*, Mühsal *f*

tribunal [traɪˈbjuːnl] *n* Gericht *nt*; (*inquiry*) Untersuchungsausschuss *m*

tributary [ˈtrɪbjutərɪ] *n* Nebenfluss *m*

tribute [ˈtrɪbjuːt] *n* (*admiration*) Zeichen *nt* der Hochachtung; **to pay ~ to sb/sth** jdm/einer Sache Tribut zollen

trick [trɪk] *n* Trick *m*; (*CARDS*) Stich *m* ♦ *vt* überlisten, beschwindeln; **to play a ~ on sb** jdm einen Streich spielen; **that should do the ~** daß müsste eigentlich klappen; **~ery** *n* Tricks *pl*

trickle [ˈtrɪkl] *n* Tröpfeln *nt*; (*small river*) Rinnsal *nt* ♦ *vi* tröpfeln; (*seep*) sickern

tricky [ˈtrɪkɪ] *adj* (*problem*) schwierig; (*situation*) kitzlig

tricycle [ˈtraɪsɪkl] *n* Dreirad *nt*

trifle [ˈtraɪfl] *n* Kleinigkeit *f*; (*COOK*) Trifle *m* ♦ *adv*: **a ~ ...** ein bisschen ...; **trifling** *adj* geringfügig

trigger [ˈtrɪgəʳ] *n* Drücker *m*; **~ off** *vt* auslösen

trim [trɪm] *adj* gepflegt; (*figure*) schlank ♦ *n* (*gute*) Verfassung *f*; (*embellishment, on car*) Verzierung *f* ♦ *vt* (*clip*) schneiden; (*trees*) stutzen; (*decorate*) besetzen; (*sails*) trimmen; **~mings** *npl* (*decorations*) Verzierung *f*, Verzierungen *pl*; (*extras*) Zubehör *nt*

Trinity [ˈtrɪnɪtɪ] *n*: **the ~** die Dreieinigkeit *f*

trinket [ˈtrɪŋkɪt] *n* kleine(s) Schmuckstück *nt*

trip [trɪp] *n* (*kurze*) Reise *f*; (*outing*) Ausflug *m*; (*stumble*) Stolpern *nt* ♦ *vi* (*stumble*) stolpern; **on a ~** auf Reisen; **~ up** *vi* stolpern; (*fig*) stolpern, einen Fehler machen ♦ *vt* zu Fall bringen; (*fig*) hereinlegen

tripe [traɪp] *n* (*food*) Kutteln *pl*; (*rubbish*) Mist *m*

triple [ˈtrɪpl] *adj* dreifach

triplets [ˈtrɪplɪts] *npl* Drillinge *pl*

triplicate [ˈtrɪplɪkət] *n*: **in ~** in dreifacher Ausfertigung

tripod [ˈtraɪpɔd] *n* (*PHOT*) Stativ *nt*

trite [traɪt] *adj* banal

triumph [ˈtraɪʌmf] *n* Triumph *m* ♦ *vi*: **to ~**

(over) triumphieren (über +*acc*); **~ant** [traɪˈʌmfənt] *adj* triumphierend

trivia [ˈtrɪvɪə] *npl* Trivialitäten *pl*

trivial [ˈtrɪvɪəl] *adj* gering(fügig), trivial

trod [trɔd] *pt of* **tread**; **~den** *pp of* **tread**

trolley [ˈtrɔlɪ] *n* Handwagen *m*; (*in shop*) Einkaufswagen *m*; (*for luggage*) Kofferkuli *m*; (*table*) Teewagen *m*; **~ bus** *n* Oberleitungsbus *m*, Obus *m*

trombone [trɔmˈbəun] *n* Posaune *f*

troop [truːp] *n* Schar *f*; (*MIL*) Trupp *m*; **~s** *npl* (*MIL*) Truppen *pl*; **~ in/out** *vi* hinein-/hinausströmen; **~ing the colour** *n* (*ceremony*) Fahnenparade *f*

trophy [ˈtrəufɪ] *n* Trophäe *f*

tropic [ˈtrɔpɪk] *n* Wendekreis *m*; **~al** *adj* tropisch

trot [trɔt] *n* Trott *m* ♦ *vi* trotten; **on the ~** (*BRIT: fig: inf*) in einer Tour

trouble [ˈtrʌbl] *n* (*problems*) Ärger *m*; (*worry*) Sorge *f*; (*in country, industry*) Unruhen *pl*; (*effort*) Mühe *f*; (*MED*): **stomach ~** Magenbeschwerden *pl* ♦ *vt* (*disturb*) stören; **~s** *npl* (*POL etc*) Unruhen *pl*; **to ~ to do sth** sich bemühen, etw zu tun; **to be in ~** Probleme *or* Ärger haben; **to go to the ~ of doing sth** sich die Mühe machen, etw zu tun; **what's the ~?** was ist los?; (*to sick person*) wo fehlts?; **~d** *adj* (*person*) beunruhigt; (*country*) geplagt; **~-free** *adj* sorglos; **~maker** *n* Unruhestifter *m*; **~shooter** *n* Vermittler *m*; **~some** *adj* lästig, unangenehm; (*child*) schwierig

trough [trɔf] *n* Trog *m*; (*channel*) Rinne *f*, Kanal *m*; (*MET*) Tief *nt*

trousers [ˈtrauzəz] *npl* Hose *f*

trout [traut] *n* Forelle *f*

trowel [ˈtrauəl] *n* Kelle *f*

truant [ˈtruənt] *n*: **to play ~** (*BRIT*) (die Schule) schwänzen

truce [truːs] *n* Waffenstillstand *m*

truck [trʌk] *n* Lastwagen *m*; (*RAIL*) offene(r) Güterwagen *m*; **~ driver** *n* Lastwagenfahrer *m*; **~ farm** (*US*) *n* Gemüsegärtnerei *f*

trudge [trʌdʒ] *vi* sich (mühselig) dahinschleppen

true [truː] *adj* (*exact*) wahr; (*genuine*) echt; (*friend*) treu

truffle ['trʌfl] *n* Trüffel *f or m*

truly ['truːlɪ] *adv* wirklich; **yours ~** Ihr sehr ergebener

trump [trʌmp] *n* (*CARDS*) Trumpf *m*

trumpet ['trʌmpɪt] *n* Trompete *f*

truncheon ['trʌntʃən] *n* Gummiknüppel *m*

trundle ['trʌndl] *vt* schieben ♦ *vi*: **to ~ along** entlangrollen

trunk [trʌŋk] *n* (*of tree*) (Baum)stamm *m*; (*ANAT*) Rumpf *m*; (*box*) Truhe *f*, Überseekoffer *m*; (*of elephant*) Rüssel *m*; (*US: AUT*) Kofferraum *m*; **~s** *npl* (*also:* **swimming ~s**) Badehose *f*

truss [trʌs] *vt* (*also:* **~ up**) fesseln

trust [trʌst] *n* (*confidence*) Vertrauen *nt*; (*for land etc*) Treuhandvermögen *nt* ♦ *vt* (*rely on*) vertrauen +*dat*, sich verlassen auf +*acc*; (*hope*) hoffen; (*entrust*): **to ~ sth to sb** jdm etw anvertrauen; **~ed** *adj* treu; **~ee** [trʌs'tiː] *n* Vermögensverwalter *m*; **~ful** *adj* vertrauensvoll; **~ing** *adj* vertrauensvoll; **~worthy** *adj* vertrauenswürdig; (*account*), glaubwürdig

truth [truːθ] *n* Wahrheit *f*; **~ful** *adj* ehrlich

try [traɪ] *n* Versuch *m* ♦ *vt* (*attempt*) versuchen; (*test*) (aus)probieren; (*JUR: person*) unter Anklage stellen; (*: case*) verhandeln; (*courage, patience*) auf die Probe stellen ♦ *vi* (*make effort*) versuchen, sich bemühen; **to have a ~** es versuchen; **to ~ to do sth** versuchen, etw zu tun; **~ on** *vt* (*dress*) anprobieren; (*hat*) aufprobieren; **~ out** *vt* ausprobieren; **~ing** *adj* schwierig

T-shirt ['tiːʃəːt] *n* T-Shirt *nt*

T-square ['tiːskwɛəʳ] *n* Reißschiene *f*

tub [tʌb] *n* Wanne *f*, Kübel *m*; (*for margarine etc*) Becher *m*

tubby ['tʌbɪ] *adj* rundlich

tube [tjuːb] *n* Röhre *f*, Rohr *nt*; (*for toothpaste etc*) Tube *f*; (*underground*) U-Bahn *f*; (*AUT*) Schlauch *m*

tuberculosis [tjubəːkjuˈləusɪs] *n* Tuberkulose *f*

tube station *n* (*in London*) U-Bahnstation *f*;

tubing ['tjuːbɪŋ] *n* Schlauch *m*; **tubular** ['tjuːbjuləʳ] *adj* röhrenförmig

TUC (*BRIT*) *n abbr* = **Trades Union Congress**

tuck [tʌk] *n* (*fold*) Falte *f*, Einschlag *m* ♦ *vt* (*put*) stecken; (*gather*) fälteln, einschlagen; **~ away** *vt* wegstecken; **~ in** *vt* hineinstecken; (*blanket etc*) feststecken; (*person*) zudecken ♦ *vi* (*eat*) hineinhauen, zulangen; **~ up** *vt* (*child*) warm zudecken; **~ shop** *n* Süßwarenladen *m*

Tuesday ['tjuːzdɪ] *n* Dienstag *m*

tuft [tʌft] *n* Büschel *m*

tug [tʌg] *n* (*jerk*) Zerren *nt*, Ruck *m*; (*NAUT*) Schleppdampfer *m* ♦ *vt, vi* zerren, ziehen; (*boat*) schleppen; **~ of war** *n* Tauziehen *nt*

tuition [tjuːˈɪʃən] *n* (*BRIT*) Unterricht *m*; (*: private ~*) Privatunterricht *m*; (*US: school fees*) Schulgeld *nt*

tulip ['tjuːlɪp] *n* Tulpe *f*

tumble ['tʌmbl] *n* (*fall*) Sturz *m* ♦ *vi* fallen, stürzen; **~ to** *vt fus* kapieren; **~down** *adj* baufällig; **~ dryer** (*BRIT*) *n* Trockner *m*; **~r** ['tʌmbləʳ] *n* (*glass*) Trinkglas *nt*

tummy ['tʌmɪ] *n* (*inf*) Bauch *m*; **~ upset** *n* Magenverstimmung *f*

tumour ['tjuːməʳ] (*US* **tumor**) *n* Geschwulst *f*, Tumor *m*

tumultuous [tjuːˈmʌltjuəs] *adj* (*welcome, applause etc*) stürmisch

tuna ['tjuːnə] *n* T(h)unfisch *m*

tune [tjuːn] *n* Melodie *f* ♦ *vt* (*MUS*) stimmen; (*AUT*) richtig einstellen; **to sing in ~/out of ~** richtig/falsch singen; **to be out of ~ with** nicht harmonieren mit; **~ in** *vi* einschalten; **~ up** *vi* (*MUS*) stimmen; **~ful** *adj* melodisch; **~r** *n* (*RAD*) Tuner *m*; (*person*) (Instrumenten)stimmer *m*; **piano ~r** *n* Klavierstimmer(in) *m(f)*

tunic ['tjuːnɪk] *n* Waffenrock *m*; (*loose garment*) lange Bluse *f*

tuning ['tjuːnɪŋ] *n* (*RAD, AUT*) Einstellen *nt*; (*MUS*) Stimmen *nt*; **~ fork** *n* Stimmgabel *f*

Tunisia [tjuːˈnɪzɪə] *n* Tunesien *nt*

tunnel ['tʌnl] *n* Tunnel *m*, Unterführung *f* ♦ *vi* einen Tunnel anlegen

turbulent ['təːbjulənt] *adj* stürmisch

tureen [tə'riːn] *n* Terrine *f*

turf [təːf] *n* Rasen *m*; (*piece*) Sode *f* ♦ *vt* mit Grassoden belegen; **~ out** (*inf*) *vt* rauswerfen

turgid ['təːdʒɪd] *adj* geschwollen

Turk [təːk] *n* Türke *m*, Türkin *f*

Turkey ['təːkɪ] *n* Türkei *f*

turkey ['təːkɪ] *n* Puter *m*, Truthahn *m*

Turkish ['təːkɪʃ] *adj* türkisch ♦ *n* (*LING*) Türkisch *nt*

turmoil ['təːmɔɪl] *n* Aufruhr *m*, Tumult *m*

turn [təːn] *n* (*rotation*) (Um)drehung *f*; (*performance*) (Programm)nummer *f*; (*MED*) Schock *m* ♦ *vt* (*rotate*) drehen; (*change position of*) umdrehen, wenden; (*page*) umblättern; (*transform*): **to ~ sth into sth** etw in etw *acc* verwandeln; (*direct*) zuwenden ♦ *vi* (*rotate*) sich drehen; (*change direction: in car*) abbiegen; (*: wind*) drehen; (*~ round*) umdrehen, wenden; (*become*) werden; (*leaves*) sich verfärben; (*milk*) sauer werden; (*weather*) umschlagen; **to do sb a good ~** jdm etwas Gutes tun; **it's your ~** du bist dran *or* an der Reihe; **in ~, by ~s** abwechselnd; **to take ~s** sich abwechseln; **it gave me quite a ~** das hat mich schön erschreckt; **"no left ~"** (*AUT*) „Linksabbiegen verboten"; **~ away** *vi* sich abwenden; **~ back** *vt* umdrehen; (*person*) zurückschicken; (*clock*) zurückstellen ♦ *vi* umkehren; **~ down** *vt* (*refuse*) ablehnen; (*fold down*) umschlagen; **~ in** *vi* (*go to bed*) ins Bett gehen ♦ *vt* (*fold inwards*) einwärts biegen; **~ off** *vi* abbiegen ♦ *vt* ausschalten; (*tap*) zudrehen; (*machine, electricity*) abstellen; **~ on** *vt* (*light*) anschalten, einschalten; (*tap*) aufdrehen; (*machine*) anstellen; **~ out** *vi* (*prove to be*) sich erweisen; (*people*) sich entwickeln ♦ *vt* (*light*) ausschalten; (*gas*) abstellen; (*produce*) produzieren; **how did the cake ~ out?** wie ist der Kuchen geworden?; **~ over** *vi* (*person*) sich umdrehen ♦ *vt* (*object*) umdrehen, wenden; (*page*) umblättern; **~ round** *vi* (*person, vehicle*) sich herumdrehen; (*rotate*) sich drehen; **~ up** *vi* auftauchen ♦ *vt* (*collar*) hochklappen,

hochstellen; (*nose*) rümpfen; (*increase: radio*) lauter stellen; (*: heat*) höher drehen; **~ing** *n* (*in road*) Abzweigung *f*; **~ing point** *n* Wendepunkt *m*

turnip ['təːnɪp] *n* Steckrübe *f*

turnout ['təːnaut] *n* (Besucher)zahl *f*

turnover ['təːnəuvə*r*] *n* Umsatz *m*; (*of staff*) Wechsel *m*

turnpike ['təːnpaɪk] (*US*) *n* gebührenpflichtige Straße *f*

turn-: ~stile ['təːnstaɪl] *n* Drehkreuz *nt*; **~table** ['təːnteɪbl] *n* (*of record player*) Plattenteller *m*; (*RAIL*) Drehscheibe *f*; **~-up** ['təːnʌp] (*BRIT*) *n* (*on trousers*) Aufschlag *m*

turpentine ['təːpəntaɪn] *n* Terpentin *nt*

turquoise ['təːkwɔɪz] *n* (*gem*) Türkis *m*; (*colour*) Türkis *nt* ♦ *adj* türkisfarben

turret ['tʌrɪt] *n* Turm *m*

turtle ['təːtl] *n* Schildkröte *f*; **~ neck (sweater)** *n* Pullover *m* mit Schildkrötkragen

tusk [tʌsk] *n* Stoßzahn *m*

tussle ['tʌsl] *n* Balgerei *f*

tutor ['tjuːtə*r*] *n* (*teacher*) Privatlehrer *m*; (*college instructor*) Tutor *m*; **~ial** [tjuː'tɔːrɪəl] *n* (*UNIV*) Kolloquium *nt*, Seminarübung *f*

tuxedo [tʌk'siːdəu] (*US*) *n* Smoking *m*

TV [tiː'viː] *n abbr* (= *television*) TV *nt*

twang [twæŋ] *n* scharfe(r) Ton *m*; (*of voice*) Näseln *nt*

tweezers ['twiːzəz] *npl* Pinzette *f*

twelfth [twɛlfθ] *adj* zwölfte(r, s)

twelve [twɛlv] *num* zwölf; **at ~ o'clock** (*midday*) um 12 Uhr; (*midnight*) um null Uhr

twentieth ['twɛntɪɪθ] *adj* zwanzigste(r, s)

twenty ['twɛntɪ] *num* zwanzig

twice [twaɪs] *adv* zweimal; **~ as much** doppelt so viel

twiddle ['twɪdl] *vt, vi*: **to ~ (with) sth** an etw *dat* herumdrehen; **to ~ one's thumbs** (*fig*) Däumchen drehen

twig [twɪg] *n* dünne(r) Zweig *m* ♦ *vt* (*inf*) kapieren, merken

twilight ['twaɪlaɪt] *n* Zwielicht *nt*

twin [twɪn] *n* Zwilling *m* ♦ *adj* Zwillings-; (*very similar*) Doppel- ♦ *vt* (*towns*) zu

Partnerstädten machen; **~-bedded room**
n Zimmer nt mit zwei Einzelbetten; **~ beds**
npl zwei (gleiche) Einzelbetten pl
twine [twaɪn] n Bindfaden m ♦ vi (plants)
sich ranken
twinge [twɪndʒ] n stechende(r) Schmerz m,
Stechen nt
twinkle ['twɪŋkl] n Funkeln nt, Blitzen nt ♦ vi
funkeln
twinned adj: **to be ~ with** die Partnerstadt
von ... sein
twirl [twəːl] n Wirbel m ♦ vt, vi
(herum)wirbeln
twist [twɪst] n (~ing) Drehung f; (bend) Kurve
f ♦ vt (turn) drehen; (make crooked)
verbiegen; (distort) verdrehen ♦ vi (wind)
sich drehen; (curve) sich winden
twit [twɪt] (inf) n Idiot m
twitch [twɪtʃ] n Zucken nt ♦ vi zucken
two [tuː] num zwei; **to put ~ and ~ together**
seine Schlüsse ziehen; **~-door** adj
zweitürig; **~-faced** adj falsch; **~-fold** adj,
adv zweifach, doppelt; **to increase ~fold**
verdoppeln; **~-piece** adj zweiteilig; **~-
piece (suit)** n Zweiteiler m; **~-piece
(swimsuit)** n zweiteilige(r) Badeanzug m;
~-seater n (plane, car) Zweisitzer m;
~some n Paar nt; **~-way** adj (traffic)
Gegen-
tycoon [taɪ'kuːn] n: **(business) ~**
(Industrie)magnat m
type [taɪp] n Typ m, Art f; (PRINT) Type f ♦ vt,
vi Maschine schreiben, tippen; **~-cast** adj
(THEAT, TV) auf eine Rolle festgelegt; **~-face**
n Schrift f; **~script** n
maschinegeschriebene(r) Text m; **~writer**
n Schreibmaschine f; **~written** adj
maschinegeschrieben
typhoid ['taɪfɔɪd] n Typhus m
typical ['tɪpɪkl] adj: **~ (of)** typisch (für)
typify ['tɪpɪfaɪ] vt typisch sein für
typing ['taɪpɪŋ] n Maschineschreiben nt
typist ['taɪpɪst] n Maschinenschreiber(in)
m(f), Tippse f (inf)
tyrant ['taɪərnt] n Tyrann m
tyre ['taɪə*] (US **tire**) n Reifen m; **~ pressure**
n Reifendruck m

U, u

U-bend ['juːbɛnd] n (in pipe) U-Bogen m
udder ['ʌdə*] n Euter nt
UFO ['juːfəu] n abbr (= unidentified flying
object) UFO nt
ugh [əːh] excl hu
ugliness ['ʌglɪnɪs] n Hässlichkeit f
ugly ['ʌglɪ] adj hässlich; (bad) böse, schlimm
UHT abbr (= ultra heat treated): **UHT milk**
H-Milch f
UK n abbr = **United Kingdom**
ulcer ['ʌlsə*] n Geschwür nt
Ulster ['ʌlstə*] n Ulster nt
ulterior [ʌl'tɪərɪə*] adj: **~ motive**
Hintergedanke m
ultimate ['ʌltɪmət] adj äußerste(r, s),
allerletzte(r, s); **~ly** adv schließlich, letzten
Endes
ultrasound ['ʌltrəsaund] n (MED) Ultraschall
m
umbilical cord [ʌm'bɪlɪkl-] n Nabelschnur f
umbrella [ʌm'brɛlə] n Schirm m
umpire ['ʌmpaɪə*] n Schiedsrichter m ♦ vt, vi
schiedsrichtern
umpteenth [ʌmp'tiːnθ] (inf) adj zig; **for the
~ time** zum x-ten Mal
UN n abbr = **United Nations**
unable [ʌn'eɪbl] adj: **to be ~ to do sth** etw
nicht tun können
unacceptable [ʌnək'sɛptəbl] adj
unannehmbar, nicht akzeptabel
unaccompanied [ʌnə'kʌmpənɪd] adj ohne
Begleitung
unaccountably [ʌnə'kauntəblɪ] adv
unerklärlich
unaccustomed [ʌnə'kʌstəmd] adj nicht
gewöhnt; (unusual) ungewohnt; **~ to** nicht
gewöhnt an +acc
unanimous [juː'nænɪməs] adj einmütig;
(vote) einstimmig; **~ly** adv einmütig;
einstimmig
unarmed [ʌn'ɑːmd] adj unbewaffnet
unashamed [ʌnə'ʃeɪmd] adj schamlos
unassuming [ʌnə'sjuːmɪŋ] adj bescheiden

unattached [ʌnə'tætʃt] *adj* ungebunden

unattended [ʌnə'tendɪd] *adj* (*person*) unbeaufsichtigt; (*thing*) unbewacht

unauthorized [ʌn'ɔːθəraɪzd] *adj* unbefugt

unavoidable [ʌnə'vɔɪdəbl] *adj* unvermeidlich

unaware [ʌnə'weəʳ] *adj*: **to be ~ of sth** sich *dat* einer Sache *gen* nicht bewusst sein; **~s** *adv* unversehens

unbalanced [ʌn'bælənst] *adj* unausgeglichen; (*mentally*) gestört

unbearable [ʌn'beərəbl] *adj* unerträglich

unbeatable [ʌn'biːtəbl] *adj* unschlagbar

unbeknown(st) [ʌnbɪ'nəun(st)] *adv*: **~ to me** ohne mein Wissen

unbelievable [ʌnbɪ'liːvəbl] *adj* unglaublich

unbend [ʌn'bend] (*irreg: like* **bend**) *vt* gerade biegen ♦ *vi* aus sich herausgehen

unbias(s)ed [ʌn'baɪəst] *adj* unparteiisch

unborn [ʌn'bɔːn] *adj* ungeboren

unbreakable [ʌn'breɪkəbl] *adj* unzerbrechlich

unbridled [ʌn'braɪdld] *adj* ungezügelt

unbroken [ʌn'brəukən] *adj* (*period*) ununterbrochen; (*spirit*) ungebrochen; (*record*) unübertroffen

unburden [ʌn'bəːdn] *vt*: **to ~ o.s.** (jdm) sein Herz ausschütten

unbutton [ʌn'bʌtn] *vt* aufknöpfen

uncalled-for [ʌn'kɔːldfɔːʳ] *adj* unnötig

uncanny [ʌn'kænɪ] *adj* unheimlich

unceasing [ʌn'siːsɪŋ] *adj* unaufhörlich

unceremonious [ʌnserɪ'məunɪəs] *adj* (*abrupt, rude*) brüsk; (*exit, departure*) überstürzt

uncertain [ʌn'səːtn] *adj* unsicher; (*doubtful*) ungewiss; (*unreliable*) unbeständig; (*vague*) undeutlich, vag(e); **~ty** *n* Ungewissheit *f*

unchanged [ʌn'tʃeɪndʒd] *adj* unverändert

unchecked [ʌn'tʃekt] *adj* ungeprüft; (*not stopped: advance*) ungehindert

uncivilized [ʌn'sɪvɪlaɪzd] *adj* unzivilisiert

uncle ['ʌŋkl] *n* Onkel *m*

uncomfortable [ʌn'kʌmfətəbl] *adj* unbequem, ungemütlich

uncommon [ʌn'kɔmən] *adj* ungewöhnlich; (*outstanding*) außergewöhnlich

uncompromising [ʌn'kɔmprəmaɪzɪŋ] *adj* kompromisslos, unnachgiebig

unconcerned [ʌnkən'səːnd] *adj* unbekümmert; (*indifferent*) gleichgültig

unconditional [ʌnkən'dɪʃənl] *adj* bedingungslos

unconscious [ʌn'kɔnʃəs] *adj* (*MED*) bewusstlos; (*not meant*) unbeabsichtigt ♦ *n*: **the ~** das Unbewusste; **~ly** *adv* unbewusst

uncontrollable [ʌnkən'trəuləbl] *adj* unkontrollierbar, unbändig

unconventional [ʌnkən'venʃənl] *adj* unkonventionell

uncouth [ʌn'kuːθ] *adj* grob

uncover [ʌn'kʌvəʳ] *vt* aufdecken

undecided [ʌndɪ'saɪdɪd] *adj* unschlüssig

undeniable [ʌndɪ'naɪəbl] *adj* unleugbar

under ['ʌndəʳ] *prep* unter ♦ *adv* darunter; **~ there** da drunter; **~ repair** in Reparatur

underage [ʌndər'eɪdʒ] *adj* minderjährig

undercarriage ['ʌndəkærɪdʒ] (*BRIT*) *n* (*AVIAT*) Fahrgestell *nt*

undercharge [ʌndə'tʃɑːdʒ] *vt*: **to ~ sb** jdm zu wenig berechnen

undercoat ['ʌndəkəut] *n* (*paint*) Grundierung *f*

undercover [ʌndə'kʌvəʳ] *adj* Geheim-

undercurrent ['ʌndəkʌrnt] *n* Unterströmung *f*

undercut [ʌndə'kʌt] (*irreg: like* **cut**) *vt* unterbieten

underdeveloped ['ʌndədɪ'veləpt] *adj* Entwicklungs-, unterentwickelt

underdog ['ʌndədɔg] *n* Unterlegene(r) *mf*

underdone [ʌndə'dʌn] *adj* (*COOK*) nicht gar, nicht durchgebraten

underestimate ['ʌndər'estɪmeɪt] *vt* unterschätzen

underexposed ['ʌndərɪks'pəuzd] *adj* unterbelichtet

underfoot [ʌndə'fut] *adv* am Boden

undergo [ʌndə'gəu] (*irreg: like* **go**) *vt* (*experience*) durchmachen; (*test, operation*) sich unterziehen +*dat*

undergraduate ['ʌndə'grædjuɪt] *n* Student(in) *m(f)*

underground ['ʌndəgraund] *n* U-Bahn *f*

♦ adj Untergrund-

undergrowth ['ʌndəgrəʊθ] n Gestrüpp nt, Unterholz nt

underhand(ed) [ʌndə'hænd(ɪd)] adj hinterhältig

underlie [ʌndə'laɪ] (irreg: like **lie**) vt zugrunde or zu Grunde liegen +dat

underline [ʌndə'laɪn] vt unterstreichen; (emphasize) betonen

underling ['ʌndəlɪŋ] n Handlanger m

undermine [ʌndə'maɪn] vt untergraben

underneath [ʌndə'niːθ] adv darunter ♦ prep unter

underpaid [ʌndə'peɪd] adj unterbezahlt

underpants ['ʌndəpænts] npl Unterhose f

underpass ['ʌndəpɑːs] (BRIT) n Unterführung f

underprivileged [ʌndə'prɪvɪlɪdʒd] adj benachteiligt, unterprivilegiert

underrate [ʌndə'reɪt] vt unterschätzen

undershirt ['ʌndəʃəːt] (US) n Unterhemd nt

undershorts ['ʌndəʃɔːts] (US) npl Unterhose f

underside ['ʌndəsaɪd] n Unterseite f

underskirt ['ʌndəskəːt] (BRIT) n Unterrock m

understand [ʌndə'stænd] (irreg: like **stand**) vt, vi verstehen; **I ~ that ...** ich habe gehört, dass ...; **am I to ~ that ...?** soll das (etwa) heißen, dass ...?; **what do you ~ by that?** was verstehen Sie darunter?; **it is understood that ...** es wurde vereinbart, dass ...; **to make o.s. understood** sich verständlich machen; **is that understood?** ist das klar?; **~able** adj verständlich; **~ing** n Verständnis nt ♦ adj verständnisvoll

understatement ['ʌndəsteɪtmənt] n (quality) Untertreibung f; **that's an ~!** das ist untertrieben!

understood [ʌndə'stʊd] pt, pp of **understand** ♦ adj klar; (implied) angenommen

understudy ['ʌndəstʌdɪ] n Ersatz(schau)spieler(in) m(f)

undertake [ʌndə'teɪk] (irreg: like **take**) vt unternehmen ♦ vi: **to ~ to do sth** sich verpflichten, etw zu tun

undertaker ['ʌndəteɪkə'] n Leichenbestat-

ter m

undertaking ['ʌndəteɪkɪŋ] n (enterprise) Unternehmen nt; (promise) Verpflichtung f

undertone ['ʌndətəʊn] n: **in an ~** mit gedämpfter Stimme

underwater ['ʌndə'wɔːtə'] adv unter Wasser ♦ adj Unterwasser-

underwear ['ʌndəwɛə'] n Unterwäsche f

underworld ['ʌndəwəːld] n (of crime) Unterwelt f

underwriter ['ʌndəraɪtə'] n Assekurant m

undesirable [ʌndɪ'zaɪərəbl] adj unerwünscht

undies ['ʌndɪz] (inf) npl (Damen)unterwäsche f

undisputed ['ʌndɪs'pjuːtɪd] adj unbestritten

undo [ʌn'duː] (irreg: like **do**) vt (unfasten) öffnen, aufmachen; (work) zunichte machen; **~ing** n Verderben nt

undoubted [ʌn'daʊtɪd] adj unbezweifelt; **~ly** adv zweifellos, ohne Zweifel

undress [ʌn'drɛs] vt ausziehen ♦ vi sich ausziehen

undue [ʌn'djuː] adj übermäßig

undulating ['ʌndjuleɪtɪŋ] adj wellenförmig; (country) wellig

unduly [ʌn'djuːlɪ] adv übermäßig

unearth [ʌn'əːθ] vt (dig up) ausgraben; (discover) ans Licht bringen

unearthly [ʌn'əːθlɪ] adj (hour) nachtschlafen

uneasy [ʌn'iːzɪ] adj (worried) unruhig; (feeling) ungut

uneconomic(al) ['ʌniːkə'nɒmɪk(l)] adj unwirtschaftlich

uneducated [ʌn'ɛdjukeɪtɪd] adj ungebildet

unemployed [ʌnɪm'plɔɪd] adj arbeitslos ♦ npl: **the ~** die Arbeitslosen pl

unemployment [ʌnɪm'plɔɪmənt] n Arbeitslosigkeit f

unending [ʌn'ɛndɪŋ] adj endlos

unerring [ʌn'əːrɪŋ] adj unfehlbar

uneven [ʌn'iːvn] adj (surface) uneben; (quality) ungleichmäßig

unexpected [ʌnɪks'pɛktɪd] adj unerwartet; **~ly** adv unerwartet

unfailing [ʌn'feɪlɪŋ] adj nie versagend

unfair [ʌn'fɛə'] adj ungerecht, unfair

unfaithful [ʌn'feɪθful] adj untreu

unfamiliar [ʌnfə'mɪlɪəʳ] *adj* ungewohnt; (*person, subject*) unbekannt; **to be ~ with** nicht kennen +*acc*, nicht vertraut sein mit

unfashionable [ʌn'fæʃnəbl] *adj* unmodern; (*area etc*) nicht in Mode

unfasten [ʌn'fɑːsn] *vt* öffnen, aufmachen

unfavourable [ʌn'feɪvrəbl] (*US* **unfavorable**) *adj* ungünstig

unfeeling [ʌn'fiːlɪŋ] *adj* gefühllos, kalt

unfinished [ʌn'fɪnɪʃt] *adj* unvollendet

unfit [ʌn'fɪt] *adj* ungeeignet; (*in bad health*) nicht fit; **~ for sth** zu *or* für etw ungeeignet

unfold [ʌn'fəʊld] *vt* entfalten; (*paper*) auseinander falten ♦ *vi* (*develop*) sich entfalten

unforeseen ['ʌnfɔː'siːn] *adj* unvorhergesehen

unforgettable [ʌnfə'getəbl] *adj* unvergesslich

unforgivable [ʌnfə'gɪvəbl] *adj* unverzeihlich

unfortunate [ʌn'fɔːtʃənət] *adj* unglücklich, bedauerlich; **~ly** *adv* leider

unfounded [ʌn'faʊndɪd] *adj* unbegründet

unfriendly [ʌn'frendlɪ] *adj* unfreundlich

ungainly [ʌn'geɪnlɪ] *adj* linkisch

ungodly [ʌn'gɒdlɪ] *adj* (*hour*) nachtschlafend; (*row*) heillos

ungrateful [ʌn'greɪtful] *adj* undankbar

unhappiness [ʌn'hæpɪnɪs] *n* Unglück *nt*, Unglückseligkeit *f*

unhappy [ʌn'hæpɪ] *adj* unglücklich; **~ with** (*arrangements etc*) unzufrieden mit

unharmed [ʌn'hɑːmd] *adj* wohlbehalten, unversehrt

UNHCR *n abbr* (= *United Nations High Commission for Refugees*) Flüchtlingshochkommissariat der Vereinten Nationen

unhealthy [ʌn'helθɪ] *adj* ungesund

unheard-of [ʌn'hɜːdɔv] *adj* unerhört

unhurt [ʌn'hɜːt] *adj* unverletzt

unidentified [ʌnaɪ'dentɪfaɪd] *adj* unbekannt, nicht identifiziert

uniform ['juːnɪfɔːm] *n* Uniform *f* ♦ *adj* einheitlich; **~ity** [juːnɪ'fɔːmɪtɪ] *n* Einheitlichkeit *f*

unify ['juːnɪfaɪ] *vt* vereinigen

unilateral [juːnɪ'lætərəl] *adj* einseitig

uninhabited [ʌnɪn'hæbɪtɪd] *adj* unbewohnt

unintentional [ʌnɪn'tenʃənəl] *adj* unabsichtlich

union ['juːnjən] *n* (*uniting*) Vereinigung *f*; (*alliance*) Bund *m*, Union *f*; (*trade ~*) Gewerkschaft *f*; **U~ Jack** *n* Union Jack *m*

unique [juː'niːk] *adj* einzig(artig)

UNISON ['juːnɪsn] *n* Gewerkschaft der Angestellten im öffentlichen Dienst

unison ['juːnɪsn] *n* Einstimmigkeit *f*; **in ~** einstimmig

unit ['juːnɪt] *n* Einheit *f*; **kitchen ~** Küchenelement *nt*

unite [juː'naɪt] *vt* vereinigen ♦ *vi* sich vereinigen; **~d** *adj* vereinigt; (*together*) vereint; **U~d Kingdom** *n* Vereinigte(s) Königreich *nt*; **U~d Nations (Organization)** *n* Vereinte Nationen *pl*; **U~d States (of America)** *n* Vereinigte Staaten *pl* (von Amerika)

unit trust (*BRIT*) *n* Treuhandgesellschaft *f*

unity ['juːnɪtɪ] *n* Einheit *f*; (*agreement*) Einigkeit *f*

universal [juːnɪ'vɜːsl] *adj* allgemein

universe ['juːnɪvɜːs] *n* (Welt)all *nt*

university [juːnɪ'vɜːsɪtɪ] *n* Universität *f*

unjust [ʌn'dʒʌst] *adj* ungerecht

unkempt [ʌn'kempt] *adj* ungepflegt

unkind [ʌn'kaɪnd] *adj* unfreundlich

unknown [ʌn'nəʊn] *adj*: **~ (to sb)** (jdm) unbekannt

unlawful [ʌn'lɔːful] *adj* illegal

unleaded ['ʌn'ledɪd] *adj* bleifrei, unverbleit; **I use ~** ich fahre bleifrei

unleash [ʌn'liːʃ] *vt* entfesseln

unless [ʌn'les] *conj* wenn nicht, es sei denn; **~ he comes** es sei denn, er kommt; **~ otherwise stated** sofern nicht anders angegeben

unlike [ʌn'laɪk] *adj* unähnlich ♦ *prep* im Gegensatz zu

unlikely [ʌn'laɪklɪ] *adj* (*not likely*) unwahrscheinlich; (*unexpected: combination etc*) merkwürdig

unlimited [ʌn'lɪmɪtɪd] *adj* unbegrenzt

unlisted ['ʌn'lɪstɪd] (*US*) *adj* nicht im

Telefonbuch stehend

unload [ʌn'ləʊd] *vt* entladen

unlock [ʌn'lɒk] *vt* aufschließen

unlucky [ʌn'lʌkɪ] *adj* unglücklich; (*person*) unglückselig; **to be ~** Pech haben

unmarried [ʌn'mærɪd] *adj* unverheiratet, ledig

unmask [ʌn'mɑːsk] *vt* entlarven

unmistakable [ʌnmɪs'teɪkəbl] *adj* unverkennbar

unmitigated [ʌn'mɪtɪgeɪtɪd] *adj* ungemildert, ganz

unnatural [ʌn'nætʃrəl] *adj* unnatürlich

unnecessary [ʌn'nesəsərɪ] *adj* unnötig

unnoticed [ʌn'nəʊtɪst] *adj*: **to go ~** unbemerkt bleiben

UNO ['juːnəʊ] *n abbr* = **United Nations Organization**

unobtainable [ʌnəb'teɪnəbl] *adj*: **this number is ~** kein Anschluss unter dieser Nummer

unobtrusive [ʌnəb'truːsɪv] *adj* unauffällig

unofficial [ʌnə'fɪʃl] *adj* inoffiziell

unpack [ʌn'pæk] *vt*, *vi* auspacken

unparalleled [ʌn'pærəleld] *adj* beispiellos

unpleasant [ʌn'pleznt] *adj* unangenehm

unplug [ʌn'plʌg] *vt* den Stecker herausziehen von

unpopular [ʌn'pɒpjʊlər] *adj* (*person*) unbeliebt; (*decision etc*) unpopulär

unprecedented [ʌn'presɪdentɪd] *adj* beispiellos

unpredictable [ʌnprɪ'dɪktəbl] *adj* unvorhersehbar; (*weather, person*) unberechenbar

unprofessional [ʌnprə'feʃənl] *adj* unprofessionell

UNPROFOR *n abbr* (= *United Nations Protection Force*) UNPROFOR *f*

unqualified [ʌn'kwɒlɪfaɪd] *adj* (*success*) uneingeschränkt, voll; (*person*) unqualifiziert

unquestionably [ʌn'kwestʃənəblɪ] *adv* fraglos

unravel [ʌn'rævl] *vt* (*disentangle*) ausfasern, entwirren; (*solve*) lösen

unreal [ʌn'rɪəl] *adj* unwirklich

unrealistic ['ʌnrɪə'lɪstɪk] *adj* unrealistisch

unreasonable [ʌn'riːznəbl] *adj* unvernünftig; (*demand*) übertrieben

unrelated [ʌnrɪ'leɪtɪd] *adj* ohne Beziehung; (*family*) nicht verwandt

unrelenting [ʌnrɪ'lentɪŋ] *adj* unerbittlich

unreliable [ʌnrɪ'laɪəbl] *adj* unzuverlässig

unremitting [ʌnrɪ'mɪtɪŋ] *adj* (*efforts, attempts*) unermüdlich

unreservedly [ʌnrɪ'zɜːvɪdlɪ] *adv* offen; (*believe, trust*) uneingeschränkt; (*cry*) rückhaltlos

unrest [ʌn'rest] *n* (*discontent*) Unruhe *f*; (*fighting*) Unruhen *pl*

unroll [ʌn'rəʊl] *vt* aufrollen

unruly [ʌn'ruːlɪ] *adj* (*child*) undiszipliniert; schwer lenkbar

unsafe [ʌn'seɪf] *adj* nicht sicher

unsaid [ʌn'sed] *adj*: **to leave sth ~** etw ungesagt lassen

unsatisfactory ['ʌnsætɪs'fæktərɪ] *adj* unbefriedigend; unzulänglich

unsavoury [ʌn'seɪvərɪ] (*US* **unsavory**) *adj* (*fig*) widerwärtig

unscathed [ʌn'skeɪðd] *adj* unversehrt

unscrew [ʌn'skruː] *vt* aufschrauben

unscrupulous [ʌn'skruːpjʊləs] *adj* skrupellos

unsettled [ʌn'setld] *adj* (*person*) rastlos; (*weather*) wechselhaft

unshaven [ʌn'ʃeɪvn] *adj* unrasiert

unsightly [ʌn'saɪtlɪ] *adj* unansehnlich

unskilled [ʌn'skɪld] *adj* ungelernt

unspeakable [ʌn'spiːkəbl] *adj* (*joy*) unsagbar; (*crime*) scheußlich

unstable [ʌn'steɪbl] *adj* instabil; (*mentally*) labil

unsteady [ʌn'stedɪ] *adj* unsicher

unstuck [ʌn'stʌk] *adj*: **to come ~** sich lösen; (*fig*) ins Wasser fallen

unsuccessful [ʌnsək'sesful] *adj* erfolglos

unsuitable [ʌn'suːtəbl] *adj* unpassend

unsure [ʌn'ʃʊər] *adj* unsicher; **to be ~ of o.s.** unsicher sein

unsuspecting [ʌnsəs'pektɪŋ] *adj* nichts ahnend

unsympathetic ['ʌnsɪmpə'θetɪk] *adj* gefühllos; (*response*) abweisend; (*unlikeable*) unsympathisch

untapped [ʌn'tæpt] *adj* (*resources*) ungenützt

unthinkable [ʌn'θɪŋkəbl] *adj* unvorstellbar

untidy [ʌn'taɪdɪ] *adj* unordentlich

untie [ʌn'taɪ] *vt* aufschnüren

until [ən'tɪl] *prep, conj* bis; **~ he comes** bis er kommt; **~ then** bis dann; **~ now** bis jetzt

untimely [ʌn'taɪmlɪ] *adj* (*death*) vorzeitig

untold [ʌn'təʊld] *adj* unermesslich

untoward [ʌntə'wɔːd] *adj* widrig

untranslatable [ʌntrænz'leɪtəbl] *adj* unübersetzbar

unused [ʌn'juːzd] *adj* unbenutzt

unusual [ʌn'juːʒʊəl] *adj* ungewöhnlich

unveil [ʌn'veɪl] *vt* enthüllen

unwanted [ʌn'wɒntɪd] *adj* unerwünscht

unwavering [ʌn'weɪvərɪŋ] *adj* standhaft, unerschütterlich

unwelcome [ʌn'welkəm] *adj* (*at a bad time*) unwillkommen; (*unpleasant*) unerfreulich

unwell [ʌn'wel] *adj*: **to feel** *or* **be ~** sich nicht wohl fühlen

unwieldy [ʌn'wiːldɪ] *adj* sperrig

unwilling [ʌn'wɪlɪŋ] *adj*: **to be ~ to do sth** nicht bereit sein, etw zu tun; **~ly** *adv* widerwillig

unwind [ʌn'waɪnd] (*irreg: like* **wind²**) *vt* abwickeln ♦ *vi* (*relax*) sich entspannen

unwise [ʌn'waɪz] *adj* unklug

unwitting [ʌn'wɪtɪŋ] *adj* unwissentlich

unworkable [ʌn'wəːkəbl] *adj* (*plan*) undurchführbar

unworthy [ʌn'wəːðɪ] *adj* (*person*): **~ (of sth)** (einer Sache *gen*) nicht wert

unwrap [ʌn'ræp] *vt* auspacken

unwritten [ʌn'rɪtn] *adj* ungeschrieben

KEYWORD
---

up [ʌp] *prep*: **to be up sth** oben auf etw *dat* sein; **to go up sth** (auf) etw *acc* hinaufgehen; **go up that road** gehen Sie die Straße hinauf

♦ *adv* **1** (*upwards, higher*) oben; **put it up a bit higher** stell es etwas weiter nach oben; **up there** da oben, dort oben; **up above** hoch oben

2: **to be up** (*out of bed*) auf sein; (*prices, level*) gestiegen sein; (*building, tent*) stehen

3: **up to** (*as far as*) bis; **up to now** bis jetzt

4: **to be up to** (*depending on*): **it's up to you** das hängt von dir ab; (*equal to*): **he's not up to it** (*job, task etc*) er ist dem nicht gewachsen; (*inf: be doing: showing disapproval, suspicion*): **what is he up to?** was führt er im Schilde?; **it's not up to me to decide** die Entscheidung liegt nicht bei mir; **his work is not up to the required standard** seine Arbeit entspricht nicht dem geforderten Niveau

♦ *n*: **ups and downs** (*in life, career*) Höhen und Tiefen *pl*

---

up-and-coming [ʌpənd'kʌmɪŋ] *adj* aufstrebend

upbringing ['ʌpbrɪŋɪŋ] *n* Erziehung *f*

update [ʌp'deɪt] *vt* auf den neuesten Stand bringen

upgrade [ʌp'greɪd] *vt* höher einstufen

upheaval [ʌp'hiːvl] *n* Umbruch *m*

uphill ['ʌp'hɪl] *adj* ansteigend; (*fig*) mühsam ♦ *adv*: **to go ~** bergauf gehen/fahren

uphold [ʌp'həʊld] (*irreg: like* **hold**) *vt* unterstützen

upholstery [ʌp'həʊlstərɪ] *n* Polster *nt*; Polsterung *f*

upkeep ['ʌpkiːp] *n* Instandhaltung *f*

upon [ə'pɒn] *prep* auf

upper ['ʌpə'] *n* (*on shoe*) Oberleder *nt* ♦ *adj* obere(r, s), höhere(r, s); **to have the ~ hand** die Oberhand haben; **~-class** vornehm; **~most** *adj* oberste(r, s), höchste(r, s); **what was ~most in my mind** was mich in erster Linie beschäftigte; **~ sixth** (*BRIT: SCOL*) *n* Abschlussklasse *f*

upright ['ʌpraɪt] *adj* aufrecht

uprising ['ʌpraɪzɪŋ] *n* Aufstand *m*

uproar ['ʌprɔː'] *n* Aufruhr *m*

uproot [ʌp'ruːt] *vt* ausreißen

upset [*n* 'ʌpset, *vb, adj* ʌp'set] (*irreg: like* **set**) *n* Aufregung *f* ♦ *vt* (*overturn*) umwerfen; (*disturb*) aufregen, bestürzen; (*plans*) durcheinander bringen ♦ *adj* (*person*) aufgeregt; (*stomach*) verdorben

upshot ['ʌpʃɒt] n (End)ergebnis nt
upside-down ['ʌpsaɪd-] adv verkehrt herum
upstairs [ʌp'steəz] adv oben; (go) nach oben ♦ adj (room) obere(r, s), Ober- ♦ n obere(s) Stockwerk nt
upstart ['ʌpstɑːt] n Emporkömmling m
upstream [ʌp'striːm] adv stromaufwärts
uptake ['ʌpteɪk] n: **to be quick on the ~** schnell begreifen; **to be slow on the ~** schwer von Begriff sein
uptight [ʌp'taɪt] (inf) adj (nervous) nervös; (inhibited) verklemmt
up-to-date ['ʌptə'deɪt] adj (clothes) modisch, modern; (information) neueste(r, s)
upturn ['ʌptɜːn] n Aufschwung m
upward ['ʌpwəd] adj nach oben gerichtet; **~(s)** adv aufwärts
uranium [juə'reɪnɪəm] n Uran nt
urban ['ɜːbən] adj städtisch, Stadt-; **~ clearway** n Stadtautobahn f
urchin ['ɜːtʃɪn] n (boy) Schlingel m; (sea ~) Seeigel m
urge [ɜːdʒ] n Drang m ♦ vt: **to ~ sb to do sth** jdn (dazu) drängen, etw zu tun
urgency ['ɜːdʒənsɪ] n Dringlichkeit f
urgent ['ɜːdʒənt] adj dringend
urinal ['juərɪnl] n (public) Pissoir nt
urinate ['juərɪneɪt] vi urinieren
urine ['juərɪn] n Urin m, Harn m
urn [ɜːn] n Urne f; (tea ~) Teemaschine f
US n abbr = **United States**
us [ʌs] pron uns; see also **me**
USA n abbr = **United States of America**
usage ['juːzɪdʒ] n Gebrauch m; (esp LING) Sprachgebrauch m
use [n juːs, vb juːz] n (employment) Gebrauch m; (point) Zweck m ♦ vt gebrauchen; **in ~** in Gebrauch; **out of ~** außer Gebrauch; **to be of ~** nützlich sein; **it's no ~** es hat keinen Zweck; **what's the ~?** was solls?; **~d to** (accustomed to) gewöhnt an +acc; **she ~d to live here** (formerly) sie hat früher mal hier gewohnt; **~ up** vt aufbrauchen, verbrauchen; **~d** adj (car) Gebraucht-; **~ful** adj nützlich; **~fulness** n Nützlichkeit f; **~less** adj nutzlos, unnütz; **~r** n Benutzer m; **~r-friendly** adj (computer)

benutzerfreundlich
usher ['ʌʃə'] n Platzanweiser m; **~ette** [ʌʃə'ret] n Platzanweiserin f
usual ['juːʒuəl] adj gewöhnlich, üblich; **as ~** wie üblich; **~ly** adv gewöhnlich
usurp [ju'zɜːp] vt an sich reißen
utensil [ju'tensl] n Gerät nt; **kitchen ~s** Küchengeräte pl
uterus ['juːtərəs] n Gebärmutter f
utilitarian [juːtɪlɪ'teərɪən] adj Nützlichkeits-
utility [ju'tɪlɪtɪ] n (usefulness) Nützlichkeit f; (also: **public ~**) öffentliche(r) Versorgungsbetrieb m; **~ room** n Hauswirtschaftsraum m
utilize ['juːtɪlaɪz] vt benützen
utmost ['ʌtməʊst] adj äußerste(r, s) ♦ n: **to do one's ~** sein Möglichstes tun
utter ['ʌtə'] adj äußerste(r, s), höchste(r, s), völlig ♦ vt äußern, aussprechen; **~ance** n Äußerung f; **~ly** adv äußerst, absolut, völlig
U-turn ['juː'tɜːn] n (AUT) Kehrtwendung f

V, v

v. abbr = **verse; versus; volt;** (= vide) **see**
vacancy ['veɪkənsɪ] n (BRIT: job) offene Stelle f; (room) freie(s) Zimmer nt; **"no vacancies"** „belegt"
vacant ['veɪkənt] adj leer; (unoccupied) frei; (house) leer stehend, unbewohnt; (stupid) (gedanken)leer; **~ lot** (US) n unbebaute(s) Grundstück nt
vacate [və'keɪt] vt (seat) frei machen; (room) räumen
vacation [və'keɪʃən] n Ferien pl, Urlaub m; **~ist** (US) n Ferienreisende(r) f(m)
vaccinate ['væksɪneɪt] vt impfen
vaccine ['væksiːn] n Impfstoff m
vacuum ['vækjʊm] n Vakuum nt; **~ bottle** (US) n Thermosflasche f; **~ cleaner** n Staubsauger m; **~ flask** (BRIT) n Thermosflasche f; **~-packed** adj vakuumversiegelt
vagina [və'dʒaɪnə] n Scheide f
vague [veɪg] adj vag(e); (absent-minded) geistesabwesend; **~ly** adv unbestimmt,

vag(e)

vain [veɪn] *adj* eitel; (*attempt*) vergeblich; **in ~** vergebens, umsonst

valentine ['væləntaɪn] *n* (*also:* **~ card**) Valentinsgruß *m*; **V~'s Day** *n* Valentinstag *m*

valet ['vælɪt] *n* Kammerdiener *m*

valiant ['væliənt] *adj* tapfer

valid ['vælɪd] *adj* gültig; (*argument*) stichhaltig; (*objection*) berechtigt; **~ity** [və'lɪdɪtɪ] *n* Gültigkeit *f*

valley ['vælɪ] *n* Tal *nt*

valour ['vælə*] (*US* **valor**) *n* Tapferkeit *f*

valuable ['væljuəbl] *adj* wertvoll; (*time*) kostbar; **~s** *npl* Wertsachen *pl*

valuation [vælju'eɪʃən] *n* (*FIN*) Schätzung *f*; Beurteilung *f*

value ['vælju:] *n* Wert *m*; (*usefulness*) Nutzen *m* ♦ *vt* (*prize*) (hoch) schätzen, werthalten; (*estimate*) schätzen; **~ added tax** (*BRIT*) *n* Mehrwertsteuer *f*; **~d** *adj* (hoch) geschätzt

valve [vælv] *n* Ventil *nt*; (*BIOL*) Klappe *f*; (*RAD*) Röhre *f*

van [væn] *n* Lieferwagen *m*; (*BRIT: RAIL*) Waggon *m*

vandal ['vændl] *n* Rowdy *m*; **~ism** *n* mutwillige Beschädigung *f*; **~ize** *vt* mutwillig beschädigen

vanguard ['vængɑ:d] *n* (*fig*) Spitze *f*

vanilla [və'nɪlə] *n* Vanille *f*; **~ ice cream** *n* Vanilleeis *nt*

vanish ['vænɪʃ] *vi* verschwinden

vanity ['vænɪtɪ] *n* Eitelkeit *f*; **~ case** *n* Schminkkoffer *m*

vantage ['vɑ:ntɪdʒ] *n*: **~ point** gute(r) Aussichtspunkt *m*

vapour ['veɪpə*] (*US* **vapor**) *n* (*mist*) Dunst *m*; (*gas*) Dampf *m*

variable ['veərɪəbl] *adj* wechselhaft, veränderlich; (*speed, height*) regulierbar

variance ['veərɪəns] *n*: **to be at ~ (with)** nicht übereinstimmen (mit)

variation [veərɪ'eɪʃən] *n* Variation *f*; (*in prices etc*) Schwankung *f*

varicose ['værɪkəus] *adj*: **~ veins** Krampfadern *pl*

varied ['veərɪd] *adj* unterschiedlich; (*life*) abwechslungsreich

variety [və'raɪətɪ] *n* (*difference*) Abwechslung *f*; (*varied collection*) Vielfalt *f*; (*COMM*) Auswahl *f*; (*sort*) Sorte *f*, Art *f*; **~ show** *n* Varietee *nt*, Varieté *nt*

various ['veərɪəs] *adj* verschieden; (*several*) mehrere

varnish ['vɑ:nɪʃ] *n* Lack *m*; (*on pottery*) Glasur *f* ♦ *vt* lackieren

vary ['veərɪ] *vt* (*alter*) verändern; (*give variety to*) abwechslungsreicher gestalten ♦ *vi* sich (ver)ändern; (*prices*) schwanken; (*weather*) unterschiedlich sein

vase [vɑ:z] *n* Vase *f*

Vaseline ['væsɪli:n] ® *n* Vaseline *f*

vast [vɑ:st] *adj* weit, groß, riesig

VAT [væt] *n abbr* (= *value added tax*) MwSt *f*

vat [væt] *n* große(s) Fass *nt*

vault [vɔ:lt] *n* (*of roof*) Gewölbe *nt*; (*tomb*) Gruft *f*; (*in bank*) Tresorraum *m*; (*leap*) Sprung *m* ♦ *vt* (*also:* **~ over**) überspringen

vaunted ['vɔ:ntɪd] *adj*: **much~** viel gerühmt

VCR *n abbr* = **video cassette recorder**

VD *n abbr* = **venereal disease**

VDU *n abbr* = **visual display unit**

veal [vi:l] *n* Kalbfleisch *nt*

veer [vɪə*] *vi* sich drehen; (*of car*) ausscheren

vegan ['vi:gən] *n* Vegan *m*, radikale(r) Vegetarier(in) *m(f)*

vegeburger ['vedʒbɜ:gə*] *n* vegetarische Frikadelle *f*

vegetable ['vedʒtəbl] *n* Gemüse *nt* ♦ *adj* Gemüse-; **~s** *npl* (*CULIN*) Gemüse *nt*

vegetarian [vedʒɪ'teərɪən] *n* Vegetarier(in) *m(f)* ♦ *adj* vegetarisch

vegetate ['vedʒɪteɪt] *vi* (dahin)vegetieren

veggieburger ['vedʒɪbɜ:gə*] *n* = **vegeburger**

vehement ['vi:ɪmənt] *adj* heftig

vehicle ['vi:ɪkl] *n* Fahrzeug *nt*; (*fig*) Mittel *nt*

veil [veɪl] *n* (*also fig*) Schleier *m* ♦ *vt* verschleiern

vein [veɪn] *n* Ader *f*; (*mood*) Stimmung *f*

velocity [vɪ'lɔsɪtɪ] *n* Geschwindigkeit *f*

velvet ['velvɪt] *n* Samt *m* ♦ *adj* Samt-

vendetta [ven'detə] *n* Fehde *f*; (*in family*)

Blutrache f

vending machine ['vendɪŋ-] n Automat m

vendor ['vendə'] n Verkäufer m

veneer [və'nɪə'] n Furnier(holz) nt; (fig) äußere(r) Anstrich m

venereal disease [vɪ'nɪərɪəl-] n Geschlechtskrankheit f

Venetian blind [vɪ'niːʃən-] n Jalousie f

vengeance ['vendʒəns] n Rache f; **with a ~** gewaltig

venison ['venɪsn] n Reh(fleisch) nt

venom ['venəm] n Gift nt

vent [vent] n Öffnung f; (in coat) Schlitz m; (fig) Ventil nt ♦ vt (emotion) abreagieren

ventilate ['ventɪleɪt] vt belüften; **ventilator** ['ventɪleɪtə'] n Ventilator m

ventriloquist [ven'trɪləkwɪst] n Bauchredner m

venture ['ventʃə'] n Unternehmung f, Projekt nt ♦ vt wagen; (life) aufs Spiel setzen ♦ vi sich wagen

venue ['venjuː] n Schauplatz m

verb [vɜːb] n Zeitwort nt, Verb nt; **~al** adj (spoken) mündlich; (translation) wörtlich; **~ally** adv mündlich

verbatim [vɜː'beɪtɪm] adv Wort für Wort ♦ adj wortwörtlich

verbose [vɜː'bəus] adj wortreich

verdict ['vɜːdɪkt] n Urteil nt

verge [vɜːdʒ] n (BRIT) Rand m ♦ vi: **to ~ on** grenzen an +acc; **"soft ~s"** (BRIT: AUT) „Seitenstreifen nicht befahrbar"; **on the ~ of doing sth** im Begriff, etw zu tun

verify ['verɪfaɪ] vt (über)prüfen; (confirm) bestätigen; (theory) beweisen

veritable ['verɪtəbl] adj wirklich, echt

vermin ['vɜːmɪn] npl Ungeziefer nt

vermouth ['vɜːməθ] n Wermut m

versatile ['vɜːsətaɪl] adj vielseitig

verse [vɜːs] n (poetry) Poesie f; (stanza) Strophe f; (of Bible) Vers m; **in ~** in Versform

version ['vɜːʃən] n Version f; (of car) Modell nt

versus ['vɜːsəs] prep gegen

vertebrate ['vɜːtɪbrɪt] adj Wirbel-

vertical ['vɜːtɪkl] adj senkrecht

vertigo ['vɜːtɪgəu] n Schwindel m

very ['verɪ] adv sehr ♦ adj (extreme) äußerste(r, s); **the ~ book which** genau das Buch, welches; **the ~ last ...** der/die/das allerletzte ...; **at the ~ least** allerwenigstens; **~ much** sehr

vessel ['vesl] n (ship) Schiff nt; (container) Gefäß nt

vest [vest] n (BRIT) Unterhemd nt; (US: waistcoat) Weste f

vested interests ['vestɪd-] npl finanzielle Beteiligung f; (people) finanziell Beteiligte pl; (fig) persönliche(s) Interesse nt

vestige ['vestɪdʒ] n Spur f

vestry ['vestrɪ] n Sakristei f

vet [vet] n abbr (= veterinary surgeon) Tierarzt m/-ärztin f

veteran ['vetərn] n Veteran(in) m(f)

veterinarian [vetrɪ'neərɪən] (US) n Tierarzt m/-ärztin f

veterinary ['vetrɪnərɪ] adj Veterinär-; **~ surgeon** (BRIT) n Tierarzt m/-ärztin f

veto ['viːtəu] (pl **~es**) n Veto nt ♦ vt sein Veto einlegen gegen

vex [veks] vt ärgern; **~ed** adj verärgert; **~ed question** umstrittene Frage f

VHF abbr (= very high frequency) UKW f

via ['vaɪə] prep über +acc

viable ['vaɪəbl] adj (plan) durchführbar; (company) rentabel

vibrant ['vaɪbrnt] adj (lively) lebhaft; (bright) leuchtend; (full of emotion: voice) bebend

vibrate [vaɪ'breɪt] vi zittern, beben; (machine, string) vibrieren; **vibration** [vaɪ'breɪʃən] n Schwingung f; (of machine) Vibrieren nt

vicar ['vɪkə'] n Pfarrer m; **~age** n Pfarrhaus nt

vice [vaɪs] n (evil) Laster nt; (TECH) Schraubstock m

vice-chairman [vaɪs'tʃeəmən] n stellvertretende(r) Vorsitzende(r) m

vice-president [vaɪs'prezɪdənt] n Vizepräsident m

vice squad n ≈ Sittenpolizei f

vice versa ['vaɪsɪ'vɜːsə] adv umgekehrt

vicinity [vɪ'sɪnɪtɪ] n Umgebung f; (closeness) Nähe f

vicious ['vɪʃəs] *adj* gemein, böse; ~ **circle** *n* Teufelskreis *m*

victim ['vɪktɪm] *n* Opfer *nt*

victor ['vɪktə'] *n* Sieger *m*

Victorian [vɪk'tɔːrɪən] *adj* viktorianisch; *(fig)* (sitten)streng

victorious [vɪk'tɔːrɪəs] *adj* siegreich

victory ['vɪktərɪ] *n* Sieg *m*

video ['vɪdɪəʊ] *adj* Fernseh-, Bild- ♦ *n* (~ *film*) Video *nt*; *(also:* ~ **cassette**) Videokassette *f*; *(also:* ~ **cassette recorder**) Videorekorder *m*; ~ **tape** *n* Videoband *nt*; ~ **wall** *n* Videowand *m*

vie [vaɪ] *vi* wetteifern

Vienna [vɪ'ɛnə] *n* Wien *nt*

Vietnam ['vjet'næm] *n* Vietnam *nt*; **~ese** *adj* vietnamesisch ♦ *n inv (person)* Vietnamese *m*, Vietnamesin *f*

view [vjuː] *n (sight)* Sicht *f*, Blick *m*; *(scene)* Aussicht *f*; *(opinion)* Ansicht *f*; *(intention)* Absicht *f* ♦ *vt (situation)* betrachten; *(house)* besichtigen; **to have sth in** ~ etw beabsichtigen; **on** ~ ausgestellt; **in** ~ **of** wegen +*gen*, angesichts +*gen*; **~er** *n (PHOT: small projector)* Gucki *m*; *(TV)* Fernsehzuschauer(in) *m(f)*; **~finder** *n* Sucher *m*; **~point** *n* Standpunkt *m*

vigil ['vɪdʒɪl] *n* (Nacht)wache *f*; **~ant** *adj* wachsam

vigorous ['vɪgərəs] *adj* kräftig; *(protest)* energisch, heftig

vile [vaɪl] *adj (mean)* gemein; *(foul)* abscheulich

villa ['vɪlə] *n* Villa *f*

village ['vɪlɪdʒ] *n* Dorf *nt*; **~r** *n* Dorfbewohner(in) *m(f)*

villain ['vɪlən] *n* Schurke *m*

vindicate ['vɪndɪkeɪt] *vt* rechtfertigen

vindictive [vɪn'dɪktɪv] *adj* nachtragend, rachsüchtig

vine [vaɪn] *n* Rebstock *m*, Rebe *f*

vinegar ['vɪnɪgə'] *n* Essig *m*

vineyard ['vɪnjɑːd] *n* Weinberg *m*

vintage ['vɪntɪdʒ] *n (of wine)* Jahrgang *m*; ~ **car** *n* Oldtimer *m (zwischen 1919 und 1930 gebaut)*; ~ **wine** *n* edle(r) Wein *m*

viola [vɪ'əʊlə] *n* Bratsche *f*

violate ['vaɪəleɪt] *vt (law)* übertreten; *(rights, rule, neutrality)* verletzen; *(sanctity, woman)* schänden; **violation** [vaɪə'leɪʃən] *n* Übertretung *f*; Verletzung *f*

violence ['vaɪələns] *n (force)* Heftigkeit *f*; *(brutality)* Gewalttätigkeit *f*

violent ['vaɪələnt] *adj (strong)* heftig; *(brutal)* gewalttätig, brutal; *(contrast)* krass; *(death)* gewaltsam

violet ['vaɪələt] *n* Veilchen *n* ♦ *adj* veilchenblau, violett

violin [vaɪə'lɪn] *n* Geige *f*, Violine *f*; **~ist** *n* Geiger(in) *m(f)*

VIP *n abbr (= very important person)* VIP *m*

virgin ['vəːdʒɪn] *n* Jungfrau *f* ♦ *adj* jungfräulich, unberührt; **~ity** [vəː'dʒɪnɪtɪ] *n* Unschuld *f*

Virgo ['vəːgəʊ] *n* Jungfrau *f*

virile ['vɪraɪl] *adj* männlich; **virility** [vɪ'rɪlɪtɪ] *n* Männlichkeit *f*

virtually ['vəːtjʊəlɪ] *adv* praktisch, fast

virtual reality ['vəːtjʊəl-] *n (COMPUT)* virtuelle Realität *f*

virtue ['vəːtjuː] *n (moral goodness)* Tugend *f*; *(good quality)* Vorteil *m*, Vorzug *m*; **by** ~ **of** aufgrund *or* auf Grund +*gen*

virtuous ['vəːtjuəs] *adj* tugendhaft

virulent ['vɪrʊlənt] *adj (poisonous)* bösartig; *(bitter)* scharf, geharnischt

virus ['vaɪərəs] *n (also COMPUT)* Virus *m*

visa ['viːzə] *n* Visum *nt*

vis-à-vis [viːzə'viː] *prep* gegenüber

viscous ['vɪskəs] *adj* zähflüssig

visibility [vɪzɪ'bɪlɪtɪ] *n (MET)* Sicht(weite) *f*

visible ['vɪzəbl] *adj* sichtbar; **visibly** *adv* sichtlich

vision ['vɪʒən] *n (ability)* Sehvermögen *nt*; *(foresight)* Weitblick *m*; *(in dream, image)* Vision *f*

visit ['vɪzɪt] *n* Besuch *m* ♦ *vt* besuchen; *(town, country)* fahren nach; **~ing hours** *npl (in hospital etc)* Besuchszeiten *pl*; **~or** *n (in house)* Besucher(in) *m(f)*; *(in hotel)* Gast *m*; **~or centre** *n* Touristeninformation *f*

visor ['vaɪzə'] *n* Visier *nt*; *(on cap)* Schirm *m*; *(AUT)* Blende *f*

vista ['vɪstə] *n* Aussicht *f*

visual ['vɪzjuəl] adj Seh-, visuell; ~ **aid** n Anschauungsmaterial nt; ~ **display unit** n Bildschirm(gerät n) m; ~**ize** vt sich +dat vorstellen; ~**ly-impaired** adj sehbehindert

vital ['vaɪtl] adj (important) unerlässlich; (necessary for life) Lebens-, lebenswichtig; (lively) vital; ~**ity** [vaɪˈtælɪtɪ] n Vitalität f; ~**ly** adv: ~**ly important** äußerst wichtig; ~ **statistics** npl (fig) Maße pl

vitamin ['vɪtəmɪn] n Vitamin nt

vivacious [vɪˈveɪʃəs] adj lebhaft

vivid ['vɪvɪd] adj (graphic) lebendig; (memory) lebhaft; (bright) leuchtend; ~**ly** adv lebendig; lebhaft; leuchtend

V-neck ['viːnɛk] n V-Ausschnitt m

vocabulary [vəˈkæbjulərɪ] n Wortschatz m, Vokabular nt

vocal ['vəukl] adj Vokal-, Gesang-; (fig) lautstark; ~ **cords** npl Stimmbänder pl

vocation [vəuˈkeɪʃən] n (calling) Berufung f; ~**al** adj Berufs-

vociferous [vəˈsɪfərəs] adj lautstark

vodka ['vɒdkə] n Wodka m

vogue [vəug] n Mode f

voice [vɔɪs] n Stimme f; (fig) Mitspracherecht nt ♦ vt äußern; ~ **mail** n (TEL) Voicemail f

void [vɔɪd] n Leere f ♦ adj (invalid) nichtig, ungültig; (empty): ~ **of** ohne, bar +gen; see **null**

volatile ['vɒlətaɪl] adj (gas) flüchtig; (person) impulsiv; (situation) brisant

volcano [vɒlˈkeɪnəu] n Vulkan m

volition [vəˈlɪʃən] n Wille m; **of one's own** ~ aus freiem Willen

volley ['vɒlɪ] n (of guns) Salve f; (of stones) Hagel m; (tennis) Flugball m; ~**ball** n Volleyball m

volt [vəult] n Volt nt; ~**age** n Spannung f

volume ['vɒljuːm] n (book) Band m; (size) Umfang m; (space) Rauminhalt m; (of sound) Lautstärke f

voluntarily ['vɒləntrɪlɪ] adv freiwillig

voluntary ['vɒləntərɪ] adj freiwillig

volunteer [vɒlənˈtɪər] n Freiwillige(r) mf ♦ vi sich freiwillig melden; **to ~ to do sth** sich anbieten, etw zu tun

vomit ['vɒmɪt] n Erbrochene(s) nt ♦ vt spucken ♦ vi sich übergeben

vote [vəut] n Stimme f; (ballot) Abstimmung f; (result) Abstimmungsergebnis nt; (franchise) Wahlrecht nt ♦ vt, vi wählen; ~ **of thanks** n Dankesworte pl; ~**r** n Wähler(in) m(f); **voting** ['vəutɪŋ] n Wahl f

voucher ['vautʃər] n Gutschein m

vouch for [vautʃ-] vt bürgen für

vow [vau] n Versprechen nt; (REL) Gelübde nt ♦ vt geloben

vowel ['vauəl] n Vokal m

voyage ['vɔɪdʒ] n Reise f

vulgar ['vʌlgər] adj (rude) vulgär; ~**ity** [vʌlˈgærɪtɪ] n Vulgarität f

vulnerable ['vʌlnərəbl] adj (easily injured) verwundbar; (sensitive) verletzlich

vulture ['vʌltʃər] n Geier m

W, w

wad [wɒd] n (bundle) Bündel nt; (of paper) Stoß m; (of money) Packen m

waddle ['wɒdl] vi watscheln

wade [weɪd] vi: **to ~ through** waten durch

wafer ['weɪfər] n Waffel f; (REL) Hostie f; (COMPUT) Wafer f

waffle ['wɒfl] n Waffel f; (inf: empty talk) Geschwafel nt ♦ vi schwafeln

waft [wɒft] vt, vi wehen

wag [wæg] vt (tail) wedeln mit ♦ vi wedeln

wage [weɪdʒ] n (also: ~**s**) (Arbeits)lohn m ♦ vt: **to ~ war** Krieg führen; ~ **earner** n Lohnempfänger(in) m(f); ~ **packet** n Lohntüte f

wager ['weɪdʒər] n Wette f ♦ vt, vi wetten

waggle ['wægl] vi wackeln

wag(g)on ['wægən] n (horse-drawn) Fuhrwerk nt; (US: AUT) Wagen m; (BRIT: RAIL) Wag(g)on m

wail [weɪl] n Wehgeschrei nt ♦ vi wehklagen, jammern

waist [weɪst] n Taille f; ~**coat** (BRIT) n Weste f; ~**line** n Taille f

wait [weɪt] n Wartezeit f ♦ vi warten; **to lie in** ~ **for sb** jdm auflauern; **I can't ~ to see**

him ich kanns kaum erwarten ihn zu sehen; **"no ~ing"** (BRIT: AUT) „Halteverbot"; **~ behind** *vi* zurückbleiben; **~ for** *vt fus* warten auf +*acc*; **~ on** *vt fus* bedienen; **~er** *n* Kellner *m*; **~ing list** *n* Warteliste *f*; **~ing room** *n* (MED) Wartezimmer *nt*; (RAIL) Wartesaal *m*; **~ress** *n* Kellnerin *f*

waive [weɪv] *vt* verzichten auf +*acc*

wake [weɪk] (*pt* **woke, waked,** *pp* **woken**) *vt* wecken ♦ *vi* (*also:* **~ up**) aufwachen ♦ *n* (NAUT) Kielwasser *nt*; (*for dead*) Totenwache *f*; **to ~ up to** (*fig*) sich bewusst werden +*gen*

waken ['weɪkn] *vt* aufwecken

Wales [weɪlz] *n* Wales *nt*

walk [wɔːk] *n* Spaziergang *m*; (*gait*) Gang *m*; (*route*) Weg *m* ♦ *vi* gehen; (*stroll*) spazieren gehen; (*longer*) wandern; **~s of life** Sphären *pl*; **a 10-minute ~** 10 Minuten zu Fuß; **to ~ out on sb** (*inf*) jdn sitzen lassen; **~er** *n* Spaziergänger *m*; (*hiker*) Wanderer *m*; **~ie-talkie** ['wɔːkɪ'tɔːkɪ] *n* tragbare(s) Sprechfunkgerät *nt*; **~ing** *n* Gehen *nt*; (*hiking*) Wandern *nt* ♦ *adj* Wander-; **~ing shoes** *npl* Wanderschuhe *pl*; **~ing stick** *n* Spazierstock *m*; **W~man** ['wɔːkmən] ® *n* Walkman *m* ®; **~out** *n* Streik *m*; **~over** (*inf*) *n* leichte(r) Sieg *m*; **~way** *n* Fußweg *m*

wall [wɔːl] *n* (*inside*) Wand *f*; (*outside*) Mauer *f*; **~ed** *adj* von Mauern umgeben

wallet ['wɒlɪt] *n* Brieftasche *f*

wallflower ['wɔːlflauə*r*] *n* Goldlack *m*; **to be a ~** (*fig*) ein Mauerblümchen sein

wallop ['wɒləp] (*inf*) *vt* schlagen, verprügeln

wallow ['wɒləu] *vi* sich wälzen

wallpaper ['wɔːlpeɪpə*r*] *n* Tapete *f*

walnut ['wɔːlnʌt] *n* Walnuss *f*

walrus ['wɔːlrəs] *n* Walross *nt*

waltz [wɔːlts] *n* Walzer *m* ♦ *vi* Walzer tanzen

wan [wɒn] *adj* bleich

wand [wɒnd] *n* (*also:* **magic ~**) Zauberstab *m*

wander ['wɒndə*r*] *vi* (*roam*) (herum)wandern; (*fig*) abschweifen

wane [weɪn] *vi* abnehmen; (*fig*) schwinden

wangle ['wæŋgl] (BRIT: *inf*) *vt:* **to ~ sth** etw richtig hindrehen

want [wɒnt] *n* (*lack*) Mangel *m* ♦ *vt* (*need*) brauchen; (*desire*) wollen; (*lack*) nicht haben; **~s** *npl* (*needs*) Bedürfnisse *pl*; **for ~ of** aus Mangel an +*dat*; mangels +*gen*; **to ~ to do sth** etw tun wollen; **to ~ sb to do sth** wollen, dass jd etw tut; **~ed** *adj* (*criminal etc*) gesucht; **"cook ~ed"** (*in adverts*) „Koch/Köchin gesucht"; **~ing** *adj:* **to be found ~ing** sich als unzulänglich erweisen

wanton ['wɒntən] *adj* mutwillig, zügellos

war [wɔː*r*] *n* Krieg *m*; **to make ~** Krieg führen

ward [wɔːd] *n* (*in hospital*) Station *f*; (*of city*) Bezirk *m*; (*child*) Mündel *nt*; **~ off** *vt* abwenden, abwehren

warden ['wɔːdn] *n* (*guard*) Wächter *m*, Aufseher *m*; (BRIT: *in youth hostel*) Herbergsvater *m*; (UNIV) Heimleiter *m*; (BRIT: *also:* **traffic ~**) ≈ Verkehrspolizist *m*, ≈ Politesse *f*

warder ['wɔːdə*r*] (BRIT) *n* Gefängniswärter *m*

wardrobe ['wɔːdrəub] *n* Kleiderschrank *m*; (*clothes*) Garderobe *f*

warehouse ['wɛəhaus] *n* Lagerhaus *nt*

wares [wɛəz] *npl* Ware *f*

warfare ['wɔːfɛə*r*] *n* Krieg *m*; Kriegsführung *f*

warhead ['wɔːhed] *n* Sprengkopf *m*

warily ['wɛərɪlɪ] *adv* vorsichtig

warlike ['wɔːlaɪk] *adj* kriegerisch

warm [wɔːm] *adj* warm; (*welcome*) herzlich ♦ *vt, vi* wärmen; **I'm ~** mir ist warm; **it's ~** es ist warm; **~ up** *vt* aufwärmen ♦ *vi* warm werden; **~-hearted** *adj* warmherzig; **~ly** *adv* warm; herzlich; **~th** *n* Wärme *f*; Herzlichkeit *f*

warn [wɔːn] *vt:* **to ~ (of or against)** warnen (vor +*dat*); **~ing** *n* Warnung *f*; **without ~ing** unerwartet; **~ing light** *n* Warnlicht *nt*; **~ing triangle** *n* (AUT) Warndreieck *nt*

warp [wɔːp] *vt* verziehen; **~ed** *adj* wellig; (*fig*) pervers

warrant ['wɒrənt] *n* (*for arrest*) Haftbefehl *m*

warranty ['wɒrəntɪ] *n* Garantie *f*

warren ['wɒrən] *n* Labyrinth *nt*

Warsaw ['wɔːsɔː] *n* Warschau *nt*

warship ['wɔːʃɪp] *n* Kriegsschiff *nt*

wart [wɔːt] *n* Warze *f*

wartime ['wɔːtaɪm] n Krieg m

wary ['weərɪ] adj misstrauisch

was [wɒz] pt of **be**

wash [wɒʃ] n Wäsche f ♦ vt waschen; (dishes) abwaschen ♦ vi sich waschen; (do ~ing) waschen; **to have a ~** sich waschen; **~ away** vt abwaschen, wegspülen; **~ off** vt abwaschen; **~ up** vi (BRIT) spülen; (US) sich waschen; **~able** adj waschbar; **~basin** n Waschbecken nt; **~ bowl** (US) n Waschbecken nt; **~ cloth** (US) n (face cloth) Waschlappen m; **~er** n (TECH) Dichtungsring m; (machine) Waschmaschine f; **~ing** n Wäsche f; **~ing machine** n Waschmaschine f; **~ing powder** (BRIT) n Waschpulver nt; **~ing-up** n Abwasch m; **~ing-up liquid** n Spülmittel nt; **~-out** (inf) n (event) Reinfall m; (person) Niete f; **~room** n Waschraum m

wasn't ['wɒznt] = **was not**

wasp [wɒsp] n Wespe f

wastage ['weɪstɪdʒ] n Verlust m; **natural ~** Verschleiß m

waste [weɪst] n (wasting) Verschwendung f; (what is ~d) Abfall m ♦ adj (useless) überschüssig, Abfall- ♦ vt (object) verschwenden; (time, life) vergeuden ♦ vi: **to ~ away** verfallen, verkümmern; **~s** npl (land) Einöde f; **~ disposal unit** (BRIT) n Müllschlucker m; **~ful** adj verschwenderisch; (process) aufwändig, aufwendig; **~ ground** (BRIT) n unbebaute(s) Grundstück nt; **~land** n Ödland nt; **~paper basket** n Papierkorb m; **~ pipe** n Abflussrohr nt

watch [wɒtʃ] n Wache f; (for time) Uhr f ♦ vt ansehen; (observe) beobachten; (be careful of) aufpassen auf +acc; (guard) bewachen ♦ vi zusehen; **to be on the ~ (for sth)** (auf etw acc) aufpassen; **to ~ TV** fernsehen; **to ~ sb doing sth** jdm bei etw zuschauen; **~ out** vi Ausschau halten; (be careful) aufpassen; **~ out!** pass auf!; **~dog** n Wachhund m; (fig) Wächter m; **~ful** adj wachsam; **~maker** n Uhrmacher m; **~man** (irreg) n (also: **night ~man**) (Nacht)wächter m; **~ strap** n Uhrarmband nt

water ['wɔːtər] n Wasser nt ♦ vt (be)gießen; (river) bewässern; (horses) tränken ♦ vi (eye) tränen; **~s** npl (of sea, river etc) Gewässer nt; **~ down** vt verwässern; **~ closet** (BRIT) n (Wasser)klosett nt; **~colour** (US **watercolor**) n (painting) Aquarell nt; (paint) Wasserfarbe f; **~cress** n (Brunnen)kresse f; **~fall** n Wasserfall m; **~ heater** n Heißwassergerät nt; **~ing can** n Gießkanne f; **~ level** n Wasserstand m; **~lily** n Seerose f; **~line** n Wasserlinie f; **~logged** adj (ground) voll Wasser; **~ main** n Haupt(wasser)leitung f; **~mark** n Wasserzeichen nt; (on wall) Wasserstandsmarke f; **~melon** n Wassermelone f; **~ polo** n Wasserball(spiel) nt; **~proof** adj wasserdicht; **~shed** n Wasserscheide f; **~skiing** n Wasserskilaufen nt; **~ tank** n Wassertank m; **~tight** adj wasserdicht; **~way** n Wasserweg m; **~works** npl Wasserwerk nt; **~y** adj wäss(e)rig

watt [wɒt] n Watt nt

wave [weɪv] n Welle f; (with hand) Winken nt ♦ vt (move to and fro) schwenken; (hand, flag) winken mit ♦ vi (person) winken; (flag) wehen; **~length** n (also fig) Wellenlänge f

waver ['weɪvər] vi schwanken

wavy ['weɪvɪ] adj wellig

wax [wæks] n Wachs nt; (sealing ~) Siegellack m; (in ear) Ohrenschmalz nt ♦ vt (floor) (ein)wachsen ♦ vi (moon) zunehmen; **~works** npl Wachsfigurenkabinett nt

way [weɪ] n Weg m; (method) Art und Weise f; (direction) Richtung f; (habit) Gewohnheit f; (distance) Entfernung f; (condition) Zustand m; **which ~? - this ~** welche Richtung? - hier entlang; **on the ~** (en route) unterwegs; **to be in the ~** im Weg sein; **to go out of one's ~ to do sth** sich besonders anstrengen, um etw zu tun; **to lose one's ~** sich verirren; **"give ~"** (BRIT: AUT) „Vorfahrt achten!"; **in a ~** in gewisser Weise; **by the ~** übrigens; **in some ~s** in gewisser Hinsicht; **"~ in"** (BRIT) „Eingang"; **"~ out"** (BRIT) „Ausgang"

waylay [weɪ'leɪ] (irreg: like lay) vt auflauern

+*dat*

wayward ['weɪwəd] *adj* eigensinnig

W.C. (*BRIT*) *n* WC *nt*

we [wi:] *pl pron* wir

weak [wi:k] *adj* schwach; **~en** *vt* schwächen
♦ *vi* schwächer werden; **~ling** *n*
Schwächling *m*; **~ness** *n* Schwäche *f*

wealth [wɛlθ] *n* Reichtum *m*; (*abundance*)
Fülle *f*; **~y** *adj* reich

wean [wi:n] *vt* entwöhnen

weapon ['wɛpən] *n* Waffe *f*

wear [wɛəʳ] (*pt* **wore**, *pp* **worn**) *n* (*clothing*):
sports/baby ~ Sport-/Babykleidung *f*; (*use*)
Verschleiß *m* ♦ *vt* (*have on*) tragen; (*smile
etc*) haben; (*use*) abnutzen ♦ *vi* (*last*) halten;
(*become old*) (sich) verschleißen; **evening ~**
Abendkleidung *f*; **~ and tear** Verschleiß *m*;
~ away *vt* verbrauchen ♦ *vi* schwinden; **~
down** *vt* (*people*) zermürben; **~ off** *vi* sich
verlieren; **~ out** *vt* verschleißen; (*person*)
erschöpfen

weary ['wɪərɪ] *adj* müde ♦ *vt* ermüden ♦ *vi*
überdrüssig werden

weasel ['wi:zl] *n* Wiesel *nt*

weather ['wɛðəʳ] *n* Wetter *nt* ♦ *vt* verwittern
lassen; (*resist*) überstehen; **under the ~** (*fig:
ill*) angeschlagen (*inf*); **~-beaten** *adj*
verwittert; **~cock** *n* Wetterhahn *m*; **~
forecast** *n* Wettervorhersage *f*; **~ vane** *n*
Wetterfahne *f*

weave [wi:v] (*pt* **wove**, *pp* **woven**) *vt*
weben; **~r** *n* Weber(in) *m(f)*; **weaving** *n*
(*craft*) Webkunst *f*

Web [wɛb] *n*: **the ~** das Web

web *n* Netz *nt*; (*membrane*) Schwimmhaut
f; **~ site** *n* (*COMPUT*) Website *f*, Webseite *f*

wed [wɛd] (*pt*, *pp* **wedded**) *vt* heiraten ♦ *n*:
the newly-~s *npl* die Frischvermählten *pl*

we'd [wi:d] = **we had**; **we would**

wedding ['wɛdɪŋ] *n* Hochzeit *f*; **silver/
golden ~ anniversary** Silberhochzeit *f/*
goldene Hochzeit *f*; **~ day** *n* Hochzeitstag
m; **~ dress** *n* Hochzeitskleid *nt*; **~ ring** *n*
Trauring *m*, Ehering *m*

wedge [wɛdʒ] *n* Keil *m*; (*of cheese etc*) Stück
nt ♦ *vt* (*fasten*) festklemmen; (*pack tightly*)
einkeilen

Wednesday ['wɛdnzdɪ] *n* Mittwoch *m*

wee [wi:] (*SCOTTISH*) *adj* klein, winzig

weed [wi:d] *n* Unkraut *nt* ♦ *vt* jäten; **~-killer**
n Unkrautvertilgungsmittel *nt*

weedy ['wi:dɪ] *adj* (*person*) schmächtig

week [wi:k] *n* Woche *f*; **a ~ today/on
Friday** heute/Freitag in einer Woche; **~day**
n Wochentag *m*; **~end** *n* Wochenende *nt*;
~ly *adj* wöchentlich; (*wages, magazine*)
Wochen- ♦ *adv* wöchentlich

weep [wi:p] (*pt*, *pp* **wept**) *vi* weinen; **~ing
willow** *n* Trauerweide *f*

weigh [weɪ] *vt*, *vi* wiegen; **to ~ anchor** den
Anker lichten; **~ down** *vt* niederdrücken; **~
up** *vt* abschätzen

weight [weɪt] *n* Gewicht *nt*; **to lose/put on
~** abnehmen/zunehmen; **~ing** *n* (*allowance*)
Zulage *f*; **~-lifter** *n* Gewichtheber *m*;
~lifting *n* Gewichtheben *nt*; **~y** *adj* (*heavy*)
gewichtig; (*important*) schwerwiegend,
schwer wiegend

weir [wɪəʳ] *n* (Stau)wehr *nt*

weird [wɪəd] *adj* seltsam

welcome ['wɛlkəm] *n* Willkommen *nt*,
Empfang *m* ♦ *vt* begrüßen; **thank you -
you're ~!** danke - nichts zu danken

welder ['wɛldəʳ] *n* (*person*) Schweißer(in)
m(f)

welding ['wɛldɪŋ] *n* Schweißen *nt*

welfare ['wɛlfɛəʳ] *n* Wohl *nt*; (*social*) Fürsorge
f; **~ state** *n* Wohlfahrtsstaat *m*; **~ work** *n*
Fürsorge *f*

well [wɛl] *n* Brunnen *m*; (*oil ~*) Quelle *f* ♦ *adj*
(*in good health*) gesund ♦ *adv* gut ♦ *excl*
nun!, na schön!; **I'm ~** es geht mir gut; **get
~ soon!** gute Besserung!; **as ~** auch; **as ~
as** sowohl als auch; **~ done!** gut gemacht!;
to do ~ (*person*) gut zurechtkommen;
(*business*) gut gehen; **~ up** *vi*
emporsteigen; (*fig*) aufsteigen

we'll [wi:l] = **we will**; **we shall**

well: **~-behaved** ['wɛlbɪ'heɪvd] *adj*
wohlerzogen; **~-being** ['wɛl'bi:ɪŋ] *n* Wohl
nt; **~-built** ['wɛl'bɪlt] *adj* kräftig gebaut; **~-
deserved** ['wɛldɪ'zɜ:vd] *adj* wohlverdient;
~-dressed ['wɛl'drɛst] *adj* gut gekleidet;
~-heeled ['wɛl'hi:ld] (*inf*) *adj* (*wealthy*) gut

gepolstert

wellingtons ['welɪŋtənz] npl (also: **wellington boots**) Gummistiefel pl

well: **~-known** ['wel'nəun] adj bekannt; **~-mannered** ['wel'mænəd] adj wohlerzogen; **~-meaning** ['wel'mi:nɪŋ] adj (person) wohlmeinend; (action) gut gemeint; **~-off** ['wel'ɔf] adj gut situiert; **~-read** ['wel'red] adj (sehr) belesen; **~-to-do** ['weltə'du:] adj wohlhabend; **~-wisher** ['welwɪʃəʳ] n Gönner m

Welsh [welʃ] adj walisisch ♦ n (LING) Walisisch nt; **the ~** npl (people) die Waliser pl; **~ Assembly** n walisische Versammlung f; **~man/woman** (irreg) n Waliser(in) m(f)

went [went] pt of **go**

wept [wept] pt, pp of **weep**

were [wəːʳ] pt pl of **be**

we're [wɪəʳ] = **we are**

weren't [wəːnt] = **were not**

west [west] n Westen m ♦ adj West-, westlich ♦ adv westwärts, nach Westen; **the W~** der Westen; **W~ Country** (BRIT) n: **the W~ Country** der Südwesten Englands; **~erly** adj westlich; **~ern** adj westlich, West- ♦ n (CINE) Western m; **W~ Indian** adj westindisch ♦ n Westindier(in) m(f); **W~ Indies** npl Westindische Inseln pl; **~ward(s)** adv westwärts

wet [wet] adj nass; **to get ~** nass werden; **"~ paint"** „frisch gestrichen"; **~ blanket** n (fig) Triefel m; **~ suit** n Taucheranzug m

we've [wi:v] = **we have**

whack [wæk] n Schlag m ♦ vt schlagen

whale [weɪl] n Wal m

wharf [wɔːf] n Kai m

wharves [wɔːvz] npl of **wharf**

KEYWORD

what [wɔt] adj **1** (in questions) welche(r, s), was für ein(e); **what size is it?** welche Größe ist das?
2 (in exclamations) was für ein(e); **what a mess!** was für ein Durcheinander!
♦ pron (interrogative/relative) was; **what are you doing?** was machst du gerade?; **what are you talking about?** wovon reden Sie?;

what is it called? wie heißt das?; **what about ...?** wie wärs mit ...?; **I saw what you did** ich habe gesehen, was du gemacht hast
♦ excl (disbelieving) wie, was; **what, no coffee!** wie, kein Kaffee?; **I've crashed the car - what!** ich hatte einen Autounfall - was!

whatever [wɔt'evəʳ] adj: **~ book** welches Buch auch immer ♦ pron: **do ~ is necessary** tu, was (immer auch) nötig ist; **~ happens** egal, was passiert; **nothing ~** überhaupt or absolut gar nichts; **do ~ you want** tu, was (immer) du (auch) möchtest; **no reason ~** or **whatsoever** überhaupt or absolut kein Grund

whatsoever [wɔtsəu'evəʳ] adj see **whatever**

wheat [wi:t] n Weizen m

wheedle ['wi:dl] vt: **to ~ sb into doing sth** jdn dazu überreden, etw zu tun; **to ~ sth out of sb** jdm etw abluchsen

wheel [wi:l] n Rad nt; (steering ~) Lenkrad nt; (disc) Scheibe f ♦ vt schieben; **~barrow** n Schubkarren m; **~chair** n Rollstuhl m; **~clamp** n (AUT) Parkkralle f

wheeze [wi:z] vi keuchen

KEYWORD

when [wen] adv wann
♦ conj **1** (at, during, after the time that) wenn; (in past) als; **she was reading when I came in** sie las, als ich hereinkam; **be careful when you cross the road** seien Sie vorsichtig, wenn Sie über die Straße gehen
2 (on, at which) als; **on the day when I met him** an dem Tag, an dem ich ihn traf
3 (whereas) wo ... doch

whenever [wen'evəʳ] adv wann (auch) immer; (every time that) jedes Mal wenn
♦ conj (any time) wenn

where [weəʳ] adv (place) wo; (direction) wohin; **~ from** woher; **this is ~ ...** hier ...; **~abouts** ['weərəbauts] adv wo ♦ n Aufenthaltsort m; **nobody knows his ~abouts** niemand weiß, wo er ist; **~as**

[wɛərˈæz] *conj* während, wo ... doch; **~by** *pron* woran, wodurch, womit, wovon; **~upon** *conj* worauf, wonach; (*at beginning of sentence*) daraufhin; **~ver** [wɛərˈɛvəʳ] *adv* wo (immer)

wherewithal [ˈwɛəwɪðɔːl] *n* nötige (Geld)mittel *pl*

whet [wɛt] *vt* (*appetite*) anregen

whether [ˈwɛðəʳ] *conj* ob; **I don't know ~ to accept or not** ich weiß nicht, ob ich es annehmen soll oder nicht; **~ you go or not** ob du gehst oder nicht; **it's doubtful/ unclear ~ ...** es ist zweifelhaft/nicht klar, ob ...

KEYWORD

which [wɪtʃ] *adj* **1** (*interrogative: direct, indirect*) welche(r, s); **which one?** welche(r, s)?
2: **in which case** in diesem Fall; **by which time** zu dieser Zeit
♦ *pron* **1** (*interrogative*) welche(r, s); (*of people also*) wer
2 (*relative*) der/die/das; (*referring to people*) was; **the apple which you ate/which is on the table** der Apfel, den du gegessen hast/der auf dem Tisch liegt; **he said he saw her, which is true** er sagte, er habe sie gesehen, was auch stimmt

---

whichever [wɪtʃˈɛvəʳ] *adj* welche(r, s) auch immer; (*no matter which*) ganz gleich welche(r, s); **~ book you take** welches Buch du auch nimmst; **~ car you prefer** egal welches Auto du vorziehst

whiff [wɪf] *n* Hauch *m*

while [waɪl] *n* Weile *f* ♦ *conj* während; **for a ~** eine Zeit lang; **~ away** *vt* (*time*) sich *dat* vertreiben

whim [wɪm] *n* Laune *f*

whimper [ˈwɪmpəʳ] *n* Wimmern *nt* ♦ *vi* wimmern

whimsical [ˈwɪmzɪkəl] *adj* launisch

whine [waɪn] *n* Gewinsel *nt*, Gejammer *nt* ♦ *vi* heulen, winseln

whip [wɪp] *n* Peitsche *f*; (*POL*) Fraktionsführer *m* ♦ *vt* (*beat*) peitschen; (*snatch*) reißen;

~ped cream *n* Schlagsahne *f*

whip-round [ˈwɪpraund] (*BRIT: inf*) *n* Geldsammlung *f*

whirl [wə:l] *n* Wirbel *m* ♦ *vt, vi* (herum)wirbeln; **~pool** *n* Wirbel *m*; **~wind** *n* Wirbelwind *m*

whirr [wə:ʳ] *vi* schwirren, surren

whisk [wɪsk] *n* Schneebesen *m* ♦ *vt* (*cream etc*) schlagen; **to ~ sb away** *or* **off** mit jdm davon sausen

whisker [ˈwɪskəʳ] *n*: **~s** (*of animal*) Barthaare *pl*; (*of man*) Backenbart *m*

whisky [ˈwɪskɪ] (*US, IRISH* **whiskey**) *n* Whisky *m*

whisper [ˈwɪspəʳ] *n* Flüstern *nt* ♦ *vt, vi* flüstern

whistle [ˈwɪsl] *n* Pfiff *m*; (*instrument*) Pfeife *f* ♦ *vt, vi* pfeifen

white [waɪt] *n* Weiß *nt*; (*of egg*) Eiweiß *nt* ♦ *adj* weiß; **~ coffee** (*BRIT*) *n* Kaffee *m* mit Milch; **~-collar worker** *n* Angestellte(r) *m*; **~ elephant** *n* (*fig*) Fehlinvestition *f*; **~ lie** *n* Notlüge *f*; **~ paper** *n* (*POL*) Weißbuch *nt*; **~wash** *n* (*paint*) Tünche *f*; (*fig*) Ehrenrettung *f* ♦ *vt* weißen, tünchen; (*fig*) rein waschen

whiting [ˈwaɪtɪŋ] *n* Weißfisch *m*

Whitsun [ˈwɪtsn] *n* Pfingsten *nt*

whittle [ˈwɪtl] *vt*: **to ~ away** *or* **down** stutzen, verringern

whizz [wɪz] *vi*: **to ~ past** *or* **by** vorbeizischen, vorbeischwirren; **~ kid** (*inf*) *n* Kanone *f*

KEYWORD

who [hu:] *pron* **1** (*interrogative*) wer; (*acc*) wen; (*dat*) wem; **who is it?, who's there?** wer ist da?
2 (*relative*) der/die/das; **the woman/man who spoke to me** die Frau/der Mann, die/ der mit mir sprach

---

whodu(n)nit [hu:ˈdʌnɪt] (*inf*) *n* Krimi *m*

whoever [hu:ˈɛvəʳ] *pron* wer/wen/wem auch immer; (*no matter who*) ganz gleich wer/ wen/wem

whole [həul] *adj* ganz ♦ *n* Ganze(s) *nt*; **the ~ of the town** die ganze Stadt; **on the ~** im

Großen und Ganzen; **as a ~** im Großen und Ganzen; **~food(s)** ['haʊlfuːd(z)] *n(pl)* Vollwertkost *f*; **~hearted** [haʊl'haːtɪd] *adj* rückhaltlos; **~heartedly** *adv* von ganzem Herzen; **~meal** *adj* (*bread, flour*) Vollkorn-; **~sale** *n* Großhandel *m* ♦ *adj* (*trade*) Großhandels-; (*destruction*) Massen-; **~saler** *n* Großhändler *m*; **~some** *adj* bekömmlich, gesund; **~wheat** *adj* = **wholemeal**
wholly ['haʊlɪ] *adv* ganz, völlig

KEYWORD

whom [huːm] *pron* **1** (*interrogative*: *acc*) wen; (: *dat*) wem; **whom did you see?** wen haben Sie gesehen?; **to whom did you give it?** wem haben Sie es gegeben? **2** (*relative*: *acc*) den/die/das; (: *dat*) dem/ der/dem; **the man whom I saw/to whom I spoke** der Mann, den ich sah/mit dem ich sprach

whooping cough ['huːpɪŋ-] *n* Keuchhusten *m*
whore [hɔːʳ] *n* Hure *f*
whose [huːz] *adj* (*possessive*: *interrogative*) wessen; (: *relative*) dessen; (*after f and pl*) deren ♦ *pron* wessen; **~ book is this?, ~ is this book?** wessen Buch ist dies?; **~ is this?** wem gehört das?

KEYWORD

why [waɪ] *adv* warum, weshalb ♦ *conj* warum, weshalb; **that's not why I'm here** ich bin nicht deswegen hier; **that's the reason why** deshalb ♦ *excl* (*expressing surprise, shock*) na so was; (*explaining*) also dann; **why, it's you!** na so was, du bist es!

wick [wɪk] *n* Docht *m*
wicked ['wɪkɪd] *adj* böse
wicker ['wɪkəʳ] *n* (*also:* **~work**) Korbgeflecht *nt*
wicket ['wɪkɪt] *n* Tor *nt*, Dreistab *m*
wide [waɪd] *adj* breit; (*plain*) weit; (*in firing*) daneben ♦ *adv*: **to open ~** weit öffnen; **to shoot ~** danebenschießen; **~-angle lens** *n*

Weitwinkelobjektiv *nt*; **~-awake** *adj* hellwach; **~ly** *adv* weit; (*known*) allgemein; **~n** *vt* erweitern; **~ open** *adj* weit geöffnet; **~spread** *adj* weitverbreitet, weit verbreitet
widow ['wɪdəʊ] *n* Witwe *f*; **~ed** *adj* verwitwet; **~er** *n* Witwer *m*
width [wɪdθ] *n* Breite *f*, Weite *f*
wield [wiːld] *vt* schwingen, handhaben
wife [waɪf] (*pl* **wives**) *n* (Ehe)frau *f*, Gattin *f*
wig [wɪg] *n* Perücke *f*
wiggle ['wɪgl] *n* Wackeln *nt* ♦ *vt* wackeln mit ♦ *vi* wackeln
wild [waɪld] *adj* wild; (*violent*) heftig; (*plan, idea*) verrückt; **~erness** ['wɪldənɪs] *n* Wildnis *f*, Wüste *f*; **~-goose chase** *n* (*fig*) fruchtlose(s) Unternehmen *nt*; **~life** *n* Tierwelt *f*; **~ly** *adv* wild, ungestüm; (*exaggerated*) irrsinnig; **~s** *npl*: **the ~s** die Wildnis *f*
wilful ['wɪlful] (*US* **willful**) *adj* (*intended*) vorsätzlich; (*obstinate*) eigensinnig

KEYWORD

will [wɪl] *aux vb* **1** (*forms future tense*) werden; **I will finish it tomorrow** ich mache es morgen zu Ende **2** (*in conjectures, predictions*): **he will** *or* **he'll be there by now** er dürfte jetzt da sein; **that will be the postman** das wird der Postbote sein **3** (*in commands, requests, offers*): **will you be quiet!** sei endlich still!; **will you help me?** hilfst du mir?; **will you have a cup of tea?** trinken Sie eine Tasse Tee?; **I won't put up with it!** das lasse ich mir nicht gefallen! ♦ *vt* wollen ♦ *n* Wille *m*; (*JUR*) Testament *nt*

willing ['wɪlɪŋ] *adj* gewillt, bereit; **~ly** *adv* bereitwillig, gern; **~ness** *n* (Bereit)willigkeit *f*
willow ['wɪləʊ] *n* Weide *f*
willpower ['wɪl'paʊəʳ] *n* Willenskraft *f*
willy-nilly ['wɪlɪ'nɪlɪ] *adv* einfach so
wilt [wɪlt] *vi* (ver)welken
wily ['waɪlɪ] *adj* gerissen
win [wɪn] (*pt, pp* **won**) *n* Sieg *m* ♦ *vt, vi*

gewinnen; **to ~ sb over** or **round** jdn
gewinnen; jdn dazu bringen
wince [wɪns] *vi* zusammenzucken
winch [wɪntʃ] *n* Winde *f*
wind¹ [wɪnd] *n* Wind *m*; (*MED*) Blähungen *pl*
wind² [waɪnd] (*pt, pp* **wound**) *vt* (*rope*)
winden; (*bandage*) wickeln ♦ *vi* (*turn*) sich
winden; **~ up** *vt* (*clock*) aufziehen; (*debate*)
(ab)schließen
windfall [ˈwɪndfɔːl] *n* unverhoffte(r)
Glücksfall *m*
winding [ˈwaɪndɪŋ] *adj* (*road*) gewunden
wind instrument [ˈwɪnd-] *n* Blasinstrument
nt
windmill [ˈwɪndmɪl] *n* Windmühle *f*
window [ˈwɪndəu] *n* Fenster *nt*; **~ box** *n*
Blumenkasten *m*; **~ cleaner** *n*
Fensterputzer *m*; **~ envelope** *n*
Fensterbriefumschlag *m*; **~ ledge** *n*
Fenstersims *m*; **~ pane** *n* Fensterscheibe *f*;
~-shopping *n* Schaufensterbummel *m*; **to
go ~-shopping** einen Schaufensterbummel
machen; **~sill** *n* Fensterbank *f*
wind: **~pipe** *n* Luftröhre *f*; **~ power** *n*
Windenergie *f*; **~screen** (*BRIT*) *n*
Windschutzscheibe *f*; **~screen washer** *n*
Scheibenwaschanlage *f*; **~screen wiper** *n*
Scheibenwischer *m*; **~shield** (*US*) *n* =
windscreen; **~swept** *adj* vom Wind
gepeitscht; (*person*) zerzaust; **~y** *adj* windig
wine [waɪn] *n* Wein *m*; **~ bar** *n* Weinlokal *nt*;
~ cellar *n* Weinkeller *m*; **~glass** *n*
Weinglas *nt*; **~ list** *n* Weinkarte *f*; **~
merchant** *n* Weinhändler *m*; **~ tasting** *n*
Weinprobe *f*; **~ waiter** *n* Weinkellner *m*
wing [wɪŋ] *n* Flügel *m*; (*MIL*) Gruppe *f*; **~s** *npl*
(*THEAT*) Seitenkulisse *f*; **~er** *n* (*SPORT*)
Flügelstürmer *m*
wink [wɪŋk] *n* Zwinkern *nt* ♦ *vi* zwinkern,
blinzeln
winner [ˈwɪnər] *n* Gewinner *m*; (*SPORT*)
Sieger *m*
winning [ˈwɪnɪŋ] *adj* (*team*) siegreich,
Sieger-; (*goal*) entscheidend; **~ post** *n* Ziel
nt; **~s** *npl* Gewinn *m*
winter [ˈwɪntər] *n* Winter *m* ♦ *adj* (*clothes*)
Winter- ♦ *vi* überwintern; **~ sports** *npl*

Wintersport *m*; **wintry** [ˈwɪntrɪ] *adj* Winter-,
winterlich
wipe [waɪp] *n*: **to give sth a ~** etw
(ab)wischen ♦ *vt* wischen; **~ off** *vt*
abwischen; **~ out** *vt* (*debt*) löschen;
(*destroy*) auslöschen; **~ up** *vt* aufwischen
wire [ˈwaɪər] *n* Draht *m*; (*telegram*)
Telegramm *nt* ♦ *vt* telegrafieren; **to ~ sb**
jdm telegrafieren; **~less** [ˈwaɪəlɪs] (*BRIT*) *n*
Radio(apparat *m*) *nt*
wiring [ˈwaɪərɪŋ] *n* elektrische Leitungen *pl*
wiry [ˈwaɪərɪ] *adj* drahtig
wisdom [ˈwɪzdəm] *n* Weisheit *f*; (*of decision*)
Klugheit *f*; **~ tooth** *n* Weisheitszahn *m*
wise [waɪz] *adj* klug, weise ♦ *suffix*:
timewise zeitlich gesehen
wisecrack [ˈwaɪzkræk] *n* Witzelei *f*
wish [wɪʃ] *n* Wunsch *m* ♦ *vt* wünschen; **best
~es** (*on birthday etc*) alles Gute; **with best
~es** herzliche Grüße; **to ~ sb goodbye** jdn
verabschieden; **he ~ed me well** er
wünschte mir Glück; **to ~ to do sth** etw
tun wollen; **to ~ for** *vt fus* sich *dat* wünschen;
~ful thinking *n* Wunschdenken *nt*
wishy-washy [ˈwɪʃɪˈwɒʃɪ] (*inf*) *adj* (*ideas,
argument*) verschwommen
wisp [wɪsp] *n* (*Haar*)strähne *f*; (*of smoke*)
Wölkchen *nt*
wistful [ˈwɪstful] *adj* sehnsüchtig
wit [wɪt] *n* (*also:* **~s**) Verstand *m no pl*;
(*amusing ideas*) Witz *m*; (*person*) Witzbold *m*
witch [wɪtʃ] *n* Hexe *f*; **~craft** *n* Hexerei *f*

KEYWORD

with [wɪð, wɪθ] *prep* **1** (*accompanying, in the
company of*) mit; **we stayed with friends**
wir übernachteten bei Freunden; **I'll be
with you in a minute** einen Augenblick,
ich bin sofort da; **I'm not with you** (*I don't
understand*) das verstehe ich nicht; **to be
with it** (*inf: up-to-date*) auf dem Laufenden
sein; (: *alert*) (voll) da sein (*inf*)
2 (*descriptive, indicating manner etc*) mit; **the
man with the grey hat** der Mann mit dem
grauen Hut; **red with anger** rot vor Wut

withdraw [wɪθˈdrɔː] (*irreg: like* **draw**) *vt*

zurückziehen; (*money*) abheben; (*remark*) zurücknehmen ♦ *vi* sich zurückziehen; **~al** *n* Zurückziehung *f*; Abheben *nt*; Zurücknahme *f*; **~n** *adj* (*person*) verschlossen

wither ['wɪðə*r*] *vi* (ver)welken

withhold [wɪθ'həʊld] (*irreg: like* hold) *vt*: **to ~ sth (from sb)** (jdm) etw vorenthalten

within [wɪð'ɪn] *prep* innerhalb +*gen* ♦ *adv* innen; **~ sight of** in Sichtweite von; **~ the week** innerhalb dieser Woche; **~ a mile of** weniger als eine Meile von

without [wɪð'aʊt] *prep* ohne; **~ sleeping** *etc* ohne zu schlafen *etc*

withstand [wɪθ'stænd] (*irreg: like* stand) *vt* widerstehen +*dat*

witness ['wɪtnɪs] *n* Zeuge *m*, Zeugin *f* ♦ *vt* (*see*) sehen, miterleben; (*document*) beglaubigen; **~ box** *n* Zeugenstand *m*; **~ stand** (*US*) *n* Zeugenstand *m*

witticism ['wɪtɪsɪzəm] *n* witzige Bemerkung *f*

witty ['wɪtɪ] *adj* witzig, geistreich

wives [waɪvz] *pl of* **wife**

wk *abbr* = **week**

wobble ['wɒbl] *vi* wackeln

woe [wəʊ] *n* Kummer *m*

woke [wəʊk] *pt of* **wake**

woken ['wəʊkn] *pp of* **wake**

wolf [wʊlf] (*pl* **wolves**) *n* Wolf *m*

woman ['wʊmən] (*pl* **women**) *n* Frau *f*; **~ doctor** *n* Ärztin *f*; **~ly** *adj* weiblich

womb [wu:m] *n* Gebärmutter *f*

women ['wɪmɪn] *npl of* **woman**; **~'s lib** (*inf*) *n* Frauenrechtsbewegung *f*

won [wʌn] *pt, pp of* **win**

wonder ['wʌndə*r*] *n* (*marvel*) Wunder *nt*; (*surprise*) Staunen *nt*, Verwunderung *f* ♦ *vi* sich wundern ♦ *vt*: **I ~ whether ...** ich frage mich, ob ...; **it's no ~ that** es ist kein Wunder, dass; **to ~ at** sich wundern über +*acc*; **to ~ about** sich Gedanken machen über +*acc*; **~ful** *adj* wunderbar, herrlich

won't [wəʊnt] = **will not**

woo [wu:] *vt* (*audience etc*) umwerben

wood [wʊd] *n* Holz *nt*; (*forest*) Wald *m*; **~ carving** *n* Holzschnitzerei *f*; **~ed** *adj* bewaldet; **~en** *adj* (*also fig*) hölzern;

~pecker *n* Specht *m*; **~wind** *n* Blasinstrumente *pl*; **~work** *n* Holzwerk *nt*; (*craft*) Holzarbeiten *pl*; **~worm** *n* Holzwurm *m*

wool [wʊl] *n* Wolle *f*; **to pull the ~ over sb's eyes** (*fig*) jdm Sand in die Augen streuen; **~len** (*US* **woolen**) *adj* Woll-; **~lens** *npl* Wollsachen *pl*; **~ly** (*US* **wooly**) *adj* wollig; (*fig*) schwammig

word [wə:d] *n* Wort *nt*; (*news*) Bescheid *m* ♦ *vt* formulieren; **in other ~s** anders gesagt; **to break/keep one's ~** sein Wort brechen/halten; **~ing** *n* Wortlaut *m*; **~ processing** *n* Textverarbeitung *f*; **~ processor** *n* Textverarbeitung *f*

wore [wɔ:*r*] *pt of* **wear**

work [wə:k] *n* Arbeit *f*; (*ART, LITER*) Werk *nt* ♦ *vi* arbeiten; (*machine*) funktionieren; (*medicine*) wirken; (*succeed*) klappen; **~s** *n sg* (*BRIT: factory*) Fabrik *f*, Werk *nt* ♦ *npl* (*of watch*) Werk *nt*; **to be out of ~** arbeitslos sein; **in ~ing order** in betriebsfähigem Zustand; **~ loose** *vi* sich lockern; **~ on** *vi* weiterarbeiten ♦ *vt fus* arbeiten an +*dat*; (*influence*) bearbeiten; **~ out** *vi* (*sum*) aufgehen; (*plan*) klappen ♦ *vt* (*problem*) lösen; (*plan*) ausarbeiten; **it ~s out at £100** das gibt *or* macht £100; **~ up** *vt*: **to get ~ed up** sich aufregen; **~able** *adj* (*soil*) bearbeitbar; (*plan*) ausführbar; **~aholic** [wə:kə'hɒlɪk] *n* Arbeitssüchtige(r) *f(m)*; **~er** *n* Arbeiter(in) *m(f)*; **~ experience** *n* Praktikum *nt*; **~force** *n* Arbeiterschaft *f*; **~ing class** *n* Arbeiterklasse *f*; **~ing-class** *adj* Arbeiter-; **~man** (*irreg*) *n* Arbeiter *m*; **~manship** *n* Arbeit *f*, Ausführung *f*; **~sheet** *n* Arbeitsblatt *nt*; **~shop** *n* Werkstatt *f*; **~ station** *n* Arbeitsplatz *m*; **~-to-rule** (*BRIT*) *n* Dienst *m* nach Vorschrift

world [wə:ld] *n* Welt *f*; **to think the ~ of sb** große Stücke auf jdn halten; **~ly** *adj* weltlich, irdisch; **~-wide** *adj* weltweit

World-Wide Web ['wə:ld'waɪd-] *n* World Wide Web *nt*

worm [wə:m] *n* Wurm *m*

worn [wɔ:n] *pp of* **wear** ♦ *adj* (*clothes*) abgetragen; **~-out** *adj* (*object*) abgenutzt;

(person) völlig erschöpft

worried ['wʌrɪd] *adj* besorgt, beunruhigt

worry ['wʌrɪ] *n* Sorge *f* ♦ *vt* beunruhigen ♦ *vi* *(feel uneasy)* sich sorgen, sich *dat* Gedanken machen; **~ing** *adj* beunruhigend

worse [wə:s] *adj* schlechter, schlimmer ♦ *adv* schlimmer, ärger ♦ *n* Schlimmere(s) *nt*, Schlechtere(s) *nt*; **a change for the ~** eine Verschlechterung; **~n** *vt* verschlimmern ♦ *vi* sich verschlechtern; **~ off** *adj (fig)* schlechter dran

worship ['wə:ʃɪp] *n* Verehrung *f* ♦ *vt* anbeten; **Your W~** *(BRIT: to mayor)* Herr/ Frau Bürgermeister; (: *to judge)* Euer Ehren

worst [wə:st] *adj* schlimmste(r, s), schlechteste(r, s) ♦ *adv* am schlimmsten, am ärgsten ♦ *n* Schlimmste(s) *nt*, Ärgste(s) *nt*; **at ~** schlimmstenfalls

worth [wə:θ] *n* Wert *m* ♦ *adj* wert; **it's ~** it es lohnt sich; **to be ~ one's while (to do sth)** die Mühe wert sein(, etw zu tun); **~less** *adj* wertlos; *(person)* nichtsnutzig; **~while** *adj* lohnend, der Mühe wert; **~y** *adj* wert, würdig

---

KEYWORD

would [wud] *aux vb* **1** *(conditional tense)*: **if you asked him he would do it** wenn du ihn fragtest, würde er es tun; **if you had asked him he would have done it** wenn du ihn gefragt hättest, hätte er es getan
2 *(in offers, invitations, requests)*: **would you like a biscuit?** möchten Sie ein Plätzchen?; **would you ask him to come in?** würden Sie ihn bitte hineinbitten?
3 *(in indirect speech)*: **I said I would do it** ich sagte, ich würde es tun
4 *(emphatic)*: **it WOULD have to snow today!** es musste ja ausgerechnet heute schneien!
5 *(insistence)*: **she wouldn't behave** sie wollte sich partout nicht anständig benehmen
6 *(conjecture)*: **it would have been midnight** es mag ungefähr Mitternacht gewesen sein; **it would seem so** es sieht wohl so aus

7 *(indicating habit)*: **he would go there on Mondays** er ging jeden Montag dorthin

---

would-be ['wudbɪ:] *(pej) adj* Möchtegern-

wouldn't ['wudnt] = **would not**

wound¹ [wu:nd] *n (also fig)* Wunde *f* ♦ *vt* verwunden, verletzen *(also fig)*

wound² [waund] *pt, pp of* **wind**²

wove [wəuv] *pt of* **weave**; **~n** *pp of* **weave**

wrangle ['ræŋgl] *n* Streit *m* ♦ *vi* sich zanken

wrap [ræp] *vt* einwickeln; **~ up** *vt* einwickeln; *(deal)* abschließen; **~per** *n* Umschlag *m*, Schutzhülle *f*; **~ping paper** *n* Einwickelpapier *nt*

wrath [rɔθ] *n* Zorn *m*

wreak [ri:k] *vt (havoc)* anrichten; *(vengeance)* üben

wreath [ri:θ] *n* Kranz *m*

wreck [rɛk] *n (ship)* Wrack *nt*; *(sth ruined)* Ruine *f* ♦ *vt* zerstören; **~age** *n* Trümmer *pl*

wren [rɛn] *n* Zaunkönig *m*

wrench [rɛntʃ] *n (spanner)* Schraubenschlüssel *m*; *(twist)* Ruck *m* ♦ *vt* reißen, zerren; **to ~ sth from sb** jdm etw entreißen *or* entwinden

wrestle ['rɛsl] *vi*: **to ~ (with sb)** (mit jdm) ringen; **~r** *n* Ringer(in) *m(f)*; **wrestling** *n* Ringen *nt*

wretched ['rɛtʃɪd] *adj (inf)* verflixt

wriggle ['rɪgl] *n* Schlängeln *nt* ♦ *vi* sich winden

wring [rɪŋ] *(pt, pp* **wrung***) vt* wringen

wrinkle ['rɪŋkl] *n* Falte *f*, Runzel *f* ♦ *vt* runzeln ♦ *vi* sich runzeln; *(material)* knittern; **~d** *adj* faltig, schrumpelig

wrist [rɪst] *n* Handgelenk *nt*; **~watch** *n* Armbanduhr *f*

writ [rɪt] *n* gerichtliche(r) Befehl *m*

write [raɪt] *(pt* **wrote***, pp* **written***) vt, vi* schreiben; **~ down** *vt* aufschreiben; **~ off** *vt (dismiss)* abschreiben; **~ out** *vt (essay)* abschreiben; *(cheque)* ausstellen; **~ up** *vt* schreiben; **~-off** *n*: **it is a ~off** das kann man abschreiben; **~r** *n* Schriftsteller *m*

writhe [raɪð] *vi* sich winden

writing ['raɪtɪŋ] *n (act)* Schreiben *nt*; *(handwriting)* (Hand)schrift *f*; **in ~** schriftlich;

~ **paper** n Schreibpapier nt
written ['rɪtn] pp of **write**
wrong [rɒŋ] adj (incorrect) falsch; (morally)
unrecht ♦ n Unrecht nt ♦ vt Unrecht tun
+dat; **he was ~ in doing that** es war nicht
recht von ihm, das zu tun; **you are ~
about that, you've got it ~** da hast du
Unrecht; **to be in the ~** im Unrecht sein;
what's ~ with your leg? was ist mit
deinem Bein los?; **to go ~** (plan) schief
gehen; (person) einen Fehler machen; **~ful**
adj unrechtmäßig; **~ly** adv falsch; (accuse)
zu Unrecht
wrong number n (TEL): **you've got the ~**
Sie sind falsch verbunden
wrote [rəut] pt of **write**
wrought [rɔ:t] adj: **~ iron** Schmiedeeisen nt
wrung [rʌŋ] pt, pp of **wring**
wry [raɪ] adj ironisch
wt. abbr = **weight**
WWW n abbr (= World Wide Web): **the ~** das
WWW.

X, x

Xmas ['ɛksməs] n abbr = **Christmas**
X-ray ['ɛksreɪ] n Röntgenaufnahme f ♦ vt
röntgen; **~~s** npl Röntgenstrahlen pl
xylophone ['zaɪləfəun] n Xylofon nt,
Xylophon nt

Y, y

yacht [jɒt] n Jacht f; **~ing** n (Sport)segeln nt;
~sman (irreg) n Sportsegler m
Yank [jæŋk] n (inf) Ami m
yap [jæp] vi (dog) kläffen
yard [jɑ:d] n Hof m; (measure) (englische)
Elle f, Yard nt (0,91 m); **~stick** n (fig)
Maßstab m
yarn [jɑ:n] n (thread) Garn nt; (story)
(Seemanns)garn nt
yawn [jɔ:n] n Gähnen nt ♦ vi gähnen; **~ing**
adj (gap) gähnend
yd. abbr = **yard(s)**

yeah [jɛə] (inf) adv ja
year [jɪər] n Jahr nt; **to be 8 ~s old** acht
Jahre alt sein; **an eight-year-old child** ein
achtjähriges Kind; **~ly** adj, adv jährlich
yearn [jə:n] vi: **to ~ (for)** sich sehnen (nach);
~ing n Verlangen nt, Sehnsucht f
yeast [ji:st] n Hefe f
yell [jɛl] n gellende(r) Schrei m ♦ vi laut
schreien
yellow ['jɛləu] adj gelb ♦ n Gelb nt
yelp [jɛlp] n Gekläff nt ♦ vi kläffen
yes [jɛs] adv ja ♦ n Ja nt, Jawort nt; **to say ~**
Ja or ja sagen; **to answer ~** mit Ja
antworten
yesterday ['jɛstədɪ] adv gestern ♦ n Gestern
nt; **~ morning/evening** gestern Morgen/
Abend; **all day ~** gestern den ganzen Tag;
the day before ~ vorgestern
yet [jɛt] adv noch; (in question) schon; (up to
now) bis jetzt ♦ conj doch, dennoch; **it is
not finished ~** es ist noch nicht fertig; **the
best ~** das bisher Beste; **as ~** bis jetzt; (in
past) bis dahin
yew [ju:] n Eibe f
yield [ji:ld] n Ertrag m ♦ vt (result, crop)
hervorbringen; (interest, profit) abwerfen;
(concede) abtreten ♦ vi nachgeben; (MIL)
sich ergeben; **"~"** (US: AUT) „Vorfahrt
gewähren"
YMCA n abbr (= Young Men's Christian
Association) CVJM m
yob [jɒb] (BRIT: inf) n Halbstarke(r) f(m)
yoga ['jəugə] n Joga m
yog(h)urt ['jəugət] n Jog(h)urt m
yoke [jəuk] n (also fig) Joch nt
yolk [jəuk] n Eidotter m, Eigelb nt

KEYWORD

you [ju:] pron **1** (subj, in comparisons: familiar
form: sg) du; (: pl) ihr; (in letters also) du,
ihr; (: polite form) Sie; **you Germans** ihr
Deutschen; **she's younger than you** sie ist
jünger als du/Sie
2 (direct object, after prep +acc: familiar form:
sg) dich; (: pl) euch; (in letters also) dich,
euch; (: polite form) Sie; **I know you** ich
kenne dich/euch/Sie

3 (*indirect object, after prep +dat: familiar form: sg*) dir; (: *pl*) euch; (*in letters also*) dir, euch; (: *polite form*) Ihnen; **I gave it to you** ich gab es dir/euch/Ihnen
4 (*impers: one: subj*) man; (: *direct object*) einen; (: *indirect object*) einem; **fresh air does you good** frische Luft tut gut

you'd [juːd] = **you had**; **you would**
you'll [juːl] = **you will**; **you shall**
young [jʌŋ] *adj* jung ♦ *npl*: **the ~** die Jungen *pl*; **~ster** *n* Junge *m*, junge(r) Bursche *m*, junge(s) Mädchen *nt*
your [jɔːʳ] *adj* (*familiar: sg*) dein; (: *pl*) euer, eure *pl*; (*polite*) Ihr; *see also* **my**
you're [juəʳ] = **you are**
yours [jɔːz] *pron* (*familiar: sg*) deine(r, s); (: *pl*) eure(r, s); (*polite*) Ihre(r, s); *see also* **mine²**
yourself [jɔːˈself] *pron* (*emphatic*) selbst; (*familiar: sg: acc*) dich (selbst); (: *dat*) dir (selbst); (: *pl*) euch (selbst); (*polite*) sich (selbst); *see also* **oneself**; **yourselves** *pl pron* (*reflexive: familiar*) euch; (: *polite*) sich; (*emphatic*) selbst; *see also* **oneself**
youth [juːθ] *n* Jugend *f*; (*young man*) junge(r) Mann *m*; **~s** *npl* (*young people*) Jugendliche *pl*; **~ club** *n* Jugendzentrum *nt*; **~ful** *adj* jugendlich; **~ hostel** *n* Jugendherberge *f*
you've [juːv] = **you have**
YTS (*BRIT*) *n abbr* (= *Youth Training Scheme*) staatliches Förderprogramm für arbeitslose Jugendliche
Yugoslav [ˈjuːgəʊslɑːv] *adj* jugoslawisch ♦ *n* Jugoslawe *m*, Jugoslawin *f*; **~ia**

[juːgəʊˈslɑːvɪə] *n* Jugoslawien *nt*
yuppie [ˈjʌpɪ] (*inf*) *n* Yuppie *m* ♦ *adj* yuppiehaft, Yuppie-
YWCA *n abbr* (= *Young Women's Christian Association*) CVJF *m*

Z, z

zany [ˈzeɪnɪ] *adj* (*ideas, sense of humour*) verrückt
zap [zæp] *vt* (*COMPUT*) löschen
zeal [ziːl] *n* Eifer *m*; **~ous** [ˈzeləs] *adj* eifrig
zebra [ˈziːbrə] *n* Zebra *nt*; **~ crossing** (*BRIT*) *n* Zebrastreifen *m*
zero [ˈzɪərəʊ] *n* Null *f*; (*on scale*) Nullpunkt *m*
zest [zest] *n* Begeisterung *f*
zigzag [ˈzɪgzæg] *n* Zickzack *m*
Zimbabwe [zɪmˈbɑːbwɪ] *n* Zimbabwe *nt*
Zimmer frame [ˈzɪmə-] *n* Laufgestell *nt*
zip [zɪp] *n* Reißverschluss *m* ♦ *vt* (*also*: **~ up**) den Reißverschluss zumachen +*gen*
zip code (*US*) *n* Postleitzahl *f*
zipper [ˈzɪpəʳ] (*US*) *n* Reißverschluss *m*
zit [zɪt] (*inf*) *n* Pickel *m*
zodiac [ˈzəʊdɪæk] *n* Tierkreis *m*
zombie [ˈzɒmbɪ] *n*: **like a ~** (*fig*) wie im Tran
zone [zəʊn] *n* (*also MIL*) Zone *f*, Gebiet *nt*; (*in town*) Bezirk *m*
zoo [zuː] *n* Zoo *m*
zoology [zuːˈɒlədʒɪ] *n* Zoologie *f*
zoom [zuːm] *vi*: **to ~ past** vorbeisausen; **~ lens** *n* Zoomobjektiv *nt*
zucchini [zuːˈkiːnɪ] (*US*) *npl* Zucchini *pl*

GERMAN IRREGULAR VERBS

*with 'sein'

infinitive	present indicative (2nd, 3rd sg)	imperfect	past participle
aufschrecken*	schrickst auf, schrickt auf	schrak or schreckte auf	aufgeschreckt
ausbedingen	bedingst aus, bedingt aus	bedang or bedingte aus	ausbedungen
backen	bäckst, bäckt	backte or buk	gebacken
befehlen	befiehlst, befiehlt	befahl	befohlen
beginnen	beginnst, beginnt	begann	begonnen
beißen	beißt, beißt	biss	gebissen
bergen	birgst, birgt	barg	geborgen
bersten*	birst, birst	barst	geborsten
bescheißen*	bescheißt, bescheißt	beschiss	beschissen
bewegen	bewegst, bewegt	bewog	bewogen
biegen	biegst, biegt	bog	gebogen
bieten	bietest, bietet	bot	geboten
binden	bindest, bindet	band	gebunden
bitten	bittest, bittet	bat	gebeten
blasen	bläst, bläst	blies	geblasen
bleiben*	bleibst, bleibt	blieb	geblieben
braten	brätst, brät	briet	gebraten
brechen*	brichst, bricht	brach	gebrochen
brennen	brennst, brennt	brannte	gebrannt
bringen	bringst, bringt	brachte	gebracht
denken	denkst, denkt	dachte	gedacht
dreschen	drisch(e)st, drischt	drosch	gedroschen
dringen*	dringst, dringt	drang	gedrungen
dürfen	darfst, darf	durfte	gedurft
empfehlen	empfiehlst, empfiehlt	empfahl	empfohlen
erbleichen*	erbleichst, erbleicht	erbleichte	erblichen
erlöschen*	erlischt, erlischt	erlosch	erloschen
erschrecken*	erschrickst, erschrickt	erschrak	erschrocken
essen	isst, isst	aß	gegessen
fahren*	fährst, fährt	fuhr	gefahren
fallen*	fällst, fällt	fiel	gefallen

infinitive	present indicative (2nd, 3rd sg)	imperfect	past participle
fangen	fängst, fängt	fing	gefangen
fechten	fichtst, ficht	focht	gefochten
finden	findest, findet	fand	gefunden
flechten	flichtst, flicht	flocht	geflochten
fliegen*	fliegst, fliegt	flog	geflogen
fliehen*	fliehst, flieht	floh	geflohen
fließen*	fließt, fließt	floss	geflossen
fressen	frisst, frisst	fraß	gefressen
frieren	frierst, friert	fror	gefroren
gären*	gärst, gärt	gor	gegoren
gebären	gebierst, gebiert	gebar	geboren
geben	gibst, gibt	gab	gegeben
gedeihen*	gedeihst, gedeiht	gedieh	gediehen
gehen*	gehst, geht	ging	gegangen
gelingen*	——, gelingt	gelang	gelungen
gelten	giltst, gilt	galt	gegolten
genesen*	gene(se)st, genest	genas	genesen
genießen	genießt, genießt	genoss	genossen
geraten*	gerätst, gerät	geriet	geraten
geschehen*	——, geschieht	geschah	geschehen
gewinnen	gewinnst, gewinnt	gewann	gewonnen
gießen	gießt, gießt	goss	gegossen
gleichen	gleichst, gleicht	glich	geglichen
gleiten*	gleitest, gleitet	glitt	geglitten
glimmen	glimmst, glimmt	glomm	geglommen
graben	gräbst, gräbt	grub	gegraben
greifen	greifst, greift	griff	gegriffen
haben	hast, hat	hatte	gehabt
halten	hältst, hält	hielt	gehalten
hängen	hängst, hängt	hing	gehangen
hauen	haust, haut	haute	gehauen
heben	hebst, hebt	hob	gehoben
heißen	heißt, heißt	hieß	geheißen
helfen	hilfst, hilft	half	geholfen
kennen	kennst, kennt	kannte	gekannt
klimmen*	klimmst, klimmt	klomm	geklommen
klingen	klingst, klingt	klang	geklungen
kneifen	kneifst, kneift	kniff	gekniffen
kommen*	kommst, kommt	kam	gekommen
können	kannst, kann	konnte	gekonnt
kriechen*	kriechst, kriecht	kroch	gekrochen
laden	lädst, lädt	lud	geladen
lassen	lässt, lässt	ließ	gelassen
laufen*	läufst, läuft	lief	gelaufen
leiden	leidest, leidet	litt	gelitten

infinitive	present indicative (2nd, 3rd sg)	imperfect	past participle
leihen	leihst, leiht	lieh	geliehen
lesen	liest, liest	las	gelesen
liegen*	liegst, liegt	lag	gelegen
lügen	lügst, lügt	log	gelogen
mahlen	mahlst, mahlt	mahlte	gemahlen
meiden	meidest, meidet	mied	gemieden
melken	melkst, melkt	melkte	gemolken
messen	misst, misst	maß	gemessen
misslingen*	——, misslingt	misslang	misslungen
mögen	magst, mag	mochte	gemocht
müssen	musst, muss	musste	gemusst
nehmen	nimmst, nimmt	nahm	genommen
nennen	nennst, nennt	nannte	genannt
pfeifen	pfeifst, pfeift	pfiff	gepfiffen
preisen	preist, preist	pries	gepriesen
quellen*	quillst, quillt	quoll	gequollen
raten	rätst, rät	riet	geraten
reiben	reibst, reibt	rieb	gerieben
reißen*	reißt, reißt	riss	gerissen
reiten*	reitest, reitet	ritt	geritten
rennen*	rennst, rennt	rannte	gerannt
riechen	riechst, riecht	roch	gerochen
ringen	ringst, ringt	rang	gerungen
rinnen*	rinnst, rinnt	rann	geronnen
rufen	rufst, ruft	rief	gerufen
salzen	salzt, salzt	salzte	gesalzen
saufen	säufst, säuft	soff	gesoffen
saugen	saugst, saugt	sog	gesogen
schaffen	schaffst, schafft	schuf	geschaffen
scheiden	scheidest, scheidet	schied	geschieden
scheinen	scheinst, scheint	schien	geschienen
schelten	schiltst, schilt	schalt	gescholten
scheren	scherst, schert	schor	geschoren
schieben	schiebst, schiebt	schob	geschoben
schießen	schießt, schießt	schoss	geschossen
schinden	schindest, schindet	schindete	geschunden
schlafen	schläfst, schläft	schlief	geschlafen
schlagen	schlägst, schlägt	schlug	geschlagen
schleichen*	schleichst, schleicht	schlich	geschlichen
schleifen	schleifst, schleift	schliff	geschliffen
schließen	schließt, schließt	schloss	geschlossen
schlingen	schlingst, schlingt	schlang	geschlungen

infinitive	present indicative (2nd, 3rd sg)	imperfect	past participle
schmeißen	schmeißt, schmeißt	schmiss	geschmissen
schmelzen*	schmilzt, schmilzt	schmolz	geschmolzen
schneiden	schneidest, schneidet	schnitt	geschnitten
schreiben	schreibst, schreibt	schrieb	geschrieben
schreien	schreist, schreit	schrie	geschrie(e)n
schreiten	schreitest, schreitet	schritt	geschritten
schweigen	schweigst, schweigt	schwieg	geschwiegen
schwellen*	schwillst, schwillt	schwoll	geschwollen
schwimmen*	schwimmst, schwimmt	schwamm	geschwommen
schwinden*	schwindest, schwindet	schwand	geschwunden
schwingen	schwingst, schwingt	schwang	geschwungen
schwören	schwörst, schwört	schwor	geschworen
sehen	siehst, sieht	sah	gesehen
sein*	bist, ist	war	gewesen
senden	sendest, sendet	sandte	gesandt
singen	singst, singt	sang	gesungen
sinken*	sinkst, sinkt	sank	gesunken
sinnen	sinnst, sinnt	sann	gesonnen
sitzen*	sitzt, sitzt	saß	gesessen
sollen	sollst, soll	sollte	gesollt
speien	speist, speit	spie	gespie(e)n
spinnen	spinnst, spinnt	spann	gesponnen
sprechen	sprichst, spricht	sprach	gesprochen
sprießen*	sprießt, sprießt	spross	gesprossen
springen*	springst, springt	sprang	gesprungen
stechen	stichst, sticht	stach	gestochen
stecken	steckst, steckt	steckte *or* stak	gesteckt
stehen	stehst, steht	stand	gestanden
stehlen	stiehlst, stiehlt	stahl	gestohlen
steigen*	steigst, steigt	stieg	gestiegen
sterben*	stirbst, stirbt	starb	gestorben
stinken	stinkst, stinkt	stank	gestunken
stoßen	stößt, stößt	stieß	gestoßen
streichen	streichst, streicht	strich	gestrichen
streiten*	streitest, streitet	stritt	gestritten
tragen	trägst, trägt	trug	getragen
treffen	triffst, trifft	traf	getroffen
treiben*	treibst, treibt	trieb	getrieben

infinitive	present indicative (2nd, 3rd sg)	imperfect	past participle
treten*	trittst, tritt	trat	getreten
trinken	trinkst, trinkt	trank	getrunken
trügen	trügst, trügt	trog	getrogen
tun	tust, tut	tat	getan
verderben	verdirbst, verdirbt	verdarb	verdorben
verdrießen	verdrießt, verdrießt	verdross	verdrossen
vergessen	vergisst, vergisst	vergaß	vergessen
verlieren	verlierst, verliert	verlor	verloren
verschleißen	verschleißt, verschleißt	verschliss	verschlissen
wachsen*	wächst, wächst	wuchs	gewachsen
weben	webst, webt	webte or wob	gewoben
wägen	wägst, wägt	wog	gewogen
waschen	wäschst, wäscht	wusch	gewaschen
weichen*	weichst, weicht	wich	gewichen
weisen	weist, weist	wies	gewiesen
wenden	wendest, wendet	wandte	gewandt
werben	wirbst, wirbt	warb	geworben
werden*	wirst, wird	wurde	geworden
werfen	wirfst, wirft	warf	geworfen
wiegen	wiegst, wiegt	wog	gewogen
winden	windest, windet	wand	gewunden
wissen	weißt, weiß	wusste	gewusst
wollen	willst, will	wollte	gewollt
wringen	wringst, wringt	wrang	gewrungen
zeihen	zeihst, zeiht	zieh	geziehen
ziehen*	ziehst, zieht	zog	gezogen
zwingen	zwingst, zwingt	zwang	gezwungen

GERMAN SPELLING CHANGES

In July 1996, all German-speaking countries signed a declaration concerning the reform of German spelling, with the result that the new spelling rules are now taught in all schools. To ensure that you have the most up-to-date information at your fingertips, the following list contains the old and new spellings of all German headwords and translations in this dictionary which are affected by the reform.

ALT/OLD	NEU/NEW	ALT/OLD	NEU/NEW
abend	**Abend**	aufsein	**auf sein**
Abfluß	**Abfluss**	aufwendig	**aufwendig**
Abflußrohr	**Abflussrohr**		or **aufwändig**
Abschluß	**Abschluss**	auseinanderbrechen	**auseinander brechen**
Abschlußexamen	**Abschlussexamen**	auseinanderbringen	**auseinander bringen**
Abschlußfeier	**Abschlussfeier**	auseinanderfallen	**auseinander fallen**
Abschlußklasse	**Abschlussklasse**	auseinanderfalten	**auseinander falten**
Abschlußprüfung	**Abschlussprüfung**	auseinandergehen	**auseinander gehen**
Abschuß	**Abschuss**	auseinanderhalten	**auseinander halten**
Abschußrampe	**Abschussrampe**	auseinandernehmen	**auseinander nehmen**
Abszeß	**Abszess**	auseinandersetzen	**auseinander setzen**
achtgeben	**Acht geben**	Ausfluß	**Ausfluss**
Adreßbuch	**Adressbuch**	Ausguß	**Ausguss**
Alleinerziehende(r)	**Alleinerziehende(r)**	Auslaß	**Auslass**
	or **allein Erziehende(r)**	Ausschluß	**Ausschluss**
alleinstehend	**allein stehend**	Ausschuß	**Ausschuss**
allgemeingültig	**allgemein gültig**	Ausschuß(artikel)	**Ausschuss(artikel)**
allzuoft	**allzu oft**	aussein	**aus sein**
allzuviel	**allzu viel**	außerstande	**außer Stande**
Alptraum	**Alptraum**	Autobiographie	**Autobiographie**
	or **Albtraum**		or **Autobiografie**
Amboß	**Amboss**	Baß	**Bass**
Amtsanschluß	**Amtsanschluss**	Baßstimme	**Bassstimme**
(Amts)mißbrauch	**(Amts)missbrauch**		or **Bass-Stimme**
andersdenkend	**anders denkend**	Ballettänzer(in)	**Balletttänzer(in)**
aneinandergeraten	**aneinander geraten**		or **Ballett-Tänzer(in)**
aneinanderreihen	**aneinander reihen**	beeinflußbar	**beeinflussbar**
Anlaß	**Anlass**	beiseitelegen	**beiseite legen**
anläßlich	**anlässlich**	bekanntgeben	**bekannt geben**
Anschluß	**Anschluss**	bekanntmachen	**bekannt machen**
Anschlußflug	**Anschlussflug**	Beschluß	**Beschluss**
As	**Ass**	Beschuß	**Beschuss**
aufeinanderfolgen	**aufeinander folgen**	bessergehen	**besser gehen**
aufeinanderfolgend	**aufeinander folgend**	Bettuch	**Betttuch**
aufeinanderlegen	**aufeinander legen**		or **Bett-Tuch**
aufeinanderprallen	**aufeinander prallen**	(Bevölkerungs)überschuß	
Aufschluß	**Aufschluss**		**(Bevölkerungs)überschuss**
aufschlußreich	**aufschlussreich**	bewußt	**bewusst**
aufsehenerregend	**Aufsehen erregend**	bewußtlos	**bewusstlos**

ALT/OLD	NEU/NEW	ALT/OLD	NEU/NEW
Bewußtlosigkeit	**Bewusstlosigkeit**	durchnummerieren	**durchnummerieren**
Bewußtsein	**Bewusstsein**	ehrfurchtgebietend	**Ehrfurcht gebietend**
bezug	**Bezug**	Einfluß	**Einfluss**
Bibliographie	**Bibliographie**	Einflußbereich	**Einflussbereich**
	or **Bibliografie**	einflußreich	**einflussreich**
Biographie	**Biographie**	einigemal	**einige Mal**
	or **Biografie**	einiggehen	**einig gehen**
Biß	**Biss**	Einlaß	**Einlass**
biß	**biss**	ekelerregend	**Ekel erregend**
bißchen	**bisschen**	Elsaß	**Elsass**
blaß	**blass**	Engpaß	**Engpass**
bläßlich	**blässlich**	Entschluß	**Entschluss**
bleibenlassen	**bleiben lassen**	entschlußfreudig	**entschlussfreudig**
Bluterguß	**Bluterguss**	Entschlußkraft	**Entschlusskraft**
Boß	**Boss**	epochemachend	**Epoche machend**
braungebrannt	**braun gebrannt**	Erdgeschoß	**Erdgeschoss**
breitmachen	**breit machen**	Erdnuß	**Erdnuss**
Brennessel	**Brennnessel**	Erdnußbutter	**Erdnussbutter**
	or **Brenn-Nessel**	erfolgversprechend	**Erfolg versprechend**
Büroschluß	**Büroschluss**	Erguß	**Erguss**
Butterfaß	**Butterfass**	Erlaß	**Erlass**
Cashewnuß	**Cashewnuss**	ernstgemeint	**ernst gemeint**
Chicorée	**Chicorée**	erstemal	**erste Mal**
	or **Schikoree**	Eß–	**Ess–**
Choreograph(in)	**Choreograph(in)**	erstenmal	**ersten Mal**
	or **Choreograf(in)**	eßbar	**essbar**
Computertomographie	**Computertomographie**	Eßbesteck	**Essbesteck**
	or **Computertomografie**	Eßecke	**Essecke**
dabeisein	**dabei sein**	Eßgeschirr	**Essgeschirr**
dafürkönnen	**dafür können**	Eßkastanie	**Esskastanie**
dahinterkommen	**dahinter kommen**	Eßlöffel	**Esslöffel**
darauffolgend	**darauf folgend**	Eßlöffel(voll)	**Esslöffel (voll)**
dasein	**da sein**	(Eß)stäbchen	**(Ess)stäbchen**
daß	**dass**		*or* **(Ess–)Stäbchen**
Dekolleté	**Dekolleté**	Eßtisch	**Esstisch**
	or **Dekolletee**	Eßwaren	**Esswaren**
Delphin	**Delphin**	Eßzimmer	**Esszimmer**
	or **Delfin**	Expreß	**Express**
dessenungeachtet	**dessen ungeachtet**	Expreß–	**Express–**
dichtbevölkert	**dicht bevölkert**	Expreßgut	**Expressgut**
diensthabend	**Dienst habend**	Expreßzug	**Expresszug**
differential	**differential**	Exzeß	**Exzess**
	or **differenzial**	Facette	**Facette**
Differentialrechnung	**Differentialrechnung**		*or* **Fassette**
	or **Differenzialrechnung**	Fährenanschluß	**Fährenanschluss**
Diktaphon	**Diktaphon**	Fairneß	**Fairness**
	or **Diktafon**	fallenlassen	**fallen lassen**
dreiviertel	**drei Viertel**	Faß	**Fass**
durcheinanderbringen	**durcheinander bringen**	faßbar	**fassbar**
durcheinanderreden	**durcheinander reden**	Fehlschuß	**Fehlschuss**
durcheinanderwerfen	**durcheinander werfen**	fernhalten	**fern halten**

ALT/OLD	NEU/NEW
fertigbringen	**fertig bringen**
fertigmachen	**fertig machen**
fertigstellen	**fertig stellen**
fertigwerden	**fertig werden**
festangestellt	**fest angestellt**
Fitneß	**Fitness**
fleischfressend	**Fleisch fressend**
floß	**floss**
Fluß	**Fluss**
Fluß–	**Fluss–**
	or **Fluss-**
flußabwärts	**flussabwärts**
Flußbarsch	**Flussbarsch**
Flußbett	**Flussbett**
Flußdiagramm	**Flussdiagramm**
flüssigmachen	**flüssig machen**
Flußufer	**Flussufer**
Fön ®	**Fön ®**
	or **Föhn ®**
fönen	**föhnen**
Fönfrisur	**Föhnfrisur**
Friedensschluß	**Friedensschluss**
Frischvermählte	**frisch Vermählte**
Frischvermählten	**frisch Vermählten**
frißt	**frisst**
fritieren	**frittieren**
Gebiß	**Gebiss**
Gebührenerlaß	**Gebührenerlass**
gefangen(gehalten)	**gefangen (gehalten)**
gefangenhalten	**gefangen halten**
gefangennehmen	**gefangen nehmen**
gefaßt	**gefasst**
geheimhalten	**geheim halten**
gehenlassen	**gehen lassen**
Gemeinschaftsanschluß	
	Gemeinschaftsanschluss
Gemse	**Gämse**
gemußt	**gemusst**
genaugenommen	**genau genommen**
Genuß	**Genuss**
genüßlich	**genüsslich**
Genußmittel	**Genussmittel**
Geograph	**Geograph**
	or **Geograf**
Geographie	**Geographie**
	or **Geografie**
geographisch	**geographisch**
	or **geografisch**
geringachten	**gering achten**
Geschäftsschluß	**Geschäftsschluss**
Geschoß	**Geschoss**
gewinnbringend	**Gewinn bringend**
gewiß	**gewiss**
Gewißheit	**Gewissheit**
gewußt	**gewusst**
glattrasiert	**glatt rasiert**
glattstreichen	**glatt streichen**
gleichbleibend	**gleich bleibend**
gleichgesinnt	**gleich gesinnt**
Glimmstengel	**Glimmstängel**
Grammophon	**Grammophon**
	or **Grammofon**
(Grammophon)nadel	**(Grammophon)nadel**
	or **(Grammofon)nadel**
Graphiker(in)	**Graphiker(in)**
	or **Grafiker(in)**
graphisch	**graphisch**
	or **grafisch**
gräßlich	**grässlich**
Greuel	**Gräuel**
Greueltat	**Gräueltat**
greulich	**gräulich**
Grundriß	**Grundriss**
Guß	**Guss**
Gußeisen	**Gusseisen**
gutaussehend	**gut aussehend**
gutgehen	**gut gehen**
gutgehend	**gut gehend**
gutgemeint	**gut gemeint**
guttun	**gut tun**
haftenbleiben	**haften bleiben**
halboffen	**halb offen**
haltmachen	**Halt machen**
Hämorrhoiden	**Hämorrhoiden**
	or **Hämorriden**
Handvoll	**Hand voll**
hängenbleiben	**hängen bleiben**
hängenlassen	**hängen lassen**
hartgekocht	**hart gekocht**
Haselnuß	**Haselnuss**
Haß	**Hass**
häßlich	**hässlich**
Häßlichkeit	**Hässlichkeit**
haushalten	**haushalten**
	or **Haus halten**
heiligsprechen	**heilig sprechen**
Hexenschuß	**Hexenschuss**
hierbehalten	**hier behalten**
hierbleiben	**hier bleiben**
hierlassen	**hier lassen**
hierzulande	**hierzulande**
	or **hier zu Lande**
hochachten	**hoch achten**

ALT/OLD	NEU/NEW	ALT/OLD	NEU/NEW
hochbegabt	**hoch begabt**	kompromißlos	**kompromisslos**
hochdotiert	**hoch dotiert**	Kompromißlösung	**Kompromisslösung**
hochentwickelt	**hoch entwickelt**	Kongreß	**Kongress**
(hoch)geschätzt	**(hoch) geschätzt**	Kongreßzentrum	**Kongresszentrum**
(hoch)schätzen	**(hoch) schätzen**	Kontrabaß	**Kontrabass**
(Honorar)vorschuß	**(Honorar)vorschuss**	kraß	**krass**
Imbiß	**Imbiss**	Kreppapier	**Krepppapier**
Imbißhalle	**Imbisshalle**		*or* **Krepp–Papier**
Imbißraum	**Imbissraum**	kriegführend	**Krieg führend**
Imbißstube	**Imbissstube**	krummnehmen	**krumm nehmen**
	or **Imbiss–Stube**	Kurzbiographie	**Kurzbiographie**
immerwährend	**immer während**		*or* **Kurzbiografie**
imstande	**imstande**	kurzhalten	**kurz halten**
	or **im Stande**	Kurzschluß	**Kurzschluss**
ineinandergreifen	**ineinander greifen**	Kuß	**Kuss**
ineinanderschieben	**ineinander schieben**	Ladenschluß	**Ladenschluss**
Intercity–Expreßzug	**Intercity–Expresszug**	Laufpaß	**Laufpass**
ißt	**isst**	leerlaufen	**leer laufen**
Jahresabschluß	**Jahresabschluss**	leerstehend	**leer stehend**
jedesmal	**jedes Mal**	leichtfallen	**leicht fallen**
Joghurt	**Joghurt**	leichtmachen	**leicht machen**
	or **Jogurt**	Lenkradschloß	**Lenkradschloss**
kahlgeschoren	**kahl geschoren**	letztemal	**letzte Mal**
kaltbleiben	**kalt bleiben**	liebgewinnen	**lieb gewinnen**
Kammuschel	**Kammmuschel**	liebhaben	**lieb haben**
	or **Kamm–Muschel**	liegenbleiben	**liegen bleiben**
Känguruh	**Känguru**	liegenlassen	**liegen lassen**
Karamel	**Karamell**	Litfaßsäule	**Litfasssäule**
Karamelbonbon	**Karamellbonbon**		*or* **Litfass–Säule**
Katarrh	**Katarr**	Lithographie	**Lithographie**
	or **Katarr**		*or* **Lithografie**
Kellergeschoß	**Kellergeschoss**	Luftschloß	**Luftschloss**
kennenlernen	**kennen lernen**	maschineschreiben	**Maschine schreiben**
keß	**kess**	maßhalten	**Maß halten**
klarsehen	**klar sehen**	Megaphon	**Megaphon**
klarwerden	**klar werden**		*or* **Megafon**
klassenbewußt	**klassenbewusst**		
Klassenbewußtsein	**Klassenbewusstsein**	Meldeschluß	**Meldeschluss**
klatschnaß	**klatschnass**	meßbar	**messbar**
kleinhacken	**klein hacken**	Meßbecher	**Messbecher**
kleinschneiden	**klein schneiden**	Meßgerät	**Messgerät**
klitschnaß	**klitschnass**	Mikrophon	**Mikrophon**
knapphalten	**knapp halten**		*or* **Mikrofon**
Kokosnuß	**Kokosnuss**	Miß–	**Miss–**
Koloß	**Koloss**	mißachten	**missachten**
Kombinationsschloß	**Kombinationsschloss**	Mißachtung	**Missachtung**
Kommuniqué	**Kommuniqué**	Mißbehagen	**Missbehagen**
	or **Kommunikee**	Mißbildung	**Missbildung**
Kompaß	**Kompass**	mißbilligen	**missbilligen**
Kompromiß	**Kompromiss**	Mißbilligung	**Missbilligung**
kompromißbereit	**kompromissbereit**	Mißbrauch	**Missbrauch**
		mißbrauchen	**missbrauchen**

ALT/OLD	NEU/NEW	ALT/OLD	NEU/NEW
Mißerfolg	**Misserfolg**	Nebenanschluß	**Nebenanschluss**
Mißfallen	**Missfallen**	nebeneinanderlegen	**nebeneinander legen**
mißfallen	**missfallen**	nebeneinanderstellen	**nebeneinander stellen**
Mißgeburt	**Missgeburt**	Nebenfluß	**Nebenfluss**
Mißgeschick	**Missgeschick**	Necessaire	**Necessaire**
mißgestaltet	**missgestaltet**		or **Nessessär**
mißglücken	**missglücken**	Negligé	**Negligé**
mißgönnen	**missgönnen**		or **Negligee**
Mißgriff	**Missgriff**	Netzanschluß	**Netzanschluss**
Mißgunst	**Missgunst**	neuentdeckt	**neu entdeckt**
mißgünstig	**missgünstig**	nichtsahnend	**nichts ahnend**
mißhandeln	**misshandeln**	nichtssagend	**nichts sagend**
Mißhandlung	**Misshandlung**	Nonstop-	**Nonstop-**
Mißklang	**Missklang**		or **Non-Stop-**
Mißkredit	**Misskredit**	notleidend	**Not leidend**
mißlich	**misslich**	numerieren	**nummerieren**
mißlingen	**misslingen**	Nuß	**Nuss**
mißlungen	**misslungen**	Nußbaum	**Nussbaum**
Mißmut	**Missmut**	Nußknacker	**Nussknacker**
mißmutig	**missmutig**	Nußschale	**Nussschale**
mißraten	**missraten**		or **Nuss-Schale**
Mißstand	**Missstand**	obenerwähnt	**oben erwähnt**
	or **Miss-Stand**	obengenannt	**oben genannt**
Mißtrauen	**Misstrauen**	Obergeschoß	**Obergeschoss**
mißtrauen	**misstrauen**	offenbleiben	**offen bleiben**
Mißtrauensantrag	**Misstrauensantrag**	offenhalten	**offen halten**
Mißtrauensvotum	**Misstrauensvotum**	offenlassen	**offen lassen**
mißtrauisch	**misstrauisch**	offenstehen	**offen stehen**
Mißverhältnis	**Missverhältnis**	Ölmeßstab	**Ölmessstab**
Mißverständnis	**Missverständnis**		or **Ölmess-Stab**
mißverstehen	**missverstehen**	Orthographie	**Orthographie**
Mißwirtschaft	**Misswirtschaft**		or **Orthografie**
mittag	**Mittag**	orthographisch	**orthographisch**
Mop	**Mopp**		or **orthografisch**
Muß	**Muss**	paarmal	**paar Mal**
mußte	**musste**	Panther	**Panther**
nachhinein	**Nachhinein**		or **Panter**
Nachlaß	**Nachlass**	Paragraph	**Paragraph**
nahegehen	**nahe gehen**		or **Paragraf**
nahekommen	**nahe kommen**	Paranuß	**Paranuss**
nahelegen	**nahe legen**	Parlamentsbeschluß	**Parlamentsbeschluss**
naheliegen	**nahe liegen**	Paß	**Pass**
naheliegend	**nahe liegend**	Paß-	**Pass-**
näherkommen	**näher kommen**	Paßamt	**Passamt**
näherrücken	**näher rücken**	Paßbild	**Passbild**
nahestehen	**nahe stehen**	Paßkontrolle	**Passkontrolle**
nahestehend	**nahe stehend**	Paßstelle	**Passstelle**
nahetreten	**nahe treten**		or **Pass-Stelle**
naß	**nass**	Paßstraße	**Passstraße**
naßkalt	**nasskalt**		or **Pass-Straße**
Naßrasur	**Nassrasur**	patschnaß	**patschnass**

618

ALT/OLD	NEU/NEW	ALT/OLD	NEU/NEW
pflichtbewußt	pflichtbewusst	rotglühend	rot glühend
Phantasie	Phantasie	Rückschluß	Rückschluss
	or Fantasie	Rußland	Russland
Phantasie–	Phantasie–	Safe(r) Sex	Safe(r) Sex
	or Fantasie–		or Safe(r)-sex
phantasielos	phantasielos	Salzfaß	Salzfass
	or fantasielos	sauberhalten	sauber halten
phantasiereich	phantasiereich	Saxophon	Saxophon
	or fantasiereich		or Saxofon
phantasieren	phantasieren	Schattenriß	Schattenriss
	or fantasieren	schiefgehen	schief gehen
phantasievoll	phantasievoll	Schiffahrt	Schifffahrt
	or fantasievoll		or Schiff-Fahrt
phantastisch	phantastisch	Schiffahrtslinie	Schifffahrtslinie
	or fantastisch	Schlangenbiß	Schlangenbiss
platschnaß	platschnass	schlechtgehen	schlecht gehen
plazieren	platzieren	schlechtmachen	schlecht machen
Pornographie	Pornographie	Schlegel	Schlägel
	or Pornografie	Schloß	Schloss
pornographisch	pornographisch	schloß	schloss
	or pornografisch	Schluß	Schluss
Portemonnaie	Portemonnaie	Schluß–	Schluss–
	or Portmonee	(Schluß)folgerung	(Schluss)folgerung
Potential	Potential	Schlußlicht	Schlusslicht
	or Potenzial	Schlußrunde	Schlussrunde
potentiell	potentiell	Schlußrundenteilnehmer	
	or potenziell		Schlussrundenteilnehmer
preisbewußt	preisbewusst	Schlußstrich	Schlussstrich
Preßluft	Pressluft		or Schluss-Strich
Preßluftbohrer	Pressluftbohrer	Schlußverkauf	Schlussverkauf
Preßlufthammer	Presslufthammer	Schmiß	Schmiss
Prozeß	Prozess	Schnappschloß	Schnappschloss
Prüfungsausschuß	Prüfungsausschuss	Schnappschuß	Schnappschuss
radfahren	Rad fahren	Schnellimbiß	Schnellimbiss
(Raketen)abschuß	(Raketen)abschuss	schneuzen	schnäuzen
Rassenhaß	Rassenhass	schoß	schoss
rauh	rau	Schößling	Schössling
Rauhreif	Raureif	Schrittempo	Schritttempo
Raumschiffahrt	Raumschifffahrt		or Schritt-Tempo
	or Raumschiff-Fahrt	Schuß	Schuss
Rausschmiß	Rausschmiss	Schußbereich	Schussbereich
Rechnungsabschluß	Rechnungsabschluss	Schußlinie	Schusslinie
reinwaschen	rein waschen	Schußverletzung	Schussverletzung
Reisepaß	Reisepass	Schußwaffe	Schusswaffe
Reißverschluß	Reißverschluss	Schußweite	Schussweite
richtigstellen	richtig stellen	schwererziehbar	schwer erziehbar
Riß	Riss	schwerfallen	schwer fallen
Rolladen	Rollladen	schwermachen	schwer machen
	or Roll–Laden	schwernehmen	schwer nehmen
Roß	Ross	schwertun	schwer tun
Roßkastanie	Rosskastanie	schwerverdaulich	schwer verdaulich

	NEU/NEW	ALT/OLD	NEU/NEW
	schwer verletzt		or telegrafieren
...raph	Seismograph	Thunfisch	Thunfisch
	or Seismograf		or Tunfisch
selbständig	selbständig	tiefausgeschnitten	tief ausgeschnitten
	or selbstständig	tiefgehend	tief gehend
Selbständigkeit	Selbständigkeit	tiefgekühlt	tief gekühlt
	or Selbstständigkeit	tiefgreifend	tief greifend
selbstbewußt	selbstbewusst	tiefschürfend	tief schürfend
Selbstbewußtsein	Selbstbewusstsein	Tip	Tipp
selbstgemacht	selbst gemacht	topographisch	topographisch
selbstverständlich	selbst verständlich		or topografisch
selbstverwaltet	selbst verwaltet	totenblaß	totenblass
seßhaft	sesshaft	totgeboren	tot geboren
Showbusineß	Showbusiness	Trugschluß	Trugschluss
Sicherheitsschloß	Sicherheitsschloss	tschüs	tschüs
sitzenbleiben	sitzen bleiben		or tschüss
sitzenlassen	sitzen lassen	übelgelaunt	übel gelaunt
Skipaß	Skipass	übelnehmen	übel nehmen
sogenannt	so genannt	übelriechend	übel riechend
Sommerschlußverkauf		übelwollend	übel wollend
	Sommerschlussverkauf	Überdruß	Überdruss
sonstjemand	sonst jemand	übereinanderlegen	übereinander legen
sonstwo	sonst wo	Überfluß	Überfluss
sonstwoher	sonst woher	Überschuß	Überschuss
sonstwohin	sonst wohin	überschwenglich	überschwänglich
Spannbettuch	Spannbetttuch	übrigbleiben	übrig bleiben
	or Spannbett-Tuch	übriggeblieben	übrig geblieben
spazierenfahren	spazieren fahren	übriglassen	übrig lassen
spazierengehen	spazieren gehen	Umriß	Umriss
Sprößling	Sprössling	unbewußt	unbewusst
steckenbleiben	stecken bleiben	Unbewußte	Unbewusste
steckenlassen	stecken lassen	unerläßlich	unerlässlich
stehenbleiben	stehen bleiben	unermeßlich	unermesslich
stehenlassen	stehen lassen	unfaßbar	unfassbar
Stengel	Stängel	ungewiß	ungewiss
Stenographie	Stenographie	Ungewißheit	Ungewissheit
	or Stenografie	unmißverständlich	unmissverständlich
stenographieren	stenographieren	unpäßlich	unpässlich
	or stenografieren	unselbständig	unselbständig
Stenograph(in)	Stenograph(in)		or unselbstständig
	or Stenograf(in)	unterbewußt	unterbewusst
stereophonisch	stereophonisch	Unterbewußte	Unterbewusste
	or stereofonisch	Unterbewußtsein	Unterbewusstsein
Stewardeß	Stewardess	Untergeschoß	Untergeschoss
Stilleben	Stillleben	Untersuchungsausschuß	
	or Still-Leben		Untersuchungsausschuss
stillegen	stilllegen	unvergeßlich	unvergesslich
Streifschuß	Streifschuss	Varieté	Varieté
strenggenommen	streng genommen		or Varietee
Streß	Stress	verantwortungsbewußt	
telegraphieren	telegraphieren		verantwortungsbewusst

ALT/OLD	NEU/NEW	ALT/OLD	NEU/NEW
Verdruß	**Verdruss**	wiedergutzumachen	**wieder gutzumachen**
vergeßlich	**vergesslich**	wiederherstellen	**wieder herstellen**
Vergeßlichkeit	**Vergesslichkeit**	wiedersehen	**wieder sehen**
Vergißmeinnicht	**Vergissmeinnicht**	wiedervereinigen	**wieder vereinigen**
vergißt	**vergisst**	wiederverwenden	**wieder verwenden**
verhaßt	**verhasst**	wiederverwerten	**wieder verwerten**
Verlaß	**Verlass**	wieviel	**wie viel**
verläßlich	**verlässlich**	Wißbegier(de)	**Wissbegier(de)**
verlorengehen	**verloren gehen**	wißbegierig	**wissbegierig**
vermißt	**vermisst**	wohltun	**wohl tun**
Verschluß	**Verschluss**	wußte	**wusste**
vertrauenerweckend	**Vertrauen erweckend**	Xylophon	**Xylophon**
vielsagend	**viel sagend**		or **Xylofon**
vielversprechend	**viel versprechend**	Zahlenschloß	**Zahlenschloss**
(voll)fressen	**(voll) fressen**	zeitlang	**Zeit lang**
vollgepfropft	**voll gepfropft**	zielbewußt	**zielbewusst**
vollpfropfen	**voll pfropfen**	Zuckerguß	**Zuckerguss**
vollstopfen	**voll stopfen**	zufriedengeben	**zufrieden geben**
volltanken	**voll tanken**	zufriedenstellen	**zufrieden stellen**
vorgefaßt	**vorgefasst**	zufriedenstellend	**zufrieden stellend**
Vorhängeschloß	**Vorhängeschloss**	zugrunde	**zugrunde**
vorhinein	**Vorhinein**		or **zu Grunde**
vorliebnehmen	**vorlieb nehmen**	zugunsten	**zugunsten**
Vorschuß	**Vorschuss**		or **zu Gunsten**
vorwärtsbewegen	**vorwärts bewegen**	zuleide	**zuleide**
vorwärtsdrängen	**vorwärts drängen**		or **zu Leide**
vorwärtsgehen	**vorwärts gehen**	zumute	**zumute**
vorwärtskommen	**vorwärts kommen**		or **zu Mute**
Waggon	**Waggon**	Zündschloß	**Zündschloss**
	or **Wagon**	Zungenkuß	**Zungenkuss**
Walnuß	**Walnuss**	zunutze	**zunutze**
Walroß	**Walross**		or **zu Nutze**
wasserabstoßend	**Wasser abstoßend**	Zusammenschluß	**Zusammenschluss**
wäßrig	**wässrig**	zuschulden	**zuschulden**
Weißrußland	**Weißrussland**		or **zu Schulden**
weitblickend	**weitblickend**	Zuschuß	**Zuschuss**
	or **weit blickend**	zustande	**zustande**
weitreichend	**weitreichend**		or **zu Stande**
	or **weit reichend**	zustande bringen	**zustande bringen**
weitverbreitet	**weitverbreitet**		or **zu Stande bringen**
	or **weit verbreitet**	zustande kommen	**zustande kommen**
wiederaufbauen	**wieder aufbauen**		or **zu Stande kommen**
wiederaufbereiten	**wieder aufbereiten**	zutage	**zutage**
wiederaufnehmen	**wieder aufnehmen**		or **zu Tage**
wiederbeleben	**wieder beleben**	zuviel	**zu viel**
wiedereinsetzen	**wieder einsetzen**	zuwege	**zuwege**
wiedererkennen	**wieder erkennen**		or **zu Wege**
wiedererwachen	**wieder erwachen**	zuwenig	**zu wenig**
wiedergutmachen	**wieder gutmachen**		